A MIDNIGHT MEETING.—REV. BAPTIST NOEL SPEAKING.

LONDON LABOUR
AND THE LONDON POOR

BY
HENRY MAYHEW

WITH A NEW INTRODUCTION BY
JOHN D. ROSENBERG
Professor of English, Columbia University

IN FOUR VOLUMES
VOLUME IV
*Those That Will Not Work, comprising
Prostitutes, Thieves, Swindlers and Beggars,
by several contributors*

DOVER PUBLICATIONS, INC.
NEW YORK

Copyright © 1968 by DOVER PUBLICATIONS, INC.
All rights reserved under Pan American and
International Copyright Conventions.

Published in Canada by General Publishing Company, Ltd.,
30 Lesmill Road, Don Mills, Toronto, Ontario.

Published in the United Kingdom by Constable and Company, Ltd.,
10 Orange Street, London WC 2.

This Dover edition, first published in 1968, is an unabridged republication of the work as published by Griffin, Bohn, and Company in 1861–1862, to which has been added a new Introduction by John D. Rosenberg.

Library of Congress Catalog Card Number: 68-19549

MANUFACTURED IN THE UNITED STATES OF AMERICA

DOVER PUBLICATIONS, INC.
180 VARICK STREET
NEW YORK, N. Y. 10014

ADVERTISEMENT.

It would be a work of supererogation to extol the utility of such a publication as "London Labour and the London Poor," so apparent must be its value to all classes of society. It stands alone as a photograph of life as actually spent by the lower classes of the Metropolis. That one half of the world does not know how the other half lives is an axiom of antiquity, but the truthful revelations and descriptions of the London street folk, workers and non-workers, and the means by which they exist, will go a great way to enlighten the educated classes respecting matters which have hitherto been involved in mystery and uncertainty.

The class of individuals treated of in this volume are the Non-Workers, or in other words, the Dangerous Classes of the Metropolis; and every endeavour has been made to obtain correct information, not only through the assistance of the police authorities, but by an expenditure of much time and research among the unfortunates themselves. Their favourite haunts, and the localities in London wherein they chiefly congregate, as well as their modes of existence, are accurately described; in addition to which have been inserted very many deeply interesting autobiographies, faithfully transcribed from their own lips, which go far to unveil the intricate schemes of villany and crime that abound in the Metropolis, and prove how much more rational and effective are preventive measures than such as are merely correctional.

Every phase of vice has been investigated and treated of, in order that all possible information that can prove interesting to the moralist, the philanthropist, and the statist, as well as to the general public, might be afforded. In a word the veil has been raised, and the skeleton exposed to the view of the public.

In order to inspire hope and confidence in those who would shudder and lose heart in the perusal of such a record of crime and misery, the volume is prefaced by a comprehensive account of the agencies in operation within the Metropolis for the suppression of crime and vice, in which is detailed the aim and scope of the numerous religious and philanthropic associations now actively following the footsteps of that Divine Saviour, Whose chief mission was to the poor and guilty.

These brave workers now abound in all the dark places of the Metropolis, and the fruits of their labours, particularly in the case of youthful criminals, are becoming, through the blessing of Providence, abundantly apparent.

A vast amount of statistical information, compiled from authentic records, is contained in the body of the work, and in the Appendix, and a few illustrations are introduced, graphically showing the extremes of vice and crime

The publishers have to thank Sir Richard Mayne and the authorities at Scotland Yard, as well as the Secretaries of the various charitable societies, for much valuable information and assistance.

Stationers' Hall Court;
December, 1861.

CONTENTS.

THE AGENCIES AT PRESENT IN OPERATION WITHIN THE METROPOLIS, FOR THE SUPPRESSION OF VICE AND CRIME.
By the Rev. William Tuckniss, B.A.

	PAGE		PAGE
Universal Desire for Investigation	xi	Preventive Agencies—*continued*.	
Mere Palliatives insufficient to Check the Growth of Crime	xi	House of Charity	xxviii
		Foundling Hospital	xxviii
Decrease of Crime doubtful	xii	Society for the Suppression of Mendicity	xxviii
General Desire to Alleviate Misery	xiii		
Guthrie on Great Cities	xiv	Association for Promoting the Relief of Destitution	xxviii
Social Position of London	xv		
Agencies at Work in London	xvii	Association for the Aid and Benefit of Dressmakers and Milliners	xxix
Their Number and Income	xvii		
Curative Agencies	xviii		
British and Foreign Bible Society	xix	Young Women's Christian Association and West-end Home	xxix
Society for Promoting Christian Knowledge	xix	Society for Promoting the Employment of Women	xxx
Institution for Reading the Word of God in the Open Air	xix	Metropolitan Early Closing Association, &c.	xxx
Theatre Services	xix	Repressive and Punitive Agencies	xxx
London City Mission	xx	Society for the Suppression of Vice	xxxi
Church of England Scripture Readers' Society	xxii		
Religious Tract Society	xxiii	The Associate Institution	xxxi
Pure Literature Society	xxiii	Society for Promoting the Observance of the Lord's Day	xxxiv
Preventive Agencies	xxiv		
National Temperance Society	xxiv	Society for the Prevention of Cruelty to Animals	xxxiv
United Kingdom Alliance	xxiv	Reformative Agencies	xxxiv
Free Drinking Fountain Association	xxv	Reformatory and Refuge Union	xxxiv
Ragged School Union	xxv	Reformative Agencies for Fallen Women	xxxv
Society for Improving the Condition of the Labouring Classes	xxv		
		Magdalen Hospital	xxxvi
Female Servants' Home Society	xxvi	London by Moonlight Mission	xxxvii
Female Aid Society	xxvii	Society for the Rescue of Young Women and Children	xxxvii
Training Institutions for Servants	xxvii		
Field Lane Night Refuges	xxvii	London Female Preventive and Reformatory Institution	xxxvii
Dudley Stuart Night Refuge	xxvii		
Houseless Poor Asylum	xxviii	Concluding Remarks	xxxviii

INTRODUCTION AND CLASSIFICATION. By Henry Mayhew 1

Workers and Non-workers	2	Those that need not Work	27
Classification of ditto	11	Those who derive their Income from Rent	27
Those who will Work	12		
Enrichers	13	Those who derive their Income from Dividends	27
Auxiliaries	16		
Benefactors	19	Those who derive their Income from Yearly Stipends	27
Servitors	20		
Those who cannot Work	22	Those who derive their Income from obsolete or nominal Offices	27
Those who are provided for	22		
Those who are unprovided for	22	Those who derive their Income from Trades in which they do not appear	27
Those who will not Work	23		
Vagrants or Tramps	23		
Professional Beggars	23	Those who derive their Income by favour from others	27
Cheats and their Dependants	24		
Thieves and their Dependants	25	Those who derive their support from the head of the family	27
Prostitutes and their Dependants	27		

THE NON-WORKERS. By Henry Mayhew 28

PROSTITUTES.

THE PROSTITUTE CLASS GENERALLY. By Henry Mayhew and Bracebridge Hemyng .. 35

	PAGE
Prostitution in Ancient States ..	37
The Jews, &c.	39
Ancient Egypt	43
Ancient Greece	45
Ancient Rome	49
The Anglo-Saxons	34
Prostitution among the Barbarous Nations	58
African Nations	58
Australia	67
New Zealand	71
Islands of the Pacific	76
North American Indians ..	84
South American Indians ..	90
Cities of South America ..	93
West Indies	94
Java	96
Sumatra	99
Borneo	103
Prostitution among the Semi-civilized Nations	104
Celebes	107
Persia	108
The Affghans	111
Kashmir	115
India	117
Ceylon	125
China	129
Japan	136
Prostitution among the Semi-Civilized Nations—continued.	
The ultra-Gangetic Nations ..	139
Egypt	141
Northern Africa	149
Arabia, Syria, and Asia Minor	151
Turkey	155
Circassia	158
The Tartar Races	160
Prostitution among the Mixed Northern Nations	163
Russia	165
Siberia	167
Iceland and Greenland ..	172
Lapland and Sweden	174
Norway	177
Denmark	179
Prostitution in Civilized States ..	181
Spain	191
Amsterdam	195
Belgium	195
Hamburg	196
Prussia—Germany	198
Berlin	198
Austria	200
Modern Rome	201
Turin	203
Berne	204
Paris	205

PROSTITUTION IN LONDON. By Bracebridge Hemyng 210

	PAGE
General Remarks	210
Seclusives, or those that Live in Private Houses and Apartments ..	215
The Haymarket	217
Degree of Education among Prostitutes	218
Board Lodgers	220
Autobiographies	220
Those who Live in low Lodging Houses	223
Swindling Sall	223
Lushing Loo	224
Sailors' Women	226
Visit to Ratcliff Highway ..	228
Visit to Bluegate Fields, &c. ..	231
Soldiers' Women	233
Visit to Knightsbridge ..	235
Thieves' Women	236
Visit to Drury Lane, &c. ..	236
Park Women	242
Examples	242
The Dependants of Prostitutes ..	246
Bawds	246
Followers of Dress Lodgers ..	247
Keepers of Accommodation Houses	249
Procuresses, Pimps, and Panders ..	250
Fancy Men	252
Bullies	253
Clandestine Prostitutes	
Female Operatives	255
Maid Servants	257
Ladies of Intrigue and Houses of Assignation	
Cohabitant Prostitutes	259
Narrative of a Gay Woman ..	260
Criminal Returns	263
Traffic in Foreign Women ..	269

THIEVES AND SWINDLERS.—By John Binny.

	PAGE
Introduction	273
Sneaks, or Common Thieves ..	277
Juvenile Thieves	277
Stealing from Street Stalls ..	277
Stealing from the Till ..	278
Sneaks or Common Thieves—continued.	
Stealing from the Doors and Windows of Shops	279
Stealing from Children ..	281
Child Stripping	281

THIEVES AND SWINDLERS—*continued.*

	PAGE
SNEAKS OR COMMON THIEVES—*continued*	
Stealing from Drunken Persons	282
Stealing Linen, &c.	283
Robberies from Carts	284
Stealing Lead from House-tops, Copper from Kitchens, &c.	285
Robberies by false Keys	286
Robberies by Lodgers	288
Robberies by Servants	289
Area and Lobby Sneaks	290
Stealing by Lifting Windows, &c.	292
Attic or Garret Thieves	293
A Visit to the Rookery of St. Giles	294
Narrative of a London Sneak	301
PICKPOCKETS AND SHOPLIFTERS	303
Common Pickpockets	306
Omnibus Pickpockets	309
Railway Pickpockets	310
A Visit to the Thieves' Dens in Spitalfields	311
Narrative of a Pickpocket	316
HORSE AND DOG STEALERS	325
Horse Stealing	325
Dog Stealing	325
HIGHWAY ROBBERS	326
A Ramble among the Thieves' Dens in the Borough	330
HOUSEBREAKERS AND BURGLARS	334
Narrative of a Burglar	345
Narrative of another Burglar	349
PROSTITUTE THIEVES	355
Prostitutes of the Haymarket	356
Common Street Walkers	360
Hired Prostitutes	361
Park Women	362
Soldiers' Women	363
Sailors' Women	365
FELONIES ON THE RIVER THAMES	366
Mudlarks	366
Sweeping Boys	367
Sellers of Small Wares	367
Labourers on board Ship	367
Dredgermen or Fishermen	368
Smuggling	368
Felonies by Lightermen	368
The River Pirates	369
Narrative of a Mudlark	370
RECEIVERS OF STOLEN PROPERTY	373
Dolly Shops	373
Pawnbrokers, &c.	374
Narrative of a Returned Convict	376
COINING	377
Coiners	378
Forgers	380
CHEATS	383
Embezzlers	383
Magsmen or Sharpers	385
Swindlers	388

BEGGARS.—By ANDREW HALLIDAY.

	PAGE
INTRODUCTION	393
ORIGIN AND HISTORY OF THE POOR LAWS.	394
Statistics of the Poor Laws	397
Report of the Poor Law Board	397
STREET BEGGARS IN 1816	398
MENDICANT PENSIONERS	399
MENDICITY SOCIETY	399
Examples of Applications	401
BEGGING LETTER WRITERS	403
Decayed Gentlemen	404
Broken-down Tradesmen	405
Distressed Scholar	405
The Kaggs' Family	406
ADVERTISING BEGGING LETTER WRITERS	410
ASHAMED BEGGARS	412
THE SWELL BEGGAR	413
CLEAN FAMILY BEGGARS	413
NAVAL AND MILITARY BEGGARS	415
Turnpike Sailor	415
Street Campaigners	417
FOREIGN BEGGARS	419
The French Beggar	419
Destitute Poles	420
Hindoo Beggars	423
Negro Beggars	425
DISASTER BEGGARS	427
A Shipwrecked Mariner	428
Blown-up Miners	429
Burnt-out Tradesmen	429
Lucifer Droppers	431
Bodily Afflicted Beggars	431
Seventy years a Beggar	432
Having swollen Legs	433
Cripples	433
A Blind Beggar	433
Beggars subject to Fits	434
Being in a Decline	435
Shallow Coves	435
Famished Beggars	436
The Choking Dodge	437
The Offal Eater	437
PETTY TRADING BEGGARS	438
An Author's Wife	440
DEPENDANTS OF BEGGARS	441
Referees	445
DISTRESSED OPERATIVE BEGGARS	446
Starved-out Manufacturers	446
Unemployed Agriculturists	446
Frozen-out Gardeners	446
Hand-loom Weavers, &c.	447

APPENDIX.

MAPS AND TABLES

ILLUSTRATING THE CRIMINAL STATISTICS OF EACH OF THE COUNTIES OF ENGLAND AND WALES IN 1851.

	PAGE		PAGE
Map showing the Density of the Population	451	Map showing Committals for Assault with Intent to Ravish and Carnally Abuse	481
Table of ditto	452	Table of ditto	482
Map showing the Intensity of Criminality	455	Map showing Commitals for Disorderly Houses	485
Table of ditto	456	Table of ditto	486
Map showing the Intensity of Ignorance	459	Map showing Concealment of Births	489
Table of ditto	460	Table of ditto	490
Table of Ignorance among Criminals	462	Map showing attempts at Miscarriage	493
Table of Degrees of Criminality	464	Table of ditto	494
Comparative Educational Tables	465	Map showing Assaults with Intent	497
Map showing the Number of Illegitimate Children	467	Table of ditto	498
Table of ditto	468	Map showing Committals for Bigamy	499
Map showing the Number of Early Marriages	471	Table of ditto	500
Table of ditto	472	Map showing Committals for Abduction	501
Map showing the Number of Females	475	Table of ditto	502
Table of ditto	476	Map showing the Criminality of Females	503
Map showing Commitals for Rape	477	Table of ditto	504
Table of ditto	479		

LIST OF ILLUSTRATIONS.

A MIDNIGHT MEETING—REV. BAPTIST NOEL SPEAKING	*Frontispiece*
GREEK DANCING GIRL—HETAIRA—AGE OF SOCRATES	*Page* 45
ROMAN BROTHEL—IMPERIAL ERA	47
WOMEN OF THE BOSJES RACE	59
GIRLS OF NUBIA—MAKING POTTERY	65
WOMAN OF THE SACS, OR "SAU-KIES," TRIBE OF AMERICAN INDIANS	85
DYAK WOMEN—BORNEO	103
CHINESE WOMAN—PROSTITUTE	129
SCENE IN THE GARDENS OF 'CLOSERIE DES LILAS'—PARIS	213
A NIGHT HOUSE—KATE HAMILTON'S	217
THE NEW CUT—EVENING	223
THE HAYMARKET—MIDNIGHT	261
BOYS EXERCISING AT TOTHILL FIELDS' PRISON	301
CELL, WITH PRISONER AT CRANK LABOUR IN THE SURREY HOUSE OF CORRECTION	345
FRIENDS VISITING PRISONERS	377
LIBERATION OF PRISONERS FROM COLDBATH FIELDS' HOUSE OF CORRECTION	387

INTRODUCTION.

THE AGENCIES AT PRESENT IN OPERATION WITHIN THE METROPOLIS FOR THE SUPPRESSION OF VICE AND CRIME.

One of the most remarkable and distinctive features of the present age is the universal desire for analytical investigations. Almost every branch of social economy is treated with a precision, and pursued with an accuracy, that pertains to an exact science. Demonstration has been reduced to a mathematical certainty; figures and statistics everywhere abound, and supply data for further research.

Too often, however, it happens that the solution of the social problem, or the collation of facts tending to throw light upon the moral and religious condition of our country, forms the goal, and not the starting point of our labours.

Having accomplished a diligent, and often a laborious, search, and succeeded in eliminating truth from a mass of contradictory evidence, men are generally satisfied with the mere pleasure derived from success. Their knowledge, the hard pursuit of which has called forth immense energy and perseverance, and entrenched largely on their time and capital, is no longer the means to an end, but the end itself. Having gathered a few pebbles from the exhaustless arcana of social philosophy, they complacently enjoy their newly-found treasures, without a thought of the practical uses to which they may be applied.

Other men are found who enter into their labours, and use the materials thus collected as the basis of further philanthropic investigations.

While thus perpetually rising higher in the scale of intelligence, and arriving at closer approximations to truth, men too often neglect to turn their discoveries to any utilitarian or practical purpose, and rest content with merely theoretical results.

Thus it is that while an inductive philosophy is built up from a series of statistics and particulars, very little is being done to reduce this knowledge to practice. The science of investigation is admirable as far as it goes, and the pursuit of truth is at all times an object worthy of human ambition; but it must become the pioneer to tangible results, or its utility will by no means be apparent; and indeed it becomes a question, in an active state of existence, how far knowledge, which is final in its character and valuable merely for its own sake, is calculated to reward the efforts expended on its acquisition. It is true that the old philosophers held a contemplative life to be the highest development of human happiness, but their dreamy and fluctuating views are hardly likely to carry weight in an age of bustling activity; and it is equally certain that the bare, quiescent contemplation of evil in all its endless ramifications and hideous consequences, apart from all remedial efforts, is not likely to prove satisfactory to the philanthropist, nor consolatory to the Christian.

It is only so far as knowledge opens up to us the path of usefulness, and directs us how and where to plant our energies for the benefit of the human race, that it becomes really valuable. If, however, knowledge be power, and if the discovery of an evil be half-way towards its cure, then have we a right to expect that our humanitarian and other appliances for the alleviation of misery and the prevention of crime, should at least keep pace with modern developments of social science

Hitherto men have been content to declaim against these evils, wherever they existed, without suggesting any feasible remedies.

For a length of time our philanthropic schemes have partaken too much of the character of mere surface appliances, directed to the amelioration of existing evils, but in no way likely to effect their extirpation. We have been dealing with effects rather than with first causes, and in our zeal to absorb, divert, or diminish the former, the latter have generally escaped detection. When too late, we have discovered that mere palliatives will not suffice, and that they are powerless to resist the steady growth of crime in all its subtle developments. For, as well might we attempt to exhaust the perennial flow of a spring by the application of sponges, as prescribe external alleviations for our social disorders.

Our homes, penitentiaries, and industrial reformatories will continue to do their work of mercy upon an infinitesimal scale, and will snatch solitary individuals from impending destruction; but in the meantime the reproductive process goes on, and fresh victims are hurried upon the stage of suffering and of guilt, from numberless unforeseen and unsuspected channels, thus causing a continuous succession of want, profligacy, and wretchedness.

We have affected surprise, that, notwithstanding all our benevolent exertions, and the completeness and efficiency of our reclaiming systems, the great tide of our social impurities continues to roll on with increasing velocity. Happily, however, for future generations, there is a manifest tendency in the present age to correct these fatal mistakes, and to return to first principles.

The science of anatomy is not confined to hospitals and dissecting-rooms, nor restricted in its application to the human frame. Social science conferences, and other associations are laying bare the deeply-imbedded roots of our national evils, and are preparing the way for their extirpation. Men are getting tired of planting flowers and training creepers to hide their social upases, and are beginning to discover that it is both sounder policy and truer economy to uproot a noxious weed than to pluck off its poisonous berries.

We have flattered ourselves that education and civilization, with all their humanizing and elevating influences, would gradually permeate all ranks of society; and that the leaven of Christianity would ultimately subdue the power of evil, and convert our outer world into an Elysium of purity and unselfishness. The results, however, of past years have hardly answered these sanguine expectations; and our present experience goes far to prove, that while there has undoubtedly been progress for good, there has been a corresponding progress for evil; for although the criminal statistics of some localities exhibit a sensible diminution in certain forms of vice, we must not forget that an increase of education and a growing intelligence bring with them superior facilities for the successful perpetration and concealment of crime.

All the latest developments of science and skill being pressed into the service of the modern criminal, his evasion of justice must often be regarded less as the result of caution, or of a fortuitous combination of favourable circumstances, than of his knowledge of chemical properties and physical laws. So far indeed from our being able to augur favourably from the infrequency of convictions, the fearful tragedies which are occasionally brought to the surface of society, coupled in many instances with a surprising fertility of resource and ingenuity of method, are indicative of an under current of crime—the depth and foulness of which defy all computation. We may add further, that the immense difficulty of obtaining direct evidence in cases of criminal prosecution, and the *onus probandi* that the law, not unfairly, throws upon the accusers, are sufficient to hush up any cases of mere suspicion; so that at present we possess no adequate data by which to gauge the real dimensions of crime, or to judge respecting its insidious growth and power. It is not, however so much with crime in the abstract, as with the most prolific sources of vice that the philanthropist has to deal; and it is a highly suggestive and encouraging fact that, in these days, men are concerned in investigating the various causes of crime, and in exposing its reflex influence upon society. Just in proportion as they adhere to this course, which is distinguished alike by prudence and sagacity, will they become instrumental in effecting a radical reformation of existing evils, and in restoring society to a more healthy and vigorous condition. " What we want in all such cases is no false rhetoric and no violent outbursts of passion, but clear statements of that vivid truth which contains the intrinsic elements o reformation amongst mankind. The true philanthropist is the man whose judgment is on a par with his feelings, and who recognizes the fact that there is some particle of meaning in every particle of suffering around us.

"Some of this wretchedness is remediable, the result of actual causes which may be altered, though much is beyond human control. In an age like this, however we may toil to overtake the urgent need of our own time, the difficulty is, at the same time, calmly and deliberately to satisfy the fresh wants which may daily arise —keeping pace with them. With the heavy defalcations from past years weighing upon them, our statesmen and economists are often bewildered at the magnitude of their engagements; while the best and wisest amongst us are crushed and appalled by the new and giant evils which are continually being brought to light. Earnest thought, however, is the true incentive to action,"* and we would thankfully recognize as one visible result of the increasing attention given to matters of public interest, a growing disposition on the part of all who are qualified by position and authority, to grapple manfully with the various phases of wretchedness and crime now contributing their influence upon our social condition.

Nowhere are these hopeful indications more manifest than in this giant metropolis, where the various conditions of ordinary life seem to be intensified by their direct contact with good and evil; and where Christianity appears to be struggling to maintain its independent and aggressive character, amid much that is calculated to retard its progress and check its influence.

It is here, within the crowded areas and noisome purlieus of this greatest of great cities, that we may gather lessons of life to be gained nowhere else—and of which those can form a very inadequate conception, who dwell only in an atmosphere of honied flowers and rural pleasures.

It is here especially that the sorrows and sufferings of humanity have evoked an active and pervasive spirit of benevolence, which has infected all ranks and penetrated every class of society; so that the high born and the educated, the gentle and the refined, vie with each other in a restless energy to alleviate human misery and to assuage some of the groans of creation. This disposition to relieve distress in every shape, and to mitigate the ills of a common brotherhood, proclaims at once its divine origin, and is, in fact, the nearest assimilation to the character of Him who "went about doing good."

The germ of this heaven-born principle has survived the fall; and though its highest development is one of the distinguishing marks of the true Christian, its existence is discernible in all who have not sinned away the last faint outlines o1 the Divine image.

Some philosophers, indeed, would persuade us that there is no such thing in existence as a principle of pure, unmixed benevolence; that every exercise of charity is simply another mode of self-gratification, and every generous impulse a mere exhibition of selfishness.

Undoubtedly there is a "luxury in doing good," and the ability to contribute to the happiness of others is one of the purest sources of human gratification; but we question whether an act, resulting from mere self-love, is capable of yielding any solid satisfaction to the agent; and we therefore hold the existence of

* *Meliora*, No. viii., p. 317.

genuine benevolence, believing that it is a principle innate in the human breast, and requiring only to be developed and consecrated by religious influence to become one of the most powerful levers for the evangelization of the world.

Unhappily there are too many who have schooled themselves to the practice of inhumanity, and closed up the springs of spontaneous sympathy, thus depriving the heart of its rightful heritage, and restricting the sphere of its operations to self. Those who thus sever themselves from all external influences are left at length in undisturbed possession of a little world of their own creation. No longer linked to their fellow-men in the bonds of true fellowship, their orbit of activity becomes narrower, until at length every avenue to the heart is hermetically sealed, except such as minister to self-gratification and indulgence. The man who has thus estranged himself from the rest of creation, and become isolated from all the ties of a common humanity, is indeed an object of unqualified pity, because he has destroyed one of the purest springs of happiness.

He who, on the other hand, is most fully alive to the claims of universal brotherhood, and whose heart is most

> " At leisure from itself,
> To soothe and sympathize,"

is the highest type of man, and the best representative of his race. This spirit of brotherhood if recognised by the world, would " hush the thunder of battle, and wipe away the tears of nations. It would sweep earth's wildernesses of moral blight, causing them to blossom as the rose."

Those persons who accustom themselves to speak of London as a mere seething caldron of crime, or as a very charnel-house of impurity, without any redeeming character or hopeful element, are surely as wide of the mark as they who under-rate its vast resources for crime, or take a superficial view of its predominant vices.

It would, perhaps, be a curious and not unprofitable subject of inquiry how far the metropolis contributes its influence for good or evil upon the provinces, and to what extent the country is capable of reciprocating this influence. Probably, allowance being made for the difference of population, the law of giving and receiving is pretty evenly adjusted. Those forms of vice which seem to be more indigenous to our great cities are steadily imported into the country, while on the other hand, the hamlet and the village transmit to the town those particular vices in which they appear to be constitutionally most prolific.

It is in the crowded city, however, that the seeds of good or evil are brought to the highest state of maturity, and virtue and vice most rapidly developed, under the forcing influences that everywhere abound.

" Great cities," says Dr. Guthrie, " many have found to be great curses. It had been well for many an honest lad and unsuspecting country girl, that hopes of higher wages and opportunities of fortune—that the gay attire and polished tongue, and gilded story of some old acquaintance—had never turned their steps cityward, nor turned them from the rude simplicity, but safety of their rustic home. Many a foot that once lightly pressed the heather or brushed the dewy grass, has wearily trodden in darkness, and guilt, and remorse, on these city pavements. Happy had it been for many that they had never exchanged the starry skies for the lamps of the town, nor had left their lonely glens, or quiet hamlets, or solitary shores, for the throng and roar of our streets. Well for them that they had heard no roar but the rivers, whose winter flood it had been safer to breast; no roar but oceans, whose stormiest waves it had been safer to ride, than encounter the flood of city temptations, which has wrecked their virtue and swept them into ruin.

" Yet I bless God for cities. The world had not been what it is without them.

The disciples were commanded to 'begin at Jerusalem,' and Paul threw himself into the cities of the ancient world, as offering the most commanding positions of influence. Cities have been as lamps of light along the pathway of humanity and religion. Within them science has given birth to her noblest discoveries Behind their walls freedom has fought her noblest battles. They have stood on the surface of the earth like great breakwaters, rolling back or turning aside the swelling tide of oppression. Cities, indeed, have been the cradles of human liberty. They have been the radiating, active centres of almost all church and state reformation. The highest humanity has been developed in cities. Somehow or other, amid their crowding and confinement, the human mind finds its fullest freest expansion. Unlike the dwarfed and dusty plants which stand in our city gardens, languishing like exiles for the purer air and freer sunshine, that kiss their fellows far away in flowery fields and green woodland, on sunny banks and breezy hills, man reaches his highest condition amid the social influences of the crowded city. His intellect receives its brightest polish, where gold and silver lose theirs, tarnished by the scorching smoke and foul vapours of city air. The mental powers acquire their full robustness, where the cheek loses its ruddy hue, and the limbs their elastic step, and pale thought sits on manly brows, and as aërolites— those shooting stars which, like a good man on his path in life, leave a train of glory behind them on the dusky sky—are supposed to catch fire by the rapidity of their motion, as they rush through the higher regions of our atmosphere, so the mind of man fires, burns, shines, acquires its most dazzling brilliancy, by the very rapidity of action into which it is thrown amid the bustle and excitements of city life. And if, just as in those countries where tropical suns, and the same skies, ripen the sweetest fruit and the deadliest poisons—you find in the city the most daring and active wickedness, you find there also, boldly confronting it, the most active, diligent, warm-hearted, self-denying and devoted Christians." *

London then may be considered as the grand central focus of operations, at once the emporium of crime and the palladium of Christianity. It is, in fact the great arena of conflict between the powers of darkness and the ministry of heaven. Here, within the area of our metropolis, the real struggle is maintained between the two antagonistic principles of good and evil. It is here that they join issue in the most deadly proximity, and struggle for the vantage-ground.

Here legions of crime and legions of vices unite and form an almost impenetrable phalanx, while the strong man armed enjoys his goods in peace—no, not in peace, for here too the banner of the cross is most firmly planted, and Christianity wins its freshest laurels. Here is the stronghold, the occupation of which by the everlasting gospel, has given vigour, support, and consistency to the religion of the world. Here is concentrated that fervent and apostolic piety that has made itself felt to the remotest corner of the earth; and here is the nucleus of missionary enterprise, and the radiating centre of active benevolence.

"The Christian power that has moved a sluggish world on, the Christian benevolence and energy that have changed the face of society, the Christian zeal that has gone forth, burning to win nations and kingdoms for Jesus," have received their birth or development in London.

Since, then, this busy mart of the world, in which the most opposite and dissimilar wares are exhibited, is made up of such composite materials and conflicting elements, it is only fair that while estimating its capabilities for crime, and endeavouring to plumb its depths of depravity, ignorance, and suffering, we should, when possible, faithfully depict their opposites, and take cognizance of such instrumentalities as present the best antidotes and alleviations.

It is questionable, indeed, how far the cause of religion and morality would be

* *The City, its Sins and its Sorrows*, p. 8.

promoted by a ghastly array of facts, representing the dimensions of crime in all its naked deformity, or by any exhibition, however truthful, of vice and wretchedness under their most repulsive aspects, and without any cheering reference to corrective and remedial agencies. The effect produced upon the mind, in such a case, would be, in the generality of instances, blank despair; and the only influence thus excited would partake strongly of that morbid sympathy and unhealthy excitement, awakened by delineations of fictitious distress.

To unravel the dark catalogue of London profligacy, and present to the eye of the reader the wearisome expanse of guilt and suffering, unrelieved by any indications of improvement, would be like exhibiting the convulsive death-agony of a drowning man without the friendly succour of a rope, or like conjuring up the horrors of a shipwreck without the mental relief afforded by a life-boat.

We need the day star of hope to guide us through the impenetrable gloom of moral darkness. The olive branch of mercy and the rainbow of promise are as needful tokens of social and religious improvement, as of abated judgments and returning favour.

After being required to give attention to figures and statistics representing crime in the aggregate, the mental eye requires alleviation from the gross darkness it has encountered, and looks impatiently for some streak of light in the moral horizon, indicative of approaching day. To view London crime and misery, without their encouraging counterparts, would be like groping our way through the blackness of midnight, unrelieved by the faintest glimmer of light.

Just, however, as stars shine brightest in the darkest nights, so may we discover some element of hope under the most appalling exhibitions of human depravity, which thus serve as a background to portray in bolder relief, and by force of contrast, the redeeming qualities of Christianity.

As a work of absorbing interest and utility to the British philanthropist, Mr. Mayhew's wonderful book, "London Labour and London Poor," stands probably unrivalled. The mass of evidence and detail, accumulated after the most careful and indefatigable research, and the personal interest which is sustained throughout, by the relation of facts and occurrences, gleaned from the author's own private observation, or in which he took an active share, render his work both invaluable to the legislator and acceptable to the general reader.

While, however, the former will refer to it as a book of reference, the latter would probably rise from its perusal, with a sickening apprehension of London depravity, and unless fortified by a previous knowledge of counteracting agencies would probably form a too lugubrious and desponding view of its social aspects. As any such impression, derived from *ex-parte* statements, would be highly detrimental to the cause of truth and religious progress, and might contribute to the relaxation of individual effort, the publishers have naturally hesitated to allow one of the most startling and vivid records of crime to go forth to the world, without directing attention to the most approved and popular agencies, for the correction of such abuses, as have been faithfully delineated in the course of the work.

The following brief summary of charitable and religious organizations, having for their object the repression of crime and the diffusion of vital Christianity, is intended therefore to form a supplement, or prefatory essay, to the fourth and concluding volume of *London Labour and London Poor*.

It would be impossible, within the narrow limits that have been assigned to this essay, to do more than touch in a cursory and incidental manner upon some of the principal agencies now at work within the metropolis, for the suppression of vice and crime; the object being not so much to exhibit the results which have rewarded such instrumentalities, great and incalculable as they are, as to indicate the best channels of usefulness, towards which public attention should be constantly directed; not to foster pride and self-complacency by tracing the progress we have already made, in the race of Christian philanthropy, but rather to show how we may, by rendering efficient support to existing organizations, advance still further towards the goal, and rise to higher degrees of service in that ministry of love, which aims at nothing less than the regeneration of society, and the restoration of its unhappy prodigals to a condition of present and eternal peace.

What we want is not so much the elaboration of new schemes and the introduction of untried agencies, as a more unanimous and hearty co-operation in sustaining such as are at present in existence, many of which though fully deserving of a large measure of confidence and support, are grown effete solely from want of funds to maintain them in efficiency.

It has been truthfully remarked that there is hardly a woe or a misery to which men are liable, whether resulting from accidental causes or from personal culpability, which has not been assuaged or mitigated by benevolent exertions. Experience indeed would go far to prove that there are everywhere around us two mighty conflicting elements at work, each having no other object than to pull down and destroy the other. Every vice has its corresponding virtue, every form of evil its counteracting influence for good, every Mount Ebal, its Gerizim; the one being designed to act as an antidote or corrective to the other, and to restore the type of heaven which the other has defaced. The highest glory of our land—a glory far removed from territorial acquisitions and national aggrandisement, and that which makes it pre-eminently the admiration and envy of all other countries— are its benevolent and charitable endowments. There is not another nation in the world, where eleemosynary institutions have obtained such a permanent hold upon the sympathies of all classes of society, nor where such vast sums are realized by voluntary and private contributions.

"Palatial buildings, hospitals, reformatories, asylums, penitentiaries, homes and refuges, there are, for the sick, the maimed, the blind, the crippled, the aged, the infirm, the deaf, the dumb, the hungry, the naked, the fallen and the destitute; and it is to the support of such institutions, and the works which they carry on, that the nobles of the land, and our prosperous merchants devote a large proportion of their wealth." No less than 530 charitable societies exist in London alone, and nearly £2,000,000 of money is annually spent by them, while probably the amount of alms bestowed altogether is not less than £3,500,000.*

How far these resources, vast and extended as they really are, are capable of satisfying present demands, may be best inferred from the state of our criminal population, which is still to be counted by tens of thousands, even while our prisons, refuges, and reformatories are filled to overflowing.

"In spite," says the author just quoted, "of our prison discipline, our classification system, our silent system, and our separate system, all these efforts that we make, and perhaps boast that we make, to turn back the law-breaker to honest paths, nearly 30,000 criminals are each year sent to prison, who only know the higher classes as objects of plunder, and the maintenances of law and order as things; if possible to be destroyed, and if not avoided." £170,000 are annually expended in London for the reformation of such offenders, and every modern appliance that mercy or ingenuity can devise is brought to bear upon our prison system, with what results may be clearly ascertained by the large and increasing number of re-commitments—which form a proportion of something like 30 per cent. on such as have been previously incarcerated; while these, be it remembered, represent only the number of those who render themselves amenable to justice by detection; there being no means of ascertaining how many continue their avocations with impunity.

Results like these are sufficiently disheartening to the philanthropist, and em-

* Any person wishing for further information respecting these Societies, may obtain it from a work published by Messrs. Low and Son, entitled "London Charities."

barrassing to the statesman, and serve to show that however necessary it may be to devise methods for criminal reformation, it is even more incumbent upon us, and far more remunerative in the end, to carry out the principles of prevention.

The various agencies, at work in London, for the suppression of vice and crime, may be treated under the following heads, which will serve to indicate their relative value and proportionate influence; and though, in their popular sense, many of the words used, may appear to be only convertible terms, it is intended, for the sake of perspicuity and arrangement, to assign to each a distinctive and separate meaning.

Thus the word *curative* is used, not in its loose, remedial sense, as applying to expedients calculated to produce a diminution of crime, but must be understood as tending to the entire and absolute change of the human will, and the renovation of a corrupt nature—such a thorough change, in fact, as is implied in the word *cure*.

Agencies for the suppression of vice and crime.
1. Curative (radical).
2. Preventive (obstructive).
3. Repressive and punitive (compulsory).
4. Reformative (remedial).

1. *Curative Agencies.*

Under this head *religion* naturally occupies the foremost place; since, by its restraining influence and converting power, it presents the only true antidote, and the only safe barrier to the existence or progress of crime; all other specifics, however valuable, being liable to the imputation of failure, and their influence being either more or less efficacious, according to the various phases of moral disease exhibited by different mental and physical constitutions.

While applying political expedients for the cure of such disorders, it must ever be borne in mind, that the origin of all evil is to be found in the corruption of the human heart, and in its entire alienation from God; and it is only so far as these intrinsic defects can be remedied, that any permanent influence will be produced. That power, therefore, which seizes upon the citadel of the heart, controlling its affections, regulating its principles of action, and subduing its vicious propensities or illicit motions, is the only sovereign remedy for crime. In its natural state the heart may be compared to a fountain discharging only turbid and bitter waters; but while various agencies are employed to sweeten, disguise, or check this poisoned current, religion is the only influence which purifies the fountain head, and dries up the noxious springs, by placing a wholesome check upon the first motive principles of action—the thoughts.

The truth of these remarks is even more strikingly exemplified in the sudden and complete transformations of character, effected by the all-mighty influence of religion. The moral demoniac finds no difficulty in bursting the chains and fetters, in which society has attempted to bind him. He is never changed, only curbed, pacified, or restrained by such artificial modes of treatment. The wound may be cauterised, cicatrised, or mollified, but the poison, if left in the system, is sure to rankle and exhibit itself afresh. Religion, however, casts out the unclean spirit, restores human nature to its right mind, and asserts the supremacy of reason over that of passion and caprice.

Next in value and importance to religion itself, are those subordinate instrumentalities calculated to exhibit or extend its influence, and which bear the same relation to it as the means do to the end. Such are the various agencies, in that divinely-appointed machinery for the regeneration of mankind, the universal spread of "truth and justice, religion and piety" throughout the world, and for the formation and support of the spiritual Church of Christ.

The most powerful and efficacious of all levers for the social, moral, and spiritual elevation of mankind is the *Word of God*. Into whatever quarters of the habitable globe the sacred volume is diffused, there is a corresponding spread of civilisation, and a sensible improvement in the scale of humanity; and those countries are most socially, morally, and politically debased, in which its circulation is debarred or restricted.

Here it is only right to mention those societies which are directly concerned in diffusing the Scriptures.

The British and Foreign Bible Society is one of the most honoured and influential channels for promoting the circulation of the Word of God, "without note or comment." It dates its origin from 1804, and since this period it has, either directly or indirectly, been instrumental in translating the Scriptures into 160 different languages or dialects, including 190 separate versions. Connected with this Society, there are in the United Kingdom 3728 auxiliary branches or associations.

The number of issues from London alone, during the last financial year, amount to 594,651 copies of the Old Testament, and 544,901 copies of the New Testament. The grants made during the same time amounted to £58,551 17s. 7d. The total receipts of the Society derived from subscriptions, and from the sale of publications, amounted last year to £206,778 12s. 6d.

Next to the Bible Society, the *Society for Promoting Christian Knowledge* is most directly concerned in the propagation of the Scriptures. It was founded in 1698. During the past year 157,358 Bibles, and 78,234 New Testaments have been issued, besides prayer-books, tracts, and other publications. In addition to the dissemination of religious works, its objects include the extension of the Episcopate in the colonies, by contributing to the erection of new sees, and the support of colleges and educational institutions. The receipts for the past year amounted to £31,697 19s. 7d. besides £81,516 6s. 8d. received for the sale of publications.

In addition to these larger instrumentalities for the circulation of the Scriptures, it has been reserved for modern zeal and piety to discover a "missing link" in the operations hitherto in use, and this void has been admirably supplied by the "Bible women" of the nineteenth century. The appointment of these female colporteurs has been attended with the most beneficial and encouraging results, for not only has the sale of Bibles been facilitated among classes almost inaccessible to such influences, but opportunities have been afforded of permanently benefiting some of the most wretched and morally debased of our population. The introductions, gained by means of this traffic, have been turned to the best account, and a kindly influence has been established over the families thus visited, which has been often attended with the most favourable results.

"The lowest strata of society are thus reached by an agency which takes the Bible as the starting point of its labours, and makes IT the basis of all the social and religious improvements which are subsequently attempted. Small in its beginnings, the work, by its proved adaptation and results, has greatly enlarged its dimensions, enlisting the sympathy and liberality of the Christian public; and in almost all the metropolitan districts affording scope for the agency, the Bible women are to be found prosecuting their arduous labours, with immense advantage to the poor. At the present time there are 152 of these agents employed. During the past year the Bible women in London disposed of many thousand copies of the Scriptures amongst classes, which, to a very great extent, were beyond the reach of the ordinary means used to effect this work; and this circulation was attained not by the easy method of gift, but by sale, the very poorest of the population being willing, when brought under kind and persuasive influence, to pay for the Bible or Testament by small weekly instalments."

Another kindred agency of recent appointment is the "*Institution for reading aloud the Word of God in the open air*," in connection with which are the "*Bible*

Carriages," or locomotive depôts, now employed for extending the sale of the Scriptures in various parts of London, and which have succeeded in drawing a large number of purchasers, attracted, no doubt, by the novelty and singularity of the means adopted.

While enumerating the religious agencies concerned in the repression of crime in London, allusion need only be made incidentally to such as necessarily spring out of an organized, ecclesiastical, or parochial machinery consisting of clergy, churches, chapels, schools, &c., and to the various societies and associations designed to extend and give support to this machinery; the object of this essay being rather to draw public attention to such auxiliary and supplemental organisations, as are less generally known, or are of more recent origin.

One of the most remarkable movements of modern times in connection with preaching, has been the establishment of *Theatre services*, which owe their existence to the present Earl of Shaftesbury. So irregular and unconstitutional a proceeding provoked, as might naturally have been expected, a large amount of censure and unfriendly criticism. Ecclesiastical dignities were at first somewhat scandalized by such an innovation of church discipline, and evidently regarded the movement as one calling rather for reluctant toleration, than as being entitled to episcopal sanction—a feeling which was probably largely shared by the more sober and orthodox portion of the community.

There appeared to be, at first sight, it must be confessed, a singular incongruity, if not an absolute impropriety, in converting the stage of a playhouse into a temple for the provisional celebration of divine worship, and using an edifice habitually consecrated to amusement, for the alternate promulgation of sacred verities and pantomimic representations. Apart, however, from the repulsive features of the proceeding arising from local associations, and from the periodical juxtaposition of objects the most hostile and dissimilar, there appeared to be no graver objection to the arrangement. The end was here, at least, supposed not only to justify, but even to sanctify the means, and the defence of this mal-appropriation was not unfairly said to consist in the inadequacy of church accommodation, and in the cheap facilities thus afforded, for bringing under the occasional ministry of the word of life, classes, who from long habits of neglect, prejudice, and an utter disrelish of religious ordinances, had become isolated from the ordinary channels of instruction and improvement. The movement having now had a fair trial, and the results being found to answer the expectations of the originators, it may be regarded as no longer a hazardous experiment, but as a part of the recognised machinery employed for the evangelisation of the masses.

These special services for the working classes are now regularly conducted in the various theatres and buildings temporarily appropriated to divine worship. The attendance has been uniformly good, and that of a class who habitually absent themselves from religious ordinances, and could not therefore be reached by any of the usual instrumentalities. Considering the unpromising materials of which these singular congregations are composed, and the unfavourable antecedents of most of the audience, it is something to be able to state that on such occasions they are, for the most part, orderly and well conducted, while the continued good attendance at these services marks the appreciation in which they are held. During the Sabbath, then, at least, a wonderful outward transformation is effected in the pursuits and general demeanor of the frequenters, who meet together, week after week, to hear the Gospel message expounded in the very edifice, which during the previous six days has resounded with their oaths, ribaldries, and licentious language. Is there not room for at least a charitable hope, that when the heralds of salvation carry their proclamations into the very heart of the enemy's territory, and aggressively plant the banner of the cross, where only the cloven foot is wont to be seen, some victories will be achieved over the world, the flesh, and the devil and that some who usually meet to scoff and jeer, will return home savingly impressed with what they have heard?

In strict conformity with the objects contemplated by this arrangement, and arising out of the same temporary necessity, is *The Open-Air Mission*, which was established in 1853 "for the purpose of stirring up the Church of Christ, especially the lay elements, to go out into the streets and lanes of the city, the towns and villages of the provinces, the great gatherings that periodically occur at races, fairs, executions, &c.; to go into lodging-houses, workhouses, and hospitals, and in fact wherever persons are to be met with and spoken to about sin and salvation." Since the formation of the Society, open-air preaching has become as it were a standing institution, and is recognized as an indispensable agency in working densely-populated districts. Ministers and laymen are to be found on every hand using this divinely-appointed and apostolic agency to "bring in the poor, the maimed, the halt, and the blind," and God has eminently blessed their labours.

From May 1st, 1860, to March 31st, 1861, the London City Missionaries conducted 4,489 outdoor meetings, at which the average attendance was 103, and the gross attendance 465,070. Numerous associations have been formed in connection with this Society for Open-Air Preaching, in various parts of London, and during the summer, eighteen stations are occupied for this purpose by the students at the Church Missionary College, under the direction of the Islington Church Home Mission. A course of Sunday afternoon services is also regularly held by the appointment of the rector in Covent Garden Market, which are generally well attended and appear admirably calculated to benefit the classes whose welfare is designed. The Bishop of London and other dignities of the Church have been the preachers on such occasions, and have thus lent their countenance to the proceeding.

In reference to all such agencies as open-air services, prayer meetings, tract distributions, Bible readings, &c., it may be safely asserted, that never in the entire history of the Church was there a period, when such extraordinary efforts have been made to evangelise the poor and the criminal population of London; or when a similar activity has been displayed in ministering to the social and spiritual wants of the community.

One of the oldest and most privileged institutions within the metropolis, for bringing the influences of religion to bear upon the dense masses of our population is the *London City Mission*. It was founded in 1835, and its growth has steadily progressed up to the present date. The object of the mission is to "extend the knowledge of the Gospel, among the inhabitants of London and its vicinity (especially the poor), without any reference to denominational distinctions, or the peculiarities of Church government. To effect this object, missionaries of approved character and qualifications are employed, whose duty it is to visit from house to house in the respective districts assigned to them, to read the Scriptures, engage in religious conversation, and urge those who are living in the neglect of religion to observe the Sabbath and attend public worship. They are also required to see that all persons possess the Scriptures, to distribute approved religious tracts, and to aid in obtaining Scriptural education for the children of the poor. By the approval of the committee they also hold meetings for reading and expounding the Scriptures and prayer, and adopt such other means as are deemed necessary for the accomplishment of the mission."

The London City Mission maintains a staff of 389 missionaries, who are employed in the various London and suburban districts; and thus the entire city is more or less compassed by this effective machinery, and brought under the saving influences of the Gospel. The very silent and unobtrusive character of the work thus effected, precludes anything like an accurate estimate of results, or a showy parade of success.

It works secretly, quietly, and savingly, in districts too vast to admit of pastoral supervision, and in neighbourhoods too outwardly unattractive and unpropitious, to win the attention of any who are not animated with a devoted love of souls. The influence which is thus exerted in a social and religious point of view is inestimable, and the benefits conferred by this mission, are of an order that would be best understood and appreciated by the community, if they were for a time to be suddenly withdrawn.

In addition to the regular visitation of the poor, the missionaries are employed in conducting religious services in some of the "worst spots that can be found in the metropolis, and the audiences have been, in such cases, ordinarily the most vicious and debased classes of the population."

Six missionaries are appointed, whose exclusive duty it is to visit the various public-houses and coffee-shops in London, and to converse with the *habitués* on subjects of vital importance. There are also three missionaries to the London cabmen, a class greatly needing their religious offices, and by their occupation almost excluded from any social or elevating influences.

The following summary of missionary work, and its results for 1861, is sufficiently encouraging, as pointing in some instances, at least, to a sensible diminution of crime, and as being suggestive of a vast amount of good effected by this pervasive evangelistic machinery.

Number of Missionaries employed	381
Visits paid	1,815,332
Of which to the sick and dying	237,599
Scriptures distributed	11,458
Religious Tracts given away	2,721,73
Books lent	54,00
In-door Meetings and Bible Classes held	41,777
Gross attendance at ditto	1,467,006
Out-door Services held	4,489
Gross attendance at ditto	465,070
Readings of Scripture in visitation	584,166
Communicants	1,535
Families induced to commence family prayer	681
Drunkards reclaimed	1,230
Unmarried couples induced to marry	361
Fallen females rescued or reclaimed	681
Shops closed on the Sabbath	212
Children sent to school	10,158
Adults who died having been visited by the Missionary *only*	1,796

The income of the London City Mission, during the past year, amounted to 35,018*l*. 6*s*. 10*d*.; 5,763*l*. 15*s*. 7*d*. having been contributed by country associations.

Next to the London City Mission, the *Church of England Scripture Readers' Society* is one of the most extensive and important channels for disseminating a religious influence among the masses by means of a parochial lay agency.

It is the special duty of the Scripture readers to visit from house to house; to read the Scriptures to all with whom they come in contact; to grapple with vice and crime *where they abound;* and to shrink from no effort to arrest their career.

"To overtake and overlook the growing multitudes which crowd our large and densely-peopled parishes," was a work universally admitted to be beyond the present limits of clerical effort; and this *desideratum* has been supplied, at least to some extent, by the appointment of a lay agency, acting under the direction and control of the parochial clergy. By this means "cases are brought to light and doors opened to the pastoral visit, which were either closed against it or not discovered before; and an amount of information concerning the religious condition of the parish is obtained, such as the minister, single-handed, or with the aid of a curate, never had before." The following results, which are reported as having attended the labours of a single Scripture reader, during a period of fourteen years, will serve as an illustration of the nature of those services rendered by this instrumentality:—

Visits paid to the poor	23,986
Infants and adults baptized on his recommendation	3,510
Children and adults persuaded to attend school	2,411
Persons led to attend church for the first time	307
Persons confirmed during visitation	429
Communicants obtained by ditto	269
Persons living in sin induced to marry	48

One hundred and twenty-five grants are now made by the Society for the maintenance of Scripture readers in eighty-seven parishes and districts in the metropolis, embracing a population of upwards of a million.

The Society's income for the past year amounted to 9,850l 2s. 10d.

Second only in importance to personal evangelistic effort is the influence of a *Religious Press*. Public opinion being often fluctuating, and its general estimates of morality being, to a considerable extent, formed by the current literature of the age, it is essential that this mighty and controlling power should be exerted on the side of religion and virtue.

Works of a high moral tone, inculcating correct principles and instilling lessons of practical piety, conduce, therefore, in the highest degree, to a wholesome state of society, and to the preservation of public morals.

The two great emporiums of religious literature, most directly concerned in producing these results, are the *Religious Tract Society* and the *Society for the Promotion of Christian Knowledge*. The latter has already been referred to, as one of the main channels for the diffusion of the Scriptures.

None of the works issued by the *Religious Tract Society* can compete in point of interest or usefulness with those widely-circulated and deservedly-popular serials the Leisure Hour, the Sunday at Home, and the Cottager, a periodical lately published, and admirably adapted for the homes of the working classes.

The publications issued by the Society during the past year amounted to 41,883,921; half of which number were English tracts and handbills; 537,729 were foreign tracts; and 13,194,155 fall under the head of periodicals.

The entire number of both English and foreign publications issued by the Society, since its foundation in 1799, amount to 912,000,000.

Grants of books and tracts are annually made by the Society for schools and village libraries, prisons, workhouses, and hospitals, for the use of soldiers, sailors, emigrants, and for circulation at fairs and races, by city missionaries and colporteurs.

The total number of such grants during the past year amounted to 5,762,241; and were of the value of £6,116 14s. 4d.

The entire receipts of the Society from all sources for the past year amounted to £103,127 16s. 11d.; the benevolent contributions being £9,642 9s. 2d.

Other channels for the supply and extension of religious literature are the *Weekly Tract Society*, the *English Monthly Tract Society*, and the *Book Society*, which latter aims especially at promoting religious knowledge among the poor.

As a supplemental agency for the collection and dissemination of a wholesome literature, the *Pure Literature Society*, established 1854, is deserving of especial commendatory notice.

The following is a list of the periodicals recommended by the Society; and the circulation of which it seeks to facilitate:—

For Adults:—Leisure Hour, British Workman, Good Words, Old Jonathan, Youth's Magazine, Appeal, Bible-Class Magazine, Christian Treasury, Churchman's Penny Magazine, Evening Hour, Family Treasury, Family Paper, Friendly Visitor, Mother's Friend, Servant's Magazine, Sunday at Home, The Cottager, Tract Magazine.

For Children:—Young England, Band of Hope Review, Child's Own Magazine, Child's Companion, Child's Paper, Children's Friend, Children's Paper, Our Children's Magazine, Sabbath School Messenger, Sunday Scholar's Companion.

Upwards of 140,000 periodicals are sent out annually by the Society in monthly parcels.

The Society's income during the past year amounted to £2,783 12s. 2d.

2. *Preventive Agencies.*

Under this division are not included those measures which have for their object the forcible suppression of crime, which will be considered under a separate head, nor yet such as are calculated to extinguish those criminal propensities, which are ever lying dormant in the human heart, for these, as has been already shown, can only be effectually subdued, or eradicated by the influences of religion. By preventive agencies are rather to be understood, those instrumentalities best adapted to effect the removal of peculiar forms of temptation, or to abridge the power of special producing causes of vice; whatever means, in fact, are efficacious in removing hindrances to the development of virtue, and in fostering principles of morality. Human nature, owing to the force of adverse circumstances, being often placed at a disadvantage, it is the peculiar province of preventive agencies to give it a fair chance of escape, by extricating it from its perilous position, and surrounding it with virtuous influences and humanizing appliances. Under this head, moreover, are included all such measures as conduce to the social and moral improvement of the community, either by presenting an indirect barrier to the progress of crime, or by the employment of counteracting agencies.

In this connexion the *Temperance Associations* are deserving of especial prominence. Drunkenness being the most fruitful source of all crime, and the primary cause of want and wretchedness, it follows that whatever instrumentalities are capable of arresting its progress, or curtailing its influence, are in every way worthy the consideration of the philanthropist and the statesman. The utility of temperance societies has often been called in question; but it must be admitted, that as an instrumental agency for the suppression of drunkenness, and consequently for the diminution of crime, the influence of such associations is unlimited. Whether or not the entire-abstinence system is based on philosophical arguments, or is deducible from Scripture teaching, is little to the point, provided the fruits it has yielded are unquestionably salutary in their effects upon society, and conducive to the present and eternal happiness of millions of individuals, who, but for this timely interference would have continued in their mad career of dissipation, without the power to break off the thraldom, or to dispel the infatuation in which they were held.

The National Temperance Society, formed in 1842, is now in active operation, and seeks by means of meetings, lectures, and publications, to disseminate its principles, and to draw attention to the objects it is endeavouring to promote.

The United Kingdom Alliance, for the legislative suppression of the liquor traffic, is a step in advance of the ordinary temperance movement, and aims at nothing short of the entire extinction of a commerce in intoxicating drinks. This body has already secured a large number of influential adherents, and appears to be rapidly gaining ground. A monster meeting has lately been held in Manchester in furtherance of the Society's proximate aims, which are to introduce a permissive Bill into Parliament, to delegate to local authorities the power to prohibit such traffic within their respective neighbourhoods.

The passing of this Act will in effect resolve the question of abolition or toleration into one of public opinion; and districts, if so inclined, will possess the power of deciding whether or no the sale of intoxicating drinks shall be carried on within their own parochial boundaries.

As a counteracting agency to the beer-shop and the gin-palace, *The Metropolitan Free Drinking Fountain Association,* formed two years ago, is deserving of special notice. It has for its objects the erection and maintenance of drinking fountains in the various crowded thoroughfares of the metropolis, thus humanely furnishing the means of alleviating that feverish thirst, which during the hot season impels so many to an excessive use of intoxicating drinks.

The Ragged Schools hold a prominent place among the indirectly preventive agencies for the suppression of crime in the metropolis; for since ignorance is generally the parent of vice, any means of securing the benefits of education to those who are hopelessly deprived of it, must operate in favour of the well being of society.

The Ragged School Union has been formed with a view to develope and give consistency to this movement, which it does by collecting and diffusing information respecting schools now in existence, and by pecuniary grants towards their foundation and support.

The number of buildings now in existence in London, appropriated to these educational purposes, is 176. The day-schools are 151 in number, and are attended by 17,230 scholars. The evening-schools number 215, and the scholars 9,840; Sunday-schools 207, and scholars 25,260. The number of scholars placed in situations last year amounted to 1,800.

Penny Banks, Clothing Clubs, Reading Rooms, Mother's Meetings, and Shoe-Black Brigades have been established in connexion with this movement, and contribute their influence to the general well-being of those attending the schools, as well as to that of society at large.

In connexion with the Union are 16 refuges for the homeless and destitute, accommodating 700 inmates.

The receipts of the Union amounted last year to £5,739 7s. 8d.; and probably no money was ever laid out at better interest, than that contributed by the benevolent public towards the rescue and moral training of these embryo criminals. Difficult as the principle of Government intervention no doubt is, that would be a wise, politic, humane, and economical course which should sever this Gordian knot, by constituting the State the lawful guardian of such as are deprived of all that is understood by the terms home influence, and moral training.

Another agency contributing largely to the prevention of crime is *the Society for Improving the Condition of the Labouring Classes,* not so much, however, in the transformations and improvement of buildings effected under its own immediate control, which are rather designed to serve as models to those desirous of carrying out these principles of reform, as by drawing public attention to one of the most interesting and painful subjects that can occupy the mind of the philanthropist, viz., the inadequate provision of decent, and proper house accommodation for the industrial classes, which is now universally admitted to be productive of the worst social disorders.

The important provisions of the Common Lodging-Houses Act, passed in 1851 under the auspices of Lord Shaftesbury, and the system of registration thus enforced, have also been attended with great benefits, and have conduced not a little to the promotion of social and sanatory reform, by bringing legal enactments to bear upon the disorders, indecencies, and impurities of low and crowded lodging-houses.

There is no class of preventive agencies in the metropolis, which on every principle of justice and humanity have stronger claims on the sympathy of the benevolent than such as interpose their friendly shelter and kind offices, to **rescue** those who are suddenly reduced to positions of great extremity and temptation. It is doubtless an act of mercy to rescue a drowning man, and such charitable deeds are performed by those who labour for the reformation of the criminal; but it is a higher act of charity, and a wiser and more Christian course to prevent his falling into the stream; experience, however, proves that it is easier to enlist sympathy on behalf of one who is already being swept away by the current of crime, than to rescue one who is bordering on destruction, and perhaps bravely battling with temptation. This is perhaps only natural; our perception of danger in the one case is far greater than in the other, and our commiseration is awakened at sight of the death agony of the drowning wretch, but is hardly stirred on behalf of him who walks on the slippery brink.*

It is unhappily a fact too well authenticated to need further demonstration, that owing perhaps to sudden reverses of fortune, to the removal of natural protectors, or to the force of some overwhelming temptation, many persons are unwillingly, and almost unavoidably, pressed into the ranks of crime, who but for the extremity in which they were placed, would have continued to walk erect in the path of honour and virtue. Let none then who move in the calm sunlight of prosperity, presume to judge those who stumble in the dark night of trial.

"The path of a man, even of a man on the highway to heaven, is never one of perfect safety. There are many dangerous passes in the journey of life. The very next turn, for anything we know, may bring us on one. Turn that projecting point, which hides the path before you, and you are suddenly in circumstances which demand that reason be strong, and conscience be tender, and hope be bright, and faith be vigorous."

Happily there are persons whose qualities of head and heart have enabled them by precautionary measures to provide against the weakness of human nature, and to offer assistance to those who are placed in such critical positions.

There is no class more essential to the well-being and comfort of society, and none, it is to be feared, more exposed to dangers and temptations, than domestic servants. It is calculated that in London alone there are upwards of one hundred thousand females engaged in domestic service, and that ten thousand of these are continually in a transition state, and therefore out of employment. When it is borne in mind that vast numbers of these young women have migrated, at an early age, from various parts of the country in search of a livelihood, that many of them are orphans and friendless, or at least wholly destitute of friends and resources in London, that they are moreover inexperienced, unsuspecting, and ignorant of the snares and temptations that surround them, it cannot be a matter of surprise that the reports of all the London penitentiaries should bear witness to the fact, that a large majority of the fallen women who are received into these institutions came originally from the ranks of domestic service. It would be superfluous to attempt to prove the value of associations formed to counteract these evils, by offering advice, shelter, and protection to servants who are out of situations or seeking employment. One of the oldest and best organizations of this kind is the *Female Servants' Home Society*,† which has now been in active operation four-and-twenty years. Its objects are to provide a safe *home* for respectable female servants when

---

* The following circumstance may be regarded as an illustration of this assertion:—
A girl is reported to have applied for admission into one of the older Institutions in London for the rescue of the fallen. On examination, however, it was ascertained that she had *not fallen low enough* to merit the assistance she craved, and she was accordingly rejected because her moral character was not sufficiently depraved. Here, at least, the greater the sinner, the greater the compassion!

† The Homes are situated in Nutford Place, Edgware Road; Hatton Garden, Holborn; Blackfriars Road; and Woodland Terrace, Greenwich. The Society is very inadequately supported, and is greatly in need of funds to maintain its efficiency.

out of place, or for those seeking situations. The Homes, four in number, are under the control of experienced and pious matrons, who establish a kind and motherly influence over the inmates, and are indefatigable in endeavouring to promote their welfare. The Homes are regularly visited by Christian ladies, and a service is conducted every week by the chaplain. A registry, free to the servants, is attached to each Home, where for a trifling fee of half-a-crown, or by an annual subscription of one guinea, every facility is afforded to employers of procuring efficient and trustworthy servants.

Since the formation of the Society, upwards of 7,000 servants have been received into the Homes, and 37,000 have availed themselves of the registry provided, while in numberless instances young and friendless girls have been rescued from positions of extreme and imminent danger.

A kindred institution to the above is *The Female Aid Society*, established in 1836. Its objects, which are threefold, are thus defined:—

1st. "It provides a home for female servants, where they may reside with comfort, respectability, and economy, while seeking for situations;" and in connexion with which is a register for the convenience of servants and employers.

2nd. "It receives into a home, for purposes of protection and instruction, young girls to be trained for service and other employments, who, from circumstances of poverty, orphanage, or sinful conduct in those who should preserve them from evil, are exposed to great temptations, and are in want of a home where there is proper guardianship and example."

3rd. "A home and rescue is offered to women who, weary of sin, are desirous of leaving a life of awful depravity and misery;" and no depth of past degradation, provided there is any sign of amendment, presents a barrier to their reception, shelter being freely offered to the very outcast among the outcasts, to inmates of refractory wards, of workhouses, and to women freshly discharged from prison. Since the formation of the Society 4,116 servants have been admitted into the Home, and 7,622 placed in service; 2,008 young women have enjoyed the protection of the Friendless' Home, and 2,205 have been received as penitents. Want of funds, however, has obliged the Society to curtail its operations.

The Girls' Laundry and Training Institution for Young Servants is an industrial home, affording shelter, protection, and instruction in household duties to forty young girls, who are thus carefully trained and prepared for domestic service.

Other institutions for the accommodation, temporary relief, and permanent benefit of servants are, *The National Guardian Institution, The Marylebone Philanthropic Servants' Institution and Pension Society, The Provisional Protection Society, The General Domestic Servants' Benevolent Institution,* and *The Servants' Provident and Benevolent Society.*

Among the London preventive agencies must be classed the various homes, refuges, and asylums for the relief of the utterly destitute and friendless of good character, and which severally offer food, shelter, and protection to those needing their assistance.

The Field Lane Night Refuges provide accommodation nightly for 200 men and women; and by this instrumentality many are rescued from death and crime, and are enabled to regain their positions in life, or to maintain themselves in respectability. During the past year 31,747 lodgings were afforded to persons of both sexes. Many of those thus assisted were poor needlewomen, who, during an inclement winter, had been, together with their families, turned into the street, having been stript of everything for rent.

The Dudley Stuart Night Refuge, founded by Lord Dudley Stuart in 1852, provides for the reception of the utterly destitute during the winter months. Accommodation is offered to 95 persons in two warm, spacious, and well-ventilated apartments. The relief afforded consists of a night's lodging, bread night and morning, and medical attendance, if required. This charity has, since its foundation, alleviated a vast amount of suffering. It admits those against whom every other door is closed, and requires no recommendation beyond the utter destitution of the applicants. Upwards of 8,000 men, women, and children were admitted and relieved during last winter.

The Houseless Poor Asylum is the oldest night-refuge in London, and was opened to "afford nightly shelter and sustenance to the absolutely destitute working classes, who are suddenly thrown out of employment during the inclement winter months." Accommodation is provided for 700; and since the opening of the Asylum 1,449,047 nights' lodgings and 3,515,951 rations of bread have been supplied.

The House of Charity provides for the reception of distressed persons of good character, who, from various accidental causes, require a temporary home, protection, and food. Nearly 3000 persons of both sexes have been thus accommodated for an average period of a month or five weeks.

The Foundling Hospital, first opened in 1741, for the reception of illegitimate children, has undergone considerable changes and improvements, and now shelters, maintains, and educates 460 children, who, at the age of fifteen, are apprenticed or otherwise provided for, and are thus humanely rescued from the early and contaminating influence of vicious associations. No child is eligible for this charity unless there is satisfactory proof of the mother's previous good character and present necessity, of desertion by the father, and that the reception of the child will, in all probability, be the means of replacing the mother in the course of virtue, and the way of an honest livelihood.

The Society for the Suppression of Mendicity was instituted in 1818, "for the purpose of checking the practice of public mendicity, with all its baneful and demoralizing consequences; by putting the laws in force against imposters who adopt it as a trade, and by affording prompt and effectual assistance to those whom sudden calamity or unaffected distress may cast in want and misery upon the public attention."

A just discrimination between cases of real and fictitious distress, and a judicious adaptation of relief to deserving cases, is a necessary, but very difficult, part of true benevolence. The frauds which are successfully practised by systematic sharpers upon a charitable, but over-credulous public, and the existence of an immense amount of genuine and unrelieved suffering, are sufficient proofs of the value and importance of any agency designed to counteract these abuses, and to accord a just measure of benevolence.

By means of printed tickets supplied to subscribers, beggars can be directed to the Society's offices, where their cases are fully investigated, and treated according to desert, a sure provision being thus made against imposture.

Since the formation of the Society 51,016 registered cases have been disposed of, and food, money, and clothing dispensed to deserving applicants, while employment has been provided for such as were found able to work.

The Association for Promoting the Relief of Destitution in the Metropolis is likewise a safe channel for the exercise of public benevolence. It is carried on under the direction of the bishop and clergy, and the efforts of the Association are directed to the origination and support of local undertakings, thus forming a connection and a centre of union between the various parochial visiting societies.

The present condition of that large class of female workers in London, comprehended under the terms milliners and dressmakers, is one of the saddest reproaches upon a country whose benevolent objects are so numerous, and so extensive, and one of the severest comments upon the heartlessness and artificialism of that society, which takes no cognizance of those who are most largely concerned in administering to its necessities. The miseries of this shamefully under-paid and cruelly over-worked class of white slaves have been too often eloquently animadverted upon, to need any further denunciations of the system, under which they are hopelessly and unfeelingly condemned to labour.

The impossibility of supporting life on the wretched pittance accorded to their labours, is the oft-heard, and the unanswerably extenuating plea for their recourse to criminal avocations.

While, however, the State shrinks from the task of ameliorating their condition by any legislative interference, it is satisfactory to know that public benevolence in this wide field is not wholly unrepresented.

The *Association for the Aid and Benefit of Dressmakers and Milliners* is a noble breakwater against the inroads of oppression, and a valuable counteracting agency to the force of temptation.

Its objects, briefly stated, are to obtain some remission of labour and other concessions from employers, and to afford pecuniary and medical assistance in cases of temporary distress or illness. A registry and provident fund are provided in connexion with the association.

Actuated by the same humane intention, although different in object, is the *Needlewomen's Institution*, established in 1850, "with the twofold view of affording those who had suffered under the oppression of middle men and slop-sellers, the opportunity of maintaining themselves, by supplying them with regular employment at remunerative prices, in airy work-rooms, and if desired, lodging at a moderate charge."

Another institution of very recent origin directed to the religious and social improvement of the same unhappy class, is the *Young Women's Christian Association and West London Home*, for young women engaged in houses of business. Its objects are twofold, 1st, "to supply a place where young women so employed, can profitably spend their *Sundays and week-day evenings*," thus counteracting the evil influence of badly conducted houses of business; and 2nd, "the home is intended to provide a residence for young people coming from the country to seek employment, and for those who are changing their situations, or who from over-work and failing health require rest for a time." The rooms of the Association are open every evening from seven until ten o'clock, when educational and religious classes are held for the benefit of those attending.

Thus, "where occasional spasms of sympathy, the well-merited castigations of the press, and the voice of popular opinion had unitedly failed to shake the throne of the god of Mammon, erected on skeletons, and cemented with the blood of women and children, it was reserved for a Christian lady to strike out a plan which has already been productive of an immensity of good, and has commended itself to the approval of all who are labouring to promote the welfare of this oppressed and neglected class. The better to appreciate the importance of this noble and truly womanly enterprise, only let the solemn and fearful fact be borne in mind, that in London *alone* 1,000 poor girls are yearly crushed out of life from over-toil and grinding oppression, while 15,000 are living in a state of semi-starvation. Ah! who can wonder that our streets swarm with the fallen and the lost, when SIN OR STARVE is the dire alternative! Who cannot track the *via doloroso* between the 15,000 starving and the thrice that number living by sin as a trade!

"Here, then, is an Institution that meets the wants of the case. It not only catches them before they go over the precipice, and lovingly shelters them from the fierce blasts of temptation, beating remorselessly on many a young and shrinking heart, but ensures them a '*Home*,' where soul and body alike may find rest and peace."*

---

* Any one desiring further information respecting this truly admirable movement, will do well to procure a little pamphlet, entitled, "A Brief Sketch of the Origin, Aim, and Mode of

The *Society for Promoting the Employment of Women* has lately been called into existence, by the emergencies of the present age, the object of which is to develop and extend the hitherto restricted field of female labour, by the establishment of industrial schools and workshops, where girls may be taught those trades and occupations which are at present exclusively monopolised by men. Those "educated in this school will be capable of becoming clerks, cashiers, railway-ticket ·ellers, printers," &c.

These and similar measures which tend to open up resources to women in search of a livelihood, will have the happiest effect in diverting numbers into paths of honest industry, who now labour under strong temptations to abandon themselves to a life of criminal ease and self-indulgence.

The remaining agencies indirectly tending to the prevention of crime, are the *Metropolitan Early Closing Association,* for abridging the hours of business, so as to afford to assistants time for recreation, and for physical, intellectual, and moral improvement; the *Metropolitan Evening Classes for Young Men,* for furnishing the means of instruction and self-improvement; and the *Young Men's Christian Association,* for promoting the spiritual and mental improvement of young men, "by means of devotional meetings, classes for Biblical instruction, and for literary improvement, the delivery of lectures, the diffusion of Christian literature, and a library for reference and circulation." This last instrumentality has been widely blessed, and its beneficial influence is now extended, by means of branch associations, to most of the provincial towns.

3. *Repressive and Punitive Agencies.*

The various instrumentalities falling under this head appear deserving of separate consideration, and cannot therefore be appropriately included under either of the previous divisions, being neither curative in their character, nor preventive to any appreciable extent. They evidently presuppose the existence of crime, and merely seek to diminish its influence, or curtail its power by the application of legal provisions and compulsory measures, intended on the one hand to indemnify society against the infraction of its rights, and on the other to intimidate or restrain the criminal offender. The absolute reformation of the viciously disposed can hardly be expected to result from the use of such means, and belongs properly to another class of agencies. It may indeed be achieved by punitive measures, but in this case reformation of character is rather a startling accident than an essential property of the system pursued. Experience has abundantly established the utility of legal provisions as a "terror to evil doers;" but the statistics of our police-courts will by no means warrant the assumption that penal measures have *per se* been successful in reclaiming the offender. It is not intended, however, while speaking of repressive and punitive agencies, to include in this category the strictly legal efforts employed by the State to deter and correct the criminal who renders himself amenable to justice. This subject will be found fully and distinctly treated by Mr. Mayhew, in a work now in the press, entitled " Prisons of London, and Scenes of Prison Life."

The inquiry pursued in the course of this Essay is not designed to comprehend such constitutional measures as are employed by either Church or State, for the suppression of vice and crime; but rather to draw from their obscurity, and to give prominence to those resources and expedients which society itself adopts, for the defence and preservation of its own interests.

Conducting the Young Women's Christian Association, and West London Home for Young Women engaged in Houses of Business, 49, Great Marlborough-street, Regent-street, London; in a Letter to the Earl of Roden, President of the Association."

The Society for the Suppression of Vice, which was established in 1802, has for its objects the repression of attempts " to spread infidelity and blasphemy by means of public lectures, and printed publications." The operations of the Society have also been directed to the suppression of disorderly houses, the punishment of fortune-tellers, and other important objects. " It is represented that by means of this Society many convictions have taken place, and persons have been sentenced to imprisonment for selling obscene publications and prints," while their works have been either seized or destroyed. With such admirable intentions and useful objects, to commend it to benevolent support, and with the entire voice of public opinion in its favour, the only wonder is that this Society does not carry on its operations with greater publicity, vigilance, and efficiency. Unhappily the loathsome traffic in Holywell Street literature is still carried on with bold and unblushing effrontery, and its existence, although greatly diminished in the country, is too notorious and too patent, in certain portions of the metropolis, to need any extraordinary efforts to promote exposure and punishment.

The demoralizing influence of low theatres, and the licentious corruptions of the Coal Hole, and Posés Plastiques, might surely afford scope for vigorous prosecutions under the Society's auspices; and yet these dens, in which the vilest passions of mankind are stimulated, and every sentiment of religion, virtue, and decency grossly outraged, or publicly caricatured, are allowed to emit their virulent poison upon all ranks of society without the slightest let or hindrance! Only let a man smitten by the plague or with any other infectious disease, obtrude himself by unnecessary contact upon the public, and his right to free agency would be summarily disposed of, by speedy incarceration within the walls of a hospital; but provided only the disorder be a moral one—and therefore far more to be dreaded, in its pestiferous influence and baneful effects upon society— it is forsooth to be tolerated as a necessary evil! *Proh tempora et mores!*

The Associate Institution, formed in 1844, has been in active operation fifteen years, and has been instrumental in effecting a large amount of good, by improving and enforcing the laws for the protection of women. It has maintained a strenuous crusade against houses of ill-fame, and has since its establishment conducted upwards of 300 prosecutions, in most of which it has been successful in bringing condign punishment upon the heads of those, who have committed criminal assaults upon women and children, or who have decoyed them away for immoral purposes.

Important as these results have been, a larger amount of good has probably been achieved by means of lectures and meetings held in various parts of the country by Mr. J. Harding, the Society's travelling secretary, whose faithful and stirring appeals and bold denunciations of vice have contributed not a little to the spread of sounder and more wholesome views on social questions, and to the removal of that ignorance of profligate wiles and artifices, which, in so many cases, proves fatal to the unsuspecting and unwary.

Two Bills prepared by this Association, one for the protection of female children between 12 and 13 years of age, and the other to simplify and facilitate the prosecution of persons charged with keeping houses of ill fame, were this year submitted to parliament, but unhappily without success, having been lost either on technical grounds, or for want of support. It is refreshing to turn from the supineness of statesmen to the energy and decision manifested by private associations in resisting the encroachments of vice. The *East London Association*, composed of a committee partly clerical and partly lay, and including most of the influential parochial clergy in the district, was instituted four years ago for the purpose of checking " that class of *public offences*, which consists in acts of indecency, profaneness, drunkenness, and prostitution."

Its modes of action are as follows:—

1. To create and foster public opinion in reprobation of the above-named acts.

2. To bring such public opinion to bear upon all exercising social influence, with a view to discountenance the perpetrators and abettors thereof.

3. To secure the efficient application by the Police of the laws and regulations for the suppression of the class of public offences above named; and to obtain, if necessary, the institution of legal proceedings.

4. To procure the alteration of the law, wheresoever needful to the object contemplated, and especially to the obtaining further restrictions in granting Licenses for Music and Dancing to houses where intoxicating liquors are sold.

5. To find Houses of Refuge and means of restoration for the victims of seduction by honest employment, emigration, &c.

It is satisfactory to state that already, and with the very limited funds placed at the disposal of this Association, no fewer than " seventy-five houses in some of the worst streets in the east of London, hitherto devoted to the vilest purposes, have been cleared of their inmates; one of these houses having had thirty rooms, which were occupied by prostitutes; that more than one house ostensibly open for public accommodation, but really for ensnaring females for prostitution, has been closed; and that in one instance of peculiar atrocity, the owner of the house has been convicted and punished. Handbills have also been issued, containing extracts from the Police Acts, to show the power of remedy for offences against public decency, such as swearing, the use of improper language, and the exhibition of improper conduct in the streets."

Such are the objects and results of this Association, and such the praiseworthy example set to other London districts, which if vigorously followed would result, at least, in the repression of vice, and in a marked diminution of crime.

"It is chiefly from the reserve which, rather by implication than by compact, has so long been preserved in those influential quarters where the power to correct and guide public opinion is maintained, that the crying social evil of our day has attained such dimensions, and exhibited itself in such dangerous and revolting forms as we have referred to. Preachers, moralists, and public writers have been deterred by the difficulty and delicacy of the subject from their obvious duty of protecting the social interests, and a sluggish legislature, ever inert in introducing such measures as are calculated to foster and conserve the public virtue, has thus lacked the external pressure which might have aroused it to vigilance and forethought in the discharge of its duties. Recently, however, there have been clear indications that a distrust of the old plan is spreading. With manifest reluctance, but not without interest, has public attention fastened itself on a subject in which not merely the happiness of individuals, and the peace of families, but the national prosperity and the concerns of social life, are felt to be bound up. Inquiries as to the best mode of doing something to stem the tide of immorality which is coursing onwards are made in quarters where indifference, if not acquiescence, was formerly manifested. Public opinion is ever slowly formed, but is seldom wrong at the last in detecting the true source of generic evils, and in applying to them the best remedies. Example, also, is as contagious on the side of virtue as of vice; and where an initiative step, taken by another, appeals to our intuitive sense of right and duty, it is seldom that the courageous right-doer has to wait long for the expression of sympathy and the proffer of aid.

"It is only recently that the great sin of our land has received a measure of the attention it has long and loudly called for.

"First in one quarter, and then in another, has the subject been discussed with tolerable delicacy, and with an approximate fidelity.

"The discussion has done good. Men have thought about the subject, have been led to measure the fearful dimensions of this evil, to observe its progress and influence within their own neighbourhoods, and have come at last to deplore the existence of that which they have too long tolerated or connived at. Where remedial measures have been attempted, they have not lacked for countenance and support; and, in some quarters, at least, there have been indications of a desire to pass from the feebler stage of alleviation to the more potential remedy of prevention. Whilst it seems to be admitted on all hands, that to aim at the forcible extinction of immorality would be Utopian and disappointing, the repression and diminution of crime is felt to be an imperious obligation upon all who are vested with any power and influence for that end.

"We cannot help regarding the measures which have been recently adopted by certain parochial authorities in the metropolis as at once a proof of the benefit which has arisen from the partial discussion of this subject in the various public channels into which it has gained admittance; and we regard it, further, as a cheering sign that a deepening conviction is spreading on all sides respecting the absolute necessity of a well-organised antagonism to evil, in place of our former supine indifference, or more culpable acquiescence. Some of the most influential metropolitan vestries have commenced a crusade against the keepers of bad houses in their respective parishes, and, by the vigour and promptitude characterizing their prosecutions, seem determined to hunt down the hosts of abandoned householders who are mainly concerned in extending and facilitating immorality.

"Aristocratic St. James's, and more plebeian Lambeth, have alike joined in these laudable measures; and it is to be noticed, with extreme satisfaction, that the steps thus taken have been almost invariably successful, and that severe punishments have been inflicted upon the wretches who were the objects of these prosecutions. Such a movement cannot be sufficiently applauded, and fervently is it to be trusted that the example thus shown in these influential centres may not only reach to every other parish in the metropolis, but may also stir up the parochial authorities in every city and town in the land to a like course of procedure. This is to strike at the main root of the evil. In vain are all our Reformatories and Refuges, in vain the endeavours of Christian people to repress the evil by exertions for the rescue even of a large number of its victims, if the floodgates of vice be allowed, by public neglect, to remain open, ever to pour out into our streets fresh streams of wickedness and pollution. There are, no doubt, persons who think that measures, such as those now under consideration, will not materially check the traffic in vice, but will only lead to its being more subtly and secretly practised. Even that result, if brought about, would be something gained, something as a protest on the side of public purity and virtue, and something in the amount of warning and terror brought home to guilty breasts, leading them to dread retribution in future, whenever offended justice could detect them in their malpractices. But in truth there is no limit to the amount of good which would result from these repressive measures becoming universal and well-sustained.

"Many persons would be saved from future ruin, a manifest check would be given to the further development of iniquity, and the example of authority thus generally exercised in aid of the cause of virtue, would greatly tend to the spread of sounder views of social duty in regard to this matter."*

One of the greatest scandals on a country professedly Christian, is the extent to which Sabbath desecration pervades the metropolis. Although the traffic now openly pursued in the streets, or carried on with impunity in shops, is strictly illegal, yet the technicalities which are too often allowed to obstruct the ends of justice, and the smallness of the fines inflicted, even where summary conviction follows, concur to render the law, in this particular, a mere dead letter.

The permission to sell on Sunday, originally extended only to vendors of perishable articles, is now claimed by whole troops of costermongers, who, pre-

* "The Magdalen's Friend and Female Homes' Intelligencer, No. 12, vol. ii."

suming upon the license they have so long enjoyed, no longer hesitate to ply their usual calling in the most public and offensive manner, frequently pursuing their traffic in the open streets during the hours of divine service, and disturbing whole congregations by their noisy vociferations around the very doors of our churches.

These evils call loudly for more stringent legal measures, and it is to be hoped the time is not far distant when some improvement will take place.

As one means of directing public attention to this subject, by the circulation of appeals and tracts, and of promoting the introduction of salutary legal provisions for the repression of such acts of desecration, the *Society for Promoting the Due Observance of the Lord's Day* is entitled to a large measure of support. The efforts made by the Society to awaken public opposition to the obnoxious provisions of Lord Chelmsford's Sunday Trading Bill, were probably mainly instrumental in securing its rejection.

One of the noblest repressive agencies within the metropolis is the *Royal Society for the Prevention of Cruelty to Animals*, established in 1824, which employs a number of agents to frequent the markets and public thoroughfares, for the purpose of bringing to punishment persons detected in the commission of acts of cruelty to animals. It seeks, moreover, by means of suitable tracts, to diffuse among the public a just sense of the duty of humanity and forbearance towards the lower orders of creation. Allusion was made during the present year to the objects embraced by this Society from upwards of two thousand London pulpits, which will doubtless have the effect of directing the attention of the benevolent public to an instrumentality which has already achieved a large amount of good; and only requires to be better known to enjoy a corresponding measure of support.

4. *Reformative Agencies.*

Must be understood as referring solely to individuals, and include all such measures as are employed to effect an external change of character, and render those, who are vicious and depraved, honest and respectable members of society.

While, however, agencies of this kind are reformative in their relation to persons, they have also a preventive aspect, when viewed in their bearings upon the entire community; for the reformation of every vicious man is a social boon, inasmuch as it removes one individual from a course of vice, and thus diminishes the aggregate of crime.

As a nucleus of reformatory operations, and a "centre of information and encouragement," the *Reformatory and Refuge Union* was established in 1856. It seeks to diffuse information respecting the various agencies at present in existence, and to encourage and facilitate the establishment of new institutions. In connection with the Union is a "*Female Mission*" for the rescue of the fallen. The Mission maintains a staff of female missionaries, whose business it is to distribute tracts among the fallen women of the metropolis, to converse with them in the streets, and visit them in their houses, in the hospitals, or in the workhouses. These missionaries, "as a rule, leave their homes between eight and nine o'clock at night, remaining out till nearly twelve, and occasionally till one in the morning. They are located in different parts of London, near to the nightly walks and haunts of those they desire to benefit. They have the means of rescuing a large number who have been placed in the Homes or restored to their friends."

There are upwards of fifty metropolitan institutions for the reception of the destitute and the reformation of the criminal, or those who are exposed to temptation, capable of accommodating collectively about 4,000 persons of both sexes.

Nine of these institutions are designed especially for the reception and training of juvenile criminals, sentenced under the "Youthful Offenders' Act," and two for vagrants sentenced to detention under the "Industrial School Act." Three are exclusively appropriated to the benefit of discharged prisoners, and the rest are chiefly employed in the rescue and reformation of destitute or criminal children.*

Most of these institutions, with the exception of such as are certified by Act of Parliament, and aided by Government subsidies, are supported entirely by voluntary contributions and by the earnings of the inmates, who are either admitted free on application, or by payment of a small sum towards the expense of maintenance.

Such is the benevolent machinery now at work within the metropolis for the reformation of our criminal population, and for the preservation of those who are in a fair way of becoming the moral pests and aliens of society.

The results, both in a religious, social, and sanatory point of view, achieved by these different agencies, are beyond all human calculation; and it is mainly to their beneficial and restraining influence that the peace, safety, and well-being of society may be attributed.

The other *Reformative Agencies* are those adapted to the rescue and reformation of fallen women, or such as have been led astray from the paths of virtue.

There are twenty-one institutions in London devoted to these objects, and unitedly providing accommodation for about 1,200 inmates. Ten of these are in connexion with the Church of England, and in the remaining eleven the religious instruction is unsectarian and evangelical. Three, viz., *The Female Temporary Home*, *The Trinity Home*, and *The Home of Hope*, are designed for the reception of the better educated and higher class of fallen women. One, viz., *The London Society for the Protection of Young Females*, is limited to girls under fifteen years of age; and another, *The Marylebone Female Protection Society*, affords shelter exclusively to those who have recently been led astray, and whose previous good character will bear the strictest investigation.

It may be fairly assumed that the objects of all these institutions are substantially the same, viz., the reformation of character, and the restoration of the individual to religious and social privileges. While, however, the end is in most cases one and the same, the methods and subordinate means adopted to insure its attainment, are often strikingly dissimilar, and present distinctive and almost opposite features. Thus one class of institutions, in imitation of our Lord's merciful forbearance towards the sinner, make their treatment pre-eminently one of love, and seek by means the most gentle and attractive to win back the stubborn wills and depraved natures of those entrusted to their care. Kindness is the only instrument used in laying siege to the hard heart, and in mollifying the seared conscience. Stern discipline, irritating restraints, and rigorous exactions, form no part of a system which is built up on the model prescribed by Him, who "spake as never man spake."

That a mode of treatment which affords such a remarkable coincidence, and such a striking parallel to the divine method of dealing with the sinner, so eloquently taught under the parable of the Prodigal Son, should be found by experience to be the only really efficacious one, can hardly be a matter of surprise. The fact is too notorious to require any proof that in numberless instances

'Law and terrors do but harden'

the heart which can be easily subdued by the exhibition of Christian kindness. Here is the omnipotent weapon which has achieved such moral victories, when

* Those who wish for further information respecting these Institutions are referred to a handbook containing authentic accounts of the various Metropolitan Reformatories, Refuges, and Industrial Schools, published by the Reformatory and Refuge Union. A magazine, edited by a clergyman, price 3*d.* monthly, designed to awaken and sustain public sympathy on behalf of the fallen, and to draw attention to the most prolific causes, contributing to the extension of the social evil.

wielded by gentle and loving women, like Miss Marsh, Mrs. Wightman, and Mrs. Sheppard.

The opposite mode of treatment, however successful it may be in the restoration of external character, or in the subjugation of turbulent passions, is defective, inasmuch as it fails to influence the heart, and therefore at best contributes only to an incomplete and partial cure. The almost penal character of the system pursued in many of the older penitentiaries is founded on the misconception, that the injury sustained by society in the departure from virtue of her female members, can only be atoned for by some personal mulct inflicted on the offender. While, therefore, the ultimate object is the reformation of lost character, this is too often overlooked or rendered subsidiary to the proximate one of propitiating society; and the austere regimen by which the latter point is secured, is generally found to be subversive of the other. When, however, as is too frequently the case, society is the *tempter*, the offence may surely be condoned by a less rigorous process! Society may indeed well waive the right to compensation for supposed damages, when it can be proved that she is at least *particeps criminis*, and when, moreover, she has a personal interest in the speedy restoration of her unhappy prodigals. The retributive suffering, which, in the majority of cases, so surely overtakes the female delinquent, may be urged as another reason for dealing leniently with the erring; but the strongest justification of such a method is undoubtedly derived from the success attending it, and from the Divine sanction which it has received.

The impediments which the old penitentiary system of close confinement, criminal fare, and hard labour, have unfortunately presented to the rescue of fallen women is too well known to those who are accustomed to deal with this class. Frequently are the urgent entreaties of the missionary to forsake an abandoned course of life, and seek shelter in some institution, met with either rancorous denunciations against the penal system, or by polite but firm refusals to submit to the discipline, which is supposed to extend to all reformatory asylums.

Gradually, however, this prevailing opinion is being cleared away, and the fallen women themselves are not slow to distinguish between the two opposite methods of treatment, a fact which is rendered clearly apparent by the overwhelming number of applications for admission into those Homes which are characterized by a more humane and gentle regimen.

The oldest reformatory institution in the metropolis for the reception of fallen women is *The Magdalen Hospital*, founded in 1758. During the last 100 years of its existence nearly 9,000 women have been admitted, about two-thirds of whom have been restored to friends or relations. At the time when this charity was first instituted "the notion of providing a house for the reception and maintenance of 'Penitent Prostitutes' seems not to have suggested itself to the public mind. Even good and actively benevolent men appear to have been startled at the novelty of the proposition, while they doubted the wisdom, and still more the success of such an attempt. The newspapers of that period contained both arguments against, and ridicule of the plan and its promoters. God, however, blessed the undertaking, and raised up friends and supporters in every direction."

So that eighteen years after its incorporation its friends were able to use the following cheering language.

"We see many fellow-creatures, by means of this happy asylum, rescued from sorrow in which they had been involved by all the iniquitous stratagems of seduction; in which condition they had been detained by a species of horrid necessity; from which they had no probable or possible retreat; and in which they must, therefore, according to all human appearance, have perished. We see them restored to their God, to their parents, to their friends, their country, and themselves. What charitable heart, what truly Christian hand can withhold its best endeavours to promote an undertaking so laudable, so beneficent? Who would not desire to add to the number of souls preserved from the deepest guilt—of bodies rescued from shame, misery, and death? Who would not wish to wipe the tear from a parent's eyes—to save the hoary head from being brought down with sorrow to the grave?"

An interval of half a century elapsed after the foundation of the Magdalen Asylum before the establishment of any similar institution. Within the last ten years, however, public attention has been directed with increasing interest to this subject, and numerous efforts have been made to provide more ample accommodation for those who are desirous of escaping from their wretched mode of life.

The *London by Moonlight Mission*, inaugurated some years ago by Lieutenant Blackmore, has been followed in our own day by the *Midnight Meeting Movement*, which has excited a world-wide sympathy and interest, and has been very generally approved even in quarters where encouragement could be least expected. The commencement of these meetings in London was the signal for similar experiments in Manchester, Liverpool, Nottingham, Edinburgh, Glasgow, Dundee, Dublin, and other large towns.

Twenty-two of these meetings have now been held, and attended by upwards of 4,000 women, more than 600 of whom have been rescued, and either restored to friends, or placed in situations, where they are giving satisfactory evidence of outward reformation, and many of them of a thorough change of character.

The largest association in London for the reformation of fallen women, is the *Society for the Rescue of Young Women and Children*. The Society has at present eleven homes in various parts of London, and one at Dover. Four of these are "Family Homes" for the reception of *preventive* cases, or young girls who have *not* strayed from the path of virtue, but are addicted to crime, or are in circumstances of danger. One is a Home for orphan children, from nine to thirteen years of age; and the remaining seven are for fallen cases.

Upwards of 2,700 women and children have been admitted into these Homes since the Society's formation in 1853, the greater part of whom have given satisfactory proof of having been reclaimed and permanently benefitted. The Society's income for the past year amounted to £6,789 17s. 2d. The Homes are under the care of pious and experienced matrons, who labour incessantly to promote the spiritual and social welfare of their charges.

Another institution of recent origin, but of rapidly increasing growth, is the *London Female Preventive and Reformatory Institution*, which already numbers four Homes, and has admitted, during the past year, upwards of 250 inmates.

The following are the objects embraced by the Institution:—

"I. To seek the destitute and fallen by voluntary missionary effort.

"II. To afford temporary protection to friendless young women, whose circumstances expose them to danger; also to effect the rescue of fallen females, especially those decoyed from the country, by admitting them to the benefits of this Institution.

"III. To restore, when practicable, the wanderer to her family and friends, whether in town or country.

"IV. To qualify those admitted into the Institution for various departments of domestic service, to obtain suitable situations for them, and provide them with clothing.

"V. To aid such as for approved reasons wish to emigrate.

"VI. Above all, to seek the spiritual welfare of the inmates."

The two last-named Societies and the *Home of Hope*, which is another Refuge identical in character and spirit with that last named, have received most of the cases rescued by the midnight meetings.

Great and encouraging as are the results effected by these institutions, and wide as the sympathy is which they have awakened, it is clear that the means of rescue are as yet wholly disproportioned to the numbers claiming assistance.

Calculating the number of fallen women in London at *eighty thousand*, which is probably not far wide of the truth, and computing the number at present in the different institutions to be 1,000, the chance of rescue through the only recognized medium for female reformation is offered to *one woman in every eighty!*

This is *the high-water* mark of public charity, and the utmost provision made by Society for the rescue of these 80,000 outcasts! And yet there are special reasons which seem to give them a strong claim upon the sympathy and compassion of the benevolent public. The brief term of their existence, the average length of which is at best but a few years, and the fact that large numbers of them are driven upon the streets by a stern necessity, and compelled to live by sin as a trade, while everything contributes to prevent their escape from the mode of life into which they have been involuntarily forced, are surely considerations calculated to stimulate Christian effort on their behalf. But more than this,—it is well known that they are hanging as it were over the mouth of the bottomless pit.

"Their life-blood is ebbing at a fearful rate, and their souls are drifting madly to eternity. Their fate is certain; their doom impends: and, for their death-bed, there is not even the faintest glimmer of hope which charity can bequeath to the dying sinner. All others *may* find peace at last; but these, suddenly overtaken by death, and perishing *in* and *by* their sins, *must* be irrevocably lost. And who are they on whose warm vitals the 'worm feeds sweetly,' even on this side the grave, and around whose heads the unquenchable fire prematurely burns? Who are those whose souls, in countless numbers, are now glutting the chambers of hell? Not swarthy Indians nor sable Africans, whose deeds of violence and superstition have spread horror and astonishment among civilized nations, but delicately-nurtured Saxon women, who in infancy were lovingly fondled in the arms of Christian mothers, and received 'into the ark of Christ's Church' in baptism, before a praying congregation; young girls, for whom pious sponsors promised that they should be 'virtuously brought up to lead a godly and a Christian life,' and who, in the faithful discharge of this promise, were trained in our Sabbath-schools, and 'taken to the Bishop to be confirmed by him.' They have sung the same hymns which we now sing; our congregational melodies are still familiar to them. They have read the same Scriptures which we now read, worshipped in the same temple in which we assemble, offered up the same prayers, listened to the same exhortations, and looked forward to the same glorious fruition of future blessedness. But where are they now? What are their hopes and expectations, and what the probable end of their existence? Let those answer these questions who sneeringly ask why such prodigious efforts are made to rescue the fallen.

"It not unfrequently happens, however, that the benevolent promoters of such schemes are perplexed and disheartened by those who assume a tone of expediency and argue thus: 'Yes, it is all very true; and we can sympathise with your efforts, and pity the poor unhappy objects of your solicitude; but, then, this is a necessary evil, and any attempts to remove it are altogether mistaken, and are sure to end in failure, or to produce greater mischief. Besides, the demand will always create the supply, and for every fallen woman you snatch from the streets, an innocent, and hitherto virtuous girl, must be sacrificed. No, we are sorry for them, but better let them perish than save them at the sacrifice of other victims.'

"First then, this is a '*necessary* evil.' Falsehood is sufficiently patent upon the face of this foolish and monstrous assertion. Could the Creator have pronounced his work 'very good' with such an inseparable appendage to social life? Again, how comes it that a '*necessary* evil' only exhibits itself in *certain localities*, and under particular circumstances, disappearing altogether in uncivilized countries, and gathering strength and virulence in the most refined states of society? Will any modern philosopher favour us with a solution of this difficulty?

But 'the demand will always create the supply.' Inexorable logic apparently, and incontrovertible if the supply were limited to the demand. This, however, we deny. Thousands are driven to prostitution as the only alternative from starvation. *Necessity*, and not the demand, here creates the supply, and it is well known that the supply *suggests* the demand. Is, then, the balance of vice so exact and undeviating, that the gap occasioned by the removal of one victim must be speedily filled by another? Is the equilibrium of profligacy so nicely adjusted, that it would be dangerous to assert the prerogative of virtue; and shall we desire its unhappy votaries to continue in sin that virtue may abound? Shall we drive back anxious souls, striving to 'flee from the wrath to come,' with the cold-blooded assurance that, 'for the good of society, they had better remain where they are? Will it satisfy an immortal spirit, to be told that she helps to maintain the proper equilibrium of vice; or that, by standing in the gap, she is a benefactor to the innocent of her own sex, who would otherwise be sacrificed? Shall we assign as our reason for not preaching the Gospel to 'every creature,' that the state of society would be unhinged by curtailing a necessary evil, or that greater injuries would result from any attempt to rescue perishing souls? Shall we mock Him who has said 'All souls are mine,' by elevating a doctrine of human expediency above the authority of a distinct command? Let us be sure that, in a case so intimately affecting the honour and glory of God, to 'obey is better than sacrifice, and to hearken than the fat of rams.' In vain may we plead political necessity as a plausible pretext for disobedience.

"We are not afraid, however, to meet this argument on philosophical grounds; and we affirm, confidently, that the rescue of every fallen woman is a social boon. Admitting the *possibility* that, eventually, her place will be supplied by another—for we can approach no nearer to the truth—is it not better to remove a *present* evil than to provide for a *remote* contingency? Supposing that in the long vista of future years, the immolation of a fresh victim is the price of every individual rescue, do we overlook the fact, that *in the mean time* a powerful temptation is removed, and that not merely *units*, but probably *hundreds*, of the young of the opposite sex are delivered from the toils of the strange woman? Is nothing achieved by the temporary removal of one tempter from the streets, and is society a loser in the end, by the reformation of one whose sole occupation is to waylay and ruin the youth of the opposite sex? Let our moral economists escape from this dilemma if they can; the philanthropist and the Christian need no further arguments to convince them that they have not only the law of God, but the inexorable logic of common sense on their side.

"Who can tell the pestiferous influence exercised on society by one single fallen woman? Who can calculate the evils of such a system? Woman, waylaid, tempted, deceived, becomes in turn the terrible avenger of her sex. Armed with a power which is all but irresistible, and stript of that which can alone restrain and purify her influence, she steps upon the arena of life qualified to act her part in the reorganization of society. The *lex talionis*—the law of retaliation—is hers. Society has made her what she is, and must be now governed by her potent influence. The weight of this influence is untold: view it in the dissolution of domestic ties, in the sacrifice of family peace, in the cold desolation of promising homes; but, above all, in the growth of practical Atheism, and in the downward tendency of all that is pure and holy in life! One and another who has been educated in an atmosphere redolent of virtue and principle, and has given promise of high and noble qualities, falls a victim to the prevalence of meretricious allurements and carries back to his hitherto untainted home the noxious influence he has imbibed. Another and another, within the range of that influence, is made to suffer for his sacrifice of moral rectitude, and they, in their turn, become the agents, and the originators of fresh evils. Who, in contemplating this pedigree of profligacy resulting from a solitary temptation, will venture to affirm that the temporary withdrawal of a single prostitute is not a social blessing? Surely for such *immediate results* we are justified in dispensing with considerations of *future expediency;* and, acting upon the first principles of Christian ethics, may help to reform the vicious and profligate, leaving it in the hands of a merciful God to avert the contingency of ruin overtaking the as yet unfallen woman."*

In reference to all such Christian efforts to reclaim the fallen, it has been truly said that "You may ransack the world for objects of compassion. You may scour the earth in search of suffering humanity, on which to exercise your philanthropy; you may roam the countless hospitals and asylums of this vast city; you may penetrate the dens and caves of all other profligacy; you may lavish your bounty upon a transatlantic famine, or dive into Neapolitan dungeons, or scatter the Bible broadcast throughout the great moral wildernesses of heathendom: but in all the million claims upon your faith, upon your feeling as a man, upon your benevolence as a Christian, you will never fulfil a mission dearer to Christ, you will never promote a charity more congenial to the spirit of this gospel; you will never more surely wake up joy in heaven, and force tears into the eyes of sympathising angels, than when you can bring a Magdalene face to face with her Redeemer, and thrill her poor heart, even to breaking, with the plaintive music of that divine voice, calling her by name—MARY."

* "Magdalen's Friend," vol. ii. p. 131.

LONDON LABOUR

AND THE

LONDON POOR.

THOSE THAT WILL NOT WORK.

INTRODUCTION.

I ENTER upon this part of my subject with a deep sense of the misery, the vice, the ignorance, and the want that encompass us on every side—I enter upon it after much grave attention to the subject, observing closely, reflecting patiently, and generalizing cautiously upon the phenomena and causes of the vice and crime of this city—I enter upon it after a thoughtful study of the habits and character of the "outcast" class generally—I enter upon it, moreover, not only as forming an integral and most important part of the task I have imposed upon myself, but from a wish to divest the public mind of certain "idols" of the platform and conventicle—"idols" peculiar to our own time, and unknown to the great Father of the inductive philosophy—and "idols," too, that appear to me greatly to obstruct a proper understanding of the subject. Further, I am led to believe that I can contribute some new facts concerning the physics and economy of vice and crime generally, that will not only make the solution of the social problem more easy to us, but, setting more plainly before us some of its latent causes, make us look with more pity and less anger on those who want the fortitude to resist their influence; and induce us, or at least the more earnest among us, to apply ourselves steadfastly to the removal or alleviation of those social evils that appear to create so large a proportion of the vice and crime that we seek by punishment to prevent.

Such are the *ultimate* objects of my present labours: the result of them is given to the world with an earnest desire to better the condition of the wretched social outcasts of whom I have now to treat, and to contribute, if possible, my mite of good towards the common weal.

But though such be my ultimate object, let me here confess that my immediate aim is the elimination of the truth; without this, of course, all other principles must be sheer sentimentality—sentiments being, to my mind, opinions engendered by the feelings rather than the judgment. The attainment of the truth, then, will be my primary aim; but by the truth, I wish it to be understood, I mean something *more* than the bare facts. Facts, according to my ideas, are merely the elements of truths, and not the truths themselves; of all matters there are none so utterly useless by themselves as your mere matters of fact. A fact, so long as it remains an isolated fact, is a dull, dead, uninformed thing; no object nor event by itself can possibly give us any knowledge, we must compare it with some other, even to distinguish it; and it is the distinctive quality thus developed that constitutes the essence of a thing—that is to say, the point by which we cognize and recognise it when again presented to us. A fact must be assimilated with, or discriminated from, some other fact or facts, in order to be raised to the dignity of a truth, and made to convey the least knowledge to the mind. To say, for instance, that in the year 1850 there were 26,813 criminal offenders in England and Wales, is merely to oppress the brain with the record of a fact that, *per se*, is so much mental lumber. This is the very mummery of statistics; of what rational good can such information by itself be to any person? who can tell whether the number of offenders in that year be large or small, unless they compare it with the number of some other year, or in some other country? but to do this will require another fact, and even then this second fact can give us but little real knowledge. It may teach us, perhaps, that the past year was more or less criminal than some other year, or that the people of this country, in that year, were more or less disposed to the infraction of the laws than some other people abroad; still, what will all this avail us? If the year which we select to contrast criminally with that of 1850 be not itself compared with other years, how are we to know whether the number of criminals appertaining to it be above or below the average? or, in other words, how can the one be made a measure of the other?

To give the least mental value to facts, therefore, we must generalize them, that is to say, we must contemplate them in connection with other facts, and so discover their agreements and differences, their antecedents, concomitants, and consequences. It is true we may frame erroneous and defective theories in so doing; we may believe things which are similar in appearance to be similar in their powers and properties also; we may distinguish between things having no real difference; we may mistake concomitant events for consequences; we may generalize with too few particulars, and hastily infer that to be common to all which is but the special attribute of a limited number; nevertheless, if theory may occasionally teach us wrongly, facts without theory or generalization cannot possibly teach us at all. What the process of digestion is to food, that of generalizing is to fact; for as it is by the assimilation of the substances we eat with the elements of our bodies that our limbs are enlarged and our whole frames strengthened, so is it by associating perception with perception in our brains that our intellect becomes at once expanded and invigorated. Contrary to the vulgar notion, theory, that is to say, theory in its true Baconian sense, is not opposed to fact, but consists rather of a *large* collection of facts; it is not true of this or that thing alone, but of *all* things belonging to the same class—in a word, it consists not of *one* fact but an *infinity*. The theory of gravitation, for instance, expresses not only what occurs when a stone falls to the earth, but when every other body does the same thing; it expresses, moreover, what takes place in the revolution of the moon round our planet, and in the revolution of our planet and of all the other planets round our sun, and of all other suns round the centre of the universe; in fine, it is true not of one thing merely, but of every material object in the entire range of creation.

There are, of course, two methods of dealing philosophically with every subject —deductively and inductively. We may either proceed from principles to facts, or recede from facts to principles. The one explains, the other investigates; the former applies known general rules to the comprehension of particular phenomena, and the latter classifies the particular phenomena, so that we may ultimately come to comprehend their unknown general rules. The deductive method is the mode of *using* knowledge, and the inductive method the mode of *acquiring* it.

In a subject like the crime and vice of the metropolis, and the country in general, of which so little is known — of which there are so many facts, but so little comprehension—it is evident that we must seek by induction, that is to say, by a careful classification of the known phenomena, to render the matter more intelligible; in fine, we must, in order to arrive at a *comprehensive* knowledge of its antecedents, consequences, and concomitants, contemplate as large a number of facts as possible in as many different relations as the statistical records of the country will admit of our doing.

With this brief preamble I will proceed to treat generally of the class that will not work, and then particularly of that portion of them termed prostitutes. But, first, who are those that *will* work, and who those that *will not* work? This is the primary point to be evolved.

OF THE WORKERS AND NON-WORKERS.

THE essential quality of an animal is that it seeks its own living, whereas a vegetable has its living brought to it. An animal cannot stick its feet in the ground and suck up the inorganic elements of its body from the soil, nor drink in the organic elements from the atmosphere. The leaves of plants are not only their lungs but their stomachs. As *they* breathe they acquire food and strength, but as animals breathe *they* gradually waste away. The carbon which is *secreted* by the process of respiration in the vegetable is excreted by the very same process in the animal. Hence a fresh supply of *carbonaceous* matter must be sought after and obtained at frequent intervals, in order to repair the continual waste of animal life.

But in the act of seeking for substances fitted to replace that which is lost in respiration, nerves must be excited and muscles moved; and recent discoveries have shown that such excitation and motion are attended with decomposition of the organs in which they occur. Muscular action gives rise to the destruction of muscular tissue, nervous action to a change in the nervous matter; and this destruction and decomposition necessarily involve a fresh supply of *nitrogenous* matter, in order that the loss may be repaired.

Now a tree, being inactive, has little or no waste. All the food that it obtains goes to the invigoration of its frame; not one atom is destroyed in seeking more: but the essential condition of animal life is muscular action; the essential condition of muscular action is the destruction of muscular tissue; and the essential condition of the destruction of muscular tissue is a supply of food fitted for the reformation of it, or—*death*. It is impossible for an animal—like a vegetable—to stand still and not destroy. If the limbs are not moving, the heart is beating, the lungs playing, the bosom heaving. Hence an animal, in order to continue its existence, must obtain its subsistence either by its own exertions or by those of others—in a word, it must be *autobious* or *allobious*.

The procuration of sustenance, then, is the necessary condition of animal life, and constitutes the sole apparent reason for the addition of the locomotive apparatus to the vegetative functions of sentient nature; but the faculties of comparison and volition have been further added to the animal nature of Man, in order to enable him, among other things, the better to gratify his wants—to give him such a mastery over the elements of material nature, that he may force the external world the more readily to contribute to his support. Hence the derangement of either one of those functions must degrade the human being—as regards his means of sustenance—to the level of the brute. If his intellect be impaired, and the faculty of perceiving "the fitness of things" be consequently lost to him—or, this being sound, if the power of moving his muscles in compliance with his will be deficient—then the individual becomes no longer capable, like his fellows, of continuing his existence by his own exertions.

Hence, in every state, we have two extensive causes of allobiism, or living by the labour of others; the one intellectual, as in the case of lunatics and idiots, and the other physical, as in the case of the infirm, the crippled, and the maimed—the old and the young.

But a third, and a more extensive class, still remains to be particularized. The members of every community may be divided into the *energetic* and the *an-ergetic;* that is to say, into the hardworking and the non-working, the industrious and the indolent classes; the distinguishing characteristic of the *anergetic* being the extreme irksomeness of all labour to them, and their consequent indisposition to work for their subsistence. Now, in the circumstances above enumerated, we have three capital causes why, in every State, a certain portion of the community must derive their subsistence from the exertions of the rest; the first proceeds from some *physical* defect, as in the case of the old and the young, the super-annuated and the sub-annuated, the crippled and the maimed; the second from some *intellectual* defect, as in the case of lunatics and idiots; and the third from some *moral* defect, as in the case of the indolent, the vagrant, the professional mendicant, and the criminal. In all civilized countries, there will necessarily be a greater or less number of human parasites living on the sustenance of their fellows. The industrious must labour to support the lazy, and the sane to keep the insane, and the able-bodied to maintain the infirm.

Still, to complete the social fabric, another class requires to be specified. As yet, regard has been paid only to those who must needs labour for their living, or who, in default of so doing, must prey on the proceeds of the industry of their more active or more stalwart brethren. There is, however, in all civilized society, a farther portion of the people distinct from either of those above mentioned, who, being already provided—no matter how—with a sufficient stock of sustenance, or what will exchange for such, have no occasion to toil for an additional supply.

Hence all society would appear to arrange itself into four different classes:—

    I. Those that Will Work.
    II. Those that Cannot Work.
    III. Those that Will Not Work.
    IV. Those that Need Not Work.

Under one or other section of this quadruple division, every member, not only of our community, but of every other civilized State, must necessarily be included; the rich, the poor, the industrious, the idle, the honest, the dishonest, the virtuous, and the vicious—each and all must be comprised therein.

Let me now proceed specially to treat of each of these classes—to distribute under one or other of these four categories the diverse modes of living peculiar to the members of our own community, and so to enunciate, for the first time, the natural history, as it were, of the industry and idleness of Great Britain in the nineteenth century.

It is no easy matter, however, to classify the different kinds of labour scientifically. To arrange the several varieties of work into "orders," and to group the manifold species of arts under a few comprehensive genera—so that the mind may grasp the whole at one effort—is a task of a most perplexing character. Moreover, the first attempt to bring any number of diverse phenomena within the rules of logical division is not only a matter of considerable difficulty, but one, unfortunately, that is generally unsuccessful. It is impossible, however, to proceed with the present inquiry without making some attempt at systematic arrangement; for of all scientific processes, the classification of the various phenomena, in connection with a given subject, is perhaps the most important; indeed, if we consider that the function of cognition is essentially *discriminative*, it is evident, that without distinguishing between one object and another, there can be no knowledge, nor, indeed, any perception. Even as the seizing of a particular difference causes the mind to *apprehend* the special character of an object, so does the discovery of the agreements and differences among the several phenomena of a subject enable the understanding to *comprehend* it. What the generalization of events is to the ascertainment of natural laws, the generalization of things is to the discovery of natural systems. But classification is no less dangerous than it is important to science; for in precisely the same proportion as a correct grouping of objects into genera and species, orders and varieties, expands and assists our understanding, so does any erroneous arrangement cripple and retard all true knowledge. The reduction of all external substances into four elements by the ancients—earth, air, fire, and water—perhaps did more to obstruct the progress of chemical science than even a prohibition of the study could have effected.

But the branches of industry are so multifarious, the divisions of labour so minute and manifold, that it seems at first almost impossible to reduce them to any system. Moreover, the crude generalizations expressed in the names of the several arts, render the subject still more perplexing.

Some kinds of workmen, for example, are called after the *articles they make*—as saddlers, hatters, boot-makers, dress-makers, breeches-makers, stay-makers, lace-makers, button-makers, glovers, cabinet-makers, artificial-flower-makers, ship-builders, organ-builders, boat-builders, nailers, pin-makers, basket-makers, pump-makers, clock and watch makers, wheel-wrights, ship-wrights, and so forth.

Some operatives, on the other hand, take their names not from what they make, but from the *kind of work they perform*. Hence we have carvers, joiners, bricklayers, weavers, knitters, engravers, embroiderers, tanners, curriers, bleachers, thatchers, lime-burners, glass-blowers, seamstresses, assayers, refiners, embossers, chasers, painters, paper-hangers, printers, book-binders, cab-drivers, fishermen, graziers, and so on.

Other artizans, again, are styled after the *materials upon which they work*, such as tinmen, jewellers, lapidaries, goldsmiths, braziers, plumbers, pewterers, glaziers, &c. &c.

And lastly, a few operatives are named after the *tools they use;* thus we have ploughmen, sawyers, and needlewomen.

But these divisions, it is evident, are as unscientific as they are arbitrary; nor would it be possible, by adopting such a classification, to arrive at any practical result.

Now, I *had* hoped to have derived some little assistance in my attempt to reduce the several varieties of work to system from the arrangement of the products of industry and art at "the Great Exhibition." I knew, however, that the point of classification had proved the great stumbling block to the French Industrial Exhibitions. In the Exposition of the Arts and Manufactures of France in 1806, for instance, M. Costaz adopted a topographical arrangement, according to the departments of the kingdom whence the specimens were sent. In 1819, again, finding the previous arrangement conveyed little or no knowledge, depending, as it did, on the mere local association of the places of manufacture, the same philosopher attempted to classify all arts into a sort of natural system, but the separate divisions amounted to thirty-nine, and were found to be confused and inconvenient. In 1827 M. Payon adopted a classification into five great divisions, arranging the arts according as they are chemical, mechanical, physical, economical, or "miscellaneous" in their nature. It was found, however, in practice, that two, or even three, of these characteristics often belonged to the same manufacture. In

1834 M. Dupin proposed a classification that was found to work better than any which preceded it. He viewed man as a locomotive animal, a clothed animal, a domiciled animal, &c., and thus tracing him through his various daily wants and employments, he arrived at a classification in which all arts are placed under nine headings, according as they contribute to the alimentary, sanitary, vestiary, domiciliary, locomotive, sensitive, intellectual, preparative, or social tendencies of man. In 1844 and 1849 attempts were made towards an eclectic combination of two or three of the above-mentioned systems, but it does not appear that the latter arrangements presented any marked advantages.

Now, with all the experience of the French nation to guide us, I naturally expected that especial attention would be directed towards the point of classification with us, and that a technological system would be propounded, which would be found at least an improvement on the bungling systems of the French. It must be confessed, however, that no nation could possibly have stultified itself so egregiously as we have done in this respect. Never was there anything half so puerile as the classification of the works of industry in our own Exhibition!

But this comes of the patronage of Princes; for we are told that at one of the earliest meetings at Buckingham Palace his Royal Highness *propounded* the system of classification according to which the works of industry *were to be* arranged. The published minutes of the meeting on the 30th of June, 1849, inform us—

"His Royal Highness communicated his views regarding the formation of a Great Collection of Works of Industry and Art in London in 1851, for the purposes of exhibition, and of competition and encouragement. His Royal Highness considered that such a collection and exhibition should consist of the following divisions:—

Raw Materials.
Machinery and Mechanical Inventions.
Manufactures.
Sculpture and Plastic Art generally."

Now, were it possible for monarchs to do with natural laws as with social ones, namely, to blow a trumpet and declaring "*le roi le veut*," to have their will pass into one of the statutes of creation, it might be advantageous to science that Princes should seek to lay down orders of arrangement and propound systems of classification. But seeing that Science is as pure a republic as Letters, and that there are no "Highnesses" in philosophy—for if there be any aristocracy at all in such matters, it is at least an aristocracy of intellect — it is rather an injury than a benefit that those who are high in authority should interfere in these affairs at all; since, from the very circumstances of their position it is utterly impossible for them to arrive at anything more than the merest surface knowledge on such subjects. The influence, too, that their mere "authority" has over men's minds is directly opposed to the perception of truth, preventing that free and independent exercise of the intellect from which alone all discovery and knowledge can proceed.

Judging the quadruple arrangement of the Great Exhibition by the laws of logical division, we find that the three classes—Raw Materials, Machinery, and Manufactures—which refer more particularly to the Works of Industry, are neither distinct nor do they include the whole. What is a raw material, and what a manufacture? It is from the difficulty of distinguishing between these two conditions that leather is placed under Manufactures, and steel under Raw Materials—though surely steel is iron *plus* carbon, and leather skin *plus* tannin; so that, technologically considered, there is no difference between them. If by the term raw material is meant some natural product in its crude state, then it is evident that "Geological maps, plans, and sections; prussiate of potash, and other mixed chemical manufactures; sulphuric, muriatic, nitric, and other acids; medicinal tinctures, cod liver oil, dried fruits, fermented liquors and spirits, preserved meats, portable soups, glue, and the alloys" cannot possibly rank as *raw* materials, though one and all of these articles are to be found so "classified" at the Great Exhibition; but if the meaning of a "raw material" be extended to any product which constitutes the substance to be operated upon in an industrial art, then the answer is that leather, which is the material of shoes and harness, is no more a manufacture than steel, which is placed among the raw materials, because forming the constituent substance of cutlery and tools. So interlinked are the various arts and manufactures, that what is the product of one process of industry is the material of another—thus, yarn is the product of spinning, and the material of weaving, and in the same manner the cloth, which is the product of weaving, becomes the material of tailoring.

But a still greater blunder than the non-distinction between products and materials lies in the confounding of *processes* with *products*. In an Industrial Exhibition to reserve no special place for the processes of industry is very much like the play of Hamlet with the part of Hamlet omitted; and yet it is evident that, in the quadruple arrangement before mentioned, those most important industrial operations which consist merely in arriving at the same result by simpler means—as, for instance, the hot blast in metallurgical operations—can find no distinct expression. The consequence is that methods of work are arranged under the same head as the work itself; and the "Executive" have been obliged to group under the first subdivision of *Raw Materials* the following inconsistent jumble:—Salt deposits; ventilation; safety lamps and other methods of lighting; methods of lowering and raising miners, and draining; methods of roasting, smelting, or otherwise reducing ores; while under the second subdivision of Raw Materials chemical and pharmaceutical *processes* and *products* are indiscriminately confounded.

Another most important defect is the omission of all mention of those industrial processes which have *no special or distinct products of their own*, but which are rather engaged *in adding to the beauty or durability of others;* as, for instance, the bleaching of some textile fabrics, the embroidering of others, the dyeing and printing of others; the binding of books; the cutting of glass; the painting of china, &c. From the want of an express division for this large portion of our industrial arts, there is a jumbling and a bungling throughout the whole arrangement. Under the head of *manufactures* are grouped printing and bookbinding, the "dyeing of woollen, cotton, and linen goods," "embroidery, fancy, and industrial work," the cutting and engraving of glass; and, lastly, the art of "decoration generally," including "ornamental, coloured decoration," and the "imitations of woods, marbles, &c.,"—though surely these are one and all *additions* to manufactures rather than *manufactures* themselves. Indeed, a more extraordinary and unscientific hotch-potch than the entire arrangement has never been submitted to public criticism and public ridicule.

Amid all this confusion and perplexity, then, how are we to proceed? Why, we must direct our attention to some more judicious and more experienced guide. In such matters, at least, as the Exposition of the Science of Labour, it is clear that we must "put not our trust in princes."

That Prince Albert has conferred a great boon on the country in the establishment of the Great Exhibition (for it is due not only to his patronage but to his own personal exertions), no unprejudiced mind can for a moment doubt; and that he has, ever since his first coming among us, filled a most delicate office in the State in a highly decorous and commendable manner, avoiding all political partizanship, and being ever ready to give the influence of his patronage, and, indeed, co-operation, to anything that appeared to promise an amelioration of the condition of the working classes of this country, I am most glad to have it in my power to bear witness; but that, *because of this,* we should pin our faith to a "hasty generalization" propounded by him, would be to render ourselves at once silly and servile.

If, with the view of obtaining some more precise information concerning the several branches of industry, we turn our attention to the Government analysis of the different modes of employment among the people, we shall find that for all purposes of a scientific or definite character the Occupation Abstract of the Census of this country is comparatively useless. Previous to 1841, the sole attempt made at generalization was the division of the entire industrial community into three orders, viz.:—

I. *Those employed in Agriculture.*
  1. Agricultural Occupiers.
    a. Employing Labourers.
    b. Not employing Labourers.
  2. Agricultural Labourers.

II. *Those employed in Manufactures.*
  1. Employed in Manufactures.
  2. Employed in making Manufacturing Machinery.

III. *All other Classes.*
  1. Employed in Retail Trade or in Handicraft, as Masters or Workmen.
  2. Capitalists, Bankers, Professional, and other educated men.
  3. Labourers employed in labour not Agricultural—as Miners, Quarriers, Fishermen, Porters, &c.
  4. Male Servants.
  5. Other Males, 20 years of age.

The defects of this arrangement must be self-evident to all who have paid the least attention to economical science. It offends against both the laws of logical division, the parts being neither distinct nor equal to the whole. In the first place, what is a manufacturer? and how is such an one to be distinguished from one employed in handicraft? How do the workers in metal, as the "tin manufacturers," "lead manufacturers," "iron manufacturers"—who are one and all classed under the head of manufacturers—differ, in an economical point of view, from the workers in wood, as the carpenters and joiners, the cabinet-makers, ship-builders, &c., who are all classed under the head of handicraftsmen? Again, according to the census of 1831, a brewer is placed among those employed in retail trade or in handicrafts, while a vinegar maker is ranked with the manufacturers. According to Mr. Babbage, *manufacturing* differs from mere *making* simply in the quantity produced—he being a manufacturer who makes a greater number of the same articles; manufacturing is thus simply production in a large way, in connection with the several handicrafts. Dr. Ure, however, appears to consider such articles manufactures as are produced by means of machinery, citing the word which originally signified production by hand (being the Latin equivalent for the Saxon *handicraft*) as an instance of those singular verbal corruptions by which terms come to stand for the very opposite to their literal meaning. But with all deference to the Doctor, for whose judgment I have the highest respect, Mr. Babbage's definition of a manufacturer, viz., as a producer on a large scale, appears to me the more correct; for it is in this sense that we speak of manufacturing chemists, boot and shoe manufacturers, ginger-beer manufacturers, and the like.

The Occupation Abstract of the Census of 1841, though far more comprehensive than the one preceding it, is equally unsatisfactory and unphilosophical. In this document the several members of Society are thus classified:—

I. *Persons engaged in Commerce, Trade, and Manufacture.*
II. *Agriculture.*
III. *Labour, not Agricultural.*
IV. *Army and Navy Merchant Seamen, Fishermen, and Watermen.*
V. *Professions and other pursuits requiring education.*
VI. *Government, Civil Service, and Municipal and Parochial Officers.*
VII. *Domestic Servants.*
VIII. *Persons of Independent Means.*
IX. *Almspeople, Pensioners, Paupers, Lunatics, and Prisoners.*
X. *Remainder of Population, including Women and Children.*

Here it will be seen that the defects arising from drawing distinctions where no real differences exist, are avoided, those engaged in handicrafts being included under the same head as those engaged in manufacture; but the equally grave error of confounding or grouping together occupations which are essentially diverse, is allowed to continue. Accordingly, the first division is made to include those who are engaged in trade and commerce as well as manufacture, though surely—the one belongs strictly to the distributing, and the other to the producing class—occupations which are not only essentially distinct, but of which it is absolutely necessary for a right understanding of the state of the country that we know the proportion that the one bears to the other. Again, the employers in both cases are confounded with the employed, so that, though the capitalists who supply the materials, and pay the wages for the several kinds of work are a distinct body of people from those who *do* the work, and a body, moreover, that it is of the highest possible importance, in an economical point of view, that we should be able to estimate numerically,—no attempt is made to discriminate the one from the other. Now these three classes, distributors, employers, and operatives, which in the Government returns of the people are jumbled together in one heterogeneous crowd, as if the distinctions between Capital, Labour, and Distribution had never been propounded, are precisely those concerning which the social inquirer desires the most minute information.

The Irish census is differently arranged from that of Great Britain. There the several classes are grouped under the following heads:—

I. *Ministering to Food.*
   1. As Producers.
   2. As Preparers.
   3. As Distributors.
II. *Ministering to Clothing.*
   1. As Manufacturers of Materials.
   2. As Handicraftsmen and Dealers.
III. *Ministering to Lodging, Furniture, Machinery, &c.*
IV. *Ministering to Health.*
V. *Ministering to Charity.*
VI. *Ministering to Justice.*
VII. *Ministering to Education.*
VIII. *Ministering to Religion.*
IX. *Various Arts and Employments, not included in the foregoing.*
X. *Residue of Population,* not having specified occupations, and including unemployed persons and women.

This, however, is no improvement upon the English classification. There is the same want of discrimination, and the same disregard of the great "economical" divisions of society.

Moreover, to show the extreme fallacy of such a classification, it is only necessary to make the following extract from the Report of the Commissioners for Great Britain:—

"We would willingly have given a classification of the occupations of the inhabitants of Great Britain into the various wants to which they respectively minister, but, in attempting this, we were stopped by the various anomalies and uncertainties to which such a classification seemed necessarily to lead, from the fact that many persons supply more than one want, though they can only be classed under one head. Thus to give but a single instance—*the farmer and grazier may be deemed to minister quite as much to clothing by the fleece and hides as he does to food by the flesh of his sheep and cattle.*"

He, therefore, who would seek to elaborate the natural history of the industry of the people of England, must direct his attention to some social philosopher, who has given the subject more consideration than either princes or Government officials can possibly be expected to devote to it. Among the whole body of economists, Mr. Stuart Mill appears to be the only man who has taken a comprehensive and enlightened view of the several functions of society. Following in the footsteps of M. Say, the French social philosopher, he first points out concerning the products of industry, that labour is not creative of objects but of utilities, and then proceeds to say:—

"Now the utilities produced by labour are of three kinds; they are—

"First, utilities *fixed and embodied in outward objects;* by labour employed in investing external *material* things with properties which render them serviceable to human beings. This is the common case, and requires no illustration.

"Secondly, utilities *fixed and embodied in human beings;* the labour being in this case employed in conferring on human beings qualities which render them serviceable to themselves and others. To this class belongs the labour of all concerned in education; not only schoolmasters, tutors, and professors, but governments, so far as they aim successfully at the improvement of the people; moralists and clergymen, as far as productive of benefit; the labour of physicians, as far as instrumental in preserving life and physical or mental efficiency; of the teachers of bodily exercises, and of the various trades, sciences, and arts, together with the labour of the learners in acquiring them, and all labour bestowed by any persons, throughout life, in improving the knowledge or cultivating the bodily and mental faculties of themselves or others.

"Thirdly, and lastly, utilities *not fixed or embodied in any object*, but consisting in a mere *service rendered*, a pleasure given, an inconvenience or pain averted, during a longer or a shorter time, but without leaving a *permanent* acquisition in the improved qualities of any person or thing; the labour here being employed in producing an utility *directly*, not (as in the two former cases) in *fitting some other* thing to afford an utility. Such, for example, is the labour of the musical performer, the actor, the public declaimer or reciter, and the showman.

"Some good may, no doubt, be produced beyond the moment, upon the feeling and disposition, or general state of enjoyment of the spectators; or instead of good there may be harm, but neither the one nor the other is the effect intended, is the result for which the exhibitor works and the spectator pays, but the immediate pleasure. Such, again, is the labour of the army and navy; they, at the best, prevent a country from being conquered, or from being injured or insulted, which is a service, but in all other respects leave the country neither improved nor deteriorated. Such, too, is the labour of the legislator, the judge, the officer of justice, and all other agents of Government, in their ordinary functions, apart from any influence they may exert on the improvement of the national mind. The service which they render is to maintain peace and security; these compose the utility which they produce. It may appear to some that carriers, and merchants or dealers, should be placed in this same class, since their labour does not add any properties to objects, but I reply that it does, it adds the property of being in the place where they are wanted, instead of being in some other place, which is a very useful property, and the utility it confers is embodied in the things themselves, which now actually are in the place where they are required for use, and in consequence of that increased utility could be sold at an increased price proportioned to the labour expended in conferring it. This labour, therefore, does not belong to the third class, but to the first."

To the latter part of the above classification, I regret to say I cannot assent. Surely the property of being in the place where they are wanted, which carriers and distributors are said to confer on external objects, cannot be said to be fixed—if, indeed, it be strictly *embodied* in the objects, since the very act of distribution consists in the alteration of this local relation, and transferring such objects to the possession of another. Is not the utility which the weaver fixes and embodies in a yard of cotton, a very different utility from that effected by the linendraper in handing the same yard of cotton over the counter in exchange for so much money? and in this particular act, it would be difficult to perceive what is fixed and embodied, seeing that it consists essentially in an exchange of commodities.

Mr. Mill's mistake appears to consist in not discerning that there is another class of labour besides that employed in producing utilities *directly*, and that occupied in *fitting other things* to afford utilities: viz., that which is engaged in *assisting* those who are so occupied in fitting things to be useful. This class consists of such as are engaged in aiding the producers of permanent material utilities either *before* or during production, and such as are engaged in aiding them *after* production. Under the first division are comprised capitalists, or those who supply the materials and tools for the work, superintendents and managers, or those who direct the work, and labourers, or those who perform some minor office connected with the work, as in turning the large wheel for a turner, in carrying the bricks to a bricklayer, and the like; while in the second division, or those who are engaged in assisting producers *after* production, are included carriers, or those who remove the produce to the market, and dealers and shopmen, or those who obtain purchasers for it. Now it is evident that the function of all these classes is merely *auxiliary* to the labour of the producers. consisting principally of so many modes of economizing their time and labour. Whether the gains of some of these auxiliary classes are as disproportionately large, as the others are disproportionately small, this is not the place to inquire. My present duty is merely to record the fact of the existence of such classes, and to assign them their proper place in the social fabric, as at present constituted.

Now, from the above it will appear, that there are four distinct classes of workers:—

I. ENRICHERS, or those who are employed in producing utilities fixed and embodied in material things, that is to say, in producing exchangeable commodities or riches.

II. AUXILIARIES, or those who are employed in aiding the production of exchangeable commodities.

III. BENEFACTORS, or those who are employed in producing utilities fixed and embodied in human beings, that is to say, in conferring upon them some permanent good.

IV. SERVITORS, or those who are employed in rendering some service, that is to say, in conferring some temporary good upon another.

Class 1 is engaged in investing *material* objects with qualities which render them serviceable to others.

Class 2 is engaged in aiding the operations of Class 1.

Class 3 is engaged in conferring on *human beings* qualities which render them serviceable to themselves or others.

Class 4 is engaged in giving a pleasure, averting a pain (during a longer or shorter period), or preventing an inconvenience, by performing some office for others that they would find irksome to do for themselves.

Hence it appears that the operations of the first and third of the above classes, or the Enrichers and Benefactors of Society, tend to leave some *permanent acquisition* in the improved qualities of either persons or things,—whereas the operations of the second and fourth classes, or the Auxiliaries and Servitors, are limited merely to promoting either the labours or the pleasures of the other members of the community.

Such, then, are the several classes of Workers; and here it should be stated that, I apply the title Worker to all those who do *anything* for their living, who perform any act whatsoever that is considered worthy of being paid for by others, without regard to the question whether such labourers tend to add to or decrease the aggregate wealth of the community. I consider all persons doing or giving something for the comforts they obtain, as self-supporting individuals. Whether that something be really an equivalent for the emoluments they receive, it is not my vocation here to inquire. Suffice it some real or imaginary benefit is conferred upon society, or a particular individual, and what is thought a fair and proper reward is given in return for it. Hence I look upon soldiers, sailors, Government and parochial officers, capitalists, clergymen, lawyers, wives, &c., &c., as self-supporting —a certain amount of labour, or a certain desirable commodity, being given by each and all in exchange for other commodities, which are considered less desirable to the individuals parting with them, and more desirable to those receiving them.

Nevertheless, it must be confessed that, economically speaking, the most important and directly valuable of all classes are those whom I have here denominated Enrichers. These consist not only of Producers, but of the Collectors and Extractors of Wealth, concerning whom a few words are necessary.

There are three modes of obtaining the materials of our wealth—(1) by collecting, (2) by extracting, and (3) by producing them. The industrial processes concerned in the collection of the materials of wealth are of the rudest and most primitive kind—being pursued principally by such tribes as depend for their food, and raiment, and shelter, on the spontaneous productions of nature. The usual modes by which the collection is made is by gathering the vegetable produce (which is the simplest and most direct form of all industry), and when the produce is of an animal nature, by hunting, shooting, or fishing, according as the animal sought after inhabits the land, the air, or the water. In a more advanced state of society, where the erection of places of shelter has come to constitute one of the acts of life, the felling of trees will also form one of the modes by which the materials making up the wealth of the nation are collected. In Great Britain there appears to be fewer people connected with the mere *collection* of wealth than with any other general industrial process. The fishermen are not above 25,000, and the wood-cutters and woodmen not 5000; so that even with gamekeepers, and others engaged in the taking of game, we may safely say that there are about 30,000 out of 18,000,000, or only one-six hundredth of the entire population, engaged in this mode of industry—a fact which strongly indicates the artificial character of our society.

The *production* of the materials of wealth, which indicates a far higher state of civilization, and which consists in the several agricultural and farming processes for increasing the natural stock of animal and vegetable food, employs upwards of one million; while those who are engaged in the *extraction* of our treasures from the earth, either by mining or quarrying, both of which processes—depending, as they do, upon a knowledge of some of the subtler natural powers — could only have been brought into operation in a highly advanced stage of the human intellect, number about a quarter of a million. Altogether, there appear to be about one million and a half of individuals engaged in the industrial processes connected with the collection, extraction, and production of the materials of wealth; those who are employed in operating upon these materials, in the fashioning of them into manufactures, making them up into commodities, as well as those engaged in the distribution of them—that is to say, the transport and sale of them when so fashioned or made up—appear to amount to another two millions and a half, so that the industrial classes of Great Britain, taken altogether, may be said to amount to four millions. For the more perfect comprehension, however, of the several classes of society, let me subjoin a table in round numbers, calculated from the census of 1841, and including among the first items both the employers as well as employed :—

Engaged in Trade and Manufacture	3,000,000
,, Agriculture	1,500,000
,, Mining, Quarrying, and Transit	750,000
Total Employers and Employed	5,250,000
Domestic Servants	1,000,000
Independent persons	500,000
Educated pursuits (including Professions and Fine Arts)	200,000
Government Officers (including Army, Navy, Civil Service, and Parish Officers)	200,000
Alms-people (including Paupers, Prisoners, and Lunatics)	200,000
	7,350,000
Residue of Population (including 3,500,000 wives and 7,500,000 children)	11,000,000
	18,350,000

Now, of the 5,250,000 individuals engaged in Agriculture, Mining, Transit, Manufacture and Trade, it would appear that about one million and a quarter may be considered as employers; and, consequently, that the remaining four millions may be said to represent the numerical strength of the operatives of England and Scotland. Of these about one million, or a quarter of the whole, may be said to be engaged in producing the materials of wealth; and about a quarter of a million, or one-sixteenth of the entire number, in extracting from the soil the substances upon which many of the manufacturers have to operate.

The artizans, or those who are engaged in the several handicrafts or manufactures operating upon the various materials of wealth thus obtained, are distinct from the workmen above-mentioned, belonging to what are called skilled labourers, whereas those who are employed in the collection, extraction, or growing of wealth, belong to the unskilled class.

An artisan is an *educated* handicraftsman, following a calling that requires an apprenticeship of greater or less duration in order to arrive at perfection in it; whereas a labourer's occupation needs no education whatever. Many years must be spent in practising before a man can acquire sufficient manual dexterity to make a pair of boots or a coat; dock labour or porter's work, however, needs neither teaching nor learning, for any man can carry a load or turn a wheel. The artisan, therefore, is literally a handicraftsman—one who by practice has acquired manual dexterity enough to perform a particular class of work, which is consequently called "skilled." The natural classification of artisans, or skilled labourers, appears to be according to the materials upon which they work, for this circumstance seems to constitute the peculiar quality of the art more than the tool used—indeed, it appears to be the principal cause of the modification of the implements in different handicrafts. The tools used to fashion, as well as the instruments and substances used to join the several materials operated upon in the manufactures and handicrafts, differ according as those materials are of different kinds. We do not, for instance, attempt to saw cloth into shape nor to cut bricks with shears; neither do we solder the soles to the upper leathers of our boots, nor nail together the seams of our shirts. And even in those crafts where the means of uniting the materials are similar, the artisan working upon one kind of substance is generally incapable of operating upon another. The tailor who stitches woollen materials together would make but a poor hand at sewing leather. The two substances are joined by the same means, but in a different manner, and with different instruments. So the turner, who has been accustomed to turn wood, is unable to fashion metals by the same method.

The most natural mode of grouping the artisans into classes would appear to be according as they pursue some *mechanical* or *chemical* occupation. The former are literally mechanics or handicraftsmen—the latter chemical manufacturers. The handicraftsmen consist of (1) The workers in silk, wool, cotton, flax, and hemp—as weavers, spinners, knitters, carpet-makers, lace-makers, rope-makers, canvas-weavers, &c. (2) The workers in skin, gut, and feathers—as tanners, curriers, furriers, feather dressers, &c. (3) The makers up of silken, woollen, cotton, linen, hempen, and leathern materials—as tailors, milliners, shirtmakers, sail-makers, hatters, glove-makers, saddlers, and the like. (4) The workers in wood, as the carpenters, the cabinet-makers, &c. (5) The workers in cane, osier, reed, rush, and straw—as basket-makers, straw-plait manufacturers, thatchers, and the like. (6) The workers in brick and stones—as bricklayers, masons, &c. (7) The workers in glass and earthenware—as potters, glass-blowers, glass-cutters, bottle-makers, glaziers, &c. (8) The workers in metals—as braziers, tinmen, plumbers, goldsmiths, pewterers, coppersmiths, iron-founders, blacksmiths, whitesmiths, anchorsmiths, locksmiths, &c. (9) The workers in paper—as the paper-makers, cardboard-makers. (10) The chemical manufacturers—as powder-makers, white-lead-makers, alkali and acid manufacturers, lucifer-match-makers, blacking-makers, ink-makers, soap-boilers, tallow-chandlers, &c. (11) The workers at the superlative or extrinsic arts—that is to say, those which have no manufactures of their own, but which are engaged in adding to the utility or beauty of others—as printing bookbinding, painting, and decorating, gilding, burnishing, &c.

The circumstances which govern the classification of *trades* are totally different from those regulating the division of work. In trade the convenience of the purchaser is mainly studied, the sale of such articles being associated as are usually required together. Hence the master coachmaker is frequently a harness manufacturer as well, for the purchaser of the one commodity generally stands in need of the other. The painter and house-decorator not only follows the trade of the glazier, but of the plumber, too; because these arts are one and all connected with the "doing up" of houses. For the same reason the builder combines the business of the plasterer with that of the bricklayer, and not unfrequently that of the carpenter and joiner in addition. In all of these businesses, however, a distinct set of workmen are required, according as the materials operated upon are different.

We are now in a position to proceed with the arrangement of the several members of society into different classes, according to the principles of classification which have been here laid down. The difficulties of the task, however, should be continually borne in mind; for where so many have failed it cannot be expected that perfection can be arrived at by any one individual; and, slight as the labour of such a task may at the first glance appear to some, still the system here propounded has been the work and study of many months.

CLASSIFICATION

OF

THE WORKERS AND NON-WORKERS

OF GREAT BRITAIN.

THOSE WHO WILL WORK.

I. ENRICHERS, as the Collectors, Extractors, or Producers of Exchangeable Commodities.

II. AUXILIARIES, as the Promoters of Production, or the Distributors of the Produce.

III. BENEFACTORS, or those who confer some permanent benefit, as Educators and Curators engaged in promoting the physical, intellectual, or spiritual well-being of the people.

IV. SERVITORS, or those who render some temporary service, or pleasure, as Amusers, Protectors, and Servants.

THOSE WHO CANNOT WORK.

V. THOSE WHO ARE PROVIDED FOR BY SOME PUBLIC INSTITUTION, as the Inmates of workhouses, prisons, hospitals, asylums, almshouses, dormitories, and refuges.

VI. THOSE WHO ARE UNPROVIDED FOR, and incapacitated for labour, either from want of power, from want of means, or from want of employment.

THOSE WHO WILL NOT WORK.

VII. VAGRANTS.

VIII. PROFESSIONAL BEGGARS.

IX. CHEATS.

X. THIEVES.

XI. PROSTITUTES.

THOSE WHO NEED NOT WORK.

XII. THOSE WHO DERIVE THEIR INCOME FROM RENT.

XIII. THOSE WHO DERIVE THEIR INCOME FROM DIVIDENDS.

XIV. THOSE WHO DERIVE THEIR INCOME FROM YEARLY STIPENDS.

XV. THOSE WHO DERIVE THEIR INCOME FROM OBSOLETE OR NOMINAL OFFICES.

XVI. THOSE WHO DERIVE THEIR INCOME FROM TRADES IN WHICH THEY DO NOT APPEAR.

XVII. THOSE WHO DERIVE THEIR INCOME BY FAVOUR FROM OTHERS.

XVIII. THOSE WHO DERIVE THEIR SUPPORT FROM THE HEAD OF THE FAMILY.

THOSE WHO WILL WORK.

I. *Enrichers*, or those engaged in the collection, extraction, or production of exchangeable commodities.

   A. COLLECTORS.
      1. Fishermen.
      2. Woodmen.
      3. Sand and Clay-collectors.
      4. Copperas, Cement-stones, and other finders.

   B. EXTRACTORS.
      1. Miners.
         a. Coal.
         b. Salt.
         c. Iron, Lead, Tin, Copper, Zinc, Manganese.
      2. Quarryers.
         a. Slate.
         b. Stone.

   C. GROWERS.
      1. Farmers.
         a. Capitalist Farmers.
            i. Yeomen, or Proprietary Farmers.
            ii. Tenant Farmers.
         b. Peasant Farmers.
            i. Peasant Proprietors; as the Cumberland "Statesmen."
            ii. "Metayers," or labourers paying the landlord a certain portion of the produce as rent for the use of the land.
            iii. "Cottiers," or labouring Tenant Farmers.
      2. Graziers.
      3. Gardeners, Nurserymen, Florists.

   D. MAKERS OR ARTIFICERS.
      1. Mechanics.
         a. Workers in Silk, Wool, Worsted, Hair, Cotton, Flax, Hemp, Coir.
         b. Workers in Skin, Gut, and Feathers.
         c. Workers in Woollen, Silken, Cotton, Linen, and Leathern Materials.
         d. Workers in Wood, Ivory, Bone, Horn, and Shell.
         e. Workers in Osier, Cane, Reed, Rush, and Straw.
         f. Workers in Stone and Brick.
         g. Workers in Glass and Earthenware.
         h. Workers in Metal.
         i. Workers in Paper.
      2. Chemical Manufacturers.
         a. Acid, Alkali, Alum, Copperas, Prussian-Blue, and other Manufacturers.
         b. Gunpowder Manufacturers, Percussion-Cap, Cartridge, and Firework Makers.
         c. Brimstone and Lucifer-match Manufacturers.
         d. White-lead, Colour, Black-lead, Whiting, and Blue Manufacturers.
         e. Oil and Turpentine Distillers, and Varnish Manufacturers.
         f. Ink Manufacturers, Sealing-wax and Wafer Makers.
         g. Blacking Manufacturers.
         h. Soap Boilers and Grease Makers.
         i. Starch Manufacturers.
         j. Tallow and Wax Chandlers.
         k. Artificial Manure Manufacturers.

  l. Artificial Stone and Cement Manufacturers.
m. Asphalte and Tar Manufacturers.
n. Glue and Size Makers.
  o. Polishing Paste, and Glass and Emery Paper Makers.
  p. Lime, Coke, and Charcoal Burners.
  q. Manufacturing Chemists and Drug Manufacturers.
  r. Workers connected with Provisions, Luxuries, and Medicines.
    i. Bakers, and Biscuit Makers.
    ii. Brewers.
    iii. Soda-water and Ginger-beer Manufacturers.
    iv. Distillers and Rectifiers.
    v. British Wine Manufacturers
    vi. Vinegar Manufacturers.
    vii. Fish and Provision Curers.
    viii. Preserved Meats and Preserved Fruit Preparers.
    ix. Sauce and Pickle Manufacturers.
    x. Mustard Makers.
    xi. Isinglass Manufacturers.
    xii. Sugar Bakers, Boilers, and Refiners.
    xiii. Confectioners and Pastry-cooks.
    xiv. Rice and Farinaceous Food Manufacturers.
    xv. Chocolate, Cocoa, and other Manufacturers of Substitutes for Tea.
    xvi. Cigar, Tobacco, and Snuff Manufacturers.
    xvii. Quack, and other Medicine Manufacturers, as Pills, Powders, Syrups, Cordials, Embrocations, Ointments, Plaisters, &c.

3. Workers connected with the Superlative Arts, that is to say, with those arts which have no products of their own, and are engaged either in adding to the beauty or usefulness of the products of other arts, or in inventing or designing the work appertaining to them.
 a. Printers.
 b. Bookbinders.
 c. Painters, Decorators, and Gilders.
 d. Writers and Stencillers.
 e. Dyers, Bleachers, Scourers, Calenderers, and Fullers.
 f. Print Colourers.
 g. Designers of Patterns.
 h. Embroiderers (of Muslin, Silk, &c.), and Fancy Workers.
 i. Desiccators, Anti-dry-rot Preservers, Waterproofers.
 j. Burnishers, Polishers, Grinders, Japanners, and French Polishers.
 k. Engravers, Chasers, Die-Sinkers, Embossers, Engine-Turners, and Glass-Cutters.
 l. Artists, Sculptors, and Carvers of Wood, Coral, Jet, &c.
 m. Modellers and Moulders.
 n. Architects, Surveyors, and Civil Engineers.
 o. Composers.
 p. Authors, Editors, and Reporters.

 *** Operatives are divisible, *according to the mode in which they are paid,* into—
  1. Day-workers.
  2. Piece-workers.
  3. "Lump" or Contract-workers; as at the docks.
  4. Perquisite-workers; as waiters, &c.
  5. "Kind" or Truck-workers; as the farm servants in the North of England, Domestic Servants and Milliners, Ballast-heavers, and men paid at "Tommy-shops."
  6. Tenant-workers; or those who lodge with or reside in houses belonging to their employers. The Slop-working Tailors generally lodge with the "Sweaters," and the "Hinds" of Northumberland, Cumberland, and Westmoreland have houses found them by their employers. These "Hinds" have to keep a

"Bondager," that is, a female in the house ready to answer the master's call, and to work at stipulated wages.

7. Improvement-workers; or those who are considered to be remunerated for their work by the instruction they receive in doing it; as "improvers" and apprentices.

8. Tribute-workers, as the Cornish Miners, Whalers, and Weavers in some parts of Ireland, where a certain proportion of the proceeds of the work done belongs to the workmen.

The wages of "society-men" among operatives are settled by *custom*, the wages of "non-society-men" are settled by *competition*.

Operatives are also divisible, *according to the places at which they work*, into—

1. Domestic workers, or those who work at home.
2. Shop or Factory workers, or those who work on the employer's premises.
3. Out-door workers, or those who work in the open air; as bricklayers, agricultural labourers, &c.
4. Jobbing-workers, or those who go out to work at private houses.
5. Rent-men, or those who pay rent for
   a. A "seat" at some domestic worker's rooms.
   b. "Power," as turners, and others, when requiring the use of a steam-engine. Some operatives have to pay rent for tools or "frames," as the sawyers and "stockingers," and some for gas when working on their employer's premises.

Operatives are further divisible, *according to those whom they employ to assist them*, into—

1. Family workers, or those who avail themselves of the assistance of their wives and children, as the Spitalfields Weavers.
2. "Sweaters" and Piece-master workers, or those who employ other members of their trade at less wages than they themselves receive.
3. "Garret-master" workers, or those who avail themselves of the labour (chiefly) of apprentices.

Operatives are moreover divisible, *according to those by whom they are employed*, into—

1. "Flints" and "Dungs;" "Whites" and "Blacks," according as they work for employers who pay or do not pay "society prices."
2. Jobbing piece-workers, or those who work single-handed for the public (without the intervention of an "employer") and are paid by the *piece*. These mostly do the work at their own homes, as cobblers, repairers, &c.
3. Jobbing day-workers, or those who work single-handed for the public (without the intervention of an "employer") and are paid by the *day*. These mostly go out to work at persons' houses and frequently have their food found them. Among the tailors and carpenters this practice is called "whipping the cat."
4. "Co-operative men," or those who work in "association" for their own profit, obtaining their work directly from the public, without the intervention of an "employer."

Lastly, Operatives admit of being arranged into two distinct classes, viz., the superior, or higher-priced, and the inferior, or lower-priced.

The superior, or higher-priced, operatives consist of—

1. The skilful.
2. The trustworthy.
3. The well-conditioned.

The inferior, or lower-priced operatives, on the other hand, are composed of—

1. The unskilful; as the old or superannuated, the young (including apprentices and "improvers"), the slow, and the awkward.

2. The untrustworthy; as the drunken, the idle, and the dishonest. Some of the cheap workers, whose wages are minimized almost to starvation point, so that honesty becomes morally impossible, have to deposit a certain sum of money, or to procure two householders to act as security for the faithful return of the work given out to them.
3. The inexpensive, consisting of—
    a. Those who can live upon less; as single men, foreigners, Irishmen, women, &c.
    b. Those who derive their subsistence from other sources; as Wives, Children, Paupers, Prisoners, Inmates of Asylums, Prostitutes, and Amateurs (or those who work at a business merely for pocket-money).
    c. Those who are in receipt of some pecuniary or other aid; as Pensioners, Allottees of land, and such as have out-door relief from the workhouse.

II. *Auxiliaries*, or those engaged in promoting the enrichment and distributing the riches of the community.
  A. PROMOTERS OF PRODUCTION.
   1. Employers, or those who find the materials, implements, and appurtenances for the work, and pay the wages of the workmen.
      a. Administrative Employers, or those who supply wholesale or retail dealers. These are subdivisible into—
         i. Standard Employers, or those who work at the regular standard prices of the trade.
         ii. "Cutting" Employers, or those who work at less than the regular prices of the trade; as Contractors, &c.
      b. Executive Employers, or those who work directly for the public without the intervention of a wholesale or retail dealer; as Builders, &c.
      c. Distributive Employers, or those who are both producers and retail traders.
         i. Those who retail what they produce; as Tailors, Shoemakers, Bakers, Eating-house Keepers, Street Mechanics, &c.
         ii. Those who retail other things (generally provisions), and compel or expect the men in their employ to deal with them for those articles, as the Truck-Masters and others.
         iii. Those who retail the appurtenances of the trade to which they belong, and compel or expect the men in their employ to purchase such appurtenances of them; as trimmings in the tailors' trade, thread among the seamstresses, and the like.
      d. Middlemen Employers, or those who act between the employer and the employed, obtaining work from employers, and employing others to do it; as Sub-contractors, Sweaters, &c. These consist of—
         i. Trade-working Employers, or those who make up goods for other employers in the trade.
         ii. Garret-masters, or those who make up goods for the trade on the smallest amount of capital, and generally on speculation.
         iii. Trading Operative Employers, or those who obtain work in considerable quantities, and employ others at reduced wages to assist them in it; as "Sweaters," "Seconders," &c. These are either—
            α. Piece Masters; as those who take out a certain piece of work and employ others to help them at reduced wages.
            β. "Lumper" Employers, or those who contract to do the work by the lump, which is usually paid for by the piece, and employ others at reduced wages in order to complete it.
   ₊ Employers are known among operatives as "honourable" or "dishonourable," according as the wages they pay are those, or less than those, of the Trade Society.
   2. Superintendents, or those who look after the workmen on behalf of employers.

  a. Managers.
  b. Clerks of the Works.
  c. Foremen.
  d. Overlookers.
  e. Tellers and Meters, or those who take note of the number and quantity of the articles delivered.
  f. Provers, or those whose duty it is to examine the quality or weight of the articles delivered.
  g. Timekeepers, or those who note the time of the operatives coming to and quitting labour.
  h. Gatekeepers, or those who see that no goods are taken out.
  i. Clerks, or those who keep accounts of all sales and purchases, incomings, and outgoings of the business.
  j. Pay Clerks, or those who pay the workmen their wages.
 3. Labourers.
  a. Acting as motive powers.
   i. Turning wheels, working pumps, blowing bellows.
   ii. Wheeling, dragging, pulling, or hoisting loads.
   iii. Shifting (scenes), or turning (corn).
   iv. Carrying (bricks, as hodmen).
   v. Driving (piles), ramming down (stones, as paviours).
   vi. Pressing (as fruit, for juice ; seeds, for oil).
  b. Uniting or putting one thing to another.
   i. Feeding (furnace), laying-on (as for printing machines).
   ii. Filling (as "fillers-in" of sieves at dust-yards).
   iii. Oiling (engines), greasing (railway wheels), pitching or tarring (vessels), pasting paper (for bags).
   iv. Mixing (mortar), kneading (clay).
   v. Tying up (plants and bunches of vegetables).
   vi. Folding (printed sheets).
   vii. Corking (bottles), or caulking (ships).
  c. Separating one thing from another.
   i. Sifting (cinders), screening (coals).
   ii. Picking (fruit, hops, &c.), shelling (peas), peeling, barking, and threshing.
   iii. Winnowing.
   iv. Weeding and stoning.
   v. Reaping and mowing.
   vi. Felling, lopping, hewing, chopping (as fire-wood), cutting (as chaff), shearing (sheep).
   vii. Sawing.
   viii. Blasting.
   viii. Breaking (stones), crushing (bones and ores), pounding (drugs).
   ix. Scouring (as sand from castings), scraping (ships).
  d. Excavating, sinking, and embanking.
   i. Tunnelling.
   ii. Sinking foundations.
   iii. Boring.
   iv. Draining, trenching, ditching, and hedging.
   v. Embanking.
   vi. Road-making, cutting.

B. DISTRIBUTORS OF PRODUCTION.
 1. Dealers, or those who are engaged in the buying and selling of commodities on their own account.
  a. Merchants or Importers, and Exporters.
  b. Wholesale Traders.
  c. Retail Traders.
  d. Contracting Purveyors, or those who supply goods by agreement.
  e. Contractors for work or repairs ; as Road Contractors, and others.

  f. Contractors for privileges, as the right of Printing the Catalogue of the Great Exhibition, or selling refreshments at Railway Stations, &c.
  g. Farmers of revenues from dues, tolls, &c.
  h. Itinerants, or those who seek out the Customers, instead of the Customers seeking out them.
   i. Hawkers, or those who cry their goods.
   ii. Pedlars, or those who carry their goods round.

2. Agents, or those who are engaged in the buying or selling of commodities for others, as Land Agents, House and Estate Agents, Colonial and East India Agents, &c., &c.
  a. Supercargoes.
  b. Factors, or Consignees.
  c. Brokers, Bill, Stock, Share, Ship, Sugar, Cotton, &c.
  d. Commission Salesmen, or Unlicensed Brokers.
  e. Buyers, or those who purchase materials or goods for Manufacturers, or Dealers.
  f. Auctioneers, or those who sell goods on Commission to the highest bidder.

3. Lenders and Lettors-out, or those who receive a certain sum for the loan or use of a thing.
  a. Lenders or Lettors-out of commodities, as—
   i. Job-horses, carriages, chairs and seats in parks, gardens, &c.
   ii. Plate, linen, furniture, piano-fortes, flowers, fancy dresses, Court suits, &c.
   iii. Books, newspapers, prints, and music.
  b. Lettors-out of tenements and storage room, as—
   i. Houses.
   ii. Lodgings.
   iii. Warehouse-room for imports, &c., as at wharfs.
   iv. Warehouse-room for furniture and other goods.
  c. Lenders of money, as—
   i. Mortgagees.
   ii. Bankers.
   iii. Bill-discounters.
   iv. Loan offices with and without policies of assurance.
   v. Building and investment societies.
   vi. Pawnbrokers.
   vii. Dolly shopmen.

⁎⁎* The several modes of distributing goods or money are—
1. By private contract or agreement.
2. By a fixed or ticketed price.
3. By competition, as at Auctions.
4. By games of chance, as Lotteries (with the "Art Union"), Raffles (at Fancy Fairs), Tossing (with piemen and others), Prizes for skill (with throwing sticks, &c.), Betting, Racing, &c.

The places at which goods are distributed are—
1. Fairs, or annual gatherings of buyers and sellers.
2. Markets, or weekly gatherings of buyers and sellers.
3. Exchanges, or daily gatherings of merchants and agents.
4. Counting-houses, or the places of business of wholesale traders.
5. Shops, or the places of business of retail traders.
6. Bazaars, or congregations of shops.

4. Trade Assistants.
  a. Shopmen and Warehousemen.
  b. Shopwalkers.
  c. Cashiers or Receivers.
  d. Clerks.
  e. Accountants.
  f. Rent-Collectors.
  g. Debt-collectors.

  h. Travellers, Town as well as Commercial.
  i. Touters.
  j. Barkers (outside shops).
  k. Bill deliverers.
  l. Bill-stickers.
  m. Boardmen.
  n. Advertizing-van Men.

 5. Carriers.
  a. Those engaged in the external transit of the Kingdom.
   i. Mercantile Sailing Vessels.
   ii. Mercantile Steam Vessels.
  b. Those engaged in the internal Transit of the Kingdom.
   i. Those engaged in the coasting trade from port to port.
   ii. Those engaged in carrying inland from town to town, as—
    a. Those connected with land carriage; as railroad men, stage coachmen, mail coachmen, and mail cartmen, post boys, flymen, waggoners, country carriers, and drovers.
    β. Those connected with water carriage; as navigable river and canal men, bargemen, towing men.
   iii. Those engaged in carrying to and from different parts of the same town by land and water.
    a. Passengers; as Omnibus-men, Cabmen, Glass and Job Coachmen, Fly Men, Excursion-van Men, Donkey-boys, Goat-carriage boys, Sedan and Bath Chair Men, Guides.
    β. Goods; as Waggoners, Draymen, Carters, Spring-Van Men, Truckmen, Porters (ticketed and unticketed, and public and private men).
    γ. Letters and Messages; as Messengers, Errand Boys, Telegraph Men, and Postmen.
    δ. Goods and Passengers by water; as Bargemen, Lightermen, Hoymen, Watermen, River Steamboat Men.
  c. Those engaged in the lading and unlading and the fitting of vessels, as well the packing of goods.
   i. Dock and wharf labourers.
   ii. Coal whippers.
   iii. Lumpers, or dischargers of timber ships.
   iv. Timber porters and rafters.
   v. Corn porters.
   vi. Ballast heavers.
   vii. Stevedores, or stowers.
   viii. Riggers.
   ix. Packers and pressers.

III. *Benefactors*, or those who confer some *permanent* benefit by promoting the physical, intellectual, or spiritual well-being of others.

 A. EDUCATORS.
  1. Professors.
  2. Tutors.
  3. Governesses.
  4. Schoolmasters.
  5. Ushers.
  6. Teachers of Languages.
  7. Teachers of Sciences.
  8. Lecturers.
  9. Teachers of "Accomplishments"; as Music, Singing, Dancing, Drawing, Wax-Flower Modelling, &c.
  10. Teachers of Exercises; as Gymnastics.
  11. Teachers of Arts of Self-Defence; as Fencing, Boxing, &c.
  12. Teachers of Trades and Professions.

B. CURATORS.
    1. Corporeal.
        a. Physicians.
        b. Surgeons.
        c. General Practitioners.
        d. Homœopathists.
        e. Hydropathists.
    2. Spiritual.
        a. Ministers of the Church of England.
        b. Dissenting Ministers.
        c. Catholic Ministers.
        d. Missionaries.
        e. Scripture Readers.
        f. Sisters of Charity.
        g. Visitants.

IV. *Servitors*, or those who render some *temporary* service or pleasure to others.
    A. AMUSERS, or those who contribute to our entertainment.
        1. Actors.
        2. Reciters.
        3. Improvisers.
        4. Singers.
        5. Musicians.
        6. Dancers.
        7. Riders, or Equestrian Performers.
        8. Fencers and Pugilists.
        9. Conjurers.
        10. Posturers.
        11. Equilibrists.
        12. Tumblers.
        13. Exhibitors or Showmen.
            a. Of Curiosities.
            b. Of Monstrosities.
    B. PROTECTORS, or those who contribute to our security against injury.
        1. Legislative.
            a. The Sovereign.
            b. The Members of the House of Lords.
            c. The Members of the House of Commons.
        2. Judicial.
            a. The Judges in Chancery, Queen's Bench, Common Pleas, Exchequer, Ecclesiastical, Admiralty, and Criminal Courts.
            b. Masters in Chancery, Commissioners of the Bankruptcy, Insolvent Debtors, Sheriffs, and County Courts, Magistrates, Justices of the Peace, Recorders, Coroners, Revising Barristers.
            c. Barristers, Pleaders, Conveyancers, Attorneys, Proctors.
        3. Administrative or Executive.
            a. The Lords Commisioners of the Treasury; the Secretaries of State for Home, Foreign, and Colonial Affairs; the Chancellor and Comptroller of the Exchequer; the Privy Council, and the Privy Seal; the Board of Trade, the Board of Control, and the Board of Health; the Board of Inland Revenue, the Poor-Law Board, and the Board of Audit; the Commissioners of Woods and Forests: the Ministers and Officials in connection with the Army and Navy, the Post Office, and the Mint; the Inspectors of Prisons, Factories, Railways, Workhouses, Schools, and Lunatic Asylums; the Officers in connection with the Registration and Statistical Departments; and the other Functionaries appertaining to the *Government at home*.
            b. The Ambassadors, Envoys Extraordinary, Ministers Plenipotentiary, Secretaries of Legation, Chargés d'Affaires, Consuls, and other Ministers and Functionaries appertaining to the *Government abroad*.

c. The Governors and Commanders of British Colonies and Settlements.
   d. The Lord Lieutenants, Custodes Rotulorum, High and Deputy Sheriffs, High Bailiffs, High and Petty Constables, and other Functionaries of *the Counties.*
   e. The Mayors, Aldermen, Common Councilmen, Chamberlains, Common Sergeants, Treasurers, Auditors, Assessors, Inspectors of Weights and Measures, and other Functionaries of *the Cities or incorporated Towns.*
   f. The Churchwardens, the Commissioners of Sewers and Paving, the Select and Special Vestrymen, the Vestry Clerks, the Overseers or Guardians of the Poor, the Relieving Officers, the Masters of the Workhouses, the Beadles, and other *Parochial Functionaries.*
   g. The Masters and Brethren of the Trinity Corporation, the Pier and Harbour Masters, Conservators of Rivers, and other Functionaries connected with Navigation, and the Trustees and Commissioners in connection with the Public Roads.
   h. The Naval and Military Powers; as the Army, Navy, Marines, Militia, and Yeomanry.
   i. The Civil Forces; as Policemen, Patrole, and Private Watchmen.
   j. Sheriffs' Officers, Bailiffs' Followers, Sponging-house Keepers.
   k. Governors of Prisons, Jailers, Turnkeys, Officers on board the Hulks and Transport Ships, Hangmen.
   l. The Fiscal Forces; as the Coast Guard, Custom-house Officers, Excise Officers.
   m. Collectors of Imposts; as Tax and Rate Collectors, Turnpike Men, Toll Collectors of Bridges and Markets, Collectors of Pier and Harbour dues, and Light, Buoy, and Beacon dues.
   n. Guardians of special localities; as Rangers, and Park-keepers, Arcade-keepers, Street-keepers, Square-keepers, Bazaar-keepers, Gate and Lodge-keepers, Empty-house-keepers.
   o. Conservators; as Curators of Museums, Librarians, Storekeepers, and others.
   p. Protective Associations; as Insurance Companies against Loss by fire, shipwreck, storms, railway accidents, death of cattle, Life Assurance Societies, Provident or Benefit Clubs, Guarantee Societies, Trade Protection Societies, Fire Brigade and Fire-escape Men, Humane Society Men, and Officers of the Societies for the Suppression of Mendicity, Vice, and cruelty to Animals.

SERVANTS, or those who contribute to our comfort or convenience by the performance of certain offices for us.

1. Private Servants, regularly engaged.
    a. Stewards.
    b. Farm Bailiffs.
    c. Secretaries.
    d. Amanuenses.
    e. Companions.
    f. Butlers.
    g. Valets.
    h. Footmen, Pages, and Hall Porters.
    i. Coachmen, Grooms, "Tigers," and Helpers at Stables.
    j. Huntsmen and Whippers-in.
    k. Kennelmen.
    l. Gamekeepers.
    m. Gardeners.
    n. Housekeepers.
    o. Ladies' Maids.
    p. Nursery Maids and Wet Nurses.
    q. House Maids and Parlour Maids.
    r. Cooks and Scullery Maids.
    s. Dairy Maids.
    t. Maids of all work.

2. Private Servants temporarily engaged.
   a. Couriers.
   b. Interpreters.
   c. Monthly Nurses and Invalid Nurses.
   d. Waiters at Parties.
   e. Charwomen.
   f. Knife, boot, window, and paint Cleaners, Pot scourers, Carpet beaters.
3. Public Servants.
   a. Waiters at hotels and public gardens.
   b. Masters of the Ceremonies.
   c. Chamber-Maids.
   d. Boots.
   e. Ostlers.
   f. Job Coachmen.
   g. Post-boys.
   h. Washerwomen.
   i. Dustmen.
   j. Sweeps.
   k. Scavengers.
   l. Nightmen.
   m. Flushermen.
   n. Turncocks.
   o. Lamplighters.
   p. Horse Holders.
   q. Crossing Sweepers.

THOSE WHO CANNOT WORK.

V. *Those that are provided for by some Public Institution.*
   A. THE INMATES OF WORKHOUSES.
   B. THE INMATES OF PRISONS.
      1. Debtors.
      2. Criminals (Some of these, however, are made to work by the authorities).
   C. THE INMATES OF HOSPITALS.
      1. The Sick.
      2. The Insane; as Lunatics and Idiots.
      3. Veterans; as Greenwich and Chelsea Hospital men.
      4. The Deserted Young; as the Foundling Hospital children.
   D. THE INMATES OF ASYLUMS AND ALMSHOUSES.
      1. The Afflicted; as the Deaf, and Dumb, and Blind.
      2. The Destitute Young; as Orphans.
      3. The Decayed Members of the several Trades or Sects.
         a. Trade and Provident Asylums and Almshouses.
         b. Sectarian Asylums and Almshouses—as for aged Jews, Widows of Clergymen, &c.
   E. THE INMATES OF THE SEVERAL REFUGES AND DORMITORIES FOR THE HOUSELESS AND DESTITUTE.

VI. *Those who are Unprovided for.*
   A. THOSE WHO ARE INCAPACITATED FROM WANT OF POWER.
      1. Owing to their Age.
         a. The Old.
         b. The Young.
      2. Owing to some Bodily Ailment.
         a. The Sick.
         b. The Crippled.
         c. The Maimed.

d. The Paralyzed.
   e. The Blind.
  3. Owing to some Mental Infirmity.
   a. The Insane.
   b. The Idiotic.
   c. The Untaught, or those who have never been brought up to any industrial occupation; as Widows and those who have "seen better days."
B. Those who are incapacitated from Want of Means.
  1. Having no tools; as is often the case with distressed carpenters.
  2. Having no clothes; as servants when long out of a situation.
  3. Having no stock-money; as impoverished street-sellers.
  4. Having no materials; as the "used-up" garret or chamber masters in the boot and shoe or cabinet-making trade.
  5. Having no place wherein to work; as when those who pursue their calling at home are forced to become the inmates of a nightly lodging-house.
C. Those who are incapacitated from Want of Employment.
  1. Owing to a glut or stagnation in business; as among the cotton-spinners, the iron-workers, the railway-navigators, and the like.
  2. Owing to a change in fashion; as in the button-making trade.
  3. Owing to the introduction of machinery; as among the sawyers, hand-loom weavers, pillow-lace makers, threshers, and others.
  4. Owing to the advent of the slack season; as among the tailors and mantua-makers, and drawn-bonnet-makers.
  5. Owing to the continuance of unfavourable weather.
   a. From the prevalence of rain; as street-sellers, and others.
   b. From the prevalence of easterly winds; as dock-labourers.
  6. Owing to the approach of winter; as among the builders, brickmakers, market-gardeners, harvest-men.
  7. Owing to the loss of character.
   a. Culpably; from intemperate habits, or misconduct of some kind.
   b. Accidentally; as when a servant's late master goes abroad, and a written testimonial is objected to.

THOSE WHO WILL NOT WORK.

VII. *Vagrants or Tramps.*

Under this head is included all that multifarious tribe of "sturdy rogues," who ramble across the country during the summer, sleeping at the "casual wards" of the workhouses, and who return to London in the winter to avail themselves of the gratuitous lodgings and food attainable at the several metropolitan refuges.

VIII. *Professional Beggars and their Dependents.*
  A. Naval and Military Beggars.
   1. Turnpike Sailors.
   2. Spanish Legion Men, &c.
   3. Veterans.
  B. "Distressed-Operative" Beggars.
   1. Pretended Starved-out Manufacturers, as the Nottingham "Driz" or Lace-Men.
   2. Pretended Unemployed Agriculturists.
   3. Pretended Frozen-out Gardeners.
   4. Pretended Hand-loom Weavers, and others deprived of their living by Machinery.
  C. "Respectable" Beggars.
   1. Pretended Broken-down Tradesmen, or Decayed Gentlemen.
   2. Pretended Distressed Ushers, unable to take situation for want of clothes.

3. "Clean-Family Beggars" with children in very white pinafores, their faces newly washed, and their hair carefully brushed.
4. Ashamed Beggars, or those who "stand pad with a fakement" (remain stationary, holding a written placard), and pretend to hide their faces.

D. "Disaster" Beggars.
1. Shipwrecked Mariners.
2. Blown-up Miners.
3. Burnt-out Tradesmen.
4. Lucifer Droppers.

E. Bodily Afflicted Beggars.
1. Having real or pretended sores, vulgarly known as the "scaldrum dodge."
2. Having swollen legs.
3. Being crippled, deformed, maimed, or paralyzed.
4. Being blind.
5. Being subject to fits.
6. Being in a decline, and appearing with bandages round the head.
7. "Shallow coves," or those who exhibit themselves in the streets half clad, especially in cold weather.

F. Famished Beggars.
1. Those who chalk on the pavement, "I am starving."
2. Those who "stand pad" with a small piece of paper similarly inscribed.

G. Foreign Beggars.
1. Frenchmen who stop passengers in the street and request to know if they can speak French, previous to presenting a written statement of their distress.
2. Pretended Destitute Poles.
3. Hindoos and Negroes, who stand shivering by the kerb.

H. Petty Trading Beggars.
1. Tract sellers.
2. Sellers of lucifers, boot-laces, cabbage-nets, tapes, and cottons.

⁎ The several varieties of beggars admit of being sub-divided into—
    a. Patterers, or those who beg on the "blob," that is, by word of mouth.
    b. Screevers, or those who beg by *screeving*, that is, by written documents, setting forth imaginary cases of distress, such documents being either—
        i. "Slums" (letters).
        ii. "Fakements" (petitions).

I. The Dependents of Beggars.
1. Screevers Proper, or the writers of slums and fakements for those who beg by screeving.
2. Referees, or those who give characters to professional beggars when a reference is required.

IX. *Cheats and their Dependents.*

A. Those who Cheat the Government.
1. Smugglers defrauding the Customs.
2. "Jiggers" defrauding the Excise by working illicit stills, and the like.

B. Those who Cheat the Public.
1. Swindlers, defrauding those of whom they buy.
2. "Duffers" and "horse-chaunters," defrauding those to whom they sell.
3. "Charley-pitchers" and other low gamblers, defrauding those with whom they play.
4. "Bouncers and Besters" defrauding, by laying wagers, swaggering, or using threats.
5. "Flatcatchers," defrauding by pretending to find some valuable article—as Fawney or Ring-Droppers.

6. Bubble-Men, defrauding by instituting pretended companies—as Sham Next-of-Kin-Societies, Assurance and Annuity Offices, Benefit Clubs, and the like.
7. Douceur-Men, defrauding by offering for a certain sum to confer some boon upon a person as—
   a. To procure Government Situations for laymen, or benefices for clergymen.
   b. To provide Servants with Places.
   c. To teach some lucrative occupation.
   d. To put persons in possession of some information "to their advantage."
8. Deposit-Men, defrauding by obtaining a certain sum as security for future work or some promised place of trust.

C. The Dependents of Cheats are—
1. "Jollies," and "Magsmen," or accomplices of the "Bouncers and Besters."
2. "Bonnets," or accomplices of Gamblers.
3. Referees, or those who give false characters to swindlers and others.

X. *Thieves and their Dependents.*

A. Those who Plunder with Violence.
1. "Cracksmen"—as Housebreakers and Burglars.
2. "Rampsmen," or Footpads.
3. "Bludgers," or Stick-slingers, plundering in company with prostitutes.

B. Those who "Hocus," or Plunder their Victims when Stupified.
1. "Drummers," or those who render people insensible.
   a. By handkerchiefs steeped in chloroform.
   b. By drugs poured into liquor.
2. "Bug-hunters," or those who go round to the public-houses and plunder drunken men.

C. Those who Plunder by Manual Dexterity, by Stealth, or by Breach of Trust.
1. "Mobsmen," or those who plunder by manual dexterity—as the "light-fingered gentry."
   a. "Buzzers," or those who abstract handkerchiefs and other articles from gentlemen's pockets.
      i. "Stook-buzzers," those who steal handkerchiefs.
      ii. "Tail-Buzzers," those who dive into coat-pockets for sneezers (snuff-boxes,) skins and dummies (purses and pocket-books).
   b. "Wires," or those who pick ladies' pockets.
   c. "Prop-nailers," those who steal pins and brooches.
   d. "Thimble-screwers," those who wrench watches from their guards.
   e. "Shop-lifters," or those who purloin goods from shops while examining articles.
2. "Sneaksmen," or those who plunder by means of stealth.
   a. Those who purloin goods, provisions, money, clothes, old metal, &c.
      i. "Drag Sneaks," or those who steal goods or luggage from carts and coaches.
      ii. "Snoozers," or those who sleep at railway hotels, and decamp with some passenger's luggage or property in the morning.
      iii. "Star-glazers," or those who cut the panes out of shop-windows.
      iv. "Till Friskers," or those who empty tills of their contents during the absence of the shopmen.
      v. "Sawney-Hunters," or those who go purloining bacon from cheesemongers' shop-doors.
      vi. "Noisy-racket Men," or those who steal china and glass from outside of china-shops.
      vii. "Area Sneaks," or those who steal from houses by going down the area steps.
      viii. "Dead Lurkers," or those who steal coats and umbrellas from passages at dusk, or on Sunday afternoons.
      ix. "Snow Gatherers," or those who steal clean clothes off the hedges.
      x. "Skinners," or those women who entice children and sailors to go with them and then strip them of their clothes.

  xi. "Bluey-Hunters," or those who purloin lead from the tops of houses.
  xii. "Cat and Kitten Hunters," or those who purloin pewter quart and pint pots from the top of area railings.
  xiii. "Toshers," or those who purloin copper from the ships along shore.
  xiv. Mudlarks, or those who steal pieces of rope and lumps of coal from among the vessels at the river-side.
 b. Those who steal animals.
  i. Horse Stealers.
  ii. Sheep, or "Woolly-bird," Stealers.
  iii. Deer Stealers.
  iv. Dog Stealers.
  v. Poachers, or Game Stealers.
  vi. "Lady and Gentlemen Racket Men," or those who steal cocks and hens.
  vii. Cat Stealers, or those who make away with cats for the sake of their skins and bones.
 c. Those who steal dead bodies—as the "Resurrectionists."
3. Those who plunder by breach of trust.
 a. Embezzlers, or those who rob their employers.
  i. By receiving what is due to them, and never accounting for it.
  ii. By obtaining goods in their employer's name.
  iii. By purloining money from the till, or goods from the premises.
 b. Illegal Pawners.
  i. Those who pledge work given out to them by employers.
  ii. Those who pledge blankets, sheets, &c., from lodgings.
 c. Dishonest servants, those who make away with the property of their masters.
 d. Bill Stealers, or those who purloin bills of exchange entrusted to them, to get discounted.
 e. Letter Stealers.

D. "SHOFUL MEN," OR THOSE WHO PLUNDER BY MEANS OF COUNTERFEITS.
 1. Coiners or fabricators of counterfeit money.
 2. Forgers of bank notes.
 3. Forgers of checks and acceptances.
 4. Forgers of wills.

E. DEPENDENTS OF THIEVES.
 1. "Fences," or receivers of stolen goods.
 2. "Smashers," or utterers of base coin or forged notes.

XI. *Prostitutes and their Dependents.*

A. PROFESSIONAL PROSTITUTES.
 1. Seclusives, or those who live in private houses or apartments.
  a. Kept Mistresses.
  b. "Prima Donnas," or those who belong to the "first class," and live in a superior style.
 2. Convives, or those who live in the same house with a number of others.
  a. Those who are independent of the mistress of the house.
  b. Those who are subject to the mistress of a brothel.
   i. "Board Lodgers," or those who give a portion of what they receive to the mistress of the brothel, in return for their board and lodging.
   ii. "Dress Lodgers," or those who give either a portion or the whole of what they get to the mistress of the brothel in return for their board, lodging, and clothes.
 3. Those who live in low lodging-houses.
 4. Sailors' and soldiers' women.
 5. Park women, or those who frequent the parks at night, and other retired places.

    6. Thieves' women, or those who entrap men into bye streets for the purpose of robbery.
    7. The Dependents of Prostitutes :
        a. "Bawds," or Keepers of Brothels.
        b. Followers of Dress Lodgers.
        c. Keepers of Accommodation Houses.
        d. Procuresses, Pimps, and Panders.
        e. Fancy-Men.
        f. Magsmen and Bullies.
  B. CLANDESTINE PROSTITUTES.
    1. Female Operatives.
    2. Maid Servants.
    3. Ladies of Intrigue.
    4. Keepers of Houses of Assignation.
  C. COHABITANT PROSTITUTES.
    1. Those whose paramours cannot afford to pay the marriage fees.
    2. Those whose paramours do not believe in the sanctity of the ceremony.
    3. Those who have married a relative forbidden by law.
    4. Those whose paramours object to marry them for pecuniary or family reasons.
    5. Those who would forfeit their income by marrying, as officers' widows in receipt of pensions, and those who hold property only while unmarried.

THOSE WHO NEED NOT WORK.

XII. *Those who derive their income from rent.*
  A. LANDLORDS OF ESTATES.
  B. LANDLORDS OF HOUSES.

XIII. *Those who derive their income from dividends.*
  A. FUNDHOLDERS.
  B. SHAREHOLDERS.
    1. In Mines.
    2. In Canals.
    3. In Railways.
    4. In Public Companies.

XIV. *Those who derive their income from yearly stipends.*
  A. ANNUITANTS.
  B. PENSIONERS.

XV. *Those who hold obsolete or nominal offices.*
  SINECURISTS.

XVI. *Those who derive their incomes from trades in which they never appear.*
  A. SLEEPING PARTNERS.
  B. ROYALTY MEN.

XVII. *Those who derive their incomes by favour from some other.*
  A. PROTEGÉS.
  B. DEPENDENTS.

XVIII. *Those who derive their support from the head of the family.*
  A. WIVES.
  B. CHILDREN.

OF THE NON-WORKERS.

THE exposition of the several members of society being finished, I now come to treat of that inoperative moiety of it, which more especially concerns us here. The non-workers, we have seen, consist of three broadly marked and distinct orders, viz:—

The incapacitated, or compulsory non-workers.
The indisposed, or voluntary non-workers.
The independent, or privileged non-workers.

It would be of the highest possible importance, could we ascertain with any precision the number of people existing in this country, who do no manner of work for their support ; and I was anxious to have concluded the preceding account of the several divisions of society, with an estimate of the numbers appertaining to each of the four great classes, as well as the incomes accruing to them. I found, however, on consulting the official documents with this view, that the government returns were in such an economical tangle—distributor being confounded with employer, and employer again jumbled up with the employed—that any attempt to unravel the twisted yarn would have cost an infinity of trouble, and have been almost worthless after all ; and it was from a long experience as to the incompetency of the official returns to aid the social inquirer in solving the great economical problems concerning the production and distribution of wealth, that I was induced to suggest to Sir George Grey (to whom I had been indebted for much courtesy and valuable information, and who, from the commencement of my investigations, had shown a readiness to afford me every assistance), that, in the ensuing census, an attempt should be made to obtain some definite account of the numbers of employers and employed, and I am happy to say that, in conformity with my suggestion, the next "Abstract of the Occupations of the People," will at least teach us the proportion between these two main elements of our social state ; so that if the Distributors are but kept distinct from the Promoters and Producers of the wealth of the country, one important step towards a right understanding of the subject will assuredly have been made*.

It should, however, be borne in mind, that, though the distribution, the promotion, and the production of the riches or exchangeable commodities of a country are usually distinct offices in every civilized nation, they are not invariably separate functions, even in our own. The exceptions to the economical rule with us appear to be as follows :—

1. Sometimes the producers themselves supply the materials, tools, shelter, and subsistence, that they require for their work, though this is usually done by some capitalist ; and having finished the work, proceed themselves to find purchasers for it likewise (though this is generally the office of the distributor or dealer). Street artizans, or those who make the goods they sell in the streets, may be cited as instances of a class uniting in itself the three functions of producer, capitalist (supplying the materials, &c.), and distributor.

2. Sometimes the capitalist employer is also the distributor of the commodities, such being the case with bakers, tailors,

---

* Mr. Mill's mistake in ranking the Employers and Distributors among the Enrichers, or those who increase the exchangeable commodities of the country, arose from a desire to place the dealers and capitalists among the productive labourers, than which nothing could be more idle, for surely they do not add, *directly*, one brass farthing, as the saying is, to the national stock of wealth. A little reflection would have shown that gentleman that the true function of employers and dealers was that of the *indirect aiders* of production rather than the direct producers. The economical scale of production appears to be as follows :—(1) The Employer, providing the materials, tools, and shelter necessary for the due performance of the work, together with the food for the subsistence of the artificer during the work. (2) The Labourer, fitting or preparing the materials for the artificer. (3) The Artificer or workman, positively doing the work and creating a new product. (4) The Superlative Artizan, engaged in adding to the beauty or utility of such product. (5) The Distributor or Dealer, engaged in carrying and disposing of the product in the best market. The functions of Nos. 1 and 2 generally precede production, those of Nos. 4 and 5 usually succeed it ; while No. 3 is the absolute producer. The labours of No. 4, however, are so intimately associated with the produce—sometimes designing the work, and sometimes "finishing" it—that it seems but right that the superlative artizan should be ranked with the artificer ; the mere labourer, however, who turns the wheel for the turner, or carries the bricks to the bricklayer and the like, cannot strictly be ranked as a *producer* any more than a porter or dock labourer.

and the like, who themselves "purvey" what they employ others to produce.

3. Sometimes the craft does not admit of a distributor being attached to it; the employer himself undertaking to supply the wants of the public; this is the case with the building and decoration of houses.

4. Sometimes the work is done directly for the public, without the intervention of either a distributor or trading-employer; such is the case with the jobbing, day, or piece workers—among the seamstresses and journeymen tailors, for instance—who "make up ladies' and gentlemen's own materials," either at home or at the houses of those for whom the work is done.

5. Sometimes the artificers or working men are their own capitalists; providing the materials, tools, shelter, and subsistence requisite for the work, as is the case with the garret and chamber-masters in the slop cabinet and shoe trades, and among the members of co-operative associations.

6. Sometimes the artificers are both employers and employed; being supplied with their materials and subsistence from a capitalist, and supplying them again to other artificers working under them; this is the case with sweaters, piece-working masters, first hands, and the like.

7. Sometimes the capitalist employer, on the other hand, is, or rather assumes to be, the proprietor of both the capital and labour; as is the case with the slave-owners, masters of serfs, bondmen, villeins, and the like; though this state of things, thank God, no longer exists in this country.

8. Sometimes the capitalist supplies all the requisites of production, excepting the subsistence of the artificer, who is remunerated by a certain share of the profits (if any); this is often the case with publishers and authors.

9. Sometimes the capitalist supplies only the materials and subsistence, but not the tools, of the artificers, and sometimes he compels them to pay him a rent for them out of their wages; as is the case with the employers of the sawyers and stockingers.

10. Sometimes the capitalist supplies the materials, tools, and subsistence of the artificers, but not the appliances of their work; and sometimes he compels them to purchase such appliances of him at an exorbitant profit; as the trimmings in the tailors' trade, thread with the seamstresses, and the like.

11. Sometimes the capitalist supplies the materials, tools, subsistence, and shelter of the artificers, but not their gas-light, and compels them to pay a rent for the same out of their wages.

12. Sometimes the capitalist supplies the materials, tools, appliances, and subsistence, but not the shelter, necessary for the due performance of the work, the artificers, in such cases, doing the work at their own homes.

But all this concerns the workers more directly than the non-workers of society, and it is mentioned here merely with the view of completing the classification before given. Our more immediate business in this place lies with the inoperative, rather than the operative, members of the community. Nor is it with the entire body of these that we have to deal, but rather with that third order of the non-working class who are unwilling, though able, to work, as contradistinguished from those who are willing, but unable, to do so. The non-workers are a peculiar class, including orders diametrically opposed to each other: the very rich and the very poor, in the first place, and the honest and dishonest in the second. The dishonest members of society constitute those who are known more particularly as the criminal class. Hence to inquire into their means of living and mode of life, involves an investigation into the nature and the extent of crime in this country. Crime, sin, and vice are three terms used for the infraction of three different kinds of laws—social, religious, and moral. Crime is the transgression of some social law, even as sin is the transgression of some religious law, and vice the breach of some moral one. These laws, however, often differ only in emanating from different authorities; while infractions of them are merely offences against different powers. To thieve is to offend at once socially, religiously, and morally; for not only does the social, but the religious and moral law, each and all, enjoin that we should respect the property of others.

But there are other crimes or offences against the social powers, besides such as are committed by those who will not work. The crimes perpetrated by those who object to labour for their living, are habitual crimes; whereas those perpetrated by the other classes of society are accidental crimes, arising from the pressure of a variety of circumstances. Here, then, we have a most important fundamental distinction: all crimes, and consequently all criminals, are divisible into two different classes, the professional and the casual; that is to say, there are two distinct orders of people continually offending against the laws of society, viz., those who do so as a regular means of living, and those who do so from some accidental cause. It is impossible to arrive at any accurate knowledge on the subject of crime generally, without making this first analysis of the several species of offences according to their causes; that is to say, arranging them into opposite groups or classes, according as they arise from an habitual indisposition to labour on the part of some of the offenders, or from the temporary pressure of circumstances upon others. The official returns, however, on this subject are as unphilosophic as the generality of such documents, and consist of a crude mass of undigested facts, being a statistical illustration of the "rudis indigestaque moles," in connection with a criminal chaos.

At present the several crimes of the country are officially divided into four classes:—
   I. Offences against persons; including murder, rape, bigamy, assaults, &c.
  II. Offences against property.
     A. With violence; including burglary, robbery, piracy, &c.
     B. Without violence; including embezzlement, cattle-stealing, larceny, and fraud.
     C. Malicious offences against property; including arson, incendiarism, maiming cattle, &c.
 III. Forgery and offences against the currency; including the forging of wills, bank-notes, and coining, &c.
 IV. Other offences; including high-treason, sedition, poaching, smuggling, working illicit stills, perjury, &c.

M. Guerry, the eminent French statist, adopts a far more philosophic arrangement, and divides the several crimes into—
   I. Crimes against the State; as high treason, &c.
  II. Crimes against personal safety; as murder, assault, &c.
 III. Crimes against morals (with and without violence); as rape, bigamy, &c.
 IV. Crimes against property (proceeding from cupidity or malice); as larceny, embezzlement, incendiarism, and the like.

The same fundamental error which renders the government classification comparatively worthless, deprives that of the French philosopher of all practical value. It gives us no knowledge of the character of the people committing the crimes; being merely a system of criminal mnemonics, as it were, or easy method of remembering the several varieties of offences. The classes in both systems are but so many mental pigeon-holes for the orderly arrangement and partitioning of the various infractions of the law; further than this they cannot help us.

Whatever other information the inquirer may want, he must obtain for himself; if he wish to learn from the crimes something as to their causes, as well as the nature of the criminals, he must begin *de novo*, and, using the official facts, but rejecting the official system of classification, proceed to arrange all the several offences into two classes, according as they are of a professional and casual character, committed by habitual or occasional offenders. Adopting this principle, it will be found that the *non-professional* crimes consist mainly of murder, assaults, incendiarism, ravishment, bigamy, embezzlement, high treason, and the like; for it is evident that none can make a trade or profession of the commission of these crimes, or resort to them as a regular means of living*.

The *professional* crimes, on the other hand, will be generally found to include burglary, robbery, poaching, coining, smuggling, working of illicit stills, larceny from the person, simple larceny, &c., because each and every of these are regular crafts, requiring almost the same apprenticeship as any other mode of life. Burglary, coining, working illicit stills, and picking pockets, are all *arts* to which no man, without some previous training, can take. Hence to know whether the number of these dishonest *handicrafts*—for such they really are—be annually on the increase or not, is to solve a most important portion of the criminal problem; it is to ascertain whether crime pursued as a profession or business, is being augmented among us—to discover whether the criminal class, as a distinct portion of our people is, or is not, on the advance. The non-professional crimes will furnish us with equally curious results, showing a yearly impress of the character of the times; for being only occasional offences, of course the number of such offenders at different years will give us a knowledge of the intensity of the several occasions inducing the crimes in such years.

The accidental crimes, classified according to their causes, may be said to consist of—
   I. Crimes of malice, exercised either against the person or the property of the object.

---

* At one time, however, murder became a *trade* in this country, namely, when the dead bodies of human beings grew to be of such value that the burking of the living was resorted to by the "resurrectionists," as a means of keeping up the supply.

II. Crimes of lust and perverted appetites; as rape, &c.
III. Crimes of shame; as concealing the births of infants, attempts to procure miscarriage, and the like.
IV. Crimes of temptation, ⎫ with, or without breach of
V. Crimes of cupidity, ⎬ trust.
VI. Crimes of want, ⎭
VII. Crimes of political prejudices.

With the class of casual or accidental criminals, however, we are not at present concerned. Those who resort to crime as a means of support, when in a state of extreme want, for instance, cannot be said to belong to the *voluntary* non-workers, for many of these would willingly work to increase their sustenance, if that end were attainable by such means, but the poor shirt-workers, slop-tailors, and the like, have not the power of earning more than the barest subsistence by their labour, so that the pawning of the work entrusted to them by their employers, becomes an act to which they are immediately impelled for "dear life," on the occurrence of the least illness or mishap among them. Such *offenders*, therefore, belong more properly to those who cannot work for their living, or rather, who cannot live by their working, and though they offend against the laws in the same manner as those that will not work, they cannot certainly be said to be of the same class.

The *voluntary* non-workers are a distinct body of people. In the introductory chapter to the first volume of the "Street-folk," they have been shown to appertain to even the rudest nations, being as it were the human parasites of every civilized and barbarous community. The Hottentots have their "*Sonquas*," and the Kafirs their "*Fingoes*," as we have our "Prigs" and "Cadgers." Those who will not work for the food they consume, appear to be part and parcel of a State—an essential element of the social fabric as much as those who cannot, or need not work for their living. Go where you will, to what corner of the earth you please, search out or propound what new-fangled or obsolete form of society you may, there will be some members of it more apathetic than the rest, who object to work—some more infirm than the rest, who are denied the power to work—and some more thrifty than the rest, who from their past savings have no necessity to work for the future. These several forms are but the necessary consequences of specific differences in the constitution of different beings. Circumstances may tend to give an unnatural development to either one or other of the classes; the criminal class, the pauper class, or the wealthy class, may be in excess in one form of society, as compared with another, or they may be repressed by certain social arrangements; nevertheless, to a greater or less degree, there they will and *must* ever be.

Since, then, there *is* an essentially distinct class of people who *will* not work for their living, and since work is a necessary condition of the human organism, the question becomes, How do such people live? There is but one answer:—If they do not labour to procure their own food, of course they must live on the food procured by the labour of others. But how do they obtain possession of the food belonging to others? There are but two means: it must either be given to them by, or be taken from, the industrious portion of the community. Consequently, the next point to be settled is, what are the means by which those who *object* to work get their food given to them, and what the means by which they are enabled to take it from others. Let us begin with the last mentioned.

The means by which the criminal classes obtain their living constitute the essential points of difference among them, and form indeed the methods of distinction among themselves. The "Rampsmen," the "Drummers," the "Mobsmen," the "Sneaksmen," and the "Shofulmen,"* which are the terms by which they themselves designate the several branches of the "profession," are but so many expressions indicating the several modes of obtaining the property of which they become possessed.

The "*Rampsman*" or "*Cracksman*" plunders by force; as the burglar, footpad, &c.
The "*Drummer*" plunders by stupefaction; as the hocusser.
The "*Mobsman*" plunders by manual dexterity; as the pickpocket.
The "*Sneaksman*" plunders by stealth; as the petty-larceny men and boys.
The "*Shofulman*" plunders by counterfeits; as the coiner.

Now each and all of these are distinct species of the genus, having often little or no connection with the others. The "Cracksman," or housebreaker, would no more think of associating with the "Sneaksman" than a barrister would dream of sitting down to dinner with an attorney; the perils braved by the housebreaker or the footpad make the cowardice of the sneaksman contemptible to him; and the one is distinguished by a

* The word Shoful is derived from the Danish *skuffe*, to shove, to deceive, cheat; the Saxon form of the same verb is *Scufan*, whence the English *Shove*.

kind of bulldog insensibility to danger, while the other is marked by a low cat-like cunning. The "Mobsman," on the other hand, is more of a handicraftsman than either, and is comparatively refined by the society he is obliged to keep. He usually dresses in the same elaborate style of fashion as a Jew on a Saturday (in which case he is more particularly described by the prefix "swell"), and "mixes" generally in the "best of company," frequenting—for the purposes of his business—all the places of public entertainment, and often being a regular attendant at church and the more elegant chapels, especially during charity sermons. The Mobsman takes his name from the gregarious habits of the class to which he belongs, it being necessary, for the successful picking of pockets, that the work be done in small gangs or mobs, so as to "cover" the operator. Among the Sneaksmen, again, the purloiners of animals, such as the horse stealers, the sheep stealers, the deer stealers, and the poachers, all belong to a particular tribe (with the exception of the dog stealers)—they are agricultural thieves; whereas the others are generally of a more civic character. The Shofulmen, or coiners, moreover constitute a distinct species, and upon them, like the others, is impressed the stamp of the peculiar line of roguery they may chance to follow as a means of subsistence.

Such are the more salient features of that portion of the voluntary non-workers who live by *taking* what they want from others. The other moiety of the same class who live by getting what they want *given* to them, is equally peculiar. These consist of the "Flatcatchers," the "Hunter" and "Charley* Pitchers," the "Bouncers" and "Besters," the "Cadgers," the Vagrants, and the Prostitutes.

The "*Flatcatchers*" obtain what they want by false pretences ; as swindlers, duffers, ring droppers, and cheats of all kinds.

The "*Hunter*" and "*Charley Pitchers*" obtain what they want by gaming ; as thimblerig men, &c.

The "*Bouncers*" and "*Besters*" obtain what they want by betting, intimidating, or talking people out of their property.

The "*Cadgers*" obtain what they want by begging, and exciting false sympathy.

The *Vagrants* obtain what they want by declaring on the casual ward of the parish workhouse.

* A Charley Pitcher seems to be one who pitches to the *Ceorla*, or countryman, and hence is equivalent to the term *Yokel*-hunter.

The *Prostitutes* obtain what they want by the performance of an immoral act.

Each of these, again, are unmistakeably distinguished from the rest. The "Flatcatchers" are generally remarkable for great shrewdness, especially in the knowledge of human character and ingenuity in designing and carrying out their several schemes. The "Charley Pitchers" appertain more to the conjuring or sleight-of-hand and blackleg class. The "Cadgers," again, are to the class of cheats what the "Sneaksmen" are to the thieves, the lowest of all, being the least distinguished for those characteristics which mark the other members of the same body. As the "Sneaksmen" are the least daring and expert of all the thieves, so are the "Cadgers" the least intellectual and cunning of all the cheats. A "shallow cove," that is to say, one who exhibits himself half naked in the streets as a means of obtaining his living, is looked upon as the most despicable of all, since the act requires neither courage, intellect, nor dexterity for the execution of it. The Vagrants, on the other hand, are the wanderers—the English Bedouins—those who, in their own words, "love to shake a free leg"—the thoughtless and the careless vagabonds of our race; while the Prostitutes, as a body, are the shameless among our women.

Such, then, are the characters of the voluntary non-workers, or professionally criminal class, the vagrants, beggars, cheats, thieves, and prostitutes — each order expressing some different mode of existence adopted by those who object to labour for their living. The vagrants, who love a roving life, exist principally by declaring on the parish funds for the time being ; the beggars, as deficient in courage and intellect as in pride, prefer to live by soliciting alms of the public ; the cheats, possessed of considerable cunning and ingenuity, choose rather to subsist by continual fraud and deception ; the thieves, distinguished generally by a hardihood and comparative disregard of danger, find greater delight in risking their liberty by taking what they want, instead of waiting to have it given them ; while the prostitutes, as deficient in shame as the beggars are in pride, prefer to live by using their charms for the vilest of purposes.

The exposition of the *causes* why the several species of voluntary non-workers object to labour for their living, I shall reserve for a future occasion ; that they do *object* to work is patent in the fact that they might sustain themselves by their industry if they chose (for those who are unable to do so, and are consequently driven to dishonesty, have been purposely removed from the class).

The number of individuals belonging to the professional criminal class, we are not yet in a position to ascertain; but few dependable facts have been collected on the subject, and even these have been obtained so many years back that, with the increase of population, they have become almost worthless, except in a historic point of view. Such as they are, however, it will be as well to add them to this introduction to the class of voluntary non-workers, as the best information at present existing upon the subject.

TABLE SHOWING THE NUMBER OF DEPREDATORS, OFFENDERS, AND SUSPECTED PERSONS WHO HAVE BEEN BROUGHT WITHIN THE COGNIZANCE OF THE POLICE IN THE YEAR 1837, COMPREHENDING :—

1. Persons who have no visible means of subsistence, and who are believed to live wholly by violation of the law, as by habitual depredation, by fraud, by prostitution, &c.
2. Persons following some ostensible and legal occupation, but who are known to have committed an offence, and are believed to augment their gains by habitual or occasional violation of the law.
3. Persons not known to have committed any offences, but known as associates of the above classes, and otherwise deemed to be suspicious characters.

Character and description of Offenders.		Metropolitan Police District.			
		1st Class.	2nd Class.	3rd Class.	Total all Classes.
RAMPSMEN †	Burglars	77	22	8	107
	Housebreakers	59	17	34	110
	Highway robbers	19	8	11	38
		155	47	53	255
MOBSMEN	Pickpockets	544	75	154	773
SNEAKSMEN	Common thieves	1667	1338	652	3657
ANIMAL STEALERS	Horse stealers	7	4		11
	Cattle stealers				
	Dog stealers	45	48	48	141
		52	52	48	152
SHOFULMEN	*Forgers		3		3
	*Coiners	25	1	2	28
	Utterers of base coin	202	54	61	317
		227	58	63	348
FLATCATCHERS	*Obtainers of goods by false pretences	33	108		141
	*Persons committing frauds of any other description	23	118	41	182
		56	226		323
	Receivers of stolen goods	51	158	134	343
	*Habitual disturbers of the public peace	723	1866	179	2768
	Vagrants	1089	186	20	1295
CADGERS	*Begging-letter writers	12	17	21	50
	Bearers of begging-letters	22	40	24	86
		34	57	45	136
PROSTITUTES	*Prostitutes, well-dressed, living in brothels	813	62	20	895
	*Prostitutes, well-dressed, walking the streets	1460	79	73	1612
	Prostitutes, low, infesting low neighbourhoods	3533	147	184	3864
		5806	288	277	6371
	*Classes not before enumerated	40	2	438	470
	Total	10,444	4353	2104	16,901

* Those marked thus * are of a non-migratory character.
† The titles of the classes as here given do not form part of the original table.

The estimate made for five of the principal provincial towns in the same year was as follows:—

TABLE SHOWING THE NUMBER OF DEPREDATORS, OFFENDERS, AND SUSPECTED PERSONS BROUGHT WITHIN THE COGNIZANCE OF THE POLICE OF THE UNDERMENTIONED DISTRICTS, IN THE YEAR 1837.

District or Place.	Number of Depredators, Offenders, and Suspected Persons.				Average Length of Career.	Proportion of known bad Characters to the Population.
	1st Class.	2nd Class.	3rd Class.	Total.		
Metropolitan Police District	10,444	4353	2104	16,901	4 yrs.	1 in 89
Borough of Liverpool	3,580	916	215	4,711	......	1 in 45
City and County of Bristol	1,935	1190	356	3,481	......	1 in 31
City of Bath	284	470	847	1,601	......	1 in 37
Town and County of Newcastle-on-Tyne	1,730	222	62	2,014	$2\frac{1}{4}$ yrs.	1 in 27
Total	17,973	7151	3584	28,708		

By the above table it will be seen that, in 1837, there were 28,708 persons of known bad character, infesting five of the principal towns in England: nearly 18,000 of the entire number had no visible means of subsistence, and were believed to live wholly by depredation; 7000 were believed to augment their gains by habitual or occasional violation of the law; and 3500 were known to be associates of the others, and otherwise deemed suspicious characters. According to the average proportion of these persons to the population, there would have been in the other large towns nearly 32,000 persons of a similar class, and upwards of 69,000 of such persons dispersed throughout the rest of the country. Adding these together, we have as many as 130,000 individuals of known bad character in England and Wales, *without* the walls of the prisons.

To form an accurate notion of the total number of the criminal population at the above period, we must add to the preceding amount the number of persons resident *within* the walls of the prisons. These, at the time of taking the last census, amounted to 19.888, which, added to the 130,000 above enumerated, gives within a fraction of 150,000 individuals for the entire criminal population of the country, as known to the police in 1837.

Let us now, for a moment, turn our attention to the number and cost of the honest and dishonest poor throughout England and Wales. Mr. Porter, usually no mean authority upon all matters of a statistical nature, tells us, in his "Progress of the Nation," p. 530, that "the proportion of persons in the United Kingdom who pass their time without applying to any gainful occupation is quite *inconsiderable!* Of 5,800,000 males of 20 years and upwards living at the time of the census of 1831, there were said to be engaged in some calling or profession 5,450,000, thus leaving unemployed only 350,000, or rather less than six per cent." "The number of unemployed adult males in Great Britain in 1841," he afterwards informs us, "was only 274,000 and odd."

But this statement gives us no accurate idea of the number of persons subsisting by charity or crime, for the author of the "Progress of the Nation," strange to say, wholly excludes from his calculation the mass of individuals maintained by the several parishes, as well as the criminals, almspeople, and lunatics throughout the country! Now, according to the Report of the Poor-law Commissioners, the number of paupers receiving in and out-door relief, in 1848, was no less than 1,870,000 and odd. The number of criminals and suspicious characters throughout the country, in 1837, we have seen, was 150,000. In 1844 the number of lunatics in county asylums was 4000 and odd; while, according to the occupation abstract of the population returns there were in 1841 upwards of 5000 almspeople, 1000 beggars, and 21,000 pensioners. These, formed into one sum, give us no less than 2,000,000 of individuals living upon the income of the remainder of the population. By the above computation, therefore, we see that, out of a total of 16,000,000 souls, in England and Wales, one-eighth, or twelve per cent. of the whole, continue their existence either by pauperism, mendicancy, or crime.

Now, the cost of this immense mass of vice and want is even more appalling than the number of individuals subsisting in such utter degradation. The total amount of money levied in 1848 for the relief of the poor throughout England and Wales, was 7,400,000*l*. But, exclusive of this amount, the magnitude of the sum that we give voluntarily towards the support and education of the poorer classes, is unparalleled in the history of any other nation, or of any other time. According to the summary of the returns annexed to the voluminous reports of the Charity Commissioners, the rent of the land and other fixed property, together with the interest of the money left for charitable purposes in England and Wales, amounts to 1,200,000*l*. a year; and it is believed that, by proper management, this return might be increased to an annual income of at least two millions of money. "And yet," says Mr. M'Culloch, "there can be no doubt that even this large sum falls far below the amount expended every year in voluntary donations to charitable establishments. Nor can any estimate be formed," he adds, " of the money given in charity to individuals, but in the aggregate it cannot fail to amount to an immense sum." All things considered, therefore, we cannot be very far from the truth, if we assume the sums *voluntarily* subscribed towards the relief of the poor to equal, in the aggregate, the total amount raised by assessment for the same purpose (the income from voluntary subscriptions to the *metropolitan* charities alone equals 1,000,000*l*. and odd); so that it would appear that the well-to-do amongst us expend the vast sum of 15,000,000*l*. per annum in mitigating the miseries of their less fortunate brethren.

But though it may be said that we give altogether 15,000,000*l*. a year to alleviate the distress of those who want or suffer, we must remember that this vast sum expresses not only the liberal extent of our sympathy, but likewise the fearful amount of want and suffering, on the one hand, and of excess and luxury on the other, that there must be in the land. If the poorer classes require fifteen millions to be added in charity every year to their aggregate income in order to relieve their pains and privations, and the richer can afford to have the same immense sum taken from theirs, and yet scarcely feel the loss, it shows at once how much the one class must have in excess and the other in deficiency. Whether such a state of things is a necessary evil connected with the distribution of wealth, this is not the place for me to argue. All I have to do here is to draw attention to the fact. It is for others to lay bare the cause, and, if possible, discover the remedy.

There still remains, however, to be added to the sum expended in voluntary or compulsory relief of the poor, the cost of our criminal and convict establishments at home and abroad. This, according to the Government estimates, amounts to very nearly 1,000,000*l*.; then there is the value of the property appropriated by the 150,000 habitual criminals, and this, at 10*s*. a week per head, amounts to very nearly 4,000,000*l*.; so that, adding these items to the sum before-mentioned, we have, in round numbers, the enormous amount of 20,000,000*l*. per annum as the cost of the paupers and criminals of this country; and, reckoning the national income, with Mr. M'Culloch and others, at 350,000,000*l*., it follows that the country has to give upwards of five per cent. out of its gross earnings every year to support those who are either incapable or unwilling to obtain a living for themselves.

OF THE PROSTITUTE CLASS GENERALLY.

WE have now seen that the two modes of obtaining a living other than by working for it are, by forcibly or stealthily appropriating the proceeds of another's labour, or else by seducing the more industrious or thrifty to part with a portion of their gains. Prostitution, professionally resorted to, belongs to the latter class, and consists, when adopted as a means of subsistence without labour, in inducing others, by the performance of some immoral act, to render up a portion of their possessions. Literally construed, prostitution is the putting of anything to a vile use; in this sense perjury is a species of prostitution, being an unworthy use of the faculty of speech; so, again, bribery is a prostitution of the right of voting; while prostitution, specially so called, is the using of her charms by a woman for immoral purposes. This, of course, may be done either from mercenary or voluptuous motives; be the cause, however, what it may, the act remains the same, and consists in the base perversion of a woman's charms—the surrendering of her virtue to criminal indulgence. Prostitution has been defined to be the illicit intercourse of the sexes; but illicit is unlicensed, and the mere sanctioning of an immoral act could not dignify it into a moral one. Such a definition would make the criminality of the act to consist solely in the absence of the priest's licence.

In Persia there are no professional prostitutes permitted; but though the priest's sanction there precedes the surrendering of the woman's virtue in every instance, still the same immoral perversion takes place—it being customary for couples to be wedded for a small sum by the priest in the evening, and divorced by him, for an equally small sum, in the morning. Here, then, we find the licensed intercourse assuming the same immoral cast as the unlicensed; for surely none will maintain that these nuptial ephemeræ are sanctified, because accompanied with a priestly licence. Nor can we, on the other hand, assert that the mere fact of continence in the association of the sexes, the persistence of the female to one male, or the continued endurance of an unsanctioned attachment, can ever be raised into anything purer than cohabitation, or the chastity of unchastity.

Prostitution, then, does not consist solely in promiscuous intercourse, for she who confines her favours to one may still be a prostitute; nor does it consist in illicit or unsanctioned intercourse, for, as we have seen, the intercourse may be sanctioned and still be prostitution to all intents and purposes. Nor can it be said to consist solely in the mercenary motives so often prompting to the commission of the act; for fornication is expressly that form of prostitution which is the result of illicit attachment.

In what, then, it may be asked, *does* prostitution consist? It consists, I answer, in what the word literally expresses —putting a woman's charms to vile uses. The term *whore* has, strictly, the same signification as that of *prostitute;* though usually supposed to be from the Saxon verb *hyrian*, to hire, and, consequently, to mean a woman whose favours can be procured for a reward. But the Saxon substantive *hure*, is the same word as the first syllable of *hor-cwen*, which signifies literally a filthy quean, a *har*-lot. Now the term *hor*, in *hor-cwen*, is but another form of the Saxon adjective *horig*, filthy, dirty, the Latin equivalent of which is *sor*-didus; hence the substantive *horines* means filthiness, and *horingas*, adulterers (or filthy people), and *hornung*, adultery, fornication, whoredom (or filthy acts). Prostitution and whoredom, then, have both the same meaning, viz., perversion to vile or *filthy* uses; and consist in the surrendering of a woman's virtue in a manner that excites *our moral disgust*. The offensiveness of the act of unchastity to the moral taste or sense constitutes the very essence of prostitution; and it is this moral offensiveness which often makes the licensed intercourse of the sexes, as in the marriage of a young girl to an old man, for the sake of his money, as much an act of prostitution as even the grossest libertinism.

The next question consequently becomes, what are the invariable antecedents which excite the moral disgust in every act of prostitution? or are there any such invariable antecedents characterizing each offensive perversion of a woman's charms? Is the offensiveness a mere matter of taste, differing according as the moral palates of the individuals or races may differ one from the other, and ultimately referable to some peculiar form of organization, convention, fashion, or geography? or is it a part of the inherent constitution of things?—in a word, is there an abstract chastity and unchastity; an erotic τὸ καλὸν and τὸ κακὸν; an universal standard of moral beauty and ugliness in woman—that, go where you will, is the same to all natures and in all countries? or is the vice of one set of people the virtue of another, as this race admires white teeth and that black?

This is a matter lying, as it were, across the very threshold of the subject, and which must necessarily, according as one or other view be taken, give a wholly different cast, not only to all our thoughts in connection with the evil, but to all our plans for the remedy of it. If prostitution be loathsome to us, merely because it is the moral fashion of our people that it should be so, then by popularizing new forms of thought and feeling among us may we remove all opprobrium from the act, and so put an end to all the moral evil in connection with it; but if it be naturally and innately offensive to every healthy mind, then can it be remedied solely by improving the tone of the thoughts and feelings of the depraved, and restoring the lost moral sense, as well as directing the perverted taste to more wholesome and beautiful objects.

To solve this part of the problem, then, it will be necessary that we should take as comprehensive a view of the subject as possible, collecting a large and multifarious body of facts, and examining the matter from almost every conceivable point of view. It will be necessary that we should regard it by the light of the early ages of society—that we should contemplate it amid all the primitive rudeness of barbaric life—and ultimately that we should study it under the many varied phases that it assumes in civilized communities.

For the better performance of this task I have availed myself of the services and assistance of my friend, Mr. Horace St. John, whom I shall now leave to lay before the reader the many curious and interesting facts which he has collected at my request in connection with the ancient and foreign part of the subject, after which I shall return to the consideration of that branch of the general inquiry connected more immediately with the prostitution of this country.

OF PROSTITUTION IN ANCIENT STATES: GENERAL VIEW.

IN the following inquiry, though the chief object will be to ascertain the extent and character of the prostitute class of women, it will be necessary to indicate generally the condition of the sex in various ages, and among different nations. This will afford a comparative view of the subject. It is impossible to form a judgment on the condition of this class, and its influence on society, without learning in what degree of estimation morality is viewed by a people; what position in the social scale is occupied by their women; at what price chastity is held; and what are the relative stations of the sexes. To afford a correct idea of this, in plain, popular language, is the task to which we now apply ourselves; and we commence with the ancient states whose institutions have, in a greater or less degree, influenced those of all others, in every later age. It is necessary to maintain a distinction between those countries where marriage was an institution, and those—if they are not quite fabulous—at least savage communities where the intercourse of men with women is looser than that of beasts.

Far as we can trace the history of society we discover no state without the blemish of prostitution. In some it was more, in others less prevalent; but in all it existed in one form or another. In examining the manners of the ancient nations, Hebrews, Egyptians, Greeks, Romans, Celts, and Anglo Saxons, we find women who degraded themselves from vanity, lust, or for gain; and, among the old communities of the East, less known to us, public immorality was a characteristic. We shall show this to have been the case, and, basing our statements on the most creditable authority, indicate the principal features of each system. The information, it is true, which has been bequeathed to us, and elucidated by the learning and diligence of numerous scholars, is far from complete; but enough may be collected among the antiquities of Israel, Greece, Rome, and Egypt, to establish a fair opinion. The general design of this inquiry will be to draw a view of the position occupied by the female sex in different ages and countries, to measure the estimation in which it was held, to fix the accepted standard of morality, to ascertain the recognised significance of the marriage contract, the laws relating to polygamy and concubinage, the value at which feminine virtue and modesty were held, and thus to consider the prostitute in relation to the system of which she formed a part. *She* will be the particular object of investigation; but the others are by no means unimportant. They are, indeed, necessary to a just and comprehensive view of the question before us. In a society where men lived in brutal promiscuousness with the women, prostitution could scarcely exist; where chastity was lightly esteemed, and marriage held to be a loose contract for social purposes, adultery could hardly be very full of shame. In this, therefore, as in all other inquiries, it is necessary to view the actual object in relation to others which are invariably connected with it. There is no universal, unvarying standard, by which even prostitution can be measured. Circumstances, not belonging, yet not entirely foreign to it, are to be considered. Consequently, while we hold that in view as the main ground of research, we shall, where materials allow, draw a sketch of the situation occupied by the female sex, and of the other traits of civilization to which we have referred.

In a general view, Greece and Rome, with the great city of Babylon, stand most prominently forward with their system of prostitution. Closer inquiry, however, induces us to hesitate before assigning them that distinction. Of the two classical states especially, it is because our information is more immediate and complete, that their public immorality is more remarkable. The poets of the earlier, and the historians of the later, period, have transmitted to us numerous accounts of the manners and customs of Greece and Rome; their painters have left us views,—their architects and sculptors, monuments of their civilization. Their moralists and satirists have enlarged on the prevalent vices, and from all these sources we are enabled to derive clearer ideas of their women, and especially their prostitution. Besides, in a polished state, with pure manners the prostitute class will always be more distinct, and therefore more conspicuous.

Babylon, far more than a thousand years ago, was a proverb of immorality. Her name and the name of Whore have been associated ideas, not on account only of the idolatry practised by her people, but on account of their licentious manners. Concerning Egypt, though Diodorus and Herodotus wrote of it, little is known; of the marriage ceremony absolutely nothing. The prostitutes are not described; but, from every trace and record of their civilization which has been preserved, it is evident that a large class addicted itself to this calling. Who were the public musicians, disreputable in the eyes of all other persons?—who were the dancers who performed their wanton feats at the entertainments of the rich, and stripped themselves half, or entirely, naked before their couches?—who were the drunken women, who bared their bodies, and capered in that state on the Nile boats, during the festival of Bubastis?—who were they who assisted at the sacerdotal orgies, which defiled the temples of ancient Egypt? —who could they have been, but women of abandoned character, who prostituted themselves for vile purposes, for gain or pleasure?

Among the Jews, again, the continually reiterated allusions to harlots, in the Scriptures, the abominations perpetually charged to their account, the threats pronounced upon their wickedness, the frequent allusions to their licentious manners, indicate a wide prevalence of this system. Among a people so commonly guilty of nameless crimes, we cannot expect to find chastity a peculiar virtue. Indeed, it is seldom such vices are practised until all the inferior offences against decency have become insipid through satiety. The writers, therefore, who parade before us the civilization of the Jews, as an example of public morality, base their conclusions on a strange interpretation of facts. To contrast them with the manners of Attic Greece, is a pure satire on common sense. Sparta was licentious, but not in the low and gross manner of the Jews. Athens harboured a licentious class; but none like those bestial voluptuaries among the Hebrews, in whom lust became a loathsome passion. Although, therefore, the actual manners of ancient Israel have been less vividly described than those of Greece, it is evident from the tenour of Scripture history, that morality there was less pure than in the Attic state.

Rome, under the republic, was, perhaps, still farther removed from the charge of corruption. Prostitutes it had, and brothels; but its women were generally virtuous. The chastity of the Roman matron has passed into a proverb. It was, however, if we may credit the historian Tacitus, exceeded by the modesty of the women in ancient Germany. Among them morals appear purged of licentiousness. Polygamy was forbidden, and practised only by the petty kings who set themselves above the law. The manners of the people, rather than the enactments of their code, prohibited divorce. Adultery, rare as it was, ranked as an inexpiable crime; while seduction was condemned, and prostitution unknown. It was not, however, the severity of the law which enforced the virtue; it was the virtue that imparted its spirit to the law. From the morals of ancient Germany, the lawgivers of society might learn many useful lessons. Bars and bolts, multiplied walls, troops of eunuchs, jealous lattices, and the dread of punishment, failed to guard the harems of the East; while the hut of the German barbarian, open on all sides, was impregnable against the seducer. The poor toy of the Persian's seraglio, protected by a hundred devices, often eluded them all; but the German women were the guardians of their own honour. They may be described as possessing all the virtues, without the vices, of the stern Spartan stock; and, living on terms of equality with the men, held their virtue at too dear a price to prostitute it for admiration, or lust, or money. Civilization, in this respect, has done the Germans a very ill office.

Allied to these fierce wanderers in the Hyrcynian wood were the Saxons, from whom our ancestors descended. We shall find among them, on their native soil, similar manners, especially in the circumstance of the adulteress being whipped without mercy through the village. Among them prevailed, however, an enlightened reverence for the female sex, which contrasted strongly with the ideas of many surrounding nations, who looked on a woman as a creature merely dedicated to the service and gratification of man. They brought over to England institutions susceptible of being moulded to a different form. They became more refined and less moral. Whenever, indeed, rude men, who have not given themselves up to the indulgence of their low physical appetites, turn from the chase, from war, and similar rough occupations, to the framing of laws, to the formation of society, to any intellectual exercise, it appears natural that other propensities should be awakened in them, and of these the sensual always form a part. It is, consequently, interesting to study the progress of manners from stage to stage of civilization, from the rudest tribe to the most refined community.

We shall occupy ourselves first with the Hebrew republic, and then with the monarchy which succeeded it. From Israel we proceed to Egypt, related to it in various ways. Thence our attention will be directed to Greece, which offered models to the statesmen and public economists of all time. The contrast between the Ionic and the Doric states will be presented. Then we shall proceed to Rome, which will lead us to the Anglo-Saxons, others being incidentally noticed by the way.

In all, as far as our limits and our materials will allow, a sketch of the condition of women, the national ideas of feminine virtue, the laws of marriage, and the extent of prostitution, will be given; and thus the reader will be prepared to enter on the wider field of modern society abroad. This will be divided into the barbarous and the civilized; and of the barbarous, the hunters, fishers, shepherds, and tillers of the soil, may be separately noticed.

The account of every ancient people will not be equally complete, because the sources of information are not so. Thus of Egypt, its marriage-customs are wholly unknown; of the Anglo-Saxons, although the learning and industry of Sharon Turner have been employed upon them, our knowledge is extremely imperfect. Even Rome and Greece, though they present us with the general features of their social systems, disappoint us when we search into details. Nevertheless, the reader may be enabled, as we have before said, to form a just idea of the condition of women in antiquity; for the researches of modern scholars have succeeded, at least, in laying bare the principal roots of the ancient system, upon which all the institutions of existing society are, in one form or another, established.

Of Prostitution among the Jews and other Ancient Nations.

A SLIGHT and rapid view of the subject in connection with the Jews, and more obscure nations of antiquity, is all that can here be attempted. With reference to the republic of the Hebrew race, though the ingenuity of modern writers has built up very pleasing theories, described as the manners and customs of the Jews, we can look nowhere for information except to the Bible, and, in a later age, to Josephus.

The position of woman among the Jews was by no means exalted. She was seldom consulted by her friends, when an union with her was desired by a wealthy suitor. Indeed, in the patriarchal times she was regarded more as her husband's property than as his companion. Such must invariably be the case where polygamy and concubinage are institutions of society. At a still earlier period the customs of society were even more at variance with our ideas. Of course the sons of Adam must have married their sisters, and the practice continued after the necessity for it had ceased. Abraham formed such an union without exciting surprise. The patriarchs permitted men to wed two sisters at once, but the law of Moses brought a reform of marriage customs among the Jews *. They discontinued the intercourse between blood-relatives long before it was abandoned by the surrounding nations. Marriages with sisters not by the same mother were forbidden in the Mosaic code. Previously, however, none were unlawful except those of a man with his mother, or mother-in-law, or full sister. In the new dispensation the widow of a deceased brother was placed within the prohibited degree of consanguinity.

The laws against adultery were severe; death was ordained for both the guilty persons, and the punishment appears always to have been by stoning. Many victims, doubtless, perished under this cruel code; but the example of Jesus Christ gave a new lesson to mankind. The woman was brought before him, and the Jews claimed her condemnation. They asked him "should she be stoned." Had he said no, they might have charged him with favouring adultery, and denying the Mosaic law; had he said yes, the Romans might have impeached him, for they had assumed the distribution of justice, and abolished the punishment of death for adultery. But he evaded their malice, and gave the law of mercy. "Let him that is without sin among you cast the first stone." They all went out, and when he was alone with her he said, "Hath no man condemned thee?" She answered, "No man, Lord." And he again said, "*Neither do I condemn thee—go, and sin no more.*"

That sentence should ever be in remembrance when we frame our moral code.

---
* The marriage institution is mentioned early in Genesis vi. 1, 2, "And it came to pass, when men began to multiply on the face of the earth, and daughters were born unto them,

"That the sons of God saw the daughters of men that they were fair; and they took them wives of all which they chose."

Adultery, however, was a crime only to be committed with a married woman, or one who was betrothed. The man's marriage placed him under no obligation to abstain from intercourse with other than his wife. Wives to the number of four were allowed, while concubinage was unlimited. The first wife, however, was superior to the others. Jealousy, therefore, among the Jewish women could not have been a powerful feeling. Indeed we find strong proofs to the contrary. When Sarah found herself barren, she gave Hagar, her Egyptian maid, to Abraham, as a concubine or inferior wife. Other women, frequently, on discovering themselves to be sterile, begged their husbands to procure another companion of the bed, that they might not die childless. Similar instances are common in the social history of the East.

Marriage with an idolater was forbidden; but a man might marry a proselyte captive. When he saw a beautiful woman among his prisoners of war, he was to take her home, shave her head, pare her nails, change her raiment into that of a free person, and as he had *humbled* her, was forbidden to make merchandise of her again. The possession, nevertheless, of two wives by a private individual was a rare thing. Popular feeling was generally averse to it. The personages who most commonly practised it were the great men and kings, who were most expressly prohibited. In the Book of Deuteronomy, when the degraded Israelites had clamoured for a king, the law was given, "Neither shall he multiply wives to himself, so that his heart turn not away." No command was more frequently broken in the palaces of Israel. David had an immense harem; it seemed to be reckoned among the regalia. Solomon, who married Pharaoh's daughter, had seven hundred wives — princesses — and three hundred concubines; but we find that he "did evil in the sight of the Lord," and that "his heart was turned away."

Respecting the children born to these parents there was a change in the law. In *Genesis* a man was allowed to transfer the inheritance to a favourite child; but, probably from the many flagitious actions committed, it was in Deuteronomy ordained, that if a man had two wives, of whom he hated one and loved the other—each bearing a child, the first-born, whether of the loved or the hated woman, should enjoy the right of inheritance.

From all the passages in Scripture referring to this subject, it appears that women among the Jews held but an inferior position, being made the subject of barter, and that marriage was not a sacred but a civil institution,—a legal bond, which might be broken by a legal act. Matches were usually made by the woman's kindred, she herself being a secondary actor in the transaction.

Throughout the Bible, notwithstanding, we find women held by the inspired writers in great respect, their treatment by the rebellious Jews, as they sank through various degrees of corruption, being continually set forth among the abominations practised by that flagitious people.

In the Scriptures we discover innumerable references to women, and to prostitutes in particular; but, collecting and comparing them all, we find for our present purpose materials by no means abundant: there is no exact information. Prostitutes, we know, existed, and we are told in what estimation they were held; that they stood at the corners of streets, that they practised many seductive arts, and sold themselves at a very cheap rate: but how many they were, how they lived, what was the nature of their places of resort, we are left uninformed, or guided only by obscure allusions. Nevertheless, sufficient is known upon which to base a view of the condition of women, and the extent of morality among the most ancient nation recognised in history.

In the book of Genesis, whence we obtain our first glimpses of the social history of mankind, we find interesting, though imperfect, sketches of a curious state of society. We meet, even so early as this, with a woman wearing a veil, not taking her meals in company with men, living in separate apartments, and presenting a model of the system still prevalent in the East. Simplicity and luxury in strange combination characterized the manners of that remote age. Their morals appear to have been at all times gross; and one of the principal tasks of legislation was to restrain the licentiousness to which the people were so prone to abandon themselves. Many barbarous races present at this day social institutions similar to those of the Jews, whence many writers have traced them to that stock. It is more probable, however, that similar manners grow out of a similar condition.

Several writers, we know, contend for the purity of manners among the Jews, and point to the rigid laws which ruled them. The social history of mankind, however, if it proves anything, proves this, that it is not by any means the nation with the severest code which is the most virtuous. Examples of the contrary might be multiplied. No state, savage or civilized, could ever have more rigorous laws than Achin and Japan, and nowhere have the people been more flagitious. While the Draconic code was in force, morals in Greece went to rot. Consequently, if we are to consider the Jews to have been a moral people, it must certainly not be on the ground of their severe laws. Arguing from that, a contrary inference should be drawn. The direct evidence, however, tends the other way. Chastity appears to have been by no means a favourite virtue. Not to allude to the unnatural abominations mentioned in the Bible, it is certain that there existed a considerable class of public women, who prostituted themselves to any one for a certain reward.

The story of Tamar is a curious illustration of this subject. To impose on Judah, and bear a child by him, and in spite of him, she assumes the habit and appearance of a regular prostitute. She then goes out, and sitting down by the highway covers her face. Judah thought her to be a harlot, "because she covered her face," which, as the commentators tell us, was the custom for such women to do, as among the same class of females in Persia, in mimicry of a shame they did not feel. Judah speaks to her, and says, "Go to, I pray thee, let me come in unto thee." She answers, "What wilt thou give me, that thou mayest come in unto me ?'" He promises to give her a kid from his flock, but she demands a pledge; this he gave, and went with her.

The circumstance is related in a manner which seems to show that the practice was common with men, nor does any particular disgrace appear to attach to it. When, however, Judah learns that his daughter-in-law Tamar is "with child by whoredom," he condemns her to the punishment of death by burning, on the secret being at length revealed to him *. We have here a singular illustration of manners among the primitive tribes of that great family of mankind. The corruption of manners reached, it is probable, a high degree before the laws were given.

Where concubinage was practised, feminine virtue could not be held as a precious possession. The intercourse accordingly of a married man with an unmarried woman was esteemed simply as a proof of deficient chastity. At the same time, the encouragement of prostitution, or "the feeding of whores," is denounced as the conduct of foolish and profligate men, who unwisely waste their substance. The

---

* The passage here alluded to is as follows:—

"Then said Judah to Tamar his daughter in law, Remain a widow at thy father's house, till Shelah my son be grown: for he said, Lest peradventure he die also, as his brethren did. And Tamar went and dwelt in her father's house.

"And in process of time the daughter of Shuah Judah's wife died; and Judah was comforted, and went up unto his sheepshearers to Timnath, he and his friend Hirah the Adullamite.

"And it was told Tamar, saying, Behold thy father in law goeth up to Timnath to shear his sheep.

"And she put her widow's garments off from her, and covered her with a vail, and wrapped herself, and sat in an open place, which is by the way to Timnath; for she saw that Shelah was grown, and she was not given unto him to wife.

"When Judah saw her, he thought her to be an harlot; because she had covered her face.

"And he turned unto her by the way, and said, Go to, I pray thee, let me come in unto thee; (for he knew not that she was his daughter in law.) And she said, What wilt thou give me, that thou mayest come in unto me?

"And he said, I will send thee a kid from the flock. And she said, Wilt thou give me a pledge, till thou send it?

"And he said, What pledge shall I give thee? And she said, Thy signet, and thy bracelets, and thy staff that is thine hand. And he gave it her and came in unto her, and she conceived by him.

"And she arose, and went away, and laid by her vail from her, and put on the garments of her widowhood.

"And Judah sent the kid by the hand of his friend the Adullamite, to receive his pledge from the woman's hand: but he found her not.

"Then he asked the men of that place, saying, Where is the harlot, that was openly by the way side? And they said, There was no harlot in this place.

"And he returned to Judah, and said, I cannot find her; and also the men of the place said, that there was no harlot in this place.

"And Judah said, Let her take it to her, lest we be shamed: behold, I sent this kid, and thou hast not found her.

"And it came to pass about three months after, that it was told Judah, saying, Tamar thy daughter in law hath played the harlot; and also, behold, she is with child by whoredom. And Judah said, Bring her forth, and let her be burnt.

"When she was brought forth, she sent to her father in law, saying, By the man, whose these are, am I with child: and she said, Discern, I pray thee, whose are these, the signet, and bracelets, and staff.

"And Judah acknowledged them, and said, She hath been more righteous than I; because that I gave her not to Shelah my son. And he knew her again no more."—Gen. xxxviii. 11–26.

class of prostitutes was held in very low esteem; they were, in general, foreigners and heathens, and are spoken of usually as "strange women." Delilah, who beguiled Sampson, was probably a Philistine, though it is not certain that she was not an Israelite. At any rate, there appear to have been many Jewish women, of the lowest order, who followed this degrading occupation. To render them as few as possible, a law was passed forbidding men, under severe penalties, from bringing up their daughters to prostitution for gain. Legislation, however, could not entirely restrain the vicious from such a course of life.

Apparently the prostitutes, among the Jews, sometimes obtained husbands. Priests, however, were forbidden on any account to marry a harlot, or indeed any woman with even a breath of imputation on her fame. For the daughter of a priest, who took to the calling of a prostitute, the punishment was death by burning. For any woman it was infamous, but in spite of what was laid down in the law, or by the public opinion of the Jews, cities never wanted prostitutes, and women walked the streets, or stood in groups at the corners, ready to entrap the young men who came forth in quest of pleasure. Among the exhortations of parents to their sons, and of patriarchs to youth, we always find an injunction to beware of strange women, which implies a considerable prevalence of the system. The readers of the Bible will at once remember the many passages of this kind contained in that volume*.

With respect to prostitution among the Jews, an illustration is afforded by the story of the two mothers who came before Solomon for judgment. They were *harlots*, though bearing children, and they said they dwelt in one house, and "there was no stranger with us in the house." Another is afforded by the account of the two men whom Joshua sent out as spies. They came into a harlot's house at Rabbah—a brothel, in fact, where, as at Rome in the Imperial age, the woman sat impudently, without a veil, at the door, and solicited the passers by. They wore peculiar clothing. In addition to the vile customs of the East, we find, "Thou shalt not bring into the temple the price of a whore." This was to guard against the introduction of a practice not uncommon among some ancient and modern nations, of the priests enriching themselves and their temple by hiring out prostitutes*.

Another state, known to us from Scripture, is Babylon, surnamed the Whore, as well from its profligacy as its idolatry. The one, indeed, was accompanied by the other. Luxury and debauch were carried to the highest excess. The Temple of Venus,—a goddess known there as Mylitta,—was sacred to prostitution. The priests had, in immemorial time, invented a law that every woman should once in her life present herself at the temple, and prostitute her body to any stranger who might desire it. Consecrated by religion, this act appeared odious to few of the Babylonian citizens. The woman came, dressed brilliantly, and crowned with a garland of flowers; she sat down with her companions in a place where the strangers who filled the galleries might observe and make choice of their victims. Numbers were found always ready enough to enjoy the privilege procured for them by the priests. When a man had selected one of the women who pleased him most, he came down, and making her a present of money, which she was compelled to take, took her hand and said, "I implore in thy favour the goddess Mylitta!" He then led her to a retired spot and consummated the transaction. Having once entered the temple it was impossible for any ordinary woman to return home without having prostituted herself. Nevertheless, the priests allowed some ladies of rank and wealth to make a bargain for their chastity, which they probably desired to dispose of more agreeably to their own caprice. These few privileged persons went through the ceremonies without performing the usual act of prostitution. At the taking of Babylon by Cyrus, men were found ready to hire out their daughters and prostitute them for profit, while in the Alexandrian age men sent their wives to strangers for a sum of money†.

Throughout the countries of the East, upon the history of which at that early period any light has been thrown, we discover the prevalence of similar customs. The most celebrated appear the most licentious, but probably only because they have

---

* All this is based on the authority of the Bible. Elucidations also have been afforded by "The Book of the Religion &c., of the Jews," from the Hebrew, by Gamaliel ben Peldahzur; "The Laws and Polity of the Jews," Sigonius, "Republica Hebræorum;" and the various commentators.

* Mary Magdalene, of Magdala, was not the sinner, the woman of the city, who washed the feet of Jesus. She appears to have been a reputable person, while the other had been a prostitute. What a lesson is read to us by Christ's behaviour to her!

† See Goguet, "Origine des Loix," with Herodotus, Strabo, and Quintus Curtius.

been the most strictly investigated. The wealthy and luxurious capitals, in which the spoils of great conquests were piled up, never failed to supply a sufficient number of abandoned women, supported by the looser sort of men, in various degrees of position, from penury to splendour. Though circumstances of time and place, of religion and civilization, imparted peculiar characteristics to the prostitute class of each age and country, the general features of the system were invariably the same, and the prostitutes of Babylon resembled very much the prostitutes of New Orleans and London. We turn next to ancient Egypt, a country of whose laws and manners we have had interesting, if not complete, accounts bequeathed us.

OF PROSTITUTION IN ANCIENT EGYPT.

TURNING to ancient Egypt, we find, in the records of that singular people, little directly bearing on the question before us. Herodotus, and Diodorus the Sicilian, are almost the sole lights which guide us in our researches among them. Recently, the labours of a learned antiquarian have tended to increase our acquaintance with the people of old Egypt, by translating into language the volumes of information engraved or painted on the walls of tombs, temples, palaces, and monuments, so numerous in the cities on the banks of the Nile. We have thus had broad glimpses of the ancient history, the geography, population, government, the arts, the industry, and the manners of that country at that period; but the extent of the prostitute system has not been touched upon. Nevertheless, as one of the most ancient civilizations known to history, Egyptian society deserves some attention, and it is worth while to glance at the general condition of its women, especially as a few facts throw light on the especial point of our inquiry.

The position of a woman in ancient Egypt was in some respects remarkable. Entire mistress of the household, she exercised considerable influence over her husband, and was not subjected to any intolerable tyranny. In all countries, however, where concubinage is allowed, the condition of the sex must be in a degree degraded. Herodotus tells us that the Egyptians married only one wife, Diodorus that they married as many as they pleased, the restriction applying only to the sacerdotal order. The contradiction may be reconciled by supposing that the former writer described the general practice, and the latter the permission granted by the law; or, which is more probable, that he confounded concubinage with polygamy. From frequent allusions to this system we know it was tolerated. Wise laws, however, held a check upon the practice. Every child, the fruit of whatever union, was to be reared by its parents, infanticide being severely punished. Illegitimacy was a term not recognised. The son of the free, and the son of the bondwoman, had an equal right to inheritance, the father alone being referred to, since the mother was viewed as little more than a nurse to her own offspring. Women in Egypt bore numerous children, which rendered many concubines a burden too heavy for any but the wealthy to bear; nevertheless, some did indulge themselves in this manner, procuring young girls from the slave-merchants who came from abroad, or captives taken in the field.

In a country where the marriage of brother and sister was allowed, we might expect to find curious laws relating to the subject before us. But they were not curious, in any particular degree. Adultery was punished in the woman by the amputation of her nose, in the man by a thousand blows with a stick. The wealthier men were extremely jealous, forcing their wives to go barefooted, that they might not wander in the streets. Eunuchs, also, were maintained by some. Among classes of a lower grade, the women enjoyed peculiar freedom, being allowed to take part in certain public festivals, on which occasions they wore a transparent veil. Among all sorts and conditions of the sex, the drinking of wine was permitted, as it was by the Greeks, though not by the Romans; and ladies are occasionally represented on the monuments, exhibiting all the evidences of excess.

These observations apply to the respectable female society of ancient Egypt. There existed, however, another class, nowhere indeed indicated under the term harlot, or prostitute, but evidently such from the accounts we have received. If the descriptions transmitted to us of the ordinary female society be correct, the women to whom we allude could have been no other than public prostitutes. Such were, in all probability, those who enlivened the festival of Bubastis, and danced at the private entertainments. What ideas of decency prevailed among them, may be imagined from the brief though curious account afforded by Herodotus. When the time of the festival arrived, men and women embarked promiscuously, and in great numbers, on board the vessels which conveyed them up or down the river. During the voyage, they played on various instruments, and whenever they arrived at a city moored the boats. Then some of the women, who could have been no other than the Almé of those days*, played furiously all kinds of music, flung off their garments, challenged the women of the town with gross insulting language, and outraged decency by their gestures and postures. An immense concourse of people assembled on the occasion, and a large proportion of them belonged to the female sex. "Some of them" only, according to our author, took part in the exhibitions of profligacy we have noticed.

The public dancers and musicians of the female sex were also, in all probability, members of the sisterhood we allude to. They were, it is well known, held in extremely low estimation: they were clothed, like the prostitutes of ancient Greece, in a single light garment; indeed, from the monuments, it is questionable whether they did not, like those in the Roman saturnalia of Flora, dance entirely naked at some of the more dissolute private festivals of the wealthy. At any rate, their forms are represented so completely undraped, that any garment they wore must have been a light veil which clung to the skin, and was transparent. But from what we are told of the festival of Bubastis, it is by no means improbable that they were actually nude.

In that remote period, fancifully called the age of Sesostris, chastity does not appear to have been the capital virtue of society among the Egyptians. At least, we must draw this inference if we are to attach any significance to traditions or fables, which generally reflect some phase of truth. Sesostris, it is said, having offended the gods, was struck blind, and ordered to find a woman who had been strictly faithful to her husband. He was very long in performing the task, being furnished with an unerring rule of judgment. Of course the account is an idle fable, yet it is not altogether unworthy of notice, for it indicates an opinion as to the chastity of that period†.

OF PROSTITUTION IN ANCIENT GREECE.

IN the heroic ages of Greece, we find women —on the authority, indeed, of poets, the sole historians of those times—enjoying a considerable share of liberty, held in much respect, accustomed to self-reliance, and allowed freely to mingle with others of their own sex and with men. A modest simplicity of manners is ascribed to them, which is wholly foreign to modern ideas of refinement. What education they received is not well known, though they appear to have been trained to practise many of the useful as well as the elegant arts of life; but with respect to the morality prevalent among them little exact information can be gained. As in the Bible, however, frequent allusion is made to harlots and strange women, waiting at the corners of the streets, so in the poets of antiquity, passages occur which point to the existence of a class, dedicating itself to serve, for gain, the passions of men who could not afford marriage, or would not be bound by its restrictions. The science of statistics, however, does not seem to have been cultivated in those days. We are not told with certainty of the population of cities, or even whole countries, and men were not then found to calculate how many in a hundred were immoral, or to compare the prostitute with the honourable classes of women.

With the commencement of the strictly historical age, though statistics are still wanting, there have been collected materials from which we may gather fair ideas of the *status* of women, and the position and extent of the prostitute class among them. Beginning with Sparta, a very peculiar system displays itself. Among the citizens of that celebrated Doric state, women were regarded as little more than agencies for the production of other citizens. The handsome bull-stranglers of Lacedæmon held exceedingly lax notions of morality, and would have considered a delicately chaste woman as one characterized by a singular natural weakness. Taught to consider themselves more in their capacity of citizens than of women, their duty to their husbands, or to their own virtue, occupied always the second place. Their education inculcated the practice of immorality. All ideas of modesty were by a deliberate public training obliterated from their minds. Scourged with the whip when young, taught to wrestle, box, and race naked before assemblages of men, their wantonness and licentiousness passed every bound. Marriage, indeed, was an institution of the state; but no man could call his wife his own. On occasions when the male population was away in the field, the women complained that there was no chance of children being born, and young men were sent back from the camp, to become the husbands of the

---

* Dr. Beloe also takes this view.

† Diodorus Siculus, i. 59. See also 'the Euterpe of Herodotus, and Sir G. Wilkinson's Ancient Egypt.

GREEK DANCING-GIRL—HETAIRA: *Age of Socrates.*

[From "*Costume Antico e Moderno.*"—Milan, 1616.]

whole female population, married and single.

In times of peace, also, the public laws gave every woman a chance of becoming what we should in these days term a public prostitute. A man without a wife might insist on borrowing for a certain time the wife of another. Should her husband resist, the law was called in to enforce the demand. It is asserted, indeed, by some, that adultery was unknown in Sparta. There was no such offence, in truth, recognised in the code. It was common, legal, and occurred every day. At the same time, however, it is to be remembered, that the severe laws of Sparta, recognising no concessions to the weaker passions of men, allowed these things only for state purposes, that citizens might be brought forth. There appears to have been no class of prostitutes gaining a livelihood by selling their persons to the pleasures of men: the rigorous code of the state forbade such sensual indulgences. Women were not allowed, apparently, to walk the streets. The young were strictly watched by the elders, the elders jealously observed by the young; and any proneness to a practice subversive of that vigorous health in the population, considered essential to preserve the manhood of Sparta, would have been denounced as an attempt to introduce luxury and effeminacy—the vices, in their eyes, of slaves. To assert that in the whole state no virtuous women, and no public prostitutes, in our sense of the word, could be found, would be rash; but it is certain that no authority which has come down to us represents chastity as a Spartan virtue, or prostitution for money, or from predilection, one of their social institutions.

In Athens a wholly different picture is presented. There, and generally among the Ionians, the duty of the wife was to preserve a chastity as delicate and pure as any which is required in our strictest social circle. There, at the same time, the courtezan class existed, and men of all descriptions and all ages encouraged prostitution, to which a considerable class of women devoted themselves. This is a complete contrast with Sparta.

The young girls of Attica were early trained to all the offices of religion; they acquired considerable knowledge; their intellectual qualities were to some degree developed: they were educated to become housekeepers, wives, and mothers, such as we describe under those heads. Exercising considerable influence over their male relatives, they possessed consequently considerable weight in the community, and altogether held a higher position than the women of Sparta. They led secluded lives, yet they enjoyed many opportunities of intercourse with the other sex; and though, in their theatres, and in their temples, indecency of the grossest description was frequently displayed to their sight, they seem otherwise to have been somewhat refined in this respect. In Sparta, the virgins never hesitated to expose themselves naked before any circle of spectators: in Athens they observed at least the public forms of decorum, and, with the exception of the Hetairæ or prostitute class, were sufficiently modest in their conversation and in their behaviour.

Accustomed to be present at public spectacles, to converse with men, to share in the performance of ceremonies at religious or civic festivals, the women of Athens occupied a position somewhat approaching that which we believe is proper to their sex. Marriages, as among us, were contracted, some from sentiment, others from interest. We are led to form a high idea of the general morality prevailing in the Attic states of Greece at an early period, from the exalted view of love, of chastity, of matronly duties, urged in the writers of the time. This seems a fair measure to employ, since, in a later age, when morals were more corrupt, and the regular class of prostitutes might be confounded with the general society, the style and sentiment of poets and others formed an exact reflex of the prevailing state of morality.

Traditions point to a period in the social history of Greece, when men and women dispensed altogether with the ceremony of marriage, living not only out of wedlock, but promiscuously, without an idea of any permanent compact between two individuals of opposite sexes. If such a state of things ever existed, it must have been before any regular society was formed, and it is therefore vain to dwell upon it. Polygamy, we know, long continued in practice among the Greeks, though it was a privilege and a propensity chiefly followed by the powerful and rich. In Athens marriage was held sacred. The character of a bachelor was disreputable. So, indeed, was it in Sparta, where young men remaining single after a certain period might be punished for the neglect of a duty exacted from them by the severe laws of the state. In both states, but in different degrees, the prohibition of marriage within certain limits of consanguinity extended; but when once the union took place, it was, in Athens, a crime of great enormity to defile its sanctity. The influence of the wife was, in the household, powerful; and commanding, as she did, the respect of men, the advantages of her position were so great, that to risk their loss by a transgression of the moral law, was not a common occurrence. We may therefore assign to the women of Athens a high average of morality, and consider them as having been held in remarkable estimation.

An important point in the manners of every people is the institution of marriage. From an inquiry into its estimation, whether it be held a religious rite, or a civil contract, or both, with various other circumstances in connection with these, we are aided in forming a just idea of the prevalent civilization. In the Doric states of Greece, it was esteemed as little more than a prudent ceremony, binding man and woman together for purposes of state. As among the savages of Australasia, it was the custom for a man to bear a woman forcibly from among her companions, when he took her to the bridesmaid's house, and, her hair being cut short and her clothes changed, she was delivered to him as wife. His intercourse with her however, was, for some time clandestine, and he shunned being seen in her society. This was the case with the wealthier maidens. The portionless girls were, from time to time, shut up in a dark edifice, and the youths, being introduced, accepted each the woman he happened to seize upon. A penalty was imposed on any one refusing to abide by the decision of chance.

Occasionally public ceremonies were enacted at the marriages of the rich; but from all testimony it appears certain that the union of man with woman at Sparta was entirely of a civil, and by no means of a sacred character. Private interest, sentiment, and happiness were indeed, in this, as in all other matters, subordinate to the public exigencies. When a woman had no children by her own husband, she was not only allowed, but required by the law to cohabit with another man. Anaxandrides, to procure an heir, had, contrary to all custom, two wives. The state excused no licentiousness for its own sake, but any amount for a public object *.

In Attic Greece, the ceremony of marriage was viewed in a more poetical light, and divinity was supposed to preside over it. We have already alluded to the notion of the promiscuous intercourse among them at a remote period; but, passing from this fable, we find traces of polygamy long discernible.

Heracles maintained a regular seraglio. Egeus, Pallas, Priam, Agamemnon, and nearly all the chiefs, possessed harems, but these were irregularities, contrary to law and custom, and only in fashion among royal personages. The story of the two wives of Socrates seems a pure invention.

In the Athenian Republic, marriage, being held in reverence, was protected by the law. In the later and better known ages, consanguinity within certain limits was a bar to such union. Men, however, might marry half-sisters by the fathers' side, though few availed themselves of the permission. Betrothed long before marriage by their parents, the young man and woman were nevertheless allowed on most occasions to consult their own inclinations. Numerous religious rites preceded the actual ceremony, and heavenly favour was invoked upon it. The marriage was performed at the altar in the temple, where sacrifice was made, and a mutual oath of fidelity strengthened by every sacred pledge. Adultery was held a debasing crime, and divorce discreditable to man and wife *.

In connection with the subject of marriage is that of infanticide. It prevailed among the Greeks, under the sanction of philosophy. Among the Thebans and the Tyrrhenians it was, however, unknown. Why? Because they were more humane, or moral? Not by any means. They were among the most profligate societies of antiquity. It is generally shame which induces to child-murder women bearing offspring from illicit intercourse with men. Where no disgrace attaches to illegitimate offspring, the principal incentive to destroy them is taken away; and in Tyre, where female slaves served naked at the table of the rich, and even ladies joined the orgies in that condition, modesty was by no means a common grace of their sex.

The Thebans, a very gross people, made infanticide a capital crime; but allowed the poor to impose on the state, under certain circumstances, the burden of their children. In Thrace, the infant, placed in an earthen pot, was left to be devoured by wild beasts, or to perish of cold and hunger †.

In Sparta, clandestine infanticide was a crime; but the state often performed what it declared a duty, by condemning weakly and delicate infants to be flung into a pit. In Athens, on the contrary; it was left for desperate women, and cold-blooded men,

---

* Manners and Customs of Ancient Greece, by J. A. St. John.

* Manners and Customs of Ancient Greece, by J. A. St. John.
† Mackinnon's History of Civilization.

ROMAN BROTHEL.—IMPERIAL ERA. (DUFOUR.)

privately to accomplish the act, exposing their children in public places to perish, or to claim charity from some wayfarer. Frequently the rich had recourse to this, for concealing an intrigue, and left a costly dowry of gold and jewels in the earthen jar where they deposited the victim. The temple steps sometimes received the foundling; but occasionally they were left to die in desert places.

In the flourishing period of the Republic, however, poverty was so rare, indeed so unknown, that it seldom exacted these sacrifices from the humbler people. Infanticide was then left to the wholly unnatural who refused the burden, or the guilty who dreaded the shame, of a child.

But in the female society of that state, there was, as we have said, a sisterhood which exercised no inconsiderable influence on public manners. These were the Hetairæ, or prostitutes, who occupied much the same position which the same class does in most civilized communities of modern times. The youthful, beautiful, elegant, polished, and graceful, commanded, while their attractions lasted, the favours and the deference of wealthy and profligate young men, and, when their persons had faded, sank by degrees, until they dragged themselves in misery through the streets, glad to procure a meal by indiscriminate prostitution, with all who accepted their company. When children were born to them, infanticide usually—especially in the case of girls—relieved them of the burden.

The position the prostitute class of Athens occupied in relation to the other women in the community was peculiar. They entered the temples during the period of one particular festival—and in modern countries the church is never closed against them; but they were not, as among us, allowed to occupy the same place at the theatre with the Athenian female citizen. Yet this was not altogether to protect the virtue of the woman; it was to satisfy the pride of the citizen, since every stranger suffered an equal exclusion from these "reserved seats." Notwithstanding this, however, the courtezans occasionally visited the ladies in their own houses, to instruct them in those accomplishments in which, from the peculiar tenor of their lives, they were most practised, while it appears that both classes mingled at the public baths.

The Hetairæ, or prostitute class, exercised undoubtedly an evil influence on the society of Athens. They indulged the sensual tastes and the vanity of the young, encouraged among them a dissolute manner of life, and, while the power of their attractions lasted, led them into expensive luxury, which could not fail of an injurious effect on the community. The career of the prostitute was, as it is in all countries, short, and miserable at its close. While their beauty remained unfaded they were puffed up with vanity, carried along by perpetual excitement, flattered by the compliments of young men, and by the conversation of even the greatest philosophers, and maintained in opulence by the gifts of their admirers. Premature age, however, always, except in a few celebrated cases, assailed them. They became old, ugly, wrinkled, deformed, and full of disease, and might be seen crawling through the market places, haggling for morsels of provision, amid the jeers and insults of the populace.

In some instances, indeed, there occurred in Athens what occasionally happens in all countries. Men took as wives the prostitutes with whom they had associated. Even the wise Plato became enamoured of Archæanassa, an Hetaira of Ctesiphon. For many of these women were no less renowned for the brilliancy of their intellectual qualities than for their personal charms. Of Phryne, whose bosom was bared before the judges by her advocate, and who sat as a model to the greatest of ancient sculptors, all the world has heard. Her statue, of pure gold, was placed on a pillar of white marble at Delphi. Aspasia exercised at Athens influence equal to that of a queen, attracting round her all the characters of the day, as Madame Roland was wont to do in Paris. Socrates confessed to have learned from her much in the art of rhetoric. Yet these women, harsh as the judgment may appear, were common whores, though outwardly refined, and mentally cultivated. Instances, indeed, of high public virtue displayed by members of that sisterhood, distinguished among the Hetairæ of ancient Greece, are on record, and sufficient accounts of them have been transmitted to us to show that they were among the male society a recognised and respected class, while by the women they were neither abhorred nor considered as a pollution to the community. Still, prostitutes they were, to all intents and purposes.

The mean, the poor, and faded, were chiefly despised for their ugliness and indigence, not for their incontinence. It was, in the Homeric ages, as we learn from the Odyssey, held disgraceful for "a noble maiden" to lose her chastity. But in Athens, at a later time, chastity in an unmarried woman was not held a virtue, the loss of which degraded her utterly below the consideration of all other classes, or debarred her for ever from any intercourse with the honourable of her own sex. The Hetaira was not, it is true, admitted to mingle freely in the society of young women; but she was not shut out from all communication with them; while among men, if her natural attractions or accomplishments were great, she exercised peculiar influence. Consequently, it appears that in Athens the superior public prostitute had a *status* higher than that of any woman of similar character in our own day. If we look for a comparison to illustrate our meaning, we may find it in many of the ladies who at various periods have frequented our court—known but not acknowledged prostitutes*.

In the public judgments of Athens we find, it is true, a penalty or fine imposed on "whoredom,"† from which, however, the people escaped by a variation of terms, calling a whore a mistress, as Plutarch tells us. Solon, however, recognised prostitution as a necessary, or at least an inevitable evil, for he first built a temple to Aphrodite Pandemos, which, truly rendered, means Venus the Prostitute; and his view was justified by the declaration that the existence of a prostitute class was necessary, in order, as Cato also thought, that the wives and daughters of citizens might be safe from the passion which young men would, in one way or the other, satiate upon the other sex. Though procurers, therefore, were punishable by law, and the Hetairæ were obliged to wear coloured or flowered garments, it was enacted in the civil code of Athens, that "persons keeping company with common strumpets shall not be deemed adulterers, for such shall be common for the satiating of lust."

Brothels, consequently, existed in moderate numbers at Athens, and the young men were not discouraged from attending them occasionally. There were also particular places in the city where the prostitutes congregated, and a Temple of Venus, which was their peculiar resort. We find in the poets passages, indeed, advocating the support of whores ‡.

Still, respected and beloved as the Hetairæ were among their friends and lovers, recognised by the law, and protected by it, general public respect was denied them, for the Athenians estimated above their brilliant charms the modest virtues of inferior women*.

One of the most remarkable features in the public economy of Athens was the tax upon prostitutes, introduced also in Rome by Caligula. It was annually farmed out by the Senate to individuals who knew accurately the names of all who followed this calling. It is to be regretted that their statistics have not been furnished to us. Every woman, it appears, had a fixed price, which she might charge to the men to whom she prostituted her person, and the amount of the tax varied according to their profits. Apparently, they were principally "strangers" who filled the ranks of the Hetairæ, for we find that if persons enjoying the rank and privilege of citizens took to the occuption, a tax was imposed on them as on the ordinary prostitutes, and they were punished by exclusion from the public sacrifices, and from the honourable offices of state. The same writer informs us, on the authority of Demosthenes, that a citizen who cohabited with an alien paid a penalty, in case he was convicted, of a thousand drachmas, but the penalty could not often have been enforced, as the laws of Solon recognised prostitution; it was a feature in the manners of the city, and brothels were fearlessly kept, and entered without shame. Numerous evidences of this have been supplied us†. To preserve a respect for chastity, however, and to inculcate a horror for the prostitute's occupation, the same code allowed men to sell their sisters or daughters when convicted of an act of fornication, which, in Athens, as elsewhere, frequently was the first step in the regular career of these women ‡.

The dishonour thus accruing to the general body of prostitutes, though a small class of them enjoyed many superior advantages from their wealth, and the polish of their manners, served at Athens, in some degree, to preserve public morality. The system never seems to have reached the height which it has gained in many of our modern cities, where married women often follow the occupation, and live upon its gains §.

In Corinth, however, prostitutes abounded, and the Temple of Venus in that city was sometimes thronged by a thousand of them. They were usually

---

* This view is chiefly drawn from information collected in Manners and Customs of Ancient Greece, by J. A. St. John.
† Potter's Antiquities of Greece.
‡ Ibid.

* Hase On the Ancient Greeks.
† Boeck's Public Economy of Athens.
‡ Potter's Antiquities of Greece
§ Hase On the Ancient Greeks.

the most beautiful women of the state, presented or sold to the temple, who prostituted themselves for hire. They were of a superior kind, admitting to their embraces none but men who would pay munificently, and in this manner many of them are said to have accumulated large fortunes*.

Tabular statements, and numerical estimates, have been wanting to complete this glance at the system in ancient Greece; but it may, nevertheless, afford a just idea of the extent and character of the prostitute class there.

Of Prostitution in ancient Rome.

If our knowledge of ancient Greece, with reference to its moral economy, is slight, ancient Rome is still less understood. Nothing, indeed, like a detailed account of its social institutions has been preserved; its scheme of manners is incompletely comprehended; and only an outline picture of its private life can be formed from passages supplied by hundreds of authors, from allusions in the poets and in the satirical writers. German scholars have laboured industriously in the field of classical politics; but the social economy of Rome has been neglected, or, which is worse, obscured by them. We are, therefore, enabled only to afford a general sketch of the subject in connection with the great Republic, and the imperial system which grew out of its decay.

Examining the condition of the female sex, especially with reference to prostitutes, we must in Rome, as in all other states, distribute our observations over several distinct periods—for such there were in the social history of the nation.

In the more honourable days of the Republic, women occupied a high status. While the state was extremely young we find them, indeed, in perpetual tutelage; but gradually, as institutions were improved and manners refined, they rose to independence, and formed an influential element in society. The matron, in particular, stood in her due position. Respected, accomplished, allowed to converse with men, she was, in the most flourishing era of Roman history, a model for her sex. She presided over the whole household, superintended the education of the children, while they remained in tender years, and shared the honours of her husband. Instead of confined apartments being allotted to her as a domestic prison, the best chambers in the house were assigned, while the whole of it was free to her. Other circumstances in her condition combined to invest her with dignity; and the consequence was, that the Roman matron seldom or never transgressed against the moral or social law. No divorce is recorded before the year 234 B.C.; and that instance was on account of the woman's barrenness—a plea allowed by the law, but universally reprobated by the people. Yet the obstacles to this dissolution of the marriage compact were by no means formidable. Under the imperial régime, when there was less facility, divorces were more frequent.

The Roman law of marriage was strict. Degrees of consanguinity were marked, though within narrower limits than among us, within which marriage was not only illegal, but wholly void, and any intercourse, by virtue of it, denounced as incest by the law. Public infamy attached to it—not only the odium of opinion, but a formal decree by the prætor. Adultery was held as a base, inexpiable crime. It was interdicted under every penalty short of death, and even this was allowed under certain circumstances to be inflicted by the husband. Wedded life, indeed, was held sacred by every class from the knights to the slaves, though among these social aliens actual marriage could not take place. Celibacy was not only disreputable, but, in a particular degree, criminal; while barrenness brought shame upon the woman who was cursed with it. In an equal, or a greater ratio, was parentage honourable. Polygamy was illegal; but the social code allowed one wife and several concubines, occupying a medium position, finely described by Gibbon, as below the honours of a wife, and above the infamy of a prostitute. Such institutions were licensed that common whoredom might be checked; though the children born of such intercourse were refused the rank of citizens. Often, indeed, they were a burden to the guilty as well as to the poor; and infanticide, which was declared in 374 B.C. a capital crime, was resorted to as a means of relief.

If we examine our question in connection with marriage among the ancient Romans we find a curious system. First, there were certain conditions to constitute *connubium*, without which no legal union could be formed. There was only connubium between Roman citizens*; there

---

* Boeck. Potter. Mitford's notions of the Hetairæ appear to have been somewhat fanciful.

* Occasional exceptions occurred. At one time there was no connubium between the plebeian and the patrician; but the Lex Canuleia allowed it.

was none where either of the parties possessed it already with another; none between parent and child, natural or by adoption; none between grandparents and grandchildren; none between brothers and sisters, of whole or half blood; none between uncle and niece, or aunt and nephew: though Claudius legalized it by his marriage with Agrippina, the practice never went beyond the example. Unions of this kind taking place were void, and the father could claim no authority over his children. Mutual consent was essential—of the persons themselves, and of their friends. One wife only was allowed, though marriage after full divorce was permitted.

There were two kinds of marriage,—that *cum*, and that *sine conventione*. In the former the wife passed into her husband's family, and became subject to him; in the latter she abdicated none of her old relations, and was equal to her husband. There was no ceremony absolutely essential to constitute a marriage. Cohabitation during a whole year made a legal and lasting union; but the woman's absence during three nights annually released her from the submission entailed by the marriage *cum conventione*. Certain words, also, with religious rites, performed in presence of ten witnesses, completed a marriage; but certain priestly offices, such as those of the *flamen dialis*, could only be performed for those whose parents had been wedded in a similar way*. The sponsalia, or contracts between the man and his wife's friends, were usual, but not essential, and could be dissolved by mutual consent. The Roman idea of marriage was, in a word, the union of male and female for life, bringing a community of fortune, by a civil, not a sacred contract. Yet from the ceremonies *generally* observed, it is evident that an idea, though unrecognised, of a religious union, existed among the Romans in their more pious age.

With respect to property, its arrangement depended on settlements made beforehand. Divorce was at one time procured by mutual consent, though afterwards it became more difficult, but never impossible.

There was in Rome a legal concubinage between unmarried persons, resembling the morganatic or "left-handed" marriage, giving neither the woman nor her children any rights acquired from the husband.

* The sacerdotal functionary, termed *flamen dialis*, like the high-priest of the Jews, could only wed a virgin of unblemished honour, and when she died, could not marry again, but was forced to resign his office.

Widowers often took a concubine, without infamy *.

The law of Romulus, enacting that no male child should be exposed, and that the first daughter should always be preserved, while every other should be brought up, or live on trial, as it were, for three years, has misled some writers into giving the Romans credit for a loftier humanity. No parent, it is argued, would destroy a three years' old child. Nevertheless, it is certain that, in the imperial age, at least, infanticide and child-dropping were frequent occurrences. Deformed or mutilated infants, having been shown to five witnesses, might be destroyed at once. The Milky Column, in the Herb-market, was a place where public nurses sat to suckle or otherwise tend the foundlings picked up in various parts of the city. In the early Christian age it was a reproach to the Romans that they cast forth their sons, as Tertullian expresses it, to be picked up and nourished by the fisherwomen who passed. Mothers would deny their children when brought home to their houses. Some strangled them at once. Various devices were adopted among them, as among other nations of antiquity, to check the overflow of population, as well as to hide the crimes of the guilty. Thus the Phœnicians passed children through fire, as a sacrifice; the Carthaginians offered them up at the altar; the Syrians flung them from the lofty propylæa of a temple †. One observation, however, applies to the Romans, and, we believe, to every other nation, savage or civilized, in every age of the world—exceptions being invariably allowed. Cruel as may have been the laws sanctioning infanticide, when once the child was received into the bosom of the family it was cared for with tenderness, and, generally, with discretion. It is not sentiment, but justice, which induces us to say that the mother, having once accepted her charge, has seldom been guilty of wilful neglect. The abandoned and dissolute, especially in those societies where fashion has made the performance of maternal duty ridiculous, if not disreputable, have consigned their offspring to others; but women in their natural state usually fulfil this obligation.

In Rome, from various causes, public decency was, at least during the republican period, more rigidly observed, and licen-

* See Julian Law, Ulpian, Gaius, Tacitus, Suetonius, and Dion Cassius, from whom, with various others, Smith's Dictionary is compiled.

† Dion. Halicar.; Apuleius; Festus; Lactarra Columna; Tertullian's Apolog.; Ambrose's Hexam.; Lucian, De Syriâ Deâ.

tiousness less common and less tolerated than in Sparta or even the later age of Athens. None of its institutions rivalled the dissolute manners of Crete or Corinth. One cause of prostitution being less common was the licence of concubinage, which was to the rich a preferable and a safer plan of self-indulgence. It existed, however, in the State, and employed a considerable class of women, though we are told the accomplished prostitute was known as a Grecian import. Nevertheless, the frequent allusions of the laws to these women prove that they formed no insignificant element in the society of the capital.

Lenocinium, or the keeping of female slaves to hire them out as prostitutes for profit, was an offence rather against the moral than the written law of Rome. The lenones, in many instances, kept brothels or houses open for the trade of prostitution. They purchased in the market handsome girls, for each of whom a sum equal to about 250*l.* of English currency was given—from which we infer that the rates charged in the superior establishments of this kind were somewhat high. Free women were also kept for the same purpose, upon a mutual agreement. The practice was not actually interdicted, but branded as infamous by the prætor's declaration. No woman, however, whose father, grandfather, or husband had been a Roman knight was allowed to prostitute herself for gain. The independent prostitutes, or those who occupied houses of their own, were compelled to affix on the door a notice of their calling, and the price they demanded. They were also required, when they signified to the prætor, as they were bound to do, their intention of following this disgraceful occupation, to drop their real names, which they resumed whenever they abandoned that mode of life. Cato, the censor, recognised prostitution as Solon did, and Cicero declared no State ever existed without it. Notwithstanding this, the occupation of the prostitute was, in the republican age, so infamous that a comparatively small class practised it; but under the emperors it grew so prevalent, that during the reign of the few of them who even pretended to morality, the severest edicts appeared called for against it. Caligula, however, made a profit from the system. The lenones were subject to a tax, which fell, of course, as in Athens, upon the prostitutes themselves. No check, therefore, was offered by him to prostitution. But Theodosius and Valentinian sought, by formidable penalties, to prevent parents from prostituting their children, and masters their slaves, for gain.

Lenocinium was interdicted under pain of the scourge, banishment, and other punishments. In one age public opinion, in the other the whip, held guardianship over the morals of the State.

The owners of houses who allowed lenocinium to be carried on on their premises were liable to forfeit the property, besides paying a price of ten pounds weight of gold. Such edicts, however, only drove immorality into the dark. When the prostitutes could not find enough brothels to harbour them— and, indeed, at all times the poorer sort were excluded from these large establishments— places of refuge were still open. The *fornices* of Rome were long galleries, divided into a double row of cells—some broad and airy, others only small dark arches, situated on a level with the street, and forming the substructure of the houses above. Some of them, as those of the Formian villa of Cicero, were tastefully stuccoed, and painted in streaks of pink, yellow, and blue. In these long lines of cells the prostitutes of the poorer class were accustomed to assemble, and thence was derived the ecclesiastical term fornication, with its ordinary English meaning. Allusions to this practice occur in the works of Horace and Juvenal, as well as other writers. Some of the arches appear to have been below the surface of the ground, as we find a decree of Theodosius against the subterranean brothels of Rome.

The great satirist who has left us his vivid, though exaggerated picture of manners in the imperial age, supplies some allusions in elucidation of our subject. He speaks of the "transparent garments" worn by prostitutes, as by the dancers of ancient Egypt; of the "foreign women" who swarmed in its "foul brothels;" of the "gay harlots' chariots" dashing through the streets; and of the porticos and covered walks forming for these women places of promenade. We learn that some of them were forced, as a punishment for disorderly behaviour, to wear the male toga, while most were distinguished by a yellow headdress. The fornices were publicly opened and closed at certain hours. The women stood at the doors of their cells, in loose, light attire, their bosoms exposed, and the nipples gilt. Thus Messelana stood at the door of the lupanaria, with her breast adorned with this singular ornament*.

At various periods efforts were made to suppress the prostitutes' calling, but never with success. The lawmakers of the imperial age gave no example of the morality

* See Satire vi. 121-2.

which their edicts pretended to uphold. Thus, the bawds who inveigled or ravished girls from their homes, to obtain a livelihood by their prostitution, became liable to "extreme penalties," though what these were we know not. The law of lenocinium was more widely interpreted, as manners became more corrupt. If a husband permitted his wife to prostitute herself that he might share the gains, it was lenocinium. Justinian allowed a woman the privilege of divorce, if her husband endeavoured to tempt her into such adultery: he was forced also to restore her dowry. On the other hand, if a woman committed the crime, it was lenocinium for the husband to receive her again, to spare the adulterer if caught in the act, or to refrain from prosecuting him if otherwise detected. If a man married a woman convicted of adultery, discovered a crime of this kind and was bribed to hold his peace, commenced a prosecution for adultery and withdrew it, or lent his house for rape or prostitution, the Julian law made him guilty of lenocinium, and penalties of various kinds were attached to the offence in its different modifications.

Lupanaria, or common brothels, were at all times considered infamous. Young men seem to have been more careful to visit them in secret than at Athens, where they visited and left them in the light of open day, and were encouraged to do so by the poets. There was, however, another class of disreputable places of assembly, to which a similar exists in most modern cities. These were the lower order of *popinæ*, or houses of entertainment, not absolutely recognised as "stews," but generally known to be the resorts of prostitutes and their companions. In Pompeii there appears to have existed a class of the same description, for in one of the wine-houses discovered there, an inner room is situated behind the shop, the walls of which are covered with lewd and filthy pictures. Pornography, or obscene painting, was much practised at Rome, and doubtless afforded much pleasure to the company who nightly assembled in the Ganeæ, or regular brothels.

As among the Greeks, instances of men willing to marry prostitutes occurred among the Romans. It was found necessary to check the practice by rendering it disreputable. The penalty of public infamy was denounced against all freemen contracting such an union; while a senator, and the son of a senator, were especially forbidden.

The prostitutes of Rome, like those of many other countries, varied their principal calling by others which rendered them more attractive to the dissolute youth of the city. They cultivated the arts of dancing, singing, and playing on musical instruments. They performed lascivious dances at their places of assembly, playing on the flute, and practising all those tricks of seduction employed so successfully by the Almé of Egypt.

Difficulties have arisen before many inquirers into the social condition of the ancient Romans, as to whence the prostitutes came, seeing that they were chiefly strangers. Some light, we think, is thrown on the subject by the fact that the Ambubaiæ were Syrian musicians, who performed dances in Rome, and, like the Bayaderes of India, the Almé of Egypt, and the dancers of Java, led a life of prostitution. They continued long to be imported; for, in the History of Gibbon, we find particular notice of the lascivious dances performed by the Syrian damsels round the altars on the Palatine Hill, to please the bestial senses of Elagabalus. During the public pantomimes, the prostitutes danced naked before the people; and, at the Floralian festival, the actresses at the theatre, who are known to have been common prostitutes, were compelled to strip, and perform indecent evolutions for the delight of the audience. This refers, however, to the imperial age. It was at no time a task of much inconvenience to divest themselves of clothing, for the harlots never encumbered themselves with much. In this they resembled the Hetairæ of Greece, whose thin slight garment was so insufficient for the purposes of decency, that it was designated as "naked." This was not, however, from hardiness or simplicity, but merely to promote the profit of their calling. In other respects the luxury of the wealthy prostitutes was boundless, and they were borne through the streets on the rich and elegant lactræ or portable couches, softly pillowed on which they reposed their limbs in voluptuous indolence. In the reign of Domitian a decree was passed that no whore should in future make use of these couches, which were reserved as an especial luxury to the privileged classes of Rome.

The edicts against prostitution increased in severity under various emperors. The severity of Constantine enacted that a man guilty of rape should die, whether he accomplished his purpose by violence, or by gentle and gradual seduction. The virgin who confessed her consent, instead of procuring a mitigation of this sentence, exposed herself to share the penalty. Slaves who were accomplices in the crime of procuring young women for prostitution, were punished by being burnt, or having boiling metal poured down their throats. The consequence of such a savage law was, that it could not be generally applied; nor was it enforced by the example of the emperor, who, once rigidly strict, turned dissolute and luxurious towards the close of his reign.

It will be seen, from the information here collected, that no actual knowledge exists of the precise extent of the prostitute system in Rome. Facts, and some of these extremely curious, have been preserved in connection with it; but the statistics of the question are wholly lost, if, indeed, they ever existed. On this account, it appeared possible to do no more than bring those facts together, and, throwing them into a general sketch of the morality prevailing at different periods in the social history of that state, to draw thence an idea of the truth. Under the comparatively virtuous Republic, a line could certainly be drawn between the profligate and the moral classes of the community. Under some of the emperors such a distinction was wholly impossible. The vulgar prostitute was commonly met at the tables of the rich, and the palace itself was no more than an imperial brothel. A few notes on the history of the empire will justify these remarks.

In the early period of the decline, the licentious amours of Faustina were excused, even encouraged, by her husband, and the nobles paid homage in the temples before the image of an adultress. In the eyes of Commodus virtue was criminal, since it implied a reflection upon his profligacy. Dissolving his frame in lust amid 300 concubines and boys, he violated by force the few modest women remaining near his court. Julia, the wife of Severus, though flattered in life and death by public writers, was no better than a harlot. We have already noticed the pleasures of Elagabalus, who committed rape upon a vestal virgin, and condescended to the most bestial vice. The nobles readily followed his example, and the people were easily led into the fashion. Maximin drowned every coy maiden who refused his embraces. In process of time, the most degrading features of Asiatic profligacy were introduced into Rome, and eunuchs crowded the palaces of the emperor and his nobles. History alludes to no more vulgar prostitute than the Empress Theodora, who played comedies before the people of Constantinople, and prostituted her person—of unparalleled beauty as it was—night after night to a promiscuous crowd of citizens and strangers, of every rank and description. She exhibited herself naked in the theatre. Her sympathy for the prostitute class may be indicated by almost the only virtuous action recorderecl of her;—inducing her husband Justinian to found a monastery on the shores of the Bosphorus, where 500 miserable women, collected from the streets and brothels, were offered a refuge. When we remember the usual relative proportion of objects relieved by charity, to the numbers from which they are selected, this indicates a considerable trade in prostitution then carried on in Constantinople. When, however, such a social system prevailed, no inquiry could fix the professional class of harlots, since moral women, if any existed, were certainly exceptions.

It is always necessary, while inquiring into the morality of any people, to inquire into the extent to which the practice of procuring abortion was carried, and how it was viewed. Montesquieu justly observes, that it is by no means unnatural, though it may be criminal, for a prostitute, should she by chance conceive a child, to seek to be relieved from the burden. She has no means of support except one which she cannot possibly follow and at the same time fulfil the duties of a mother. These considerations, perhaps, had some weight with the legislators of Rome, as well as those reasons of political prudence which in various ancient states recognised infanticide. That it was practised to some extent there, is shown by frequent allusions in various works. It has been asserted, indeed, that the custom of procuring abortion prevailed to such an extent, that, combined with celibacy, it materially affected the population of the state, but this appears a false view. There are no accounts to support such an idea. It is not known at what particular time a law was introduced against it. Certainly it was held in a different light than it is by our religion, and our civilization. Plato's republic permits it. Aristotle also allows it to be practised under certain circumstances, but only before the child is quick in the womb. So, also, among the Romans, it seems long to have been unrestrained by law, though it is impossible to believe that the natural instincts of women would not deter them, except in desperate situations, from such unnatural offences.

Such is the view of the prostitute system, with a sketch of general morality, which the facts preserved by history enable us to offer. It appears from these facts, that, during the more flourishing period of the Roman state, the prostitutes formed a class, to which the principal immorality of the female society was confined, while in the later or imperial age profligacy ran loose among the people, so that the distinction between the regular harlot and the unrecognised prostitute was all but lost. Chastity, under the Republic, was a peculiar Roman virtue, and the prostitutes were usually foreigners, while we do not find that they ever mixed with reputable women who had characters to lose*

OF PROSTITUTION AMONG THE ANGLO-SAXONS.

WE leave the countries of classical antiquity and arrive at the Anglo-Saxons of our own history, in whom the reader will feel a peculiar interest. Unfortunately, our usual observations with reference to ancient times, apply to them also. Extremely imperfect records exist of their manners, laws, and institutions. The learned and industrious Sharon Turner has collected most of the facts known, yet neither the word prostitution, nor any term analogous to it, is to be found in his work. In the Leges Anglo-Saxonicæ, we find laws and regulations in reference to the chastity of the women, but nothing which indicates the existence of a class professionally addicted to prostitution. Nevertheless, it is improbable that such a class was utterly unknown, for the modern historians, as well as the old chroniclers, who have described the era, allude repeatedly to the licentious manners of the period. Gluttoning and deep drinking may, however, have excused the epithet, without supposing any prevalence of immorality.

Sharon Turner refers us to the Maories of New Zealand, for a parallel to the manners and condition of Great Britain, when first invaded by the Romans. As far as profligacy goes, the comparison appears correct.

Among the Britons, however, prevailed the extraordinary and pernicious institution of small societies of ten or twelve men, with a community of women among them.

* Taylor's Elements of the Civil Law; Becker's Private Life of the Greeks and Romans; Suetonius, with Burmann's Notes; the Codes of Justinian and Constantine; Smith's Dictionary of Antiquities; Adams's Antiquities; Fergusson's Roman Republic; Niebuhr's History; Gibbon's Decline and Fall, supply facts for the above; while the writings of Horace, Juvenal, Lactantius, Dion Cassius, the Augustine History, and numerous other authors, afford scattered notices, not easy to collect or digest.

Ceremonies of marriage, indeed, took place, but for no other purpose than to provide that each woman's husband should maintain all her children, whoever their fathers might be. In some of their religious ceremonies women officiated naked, and in all their modes of life a coarse licentiousness obtained.

The Romans introduced a more refined luxury, and manners became less coarse, though no less profligate. The Saxons, however, then transported themselves to these islands from the Cymbric Peninsula, and the civilization of the country passed through a complete revolution. In their original country they had displayed a system of manners peculiar to themselves, and the other wild races inhabiting the mighty woods of Germany. Their laws against adultery were of the most savage character. When a woman was guilty of it, she was compelled to hang herself, her body was burned, and the execution of the adulterer took place over the pile of her ashes. Among some communities the punishment was still more severe, and infinitely more barbarous. The guilty creature was whipped from village to village by a number of women, who tore off her garments to the waist, and pierced her with their knives. Company after company of them pursued her until she sank under the shame, torture, and loss of blood. Chastity, indeed, was very generally regarded among these rude people, but their ideas were very foreign from ours. The degrees of consanguinity within which marriage was prohibited were extremely narrow, a son being permitted to marry his father's widow, provided she was not his own mother.

In their marriage customs the Anglo-Saxons displayed considerable regard for the female sex, although the wife was taken rather as the property than as the companion of the husband. The original laws of Ethelbert, indeed, as we have said, made the transaction wholly one of purchase; but in the reign of Edmund a more refined code was established. The betrothal usually took place some time before the actual ceremony. This was held as a sacred tie, the high-priest being at the marriage to consecrate it, and pray for a blessing on the wedded pair*.

* To show that a prostitute class existed, among women without means of support, we might mention instances of wills in which mothers left property to their daughters, on condition that they should marry or keep themselves chaste, and not earn money by prostitution.

The manners of the Anglo-Saxons, after their settlement in England, underwent considerable improvement. They became, indeed, to a degree civilized. Their women were no longer the savages of Germany. They occupied a position wholly different from that of their sex among the more polished and luxurious nations of the East. It was, we may say, similar to that which they at present fill among us. They were recognised as members of the body politic, could bequeath and inherit property, could appeal to the law against any man; they possessed, in a word, the rights, the duties, and the public relations of citizens. Of course, in all these particulars, their position was modified by the natural restraints imposed on their sex. This refers to the more improved period of their civilization. In the laws of Ethelbert a man was permitted to buy a wife, provided he did it openly. By Edmund's time, however, the practice was changed, and the woman's consent, as well as that of her friends, was necessary. The man was also pledged before the law to support and respect her. She carried public protection into her new home. Considerable honour, consequence, and independence were there pre-enjoyed by the female sex. Nevertheless there continued long to be in the transaction much of a business character, and the consent of the woman was frequently no more than submission to the terms of a bargain struck between her lover and her parents. By some husbands, indeed, a wife seems to have been considered as little more than a property. We find adultery, for instance, allowed to be compounded. "If a freeman cohabit with the wife of a freeman he must pay the fine, and obtain another woman with his own money, and lead her to the other." In other words, when he has destroyed the value of one wife, he must buy a fresh one for the injured husband.

This would seem to indicate that women were to be had for money. Adultery, indeed, was at all times an affair of payments. It was punished only by various fines, varying according to the rank of the woman. The chastity of the high noble's wife was valued at six pounds, that of a churl's attendant at six shillings.

In the Leges Anglo-Saxonicæ we find many regulations laid down respecting rape and fornication, which imply the occasional practice of those crimes. From the tone of the enactments on the subject, it seems impossible reasonably to doubt that a class of women existed who prostituted themselves for gain or pleasure to the other sex. None such, it is true, is directly indicated. We find, however, a rule of the venerable Bede, that any "slave woman" or "servile" turning her eyes immodestly on men, is to be severely chided. Blount also, quoted in Brand's "Popular Antiquities," with the historian Henry, describes the punishment of the cucking stool, as inflicted by the Anglo-Saxons, both in Germany and in England, upon scolds, disorderly women, and strumpets, who in the more barbarous society on the Continent were suffocated in marshes. In Cornwall harlots were long punished in the ludicrous and degrading manner described by Brand.

In the absence of any ground upon which to stand, we cannot describe a particular class among the Anglo-Saxons as addicted to prostitution, but from the whole colour of their civilization, from the rudest to the most refined period, it is evident the practice was followed, in a greater or less degree*.

OF PROSTITUTION AMONG THE BARBAROUS NATIONS.

INTRODUCTION.

IN surveying the social aspects of the barbarian world, we discover many striking phenomena. The relations of the sexes, among uneducated races, appear modified by every circumstance of their position; but everywhere the natural ascendancy of the strong over the weak is displayed. A few savage communities allow women a position nearly level with that of the men; but wherever this is the case, a degree of civilization has been attained.

If we divide mankind into two classes—the civilized and the savage—forming an ideal of both extremes, we shall not find one tribe or community to occupy either pole of our supposed sphere. No one requires to be told that every part of the human race is still below the perfect development of its good attributes; but the observation is equally true, though less generally accepted, that every family of creatures showing our nature has advanced beyond the utterly savage state. When we find men wandering not only unclothed, but unhoused, over the earth, and following only their animal propensities, we may

* Consult Sharon Turner; the various old chroniclers; the Leges Anglo-Saxonicæ, ed. Wilkins; Brand's Popular Antiquities, &c.

regard them as wholly untaught. At present no such tribe is known. Every human being that has come under our notice has progressed beyond the simple gratification of his appetites. The love of ornament and the practice of exchange have raised him one step in the scale.

The Africans, the Australians, the New Zealanders, the ruder tribes of the Pacific Isles, the Dyaks of Borneo, and the natives of Sumatra and Celebes, with the Indians of North and South America, may be included under the appellation *barbarous*. They vary, however, in the characteristics of their barbarism, as the nations of Europe vary in the characteristics of their civilization. They are even divided into classes. (1) The hunters, with little property in the soil, precarious means of existence, and migratory habits; the fishers, who are only the hunters of the sea; (2) the pastoral tribes, with property in herds and flocks, nomade, and therefore little property in the soil; (3) the agricultural tribes, permanently or temporarily fixed to localities, whose means of life are less precarious, and whose habits are more regular than those of the two former. The third is the most educated, the second the most innocent, the first the most simple state. It is among the shepherds that women enjoy most consideration, and that morality is highest. The hunters are more savage, and the tillers of the earth more sensual.

In judging the condition of the female sex, it is always necessary to hold in view the general state of manners. When we inquire how husbands behave to their wives, and how parents treat their daughters, we must ask also how they live themselves. Where the male sex is degraded the female will be so. On the other hand, the refinement of any people may be estimated by the condition of its women. The islanders of Celebes are among the most elevated of barbarian races, and the sexes are nearly on an equality. The hordes of Western Africa are the most gross and ferocious of savages, and their women are treated as reptiles. The Indians of North America offer, apparently, an exception to this rule, for their lofty, proud, and polished warriors behave contemptuously to the squaws in their wigwam, who crouch to the earth while their lords stand haughtily before the most powerful conquerors. But the Choctaws and the Cherokees are in reality as far removed from true civilization as the dwellers in New Zealand. The amenities and not the arts of life civilize men. Wherever in the Indian village the gentler influences of humanity prevail, the feebler sex is treated with respect and affection.

The points of contrast between barbarian and civilized races display themselves strongly in relation to the condition of the female sex. Throughout the savage portions of Africa one system of manners prevails. The men occupy the lowest stage of the social scale. They are neither hunters, fishers, shepherds, nor tillers of the soil; but mix up several occupations, though none of an elevating character. Some raise a few materials of food; others collect ivory in the woods; others live on the profits of the slave-trade; but the greater number subsist on the refuse of what they gain in the service of their petty kings. They have been sophisticated from the simplicity of savages without acquiring one grace from civilization. Subject to the gross caprice of princes more miserable than themselves, they have remained beyond the reach of every humanizing influence, and, as a natural consequence, their women are debased. Polygamy produces its worst results. The wife is an object of barter; a slave, whose labour assists to support her owner. In some parts diligence is more valued than chastity. In others the husband makes a profit from his wife's prostitution. The slave trade has assisted largely towards this melancholy state of manners. The finer sentiments of humanity are altogether lost, and the contempt for life, as well as for all that is amiable or pure, has reduced men far below the level of the brute creation. We speak literally in saying that a nobler, happier spectacle is presented among the antelope and elephant herds than among the swarms of men and women corrupting in Africa. In the few parts where the male sex has risen from this debasement, the female has been equally improved. The barbarous Edeeyahs offer an example.

The savages of Australia differ in many respects from those of Western Africa. They are even less educated, but they are also less ferocious; their women are their abject servitors, but there is more humanity in their treatment. They have scarcely approached so near to the forms of regular society, as to systematize the intercourse of the sexes. Nevertheless, among some tribes we not only find the institution of marriage respected, but wives guarded with Turkish jealousy. Among a people which does not dwell in regular habitations, or even lodge in roomy tents, it is scarcely possible to imagine the sanctity of a man's harem; but it is true, notwithstanding, that a similar seclusion is enforced. The Australian woman, in the desert and under the open sky, is hedged round by her husband's jealousy as securely as the ancient German was in her unwalled shelter of thatch.

It is seldom, however, that among barbarous races we find the sentiment of chastity in its abstract sense. Women are generally treated as though their inclinations were licentious, and in this consists one great line of distinction between civilization and barbarism. With the one, moral influence—with the other, material force, is employed as the guardian of female honour. The result is important to be noticed. Women are depraved by the rude and gross means devised to keep them virtuous. Where the moral sentiment is feebly developed, guilt is created by the efforts made to prevent it. The wife perpetually watched, as though her heart were full of adultery, becomes an adulteress. The young girl continually guarded, with the avowed object of compelling her to be chaste, loses insensibly any natural feeling she may have possessed, and covets the opportunity to sin.

In the South Sea Islands this truth is illustrated; in New Zealand it is still more strongly proved. It is taken for granted that a woman will prostitute herself if she can. The state of morality is consequently so low that it is difficult for parents to preserve a daughter's virtue until she is given in marriage. To prevent her holding *vicious* intercourse she is forbidden to hold *any* intercourse with the opposite sex.

Another characteristic of civilized races is the separation of the vicious from the moral classes; they systematize the offences against society. Every class of vile persons becomes, as it were, an isolated community; the prostitute is segregated from the rest of her sex. In some barbarian states, as in Dahomey, the same division is effected; but the kings of that country have sought to mimic the forms of educated communities. The professional is distinguished from the habitual prostitute only by her open assumption of the title; but the immorality of the female sex in Dahomey is far from being represented by the order of confessed harlots.

The inhabitants of some islands, and the shores of bays and roadsteads, have discovered that in prostituting their women to the crews of trading ships they have a readier means of subsistence than was offered by their former industry. This has produced a frightful system of vicious commerce, which still prevails to a great extent in the Pacific, as well as in New Zealand and the ports of Africa. It is for Europeans to repair the evil created by the incontinence of their predecessors. Many captains of vessels have already effected much good by forbidding women to come on board.

In proportion as nations approach the higher stages of civilization does the respect for human life increase. Infanticide is practised with the least remorse by the most savage tribes. Among those communities with whom the means of existence are precarious this crime is most common. Wherever barbarians have been induced to labour, and secured in the enjoyment of their earnings, the natural feelings of the breast have revived; and mothers who have slain six infants cherish the seventh as a sacred possession. Missionary enterprise has produced much good in this respect; while the beneficent rule of our Indian government has bestowed incalculable blessings on the people of the East, among whom the system of infanticide is daily becoming rarer, and the condition of women more elevated.

The same may be remarked of that unnatural practice upon which, as indeed on all kindred subjects, writers are reluctant to touch—that, we mean, of destroying the unborn fruits of union. The savage regards it as an act rather meritorious for its ingenuity than abominable for its unnatural character. The cause that encourages infanticide encourages this, which, indeed, is the less horrible crime. The woman is less reluctant to extinguish the vitality of a being which has become to her dear only in anticipation, than to quench a life which has once been embodied before her eyes, and warmed in her bosom. The operation, so dangerous to females in civilized communities, is, like childbirth, far easier among savages. The native of the Bornean woods, without any of the delicacy engendered by luxury, may one moment be without a pang giving birth to an infant, and the next be washing it in a neighbouring brook. The Malayan lady, bred in a city in indolence and comfort, suffers agony under which she sometimes perishes before her offspring has breathed. So it is with the practice of destroying the unborn child. Civilization lessens in all creatures their means of independent life, and their powers of endurance; but it also enables them to discover or compound the elements by which these artificial ills may be remedied.

In proportion as the intercourse of the sexes is loose is the difficulty of learning the actual extent of immoral practices. The prostitute class, as we proceed from the pure savage to the highest point of civilization, becomes more and more distinct—being more conspicuous because more isolated. This is accompanied by another process, which is a superior standard by which to measure the social elevation of a people. Women respect themselves in proportion as men respect them. Where locks and bolts, scourges and cudgels, are the guardians of female chastity, it is only preserved when there is no opportunity to lose it. When the protecting influence springs from within, the woman moves a virtuous being, defended even from a licentious glance by the impenetrable cloud which her native modesty and virtue diffuse around her.

Of Prostitution among African Nations.

In the wide field of inquiry presented by the barbarian races of our own time, Africa occupies a prominent place. Some of the most wild and savage tribes of the human family are to be found on that immense peninsula. Many degrees in the inferior scale of civilization are represented, from the uncouth Hottentots of the south to the wandering Arabs of the desert, in whose blameless lives we have a picture of original simplicity—not far removed from the real refinement, though very far from the vices, of the most polished among the communities of Europe. The inquiry we have made into the condition of women and the state of manners in Africa, has confirmed us in our opinion, which is supported also by many circumstances observed among other races of men. The medium of refinement is accompanied by the least immorality. As in our own, among other civilized states, the ratio of profligacy is greatest at the opposite poles of society—the wealthiest and the most indigent—so in Africa it is among the basest savages and among the most highly polished communities that immorality prevails to the greatest extent. The brutal hordes on the western coast, with the populations of the half-civilized cities of the north, abound in vices, while the barbarian though innocent communities, with the wandering dwellers in the desert, are characterised by manners far more pure.

In ranging over Africa in search of facts to complete the present inquiry, we meet with numerous tribes belonging to seven separate races of mankind: the Hottentot, the Kaffir, the Negro, the Moor, the Abyssinian, the Arab, and the Copts or descendants of the true Egyptian stock. Among each of these we perceive some varieties of manners; but everywhere in Africa one circumstance is prominent—the degraded condition of the female sex. The women of Cairo and Algiers are in comparison treated with little more refinement than those of some purely savage states; but we shall not include such communities among the barbarian races, reserving Egypt and some of the other countries characterised by a mongrel civilization for separate notices. We may, as far as our present inquiry goes, present the subject clearly and without confusion by making a geographical arrangement, and, commencing from the south, pass over the continent, until we encounter a form of civilization in the valley of the Lower Nile.

The condition of women generally in heathen countries is degraded. As we proceed through Africa this truth will be strongly illustrated. Commencing with the Hottentots of the south, we find them a dissolute profligate race, who have been so from the earliest period. It was remarked in 1655 by Van Riebeck, when the chiefs, departing on a distant expedition, were urged to leave their women behind, they replied "that their wives must be with them everywhere so as to be kept from the other men." It was remarked also in 1840 by Colonel Napier, who describes them as proverbially unchaste. Polygamy, at the early period referred to, was prevalent. Men bought their wives—sometimes from their wealthier, sometimes from their poorer, neighbours; but all alliances between persons of near kindred were held in utter abhorrence. Indecency and lewdness are their characteristics, for though now accustomed to clothing, it is no uncommon thing for them, when drunk at their festivals, to strip naked and perform lascivious dances, to music of the rudest harmony. Many among them appear to prostitute themselves readily to strangers, some from inclination, others for money, many for a gift of finery; but in what numbers this disreputable class exists we have no means of knowing*. A superior order, however, is scattered among these degraded creatures, and many lively, intelligent, and well-conducted women have attracted the notice of travellers.

The pastoral Kaffirs are perhaps a more moral though a more ferocious people than the Hottentots. They are, indeed, superior in mental and physical characteristics, being more addicted to arms, and less to debauch. They also, however, practise polygamy, and buy their wives for so many

* Napier's Excursions in Southern Africa.

WOMAN OF THE BOSJES RACE.

[*From a Daguerreotype by* BEARD.]

head of cattle. Among them, as well as among the Bechuanas, the girls undergo a probation before marriage, during which they live apart, and hold no intercourse with their tribe except through an old woman. Sichele, king of the Bechuanas, had numerous wives, of whom one was a favourite; but he granted each a separate hut, so that his palace was a kind of village surrounded by a fence. They punish theft in a woman by twisting dry grass round her fingers and burning them to the bone. Wandering from place to place in tent-shaped temporary huts, they carry their women with them, and condemn them to domestic labour. Even the chief's wives assist in grinding the corn, and tending their husband's nomade household. Divorce is easy, on very slight grounds. We occasionally hear of women committing what is termed fornication, but no professed class of prostitutes has been described. As among all nations practising polygamy, marriage is not held as a sacred tie; but adultery on the wife's part is severely punished as an infraction of the social law. The bonds of natural affection appear extremely weak among the Kaffir tribes. Men are inspired by an inclination, not an attachment, to their wives, and mothers possess less affection for their children than is observed even in the Australian savage. The weak and sickly are sometimes abandoned, to save the expense or trouble of their support. Mrs. Ward knew of a woman who, having a little daughter in a decline, buried it alive, to be rid of the burden. The little creature, imperfectly interred, burst from its grave and ran home. Again it was forced into the hole, again it escaped, and a third time it was removed to the earth; once more, however, it struggled till free, and, flying to its mother's hut, was at last received, and ultimately recovered. Such instances of inhumanity are not rare among the Kaffir tribes, whose passion for blood and war seems to have blunted some of their natural sentiments. Husbands, when their wives are sick, frequently drag them into a neighbouring thicket, where they are left to die, and women continually do the same with their poor offspring. It is important, however, to mention, that in the instances of Kaffirs converted to Christianity their manners undergo a most favourable modification. One of them was known to Mrs. Ward who had refused to take a second wife, in deference to the moral law laid down by the interpreters of his adopted religion; and, where the conversion is sincere, they always manifest an inclination to practise the manners of the white men*.

In the rude maritime region extending from the countries on the border of the Cape territory as far as the Senegal, a set of characteristic features is universally marked on the people, varied though their nationality be. Differences, of course, prevail among the numerous tribes in the several states; but the impress of African civilization is there all but uniform.

Those between the tropics, especially, are absorbed in licentiousness. Morality is a strange idea to them. Polygamy is universally practised, and in most places without limitation; while nowhere is a man restrained by the social law from intercourse with any number of females he chooses. The result is that women are, for the most part, looked upon as a marketable commodity; that the pure and exalted sentiment of love is utterly unknown; and that even the commonest feelings of humanity appear absent from among them. Husbands, for instance, on the Gold Coast, are known to prostitute their wives to others for a sum of money. This is an open transaction. In other places, however, where the adulterer pays a fine to the husband he has injured, we find men allowing their wives an opportunity to be unfaithful, in order to obtain the price of the crime. Throughout, indeed, the gloomy and savage states, sheltered by the woods bordering the Niger, and over the whole western coast, mankind appears in its uncouthest form. Human nature, degraded by perpetual war against itself, rots at the feet of a gross superstition. As we have said, the result is developed in various modifications of barbarian manners.

When Laird, in 1832, visited the Niger, he found the condition of the female sex upon its borders most humiliating. In the dominions of King Boy polygamy was unlimited, and the wives reduced to slavery in their own homes. The people dwelling on the banks of the Lower Niger may be described, in fact, as among the most idle, ignorant, and profligate in Africa. The prince himself set the example to his subjects. He possessed 140 wives and concubines, of whom one was no more than thirteen years of age, whom he had purchased for a few muskets and a piece of cloth. Half a dozen enjoyed the distinction of favourites; one of them was more than 25 stones in weight. The mo-

* Harriet Ward's Five Years in Kaffir Land; Barrow's Travels; Methuen's Life in the Wilderness.

ther of this pluralist was maintained in her son's palace, where she amused the court by dances of the most revolting and obscene description. No care was, in any respect, taken to preserve a sense of virtue in the king's harem; but adultery was, nevertheless, punished with death. This appears the case in most countries where shame holds no check on immorality; it may, indeed, be taken in some measure as an index to the state of manners where crimes against chastity are visited with public infamy alone, or with legal penalties. In the dominions of Boy, one wife, at least, was expected to attend her husband, even when dead. The chosen victim was bound and thrown into the river; a mode of death preferable to that practised at Calabar, on the coast, where the miserable woman is buried alive. In the kingdom of Fundals, when a chief died leaving fifteen women in his harem, the king selected one to be hung over the tomb, and transferred the rest to his own palace; nevertheless, a few of these enjoyed an independent existence. One lively intelligent woman possessed an estate of land and 200 slaves, whom she employed in trade. Industry flourished, there being small competition, as a more idle demoralized people than the dwellers on the Niger as far as Ebo cannot be imagined.

Above that place, where the land is less marshy and more favourable to cultivation, the natives are more intelligent, more addicted to agriculture, more manly in their habits, and in proportion more kind and respectful to their women. Polygamy, it is true, prevails, as it does all over Western Africa, but the sex is somewhat raised above a mere instrument of sensual gratification. In other directions the old features are resumed. The Bambarras, a Pagan people, marry as many wives as they can support; and the Mandingoes, who are only allowed four, treat them as slaves, though they love their children.

The native of Western Africa, in most cases, looks upon his wife, in one respect as a source of pleasure, in another as a source of gain, reckoning her as property to the amount she can earn by labour. In the institution of marriage, therefore, it may easily be conceived that no sacred tie is acknowledged. It is merely a civil contract, to be dissolved at will. The man sends a present to the woman's father; if a virgin, she exchanges her leathern girdle for a cloth wrapped about the loins, and a little merry-making consummates the transaction. This account applies especially to the Tilatates. In Yarriba and Bughor, when a woman finds herself *enceinte*, she is obliged to inform her husband, or suffer a public whipping when the discovery is made. This custom refers, there is no doubt, to a feature in the morals of the people. Mothers, also, are forced to suckle their children until three years old, and punished if, during that period, they cohabit with a man.

Strange inconsistencies occasionally display themselves in the manners of these unintellectual barbarians. They have introduced a feature of Asiatic luxury, by having eunuchs to guard their seraglios, while instances occur in which the uncouth savage professes a sentiment of attachment. The King of Attah told Lander that he loved him as he loved the wife who shared his bed. Yet he was a polygamist, and a sensualist. In Abookir the prince was continually multiplying the inmates of his harem, and having many daughters, had numbers of wives younger than they. Girls of eleven years old are there considered marriageable.

Regarded as a mere social contract, temporary or otherwise, marriage, in this region, is held among the most ordinary occurrences of life. A man arriving at the age of 20 takes one wife, and then another, increasing the number from four to 100, as his circumstances allow. Many women, even under this system, cannot procure husbands. This, however, we must not ascribe so much to a vast preponderance of the female sex over the male, as to the fact that thousands of men take no permanent partners at all. It may, perhaps, be safe to assert that, of the single men, none remain without intercourse with women, and of the unmarried women, that not one preserves her chastity. The idea of that virtue appears foreign to those races. Adultery, indeed, is held a crime, but not so much against morals as against the husband. A wife suspected of it is compelled to drink a decoction called Sassy water, which poisons her, unless she bribes the priest to render it harmless by dilution, in which case she is pronounced innocent. The widow, even, who has been known to live on bad terms with her husband is forced, among the tribes on the banks of the Lower Niger, to undergo this ordeal. An illicit connection with the king's wife, however, is punished with death to both parties, while among the chiefs the fine of a slave is exacted. Every woman, except the consort of royalty, has thus her market value, which is greatly increased if her friends fatten her up to a colossal size. Men frequently buy slender girls at a cheap rate, and feed them to a proper obesity before taking them as companions. Marriage, or concubinage, may be entered on at the age of thirteen, and so universal is the system in this part of Africa, that the sex seems absolutely wedded to its degradation.

Among the people of Ibu a singular custom exists. When twins are born they are immediately exposed to wild beasts. The mother, compelled to go through a long course of purification and penance, is thenceforward an outlaw, disgraced among the women, who hold up two fingers as she passes, to remind her of the misfortune:— she is at once divorced from her husband.

Though thus reduced to slavery by the other sex, women, among these tribes, enjoy a certain degree of freedom, which is a mitigation of their miserable state. Married without their own consent, they are sold to a husband for from 26s. and upwards, and thenceforward become his servants. Yet the favourite wives of the rich, exempt from toil, are allowed to amuse themselves in various ways, and even to walk about unveiled, under the guard of an eunuch. Men never eat with their wives, and often treat them brutally, bewailing the loss of a slave far more than the death of a wife, unless she happens to please the caprice of the hour. It is among the poorest that most freedom is allowed, and among those tribes who have intercourse with Europeans that most ferocity prevails. Some dig the soil, some attend to the household, some support their husbands by the profits of a petty retail trade, while others, kept for his gratification, are allowed to idle. These favoured ones are often slaves. A handsome young one often sells for from 60,000 to 120,000 cowries (from 3l. 15s. to 7l. 10s.*), while the price of a common wife is only 20,000 cowries (25s.). Frequently, the man's inclination changes its direction, and he sells one girl to purchase another. With many of the kings and chiefs a continual trade in women is common. King Bell, of the Cameroons, for instance, had more than 100 wives, and his wealth was increased by their numbers. In his dominions the young maidens had considerable liberty, sporting in the fields, and enjoying, for a few years, comparative independence of the men†.

In the kingdom of Dahomey, on the Guinea Coast, we find some of the most remarkable institutions with respect to women which exist in the world. It has been the centre of the slave trade. Few of the comparatively fair aboriginal race exist, but in their place has been gathered a mixed population, incontestably one of the most profligate in Africa. Entering its seaport town the traveller is at once struck by the remarkable immodesty of the female population. Throughout the country the same characteristic is observable, though in a modified degree. Sir John Malcolm observed of the subjects of the Imaum of Muscat — manners they have none, and their habits are disgusting. The same description has been judiciously applied to the people of Dahomey. They are profligates, from the highest to the lowest—a bloody-minded savage race, delighting in human suffering, and finding their national pleasure in customs the most revolting and cruel that ever obtained in the world.

The king practises all these, and is superior in brutality and filthiness to any of his subjects. This has been a characteristic of the throne in Dahomey. He has thousands of wives, while his chiefs have hundreds, and the common people tens. The royal favourites are considered too sacred to be looked upon by vulgar eyes. Whenever they proceed along the public road, a bell is rung to warn all passengers of their approach, and every one must then turn aside or hide his face. If one of them commits adultery, she is, with her paramour, put to death. The harem is sacred against strangers, but the privileged nobility attend the royal feasts, where the king's wives sit, attired in showy costumes of the reign of Charles II., drinking rum and leading the debauch. Those of an inferior class, or the concubines, are employed in trade, the profits of which accrue to their master. Every unmarried woman in Dahomey is virtually the property of the sovereign, who makes his choice among them. No one dares to dispute his will, or to claim a maiden towards whom he has signified his inclination.

When the king desires to confer honour on any favourite, he chooses a wife for him, and presents her publicly. In this case she performs the ceremony of handing to her husband a cup of rum, which is a sign of union. Otherwise no rite or ceremony whatever is essential. However, the man must finally take his wife or concubine, in the usual business manner, for if he seduces a maiden he must marry her, or pay to her parent or master 160,000 cowries (equal to 7l. 10s. of our money). Failing in this, he may be sold as a slave. This punishment also is inflicted on those who

---

* Cowries are valued at fifteen pence to the thousand.

† Bowdich's Essay; Thompson and Allen's Expedition to the Niger; Laird's Voyage.

commit adultery with a common person's wife. The rich often buy a number of concubines, live with them for a short time, and then sell them at a profit. It is in Dahomey, too, that the practice prevails of throwing a wife in the way of committing adultery for the sake of the penalty which her husband may exact from the criminal. It is commonly known that the king of Dahomey supports an army of several thousand Amazonian soldiers. These women dress in male attire, and are not allowed to marry, or supposed to hold intercourse with the other sex. They declare themselves, indeed, to have changed their nature. "We are men," they say, "and no women." In all things—courage and ferocity among the rest—they seek to preserve the character. They dwell in barracks, under the care of eunuchs; they practise wild war-dances, and, officered by their own sex, scorn the allurements of any weaker passion; they are, therefore, for the most part chaste. Vanity and superstition combine to guard their virtue. They boast of never encountering a man except in the field of battle. Thus their pride is enlisted in the service of their chastity. A charm is placed under the threshold of their common dwelling, as it is under that of the palace harem, which is supposed to strike with disease the bowels of any guilty woman who may cross it. So strong is this belief, that many incontinent Amazons have voluntarily revealed their crime, though well aware that the punishment of death will be, without mercy, dealt upon them as well as their lovers*.

Most men have a favourite wife, and her privilege is valuable so long as her husband lives; but on his decease it entails a terrible obligation. The dying chief invites one or more of his principal wives to die with him, and these, with a number of slaves, varying according to his rank, are sacrificed at his tomb.

In consequence of the immense number of wives and concubines kept by the king and his wealthier subjects, numbers of the common people are forced to be content with the company of prostitutes, who are licensed in Dahomey, and subject to a particular tax. There is a band of them, according to Dalzel, who appears worthy of belief, in every village, though confined to a certain quarter, and they prostitute themselves to any who desire it, at a moderate fixed price. The profits thus obtained are often insufficient for their support, and they eke out their gains by breeding fowls, and other industrial occupations. Women also hire themselves out to carry heavy burdens, and they no doubt belong to the prostitute class. Norris saw 250 of these unfortunate women collected in a troop on a public occasion. The object of this institution, according to the king, was to save the respectable people from seduction. There were many men who could not get wives, and, unless prostitutes existed, they would seduce the wives or daughters of others. At Whyddah, on the coast, Mr. John Duncan was assailed by numbers of women who offered to "become his wives," or, in other words, to prostitute themselves to him, for a drop of rum. Many of the poorer class strolled about naked, ready to accept any one for a miserable gratuity. In that city it was the custom when a man committed adultery, to press him into the king's army. Formerly he was sacrificed, but the practice was abolished—prisoners of war furnishing "the annual customs" with victims. Whatever the punishment was, however, it was ineffectual to suppress the crime, as depravity was the general characteristic of the people. At Zapoorah, beyond Dahomey, a chief offered one of his wives for sale, and parents asked a price for their children; while at Gaffa, still further, the men are more jealous, and the women more modest. Adultery with the king's wife was punished by impalement on a red-hot stake.

The dirty, lazy, and dull people of the Fantee coast, near Dahomey, wear the same moral aspect as the subjects of that kingdom. Women support the men. Parents would sell their children, husbands their wives, and women themselves, for a trifling sum. One woman was so desirous of changing her companion, that she took possession of a recent traveller's bed, and could only be expelled by force. Marriage is a mere purchase—of from six to twenty wives and concubines. The rich support their harems at a great cost. The common price is sixteen dollars. Maidens are seldom bought when beyond fifteen or sixteen years of age, so that many men have wives younger than their daughters. The indivi-

* A letter, published in the *Times* in August last, announces the disastrous defeat of the celebrated body of fighting women in the pay of the King of Dahomey. The Amazons had advanced to the attack of Abbeokuta, a town in the Bight of Benin, with the object of surprising and carrying off the inhabitants, to supply the demand for slaves; but the latter, being apprised of the approach of the female warriors, turned out in force, repulsed them from the town, and in the course of pursuit effected great slaughter amongst their ranks. More than 1000 are reported to have been left dead on the field.

dual committing adultery is forced to buy his paramour at her original price. Contrary to the custom of Ibu and Bony, the mother of twins is, among the Fantees, held in great respect.

Along the coast of Benin manners, in most respects similar to these, prevail—public dancers acting as prostitutes in most of the native towns, and offering themselves for a wretched price. Every woman holds it an honour to be the king's companion even for one night *.

In Ashantee, where polygamy, as elsewhere in Africa, prevails, adultery is common, especially among the king's wives, who, when discovered, are hewn to pieces. The manners of the people are profligate beyond anything of which in England we can realize an idea. In the country of the Kroomen, eastward on the Guinea Coast, where nearly all the labour devolves on women, men become independent by the possession of from twenty to forty wives. One practice prevailing there is characterized by an unusual depravity. The son, inheriting his father's property, inherits also his wives, his own mother then becoming his slave. In the interior, on the banks of the Asinnee, we find a people among whom the men are industrious, and the women treated with respect. The consequence is a far higher standard of morality †.

It is remarkable to find among the Edeeyahs of Fernando Po a strong contrast to these general characteristics of manners and morality in Western Africa. Generous, hospitable, humane, practising no murder, possessing no slaves, with only innocent rites, they treat their women with comparative consideration, and assign them far less than the usual amount of hard labour. To cook food, bear palm oil to market, and press the nuts, are their principal occupations. Polygamy is allowed, and when a man undertakes a journey, he is accompanied by one or more of his wives, who are much attached to their husbands and children.

The first wife taken by a man must be betrothed to him at least two years before marriage. During that period the lover must perform all the duties which otherwise would have been performed by her. He must go, indeed, through a probation resembling the servitude of Jacob for Rachel. Meanwhile the maiden is kept in a hut, concealed from the sight of the people. These courtships often begin while the girl is no more than thirteen or fourteen, and her lover only a youth; but if he seduces her before the two years are elapsed, he is severely punished. That time having expired the young wife is still kept in the hut, where she receives her husband's visits until it is evident she is about to become a mother—or if not, for eighteen months. When she first appears publicly as a married woman, all the virgins of her tribe salute her and dance about her. These customs indicate far more purity and elevation of manners among the Edeeyahs than among any other people in Western Africa. They are only observed, however, with regard to the first wife, all the others being virtually no more than concubines governed by her. Some chiefs have upwards of a hundred, and the king more than twice that number.

Adultery is severely punished, but, nevertheless, not very rare. For the first offence both parties lose one hand. For the second the man, with his relatives, is heavily fined, and otherwise chastised, while the woman, losing the other hand, is driven as an outlaw into the woods. This exile is more terrible to the Edeeyahs than the mutilation *.

In examining the condition of Africa, in the light we have chosen, it would entail a tiresome repetition to pass in review all the various groups of states sunk in barbarism. The natives are generally barbarian. Elevated slightly above the hunting or pure savage state, they have subdued some animals to their use, and practise some ingenious arts; but their manners are baser than those of any race below them in point of art and luxury. We have seen that in the West, with a few rare exceptions, profligacy is the universal feature of society. In the East it is almost equally so. Our knowledge of that coast, it is true, is less full than of the West; but travellers afford sufficient information to justify an opinion on the general state of manners. In Zulu, as an example of the rest, the king has a seraglio of fifteen hundred women, who are slaves to his caprice. His mother was in that condition when Isaacs visited the country. She endured corporal chastisement from her son. A number of women and boys, belonging to the royal harem, and suspected of illicit

* Dahomey and the Dahomans, by J. E. Forbes; Dalzel's History of Dahomey; M'Leod's Account; John Duncan's Travels; Adams's Remarks on the West Coast; Adams's Sketches; Meredith's Account of the Gold Coast.
† Dupuis' Observations.

* Thompson and Allen's Expedition up the Niger.

intercourse, were massacred by the prince's orders. Adultery, indeed, was a thing of continual occurrence in the palace. Marriage is held among the people not as a sacred tie but as a state of friendship. All the people, however, are polygamists, and the laws of morality refer only to wives. With others the intercourse of the sexes is unrestrained. Men do not cohabit with their wives on the first night after their wedding. This ceremony among the rich is accompanied by a grand feast, though, as in other parts of Africa, the wife is bought—at the most for ten cows. A man cannot sell but may dismiss his wife, over whom also he has the power of life and death. Adultery is always capitally punished, that is, when discovered; for with eighty or ninety women in his possession, it is not always possible for the husband to watch their conduct—especially as they labour for his support. Girls are not allowed to marry or become concubines until the age of fourteen, until which period they go without clothing. The degrees of consanguinity, within which marriage is strictly prohibited, are very wide—an union being permitted only between the most distant relations.

It is necessary to observe that in the Zulu kingdom profligacy is more general among the men than among the women, for wives hold the marriage tie in great estimation. It is the unlimited power of the male sex over the other which forces it to become the prey of sensuality. Throughout the Eastern region, indeed, women are the mere instruments of pleasure, being bought and sold like cattle—forced to toil and live in drudgery for the benefit of their masters and husbands*.

Among the nomade and stationary tribes of the Sahara, who are not aboriginal to that region, we have a different system of manners. In the Arabian communities you may find women ready to perform indecent actions, and even to prostitute themselves for money; but these are of the low classes. Cases of adultery are rare.

The Mohammedans believe that a man cannot have too many wives, or, at least, too many concubines. They declare it assists their devotion; but the feeling is one merely sensual. Pure sentiment is a thing in which they can scarcely believe. Rich men who are accustomed to travel in pursuit of trade, have one family at Ghadames, another, perhaps, at Ghat, and another at Soudan, and live with each of them by turns. These women stand in great fear of their husbands. The rich are veiled, and live in retirement; the poor do not; but all will unveil their faces to a stranger, if it can be done with safety. The white, or respectable women of Ghadames, never descend into the streets, or even into the gardens of their houses. The flat roof of their dwelling is their perpetual promenade, and a suite of two or three rooms their abode. It is said that in these retreats many of the women privately rule their husbands, though no men will confess the fact. Among the Marabouts it is held disgraceful to be unmarried, but shameful also to be under the wife's control.

The negresses and half-castes who may be seen in the streets of the cities of the Sahara, are generally slaves. The women of the Touarik tribes, however, are by no means so. They belong to a fierce and warlike tribe, half vagrant, half stationary, and are bound by few restrictions. Their morals are described as superior to those of the lower class of women in Europe; though exceptions, of course, are found. One Touarik woman offered to prostitute herself to Richardson for a sum of money; or, as it was expressed, to become his wife.

Polygamy, though universally allowed in the Sahara, is not carried to an extent at all equal to that prevailing in the savage regions on the east and west. Three wives usually occupy the harem of a rich man. Marriage is, as usual with people of that religion, a civil contract with a shade of sanctity upon it, but celebrated with great feasts and rejoicings. The bridegroom is expected to live in retirement during two or three weeks. He occasionally walks about the town at evening alone, dressed in gay clothes of blue and scarlet, and bearing a fine long stave of brass or polished iron. He never speaks or is spoken to, and vanishes on meeting any one.

The manners of the communities in the Sahara are imperfectly known; but from the accounts we have received they appear to be of a far more elevated order than those of any other part of Africa. It is true that customs prevail which shock our ideas of decency. A chief, for instance, offered Richardson his two daughters as wives. It is also true that many women exist who follow the profession of prostitutes, though we have no distinct account of them. But immorality is usually among them a secret crime. Their general customs with regard to sexual intercourse are at least as pure as those of Europe. Among the wandering tribes of the desert the hardship of their lives, continual occu-

---

* Isaacs' Travels on the East Coast; Captain Owen's Voyage.

GIRLS OF NUBIA (MAKING POTTERY).

[*From* St. John's "*Oriental Album.*"]

pation, varied scenes of excitement, and contempt for sensual enjoyments, contribute to preserve chastity among their virtues; while the Marabouts of the cities are of a generally moral character. Intoxication never happens among the women. Still, the condition of the sex is degraded; for they are, with exceptions, regarded only as the materials of a man's household, and ministers to the sensual enjoyments of his life[*]. The Mohammedans of Central Africa, bigoted as to dogmas, are nevertheless more liberal to women, who enjoy more consideration among them than in the more important strongholds of that religion[†].

The wandering Arabs of Algeria hold marriage as a business transaction, though the estimation of the sex is not low. The lover brings to the woman's home ten head of cattle, with other presents, which usually form her dowry. The father asks, "How much does she whom you are going to have for wife cost you?" He replies, "A prudent and industrious woman can never be too dear." She is dressed, placed on a horse, and borne to her new home amid rejoicing. She then drinks the cup of welcome, and thrusting a stick into the ground, declares, "As this stick will remain here until some one forces it away, so will I." She then performs some little office to show she is ready for the duty of a wife, and the ceremony is ended[‡].

Transferring our observations to Abyssinia, we find in its several divisions different characteristics of manners. In Tajura, on the Red Sea, profligacy is a conspicuous feature of society. Men live with their wives for a short period, and then sell them, maintaining thus a succession of favourites in their harems. Parents, also, are known not only to sell their daughters as wives, but to hire them out as prostitutes. One chief offered a traveller his daughter either as a temporary or a permanent companion; he showed another whom he would have sold for 100 dollars. One woman presented herself, stating, as a recommendation, that she had already lived with five men. These are nothing but prostitutes, whatever the delicacy of travellers induces them to term them. Unfortunately the inquiries made into this system are very slight, affording us no statistics or results of any kind. We are thus left to judge of morality in Tajura by the fact that syphilis afflicts nearly the whole population, man and woman, sultan and beggar, priests and their wives included.

In the Christian kingdom of Shoa, the Christian king has one wife, and 500 concubines; seven in the palace, thirteen at different places in the outskirts, and the rest in various parts of his dominions. He makes a present to the parents of any women he may desire, and is usually well paid in return for the honour. The governors of cities and provinces follow this example, keeping establishments of concubines at different places. Scores of the royal slaves are cast aside, and their place supplied by others.

In Shoa there are two kinds of marriage; one a mere agreement to cohabitation, another a holy ceremony; the former is almost universally practised. The men and women declare before witnesses that they intend to live happily together. The connection thus easily contracted is easily broken; mutual consent only is necessary to a divorce. In Shoa a wife is valued according to the amount of her property. The heiress to a house, a field and a bedstead, is sure to have a husband. When they quarrel and part, a division of goods takes place. Holy ceremonies are very rare, and not much relished. A wedded couple, in one sense of the term, is a phenomenon. Instances of incontinence are frequent; while the caprice of the men leads them often to increase the number of their concubines. These are procured as well from the Christians as from the Mohammedans and Pagans; but the poor girls professing these religions are forced to a blind profession of Christianity. Favourite slaves and concubines hold the same position with married women; while illegitimate and legitimate children are treated by the law with no distinction. Three hundred of the king's concubines are slaves, taken in war or purchased from dealers. They are guarded by fifty eunuchs, and live in seclusion; though this by no means prevents the court from overflowing with licentiousness. Numerous adulteries take place, and this example is followed by the people; among whom a chaste married couple is not common.

Women in Abyssinia, which is an agricultural country, mix freely with the men, and dance in their company; though a few jealous husbands or cautious parents seclude them. Morality is at an extremely low ebb. At the Christmas saturnalia, gross and disgusting scenes occur, as well as at other feasts. What else can be ex-

---

[*] Richardson's Travels in the Sahara.
[†] Account of Africa, by Jameson, Wilson, and Hugh Murray.
[‡] Count St. Marie's Visit to Algeria.

pected in a country where 12,000 priests live devoted, in theory at least, to celibacy; and where, at the annual baptisms, these priests, with men, women, and children strip naked, and rush in promiscuous crowds into a stream, where they are baptised according to the Christian religion! The sacerdotal class of Shoa is notoriously drunken and profligate. Another cause of corruption is the caprice which induces men to abandon their concubines after short cohabitation with them. These women, discarded and neglected, devote themselves to an infamous profession, and thus immorality is perpetuated through every grade of their society: in a word, the morals of Shoa are of the lowest description. In the Mohammedan states in its neighbourhood the condition of the sex is no better. If there is less general prostitution, it is because every woman is the slave of some man's lust, and is imprisoned under his eye. He is jealous only of her person; scarcely attributing to her a single quality which is not perceptible to his senses*.

In the southern provinces of Kordofan, under the government of Egypt, south of the Nubian Mountains, immense labour is imposed on the unmarried girls; yet the sentiment of love is not altogether unknown to them, and men fight duels with whips of hippopotamus hide on account of a disputed mistress. The wife is nevertheless a virtual slave, and still more degraded should she prove barren; the husband, in that case, solaces himself with a concubine, who, if she bears a child, is elevated to the rank of wife. It is common among the rich for a man to make his wife a separate allowance after the birth of her second child, when she goes to live in a separate hut. All their bloom is gone by the time they are twenty-four years old, and thenceforward they enjoy no estimation from the men. Yet, improvident in their hearts, the young girls of Kordofan are merry; and, whether at work or idle, spend the day in songs and laughter; while in the evening they assemble and dance to the music of the Tarabuka drum. Their demeanour, in general, is modest, and their lives are chaste. Married women, on the contrary, especially those who are neglected by their husbands, occupy themselves in gossip, and find solace in criminal intrigues. In some parts of the country,

indeed, men consider it an honour for their wives to have intercourse with others; and the women are often forwarded in their advances. Female slaves often have liberty when they bear children to their proprietors.

Women eat when the men have done, and pretty dancers attend at the feasts to amuse their employers. These girls, like the Ghawazee of Lower Egypt, are usually prostitutes, and very skilful in the arts of seduction. Numbers of this class fled from Egypt into Kordofan, on one occasion, when Mohammed Ali, in one of his affected fits of morality, endeavoured to suppress their calling altogether.

Marriage, it may be scarcely necessary to say, is concluded without the woman's consent. The man bargains for her, pays her price, takes her home, strips off her virginal girdle, which is the only garment of unmarried girls, and covers her with a cloth about her loins; a feast and a dance occasionally celebrate the event. When a wife is ill-treated beyond endurance, she demands a divorce; and, taking her female offspring, with her dowry, returns home. Trifles often produce these separations. That her husband has not allowed her sufficient pomatum to anoint her person with, is not unfrequently the ground of complaint. Few men in Kordofan have more than two wives; but most have concubines besides, whom the more opulent protect by a guard of eunuchs.

These remarks apply to the agricultural or fixed population. The Baghaira, or wandering pastoral tribes of Kordofan, are a modest, moral race—naked, but not on that account indecent*.

A chief of the Berbers offered a late traveller the choice of his two daughters for a bedfellow. They were already both married. Women there, however, as well as in Dongola, are, many of them, ready to prostitute themselves for a present. A virgin, whether as wife or concubine, may be purchased for a horse. "Why do you not marry?" said a traveller to a young Berber. He pointed to a colt and answered "When that is a horse I shall marry."†

The condition of women and state of manners on the upper borders of the Nile, we find described in Ferdinand Werne's account of his recent voyage to discover the sources of the White Stream. The system in Khartum may be indicated by one sentence in the traveller's own language. He speaks of desiring that the pay

---

* These views of Abyssinian society are afforded by Bruce, and lately by Gogat, and have been contradicted by Mr. Salt. They are fully corroborated, however, by the more recent and valuable authority of Sir Cornwallis Harris.

* Ignatius Palme's Travels in Kordofan.
† Expedition to Dongola and Sennaar.

might be advanced to prevent starvation from visiting the soldiers' families, "which, from the low price of female slaves, were numerous." It may, without resort to hyperbole, be said, that the female monkeys peopling the neighbouring woods occupy a far nobler and more natural position. Among the barbarians on the banks of the river further up, the state of manners is in a great degree more pure. The Keks, for example, are described as leading a blameless life. The travellers saw no marriageable maidens or children, married women alone appearing. The most singular social economy prevails among them. The women live, during a considerable part of the year, in villages apart from the men, who possess only temporary huts. Their wives have regular substantial habitations, which are common to both sexes during the rainy season. A man dare not approach the "harem village," except at the proper period, though some of the women occasionally creep into their husbands' village. Polygamy is allowed, but only practised by the chiefs, since all the wives are bought, which renders the indulgence costly.

Among some of the tribes on the banks of the White Nile women will sell their children if they can do so with profit. Everywhere in that region the maidens mingle naked with the men, but appear by no means immodest. When married they wear an apron. All exhibit a sense of shame at exhibiting themselves unclothed before strangers. Beyond the Mountains of the Moon, however, Werne found people, among whom the unmarried men and women were separated. They were completely naked, but chaste and decent nevertheless. A heavy price was always asked for a girl, which prevented common polygamy, though their social code permitted it*.

It must be evident that, in an inquiry like the present, a view of the manners and morals of Africa with regard to the female sex must be incomplete. In the first place, our information is very limited; in the second, we are confined for space— for otherwise these sketches could be extended to an indefinite extent. We have, however, taken observations in Southern, in Western, in Eastern, in Northern, and Central Africa. Kingdoms and communities, indeed, there are which we have not included in our description. Of these some wear features so similar to others we have noticed, that to particularise them is unnecessary in a general view. Of others,

* Werne's Expedition up the White Nile.

such as Egypt, Nubia, Barca, Tripoli, Algiers, and Morocco, we shall treat in a future division of the subject, because they are not included, by the character of their civilization, among the communities of which we have hitherto spoken. The reader will, we trust, have been enabled to form a fair idea of the average of morals among the savages and semi-savages of Africa. With modern barbarians, as with ancient states, tabular statistics are impossible: but from a description in general terms, we cannot always refuse to ground a confident opinion.

Women in Australia.

In Australia we have a family of the human race still more uneducated, though not more barbarous, than that which inhabits the woods of the African continent. There is among them less approach to the arts of civilization, less ingenuity, less intelligence, but there is more simplicity. Their customs are not so brutal as those prevailing on the banks of the Joliba or the Senegal. Nevertheless they are true savages, and the condition of their women is consistent with all the other features of their irreclaimed state. Of the Australians, however, as of all races imperfectly known, there obtains in this country a vulgar idea drawn from the old accounts, which are little better than caricatures. They have been represented as a hideous race, scarcely elevated above the brute, blood-thirsty, destitute of human feeling, without any redeeming characteristics, and, moreover, incapable of civilization. Such a description is calculated only to mislead. The aborigines of Australia are certainly a low, barbarous, and even a brutal race, but the true picture of their manners, which form the expression of their character, is not without encouraging traits.

Considering the great extent of New Holland, it is surprising to find such an uniformity of character and customs, as we actually discover among its nations. The language, varied by dialects, the habits, social laws, and ideas of the people, are extremely similar, whether we visit them in that province called the Happy or in the districts around Port Essington. Consequently, though it occupy a large space on the map, this region will not require any very extended notice. An idea of the condition and morality of its women may be afforded by one general view, with reference to the various local peculiarities noticed by travellers.

The native inhabitants of Australia are generally nomadic. They dwell in temporary villages scattered over vast surfaces of country, and move from place to place, as the supply of provisions, spontaneously provided by the earth, is more or less abundant. Separated as they are into small isolated communities—rarely numbering more than eighty members—they resort to the borders of lakes and streams, which dry up at certain seasons, and force them to seek elsewhere a home. A rude copy of the patriarchal form of government prevails among them—old men being the rulers of the tribe.

The condition of women among these primitive savages is extremely low. They are servants of the stronger sex. In some of their dialects wife and slave are synonymous. All the labour devolves on her, and, as no form of agriculture is practised, this consists principally in the search for the means of life. She collects the daily food, she prepares the camp or the hut at night, she piles fire-wood, draws water, weaves baskets, carries all burdens, and bears the children on her back, and the return for all this willing devotion is frequently the grossest ill-usage.

There is no form of marriage ceremony observed. A man gets a wife in various ways. Sometimes she is betrothed to him while an infant—even before her birth, and sometimes she devolves to him with other property. The eldest surviving brother, or next male relative, inherits the women of a whole family. Thus many households are supplied. Others steal their wives from hostile tribes, and frequent wars arise from such proceedings. Polygamy is universally allowed, but not by any means generally practised; for there are few parts of Australia where the female sex is not outnumbered by the male. Plurality of wives consequently implies wealth and distinction—each additional one being regarded as a new slave, an increase of property. Nor are the women jealous of polygamy. When a man has many wives, they subdivide the labour, which otherwise would devolve on one, thus lightening each others' burdens, and procuring companionship. There can indeed be little jealous feeling where affection on the part of the husband to the wife is almost a thing unknown.

The Australian wife when past the prime of life is usually a wretched object. She is often deformed and crippled by excessive toil—her body bent, her legs crooked, her ankles swollen, her face wearing an aspect of sullen apathy, produced by long hardship. When young, however, they are frequently lively and happy, not being cursed with keen feelings, and caring for little beyond the present hour. Should a young woman, nevertheless, be distinguished by peculiar beauty, she leads, while her attractions last, a miserable course of existence. Betrothed at an early age, she is perpetually watched by the future husband, and upon the least suspicion of infidelity is subjected to the most brutal treatment. To thrust a spear through her thigh or the calf of her leg is the common mode of punishment. She may, in spite of all precautions, be snatched away: whether consenting or not, she must endure the same penalty. If she be chaste, the man who has attempted to seduce her may strike her with a club, stun her, and bear her to a wood, where she is violated by force. Still she is punished, and it is, says Sir George Grey, no common sight to see a woman of superior elegance or beauty who has not some scars disfiguring various parts of her person. This period, however, is soon over, for the bloom of an Australian woman is very short-lived. When the seducer is found, he is punished in a similar manner, and if he have committed adultery with a married woman, suffers death.

The jealousy of the married men is excessive, and would be ridiculous were it not that their vigilance is absolutely called for. A careless husband would speedily suffer for his neglect. Accordingly we find the Australian savages practising in their woods or open plains restrictions not dissimilar to those adopted in the seraglios of the East. When an encampment is formed for the night every man overlooks his wives while they build one or more temporary huts, over which he then places himself as a guard. The young children and the unmarried girls occupy this portion of the village. Boys above ten years of age and all single men are forced to sleep in a separate encampment, constructed for them by their mothers, and are not allowed to visit the bivouacs of the married men. Under no circumstances is a strange native allowed to approach one of the family huts. Each of these little dwellings is placed far from the rest, so that when their inmates desire to hold converse they sing to each other from a distance. When the young men collect to dance, the maidens and wives are allowed to be spectators, but only on a few occasions to join. They have dances of their own, at which the youth of the other sex are not permitted to be present.

In spite of this excessive jealousy the idea of a husband's affection for his wife appears strange to them. Men return from journeys without exchanging a greeting with the mothers of their children, but those children they salute with many endearing terms, falling on their necks and shedding tears with every demonstration of love. A man has been known, when his wife was grievously sick, to leave her to die in the wilderness, rather than be troubled with her on his journey.

Yet the influence of women is not by any means small. In some of the tribes they obtain a position of moderate equality with the husband, are well-fed, clothed, and treated as rational beings. Everywhere the men, young and old, strive to deserve their praise; and exhibitions of vanity take place, perfectly ludicrous to those European travellers who forget that the silly dandyism of the Australian savage, with his paint and opossum skin, is only peculiar in its form of expression. Women are often present on the field of battle, to inspire their husbands by exhortations, to rouse them by clamours of revenge or appeals to their valour; and among the chief punishments of cowardice is their contempt. The man failing in any great duty of a warrior is so disgraced. Thus, if he neglect to avenge the death of his nearest relation, his wives may quit him; the unmarried girls shun him with scorn, and he is driven by their reproaches to perform his bloody and dangerous task.

Where polygamy exists it is seldom the woman's consent is required before her union with a suitor. In Australia it is never required or expected. The transaction is entirely between her father and the man who desires her for a wife, or, rather, for a concubine. She is ordered, perhaps, to take up her household bag, and go to a certain man's hut, and this may be the first notice she has of the marriage. There she is in the position of a slave to her master. If she be obedient, toil without torture is her mitigated lot; but if she rebel, the club is employed to enforce submission. She is her husband's absolute property. He may give her away, exchange her, or lend her as he pleases. Indeed, old men will sometimes offer their wives to friends, or as a mark of respect to strangers; and the offer is not uncommonly accepted.

Though we have mentioned three ways of obtaining a wife, the system of betrothal is the most general. Almost every female child is so disposed of a few days after its birth. From that moment the parents have no control whatever over her future settlement; she is in fact a bought slave. Should her betrothed die she becomes the property of his heir. Whatever her age she may be taken into the hut; cohabitation often commencing while the girl is not twelve years old, and her husband only a boy. Three days after her first husband's death the widow goes to the hut of the second.

Some restrictions, however, are imposed on the intercourse of the sexes. Thus all children take the family name of their mother, and a man may not marry a woman of his own family name. Relations nearer than cousins are not allowed to marry, and an alliance even within this degree is very rare. The Australians have, indeed, a horror of all connections with the least stigma of incest upon them, and adjudge the punishment of death to such an offence. Their laws, which are matters not of enactment but of custom, are extremely severe upon this and all other points connected with their women.

Chastity, nevertheless, is neither highly appreciated nor often practised. It is far from being prized by the women as a jewel of value; on the contrary, they plot for opportunities to yield it illicitly, and can scarcely be said to know the idea. Profligacy is all but universal among them; it is a characteristic even of the children. When some schools were formed at Perth, for the education of the natives, it was found absolutely necessary to separate children of tender years, in order to prevent scenes of vile debauch from being enacted. It should be said, however, that though indiscriminate prostitution among the women, and depraved sensuality among the men, exist in the most savage communities, disease and vice are far less characteristic of them than of those tribes which have come in contact with Europeans. In all the colonial towns there is a class of native women following the calling of prostitutes, and there the venereal disease and syphilis are most deadly and widely prevalent. The former appears to have been brought from Europe, and makes terrible havoc among them. The latter, ascribed by their traditions to the East, has been found among tribes which had apparently never held intercourse with the whites; in such cases, however, it is in a milder form.

Several causes contribute to the corruption of manners among these savage tribes. One of the principal is, the monopoly of women claimed by the old men. The patriarchs of the tribe, contrive to secure all the young girls, leaving to their more youthful brethren only common prostitutes, prisoners of war, and such women as they can ravish from a neighbouring community, or seduce from their husbands' dwellings. They also abandon to them their own wives when 30 or 40 years old, obtaining in exchange the little girls belonging to the young man's family. The youthful warrior, therefore, with a number of sisters, can usually succeed in obtaining a few wives by barter. That their personal attractions are faded is not of any high importance; since they are needed chiefly to render him independent of labour. His sensual appetites he is content to gratify, until he becomes a patriarch, by illicit intrigues with other women of the tribe. Of these there are generally some ready to sell or give away their favours. The wives, especially of the very old chiefs, look anxiously forward to the death of their husbands, when they hope, in the usual course of inheritance, to be transferred to the hut of a younger man; for, among nations in this debased state, it is not *the* woman that is prized, but *a* woman. Personal attachment is rare. The husband whose wife has been ravished away by a warrior from a neighbouring tribe may be pacified by being presented with another companion. Even in Australia Felix, which is peopled by the most intelligent, industrious, and manly of the Australian race, the young man disappointed of a wife in his own tribe sets off to another, waylays some woman, asks her to elope with him, and, on her refusal, stuns her with his club, and drags her away in triumph. Marriage, indeed, appears too dignified a term to apply to this system of concubinage and servitude which in Australia goes under that name. Travellers have found in the far interior happy families of man and wife, roaming together, with common interests, and united by affection; but such instances are rare.

A large proportion of the young men in Australia can by no means obtain wives. This arises from the numerical disparity between the sexes, which is almost universal in that region, and is chiefly attributable to the practice of infanticide. Child-killing is indeed among the social institutions of that poor and barbarous race. Women have been known to kill and eat their offspring, and men to swing them by the legs and dash out their brains against a tree. The custom is becoming rare among those tribes in constant intercourse with Europeans, but that intercourse itself has caused much of the evil. Half-castes, or the offspring of native women by European fathers, are almost invariably sacrificed. They are held in dread by the people, who fear the growth of a mixed race which may one day conquer or destroy them. Females, also, are killed in great numbers. This class of infanticide is regulated by various circumstances in different communities. Among some tribes all the girls are destroyed until a boy is born; in others, the firstborn is exposed; in others, all above a certain number perish; but everywhere the custom prevails. One of two twins—a rare birth—is almost always killed. It may be ascribed to the miserably poor condition of the people, and the degraded state of the female sex; for in a region where the aborigines have not yet learned to till the soil, and where the means of life are scanty, there will always be an inducement to check the growth of numbers by infanticide; and where women have to perform all the labour, and follow their husbands in long marches or campaigns, ministering to every want they may experience, the trouble of nursing an infant is often saved at the cost of the infant's life. Neglect also effects the same purpose.

The population, under these circumstances, has always been thin, and is apparently decreasing. Among 421 persons belonging to various tribes in Australia Felix, Eyre remarked that there were in the course of two years and a half only ten children reared. In other places one child to every six women was not an unusual average. This, however, is not all to be ascribed to infanticide. Many of the females abandon themselves so recklessly to vice that they lose all their natural powers, and become incapable of bearing offspring. Eyre found in other parts of Australia that the average of births was four to every woman. In New South Wales the proportion of women to men appears to be as two to three; while in the interior, Sturt calculated that female children outnumbered the male, while with adults the reverse was true. This indicates an awful spread of the practice of infanticide, which we cannot refuse to believe when we remember the facts which travellers of undeniable integrity have made known to us.

To suppose from this that in Australia the natural sentiments of humanity are unknown, would be extremely rash. On the contrary, we find very much that is beautiful in the character of its wild people, and are led to believe that civilization may go far towards elevating them from all their barbarous customs. Women are known to bear about their necks, as relics sacred to affection, the bones of their children, whom they have mourned for years with a pure and deep sorrow. Men have loved and respected their wives; maidens have prized and guarded their virtue; but it is too true that these are exceptions, and that the character and the condition of the female sex in Australia is that of debasement and immorality.

With respect to the prostitute class of the colonial towns, to which allusion has been made, it will be noticed in another part of this inquiry, when we examine into the manners of English and other settlers abroad.

Of prostitutes as a class among the natives themselves, it is impossible to speak separately; for prostitution of that kind implies some advance towards the forms of regular society, and little of this appears yet to be made in that region. From the sketch we have given, however, a general idea may be gained of the state of women and the estimation of virtue among a race second only to the lowest tribes of Africa in barbarity and degradation*.

Of Prostitution in New Zealand.

In the New Zealand group we find a race considerably elevated above the other inhabitants of Australasia, with a species of native civilization—a system of art, industry, and manners. Perhaps the savage of New Holland is one of the most miserable, and the New Zealander one of the most elevated, barbarians in the world. By this we do not mean that he has made any progress in refinement, or been subdued by the amiable amenities of life; but he is quick, intelligent, apt to learn, swift to imitate, and docile in the school of civilization. The Maories, in their original state, are low and brutal; but they are easily raised from that condition. They have exhibited a capacity for the reception of knowledge, and a desire to adopt what they are taught to admire—which encourage strong hopes of their reclamation. Among them, however, vice was, until recently, almost universal, and at the present day it is so, with the exception of a few tribes brought directly under the influence of educated and moral European communities. The only class which has discarded the most systematic immorality is that which has reconciled itself to the Christian religion, or been persuaded to follow the manners of the white men. The unreclaimed tribes present a spectacle of licentiousness which distinguishes them even among barbarous nations.

They show, indeed, an advance in profligacy. Their immorality is upon a plan, and recognised in that unwritten social law which among barbarians remedies the want of a written code. It is not the beastly lust of the savage, who appears merely obedient to an animal instinct, against which there is no principle of morals or sentiment of decency to contend; —it is the appetite of the sensualist, deliberately gratified, and by means similar, in many respects, to those adopted among the lowest classes in Europe. We may, indeed, compare the Maori village, unsubjected to missionary influence, with some of the hamlets in our rural provinces, where moral education of every kind is equally an exile.

The New Zealanders have been divided into the descendants of two races, the one inferior to the other; and the Malay has been taken as the superior. Ethnologists may prove a difference between them, and trace it through their manners; but these distinctions of race are not sufficiently marked to require separate investigations. The social institutions of the islanders are very generally the same, with some unimportant variations among the several tribes. We are placed in this peculiar difficulty when inquiring into the manners of New Zealand—that they appear to have undergone considerable modification since, and in consequence of, the arrival of Europeans. The natives refer to this change themselves, and in some cases charge the whites with introducing various evils into their country. Undoubtedly this is as true of New Zealand as of every other portion of the globe whither men have carried from Christendom the vices as well as the advantages of civilization. But in speaking of European settlers, a broad distinction must be borne in mind. White is not more contrasted with black, than are the regular orderly colonies established under the authority of Great Britain with the irregular scattered settlements planted by whalers, runaway or released convicts, land speculators, and other adventurers before the formal hoisting of our flag. The

---

* See Sturt's Two Expeditions, and Sturt's Expedition to Central Australia; Westgarth's Australia Felix; Leichardt's Expeditions; Hodgson's Australian Settlements; Haydon's Australia Felix; Stoke's Discoveries; Angas' Savage Life and Scenes; Sir George Grey's Journals; Eyre's Expedition; Pridden's History; Earl, Mackenzie, Mitchell, Howitt, Mudie, Macconochie, Oxley, Henderson, Cunningham, with the other travellers and residents, almost innumerable, who have described the aborigines of Australia.

influence of the one has been to enlighten and to elevate, of the other to debase and demoralize, the native population. Gambling, drinking, and prostitution were encouraged or introduced by the one, Christianity, order, and morality are spreading through the exertions of the other; and it is, therefore, unjust to confound them in one general panegyric or condemnation. Nor shall we include all the unrecognised settlements in this description. Many of the hardy whalers and others have taken to themselves Maori wives, who, sober, thrifty, and industrious, submit without complaining to rough usage and hard work, and are animated by a deep affection for their husbands. Contented with a calico gown and blanket, an occasional pipe of tobacco, and a very frugal life, they cost little to support, and appear for the most part not only willing but cheerful.

The female sex throughout New Zealand is not in such complete subjection to the male as in New Holland. With the right they have acquired the power to resist any unnatural encroachment upon their liberties, though still in a state of comparative bondage. They are influential in society, and whenever this is the case they enjoy, more or less, remission of oppression. We find them declaiming at public meetings of the people, and fiercely denouncing the warriors who may be dishonourably averse to war, or have behaved ignominiously in the field. By influencing their friends and relatives they often secure to themselves revenge for an injury, and thus security against the same in future. In various other ways their position is defended against utter abasement. They are not regarded merely as subservient to the lust and indolence of the male sex. When dead they are buried with ceremony according to the husband's rank, and formal rites of mourning are observed for them. In public and in domestic affairs their opinions are consulted, and often their hands are obtained in marriage by the most humble supplication, or the most difficult course of persuasion, by the lover. All this is evidence of a higher state than that which is occupied by females either in Africa or New Holland.

Polygamy is permitted and practised by those who can afford it. In reality, however, the man has but one wife and a number of concubines, for though the second and third may be ceremoniously wedded to him, they are in subjection to the first, and his intercourse with them is frequently checked by her. She is paramount and all but supreme, though a man of determination will sometimes divorce his first wife to punish her contumelious behaviour to his second.

It is customary for a man to marry two or more sisters, the eldest being recognised as the chief or head of the family. They all eat with the men, accompanying them, as well as their lovers and relations, before marriage, on their war expeditions or to their feasts. Betrothal takes place at a very early age—often conditionally before birth. Thus two brothers or two friends will agree that if their first children prove respectively a boy and a girl, they shall be married. When it is not settled so early, it is arranged during infancy, or at least childhood—for a girl of sixteen without an accepted lover is regarded as having outlived her attractions and all chance of an alliance. The betrothal is usually the occasion of a great feast, where wishes for the good success and welfare of the young couple are proclaimed by a company of friends. Three varieties of marriage formality are observed—differing as the girl is wanted to fill the place of first, second, third, or fourth wife. The first is a regular ceremony, the second less formal, and the last, which is merely conventional, is when a slave is raised from servitude to the marital embrace. The highest is that in which the priest pronounces a benediction, and a hope, not a prayer, for the prosperity of the married couple. The rest, which is the most approved and common, is for the man to conduct his betrothed to his hut, and she is thenceforward mistress of the place. Unless she be divorced, no one can take away her power, and no inferior wife can divide it. When they have entered the dwelling a party of friends surround it, make an attack, force their way, strip the newly-married pair nearly naked, plunder all they can find, and retire. By taking a woman to his house a man makes her his wife, or virtually, except in the case of the first, his concubine. When he merely desires to cohabit with one, without being formally united to her, he visits her habitation.

Though polygamy or concubinage has been practised in New Zealand from immemorial time, jealousy still burns among the wives as fiercely as in any Christian country where the institution is forbidden by the social law. It is the cause of bitter domestic feuds. The household, with a plurality of women, is rarely at peace. It is universally known to what an extent the jealousy of the Dutch women in Batavia carried them when their husbands indulged in the practice—common in Dutch settlements — of keeping female slaves. They watched their opportunity, and when it occurred would carry a poor girl into the woods, strip her entirely naked, smear her person all over with honey, and leave her to be tortured by the attacks of insects and vermin. A similar spirit of ferocious jealousy is characteristic of the women in New Zealand. The inferior wives consequently lead a miserable life, subjected to the severest tyranny from the chief, who makes them her handmaids, and sometimes terrifies her husband from marital intercourse with them. She exposes them to perpetual danger by endeavouring to insinuate into his mind suspicions of their fidelity, and thus the household is rendered miserable. When a man takes a journey he is usually accompanied by one of his wives, or, if he goes alone, will bring one back with him. Hence arise bitter heart-burnings and quarrels. Occasionally they lead to the death of one among the disputants, and frequently to infanticide.

So furious are the passions of the women when their jealousy is excited against their younger rivals, that many of the chiefs in New Zealand fear to enjoy the privilege allowed them by their social law. When they resolve upon it, they often proceed with a caution very amusing to contemplate. More than one anecdote in illustration of this is related in the works of recent travellers. A man having a first wife of bad temper and faded beauty, whom he fears, nevertheless, to offend altogether, is attracted by some young girl of superior charms, and offers to take her home; she accepts, and the husband prepares to execute his design. It is often long before he acquires courage to inform his wife, and only by the most skilful mixture of persuasion, management, and threats, that she is ever brought to consent. Women captured in battle, however, may be made slaves, or taken at once to their captor's bed. Thus raised from actual slavery, their condition is little improved. The tyranny of the chief wife is exercised to oppress, insult, and irritate them. Should one of them prove pregnant, her mistress — especially if herself barren — will often exert the most abominable arts to ensure her miscarriage, that the husband may be disappointed of his child, and the concubine of his favour which would thence accrue to her.

Divorces, according to the testimony of most writers, are not unfrequent in New Zealand. Among the ordinary causes are, mere decline of conjugal affection, barrenness in the wife, and a multiplication of concubines. A stepmother ill-treating the children, or a mother wantonly killing one of them, is liable to divorce. The latter is not an useless precaution, for jealous wives have been known in cold blood to murder an infant, merely to revenge themselves upon their husbands, or irritate them into divorce. A woman extravagantly squandering the common property, idling her time, playing the coquette, becoming suspected of infidelity, or refusing to admit a new wife into the house, is sometimes put away. This is effected by expelling her from the house. When it is she who seeks it, she flies to her relatives or friends. Should the husband be content with his loss, both are at liberty to marry; but if he desire to regain her, he seeks to coax her back, and, failing in that, employs force. She is compelled to submit unless her parents are powerful enough to defend her — for in New Zealand arms are the arbiters of law. When the desire to separate is mutual, it is effected by agreement, which is a complete release to both. If the husband insist on taking away the children, he may, but he is forbidden, on pain of severe punishment, from annoying his former wife any further.

There is among the New Zealanders a rite known as *Tapu*, and the person performing it is sacred against the touch of another. While in this condition no contact is allowed with any person or thing. There are, however, comparative forms of Tapu. Thus a woman, in the matter of sexual intercourse, is *tapu* to all but her husband, and adultery is severely punished. Formerly the irrevocable remedy was death, and this may still be inflicted; but jealousy is seldom strong in the New Zealand husband, who often contents himself with receiving a heavy fine from his enemy. The crime is always infamous, but not inexpiable. The husband occasionally, when his wife has been guilty, takes her out of the house, strips her, and exposes her entirely naked, then receiving her back with forgiveness. The paramour usually attempts to fly. If he be not put to death, he also is sometimes subjected to a similar disgrace. When a wife discovers any girl carrying on a secret and illicit connection with her husband, a favourite mode of revenge is, to strip and expose her in this manner. For, in New Zealand, libidinous as the conduct of the people may be, their outward behaviour is, on the whole, decorous. They indulge in few indecencies before a third person. The exposure of the person is one of the most terrible punishments which can be inflicted. A woman has hanged herself on its being said that she has been seen naked. One girl at Karawanga, on the river Thames, charged with this offence, was hung up by the heels and ignominiously flogged before all the tribe. Shame drove her mad, and she shot herself. They are otherwise obscene, and the children are adepts in indecency and immorality. One strong characteristic of their rude attempts at art is the obscenity in their paintings and carvings. In those singular specimens which crowd the rocks of Depuch Island, on the coast of New Holland, not a trace of this grossness is visible.

One of the most melancholy features in the manners of this barbarous race, is the prevalence of infanticide. The Christian converts, as well as some of the natives who hold frequent intercourse with the more respectable Europeans, have abandoned it, as well as polygamy; but, with these exceptions, it is general throughout the thinly-scattered population of New Zealand. It almost always takes place immediately after birth, before the sentiment of maternal affection grows strong in the mother's breast. After keeping a child a little while they seldom, except under the influence of frenzy, destroy it. As they have said to travellers, they do not look on them, lest they should love them. The weakly or deformed are always slain. The victim is sometimes buried alive, sometimes killed by violent compression of its head. This practice has contributed greatly to keep the population down. It is openly and unblushingly pursued, the principal victims being the females. The chief reasons for it are usually—revenge in the woman against her husband's neglect, poverty, dread of shame, and superstition. One of the most common causes is the wife's belief that her husband cares no longer for his offspring. The priests, whose low cunning is as characteristic of the class in those islands as elsewhere, frequently demand a victim for an oblation of blood to the spirit of evil, and never fail to extort the sacrifice from some poor ignorant mother. Another injurious and unnatural practice is, that of checking or neutralizing the operations of nature by procuring abortion.

Tyrone Power, in his observations on the immorality prevalent in New Zealand, remarks that some of the young girls, betrothed from an early age, are *tapu*, and thus preserved chaste. He regrets that this superstition is not more influential, since it would check the system of almost universal and indiscriminate prostitution, which prevails among those not subject to this rite. Except when the woman is *tapu*, her profligacy is neither punished nor censured. Fathers, mothers, and brothers will, without a blush, give, sell, or lend on hire, the persons of their female relatives. The women themselves willingly acknowledge the bargain, and Mr. Power declares the most modest of them will succumb to a liberal offer of money. Nor is anything else to be expected in any general degree. The children are educated to obscenity and vice. Their intercourse is scarcely restrained, and the early age at which it takes place has proved physically injurious to the race. Even those who are betrothed in infancy and rendered *tapu* to each other, commence cohabitation before they have emerged, according to English ideas, from childhood. Except in the case of those couples thus pledged before they can make a choice of their own, the laws which in New Zealand regulate the intercourse of the sexes with regard to preparations for marriage, approach in spirit to our own. A man desiring to take as wife a woman who is bound by no betrothment has to court her, and sometimes does so with supplication. The girls exhibit great coyness of manner, and are particular in hiding their faces from the stranger's eye. When they bathe it is in a secluded spot; but they exercise all the arts which attract the opposite sex. When one or two suitors woo an independent woman, the choice is naturally given to the wealthiest; but should she decline to fix her preference on either, a desperate feud occurs, and she is won by force of arms. Sometimes a young girl is seized by two rivals, who pull on either side until her arms are loosened in the sockets, and one gives way.

Perhaps, under these circumstances, the system of betrothal is productive of useful results, since it prevents the feuds and conflicts which might otherwise spring from the rivalry of suitors. The girl thus bound must submit to marriage with the man, whatever may be her indifference or aversion to him. Occasionally, indeed, some more youthful, or otherwise attractive, lover gains her consent to an elopement. If caught, however, both of the culprits are severely whipped. Should the young suitor be of poor and mean condition, he runs the chance of being robbed and murdered for his audacity. When, on the contrary, a powerful chief is desirous of obtaining a maiden who is betrothed, he has little difficulty in effecting his object, for in New Zealand the liberty of the individual is proportionate to his strength. It is a feudal system, where the strong may evade the regulations of the social law, and the weak must submit. Justice, however, to the missionaries in those islands requires us to add, that in the districts where their influence is strong, a beneficial change in this, as in other respects, has been produced upon the people. They acknowledge more readily the supremacy of law; they prefer a judicial tribunal to the trial of arms; they restrain their animal passions in obedience to the moral code which has been exhibited to them; and many old polygamists have put away all their wives but one, contented to live faithfully with her.

Among the heathen population chastity is not viewed in the same light as with us. It not so much required from the *woman* as from the *wife*, from the *young girl* as from the *betrothed maiden*. In fact, it signifies little more than faithful conduct in marriage, not for the sake of honour or virtue, but for that of the husband. With such a social theory, we can expect no general refinement in morality. Indeed, the term is not translatable into the language of New Zealand. Modesty is a fashion, not a sentiment, with them. The woman who would retire from the stranger's gaze may, previous to marriage or betrothal, intrigue with any man without incurring an infamous reputation. Prostitution is not only a common but a recognised thing. Men care little to receive virgins into their huts as wives. Husbands have boasted that their wives had been the concubines of Europeans; and one declared to Polack that he was married to a woman who had regularly followed the calling of a prostitute among the crews of ships in the harbour. This he mentioned with no inconsiderable pride, as a proof of the beauty of the prize he had carried away.

Formerly many of the chiefs dwelling on the coast were known to derive a part of their revenue from the prostitution of young females. It was, indeed, converted into a regular trade, and to a great extent with the European ships visiting the group. The handsomest and plumpest women in the villages were chosen, and bartered for certain sums of money or articles of merchandise, some for a longer, some for a shorter period. The practice is now, if not abolished, at least held in great reprobation, as the following anecdote will show. It exhibits the depraved manners of the people in a striking light, and is an illustration of that want of affection between married people which has been remarked as a characteristic of the New Zealanders. A chief from Wallatani, in the Bay of Plenty, went on an excursion to the Bay of Islands, and was accompanied by his wife and her sister. There he met a chief of the neighbourhood, who possessed some merchandise which he coveted. He at once offered to barter the chastity of his wife for the goods, and the proposal was accepted. The woman told her sister of the transaction, and she divulged the secret. So much reproach was brought upon the chief among his people, that he shot his wife's sister to punish her incontinent tongue.

Jerningham Wakefield describes the arrival of the whalers in port. He mentions as one of the most important transactions following this event, the providing of the company with "wives for the season." Some had their regular helpmates, but others were forced to hire women. Bargains were formally struck, and when a woman failed to give satisfaction, she was exchanged for another. She was at once the slave and the companion of her master. This is neither more nor less than a regular system of prostitution; but it is gradually going out of fashion, and is only carried on in a clandestine manner in the colonies properly so called. Indeed this is, unfortunately, one of the chief products of imperfect civilization—that vice, which before was open, is driven into the dark; it is not extirpated, but is concealed. A man offered his wife to the traveller Earl, and the woman was by no means loth to prostitute herself for a donation. Barbarians readily acquire the modes of vice practised by Europeans. In the criminal calendar of Wellington for 1846, we find one native convicted and punished for keeping a house of ill-fame.

Extraordinary as it may appear, prostitution in New Zealand has tended to cure one great evil. It has largely checked the practice of infanticide. For, as the female children were usually destroyed, it was on the supposition that, instead of being valuable, they would be burdensome to their parents. This continued to be the case until the discovery was made that by prostituting the young girls considerable profits might be made. It is to Europeans that the introduction of this idea is chiefly owing. The females were then, in many cases, carefully reared, and brought up to this dishonourable calling without reluctance. No difficulty was ever experienced from their resistance, as they would probably have become prostitutes of their own free will, had they not been directed to the occupation. Slavery, which has from the earliest time existed in New Zealand, has supplied the materials of prostitution, female servants being consigned to it. When possessed of any attractions they are almost invariably debauched by their masters, and frequently suffer nameless punishments from the jealous head wife. Concubinage does not, as in some other countries, release a woman from servitude, but she enjoys a privilege which is denied to the chief wife—she may marry again after her master's death.

Formerly the general custom, however, was for a wife to hang, drown, strangle, or starve herself on the death of her husband. Her relatives often gave her a rope of flax, with which she retired to a neighbouring thicket and died. It was not a peremptory obligation, but custom viewed it as almost a sacred duty. Sometimes three of the wives destroyed themselves, but generally one victim sufficed. Self-immolation is now, indeed, becoming very rare; but it is still the practice for the widow, whether she loved her husband or not, to lament him with loud cries, and lacerate her flesh upon his tomb. Whenever she marries again a priest is consulted to predict whether she will survive the second husband or not. Occasionally we find instances of real attachment between man and wife, such as would sanctify any family hearth; while examples have occurred of women hanging themselves for sorrow, on the death of a betrothed lover.

These, however, are only indications that humanity is not in New Zealand universally debased below the brute condition. The general colour of the picture is dark. Women are degraded; men are profligate; virtue is unknown in its abstract sense; chastity is rare; and prostitution a characteristic of female society. Fathers, mothers, and brothers—usually the guardians of a young woman—prostitute her for gain, and the women themselves delight in this vice. There is, nevertheless, some amelioration observable in the manners of the people, produced by the influence of the English colonies. Those colonies themselves, however, are not free from the stain, as will be shown when we treat of communities of that description in general.*

Of Prostitution in the Islands of the Pacific.

Among the innumerable islands which are scattered over the surface of the Pacific,

* Tyrone Power's Pen and Pencil Sketches; Angas's Savage Life and Scenes; Handbook of New Zealand, by a Magistrate of the Colony; Dieffenbach's Travels; Brown on the Aborigines; Jerningham Wakefield; Earl's Travels, &c., &c.

we discover various phases of manners developed under different influences. In some of the lonely groups lying out of the usual course of trade or travel, comnities exist whose social habits remain entirely pure—that is, unchanged by intercourse with foreigners. In others continual communication through a long period, with white men, has wholly changed the characteristic aspects of the people—given them a new religion, a new moral code, new ideas of decency and virtue, new pleasures, and new modes of life. The same process appears likely, at a future day, to obliterate the ancient system of things. In all the islands of this class, indeed, the reform of manners is not so thorough as the florid accounts of the missionaries would induce us to believe; but those pioneers of civilization have done enough, without assuming more than their due, to deserve the praise of all Christendom. To have restrained the fiercest passions of human nature among ignorant and wilful savages; to have converted base libidinous heathens into decent Christians; to have checked the practice of polygamy; and in many places to have extinguished the crime of infanticide;—these are achievements which entitle the missionaries to the applause and respect of Europe; but it is no disparagement of their labours to show, where it is true, that immense things yet remain to be performed before the islanders of the Pacific are raised to the ordinary level of civilized humanity.

The main family of the Pacific—the Society, the Friendly, the Sandwich, the Navigators', and the Marquesas Islands—present a state of society interesting and curious. Inhabiting one of the most beautiful regions on the face of the earth, with every natural advantage, the inhabitants of those groups were originally among the most degraded of mankind. Superior to the savage hordes of Africa and the wandering tribes of Australia, they are in physical and intellectual qualities inferior to the natives of New Zealand, though excelling them in simplicity and willingness to learn.

Tahiti may be considered the capital of Polynesia, as it is the head of its politics, trade, and general civilization. Before the settlement of the missionaries and the introduction of a new social scheme, its manners were barbarous and disgusting. The condition of the female sex corresponded to this order of things. It was humiliated to the last degree. Most of the men, by a sacred rite, were rendered too holy for any intercourse with the women except such as was pleasant to their own lusts. It was similar to the *tapu* of the New Zealanders, but was not, as among them, common to all. It was an exclusive privilege of the males. In consequence of this, women lived in a condition of exile from all the pleasures of life. They never sat at meals with their husbands, dared not eat the flesh of pigs, of fowls, of certain fish, or touch the utensils used by the men. They never entered the houses of their "*tabooed*" lords, dwelling in separate habitations, which these might enter when they chose. Those of the royal blood, however, were excepted from the action of this law. They might mingle with the other sex, might inherit the throne, and enjoy the advantages of society. With almost all others, beggary, toil, and degradation was the universal lot.

Marriage under such circumstances could not be looked upon as a sacred tie, or even a dignified state. It was held to serve only the purposes of nature and the pleasures of the men. With all, indeed, except the rich, it was a mere unceremonious bargain, in which the woman was purchased, though the parents usually made a present to their son-in-law. Among the nobler orders of society there was a little more parade, though an equal absence of sanctity. A person with a beautiful daughter brought her to some chief, saying, "Here is a wife for you." If she pleased him he took her from her father's hands, placed her under the care of a confidential servant, and had her fattened, until old and plump enough for marriage. All her friends assembled with his at the temple, and proceeded to the altar. The bride, with a rope hanging about her neck, was accompanied by a man bearing a bunch of the fragrant fern. Prayers were muttered, and blessing invoked upon the union. Then the names of their ancestors were whispered, and at each one of the leaves was torn. The nearest kinsman of the woman next loosened the rope from about her neck, and delivered her over to the bridegroom, bidding him take her home. Presents of various kinds were made to the newly-married pair, but, with all this ceremony, the tie was merely one of convenience. Within a month the man might tire of his partner and wish to be rid of her. All he had to do was to desire her departure, saying, "It is enough —go away." She immediately left him, and almost invariably became a prostitute. This process might be repeated as often as he pleased. The caprice of the male sex thus threw numbers of the females into a necessity of supporting themselves by the public hire of their persons. For, although polygamy existed, it was practised only by the rich, since the facility of divorce rendered it more convenient to take one wife, dwell with her a short time, and abandon her for another, than to be troubled or burdened with several at the same time. The wealthy, however, took numerous concubines—indulging in this luxury more than any of the other islanders. In all their customs and national characteristics, if we desire to view them in their original form, we must contemplate the people of those islands as they were twenty years ago. A great change is now apparent among them. The accounts, therefore, published at that period, though improved by later inquiries, afford us the information we are in search of. We are not surprised to find an indolent licentious people, as they were, when under no restraint, addicted to the most odious forms of vice. One natural result of their manner of life was infanticide. It was practised to a frightful extent, and was encouraged by a variety of causes. In the first place, poverty and idleness often induced parents to destroy their children — choosing to suffer that short pang of natural sorrow than the long struggles with starvation which awaited the indigent—even in those prolific islands. Next the common licentiousness produced innumerable bastards, which were generally killed. Thirdly, the social institutions of the country, with the division of classes, contributed to increase the prevalence of the custom—for the fruit of all unequal matches was cast aside. Superstition also aided it, for the priests demanded for their gods frequent oblations of infant blood. The missionary Williams was informed that, from the constant occurrence of wars, women, being abandoned by their husbands, slew their children, whom they knew not how to support. When a man married a girl of inferior rank, two, four, or six of her children were sacrificed before she could claim equality with him, and should she bear any more they were spared. Vanity, too, exercised its influence, for, as nursing impaired the beauty of the women, they sought to preserve their attractions by sparing themselves the labour. Perhaps, however, we should not lay it to the charge of vanity. The miserable women of these islands found in the flower of their persons the only chance of attachment or respect from their husbands. When this had faded, nothing could save them from neglect.

Whatever the cause, the extent of the practice was fearful. Three-fourths of the children were destroyed, and sometimes in the most atrocious manner. A wet cloth placed on the infant's mouth, the hands clenched round its throat, or the earth heaped over it while alive in a grave, were among the most humane. Others broke the infant's joints, one by one, until it expired. This was usually the plan of the professional child-killers, of whom there was a class—male and female—though the parents often performed the office themselves. Before the establishment of Christianity, Williams declares he never conversed with a woman who had not destroyed one or two of her offspring. Many confessed to him, as well as to Wilmer, that they had killed, some three, some five, some nine, and one seventeen.

Connected with infanticide was one of the most extraordinary institutions ever established in a savage or a civilized country. This was the Areoi Society. It was at once the source of their greatest amusements and their greatest sorrow, and was strictly confined to the Society group, though indications of a similar thing have been discovered in the Ladrones. The delicacy of the missionary writers—in many instances extremely absurd—has induced them to neglect informing us in detail of the practices and regulations adopted by this society; but enough is known from them, and from less timid narrators, to allow of a tolerably full sketch.

From the traditions of the people it appears that the society was of very ancient date: they said there had been Areois as long as there had been men. Its origin is traced to two heroes—brothers, who, in consequence of some adventures with the gods, were deified, and made kings of the Areoi, which included all who would adhere to them as their lords in heaven. Living in celibacy themselves, they did not enjoin the same on their followers; but required that they should leave no descendants. Thus the great law of the Areois was that all their children should be slain. What the real origin of the institution was it is impossible to discover. This legend, however, indicates a part of its nature.

The Areois formed a body of privileged libertines, who spent their days travelling from province to province, from island to island, exhibiting a kind of licentious dramatic spectacle to the people, and everywhere indulging the grossest of their passions. The company located itself in a particular spot as its head-quarters, and at certain seasons departed on an excursion through the group. Great parade was made on the occasion of their setting out. They bore with them portable temples for the worship of their tutelar gods, and, wherever they halted, performed their pantomimes for the amusement of the people. The priests and others—all classes and things—were ridiculed by them in their speeches, with entire impunity, and they were entertained by the chiefs with sumptuous feasts. There were, however, seven classes of the Areois, of which the first was select and small, while the seventh performed the lower and more laborious parts in their entertainments. Numbers of servants followed them to prepare their food and their dresses, and were distinguished by the name of Fanannan; these were not obliged to destroy their children.

Every Areoi had his own wife, who was sacred from attack. Improper conduct towards her was severely punished, sometimes by death. Towards the wives of other persons, however, no respect was shown; for after one of their vile and obscene spectacles, the members of the fraternity would rush abroad, and commit every kind of excess among the humble people. At their grand feasts, to which the privileged orders only were admitted, numbers of handsome girls were introduced, who prostituted themselves for small gifts to any member of the association.

The practice of destroying all their children, which was compulsory among the Areois, licensed them to every kind of excess. The moment a child was born its life was extinguished—either strangled, stabbed with a sharp bamboo, or crushed under the foot. The professional executioner waited by the woman's couch, and, immediately the infant came into the world, seized it, hurried it away, and in an instant flung it dead into some neighbouring thicket, or a pit prepared beforehand.

Infanticide was by no means confined to the Areois; it was an universal practice. Generally the sacrifice took place immediately after the birth; for, with the exception of those children demanded by the priests to offer in the temple, it was seldom that an infant allowed to live half an hour was destroyed. Whenever the execution was performed, it was previously resolved upon. The females were killed oftener than the males, and thus sprang up a great disproportion between the sexes, which was evidently owing to this and their often unnatural customs, as, since their abolition, the sexes are nearly equal.

Adultery was sometimes punished with death, but not under the public law. It was optional with the husband to pursue the criminal, or content himself with procuring another wife. A strange state of manners is exhibited by the account we have of the early missionaries arriving in Tahiti. The King Pomare came down to meet them with his wife Idia. This woman, though married to the prince, remaining on friendly terms with him, offering him advice, and influencing his actions by her counsel, was then cohabiting with one of her own servants, who had for some time been her paramour. The King, meanwhile, had taken his wife's youngest sister as a concubine; but she had deserted him for a more youthful lover, whereupon he contented himself with a girl belonging to the poorer class. Women, indeed, and men of the royal blood, were above the law.

Abandoned wives, and girls who could find no husbands, usually became prostitutes, as distinguished from those who pursued a profligate life from sheer sensuality. They hired themselves out to the young men whom the monopoly of women by the rich constrained to be contented with such companions. We have no information whether they were subject to any especial regulations; what the terms of contract were between them and their temporary cohabitants; how they supported themselves in old age; or, indeed, of anything concerning them, except the general nature of their calling. A large class of these prostitutes dwelt near the ports and anchoring grounds, deriving their means of subsistence from open or clandestine intercourse with the sailors, who willingly paid them with little articles of ornament or utility from Europe.

One of the missionaries of the first company desired to marry a Tahiti woman. His brethren, however, strongly objected to the act; first, because she was a heathen, second, because she was a prostitute. There could not be then found on the island, as they declared themselves on belief, a single undebauched girl above twelve years of age; therefore, in accordance with the Scripture prohibition against marrying a "heathen harlot," they forbade him forming the connection. Nevertheless he persisted, took the prostitute as wife, and is supposed to have been murdered with her connivance.

Inconstancy among wives, and profligacy among unmarried women, was then a characteristic almost universal in Tahiti. The wide-spread practice of procuring abortion concealed many of the intrigues which took place, and the last crime which began visibly to decrease was that of adultery.

Nor could this be a matter of wonder. The education of the people was in a school of licentiousness. The most effective lessons in obscenity were afforded by the priests in the temples, and children of tender years indulged in acts of indescribable depravity. Thus in few parts of the world could be discovered a more corrupt system of manners, a more complete absence of morals, than in Tahiti.

Under the influence of the missionaries a great and beneficial change was produced. French priests have now in a measure superseded them; but even their exertions have not been able to neutralize the good effects of the new code of morals introduced by the English friends of civilization.

As to the actual amount, however, of the good which has been effected, the accounts are contradictory. From the missionaries themselves we learn that Christianity has been firmly established; that the female sex has been elevated to an honourable position; that the Christian rite of marriage is now generally observed; that infanticide is wholly abolished; and that the manners of the people have become comparatively pure. The picture, indeed, drawn by these artists, is vivid and full of charms. We cannot, however, accept it without reserve; for such writers have in many parts of the world been too eager to ring their peals of triumph over the appearance of reform, without inquiring into its substantial and durable nature.

Other accounts insist on the truth of a totally different view. A recent author, a merchant, many years resident in Tahiti, describes the result of missionary labour as a mere skinning over of the corruption which exists. "Even now," he says, speaking of that island, "a people more ready to abandon themselves to sensuality cannot be found under the canopy of heaven." And further, in noticing the state of the youthful population, he asserts, "It is a rare thing for a woman to preserve her chastity until the age of puberty." Delicacy, he proceeds to tell us, is a thing unknown. There is hardly a man who would not wink at his wife's prostitution, or even abet it, to support himself. The same system of corrupt manners is general throughout the islands. The missionaries, by making adultery and fornication offences punishable by fines—so many dollars each—have set up a species of licence for immorality. The penalty is either eluded or laughed at. Sometimes the woman's paramour pays the penalty, and continues with her. The morals of the people, therefore, have not been radically reformed. Public decency is observed, but private manners are disgusting. The Tahitians have thus learned hypocrisy, for they now practise secretly what was formerly a recognised custom. The men are jealous of their own race, but will bargain for their wives with Europeans. One was asked the reason of this distinction. He instantly made answer, that when a white man took one of their wives he made her a present, passed on his way, and thought no more of her; but it was very different with their own people, for they would be continually hovering about the woman. The legal penalty for adultery by a single man is a fine of ten hogs to the husband. If it is committed by a married man he pays the ten hogs, while his paramour pays his wife another ten to compensate her for the injury she has suffered; thus the bargain is equal. Divorce is optional on either hand. For prostitution, or fornication of any kind, the missionaries enacted a fine. In a climate, however, where the girl ripens into puberty at the age of eight or nine, this becomes a licence, and immorality is very slightly checked. The depopulation of the group, which is still going on, is mainly owing, says the same author, to physical privations acting on moral depravity; for indigence is the lot of the people, and licentiousness now, as formerly, their besetting sin.

We believe this to be an unfair account of the state of things now existing in Tahiti. The writer* is possessed of a strong prejudice against the missionaries, and we are inclined to apply to him, with some modification, the observations of Commodore Wilkes, commander of the recent American exploring expedition in reference to that island. He tells us there is a class of traders who defame the missionaries, as well as a profligate class who hate them, because they forbid intoxicating liquors, have abolished lascivious dances, and prevent women going on board ship to prostitute themselves. One charge against the missionaries is, however, proved: they are guilty of a misjudging zeal amounting to fanaticism, forbidding the women to wear chaplets of flowers, because it is a sinful vanity; such a restriction is worse than ridiculous. The Commodore, however, whom we accept as a judicious and a trustworthy authority, already shows that much good has been effected. The population is now almost stationary—the births and deaths among all ages and both sexes were in 1839 naturally proportionate; Christian marriage is established as the national custom, and polygamy abolished; if infanticide be ever practised, it is as a secret crime; and as for immorality, though by no means extirpated, it has been considerably reduced. "Licentiousness," says Wilkes, "does still exist among them, but the foreign residents and visitors are in a great degree the cause of its continuance, and an unbridled intercourse with them serves to perpetuate it. Severe laws have been enacted, but they cannot be put in force in cases where one of the parties is a foreigner." He proceeds to deny that the island is conspicuous in this respect, and believes it would show advantageously in contrast with many countries usually styled civilized.

In the distant Sandwich group a similar system of manners existed before the abolition of idolatry in 1819. There was, however, one singular custom: children bore the rank of their mother, not their father, probably from the reason assigned by other savage races for different laws. that the parentage was never certain. Polygamy was practised, but if the king had a daughter by a noble wife she succeeded to the throne, though he should have numerous sons by the others; in fact, they were no more than concubines, though their offspring were not invariably destroyed, unless the mothers belonged to the humbler class of people; all the king's illegitimate children, however, were immediately killed. Adultery was punished with death; but intrigues were frequent, and infanticide was practised to a terrible extent. Since the enactment of the laws restraining sexual intercourse, the crime has become comparatively rare, and the progress of depopulation has been arrested.

We must, however, first view the people as they were before these reforms occurred: there was little check upon the intercourse of the sexes, except with regard to married women; the young girls being abandoned almost entirely to a dissolute mode of life, the marriage contract was a loose tie, easily broken, without anything of a sacred or even honourable character. Husbands continually abandoned their wives, who invariably destroyed the children thus left to them in their virtual widowhood, and took to prostitution as a means of life. The practice of procuring abortion was also resorted to, even more than infanticide, and women were sometimes killed by the operation; nevertheless, bastard children are sometimes reared, and the language of

---

* Rovings in the Pacific, by a Merchant long Resident in Tahiti, 1851.

the islanders supplies a delicate designation for one of this brood: it is called "one that comes."

Although the condition of the female sex was degraded, and although the women were for the most part subjected to the will of the chiefs, a few remained to be wedded among the poor, and to follow their own inclinations in the choice of partners. The word "courting" is used among them, or at least a synonymous term, signifying, literally, "we must be crept to." This indicates some elevation in their social intercourse, but appears to have been a recent introduction. When a man wished to marry a girl, some previous intimacy was supposed. According to their former customs he goes to her, and offers her a present. If she was willing to receive him, the gift was accepted; if not, he went his way. The parents were then consulted. When they consented he at once took home his bride, and all was consummated. When they refused he either abandoned his suit or persuaded his lover to elope with him; or, if possessed of sufficient property and power, forces her away. When once settled in union the wives were usually faithful, though previously they indulged in the utmost profligacy without any check.

The infanticide of the Sandwich Islands presented details still more horrible than the worst of those described in connection with Tahiti. Children six or seven years old, who so far had been carefully nursed, were sometimes sacrificed when their parents became desperate or indolent. An American traveller relates an affecting incident of a man who desired to be rid of his child, while the mother endeavoured to save it. Long altercations took place between them, until the father one day, to put an end to the debate, seized his little son, threw him over his knees, and with a single blow broke his back. The circumstance was related to the king, with a demand for punishment upon the offender. "Whose child was it?" he asked. They answered, "His own." "Then that is nothing," he said, "to you or to me." Usually the office was performed by female child-stranglers, who made it their profession. In a country where marriage, especially among the rich, was simply a compact for temporary or permanent cohabitation, abundance of employment was naturally afforded to those people. The chiefs, it is true, married in the temple, but the addition of ceremonies added not a whit of sanctity or durability to the bond. The first Christian wedding took place in Oalm in 1822, and the rite has since that period been established by law. The edict of 1819, indeed, proclaimed a revolution in the social system of the group. But it is not easy to reform the manners of a whole people. It is a slight task to publish laws, but difficult to enforce them, especially when they assail the most deeply-rooted prejudices, the sentiments, the passions, the religions, and the pleasures, of a numerous community. Idolatry, infanticide, polygamy, concubinage, and prostitution were all prohibited by the declaration of 1819, but are still practised, though in secret, but by no means so extensively as in former times. The financial laws check infanticide. If a man has four children, he is exempt from labour taxes to the king and to his landlord; if five, from the poll-tax also; if six, from all taxes whatsoever. Indeed, the condition of the females has been considerably raised, so that, instead of being the slaves, they are now, at least in some degree, the companions of the men.

Of the actual state of the sex, and the characteristic of manners in the Sandwich group, a fair sketch may be gathered from the facts scattered through the large work of Commodore Wilkes; he went through many districts, and examined minutely the progress of the people under the new code. In one district of Dahu, a small island in the group, no instance of infanticide had occurred (1840) during ten years; the law against the illicit intercourse of the sexes had not tended to increase the practice, and the population, which had been almost swept away, was recovering. In the valley of Halalea the population had been decreasing at the rate of one per cent. for nine years. In 1837, it was 3024—1609 males, 1415 females; and in 1840, 2935—1563 males, 1372 females. The general licentiousness of manners, causing barrenness in the women, with the practice of infanticide and abortion, prevented any increase. In Waiaulea the population of 2640 decreased by 225 in four years; and instances were known of women having six, seven, or even ten children, in as many years, without rearing one of them; the bastards were almost always destroyed, but the new law operated very beneficially to check the intercourse of the sexes; and only one case was known of a woman destroying her child, through fear of the penalty attaching to fornication. It appears probable, however, that the regulation compelling all unmarried women, found pregnant, to work on the public roads, must encourage many unnatural practices; in Hawaii itself, the principal island, where large numbers of men and women formerly lived in promiscuous intercourse—as one woman common to several men—great improvement is visible, and public manners have undergone much change; licentiousness, notwithstanding, is still a prominent characteristic of the people. These observations may be applied generally to the whole of the Sandwich group.

Of the Tonga or Friendly Islands no description equals in completeness, and none exceeds in general accuracy, that by Mariner, compiled by John Martin. According to him, the female sex was not degraded there, old persons of both sexes being entitled to equal reverence; women in particular were respected as such, considered to form part of the world's means of happiness, and protected by that law of manly honour which prohibits the strong from maltreating the weak. There were many regulations respecting rank which do not belong to this inquiry; but others of the same kind must be alluded to. The young girl, betrothed or set apart to be the wife or concubine of a noble, acquired on that account a certain position in the community. The rich women occupied themselves with various forms of elegant industry, not as professions, but accomplishments; while others made a trade of it.

The chastity of the Tonga people should be measured, in Mr. Martin's opinion, rather by their own than by others' ideas of that virtue. Among them it was held the positive duty of a married woman to be faithful to her husband. By married woman was meant one who cohabited with a man, lived under his roof and protection, and ruled an establishment of his. Her marriage was frequently independent of her own will, she being betrothed by her parents, while very young, to some chief or other person. About a third were thus disposed of, the rest marrying by their own consent. She must remain with her husband whether she pleased or not, until he chose to divorce her.

About two-thirds of the females were married, and of these about half continued with their husbands until death; that is, about a third remained married till either they or their partners died. Of the others two-thirds were married, and were soon divorced, marrying again two, three, or four times; a few never contracted any marriage at all; and a third were generally unmarried. Girls below puberty were not taken into this account.

During Mariner's residence of four years in the islands, where he enjoyed privileges of social intercourse which no native was allowed, he made numerous inquiries, and was led to believe that infidelity among the married women was very rare. He remembered only three successful instances of planned intrigue, with one other which he suspected. Great chiefs might kill their wives taken in adultery, while inferior men beat them. They were under the surveillance of female servants, who continually watched their proceedings. Independently of this also, he considered them inclined to conjugal virtue.

A man desiring to divorce his wife, had to do no more than bid her go, when she became perfect mistress of herself, and often married again in a few days. Others remained single, admitting a man into their houses occasionally, or lived as the mistress of various men from time to time—that is to say, became wandering libertines or prostitutes. Unmarried women might have intercourse with whom they pleased without opprobrium, but they were not easily won. Gross prostitution was unknown among them. The conduct of the men was very different. It was thought no reproach, as a married man, to hold intercourse with other females; but the practice was not general. It was checked by the jealousy of the wife. Single men were extremely free in their conduct; but seldom made attempts on married women. Rape occasionally happened. Captives taken in war had, as a thing of course, to submit, and incurred no dishonour through it. Few of the young men would refuse to seduce an unmarried girl of their own nation, had they the opportunity. Nevertheless, in comparison with the islanders in the surrounding sea, they were rather a chaste than a libertine people.

Commodore Wilkes declares himself glad to confirm the account in "Mariner's Tonga Islands" as an "admirable and accurate description." The women are said to be virtuous, and the general state of morals superior far to that of Tahiti. The venereal disease is much less extensively prevalent.

In the Marquesas the curious social phenomenon of polyandrism exists—several men cohabiting with one woman. This is in consequence of the preponderance of the male over the female sex. A young girl may become attached to a youth, and live with him for a short time. A man may then become attached to her, and transfer her, with her lover, to his house, where he supports them both. Infanticide is unknown, but procuring abortion not uncommon. The marriage tie, though a mere private compact signified by an exchange of presents, is, in spite of polyandrism, distinct, binding, and enduring—the parties abiding by the agreement they have made, until another formal agreement to dissolve it. In other parts of the Pacific the contrary system is carried out to an extravagant extent. In the Isle of Rotumah the land is divided into various estates, the property of certain chiefs. Each of these lords of the soil has absolute control over all the women in his district, and not one can marry without his consent. Should he not desire her for himself he allows her to contract the engagement, on receiving a present from the bridegroom. Gifts are exchanged on either side, bowls of cava are drunk, and the ceremony is over. The wife, in this island, has singular power. She may, a few days after the marriage, desire her husband to leave her. He does so for three or four months, and then returns to spend two or three days in her society. She may then request him again to quit the house; and this is repeated until she consents to live with him permanently. Occasionally, when all the preliminaries of the match are arranged, the girl will suddenly revoke her resolution, and refuse to leave her parents' house. The man may be equally desirous of leaving her at home, and in this case she is henceforward a privileged libertine, and usually lives well upon the gains of prostitution. But if, previously to the contract, she lose her virginity, the punishment is death, which is also inflicted for adultery.

A similar system with respect to the chief's authority prevails in the Feejee group. All the young girls in his district are at his mercy; he may take them all as concubines if he pleases. When they are allowed to marry they become slaves, living in complete subjection to their husbands, who flog them at will. They are denied the privilege of entering a temple, and are bought, sold, and exchanged, like cattle. Inclined as they are to licentiousness, they have certain ideas of modesty, and wear a girdle round the loins; any girl seen without this covering is put to death.

In the wild isles of the Kingsmill group in the Western Pacific, polygamy prevails; but more consideration is paid to the female sex than in any other part of that great insular region. All the hard labour is performed by the men; the women pursuing only those occupations which are truly domestic and feminine. Men, indeed, beat their wives, but in a similar manner to the lower classes here. If she be vigorous or bold enough, she returns blow for blow, and there is no appeal for him against her retaliation. Chastity is scarcely esteemed a virtue, nor is it considered essential by a man requiring a wife. After marriage, however, continence is strictly required. The adulteress is either put to death or expelled; but, in spite of these punishments, offences of this class are not uncommon. They are encouraged by the laws which forbid the younger brothers of a chief, who are not holders of land, from marriage; for it may be laid down as an axiom that all restrictions upon lawful intercourse with women multiply illicit connections. The adulteress and the prostitute in the Kingsmill Isles, as elsewhere, form the resources of those to whom celibacy is enjoined.

A wife is not bought, but the parents of both contribute to the household stock of the newly-married pair. It would be indecent in the young man to inquire of the girl's father what is the amount of her dowry. The marriage ceremony is only a feast, which is continued during three days. Children are sometimes betrothed during infancy, and in this case no marriage ceremony is required: as soon as they are sufficiently old they are sent to live together. When this is not the case, the young man makes an offer first to the girl, and, if accepted, next to her parents; but usually carries her off if they do not consent.

On the neighbouring isle of Maluni all the women who are married have been betrothed during childhood; the rest, without exception, being prostitutes, living with the single men, and receiving payment from them.

This is, as usual, in consequence of the rich men having so many wives that only a few women are left to live in common with the poorer sort. Infanticide is not practised, but abortion is continually procured. A woman has seldom more than two, and never more than three children. After the third is born she invariably calls in the aid of a woman to prevent another birth. This is not attended with any shame, but is, on the contrary, considered prudent; with the unmarried females it is invariable.

In the Samoan or Navigators' group women now enjoy equal privileges with the men, and no indiscriminate intercourse of the sexes is permitted. Polygamy has been very much checked, but is generally regretted. The people say, with a simplicity which takes away its profanity from the expression, "Why should God be so unreasonable as to require them to give up all their wives for his convenience?" Among the unconverted tribes it still prevails as formerly. Girls are betrothed early, and tabooed until marriage, which preserves the general chastity. Infanticide never occurs. Adultery is severely punished, and seldom committed; the marriage ceremony is only a trifling form of exchanging presents. The power of divorce may be exercised by the husband under certain circumstances, but not by the wife. Altogether their morals are of a superior order; and their libertine disposition exercises itself chiefly in the performance of lascivious dances. Everywhere, however, in these seas, except where the power of the missionaries is supreme, the whaling ships, on arriving at a port, attract numbers of prostitutes, who offer themselves to the sailors at various prices. When Coulter made his voyage, not many years ago, the vessel was assailed at the Kingsmill Islands by dozens of these women, who came, some attended by their fathers, mothers, or brothers, to entice the sailors. Some of them were very beautiful, and nearly naked. When he was in bed, in a house on shore, several young girls came in with scarcely any clothing, and asked him to choose a companion, or "wife." In other places hundreds of prostitutes swarmed down to the beach, performing the most obscene antics. It was so when La Perouse visited the region; it is so now. It was remarked by Cook, and it was remarked by the most recent voyager.

To pass up and down through that prodigious wilderness of sea, visiting each group in succession, and noticing the peculiar manners of all the various insular communities which there exist, would exceed the limits of an ordinary work. Nor would it continue to interest the reader; for there is an unavoidable monotony in the subject, when extended too greatly in reference to one region. What we have described will show that, among the innumerable islands of the Pacific, the original condition of women, before the partial establishment of Christianity, was pitifully degraded, and that the labours of the missionaries have been fruitful in good results. Wherever Christianity has been received, much outward improvement, at least, is visible. And there is something in this. When crime is perpetrated in secret, it is so because it is dangerous or disgraceful; and in proportion as it is either the one or the other the inducement to it will diminish. There is an immense field open in the Pacific; but the exertions of future missionaries may be encouraged by contemplating the good results which have sprung from the labours of those who have gone before them*.

OF PROSTITUTION AMONG THE NORTH-AMERICAN INDIANS.

VARIOUS as are the phases of civilization in different parts of the earth, no race is more peculiar than the North American Indian. It is alone. It stands apart from the rest of the human family. It resembles no other. In manners, customs, laws, ideas, and religion, the nation occupies its own ground, related by no tie with any of the innumerable tribes of the human family inhabiting the remaining divisions of the world. It has, indeed, exercised the ingenuity of ethnographical philosophers to trace among the North American Indians an identity of social institutions with the people of ancient Israel; but the comparison appears forced except in a few particulars, which seem rather matters of accident, and by no means the prominent characteristics of the Red or the Jewish race.

Until the complete establishment of a civilized society in North America, and before the settlement of peace, our knowledge of the Indian race was most imperfect. We depended on the relations of certain imaginative travellers, who wrote not so much to inform as to startle the reader—a practice not altogether abandoned at the present day. Carver, indeed, with a few others, brought home honest accounts of what he saw, but was not always careful to separate that from what he heard; and thus, even his picture is strangely coloured in some of its details. Later and more scrupulous travellers, however, have investigated the manners of the Indian race, and our acquaintance with it is gradually becoming familiar. Catlin and the various historians have added to our knowledge; so that a clear outline, at least of their social institutions, may be drawn. There are three classes of

* See Stuart's Voyage to the South Seas; Walpole's Four Years in the Pacific; Ellis's Tour through Hawaii; Ellis's Polynesian Researches; Herman Melville's Omoo and Typee; Progress of the Gospel in Polynesia; Montgomery's Narrative of Bennett and Tyerman's Voyage; Williams's Missionary Enterprise; Mariner's Tonga Islands; Wilkes's United States Exploring Expedition; Three Years in the Pacific, by Ruschenberger; Rovings in the Pacific, by a Merchant; Sir George Simpson's Voyage round the World; Coulter's Travels in South America; and Coulter's Voyage in the Pacific.

WOMAN OF THE SACS, OR "SÁU-KIES" TRIBE OF AMERICAN INDIANS.

[*Copied, by permission, from a Portrait taken by* Mr. Catlin, *during his residence among the Red Indians.*]

writers on the subject:—those who paint the red man as poetry incarnate; those who describe him as a vile and drunken barbarian; and those who have the sense to discriminate between the Indian of the seaport town corrupted in the dram-shop, and the Indian of the woods, displaying the original characteristics of his race. It is from such authorities we shall draw our view of the condition of women and the state of morals among them.

A race divided into several nations, and subdivided into innumerable tribes, might be supposed to present a similar diversity of manners. Not so, however. The social institutions of the North-American Indian are generally uniform, though of course there are many varieties of detail in their habits and customs. Yet these are neither so numerous nor so striking as to render it impossible to sketch the whole in a general view.

The Indian loves society. He is never found wandering alone. He is attached also to the company of women. Priding himself, however, on his stoicism, he never, at any period of his history, condescended to voluptuousness. His sense of manly pride prevented him from becoming immodest or indecent. This feeling at the same time inspired him with the idea that everything except the hunt and the warpath was below the dignity of man. The sentiments, therefore, which saved the female sex from becoming the mere food of lust, consigned it to an inferior position. The Indian women formed the labouring class. Such a result was inevitable. The warrior would only follow the chase or fight. There was labour to be performed. No men were to be employed for hire. Whatever, therefore, was to be done must be done by the females. The wife is, consequently, her husband's slave. She plants the maize, tobacco, beans, and running vines; she drives the blackbird from the corn, prepares the store of wild fruits for winter, tears up the weeds, gathers the harvest, pounds the grain, dries the buffalo meat, brings home the game, carries wood, draws water, spreads the repast, attends on her husband, aids in canoe building, and bears the poles of the wigwam from place to place. Among the trading communities she is especially valuable,—joining in the hunt, preparing the skins and fur, and filling the wigwam with the riches of the prairie, which the men exchange for the means of a luxurious life. When the hunter kills game he leaves it under a tree, perhaps many miles from the " smokes" of his tribe, returns home, and sends his wife to fetch it. Making garments of skins, sewing them with sinews and thorns; weaving mats and baskets; embroidering with shells, feathers, and grass; preparing drugs and administering medicine; and building huts—are among the other offices of the sex. To educate them for this life of industry, the girls are trained by the severe discipline of toils; taught to undergo fatigue, to be obedient, and to suffer without complaining.

Considered as the slaves of the men, it is natural to find a plurality of wives allowed by the Indian social law; accordingly from Florida to the St. Lawrence polygamy is permitted, though some tribes further north have not adopted the practice. Elsewhere also, in other directions, more than one woman is taken into the chief's wigwam. They are his servants, and he counts them as we count our horses and cattle; some of the great Mandan warriors have seven or eight; indeed, among all the communities which Catlin had an opportunity of visiting, polygamy was allowed, and it was no uncommon thing for him to find six, eight, ten, twelve, or even fourteen wives in the same lodge. The practice is of an antiquity too remote to fix, and is considered not only as necessary, but as honourable and just; they are servants, and a man's wealth is partly measured by this standard. This is one of the man's inducements to follow the custom, though it cannot be denied that some of these stoic warriors delight in a harem from the same motives as the Turk or the Hindu. It is allowed, we say, to all, but is principally confined to the great chiefs and medicine men, the others being too humble or too poor to obtain girls from their fathers: there are, indeed, few instances in which an ordinary man has more than one squaw, and it might be supposed that his wigwam was most peaceful; but it is not so. The jealousy of the Indian women is not of the same kind as with Europeans; it is watchful of strangers, not of regular wives, and six or seven of these dwell in great harmony under the same roof. So well established is this usage among them, that civilization meets more resistance in attempting to break it down, than in any other of its efforts; indeed, in overthrowing polygamy among the North-American Indians, or the remnant which is left of them, we shall overthrow their whole social economy and change their national character, and this it will be long before we are able to do. Probably the custom will continue as long as the race exists, and be only extinguished with it. Instances, indeed, have occurred, in which an Indian has sworn obedience to our social law, but many examples also are known of a return to the old habit. Sir George Simpson relates an anecdote of one who came into the settled parts, learned to read and write, adopted the principle of monogamy, and, returning among his countrymen, sought to persuade them to follow the same practice, and acquire the same accomplishments. They held long arguments with him upon the subject, debated gravely, and, in the end, instead of being converted by him, won him back to their ancient institution. He took a great number of wives, forswore books, and alluded no more to his designs of social reform. Some shame, however, possessed his mind, so that, when some Europeans were in the village, he kept in his wigwam and would not see them.

A chief named Five Crows, of the Cayux tribe, offered also to renounce polygamy, but it was from impulse only, and not from the discovery of any social principle. He had five wives, and great wealth in horses, cattle, and slaves. Falling in love, however, with a young Christian girl, the daughter of a gentleman in the service of the Hudson's Bay Company, he dismissed his old companions, and with great parade and confidence presented himself, made the proposal, but, to his infinite astonishment as well as mortification, was rejected; in a transport of spite, he immediately married one of his own slave girls. Generally, however, the American Indians are far less susceptible of the sentiment of love, still less of sensuality, than natives of Asiatic blood, and women among them are usually viewed with indifference; instances of the contrary occur and will be alluded to.

Whether polygamists or otherwise, the American Indians universally recognise the marriage contract. There is no such thing among them as a tribe practising promiscuous intercourse; the reports of such are idle tales. Such a community would become extinct, in the inevitable course of nature. The circumstances of the contract vary, however, in different parts, and among different societies. In fertile districts polygamy is more common; in barren tracts most of the men of all classes have only one wife. In some communities the man takes his squaw for life, and only divorces her for a recognised cause; in others, no more than a temporary union is expected. Everywhere, however, the condition of the sex is humiliating, if not miserable, and marriage is no more than the conjunction of a master with his servant. Thus the noblest institution of society is perverted into a form of slavery. That polygamy is practised cannot, nevertheless, be lamented in a social view. The frequency of wars among the American Indians, in their original state, caused a disproportion of the sexes, which allowed many of the men to take several wives, without preventing all from having one. Had this custom not been prevalent, one alternative only would have remained to the superfluous women—they would have become common prostitutes.

The conditions and forms of the marriage contract are various only in the inferior details—the general tenour of them being that a man procures a woman from her father as a purchase, and acquires in her a property over which he has the control of a master. Some restrictions, however, are laid upon the intercourse of the sexes. Marriage cannot be contracted among any of the tribes which originally dwelt east of the Mississippi, or indeed anywhere between kindred of a certain degree. The Iroquois warrior may choose a partner from the same tribe, but not the same cabin, or group of wigwams. For it is to be recollected that, among the tribes, especially of the Algonquin race, the whole family, or clan of several families, dwell together, bearing a common designation. One of that nation must look for a wife beyond those who bear the same token or family symbol. The Cherokee would marry at once a mother and her daughter, but never a woman of his own immediate kindred. The Indians of the Red River frequently take two or more sisters to wife at once.

The manners of the Algonquin race are generally similar. The young man desiring a wife offers a gift—or, if he be poor, his friends do it for him—to the girl's father. If this be accepted, the marriage is complete. He goes to dwell in the woman's house for a year, surrendering the gains of one hunting season to her family, and then taking her away to a wigwam of his own.

The contract is, with all the other tribes, usually made with the girl's father; she is virtually bought and sold. In many cases she is never consulted at all, and the whole is a mere mercenary transaction. Instances do occur, also, where the parties approach each other, express mutual affection, make arrangements, and swear vows, sacred and inviolable as vows can be; but the marriage is never consummated without payment to the bride's father. In the interior of Oregon the permission of the chief is first asked, then the approval of the parents, then the assent of the girl; but if she object, her decision is conclusive. If she consent, the man gives from one to five horses to her father; they have a feast, and the ceremony is complete. Espousals often take place during infancy, but neither is absolutely bound by this engagement. The influence of the parents is, however, so powerful, that their will is seldom or never resisted; so that a bargain is often concluded, and a price paid; while the girl is a child. Occasionally the female courts the male—that is, proposes to become his squaw, and promises to be faithful, good-tempered, and obedient, if he will take her to his hut. He seldom refuses, for polygamy is permitted, and a husband may in this region put away his wife when he pleases. He usually allows each to have a separate fire.

The missionaries in Oregon have had some success, and have displayed more prudence than some of their brethren of the same profession in the island of Tahiti. Men who had a plurality of wives were required, on their conversion, to maintain them; while those who had only one were forbidden to take more.

On the Red River, when a young man desires a girl as wife, he addresses her father, and, if accepted by him, dwells in his wigwam for a year—as among the Algonquins—and then takes her home. This is only observed with the first; he adds to the number, if he is wealthy, as fast as he can. Few of the women are thus left single, and scarcely any common prostitutes are found. Some will occasionally bear children before marriage; and the zeal of the missionary West was displayed in somewhat of a fanatical spirit by his refusing to baptize a child not born in formal wedlock. We may, however, forgive this eccentric spirit for the motive which created it; and must admit that, as Sir George Simpson bears witness, the Indians of Oregon are vastly reformed, and chiefly by missionary influence.

Among the curious customs preceding marriage in other parts of North America, is that of the lover going at midnight into the tent of the woman he desires, and, lighting a splinter of wood, holding it to her face. If she wake and leave the torch burning, it is a sign for him to be gone; if she blow it, he is accepted, and we are told that this frequently leads to immoral intercourse. Catlin knew a young chief of the Mandans on the Upper Missouri, who took four wives in one day, paying for each a horse or two. They were from twelve to fifteen years old, and sat happily in his wigwam, perfectly contented to dwell under his commands. He was applauded for the act. This extreme youth in the bride is common among the tribes; children pass from infancy to womanhood by a single bound—we are assured, on good testimony, that mothers twelve years of age are not unfrequent. The youths are led by precept and example to adopt marriage; celibacy beyond the age of puberty being very rare, especially in those communities which have come into familiar contact with Europeans. It appears indeed that this plan is resorted to by the men to secure virgins as their wives, for among few barbarous nations is the chastity of unmarried woman safe very long after she has reached a marriageable age. To have no husband is esteemed by the females a misfortune and a disgrace, while to have no wife entails great discomfort on a man.

It has already been shown that, when married, the woman becomes her husband's servitor; that she is, in many cases, the humiliated drudge, in all, the humble attendant on her master; that she waits on him in submissive silence while he eats, and approaches him with the deference due from an inferior to a superior being. Those who infer, however, from these circumstances that the sentiments of conjugal, filial, and parental affection are unknown to the Indian race, think erroneously of them. Strong and tender attachments continually spring up between the sexes. The lover sings of the girl he has chosen, and takes her home with the delight of gratified affection. The husband, too, when he devolves upon his wife all the labours of the wigwam, is no more conscious that he is using her harshly than she is that she occupies an unnatural position. Ideas and sentiments are often no more than things of habit, and with the Indian chief strong love is not inconsistent with his walking in lordly indolence along the forest path while she is bearing the heavy wigwam poles behind. Heckewelder relates a singular instance of indulgence, which, it must be confessed, is rare among the barbarians of North America. There was a scarcity in the district inhabited by a certain tribe, and an Indian woman, being sick, expressed a strong desire for a mess of Indian corn. Her husband having been told that a trader at Lower Sandarsky had a little, set off on horseback for that place, a hundred miles distant, gave his steed in exchange for a hatful of grain, returned home on foot, and gratified his wife by the treat he had thus procured. It is seldom that the most polished society presents a similar instance of kindliness. Many pictures of domestic happiness are exhibited among the Indians. The Blackfeet, Sanee, and Blood Indians, reckon it among their chief desires that their wives may live long and look young. Smoke sometimes rises for forty years from the same hearth, with one couple presiding over it. On the other hand, the husband's infidelity or harshness sometimes drives his wife to suicide, for the woman has no protector. The life of hardship they lead soon strips them of all their personal beauty, when they are entirely consigned to toil. In spite of this, they are well fed, healthy, and robust, unlike the women of Australia who are stinted in food, and often deformed or crippled by the severity of their labour. Nature has been very indulgent to them. Scarcely any have more than five, and few more than three children. Easy travail takes away one affliction from their lot. The pains of delivery are seldom prolonged for more than a quarter of an hour, and she who groans under the acutest pang is prophesied, with a taunt, to be the mother of cowards. Death, however, occasionally ensues. The Indian mother loves her children dearly, never trusting it to a hireling nurse—which indeed could not be found; for no woman would put away her own infant to suckle another's. Bearing the cradle on her back she performs her daily task, and if she die the nursling is laid in her grave. One curious and beautiful custom is that of carrying the cradle of a dead nursling child for a whole year, and all are familiar with the story of the Canadian mother bedewing the grave of her child with milk from her bosom. Infanticide is a rare and secret crime, not by any means to be enumerated among the characteristics of their manners.

Marriage among the North-American Indians is contracted for the happiness and comfort of the man. He is bound to live with his wife only so long as these are enjoyed. Adultery, indolence, intemperance, and sterility are among the causes of divorce. It takes place without formality by simple separation or desertion; and where there are no children is very easy. Their offspring forms their most powerful bond; for, where the mother is discarded, the unwritten law of the red man allows her to keep the children whom she has borne or nursed. The husband detecting his wife in adultery may cut off her nose, or take off part of her scalp. He sometimes kills her with her paramour at once; and the only blame attached to him on the occasion is, descending from his dignity to feel so strongly the loss of one woman, when another may easily be procured to supply her place.

The idea of chastity as a positive virtue is but feebly developed among them. With the men, indeed, it is a Spartan quality, as opposed to effeminacy; otherwise, the promiscuous sleeping of whole families in the same chamber, with various other circumstances, would tend much to immorality. Nevertheless, among some tribes, as that of the Mandans, the women are delicate and modest; and in the wigwams of the respectable families virtue is as cherished, and as unapproachable, as anywhere in the world. Generally the Indians are decent, and, with the exception of those customs which form the basis of their manners, and result directly from their national character, might be won over without difficulty to the amenities of civilized life. Many of the squaws, of course, in North America, as elsewhere, are immodest, and seek occasion to engage in an intrigue. With the unmarried girls the same is the case. A bastard child may be born without entailing great shame upon its mother, though the seducer is greatly despised; but such an occurrence is rare, not altogether, however, because the females are too chaste, but because they are too cautious, and employ means to procure abortion. This practice is sometimes resorted to by the squaws, though discountenanced by the men, except when they are on the march, or hotly pressed by an enemy.

From a notice of their punishments in Hunter's narrative of his captivity, it would appear that the last act of depravity is not unknown among the Indians. Adultery, he tells us, where not perpetrated by the husband's consent, is punishable with divorce. We might doubt the testimony of this writer, but that Wilkes found Indians in the far north, within the range of the Hudson's Bay territories, who would gamble away their wives, and prostitute them for money. These men he believed to be degraded from their original condition, but various authors speak of a similar practice. Carver relates that, among the Manedowessis, it was a custom when a young woman could not get a husband, for her to assemble all the chief warriors of the tribe in a spacious wigwam, to give them a feast, and then, retiring behind a screen, to prostitute herself to each in succession. This gained her great applause, and always insured her a husband. It was, however, nearly obsolete when he wrote, and appears now to be altogether extinct.

Many of the Europeans dwelling on the Red River were accustomed to take concubines during the period of their residence there. The Indians, who are civilized, as it is called, in the provinces of Nova Scotia, New Brunswick, and Canada, have thus learned also the worst vices of Europe. Maclean, a very recent writer, declares that the Christianized tribes in the Hudson's Bay territories have been deteriorated by intercourse with the whites, become drunken, sensual, and depraved. The venereal disease commits frightful ravages among them. Most of their diseases arise from excess of one kind or another. He says that the men employed by the Company are chiefly reconciled to their hard employment and poor remuneration by the immorality of the women, of whom large numbers follow the occupation of prostitutes, and sell themselves for the vilest price. On the north-west coast, chastity is scarcely even a name; indeed, there is no word in the language of the people to express that idea. The sea tribes are, indeed, in all cases, the most licentious; which appears to justify the remark, that intercourse with a strange unsettled population has demoralized them.

At some parts of the coast where the trading ships touch for supplies, hundreds of women come down, and, by an indecent display of their persons, endeavour to obtain permission to go on board. When Sir George Simpson arrived at one of these ports a man asked for the captain's wife, and offered his own in exchange. In that part of the country the tyranny over the female sex is even more severe than in the interior. When a man takes a wife, he purchases her as his perpetual property; and if they separate, whether from an offence of hers or his, she must never marry again. She usually takes to clandestine prostitution as a means of living. But such instances as the foregoing are not confined to the coast. In the interior the traveller may observe, wherever a large concourse of Indians is assembled, a number of beautiful and voluptuous-looking women continually mixing in the throng, and throwing their glances upon strangers, or the single young men of the tribe. The Indians have now been removed to a territory beyond the Mississippi; and it is probable their corruption will rapidly increase in proportion to their congregation.

One peculiar feature of the system, introduced of course since Europeans visited the country, remains to be noticed. Many of the white traders, among the tribes of the Upper Missouri, find it good policy to connect themselves by marriage with powerful families, and they procure then the most beautiful girls of the noblest tribes, who aspire with delight to such a station, which usually elevates them above their servile occupations to a life of indolence, ease, and pleasure. These engagements, however, are scarcely marriages—at least in the European sense of the term—ceremonies of any kind being seldom performed. A large price in Indian estimation is paid for the girl, and she is transferred at once to the trader's house; with equal facility he may annul the contract, leaving his companion to be candidate for another mate, for which her father is not sorry, as he may procure an additional horse again in exchange for her: this is no more than a system of virtual prostitution, in which the woman is hired out as a temporary companion, merely for the pecuniary gain. The trader may procure the handsomest girl in the tribe for two horses; for a gun with a supply of powder and ball; for five or six pounds of beads; for a couple of gallons of whiskey; or a handful of awls. Such is the price at which the Indian chief will prostitute his daughter. Occasionally, it must be added, the couple thus united live together permanently as man and wife, the possibility of which is, indeed, almost always supposed.

The Indians of New Caledonia, though not belonging to the same stock with the red race of North America, may be noticed here: they are extremely profligate; the venereal disease is common among them; and the blessing of a healthy climate is rendered nugatory by the intemperance of the people. Among them, nevertheless, women are held in more estimation than among the red tribes, for the men are not possessed by that sense of lordly dignity which disdains at once to become sensual, and to share the labours of the inferior sex. Women assist in the councils, and those of high rank are even admitted to the feasts. During the fishing season each sex is equally employed, and so in all their other tasks. Lewdness could not be carried to greater excess than it is among them: both men and women are addicted to the vilest crimes; they abandon themselves in youth to the indulgence of their most unbridled lust, and the country owes its rapid decrease of population to the universal depravity of the people. No man marries until his animal appetite is satiated upon the voluntary prostitutes who abound, and then his wife, if dissatisfied with the restraints of matrimony, may refuse to dwell with him; the union is consequently broken by mutual consent, for a certain time or for ever. Meanwhile they addict themselves to their former pleasures, but the woman is nominally prohibited, by law, under pain of death, from cohabiting with any man during this period of separation from her husband; he seldom cares, however, to enforce his right, and she seldom fails to break the law. Polygamy is allowed, but only one woman is actually a wife—the rest are mere concubines; the chief one may be supplanted by a new favourite, when the old one yields without a murmur, though occasionally a woman of violent passions will destroy herself.

To illustrate the general subject of the condition of women among the North-American Indians, we may notice an incident described by the observant traveller Catlin. When, among the Sioux, he proposed to paint the portrait of a woman, his condescension was regarded by the warriors of the community first as incredible and then as ridiculous. It appeared marvellous that he should think of conferring on the females the same honour he had conferred on the medicine men and braves; those whom he selected were laughed at by hundreds of others who were, nevertheless, jealous of the distinction. The men who had been painted said that if the artist was going to paint women and children the sooner he destroyed their portraits the better; the women had never taken scalps, never done anything but make fires and dress, with other occupations equally servile: at length, he explained that the portraits of the men were wanted to show the chiefs of the white nation who were great and worthy among the Sioux nation, while the women were only wanted to show how they looked and how they dressed: by this means he attained his object. Mr. Catlin considers that, on the whole, the Old World has no superior morality or virtue to hold up as an example to the American Indian races. The degradation of the women, however, is denied by none, though a woman of superior courage or contrivance sometimes places herself above the degrading laws which depress the rest of her sex. Thus one whom Catlin saw joined boldly in a dance — though females are only allowed to join in a few of these—played off great feats before the warriors, and for her audacity no less than for her skill was greeted with thundering peals of applause, besides a pile of gifts *.

* See Bancroft's History of the United States;

Of Prostitution among the Indians of South America.

The plan and purpose of this inquiry will by this time have become obvious to every reader. It is to afford a comparative view of the state of manners throughout the world, with reference to public morals, the condition and the character of the female sex. We have chosen to treat of the barbarians in a separate division of the inquiry, and for this reason have left a large portion of Africa, and by far the greatest portion of North America, for future pages. With respect to South America, its various states will be classed among those half-barbarous communities, which we shall take as the link between the savage and the civilized portions of the globe; for, in spite of the dreams in which some romantic travellers have indulged, Lima is only fit to be compared with Algiers, and Brazil with Morocco. Leaving, therefore, these half-caste societies, as we shall next turn to them in a separate notice, we may briefly treat of the Indian race which still, though in numbers awfully reduced, clings to its native soil in South America.

A very brief description will suffice. Remembering the difference of character between the Indian of the North and the Indian of the South, we may, in most respects, apply our last notices to the present subject. The barbarians with whom we have now to deal are not possessed by that rigid masculine vanity which inspires them with a contempt not only of the female sex, but of the pleasures they furnish to men of more sensual temperaments and more effeminate mould. They have less pride, but not more manliness than the Indians of the Red Race. There is no comparison, in point of mental and moral character, between the savage of the Brazilian forest and the stately Huron or Iroquois, or the warrior of the Algonquin race.

Two classes of Indians exist in South

Catlin's Eight Years' Travels; Carver's Travels in North America; Wilkes's United States' Exploring Expedition; Mackenzie's Memoirs, Official and Personal; West's Residence in the Red River Colony; West's Mission to the Indians of New Brunswick; Hunter's Memoirs of his Captivity; Drake's Book of the Indians; Halkett's Historical Notes; Buchanan's Sketches of History; Sir James Alexander's Acadie; Maclean's Twenty-Five Years' Service in Hudson's Bay; Sir George Simpson's Voyage round the World; Robertson's History of America; Robertson's History of Missions to the Indians; Cleveland's Voyages and Enterprises.

America—the pure native, and the breed corrupted by intercourse with Europeans, half-castes, and the rest of that variety of colours which have been produced between the white and the original tenant of the soil. The first is now an exceedingly small family, and some accounts have represented it as eminent for virtue and simplicity. We know that romantic pictures have been drawn of the golden days when Montezuma reigned in the Valley of Mexico, and gave laws to the free population of the country; but sober research has dissipated the idea that he was the governor of a civilized and polished nation. Superior, indeed, the Mexicans were to the savages who occupied so large a portion of the New World, but they were deficient in many of the arts, and gross in many of the manners which assist in comparing the standard of a people's progress. This much has been ascertained, though it is little. At the present day, the great characteristics of the barbarian state are strongly exhibited in this as in other parts of South America. The miserable remnant of the Indian race grows yearly more debased, learning little from its European preceptors except profligacy and the coarsest arts of vice. Throughout the region women are degraded. The men generally sleep and lounge, or occupy themselves with easy tasks, but more from indolence than pride, while the women perform the labours of the house and of the field. Such is almost the universal practice of Indian manners in South America. Instances of the contrary, indeed, there are. King found among the Chedirrione tribes of the Argentine Republic, a primitive state of society, no less innocent than simple. The women were modest, the men kind to them, and labour was justly shared. All property was in common, and the members of the community lived in perfect brotherhood. This, however, is only one cheerful spot upon the surface of South-American manners. In the Central Region the females are degraded, and chastity a rare virtue. Women may bear children before marriage without shame, and the intercourse of the sexes is unrestrained.

Among the Indians of Brazil a curious system of manners existed before the establishment of European power, and many traces of it still exist. No man might marry until he had killed an enemy. When a girl reached the age of puberty her hair was cut off, her back tattooed, and she wore a necklace of the teeth of wild beasts until her hair grew again. Bands of cotton were fastened about her waist and the fleshy parts of her arms, to signify her maidenhood. It was said that if any but a pure virgin wore these emblems, the evil spirit would bear her away; but the national belief was not sufficiently strong to render this a defence of chastity, for it was lost without reproach or fear, and incontinence was regarded as no offence. Sleeping in crowds, in large common dormitories produced a pernicious effect on the people, destroyed all ideas of decency, and caused universal lewdness. When a man tired of his wife, he put her away and took another; indeed, as many as he pleased. Although unrestrained polygamy was allowed, the first wife, however, continued to enjoy some privileges, as having a separate berth to sleep in, and a separate plot of ground to cultivate for her own use. Nevertheless she was bitterly jealous of those who supplanted her, and frequently, when altogether neglected by her husband, abandoned herself altogether to vice, and became a clandestine prostitute to any of the young men who would flatter or pay her for the favour.

Being regarded, more or less, as property, a man's wives formed part of his estate, and were bequeathed on his death to his brother or nearest kinsman. The women thus procured were seldom treated with any delicacy or consideration, yet they found sources of happiness, and were often lively and gay to the last degree. When utterly miserable the female sex does not delight to clothe itself in gaudy attire, or adorn itself with sparkling trinkets, as in Brazil, where masculine vanity ran so high that it declared certain ornaments to be the exclusive privilege of men.

In the neighbouring regions there was some variety among the different tribes. The Tyrinambas used their women fairly, though they somewhat overloaded them with employment. They were, however, generally happy, and were principally employed in spinning and weaving—for the industrial arts had reached that stage among them. They also cultivated the ground. On this subject a curious and not unpoetical idea prevailed among some of the Indians of South America. It was, that as females only bore children, so the grain planted by their hands would fructify in a more plentiful increase than that sown by men. Female porters, also, formed a considerable class.

In Paraguay the wars that spread havoc among the miserable people gave rise to a flagitious custom, which destroyed the population more rapidly than pestilence or the sword. No woman ever reared more than one child. The difficulty of subsistence was one cause which induced this custom. The practice of producing abortion was adopted in preference to infanticide, since it inflicted a less violent shock on the natural feelings of the woman. Remonstrated with upon the horror of the crime, one mother replied that an infant was a great incumbrance, that parturition took away from the grace of the figure, rendering her less attractive to the men, and moreover that abortion was easier than delivery. The manner of procuring it was singular. The woman lay down on her back, and was beaten by two aged crones till the result was certain. Many died in consequence of this barbarous process, while others contracted a disease which afflicted them through life. Men and women were equally debauched. Their gregarious habits afforded unlimited opportunities for intrigue, and husbands cared little to whom their wives prostituted themselves, though they regarded them as absolute property, branding them on the thigh or bosom with a hot iron as they did their horses. One peculiar custom obtained among them — the married spoke in a dialect different from that employed by the unmarried people.

Contrasted with this community was the Abifrone, a tribe inhabiting the same region, more long-lived, healthy, and numerous, because they were temperate and chaste. Morality was characteristic of them, and prudence also. The men seldom or never married before the age of thirty, or the women before that of twenty, and were usually continent before contracting that engagement. A wife was purchased from her parents, and was entirely at their disposal, unless bold enough to run away. There was some poetry in the rite of marriage. If the suit was accepted, eight maidens carried a canopy of fine tissue over the bride, who walked in silence, and with downcast eyes, to her husband's tent. There he received her with signs of love; she then returned, bearing the few domestic articles necessary to their simple mode of life, and her new master dwelt in her father's house with her until she had borne a child, or he had sufficiently proved his affection towards her. Women were obliged to suckle their children for three years, and forbidden to hold connubial intercourse during that period. This induced the practice of procuring abortion, for the wife feared her husband would forget and abandon her after the long interval. Depopulation was thus caused. Infanticide, also, was practised, but the boys were selected as victims rather than the girls, who were valuable to their parents. The intercourse of the sexes before marriage was rigidly watched; the maidens were educated in habits of industry, and taught to prize their virtue. When the missionaries came among them preaching against polygamy and divorce, the women of this tribe were eager listeners.

Transferring our attention to another part of the South-American Continent, we find among the Sambos of the Mosquito Shore some curious customs. They are not of the Indian race, but closely allied with them in their social habits: when a man commits adultery the injured husband shoots a beeve, takes a horse, or carries off something of value, no matter to whom it may belong, and the proprietor must obtain restitution from the adulterer. Polygamy is practised among them, but one wife is superior to the rest; they marry very young; the Indians of the same country have a plurality of wives, but each must have a separate hut; if the husband makes a present to one, he must make one of equal value to each of the others, and he must spend his time with them equally, week by week.

In Venezuela, among the native tribes, marriage is frequently dispensed with altogether, and cohabitation takes place for a temporary period, or permanently, as the sentiments of the man may incline. This is the case even among the Christianized people, but no blame can be attached to them, poor as they are; for the priests, grasping everywhere, charge such high fees, that marriage is a privilege of the rich.

The same characteristics prevail all over South America, in Chili, Peru, Mexico, and among the Araucanian tribes: the men idle, the women labour; and the national idea is, that one sex is born to command, the other to obey. The Araucanians carry this principle to excess, and do not allow their wives to eat until they are satisfied. When a man desires to have a girl as his wife, he proposes for her to the father; if the father consent, the girl, without being informed of the bargain, is sent out on some pretended errand, when she is seized by her purchaser and carried home to his tent or hut. There a feast is prepared; their friends assemble; her price is paid in horses, cattle, or money, and the ceremony is concluded by a debauch. Immorality among them is rather secret than recognised; in Peru it is affirmed that, among the native Indians, instances of infidelity between man and wife are very rare, for where polygamy is sanctioned and regulated by law, it is by no means inconsistent with chastity.

In New Andalusia the men and women go all but naked, wearing only slight girdles, and appearing strangers to the sentiment of decency. The condition of the female sex is that of privation and labour; yet, though overwhelmed with toil, they appear happier, because naturally more buoyant of heart than the squaws of North America. Even among the Indians on the banks of the Xingu, where the lordly husband lies all day in a hammock, and requires literally to be fed by his faithful wife, the women sing, dance, and seem to enjoy their lives most heartily. So, throughout the whole region, humiliation and slavery form their lot, but their spirit yields willingly to the yoke, which consequently does not pain them.

The regular prostitute class of South America belongs to the half-civilized communities, and will be noticed in our reference to them *.

Of Prostitution in the Cities of South America.

When we visit the semi-civilized communities of South America, instead of the barbarian tribes still running wild in its deserts of forest, the state of morals we discover presents a contrast by no means favourable to the half-educated States, where a hybrid compromise seems to have been made between refinement and barbarism. The general characteristic of South-American society is profligacy. Almost every city on that continent is demoralized and debauched; Brazil, Mexico, Peru, Chili, all present features very similar, and differing only in the inferior details. Professional prostitutes, indiscriminate in their companionship, form only a small part of the system. Immorality takes many other forms. This, however, we learn only from the general terms in which traveller after traveller has described those regions, especially the cities. Absolute information we have none, except with respect to the station occupied by women, and their moral demeanour in society. Statistics are entirely wanting. All writers seem by mutual consent to have avoided our subject, and left us to conjecture the extent and character of prostitution in Mexico, Rio Janeiro, Lima, and the various other cities of South America.

In Mexico, the women of the upper or idle classes are described as elegant, polished, and fascinating, perfectly easy in society, and attached above all things to the gaieties of life. Their morals appear to be similar to those of the female sex in the older cities of Spain—that is, there are many profligates among them; but a large number are well-conducted, virtuous women, not very timid in society, but not immodest. Among the lower classes the average of Spain may also be adopted—if we may ground an opinion on the vague accounts we receive from travellers.

In Lima, society is far more profligate. The women are superior to the men in little more than affection for their children; in other respects their general conduct is loose. They are devoured with that passion for intrigue—not amounting in many cases to actual adultery—which has been a famous trait in the manners of that country in Europe whence South America has derived all its impress of civilization. One remark which is true of Lima, applies also to the other cities. The veil, which in some countries is worn as the guard of virtue, is here the screen of vice. It is inviolable. The woman so draped may pass her own husband unrecognised, so that she can play truant as she pleases. Two or three females of good station often pay visits at the houses of strange men, without being known. Men sometimes take up with their own wives in the streets, or at some place of public entertainment, or on the alameda, or city promenade, without being aware who their companions are.

The state of manners indicated by frequent allusions to these facts is far from pure. We have also a few other glimpses into the society of Mexico and Lima. In the former there were, in 1842, 491 persons —312 men, and 179 women—committed to prison for "prostitution, adultery, bigamy, sodomy, and incest;" besides 65 men, and 21 women, for "rape and incontinence." So far for the capital of Mexico.

* Short and general as this sketch is, the facts it contains, or is based upon, are drawn from Dunlop's Travels in Central America; Captain Basil Hall's Journal; King's Twenty-Four Years in the Argentine Republic; Robertson's Letters on Paraguay; Robertson's Letters on South America; Stephenson's Incident of Travel in Central America; Norman's Rambles in Yucatan; Waterton's Wanderings in South America; Southey's History of Brazil; Young's Residence on the Mosquito Shore; Gardiner's Travels in Brazil; Hawkshaw's Reminiscences; Stephenson's Historical and Descriptive Narrative; Humboldt's Personal Narrative; Prince Adalbert's Travels; Macgregor's Progress of America.

In Lima, the chief city of Peru, the number of illegitimate children annually born is about 860; and of new-born infants exposed and found dead, 460. Two-thirds of the former, and four-fifths of the latter, belong to the coloured population—which is, indeed, in a proportionate majority. A dead child is picked up without any sensation being excited among the inhabitants of the locality in which it is found. Frequently it is cast away unburied. Ischudi has seen these little carcasses dragged about by vultures, in the public streets.

The white creoles are noted for sensuality, as well as a brutal want of sentiment towards their offspring. The dances in which they indulge are some of them of indescribable obscenity, and the whole population is addicted to demoralizing pleasures. In Lima, however, though delicate modest women are rare, actual adultery is not often committed by that sex. The men seem to obey the exhortation of Cato, who encouraged prostitutes, while he abhorred unfaithful wives—" Courage, my friends; go and see the girls, but do not corrupt the married women." Concubinage is more common, or rather, perhaps, more public than in Europe, and the father is usually very fond and careful of his natural children. Where marriage is contracted, it is, all over the Continent, fulfilled at an early age. In Brazil the neglect of this institution and the profligate intercourse of the sexes have diminished the population to an immense extent. In Rio Janeiro, however, we are told that the manners of the people have much improved since they have become more republican in their manners and ideas. The women there are shy and retired, but ignorance and awkwardness more than modesty may be assigned as the cause. While slavery was a public institution, which the government desired to abolish, the only restriction in the intercourse of the sexes was among the slaves. Procreation among them was as far as possible prevented; the women and the men in Janeiro were locked up at night in separate apartments, and carefully watched during the day.

In Chili, also, a reform of manners has commenced since the reduction of the military power, which is proverbially demoralizing. The higher classes of females have a character for modesty and virtue, but the men generally indulge themselves in vicious pleasures to a very considerable extent. It is, perhaps, in Brazil that society is most corrupt, for there the common decencies of life are, among the inferior orders, grossly disregarded. Matheson, the traveller, slept in the same room with a young married couple; girls are sold as concubines, and children are hired out by their mothers to prostitution. The youth of that sex bathe, while very young, entirely naked, and afterwards with scarcely any clothing, before the public eye, so that altogether the manners of the people are wanting in decency.

Travellers agree in assigning as one chief cause of this general demoralization, the profligate conduct of the Roman Catholic clergy; their lives are, in many cases—and of course there are many exceptions also — exceedingly scandalous. Numbers of them, bound by their vows to celibacy, live with concubines, and are not even faithful or constant to them. Where the priests have such influence, and indulge in such practices, we may expect to find a low state of morals. That this is the case in the cities of the South America most travellers agree in declaring; but unfortunately their notices are only vague generalities, and we have no positive information as to the extent and character of prostitution in those cities[*].

Of Prostitution in the West Indies.

A very slight notice of the West Indies will suffice, until we arrive at that division of our inquiry which includes the half-civilized communities, and the colonial societies related to Great Britain. Of the barbarous race scarcely a vestige remains, and of the negro population a general view is all that is required, except with reference to the prostitution carried on under the encouragement of the European settlers, which we shall hereafter describe. When Columbus first visited the beautiful islands of the West Indian group, he found two classes of people inhabiting them—the savage and cannibal Caribs, who delighted in war, and preyed upon the weaker and more effeminate tribes; and the comparatively innocent and simple communities, whose unwarlike habits rendered them victims to their more powerful neighbours. The characteristics of these distinct populations were strongly illustrated in their

[*] Macgregor's Progress of America; Kidder's Residence in Brazil; Walpole's Four Years in the Pacific; Ruschenberger's Three Years in the Pacific; Rovings in the Pacific, by a Merchant; Mayer's Mexico as it is; Matheson's Travels in Brazil; Wilkes's Exploring Expedition; Caldcleugh's Travels in South America; Robertson's Letters on South America.

treatment of women. The mild and peaceful islanders admitted the female sex to a participation in the delights and enjoyments of life, allowed their women to mingle with them in the dance, to inherit power, to wear what ornaments they fancied; and shared, indeed, with them all the opportunities of happiness which belonged to their savage condition. Among the cannibal Caribs, on the other hand, a different fashion prevailed. The handsomest and youngest of female captives taken in war were preserved as slaves and companions, while their other prisoners were devoured. The lot of these exiles, however, was little superior to that of the Carib women themselves. The nation was low and barbarous, and accordingly treated its women with harshness and indignity. Proud of their superior power and courage, the men looked down on the females as on an inferior sex, whose degradation was natural and just. Although a wife was awarded as the prize of valour, she was regarded as property acquired. She was her husband's slave. All the drudgery of his habitation fell on her. She bore his implements for war or for the chase. She carried home the game he had killed; and never sat down to a meal with him, or even dared to eat in his presence. She approached him with abject humility, and if she ever complained of ill usage, it was at the peril of her life. Nevertheless, the child born of this slave was loved and tended with wonderful care. This description, however, must apply to the weaker race of women, not to those Amazons described by Columbus, who, well-trained to war, rivalled in power of muscle and vigour of limb the bull-stranglers of Sparta.

These, however—the original inhabitants of the West-Indian Islands—have disappeared, and been succeeded by another race or compound of races, among which the Negroes only claim our notice at present. Among the blacks of Antigua, as an example of the rest, immorality is a characteristic which may be traced to the institution of slavery. Infanticide is frequently practised by them, especially since the Emancipation Act was passed. The reason of this circumstance, which at first seems strange, is very clear. Under the institution of slavery, negroes were not allowed to marry, or, at least, their marriages were never held as binding before the law. They therefore cohabited, and their unions lasted usually only so long as the caprice of affection, or the heat of a criminal appetite existed. Women, therefore, continually had five, six, seven, eight, or nine children by various fathers, and no disgrace was attached to the fact. A new system was introduced by the abolition of the slave system. The sentiments of shame and modesty have been cultivated in their minds; and the idea of female virtue has at least been awakened, so that they often seek to escape the consequences of an illicit amour by destroying the offspring.

One of the demoralizing effects of slavery was the encouragement of a species of concubinage. Rewards, indeed, were held out by some masters to such of the negroes as lived faithfully with a single partner; but the prevalence of vice was all but universal. A permanent engagement between a man and a woman was seldom formed. Two females frequently lived with one man, and of these one was considered his wife and the other his mistress.

When the negroes were emancipated, in 1834, many of them were anxious to be legally married. Numbers had been already united in wedlock by the missionary preachers; yet, though complete in its character, and regarded as a sacred tie, this act was not held as binding by the law, and many of the emancipated negroes, putting away the partners of their compulsory servitude, took new companions to their homes.

The offence of bigamy was not uncommon among them, and still continues to be so. It is prohibited under a severe enactment, but many devices are adopted to elude the law. Concubinage is less openly practised than formerly, but the tie of marriage is by no means generally respected. Chastity is indifferently regarded; and where the men do not prize it in women, women will be at little pains to preserve it for the men. Women are sometimes married who have been living in concubinage with several persons, and become the mothers of numerous children.

The condition of the free female negroes is by no means so degraded as in the original country of the blacks. Women enjoy an independent existence, and live as they please, though many of them labour. Their character is not distinguished by morality. Decency was entirely obliterated from their ideas, and they are only beginning to recover it. Women who were daily stripped and exposed to receive a whipping from the hands of men, could not be expected long to retain the sense of feminine shame; and this process, acting upon one generation after another, has left its impress on the character of the negro population. Human nature, also, was outraged by the gross tyranny of the planters. The intercourse of the sexes was regulated, not with a view to the morals of the negroes, but to the propagation of the species. They were coupled like beasts, to increase the number of slaves on the estate. In consequence of this the degradation of the negro population was so complete that, after it was emancipated, a woman considered it more honourable to become the mistress of a white, than the wife of a black man. In all the islands, indeed, this vile system was carried on. In St. Lucia, however, the intercourse was almost unrestrained, and consequently became in a degree promiscuous; for moral law there was none. The St. Lucia negro, in fact, is, even at this day, averse to matrimony, and inclined to support concubines, to none of whom is he faithful, even for an interval of time. Yet he is thoroughly attached to his children. It has been observed, that if any improvement in the morality of the island has taken place, it is more in the tone than in the temper, in the appearance than in the reality. Infanticide is never practised, or only as a rare and secret crime. It is prevented, however, not by moral restraint, but by the motherly feelings of the women—by the absence of reproach on bastardy, and the facility for rearing children.

In Santa Cruz the same low condition of manners is observable in the negro population; though in Jamaica the negroes are generally married, and are, on the whole, faithful to the engagement. This, however, is the result of the Emancipation Act. Previously to that mighty social reform, marriage, or a connubial contract of any kind, was rare; and the intercourse of the sexes was loose, profligate, and lewd. The men lived either with several concubines at once, or replaced one by another, as their inclination prompted. When the missionaries endeavoured to change this state of things, any couples which submitted to their teaching were sure to be ridiculed and jeered by the servile and demoralized populace. When slavery was abolished, so far had the corruption of manners proceeded, that numbers of the women, in the delirium of their new liberty, abandoned themselves to their vicious appetites, and became common prostitutes.

The example of Europeans has not by any means displayed to the negroes any instruction in morality; on the contrary, it has, to a great extent, encouraged their vices. This we shall show in a future division of the subject. We therefore leave at present the other islands which form the plantation colonies of England and Spain: we shall hereafter visit the native community which has recently made itself ridiculous by enacting the forms of an empire—we allude to Hayti, or St. Domingo. The brief notice we have given is intended to apply to the rude black population, but not in respect of its relation to the white communities *.

OF PROSTITUTION IN JAVA.

In the island of Java, which is perhaps the most fertile and beautiful country in the world, a curious system of manners now prevails. Hindoos have been succeeded by Mohammedans, and these by Dutch: each of the conquering races has impressed some characteristic trait on the population, and, unfortunately, the stamp of vice is more easily set than any other. The character and condition of the female sex in Java indicate the whole state of manners there. The men are somewhat cold towards the women, a fact which some learned Theban has ascribed to their feeding more on vegetable than on animal substances, but they are neither cruel nor negligent towards them. The institution of marriage is universally known, if not universally practised or generally respected. The lot of women may be described as peculiarly fortunate; in general they are not ill-used at all, and when, as among some of the more opulent, they are secluded, they are rather withdrawn from the indiscriminate gaze of the people, than shut up in lonely secrecy, for they are by no means watched with that exaggerated jealousy which in some parts of the East renders the husband a continual spy on the actions of his wife. Though the man pays a price for his bride, he does not therefore disdain or abuse her.

The condition of the sex in Java is, indeed, an exception to the habitual custom of Asiatics. The women eat with the men, associate with them in all the offices and pleasures of life, and live on terms of mutual equality.

* Capadose's Sixteen Years in the West Indies; Antigua and the Antiguans; Breen's Historical Account of St. Lucia; Gurney's Winter in the West Indies; Bidwell's West Indies as they Are; Stewart's State of Jamaica; Lloyd's Letters from the West Indies; Bayley's Four Years' Residence; Southey's History of the West Indies; Washington Irving's Life and Voyages of Columbus; Baird's Impressions of the West Indies, &c.

Many queens have, in different States, occupied the throne. The sex is nowhere in the island, as a rule, treated with coarseness, violence, or neglect. They are industrious, and hard-working, but they labour more through desire of praise than through fear of chastisement, and are admitted to the performance of many honourable tasks. Among the wealthier classes men sometimes act tyrannically in their households; but this must be taken as the characteristic not of the race, but of individuals. Those who seclude their wives do so only from the common eye; English gentlemen have often been introduced into the most private chambers of the harem, while the wives and daughters of the greatest chiefs have appeared at the entertainments given by the European residents in Batavia, Sumarang, and other cities, where they conduct themselves usually with modesty and good grace.

Polygamy and concubinage are tolerated, that is, they are practised among the nobility of Java, who do not allow public opinion to interfere with the gratification of their desires; both of these customs are looked upon, however, rather as vicious luxuries, than as established social institutions; yet, however limited their extent, they never fail to degrade the position and to vitiate the character of the female sex. Some circumstances in the feelings of the people prevent either practice from being generally adopted, and the evil is thus, in its moral influence, mitigated. The first wife is always mistress of the household, and the others are little more than her handmaids, who contribute to her husband's gratification, but never share his rank or his wealth. No man of station will give his daughter as a second or third wife, unless to a chief of far higher nobility than himself; the inferior wives or concubines are therefore of an inferior class. Thus the artificial distinctions of classes vitiate the public morals, for a woman considers it dishonourable, not to prostitute herself, but to prostitute herself to a poor man of humble birth.

When we say that polygamy and concubinage are not general in Java, the reader must by no means infer a high state of manners to exist there. On the contrary, Java is the most immoral country in insular Asia. The woman who would be ashamed to become the second wife of a chief might not be ashamed to commit adultery with him; in general terms, both sexes are extremely profligate and depraved, though the poets and historians of the island boast of chastity as the distinguishing ornament of their women; because a married female shrieks when a strange man attempts to kiss her before her attendants and a large mixed company, they hold up their sex in Java as the standard of feminine purity and virtue.

In most islands of the Indian Archipelago, divorces are not easy to be obtained; but in Java the total separation of married people may be procured with the utmost freedom and facility. It is a privilege in which the women indulge themselves to a most wanton degree, and often so much as to fall little short of prostitution. A wife may turn away her husband by paying him a certain sum of money; he is not, indeed, absolutely bound to accept this, but usually does so, in conformity with the established opinion of society, that it is disreputable to live with a woman on such terms. Women often change their partners three or four times before they are thirty years of age; some have been seen boasting of a twelfth husband. In Java the means of subsistence abound, and are easy to be procured as well by females as by men; one sex is, therefore, in a great measure, independent of the other; women find no difficulty in living without husbands. They are not, consequently, forced to remain in a state of bondage through fear of being drifted destitute upon the world; but, unfortunately for the theories of our new female reformers, the sex in Java, though thus enfranchised, is proverbially dissolute and libertine.

This, nevertheless, in reality is no argument for those who attempt to show that the female sex, enjoying perfect liberty, makes use of its freedom to indulge in vicious pleasures. The women of Java are dissolute, not because they are free of control, but because the whole society of the island is profligate. Among the wealthier classes, especially, the utmost immorality prevails with respect to the intercourse of the sexes. In the great native towns the population is debauched to the last degree. Intrigues among the married women continually occur; and females of high rank have intercourse with paramours, to the knowledge, and almost before the faces, of their husbands. The men are tame and servile, often not daring to revenge their honour or assert the conjugal right, and they are by no means inspired with that fiery spirit of jealousy which among many Asiatics renders a wife sacred from all but her husband's eye. Females of respectable rank are often the subject of conversation. An inquiry after a man's family is held by no means insulting, but rather as a conventional act of courtesy.

Flagrant instances of the loose character of Javan manners have come to the notice of travellers. Before the island was absolutely conquered by the Dutch, one of its great princes, being desirous of purchasing the favour of the people, gave many public feasts and entertainments, at which the wives and daughters of the chiefs attended. He seduced one of his guests, a married woman, and was in the habit of passing the night with her, while her husband was engaged with his duty on the public guard. One morning, by chance, the chief returned home earlier than usual, and detected them together. He had, however, discovered the rank of the paramour, and discreetly coughed, that the prince might have an opportunity to escape. He then went into the chamber, and severely flogged his guilty wife. She fled, and complained to the king of the treatment she had received. He being in the critical position of making good his claim to a crown, dared not exercise the usual prerogative of a throne; but called for the man he had injured, made him many rich gifts, and offered him, as compensation, the handsomest woman in his own household. The husband accepted the peace-offerings, and was content to take back his adulterous wife. The relation of a subject to his prince must, at least when developed in this manner, be most unnatural.

Women in Java are usually married very young, though not before the age of puberty, which is speedily reached. The reason assigned by writers for this haste is, that their chastity is no longer safe after they have reached womanhood. Men wait for two or three years after that period, during which they may indulge in unbounded profligacy. At eighteen or twenty a girl is looked upon as verging towards the wane of life, and becomes a suspected character. No age, however, excludes a woman from the chance of a match; but scarcely any are unmarried after 22. Widows at 50 often procure husbands; for men at that period of life usually choose wives equal in years to themselves, and sometimes older.

The preliminary arrangements are made by the parents on both sides; for no intercourse could previously take place between the young people themselves without being, and often justly, the occasion of scandal. They are looked upon, as the natives themselves express it, as mere puppets in the performance. There are three kinds of connection. The first is when the rank of the parties is equal, or when the man is superior to the woman. The second is when the bride is above her husband, who is taken into the house, and adopted into the family, by his father-in-law. The third is a species of concubinage, without any rites whatever, and confirmed by the simple fact of recognised cohabitation. In such cases, as no formality is required to conclude, so none is necessary to dissolve the contract, which is, therefore, no more than a species of prostitution, for the changes of companions are extremely frequent.

In the other two, the ceremonies are similar. The young people are, in all cases, betrothed for a longer or a shorter period before their union—from one month to several years. The father of the youth, having made for his son what he considers a suitable choice, proceeds to the parents of the girl, and proposes for an alliance. If they accept the suit, a betrothal is ratified by some trifling present to the bride. Visits are made, that the intended nuptials may be publicly known. At the third stage in the progress of the transaction the price is arranged, and varies according to the rank and circumstances of the families. Sometimes it is plainly called the *purchase money;* sometimes the act of sale is covered by a more delicate term—*the deposit*. It is usually considered, however, as a settlement or provision for the bride.

The only Mohammedan feature in the whole ceremony is the exchange of vows in a mosque. This is followed by many ritual observances, more of etiquette than religion, and great parade is affected. At length the married people eat rice from one vessel, to typify their common fortune; but in some places the bride washes her husband's feet, as an acknowledgment of her subjection to him, or else he treads upon a raw egg, and she wipes his foot.

Though, as we have said, polygamy and concubinage are not generally practised, partly because too expensive, partly from a feeling against them—some of the rich chiefs indulge in them to an extravagant degree, and glory in a train of 60 children. The wives, however, as already noticed, can easily release themselves when their married state is deteriorated into real or fancied bondage. The fact of their early marriage, without knowing their future husband, or consenting to the union, causes a great number of divorces. A widow may marry again after three months and ten days have elapsed since her husband's death.

Though the intercourse of the sexes is so free that vicious inclinations may be indulged without difficulty or peril, the Javans support a large class of women—prostitutes by profession. Adultery is not considered a very heinous crime, but rather an offence against the husband's property and honour, yet it is attended sometimes with danger, and often with disagreeable results. The vocation of the trading prostitute is not, therefore, taken away. She unites in Java, as in India, the profession of a dancer with her infamous calling.

There is a large class of these dancers in the island. The people are passionately fond of this amusement, but no respectable woman will join in it. The sultans, indeed, used to have some of their most beautiful concubines trained to dance, and they were privileged in the performance of certain figures; but, otherwise, all its professors are prostitutes. Nevertheless, a Javan chief of high rank is not ashamed to be seen before a large mixed assembly tripping with one of these women.

The dancers may be found in all parts of Java, but chiefly in the north-west, towards the capital. They figure at most of the public and private entertainments. Their conduct is so dissolute that the words dancer and prostitute are, in the Javan language, synonymous; yet, on account of the wealth they often amass, petty chiefs occasionally marry them. In such cases they usually, after a few years, become tired of their quiet secluded life, divorce their husbands, and resume their old calling. The dress in which they appear to dance is very immodest, exposing almost the whole bosom, and the attitudes they assume are licentious in a high degree. Nevertheless, they seldom descend to the obscene and degrading postures practised by some of the Bayaderes in India.

The Europeans in Java have not certainly, up to a late period, at least, set to their native subjects an example of pure manners. The Dutch merchant had usually a Javan female at the head of his household, who served him as a mistress as well. Indeed, the marriage ceremony is seldom insisted on by the women; while, among the lower classes, simple cohabitation is the usual method in which the sexes are related. Yet they are by no means so gross and sensual as the wealthier sort of people. Altogether, however, the island is remarkable for the profligacy of its inhabitants. In every city prostitutes abound; and about the roads in their vicinity women may be seen straying, ready for hire. They mostly, as we have said, assume also the profession of dancers, and this, in a manner, covers the profligacy of those who employ them at their houses*.

Of Prostitution in Sumatra.

THE population of this extensive island is divided into several tribes, slightly differing in their manners and modes of life. The Rejangs, who may be supposed to represent its original habits, are still rude barbarians. With them, as with many people of the East, the scrupulous attention to external show is by no means accompanied by a similar spirit within. They drape their women from chin to foot, and dread lest a virgin should expose any part of her person; yet modesty is not at all a characteristic of the dwellers in villages and towns, to whom this description refers. Those who live in the rural communities, and are more easy in their costume, distinguish themselves by their decency and decorum. In this is exhibited a curious fact, which may be discovered in many parts of the world.

The civilization, if such it may be called, of Sumatra, is of a peculiar character. Its people are in that stage of their progress when great importance is ascribed to the multiplied formulas of etiquette. Ritual is with them more essential than principle—of which, indeed, they know little. It is wonderful to examine the intricate details of the Sumatran marriage contract. Nearly all the litigation in the country springs from that perplexing cause. Men in a barbarous state appear to be under the influence of some law which forces them into extremes. They must be at one pole or another. Either they dispense altogether with ceremonial usages, and satisfy themselves with obeying the simple dictates of nature, under plain rules for their own convenience, or they divide the sexes by a maze of convention, which prescribes a form for the most trivial occasions of life. True refinement appears to be in the medium; but this is a question still to be resolved. In some districts of Sumatra, Europeans, wearied with the endless legal quarrels arising from these complicated transactions, have prevailed on the people to simplify their code of marriage, and the result has proved beneficial.

* Raffles's History of Java; Crawfurd's Indian Archipelago; Stavorinus's Voyages; Earl's Eastern Seas, &c.

Some have supposed that the system of procuring wives by purchase, which renders marriage difficult to the poor, has retarded the growth of population. Others, however, assert, and with much appearance of reason, that in Sumatra at least the contrary is true. Children being considered as property, and daughters being especially valuable for the price they command, powerful incentives to matrimony exist. The purchase-money obtained for the girls supplies wives for the sons, and in few islands are instances of celibacy more rare. It is certain, however, that the fostering, or rendering obligatory, thrifty habits on the young, has a tendency to check population, though it may be only so far as to keep it on a level with the means of subsistence. Various European countries illustrate that truth. In Sumatra, also, we have a wealthy region thinly and badly peopled; but misgovernment, war, and barbarism may be assigned as the chief causes. Besides, it is said the women are naturally unprolific; that they cease to bear children at an early age; that ignorance of the medical art causes thousands to perish of endemic complaints.

There are three modes of forming a marriage contract. The first is that, when one man pays to another a certain sum of money in exchange for his daughter, who becomes a virtual slave. There is usually, however, a certain amount — about five dollars—held back, and, so long as this remains unpaid, friendship is supposed to exist between the families, and the girl's parents have a right to complain if she be ill-treated. If the husband wound her he is liable to a fine, and in other ways his absolute command is curtailed. When, however, on the occasion of a violent quarrel, the sum is paid, the bond of relationship is broken, and the woman is entirely in her master's power. The regulations in regard to money are numerous and intricate; but need not be explained in detail. They give occasion, however, as we have said, to endless law-suits, which are bequeathed by one generation to another.

In other cases the marriage contract is an affair of barter. One virgin is given for another, and a man who has not one of his own sometimes borrows a girl, engaging to replace or pay for her when required. A man having a son and a daughter, may give the latter in exchange for a wife to the former. A brother may barter his sister for a wife, or procure a cousin instead. If, however, she be under age, a certain allowance is made until she becomes marriageable.

Another method is practised when a parent desires to get rid of a daughter suffering from some infirmity or defect. He sells her altogether without any reserve, and she has fewer privileges than other classes of wives.

Sometimes a girl evades these laws by an elopement, and a match is formed upon mutual affection. If the fugitive couple are overtaken on the road, they may be separated; but when once they have taken sanctuary, and the man declares his willingness to comply with all the necessary forms, his wife is safely secured to him.

Many persons have assigned to whole nations, in various parts of the world, a Jewish origin, partly because the custom prevails with them of a man marrying his brother's widow. The Sumatrans, in this case, belong to them also, for the same rule is enforced by them; but if there be no brother surviving, the woman is taken by her husband's nearest male relation—the father excepted. If any of her purchase-money remains unpaid, her new master is answerable for it.

When, under this system, adultery is committed—which is not frequently the case—the husband usually passes it over, or inflicts revenge with his own hand. It is seldom such an offence is brought before the law. When a man desires to divorce his wife thus married to him, he may claim back her purchase-money, with the exception of twenty-five dollars, as she is supposed, by cohabitation with him, to have diminished in value to that amount. If, having taken a woman, he be unable to pay the whole price, though repeatedly dunned for it, the girl's parents may sue for a divorce, but they must restore all they have received. The old ceremony consisted merely in cutting a rattan cane in two, in the presence of the disunited couple, their friends, and the chiefs of the province. The woman is expected to take to her husband's house effects to the value of ten dollars. If she take more, he is chargeable to the amount. Thus the whole transaction is carried on upon mercenary grounds.

The second kind of marriage, is when a virgin's father chooses for her husband some young man whom he adopts into his family, making a feast on the occasion and receiving what we may term a premium of twenty dollars. The young man is thenceforward a property in his father-in-law's family. They are answerable for the debts he may incur; but all he has and all he earns belong to them; he is liable to be divorced when they please, and to be turned away destitute. Under certain circumstances he may redeem himself from this bondage, but pecuniary considerations are so entangled with the whole agreement that infinite confusion is the result. Several generations are sometimes bound in this manner before the contract can be legally broken by the fulfilment of all the required conditions.

The Malays of Sumalda have generally adopted the third kind of marriage, which is called *the free*. It is a more honourable compact, in which the families approach each other on the natural level of equality. A small sum is paid to the girl's parents, usually about twelve dollars, and an agreement is drawn up, that all property shall be common between husband and wife, and that, when divorce takes place by mutual consent, all shall be fairly divided. If the man only presses a separation, he gives half his effects, and loses the twelve dollars; if the woman, she then loses her right to any but her female paraphernalia. This description of contract, which is productive of most just dealing and felicity, has been adopted in many parts of the island.

The actual ceremony of marriage, though fenced about with so many ceremonial observances, is extremely simple. An entertainment is given, the couple join their hands, and some one pronounces them man and wife.

Where the female sex is a material for sale, little of what we term courtship can be expected. The manners of the country are opposed to it; strict separation is enforced between the youth of different sexes; and when a man pays the full price for a bride, he considers himself entitled to her without any manner of persuasion or solicitation to herself. Nevertheless, traces of gallantry—using that word in its proper, not its ridiculous sense—may be observed in the manners of the people. A degree of respect is shown to women, which may be favourably contrasted with the conduct of some polished nations. On the few occasions on which the young people meet, such as festivals and public gatherings in the village hall, they dance and sing, and behave with much delicacy; mutual attachments often spring out of such association, and the parents frequently promote the desire of union thus arising. In most countries, indeed, the barbarism of the law is mitigated in its influence by the universal operation of the natural human sentiments; it is no less true than strange, that mankind are usually better, not only than their rulers, but than their laws. The festivals are enlivened by dances and songs; the dances have been described as licentious and grotesque, but Marsden, the philosophical historian of Sumalda, only remarks that the figures displayed at English balls are often more immodest and absurd. The songs are usually extempore, and always turn on the subject of love.

The existence or flourishing of any sentiment among a people with whom marriage is a commercial transaction, and who allow a plurality of wives, may be considered incredible; but as, in the first instance, Nature often asserts herself and the law is accommodated to her will, so, in the second, the nature of things prevents any general extension of the practice. Polygamy is permitted; but only a few chiefs have more than one companion. The general indigence of the people is one cause of this, for the perpetual weight of necessity is more powerful than the irregular impulse of animal passion. To be a second wife is also considered by many below the dignity of a reputable person. A man sometimes prefers a divorce for his daughter when he hears that her husband is about to take another wife. In the contract which stipulates for a division of property, polygamy is impossible, for this obvious reason, that the wife must have half the husband's effects, which more than one, of course, could not do. The origin of polygamy in Sumalda and other parts of Asia has been traced by various ingenious writers to different causes; but being, as it is, the indulgence which is a privilege of wealth, it appears to have grown up with the whole system of manners; no natural reason seems to exist for it. The proportion of the sexes is nearly equal, and all the theories grounded on a different assumption fall to pieces. Wherever polygamy exists, women are purchased, and where they are thus viewed as property, wealthy men will surely distinguish themselves from their neighbours by a plurality of wives; and this happens in Rajpooratan, where the women are far less numerous than the men, as well as in other countries where they out-number them to an equal extent.

In the country parts of Sumatra, chastity, says Marsden, exists more than among any other people with which he was acquainted. The same characteristic appears to distinguish them at the present day. Interest, as well as decency, renders the parents anxious to preserve the virtue of their daughters. The price of a virgin is so far above that of a woman who has been defiled, that the girls are jealously watched, lest their value deteriorate in this respect. But the truth of the Oriental idea is sometimes illustrated—that girls should marry as soon as they are marriageable, or they soon cease to be chaste. In Sumatra they remain single for some time after that period, and occasionally lose their chastity in consequence. In such cases the seducer, if discovered, may be forced to marry the girl, and pay her price, or make good the diminution he has occasioned in her value.

Regular prostitution is little known, except in the towns. There, especially in the bazaars, women following that calling may be found mixed up with the concourse of sailors and others who support them. In the seaports especially, where the population is not only floating, but mixed from various nations, there is a great deal of profligacy, and troops of professional prostitutes ply the streets for hire. Europeans, however, who represent the general manners of the island from the experience of short visits to the maritime cities, convey a false impression of the people. The Sumatran is, as a rule, contented to marry and be faithful to his wife. This proceeds, however, it would seem, rather from some peculiar tone of temperament, than from any principles of morality; for their ideas on this subject are, at any rate, widely different from ours. Incest they hold as an offence; but except it occurs within the first degree it is regarded rather as an infraction of the conventional, than the natural law. It is sometimes punished by a fine; but sometimes also the marriage is confirmed, and the parties remain together.

The chiefs of the cannibal nations of Batta have sometimes several concubines. A man once stole a woman of this kind—the favourite of her master—and was punished by being cut to pieces, roasted, and devoured. Among the people of Bulu China, on the east coast, a man may have four wives, and as many concubines as possible. Some of the chiefs possess one of these companions in each town or village of their country. Adultery is punished by death to both criminals.

The general treatment of the sex in Sumatra is of an average character. They are not absolutely degraded, nor do they enjoy an elevated position. The poorer classes labour, and all are subject to the men; but on the whole they are far superior to Java, and, in a considerable degree, to many other Eastern countries*.

* Marsden's Sumatra; Anderson's Mission to the East Coast; Crawfurd's Indian Archipelago; Journal of the Indian Archipelago.

OF BORNEO.

THE splendid achievements in the cause of civilization which Sir James Brooke has performed, have directed an extraordinary attention to the immense island of Borneo. Like the rest of the Indian Archipelago, it is, nevertheless, little known to the English reader—no complete accounts having been yet published. Sir James Brooke, however, with Captain Keppel, Captain Mundy, Mr. Hugh Low, and others, have thrown a new light on the country, and enabled us to discern many striking features in the social system of the races which inhabit it. The uniformity of manners observable in Celebes does not exist in Borneo. The inhabitants of Borneo, for the most part, remain in an inferior stage of the barbarian state. There are, however, among them many varieties of the social law. Some are the purest savages, wandering unclothed in the depths of the forests, and subsisting alone on the spontaneous gifts of nature. Others cultivate the soil, dwell in comfortable villages, and traffic with their neighbours. The river communities are far more advanced than those who live far from the means of water-carriage; and the inhabitants of the maritime towns are more educated, and also more profligate, than any. They have been depraved by that bloody and destructive system of piracy, which was, until recently, the curse of the Archipelago; but when Sir James Brooke's policy has been maturely developed, we may expect to see vast ameliorations in their manners.

The state of morals among the Sea Dyaks, or dwellers on the coast, is low, even in comparison with the average of other Asiatic races. There is no social law to govern the intercourse of the youths of both sexes before marriage. Even the authority of parents is not recognised to any extent. The Dyak girl is supposed capable of selecting a husband for herself; and before she is betrothed to a man she may cohabit, without disgrace, with any other with whom she may please to associate. The women appear to make liberal use of this privilege. Loose as their conduct is, however, before marriage, they are subject afterwards to a more stringent code. As a man is only allowed one wife, he requires strict fidelity in her, and if she break faith with him, she is punished by a severe beating and a heavy fine. On his part, moreover, he must be continent, for the penalty is the same for either sex. Cases of adultery are not frequent in times of peace, though during war more licence

DYAK WOMAN—BORNEO.

[*From* Marryat's "*Indian Archipelago.*"]

is allowed. The Dyak women seldom engage in intrigues with Malays or other foreigners.

From their long intercourse with the Malays, who are all Mohammedans, the Dyaks might have been expected to borrow such of their customs as encourage the savage in the gratification of his animal appetites, and would enable him to live in lordly indolence on the labour of his wives. Monogamy, however, still prevails with all the tribes.

The ceremony of marriage—if such it can be called—is simple to the last degree with all except a few communities, who practise some particular rites. The consent of the woman is necessary to the match, which is made without the intervention of the parents, who, after the mutual willingness of the young people has been expressed, cannot refuse their sanction. The bride and bridegroom meet, a feast is given, and the transaction is concluded.

There are certain restrictions on the immoral intercourse of the young people, to which we have alluded. If a girl becomes pregnant, the father of her child must marry her. Such an occurrence often precedes a match. Men and women live with each other on trial, and if no signs of offspring appear, the acquaintance is discontinued. Constancy during such an intercourse is not rigidly required. Mr. Hugh Low was assured that, in some communities, the laxity of manners was carried so far, that when a chief was travelling from place to place, hospitality required that at every village he should be furnished with a girl as his companion while he rested. Such a practice is general among the Kyans who inhabit a large part of the interior of Borneo. The fear of not becoming the father of a family—a misfortune greatly dreaded by the Dyaks—is supposed to encourage the loose intercourse of the unmarried people, since, as we have said, a man always marries the woman by whom he has a child.

Among the Dyaks who dwell on the hills in the interior, a higher morality prevails. The licentious intercourse of the unmarried people is not permitted. The young and single men are obliged to sleep apart in a separate building, and the girls are carefully kept from them. Marriage is contracted at a very early age, and adultery is almost unknown. Polygamy is not allowed; but some of the chiefs indulge in a second wife or concubine—an infringement of the law which is held in great reprobation, though it cannot be prevented. The degrees of consanguinity within which marriage is prohibited extend beyond cousins. One man shocked the public feeling of his tribe by marrying his granddaughter —his wife and the girl's mother, his own child, being still alive. The people affirmed that ruin and darkness had covered the face of the sun ever since the day when that incestuous union took place. Nevertheless, as they adhere almost constantly to the practice of marrying within their own tribe, the whole commonwealth comes, in the course of time, to be united by distant ties of blood, which has been assigned as a cause for the cases of insanity not uncommon among them. This may be true, since it is a fact that many royal families, constrained to perpetual intermarriage, have dwindled into a race of imbeciles in consequence. The women put faith in medicines to render them fruitful; but they never resort to the custom of procuring abortion adopted by the Malay prostitutes on the coast. These women eat large quantities of honey, largely mixed with hot spices, which produces the desired result. It is said that among the people of the south numerous public prostitutes are to be found, though this is on the equivocal authority of a German missionary, whose testimony is much to be suspected. No word for prostitution appears to exist in the Dyak language. Among the Malays such women are numerous.

The Sibnouan females present a fair average of the manners prevailing with the various divisions of that singular race. Their women are not concealed, nor are they shy before strangers. They will bathe naked in the presence of men; yet many of the decencies of life are observed. Though the unmarried people sleep promiscuously in a common room, married couples have separate chambers. The labour of the household, with all the drudgery, is allotted to the females; they grind rice, carry burdens, fetch water, catch fish, and till the fields, but are far from occupying the degraded condition of the wives of the North-American Indians; their situation may, indeed, be compared to that of women in the humblest classes in England. They eat with the men, and take part in their concerns as well as their festivals. This is an agricultural and fishing tribe.

Among the Kayans a *naked woman* cannot under any circumstances be killed, or a woman with child.

Among the Mohammedan Malays, as we have said, there is more civilization and corruption of manners in another form. They are polygamists, indulge in concubines, encourage prostitutes, and sometimes treat their wives with great tyranny. An English physician lately received a message from one of the wives of a chief—celebrated for fostering privacy—desiring a secret interview with him at a secluded spot in the jungle. He went with the high belief that the woman was enamoured of his good looks. He met her, found her young and pretty, but with an air of firmness and dignity which showed that it was no frivolous purpose which had led her to take so dangerous a step. She complained of her miserable life, of the despotism under which she suffered, declared she would endure it no longer, and requested the doctor to furnish her with a small dose of arsenic to poison, not herself, but her husband. Of course he refused, and the poor creature went away sorely disappointed.

The rich Malays allow their wives to keep female slaves for their service. The position of these captives is, under any circumstances, unenviable; should, however, one of them, by her personal qualities, excite the jealousy of her mistress, her case is miserable, until she can procure another owner. Sometimes the slaves are used as concubines, when by law they become free, though they seldom avail themselves of their liberty, preferring to be supported by their old masters, while prostituting themselves to others. The wealthy chiefs spend large sums in the purchase of concubines. The marriage ceremony is performed according to the ritual of the Koran, but is often neglected.

The prostitutes who congregate in the seaport towns have not been particularly described. They appear to be divided into classes: those who cohabit temporarily with the Malays, are paid a certain price, and exchange their residence; those who prostitute themselves indiscriminately to all comers; and those who are supported by the sailors, and profligate Chinese, who invariably create such a class wherever they settle. Of their numbers we have no account, nor of their modes of life; but it is certain they exist in considerable numbers.*

* Brooke, Keppel, Mundy, Belcher, Low, &c.

PROSTITUTION AMONG THE SEMI-CIVILIZED NATIONS.

Introduction.

Surveying the social aspects of the globe, we discover an immense range occupied by races partially civilized, which connect the barbarian with the polished communities. Some of these, perhaps, are placed below European nations rather because they differ from, than because they are inferior to them.

The influence of every great religion is powerful in various divisions of the vast range. Buddha and Bramah have their millions of worshippers in China, India, and the intervening regions. The prophet is followed by whole nations in eastern Europe, Asia, and Africa. Christianity has numerous adherents on the plains of Syria, Palestine, and the countries of Asia Minor. An equal variety of institutions prevails among these half-educated races. British policy in India; paternal despotism in China; republican simplicity in Arabia, Celebes, and Afghanistan; religious tyranny in the empire of the Porte; and patriarchal freedom among the nomades of Asia Minor, exercise different influences on this mighty and mixed population. In some we find a singular purity of manners, as among the Bedouins of Arabia; with others, morals are more gross than among the worst savages; but in all there is a perceptible contrast between the civilized states of Europe on the one hand, and the barbarian countries of Africa, Australasia, and the Pacific on the other.

The position of the female sex among half-civilized races, as among all others, may be taken as a standard to measure their progress. It differs, in some remarkable particulars, from that occupied by women in purely savage or highly-civilized communities. In the one, where any regulations exist they are rude and coarse, and only obeyed where their action is constant, which it seldom is. In the other, men fear blame more than the law, and manners perform what legislation is unable to accomplish. In most of the countries of which we are now treating, government endeavours to rule with parental discipline the minutest concerns of life, to affix a penalty to every fault, to adjust with nicety the slightest relations of individuals with individuals, to guard morals by police and suppress profligacy by imperative decrees. So it is in China, so in Japan, and so in a less degree in the dominions of every Asiatic prince. In Egypt Mohammed Ali attempted, by one stroke of his pen, to blot out the stain of prostitution. He banished the old professors of that class, and new ones were created from the remainder of the population. In Persia a royal decree forbade prostitution, and men immediately prostituted the right of marriage to evade the law. In China the Emperors have, from time to time, fulminated proclamations against all profligate persons; but they have flung their invectives into the void, and no impression has been produced. The coarse and awkward efforts of a barbarian despot's will never produce any better result. The Draconic decree is promulgated and the offences it is intended to suppress continue to be perpetrated as before. A distinction must be drawn, however, between those communities in which severe laws are enacted to produce, and those in which they are inspired by, public morality. In the one case they are worthless, because they are in hostility to the prevailing system; in the other they are the signification, because they are the embodiment, of the national feeling. They may be symptoms, but they can never be causes, of virtuous manners.

The view of the half-civilized nations, which is here presented, includes sketches of India, of Afghanistan, Kashmir, the Hindu-Chinese races, China, Japan, Celebes, Ceylon, Persia, Egypt, the Barbary States, Syria, Palestine, Asia Minor, Arabia, and Turkey. In all of them polygamy exists, though to a very small extent in Ceylon. It will be seen that the popular ideas on this subject are somewhat exaggerated. Most persons unaccustomed to read or reflect, imagine that throughout the East all men have their harems filled with wives, who are beautiful prisoners, immured in perpetual seclusion, slaves to the will of their lord, and never allowed to move unless guarded by a fierce black eunuch, or a duenna still more dark and angry. It is left for those who are accustomed to peruse the accounts of veracious travellers, to know that polygamy, though allowed to almost all, is practically a privilege only of the rich, and not indulged in even by the majority of these. The general notions, also, of female seclusion are extravagant. Women in Turkey enjoy far more liberty than is usually imagined. So do they even in China, though very wealthy husbands, especially among the Hindus, shut up their wives and never allow a stranger's glance to fall upon their countenances. This excessive jealousy is not always disagreeable to the objects of it; indeed, in the harem where three or four wives are congregated, the youngest and most beautiful sometimes makes it her chief triumph over her mortified rivals, that she is watched, guarded, shaded even from the light, and immured beyond the sound of a man's voice, while they are far less religiously secluded. Thus the sex, influenced during ages by a peculiar system of manners, accommodates itself to them, invariably sinking or rising to the level assigned it by the civilization of the period.

Throughout the world the numerical disparity of the sexes is nowhere such as to induce the belief that polygamy is natural to certain countries. It is practised in many where the females are less numerous than the males, in consequence of infanticide. Everywhere, when extensively prevalent, it produces injurious results, diminishing the fecundity of women, and by no means preventing men from encouraging a class of professional prostitutes. There is, indeed, in this idea, something debasing to the female sex. That men should multiply their wives that they may not be induced to visit harlots, appears to degrade the institution of marriage, which was not intended for the satisfaction of sensual appetites, but for the continuation of the human species. Polygamy is opposed to increase, and thus appears unnatural; still more revolting to our ideas of civilization is the custom of polyandrism, or one wife with many husbands. It obtains in some regions of the Himalaya, among the Nairs of Malabar, and in the Cingalese kingdom of Kandy. Nowhere else do we find more than a trace of it, and it is singular to find a practice so utterly repugnant to the general sense of Orientals, prevailing close to the region in which men are most jealous and women most carefully guarded. In Hindustan some men will not divorce a wife whom they thoroughly dislike, because they will not allow her to be unveiled by a stranger; yet among the neighbouring Hindu-Chinese nations, a man will frequently prostitute his wife for gain. On the southern coast, and in Ceylon, eight men will live with one wife. This proves that institutions have no geographical distribution. Both kinds of polygamy are equally opposed to the natural increase of population.

Where nobler qualities distinguish the men of any race, we still find, as we ascend the scale of civilization, that women rise with them. In Afghanistan, in Celebes, and among the Bedouins of Arabia, the male sex is distinguished for its upright, dignified, and manly character. Chastity in women is prized, and because it is prized it is preserved. Where, on the contrary, the husband desires his wife may be faithful to him, not that she may be virtuous, but that he may not be robbed or wronged, it frequently occurs that she only keeps her vow until she has an opportunity to break it. On the whole, however, female chastity among the Hindus and Mohammedans is more general than from some popular accounts might be inferred. With the mixed races—hybrid in blood, manners, and religion—an inferior state of morality prevails.

With respect to actual prostitution the region which is most free from it is the desert country of Arabia. It flourishes most, perhaps, in India and China. The flower boats of the Pearl River, the temples of the Deccan, the kiosks of Barbary, the Ghawazee villages of Egypt, the dancing houses of Java, and the tea-gardens of Japan, were all originally consecrated to vice, which nowhere flourishes more rankly than in those countries where despotism has paralyzed the virtuous energies of men.

Almost everywhere the prostitute class, among Eastern nations, has addicted itself to other pursuits—to music and the dance—to inflame the lust which it designs itself to satisfy. In many countries also the prostitutes have been allied to the priesthood. Thus in India they have formed a sacred class; in the cities of Arabia they are encouraged by the Moolahs to frequent places of worship; elsewhere they have flourished under the auspices of government, which has placed them under the charge of inspectors and derived profit from their degradation. In such countries they carry on their profession more openly, and are more openly encouraged, than in others where their occupation is clandestine.

Some of the nations included in this division of the subject appear to have reached the last stage of their native civilization. Among these is China: her further progress will not be influenced by internal causes, but will be regulated by contact with a superior race. In India the process has already begun, and in the condition of women, and consequently, also, in their national character, the change is becoming apparent. Widow-burning is already a thing of the past; the blot of infanticide will soon be obliterated from the face of society; the prejudice which prevented the second marriage of women, and drove thousands to suicide or prostitution, is gradually yielding before reason; the barriers of caste are being broken down, and more natural relations restored to society. Women in India are the chief degradation to the sacred class of Brahmins, in whom were combined the fanaticism of idolatrous priests and the pride of nobles.

Thus the contact of English with Oriental civilization, gentle as it has been, is leading to the subjugation of the latter before the more humane and liberal principles of the former. But it is singular to find that much more difficulty is experienced in modifying the social institutions of half-educated, than in changing those of barbarous races. With the one they are based on habit, with the other on prejudice; and the pride of a little learning induces the one to cling to them, while the simplicity of the savage allows him easily to yield.

The sentiment of chastity is nowhere discovered pure except among very simple and unsophisticated, or very refined and polished nations. It is found in the Bedouin encampments of Arabia, it is found in the pastoral communities of Afghanistan, and it is found among the wandering shepherds of Asia Minor; but amid the barbaric millions of China, with their innumerable maxims of virtue, the true sentiment is very rare. So also is that of love, which belongs also to the infancy and to the maturity of nations, for in the intervening stages it becomes mingled with an alloy of interest, sensuality, or superstition.

Prostitution, however, belongs to all ages and to every nation. But it assumes various forms in the different classes of mankind: it is loose and scattered among the barbarous tribes not yet settled under the forms of regular society; it is systematized and acknowledged among the half-barbarous races; it is adopted as a sacred institution in regions where the object of the priesthood is, to enslave the souls of men through their senses; it is encouraged in States where the desire of government is to absorb the people in the pursuit of animal gratification, and thus distract their attention from public affairs; it is submitted to a strict, though awkward discipline in countries where the rulers desire to mimic the social code of civilized commonwealths; and as society progresses, though it becomes distinct and conspicuous, it exchanges the highway for the bye-street, the day for the night, withdraws from other classes of the people, and becomes a despised sisterhood, cut off from intercourse with the moral classes of women.

Various stages of this process may have been remarked in the view of the condition and character of women, and the extent and state of the prostitute system in barbarous countries. We now enter on the half-educated communities which occupy the greater part of the world's surface, and these will lead in the communities of Europe, to which they are linked, on the one hand

Of Celebes.

In a region so vast as the Indian Archipelago it would be useless to dwell separately upon every island, especially as many characteristics are common to most of them. We have taken Java and Sumatra as representing the Sunda group, and we shall take Celebes as the head of a family of isles, with Borneo as another. Incidental notices of any peculiarities in the lesser isles will suffice.

Celebes, in its political and social state, is far in advance of the other countries in insular Asia. It enjoys in many of its States a considerable degree of civilization. The idea of freedom, so rare among barbarous races, is recognised in its political system, and representative institutions have actually developed themselves into a republican form of government. Where such progress has been made in the art of civil polity, we may look with confidence for a superior social scheme, and this we actually find. It should be premised that the Indian Archipelago is peopled by two races—the brown, or Malay; and the black, or Ethiopian. The former is the more powerful, intelligent, and polished, and has therefore become the conquering race. It has subdued the Negro hordes of the various islands, and is now paramount in all the great native States. In Java, Sumatra, and Celebes, it has entirely displaced the original possessors of the soil, who dwell only in scattered communities, defended from annihilation by forests and hills, which serve in some degree to balance that native valour which has made the Malays an imperial nation, subdued in their turn by the more powerful race from Europe.

In the states of Celebes women are not excluded from their share in the public business of the commonwealth, though their influence is usually indirect. They rule their own households, give counsel to the men on all important occasions, and even, when the monarchy is elective, are frequently raised to the throne. They eat with their husbands, and from the same dish, only using the left side. They appear mixed with the other sex at public festivals, and, when intrusted with authority, preside over the councils, and are vigorous in the exercise of their prerogative. Nor is peace the only era of their reign. They have sometimes presented themselves in the field, and animated the warriors to battle by applauding the courageous and upbraiding the timid.

In the State of Wajo, which is, perhaps, the most advanced in the island, one check upon civilization exists, and that is the extravagant pride of birth. The spirit, if not the actual institution of caste, exists, and is productive of the usual evils attending an artificial division of classes. A woman of pure descent dare not mingle her blood with that of an inferior, though a man may ally himself with a girl of humbler station. The offspring of such a connection, however, carry with them an appellation denoting their imperfect parentage.

Polygamy is universally permitted among the Bugis of Celebes; but certain restrictions, unknown in other Mohammedan countries, attach to the privilege. Two wives seldom inhabit the same house, and for three or four to do so is an extremely rare circumstance. Usually each has a separate dwelling, and in this private establishment she generally supports herself, with occasional assistance from her husband. The men can easily procure a divorce, and when the consent is mutual nothing remains but to separate as quickly as possible. If the woman only, however, desire to be set free, she must produce some reasonable ground of complaint, for the mere neglect of conjugal duties is not considered a sufficient cause. Many years pass sometimes without any intercourse taking place between man and wife. Nevertheless, though many of them indulge in polygamy, concubinage, or the keeping of female slaves for sensual purposes, is rarely practised. Many of the rajahs, however, take women of inferior rank to be their companions until they marry a woman of equal birth, when their old partners are divorced.

In Wajo, the marriage state, though characterised by these extraordinary customs, is decently preserved, and more honourable than with any other Eastern nation. So equal, indeed, is the proportion of the sexes, that not only is the throne, or rather president's chair, given to them, but also the great offices of state. Four out of six of the great councillors are sometimes women. They ride about, transact business, and visit even foreigners as they please, and enjoy every advantage. Their manners are easy and self-possessed, though too listless and slow to be fascinating to an European. Their morals, as well as those of the men, are far superior to that of any other race in Eastern or Western Asia, and prostitution is all but unknown.

Far from modest, in the English sense of the term, they are yet very chaste; and, though they maintain little reserve in their conduct towards strangers, never exhibit the inclination to be indecent or licentious. Even the dancing girls, though of loose virtue, dress with the utmost modesty, but their performances are occasionally lascivious.

Throughout the beautiful and interesting island of Celebes the same state of things prevails, and wherever the women are most free, they are least licentious. The intercourse of the sexes is unrestrained; the youth meet without hindrance; and chastity is guarded more by the sense of honour and by the pride of virtue, than by the jealousy of husbands or the rigid surveillance of parents. On the whole, therefore, the condition of the sex in Celebes is elevated. That women are there perverted in some of their manners, and that they do not approach that exalted state which was accorded to them in the Attic states of Greece, is true, because the people are barbarians. It is necessary always, in considering the state and character of women in any country, to hold in view the state and character of the men also. We are to apply no unvarying standard to measure the condition of one sex, for it is only by viewing it relatively to the other that we can arrive at a sound conclusion. The Bugis of Celebes are among the most manly, enterprising, and virtuous nations of Asia; and their women are proportionably free, chaste, and happy*.

Of Prostitution in Persia.

In Persia the Oriental idea of the female sex is completely developed. Women are there the property of men and their enjoyment of life is circumscribed to suit the pleasure of their masters; among the wandering tribes, indeed, they go unveiled, and breathe the air of partial freedom; but among the fixed inhabitants of cities and villages, their lot is one of seclusion and servitude. Subservient as they are to the will and caprice of the supreme sex, the estimation in which they are held is extremely low. The lower classes consider them, indeed, valuable in proportion to the amount of household labour they perform; the higher classes look on them as the means of sensual gratification. We find, it is true, in Persian romance and poetry, eulogiums on the beauty of their women, and songs of devotion to them; but they are the objects of barter, and are consequently in a despised condition.

There is actually no station assigned to women in Persia; they are recognised only as ministers to the wants or pleasures of the male sex. They are what their husbands choose to make them. Instances occur where a favourite wife or concubine is ruler of the house, or a mother exercises strong influence over her son, but these are rare examples; women, in total seclusion, are submissive slaves. The wives of the Shah, especially, vegetate within the walls of a splendid prison; occasionally one of them is permitted to walk abroad, but then all must fly from the route she takes, and no one dare look upon her on pain of death. She is paraded in stately procession, and eunuchs run in front to clear the way, firing guns loaded with ball to frighten any bold adventurer who may be reckless enough to remain on the line of the cortege. This isolation of the sex pervades all the wealthier orders of Persian society; even brothers are not allowed to see their sisters after a certain age.

Polygamy is practised in Persia. The palace especially has a crowded harem; numbers of female officers and attendants wait on the Shah. The wives and concubines are arranged with the most rigid regard to the rules of precedence; none but those of the highest rank and most distinguished favour dare sit down in the presence of their royal lord; over all the rest the strictest discipline is preserved. The king is said sometimes to have a thousand women in his palace, and much skill is required to preserve decorum among them; some he has given away to his principal officers. The chief of them lives in splendour, wearing garments so thickly embroidered with pearls that they impede her movements; but the others are subject to much rigour, especially under the savage eunuchs whose favourite mode of chastising the female slaves is to strike them on the mouth with the heel of a slipper. However, large numbers of them lead a pleasant, while all enjoy an indolent life, lounging for hours in the warm bath, whence they emerge, with enervated frames, to spend an equal time in the coquetry of the toilette. All the arts which vanity can devise are exhausted to render their persons attractive to the Shah, whose favours are courted as much as his displeasure is feared. In the one case, the fortunate woman is elevated, for a brief period at least, to the very ideal of her hopes, while, in the other, she may be fastened in a sack and hurled from the top of a lofty tower.

* Brooke's Journals; Mundy; Keppel's Voyage of the Dido; Crawfurd's Archipelago.

The Persians generally believe themselves entitled to unlimited indulgence in the delights of the harem. Their religious law confines them to four wives, but they may have as many concubines or other female companions as they can support. The priests are expected to be the most chaste, but are usually the most licentious; it is remarked as an extraordinary circumstance of one celebrated spiritual leader, that it was affirmed that he never had connection with any other woman than his four legitimate wives.

A Persian is permitted, as well by the enactments of the law as by common usage, to take a female, not within the prohibited degrees of affinity, in three different ways: he may marry, he may purchase, or he may hire her. Persons are frequently betrothed during infancy; but the engagement is not considered binding unless contracted by both the actual parents. The girl, indeed, may, even under these circumstances, refuse her consent, but this privilege is rather nominal than real. If she resolutely refuse, she may be taken back to the recesses of her parent's harem, and there chastened until she choses to submit; and it is not long before she is whipped into compliance. The nuptial ceremony must be witnessed by at least two men, or one man and two women. An officer of the law attends to attest the contract. The written document is delivered to the wife, who carefully preserves it, for it is the deed that entitles her to the amount of her dower, which is part of her provision in case of being left a widow, and her sole dependence in case of being divorced. Her right in this respect is strictly guarded by law, and by her male friends, and it is one of which the women of Persia are extremely jealous. The marriage festival is usually very expensive, for the reputation of the husband is supposed to be measured by the splendour of his nuptials.

Though a man may, when he pleases, put away his wife, the expense and scandal attending such a proceeding make it rare. It seldom occurs, indeed, except among the poorer classes, who do not so rigidly seclude their females; among the wealthier and prouder, a man would be ashamed to expose a woman, with whom he had once associated, to be seen by others, unless in the case, of course, of a common woman. Divorce never takes place on account of adultery, which is punished with death. Bad temper and extravagance on the woman's side, and neglect or cruel usage on the husband's, may be urged by either as reasons for separation. If the husband sues for a divorce, he pays back the dowry he received with his bride; if the wife commences the proceeding, she loses her claim. In this, as in all other respects, the male sex has the advantage. A man who desires to be relieved of a disagreeable partner, sometimes uses her so cruelly that she is compelled to open the suit, by which means he gets rid of her, but keeps her money.

The Persian may have as many female slaves as he desires or is able to maintain. They earn no advantage of position by becoming his concubines instead of the sweepers of his house. They are still in slavery, and may at any time be sold again if they displease their masters. A woman so cast off is in a bad position, for she must then sink into worse degradation than before. Mohammedan jealousy, however, serves, in some respects, as a kind of protection for the woman; for a man, having once cohabited with her, will seldom allow her to fall into the hands of any other.

One very extraordinary custom prevails in Persia, and seems now peculiar to that country, though it is said to have existed in Arabia at the time of the prophet's appearance there. Mohammed tolerated it; but his successor, Omar, abolished it, as a species of legal prostitution injurious to the morals of the people. All the Turks and others, therefore, who hold his precepts in veneration, abhor and condemn the practice, but it still obtains. It is that of hiring a companion. A man and a woman agree to cohabit for a certain period— some for a few days, others for 99 years. In the one case it is simply an act of prostitution; in the other it is morally equivalent to marriage, though the woman acquires no right to property of any kind, except the price of her hire. This sum is agreed upon at the first compact; and though the man may discard his companion when he pleases, he must pay her the whole amount promised. If both are willing, the arrangement may be renewed at the expiration of the term, which is generally short. This kind of intercourse usually takes place among persons of very unequal stations. The women are generally of a low class, and are, for the most part, a peculiar sort of prostitutes, if prostitution mean the hiring out of a woman's person for money. The children springing from such a union are supported by the father. In one circumstance the custom differs from the ordinary prostitution of other countries. When a man has parted from a woman of this class, she is forbidden to form any new connection until a sufficient time has elapsed to prove whether or not she is pregnant from the last. This precaution is to hinder the chance of a man's being burdened with the support of a child of which he is not actually the father.

The characteristics of women in Persia agree with this picture of their treatment. They are degraded down to the level of their condition. Leaving a few exceptions out of sight, we find the rich and idle vain, sensual, and absorbed by animal desires; the poorer classes, licentious and intriguing.

The peculiar customs of the country cause strange occurrences to take place. A man is sometimes deceived into marrying the wrong woman, under cover of the inviolable drapery which veils her face. He is usually content to stow her away in his harem, and solace himself with a concubine, or the company of prostitutes; for though he may hold that his own wife and daughter would be polluted by the eye of a strange man, and though he may be able to fill his harem with beautiful slaves, the Persian voluptuary is not content. He must associate with the more brilliant and lively beauties, who are ready to receive him in various retired houses of the city. These houses are generally in obscure places, dull and uninviting on the outside, but fitted up in the interior with much elegance and luxury.

Formerly there was a numerous class of public dancing girls in Persia, and the beauty of their persons, and the melody of their voices, were celebrated by the most famous poets of the country. They were wealthy and popular, continuing to figure prominently at the entertainments of the people until the family of Futteh Ali Khan rose to the throne; they were then discouraged by a monarch who crowded his harim with a thousand women, and, in the midst of this multitude of concubines, issued edicts for the suppression of immorality. The dancing girls were prohibited from approaching the court, and compelled to seek a livelihood in the distant provinces of the empire. It is not to be denied that considerable reform has taken place in the manners of the people; but profligacy is still a marked characteristic of the cities in Persia.

Under the Sefi dynasty morals reached the last stage of depravity. The royal treasury was filled with the proceeds of immorality. Public brothels were licensed and became extremely numerous. A large revenue was drawn from them. In Ispahan alone no less than 30,000 prostitutes paid an annual sum to government. The governors of provinces and cities also granted the same privileges for sums of money, and there was scarcely a town of any size in Persia which had not at least one large brothel, crowded with inmates. The prostitutes were all licensed, and known by the appellation of *cahbeha*, or *the worthless*. An old traveller, whose authority is accepted by the best writers, describes the system then prevailing; it displays the corruption of manners in the open and systematic character of profligacy. As soon as the merchants' shops were closed in the cities the brothels were opened; the prostitutes then issued into the streets, dispersed themselves, and repaired to particular localities. There they sat down in rows, closely veiled; behind each company stood an old woman holding an extinguished candle in her hand. When any man approached with a sign that he desired to make a bargain, this harridan lit her taper, and led him down the line of women, removing the veil of each in her turn until he made his choice. The girl was then dispatched with him, under the guidance of a slave, to the house, which usually stood close by the way-side. All payments were made to the old woman or "*mother*" of the company.

Under the reigning family this open system has been checked, and prostitution, not being licensed, is a more secret system. Nevertheless, there abound in the cities of Persia numerous brothels, to which the men proceed after dark, and where they are entertained as they desire; numbers of women are always ready to hire themselves out to any who desire to associate with them.

The females of the wandering tribes are far more virtuous than those of the cities; they are also more happy and free, for if they share the labours of the men, they share also their pleasures and hopes; far from being secluded, they are allowed to converse even with strangers, and grace the hospitality of the tents with modest but polite attention. The men seldom have more than one wife, and abhor the practice of hiring women, though their priests have made attempts to introduce it among them. Still, even the women of these tribes are below their proper condition, and the men as they become wealthier become more corrupt; when, also, they sojourn for a while in the cities, they speedily contribute to the general profligacy, and often exceed the regular inhabitants in vice. Among those, however, in the nomade state, rape and adultery are rare, and when committed the woman suffers a cruel death at the hands of her nearest kindred. In the cities females are seldom publicly executed, but are put to death in private, or given as slaves to men of infamous occupation*.

Of Prostitution among the Afghans.

Women in Afghanistan are sold to the men. A marriage is a commercial transaction. The practice is recognised by the Moslem law, and is here, as in most parts of Asia, universally adopted. The price varies, of course, according to the condition of the bridegroom or his friends. Females, consequently, are in some measure regarded as property. They are in absolute subjection to the other sex. A husband may at any time, from mere caprice, and without assigning any reason, divorce his wife; but a woman cannot, unless she have good grounds, and sue for the separation before a magistrate. Even this is seldom done. When a widow marries, the friends of her first husband may claim the price that was originally paid for her; but usually the brother of the deceased inherits this property, and any one else usurping his privilege becomes a mortal enemy. However, the widow is not forced to take a new partner against her will. Indeed, if she have children with claims upon her care, it is considered more respectable to lead a single life.

In the lower regions of India, on the warm plains, we find marriage contracts fulfilled at a very early age. In the colder climate of Kabul they are left to a later period in life—men being wedded at twenty, women at about fifteen years of age. The time varies, however, with different classes. Among the poor, with whom the price of a wife is not easily to be amassed, the men often remain unmarried until forty, and the women till twenty-five. On the other hand, the rich frequently take brides of twelve to bridegrooms of fifteen, or even earlier, before either of them has attained puberty. Those living in towns and in Western Afghanistan marry earlier than those dwelling in the pastoral districts and in the eastern parts. These often wait until twenty-five, until the chin is thoroughly covered with beard, and the man is in all respects mature. The Ghiljies are still more prudent in this respect. In most parts of the country, nevertheless, the date of marriage is determined by the individual's ability to purchase a wife, provide a home, and support a family. Usually men form alliances within the blood of their own tribe; but many Afghans take also Tavjik and Persian women. It is not considered disreputable to take a wife from those nations; but it is held below the dignity of the Durani race to bestow a wife on a stranger, and this, consequently, is seldom or never done.

The intercourse of the sexes is regulated by various circumstances, many of them accidental. In the crowded towns, where the men have little opportunity of converse with the women, matches are generally made with views of family policy, and contracted through the agency of a go-between. When a man has fixed on any particular girl to be his wife, he sends some female relation or neighbour to see her and report to him upon her qualifications. If the account be satisfactory, the same agent ascertains from the girl's mother whether her family are favourable to the match; should all this prove well, arrangements are made for a public proposal. On an appointed day the suitor's father goes with a party of male relations to the young woman's father, while a similar deputation of females waits on her mother, and the offer is made in customary form. Various presents are also sent, the dowry is settled, a feast is prepared, and the betrothal takes place. Some time after, when both man and woman have mutually, by free consent, signed the articles of agreement—which stipulate for a provision for the wife in case of divorce—the union is completed at a festival, and the bride is delivered, on payment of her price, at the dwelling of her future master.

In the country, formalities very similar take place; but, as women there go unveiled, and the intercourse of the sexes is less restricted, the marriage generally originates in a personal attachment between the wedded pair, and the negotiations are only matters of etiquette. An enterprising lover may also obtain his mistress, without gaining the consent of her parents, by tearing away her veil, cutting off a lock of her hair, or throwing a large white cloth over her, and declaring her to be his lawful and affianced wife. After this no other suitor would propose for her, and she is usually bestowed on the bold lover, though he cannot escape paying some price for his wife. Such expedients are, therefore, seldom resorted to. When a man desires a girl for whom he cannot pay, and who reciprocates his affection, the common plan is to elope. This is,

* Malcolm's History of Persia; Javler's Three Years in Persia; Kotzebue's Embassy to Persia; Brydges' Narrative of the Embassy; Morier's Second Journey in Persia; Ker Porter's Travels; Stocqueler's Pilgrimage.

indeed, considered by her family as an outrage equivalent to the murder of one of its members, and pursued with equally rancorous revenge, but the possession of the wife is at least secured. The fugitive couple take refuge in the territories of some other tribe, and find the hospitable protection which is accorded by the Afghans to every guest, and still more to every suppliant.

Among the Eusufzies different customs prevail. A man never sees his bride until the marriage rites are completed. The Beduranis, also, maintain great reserve between the youth and the girl betrothed one to another. Sometimes a man goes to the house of his future father-in-law, and labours, as Jacob laboured for Rachael, without being allowed to see his destined wife until the day for the ceremony has arrived. With many of the Afghan tribes a similar rule is nominally laid down, but a secret intercourse is countenanced between the bridegroom and future bride. It is called Naumzud bauzee, or the sport of the betrothed. The young man steals by night to the house of his affianced, pretending to conceal his presence altogether from the knowledge of the men, who would affect to consider it a great scandal. He is favoured by the girl's mother, who privately conducts him to an interior apartment, where he is left alone with his beloved until the approach of morning. He is allowed the freest intercourse with her, he may converse with her as he pleases, he may kiss her, and indulge in all other innocent freedoms; but the young people are under the strongest cautions and prohibitions to refrain from anticipating the nuptial night. "Nature, however," says Mountstuart Elphinstone, "is too strong for such injunctions, and the marriage begins with all the difficulty and interest of an illicit amour." Cases have not unfrequently occurred in which the bride has been delivered of two or three children before being formally received into her husband's house. This, however, is regarded as extremely scandalous, and seldom happens among the more respectable Afghans. However, the custom of Naumzud bauzee prevails with men of the highest rank, and the king himself sometimes enjoys its midnight pleasures.

Though polygamy is allowed by the Mohammedan laws, it is too expensive to be practised by the bulk of the people. The legal number of wives is four; but many of the rich exceed this, and maintain a crowd of concubines besides. Two wives and two female slaves form a liberal establishment for a man of the middle class; while the poor are obliged to be content with one companion.

The social condition of the female sex in Afghanistan is low, as it must be in all countries where women are bought and sold. The wives of the rich, indeed, secluded in the recesses of the harem, are allowed to enjoy all the comforts and luxuries within reach of their husband's wealth. This, however, is more to please the man, than indulge the women, though many husbands really love their wives, and are influenced to a considerable degree by their desires. In general, however, it is to enjoy the pride of having a beautiful wife in his zenana, with all the appliances of opulence to render her gracious and dainty.

Among the poorer classes the women perform the drudgery of the house and carry water. Those of the most barbarous tribes share the labours of the field; but nowhere are they employed as in India, where there is scarcely any difference between the toils of the sexes. A man by the Mohammedan law is allowed to chastise his wife by beating. Custom, however, is more chivalrous and merciful than the written code, and lays it down as disgraceful for a man to avail himself of this privilege of his sex.

Though many women of the higher ranks learn to read, and exhibit considerable talents for literature, it is reckoned immodest for a female to write, as that accomplishment might be made use of to intrigue by correspondence with a lover.

Many families have all their household affairs, and many even their general customs, controlled by women. These sometimes correspond for their sons. It is usually the mother who enjoys this influence, but the wives also frequently rise to ascendancy; and all the advantages conferred on him by the Mohammedan law frequently fail to save a man from sinking to a secondary position in his own house. All domestic amusements indulged in by men are, among the lower and more estimable orders, shared by the women.

In towns, these envelope themselves in an ample white wrapper, like the Arab burnouse, which covers them to the feet, and altogether conceals their figure. A network in the hood, spread over the face, enables them to see, while their features are invisible to others. When on horseback, those of the upper classes wear large white cotton wrappers on their legs, which completely hides the shape of the limb. Frequently, also, they travel in hampers, large enough to allow of their reclining, which are strung like paniers over a camel's back, and covered with a case of broad cloth. They are hot almost to suffocation during the sultry season. Females are allowed to go about seated in this manner, and form a large proportion in the crowds which throng the public ways. Scrupulously concealed as their features are, they are thus subject to little restraint; and, compared with their sex in the neighbouring regions, though they do not occupy an honourable, they are by no means in an unhappy position.

In the rural districts they are still more free, and go without a veil. Walking through the village or the camp, they are subject to no other restraint than the universal opinion that it is indecent to associate with the other sex. Should a strange man approach, they immediately cover their faces. At home, they seldom enter the public room of their house if an Afghan with whom they are not intimate is there. With Armenians, Persians, and Hindoos, indeed, they do not hold this reserve; for they consider them as of no importance; and the pride of her race is, in these cases, a sufficient guardian to the woman's virtue. When their husbands are from home, also, they receive guests, and entertain them with all the liberal courtesy required by the sacred laws of hospitality.

But the modesty and chastity of the country women, especially of those belonging to the simple shepherd tribes, has been remarked and admired by almost every traveller. "There are no common prostitutes," says Mountstuart Elphinstone, "except in the towns, and very few even there, especially in the west, which is the colder region; it is considered very disreputable to frequent their company." In Afghanistan, however, as in all other parts of the East, and in many states of antiquity, the imperfect education of the women is a cause of profligacy among the men. The wives and concubines who fill a rich man's harem are usually ignorant, insipid, and unacquainted even with the forms of conversation. The prostitutes, on the other hand, are generally well versed in the science of the world, polished in their manners, practised in the arts of seduction, and afford amusement of such interest and variety that men, with four wives and numerous female slaves at their command, frequently seek the society of these accomplished women.

An able and judicious writer has observed that, as far as he recollected, he saw among no people in the East, except the Afghans, any traces of the sentiment which we call love, that is, according to European ideas. There, however, it not only exists, but is extremely prevalent. One sign of this is exhibited in the numerous elopements, which are always attended with peril, and are risked through love. It is common also for a man in humble circumstances to pledge his faith to a particular girl, and then start off to some remote town, or even to Lower India, where, by industry or trade, he might acquire wealth enough to purchase her from her friends. One traveller met at Poonah a young man who had contracted one of these engagements. He had formed an attachment with the daughter of a Mullah, who reciprocated his affection. Her father gave his consent willingly to the marriage; but said that his daughter's honour would suffer if she did not bring as large a price as the other women of her family. The young people were much afflicted, for the man owned only one horse. However, his mistress gave him a needle used for applying antimony to the eye, and with this pledge of her affection he was confidently working to accumulate the fortune which was required to purchase her. These romantic amours are most common among the country people, especially where the women are partially secluded—accessible enough to be admired, but withdrawn enough to excite the lover's attachment by some difficulty. Among the higher orders such unions are less frequent, though with them also they occasionally occur. It was an affair of love between a chief of the Turkolaunis and a Khan of the Euzufzies that gave rise to a bloody war which lasted many years. Many of the songs and tales sung and told among the Afghans have love for their plot and spirit, and that passion is expressed in the most glowing and flowery language. Such a trait in a nation's manners is highly favourable, and, joined with many others, renders the Afghan one of the most admirable races of the East.

An exceptional feature in the manners of that region is exhibited by the Moolah Zukkee, a sect of infidel pedants, who are more unprincipled, dissolute, and profligate than any other class in the country. They resemble in their conduct the Areois of the South Sea Islands, doubt the truth of a future state, are sceptical as to the existence of a God, and have released themselves from every fear of hell. They have taken full advantage of this, and indulge in the vilest lusts without check or shame. This is the more extraordinary as the Afghans are represented, on the whole, as a devout and pious people.

The inhabitants of Afghanistan are divided into the stationary and wandering population—the dwellers in tents, and the dwellers in houses. It is a curious fact that the dwellers in tents, who live chiefly to the west, are the more chaste and moral. It is among these, however, that the intercourse of the sexes is confined less by law than by public opinion. Men and women dance together, but in modest measures.

The slaves we have alluded to are divided into the home-born and the foreign. The beautiful girls are purchased for the harims of the rich; the others are sold as menials, or attendants on the rich women. The habit of buying concubines is unfortunately becoming more common. Intercourse with the voluptuaries of Persia has seduced them into many Persian vices. Naturally they are, perhaps, one of the least voluptuous nations in Asia; but their manners are becoming visibly corrupted, and this decay of their ancient simplicity is felt and regretted by themselves. Corps of prostitutes and harims full of concubines will do the work of the sword among them, and their spirit of independence, which never yielded even before English bayonets, will evaporate, if they long continue to decline in their morals and manners. Luxury has subdued more great nations than the sword.

In the Vizeeree country, to the north of the Sherauni district, one very extraordinary custom prevails; it is quite peculiar to that tribe; the women have the right of choosing their husbands. When a woman has fixed on any man whom she desires to marry, she sends the drummer of the camp to pin a handkerchief on his cap, with a pin which she has previously used to fasten up her hair. The drummer goes on his mission, cautiously watches his opportunity, and executes the feat in public, naming the woman. The man is obliged immediately to take her as his wife, if he can pay her price to her father*.

Of Prostitution in Kashmir.

In Kashmir we find the Hindu system of manners considerably modified by various circumstances. The people are not oppressed by that rigid code of etiquette, which in India isolates every caste and almost every family. Naturally addicted to pleasure, they find much of their enjoyment in the society of the female sex, and from the earliest times have been celebrated for their love of singers and dancers. Formerly, when the valley was more populous and flourishing than at present, its capital city was the scene of eternal revel, in which morals stood little in the way of those gratifications to which the sensual ideas of the richer orders inclined them. Now, under a vile and monstrous despotism, the inhabitants relieve themselves from a continual struggle with misfortune by indulging in gross vices. Formerly they were corrupted by luxury; now they decay through misery, and drown the sense of hopeless poverty in the gratification of their animal passions.

The situation of the female sex in Kashmir differs from that occupied by them among the Hindus of Bengal. They are far more free, and appear more licentious. The women of this delightful and romantic valley have long been celebrated for their grace and beauty. Their renown extended on the one side as far as the plains of Central Asia, and on the other beyond the borders of the Ganges. They were formerly much sought after by the Mogul nobility of Delhi, to whom they bore strong and handsome sons; and even after that monarchy had declined from its original opulence and power, its luxurious kings solaced themselves in their humiliation by concubines and dancing girls from Kashmir. Nor has the beauty which in those early ages attracted to the women of this country the admiration of all the East, faded in any degree. They are still described as the flowers of Oriental grace—not so slender as the Hindus of Bengal, but more full, round, voluptuous, and fascinating. Since few except those belonging to the very highest classes wear a veil, travellers have enjoyed abundant opportunities of observing the characteristics of the sex. The face is of a dark complexion, richly flushed with pink; the eyes are large, almond-shaped, and overflowing with a peculiar liquid brilliance; the features are regular, harmonious, and fine; while the person, as we have said, is plump and round, though the limbs are often models of grace. Such is the portrait we are led to draw by the accounts of the best writers. They agree, however, in adding, that among all, except the dancers, singers, and prostitutes, with probably those few women who are shut up in harems, art has done nothing to aid nature. The eyes, unsurpassed for brightness, with full orbs, and long black lashes, shine often from a dirty face, expressing a mind flooded with sensual desires, and utterly unadorned by

* See Elphinstone's Kabul; Vignes' Visit to Ghuzni; Burnes' Kabul.

education or accomplishments. Among the poorer classes, especially, filth, poverty, and degradation render many of the women repulsive, in spite of their natural beauty. It is remarkable that the inhabitants of the boats on the lakes possess among them the handsomest women in the valley.

The customs of marriage, courtship, and the general habits of the women, resemble so closely what have already been described in treating of India, that we need not enter into any particular account of them. The life of the woman belonging to a chief of high rank is a monotonous seclusion. She sits, enveloped in full wrappings of shawls and robes, amid all the luxury and brilliance of an Oriental harem, with every appliance of ease and comfort, but not the liberty which the humbler orders enjoy. Wives of all classes, indeed, are subject to their husbands, but those of the nobles are most under control. They often experience in its full bitterness the curse of slavery under a capricious despot. The authority of the man is absolute.

Mikran Singh, a chief of the valley, was a few years ago, during the reign of the Maharaja Runjit Singh, guilty of a horrible act, which illustrates in a striking manner the condition of women in that country. His wife happened to be in the Punjab, and, while there, was accused by some enemies of a criminal intrigue. She was sent to her husband in Kashmir. Her son flung his dagger at the feet of Mikran Singh, and threw himself at his knees, begging mercy for his mother. The man promised to forgive her; but, as soon as occasion offered, ordered her to be forced into a bath the temperature of which was rapidly increased with the purpose of suffocating her. She was tenacious of life, and struggled long with her tortures, filling the palace with shrill and piercing shrieks. Many people fled from the neighbourhood that they might not listen to these fearful cries. At length, to put an end to this horrid scene, the husband sent his wife a bowl of poison, which she drank and immediately died.

Women of the middle and lower classes affect no concealment, and never wear a veil. They experience less caprice from their husbands, and are perhaps more free than females in Hindustan formerly were. Widows have long been released from the disgusting obligation of burning at the funeral pyre of their husbands. The custom, indeed, was at no time very prevalent in the valley, and since the decree of abolition, published by Aurungzebe in 1669, it has never been revived. Women in Kashmir bear a fair proportion to the men, and are proverbially fruitful. The depopulation of the country is owing to no natural causes, but to the rapacious despotism under which it suffers. British government would soon, without a doubt, restore it to its ancient flourishing condition, as well as reform its manners.

Travellers in Kashmir always remark the dancing girls, for which it was formerly renowned. The village of Changus, near the ancient city of Achibul, was at one time celebrated for a colony of them. They excelled, in singing, dancing, and other accomplishments, all the other girls of the valley. When Vigne visited it some years ago, the village had fallen to decay, and its famous beauties had disappeared. Old men, however, remembered and spoke of them with regret. One, whose name was Lyli, still lived in the recollection of many. A few dancers of another class remained, but were inferior in their natural charms and arts to those of the city, and were obliged to be content with engagements in the humbler or country districts.

These women may be divided into classes. Among the highest we might find some that are virtuous and even modest, as we may among singers and actresses in Europe. Others frequent entertainments at the houses of rich men and public festivals, receiving large sums for their attendance, and occasionally consent to prostitute their persons for a valuable gift. Others are regular professional harlots, indiscriminately prostituting themselves to any who desire their society. Many of these are widows, who are forbidden to marry again, and are devoted to the service of some god, whose temple and priests they enrich by the gains of their disreputable calling.

The Watul or Gipsy tribe of Kashmir is remarkable for the loveliness of its females. Living in tents or temporary huts, these Gipsies pass from spot to spot; and many of their handsomest girls are sold as slaves to furnish the harems of the rich, or enter the train of some company of dancing girls. These are bred and taught to please the taste of the voluptuary, to sing licentious songs in an amorous tone, to dance in voluptuous measures, to dress in a peculiar style, and to seduce by the very expression of their countenances. Formerly many of these women amassed large sums in their various callings; but now that the prosperity of the valley has decreased, the youngest and most beautiful seek their fortunes in the cities of Agra and Delhi; which, though decaying, still retain traces of the imperial luxury and profligacy which once rendered them the splendid capitals of the East.

The bands of dancing girls are usually attended by divers hideous duennas and men, whose conspicuous ugliness makes the loveliness of the women appear more complete through contrast. Baron Hugel, whose ideas are purely German, did not find his sense of the beautiful satisfied by the women, and especially the public women, of Kashmir; but every other traveller, from Bernier to Vigne, expatiates upon the subject. The Baron does not, in other respects, inspire us with the idea that he is an authority on such a question.

The Nach girls are under the surveillance of the Government—which licenses their prostitution—and lead in general a miserable life. They are actual slaves, cannot sing or dance without permission from their overseer, and must yield up to him the most considerable part of their profits. Some of them still ask large sums, especially from strangers. One troop demanded from our German author a hundred rupees for an evening's performance.

The education of a superior Nach girl should commence when she is no more than five years old. Nine years, it is said, are required to perfect them in song and dance. They dress usually in trowsers of rich-coloured silk, loosely furled round the limb, fitting tight at the ancle, and confined round the waist by a girdle and tassels, which hang down to the knee. Over these is draped a tunic of white muslin, reaching half-way down the leg; but when dancing they wear a full flowing garment of soft light tissue of various colours, intermixed with gold. Some have been seen with ornaments on their persons to the value of 10,000 or 12,000 rupees. Some, also, with all these adornments, neglect to be clean, and omit perfume from among the graces of their toilette. Their songs are often full of sentiment and fancy, finely expressed, and accompanied by pleasing music. Their dances are not chaste or modest; but neither are they obscene or gross.

Among the poorer orders exist a swarm of prostitutes, frequenting low houses in the cities or boats on the lakes; but of their modes of life we have no account. Probably the manners of prostitutes differ little throughout the world. It is certain that they are largely patronised by the more demoralised part of the population. The traveller Moorcroft, who gave gratuitous advice to the poor of Serinaghur, had at one time nearly 7000 patients on his list. Of these a very large number were suffering from loathsome diseases, induced by the grossest and most persevering profligacy. Altogether the manners of Kashmir appear very corrupt*.

Of Prostitution in India.

We shall have to view the Hindus under two aspects—as they were under their former oppressors, and as they are under the administration of the Company. The change of rule has wrought, and is working, a change in the manners and institutions of the people perfectly wonderful to contemplate. Climate and position have much to do with national characteristics, but government has more. India under the English no more resembles India under the Mogul, than the England of the nineteenth century resembles the England of the Heptarchy. A beneficent revolution in her fortune has occurred, which is developing an extraordinary reform in the customs and ideas of her native race. Consequently a distinction must be observed between the old and the new state of things. It will be necessary, also, to distinguish those provinces which are absolutely under our sway from those which are independent, or only related to us by subsidiary alliances. A strong contrast is exhibited by these different communities, which, as far as the welfare of the people is concerned, differ as much from each other as the slave states of western Africa differ from the population of Cape Colony. In the one a wise and beneficent government is administered for the happiness of the people; in the other, an imbecile yet savage tyranny makes them look with jealousy on their more fortunate neighbours. This is an important consideration, and by no means irrelevant to our subject, for it illustrates the influence of laws and institutions upon the manners and morals of a nation.

The state of women among the Hindus is not elevated, and as long as their ancient teachers of religion are revered, such must be the case. The female sex is held absolutely dependent on the male, and, as among the Chinese, the father before marriage, the husband afterwards, and the son in widowhood, are the natural protectors assigned by the sacred law. Nothing is to be done by a woman of her purely independent will. She must reverence her lord, and approach him with humble re-

* Vigne's Travels in Kashmir; Hugel's Travels in Kashmir; Moorcroft's Travels in the Himalayan Provinces; Forster's Travels from Bengal to England; Hamilton's East India Gazetteer; Bernier's Travels in the Empire of the Mogul.

spect. She is bound to him while he desires it, whatever his conduct may be, and, if she rebel, is to be chastised with a rope or cane on the back part of her person, " and not on a noble part by any means."

Writers with a particular theory to support frequently quote the institutes of Menu, to show that a contempt of women is inculcated, and hard usage of them encouraged by the precepts of that singular code.

Indolence, vanity, irascible humours, evil dispositions, and lasciviousness, are enumerated as the vices which are declared natural to them. "A woman is chaste, when there is neither place, time, nor person, to afford her an opportunity to be immoral," says the "Hetopadera," which is quoted in application to the whole sex, though it applies only as Professor Wilson —the great authority on this subject—observes, to that class of idle, intemperate, profligate females, to be found in every society. Passages undoubtedly occur in the laws and in satirical compositions levelled at the whole sex; but the Hindus themselves usually describe them as amiable, modest, gentle, chaste, full of wit, and excelling in every grace. They are allowed to inherit property; they are permitted under certain circumstances to exercise power, though by indirect means; and they certainly exert great influence over the men. In no state of ancient times, except the polished republics of Greece and Rome, were women held in so much esteem as among the Hindus.

Debarred as they are from the advantages of education, not allowed to eat with their husbands, and forbidden from mixing in society, the Hindu women, of course, are degraded below their just position; but it is not true that they are abject slaves, or are generally treated with barbarity. Among the more wild and barbarous tribes, as well as the more ignorant classes in all parts of India, men frequently beat their wives; but, from the few revelations of the Zenana which have been made, it would appear that its inmates are generally treated with considerable deference and attention. The contact of Mohammedan with Hindu manners has certainly, however, had an effect on the latter, which has depreciated the rank and estimation of the female sex.

Nowhere, indeed, where polygamy is allowed, can women hold their true position. In India, however, though permitted, it was not encouraged by the religious law, and sanctioned in particular cases only, as barrenness, inconstancy, aversion, or some other similar cause. The wife, also, must be consulted, and her consent obtained to the second match. She still held the principal rank in the family, for the new comer could not take her place while she remained in the household.

In various parts of India, different customs of marriage prevail. There are, indeed, four prescribed forms—all honourable, and various only in detail. A fifth is, when the bridegroom, contrary to the sacred law, traffics for a girl. Another is, when a captive, left helpless in a man's power, is forced to become the companion of his bed. And a last is, when a girl is ravished, when surprised asleep, and taken off or deluded to the house of a new master.

Marriage is viewed as a religious duty by the Hindus. A few are exempted, under special circumstances, from the fulfilment of this sacred obligation. The rules of law enacted with respect to it apply chiefly to affairs of caste, with which we have here little to do. It is forbidden to purchase a wife for money, except under particular conditions; but the young girls have little share in their own destiny, being usually betrothed while very young. The father has the disposal of them until three years after the age of puberty, when it is reckoned disgraceful for her to be single, and then she may choose a partner for herself. Few, however, will marry a maiden so old. In Bahar the girl, betrothed while an infant, is not permitted to enter her husband's house until mature, when she is conducted thither with as much ceremony as the circumstances of the family will allow. In Bengal the couple are pledged with many rites and a profusion of expense. The bride is taken to her husband's house, remains there a little while, and then goes home for a short period, but the whole is consummated as soon after ten years of age as practicable. The timid effeminate Bengalee appears of a sensual character, and regards his wife as little more than the instrument of his pleasure. A better state of things is now beginning to prevail there, in consequence of the efforts made by the Company; but under the old system, not one female in twenty thousand was allowed to acquire the least particle of learning. The natives excuse or justify this fact,—first, by the prohibition against educating girls which are contained in their sacred books; and secondly, by declaring that many women would, did they possess those means of intrigue, run riot in profligacy and vice.

The birth of a daughter being throughout the East, and especially in Bengal, regarded as less auspicious than that of a son, indicates a low position of the sex. From that moment her parents are solicitous to settle her, so that she is often in infancy pledged for life. The character of the bridegroom is of little consequence. Matches, consequently, often prove unhappy, especially where the jealousy or despotism of the husband forces the woman to live in seclusion, and mainly within the private recesses of the zenana. This, however, is not the general custom, women being allowed to appear at festivals and jubilees. Even the wives of respectable Hindus frequently quit the interior apartments set aside for them, and go to bathe in the waters of the Ganges or some other holy stream. The poorer, of course, who assign a share of labour to their wives, cannot seclude them if they would, for the expense of confinement is not inconsiderable.

The wife waits on her husband, and is treated with very partial confidence. In the lower ranks she is employed to prepare cow-dung for fuel, to fetch water, to make purchases in the markets, and perform the drudgery of the house, though this is no more than is done by the poorer classes in Europe. The rich woman adorns herself, curls her hair, listens to the gossip of her slaves, and indulges in what amusements may be within her reach. It may be imagined that the child or wife, uneducated and without a gleam of light in her mind, amuses herself by a thousand trivial devices. The home is thus not unhappy, unless the husband be naturally harsh, or the house be ruled by a tyrannical mother-in-law, which is often the case. Matches founded upon a mutual attachment are very rare, but by no means unknown. The romances of the Hindus are in many cases founded on them. The general plan, however, is for the parties to be betrothed in childhood.

When they perform the ceremonies of marriage they are complete strangers to each other; yet Hindu wives are, on the whole, faithful. When the husband finds himself united to a woman who is hateful to him, he neglects her altogether, and takes another or a concubine, though this is against the ancient law. In many things, however, the practice of this nation, especially among the ruder classes, is opposed to that extraordinary sacred code. However, if he have no children, he adopts this plan of ensuring them, and frequently conceals the facts for a long time from his wife. Polygamy causes great troubles in the Bengalee households. A man is not allowed by law to take a new partner after fifty, but this regulation is observed by few. These customs, together with the facility of divorce—a privilege from which the female sex is excluded—contribute to the demoralization of society. A man calling his wife *mother*, by that act renounces her, and is thenceforward free from the tie. A barren wife may be superseded in the eighth year; she whose children are all dead in the birth; she who bears only daughters, in the eleventh; while she who is of an unkind disposition may be divorced without delay. The whole code, composed by the priestly order, is unjust to the sex.

Of the general character of the female sex in Hindustan very exaggerated ideas commonly prevail. It is represented as corrupted throughout by the obscenity and indecency of the public religion and the institutions framed by priests. It is true the Hindu Pantheon is a representation of the lowest vices, and that the manners of the people are by no means delicate; yet the respectable class of women appear chaste, orderly, modest, and decorous. The fair muscular race of Afghanistan has indeed been depicted in favourable contrast to the dark and slim race of Bengal, but this need suppose no characteristic depravity in the latter, for the hardy mountaineers are celebrated for their contempt of sensual pleasures. Other parts of India exhibit their peculiar features. Among the rude Mughs of Arracan—a hunting and fishing, as well as cultivating, and formerly a predatory tribe—when a man wants money he pawns his wife for a certain sum, or transfers her altogether. In the southern parts of the Peninsula and the Mysore, manners are more licentious, and women are more debased. There polygamy has always been practised by the powerful and wealthy whose means enabled them to enjoy indulgences discouraged by the precepts of the ancient law. Buchanan, travelling towards the close of the eighteenth century, found about 80 concubines secluded in the palace of Tippoo Sultan, at Seringapatam. These were attended by more than 500 handmaids. The same traveller made a diligent inquiry into the manners of the various communities he visited. Among the Teliga Divangas, followers of Siva, a man was allowed to take many wives, but not to hurt them, or divorce them, except for adultery. It was once the practice for the widow to bury herself alive with the body of her husband.

The Shaynagas of Canara were not allowed to take a second wife unless the first had died, or had no children. The Corannas permitted polygamy, and girls were purchased for money. Adultery was punished by a beating or by a divorce, in which case the guilty wife might marry whom she pleased. The Panchalaru had similar laws, and so indeed had many other tribes. One of the most general rules was that a woman could not be divorced except for faithless conduct. Widows were sometimes destroyed. Among the Bherid and many others, marriage was contracted, under obligation, before the age of puberty. If a girl remained single beyond that age, no credit was given to her virginity; she was declared incapable of marriage, and usually took resource in prostitution.

The severe laws against violating the law of chastity have not, in India, been formed so much for the protection of morals, as for preserving the boundaries of castes. Women are severely punished for holding intercourse with a man of superior caste; that is, if the intrigue be discovered, for there is no doubt that such intrigues frequently occur.

Among the Woddas the laws of marriage were by no means so stringent as among many other tribes visited by Buchanan. Women abounded. Every man had as many wives as he pleased. They all laboured for him; and if one was lazy she was divorced, though left free to marry again; she also might leave him if hardly treated, but could not contract a new engagement without his consent.

The Carruburru permitted adultresses to live with any man who would keep them, provided their husbands did not immediately desire revenge. They were despised, but not altogether cast out from the communion of social life. The children of concubines enjoyed equal rights with those of real wives. That they were a gross people is proved by the fact that adultery was sometimes winked at in an industrious woman, too valuable as a servant to lose. The more refined idea, however, which prevailed among them of not allowing a girl to marry until naturally marriageable, was looked upon by members of the higher castes as a beastly depravity.

Among the Rajpoots women are not degraded; they hold a higher position. Ladies of rank are, indeed, secluded, but more from ideas of dignity and etiquette than sentiments of jealousy or the habit of despotism. There is an air of chivalry in some of their customs. A woman of high station, threatened with danger, sometimes sent to any youth whom she might admire the present of a bracelet. He was then called her "bracelet-bound brother," and was expected to defend her under all circumstances, even at the hazard of his life.

Men, it has been remarked, make the laws—women make the manners—of a country. In Rajasthan, the few women reared exercised great influence on the actions, habitudes, and tastes of the men. The Rajpoot consults his wife on every important occasion; and, much as we are given to lament the condition of these women, it is by no means so debased as many writers would persuade us to imagine. Marriage contracts which often, as among the Jews, took place at the well, where the young girls assembled to draw water and converse, were, in frequent instances, the commencement of a happy life. The precepts of Menu have been quoted to show the contempt of the sex inculcated by the sacred books. His censures on a class, however, have been taken as his description of all womankind—but falsely; for the Rajpoot proverbs on this subject are derived from those famous institutes. The mouth of a woman, we find there, is constantly pure. Her name should be chosen graceful and euphonous, resembling a word of benediction. When they are honoured, the gods are pleased; when they are dishonoured, the gods are offended. The language of another sage was full of rich, and, perhaps, exaggerated sentiment. "Strike not, even with a blossom, a wife guilty of a hundred faults." The religious maxims laid down for married couples is equally elevated. "Let mutual fidelity continue until death." Intermarriage is prohibited in the same clan, or even tribe, though the patronymic may have been lost for centuries. Eight hundred years had divided the two branches of one famous house, yet an alliance between them was prohibited as incestuous.

Pregnant women and maidens are in Rajpootana treated with great tenderness and respect. Many women in this country can read and write. They cannot govern actually; but indirectly as regents, several of them have equalled in vigour and tyranny any of the masculine tyrants for which Asia is so celebrated. Polygamy has caused many troubles in the country; and at a remote period in its history we discover an instance of polyandrism.

One of the modified systems we have alluded to exists in Sindh and the Indian provinces of Beluchistan. Little gifted by nature, the Beluchi women are the servants of their husbands, and labour while their lords are feasting or sleeping.

Nevertheless, when, under the destructive tyranny of the Amirs, a foray was about to be undertaken, or any danger averted, the females of the village were taken into consultation, and strongly influenced the councils of the men. A strong resemblance was discovered by Pottinger between the moral and social institutions of the Beluchis, especially in reference to marriage, and those of the Jews.

A woman's husband dying, his brother is bound to marry her, and his children are heirs of the deceased. A similar enactment is to be found in the law as set forth in Deuteronomy. In cases of adultery, full expiation and atonement must be made, or both criminals put to death. The regulations with respect to divorce are very similar. The resemblance between Indian manners and those of the Jews was, as early as 1704, noticed by an anonymous French writer, who drew up a curious parallel in support of his theory.

The Muzmi, or hill tribes of Nepaul, who are not Hindus, follow the customs of Upper Thibet in most things, except polyandrism, or the plurality of husbands. Their women enjoy considerable privileges. The females of the Brahmin and India class in Central India, also, possess great influence over their husbands. If married to men of any consequence, they have a right to a separate provision, and an estate of their own. They enjoy much liberty, seldom wear a veil, give entertainments, and expend much money in jewels and clothes. In the families of the great Sindia and Holkar they wielded no mean degree of power, which they seldom exerted in the cause of peace. Their education is not by any means so limited as that of their sex in Bengal. Generally, among the Mohammedans of India, the women of high rank are somewhat secluded, though not severely restrained; but those of the lower classes, sharing as they do the labours and the pleasures of their husbands, are neither watched nor immured. Whether they are harshly used or not depends very much, as in England, on the individual character of the husband. No description will apply universally to the conduct of any race. In Bengal there were, under native rule, many female zemindars, or village revenue administrators, who were, however, subject to the influence, but not to the authority, of the male members of their family. Among the tribes of the Rajamahal Hills, on the western borders of that province, fewer restrictions still are in practice. They are not Hindus of caste, and therefore more free to obey their natural inclinations. One of their most prominent distinctions is the permission for widows to marry again. Their morality is tolerably good. When a man sees his son inclined to the company of prostitutes, he asks him if he desires to be married. If he replies in the affirmative, a neighbour is sent—unless a choice have been already made—to find a suitable girl. Both parties must agree to the match, though the girls, being wedded very young, seldom oppose their parents' will. The young man's father makes a present to the father of the bride; a marriage dinner is provided, the newly-joined couple eat off the same leaf, their hands are joined, they are exhorted not to quarrel, and the youth then takes home his wife.

One of the most remarkable and celebrated institutions of the Hindus was that of suttee, or the burning of the widow with her husband's body. The shastres, or sacred books, are full of recommendations to perform this terrible sacrifice, and promise ineffable bliss to the voluntary victim. This custom of female immolation, which distinguished especially Rajpoot manners, had its origin, according to the priests, in the example of a holy personage, who, to avenge an insult, consumed herself before an assemblage of the gods. Custom gave it sanction, as religion offered it a reward. The institution of castes, however, and the perpetual separation enjoined upon them, appear to have been the real origin of the custom. In a few instances a man might marry a woman of inferior order, but in no case could she descend. Polygamy being practised, men continually left numerous young widows, who, being forbidden under the pain of damnation, to contract a second engagement, had to choose between infamy, misery, and the funeral pile. It is said that 15,000 victims formerly perished annually in Bengal. When we remember that 60 sometimes died on one pyre, we can believe that a large number were thus destroyed; but the calculation alluded to appears, nevertheless, extravagant. It is unnecessary here to enter largely on the subject, which is familiar to every general reader. Happily the horrible practice is now effectually abolished throughout the British dominions—one among the innumerable blessings achieved for that region by the Company's administration. The contrast between the native states and the English provinces is remarkable, if for this alone. At the death of Runjit Singh a large sacrifice of women was made for his funeral, but now that the Punjab is annexed, no more will be permitted.

In Central India the custom prevailed most when the Rajpoots were in the height of their power, their influence, and their pride. The suttees were then very frequent, as is attested, among other evidences, by the number of monuments still remaining, with representations of the ceremony, which were erected in memory of the devoted wives. The Mohammedans, when they were supreme, endeavoured, as far as possible, to check the practice. The Mahrattas, by a judicious neglect and indifference, which neither encouraged by approval nor provoked by prohibition, which they were unable to enforce, rendered it very rare. When Sir John Malcolm wrote, about 1820, there had not been, as far as it was possible to know, throughout Central India, more than three or four instances annually during the last twenty years. These instances were confined to particular communities of Rajpoots and Brahmins, while no examples occurred, as under the princes of Jeydpoor, Jaidpoor, and Ondepoor, of women being forcibly dragged to the pile and thrust, an unwilling sacrifice, into the flames. Some of the greatest fanatics had entirely abandoned the custom for several generations. Where it continued most generally to be preserved was where the priests denounced the terrors of heavenly vengeance against those who dared to allow one precept of the sacred code to be set aside. These hereditary nobles of India obstructed the social reform of the country with all the bigotry usual to such a class. There was no duty, said the law, which a woman could honourably fulfil, after her husband's death, except casting herself in the same fire with him.

Formerly the horrors of the practice, in its details, could not be exaggerated, though writers occasionally enlarged upon the general results. Children of eight or ten years of age have devoted themselves sometimes, through fear of the harsh usage they experienced from their relatives. Women of 85 have been plunged into the blazing pile; and maidens not married, but only betrothed, have been made a sacrifice with the ashes of their intended husbands. In Ripa, if one wife consented to burn, all the rest were compelled to follow her example. Fearful scenes have on these occasions been witnessed by travellers. A miserable wretch, escaping twice from the pyre, has clung to their feet, imploring them to defend her, until, naked, with the flesh burned off many parts of her person, she has been finally flung upon the burning heap. Young children, bound together, have been laid struggling by the body, and appeared to be dead from fear before the wood was kindled. Among the Yogees, the wife sometimes buried herself alive with the corpse of her husband. In 1803 it was computed that 430 suttees took place within 30 miles of Calcutta—in 1804 between 200 and 300. What "Aborigines' Protection Society" can regret the revolution which has given India into the hands of England?

The painful subject of infanticide is next forced upon our contemplation. Formerly it prevailed to a great extent in India, though the exertions of the Company have now all but extirpated it from the British dominions. Various circumstances contributed in Rajpootana to encourage the destruction of female children. The Rajpoot must marry a woman of pure blood, beyond the utmost degree of affinity to him. To find partners for their daughters was, therefore, a difficult undertaking for the haughty nobility of Rajast'han. Besides, the stupendous extravagance of the nobles at their wedding feasts—which the pride of caste compelled—rendered such contracts an overwhelming expense. The majority of the female infants were therefore slain. In cases where a community was threatened with danger from an enemy, all the children, and, indeed, all the women, were slaughtered lest they should fall into strange hands. Custom sanctioned, but neither traditionary law nor religion allowed, infanticide, of which the ancient dwellers on the banks of the Indus gave an early example. It was the custom among them, says Ferishta, when a female child was born, to carry it to the market-place. There the parent, holding a knife in one hand and his infant in the other, demanded whether any one wanted a wife. If no one came forward to claim the child as a future bride, it was sacrificed. This caused a large numerical superiority of men. Such a birth was among the Rajpoots an occasion of sorrow. Its destruction was a melancholy event. Families were accustomed to boast of the suttees to which they had contributed the victims, but none ever recurred with pride to the children which had thus been slain. The choice, however, was for the girl to die, or live with a prospect of dishonour, which could not be endured by the proud people of Rajast'han. Wilkinson asserted in 1833, that the number of infants annually murdered in Malwa and Rajpootana was 20,000. In 1840 the population of Cutch was 12,000, but there were not 500 women. In 1843 a folio of more than 400 pages was presented to Parliament, full of correspondence on this subject. In many of the states, it appeared, the Rajahs were induced to offer portions to women when marrying, in order to check infanticide. In Katteewar great efforts were made, and parents were rewarded for preserving their female children. Pride of caste, the expense of marriage feasts, and poverty, were the general causes, besides a desire to conceal the fruit of illicit intrigues. In some villages there were only 12 girls to 79 boys under twelve years of age. In one hamlet of 20 people not one female was living. It is probable, nevertheless, that much exaggeration has been put forward on this subject, especially in reference to Rajpootana, as the seclusion of the females there rendered it impossible accurately to know the number of births. Undoubtedly, however, it was practised to a great extent; but by means of funds, for the reward and encouragement of those parents who reared all their children, as well as by the gradual introduction of laws, a mighty reform has been effected in India. In Odessa and the east of Bengal children were formerly sacrificed to the goddess Gunga, and for this purpose cast into the sacred river. In most countries infanticide has been chiefly the resort of the poor, but in parts of India it was the practice of the rich, being caused by pride rather than indigence. In Bengal, however, the peasantry were occasionally guilty of this device to rid themselves of a burden. A mother would sometimes expose her infant to be starved or devoured, and visit the place after three days had passed. If the child were still living—a very rare case—she took it home and nursed it.

Another unnatural crime was that of procuring abortion, which is still practised, though in a clandestine manner, since it is a breach of the law. It was formerly very prevalent. Ward was assured by a pundit, a professor, that in Bengal 100,000 children were thus destroyed in the womb every month. This was a startling exaggeration, but there is no doubt the offence was of frequent occurrence.

Whether the Hindus and other inhabitants of India are remarkable for their chasteness or immorality is a question much disputed. Unfortunately, men with a favourite theory to support, have been so extravagant in their assertions on either side that it is difficult, or even impossible, to form a just opinion on the subject. Many have represented the Hindus as a sensual, lascivious, profligate race; but we have the weighty testimony of Professor Wilson to the contrary. There is no doubt that the manners of the people have undergone a remarkable improvement since the establishment of British rule. The original institutions of the people were opposed to morality. The prohibition against the marriage of widows was a direct encouragement to prostitution. Many enlightened Hindus long ago recognised the demoralizing influence of this law, and exerted themselves to abolish it. A wealthy native in Calcutta once offered a dowry of 10,000 rupees to any woman who would brave the ancient prejudices of her race, and marry a second husband. A claim was soon made for the liberal donation. A learned Brahmin of Nagpoor, high in rank and opulence, wrote against the law. Among one tribe, the Bunyas, it was long ago abolished; not, however, from a moral persuasion of its injustice, but under the pressure of circumstances. Even then, however, in Bhopal, the hereditary dignitaries of the priestly order, naturally attached to ancient prejudices, sought to reestablish the prohibition. There were very few exceptions of this kind among all the millions of the Hindu race. Even the Mohammedans, with the precept and example of their own prophet to encourage them, held the marriage of a widow disgraceful. Temporary reform took place at Delhi, but the old custom was, until recently, supreme. The moral evils were that it led to depravity of conduct on the part of the widow, caused a frightful amount of infanticide and abortion, and induced these women by their practice to corrupt all others with whom they came in contact. Female children being married so early, hundreds and thousands were left widows before they had ripened into puberty. The crowded house—containing men of all shades of consanguinity, grandfathers, fathers-in-law, uncles, brothers-in-law, and cousins, all dwelling with the young widow in the inclosure of the family mansion—led to illicit and incestuous connections being continually formed. Pregnancies were removed by abortion. The Bombay code took cognisance of this, and punished it severely. When a woman was known to be pregnant she was narrowly watched, and if the father could be found he was compelled to support his child.

A boy might be betrothed to a child. If she died he was free from the engagement; but if he died she was condemned to remain a maiden widow, and subject to the humiliating laws attached to that condition. It is easy to imagine the demoralizing effects of such an institution. Under the old system the hardships and indignities imposed on the widow made her prefer suttee, or the sacrifice by fire, or else a retreat in a brothel. Another corrupting custom is that of early marriages. Men seldom have sentiments of affection for any woman, or, if at all, it is for some fascinating dancing girl, for their wives are chosen while too young to feel or excite the passion of love. They therefore—and the Brahmins in particular—resorted to the company of the prostitutes, who are all dedicated, more or less, to the service of some temple.

All the dancing women and musicians of Southern India formerly belonged to the Corinlar, a low caste, of which the respectable members, however, disdain connection with them.

They thus formed a separate order, and a certain number were attached to every temple of any consequence, receiving very small allowances. They were mostly prostitutes, at least to the Brahmins. Those attached to the edifices of great sanctity were entirely reserved for these priestly sensualists, who would have dismissed any one connecting herself with a Christian, a Mussulman, or a person of inferior caste. The others hired themselves out indiscriminately, and were greatly sought after. Their accomplishments seduced the men. The respectable women, ignorant, insipid, and tasteless, were neglected for the more attractive prostitutes. Under the rule of the Mohammedans, who were much addicted to this class of pleasures, the Brahmins did not dare enforce their exclusive privileges, but afterwards resumed their sway with great energy. A set of dancers was usually hired out at prices varying from twelve shillings to six pounds sterling. They performed at private entertainments as well as public festivals. Each troop was under a chief. When one became old she was turned away without provision, unless she had a handsome daughter following the same occupation, and in this case was usually treated by the girl with liberality and affection. Buchanan tells us that all he saw were of very ordinary appearance, inelegant in their dress, and dirty in their person. Many had the itch, and some were vilely diseased.

In the temples of Tulava, near Mangalore, a curious custom prevailed. Any woman of the four pure castes who was tired of her husband, or as a widow was weary of chastity, or as a maiden, of celibacy, went to the sacred building and ate some of the rice offered to the idol. She was then publicly questioned as to the cause of her resolution, and allowed the option of living within or without the precincts of the temple. If she chose the former, she got a daily allowance of food and annually a piece of cloth. She swept the holy building, fanned the image of the god, and confined her prostitution to the Brahmins. Usually some priestly officer of the revenue appropriated one of these women to himself, paying her a small fee or sum, and would flog her, in the most insulting manner, if she cohabited with any other man while under his care. Part of the daughters were given away in marriage, and part followed their mother's calling.

The Brahminy women who chose to live outside of the temple might cohabit with any men they pleased, but were obliged to pay a sixteenth part of their profits to the Brahmins. They were an infamous class. This system still obtains, though in a modified degree. In other parts of the region it prevails more or less. In Sindh every town of importance has a troop of dancing girls. No entertainment is complete without them. Under the native government this vice was largely encouraged. The girls swallowed spirits to stimulate their zeal. They are, many of them, very handsome, and are all prostitutes. To show the system of manners prevailing before the British conquest, it may be remarked that numbers of these women accumulated great fortunes, and that the voices of a band of prostitutes were louder than all other sounds at the Durbars of the debauched Amirs. In consequence of this the people of Sindh were hideously demoralized. Intrigues were carried on to an extraordinary extent in private life, and women generally were very lax. An evident reform is already perceptible.

Among the Hindus immorality is not a distinguishing characteristic, though many men of high grade pass their nights with dancers and prostitutes. In the temples of the south lascivious ceremonies still occur, but in Hindustan Proper such scenes are not often enacted. This decency of public manners appears of recent introduction, which is indeed a reasonable supposition, for the people have now aims in life, which they never enjoyed in security under their former rulers. It was for the interest of the princes that their subjects should be indolent and sensual. It is for the interest of the new government that they should be industrious and moral. Great efforts have been made with this object, and much good has resulted.

Towards the close of the last century an official report was made by Mr. Grant, and addressed to the Court of Directors. It was the result of an inquiry instituted into the morals of British India. India and Bengal were especially held in view. Much laxity of morals in private life then prevailed, and he believed that many intrigues were altogether concealed, while many that were discovered were hushed up. Receptacles for women of infamous character everywhere abounded, and were licensed. The prostitutes had a place in society, making a principal figure at all the entertainments of the great. They were admitted even into the zenanas to exhibit their dances. Lord Cornwallis, soon after his arrival in Bengal, was invited by the Nawab to one of these entertainments, but refused to go. The frightful punishments against adultery appeared enacted far more to protect the sanctity of caste than public or private virtue. A man committing the crime was threatened with the embraces, after death, of an iron figure of a woman made red hot. Connection, however, with prostitutes and dancing girls was permitted by the written law.

If that account was correct—and it is corroborated by many others—an immense amelioration must have taken place. The Hindus are now generally chaste, and the profligacy of their large cities does not exceed that of large cities in Europe. In Benares, in 1800, out of a population of 180,000, there were 1500 regular prostitutes, besides 264 Nach or dancing girls. They were all of the *Sudra*, which is a very low caste. In Dacca there were, out of a population of 35,238 Mohammedans and 31,429 Hindus, 234 Mohammedan and 539 Hindu prostitutes.

At Hurdwar it was one of the duties of the female pilgrims to the sacred stream to bathe stark naked before hundreds of men, which does not indicate any great modesty.

The better order of Nach girls are of the highest grace and fascination, with much personal charm, which they begin to lose at 20 years of age. They mostly dress in very modest attire, and many are decent in their manners.

The Gipsies of India, many of whom are Thugs, have numbers of handsome women in their camps, whom they send out as prostitutes to gain money, or seduce the traveller from his road.

It is said that many of the Europeans scattered over India encourage immorality, taking temporary companions. A large class of half-caste children has been certainly growing up in the country, whose mothers are not all the children of white men.

The institution of slavery in Malwa was principally confined to women. Almost all the prostitutes were of this class. They were purchased when children by the heads of companies, who trained them for the calling, and lived upon the gains of their prostitution. The system is even at present nearly similar, the girls being bargained away by their parents into virtual servitude. Many of the wealthy Brahmins, with from 50 to 200 slaves, employed them all day in the menial labours of the establishment, and at night dispersed them to separate dwellings, where they were permitted to prostitute themselves as they pleased. A large proportion of the profits, however, which accrued from this vile traffic formed the share of the master, who also claimed as slaves the children which might spring from this vile intercourse. The female slaves and dancing girls could not marry, and were often harshly used. Society was disorganized by the vast bastard breed produced by this system.

The Europeans at Madras, a few years ago, did not consider their liaisons with the native women so immoral as they would have been considered in England. The concubines were generally girls from the lower ranks, purchased from their mothers. Their conduct usually depends on the treatment they receive. Many of them become exceedingly faithful and attached, being bitterly jealous of any other native women interfering with their master's affections, but never complaining of being superseded by an English wife. They are often, however, extravagant gamblers, and involve their "lovers" in heavy debts.

An Indian mother will sometimes dedicate her female child to prostitution at the temple; and those who are not appropriated by the Brahmins may go with any one, though the money must be paid into a general fund for the support of the establishment.

Some of the ceremonies performed in the temples of the south, by the worshippers of the female deities, were simply orgies of the impurest kind. When a man desired to be initiated into these rites, he went with a priest, after various preliminary rites, to some house, taking nine females (one a Brahmin) and nine men — one woman for himself, and another for his sacerdotal preceptor. All being seated, numerous ceremonies were performed until twelve o'clock at night, when they gratified their inflamed passions in the most libidinous manner. The women, of course, were prostitutes by habit or profession. Men and women danced naked before thousands of spectators at the worship of the goddess Doorga. The impurities originated usually with the priests. Many of the Brahmins persuaded their disciples to allow them to gratify their lust upon their young wives, declaring it was a meritorious sacrifice. At the temple of Juggernaut, during the great festivals, a number of females were paid to dance and sing before the god daily. These were all prostitutes. They lived in separate houses, not in the temple.

The daughters of Brahmins, until eight years old, were declared by the religious code to be objects of worship, as forms of goddesses. Horrid orgies took place at the devotions paid them. Other women might be chosen as objects of adoration. A man must select from a particular class—his own wife or a prostitute: she must be stripped naked while the ceremony is performed, and this is done in a manner too revolting to describe. The clothes of the prostitutes hired to dance before the idols are so thin that they may almost be said to have been naked. Thus the immorality of the Hindoos, as far as it extended, was encouraged by their religion.

In another way some classes of Brahmins contributed to demoralize the people. A man of this profession would marry from three to 120 wives, in different parts of the country. Many, indeed, earned a living in this manner; for as often as they visited any woman, her father was obliged to make a present. Some go once after their marriage, and never go again; while others visit their wives once in three or four years. Some of the more respectable Brahmins never hold sexual intercourse with any of their wives, who dwell at home, but treat them with great respect. These neglected women often take to prostitution. The brothels of Calcutta and other large cities are crowded with such cast-off mistresses of the Brahmins. They procure abortion when pregnant. In the city of Bombay a whole quarter is inhabited chiefly by prostitutes. Riding in the environs, the European resident is frequently assailed by men, or sometimes boys, who inquire by signs or words, whether he desires a companion; should he assent, the woman is privately brought to his house in a close palanquin, or he is taken to a regular place of resort, in one of these vehicles, which are contrived for secrecy.

Among the Nairs, on the coast of Malabar, the institution of marriage has never been strictly or completely introduced.

Polyandrism is practised. A woman receives four or five brothers as her husbands, and a slipper left at the door is a signal that she is engaged with one of them. The mother is thus the only parent known, and the children inherit the property of the family in equal divisions. In some cases the Nairs marry a particular woman, who never leaves her mother's home, but has intercourse with any men she pleases, subject to the sacred law of caste. In the mountain community of Tibet the same custom prevails. It is to be regretted that our information on this subject is not more explicit and full.

The venereal disease is known in most parts of Hindustan. Some, with little reason, suppose it was carried there after the discovery of America. Had it been so, its introduction would probably have been noticed in history or by some tradition. It is not, indeed, called by any Sanscrit word, but is known by a Persian name*.

OF PROSTITUTION IN CEYLON.

IN Ceylon the influence of Christianity, accompanied by the moral law of England, is working a reform in the manners of large classes among the people. Under the original institutions of the Singhalese, they never licensed public prostitution; and whatever effect the Buddhist religion produced, it produced in the cause of virtue. The temples were never made brothels; but the character of the people is naturally sensual, and the capital vices of society widely prevail among them. The Buddhist code, indeed, abounds with precepts inculcating not only chastity, but rigid conti-

* Hamilton's East India Gazetteer; Buchanan's Journey in the Mysore, &c.; Bishop Heber's Journal; Hamilton's Description of Hindustan; British Friend of India Magazine; Asiatic Researces; Hugh Murray's Account of India; Conformité des Coutumes des Indes Orienteaux avec celles des Juifs; Tod's Travels in Western India; Tod's Annals of Rajasthan; Launcelot Wilkinson's Second Marriage of Widows in India; Papers presented to Parliament in 1803, on Infanticide; Grant's Observations on Society and Morals among our Asiatic Subjects; Davidson's Travels in Upper India; Mayne's Continental India; Campbell's British India; Hough's Christianity in India; Abbé Dubois' Letters on the Hindus; Malcolm's Memoir on Central India; Bevan's Thirty Years in India; Crawfurd's Researches concerning India; Hoffmeister's Travel's in India; Ward's Account of the Hindus; Mill's History of British India, Notes by Wilson; Ferishta's Mohammedan History; Thornton's History; Penhoen's Empire Anglais; Xavier; Raymond; Jaseigny; L'Inde.

nence. Profligacy, however, among the men, and want of chastity among the women, are general characteristics of all classes, from the highest to the humblest caste. To this day the disregard of virtue is a crying sin of the women, even of those who profess Christianity. Murders often occur from the jealousy of husbands or lovers detecting their wives or mistresses with a paramour.

In Ceylon, as in continental India, the division of castes is by the ancient and sacred law absolute, though custom sometimes infringes the enactments of the holy code. Marriage from a higher into a lower caste is peremptorily forbidden; though occasionally it is tolerated, but never approved, between a man of honourable and a woman of inferior rank. If a female of noble blood engage in a criminal intrigue with a plebeian, his life has on many occasions been sacrificed to wash out the stain, and formerly hers was also required to obliterate the disgrace. A recent and striking instance of this kind came to the knowledge of Mr. Charles Sirr. The daughter of a high-caste Kandian, enjoying the liberty which in Ceylon is allowed to women of all grades, became attached to a young man of lower caste, and entreated her parent's consent to the match, begging them to excuse her for her affection's sake, and declaring she could not live unless permitted to fulfil the design on which her heart was set. They refused, and, though the petition was again and again renewed, remained obdurate in their denial. The girl was some time after found to have sacrificed her honour to the man whom she loved, but dared not wed. He was all the while willing and desirous to marry her, and would have married her then, but her parents were inexorable. To preserve the honour of the family, the father slew his daughter with his own hand. The English authorities at once arrested the murderer, brought him to trial, and condemned him to death. He resolutely asserted his right to do as he pleased with the girl, protesting against any judicial interference of the English with his family arrangements. He was, nevertheless, executed, as a warning; and several of these examples have had a most salutary influence in restraining the passions of the natives in various parts of the island. It was undoubtedly the man's sense of honour that impelled him to murder his daughter; and she was thus the victim of caste prejudices, which in Ceylon are so rigid that a man could not force his slave to marry into a rank below him, whether free-born or otherwise.

In Ceylon, as in most other parts of Asia, marriages are contracted at a very early age. A man, by the law, "attains his majority" when sixteen years old, and thenceforward is released from paternal control; all engagements, however, which he may form previous to that time, without the consent of his friends in authority, are null and void. A girl, as soon as she is marriageable according to nature, is marriageable according to law; and her parents, or, if she be an orphan, her nearest kindred, give a feast—grand or humble, according to their means—when she is introduced to a number of unmarried male friends. If she be handsome or rich, a crowd of suitors is sure to be attracted. Free as women are in Ceylon after their marriage, they are rarely consulted beforehand on the choice of a partner. That is settled for the girl. To this custom much of the immorality prevalent in the island, as well as in all parts of the East, may without a doubt be ascribed. Where the sexes are not free to form what lawful unions they please, it may be taken as an axiom that they will have recourse to irregular intrigues.

When the feast is given at which a young girl is introduced as marriageable—a custom very similar in form and *object* to that which obtains in our own country—numerous young unmarried men of the same caste are invited to the house. In a short time after, a relative or friend of any young man who may desire to take the maiden as his wife, calls upon her family, and insinuates that a rumour of the intended union is flying abroad. If this be denied, quietly or otherwise, the matchmaker loses no time in withdrawing; but if it is answered in a jocular bantering strain, he takes his leave, with many compliments, to announce his reception to the father of the bridegroom. This personage, after a day or two, makes *his* call, inquires into the amount of the marriage dowry, and carries the negotiation a few steps further. Mutual visits are exchanged, and all arrangements made, with great precision. The mother of the young man, with several other matrons, take the girl into an inner room, where she is stripped, and her person examined, to see that it is free from any corporal defect, from ulcers, and from any cutaneous disease. Should this investigation prove satisfactory, numerous formalities succeed, and an auspicious day is fixed upon for the wedding. This takes place with much ceremony, the stars being in all things consulted. Should the bridegroom's horoscope refuse to agree with that of the bride, his younger brother may wed her for him by a species of proxy. The whole is a tedious succession of formal observances, not so much the ordinance of religion as the details of an ancient ritual etiquette. This is the Buddhaical custom; but it is immensely expensive, and cannot be followed by the very poor classes. It is also forbidden to people of extremely low caste, even though they should be wealthy enough to afford, or sufficiently improvident to risk it. Among the humble and indigent the marriage is confirmed by the mutual consent of the parents and the young couple passing a night together.

One of the most remarkable features in the social aspect of Ceylon is the institution of polyandrism, which among the Kandians is permitted and practised to a great extent. A Kandian matron of high caste is sometimes the wife of eight brothers. The custom is justified upon various grounds. Sirr expressed to a Kandian chief of no mean rank his abhorrence of this revolting practice. The man was surprised at these sentiments, and replied that on the contrary it was an excellent custom. Among the rich it prevented litigation; it saved property from minute subdivision; it concentrated family influence. Among the poor it was absolutely necessary, for several brothers could not each maintain a separate wife, or bear the expense of a whole family, which jointly they could easily do. The offspring of these strange unions call all the brothers alike their fathers, though preference is given to the eldest, and are equal heirs to the family property; should litigation, however, arise concerning the inheritance, they often all claim the senior brother as a parent, and the Kandian laws recognise this claim.

Although, when a plurality of husbands is adopted, they are usually brothers, a man may, with the woman's consent, bring home another, who enjoys all the marital rights, and is called an associated husband. In fact, the first may, subject to his wife's pleasure, bring home as many strangers as he pleases, and the children inherit their property equally. It is rare, however, to meet one of these associated husbands among the Kandians of higher and purer caste, though two or more brothers continually marry the same woman. This revolting custom is now confined to the province of Kandy, though some writers assert that it was formerly prevalent throughout the maritime districts. In these, however, monogamy is at present practised, except by the Mohammedans, who are polygamists. Statements to the contrary have been laid before us; but Sirr positively asserts that he never saw a Kandian or Singhalese who had acknowledged himself to have more than a single wife. The Muslims, though long settled in the island, preserve their peculiar characteristics, their religion, habits, and manners, which they have not communicated to the rest of the population.

There are two kinds of marriage in Kandy, the one called "Bema," the other "Deega." In the first of these the husband goes to live at his wife's residence, and the woman shares with her brothers the family inheritance. He, however, who is married after this fashion, enjoys little respect from his bride's relations; and if he gives offence to her father, or the head of the household, may be at once ejected from the abode. In reference to this precarious and doubtful lodgement there is an ancient proverb still popular in Kandy. It says that a man wedded according to the Bema process should only take to his bride's dwelling four articles of property—a pair of sandals to protect his feet, a palm-leaf to shield his head from the fiery rays of the sun, a walking staff to support him if he be sick, and a lantern to illuminate his path should he chance to be ejected during darkness. He may thus be prepared to depart at any hour of the day or night.

Deega, the other kind of marriage, is that in which the wife passes from underneath the parental roof to dwell in her husband's own house. In this case she relinquishes all claim to a share in her family inheritance, but acquires a contingent right to some of her husband's property. The man's authority is, under this form of contract, far greater than under that of Bema. He cannot be divorced without his own consent, while, in the other case, separation, as we have seen, is a summary process, entirely depending on the caprice of the woman or her family. In a country where the female population is considerably less numerous than the male, and where women generally enjoy much freedom, a certain degree of indulgence will always be granted to the fickle quality in their character. In Ceylon this liberty in the one sex involves a certain kind of slavery in the other. Women frequently seek for divorces upon the most frivolous and trifling pretexts, and as these are too easily attainable by the simple return of the marriage gifts, they continually occur. Should a child be born within nine months from the day of the final separation, the husband is bound to maintain it for the first three years of its life, after which it is considered sufficiently old to be taken from its mother. If, however, while under the marriage pledge, the woman defiles herself by adultery, the husband, if with his own eyes he was the witness of her infidelity, might with his own hands, under the native law, take away the life of her paramour. Notwithstanding this terrible privilege, it is asserted with consistency by many authorities that, in all parts of Ceylon, from the highest to the lowest caste, the want of conjugal faith in the married, and chastity in the unmarried people, is frightful to consider. When a man puts away his wife for adulterous intrigue, he may disinherit her and the whole of her offspring, notwithstanding that he may feel and acknowledge them all to be his own children. When, however, he seeks a divorce from caprice, he renounces all claim to his wife's inheritance or actual property, and must divide with her whatever may have been jointly accumulated during the period of their cohabitation. The men of Ceylon do not always, however, exercise their privileges. They are generally very indulgent husbands. Many of them, indeed, are uxorious to an offensive extreme, and forgive offences which, by most persons, are held unpardonable. A short time since a Kandian applied to the British judicial authorities to compel the return to him and his children of an unfaithful wife, who had deserted her home for that of a paramour. The husband pleaded his love for her, implored her for her children's sake to come back, and promised to forgive her offence; but she turned away from him, and coolly asked the judge if he could force her to return. He answered that unfortunately he could not, but advised her to return to the home of her lawful partner, who was ready to forgive and embrace her. She disregarded equally the entreaties of the one and the exhortation of the other, and returned to her paramour, whom she shortly afterwards deserted for another.

The numerous instances of this kind which happen in the island have encouraged a swarm of satirical effusions upon the faithlessness of the female sex; but if the women were also poets, they might echo every note of the song. In illustration of the estimate formed of them, we may quote a few lines translated from the original by Sirr. They apply to the fraudulent disposition of women, and have become proverbial among the people.

"I've seen the adumbra tree in flower, white plumage on the crow,
And fishes' footsteps on the deep have traced through ebb and flow.

If man it is who thus asserts, his words you may believe;
But all that woman says distrust—she speaks but to deceive."

The adumbra is a species of fig-tree, and the natives assert that no mortal has ever seen its bloom.

Under the native kings the Singhalese were forbidden to contract marriage with any one of nearer affinity than the second cousin; such an union was incestuous, and severely punished. Under the English government, however, many of these old restrictions have been modified. Among the Christian population, on the other hand —Catholic as well as Protestant—many traces of their old idolatry are still distinctly visible in the ceremony of marriage.

The Buddhist law allows to every man, whatever his grade, only one wife; but the ancient Kandian princes, of course, broke this law and took as many wives or concubines as they pleased.

We have alluded to the numerical difference between the sexes. The population of Ceylon is about 1,500,000, and the males exceed the females by nearly a tenth. In 1814 it was 476,000; there were 20,000 more males than females. In 1835 there was a population of 646,000 males, and 584,000 females. At both these periods the disparity was greatest in the poorest places. In the fishing villages, where wholesome food abounded, there were more females than males. The same circumstance is true at the present day. Some writers attribute this to a gracious provision of Nature, which checks the increase of the people; but Nature makes no provision against unnatural things, and starvation is a monstrous thing in a fertile country. We may with more safety assign as a cause the open or secret infanticide, which, under the old laws, was common. Female children, except the first born, born under a malignant star, were sure to be sacrificed. It was hardly considered an offence; but being, under the British rule, denounced as murder, has been gradually abolished. The easier means of life, which in Ceylon and throughout the rest of our Asiatic dominions are afforded to the people under English sway, take away the incentive of poverty to crime. The population has enormously increased, an unfailing sign of good government, if misery does not increase with it.

The social position of the Singhalese women is not so degraded as in many other parts of the East; the poor labouring hard, but as partners rather than as slaves. This superior condition does not, unhappily, elevate their moral character, for it is un-

CHINESE WOMAN (Prostitute),
ACCUSED OF DISORDERLY CONDUCT BEFORE A JUDGE.
[*From* Alexander's *Illustrations of China.*]

accompanied by other essential circumstances. Profligacy, we have said, is widely prevalent in Ceylon; yet prostitution, at least of the avowed and public kind, is not so. Under the Kandian dynasty it was peremptorily forbidden; a common harlot had her hair and ears cut off and was whipped naked. If, however, we accept the general definition of the word prostitution as any obscene traffic in a woman's person, we shall find much of it clandestinely practised. The women are skilful in procuring abortion, and thus rid themselves of the consequences which follow their intrigues. Of course, in the sea-port towns prostitution exists, but we have no account of it. It is fair, however, to notice the opinions of Sir Emerson Tennent, that the morals of the people in these and in all other parts of the islands are rapidly improving, and that marriage is *becoming* a more sacred tie*.

Of Prostitution in China.

In the immense empire of China, the civilization of which has been cast in a mould fashioned by despotism, a general uniformity of manners is prevalent. Singular as many of its customs are, they vary very little in the different provinces, for although the population be composed of a mixture of races, the iron discipline of the government forces all to bend to one universal fashion. The differences which are remarked between the practice of the people in one district, and those of another, spring only from the nature of circumstances. It is more easy, therefore, to take an outline view of this vast empire, than it is to sketch many smaller countries, where the uniformity of manners is not so absolute.

China affords a wide and interesting field for our inquiry. Were our information complete, there is perhaps no state in the world with reference to which so curious an account might be written as China, with its prostitution system. Unfortunately, however, the negligence or prudery of travellers has allowed the subject to be passed over. We know that a remarkable system of this kind does exist, that prostitutes abound in the cities of the Celestial Empire, and that they form a distinct order; we know something of the classes from which

* Sirr's Ceylon and the Singhalese; Pridham's History of Ceylon; Forbes' Eleven Years in Ceylon; Davy's Interior of Ceylon; Campbell's Excursions in Ceylon; Knox's Captivity in Ceylon; Knighton's History of Ceylon; Tennent's Christianity in Ceylon.

they are taken, how they are procured, in what their education consists, where and in what manner they live, and how and by whom they are encouraged. But this information is to be derived, not from any full account by an intelligent and observing inquirer, but from isolated facts scattered through a hundred books which require to be connected, and then only form a rough and incomplete view of the subject. Statistics we have positively none, though ample opportunities must be afforded travellers for arriving at something near the truth in such cities as Canton. However, from what knowledge we possess it is evident the social economy of the Chinese with respect to prostitution presents clear points of analogy with our own.

In conformity with the plan of this inquiry, we proceed first to ascertain the general condition of the female sex in China. Abundant information has been supplied us on this subject, as well by the written laws, and by the literature of the country, as by the travellers who have visited and described it.

As in all Asiatic, indeed in all barbarous, countries, women in China are counted inferior to men. The high example of Confucius taught the people—though their own character inclined them before, and was reflected from him—that the female sex was created for the convenience of the male. The great philosopher spoke of women and slaves as belonging to the same class, and complained that they were equally difficult to govern. That ten daughters are not equal in value to one son is a proverb which strongly expresses the Chinese sentiment upon this point, and the whole of their manners is pervaded by the same spirit. Feminine virtue, indeed, is severely guarded by the law, but not for its own sake. The well-being of the state, and the interest of the male sex, are sought to be protected by the rigorous enactments on the subject of chastity; but the morality, like the charity of that nation, is contained principally in its codes, essays, and poems, for in practice they are among the most demoralised on the earth.

The spirit of the Salic law might naturally be looked for in the political code of such a state. It is so. The throne can be occupied only by a man. An illegitimate son is held in more respect than a legitimate daughter. The constitution provides that if the principal wife fail to bear male children, the son of the next shall succeed, and if she be barren also, of the next, and so on, according to their seniority, the son of each has a contingent claim to the sovereignty.

Thus in the most important department of their public economy the national sentiment is manifested. We may now examine the laws which regulate the intercourse of the sexes, and then inquire into the actual state of manners. It will be useful to remember the truth, which has already been stated, that no language is so full of moral axioms and honourable sentiments as the Chinese, while no nation is more flagitious in its practice.

The government of China, styled paternal because it rules with the rod, regulates the minutest actions of a man's career. He is governed in everything—in the temple, in the street, at his own table, in all the relations of life. The law of marriage, for instance, is full, rigid, and explicit. The young persons about to be wedded know little or nothing of the transaction.

Parental authority is supreme, and alliances are contracted in which the man and wife do not see each others' faces until they occupy the same habitation and are mutually pledged for life. Match-making in China is a profession followed by old women, who earn what we may term a commission upon the sales they effect. When a union between two families is intended, its particulars must be fully explained on either side, so that no deceit shall be practised. The engagement is then drawn and the amount of presents determined, for in all countries where women hold this position, marriage is more or less a mercantile transaction. When once the contract is made, it is irrevocable. If the friends of the girl repent and desire to break the match, the man among them who had authority to give her away is liable to receive fifty strokes of the bamboo, and the marriage must proceed. Whatever other engagements have been entered into are null and punishable, and the original bridegroom has in all cases a decisive claim. If he, on the other hand, or the friend who represents and controls him, desire to dissolve the compact, giving a marriage present to another woman, he is chastised with fifty blows, and compelled to fulfil the terms of his first engagement, while his second favourite is at liberty to marry as she pleases. If either of the parties is incontinent after the ceremony of betrothal, the crime is considered as adultery, and so punished. But if any deceit be practised, and either family represent the person about to marry under a false description, they become liable to severe penalties, and on the part of the man most strictly.

The husband, finding that a girl had been palmed off on him by fraud, is permitted to release himself from the tie. Such incidents, nevertheless, do occasionally occur. One of rather an amusing nature is alluded to by several writers. A young man who had been promised in marriage the youngest daughter of a large family was startled when, after the ceremony was complete, he unveiled his bride, to find the eldest sister, very ugly and deeply pitted with the small pox. The law would have allowed him to escape from such an union, but he submitted, and soon afterwards consoled himself with a handsome concubine.

Although the girl, when once betrothed, is absolutely bound to the husband selected for her, he dare not, under pain of the bastinado, force her away before the specified time. On the other hand, her friends must not, under similar penalties, detain her after that time. Thus the law regulates the whole transaction, and the parents dispose as they will of their children. Occasionally, however, a young man, not yet emancipated from paternal authority, contracts a marriage according to his own inclination, and if the rites have actually been performed, it cannot be dissolved; but if he be only betrothed, and his parents have in the meanwhile agreed upon an alliance for him, he must relinquish his own design and obey their choice.

Polygamy is allowed in China, but under certain regulations. The first wife is usually chosen from a family equal in rank and riches to that of the husband, and is affianced with as much splendour and ceremony as the parties can afford. She acquires all the rights which belong to the chief wife in any Asiatic country. The man may then take as many as he pleases, who are inferior in rank to the first, but equal to each other. The term inferior wife is more applicable than that of concubine, as there is a form of espousal, and their children have a contingent claim to the inheritance. The practice, however, brings no honour, if it brings no positive shame, though now sanctioned by long habit. Originally it appears to have been condemned by the stricter moralists, and it has been observed that the Chinese term to describe this kind of companion is, curiously enough, compounded of the words *crime* and *woman*. It is a derogatory position, and such as only the poor and humble will consent to occupy. One of the national sayings, and the feeling with many of the women, is, that it is more honourable to be a poor man's wife than the concubine of an emperor. A man cannot, under the penalty of a hundred blows, degrade his first wife to this position, or raise an inferior wife to hers—no such act is valid before the law.

None but the rich can afford, and none but the loose and luxurious will practise, polygamy except when the first wife fails to bear a son. Unless some such reason exists, the opinion of moralists is against it. Men with too many wives lose the Emperor's confidence, since he accuses them of being absorbed in domestic concerns. In this case it is usual to take an inferior wife, who is purchased from the lower ranks for a sum of money, that an heir may be born to the house. The situation of these poor creatures is aggravated or softened according to the disposition of their chief, for they are virtually her servants, and are not allowed even to eat in her presence. They receive no elevation by her decease, but are for ever the mere slaves of their master's lust. At the same time their inferior position, and therefore inferior consequence, gains them some agreeable privileges. The principal wife is not allowed to indulge in conversation or any free intercourse with strangers—a pleasure which is sometimes enjoyed with little restraint by the others, as well as by the female domestics. Not much jealousy appears to be entertained by these women, who are easily to be procured. Their sons receive half as much patrimony as the sons of the mistress of the household.

The social laws of China inculcate the good treatment of wives; but the main solicitude of the legislator has been with respect to the fixity of the law, and the rights of the male or supreme sex. Leaving her parents' home, the girl is transferred into bondage. Some men, however, go to the house of their bride's father, which is contrary to the established form; but when once received across the threshold as a son-in-law, he cannot be ejected, and leaves only when he is inclined.

A man may not marry within a certain period of his chief wife's death; but if he takes a woman who has already been his concubine, the punishment is two degrees milder. So also with widows, who cannot be forced by their friends to make any new engagement at all, but are protected by the law. Women left in this position have a powerful dissuasive against a fresh union, in the entire independence which they enjoy, and which they could enjoy under no other circumstances.

With respect to the laws relating to consanguinity, the Chinese system is particularly rigid. The prohibited limits lie very widely apart. In this a change appears to have been effected under the Mantchus, for among the traces of ancient manners which become visible at a remoter period, revealed only, however, by the twilight of tradition, a profligate state of public morals is indicated. We find parents giving both their daughters in marriage to one man, while the intercourse of the sexes was all but entirely unrestrained. The strictness of the modern law is attended with some inconvenient results, for in China the number of family names is very small, while it enacted that all marriages between persons of the same family names are not only null and void, but punishable by blows and a fine. All such contracts between individuals previously related by marriage within four degrees, are denounced as incestuous. A man may not marry his father's or his mother's sister-in-law, his father's or mother's aunt's daughter, his son-in-law's or daughter-in-law's sister, his grandson's wife's sister, his mother's brother's or sister's daughter, or any blood relations whatever, to any degree, however remote. Such offences are punished with the bamboo. Death by strangling is enacted against one who marries a brother's widow, while with a grandfather's or father's wife it is more particularly infamous, and the criminal suffers the extreme disgrace of decapitation.

These regulations apply to the first wife, similar offences with regard to the inferior being visited with penalties two degrees less severe. Not only, however, are the degrees of consanguinity strictly defined, but the union of classes is under restriction. An officer of government within the third order marrying into a family under his jurisdiction, or in which legal proceedings are under his investigation, is subject to heavy punishment. The family of the girl, if they voluntarily aid him, incur the chastisement also; but if they have submitted under fear of his authority, they are exempt. To marry an absconded female, flying from justice, is prohibited. To take forcibly as a wife a freeman's daughter, subjects the offender to death by strangulation. An officer of government, or the son of any high functionary with hereditary honours, who takes as his first or inferior wife a female comedian or musician, or any member of a disreputable class, is punished by sixty strokes of the bamboo. An equal punishment is inflicted on any priest who marries at all; and, in addition to this, he is expelled his order. If he delude a woman under false pretences, he incurs the penalty of the worst incest. Slaves and free persons are forbidden to intermarry. Any person, conniving at, or neglecting to denounce, such illegal contracts, are criminals before the law.

The union after the betrothal must be completed; but it may also be broken. Seven causes, according to the law, justify a man in repudiating his first wife. These are—barrenness, lasciviousness, disregard of her husband's parents, talkativeness, thievish propensities, an envious suspicious temper, and inveterate infirmity. If, however, any of the three legal reasons against divorce can be proved by the woman, she cannot be put away—first, that she has mourned three years for her husband's family; second, that the family has become rich after having been poor before and at the time of marriage; third, her having no father or mother living to receive her. She is thus protected, in some measure, from her husband's caprice. If she commit adultery, however, he dare not retain, but must dismiss her. If she abscond against his will, she may be severely flogged; if she commit bigamy, she is strangled. When a man leaves his home, his wife must remain in it three years before she can sue for a divorce, and then give notice of her intention before a public tribunal. It is forbidden, under peremptory enactments, to harbour a fugitive wife or female servant.

A man finding his wife in the act of adultery may kill her with her paramour, provided he does it immediately, but only on that condition. If the guilty wife adds to her crime by intriguing against her husband's life, she dies by a slow and painful execution. If even the adulterer slay her husband without her knowledge, she is strangled. The privilege of putting a wife to death is not allowed for any inferior offence. To strike a husband, is punishable by a hundred blows and divorce; to disable him, with strangulation. In all these circumstances the inferior wife is punished one degree more severely. Thus offences against them are less harshly, and offences by them more rigidly, chastised. In addition to these legal visitations the bamboo is at hand to preserve discipline among the women.

One of the laws of China exhibits a peculiar feature of depravity in the people. It is enacted, that whoever lends his wife or daughter upon hire is to be severely punished, and any one falsely bargaining away his wife or his sister is to be similarly dealt with. All persons consenting to the transaction share the penalty. Nor is this an obsolete enactment against an unknown crime. Instances do not unfrequently occur of poor men selling their wives as concubines to their wealthier neighbours. Others prostitute them for gain; but these instances of profligacy usually occur in the large and crowded cities. Sometimes the woman consents, but sometimes also opposes the infamous design.

In 1832 a woman was condemned to strangulation for killing her husband by accident, while resisting an adulterer whom he had introduced for her to prostitute herself to him. These incidents occur only in the lowest class. Some men are as jealous as Turks, and maintain eunuchs to guard their wives.

Under this system many restrictions are imposed on the women of China. They form no part of what is called society, enjoying little companionship, even with persons of their own sex. Those of the better class are instructed in embroidering and other graceful but useless accomplishments. They are seldom educated to any extent, though some instances have occurred of learned women and elegant poetesses, who have been praised and admired throughout the country. Fond of gay clothes, of gaudy furniture, and brilliant decoration, they love nothing so much as display; and though assuming a demure and timid air, cannot be highly praised on this account, for their bashfulness is, in such cases, more apparent than real. Still they are generally described as faithful partners. Religious services are performed for them in the temple, to which women are admitted. The wives of the poorer sort labour in the fields, and perform all the drudgery of the house, an occupation which is held as suited to their nature. "Let my daughter sweep your house" is the expression made use of in offering a wife. It should be mentioned, however, to relieve the darkness of this picture, that husbands often present offerings at the temples, with prayers to the gods for the recovery of their sick wives. The idea may indeed suggest itself, that this is with a view to economy, as girls are costly purchases; but no man is the greater philosopher for asserting that a whole nation exists without the commonest sentiments of human nature. Indeed, many instances occur even in China of husbands and wives living as dear friends together, especially when polygamy has not been adopted in the dwelling. The obedience to old habits is not to be confounded with characteristic harshness in the individual; nor does it seem impossible, when we examine the variety of manners in the world, to believe in a strong and tender attachment between a man and the woman whom, in adherence to ancient usage, he would not allow to eat at the same table with himself. A privilege belongs to the female sex here which it enjoys in no other barbarian country. A strong authority is recognised in the widow over her son. She is acknowledged to have the right to be supported by him, and it is a proverbial saying, that "a woman is thrice dependent—before marriage on her father, after marriage on her husband, when a widow on her son."

From this view of the condition of women, and the regulations of marriage, we proceed to an important part of the subject—the infanticide for which China has been so infamously celebrated. It is impossible to conceive a more contradictory confusion of statements, than we have seen put forward with reference to this question. Weighing the various authorities, however, we are inclined to adopt a moderate view, rejecting the extravagant pictures of one, and the broad denials of the other set of writers. Infanticide, it cannot be disputed, is practised in the country, and to a considerable extent; but it is, and always will be impossible, to acquire the exact statistics, or even an approximation to the precise truth.

Two causes appear to have operated in encouraging this practice—the poverty of the lower classes, and the severity of the law with respect to the illicit intercourse of the sexes. The former is the principal cause. There is a strong maternal feeling in the woman's breast, and children are only destroyed when the indigence of the parents allows no hope of rearing them well. It is invariably the female child which is, under these circumstances, slain; for the son can always, after a few years, earn his livelihood, and be an assistance, instead of a burden, to the family. The birth of a female child is regarded as a calamity, and brings mourning into the house. One of the national proverbs expresses this fact in a striking manner, exhibiting also the inferior estimation in which that sex is viewed. It says, that to a female infant a common tile may be given as a toy, while to a male a gem should be presented.

When it is determined to destroy the offspring thus born under the roof of poverty, a choice of method is open. It may be drowned in warm water; its throat may be pinched; it may be stifled by a wet cloth tied over its mouth; it may be choked by grains of rice. Another plan is to carry the child, immediately after its birth, and bury it alive. Captain Collins, of the *Plover* sloop-of-war, relates that some of his company, while visiting the coast of China, saw a boat full of men and women, with four infants. They landed and dug two pits, in which they were about to inter their living but feeble victims, when they were disturbed. They then made off rapidly, and passed round a headland, beyond which they, no doubt, accomplished their purpose without interruption. When the missionary Smith was in the suburbs of Canton, in 1844, he was presented by a native with a work written by a mandarin, and published gratuitously at the expense of government, to discourage the practice of infanticide. When questioned upon the actual prevalence of the custom, the native said that, taking a circle with a radius of ten miles from the spot they then occupied, the number of infanticides within the space thus included would not exceed five hundred in a year. It was confined to the very poor, and originated in the difficulty of rearing and providing for their female offspring. The rich never encouraged, and the poor were ashamed, of the practice. He knew men who had drowned their daughters, but would not confess the act, speaking of their children as though they had died of disease. In Fokien province, on the contrary, infanticides were numerous. At a place called Kea-King-Chow, about five days' journey from Canton, there were computed to be 500 or 600 cases in a month. The comparative immunity of Canton from the contagion of this crime was the government foundling-hospital established there. About 500 female children, born of parents in poverty and want, were annually received, to have temporary provision and sustenance. From time to time, the more wealthy merchants and gentry visit the institution to select some of the children, whom they take home to educate as concubines or servants. The hospital has accommodation for at least 1000 infants, each of which is usually removed after three months, either to the house of some voluntary guardian, or to wet nurses in other districts. This is the only important institution of the kind in the province. Infanticide is still, even by the most favourable accounts, lamentably prevalent. The foundling-hospitals, of which there is one in every great town, do certainly oppose a check to the practice. That at Shanghae receives annually about 200 infants.

The villagers in the neighbourhood of Amoy confessed that female infanticide was generally practised among them, and their statements were expressed in a manner which left no doubt that they considered it an innocent and proper expedient for lightening the evils of poverty. Two out of every four, they said, were destroyed; but rich people, who could afford to bring them up never resorted to, because they never needed, such a means of relief. Some killed three, four, or even five out of six; it depended entirely on the circumstances of the individual. The object was effected immediately after the infant's birth. If sons, however, were born in alternate succession, it was regarded as an omen of happy fortune for the parents, and the daughters were spared. None of the villagers denied to any of their questioners the generality of the custom, but few would confess personally to the actual fact. In some districts one-half was reported as the average destruction of the female population, and in the cities some declared the crime was equally prevalent, though we may take this as the exaggeration which always attends the loose statements of ignorant men, who, having little idea of figures, are required to furnish a number, and speak at random.

Infanticide, however, is not wholly confined to the poor. It is occasionally resorted to by the rich to conceal their illicit amours. In 1838 a proclamation against it was published, but the general perpetration of the crime rendered its repression impossible, with such machinery as the Emperor has at his command. Abeel calculated that throughout a large district, the average was 39 per cent. of the female children. It is evident, however, from all these facts, that under an improved government, the crime might be altogether extinguished, not by severe enactments or vigilant police, but by rendering infanticide unnecessary in the eyes of the people.

The second cause which induces parents to destroy their children is the stringency of the law against the illicit intercourse of unmarried people; its provisions are equally characteristic and severe. To render its enforcement easier, the separation of the sexes is rigidly insisted upon. Not only are servants, but even brothers and sisters, prohibited from mixing except under regulation. Intercourse by mutual consent is punished with 70 blows, while with married people the penalty varies from 80 to 100. Violation of a female, wedded or single, is punished by strangulation. An assault, with intent to ravish, by 100 strokes of the bambu and perpetual banishment to a remote spot. Intercourse with children under twelve years of age is treated as rape. Should a child be born from one of these unlawful intrigues, its support devolves on the father; but if the transaction be thus far concealed, this evidence of it is usually sunk in the river, or flung out by the wayside. An unmarried woman found pregnant is severely punished, whether her accomplice can be discovered or not. The illicit intercourse of slaves with their masters' wives or daughters is punished with death; while officers of government, civil and military, and the sons of those who hold hereditary rank, if found indulging in criminal intrigues with females under their jurisdiction, are subjected to unmerciful castigation with the stick.

One grace is accorded to the weaker sex in China. No woman is committed to prison, except in capital cases, or cases of adultery. In all others they remain, if married, in the custody of their husbands; if single, in that of their friends. No woman quick with child can be flogged, tortured, or executed, until a hundred days after her delivery.

Women, however, of the poorer orders, whose friends do not care, or are unable, to be responsible for them, are lodged under the care of female wardens, and in reference to this we may instance a curious fact illustrative of prison discipline in China. In 1805 one of the great officers of government made a report to the Emperor, that three female warders of the prison were in the habit of engaging with traders in an illicit and disgraceful intercourse with female servants, and hiring out the female prisoners, not yet sentenced or waiting for discharge, to gain money for them by prostitution.

Sensual as the Chinese are, the punishable breach of the moral law—the intercourse of unmarried persons—is checked by the system of early marriages. Children are often betrothed in the cradle. Men seldom pass the age of twenty, or girls that of fifteen, in celibacy. The Parsees, however, of all ages, are notorious for their abandoned mode of life.

Prostitution, however, prevails to a prodigious extent. There is throughout the country a regular traffic in females. "Seduction and adultery," says Williams, "are comparatively unfrequent; but brothels and their inmates occur everywhere on land and water. One danger attending young girls going alone is, that they will be stolen for incarceration in these gates of hell."

This is in allusion to a very extraordinary system prevalent in the great cities of China. In 1832 it was calculated there were between 8000 and 10,000 prostitutes having abodes in and about Canton. Of these the greater portion had been stolen while children, and compelled to adopt that course of life. Dressed gaily, taught to affect happiness, and trained in seductive manners, they were examples of their class in Europe. Many young girls were carried away, forcibly violated, and then consigned to a brothel.

Hundreds of kidnappers, chiefly women, swarmed in the city, gaining a livelihood by the traffic in young girls and children. Nor was this the only way in which such places were supplied. In times of general scarcity or individual want, parents have been seen leading their own daughters through the streets and offering them for sale. The selling of children, says Conyngham, one of the most recent visitors to Canton, is an every-day occurrence, and is on the whole a check upon infanticide. The little victims are seen constantly passing on their way to the habitations of their purchasers gaily dressed out as though for some great ceremony or happy festival. Of these, indeed, some are disposed of as concubines, but many also are deliberately sold to be brought up as prostitutes. It is looked upon as a simple mercantile transaction, the children being transferred at once to the brothels, whence they are hired out for the profit of their masters. Some of those who are deserted or exposed to perish are reserved by the agents for these places; but the principal supply is brought by kidnappers. Proclamation after proclamation has been issued to complain of them, but with little effect. The system appears rather on the increase than otherwise.

The children thus purchased or picked up in the streets are educated with care, taught to play on various kinds of instruments, to dance, to sing, to perform in comedies or pantomimes, and to excel in many graceful accomplishments, which render them agreeable. They are often richly clothed, and adorned in such a way as to render them most attractive to the *roués* of Canton and Peking.

They do not often compress their feet, as it is a hindrance to their movements, but may be seen in the streets occasionally— though not often—with painted faces, looking boldly at the strangers who pass along. Of the houses they frequent we have no particular description; but they probably resemble much similar places of resort in civilized countries. A peculiar feature of China, however, is displayed in the floating brothels, which are the chief habitations of the prostitutes. Licentious as the native of that empire is in the general turn of his ideas, he makes a public display of his indulgence in those pleasures which in Europe men affect, at least, to conceal from general view. The floating brothels of the Pearl River are moored in conspicuous situations, and distinguished from the other boats by the superior style of their structure and decorations. The surface of the stream, indeed, is studded with beautiful junks, which are the first objects to attract the traveller's eye as he approaches the provincial city of Canton. Comparatively few of the women parade the streets, except when they form part of a public procession, so that there is at least in the heart of the town an appearance of morality.

Many of these brothel junks are called Flower Boats, and are resorted to by numbers of the class. They form, indeed, whole streets in the floating city on the Pearl River, which is one of the most remarkable features of Canton. The prostitutes themselves, like all women of the same sisterhood, lead a life of reckless extravagance—plunging while they can into all the exciting pleasures which are offered by their particular mode of life, careless of the future, and eagerly snatching at anything which may release them from the change of dulness or time for reflection. Diseases are very prevalent among them, and cause much havoc among the men who frequent their boats or houses. They endeavour to cure themselves by means of drugs and medicinal draughts, and by this means concentrate the malady upon some secret vital part, whence it shoots through the frame, but does not manifest itself until the victim is all but destroyed. With the exception of an unusual paleness and a heated appearance in the eyes, the prostitutes do not wear the aspect of disease; but they, indeed, paint themselves inordinately to mask the ravages of time or the maladies which afflict them.

The prostitutes of Canton are usually congregated in companies or troops, each of which is under the government of a man who is answerable for their conduct— if they rob, or disturb the peace, or commit any gross offence against decency, or perpetrate any other offence. National delicacy, however, has little to do with the prohibitions which restrain them from entering certain parts of the city, and forbid young men of rank and influence to hold intercourse with them. The brothel junks, of lofty build, brightly painted, and glittering with gaudy variegated flags, float in squadrons on the water, are seen and known by all, and are resorted to by numbers of the citizens. Persons pass to and from them without an attempt at disguise or concealment. Rich men, on festive occasions, make up a party of pleasure, embark in a gaily-decorated boat, send to one of the prostitute junks, engage as many of the women as they please, and spend the day in amusement with them. It is openly done, and no disgrace attaches to it. The junks themselves are fitted up in the interior—according to the class of prostitutes inhabiting them—with all the appurtenances of luxury, and on board them is a perpetual gala. It would be interesting to know how many of these boats are known to float on the Pearl River, with the average number of prostitutes in each.

But this is not the only, or the most offensive form which prostitution assumes in China. An incident which occurred at Shensee a few years ago illustrates another system, which is clandestine, though apparently carried on to a considerable extent. A young widow resided there with her mother-in-law, supporting herself and her companion by the wages of prostitution. At length her occupation failed her; she was deserted by her associates, and could procure no more rice or money by the pursuit of her vicious calling. The elder woman, however, would not hear of these excuses, ordered her daughter-in-law to obtain her usual supplies from the man she had last cohabited with, and on her declaring her inability, began to flog her. The prostitute defended herself, and at last, taking up a sickle, struck her relative dead. She was seized, tried, and condemned to be cut in pieces for the crime; but as her mother-in-law had been guilty of an illegal act in forcing her to prostitute herself, the sentence was changed to decapitation.

It is to be regretted that our sources of information on this subject are not more copious. Travellers have had opportunities of communicating more, but have refrained from doing so. We wait for a separate and full account of prostitution in China *.

* Staunton, Tee Tsing Leu Lee, Code of Criminal Law; Davis, the Chinese; Guttzlaff's China Opened; Fortune's Wanderings in the North of China; Smith's Visits to the Consular Cities of China; Montgomery Martin's China; Forbes's Five Years in China; Williams's Survey of the Chinese Empire; Tradescant Lay's Chinese as they Are; Morrison's View of China; Meadow's Desultory Notes on China; The Chinese Repository; Hugh Murray's Description of China; Thornton's History of China; Abeel's Residence in China; Cunyngham's Recollections of Service; Abel's Embassy to China; Medhurst's State of China; Auguste Harpman, Revue des Deux Mondes; Langdon's China; De Guignes, Voyage à Peking.

Of Prostitution in Japan.

Among the innumerable islands scattered over the southern and eastern oceans there are none more curious in their social aspects than Japan. We find there a kind of native civilization, influenced indeed by former intercourse with Europeans, but now complete within itself, and isolated from all other systems in the world. The mountainous, rocky, and arid country, has been fertilized from the centre to the sea by the persevering industry of a hardy race; they found it poor, and they have made it one of the richest agricultural regions in the globe. This fact serves to illustrate the national character.

The Japanese, upon whose institutions much light has been thrown by the learned and laborious researches of Mr. Thomas Rundall, of the Hakluyt Society, may be described as a punctilious, haughty, vindictive, and licentious people; but there is nothing vulgar in their composition. Truth is held in reverence, hospitality is viewed as sacred, and the bonds of friendship are regarded with extraordinary earnestness. St. Francis Xavier, the apostle of the Indies, declared "the Japans" to be the delight of his heart. There is, perhaps, more to admire than to love in their character. They are certainly elevated far above many of the nations who surround them, as well in the arts as in the amenities of life. Virtue is a recognised principle, and this indicates a phase of true civilization.

The character of the male is reflected by the female sex. Intelligent and agreeable in their manners, affectionate in their family relations, and faithful to their marriage vows, the women of Japan breathe all the pride of virtue. The man who attempts the honour of a matron sometimes encounters death in his adventure.

In illustration of this characteristic, Mr. Rundall relates an interesting anecdote. A noble, going on a journey, left his wife at home, and another man of rank made infamous proposals to her. Her scorn and indignation only inflamed him to his purpose, which he effected in spite of her denial. When her husband returned she received him with much reserve, and when he asked why, bade him wait until the morrow, when a grand feast was to be given. Among the guests was the noble who had wronged her. They sat down on the terraced roof of the house, and the festival began. After the repast the woman rose, declared the injury she had suffered, and passionately entreated to be slain, as a creature unfit to live. The guests, the husband foremost, besought her to be calm; they strove to impress her with the idea that she had done no wrong, that she was an innocent victim, though the author of the outrage merited no less punishment than death. She thanked them all kindly; she wept on her husband's shoulder—she kissed him affectionately—then, suddenly escaping from his embraces, rushed precipitately to the edge of the terrace, and cast herself over the parapet. In the confusion that ensued, the author of the mischief, still unsuspected, for the hapless creature had not indicated the offender, made his way down the stairs. When the rest of the party arrived he was found weltering in his blood by the corse of his victim. He had expiated his crime by committing suicide in the national manner, by slashing himself across the abdomen with two slashes in the form of a cross."

The condition of women in Japan varies with different classes. Those of high rank have a separate suite of rooms assigned to them, beyond which they are seldom seen. Among the middle and lower orders they enjoy more liberty, though they are careful to seclude themselves, and are distinguished in general by extraordinary reserve. Men pay them a polite respect not common among semi-barbarians, as the Japanese will continue to be until they are forced to acknowledge the duty of intercourse with the rest of mankind.

The marriage laws of Japan are curious, and vary in different classes. Among the wealthy they are occasions of extravagant parade and long ceremonies, in which the minutest detail is regulated by a peremptory law. A full description of all the marriage ceremonial would fill a small volume. A man can only take one wife; he is united to her in the temple. In addition, however, he may take as many concubines as he chooses, who are not degraded by their position. He may separate from a woman when he pleases; but one who is known to have done so must pay a large sum for the daughter of any other person whom he may desire to have. Marriages are seldom contracted before the age of fifteen. The courtship and betrothal are conducted with much formality; but sufficient opportunity is allowed to the youth of the two sexes to become acquainted each with the other.

The Japanese are not so jealous as many other Asiatics: "Indeed," says Captain Golovnin, "they are not more so than, considering the frailty of the sex, is reasonable." Nevertheless, a man may put his wife to death for whispering to a stranger; while adultery is always capitally punished, sometimes by the hand of the injured husband.

In the northern parts, it is said, that in the beginning of the seventeenth century a curious custom prevailed. When a woman was convicted of infidelity, her head was shaved. Her paramour was exposed to an equally disgraceful, but more whimsical penalty. The friends of his victim, whenever they met him, might strip him naked, and deprive him of his property. But the modesty with which youth are inspired from the cradle tends much to protect female virtue. The intercourse of the sexes, it will thus be seen, is regulated by very natural laws; the condition of the sex is somewhat high. Its virtues are prized by the men, and consequently are generally faithfully preserved.

We have said, however, that the men of Japan are licentious; since, therefore, the wives and daughters of the respectable classes are difficult to corrupt, a numerous sisterhood of prostitutes is rendered necessary. Accordingly we find them from the earliest period associating with every rank of men. In one of William Adams's letters, published under the editorship of Mr. Rundall, we find the king coming on board our countryman's vessel, bringing with him a number of female comedians. These formed large companies, and travelled from place to place, with a great store of apparel for the several parts they played. They belonged to one man, who set a price upon their intercourse with others, above which he dared not charge under pain of death. It was left to his own discretion to set a value on a girl at first; but afterwards he could not raise, though he might abate his charge. All bargains were made with him, and the woman must go whither she was directed. Men of the highest rank, when travelling through the islands, and resting at houses of entertainment, sent, without shame, for companies of these prostitutes; but the pander was never received by them, however wealthy he might be; after death he was also consigned to infamy. Bridled with a rope of straw, he was dragged in the clothes he died in through the streets into the fields, and there cast upon a dung-hill for dogs and fowls to devour.

In Kœmpfer's account of the city of Nangasaki we find a curious description of the prostitute system. The part of the town inhabited by these women was called "the bawdy-house quarter," and consisted of two streets, with the handsomest houses in Japan, situated on a rising hill. At these places the poor people of the town sold their handsome daughters while very young, that is, from ten to twenty years of age. Every bawd kept as many as she was able in one house; some had seven, others 30, who were commodiously lodged, taught to dance, sing, play on musical instruments, and write letters. The elder ones taught the younger, who in return waited on them; the most docile and accomplished were most sumptuously treated. The price of these women was regulated by law; and one wretched creature, having passed through all the degrees of degradation, occupied a small room near the door, where she acted as watch all night, and sold herself for a miserable coin. Others were set to this task as a punishment for ill behaviour. The infamy of this vile profession attached justly, not so much to the unhappy women themselves, as to their parents who educated them to it. Many, as they grew up, changed their mode of life, and were received again among the reputable and chaste. Generally well educated and politely bred, they often procured husbands, and passed from a life of daily prostitution to one of unswerving fidelity. The pander and the tanner of leather occupied the same position in society; which shows that the prejudice of class, rather than the abhorrence of an infamous calling, ruled the Japanese.

The historian classes the temples and brothels together, and not without justice. Prostitution was greatly encouraged by the priests. In their public spectacles, representing the adventures of gods and goddesses, young prostitutes, richly attired, were engaged to act. Their performances resembled those of the European ballet— dress, gesture, and action expressing that which in a drama language would represent.

Such was the prostitute system in the great cities; throughout the country a similar system prevailed. The houses of entertainment lining the main highways, with the tea-booths of the villages, were frequented by innumerable girls. These usually spent the morning in painting and dressing themselves, and about noon made their appearance standing before the door of the house, or sitting on benches, whence, with smiling face and coy address, they solicited the passengers. In some places their chattering and laughter were heard above all other sounds; two villages, called Akasaki and Goy, were celebrated on this account, all the houses being brothels, each containing from three to seven prostitutes. The Japanese seldom passed one of these "great storehouses of whores" without holding intercourse with some of these women. Kœmpfer asserts, in contradiction to Caras, who married a native, that there was in his time scarcely one house of entertainment in the islands which was not a brothel. When one inn had too many customers, it borrowed some girls from a neighbour who had some to spare. This profligate system is said, in the Japanese traditions, to have taken its rise at a remote period, during the reign of a certain martial emperor. That monarch, who was perpetually marching his armies to and fro, feared lest his soldiers should become weary of separation from their wives; he therefore licensed public and private brothels, which multiplied to such an extent that Japan came to be known as "the bawdy-house of China." This was in allusion to a period when prostitution was made in that empire an unlawful calling, and suppressed by severe laws. The people, deprived of the resources they had formerly enjoyed at home, made Japan the place of resort; so that its prostitution system flourished far and wide.

These accounts appear extravagant, and doubtless are so in some degree; all writers, however, coincide in describing the prostitution system of Japan as very extensive and flagitious. The French historian, Charleroix, repeats the statement of Kœmpfer. We have before us extracts from the autograph "diary of occurrants" written by Captain Richard Cock, who was chief of the English factory at Firando, from the year 1613 to 1623. There are many passages corroborative of the representations we have given. Of these some examples follow, which are also interesting as illustrations of Japanese manners.

"A.D. 1616, Sept. 8th (at Edo).—We dyned or rather supped at a merchant's house called Neyem Dono, where he provided caboques, or women players, who danced and sung; and when we returned home he sent every of them to lie with them that would have them all night.

"October 24 (at Yuenda, between Edo and Firando.)—We went to bed, and paid 3500 gins; and to the servants, 300 gins; and to the children, 200 gins, or about 200*l*. This extraordinary charge was for that we had extraordinary good cheer, being brought hither by a merchant of Edo, our friend, called Neyemon Edo, and every one a wench sent to him that would have her. I gave one of them an ichebo, but would not have her company.

"1617–18, January 27th (at Firando).—Skiezazon Dono set the masts of his junk this day, and made a feast in Japan fashion. 29th. Skiezazon Dono and his consorts had the feast of Baccus for their junk this day, dancing through the streets with caboques or women players, and entered into an English house in that order, most of their heads being heavier than their heels, that they could not find their way home without leading.

"March 29th (at Firando).—The kyng and the rest of the noblemen came to dyner (at the English house), and, as they said, were entertained to their own content, and had the dancing beares or caboques to fill their wine; Nifon Catanges, with a blind fiddler to sing, ditto.

"July 11th.—There came a company of players, or caboques, with apes and babons, sent from the tono, or king, to play at our house.

"December 6th (at Meaco).—Our host, Meaco's brother-in-law, invited us to dyner to a place of pleasure without the city, where the dancing girls or caboques were with a great feast; and there came an antick dance of satyrs or wild men of other Japons, until whom I gave 1000 gins (about 10s.), and a bar of plate to the good man of the house, value about 1l. 1s. 6d. So the dancing girls were sent home after us."

As not altogether inapplicable to the subject, the following passage, which shows how the courtezans of Japan proceed towards such as would cheat them, may be cited: "The caboques took Tane, an interpreter, prisoner, for fifteen tares (about 3l. 15s.) he owed them for lichery, and, not having to pay, set his body for sale, no one having the money for him."

It would appear that in obtaining possession of a female of this class by clandestine means tragical consequences may ensue; while, if done fairly, considerable expense may be involved. Mr. Wickham, one of the English factors stationed at Mesco, writing on the 15th of April, 1616, to his chief, Captain Cock, gives an account of a soldier of high reputation who ran away with a prostitute, and, fearing she would be reclaimed, was seized with a fit of frenzy, during which he first cut the throat of the girl, and afterwards ripped himself up. The writer then communicates a piece of news:—"Micaonæcamo, the nobellman that gave me my cattan or sword, hath carried away a caboque, and hath payed her master 10,000 tares (250l.). I would I had the money, and it makes no matter who hath the woman." Replying to this communication, Captain Cock quaintly observes on one point, "Yf some will be so foolish as to cut their bellies for love (or rather lust) of whores, the worst end of the staff will be their owne;" and on the other point he agrees with his correspondent that he "had rather have the money than the ware."

Vice of a more brutal kind is systematically practised by many of the Japanese nobility, as well as by the meanest orders; and houses are kept for this purpose similar to those inhabited by prostitutes.

Some parents apprentice out their daughters for a term of years to this abominable profession, and the girls then return to honourable life. The houses they frequent continually resound with music. At Jeddo, a later traveller was informed there was one brothel, or rather temple of prostitution, where 600 women were maintained. Notwithstanding this number, young men were nightly refused admittance, from the over-crowded state of the rooms. Passing through the streets of the brothel quarter Golovnin saw groups of girls standing about the doors; some of them were in the bloom of youth, and so handsome that they appeared fascinating even to the European eye.

Thus the system of professional prostitution flourishes more in Japan than in any other part of insular Asia; yet the women of other classes appear to hold a higher position, and to enjoy more respect from the men. It is remarked, however, by all writers, that the profligacy of the female sex is confined to those who are so by profession; but the male is generally licentious throughout the empire.

Of Prostitution in the Ultra-Gangetic Nations.

In this division we include what are commonly called the Hindu-Chinese nations, or the inhabitants of that immense tract lying between Hindustan and China. Geography makes several sections of them, and they present, it is true, some variety in laws, customs, and degrees of progress. But these are not more distinct than may be observed in every large country, whether called by one name or many. The same physical type is marked upon them all; and, speaking in general terms, their manners are uniform.

In one respect they are all similar. The condition of women is extremely low. A curious phenomenon is observable in relation to this subject. The Buddhists of the ultra-Gangetic countries, uninfluenced by the jealous spirit of the Hindu and Mohammedan codes, allow to the female sex great liberty; yet assign it less respect than it enjoys either in Hindustan or China, to both of which they are inferior in civilization. The freedom thus conceded to women fails to elevate them. They are held in contempt, they are taught to abase themselves in their own minds, and they employ their licence in degrading themselves still further. In few parts of the world is the effect of Asiatic despotism more plainly visible than in the countries lying between Hindustan and China. The peculiar system of government renders every one the king's serf. The men labour for the benefit of their master, having no opportunity to profit themselves by their own industry. Their support, therefore, naturally devolves on the women, who in Cochin China especially, plough, sow, reap, fell wood, build, and perform all the offices which civilization assigns to the abler sex.

The marriage contract is a mere bargain. A man buys his wife from her parents. The first is usually the chief, but he may have as many others as he chooses to purchase. A simple agreement before witnesses seals the union. The band thus easily formed is as easily dissolved. In Cochin China a pair of chopsticks or a porcupine quill is broken in two before a third person, and the divorce is complete. When only one desires a separation it is more difficult, but the law allows a man to sell his inferior wives.

The unmarried women of this region are proverbially and almost universally unchaste. They may prostitute themselves without incurring infamy or losing the chance of marriage. A father may yield his daughter to a visitor whom he desires specially to honour, or he may hire her out for a period to a stranger who may reside for a short time in his neighbourhood. The girl has no power to resist the consummation of this transaction, though she cannot be married without her own consent.

The wife, however, is considered sacred, but rather as the property of her husband than for the sake of virtue. A man's harem cannot be invaded, even by the king himself. This, at least, is the theory of the law; but absolutism never respects the high principles of a code which opposes its desires. Adultery is punished in Siam with a fine, in Cochin China with death. In Birmah, executions are very rare among females. "The sword," they say, "was not made for women." In all parts of the region, however, the bamboo is in requisition to discipline the women; and husbands are sometimes seen to fling their wives down in the open street, lay them on their faces, and flog them with a rattan.

It will thus be seen that, lying between two regions, in each of which a form of civilization has been introduced, the ultra-Gangetic, or Hindu-Chinese nations, differ from them both. Since no unmarried woman is required to be chaste, professional prostitutes do not form so large a class as might be expected. They do exist, however, and in considerable numbers. In Siam a common prostitute is incapable of giving evidence before a country justice, but this is by no means on account of her immorality. It is from other prejudices. The same disability attaches to braziers and blacksmiths*.

OF PROSTITUTION IN EGYPT.

EGYPT, as the seat of a civilization among the most ancient and remarkable that have flourished on the earth, calls for particular attention. The inquiries of the curious have in all ages been directed as well to its people as to its monuments. It has, indeed, been the subject of infinite investigation. Travellers innumerable have explored its beautiful valley; year after year adds to their number, and countless reports have been made to us of the ruins, the antiquities, the resources, the condition, the scenery, and the manners of Egypt. In all, consequently, except statistics, our knowledge is very considerable, though the inexhaustible interest of that celebrated country still leaves an open field for the romantic traveller. The dry hot climate is supposed to influence the character of the people. A remarkable system of politics also modifies the national features, so that we examine our subject, in reference to Egypt, with peculiar curiosity.

The population of Egypt is various, being composed of the four Mohammedan sects, of the Copts, the Greeks, the Armenians, Maronites, and Levantines. The mass, however, is formed of Arabs, while the general plan of manners has originated, in a great measure, from the spirit of the prophets' civil and religious code. Of the system with respect to the female sex this is more especially true; but the history of manners before Mohammed's age is too incomplete for us to know precisely how

* Craufurd's Embassy to Siam; Craufurd's Embassy to Avar; Tomkin's Journals and Letters; Finlayson's Mission; White's Journey; Latham's Natural History of the Varieties of Man.

much was originated, and how much was adopted by him. Had his scheme opposed itself wholly to the previous habits of the East, it would never have been so universally or so readily accepted. It is one characteristic of Asiatic countries that women exercise less influence on manners than in Europe. The laws made by men would, in fact, isolate them within a sphere of their own; but agencies which are irresistible counteract this effort. The tendency of social legislation is to shut them out from a share in the government of society; but the tendency of nature is in the contrary direction.

The women of Egypt are naturally adapted for the position in which they are placed—unless we suppose that long discipline has subdued them to the level of their condition. They display every attraction for Mohammedans, with few of the characteristics which fascinate an European. In youth many of them are possessed of every charm—the bosom richly developed, the whole form gracefully rounded, the face full of bloom, and the eyes overflowing with brilliance; but all these beauties speedily fade, and nowhere is old age so unsightly. The figure approaches maturity at the ninth or tenth year, and at fifteen or sixteen has reached the perfection of the Oriental ideal. With rare exceptions they have passed the flower of their lives at 24, and in this short-lived loveliness we may find one cause of polygamy and frequent divorce, among a people with whom women are the mere unspiritual ministers to the senses of man. The Mohammedan peoples even his heaven with feminine creations destined for his animal gratification. When, therefore, we find religion itself thus impregnated with a gross element, we can only expect to find the female sex regarded in a degrading point of view. The opinion prevails with some Muslims, that Paradise has no place reserved for women; but this is by no means the universal idea among them.

Though by their tame spirits and submissive humility the women of Egypt appear moulded to suit the system in which they move, their character has not, on the whole, been entirely vitiated by the process. Modesty and virtue are frequent ornaments of the harem, and distinguish the sex throughout the valley. Even among the lower or labouring orders, though the maidens may sometimes be seen bathing in the Nile, or hurrying from hovel to hovel naked, and at all times with a light and scanty garment, a demure and retiring demeanour is general. Chastity is a very prevalent virtue, except in the cities, where a crowded population is immersed in that profligacy surely bred by despotism. With respect to their modesty, travellers appear to have been led astray by their prejudices. Many of them appear to carry among the necessaries for their journey an English measure of propriety, which they invariably apply to all nations with which they come in contact. Thus the remark is commonly made, that women in Egypt hide their faces in obedience to habit, but care not what other part of the person they expose. Consequently, it is inferred they are devoid of modesty. But this by no means follows. Custom, which is one of the most powerful among the laws which regulate society, has taught them that to display the features is disgraceful, but has made no regulation for more than that. Unless, therefore, we accept the doctrine of innate ideas—which meets a refutation in every quarter of the globe—we must not cite the women of Egypt before the tribunal of our own opinions, and condemn them on that charge. On the contrary, we must confess that they are naturally a virtuous race, though the influences of their government are sufficiently injurious. Any, indeed, but an excellent people would long ago have been irredeemably depraved.

There are, in Egypt, only two classes of females—those whose opulence allows them to be wholly indolent, and whose life is entirely dreamed away in the luxury of the harem; and those to whom poverty gives freedom, with the obligation of labour. To see the wife of a bey, to examine her tastes, her conduct, her private pleasures, and daily occupations, you have the beau ideal of a voluptuous woman literally cradled in one long childhood, with all the ease, the indulgence, and the trifling of infancy. Enter the habitation of a fellah or artizan, and the hardship of the man's lot is exceeded by that of his wife. She has to do all that he can do; but if he be personally kind, her situation is morally superior to that of the petted toy nursed on the cushions of the harem. The same weakness, however, is paramount over both. The indolent lady satisfies herself with rich Eastern silks and shawls, and gems of fine water; while the poor drudge of the field adds to her toil, and stints herself in food, to purchase decorations for her person.

The polygamy which is practised in Egypt has, more than in many other countries, tended to the degradation of the female sex. It seems to be encouraged in some degree by the rigid separation of the sexes before marriage. A man takes with less scruple a wife whom he has never seen when he knows that if she disappoint him he may take another. The law allows four wives, with an unrestricted number of concubines. The Prophet, his companions, and the most devout of his descendants, so indulged themselves; but the idea is vulgar which supposes that Mohammed introduced the practice. On the contrary, he found it universal, and was the first to put a check upon it. Some of the higher moralists contend, that as four wives are sufficient for one man, so are four concubines; but few of the rich men who can afford to keep more allow themselves to be influenced by this opinion.

The Muslim lawgiver was wiser than the priestly legislators of India; for he insulted nature with less peremptory prohibitions against the union of sects. A Mohammedan may marry a Jewish or a Christian woman, when he feels excessive love for her, or cannot procure a wife of the true faith; but she does not inherit his property or impart her religion to her offspring. The children of a Jewish woman, if they are not educated to the Mohammedan, must embrace the Christian creed, which is considered better than their own. In this we find a privilege reserved by the male sex to itself, for a woman of the Prophet's faith dare not marry an infidel, unless compelled so to do by actual force. This has given rise to many apostasies, which form the subject of numerous romances.

The degrees of consanguinity within which marriage is prohibited are strictly marked. A man may not marry his mother or any other relative in a direct ascending line; his daughter or any descendant; his sister, or half-sister; his aunt, his niece, or his foster-mother. The Hanafee code enacts that a man shall not take as his wife any woman from whose breast he has received a single drop of milk; but E. Shafæee allows it unless he has been suckled by her five times within the course of the first two years. Nature, in this respect, is the principal guardian of the law, for as women in Egypt age very quickly, the men endeavour to obtain more youthful brides. A man may not marry the mother, or daughter of his wife, or his father's or his son's wife; his wives must not be sisters, or his own unemancipated slaves—if he already have a free wife. Those women whom the Muslim is forbidden to marry it is lawful for him to see, but no others except his own wives or female servants.

The marriage engagement is merely a civil transaction. The man and woman having declared in the presence of two witnesses their mutual willingness, and part of the dowry being paid, their union is legal. The bride usually signifies her consent through a deputy. If, however, she be under the age of puberty, her assent is not necessary, and she is in the hands of her friends. A boy may also be thus disposed of; but he may divorce his wife if he be not contented with her. Usually, if rich, he neglects the first, and takes a second by way of solace after his disappointment.

In one feature of its manners, modern Egypt resembles the States of ancient Greece. The character of a bachelor is ridiculous, if not disreputable. As soon as a youth has attained a proper age, with sufficient means, his friends advise him to marry. His mother, or a professional match-maker, is usually left to choose the bride. When a girl has been fixed upon with his approval, some one goes to her father to effect an arrangement. The price is fixed, with the amount of dowry, and the future ceremonials depend on the resources of the two families. Sometimes a profusion of rites is insisted upon; sometimes the simplest agreement is all that is required, for the law exacts nothing but the plain convention we have before described. The giving of a dowry is, however, indispensable. With all who can afford it, also, the sanction of religion and the witness of the law add solemnity to the occasion. The rich choose it as an opportunity to display the pride of wealth, and the poor to indulge in a little show, with that idleness which is so essential to the happiness of most Asiatics.

The condition of wives in Egypt has been much misrepresented by some popular writers, to whom the imprisonment and slavery of women offer a fertile theme for declamation. The word harem, or *harim*, indeed, meaning *sacred* or *prohibited*, applies to the women as well as to the apartments in which they dwell; but considerable liberty is allowed them. Those of the upper classes are secluded, and go veiled in the streets. They are seldom seen on foot in public, and their costume is indicative of this detail in their manners. Though, however, they have a suite of apartments assigned to them, they are not prisoners. A few Turks, jealous to exaggeration, may immure the inmates of the harem, and shut them altogether from contact with the world; but, generally, they are allowed to go out, pay visits, and control the household. The theory of the Muslims is more rigid than their practice, which, were it consistent in all its features, would swathe the female sex with convention, as the ancient inhabitants used to swathe their mummies—until the form of humanity is lost amid the very devices which seek to preserve it. To such an extravagant height do some of them carry their ideas of the sanctity of the female sex, that their tombs are closed against strangers, while others will not permit a man and a woman to be buried in the same grave. Generally, however, husbands do not object to their wives mingling with the public throng so as they religiously veil their faces. The lower orders are, of course, the least restrained. Those of the wealthiest and proudest men are most strictly secluded; but the interchange of visits between the harems is constant. With this degree of freedom the Egyptian women are content. Time has trained them to their situation, until a relaxation in their discipline is viewed less as an indulgence than a right. The wife who is allowed too much liberty imagines she is neglected, and, if others are more narrowly watched, is jealous of the superior solicitude bestowed on them. Among the rich the harem supplies all the delights of life. Rose-water, perfumes, sherbet, coffee, and sweatmeats, constitute the supreme joys of existence, with precious silks, muslins, and jewels. Among the poor, though reduced to beasts of burden, their buoyant hearts are not depressed under the load, and they sing from infancy to old age. Nevertheless their lives are full of misery, but it is the misery of a class, not only of one sex.

The Muslim woman is *proud* of her husband, and *fond* of her children. Exceptions undoubtedly occur, in which the warmth of the Oriental temperament takes the form of refined and spiritual love; but these are rare. In their offspring they find the chief resource of their lives. They may become mothers at twelve years of age, and at fifteen commonly do so. They give proof of astonishing fecundity, bearing numbers of children, though ceasing at an earlier period than among Europeans. That is the critical occasion of their lives, but they who pass it safely often survive to an extreme old age. The manners of the country render it necessary that midwives only should attend at the accouchement, which is usually easy. When a physician is called in, he must feel his patient's pulse through the sleeve of her garment, while her face is almost invariably wrapped in a veil. The utmost kindness, even in the indulgence of their most trifling whims, is shown to pregnant women. The absence of that sentiment which, according to English notions, should attach a wife to her husband, is made up by the stronger bond which binds a mother to her child. Upon this all the wealth of her affection is bestowed, and in that precious charge all her soul is centred. This feeling—the most pure and true of any that grow in the human breast—stands to the woman of Egypt in place of every other. A proverbial saying expresses the national philosophy upon this subject: "A husband is a husband; if one is lost another is to be got; but who can give me back my child?" To be childless is regarded as a signal misfortune, and with those who happen to be barren many devices are employed to remove the curse. Among these, one of the most curious is—to wash the skin with the blood of an executed criminal. Her fecundity, with her parental care, might be expected to prove itself by a flourishing population; but the blind rapacity and profligate contempt of human life exhibited by the tyrants who, in succession, have ruled Egypt, have been more than enough to neutralise the liberality of nature.

The Mohammedan is essentially an Epicurean. In him the object of nature appears perverted. Instead of the animal being made subservient to the intellectual man, the mind is devoted to gratifying the sense. His life is divided between praying, bathing, smoking, lounging, drinking coffee, and the gratification of the various appetites. Voluptuary as he is, therefore, the opulent Egyptian does not rest content with the four wives allowed him by the law. He takes as many concubines as he can afford. They are all slaves, and are absolutely at the disposal of their master, who may handle, whip, or punish them otherwise as he pleases, and incurs very slight danger by killing one of them. The same regulations as to blood affinity apply to them as to free women. A man when he takes a female slave must wait three months before he can make her his concubine. If she bear him a child which he acknowledges to be his own, it is free. Otherwise it is the inheritor of its mother's bonds. She herself cannot afterwards be sold or given away, but is entitled to emancipation on the death of her lord. He is not, however, obliged to free her at once, though, if he have not already four wives, it is considered honourable to do so. A wife sometimes brings to the establishment a few handmaidens. Over these she has control, and need not, unless she pleases, allow them to appear unveiled in their master's presence; but occasionally we find a wife presenting her husband with a beautiful slave damsel, as Sarah presented her bondwoman Hagar to Abraham. Rich men often purchase handsome white girls. Those of the humbler class are usually brown Abyssinians, for the blacks are generally employed in menial offices. Neither the concubine nor the wife is permitted to eat with the lord of the house. On the contrary, they are required to wait on him, and frequently, but not always, to serve as domestics. In consequence of this system, a great gulf lies between man and wife. His presence is viewed as a restraint in the harem, which, from all we can learn, is mostly lively and loquacious. Nor is this surprising, when we consider that the harems of aged men are so frequently filled with young girls in the fresh bloom of life, who can never learn to be fond of their husbands. The Egyptian proverb in reference to this is peculiarly apt. It describes an ugly old Turk with some beautiful youthful wives as "A paradise in which hogs feed." Ibrahim Pasha introduced into his private apartments the amusement of billiards, which at once became a favourite recreation.

Though polygamy is not only licensed but esteemed, and concubinage unlimited, few Egyptians have more than one wife, or one female slave. Not more, indeed, than one in twenty, it is said, indulge in this kind of pluralism, and it is probable that concubinage might be almost altogether abolished by the suppression of the slave trade. At present the markets are continually supplied with girls kidnapped in various countries, and these are sometimes stripped and exposed naked to the purchaser's inspection.

Satisfied as he generally is with one wife, the Egyptian Mohammedan is not by any means remarkable for continence. He may content himself with a single woman, but he may change her as often as he pleases, a privilege which is continually abused. The facility of divorce has had a most demoralising effect upon Egyptian manners.

A man may twice put away his wife and take her back without ceremony. If, however, he divorces her a third time, or deliberately unites in one act the effect of three, he cannot take her again until she has been married and divorced by another husband. The manner of divorce is sufficiently simple. The husband says, "I divorce thee," and returns his wife about one-third of the dowry, with the effects which she brought at her marriage. He may do this through sheer caprice, without assigning or proving any reason; but when a woman desires to put away her husband, she must show herself to have suffered serious ill-treatment or neglect, lose the share of her dowry, and often go into a court of justice to prove her claim. With the man this is never required, as is indicated by the common proverb: "If my husband consents, why should the Kadi's consent be necessary?"

A widow must wait three months, and a divorced woman three months and ten days, or, if pregnant, until delivery, before marrying again. The latter, in this case, must also wait an additional forty days before she can receive her new husband. Meanwhile her former proprietor must support her, either in his own house or in that of her parents. If he divorce her before the actual consummation of the marriage, he must provide for her more liberally. In case, however, of a wife being rebellious, and refusing to recognise the lawful authority of her husband, he may prove her to have offended, before a Kadi, and procure a certificate exempting him from the obligation to clothe, lodge, or maintain her. Thus she is desolate and without resource, for she dare not go to another home; but if she formally promise to be obedient in future, her husband must support or divorce her. When a wife desires to be freed from any man's restraint and is unable to dissolve the union altogether, she may make a complaint and obtain a licence to go to her father's house. In that case he, through sheer spite, generally persists in refusing to divorce her. Sometimes a man with a disagreeable mother-in-law quartered upon him, puts away his wife in order to be rid of both.

The slightness of the marriage tie, and the ease with which it may be severed, leads, as we have said, to a profligate abuse of the power thus assumed by the male sex. Numbers of men have, in the course of their lives, 10, 20, 30, or even 40 wives. Women, also, have as many as a dozen partners in succession. Some profligates have been known to marry a woman almost every month. A man without property may pick up a handsome young widow, or divorced woman, for about 10s., which he pays as dowry. He lives with her a few days or weeks, and then divorces her with the payment of about 20s., to support her in the interval during which she is prohibited from marrying again. Such conduct, however, is regarded as disreputable, so that few respectable families will trust a girl with any man who has put away many wives. The crime of adultery is laid down by the law as worthy of severe punishment. Four eye-witnesses, however, are necessary to prove the fact, and the woman may then be stoned to death. From the secluded nature of their lives, and from the nature of the offence itself, it is rarely that such testimony is to be had. Cases, therefore, scarcely ever occur before the public courts. Heavy and ignominious penalties are denounced against witnesses who make these charges and fail in the proof. Unmarried persons convicted of fornication may be punished by the infliction of one hundred stripes, and, under the law acknowledged by the Sumrh sect, may be banished for a whole year.

Egypt has in all times been famous for its public dancing girls, who were all prostitutes. The superior classes of them formed a separate tribe or collection of tribes, known as the Ghawazee. A female of this community is called Ghazeeyeh, and a man Ghazee. The common dancing girls of the country are often erroneously confounded with the Almeh—Awalim in the singular—who are properly female singers; though, whatever some authoritative writers may assert, they certainly practise dancing, as well as prostitution, especially since the exile of the Ghawazee. They perform at private entertainments, and are sometimes munificently rewarded. The Ghawazee, on the other hand, were accustomed to put aside their veils and display their licentious movements in public, before the lowest audience. The evolutions with which they were accustomed to amuse their patrons were commonly the reverse of elegant. Commencing with decency enough, they soon degenerated into obscenity, the women contorting their bodies into the most libidinous postures. The dress was graceful, but exposed a large portion of the bosom, and was frequently half thrown aside. The Ghawazee sometimes performed in the court of a house or in the open street; but were not admitted into the harems of respectable families. A party of men often met in a house, and sent for the dancers to amuse them. Their performances, on such occasions, were more than usually licentious, and their dresses less decent. A chemise of transparent texture, which scarcely hid the skin, and a pair of full trousers, was frequently all that covered them. Drinking copious draughts of brandy or some other intoxicating liquor, they soon laid aside even the affectation of modesty, and scenes took place like those with which the priests defiled the temples of India. Many of the women who thus degrade themselves are exceedingly beautiful. As a class, indeed, they are described as the handsomest in Egypt. They are distinguished, by the peculiar caste of their countenances, from all other females in the country, and there can be little doubt that they spring from a distinct race. They boast themselves of the Barmecide descent, but this is impossible to be proved. It has been conjectured that they are the lineal, as well as the professional descendants of those licentious dancers who exhibited naked—as these sometimes do—before the Egyptians in the age of the Pharaohs. Some imagine that the dancers of Gade, or Cadiz, ridiculed by Juvenal, were the prototypes of the modern Ghawazee; but it has been supposed, with more reason, that the Phœnicians introduced the practice thither from the East, where profligacy flourished at the earliest period.

It has been the pride of the Ghawazee tribes to preserve themselves distinct from all other classes of the population, to intermarry, and thus to perpetuate their blood unmingled. A few have repented their mode of life, and married respectable Arabs; but this has not often occurred. They never among themselves took a husband until they had entered on a course of prostitution. To this venal calling they were all trained from childhood, though all were not taught to dance. In this community of harlots, it is singular to find that the husband was inferior to the wife; indeed he was subject to her, performing the double office of servant and procurer. If she was a dancer he was generally her musician, and sat by quietly tinkling upon a stringed instrument, while she, his wife, exposed her person in the most indecent attitudes, and by every voluptuous artifice endeavoured to seduce the spectator. Profligacy never assumed a more infamous form than that of the husband assisting at the daily adultery of his wife. Some of the men earned a livelihood as blacksmiths or tinkers. Many of them, however, were rich, and the women, especially, were possessed of costly dresses and ornaments.

The Ghawazee generally followed the kind of life led by our gipsies, whom some, indeed, have traced to an Egyptian origin. Many, but not all, of the wanderers of this nation in the Valley of the Nile, ascribe to themselves a descent from a branch of the same family from which the Ghawazee claim to have sprung; but both traditions rest on doubtful testimony. The ordinary language of the Ghawazee is similar to that in use among the rest of the Egyptian population; but like all other unsettled, wandering tribes, they have a peculiar dialect, a species of slang, only intelligible to themselves. Most of them profess the Mohammedan faith, and they were accustomed to follow in crowds the pilgrim caravans to the sacred shrine at Mecca.

Every considerable town in Egypt formerly harboured a large body of the Ghawazee, who occupied a distinct quarter, allotted entirely to prostitutes and their companions. Low huts, temporary sheds, or tents, formed their usual habitations, since they were in the habit of frequently transplanting themselves from one district to another. Others, however, occupied and furnished handsome houses, trading also in camels, asses, and grain; possessing numerous female slaves, upon whose prostitution they also realized much profit. They crowded the camps and attended the great religious festivals, and on these occasions the Ghawazee tents were always conspicuous. Some joined the accomplishment of singing with that of the dance.

The inferior Ghawazee women resembled in their attire the common prostitutes of other classes, which also swarmed in Egypt. Many of these also, who were not Ghawazees, took the name, in order to increase the gains of their calling.

The system of marriage, to which we have slightly alluded, is worthy of more particular notice. The man who married a Ghazeeyah was a low and despised creature. The saying is proverbial in Egypt, that "the husband of a harlot is a base wretch by his own testimony." The law among the Ghawazee was, that a girl as soon as marriageable must prostitute herself to a stranger and then take a husband. He is constantly employed in looking for persons to bring to her, himself cohabiting with her only by stealth, for she would be exposed to shame and made the object of ridicule were it known that she had admitted her own husband to her embraces. Polygamy is unknown among the Ghawazee. In that community, indeed, as it existed previously to the edict of 1835, we find a system exactly the reverse of that in the midst of which it existed. The birth of a male child was looked upon as a misfortune, since he was of no value to the tribe. Women, on the contrary, were precious, because they were sought after by nearly the whole male population of Egypt. The Ghazeeyeh made it a rule never to refuse the offer of a person who could pay anything. The fashionable dancer, therefore, at country fairs, though glittering with golden ornaments, and arrayed in all the beauties of the eastern loom, would admit the visit of any rough and ragged peasant for a sum not exceeding twopence. In this manner, by seizing whatever was offered to them, they often accumulated wealth, dressed in superb attire, rich embroidery of gold, with chains of golden coins, and solid bracelets of the same costly metal. In many instances, when the Ghazeeyeh had lost or divorced her former husband, and become opulent upon the profits of her venal calling, she married some village Sheikh, who was proud of his acquisition. A virgin Ghazeeyeh was never induced to forsake her hereditary profession; but when she formed such an alliance, she made a solemn vow on the tomb of some saint, to be true to her new partner, sacrificed a sheep, and was generally faithful to her sacred engagement.

It was not only in the more populous cities and districts of Lower Egypt that the Ghawazee pursued their double calling of dancer and prostitute. Those in the Upper country were equally addicted to that immoral calling, and were, in proportion, equally encouraged. Even in the small villages a company of them was usually to be found, glittering in finery of gaudy colours, unveiled, and clothed only in those light transparent garments in which the members of the same sisterhood are represented on the monuments—a loose chemise of gauze, a scarf negligently hung about the loins, and loose trousers of the most delicate texture. Their dances were exhibitions of unrestrained indecency,—attitude, look, and movement being equally lascivious. They also sang and played on the viol, lute, tambour, lyre, or castanet. The common prostitutes of the meaner class excelled them, at least in the affectation of modesty. Many of the Ghawazee, however, appear sensible of the degradation to which they are consigned.

The dance of the Ghawazee was, to the Egyptians, what an opera ballet is in England—the representation of some episode, generally of love. Formerly there was, near Cairo, a little village called Shaarah, the Eleusis of modern Egypt, where the mystical rites of Athor were, until recently, celebrated. It was a collection of small mud huts, distinguished from those of the common people by superior cleanliness and comfort. Numbers of the Ghawazee dwelt here, and when Mr. J. A. St. John visited their abode, came out to meet him, dressed in elegant attire, with a profusion of ornaments. All were young—none were more than twenty, many not more than ten years of age. Some were exceedingly handsome, while others, to an European judge, appeared quite the reverse. In this village lived a considerable number of the Ghawazee. The greater part of their lives was passed in the coffee-house, where they lounged all day on cushions, sipping coffee, singing, and indulging in licentious conversation. In the great room a hundred might assemble, and here they were visited by the profligates of Cairo, to whom the village of Shaarah was a regular place of resort. In the towns they frequented the common coffee-houses, and in the smaller hamlets up the valley, they wandered all day among the dwellings, or reclined on benches in the open air until a boat with travellers appeared on the Nile, when they immediately hurried down to the shore and commenced their lascivious songs. The Arabs have the reputation of being extremely profligate, and when on their journeys never visited a city or village without paying a visit to the Ghawazee quarter. Indeed, the manners of the population have been debased under every vicious influence. A despotic government, an epicurean religion, and the spirit of indolence thus engendered, have encouraged among the men every species of crime against nature. The corruption which brought a curse on the Cities of the Plain is emulated in the cities of Egypt.

When Burckhardt wrote, about 1830, the number of males and females of the Ghawazee nation in Egypt was estimated at from 6000 to 8000. Their principal settlements were in the towns of the Delta in Lower Egypt, and, in the upper country, at Kenneh, where a colony of at least 300 generally resided. The scattered companies generally formed a great concourse at Tanta, in the Delta, at the three annual festivals, when a vast multitude was collected from all parts of the valley. Six hundred Ghawazee have on such occasions pitched their tents near the town. During the reign of the Memlooks, the influence of these women was, in the open country, very considerable. Many respectable persons courted their favour. They were accustomed to dwell in the towns until the brutality of the soldiers—who sometimes killed one in a fit of jealousy—drove them into the rural parts. At each of their chief places of sojourn one was invested with the title of Emir, or chief of the settlement. She was entitled to no authority over the rest, yet exercised much influence by virtue of her dignity. In Cairo itself their number was small, and they inhabited a spacious Khan, or hotel, overlooked by the castle. "In a city," says Burckhardt, "where among women of every rank chastity is so rare as at Cairo, it could not be expected that public prostitution should thrive." This is a harsh judgment on the character of the Caireen females, and, according to the accounts of most travellers, it is unjust.

Before Mohammed Ali, instigated by the priests, made his awkward crusade against the Ghawazee tribes, the public prostitutes were put under the jurisdiction of a magistrate—an aga, or captain of the dancing girls. He kept a list of them, and exacted from each a sum of money by way of tax. He also acted as a censor on the general morality of the people. One of these agas took upon himself an extension of his jurisdiction, and whenever he found a woman, no matter of what class, who had been guilty of a single act of incontinence, he added her name to the list of common prostitutes, and extorted the tax from her, unless she could offer him a sufficient bribe, and thus escape the infamy. Nor was this all. To gratify private revenge, he sometimes inserted in his list the names of respectable ladies; but was at length detected and punished with death. Whenever a party of Ghawazee was engaged, they had to pay to their chief a sum of money and procure his permission to dance. This practice was pursued by persons who farmed the tax, until Mohammed Ali was smitten by a sudden reverence for morals, and made an attempt, characteristic of his vulgar genius, to abolish the profligacy of Egypt. In June, 1834, a law was published compelling the Ghawazee throughout the country to retire from their profession. It is said that the Moolahs, or Muslim bishops, objected to them, not on account of the impurities they practised, but because it was a scandal that women belonging to the race of true believers should expose their faces to infidels for hire. An agitation was raised on the subject; a storm of sacerdotal rage assailed the palace; and the viceroy, priest-ridden, banished all the dancers to Esneh, 500 miles up the Nile. There they were herded together, with a small stipend from government to keep them from starvation. The effect of this truly barbarian device was just what might have been expected. The profligacy, which had been chiefly confined to them, broke out in other classes, and demoralization advanced several steps further. It is said that the Moolahs repent their policy, since some additional burdens have been laid on them to make up for the loss of revenue.

Under the old system, when all the known prostitutes paid a tax, the amount contributed by those of Cairo alone was 800 purses, or 4000*l*., which was a tenth of the income-tax on the whole population. This will suggest an idea of the numbers in which they existed. The Ghawazee formed the chief element in this system of prostitution, and Mohammed Ali imagined that with one stroke of the pen he could obliterate this blot on the social aspect of Egypt—he who had so worn himself out with licentious pleasures that his physicians had to persuade him to disband an army of concubines which he had kept at the expense of his miserable people. At once prostitution was denounced as a crime. The Ghazeeyeh daring to infringe the new law was condemned to fifty stripes for the first, and imprisonment with severe labour for the second, offence. The punishments of these and of all other women were illegal, according to the code of the Prophet. It has, however, been a blessing to the Mohammedan population of the East that their great lawgiver left his frame of legislation, for, invested with the authority of religion, it has been some check on the caprice of tyrants.

The men, also, who were detected encouraging the Ghawazee were made liable to the punishment of the bastinado. Legal enactments, however, cannot purify the morals of a whole community. Prostitution was abolished by law, but remained in practice as flagrant as ever. The Egyptians borrowed a device from the Persians. When a man desires to have intercourse with a woman of the prostitute class, he marries her in the evening and divorces her in the morning. The dowry he pays her is no more than she would receive were this transaction not to take place. She dare not apply for the usual stipend to maintain her afterwards. Even these connections are often kept entirely secret. The dancing has been more successfully suppressed, for many of the performances were public; but the Europeans, as well as the rich natives, frequently indulge by stealth in the prohibited amusement.

The Almehs, at least since the banishment of the Ghawazee, dance, and prostitute themselves, as well as sing—though their name implies neither practice, meaning simply "learned or accomplished women." When an entertainment of the kind is given, it is usual to choose for the scene a lonely house in the outskirts of the city, surrounded by a garden with a high wall. There, with the windows veiled, parties meet, and the dancers are introduced. Women with children at the breast come sometimes to take part in these abominable orgies; but do not usually, unless excited by the men, develop all their powers of licentious expression. Occasionally a party of soldiers breaks in on the forbidden revel, and the girls are carried off to prison, where stripes, or, perhaps, sentences of banishment, await them.

There are, however, in Egypt considerable classes of women solely devoted to prostitution, who practise none of the accomplishments in which the Almeh and Ghawazee excel. Among them is a peculiar tribe called the Halekye, whose husbands are tinkers or horse and ass doctors. They wander about the country like gipsies, and most of the women engage in prostitution. Prostitutes of the common order swarm in all the cities and towns of the valley. In and about Cairo they are particularly numerous, whole quarters being inhabited exclusively by them. Legislation is powerless to suppress their calling. Their dress differs from that of the other sorts of women only in being more gay and less disguising. Some even wear the veil and affect all the airs of modesty. Many are divorced women, or widows, or wives of men whose business has obliged them to go abroad. The wives of many of the Arabs, if neglected for a short time, slide easily into prostitution. When Ibrahim Pasha was away on the expedition to Syria, it was said that on his return the soldiers would find all their wives courtezans; but this, of course, was a satire.

Numbers of the common prostitutes in Cairo have been accustomed to sell pigeons and other birds in the different bazaars. Hence has arisen a proverb, that a person who marries in the bird-market must divorce his wife next morning. We find in these popular sayings many indications of the features which mark the system in Egypt. We have some in allusion to the shouts and disorderly conduct of persons issuing from the brothels in the morning, and others describing the career of the prostitutes themselves. "The public woman who is liberal of her favours does not wish for a procuress." "If a harlot repent she becomes a procuress."

One reason assigned for the practice of early marriages is, the proneness of the young men to be seduced by prostitutes. It is only just, however, to observe, that in

Alexandria, though it is considered the *refugium peccatorum* of the Mediterranean, the European community has preserved itself to an unusual degree uncontaminated by the general corruption of the male population.

The women of Egypt, as we have already observed, are, in point of morals, far superior to the men. They are generally silly and childish, because they are treated as soulless creatures and children; but, on the whole, their character is not so degraded by unnatural vices as that of their male rulers. These generally are coarse voluptuaries, in whom little except the animal appetite is developed.

We perceive in Egypt the illustration of some signal truths. We find there the proper fruits of Oriental despotism; we see the results of a vulgar barbarian attempt to reform public morals. We witness also the influence of its position upon the character of the female sex. Women in Egypt have been made by their social laws what the originator of those laws considered them to be—the mere servitors of man. In the prostitute system of the country we discover some singular features, which contribute to render modern Egypt, in relation to our actual subject, one of the most interesting regions in the East. The Christian population we do not notice, because it is composed of fragments of races which will be noticed in their proper countries*.

Of Prostitution among the States of Northern Africa.

A very brief notice is all that is required by the other States of northern Africa. They are distinguished from the barbarous communities of that region by having assumed the forms of regular society, which places them under a separate head, but, in relation to our subject, they present little that is characteristic. In describing the condition and morality of the female sex in other Mohammedan countries we

* Lane's Modern Egyptians; Poole's Englishwoman in Egypt; Yates's Egypt; St. John's Egypt and Mohammed Ali; St. John's Egypt and Nubia; St. John's Oriental Album; Cadalvene and Breuvery, l'Égypte; Mugin's Histoire de l'Égypte; Burckhardt's Arabic Proverbs; Expédition Française à l'Égypte; Niebuhr's Travels in Egypt, &c.; Thackeray's From Cornhill to Cairo; Warburton's Crescent and the Cross; Bayle St. John's Levantine Family; Henniker's Travels; Minutoli's Recollections of Egypt; Boaz's Modern Egypt; Clot Bey's Aperçu Général sur l'Égypte; Pueckler Muskau's Egypt and Mehemet Ali.

shall meet with nearly all the features offered by Algiers, Barca, Morocco, Tunis, and Tripoli. Nevertheless, on account of the extraordinary mixture of the population, some curious details are observed. Turks, Christians, Arabs, Jews, Berbers, and Moors mingle in the cities of those States. The last, however, form the mass, and it is to them our remarks must apply.

The Moors of northern Africa possess all the vices, and scarcely any of the virtues, of the Mohammedans of the East. They are proud, ignorant, sensual, and depraved, without any of that high spirit of honour which often, in the oriental Muslim, half redeems his character.

The treatment of women among the Moors answers exactly to this view. They are regarded as the mere material instruments of man's gratification. Accordingly their whole education is modelled so as to render them fit to serve the lust of a gross sensualist. Among the more elevated nations of Asia, men sometimes tire of their wives' company, because they are simple beauties, without animation of mind, seeking the society of educated courtezans, more for their wit and vivacity than for their meaner and more material accomplishments. But, with the Moors, the animal appetite is all that they seek to satisfy. A woman with daughters does not train them in seductive arts; she *feeds* them into a seductive appearance — as pigeons and doves are fed in certain parts of Italy. They are made to swallow daily a number of balls of paste, dipped in oil, and the rod enforces their compliance. This practice is adopted as well by the inmate of the rich man's harem as by the courtezan; for to be plump, sleek, and fair, are the objects of their common ambition. A girl who is a camel's load is the perfection of Moorish beauty. Thus intellect and sentiment are not the possessions to recommend her, but fat.

It is strange that the woman's character does not correspond altogether with her mode of life. Heavy, corpulent, and sensual, she is, nevertheless, alive to the keenest feeling. Hot impulses, untameable in their outbreak, characterize her sex. Rivarol once said, that in Paris the veins of the women were full of milk; but in Berlin, of pure blood. Pananti says that in the Moorish woman fire is the circulating fluid. Fiery hearts, indeed, are general among the women of the East; and are as remarkable in Egypt as in Morocco, where Oriental passions seem to spring from African soil.

Immured as the wives of rich men are

in splendid harems, and rigidly excluded from intercourse with the other sex, they seek their whole enjoyment in the gratification of their passions or their senses. Their time is spent at home, or at the bath, lounging on cushions, sipping coffee, smoking, gossiping, or multiplying the devices of the toilette.

The Moors are extravagantly jealous. Some have been known to slay their women before proceeding on a long journey; others have forbidden them to name even an animal of the masculine gender. They are, therefore, entirely shut up within the walls of the harem; muffled under mountains of ungraceful black drapery as they move along the streets; or secluded from the sight of the world in the impenetrable recesses of the bath. There they exhaust all the ingenuity they can command in the perfuming and decoration of their persons.

Many have wondered why women thus prevented from displaying themselves should be so untiring in the offices of vanity. The reason, however, is clear. In the Moorish harem all that a wife or concubine has to look to is the favour of her lord. If she succeed in charming him, her lot is far more happy than under any other circumstances. Besides, it is not only to please him that she labours. The mortification of her rivals is an additional source of triumph, for in the narrow sphere of the harem, where the nobler qualities of the mind have no room for development, the meanest naturally flourish most profusely.

The marriage laws of Mohammedan countries in general prevail in the Barbary States, with slight modifications. The husband has more absolute control over the wife. Few take more than one, though polygamy is universally allowed. Opulent men, however, sometimes indulge in the full complement of four, besides a number of concubines. Though the betrothal usually takes place at an extremely early age, the actual union seldom takes place until the bride is twelve or thirteen, when, as a poet of Barbary expresses it, "The rose-bud expands to imbibe the vivifying rays of love."

An extensive system of professional prostitution prevails in all the cities of these States. In Algiers and Morocco they are particularly numerous. The low drinking shops are crowded with men, and the loose characters of the town have each a companion who is a harlot. The public dancers all belong to this sisterhood. They exist in large numbers and are very much encouraged by both sexes. The women in the baths, after steeping their bodies in warm water until every nerve is relaxed, and all their limbs are softened into a voluptuous languor, lie on cushions and sip coffee, while dancers, attired in a slight costume, display their licentious arts, and Almeh sing songs equally lascivious. These prostitutes are of various classes, from the low vulgar wretches, encouraged by the French soldiers in Algiers, to the wealthy courtezans who live amid luxury and splendour.

A late traveller was introduced by a friend to "a Moorish lady." She occupied a fine house, situated, however, in a narrow and retired street. Its architecture was rich, and on the door being opened, signs of wealth became everywhere apparent. The visitor was ushered into a spacious apartment, roofed with graceful arches, and hung with rich-coloured silks. A lamp burning amid piles of freshly-gathered flowers, stood on the table. Reclining on a luxurious divan, with a tiger-skin spread at her feet, was a woman of extreme loveliness, attired in a superb costume. Though of a fair and brilliant complexion, her hair was jet black, braided with curious art and bound up with strings of pearl. Its heavy tresses were partly concealed by a tiara of crimson, figured with gold. Diamond drops hung from her ears; corals and gems sparkled round her neck.

A garment, of a fabric almost transparent, was folded over her bosom, and fastened with a golden ornament. A loose pelisse of blue brocade, confined at the waist with a cymar of embroidered silk, displayed the contour of her figure, and full trousers of muslin were furled about her limbs. Her cheek was tattooed with a blue star, and her nails were stained pink with henna. She was waited upon by a negro girl wearing a white muslin turban ornamented with a rose, the leaves and stem of which were gilded. Elegant in her manners, easy in her mode of address, this woman appeared to the uninitiated traveller the model of feminine grace. When he took his leave, however, his friend undeceived him, with an apology, and he discovered that he had been conversing with a Moorish prostitute.

This sketch of a woman, belonging to the class, may serve to show the extent to which some of them are encouraged. Indeed the society of the dancers, who are all prostitutes, is a favourite recreation with the Moors of all classes. The women, as we have said, belong to various grades, from those who debase themselves by their obscene postures in the low coffee-houses, to those who display their more elegant licentiousness to amuse the wealthy. A man, entertaining a party of friends, sends for a company of dancers to enliven them in his kiosk or pavilion. There, amid the fumes of tobacco, and sometimes of strong liquors (for the precepts of the Koran are often disregarded), these unhappy women descend from ordinary immodesty to the most degrading obscenity, until the orgies become such as no pen could describe. When the master of the feast is particularly delighted with the beauty or the dexterity of any girl, he performs a favourite act of gallantry by dropping a few golden coins into her bosom. The whole company is liberally rewarded *.

OF PROSTITUTION IN ARABIA, SYRIA, AND ASIA MINOR.

IN whatever countries the Mohammedan religion has been established, to describe the condition of women would be generally to repeat the accounts already given. Their character varies in different populations, but everywhere the laws to which they are subject are substantially the same.

In Syria and Asia Minor the marriage code is, among the Muslims, precisely similar to that of Egypt and Turkey, and so also in Arabia. In Natolia, especially, the influence of the Prophet's law is powerful, and the comparative simplicity of its inhabitants leads them to respect the boundaries laid down to their indulgences. Possessing within their own country all the materials of prosperity, they might, with virtue and industry, become once more a powerful and wealthy race; but misgovernment adds yearly to the mass of their corruption, and they perish in misery and servitude.

In such countries ambition sees no path but that of reckless crime, and mental activity only stimulates to sensual pursuits. Accordingly profligacy flourishes in the cities of Asia Minor, though in the thinly-peopled tracts there is perhaps more purity of manners than in any other Mohammedan country, except Arabia. Polygamy, permitted as it is by the law, is far from being generally adopted. In 1830, the extensive city of Brussa contained only a single man who had more than one wife. Women are secluded to some extent, but enjoy great freedom. Loved and indulged they are, but not respected; and, consequently, their morals are inferior to those of the Bedouin wives.

The Christians, who are so freely tolerated among the Mohammedan population of Asia Minor, preserve very much the customs of Europe, except in the lesser details of their life. In the rich provinces of Syria, Arabs, Greeks, and Ottomans have mingled, bringing each some characteristic habits to modify the general social scheme. The pastoral and the Christian tribes are by far the most moral.

Among the Maronites of Lebanon, who hold our faith, a rigid code exists, with purity of manners; but, as among the ancient Germans, the severe law is only the moral influence in action. The law, without the feeling which upholds it, would be powerful; which constitutes the difference between a community which frames its own code according to its own spirit, and that which receives decrees from the caprice of a ruler. If a man among the Maronites seduce a girl, he must marry her; should he refuse, fasts, imprisonments, and even blows are employed, which force him to submit. The illicit intercourse of the sexes, married or unmarried, is reprobated by the sense of the community, and the profession of prostitution is unknown. On the whole, this may be described as a simple and comparatively innocent race, removed above the profligacy which ferments around them.

The Druses, also, are distinguished by the same characteristics; they do not permit polygamy, and marry very young. A man may divorce his wife, however, by only saying, "Go;" or if she ask permission to visit her relatives, and he concede it, without enjoining her to return, she must consider herself put away. In spite of this facility such separations scarcely ever occur. An adulteress is mercilessly put to death by the hands of her friends. One who commits fornication suffers a similar punishment, but in this case the father may pardon her if he choose. The tenderness of the parent sometimes induces him to spare his child, though her guilt may stain the honour of his house; but brothers, it is said, never relent, visiting the sin of their sister with unsparing sternness.

Prostitutes and dancing girls are common in all the cities and towns of Syria, but they are never met with among any of the pastoral or nomade tribes. In Asia Minor and Palestine the same circumstance is to be observed.

There is little to remark upon in the habits or characteristics of the class, which is similar to others of the same sisterhood

* See Kennedy's Algeria and Tunis in 1845; Russel's Barbary States; Jackson's Account; St. Marie's Visit to Algeria; Pananti's Narrative; Beechey, Blaquière, &c.

in Egypt, Turkey, and other parts of the East*. Since, therefore, little could be gained by dwelling at length upon these countries, we quit them, and pass to a region which, if the spirit of romance still remains on earth, may be described as its chosen home.

In Arabia we find a system of manners at once unique and beautiful. In saying this, however, we allude to the Bedouins, or representatives of the true Arab race, who preserve their original simplicity in the rainless plains of their ancient country. In the cities of the coast, and wherever the fertility of the soil has attracted a crowded population, vice has introduced itself, and the graces of the shepherd state have quickly disappeared. In surveying the civilization of Arabia this distinction must always be held in view.

Many natural circumstances combine to influence the natural character of the Arabs in their native region. A country whose sunny and sandy plains alternate with tracts of hills and valleys of the richest bloom, has been their home. In the mountains of Yemen wet and dry seasons alternate, but over the desert hangs a sky of perpetual blue,—bright, dry, and warm; while, during the summer solstice, a sun almost vertical floods the waste of rock and sand with insufferable light, parching the face of all nature.

In this extraordinary region the Arabs live; some, as we have said, in cities or villages, some in separate families, under tents. An independent patriarchal form of government has been preserved in complete unity with their simple system of manners. Their religion is that of Mohammed, though various interpretations of his law have divided them into numerous sects. Differing, as they do, in their scheme of education from Europeans, it is difficult for us to understand their character. The boy grows up until five years old under his mother's care; then, without a graduation, he is taken to his father's side. From the companionship of women and children he passes at once into the society of men.

The Arabs hold the female sex in high estimation. They exclude women, indeed, from all public assemblies, preclude them from the use of strong liquors, and hold them from infancy to womanhood under tutelage; but they restrain themselves as well, and their general demeanour is modest, sober, and grave. Those in the fertile province of Yemen are more vivacious than those of the sterile plains. Nevertheless the men love society. Every village has its coffee-house full of gossipers, and every camp its place of rendezvous.

The women of the family occupy the interior of the house or tent; they are secluded to some extent, but not in the extravagant degree described by some writers. A man will not salute one in public, or fix his eyes upon her. Strangers, in general, are not allowed to converse with them, and they are expected to pay great deference to the ruling sex, but they are neither disguised nor immured. Veils they wear, but do not hide their faces with that religious care considered indispensable in some countries. Among many of the tent-dwellers, women drink coffee with strangers; and in some of the communities towards the south they are allowed to entertain a guest in their husband's absence. Indeed it may be said, that they are in Arabia more free than anywhere else in Islam, and proverbially abstemious in the gratification of all their appetites. All the household duties are performed by them. They fetch water, drive flocks, and wait on the men; but they are loved and respected, notwithstanding, and no claim is held so sacred as that by which a mother exacts duty from her son. There is, indeed, something admirable in the simplicity of these desert tribes, where the wife sits within her husband's tent, weaving her own garments from the wool of his flocks.

Where several families are congregated, the females visit each other, assemble together, and exchange every pleasant service. They meet in the evening to sing to the young men of the tribe, and many romantic assignations are kept in the little secluded valleys in which Arabia abounds. The well is the favourite spot of rendezvous.

The dances of the Arab girls, who perform before the men, are not only decent but elegant and romantic—totally in contrast to those of the Ghawazee. These amusements are as much for their own gratification as that of the other sex, for sometimes no males are present. Nor are they forced to exhibit when disinclined. Sometimes when the young men have offended the maidens of a tribe, they assemble night after night, but no damsels appear to dance or sing. All this indicates considerable purity of manners. The Mohammedan marriage law prevails among all the Arabs of the peninsula, though its details are modified by their system of manners. A man is

---

* The most valuable body of information on the Turkish Empire ever published was collected by the Rev. Robert Walpole, whose acquirements as a scholar are equalled by his accomplishments as a writer and a preacher.

expected, though not compelled, to take the widow of his deceased brother. A man has an exclusive right to the hand of his cousin, but is not compelled to marry her. He, however, must finally renounce his claim before she can be taken by any one else. Each may have four wives and as many concubines as he pleases. Two sisters may not be had at once; but one being divorced, the other may be taken.

The disparity between the sexes in point of number, which has been asserted by some travellers, does not appear to exist. Polygamy, a privilege of the rich, is seldom practised even by them. Many wealthy Bedouins, who could well maintain a harem, declare they could not be happy with more than one companion. The law obliges a man to pass at least one night in every week with each of his wives, and this has assisted in checking the practice.

The Mohammedans of Arabia are accused of selling their daughters; but they do not often bargain them away for profit. They naturally prefer a wealthy before a poor son-in-law, and receive a bounty from him; but they richly portion out the bride. She is further endowed by her husband. The contract drawn up before the Kadi stipulates not only what she is to receive upon her marriage, but what she may claim in case of a divorce. In many cases a sheikh of substantial fortune takes a poor son-in-law, gives him the sum necessary to be paid before the judge, and exacts from him in return only a pledge of such an amount, in the event of repudiation, that it can never take place. The wife, not being compelled to vest all her property in him, is, in some measure, free from his authority. She is, indeed, more supreme in the household than in most countries, and is even more happy, because she can insist upon a divorce if ill-used. Some men, indeed, take two wives, and some even three, but these instances are so few that, though the sexes are numerically equal, almost every man may have a wife. In the towns, soldiers and domestics are more frequently married than in Europe. No insult wounds an Arab woman more than to compare her to a fruitless tree. In this way the evils of polygamy, in the cities, are counteracted. A maiden past the marriageable age is ashamed of her virginity, and a widow without children is miserable until she finds a new partner. There are no retreats whither celibacy may fly for refuge from the taunts of the world. Every woman, consequently, is desirous to marry; but those who are taken by pluralists bear fewer children than those who have no rival under the roof. In the house of a polygamist, each woman, feeling she has to contend for favour, seeks by unnatural means to increase her own attractions, to seem more voluptuous than she is, and thus injures her natural powers. Concubinage is more common than polygamy. The sheriff of Mecca has numerous female slaves, and his high example is followed by many wealthy men in the luxurious and corrupt populations of the cities. In the desert it is more rare, and, indeed, scarcely ever practised, except where a father presents his son with a beautiful bondmaid, that he may be satisfied with her, and not enter the towns in search of prostitutes.

In Mecca, the sacred city of the Mohammedan faith, nearly all the wealthy men maintain concubines, but, if they bear children, must, unless their complement of four wives be already complete, marry them or incur public reproach. Some of these voluptuaries, who look on women only as a means to gratify their animal appetites, marry none but Abyssinian wives, because they are more servile, obsequious, and voluptuous than those of pure Arabian blood. Foreigners arriving at that city with the caravan bargain for a female slave, intending to sell her at their departure, unless she bear offspring, in which case she is elevated to the position of a wife. Under any circumstances, to sell a concubine slave, is by the respectable part of the community, regarded as disreputable. Speculators, however, sometimes buy young girls, indulge their sensuality upon them, train them up, educate them, and sell them at a profit. No distinction is made among the children, of whichever class of mothers they are born.

It is one sign of pure manners among the simple communities of Arabia, that chastity is highly prized. When the young Arab marries a girl, he sometimes stipulates in the contract that she must be a virgin. Of this he desires to assure himself by examination. If the outward signs are wanting, the bride's father has to prove the circumstance accidental; should he fail in this, the fame of her innocence may be destroyed, and she may be driven from home overwhelmed with shame. In many of the nomade communities it is the invariable rule to put away a bride immediately after the discovery of any suspicious sign, and in the hills of Yemen the laws are equally severe. The man who marries a woman disgraced by incontinence shares her infamy unless he send her back to her father.

The dwellers in towns, estimating less

highly the worth of feminine virtue, laugh at a man who dishonours his family on account of such a circumstance. A man finding that his bride is not a virgin demands compensation from her father, keeps her a short time, and then puts her away privily, as Joseph was minded to do with the mother of Jesus. Many also understand that nature has refused the sign to some females, and that it is unjust to condemn a woman on the strength of a circumstance which a hundred accidents may have caused. If adultery be committed by the wife, the law condemns her to have her throat cut by the hand of her brother or father; but in general humanity prevails against the written code, and this horrible punishment is seldom inflicted. The usual manner of visiting such an offence is by summary divorce, which is indeed easily to be obtained for trivial causes, or for no cause at all. In towns an agreement before the Kadi, in the desert a lamb slaughtered before the door of the tent, is all the ceremony needed. The simple pronunciation of the word "Go" is, in many parts, sufficient. Men of violent passions abuse this privilege, and it is said that some, not more than 40 years of age, have had as many as 50 wives; but it is utterly untrue to say that such instances are frequent. The existence of the pure and true sentiment of love, which is so rare in Mohammedan countries, is admitted to prevail in Arabia; the natural jealousy of the male sex, the superior wisdom of their regulations respecting the intercourse of the sexes prior to marriage, the independence of the women, and the lofty system of morals distinguishing the Bedouins of the desert, are totally incompatible with such a flagrant profligacy in the use of divorce. Were it the case, the complete confusion of society would ensue; whereas no region in the world presents spectacles of happier homes than the plains of Arabia, with their tents and wandering tribes. Women are comparatively free, being tolerated even in religious differences, which implies a high estimate of their intellectual qualities. The republican spirit of the desert assigns them, indeed, their natural position, and, though much is required from them as modest women, little is exacted from them as an inferior sex.

Some of the peculiar customs among the various communities of Arabia are curious enough to require notice. Before the Wahaby Conquest it was customary among the Deyr Arabs for a man to take his daughter, when marriageable, to the market-place—where all such engagements were formed—and proclaim her for disposal, crying aloud, "Who will buy the virgin?" The Bedouins of Mount Sinai still adhere to their singular practices. A man desiring matrimony makes a bargain with some one who has an unmarried daughter, and if able to settle it, sticks in his turban a sprig of green, which signifies that he is wedded to a virgin. The bride's inclinations are not beforehand consulted. She must go home with her husband, and submit for one night to his embraces. If she be not pleased, however, she may in the morning go home, when the contract is dissolved. Among the wealthier tribes of the East, no price is paid, and every girl is free to choose a partner. Modesty, with them, is regarded as the finest grace of the sex. It is genuine and unassailable. The bride even is sometimes so coy, that her husband is obliged to tie her up and whip her before she will yield to him. A widow's marriage is disreputable, and assailed with every demonstration of disrespect. This proves that divorce among them is unfrequent. Among the Nazyene, a tribe on the peninsula of Sinai, a girl, when given in marriage, flies and takes refuge among the hills, where she is supplied with food by her relations. The bridegroom goes in search, and when he finds his bride, must pass the night with her in the open air. She may repeat the flight several times, and indeed is not expected to live with her husband until a whole year has elapsed or she has become pregnant. Various other customs characterise different tribes; but in every feature of Arabian manners we discover a simplicity and purity as admirable as it is rare. Conjugal infidelity is rare in the desert. Fornication scarcely ever happens, and common prostitutes are unknown. In the crowded towns on the coast, however, there are numbers of professional prostitutes, licensed to carry on their calling, who pay considerable sums to the magistrates for the enjoyment of their privileges. In Mecca they are extremely numerous, and for the most part inhabit the poorest quarter of the city. In Dhyrdda, also, they are extremely numerous, but the population of that place is almost exclusively foreign. These women bear scarcely any children. When, during the early years of their vocation, they are capable of producing offspring, they employ artificial means to ensure abortion. The seeds of the tree whence is obtained the balm of Mecca, are used for that purpose.

In the mosques of the sacred city, prostitutes collect in great numbers, and are largely encouraged by the Moolah or priestly class, who find them a source of profit. Those of the more indigent description inhabit a particular quarter, but the others are dispersed amid the general mass of the population. They are more decent in their outward demeanour than the same class in the East and in Europe, and it requires a practised eye to detect, amid the throng of veiled women circulating in the streets and bazaars, those of the venal sisterhood. Contrary, however, to the rule which prevails in England, they are almost the only females who frequent places of worship, which is on account not of their devotion, but of their effrontery, the prejudices of Mohammedans being against it. The Bedouins near cities sometimes frequent the brothels in their neighbourhood; but these belong to the class the manners of which have been vitiated by intercourse with strangers.

In what numbers the prostitutes of the Arabian cities are found we know not, nor do we discover anything remarkable in their manners or modes of life. It would, consequently, be unprofitable to dwell on them. We have to notice, however, in connection with Arabia, two remarkable customs, one of which exhibits to us a class of male prostitutes, if such a term may be allowed, and the other a species of hospitality, now very rare, except among the grossest communities.

In the Arabian province of Hedjaz no unmarried woman may pass within the boundary or enter the mosque. As, however, many rich old widows and persons whose husbands have died by the way arrive with every pilgrim caravan, some device is necessary to procure them admission without breaking the law. A number of men, therefore, live in the frontier towns, who, upon the arrival of every concourse, hire themselves out to the women, marry them, live with them while they pass through the sacred territory, receive a munificent sum for their services, and are then divorced. If one of these individuals chooses to insist on keeping the wife he has procured, she cannot help it; but such an act would be attended with great discredit and the loss of a very profitable occupation. Eight hundred men are sometimes employed as temporary husbands, and a number of boys are continually trained that they may inherit the calling. On the various roads to the shrine of Mecca congregate a number of women, with somewhat of a sacred character attached to them. They are prostitutes, but not indiscriminate in their connections, since they offer to bear to wealthy pilgrims children, who are considered as born under a fortunate auspice.

Among the Merehedes, on the frontiers of Yemen, a custom far more revolting has existed from ancient time, and still prevails. A stranger arriving as a guest is compelled to pass the night with the wife of his host, whatever her age or condition. Should he succeed in pleasing her he is honourably treated. If not, she cuts off a piece of his garment, turns him out into the village, and leaves him to be driven away in disgrace. When the Wahabis conquered the Merehedes, they forced them to abandon this odious practice; but some misfortunes ensuing to the tribe, they were all imputed to this sacrilegious infringement of an ancient law. The custom was therefore restored. Some other female of the family, may, however, be substituted for the wife, but young virgins are never sacrificed to this barbarous hospitality *.

OF PROSTITUTION IN TURKEY.

THERE is one general system of manners pervading the Mohammedan world. In examining, therefore, the moral aspects of the various countries in which the religion of the Prophet is established, we find little in each to distinguish it from the rest. In Turkey exists the same civilization as in Egypt, though its population is more corrupt. 25,000,000 souls inhabit a region which would support twice as many, and yearly the work of decay is going on.

The Osmanlis, a race of Scythian extraction, have held Turkey during 400 years, receiving, however, large infusions of Persian and Mongolian blood. The wealthier people their harems with the beauties of Georgia and Circassia; the humbler intermarry with Servians, Bulgarians, Albanians, and Greeks, so that the original physical characteristics of the race have been greatly modified. Their moral nature has changed also, but in a less degree. Proud, sensual, and depraved in their tastes, they are too indolent to acquire even the means of gratifying their most powerful cravings. Their pride is satisfied with the recollection of

* Niebuhr's Description de l'Arabie; Burckhardt's Travels in Arabia; Burckhardt's Notes on the Bedouins, &c.; Chesney's Euphrates Expedition; Farren's Letters to Lord Lindsay; Perrier's Syrie sous Mehemet Ali; Skinner's Overland Journey; Kinnear's Cairo, Petra, and Damascus; Kelly's Syria and the Holy Land; Walpole's Memoirs; Poujolat's Voyage en Orient; Ainsworth's Travels in Asia Minor; Blondel's Deux Ans en Syrie.

former glories; their lust looks forward to the enjoyments of paradise, crowded, as they believe, with celestial creatures devoted to the delight of their senses. Immersed in an atmosphere of epicurean speculation, the Turk whom poverty does not compel to labour for his bread passes the day in lounging on cushions, smoking, sipping coffee, winking with half-closed eyes on the landscape, dreamily indifferent to all external objects. Even the poor indulge in this idleness. They measure out the amount of labour sufficient to keep them from want, and spend the rest of their lives drowsily awaiting the sensual bliss promised them by their prophet in heaven. During this lethargy passions more violent than are known to Europeans sleep in their breasts, and when these are excited, the Turk cannot be surpassed for brutal fury. All his ideas are gross. He is able to imagine no authority not armed with whip or sword. Moral power is to him an incomprehensible idea. It is, perhaps, for this reason that the Osmanlis have conquered so much, and possessed so little talent for governing what they acquired.

This notice of the Turkish character is necessary, because it corresponds exactly with their estimation of the female sex. The person alone is loved. Intellect in a Turkish woman is a quality rarely developed, because never prized. It is no part of her education to learn to read or write. To adorn herself, to dress in charming attire, to beautify her face, to perfume her hair, and soften her limbs in the bath or with fine ointments, is the object to which she applies her mind; and when, thus decorated, she lounges on a pile of cushions in the full splendour of her costume, her delight is some spectacle which will stimulate her passions and intoxicate her with excitement. Turkey is thus the empire of the senses.

Polygamy, authorized by the Prophet's code, is not now so frequently resorted to as formerly. It is growing into disrepute, and the female sex, upon which the laws relating to property have conferred much independence, are generally averse to it. Men marrying wives equal in rank to themselves frequently engage in their first marriage contract not to form a second, and the breach of this agreement is viewed as a profligate abuse of manners. The practice of polygamy was once, however, very prevalent among the higher orders, and contributed much to corrupt as well as to diminish the population. In the families of those Mohammedans who indulge in a plurality of wives, the children are fewer than in those of the Greeks, Armenians, and Jews, to whom polygamy is not permitted.

The offspring of married women, also, in the middle ranks of life is more numerous than in the wealthier harems. Indeed, the sex in Turkey is naturally prolific; but the growth of the nation has been checked by this among other causes. To account for the origin of the practice in Turkey many ingenious theories have been framed. It appears easy, however, to find its origin. The men are naturally sensual, and have never been accustomed to respect the female sex. When, therefore, an individual's wealth allowed him, he naturally made use of it to multiply the sources of that animal enjoyment, dearer to him than any other earthly pleasure. Some have supposed that polygamy was necessitated by the numerical disparity of the sexes; but this does not seem the case. In those cities and towns where the women are in greater numbers than the men, we find that they are purchased in large numbers from the neighbouring villages or in the markets, to furnish the harems of the opulent.

The social code of Turkey requires a woman to preserve herself in strict seclusion. The privacy of her apartments is so great that, unless on very rare occasions, no male is allowed to enter them except the master of the house. There are only certain days of the year in which a brother, an uncle, or a father-in-law can be admitted, or on festive occasions, such as a birthday or ceremony of circumcision.

The usages of the country do not even permit a man to see his wife before marriage. In this respect the Turks are more jealous than their written law, for the Prophet advised his friend to obtain a glimpse of the woman whom he designed to receive into his bed. She may gratify her curiosity by seeing him, but such an occurrence is not frequent. This severe separation of the sexes has given employment to a class of professional matchmakers, who, as in China, make considerable profits by their calling, and often gain money under fraudulent pretences. The beauty and temper of the woman are exaggerated to the man, who, on the other hand, is described to the lady as possessed of every heroic qualification. They are mutually deceived; they rush into a marriage, and perhaps in a few days a divorce is required. Children of three or four years are sometimes betrothed, and married when they are fourteen. This interference of the parents leads often to evil results, for the youth, who is forced to accept his father's choice, sometimes hates his bride before he sees her, and resolves to take a concubine as soon as circumstances permit.

Each family deputes an agent to promote the satisfactory settlement of the transaction, while the girl herself, under her cloudy veil, sits in her harem to await her fate. To expose her face to a strange man's gaze would be regarded as a species of prostitution. Her fortune is, therefore, decided for her. The terms of the contract are laid down in a document, which is signed by witnesses, and the woman is then called "a wife by writing." This is concluded some days before the actual rite of wedding; but the whole interval is occupied with ceremonies, rejoicing, and liberal displays of hospitality. A man in Constantinople usually reckons on spending a year's income on the occasion of his marriage. The average of this, in the middle ranks, is from 2000 to 2500 piastres.

On the appointed day the union, which is a mere civil contract, though blessed by religious rites, is concluded. The bridegroom is conducted by an Imaum, or priest, to the entrance of the bride's chamber, and there a prayer is uttered, to which all his friends make response. He is then left alone, standing outside the door. He knocks three times. A slave-maid admits him, going out herself to fetch a table with a tray of viands. While she is gone the husband endeavours to uncover his wife's face, in which, after the usual coy resistance prescribed by custom, he, of course, succeeds. Meanwhile the damsel returns, and they eat together. The meal is very quickly dispatched, and a bridal couch is spread on the floor. Then the bride is taken into a neighbouring room, where she is undressed by her mother and her friends, after which the newly-married pair are left alone. Among the most popular stories connected with Ottoman manners, is that of the sultan throwing his handkerchief to the woman he chooses as the companion of his pillow, and the imitation of this practice by great men in their harems. This, however, is a fanciful invention, repeated by some travellers who desired the world to suppose they were intimate with the secrets of the seraglio. When the sultan chooses any one of his women to pass the night with, he sends an eunuch with a present to inform her of the intended honour. She is taken to a bath, perfumed, attired in beautiful garments, and then placed in bed. The story of her creeping in at the foot of the couch is also a fable. The first chosen is the chief in rank.

The first of these fanciful accounts was probably suggested by a custom still practised among some of the Bosnian communities in western Turkey, where manners are more simple than in the eastern provinces. The young Muslim girls are there permitted to walk about in the daytime with uncovered faces. A man inclined to matrimony who happens to be pleased with the appearance of one of these maidens throws an embroidered handkerchief, or some part of his dress, over her head or neck. She then returns to her home, considers herself betrothed, and never again exposes her features in public. This is the usual preliminary to marriage; but it is probable that the lover has more than one look at his mistress before he makes the sign.

Even the sultan's concubines are purchased slaves, since no free Turkish woman can occupy that position. Occasionally he gives one away to a favourite pasha, who looks with pride upon the acquisition, and glories in the refuse of a palace. Little girls, about seven years of age, are much prized as slaves, and are often sold for upwards of a hundred guineas.

Life in the harems of Constantinople is similar to that in those of Cairo. It is a round of sensual enjoyment, in which vanity is almost the only relief to the grosser appetites of humanity. The bath is the favourite place of resort. Lady Wortley Montague has left a celebrated description of one of these palaces of indolence. The ladies, perfectly naked, walked up and down, or reclined in various attitudes on heaps of cushions, attended by pretty slaves, who handed them coffee or sherbet. They delighted in the voluptuous movements of the female dancers, of which the public class in Turkey, as in Egypt, is composed of prostitutes. It struck them with surprise and disappointment that Lady Mary did not take off her clothes as they did; but she showed them how she was cased up in her stays, so that she could not strip, which they imagined was an ingenious device of her jealous husband.

The morals of the Turkish women in general are described by most writers as very loose. The veils which were invented to preserve their virtue, favour their intrigues to dispose of it. The most watchful husband may pass his wife in the street without knowing her. Thus they live in perpetual masquerade. The places of assignment are usually at Jews' shops, where they meet their paramours, though very seldom letting them know who they are. "You may easily imagine," said Lady

Montague, "the number of faithful wives to be very small in a country where they have nothing to fear from a lover's indiscretion." This may be taken, however, as an exaggerated view, for her ladyship was accustomed to breathe the impure moral atmosphere of courts, and cared little for the character of her sex in any part of the world.

The wife in Turkey holds this check upon the caprice of her husband—her property belongs to herself, and if she be divorced she may take it away. The widow, also, is inviolable in her harem, not only against private intrusion, but against the officers of the law. If a woman's husband neglect her, that is, if he fail to visit her once a week, she may sue for a separation, which may be easily effected before a Kadi. If she commit adultery, he may also sue; but if the divorce takes place by mutual consent no formality whatever is required. As in Egypt, a man may marry a woman twice after divorcing her; but the third time he must not take her again, until she has been had and put away by another person.

Women, in Turkey, regard as an object more pitiable than any other the childless wife. With them to be barren after marriage is viewed as more disgraceful than with us to be fruitful before. All sorts of quackeries are resorted to by them to prolong and increase their powers of child-bearing, so that many kill themselves by the dangerous devices they employ. It is common to see a woman who has borne thirteen or fourteen children; some in the middle ranks bear from 25 to 30. They pray for the birth of twins, and are usually good mothers, though some have expressed themselves indifferent whether all their children lived or half of them were swept off by the plague. The single instance of superior refinement observable in Egypt is also remarkable here. Midwives only attend the bed of child-birth. There are no accoucheurs. Female practitioners also cure diseases; though an European physician is sometimes admitted to feel a pulse or even to see a patient's face.

Among the humbler classes the condition of the women resembles very nearly that of our own country. Their morality is generally superior to that of those wealthier inmates of the harems whose indolence seduces them into vice.

The dancing girls of the public class of Turkey resemble, in all respects, those of Egypt. They are prostitutes by profession; but they do not appear to be so numerous in that country as formerly. Their performances, however, are prized by all classes, and they dance as lasciviously in the harem before women, as in the Kiosk before a party of convivial men. Those who perform in public indulge in every obscenity, and vie with each other in their indecent exhibitions. Their costume is exceedingly rich both in colour and in material. Frequenting the coffee-houses by day, they pick up companions, whom they entertain with songs, or tales, or caresses until nightfall, when preliminary orgies take place, and they disperse, with their patrons, to houses in various parts of the city, generally in the more narrow, tortuous, and remote streets. The outsides of these habitations are usually of a forbidding, cheerless, dirty aspect, but the interior of those belonging to the wealthier chiefs of the dancing girls are fitted up with every appurtenance of luxury.

One of the most extraordinary features in the social institutions of Turkey is the temporary union, or marriage of convenience, which is adopted by many. It is, indeed, strictly speaking, simple prostitution. A man going on a journey, and leaving his wife behind, arrives in a strange city, where he desires to make some stay. He immediately bargains for a girl to live with him while he remains in the neighbourhood; a regular agreement is drawn up, and he supports her, and pays her friends, while he has her in his possession. The Moolahs declare this to be one valuable privilege of the male sex in Turkey; but the engagement does not appear to be valid before the law, if contracted expressly as a temporary union. But this is not necessary. The facility of divorce renders all such precaution useless. The man, therefore, takes the girl, nominally as his wife, but virtually as his mistress, until he is tired of her, or wishes to depart, when she returns to her friends and waits the occasion of a new engagement.

Such is, in outline, the social system of Turkey with reference to the female sex[*].

Of Prostitution in Circassia.

A peculiar interest attaches to the nation inhabiting that isthmus, with its stupend-

[*] Walpole's Memoirs of Turkey; Deux Années à Constantinople; Walpole's Travels; Sketches of Turkey by an American; Castellan's Mœurs des Ottomanes; Macfarlane's Constantinople in 1828; Porter's Philosophical Transactions; Lady M. W. Montague's Letters; St. John's Notes; Thornton; Walsh; Slade's Travels; Marshall; Marmont's Turkey; Arvieux's Voyages; Russel's Aleppo, &c.

ous mountains, which forms the natural barrier between Asia and Europe; and is, perhaps, still the least known region in the ancient world. The Western Caucasus comprehends an immense district commencing at the middle Kuban, and terminating with Georgia. It is peopled by various tribes, claiming a common descent, and governed by princes, elders, and nobles. The Circassians are a brave and civilized, hospitable and courteous, race, resembling the ancient Swiss; and they present a singular system of manners varying considerably with the different tribes.

There is a race, known as the Abassians, which is considered the aboriginal nation of the Caucasus,—described by Strabo as a predatory people,—pirates at sea, robbers on land; characteristics which they have to this day preserved. They are, however, in other respects, virtuous, dwelling in fixed habitations, strangers to the worst vices of civilized life, and humble in their desires. Their religion, a compound of Judaism, Christianity, and Islamism, permits polygamy; but, as a wife is expensive, they are usually contented with one, who is more the companion than the menial of her husband. The women are exceedingly industrious; employing themselves in a variety of pursuits, and tasking themselves far more than is essentially necessary in order to procure ornamental clothes. To reward them for this they are allowed full liberty, are free in their social intercourse, and, if they wear a veil, wear it only to screen their complexions from the sun. Their costume is highly elegant, and their state is indicated by the colour of their trowsers—white being that for the virgin, red for the wife, and blue for the widow.

The laws these people have made to protect their own morals, have, in some degree, answered their purpose. Illegitimate children have no claim to a share of the patrimony, and can legally claim no relationship with any one. Should they be sold as slaves there is no one bound to ransom; should they be assassinated there is no relative expected to avenge their death. Nevertheless the inherent kindness of the Abassians mitigates the effect of these harsh laws. Illegitimate children are rarely treated ill, and their legitimate brothers often make with them a voluntary partition of property.

But when a man marries a barren woman, he is allowed to take a concubine, whose children inherit no disability on this account.

When a man dies, be his rank what it may, the social law confers on his wife the superintendence of the household, and she administers the property without division until her death, when it is divided among the sons. Should any of the daughters remain unmarried, their eldest brother is bound to support them until a suitor appears, when he may make as good a bargain as he can.

Severe laws have been enacted against immorality. The man detected in illicit intercourse with a married or unmarried woman is tried before the elders of the community, who rarely fail to punish him, either by a fine or by perpetual banishment. The dishonoured wife is returned to her parents, as well as the girl, and sold as a slave. The dowry which her husband had given for her is returned to him. If the guilt have happened in the family of a prince, it can only be washed out by the blood of one, if not both, of the criminals. So bitter, indeed, is the shame which such an occurrence brings upon a house, that they who have been so disgraced often retire to some desolate part of the Caucasus, there to hide themselves from the obloquy which ever afterwards attaches to their name.

When a man desires to divorce his wife, he must declare before a council of elders the reasons for such a step; and if these be not perfectly satisfactory he is obliged to pay the parents of the women a sufficient amount to recompense them for the burden thus thrown upon their hands. Should the woman, however, marry again before two years have expired this sum is returned. Frequently a maiden having formed some romantic attachment, and hating the man chosen as her husband by her parents, flies alone into the woods, and hides until her friends proclaim themselves willing to concede her desires. Occasionally, also, two warriors select the same girl to marry, and in this case a duel is fought —sometimes with fire-arms—the victor carrying off the prize. Similar laws and usages prevail among the Circassians, except that the wealthier men among them seclude their wives, and are altogether more Turkish in their manners. On the whole, however, the patriarchal institutions of this singular and romantic people are admirable for the effect they produce, since the Circassians and Abassians are exceedingly pure in their morality.

Among the Circassians themselves, with the exception of the prouder nobles, women are not secluded. The wives and daughters of a house are often introduced to the traveller, and unmarried girls are frequently seen at public assemblies. One singular custom, however, is observed, which is that the husband never appears abroad with his wife, and scarcely ever sees her during the day. This is not from neglect or scorn, but in accordance with ancient habits, and a desire to prolong the first sentiments with which the bridegroom approaches his bride.

All Circassian women wear, until they are married, a tight corset of leather, which makes their complexion sallow, and hurts the figure, as all unnatural compression does. The consequence is that the young wives are infinitely more beautiful than the maidens; and the charms of the women of this race are celebrated throughout the world. The reason assigned for this strange custom is, that it is shameful for a virgin to have a full bosom. When a girl has been chosen and purchased, her future husband comes to the house, places her on horseback, gallops away, and conveys her home. Then, when all the people are supposed to be asleep, the bridegroom first unlooses the abominable ligatures which confine the bosom of his bride. He does not, until some time has passed, live with her openly.

An idea prevails among the vulgar in Europe, that the Circassians sell their daughters as slaves to any Turk or Persian who may desire to buy them. This is not correct. They are particularly careful as to the position and birth of the individual who desires to intermarry with them, and the sale is no more than takes place among their own people, as well as among all the nations inhabiting the Caucasus. Great precautions are taken to secure the happiness of the girls, and long negotiations frequently produce no bargain. It is true that in the bazaars of Constantinople, and the principal towns of Asia Minor and Persia, numerous girls are sold under the name of Circassians, but they are mostly Abassians, or the children of Circassian peasants, or children ravished from the neighbouring Cossacks, or slaves procured from those base Circassian traders who have given in their adhesion to Russia. Many of the girls, being trained to such ideas from childhood, prefer the Turkish harem to the life they follow among their native hills. Some come back after having obtained their liberty, and bring accounts, in the most fluent language, of the voluptuous joys they have indulged in in their luxurious prisons; but generally the race is dearly attached to its freedom.

Throughout the Caucasus we have found a high scale of manners. Prostitution, as a profession, is unknown. In one of the simple tribes, still under patriarchal rule, a girl who took up such a calling would be so shunned and abhorred by the rest of her country-women, that she would speedily be compelled to fly beyond the bounds of their territory, that is, if she escaped being sold as a slave or put to death by her indignant friends. The parental authority, more moral than legal, is a great check upon profligacy, since a man of whatever age, if he have a father living, pays obedience to him, and fears to incur his reproof. It is therefore delightful to point out a country surrounded by gross and profligate nations, where simplicity of manners still prevails, and where the female sex is as happy and as highly esteemed as it is modest, chaste, and virtuous*.

Of Prostitution among the Tartar Races.

The immense region of Central Asia, little known and seldom visited, has been the cradle of great nations, which have exercised a mighty influence on the fortunes of the world, and may again become conspicuous in history. It is, therefore, interesting, as well as important, to inquire into the characteristics of the populations which still cling to its soil. They are divided under many names, and among the most remarkable are the hordes of Kirghiz Kazaks, who wander between the borders of the Caspian Sea on the west, and the fortified line which forms the southern frontier of the Russian Empire. On the east it is divided by a similar chain of posts from the Chinese dominions, but towards the south the limits of their wanderings are unknown. Over this vast steppe a various climate prevails; but the whole is particularly marked by extremes of heat and cold, while the soil is composed of alternate deserts of sand and pasture, where rain during the greater part of the year is exceedingly scanty. A short and delicious spring, a burning and dry summer, a short and miserable autumn, which speedily darkens into a long, bitter, and gloomy winter—such are the influences to which these hordes are subject. Forests, patches of green, salt lakes, springs and rivers of fresh water, a few rich valleys, and some rocky hills, vary the aspect of the wilderness which is their

* Spenser's Western Caucasus; Klaproth's Voyages dans le Caucase; Spenser's Travels in Circassia; Wilbraham's Travels; Marigny's Three Voyages.

home; but generally it is a blank and monotonous waste. All these circumstances are enumerated, as they may be supposed to have formed, or at least to have modified, the character of the Kirghiz Kazaks. They are divided into three principal hordes—the Great, the Lesser, and the Little—amounting altogether to from 2,000,000 to 2,400,000 souls. Engaged perpetually in wandering from place to place, they have nevertheless certain spots, belonging by prescriptive rights to particular tribes, where they encamp for the coldest months of the winter. Their manners afford a faithful picture of the ancient patriarchal life, not, indeed, the poetical life of Arcadia and the pastures of Israel, but that of the Scythians, as represented by Herodotus, or the Bedouins in their original simplicity. Forming a nation of shepherds, they appear to live only on and for their flocks, accustoming themselves little to the use of arms, and, though perpetually on horseback, seldom engaging in the chase. They dwell in huts or temporary habitations of strong wickerwork, covered in with fleeces; and in the interior of these singular habitations much comfort, elegance, and even sumptuous luxury may often be found. Nevertheless they are a robust, hardy race, possessing very indistinct ideas of property, and, though addicted to sensual enjoyments, long lived, and seldom visited by epidemic diseases, except when the small-pox is brought among them from Siberia.

Their manners with respect to the character and treatment of the female sex are simple, but, in comparison with other pastoral races, somewhat coarse. In costume the woman differs little from the man. Both men and women adorn themselves with ornaments of silver, gold, or coral, or even pearls and other gems, and in this reciprocal display of vanity we discover a token of equality between the sexes. It is difficult to ascertain the religion of these hordes, but it is apparently a crude mixture of Mohammedanism and Paganism. The Muslims have attempted to disseminate their doctrines widely, but few of the Prophet's laws have been accepted so readily as that which allows a plurality of wives—which the Kirghiz indulge in whenever they can afford the amount to be paid for a bride according to the usages of their nation.

The Kirghiz are immoderately addicted to voluptuous pleasures, and are extremely idle. It is curious to remark, however, that while the men are distinguished by their indolence, the women are fond of exertion, occupying themselves, as much from inclination as from necessity, with the affairs of the household, with attendance on the flocks, and with the manufacture of garments. Their recompense is to be treated as servitors by masters who are sometimes proud and harsh; but the labour of the women is not compulsory, nor are they shut up in harems, or forbidden to mix with the other sex. The seclusion of females, indeed, is not a custom. Their manner of living exposes them to every temptation; jealousy has little power to watch, and the wife's virtue is, for the most part, left to guard itself.

Though, as we have said, the Kirghiz, when they are rich enough, eagerly avail themselves of the privilege of polygamy, few possess wealth enough to enable them to marry more than one wife. This circumstance prevents them from indulging in that pride which impels a man to shut up the partner of his pillow from every eye but his own. They who have seraglios must follow a steady and uniform course of life. The Tartar's tent offers few obstacles to curiosity or intrigue. Turks and Persians who keep a harem usually possess slaves also, whose labour permits their mistresses to lounge idly on silken cushions; but as the Kirghiz loves to be indolent, he is constrained to let his wife be as active as she pleases, and is never so happy as when she saves him the trouble of moving from his couch, by going everywhere and doing everything herself. But on horseback he is proud of motion, which accounts partly for the migratory habits of the hordes, though the nature of their country is the chief cause of their nomade manner of life. Women consequently enjoy their liberty, and to their love of industry they join a goodness of heart and a warmth of affection which extort praises from many travellers.

The great check upon polygamy is, as we have noticed, the cost of the *Kalyms*, which is to be paid for every woman. This price varies in amount, from five or six sheep, and occasionally less among the poor, to 200 or 500 or even 1000 horses among the rich. To these are added different household effects, with, on rare occasions, a few slaves, male or female. Out of these payments a considerable share goes to the Mohammedan Moolahs who frequent the steppes, and who are attracted thither no less by their profitable occupation of marrying the people than by religious zeal. The Kalym increases with the number of wives. The second costs more than the first, and the third than the second, and so forth, which enables none but a very wealthy man to keep a harem. The khan of the Little Horde, who was lord over nearly 1,000,000 men, had sixteen or seventeen wives, besides fifteen concubines, whose offspring, however, were all on an equality. This patriarch had 42 sons and about 34 daughters. Young men usually take their first wife not according to their own choice, but under their father's direction. As to girls they are always under their parents' control, and many are affianced during infancy.

The first arrangement made when a marriage is in contemplation is to fix the amount of the *kalym*, and the date on which it is to be paid. These preliminaries concluded, the Moolah consecrates the transaction by asking three times of the parents of the bride and those of the bridegroom, "Do you consent to the union of your children?" and reading prayers for the happiness of the married couple. Witnesses and arbitrators are then chosen, who may decide future disputes, should any such arise, and the nuptials are terminated by a feast and various kinds of merry-making. The man then begins to pay a kalym, or else his father does this on his behalf; and the parents of the girl occupy themselves with getting ready a trousseau for their daughter—among the articles of which it is essentially requisite to include the tent which the bride is to occupy when she is finally delivered over to her husband. While the kalym remains unpaid the marriage is suspended; though the bridegroom may pay visits to the maiden he has chosen, and even live with her, provided he engages not to take away her chastity.

Among some tribes these preliminary meetings are conducted with much ceremony; in all they are often the first interviews which the husband has with the woman who is to be his wife. When once, however, a part of the required amount is paid, neither can retract without disgrace. Ruptures, indeed, rarely, if ever, take place; partly because no young girl dare to assert a will of her own, and partly because the man does not care to rebel against a union which he is free to break when he desires.

Frequently, however, the bride and bridegroom, during their preliminary visits, anticipate the final nuptial ceremony; in which case this is usually hastened, though the whole amount of kalym may not have been paid. They are led, richly clothed if possible, into a tent, where various rites are performed. The husband then departs, but immediately comes again on horseback and demands his wife. Her parents refuse to yield her, when he enters, bears her off by force, places her across his saddle, and gallops away to his tent, which during many hours after is sacred against all intruders. This custom, however, is not universal.

If a man finds his wife not to be a virgin, he may disgrace her, send her home, and demand from her father the restitution of the kalym, or one of his other daughters who happens to be chaste, without payment.

As every woman brings with her dowry a new tent, so each wife, when a man has more than one, dwells in a separate habitation. The first is styled the "rich wife," and exercises superior authority over all the rest. Though she may have disgusted her husband, he is bound to distinguish her by respect; while the others, entirely equal among themselves, remain always in a certain dependence on her. Prudent husbands divide even the flocks belonging to the different women, that the children of each may justly inherit her property. The chief wife may quit her husband, if she can show any grave cause for separation, and return to her parents, but the others have not that privilege.

The manners of the Kirghiz women are in general simple and courteous; and the conduct of the men towards them, though often rude, gross, and contemptuous, is frequently also polite and deferential. The love songs of the desert are some of them exceedingly poetical; and the pictures drawn by Tartar improvisatoris of their mistresses are full of passion and adulation.

A man may kill his wife if he find her actually committing adultery, but not otherwise. A fine is the usual punishment of the adulterer; while the woman may be divorced, or chastised in various ways.

Generally the morals of the Kirghiz Kazaks are good. Chastity in their women is highly prized—its loss entailing disgrace; but as numbers of the men are extremely sensual, many prostitutes may usually be found in each camp, though not so many as some appear to imagine. They live usually in companies, resembling the class of suttlers in European armies; though some of superior fortune inhabit separate tents, and live in ease and plenty.

Among the Nogay Tartars, who are also nomades, the custom prevails of a man serving his father-in-law for a certain number of years. With them the weaker is absolutely the property of the stronger sex, and all contracts are transactions of sale. The father sells his daughter, the brother his sister, and girls are considered part of an inheritance as much as flocks and herds, and are equally divided among the sons. The value of a woman is measured in cows; five being the cost of an inferior, and thirty of a superior one. The man, however, though obliged to buy, is not allowed to sell his wife. If she transgress beyond his patience he turns her out of the dwelling, and she returns to her parents, who seldom fail to receive her kindly. Divorce is permitted, but is so costly that few resort to it. When a wife leaves her husband against his consent he may demand her back; but if she meanwhile commit adultery or theft, her parents must restore the kalym which was originally paid for her, and she becomes so infamous that only the poorest man will buy her.

The rich are polygamists; and as the sexes are about equal in point of numbers, many of the poor cannot get a wife of any kind. The woman is not allowed to eat with her husband; and if she expect paradise, it is with the understanding that she is to dwell there as a servitor. Marriages are not fruitful, and the population is regularly decreasing.

The Russians have introduced into the country certain virulent diseases, which aid rapidly to thin the people, who themselves have lost much in morality. Wherever they have large encampments, and settle for the winter, numbers of prostitutes spring up among them, not indeed entirely addicted and altogether destined to that calling, but employing it as a means of gain, and living on its wages for a shorter or a longer period.

Prostitution, which is unknown among the pastoral tribes of Arabia, is, in fact, very prevalent among some of the shepherd communities inhabiting the Tartar steppes. There are two classes of women who betake themselves to it—widows and divorced women—who, having no independent means of subsistence, hire out their persons under a sort of necessity, and linger through a miserable remnant of life, in dirt, rags, and contempt; and a few who addict themselves to prostitution simply under the impulse of a profligate disposition. On the whole, however, the morality of Tartars is of a superior character *.

* Levchine's Les Kirghiz Kazaks; Spencer's Travels; Klaproth's Travels, &c., &c.

OF THE MIXED NORTHERN NATIONS.

INTRODUCTORY.

PURSUING our inquiries among the northern races, to the very extreme of Polar cold, we discover many interesting peculiarities. Perhaps, however, the most important result of our research is the establishment of the fact, that the popular idea is in great measure erroneous, of hot countries having the most licentious population. Climate, indeed, may by fine degrees influence the temperament of men; but the conspicuous truth evolved from all our investigations has been that the manners of nations are regulated by their moral education, and not by the thermometer.

In Egypt, India, Persia, and the other hot regions of the African and Asiatic continents, there prevails a voluptuous spirit; but in Russia, in Siberia, among the Greenlanders, and the tribes of the snowy deserts in the utmost north, equal sensuality is to be discovered. In the warm and happy plains of Arabia, in the sultry champagnes of various parts of the East, we find shepherd communities with manners most pure and simple, and we find the same among many roving nations in the cold of Tartary and Siberia. The languor and indolence engendered by a fervent climate may, indeed, induce a thirst for exciting pleasure; but the rigour and inclemency of the north appear equally to dispose men to take refuge in sensual gratification. Ispahan was never more licentious than St. Petersburgh 50 years ago; nor are the debauchees in the burning atmosphere of Africa more gross and indiscriminate in their pursuit of animal delights than many tribes of Esquimaux, buried though they be among the frosts of an eternal winter.

Thus climate appears to exert, at least, far less influence than is popularly imagined. The horrible orgies of the Areois, in the voluptuous islands of the Pacific, were rivalled and surpassed by the Physical

Societies of Moscow; nor are the revels of Southern India more profligate than those enacted among the snowy solitudes of Siberia. Indeed, among the Hindus, we have never found perpetrated, even by the lowest class, depravities more vile than those we have discovered among tribes in Kamschatka and other parts of the Arctic regions.

One circumstance, however, appears to be undeniable. The temperament of Asiatics is more easily inflamed than that of northern races. Their mind is more active, their fancy more busy, their imagination more creative. They give even to their vices a picturesque colour, quality, and configuration, whereas the voluptuaries of cold countries are dull and drowsy sensualists, without a tinge of poetry in their composition. For this reason the ardent passions of the East have been celebrated in romance and history, while the slothful sensuality of the North has been neglected and forgotten. The world consequently has heard much of the one, and little or nothing of the other; and in course of time, by a very natural process, has imagined that the burning climates of Asia represent the passions of its inhabitants, while the snows of the opposite regions of Polar cold are characteristic of their purity and freedom from the dross of vice.

This idea, which we confess we once shared with the rest of the public, has been dissipated in our minds by the inquiries we have made. The sensuality of the East is more striking, more conspicuous, more celebrated, because it has been dressed by history and fable in more attractive forms, while that of the North is forgotten, because it has presented no theme for declamation or romance. But the people of the one resemble very much the people of the other; and even in the South, among the old and decaying nations of Europe, the same truth is discovered. Spain and Italy are supposed to be the cradles of voluptuous sentiment; but history shows how they have, in the manners of their people, passed from gradation to gradation, from variety to variety, while their climate has remained perpetually the same. Nature alters in nothing, but civilization is in continual change; and Rome, which was the sanctuary of female virtue in the heroic times of the Republic, is now, like Babylon, a city where adultery is licensed, and profligacy has the encouragement of the law.

Manners in Russia appear also to have passed through a considerable change since the days of the Empress Catherine. When it becomes civilized, it will, probably, improve still further. Its manners are now gross and profligate in the extreme, which in servile populations is invariably the case; but they have undergone considerable ameliorations since the close of the last century. In the neighbouring and kindred regions of Siberia, alterations appear only in those parts where a congregation of tribes has taken place, and the ruder are giving way to the more refined forms of society. Throughout the North, indeed, as much variety appears as in the East, and communities dwelling under the same temperature, present a perfect contrast in their morals and customs.

In Finland a very extraordinary state of manners still prevails. A recent traveller affords a curious illustration of this, showing how the ideas of decency in various countries are modified by habit. He went to a bath, and when conducted into a private chamber, found to his astonishment a tall handsome girl ready to attend him. She exhibited the utmost coolness and indifference, stripped off all his clothes, and rubbed him with herbs from head to foot as though he had been a mere log of wood, bathed him, laid him on his face, scourged him with a bundle of twigs, until he broke out into copious perspiration, dried him with towels, and all the while appeared utterly unconscious that her task was inconsistent with modesty or decent manners. In many parts of the North it is customary, as in some places in the East, and in the heroic ages in Greece, for the maidens of the house to attend a guest to his bedchamber, and assist in disposing him in comfort for the night. These practices do not in all countries, and at all times, illustrate the same national characteristics. They belong on the contrary to two extremes of social development. They indicate either a perfect simplicity or a total corruption of manners. It was genuine purity of mind and unsuspecting innocence of character that is represented in the virgin who attended Ulysses to the bath; but it was the vilest sensuality and brutality of manners that allowed the Roman Emperor of later days to be bathed and dressed by women.

Consequently in passing from the semi-civilized nations, through the races of the North, to the educated communities of Christendom, we proceed without the theory of measuring a country's manners by its geographical position. If it be civilized, it will be moral; but civilization is a false name when it is applied to a corrupt and enervated society. Art and luxury are not its highest evidences; but virtue and obedience to the exalted maxims of ethical philosophy.

Of Prostitution in Russia.

Russia, included by courtesy among civilized states, retains strong traces of its original barbarism. Resembling China in its system of government, it resembles it also in manners. What is admirable in its social characteristics arises from the natural good qualities of the people, who, notwithstanding a despotism which has wanted no feature to degrade them, please the traveller by a display of many signs of good disposition.

Russia resembles Asia in the indolence and apathy of its population. In the one region nations appear to have been enervated by heat, in the other benumbed by cold into a torpid submission to power. This is evident from the state of public manners. In Russia the inquiry is not what is essentially wrong, but what is wrong according to the police; and nothing else is condemned. Abject towards their rulers, they assume towards others the arrogance of slaves, so that a succession of tyrants may be said to exist from the emperor who tramples down sixty millions, to the peasant who oppresses his serving-boy.

No more striking proof could be mentioned of the fact that the condition and character of women form an infallible measure of civilization, than the state of the sex in Russia. It is true that our knowledge is very incomplete. Most travellers who have written on that country complain how difficult it is to describe it well, and they have generally verified their remark; still we learn enough from various authorities to enable us to judge in a general way of its characteristics.

Among the higher classes women affect and study a polish and refinement of manners, but this relates chiefly to the formalities of life. They dare not, under their own social code, make an inelegant salutation, transgress a point of etiquette, ride in an unfashionable equipage, or converse in a vulgar tone; but they may break the most sacred moral laws, may speak openly of indecent subjects, and may act and talk in a way which a modest English lady would blush to think of. The position they hold in society is in accordance with this view. Formerly marriage was little more than a bond between master and slave; but the relation has been, in that respect, improved. Women are to a certain degree independent, but it is the independence of neglect. They lead, in a word, a life very nearly resembling that of fashionable persons in our own metropolis, but their morals are not to be compared.

Little need be said of the marriage contract in Russia, since it is under the laws of the Christian church. It is, however, necessary to mention that few engagements occur between persons mutually united by affection. Interest is the usual tie; and frequently a girl is taken to the altar, where her appointed husband stands before her, all but an utter stranger. The ceremony is so theatrical that it wears no solemnity whatever. It is a drawing-room scene, directed by priests; so that the very seal of matrimony is of such a kind as to impress the woman with no idea of a holy union. The wives of the Russian nobles have accordingly little reputation for fidelity to their husbands; a characteristic observed by Clarke, long ago, as he travelled, and confirmed by Mr. Thompson, who wrote a year or two since, as well as by many other writers. Immorality and intrigue are of universal prevalence, from the palace to the private house. In a social sense they are scarcely looked upon as offences. The husband and wife, united by a bond, not of affection but of policy, look on each other from the first with coldness and indifference. Gradually each withdraws in a separate circle of life, and at length one looks without much care upon the guilt of the other. Before marriage the sexes are divided by etiquette, after marriage by mutual repulsion. The women, inferior in personal attractions, but superior in manner and acquirements to the men, receive from them little respect; and thus society, poisoned in its very springs, becomes yearly more dissolute and melancholy.

None will require to be reminded that numerous exceptions occur; that pure and strong family attachments exist in Russia; that young persons marry sometimes influenced by reciprocal feelings of affection; but from the accounts of all the writers we know who have described Russia, no other picture of its society could fairly be drawn. There is in that state licence for every crime which does not offend the government; and the more the nation is absorbed in its sensual enjoyments, the less will it be disposed to weary of servitude.

Among the peasantry sensuality is equally prevalent. They generally marry very young, but it is by no means essential that the bride should be a virgin. On the contrary, numbers of women never marry until they have had an intrigue with some other lover.

St. Petersburgh, it is said, is a city of men, there being, in a population of about 500,000, 100,000 more males than females. The native Russians are less handsome and sooner faded than the women of Germany, Finland, Livonia, Esthonia, and Courland—countries which supply the state with prostitutes. Such are the manners of the city that no woman may walk out unless accompanied by a man, not even on the great promenades, in the broad light of day.

In ten years, from 1821 to 1831, the deaths in St. Petersburgh were 61,616, being 24,229 more than the births; and during the same period there were 11,429 marriages. The native Russian women are remarkable for the ease with which they bring forth children, while the foreigners in that country are precisely the reverse. Of the former, 15 in 1000; and of the latter, 25 is the average of those who die in childbed. The average of 20 years gives 6 still-born infants out of every 1000.

The foundling hospitals of Russia, magnificent as they are, cannot but be regarded as a premium upon immorality. Those of St. Petersburgh alone cost from 600,000,000 to 700,000,000 of rubles annually; supporting from 25,000 to 30,000 children, who are received at the rate of 7000 or 8000 a year. They are called "houses of education," because a prejudice attaches to their proper name. They are not, however, intended for infants who are picked up in the streets. There is never a case of such exposure. Women who have children of which they desire to be rid, bring them usually in the twilight, and they are taken in without any questions being asked. No one can tell whether they are legitimate or illegitimate—whether the offspring of poverty, adultery, or prostitution. In cases where fear or shame might in other countries induce a woman to murder or abandon her child, the mothers bring them to the hospital, and impenetrable obscurity remains over the previous part of the transaction. It is questionable whether the crimes thus prevented would make up an amount of evil equal to that caused by the profligacy to which the licence of impunity and encouragement is thus afforded.

Violence committed on a woman, married or single, is, in Russia, punishable by the knout; but this is almost the only check which the law, written or social, imposes on immorality. It is said that judges sometimes compound with a female criminal who happens to possess beauty, and pardon her at the price of her virtue.

When a French writer, many years ago, astonished the civilized countries of Europe by the description of a private institution in Russia known as the Physical Club, his report was rejected by the majority of persons as one of those travellers' tales which had their origin in a man's impudence or credulity. Lyall, however, made extensive inquiries upon the subject, and found that there did actually exist at Moscow a society called the Physical Club, the object of which exhibited, perhaps, more depravity of manners than could be found in any other part of the world, except among the Areois of the Pacific.

This club was originated by eight men and women of high rank, who agreed to hold common intercourse with each other, and for that purpose established a society. Its members all belonged to the nobility, and they sought to exclude all but beautiful women with the bloom of youth still upon them. Admittance was very difficult to be procured. A person before being initiated was sworn to secrecy, so that the names of the members remained unknown.

At stated intervals the members of the club assembled at a large house, where, in a magnificent saloon, brilliantly lighted up, they indulged in every kind of licentious amusements, inflaming themselves with strong potations, and preparing for the hideous orgies which were to follow. Suddenly all the candles were put out, each man chose a companion, and a scene of indescribable debauch ensued. On other occasions tickets were drawn by lot, and the company paired off to bedchambers prepared for this libidinous festival. This horrible institution, transferring its pestilential influence through every circle of society in Moscow, was abolished by Catherine the Second, who hated to see the reflection of her own vices—for it is matter of history that she was a vulgar prostitute herself.

Of the prostitute system in Russia our accounts are the most scanty possible. They exist in large numbers in every city and almost in every village; and a traveller remarks that they have the character of demanding to be paid beforehand, and refusing afterwards to remain with their companion. They do not form so distinct and conspicuous a class as in some countries, for the virtue of married women and young girls in the various ranks of life is not so inaccessible as to distinguish the professional prostitute so broadly from the other classes, as in a society whose manners are less corrupt. They are, in the cities, under the perpetual surveillance of the police. In the rural districts numbers of young women, belonging to the village populations, addict themselves to prostitution for gain—some permanently, others only until they have a chance of marriage.

There is apparently no check upon this calling, unless the women become afflicted by disease. When this is discovered the prostitute is forced to discontinue for awhile her dissolute course of life, and remain in a hospital until cured. When, as very frequently happens, the wife of a soldier takes to this occupation, and becomes tainted, she is delivered to her husband, who is obliged to sign a bond, engaging for the future to restrain her from profligacy. The wives of serfs are also delivered up to their husbands, who must pay the expenses of their cure at the hospitals. If they refuse to do this, and to answer for the future conduct of their partners, the women are sent, without further ceremony, to Siberia.

Another peculiarity in the civilization of Russia is exhibited in the market of wives, which is annually held in St. Petersburgh. It is one of those things which many persons exercise their philosophy by refusing to believe; but its existence is undoubted. It is still practised, even among the upper orders, while among the humbler classes it is extremely popular. Every year, on the twenty-sixth day of May, numbers of young women assemble in a particular part of the City Summer Garden, where they are exhibited in a formal "*bride*-show." Decked with an Oriental profusion of ornaments, all the marriageable girls are arranged in lines along the shady alleys, while some friends and professional match-makers stand in attendance on each group. The men who are inclined to matrimony visit the garden, pass along the rows of maidens, inspect them leisurely, enter into conversation, and, if pleased, enter into a preliminary, but conditional, contract. Numerous matches are thus formed; but very frequently the engagement here concluded, has long, between the youthful couple, been a matter of contemplation. Those who do not possess sufficient beauty or fascination are sometimes loaded with the signs of property to induce men to take them. A mother once, desiring to match her daughter to a man of substance, hung about her neck a massive chain of gold, to which was attached six dozen silver-gilt tea-spoons, and three dozen table-spoons, besides two heavy punch-ladles of the same metal, which soon attracted the attention of the young men. In the towns, indeed, we are told that marriages among all classes are generally settled by interest. In the rural parts this is also the case, but in a less degree. There it is the custom—among the peasantry—for the bride and bridegroom to enter the church door side by side, which they take care to do with the utmost regularity, since the superstitious idea prevails, that the one who plants a foot first inside the threshold of the edifice, will be supreme over the other, and become a tyrant in the family. The serfs cannot marry without the consent of their masters. In all parts of Russia the marriage of a felon is dissolved by the sentence which condemns him; but if he be pardoned before his wife has married again, he can recover her.

It will, from this account, be seen that the manners and morals of the Russians are dissolute in an extraordinary degree. There is, perhaps, no part of Europe where the people, as a race, are so profligate. This does not imply that the society of St. Petersburgh or Moscow is not distinguished by many virtuous families; but, on the whole, all travellers concur in showing the facts upon which we have based our estimate of the national character with respect to morality *.

Of Prostitution in Siberia.

From Russia the transition is natural to the contiguous and kindred region of Siberia. Thence we may, without any apology, extend our inquiries to the remotest north—for the Arctic countries do not present themselves with sufficient prominence to occupy a separate account, and to none could they be added as a supplement more fitly than to the snowy wilderness which spreads on one side to the shores of the Frozen Sea, and on the other to the frontiers of the Chinese Empire. It may appear anomalous to include any of these tracts under the head of civilized countries; but we place them as an appendage of Russia, to which, indeed, they form an appropriate companion.

The state of manners at which the po-

* Kohl's Russia and the Russians; La Russie en 1844—par un Homme d'État; Russia under Nicolas I.; Clarke's Travels; Lyall's Character of the Russians; Voyages des Deux Français; Granville's Travels; Golovine's Russia under the Autocrat; Venables' Domestic Manners of the Russians; Bourke's St. Petersburgh and Moscow; Thompson's Life in Russia; Jesse's Notes by a Half-Pay; Erman's Travels.

pulation of these snowy tracts have arrived is extremely low. Nature has taught them many rude arts; but their civilization has not advanced far beyond its crudest elements. The severe rigours to which they are exposed have produced pressing wants, which they have ingenuity enough to satisfy, and further than this their education does not appear to go. They are rude, ignorant, and gross. Some remain with none but the faintest idea of a Deity; others preserve the ancient heathen belief of the Shamans; others have accepted a form of Christianity; but in few of them has a variation in their religious ideas resulted in a change of manners. In fact, the form, and not the spirit of our creed has been introduced among them.

Throughout the immense tracts of Siberia we find numerous tribes, and even nations, classed under various denominations; but all, in their general manners, very much resembling each other. The condition and character of the female sex among them is low; but it is not treated with that harshness or contumely which it experiences in some savage races. Although the rude Ostyak, for instance, considers his wife as no more than a domestic drudge, seldom thinks of giving her a cordial word, and loads her with tasks, he does not use her with positive severity. Among the Samoyedes, women are much less happy and more harshly treated. In the perpetual migrations of the tribes they are charged with the principal burdens, and drag after the men like a train of slaves. The wife is viewed as a necessary but almost disgusting appendage to a man's household. She is regarded as unclean under many circumstances—especially childbirth, after which her husband will not approach her for two months. When about to be delivered she experiences, instead of the kind, considerate usage which some, even of the wildest savages pay to their women in such situations, a scorn and indignity to which, by long custom, she has thoroughly learned to bend.

In many parts of Siberia, however, a better prospect is presented, and the sexes appear more on an equality. Towards the centre, away from the sea on one hand, and Russia on the other, the tribes enjoy a very independent existence, being, indeed, the most free among the subjects of the Czar. In the winter time, when the rivers are completely frozen, the young girls assemble on their snowy borders, taking care to deck themselves out with every sort of finery they can procure. Their friends also congregate, forming groups, gossip, and enjoy themselves, while the youths mix with the maidens—each selecting the partner he likes the best. It is at this time of the year that the principal matches are arranged. In all parts it is customary to pay a certain amount to the girl's parents to buy the privilege of marrying her. Should a man not be rich enough to offer the sum required, he hires himself to her father, who tasks him sometimes very heavily, and continues in servitude for three, five, seven, or ten years, according to the agreement made beforehand. At the end of that period he takes his bride, is redeemed from his servile condition, and enters the family with all the dignities and rights of a son-in-law.

Among the Ostyaks it is regarded as very disgraceful to marry a brother's widow, a mother-in-law, or, indeed, any person connected in an ascending or descending line with the wife; but it is reckoned honourable to marry several sisters. The sister of a deceased wife is considered a particular acquisition, and, indeed, is attended with a solid advantage, for a man taking the second daughter of a house pays to her father a sum only equal to half of that which he paid for the first. No one can marry a person of the same family name; but this [seems to apply to men alone, for a woman under this description who enters another household, and bears a daughter, may bestow her upon her brother. In a word, every union is lawful provided the father of the bridegroom and the father of the bride are of different families—though custom makes other distinctions, which are generally observed with as much strictness as those marked by the traditionary law.

When an Ostyak desires to marry he selects from among his companions or relatives a mediator. He then goes with a train of friends, as numerous as his influence enables him to collect, and stands before the door of the house in which the girl whom he has fixed upon resides. Her father easily guesses, on the arrival of such a cavalcade, what the object of it is, and consequently asks no questions, but invites the company in and welcomes them with a feast. Then, retiring with the mediator into another hut, he enters into a negotiation about the amount which he is to receive for his daughter. These things are quietly arranged, though the spirit of bargaining is generally active on both sides. It is not necessary to pay down the whole amount at once, but this must be done before the nuptials can take place. Sometimes, however, a man snatches away his bride before he has fully discharged his debt. In that case her father waits for an opportunity to seize her, carries her home, and keeps her in pledge until the amount be faithfully paid.

Similar customs prevail among the Samoyedes, who are polygamists, though they prefer the changing one wife for another, according to the changes in their inclination, to having two or three at once. The Tungueses, however, often keep as many as five, but even among them the majority of men marry no more than one at a time. They enter into matrimony at a very early age. It is common to see a husband fifteen years old, and a wife, or even a widow, of twelve. There is with them no feast or ceremony of any kind. The bargain is made and ratified, and the young couple proceed forthwith to their nuptial couch.

The Bulwattes, who are also polygamists, treat their women well. Among them one curious observance is,—that the consummation of every marriage must take place in a newly-built hut, where, as they say, no impure things can have been. This is, at any rate, a poetical and a somewhat refined idea. Certain feasts are essential before the union is contracted.

The Tchoutkas, beyond Nigri Kolinsk, have been baptized in large numbers. Their Christianity, however, does not incline them to remove polygamy, for they have in most cases a plurality of wives, whom they marry for a certain period—long or short, as circumstances may determine. It sometimes happens in one of these households that the wife obtains sufficient ascendancy over her husband to bind him to her, and a convention, intended from the first to be only temporary, becomes permanent. The woman who accomplishes this achievement is honoured by the rest of her sex, and is thenceforward supreme in the family. Generally speaking the women of this tribe are more happy and free than in any other part of Siberia.

Among the Tschuwasses it is customary on the occasion of a betrothal to offer a sacrifice of bread and honey to the sun, that he may look down with favour on the union. On the appointed day, while the guests are assembling, the bride hides herself behind a screen. Then she walks round the room three times, followed by a train of virgins bearing honey and bread. The bridegroom entering, snatches over her veil, kisses her, and exchanges rings. She then distributes refreshments to her friends, who salute her as "the betrothed girl," after which she is led behind the screen to put on a matron's cap. One of the concluding rites performed is that of the bride pulling off her new husband's boots—a ceremony to symbolise her promise of obedience to him. When, however, he on his part takes the cap from her head, she is divorced, and goes home to her parents.

Still more degrading is the custom of the Tchemerisses. A man, representing the girl's father, presents to her husband a whip, which he is allowed freely to use. There is only one occasion during the year when men permit their wives to eat with them. The Morduans betroth their children while very young; but the youth does not know his bride until he marries her. She is then brought to him, placed on a mat, and consigned to his charge with these words, "Here, wolf, take thy lamb." Still more singular is the custom of the Wotyahe tribes. With them it is usual for the young wife, a few days after the wedding, to go back to her father's house, resume her virgin costume, and remain sometimes during a whole year. At the end of that period the husband goes to fetch her, when she feigns reluctance, and exhibits every sign of bashfulness and modesty. The women of this community are habitually chaste and decorous in their behaviour.

The usual occupations of the men in Siberia are hunting, fishing, smoking, drinking, and bartering with the Russian traders. Those of the women are far more numerous and wearisome. They build the huts, they tend the cattle, they prepare the sledges, they harness the reindeer when their husbands are away, and drive them also occasionally; they weave mats, baskets, and cloth; they dye worsted for embroidery; they tan hides, make garments, cook the food, and, in some tribes, assist in catching fish. While they perform these varied and harassing offices without a murmur, as they usually do, their life is one of peace; but if they repine they are sure to be harshly reproved, if not severely punished. In some communities the husband is permitted the free use of his whip; but in others, as that of the Ostyaks, a husband dare not flog his wife without the consent of her father, and on account of some grievous fault. If he does she has the privilege of flying home, when her dowry must be restored, and she has her liberty complete.

Jealousy is a sentiment little known among the Ostyaks, or, indeed, any of the Siberian races. Sometimes the women wear veils, but not with that strictness observable with some nations, and more to save their eyes from the effect of the snow glare than from any other motive. Modesty, indeed, is by no means one of their characteristics. Nor is chastity very highly prized. When a Samoyede woman is about to be delivered, she is obliged to confess, in presence of her husband and a midwife, whether she has engaged in any criminal intrigue. If she tell an untruth, the national superstition is that death will assail her amid the pangs of childbirth. Should she declare herself guilty, the husband contents himself with going to the person whom her confession has accused, and exacting from him a small fine by way of compensation—for having, "without permission," carried on intercourse with a stranger's wife.

The barbarous manners of Siberia do not allow us, indeed, to expect any refined modesty among its women. Wrangell was introduced into the family of a rich and influential man—the head of a tribe. Within a low-roofed but spacious habitation he found five or six women—wives and daughters, of various ages, all completely naked. They roared with laughter when their visitor entered, and appeared excessively amused at being discovered in that condition. The dancing women of these tribes wear clothing while they display their skill, but otherwise they are as indecent as possible. Obscene and degrading postures, indeed, make up the chief merit of their performances. A late traveller, hearing of these dancers, desired some women to perform, but they appeared so modest, bashful, and diffident, that he feared to urge them. However, after considerable solicitation they consented, when he was disgusted at seeing them fling themselves with marvellous rapidity into a hundred disgraceful attitudes.

Infanticide is not practised in Siberia, except on those children who are born with deformities. These are, it is said, invariably destroyed. There is, in fact, little inducement to the crime, for the whole region is but scantily peopled, and marriages are not at all prolific.

The morals of the Siberian races are universally low. A licentious intercourse is carried on between the sexes long before marriage, early as this takes place. In the great city of Yehaterinbourgh, where religious dissensions are extremely bitter, profligacy is still more powerful, and women, from sheer lust, prostitute themselves to men of all sects, with whom, however, they would rigidly refuse to eat or drink. In all the towns numbers of prostitutes reside. They are scarcely, if at all, reprobrated by the other classes of the population, and the young men who do not wish to marry, or cannot afford to procure a wife, as well as widowers, resort to them continually. The process, in fact, which educates a Siberian prostitute to her calling, appears to be this. A young girl, in a community where general licentiousness of manners prevails, is brought up from her mother's breast with the most loose ideas. She is not taught to prize her chastity, though told that marriage is the destiny to which she must look, and warned that her husband will require her to be faithful to him. Meanwhile, however, there is little in her own mind, or in the care of her friends, to protect her virtue. She forms acquaintances, and is seduced, first by one, and then by another, until her profligacy becomes so flagrant and so public that no one will purchase her as a wife. Accordingly she follows as a means of livelihood that which she has hitherto resorted to only as a means of indulging her vicious appetite. Thousands of prostitutes are thus made, especially amid the crowded communities. In some of the small wandering tribes, the women are comparatively chaste; but on the whole the refined sentiments of virtue are unknown, and prostitution extremely prevalent. This appears strange to those who are accustomed to believe that a warm climate is essential to form a sensual race. It seems, on the contrary, that one extreme of temperature is accompanied with influences as demoralising as another, for it is certain that nations dwelling in the temperate zone are more moderate in their passions, and more abstemious in the gratification of them.

For the races inhabiting the Arctic regions, the Esquimaux may be taken as a proper type. As a race, they are dirty, poor, and immoral, but not so grovelling as the tribes of Western Africa. Though their ideas of beauty and grace are totally at variance with ours, it is wrong to suppose that they have none, for the Esquimaux woman, who tattooes her skin to charm a lover, exhibits undeniably one of those characteristics in human nature which allow opportunities to civilize individuals and nations. They are an ingenious industrious people, understanding well how to make use of those conveniences and appliances of life which have been placed by nature at their disposal; and they who make themselves comfortable and happy in the coldest and most desolate parts of the earth, must possess a certain amount of that genius which, properly developed, flourishes in civilization.

The estimation in which women are held among the Esquimaux is somewhat greater than is usual among savages. They are by no means abject drudges, those cares only being assigned to them which are purely domestic, and which are apportioned to the females among the humbler classes in all European countries. The wife makes and tends the fire, cooks the food, watches the children, is sempstress to the whole family, and orders all the household arrangements, while her husband is labouring abroad for her subsistence. When a journey is to be performed, they, it is true, bear a considerable share of the burdens, but not more than among many of the poor fishing populations of civilized countries in Europe, in some of which the man's occupation ceases when his boat touches the shore. It is a division of labour, not so much imposed as shared, and the toil is not by any means hateful to them. During the stationary residence in the winter, the life led by the women is in fact one of ease, indolence, and pleasure, for they sit at home, cross-legged on their couches, almost all the day, enjoying themselves as they please, with a fire to warm the habitation, which it is a pleasant task to attend.

The Esquimaux women are not very prolific, few bearing more than three or four children. They generally suckle them themselves, but it is not uncommon for one woman to nurse at her breast the infant of another who may be closely occupied at the time. They are more desirous of bearing male than female offspring, for parents look to their sons in old age as a means of support.

The Esquimaux are permitted by their social and hereditary law to have two wives, but the custom is by no means general. Parry describes a tribe of 219—69 being men, 77 women, and the rest children—among whom there were only twelve men who had two wives, while a few were doubly betrothed. Two instances occurred of a father and son being married to sisters. Children are usually plighted during infancy—that is, from three to seven years of age, and the boy sometimes plays with his future bride, calling her wife. When a man has two wives, there is usually a difference of six or seven years between their ages, and the senior being mistress, takes her station by the principal fire, which she entirely superintends. Her position is in every respect one of superiority; but this is seldom asserted, as the two generally live in the most perfect harmony. The marriage contract has nothing of a sacred character about it, being merely a social arrangement which may be with great facility dissolved. A man can without any ceremony repudiate his wife, to punish her for a real or supposed offence, but this is rarely done. The husband, who is usually older by many years than his partner, chastises her himself when she irritates him, though caring comparatively little for her fidelity. Absolute in his authority, according to the laws of the Esquimaux, he is sometimes, nevertheless, ruled by the women. Usually, however, he upholds his prerogative, and punishes any infringement of it in a very summary manner; but the utmost harshness commonly employed is to make the delinquent lead her master's reindeer while he rides comfortably in his sledge. Women are very careful of their husbands, partly no doubt from natural sentiments of affection, but partly also, we may believe, from knowledge of the fact that widows are not half so happy as wives, being dirty and ragged, unless they have friends willing to support them, or sufficient attractions to enable them to gain a livelihood by regular prostitution.

Respecting the virtue of the Esquimaux women and the morality of the men, little of a favourable nature is to be said. Husbands have continually offered their wives to strangers for a knife or a jacket. Some of the young men told Parry, that when two of them were about to be absent for any length of time on whaling expeditions, they often exchanged wives as a matter of temporary convenience. Instances of which have been noticed by the voyager—in some cases merely because one woman was pregnant and unable to bear the hardship of a journey. The same writer affirms that in no country is prostitution carried to a greater length. The behaviour of most of the women while the men are absent, causes a total disregard of connubial fidelity. Their departure, in fact, is usually a signal to cast aside all restraint, and, as the last excess of profligacy, children are sent out by their mothers to keep watch lest the husband should return while his habitation is occupied by a stranger*.

* Wrangell's Nord de la Siberie; Cottrell's Recollections of Siberia; Dobell's Travels; Hollman's Travels; Erman's Travels; Parry's Three Voyages; Bache's Narrative; Bache's Land Expedition; King's Journey to the Arctic Ocean;

ICELAND AND GREENLAND.

ICELAND and Greenland, differing in their people, their fortunes and their civilization, may, nevertheless, be classed together, for both belong geographically to the western world, while both present intimate relations with Europe. Iceland, a lonely, gloomy, and extensive country, is inhabited by a serious, humble, and quiet people, numbering about 55,000. Isolated from the rest of the world by dreary and tempestuous seas spreading far around it on every side, its inhabitants remain to this day almost in their primitive condition. Nine centuries have produced little change in their language, costume, or modes of life. Formerly, indeed, they were heathens, and have now been converted to Christianity. Modifications have also occurred in their manners. At one period, for instance, the law allowed the exposure of such children as their parents desired to be rid of, and the unnatural sacrifice was common. It originated with the men, and the women appear never to have become reconciled with the usage, which has now been entirely abolished, though infants perish in large numbers from insufficient and unskilful nursing. On the whole, however, the original manners of the Icelanders remain unchanged. We refer, of course, to a period since what has been termed the heroic age, when a system of society prevailed, which has been entirely swept away by a new and victorious civilization. In those ancient times, when Iceland was a republic, with institutions of a most remarkable nature, the treatment of the female sex there, and among the Scandinavian nations generally, was unequalled by any other heathen communities, except the polished state of Greece. Polygamy, though not forbidden by their religious code, was exceedingly rare. Their manners, indeed, are, in several other respects, superior to their enacted laws. Fathers, or other near male relatives, possessed unlimited power to dispose of the young girls as best suited their convenience or caprice, but seldom or ever exercised this invidious prerogative, leaving them rather to their own choice. With mild advice, indeed, they persuaded them to prudent unions, but with no harsh, inconsiderate authority. The daughter received, on her marriage, a dowry from her parents besides a present from her husband. These acquisitions formed a property which remained absolutely her own, and constituted her provision in the event of a divorce. This could take place whenever she chose to express before certain prescribed witnesses her desire for such separation. A harsh word, any ill-usage, or a hasty blow, might be pleaded as sufficient reason for her resolve; and by a liberal use of this prerogative the wives of Iceland obtained high authority over their husbands. They occasionally accompanied them to the public assemblies, which were convened in conformity with their popular institutions, and were always present at the great festivals. Sometimes they assembled in rooms assigned exclusively to them, and made merry among themselves; sometimes they mingled with the general company. With the exception of a few, whom the fearful superstition of that age condemned to death as witches, no women suffered very severe punishment. The warriors of the island delighted to celebrate their praises, and terms expressing the high qualities of the female sex were abundant in the Icelandic language, and profusely employed in its literature. At present the condition of the sexes is somewhat equal. The men of the humbler classes divide their labours with the women, but do not oppress them with any of the taskmaster's tyranny. Both are alike filthy and coarse in their habits. Among the wealthy, as well as in the middle orders, it is customary for ladies to wait at table when strangers are present; but this is considered as an employment by no means menial. The hospitality of the Icelanders, indeed, assumes some very singular forms. Their women often salute the stranger with a cordial embrace, from which on account of their uncleanliness he is generally desirous to escape as quickly as possible. When Henderson, the missionary, resided there, he visited, during his travels, the house of a respectable man, where he was liberally treated. At night, when he retired to his bedroom, the eldest daughter of the family attended him, and assisted him to undress by pulling off his stockings and pantaloons. He was unwilling to accept such services, to which he was wholly unaccustomed; but she imputed his refusal to politeness, and insisted on performing the office, declaring it was the invariable custom of her country. It is the task of the women, almost always, to unloose the sandals or latchets of their husband's shoes.

The intercourse of the sexes in Iceland is regulated by few absolute laws; but Christianity has abolished polygamy, while public opinion holds a strong check upon

---

Fisher's Voyage of Discovery; Barrow's Voyage; Shillinglau's Arctic Discoveries; Snow's Arctic Regions; Scoresby's Arctic Countries, &c., &c.

illicit communication. With the exception of those seaport populations, which have been corrupted by an influx of Danes and other foreigners, generally of disreputable character, they are, as a nation, moral. These exceptions contribute very considerably to the number of bastard children. In 1801, the population was 46,607 —; 21,476 males and 25,131 females, or in the proportion of thirteen to fifteen of men to women. The average marriages during a period of ten years, were 250, or one out of 188 of the population; the births 1350, or one in 35, and the deaths 1250. One child out of nine was illegitimate. In 1821 one out of seven was illegitimate, and in 1833 the proportion remained the same. Men usually marry between the ages of 25 and 32, women between those of nineteen and 30.

If, however, we give credit to a scandalous anecdote related by Lord Kames, in his "Sketches of Man," we must impute to the Icelanders, of a century and a half ago, a very profligate disposition. In 1707, it is said, a contagious distemper having cut off nearly all the people, the King of Denmark fell on an ingenious device to repeople the country. He caused a law to be promulgated that every young woman in Iceland might bear as many as six illegitimate children without injuring her reputation; but, says the gossipping philosopher, the young women were so zealous to repeople the country, that after a few years it was found necessary to abrogate the law. Little dependance is to be placed on such stories, though the number of illegitimate children born does certainly contradict the panegyrics on the pure morality of the Icelanders, in which some writers are fond of indulging. About one person in seven is married; but it is the custom among the poor for persons of both sexes to sleep promiscuously in small close cabins, which cannot but corrupt their manners. In the fishing towns, especially, where numerous foreigners have congregated, there are many prostitutes, who usually gain only part of their livelihood by that profession. What their numbers are it is impossible to tell; but it seems that the crews of the fishing-vessels, as well as the traders who frequent the ports from time to time, generally resort to the company of prostitutes, who present themselves in any numbers that may be required.

Extending our observations to the remote and desolate coast of Greenland, we find a population partly composed of European colonists and partly of Esquimaux, who have, however, a system of manners not identical with that of the tribes we have already noticed. They are a vain and indolent, but not a very sensual, people. What virtue they possess consists rather in the negation of active vice, than in any positive good qualities. Their women occupy an inferior, yet not a degraded, position. They take charge, indeed, of all domestic concerns, make clothes, tools and tents, build huts and canoes, prepare leather, carry home the game, clean and dry the garments, and cook the food, while their husbands catch seals; but the men often assist their wives in these occupations. Marriage is essentially a contract for mutual convenience, to be dissolved when it ceases to be agreeable to both. The woman looks out for a skilful hunter, the man for an industrious housewife. She brings him little dowry, possessing usually no more than a kettle, a lamp, some needles, a knife, and a few clothes. Parents seldom interfere with the matches of their children. It is considered proper for a girl, when a man comes to request her in marriage, to fly away and hide among the hills, whence she is dragged, with a show of violence, by her suitor. He takes her home, and if her aversion be real, she runs away again and again, until he is weary of pursuit. Formerly, it was the custom to make incisions in the soles of a bride's feet, as some tribes in Siberia and Borneo are accustomed to do to the captives, to prevent their escaping. When a woman is courted by a man whom she detests, she cuts off her hair, which is a sign of great horror and grief, and usually rids her of her suitor. Among the heathen tribes polygamy is allowed, though seldom practised. Divorces sometimes take place. All the man has to do is to assume a stern expression of countenance, and quit the home for a few days without saying when he intends to return. The woman takes the hint, packs up her few effects, and goes with her children to the house of her parents or some friend. Generally, however, they lead a reputable life, the women being docile, and the men indulgent.

Considering themselves, as they do, the only civilised people in the world, the Greenlanders feel a pride in observing the outward shows of decorum. They do not allow marriages within three degrees of affinity. It is not considered reputable for persons, though not related, who have been educated in the same house, to marry. Sometimes a man takes two sisters, or a mother and her daughter, but this is viewed with general reprobation. The marriage contract is, on the whole, very strictly observed, few divorces taking place, except between the young. "The most detestable crime of polygamy," as a Danish writer terms it, produced, where it was practised, little of that jealousy which might be expected among the wives, until the arrival of the missionaries, who preached against it, and speedily won the female sex to support their doctrine.

There was formerly in Greenland a society resembling very closely the Physical Club of Moscow, but still more obscene in its practices. This, however, has disappeared. Prostitution, nevertheless, prevails to a considerable degree, widows and divorced women almost invariably adopting it, as the only means of life, indeed, to which they can resort. There are numerous habitations in the larger communities, which can only be described as brothels; but the profession entails the worst odium on those who follow it *.

Of Prostitution in Lapland and Sweden.

A notice of the Scandinavian populations would be incomplete, unless we touched particularly on the Laplanders; especially as they contrast very strongly with their neighbours the Swedes, notwithstanding that these are far more inflated with the pride of civilization. Forming a nomade race, known in their own region as Finns, they occupy a country little favoured by the prodigality of nature. Nevertheless, where they have settled into fixed communities, we find them adopting many forms of luxury, polishing their manners, and pursuing wealth with eagerness. But these scarcely belong to the body of the Laplanders, and it is only necessary to say of them that they are a happy, virtuous people, distinguished by the affection and harmony existing between men and women.

The genuine Laplander, among his free rocks and snows, lives partly in a tent, partly in a hut; but, whichever tenement he inhabits, he is content with the most simple economy. During the summer he wanders, and is equally industrious and frugal; during the winter he remains in one place, enjoying the fruits of his labour in ease and idleness. This is a peculiar mode of life, and has much influence on the manners of the people; for, during their leisure months, they invent many pleasures, few of which are indulged in by one sex apart from the other.

The Lapland families are generally small; —three or four children being the largest number habitually seen; but what they do bring forth, the women bring forth easily; scarcely ever requiring help, and speedily leaving their couch to fulfil their usual tasks.

The general character of the Lapland race is good. From whatever cause the circumstance proceeds, it is certain that their morals are strict and virtuous. Few strong passions of any kind prevail among them, and they are more especially distinguished by their continence.

The priest of a large parish assured one traveller that there had been but one instance of an illegitimate birth during twenty years, and that illicit intercourse between the sexes was almost unknown.

Old travellers have amused their readers with accounts of the conjugal infidelity common in Lapland, and asserted that the men are in the habit of offering their wives to strangers: this appears to be wholly untrue. So far from truth is it, indeed, that adultery is a crime almost unknown among them; they are, in fact, rather jealous than otherwise of their women. The intercourse of the sexes, nevertheless, is free and agreeable; their marriages are contracted, sometimes according to the choice of the young people, sometimes by that of their parents. Prostitution is unknown among them, except in the fishing towns, where a few wretched women have taken to that mode of life; but, on the whole, they are a chaste and virtuous race.

The great difference between the institutions of Norway and those of Sweden consist in this—that in the former, manners influence the law; while in the latter, law attempts to regulate every detail of public manners.

Men, says the public law of Sweden, attain their majority at the age of 21 years, but women remain in tutelage during the whole period of their lives, unless the king grants a privilege of exemption: widows, however, are excepted. Men cannot legally marry before the age of 21. Even to this rule there is an exception, for among the peasants of the north it is lawful for a youth of eighteen to take a wife —a device adopted to increase the population of those thinly-inhabited provinces. Women may marry immediately after their

---

* Henderson's Residence in Iceland; Trail's Letters on Iceland; Kames' Sketches of Man; Gaimard's Voyages en Islande; Hooker's Tour in Iceland; Crantz's History of Greenland; Account of Greenland, Iceland, &c.; Dillon's Winter in Greenland; Barrow's Visit to Iceland; Egede's Descriptions of Greenland; Graah's Voyage to Greenland.

confirmation, which never takes place before fourteen. The nuptials are recognised by law, and are celebrated in the presence of a priest, by the gift of a ring. A man desiring to take his sister-in-law to wife, must have permission from the king. A few years ago an ordinance was abolished which required a similar formality to be gone through previous to the marriage of cousins. A man may marry without the consent of any one; but a woman must obtain the sanction of her parent or guardian. To render binding the contract, which stipulates for the rights of each with respect to property, it must be presented to the magistrates of the place, and signed by the priest, before the celebration of the wedding.

In default of such an agreement a division takes place, under rules which differ in the country and in the town. In the former, two-thirds of the property belong to the man, and one-third to the woman; in the latter, half is apportioned to each.

Marriage, when fully consummated, is not indissoluble. Divorce may be pronounced by the public tribunals of justice. First, for adultery on the part of the husband or of the wife; second, on the condemnation of one or the other, on account of a felonious crime, to loss of honour and liberty for ten years; thirdly, in cases of insanity; fourthly, for desertion, neglect, or the continued absence, without intelligence, of husband or wife. When a married person complains of having been abandoned, the magistrate fixes a certain interval during which the other may make answer; a notice is inserted in the gazette and the newspapers. If, at the expiration of this period, no reply is heard, the divorce is pronounced. The length of absence necessary to justify such a separation is left to the discretion of the judge. Fifthly, when one person is palmed off for another; sixthly, for ill-treatment; seventhly, for apostasy; eighthly, for incurable epilepsy. After the sentence of the civil tribunal, the divorce is held good in an ecclesiastical court.

A man is bound to support his natural children, and inquiries in cases of affiliation are frequent. When a girl accuses a man before a public tribunal, of being the father of her child, he may deny it upon oath, when her allegation is dismissed, unless she can prove by witnesses, or by any other evidence, that her claim is absolutely just. As such a proof is difficult to obtain, there are abundance of false oaths made at Stockholm. A girl sometimes accuses a peasant of being the parent of her child, demanding, perhaps, a sum of money equal to a sovereign of our coinage, by way of compensation. The man refuses to pay it, and offers to swear that he is not the child's father. The magistrate then seeks by persuasion to induce him to confess the truth; but he persists in his refusal until the woman modifies her claim. He continues all the while to threaten her with the oath of repudiation, unless she is contented with his offer. If she accepts a miserable trifle, he acknowledges the debt; if not, he perjures himself, and the law allows him to escape, though morally convinced, beyond all question, of his profligacy and falsehood.

The illegitimate child has no claim on the property of its father, or even on that of its mother; but if the parents marry, however short a time before the child's birth, it is saved from the stigma of bastardy. A legitimate child cannot be disinherited by its parents, unless for marrying against their consent, or being condemned for felony to a heavy and disgraceful punishment.

Death is the penalty attached to infanticide, but is almost invariably commuted to detention for a longer or shorter period, with hard labour in prison. In 1832 the House of Correction for females in Stockholm, which served for all Sweden, contained 290 women, of which 45 were condemned to hard labour for life; of these, 30 had murdered their children.

The punishments denounced against adultery endeavour to mark a distinction between particular degrees of the crime. Incest and bestiality are, however, punished only with a moderate fine. When a married man indulges in guilty intercourse with a married woman, they both suffer death by decapitation. When it is committed by a married man with a girl betrothed and pregnant by her lover, he receives 120 blows with a stick, and she 90 lashes with a whip. Punishments of this sort continually take place in a public square at Stockholm. At present, in whipping the girls on their naked persons, care is taken to protect their bosoms and their abdomens with plates of copper. Formerly, however, when this precaution was not adopted, the lash frequently lacerated the bosom and tore open the flesh, so as to expose the bowels. When adultery is committed by a married man with an affianced girl, or the reverse, a simple fine is exacted; in default of which, imprisonment on bread and water, or a public flogging, is inflicted. When one of the criminals only is married, and the other is entirely free, an inferior money penalty is adjudged.

An unmarried woman becoming a mother pays to the church penance money, to a certain amount. So also does every man: that is to say, the law enacts it; but it is, perhaps, needless to add that the priests get, in this respect, much less than is legally their due.

In 1836 prostitution was forbidden by law throughout Sweden. The public woman, being convicted, was imprisoned in a house of correction, until she had time to reclaim herself, and some one was willing to take her into service. The same, indeed, was done to any poor woman, whatever her character, who could not describe her occupation. Many little girls, some not more than eleven years old, were confined as a punishment for being without a regular avocation. Professional and open prostitution being thus severally prohibited by the law, there were, at that period, no regular brothels in Sweden; but the women of the lower orders were so corrupt, that prostitution was as common as possible. "Every servant girl," says the advocate Angelot, who wrote in 1836, "may be considered as a public prostitute, and every house of public entertainment may be described as a brothel."

So far the laws describe the manners of Sweden; that is, they indicate the profligacy they are unable to cure. The country is, perhaps, one of the most demoralized in Europe. During many years it continued to decline in population, prosperity, and character; and if during the last quarter of a century it has improved in these respects, it is because the old system of institutions is gradually wearing away.

Superficial travellers, who gather their ideas of other countries by no other light than that of the chandelier, and in no other society than that of fops and flirts, describe Sweden as a paradise of good breeding and elegance. Society is there often gay and lively, which satisfies the inquiries of such tourists. The ladies of that nation also possess many fascinations, with an apparent frankness and sincerity, which never fail to please. The women of the humbler orders wear, in the streets, the airs of modesty, and never shock the eye by exhibitions of wantonness or indecency. The intercourse of the sexes is extremely free; and therefore there are fewer signs of intrigue, because this is not necessary; but to infer from such circumstances that Sweden is a moral country, is to fall into a grievous error.

Sweden is immoral, and Stockholm is the most immoral place in Sweden. For many years it absolutely decayed under the moral disease which afflicted it. In 1830 it contained nearly 81,000 inhabitants; this number decreased in a year or two to 77,000, and the deaths during a period of ten years exceeded the births by an average of 895. Yet it is in a healthy situation; the people are well lodged; everything, indeed, is there to render it pure and salubrious; but the moral atmosphere is tainted by a continual epidemic of depravity.

The whole nation numbers about 3,000,000; but it is in the capital that the excess of profligacy is displayed. Three or four years ago the proportion of illegitimate children was as one to two and three-tenths, that is to say, one person out of every three was a bastard. Taking all Sweden, we find the proportion of the ten years, from 1800 to 1810, was one in sixteen; from 1810 to 1820, one in fourteen; from 1820 to 1830, one in fourteen and six-tenths. It was thus the town population which was to be charged with the immoral result of depravity. In Stockholm, however, statistics could not fully exhibit the general demoralization. Laing asserts his deliberate belief that the offspring of adultery and children saved from illegitimacy by the late marriage of their parents were there exceedingly numerous; and it is probable that the law forbidding young men to marry before they were 21 years of age had, in this respect, a very evil influence, as similar checks have undoubtedly had in Norway.

In 1837 the government of Sweden, finding that to prohibit prostitution was not to prevent it, and that the vice they sought to check increased in spite of their efforts, ran, at one impulse, to a contrary extreme. Formerly no public women were allowed, now they were created as a class; formerly no brothels were permitted to be kept by private individuals, now a huge brothel was instituted by the authorities. A large hotel was hired, was fitted up for the purpose, and opened to all the city. A number of unfortunate women were expected to inhabit this licensed resort of infamy, and it speedily overflowed. A code of regulations was framed for the government of the place; but the barbarity of this discipline prevented the scheme from succeeding. Prostitution, however, had been recognised by law. Therefore, though the government brothel was abandoned, others were multiplied in its place; and vice, which had rioted under a mask, appeared in her proper form, among the citizens of Stockholm. Nevertheless, numbers of the restaurants and houses of public entertainment still retain their original character as the secret resorts of prostitutes and their companions. One great cause of the immorality prevalent in Stockholm was, that no woman who could afford to do otherwise, or had any of the wretched pride of respectability, would suckle her own child. Wet nurses, therefore, were in great request. Unmarried girls were absolutely preferred, because the family was not troubled with their husbands. Their own offspring were meanwhile transferred to the foundling hospital, which remains another licence to immorality. There are in Stockholm two of these institutions, where the children are educated, on payment of a premium varying from five to ten pounds sterling of English coinage. In 1819 there were born in Sweden 14,000 illegitimate children, being nearly a seventh of the births. M. Alexandre Daumont says, that there was in Woesend, a canton of Finland, a special law which, granting to women equal rights of property with the men, improved the character of their morals. But no institutions will improve the manners of a country like Sweden, until the national sentiments are purified, for the example of the court and the nobility, says Mr. Laing, have instructed the people so far, that it is only a moral revolution which can reclaim them.

There is in Stockholm a separate hospital for the treatment of syphilis. It received in one year 701 patients, 148 being from the country and the rest from the city itself. In that year (1832) the number of unmarried persons, of both sexes, above the age of fifteen, was 33,581. Consequently, 1 person out of every 61 was afflicted by the venereal disease.

The condition of women in Sweden is low in comparison with the other countries of Europe, and offers a strong contrast with that which we discover in Norway. Tasks are assigned among the humble orders to the female sex against which true civilization would revolt. They carry sacks, row boats, sift lime, and bear other heavy labours. Among the middle classes they hold an inferior situation; but among the higher, though little respected, they are comparatively free*.

* Angelot's Legislation des États du Nord; Capel Brookes's Winter in Lapland and Sweden; Reichard's Guide des Voyageurs; Bramsen's Letters of a Prussian Traveller; Laing's Tour in Sweden; Tryzell's History of Sweden; Frankland's Visits to Courts of Russia and Sweden.

OF PROSTITUTION IN NORWAY.

LIVING under ancient laws and social arrangements distinct in their principles no less than in their forms from those which discipline society in the feudal countries of Europe, the people of Norway are among the most singular and interesting in the world. Their peculiar institutions, which never admitted of an hereditary nobility, have distributed property among all, so that nowhere is there less poverty, or more abundance of the necessaries of life. These circumstances have exerted a powerful influence on the moral character of the Norwegians. It is consequently important to inquire into their manners, since the solution of many social problems may, by such an investigation, be assisted.

There are in Norway two classes of checks upon the rapid increase of population—one arising from their public economy, the other artificial, and under the influence of law. In all countries where the poor possess the land, provident marriages prevent the growth of a pauper population, and this is the case in Norway. So far the results produced are wholly beneficial; but here other restraints are imposed, which, being somewhat extravagant, miss their object, and exert bad effects on the moral tone of the community.

A marriage in Norway is an occasion, not only of long and formal ceremonies, but of considerable expense. This circumstance has two opposite tendencies on the character of the people. It is not considered respectable to marry unless some grand display takes place, with a liberal festival, the distribution of presents, a long holiday, and other means of expenditure, which create a provident spirit and prudent habit, which stimulate industry, and contribute to the general happiness and prosperity. Spending on their wedding-day what would support them during twelve months, many young couples do, indeed, commit acts of injurious extravagance in emulation of their neighbours; but in accumulating what they thus lavish, they have acquired the custom of saving, the necessity for which puts off the period of marriage. The Lutheran church also holds another strong check upon improvident and ill-considered marriages. It compels all within its communion to observe two separate ceremonies—one the betrothal, the other the wedding. The first must precede the second by several months at least, and generally does by one, two, three, or even four or five years. This interposes a seasonable pause between the first engagement, which may have sprung out of a temporary passion, and its irrevocable ratification, which may be the prelude to a life of misery. It has been calculated that the practical result of this interval between the period when a girl becomes naturally, and that when she becomes legally marriageable, checks the growth of the population by four or five per cent. Maintained within just limits such social laws are found to act beneficially, and tend in every way to improve the condition, manners, habits, and morals of the people.

In Norway, however, they have been pushed beyond the frontiers of moderation, and in many cases cause more evils than they cure. For it is found impossible to put a bridle on human nature. Powerful impulses attract the sexes to intercourse, and it frequently occurs that the betrothed girl becomes a mother before she becomes a wife. Up among the high districts of the interior, it is said that the peasant girl rarely marries until she has borne a child. Throughout Norway, indeed, the proportion of illegitimate to legitimate children is about one to five, and in some parishes, where the restraint upon marriage is greatest, the average lies far more towards the side of immorality. In one of these districts, where there are no other obvious causes of profligacy, such as the resort of shipping, the cantonment of troops, the neighbourhood of a great manufactory, or any other of the usual demoralizing influences, the proportion of illegitimate children is nearly one to three.

This by no means implies, however, a profligate disposition in the Norwegians— male or female. The woman who bears offspring by a lover is almost invariably married to him afterwards; it is impatience of the restraint put upon them by the law which impels them to this illicit communication. The evils of illegitimacy are also, in a great measure, counteracted by liberal and wise regulations. Subsequent marriage of the parents removes the stigma of bastardy from their children. A man, even, who feels inclined to marry another woman, when his first friend has died or become indifferent to him, may legitimatize his former children, by a particular legal instrument. This, in such cases, which are rare, is commonly done, and all, consequently, share alike in their father's inheritance. Some neglect to perform this act of justice, but instances seldom or never occur of a man leaving his offspring desolate when he has any means or opportunity of providing for them, which in Norway almost every person has. Women in Norway occupy a position of superior honour. They have, perhaps, more to do with the real business of life, and more share in those occupations which require the exertion of intellect and study, than in England. They enjoy less compliment, but more respect, which all the sensible members of their sex would infinitely prefer. She, indeed, who provides for a household, under the peculiar domestic arrangements of the country, and presides over its economy, is held in high estimation. Women, in fact, hold a very just position in the society of Norway, having that influence and participation in its affairs which develope their mental and cultivate their moral qualities. Yet it is far from true that they occupy themselves entirely with the sober business, paying no attention to the elegant arts of life. Many of them adorn themselves also in those lighter accomplishments which gracefully amuse a leisure hour; but they certainly do not exhaust on song or dance, or the embroidery frame, the most valuable powers they possess. The able and observant traveller, Laing, supplies a true picture of their character and position, observing that among the wealthier merchants the state of the female sex is less natural and less to be admired than among the humble classes, which compose the general mass of society. Generally speaking, therefore, women nowhere play a more important part in the affairs of social life than in that remote and romantic part of Europe. Among the poor the division of labour between the sexes is excellent: all the indoor work is assigned to the women, all the outdoor labour to the men.

Travellers, among whom Mary Wolstonecroft is one, have nevertheless complained direly of the situation women hold in Norway. One gentleman condemns the national character, because the ladies in respectable houses often wait at their own tables; but this is a national peculiarity, hereditary among the Norwegians. It is a voluntary office; no compulsion is used to impose this or any other task upon them. All that we can infer from such a custom is, the dissimilarity of ideas on points of propriety which prevail with different nations. The English pity the women of Norway, because they sometimes wait at their own tables; the Norwegians accuse the men in England of ill-breeding, because they do not take off their hats whenever a female appears in sight, and because they dismiss the ladies after dinner.

With respect to the actual morals of

Norway, we may assign them the highest rank. The number of illegitimate births can scarcely be described, under the circumstances we have noticed, as indicating an immoral disposition in the people. Nowhere is adultery less frequent. The matrons are almost universally above suspicion, while street-walking and professional prostitution are almost unknown. The most profligate class of females appears to be the domestic servants *.

Of Prostitution in Denmark.

In the laws of Denmark in 1834 the position of the sexes, the regulations of the marriage contracts, and the restrictions on public immorality were sought to be fixed, with every distinction of detail. A man was declared under tutelage until the age of eighteen, and under a modified authority until twenty-five, after which he attained independence in all the acts of his life as a citizen. The woman was declared to remain under tutelage all her life. Even the widow must place herself under a guardian, without whose consent she can do nothing; but this person she may choose herself. She may place herself under the direction of one or many, and even distribute authority among them, but is never allowed to assert an independent existence.

To contract marriage a man must be at least twenty years old, and the woman not under sixteen. The system of legal and binding betrothments was abandoned in 1799; but previous to that period the ceremony of affiancing the bridegroom to the bride was important and almost as absolute as the last ceremony itself.

To contract a legal marriage, it is essential that both persons shall be free from the ties of any other legal engagements. Persons who are related to each other in an ascending or descending line are prohibited from marrying. Brother and sister, says the code, may not marry; but brother-in-law and sister-in-law, uncle and niece, may. A man who desires to marry his mother's or father's sister must obtain a special permission from the government.

* Laing's Residences in Norway; Wittich's Western Coast of Norway; Two Summers in Norway; Latham's Norway and the Norwegians; Elliot's Letters from the North; Mathew Jones's Travels; Clarke's Travels; Count Bjornstyere's Moral State of Norway; Buch's Travels in Norway; Price's Wild Scenes in Norway; Ross's Yacht Voyage to Norway; Kraft's Topographisk, Statistisk, Bestrifelse-iber Kongeriget Norge, Christiania, 1820, 5 vols. 8vo.

It is necessary before marriage to procure the consent of the parents or guardians or guardians of both parties; but if they refuse, their refusal may be complained of, and the judge, reproving them, may order the union to take place in spite of their opposition. At twenty-five years of age the man is released from this authority.

According to an ordonnance passed in 1734, promises of marriage may be written or verbal; a promise of marriage by written agreement must bear the handwriting, seal, and signature of him who makes it. It must be certified by two witnesses, respectable men, before there is any communication between the man and the woman. The verbal promise must also be spoken aloud in the presence of two respectable men, before any intercourse is allowed. Such engagements are binding, and the man who breaks one may be prosecuted at law.

There are, however, certain descriptions of persons whom the law does not allow to invoke the faith of such promises. Widows, who desire to act against their guardians' consent, and women of bad reputation, are in this manner excluded. A servant cannot plead a promise of marriage against her master, her master's son, or any person dwelling in the same house. A man may also repudiate, by a formal oath, the accusation of a pregnant woman who pretends he has promised her marriage, and that he is the father of the child she bears in her womb, unless she can prove her allegation by sufficient testimony.

Divorce is permitted, and may be pronounced immediately when legal cause is proved against one or other of a married pair. It may be demanded in the case of simple abandonment during seven years, or malicious intentional desertion for three years, in the case of condemnation to perpetual hard labour, of impotence existing previously to marriage, of the venereal disease contracted previously to marriage, of insanity supervening upon marriage, and of adultery. Divorce may also take place, without any judgment from the public tribunal, when both parties equally desire it.

In this case, after the married persons have declared their intention, they must be entirely separated in bed and at table during three years; when, if they persevere in their desires, the separation is legally complete. If, however, at the expiration of that period, one of them refuse to abide by the agreement, the administrative college may order it to be fulfilled, notwithstanding all such opposition. Lastly, the king may always allow a divorce to take place, for any or no cause, according to his royal pleasure.

Inquiries into the maternity or paternity of children are permitted. If a girl accuses a man of having been the father of an infant to her, he can only rebut the charge by taking a solemn oath that he had intercourse with her at the period presumed to be the date of her conception. She may then prove, if she can, by any means whatever, that he is swearing falsely; but such evidence being difficult to complete, so as to produce legal conviction, many individuals escape the burden which justly attaches to them.

He who acknowledges or is proved the father of a natural child is bound, until it attains its tenth year, to maintain it according to his rank in life. Should he refuse to pay what he has promised, he may be imprisoned on bread and water. Every twenty-four hours thus spent acquit him of about half-a-crown of his liability.

Illegitimate children have no claim upon the inheritance of their father's property; but to that of their mother, or even of their mother's parents, they are absolutely entitled. A natural child may be adopted or legitimatized by subsequent marriage, in which case it loses all the disability which attached to its former condition. In 1831 the proportion of illegitimate children in Denmark was one in nine and three-fifths. In Copenhagen, however, the frightful proportion was exhibited of one to three and a half.

The law adjudges to the child killer death without mercy. She is decapitated, and her head fixed upon a spike. The woman who does not take proper precautions before the delivery of her offspring is accounted guilty of infanticide should the infant die.

Notwithstanding the severity of the law infanticide is a very common crime in Denmark, although it contains foundling hospitals, at least in Copenhagen. Angelot saw in one of the prisons of that city a man, who, after having flung his four children into the water, went immediately before a magistrate, declaring that he could not provide them with sustenance, and had consequently thought it better to send them to God. Another of these murderers was a woman, who had cut the throats of two of her children, and was engaged in attempting to kill the third, when she was arrested. Superstition and misery, combined with the looseness of morals in the capital of Denmark, were the chief causes of these fearful crimes against nature. The criminals are condemned to the death we have mentioned, but their sentence is usually commuted to imprisonment for life in a house of correction.

The punishment denounced against unnatural crimes was formerly that of burning alive; but it is now softened to that of perpetual exile or forced labour.

The husband may be prosecuted for adultery, as well as the wife, and it is an offence which, says the code, may be punished by law; but authority seldom interferes. The ancient Danes visited the crime with death, and that at a period when murderers were only condemned to pay a fine. At present the penalty is fixed, for the first offence, at confiscation of a tenth part of the guilty person's property; for the second, banishment. For the third repetition of the crime the adulterer may be tied up in a sack and drowned. The law, however, has now become obsolete through long disuse.

Women may take to public prostitution if they receive permission from the authorities. They are not troubled afterwards unless they offend against peace or decency, or bear more children than may legally be born. The code declares that any unmarried woman who becomes the mother of two children may be prosecuted, fined, and committed to prison. Custom, however, in this, as in many other instances, is more considerate than the law, and no woman is troubled who has not born three children by three different men; even then a permission of a special character is necessary before the prosecution can be carried on. No doubt these restrictions encourage women to procure abortion, or destroy their offspring when born. Prostitutes are very numerous, and the vexatious restraints upon marriage appear to produce much immorality. In Copenhagen, however, the corruption of society cannot be altogether, or even chiefly, traced to that cause; for the manners of the city are, in a general sense, profligate.

The appearance of the women belonging to the lower classes in Copenhagen, as in Stockholm, is remarkably modest and unpresuming. Neat and tasteful in their costume, they preserve in their own homes a freshness and a comfort which indicate that they enjoy a position of some honour; for where women are not well treated, they never have a pride in keeping their clothes, habitations, or persons clean and elegant.

It seems that the condition as well as the morality of the sex has improved since the laws of the country have become more polished by civilization. The code we have described belonged to a period several years back. Since then a new constitution has been established; the nation has become more free; the penal laws, especially, have been very considerably modified; the relations of the sexes have lost some of the rudeness which characterized them before; and though civilization still remains at a low ebb, public manners have certainly undergone great improvement.

The prostitutes of Copenhagen live, some in a kind of hotel, where they take part in mixed entertainments, to which the dissolute persons of the city congregate; some in a sort of boarding-houses; others in private dwellings of their own; for they lodge in small rooms, and go with their companions to houses where temporary accommodation may be had at various charges. Their numbers would appear to be considerable; and their habits do not differ in any peculiar manner from those of the same class in other cities of the Continent, which afford materials for a more complete description*.

* Angelot's Legislations des États du Nord; Bremner's Excursions in Denmark; Feldborg's Denmark Delineated, &c., &c.

OF PROSTITUTION IN CIVILIZED STATES.

Introduction.

We have inquired into the history of the female sex under the social laws of antiquity, under the rude codes of barbarian races, and under the Mohammedan and Hindu systems. It will now be interesting to trace it through the dusky period of modern civilization from the rise of Christianity to the middle ages. Many writers afford the materials for a view of the prostitute systems of Europe during that era, and M. Rabuteaux especially has combined their researches in one wide and broad view.

The Christian Emperors of Rome endeavoured to suppress prostitution, but with little success. Constantine, Constantius, Theodosius the Younger, Valentian, and Justinian took up the task by turns, denounced penalties against offenders—those who debauched others, and those who prostituted themselves; but though the world changed its aspect, it did not change its vices. Among the northern barbarians, indeed, austere principles ruled over the people, and women occupied a higher place than is accorded them now. They were companions of the men, not toys for their pleasure, or bagatelles for their amusement. Called, at a later age, to the functions of maternity, they previously learned the use of reason, and succeeded from a virtuous maidenhood to the dignity of matron. The chastity which Tacitus describes among the barbarians of Germany continued long to be their characteristic; but their penal customs became milder as they received better maxims of social policy. A woman who debauched herself was expelled from the city—a sufficient punishment. She had no more any family. Even the ties of paternity were broken. Gradually, however, the barbarian conquerors of Europe bent to the attractions of a corrupted society, and though the laws of the Visigoths forbade prostitution, men were found to encourage and females to pursue this infamous occupation.

The free woman who prostituted herself was, for the first offence, punished with 300 strokes, and for the second reduced to slavery, given to some poor man, and prohibited from entering a town. Parents who connived at the vice of their children were flogged. If the offender was already in bonds, she was whipped, shorn of her hair, and returned to her master. Should he himself be the accomplice of her sin, he lost her, and suffered an equal penalty of the rod. Prostitutes who walked the streets and fields were flung into prison, scourged, and fined. A decree of Theodoric, king of the Goths, declared death against all who gave an asylum or any encouragement to infamous persons.

The epithet of "lost woman" applied to one of honest character was an insult punishable by law—generally by fines. A maiden or a widow was especially protected against such imputation. In France the female who accused another of infamous habits was condemned to pay five sous, or to walk in penance, only clothed in a light shift, while a matron followed, and thrust a fine-pointed instrument above her thighs, more as a humiliation than an injury. The Spanish code also recognised this offence, as well as that of general defamation.

The church was the universal censor of public manners in the middle ages. No sin was more severely denounced by the Christian law than that of licentiousness; yet it inculcated no savage persecution of the fallen. Good men could never forget, that a courtezan had washed the feet of Christ, and accordingly a humanizing spirit presided over the social code of the early fathers. They received into their communion any woman who renounced her evil life, married, and was faithful to her husband, or remained single without prostituting herself again.

Everywhere, indeed, Christianity tolerated prostitution. It was impossible to eradicate vice, and it was better one class should make a profession of it than that all should follow it as a secret occupation. Suppress courtezans, said St. Augustine, and you confuse all society by the caprice of the passions. Nevertheless, efforts were made to check the evil, though the principal rules of this "police of manners" were applied to confine the prostitutes of every town in a separate quarter, and to force on them an uniform apparel, that their shame might not be concealed, and that other women might be safe from the address of brutal libertines.

But while the woman who lost herself was forgiven by the civil and religious law, no toleration was extended to the wretch who made her such—the pander who seduced young girls and sold them for profit. The Council of Elvira refused pardon, even on his deathbed, to the wretch who was guilty of leading the innocent to prostitution. "Miserable wretch; brand of hell!" exclaimed Merot to one of these, "dost thou believe that when thy accursed soul is lost in eternal pains, God will be content? No; he will augment thy punishment;" and he added, that the young females he had ruined should inflict his tortures. All the rigour of the law, every form of public infamy, every device of humiliation, was called in to brand with additional opprobrium the depraved trader in prostitution.

In France the punishment was in general arbitrary, according to the circumstances of each case. Nevertheless law and usage regulated the degree of it. In Paris an edict was published in 1367 forbidding persons to procure girls for prostitution on pain of being exposed in the pillory, marked with a hot iron, and expelled from the city. It was renewed in 1415, and we find an instance of its application in the next year, for in the public accounts Cassin La Botte is described as receiving money for the expenses of an execution of this kind, in which some wretches were led into a public place, branded, mutilated by the ears, and set in the pillory. Sometimes the procuress was mounted on an ass, with her face towards its tail, a straw hat on her head, and an inscription on her back. In this state she was paraded through the streets, whipped, and sent to prison, or exiled. These circumstances appear to have frequently occurred as lately as 1756. We find it applied in a provincial town to some prostitutes who had infringed the local rules:—" They were led through the place, with a drum beating before them, and exposed." In England similar occurrences were common, and were accompanied by some peculiar details. The cart in which the culprit sat was preceded by two men playing music, while a crowd followed and showered filth and mud upon the offenders.

Sometimes, when the penalty was aggravated in severity, the culprit's hair was burnt. Thus, in 1399, at Paris, several men and women suffered this punishment, being pilloried and deprived of all their possessions. At Toulouse, a prostitute was conducted to the town hall, where the executioner tied her hands, stripped her naked, placed a cap, made in the form of a sugar-loaf, ornamented with feathers, on her head, hung an inscription on her back, and then took her out to a rock in the middle of the river. There she was compelled to enter an iron cage, which was plunged three times into the water, while nearly the whole population was assembled to witness the scene. Afterwards she was led to the hospital, where she remained labouring for the rest of her days. A similar custom existed at Bourdeaux. Everywhere, indeed, the same rude devices were employed to terrify the people from profligacy.

The laws of Naples were extremely severe. Before the thirteenth century we find every procuress endeavouring to corrupt innocent females punished, like an adultress, by the mutilation of her nose. The mother who prostituted her daughter suffered this punishment, until King Frederic absolved such women as trafficked with their children under the pressure of want. The same prince, however, decreed against all who were found guilty of preparing drugs or inflammatory liquors—to aid in their designs upon virtuous females —death in case of injury resulting, and imprisonment when no serious harm was effected. These laws, however, proved insufficient for their purpose, and towards the end of the fifteenth century profligacy ran riot in Naples. *Ruffiani* multiplied in its streets, procuring by force or by corruption multitudes of victims to fill the taverns and brothels of the city. Penalties of extreme severity were proclaimed against them. The *Ruffiani* were ordered to quit the kingdom, and the prostitutes were prohibited from harbouring such persons among them. Any woman who disobeyed was condemned to be burnt on the forehead with a hot iron, whipped in the most humiliating manner, and exiled.

The code of Alphonso IX., King of Castile, which belonged to the second half of the twelfth century, included procurers among infamous persons, which condemned them to " civil death." Five classes of these were enumerated :—I. Men who trafficked in debauch : these were expelled the country. II. Speculators who hired their houses to abandoned women for the exercise of their vocation: their houses were confiscated, and they were fined. III. Men or women who kept brothels and hired out prostitutes: if the females they sold were slaves, the law gave them liberty ; if they were free, their corrupter was under pain of death, forced to endow and place them in a situation to marry. IV. Death was denounced against the husband who connived at the dishonour of his wife, and against every one who seduced an honest woman to infamy. V. Girls who supported *Ruffiani* were publicly whipped, and deprived of the clothes they wore when arrested. The men themselves were, for the first offence, flogged ; for the second, expelled from the city; and for the third, sent to the galleys. Between 1552 and 1566 additional terrors were devised against this crime, and the *Ruffiani* once convicted were sentenced to ten years chained at the oar, while for a repetition of the offence they received two hundred blows, and were condemned for life to the galleys.

The incitement to vice has, indeed, been everywhere considered a crime deserving of the heavest punishment ; but prostitution itself has not been tolerated without interference. In France, especially, efforts were early made for its suppression. The laws, however, failed, on account of the number of offenders it would have been necessary to condemn, and a few examples only were made, to show that no licence was extended to debauch. The first edict published was an absolute prohibition by Charlemagne. He commanded strict search to be made throughout his dominions, in every habitation and place of resort, that every public woman, and all persons without known occupations or means of livelihood, might be exposed. Men who were found harbouring prostitutes were compelled to carry them on their shoulders to the place where they were to be whipped with rods. In case of refusal they suffered this infliction themselves. It is singular to find, that among the ancient Parisians no disgrace was equal to that of bearing on the back a debauched woman.

During three centuries and a half after Charlemagne, public immorality flowed in a tide over the country. Prostitutes multiplied in every town, and in the eleventh century Paris was as one general brothel. Everywhere harlots thronged the streets, soliciting the men who passed, dragging them by the arms into their dens, and if they resisted, abusing them in unmeasured terms. In the same house might be found a school on the upper floor and a brothel below. In 1254 an effort was made for the reformation of manners ; but the only effect was, that vice dissimulated instead of bearing its title on its face. Clandestine succeeded to public debauch. At length, however, some real good resulted from a succession of rigorous edicts. At the commencement of the fifteenth century, the scourge of society had been lightened, but there broke out wars and troubles which gave new licence to immorality. A hundred years revived the pestilence in all its virulent shapes ; and in 1503 a council was assembled at Paris to deliberate on the best means of abolishing the brothels which were crowded around them. Laws were passed, which we cannot describe in detail, especially as they are of no value to the legislators of this age, for in spite of them the moral malady of France extended, and public custom recognised what authority refused to allow.

In Paris the prostitutes resorted to places known as *clapiers*, or mole-holes, in allusion to the brutal subterranean life they led. They did not live in the houses where they received their temporary companions ; there were localities common to many, where they assembled during the day, and which the magistrates ordered to be opened and closed at stated hours. They were not permitted to carry on their orgies at night, to prostitute themselves in their own homes, or publicly to shock the decent population ; but they rebelled against all discipline, and evaded where they did not openly contradict the law. In 1307 an edict was published, assigning to prostitutes certain streets as places of abode—

Rue de l'Abreuvorix Macon, la Boucherie, la Rue Froidmantel, de Glatigny, la Cour Robert de Paris, les rues Baillohé, Tyron, Charon, and Champ Fleury. It is remarkable that the infamy of these neighbourhoods has been hereditary; for after the lapse of 500 years, after all the alterations in the city of Paris which have been effected, after all the vicissitudes of its domestic history, the same places still exhibit the same spectacles, and are inhabited by the same population. The complaint of two neighbours was enough to cause a prosecution against the keeper of a brothel. Notwithstanding every exertion which the inefficient law and police of those ages enabled rulers to make, prostitution increased, spread into prohibited streets, and throughout France was a characteristic feature of society. Nor were the palaces whence issued decrees for the reformation of public manners, superior in many instances to the brothels they denounced.

In the eleventh century a brothel and a church stood side by side at Rome; and 500 years after, under the pontificate of Paul II., prostitutes were numerous. Numerous statutes were enacted, and many precautions taken, which prove the grossness of manners at that epoch. One convicted of selling a girl to infamy was heavily fined, and if he did not pay within ten days had one foot cut off. The nobility and common people indulged habitually in all kinds of excess. Tortures, flogging, branding, banishment, were inflicted in vain on some to terrify the others, but with very incomplete success. To carry off and detain a prostitute against her will was punishable by amputation of the right hand, imprisonment, flogging, or exile. The rich, however, invariably bought immunity for themselves. In Spain, although violence offered to a public woman was an offence, few women dared to complain of having been seduced. In Naples, also, under King Roger, such a charge was never taken; but William, the successor of that prince, punished with death the crime of rape; but the victim must prove that she shrieked aloud, and prefer her complaint within eight days, or show that she was detained by force. When once a woman had prostituted herself, however, she had no right to refuse to yield her person to any one. This legislation extended to the extreme north, and obtained in Sleswig.

Among the most extraordinary acts of legislation on this subject was the bull of Clement II., who desired to endow the church with the surplus gains of the brothel. Every person guilty of prostitution was forced, when disposing of her property, either at death or during life, to assign half of it to a convent. This regulation was easily eluded and utterly inefficacious. A tribunal was also established, having jurisdiction over brothels, upon which a tax was laid continuing in existence until the middle of the sixteenth century. Efforts were made to confine this class of dwellings to a particular quarter, but without success. In Naples the same failure attended the attempt. Prostitutes, in spite of the law, established themselves in the most beautiful streets of the city, in palatial buildings, and there, with incessant clamour, congregated a horde of thieves, profligates, and vagabonds of every kind, until the chief quarter became uninhabitable. In 1577 they were ordered to quit the street of Catalana within eight days, under pain of the scourge for the women, and the galleys for such of the proprietors as were commoners, while simple banishment was threatened against "nobles."

One example of good legislation was the pragmatic law of 1470 to protect the unfortunates against the cupidity, the extortion, and the fraud of tavern keepers and others, who grew rich upon their infamy. Men went into their places of entertainment with some single girls, contracted a heavy debt, and then left their victims to pay. These were then given the choice of a disgraceful whipping or an engagement in the house. They often consented, and usually spent the remainder of their lives in dependence on their creditor, without ability to liberate themselves. By the new law masters of taverns were forbidden to give credit to prostitutes for more than a certain sum, and this only to supply her with food and clothing absolutely necessary. If he exceeded this amount he had no legal means of recovering it.

The most remarkable feature in the Neapolitan legislation on this subject was, the establishment, at an unknown but early date, of the Court of Prostitutes. This tribunal, which sat at Naples, had its peculiar constitution, and had jurisdiction over all cases connected with prostitution, blasphemy, and some other infamous offences. Towards the end of the sixteenth century it had risen to extraordinary power and was full of abuses. It practised all kinds of exaction and violence, every species of partiality and injustice, and even presumed to publish edicts of its own. The judges flung into prison numbers of young girls, whom they compelled to buy their liberty with money, and sometimes dared to seize women who, though of lax conduct, could not be included in the professional class. This was discovered, and led in 1589 to a reform of the court. Its powers were strictly defined, and its form of procedure placed under regulation, while the avenues to corruption were narrowed. The institution itself existed for nearly a hundred years after that period—until 1768, when a royal edict declared the ruler's resolution to abolish the infamous calling altogether. Vice, however, when widely spread in a nation, does not vanish at the breath of authority. Denounced by the law, prostitution continued to flourish and society to feel its influence.

Passing from the south to regions with a less voluptuous climate, we find Strasburgh as overflowing with vice as perhaps any other city in the world. Prostitutes were in the fifteenth century so numerous there that, though a distinct quarter was assigned for their residences, they invaded every locality, and swarmed in the finest streets. Speculators were accustomed to travel abroad and bring home unfortunate girls, whom they kidnapped and reduced to a state of slavery. Officers were appointed to visit the brothels and collect the tax imposed on them. More than fifty-seven of these places existed in six streets only. One contained nineteen, while other neighbourhoods were infested in an equal degree. At the commencement of the sixteenth century, so far were public manners demoralized that prostitutes horded in the clock towers and aisles of the great cathedral as well as in several smaller churches. In 1521 an ordinance appeared directing the "cathedral girls," who were called "swallows," to quit the sacred places of their retreat within fifteen days. To those who persevered in their libertine mode of life, various residences were assigned—in the suburbs. Strasburgh was now in the depth of demoralization; but the Reformation soon visited the city, awakened its people from sensual pleasures to an intellectual battle, and a speedy change was apparent. In 1536 there were only two brothels there. In 1540 public prostitution was effectually suppressed. Ten years after it was proposed to establish a house of legal debauch; but the attempt was resisted, though renewed in the third and fourth year after this.

It was little matter to the prostitutes to inhabit houses especially dedicated to their vile traffic. They cared not to wait passively at home for visitors. Wherever men congregated for pleasure or for the business of life, wherever there was any chance of provoking their desires, they thronged, sometimes impelled by the love of excitement, sometimes by the pains of hunger. They thus transformed into so many brothels wine houses, barber's shops, and students' rooms, and the perseverance of government against them was by no means equalled by their own tenacity. An edict of 1420 forbade prostitutes to enter the cabarets; another of 1558 prohibited tavern-keepers from entertaining them. Another denounced gambling, and prostitutes were only allowed when desirous of refreshment to stand without and drink what was handed to them from within. In England similar regulations was established, and barbers especially were made the object of very severe restrictions. Sempstresses and butchers were forbidden to employ any females of bad character, and others were restrained by similar laws.

All these efforts, however, to render the sisterhood of prostitutes a homeless, desolate, hopeless class—to deprive them of shelter, of comforts, and the honest means of life—failed in purifying the manners of the age. The baths became a regular resort of women belonging to this order—in Paris, in Geneva, in Venice, in Rome, in Naples, in Milan, in Ferrara, in Bologna, in Lucca, and in every other city of the Peninsula—so that there was scarcely the keeper of a bath who was not at the same time a brothel keeper, employing numbers of *Ruffiani* to procure attendance at his house. There were other cities in which baths were publicly tolerated and recognised as places of prostitution. Among these were Avignon and London. A statute of the Church of Avignon, dated 1441, interdicted the use of certain baths, known to be brothels, to the priests and clergy. An offence committed by day was not punished half so severely as one committed by night. There is only one other instance of a punishment inflicted during that age on men who violated the public law of morals. It was that of certain citizens of Anvers in Flanders, who were condemned to make a pilgrimage to expiate an offence of this kind. On one occasion, indeed, of which the date is lost, the magistrates of Bourdeaux caused a man to be hanged for forcibly violating a prostitute.

In Avignon, however, the licence of prostitution was shortly taken away. The residence of the popes in that city had attracted a concourse of strangers from all parts of the globe, and brothels sprung up in profusion in the neighbourhood of churches, at the door of the Papal palace, and side by side with prelatical residences—a display of libertinism so gross that the public acts of encouragement at once ceased, and an edict drove all the prostitutes out of the city.

In London, as we have said, as at Avignon, prostitution took refuge in the public baths—a practice of very ancient date. These places were situated in the borough of Southwark, which was not included in the city until 1550. It was a miserable quarter, full of inhabited ruins, to which some public gardens, dedicated to dog and bear baiting, alone attracted the people of the neighbourhood. In this general preliminary sketch it is not necessary to say more of London.

In various parts of Europe a continual stream of edicts was poured out against the system of prostitution; but it was only persecuting the victims, instead of eradicating the causes. In some States, as in Lombardy, men were forbidden to give them an asylum; they were prohibited from appearing among honest citizens; they were prevented from purchasing food or clothes, or borrowing money by the hire of their persons; in fact, fines, prisons, whips, still continued to attempt the reform of morals.

Hitherto, however, we have seen prostitution in some places protected, but in all restrained, though everywhere freely exercised by those persons who would brave its perils and its disgrace. It was now sought, by the direct and continuous intervention of the law, to transform it into a public institution, organized, watched, disciplined, by particular officers, and subjected to special authority. In France, and especially in Languedoc, these principles were, during the middle ages, firmly established. Louis XI. proclaimed, that from the remotest antiquity it was the custom in Languedoc to have a house and asylum for public women. The most celebrated of these were at Toulouse and Montpellier. That at Toulouse was known to exist during the twelfth century, and by an abuse of terms, not uncommon at that period, was called the Great Abbey. The Commune and the University divided the expense, and were proprietors of the building, and a good revenue was derived from it for municipal purposes. But in 1424 the receipts diminished considerably, to the great regret of the governors. The turbulent youth of Toulouse behaved to the poor girls, whom they sacrificed to their lust, with the utmost violence and brutality—beating them and their children, breaking up the furniture, and wrenching off even the doors of the house. Many attempts were made to repress these outbreaks, but the prostitutes were at length compelled to take refuge in the interior of the city. Severe regulations were imposed upon them. All who were diseased were compelled to live in solitude until cured, and some were whipped for disobedience. On one occasion, when a famine prevented the inhabitants from indulging in their ordinary pleasures, the prostitutes emigrated, but returned to their post in 1560. The magistrates, shamed by public outcry, which accused them of purchasing their robes from the tax on debauched women, abandoned the money, at this time, to the hospitals; but the administrators of these afterwards made them some compensation. In 1566 a council was called to deliberate on the best means of ridding the city from the profligacy and wickedness which had grown up through the immense licensed brothels it contained. To increase the scandal, four prostitutes were discovered in a monastery of Augustine friars. Three of these unhappy girls were hung. Shortly afterwards three others were found in a convent, and they also were sent to the gallows.

It appears that in 1587 prostitution was almost eradicated from Toulouse, though it flourished in the rural districts around. Many of the girls were forced to labour at cleansing the streets as a punishment. Two decrees of Louis XI. and Charles VIII. indicate the history of prostitution at Montpellier in the fifteenth century. A man named Panais possessed and governed the place devoted to this purpose, and dying, left a dynasty of brothel keepers—two sons, who associated with a banker. They embellished the edifice, furnished it luxuriously, constructed beautiful baths, and obtained a legal monopoly in their infamous traffic, by engaging to pay a certain tax. However, in 1458, another individual was permitted to establish himself, which he did with *éclat*, and the women deserted their old quarters for the new "hotel." A public cause was made of the quarrel, and it was decided that the original promoters should continue to enjoy their privilege. The two brothel keepers, who gained the titles of "Friends and faithful Councillors of the King of France," grew wealthy, and their trade of prostitution became one of the most important branches of enterprise in the city.

The city of Rhodes appears to have been another city of Europe where a chartered brothel existed, for the bishop, in 1307, forbade the inhabitants to receive any of the public prostitutes into their houses, which supposes that some particular retreat was open to them. There was one also at Lisbon; but it was not until 1394 that the magistrates deliberated on the propriety of erecting a building at the public expense, expressly as a brothel. Ten years later we find the inhabitants lamenting that their wives and daughters were endangered by the want of such a place, and in 1424 it was established. A tax was levied on the women to assist in defraying the cost, and fines were imposed for misconduct.

In Italy licensed brothels were very numerous. There was one at Mantua, and Venice was the very sink of prostitution. In 1421 the government enlisted women to this service to guard the virtue of the other classes. A matron was placed over them, who governed them, received their gains, and made a monthly division of profits. The names of several women, the most notorious and beautiful of the Venetian courtezans, are preserved by Nicolo Daglioni. A very small sum was paid to them by their patrons.

In Valencia a public brothel, on a colossal scale, existed towards the end of the fifteenth century. It resembled a little town surrounded with walls, and had a single gate; in front of this stood a gibbet for criminals. Near this was an office, where a man stood who addressed all who entered, and said, that if they would deposit what valuables they had with him, he would return them safely as they came out; but if they refused and were robbed within, he was not responsible. The wall inclosed four or five streets of little houses, inhabited by girls dressed in brilliant habiliments of velvet and silk. Three or four hundred of them were usually in attendance. They received only a small sum for their favours. Whether this system was then general in Spain we know not, but it is certain that common prostitutes abounded. Servants appear to have been hired for this purpose, for Philippe II., in 1575, in order to check the ravages of immorality, ordered that no female domestics under forty years of age should be hired by men. A decree of 1623 required that in all cities throughout the kingdom public brothels should be abolished.

In Geneva there was a "Queen of the Prostitutes," elected by the civic magistrates, who took an oath of office, and undertook to govern all the women engaged in her occupation. At Schelstadt a man was commissioned to a similar duty, and very strict rules were imposed on the population.

We have seen that in many places prostitution became a source of revenue, and might enlarge our details and multiply our examples; but it would be tedious to cite the laws of France, Spain, Italy, and Germany on the subject. They varied much in different times, but offer little interest.

The legislator, however, has not contented himself at all times with dividing the prostitute class from other classes of females, with shutting them up in separate quarters, or even confining them in houses of which he kept the key. In some cases he obliged them to assume a peculiar costume, or at least a conspicuous badge of infamy. They always endeavoured to resist or elude the restrictions laid upon them, and, feeling deeply the humiliation of such compulsion, sought by all means to evade it. The first regulation of this kind for the city of Paris is mentioned by the chronicler Geoffrey. He says, that the Queen of Louis VII. going one day to church, met a woman gorgeously attired, and, deceived by her appearance, gave her, "according to custom," the kiss of peace. She was a court prostitute; and when the royal lady heard this, she complained to her husband, who ordered that no mantles should in future be worn by prostitutes. From time to time new edicts on this subject appeared. One of 1360 forbade them to wear any embroidery, any gold or silver buttons, any pearls, or any trimmings of gray fur. In 1415 and 1419 golden and gilded zones were prohibited to them, as well as silver buckles to their shoes. The very fashion of their dress was afterwards regulated. These devices to distinguish prostitutes from respectable females were speedily imitated. An *aiguillette* of a certain colour, hung from the shoulder, was most generally adopted in France. In some towns silk was prohibited to them.

The Bishop of Rhodes, in 1307, forbade them to wear mantles, veils, amber necklaces, or rings of gold, while the popes of Rome followed the example. The laws of Mantua obliged prostitutes when they appeared in the streets to cover the rest of their clothes with a short white cloak, and wear a badge on their breasts. At Bergamo the cloak was yellow; in Parma, white; in Milan, at first, black woollen, and then black silk. If disobedient, they might be fined, and, in case of a second offence, publicly exposed, and whipped. Any one might strip the garments off any girl he met in the streets illegally attired. In London a similar distinction was imposed on them, and at Strasburgh a sugar-loaf bonnet was invented for their use. In Spain, besides prohibitions concerning dress, they were forbidden the use of coaches and litters, as well as prayer-carpets or cushions in the churches; even a hackney-carriage was not allowed to be hired by them.

The acts of legislation in France were almost exclusively police regulations. Forced to tolerate the prostitute class, the law endeavoured, by watching, restraining, shaming, and insulting it, to render its occupation so infamous as to terrify persons from seeking it as a means of livelihood. It does not seem that in France, during the middle ages, legislation ever passed this limit or went beyond the action of police. In Italy, however, and in Spain, this was not the case. The Roman law had left many vestiges, which have never, in reality, disappeared; the ecclesiastical prerogative was powerful, and disposed to be active. Local statutes existed in great abundance, and the combination of these authorities gave rise to a jurisdiction full of details: profuse, sometimes strange, always subtle, in parts inconsistent, and laboriously commented upon by a numerous school of jurists—a jurisprudence which elevated itself above simple measures of security and municipal rules, and instituted for prostitutes a civil and social statute of their own.

Ulpian says that a woman is a prostitute not only when she frequents regular brothels, but when she visits cabarets, or any other places, where she is careless of her honour. She is a prostitute who yields herself for base purposes to all men; but she who has connection only with one or two is not. Octavenus, however, thinks, more justly, that she is a prostitute who gives up her person in common, whether she receive money or not.

The lawgivers of the middle ages were not accustomed to insist on perfect or precise definitions. They liked to subtilize over terms. Some held Ulpian's limited view to be correct; others, with Octavenus, declared that any woman yielding to the solicitations of several men, even without being paid, was a prostitute. The Roman law defined prostitution to be the reception of numerous libertines. But how many? inquired St. Jerome. This threw divisions among the theorists. Some declared 40 men to be enough, some insisted on 60, others on 70; while a few, carrying extravagance to its utmost limits, asserted that no woman was a prostitute who had not delivered up her person to at least 3000 persons. While these ridiculous disputes engaged attention, the corruption of manners went on.

It is just to the wisdom of that age, however, to remark, that these discussions of the casuists appeared no less ridiculous to contemporary statesmen than to us; while the general public idea of prostitution was habitual debauch for vile purposes, whether mercenary or otherwise.

Some theorists, nevertheless, insisted that the nature of a hireling was inseparable from that of a prostitute. On this account the name *meretrix* had by the Latins been given to a woman of this class; but this view led to consequences which the wise legislator would not accept. If any female accepting a reward for her dishonour was to be publicly enumerated among professional harlots, many, from a single offence, must, under compulsion, follow a life of systematic vice. Others argued that two or three repetitions of this infamous sale would justify the title being applied; but this is a point on which writers have never agreed. Consequently, a long controversy arose upon the three conditions in dispute: what amount of publicity—what number of vicious connections—what kind of venality—was sufficient to stamp a woman with the name and character of a common prostitute.

Rabuteaux describes her as one who, under constraint, or by her own will, abandons herself, without choice, without passion, without even the impulse of the grossest lust, to an unchaste course of life. By want of choice he means the absence of a preference for the individual, by which, he adds, a forbearing judgment extenuates the offence of immorality. If, he insists, there be any choice of persons, there may be libertinism, there may be debauch, there may be scandal, there may be vice, but there is not prostitution in the true sense of the word. It applies to "sacred prostitution," whether gratuitous or venal, which was an unblushing and indiscriminate sacrifice of chastity; to that which the barbarous hospitality of savages, whether on the rivers of Lapland or in the deserts of Africa, gave up a woman to every guest; and to that legal kind in civilized countries which sold itself promiscuously for hire.

Such is M. Rabuteaux's idea. We differ from him. Prostitution appears to us the application to a vile purpose of that which was designed for honourable uses; and the mere satisfaction of animal lust is in itself the vilest object. There may exist in a woman's mind, even when most debauched, a preference for some, an aversion to others; but she is no less a prostitute, if she abandon herself viciously, whether to one or many.

While these theories divided the opinions of lawgivers, legislation on the subject was extremely difficult. They were forced to be contented with what they thought imperfect proof; and, to fix the infamy of a woman, accepted evidence from witnesses, even those accomplices in sin who, of all others, have lost the right to accuse. A female who chose the night for the period of her orgies; who, as a wanderer, without a companion to protect her, entered house after house; who waited on revellers in a place of entertainment; might be registered among common prostitutes: A legitimate suspicion, also, attached to her who received the visits of many young men; and, above all, who, in light or darkness, frequented a public school.

These women, when once consigned legally to the prostitute class, gained, in the middle ages, a right which they could not otherwise assert. The Roman laws adopted by the jurisprudence of that period allowed her to have a legal claim to payment when she prostituted her body, and the reason assigned was founded on a strange and subtle distinction of terms. "The courtesan's vocation," said Ulpian, "is infamous, but the wages of it are not; the act is shameful, but not the reward which is in prospect when the act is committed."

The Spanish law was still more favourable to her. When a man paid in advance, and she refused to submit according to her promise, he could not demand his money back. On one side she received a legitimate emolument; on the other, he was guilty of immoral turpitude which the law would not recognise. The code of Alphonso also permitted this interpretation; some commentators, however, allowing that the woman had a right to revoke the promise of yielding her person, but was bound to restore the amount of hire she had received. Long and vigorous controversies arose among the theologians when this was referred to them. It was also disputed in France, whether the prostitute could enforce payment when she had sold herself and an avaricious person refused to reward her. An imposing list of authorities is arrayed on either side.

Another question long debated was the use to which such gains could lawfully be applied. Alphonso the Wise, on the authority of Isaiah, forbade priests to receive offerings from such a source. Baldæus and others insisted that the church could not accept taxes from public women; but this by many was repudiated, as contrary to the principle that the wages of prostitution were lawfully acquired. The Spanish law allowed money of this kind to be given in alms, and the public opinion recognised the right to dispose of it by testament, though several popes attempted to decree a contrary usage. If, then, they 'could dispose of their gains as they pleased, could they inherit property? They could, but under limitations. In Savoy it appears that legacies to prostitutes made by soldiers who had not quitted service more than a year were null and void. In Spain no woman of this class could inherit to the disadvantage of the testator's relatives in a direct or collateral line. Many authorities only admitted the brother of the deceased to this right; but an exception was made when it was a daughter who succeeded to such property, or when the woman was herself married. A mother, however, could disinherit her daughter for leading a vicious life, but lost this privilege if she had been the accomplice of her immorality. The father had equal authority, but with one curious limitation. When, said the law, a father has sought to marry his daughter, and endowed her sufficiently, if she, against his will, refuses to marry and becomes a prostitute, he may cut her off; but if he have opposed her marriage until she reached the age of 25, and become a libertine, he cannot refuse to bequeath her his property. In the duchy of Asota, in Piedmont, a similar regulation was established; but the age was fixed at 29, and the woman, on every opportunity to marry, was bound to present herself before her father and demand his consent. If he refused it, he was not allowed to punish her when, at 30, she became a harlot.

The church, in those ages, made it a pious act to marry a prostitute, and absolved from their sins all who did so. In France a woman of this class might, at a very ancient period, save a criminal from death, by inducing him to espouse her, and Farnacius relates an anecdote which shows this custom to have existed in Spain. In a city, which he does not name, a young man mounted on an ass was being conducted to the scaffold. A courtezan was struck by his beauty, offered him his life if he would become her husband. He refused. The temptation was not strong enough to induce him to accept such a wife. He merely answered, "Let us move on," and reached the place of execution. Meanwhile, however, an account of the incident had reached the king, and he, admiring the youth's courage, pardoned him.

From this we may learn that though the church consecrated such a marriage with peculiar grace, public opinion considered it infamous.

The jurisprudence of the middle ages introduced new principles, and these unions became more rare. Many doctors of law announced that they were contrary to the sacred code.

In Spain, where concubinage was legally recognised, men of rank were forbidden to take as concubines slaves, whether born in actual bondage or emancipated, dancers, servants of taverns, go-betweens, or prostitutes. It was disputed whether the children of these women could be legitimatized by subsequent marriage. It was decided that they could, though with more difficulty than others, and their mothers became amenable to the laws against adultery.

Persecution in all barbarous ages and countries has endeavoured to perform the task of teaching and reclaiming mankind. The members of the venal sisterhood have, more than any others, experienced the harsh effects of this species of legislation. The law sought to withdraw them from vice by shutting from them every approach to virtue, to reform their minds by forbidding them the society of honest persons, to elevate them from their degradation by adding to their infamy. It refused to receive them as witnesses, even when violence was done upon their persons; though more liberal jurists cried out amid the clamour of intolerant bigotry, that the protection of justice should attend even the vilest prostitutes in the vilest dens of her resort; but the spirit of the times was vindictive, and because society was corrupt and base, it was most unsparing in its cruelty towards the victims of debasement and corruption.

In spite of every one of these rude devices of a rude society to banish immorality to habitations of its own, by badges, quarters, distinct costumes, and even separate laws, prostitutes swarmed in every city of Europe, and still more in its innumerable camps. Armies were then undisciplined bands of adventurers, and pillage was the soldier's chief purpose. Xenophon tells that the nations of Persia, Asia Minor, and India, were accompanied on their marches by their women and their children, to defend whom they fought with more courage; and Athenæus describes Chareas, causing a band of beautiful courtezans to dance before his phalanxes to the tune of flutes and psalteries. Two thousand prostitutes were driven from the camp of Scipio Africanus; and so, in the middle ages, every army drew in its train numbers of public women. Three hundred were with the army which laid siege to St. Jean d'Acre in 1189, and during the whole of the crusades the Christian armies were followed by them. Many times the leaders endeavoured to check this debauchery. Some of the girls were flogged. Sometimes the man who was found with one of them was obliged to allow her to strip him to his shirt, and lead him with a rope through the camp. On the plains of Perretola, after the defeat of the Florentines, in 1325, public dances were executed by prostitutes for the amusement of the army. In all parts of Europe similar profligacy distinguished the camp; and long after we find Jeanne d'Arc, when reviewing the army, chastised with her sword several prostitutes whom she detected among the ranks. Marshal Strozzi, with a ferocity worthy of that period, drowned 800 of them in the Loire. When the Duke of Alva invaded Flanders, there accompanied his army "400 courtezans on horseback, beautiful and grand as princesses, and 800 others on foot." These were for the pleasure of 10,000 men, all veterans.

Prostitution was authorized and disciplined, not only in the camps but in the palaces of those days. From the eleventh century to that of Francis I., a regular community of public women was attached to the court.

We have already noticed the Queen of Louis VII. kissing one of them on her way to church; and we find Charlemagne ordering his palace to be cleared of them. At the Council of Nantes, in 660, it was complained that the concubines of the nobility, instead of remaining at home, thronged to public assemblies; but the seraglios of these lords, in the ninth century, were places of prostitution. The German law imposed a fine of six sous on a man who committed violence on a female in the principal or royal "gynecées," but only three in any other. It was formerly the custom to send to one of these retreats a woman convicted of adultery; but this was at length forbidden, lest it should simply allow her an opportunity to repeat the offence. Sometimes they were only the harems of the proprietor, sometimes brothels. William IX., of Poitou, established in the eleventh century an abbey for prostitutes, where he added to his profligacy the crime of sacrilege, giving the harlots the titles of abbess and prioress, and parodying every sacred rite. The orgies of his palace, and indeed of all others of that age, are indescribable.

The title of King of the Prostitutes was given to the officer who presided over the royal brothels. In Paris, in Normandy, and in Burgundy, we find this functionary. Under the kings of France he enjoyed a high rank and many privileges; and associated with him was a woman who governed the prostitutes, and punished them with whipping when they offended. In England, also, the palace and the mansions of the nobles contained small brothels. In Henry VIII.'s palace was a room, with an inscription over the door, "Chamber of the King's Prostitutes."

Thus, throughout the world, there was, in the middle ages, profligacy and corruption, which rose to its height at the period which preceded the Reformation. From their chief places of resort in royal palaces prostitutes spread over the whole of society, invading the church, the hearth, following the camp, dividing the privileges of the wife, and ever debauching both sexes by their companionship. Rods, prisons, gallows, chains, pillories, tortures, served in no way to prevent or even to discourage them; badges and restrictions proved equally futile; but it is agreeable to find some relief to this dark spectacle of demoralization. In the age of primitive Christianity religious men endeavoured to reclaim from vice those whom they found making a trade of it. We cannot stay to dwell on the sincere apostleship which laboured, especially in the East, and was followed by fathers and hermits from the desert. Stories of conversions of this kind fill the legends of the time, and earnest attempts were made to offer an asylum to the unhappy women who had abandoned themselves to profligacy. We have noticed Theodora, the imperial harlot of Rome, collecting 500 prostitutes in a palace on the Bosphorus; but her impure hand could not perform well the offices of charity, and she applied force to fill her asylum. Many of the girls, therefore, who were shut up in her magnificent and luxurious prison, found their confinement insupportable, and committed suicide to escape it. In 1198 two Parisian priests established a nunnery for repentant women, and thirty years afterwards the House of the "Daughters of God" was instituted, and these efforts were rewarded with much genuine success. Two centuries passed without many enterprises of the sort being undertaken; but in the fifteenth century an association of public women was formed to exchange their base gains for those of piety and virtue.

In 1489 all the prostitutes of Amiens, animated by a sudden awaking of remorse, applied for a place of retreat, where they might bury their shame, and renew their honesty. This was granted, and several others were established, the inmates of which wore white garments.

In several other parts of France, and generally in Europe, the religious orders made attempts to recall some of the abandoned class of females, to redeem the virtue of their sex, and, as they laboured with sincerity, many of their enterprises were successful. But, on the whole, prostitution still increased, and, the Reformation broke over a state of society demoralized to the very core *.

OF PROSTITUTION IN SPAIN.

FEW nations have been described in more various ways and in more contradictory terms than the Spaniards. In the pages of one writer, we find them represented as in all things a great example of virtue, morality, and uncorrupted manners; in another, they are pictured as the very embodiment of vice and degradation. We have been at much pains to deduce from the history, from the achievements, and from the actual state of Spain, as these are set forth by innumerable authorities, a just opinion of its national characteristics, and the sketch we shall offer is the result.

In that country we have to divide class from class before we can fairly view its manners. On the one hand we have a peasantry ill-taught, and educated to servility; then a trading body, with another employed in professions; and thirdly, a large order of nobles, degenerated altogether from its ancient splendour, but preserving nevertheless all the pride, all the indolence, all the sensuality, which characterized it in the age of extended conquest and prosperous commerce. Upon all these classes time has left traces, and the influence of their history has been remarkably strong. A rich soil, a warm climate, an abundance of precious minerals—these circumstances have been by no means without their effect. The Roman Catholic religion, an army of priests, an arbitrary government, and the habit of respecting persons more than principles—these have a still more distinct impression on the national character. A literature once illustrious but now dead, an empire once splendid but now perished, a commerce once magnificent but now decayed, a

* Rabuteaux, ex Lascher, La Chaus, Layard, Knight, Dulaure, Chaussard, Jacob, Saint Hilaire, Hugues, Faumin, Sabatier, Beraud, &c., &c.

wealth once gorgeous and now turned to poverty, arts once noble and now degraded—in these we find an index to the Spanish national character. There is nothing virgin in the country, there is nothing progressive, there is nothing with hope: all the glory of Spain belongs to the past. The present is a wreck, and the future is a blank.

The manners of Spain present none of that simple purity which we find in Switzerland. Every influence to which the people are subject tends to corrupt them. Young women who stand at their windows, and see with delight the flagellants go by, lashing themselves until the blood splashes under their whips, cannot possess much dignity of mind. Yet such are the spectacles which in Spain have been made familiar and favourite to the populace. There is throughout Spanish society an effort to appear better than they are, which in itself is an unfailing indication of impurity. Men dare not when in company take any improper liberties with women, even those whom they might be able privately to seduce. On the stage they hoot a piece, which in France, or even England, would not be regarded as in the slightest degree indelicate. Nevertheless, in their retired rooms, ladies who are thus prudish before the world, will suffer approaches gross enough, will amuse themselves with obscene pictures, will pardon readily equivocal jokes, and listen to songs of the worst indecency. Nor will they object to behold the fandango danced, though, whatever some tolerant travellers may say, it is proverbially obscene.

In many parts of the country, and especially in Seville, the ancient national customs are still preserved, and young girls are always when in the street accompanied by a duenna. In Madrid, where manners have undergone a change, this is no longer the case; but in the more primitive cities it is more prevalent. The guardianship of such a companion, however, by no means implies absolutely a respectable character, for common prostitutes, when they do walk abroad, are often accompanied by old women who attract notice to them, and frequently engage visitors to their places of resort.

The actual intercourse of the sexes in public is reserved, except with respect to conversation. The gossip at a Tertullia, described by some tourists as delightful, is characterized by English ladies not at all inclined to satirize Spanish manners as very far from that which women in good society among us are accustomed to hear.

Children who appear fresh from the nursery indulge in remarks which to many appear positively obscene. The intellectual standard among them is low. Ladies have been known who, with all the pride of an hereditary title, could scarcely write their own names.

Good wives and good mothers are nevertheless very abundant in Spain. It has produced heroines of every kind, from the intriguers of the Camarilla to the defenders of a city. When "in love," the Spanish woman is exceedingly full of passion, and, carrying a knife, she occasionally employs it to revenge a slight. These essential characteristics of female manners are, however, gradually yielding under what we may term the common law of society in Europe. Madrid is assimilating itself to Paris, and Paris to London; so that as time progresses the peculiar features wear off, and statistics alone may at some future period form the measure of a people's morality.

In the rural parts women share with men the heaviest labours of the field. They may be observed as you pass along the highways, staggering under the weight of enormous burdens; but this is a circumstance attaching to poverty in all parts of the world, not to any nation in particular. It is among the upper and middle classes in Spain, though in many other countries the contrary is true, that women wear most strongly a national characteristic appearance. In Madrid and the other fashionable cities you are surprised by the vast number of women who crowd the streets. They have no domestic occupations; they trouble themselves little with the nurture or education of their children; they devolve on hirelings the management of their household affairs; and they relieve themselves from ennui by sauntering through the public places, dressed with the minutest elegance, carrying their fans, and bargaining on it, by every possible species of coquetry, for admiration from the passers by.

A Spanish woman is a natural coquette, and when married cannot abandon the habit familiarly known as flirtation. This gives rise to jealousy on the husband's part, which produces infinite misery.

Marriage is held in law a solemn and irrevocable contract. It is under many legal regulations, and subject to the authority of the Roman Catholic Church. In the hands of the clergy, indeed, there is vested a prodigious arbitrary power, which they are careful to exercise, lest it should become obsolete by disuse. They may still be seen interfering in matrimonial affairs; and a glance at the manners of the Spaniards some centuries ago will show that the clerical power has not decreased.

Public morality was carefully guarded under the rule of the Visigoths, only to be tolerated during the Middle Ages, since which time it has been at one time lax, at another severely regulated: at the present day we find it in a strange state of confusion.

In the year 586—601, the king of the Visigoths of Spain forbade prostitution in a most absolute manner under pain of severe punishment.

The daughter and the wife born of free parents, convicted of having delivered themselves over to abandonment, received for the first offence three hundred blows with a stick and were ignominiously driven from the city; a relapse was punished with the same corporal punishment, after which the culprit was handed over to a poor person, who was obliged to employ her in performing the most menial offices. If the parents were convicted of being accomplices and of having participated in the gain derived by their daughter's prostitution, each one received one hundred blows. The slave who gave herself up publicly to libertinage received three hundred blows, and when she was sent back to her master, her head was shaved, and she was banished from the city or sold in a place from whence she could not return. The master who refused to submit to these stipulations of the law received in public fifty blows with a stick or a whip, and the slave became the property of some poor man pointed out by the king or the judge, under condition of never being seen in the city again. If the master had participated in the debauchery of his slave, that is if he had reaped any profit, he received the same chastisement as the culprit.

This decree, made especially to repress prostitution in the cities, applied equally to women of ill fame who infested the boroughs, the villages, and the country at large.

This was at the commencement of the seventh century, and such were the severities of the laws passed by the king of the barbarians, Recard by name. The power of the Visigoths was broken a hundred years afterwards by the Arabs. The conquered fled to the hilly country, taking refuge in the mountains of the Asturias; but what laws were in force amongst them we do not know—we only know that the manners of the age were shameful. Perpetual wars, the capture and consequent pillage of villages, the license of the soldiery, helped to constitute a state of things not at all favourable for the developement of female chastity. The Christians and the Mussulmans held in captivity the women taken in battle and treated them as slaves.

The Arabs were soon in their turn conquered by the Moors, and, as the struggle was less bloody, the two people mingled and exercised a mutual influence over one another; but the influence of the Arabs was more direct. "The loose manners of the East," says M. Guardia, "and the luxury ever prevalent amongst orientals, were impalpably engrafted on the austerer habits of the Christians. Chivalry was found to be perfectly compatible with debauchery." The corruption of manners made rapid strides. Prostitution reappeared in all its forms; nor was it, as amongst the Arabs, hampered by municipal restrictions or fettered by arbitrary and severe legislation.

In the fifteenth century the old regulations were resuscitated, and immorality found itself once more compelled to bow to the dicta of priests. Nevertheless these rigorous measures proved that the remedy was worse than the evil. Secret debauchery took the place of public libertinage, and clandestine prostitution increased accordingly.

In the year 1552, Charles V. promulgated an edict against the keepers of houses of ill fame, considerably augmenting the existing punishments. Four years later this law was confirmed by Philip II.

The sequel, however, proves that laws were powerless against public corruption. Immorality is buoyant and contagious, and never so mischievous as when it is hidden.

The end of the fifteenth century witnessed a reform. Prostitution came to be regarded as a branch of the public administration, and placed under severe laws and precise regulations.

About 1623, the health of the community began to be considered, and hygienic measures were introduced. This was a great step, and one rendered the more necessary by reason of the terrible ravages committed by lues venerea, which at this epoch assumed the form of a terrible epidemic.

Three quarters of a century elapsed, and the subject was carefully studied, for in 1704 the council decided that the mayors of towns could arrest and imprison immodest women, who showed themselves in crowds upon the public promenades, and became an object of scandal and disorder. But these coercive measures often repeated were without effect. Soon the law was found to be powerless against corruption.

Since this epoch, public morality has been lax and openly disregarded. The provinces imitated the example of the capital. At the end of the eighteenth century an attempt was made to legislate, but nothing came of it. In 1822, the Cortes passed a Bill relating to public health, which, in point of fact, was nothing more or less than to establish houses of ill fame and recognise their existence. This fell to the ground through the opposition of a physician named Garcia.

In 1853, the population of Madrid was estimated at 270,000. These figures include the floating portion, which is not insignificant. Every woman who chooses to prostitute herself for money is perfectly at liberty to do so; she has to render no account of her conduct, no authorisation of any sort is necessary. The police give no passes nor is there any registry. Under these circumstances statistics are next to an impossibility. Not only does the law tolerate and acknowledge prostitution, but it actually appears to cherish and foster it, by permitting the grossest disorder, and by placing no obstacle in the way of the incessant progress of debauchery. Local authority confines itself to noticing only the most flagrant occurrences—such as a too great number of women in the promenades and public thoroughfares, or when a large number of men amongst the soldiers in garrison fall victims to the ravages of syphilis. It follows from such a state of things that the hospitals are gorged with sufferers, and frequently do not suffice to contain all those who wish to enter. The consequence is that this disease takes the most alarming forms, and does serious injury to the public health.

We cannot possibly make anything like a correct estimate of the number of women who live by prostitution in Madrid, although some manuscript notes furnished to M. Guardia, place it at about one thousand. This may only be an approximate calculation, and it is clearly putting it at its minimum rather than its maximum. Two hundred of these are kept women; though we are inclined to believe this much below the actual numbers, as manners are very loose in Madrid, and the habits of Spaniards incline in a singular degree to concubinage. Probably six hundred women live in houses of ill fame, the keepers of which exercise the most absolute authority over the unfortunates that come into their power. In every one of these houses one finds an indefinite number of young women, which varies from eight to ten. The woman who keeps the place lodges and dresses them. In many of these places there are only two or three resident women, for there are also houses of appointment and convenience. If the number of indoor pensioners is limited, those who walk about the streets are like locusts or the sand of the sea-shore, next to innumerable. They have their abode, perhaps, in their own families, or else they return to their lodgings. Most of these public women are either milliners, seamstresses, laundresses, and pastrycooks, or employed in the manufacture of tobacco. The people who keep houses of ill fame find it to their interest to preserve the health of their lodgers, which they are not, as a rule, negligent of, but yet it is a fact that syphilis is prevalent in Spain to a frightful extent. The authorities are at no pains to prevent its ramification, and the climate is only too favourable for its growth and extension. We divide the women who live by prostitution in Madrid into three classes : 1st, Those who are kept ; 2nd, Those who live in houses of ill fame ; and 3rdly, Those who are free, and merely make use of the above-mentioned houses for a short time. Within this latter category we must include about three hundred prostitutes, who constitute the lowest grade and infest the worst parts of the capital. These have been recruited perhaps from all classes, having sunk lower and lower, until every vestige of shame and modesty having totally disappeared, they traffic for the bare means of subsistence and submit to any and every degradation to obtain it. They even exercise their avocation in the streets and public places. On the other hand, prostitution has plenty of places of resort, such as cafés, public houses, and refreshment rooms.

The police are fully empowered to take into custody any woman guilty of an open breach of the law, although they may not interfere with her for plying her trade, or we might, with some justice, say her profession. Sometimes the magisterial authorities banish them from Madrid, thus getting rid of the most dangerous characters, who, however, like black sheep in the provincial flocks, only serve to carry corruption into districts hitherto uncontaminated.

There is in Madrid a hospital for foundlings, but the fecundity of Spanish prostitutes is not considerable. This is an asylum for every child found in the streets or brought by mothers who wish to get rid of their children. On an average it receives annually from 4500 to 5000 infants. It was founded in the sixteenth century by charitable people.

AMSTERDAM.

ONE is astonished—exclaim MM. Schneevooght (first physician at the hospital of Amsterdam), Van Frigt (assistant surgeon to the same hospital and the syphilitic dispensary), Van Oordt (student in the Parisian hospitals)—one is astonished that in a country where legislation adapts itself to the exigencies of modern times, among a people signalized by a practical genius, an enlightened administration has only very lately adopted the only measures to check the scourge of prostitution.

In Holland religious scruples have yielded before considerations of a higher nature. The Government of the Netherlands has at last decided to leave to the *Communes* the power of preventing by regulation the sad consequences of free and unrestrained prostitution. Supervision, independantly of the services which it renders to the public health, assists to prevent the extension of the evil of which we write.

It is easy to suppose that the capital of Holland offers peculiar facilities for the growth of this vice, which always flourishes in commercial and maritime cities, and more especially when the two are combined.

	In 1851	1852	1855
The municipal population was	221,111	240,669	250,304
Floating	3,532	5,687	7,357
Military	881	1,030	793

The number of strangers that come here, the mariners that commerce attracts, the luxury that reigns among the upper classes, the number of young men of good family, who are condemned to a life of celibacy by inadequate means, unite to relax the morals of the Dutch.

Even now the municipal authorities recoil before the difficulties thrown in their way by the independent spirit of the people, who do not like restrictions imposed by authority, however salutary they may be.

A curious book which appeared in 1648 relates an edict published in 1506, by virtue of which only agents of the municipal police were allowed to open and keep disorderly houses and in certain designated quarters.

In 1789 a commission of health was convoked, and strict precautions taken to guard against infection. It followed from this that 177 women were doctored in one year, a number nearly double that of the year before.

The author of a book about medicine, which appeared in Amsterdam in 1820, complained bitterly of the depravity of manners which led to the decrease of marriages, and of the great number of prostitutes who day and night frequented the streets and other public places to attract passengers by indecent gestures and immodest proposals: more than 800 were known to the police, of which about 200 lived in tolerated houses.

Coming back to modern times, during the year 1850 we find there were in Amsterdam 764 illegitimate births, among 21,365 unmarried inhabitants, between 16 and 30 years, of the male sex, and among 25,207 of the female sex. At the same time there were twenty disorderly houses and 400 prostitutes not inscribed, but simply known to the police.

There is a society in Amsterdam for rescuing fallen women who wish to lead a new life. It is called the Sternbeck Asylum, and is productive of great good.

To allude to the insignificant part played by the police is to avow the insufficiency of the hygienic department.

Although the girls in the tolerated houses are supposed to be compelled to submit to examination, any inspection, in reality, is voluntary on their part. Unfortunately there are a vast number of quacks in the city, who only prolong and aggravate disease, instead of curing it. There is a hospital for venereal affections, with two wards, one with 24 beds for the men, the other with 50 beds for the women, which are all at the service of those affected with syphilis. Besides this there is a syphilitic dispensary, where gratuitous attendance may be obtained.

Syphilis has increased very much lately among the soldiers in garrison. For instance take the subjoined figures, extending over five years:

1852	1853	1854	1855	1856
87	94	199	156	182

All women must be inscribed, whether living in houses or by themselves. Disorderly houses are under the supervision of the police. The keeper of one of these houses may not change his residence, under penalty of a fine of 7 florins and the loss of his licence, without communicating with the authorities, and loose women must be provided with a license. The regulations are very much the same all over the country, at Utrecht, Haarlem, &c.

BELGIUM.

IN the year 1856 the floating population of Brussels and its suburbs was 260,080, to which the garrison contributed 2414. In the same year the total registration of prostitutes, according to the law in their respect provided, numbered 638; these were divided into "filles de maison" and "éparses." Although the police regulations are remarkably stringent, their effect upon public morality is absolutely nil, although it must be admitted that their *surveillance* has a beneficial effect upon the public health. Prostitutes in Brussels, disgusted by the exercise of municipal power, fly without the walls, and withdraw to St. Josse, which, with other extra-mural spots, is much infested with them. The same state of things is observable, more or less, in Antwerp, Bruges, Ostend, Ghent, Mons, Liege, and Namur. By the Belgian regulations the circulation of prostitutes in the streets after sundown is prohibited; women under twenty-one may not be inscribed, and the medical visitation takes place twice a week by the divisional surgeon, and whenever else he may please by the superintending officer. All the éparses and third-class filles de maison are seen at the dispensary, and the first and second classes of the latter order at their domiciles. The éparses may secure this privilege by payment of an extra franc per visit.

The tariff of duties payable by houses and women is as follows:—

Every first-class maison de passe pays 25 francs per month.

Every second-class maison de passe pays 15 francs per month.

Every third-class maison de passe pays 5 francs per month.

Every first class "maison de débauche" pays 60 to 78 francs monthly, according to the number of its authorized occupants—from 6 to 10—and 2 francs extra for each such additional person.

Every such second-class house pays 20 to 32 francs for from 3 to 7 women, and 1 franc extra for every additional.

Every such third-class house pays from 8 to 16 francs for from 2 to 7 women, and 1 franc extra for each additional.

Every first-class fille éparse pays on each inspection 40 centimes;

Every second-class fille éparse pays on each inspection 30 centimes.

Every third-class fille éparse pays on inspection 15 centimes.

Upon punctuality for four successive visits these payments are returned, for inexactitude they are doubled.

Directly a male military patient is taken into hospital he is minutely questioned by the surgeon who attends him as to the exact locality of the house wherein he thinks he was infected, and the appearance of the woman. She is soon arrested; and if the result of the medical examination should prove her diseased, she is placed on the police surgeon's list and sent to hospital, where she is restrained for some time from spreading contagion.

HAMBURG.

HAMBURG, from its peculiar situation and the extent of its commerce, may be considered one of the great centres of trade at present existing in the world, and for that reason it deserves more than a cursory glance or a casual notice.

Documents drawn up during the thirteenth and fourteenth centuries relating to public women are still in a state of preservation.

There is a Code Municipal for the city of Hamburg (1292), which contains the most ancient regulations of this description.

The 17th, 18th, 19th, and 30th of this code regulates in detail the costume of women of ill-fame and the districts where they are allowed to dwell. Their number is not chronicled, but it appears to have been considerable.

The contractors or speculators in women were by successive enactments heavily taxed in 1562: the sum fixed for each woman was from 75 talents to the extraordinary sum of 569; but this is explained by an urgent want on the part of the municipality.

The provisions of the ancient code were maintained up to 1603, when laws of unexampled rigour were passed. Brothels were closed, women and their paramours were publicly exposed, and, as far as possible, outlawed.

In order to describe the state of prostitution in the 19th century we must call the attention of our readers to an enactment of the year 1807: it is of some length, and we have only extracted briefly from it.

1. Every person who lodges women must send to the pretor's office a list of the names of people living there, with their age, their birthplace, and the time of their entering the establishment.

2. When a new girl arrives she must be presented at the office.

3. When a woman leaves, the office must be informed of the fact in writing, and her new abode pointed out.

4. The landlord or landlady must particularly impress upon the lodgers not to have connection with men having a contagious malady.

5. When a woman discovers herself to be infected she must intimate the circum-

stance to her landlord, and abstain from practising her avocation, under pain of severe punishment.

6. The employer who makes the lodger infringe this regulation subjects himself to imprisonment and the pillory.

11. The landlord must look carefully after the health of his lodgers, who must submit to a surgical examination by the municipal physician every fifteen days, and follow his advice punctiliously.

17. Landlords are forbidden to attract foreign women by false promises who have not yet been debauched.

18. The same penalties are inflicted by the law upon a brothel-keeper who prevents a repentant woman from leaving her course of living.

19. Intoxicated men are not to be robbed, but to pay simply the charge put down in the general tariff.

A short time afterwards the French occupied the city, when this edict was repealed and another substituted in its place in the year 1811.

In 1834 the position of women and brothels was regulated, an account of which may be seen in the blue book.

It will be nothing new if we remark that marriage seems to be on the decrease in every populous city, and especially in Hamburg, as we had occasion to notice before.

In 1825 and 1826, among 208 marriages one can count no less than 108 women accouched three or four months after marriage.

We subjoin a table of illegitimate births in proportion to legitimate marriages:—

Years.	Legitimate Children.	Natural Children.
1701—1715	16	81
1780—1790	11	1
1790—1800	9	1
1800—1811	7	1

and from 1836—1846 one in five.

There are many foreign women in Hamburg, for among 512 women inscribed at the prefecture in 1846, 101 only were born in the city. Many girls are, in point of fact, known prostitutes, though not positively known as such to the authorities, for they must have the consent of their parents before they can be inscribed, which gives a larger number of strangers, who are fettered by no such restrictions.

Holstein, Prussia, and above all Brunswick and Hanover, contribute more than any other countries. Austria and France are unrepresented.

At Hamburg a woman who is in want of money may make more by a single act of indiscretion than by an entire week of labour.

It may be interesting to state the ages of the women inscribed in 1844 at the office of police:—

16 women	were less than	20
401 ,,	,, from	20 to 30
74 ,,	,,	30 to 40
11 ,,	,,	40 to 50

Total 502

The police regulations to prevent young girls not yet twenty from abandoning themselves are, as these statistics prove, totally insufficient.

The Hamburg women are generally, thanks to their strong constitutions, healthy and robust. It is remarkable that the public women possess better teeth than the rest of the feminine population.

Syphilis is not so virulent as in former times or in some other cities, and is, as the annexed hospital returns evidence, upon the decline amongst men.

In 1843 there were 355 men infected.
   1844 ,,   335   ,,
   1845 ,,   316   ,,

The way in which women of ill-fame at Hamburg end their career offers nothing remarkable: some marry, some adopt different professions, sufficiently lowly; they sell flowers, for instance, they keep cabarets, and not often houses of evil repute, a very small number become domestic servants, and some die in prison, where they have been sent to expiate an offence against the laws.

Registered women may accost persons of the male sex neither by day nor night, may show no light in their rooms unless behind drawn curtains, nor receive men under twenty years of age, nor be in the streets unaccompanied after 11 P.M., under penalties, both to herself and the landlord of the house she lives in, of from two to eight days' imprisonment on bread and water diet. She is also strictly forbidden, when out of doors, by any speech or gesture to indicate her object.

The examination with the speculum, which takes place at home twice a week, is conducted by a staff of three medical officers and an inspector of police, who sign the bill of health or remit the individual to the hospital forthwith, as the case may be.

Marriage seems to be on the decline in Hamburg, for in 1840 there was only one marriage among every one hundred of the population.

PRUSSIA—GERMANY.

ALTHOUGH education is almost compulsory in Prussia, it fails most egregiously to produce that which it ought to be the object of education and knowledge to obtain. Female chastity marks more closely than any other thing the moral condition of society. They may go through an entire course of scholastic discipline, but the regulation of the passions is more the result of home influence than of reading and writing, or Latin and Greek, inculcated and taught by educational sergeants or clergymen in primary schools and gymnasia. It is no uncommon event in the family of a respectable tradesman in Berlin to find upon his breakfast-table a young child, of which, whoever may be the father, he has no doubt at all about the maternal grandfather. Such accidents are so common that they are regarded, if not with indifference, as mere youthful indiscretions. In 1837 the number of females in the Prussian population between the beginning of their 16th year, and the end of their 45th year—that is within child-breeding age—was 2,983,146. The number of illegitimates born in the same year was 39,501, so that 1 in every 75 of the whole of the females of an age to bear children had been the mother of an illegitimate child. The unsettled military life of every Prussian on his entrance into the world as a man, inculcates habits of frivolity and thoughtlessness, and is peculiarly calculated to form the character of the young man for evil rather than for good.

BERLIN.

BERLIN, the richest and most important city in Germany, possesses a population of 300,000 inhabitants.

In a city like this, containing a far-famed and numerously attended university, a very large manufacturing business, and a numerous garrison, we may very justly expect to find prostitution in a flourishing condition; for money engenders habits of luxury, and luxury is the forerunner and the parent of vice.

At Berlin, during the middle ages, prostitution laboured under many restrictions. Documents bearing upon this epoch show us that prostitutes were confined to certain houses, in specified streets, and compelled, by command of the authorities, to wear a particular costume.

The first "*maison de joie*" was erected about the end of the 15th century, privileged by the corporation, and taxed to some extent.

Those prostitutes who infringed the rules imposed upon them were flogged and expelled from the city. But they were nevertheless under the protection of the authorities, who, in point of fact, looked upon them as belonging to the city, and forming a species of public property. Whosoever assaulted a courtezan was punished as a disturber of the public peace.

There were certain bath-houses at this time, which were much frequented by the richer part of the people and women of station, who gave themselves up to clandestine debauchery, which, if it was discovered by the police, subjected the participators in it to the severest punishment, of which banishment from the city formed the chief part. It is recounted in an old chronicle that, in 1322, an ambassador of the Archbishop of Mayence was killed by the common people for proposing to a bourgeoise to accompany him to one of these bathing establishments.

Concubinage was regarded as common prostitution, and absolutely forbidden. A law was passed, that people living together without having been united by the laws of the church, should be banished from Berlin.

Besides those prostitutes put under the protection of the authorities, and called "demoiselles de la ville," there were others called nomad or wandering women. They were equally notorious, and were also under control. They went from market to market, and from fair to fair, to give themselves up to fornication.

The Reformation changed all this. Severe moral principles made way among the people. A religious fervour commenced a war against that which had always been regarded with toleration, or at least a certain degree of forbearance, up to this time. They went so far as to look upon celibacy as a vice, and did all they could to compel bachelors to marry, by banishing all accessories of, and temptations to, debauchery. A sort of proscription was organized against loose women, and, in a short time, the city was nearly cleared of them. This was very laudable, no doubt, and highly praiseworthy from a strictly puritanical point of view, but its professors soon discovered that such an artificial state of things could not long hold together. Adultery increased enormously, clandestine prostitution was the order of the day, and infants were exposed continually in the public streets. This caused the most austere to come round to more moderate views: not only was the ancient state of things re-established, but, as the number of prostitutes did not suffice to satisfy the wants of the population, it was considered necessary to augment it, and this was accordingly done.

Calvinistic ideas, that is, rigid Protestantism, and common sense, have always struggled together in Germany, and the authorities have had the greatest trouble to regulate a necessary evil—the one of which we are treating. The practical views of the administration were fought against up to 1855, when a fixed system was established.

During the whole of this time the public health was entirely neglected, which one can partially understand, for syphilis did not make many ravages during the 16th century. It was not until the 17th that the necessity for checking its progress made itself felt. The first regulation bearing upon this scourge appeared in 1700. A medical visit was ordered every fifteen days; women found to be tainted were at once sent to the hospital, and, when cured, sent to a prison or workhouse, where they laboured until they had paid off the cost of curing their illness.

The moral condition of Berlin in 1717 was sad in the extreme. The houses of correction were not sufficient to hold the prisoners committed to them, clandestine debauchery had reached its height, and, to remedy this deplorable state of things, it was found necessary to increase the number of tolerated houses, the number of which, in a very little time, increased to an alarming extent. At the end of the seven years' war, more than a thousand houses of this nature might have been counted in the city, each containing on an average nine women. These houses were divided into three distinct classes, the lowest of which accommodated ruffians and blackguards of every description. The prostitutes were there dressed commonly, and like working people. The houses of the second category were devoted to the artizans and the middle classes. Those of the third class, were, of course, devoted to the rich, and contained women well dressed, and in every way qualified to seduce from the paths of virtue.

In 1796 another attempt was made to reduce the number of prostitutes, but like all former attempts of the same nature, it proved ineffectual on account of the augmentation of secret vice. This was at the end of the 18th and the beginning of the 19th century; and caused syphilis to increase very much, and the old regulations were put in force from 1815 to 1829.

In 1844 the respectable inhabitants of Berlin clamoured loudly for the suppression of houses of ill fame; and the government, in spite of the remonstrances of the police, listened to the petitioners, and, in 1845, all houses of this nature were closed, and the girls sent back to their homes, or some other place that they indicated outside the Prussian territory. This accomplished, the consequences very soon made themselves felt, and the Puritans, who were at the bottom of the measure, were compelled to confess that their precipitancy and ill-advised legislation were productive only of the worst effects. Clandestine prostitution developed enormously, syphilis extended its ramifications, and, after ten years, it was found necessary to re-establish tolerated houses.

The garrison suffered dreadfully from disease; so much so, indeed, that General Wrangel solicited the Minister of the Interior to put things on their old footing.

Illegitimate births terrified statisticians by their frequency.

Let us consider the number of natural births during three different periods. The first period shall indicate the births during the time that prostitution was tolerated and spread equally over the city. The second when it was confined to certain streets, and the third during the suppression.

Years.	Illegitimate Births.	Legitimate Births.
1st period, 1838-9, 1840-1	5,652	34,450
2nd „ 1842-3, 4, 5	10,175	54,696
3rd „ 1847-8, 9	5,053	26,782

The proportion of illegitimate births to legitimate, in the first period, is one to seven; in the second, one to five; in the third, one to six.

When prostitution was tolerated, the number of prostitutes did not vary very much; for instance:

In 1792 there were in Berlin 269;
„ 1796 „ „ 257;
of which 190 lived in 54 tolerated houses, and 67 in lodgings.

In 1808 there were 433 in lodgings; of which 230 were spread over 50 houses, and 203 lived in lodgings. Besides this there were about 467, who gave themselves up to clandestine prostitution. The population was at this time 150,000: it was during the occupation of the French.

In 1810 there were 165 prostitutes spread over 44 houses.

In 1819 there were 311 prostitutes, 198 in houses, and 113 in lodgings.

In 1837 there were 258 prostitutes spread over 34 houses.

In 1844 there were 287 prostitutes spread over 26 houses, and 18 in lodgings.

In 1849 the number of prostitutes of all classes in Berlin was estimated at 10,000.

There is a provision common to Berlin and some other towns, that the keeper of a licensed house must defray the cost of curing any person whose contraction of venereal disease in his house can be established.

Dr. Behrend is of opinion that besides the 10,000 prostitutes known to the authorities that we have before alluded to, there are 8000 clandestine ones.

It may be interesting to English readers to know that the price of admission to a certain class of tolerated houses in Berlin is 6d. for which a cup of coffee is given, the use of a private room for fifteen minutes 3s., for thirty minutes 5s., and those prices include the company of one of the women, who receives one-third for herself.

AUSTRIA.

IN Austria public brothels are not tolerated by the police, and public women are sent into the houses of correction; but this legislative enactment will not convey a true idea to a foreigner of the actual state of morality throughout the country. Strangers, and those whom for want of a better designation we will term closet moralists, who draw their conclusions from *primâ facie* evidence, would be inclined to consider the territory governed by the house of Hapsburg almost, if not entirely, free from vice, because the streets of the capital and other towns are almost free from the spectacles that disfigure the *pavé* in other well-known places of cosmopolitan pilgrimage and resort. But we shall prove the reverse to be the case not only in Vienna, but throughout the kingdom.

Austria is an amalgamation of conquered countries which require an enormous standing army to keep in subjection, hence it very naturally follows that the moral sense is deadened in many districts to an alarming extent; and this is the invariable result of military despotism, for the sense of morality which is essentially the result of education, is never so acute as in free and well-governed countries.

The extent and population of the different states that comprise the Austrian empire is thus estimated in the official reports of 1851.

Provinces.	Area in Sq. Miles.	Population, 1851.
German—Austria, Archduchy	15,052	2,390,376
—— Tyrol, Principality	10,981	859,700
—— Styria, Duchy	8,670	1,006,971
Sclavonian—Illyria, Kingdom	10,960	1,291,196
—— Bohemia, Kingdom	20,203	4,409,900
—— Moravia and Silesia, Margravate	10,239	2,238,424
—— Dalmatia, Kingdom	5,067	393.715
Magyar—Hungary, with Sclavonia, &c., and Croatia, Kingdom	89,040	10,158,939
—— Transylvania, Grand Principality	21,390	2,073,737
—— Military frontier	15,179	1,009,109
Polish—Galicia and Bukovina, Kingdom	33,538	4,936,303
Italian—Lombardo-Venetian Kingdom	17,511	5,007,472
Total	257,830	35,776,842

In the capital itself, the lowest and most moderate computation allows the number of prostitutes to be 15,000. These are under police supervision, although they are not licensed. The officers of justice have the power of making domiciliary visits, and enter their dwellings at any hour of the day or night. If they are discovered in the streets after a certain hour they may be apprehended, and this to a great extent prevents that parade and ostentation that is observable in most European cities of any size and note. We are informed on reliable authority (Wilde) that almost one in every two children born in Vienna is "illegitimate," which evidences very clearly that the more restrictions you place upon public immorality, so much the more do you increase private vice; from 1830 to 1837, the proportion of illegitimate to legitimate births was as ten to twelve in Vienna. In Austria registers of births, deaths, and marriages, are kept by each minister of the church for his parish, and also by the Jewish Rabbi for those of their own persuasion. The register of births records the year, month, and day of birth, the number of the house in which the birth occurred, the name of the child and its sex, and whether it be born in wedlock or illegitimate, the names and surnames of the parents, their religion and the names and surnames and condition of the sponsors. In the case of illegitimate children the name of the father cannot be entered unless he acknowledges the paternity. The register of marriages records the year, month, and day of the marriage, the place of solemnization, the names and surnames of the parties, their religion, age, and whether single or widowed, and the names, surnames, and condition of the witnesses.

If a woman makes an application to the lying-in hospital and states her poverty, she is simply asked are you legitimately or illegitimately with child. The success of her suit depends in a great measure upon her reply, for if she says I am pregnant illegitimately she is admitted on the spot, sometimes in the fifth or sixth month of her pregnancy, generally in the seventh. They present her with an imperial livery to wear, carefully preserving her old clothes until she departs. After delivery she has to nurse her own child, sometimes another's, and when she goes away she gets a bonus of five shillings, thus actually receiving a premium for losing her virtue. For the two first months of its existence the child is nurtured by its mother, it is then sent into the country at the public expense; and if a male it is always welcome in an Austrian peasant's family, for if they can rear it to eighteen years of age, it is rendered up to the conscription instead of the eldest son of its adopted father. Education is very general in Austria. The law of 1821 enacts that no male shall enter the marriage state who is not able to read, write, and understand casting up accounts. This is a serious restriction to connubial bliss amongst the industrial classes; but the law is still more arbitrary, it makes these qualifications as it were indispensable to a man's existence. It further says, no master of any trade shall without paying a heavy penalty employ workmen who are not able to read and write, and that small books of moral tendency shall be published and distributed at the lowest possible price to all the Emperor's subjects.

Mr. McGregor says, "The provisions of this law appear to me to be pretty generally put in force, for I have nowhere in Austria met with any one under thirty years of age who was not able to read and write, and I have found cheap publications, chiefly religious and moral tracts, almanacks, very much like 'Poor Richard's,' containing, with tables of the month, moon's age, sun's rising and setting, the fasts, feasts, holidays, markets, and fairs in the Empire, and opposite to the page of each month appropriate advice relative to husbandry and rural economy, with moral sayings and suitable maxims. The spirit of elementary instruction, if not the most enlightened, inculcates at every step, morality, the advantage of a virtuous life, the evil of vice, and the misery consequent on crime." Works of art are subjected like books to the censors, who are unremitting in the enforcement of their political, moral, and religious restrictions.

MODERN ROME.

MORTIFICATION of the flesh is one of the first principles of the Romish faith, and a stranger would expect to find any laxity of morals amongst the inhabitants of the eternal city severely punished; but in point of fact prostitution is tolerated and regulated in Rome, although there does not exist any special act relating to it.

In the Middle Ages many vices stained the fame of Rome; but it is of the present day that we are about to write. The Romish system has produced the following results, according to M. Felix Jacquot, who lived at Rome for four years on purpose to study the morality and the health of Italy.

1st. Not being able to confine prostitution to certain houses, it has spread itself among families.

2nd. Clandestine prostitution, which is most prevalent at Rome, has there produced the evils that it always engenders, houses of accommodation, seduction at home, and the extension of syphilis.

It is extremely probable that, as there are no standing regulations relative to prostitution, perhaps a sort of arbitrary power is vested in the police which opens the door to innumerable evils.

There exist at Rome five forms of clandestine prostitution: let us begin with the street walkers.

Street walker is the only name that can be given to those ignoble creatures that prostitute themselves in the evening and during the night, at the corners of the streets and in the dark angles of the public squares near the cathedral of St. Peter, and under the colonnades of Bernin, where the French soldiery are so often infected. The street walker was not much known at Rome before the revolution of 1849. She is the result of disorder, and the occupation of Rome by the French gives vitality to her existence. Some of these wretches will infect ten or even twenty men in one night, who have recourse to them to satisfy their brutal cravings and bestial desires.

We have to treat, secondly, of houses of ill-fame; but there is little to be said about them; they do not differ in any respect from those to be found in other cities. The dangers of frequenting them are precisely the same. Syphilis acquires new virulence by being fostered by the inmates, who are recruited from amongst innocent and inexperienced girls belonging to families in the city.

Thirdly, there are houses where the girls neither live nor sleep, but where they are sure to be found during certain hours of the day. The women dine there, and only return to their families at night. These houses are not numerous, probably there are not more than six or seven in the whole city. To escape the watchfulness of the police, these change their locale; whilst one or two close others open, so that there is no diminution of the evil. They rather affect quiet localities: the steep hilly streets little frequented, such as the rampart of the capitol behind the church of *St. Joseph des Menuisiers,* or those quarters where strangers who come to pass a season at Rome instal themselves. There are not many women, as a rule, in these houses; generally six and seldom more than eight. They are frequented by young girls, and notoriously by married women. As so many men are obliged to remain bachelors when they take orders, a vast number of women are compelled, against their will, to embrace a life of celibacy. Then, in a country without industry and with very little agriculture, the lower classes have positively no resources to marry upon. There is a disinclination, also, amongst all classes in Rome to have children without possessing the means to educate them as they should be educated. There is quite a passion amongst the ladies in Rome to get married, and they put every art into requisition to effect their end. An irreproachable character is one of the means employed by young unmarried ladies. But once married everything is changed, and their reserve ceases. This change is to be attributed to too much exclusiveness and the restraint imposed on naturally strong and libidinous instincts; at any rate it is a well-established fact at Rome that marriage is productive of the worst passions and the most scandalous intrigues.

These houses are subject to no visits of the sanitary police. If the authorities are cognisant of their existence they take no notice unless the neighbours complain of such immodest residents in their immediate vicinity. Their existence depends in a great measure upon the lowest members of the police force, whose secrecy is often bought by large bribes. If money is refused them, these fellows complain to their superiors, and the extermination of the offending house of accommodation generally ensues.

It is no uncommon thing in England and France to hear the clamour of drunken men and women issuing from those houses— the noise of bacchanal lyrics mingled with oaths and curses, the immodesty of the women joining with the blasphemy of the men: but in Italy it is different. There is a sort of dignity amongst the Italians even in the midst of their debauchery. An anonymous denunciation before the clergy of the parish or the justices that a man was drunk, will often expose the denounced individual to punishment.

The hospital of San Giacomo is set apart for syphilitic maladies, and there the women are treated by the physicians, but unfortunately too late.

Gay women are to be placed in the fourth category. Under this name we include all those who make the sale of their charms a profession. Some are mistresses to foreigners and to natives, and transmit infection from one to the other; the others receive the first comer for a certain stipulated sum. There are a few, however, who only receive those that are known to them or who are well introduced. This is a measure of personal safety; by it they elude the danger of infection, and escape from the supervision of the police.

Syphilis is very prevalent in Rome, more so than in France; and the influence of the climate is much felt in accelerating the approach and increasing the virulence of the disease.

Fifthly. Prostitution in families is one of the most deplorable results of the non-toleration of open houses of ill fame.

This actually goes on under the eyes of the parents: the mother will introduce you to her daughter, and the little brothers will provide you with a ladder to enter the house with.

The love of the *far niente* is so strong amongst the Italians that labour, when it can be obtained, is odious to them. "La travailleuse," says M. Jacquot, " chaude encore des baisers adultères sera bien reçue dans l'alcôve conjugale, si elle apporte un bon pécule au bout de la semaine;" and he adds with indignation, " for a long time I refused to believe in the existence of such ignominy, to-day I am only too well convinced."

An honest woman will on no account be seen in the streets after dark, and a servant will not go into the city from the suburbs after the day has disappeared.

The city of Rome contains 150,000 people; and nourishes, lodges, and takes care of more than 4000 poor people, infirm people, old people, orphans, foundlings, etc., without reckoning assistance given at their own houses to those who require it. There are different hospitals too: the Trinity of the Pelerins, the deaf and dumb asylum, the madhouse, etc. Nearly 22,000 necessitous are relieved every year. The hospital of St. Roch gives admittance to women with child without asking their name or condition, without inquiring whether or not they are married. Women in a good position, who wish to conceal the fruits of a culpable amour, can receive every attention by paying 3 scudi (or about 4s. 6d. of our money) a month. The child is taken to the *Pia casa di Santo-Spirito*. Both men and women when discharged from hospital are so weak that they cannot pursue their avocations. When this is the case they are received into the refuge for convalescents, called the Trinity of the Pelerins, that we have had occasion to refer to before. This hospital has received six hundred thousand inmates since the year 1625.

As things are at present constituted at Rome there is little more to be said respecting it, but we cannot conclude without expressing our admiration of the numeous charitable establishments that one finds there. Every infirmity is cared for with no sparing hand, and the defenceless and the destitute are not deserted by the state and the charity of private individuals.

TURIN.

TURIN is as important in every way as Rome, and deserves considerable attention. Its population, if we include the floating inhabitants, is more than 150,000.

Almost up to the present day, that is, until very lately, the supervision of the police was very imperfectly exercised, and the propagation of disease was the inevitable result. In 1855, M. Ratazzi, Minister of the Interior, wishing to establish a better organization, asked Doctor Sperino, well known in the world of letters for his works upon syphilis, to conceive a project bearing upon this important department of the public health.

These new ordonnances established a reform not only in Turin, but throughout the kingdom.

The public women who were visited before 1856 w-er at Turin 180; since a scrupulous supervision has been established, the number is increased to 750. When we compare these figures, we shall see how much this department of the sanitary police was neglected, and how necessary and efficacious the measures suggested by M. Sperino were. This is proved in a better way still by the notable diminution of disease among the garrison. When the *surveillance* of prostitution is badly exercised the disastrous results can escape the notice of the government, but the registry kept of the soldiers who go into hospital is an index always to be relied on.

After a long time, a hospital specially devoted to venereal diseases has sprung up in Turin, called the *Syphilocome*. Tainted women are here treated gratuitously. They also receive women sent from the provinces. Married women not prostitutes, who are nursing their children, are received here in chambers set apart for them. In 1856 the number of admissions was 1661. A similar institution is about to be erected at Genoa.

Prostitutes are now inscribed on the registers, and they must renew their licence annually. The cost of the licence in the first instance, and the cost of renewal, is

	f.	c.
For prostitutes belonging to tolerated houses -	2	0
For free women of the 1st class	2	0
„ 2nd „	1	0
„ 3rd „	0	60

The 88th article of the fifth section of the new regulations says, "The cost of the visits of the physicians made to independent prostitutes at their own houses is 1 f. 50 c., and those attached to different houses is fixed at—

	f.	c.
For those in houses of the 1st class - -	1	0
For those independent, who come to the sanitary office, of the 1st class -	1	0
„ 2nd „ -	0	50
„ 3rd „ -	gratis.	

In the third class we only include the destitute."

Art. 89. All the taxes imposed upon prostitutes and upon the chiefs of houses of tolerance must be paid to the director of the sanitary office, and are devoted to paying the numerous expenses attendant upon the supervision of prostituion.

Article 40 of the third section.—The heads of houses of tolerance must not, in any case, oppose the visits of the agents of police, by day or night, when the said visits are deemed necessary for the interests of public security.

41. The number of prostitutes in each house is fixed by the police.

49. In houses of the first class, three-fourths of the fixed price goes to the master, the other fourth to the prostitute.

50. The masters of houses of all kinds must pay to the officer of inspection, besides the tax for sanitary visits made to prostitutes living in the house, an annual sum, fixed as follows:

For houses in the first category, that is, where prostitutes have a fixed abode,

1st class 400f.
2nd „ 200f.
3rd „ 100f.

For houses coming within the second

category, that is, where independent prostitutes go to exercise their calling,

1st class 100f.
2nd ,, 60f.
3rd ,, 40f.

Payments for sanitary visis must be made every fifteen days, and the latter tax three months in advance; at the moment of inscription the woman is subjected to the first sanitary visit.

Women in houses of ill fame must not present themselves at the windows or stand in the doorway. Every immoral provocation on the part of the keeper is absolutely forbidden. All servants in these houses under forty-five shall be inspected by the doctors.

Every woman found in any of these houses without being furnished with a licence, and without being inscribed, shall be considered as giving herself up to clandestine prostitution.

The master of the house, in this case, shall have his licence suspended, or altogether taken away from him,

The police give every assistance in their power to those prostitutes who wish to quit their way of living.

Houses of ill fame are to be closed at certain hours determined by the police.

The rules passed in 1857 are very strict, and place loose women completely in the power of the police, without whose sanction they can do nothing. As long as they remain prostitutes they are in a complete state of servitude; but this severe supervision is productive of beneficial results, as far as the curtailing of the extension of syphilis goes; and, after all, this should be the main consideration with every legislator upon this much-vexed question.

BERNE.

THE peculiar customs of the Swiss during the middle ages give an unusual character to the immorality of this country. In the canton of Berne, it was the ordinary custom of the young men to make nocturnal visits in troops to the girls of their acquaintance, generally living in the same village. These visits were made for the purpose of contracting intimate relations, and usually succeeded in doing so. Thus intrigue almost invariably preceded marriage, and it was no unusual thing for the christening of the first-born to take place immediately after the marriage of its parents.

"The inconstancy of the human heart," says M. D'Erlach, "explains why young women often changed their lovers;" so men could go from one girl to another for years without any restriction or interruption on the part of the police.

The use of the bath was established during the middle ages, and although first erected for sanitary reasons it degenerated, as in Germany, into a rendezvous for immoral purposes, during the sixteenth and seventeenth centuries. These baths were taken in common, and this promiscuous bathing, and the peculiar dress worn, promoted the lasciviousness both of men and women.

About the end of the fifteenth century the demoralization of the people of Berne had reached its height, when the Emperor Sigismund visited it on his return to Rome. In 1528 the clergy, in spite of their professions, their oaths, and their precepts, surpassed every other class by the most scandalous profligacy. Amongst the houses of ill-fame one had acquired a shameful ascendancy. At the end of the invasion of the Republic by the French this tolerated house was established at No. 13, Rue de l'Arsenal, and it was frequented by all the great men of the day. It was afterwards moved, and placed opposite a church very much frequented by the people. Towards the end of the Helvetian Republic, it was once more translated, on account of the scandal its position occasioned, but it was finally closed in 1828 by a decree of the State Council. Until then there was not a single article of any sort against these places—not a law that bore even remotely upon houses of ill fame.

Notwithstanding the closing of this house, several others have sprung up in retired districts under the name of public baths, and are unmolested by the police, who tacitly acknowledge the fact of their existence and acquiesce in it. The girls in these establishments are engaged under various pretexts; some are supposed to be employed in the kitchen, some take care of the baths, some are housemaids, and look after the bed-rooms—an occupation, it is to be presumed, that most of them find congenial; sometimes they are imagined to be on a visit to the people of the house, at others they are relatives. The keeper of the house employs his own physician to look after the health of the girls; and these are obliged to report to the police if any of them are found infected, when the police make a personal visit, not generally conducive to the advancement of the interests of the master of the house.

Besides the women inhabiting these houses, which are not numerous, there may be 170 or 200 other prostitutes. These appear on the register, and are under the eye of the police.

There are belonging to certain families in the city, and exercising no profession, from 50 to 70 women.

Living in the city without their families, under the pretext of a profession, but without one, 120 to 130.

"These," says M. D'Erlach, "are our prostitutes, such as one meets in the streets, the squares, &c. As in other towns, they, by their looks, by their provoking deportment, by their dress, and by their glaring colours, endeavour to arrest attention, and entice the passers-by into places where beds may be obtained, or into those public baths which are well known to harbour prostitutes."

Another class of prostitutes is formed by those who actually have a profession, but unhappily one not sufficiently lucrative to enable them to exist. These, driven by the exigencies of their position, seek in prostitution that which their profession denies them. Among this class we see milliners, dressmakers, shop-girls, and servants. At Berne the household servants send the greatest number of prostitutes into this category. The reason is, that nine-tenths of them come from the country, and are placed in hotels, public-houses, tobacco-shops, &c., and, inexperienced, easily fall a prey to the temptations held out to them.

A few words concerning the places of rendezvous may be instructive. The girls in a certain position who have a profession of some sort, and have no locality adapted for meeting their lovers, have recourse to the public baths. In these baths each chamber has two bathing places: often the rooms communicate with one another by little doors, which facilitates the commerce of the sexes, about which the keeper of the baths is profoundly ignorant.

The legislature, as regards sanitary regulations, is mute. The only thing that can be done is to arrest the girls when it can be proved that they are infected, and they are then sent to prison.

We subjoin some extracts from the law of the 4th June, 1852, respecting drinking-houses and other analogous establishments:—

"Art. 37. The authorities of police and their servants can, in the exercise of their functions, open at any hour of the day or night the inns and other like establishments.

"Art. 39. In cases particularly urgent and important, the Executive Council is authorized to shut any inn or analogous establishment.

"Art. 55. The innkeeper must not permit in his house any infraction of the existing police regulations."

Innkeepers are further forbidden to allow certain rooms in their houses to be used for immoral purposes.

The City of Paris.

From time immemorial the immorality of the city of Paris has been proverbial. Every historian, no matter what period of Parisian history he may have been describing, has dwelt more or less on the characteristic profligacy of the French nation. Yet all documents relating to the middle ages must be received with some diffidence, as they were chiefly drawn up by ecclesiastics, whose interest it has often proved to distort facts and falsify statistics. Nevertheless, the levity of the French people has always been a matter for comment amongst the inhabitants of other countries; and although we may not find much to instruct us in the papers relative to prostitution in former times among the Parisians, there is much to be relied upon which is not altogether uninteresting.

The first document which we possess upon the number of prostitutes in Paris was drawn up about the year 1762. "This document," says M. Parent Duchatelet, "is not much known. We found the MS. in the archives of the Prefecture, with other papers relating to prostitution." It contains a memoir presented anonymously to the lieutenant of police of that period. It is written very carefully, and with great sagacity, showing a profound knowledge of the subject of which it treats. The writer estimates the number of prostitutes exercising their profession in the city of Paris at 25,000. A few years later, another writer, alluding to the same subject, reckons the number of all classes upon the pavement of Paris at 20,000; but neither of these give the sources from whence they derived their calculation.

The celebrated M. Boucher places the number of prostitutes before the Revolution at 30,000. These figures are, however, supposed to include gay women of every kind—actresses, shop-girls, manufacturing women, and public women, openly known as such.

It is easy to see that there is a great uncertainty in this calculation of the number of prostitutes before the Revolution, but in the year 1802, Fouché, then Minister of Police, having an idea of erecting dispensaries in every city in France, estimated, in speaking of Paris, that it actually did contain 30,000 public women.

Eight years later, in 1810, the Police Minister demanded from his subordinate officer an approximate estimate of the number of prostitutes in the city; and the return furnished to him places the number at 18,000, of whom one-half were kept-women. In 1825 the author of the "Biographie des Commissaires de Police" was of opinion that the actual number did not exceed 15,000.

It was not until after the administration of Baron Pasquier, and especially since 1816, that any reliable documents were prepared. The researches were executed with great care, and every woman who practised with sufficient publicity was placed on the returns.

According to M. Duchatelet, the total number of prostitutes inscribed on the register in 1812 was

Year	Number
1812	15,523
1813	20,113
1814	22,866
1815	22,249
1816	26,226
1817	28,953
1818	31,042
1819	31,280
1820	32,957
1821	34,966
1822	34,831
1823	32,510
1824	31,845
1825	31,483
1826	29,948
1827	29,663
1828	31,956
1829	34,118
1830	36,337
1831	39,128
1832	42,699

(This is amalgamating the monthly inscriptions during the entire year.)

This calculation extends over 21 years, and the author declares the numbers to be reliable. It is extremely interesting to the statistician to notice the fluctuations of vice during different periods of a country's history. In 1815 it will be perceived that the number sensibly diminishes, but it increases gradually and regularly from 1816 to 1822, a time at which the inscriptions are augmented by more than 2900. In 1827 they are again lowered, only to be considerably increased in 1830. These oscillations must arrest attention, but it is incontestable that prostitution has advanced with rapid and irresistible strides during each successive year that has succeeded, and to prove such to be the fact we accept from the same authority a table indicating the number of women inscribed on the registers within the following 22 years, which will bring us up to 1854, when there is a monthly average of 4200.

The total number of women inscribed on the register in 1833 was

Year	Number
1833	44,676
1834	45,382
1835	45,759
1836	45,811
1837	46,584
1838	47,881
1839	47,630
1840	47,153
1841	46,635
1842	46,089
1843	45,846
1844	46,340
1845	47,559
1846	49,915
1847	51,422
1848	51,298
1849	50,015
1850	52,291
1851	52,918
1852	51,620
1853	50,614
1854	50,790

(It must be understood that the registry is repeated every month.)

It has been asserted that Paris was the rendezvous of all debauched women in France, and that out of every ten thousand immodest women in the kingdom nine thousand at least are to be looked for in the capital. "Not only," wrote Restif de Bretonne, "will you find in Paris 'Lyonnaises, Picardes, Champenoises, Normandes, Provençales, Languedociennes,' &c., but foreigners, Germans, Swiss, Poles, Saxons, Spaniards, Italians, and even English, have resorted there, so that we may even denominate Paris the worst place in Europe."

At the time that Restif wrote, it may be almost supposed that Parisians were not to be found among the prostitutes of the capital.

Among 12,707 women inscribed at Paris since April 1816, up to April 1831—that is to say, during 15 years—24 were not able to tell what country they were born in, 31 came from different countries foreign to Europe, 451 belonged to European countries foreign to France, 12,201 were born in French departments.

Among the 31 strangers to Europe were—
18 Americans.
11 Africans.
2 Asiatics.

During the years 1845 to 1854 Great

Britain contributed 56 women to swell the ranks of the prostitutes in Paris, of which

London sent	-	-	30
Bristol	-	-	1
Brighton	-	-	3
Liverpool	-	-	1
Southampton	-	-	1
Sundry Villages	-	-	14
Ireland	-	-	4
Scotland	-	-	2
Total	-	-	56

From the 16th March, 1816, up to the 31st April, 1831, the total number of girls inscribed on the registers has been 12,607, of which Paris has furnished 4469, the chief towns 6939, and the others have come from various places. These statistics we consider sufficient to prove the fact of the emigration of prostitutes to Paris.

It has been supposed that almost all prostitutes are natural children. That this is not the case is abundantly proved by a careful analysis by M. Duchatelet, in which he evidences the contrary; out of 1183 children born in Paris not quite one-fourth were illegitimate.

The list of the professions practised at one time by women who have subsequently become prostitutes is alarming, from its extensiveness, including as it does no less than six hundred distinct trades, among which we perceive seamstresses, those in the linen trade, breeches-makers, flannel-waistcoat makers, glovers, upholstresses or tapestry-makers, darners and menders, strap-makers, botchers, milliners, embroideresses, gauze-workers, flowerists, feather-makers, those that colour or illuminate, knitters, lace-makers, fringe-makers, rope-makers, furriers, wool-workers, hair-weavers, machinists, cotton-spinners, silk-weavers, gold and silver gauze veil-makers, shawl-makers, bonnet-makers, and innumerable others; indeed, every trade may truly be said to be adequately represented in this social congress for the propagation of vice. There are also those who have once been much better off. For instance: seven had been shopkeepers in a very respectable way of business, three were midwives, one an artist, six were musicians and gave lessons on the harp and the piano, sixteen had been actresses in Paris and the provinces, and three (this is a very rare case, and an exception to the general rule,) possessed an income of 200 francs, of 500, and even 1000. It is not easy to determine what inducement a life of prostitution could hold out to these women.

The total number of women whose professions were known amounts to 3120.

The returns go far to evidence the evil effects of sedentary occupations upon the morals of young girls; then the fluctuations in the demand for labour are continually throwing the operatives out of work, and as a means of existence they naturally resort to prostitution to obtain a livelihood.

To show the extent to which education has spread amongst this class, we give the number of those who signed the register well, of those who signed badly, and of those who could not sign at all, out of 4470 girls born and brought up in Paris.

Those who could not sign	-	2332
Those who signed badly	-	1780
Those who signed well, and sometimes very well	-	110
And of those who possessed no indication to show what they were	-	248
Total	-	4470

Ignorance is the prevailing characteristic of the "femmes galantes" generally throughout the world, and we find it so in France, which is rather singular when we consider how comprehensive the scheme of education is in that country.

As far as religion goes, they are usually deficient in the knowledge of the most simple articles of belief. Sometimes they are fanatical to a degree, and always superstitious. This being the case, it will not seem wonderful that they always receive the rites of the Church on their deathbeds with the greatest confidence, satisfaction, and delight.

It is very well known that soldiers and sailors have a way of tattooing themselves on the chest, the arms, and sometimes the legs. The inscriptions are often of great size, and elaborately executed. One man will have a battle delineated on his skin, or the likeness of his sweetheart, but this of course depends upon his turn of mind. This habit has been adopted in Paris by those prostitutes who live in the houses frequented by the military. It may in the first instance have originated from a desire on their part to ingratiate themselves with their admirers. At all events, from whatever cause it may have arisen, it is now an established custom. Women occasionally have been seen in the hospital with as many as thirty lovers imprinted on the throat, the breast and other parts of the body, although it is customary for them to remove a lover who has been succeeded by one more favoured, and the means had recourse to, to effect this, are often prejudicial to the health of the girl in a fatal degree. They will not hesitate to employ sulphuric acid, which is as likely as not to raise an ulcer which has in very many cases ended in the death of the sufferer. Strange to say, the figures and inscriptions are rarely, if ever, immodest or indecent.

The shibboleth of this class is always "Vive la bagatelle!" When not actually engaged in the pursuits their avocation entails upon them, they seldom do anything. Their existence, if not altogether dreamy and inane, is certainly one marked rather by lassitude and inertness than energy and briskness. They are perpetually the prey of an irresistible craving after excitement, which devours them, and the morning and afternoon not unfrequently serves only to recruit the nerves shattered by the excesses of the night before. Reading is not a pastime with them, although some may frequently be found with books in their hands.

Most prostitutes pass under false names, and they even go so far as to change their names whenever they have an inclination to do so.

The names that the better class are fondest of are:—

Aumale	Malvina
Zulma	Virginia
Calliope	Azelina
Irma	Ismeria.
Zélie	Lodoiska
Amanda	Palmira
Pamela	Aspasia
Modeste	Lucrece
Natalie	Clara
Sidonia	Angelina
Olympia	Flavia
Flora	Celina
Thalia	Emily
Artemisia	Reine
Armande	Anais
Leocadia	Delphini
Octavia	Fanny.

The lower class do not, as may be supposed, possess so refined a taste as their more elevated sisters. We subjoin some of the most popular to be found in their vocabulary:—

Roussellette	La Bancale
Collette	La Blonde
Boulotte	La Provençale
Mourette	Belle-Cuisse
La Ruelle	Belle-Lambe
La Roche	Le Bœuf
La Courtille	Brunette
La Picarde	Bouquet
Faux Cul	Louchon
Mignarde	Peloton
Poil-ras	Cocote
Poillong	Bourdonneuse.

Leaving this subject, let us touch upon another which deserves our attention. Every prostitute has a lover; he is generally selected from among the law students, medical students, or young barristers, for their minds being cultivated and their address easy, the woman is charmed by an intellectual superiority she can never hope to attain to. A great number of prostitutes of course recruit for lovers among the shopboys and tradesmen of the city. They become so ardently attached to them that they will submit to almost any indignity. The "Paillasson" may be the greatest tyrant in his small way that ever had the power of lording it over another, but no diminution of her regard or passion will result from his ill-treatment. A great number of young men in Paris have no visible means of existence, but a prostitute will, in most instances, not only keep her lover out of the proceeds of her prostitution, but clothe, feed, and even lodge him herself. In fact it is more a madness than a passion. They will put up with anything,—wounds, curses, blows, all are forgiven and forgotten.

Introducing houses, and houses of accommodation are tolerated by the Parisian police, for it is found impossible, and perhaps impolitic, to suppress them. The refuse of the city, both men and women, are confined by the police to the lowest quarters of the city, that they may be under the immediate control of the authorities. So that the vilest and most abandoned women are allowed to mingle with thieves, ruffians, and malefactors of every description in a particular locality, instead of infesting other parts of the city.

The rank and title of "*Dame de Maison*," or keeper of a house of ill-fame, being the highest pinnacle of a prostitute's career, and the acme of their ambition, of course renders such a position a matter of much envy and anticipation to them. We can divide this class into four distinct divisions—

1st. Those who have, so to say, gone through the world, having been kept by officers in the army, or men of property, who, perhaps, are thrown over by their *ci-devant* admirers, and possessing some money, establish themselves in this way as a means of making a livelihood and obtaining a provision for their declining years.

2nd. Those old prostitutes who have exercised some economy during their youth, and are thus placed in a position to live somewhat at their ease.

3rd. Old servants and confidential women who have lived in the service of keepers of houses of ill-fame, who have an agreement with their mistress to take her business or succeed her on her death or bankruptcy. These women have a knowledge of the places where they have lived, and know perfectly well how to manage the girls who resort to these houses, and thoroughly understand the men who visit them.

4th. The fourth class is composed of women who have never been prostitutes, who often are married and have children. The appetite of gain has launched them in this career. It is to keep a furnished house that they have taken in prostitutes, or having set up a public-house they entertain loose women to make men come there.

There are in Paris some families who have kept prostitutes for several generations, having positively no other source of revenue than the keeping of introducing houses or houses of ill-fame. One sees the mother exercising her profession in one quarter of the city and her daughter in another. The daughters succeed their mother, the nieces their aunt, etc., but in general this is very rare, one not being able to indicate more than six families of this description.

There are some conditions which these people must subscribe to, and which offer some guarantee to the authorities for the good management of the house. To begin with: they must not be too young, lest they are unable to possess sufficient authority over the women under their jurisdiction; twenty-five is generally the lowest age, experience teaches us, at which a woman can become a safe manager of an immoral house. As a rule, licences are refused to those who have never been prostitutes.

Force, vigour, energy both of mind and body are requisite to a keeper of a house of ill-fame, as well as a habit of commanding, and something of a masculine manner. If to these qualities they join good antecedents, if they have not been taken before a justice of the peace, if they are honest, if they do not favour clandestine debauchery, if they are unaccustomed to get intoxicated, if they know how to read and write, if while they were prostitutes they had not a tendency to infringe the regulations, the authorisation they ask for is not refused them; but unhappily it is found too late, that licences are given to women who are unable to, or certainly do not, carry out these wholesome conditions and necessary stipulations. The desire to possess this coveted distinction, and pass from the condition of a simple prostitute to that of "dame de maison" often fills young women with the greatest anxiety, as they do not very well know how to invest their money, and they often embark in this career in a speculative manner causing their enterprise to end in bankruptcy and failure; this fills the authorities with great trouble and they are extremely particular in giving licences, frequently only giving a fourth-class one when the party applying for it could easily set up a first-class establishment.

Certain speculators will often furnish a house, and place a woman in it for immoral purposes, who will encourage other women, and it becomes a house of ill-fame; other intriguing women will also club together and establish a house of this sort, and install one of their creatures. Now these installed women are not really and truly, from their subordinate position, to be called "dames de maison" for if they do not every week pay so much money to the speculators who have employed them, they are instantly turned out and some one else comes in their place. It is easy to see that this system does not give them much authority over the women who live in their houses, and through whose instrumentality and prostitution the money is made. Without authority disorder must ensue, and then the police have to interfere. There were—

In 1824 - 163 of these houses in Paris.
  „ 1831 - 209   „   „
  „ 1832 - 220   „   „

On the 1st of January, 1852, there were 1246 women in these houses. On the 1st of December there were 1316, but making allowance for those incarcerated, either for some offence or for illness, we find the number reduced to about 1005 active women. There were—

In 1842 - 193 tolerated houses in Paris.
  „ 1847 - 177   „   „
  „ 1852 - 152   „   „

In which latter year these houses contained 1005 girls.

In 1854, Paris contained 140 tolerated houses in which 1009 women existed.

In the suburbs there were—

  In 1842 - 36 of these houses.
  „ 1847 - 53   „   „
  „ 1852 - 65   „   „

In 1852 the number of girls living in them was 417.

In 1854 there were 64 houses containing 493 women.

The number of these tolerated houses, it will be seen, does not fluctuate or change very largely, with the exception of those existing in the suburbs, in which in ten years, that is to say from 1842 to 1852, the number was increased by 29. We have shown that the summit of a prostitute's ambition is generally to keep a house of ill-fame, and such being the case it is only wonderful that the number of such houses is not larger than it is.

A vast deal of prostitution goes on in the small smoking shops, the low public-houses, the brandy shops, and the wine houses. These refuges exist all over Paris, they are innumerable, but one finds them collected especially at those points where the workmen and the industrial classes meet together, such as the larger barriers, nearly all the outside boulevards, those of the Hospital and the Temple, the 'Rue Fromenteau" and neighbouring places, the streets that touch the large bridges, etc.

So far back as 1818, the commissioners of the police consulted about this evil, and the necessity for suppressing it; for not only did it encourage secret vice and defeat the ends of the authorities, but it was a source of drunkenness and fighting, and indeed of all sorts of disorders.

In December, 1851, a decree was promulgated by Louis Napoleon which has had some effect in reducing the evil, for several drinking shops have been closed since then for offences against the decree.

It may be interesting to know that frequently girls take a dislike to their revolting avocation, and return voluntarily to their parents. From the 1st January, 1821, to the 30th December, 1827, 254 girls whose names were erased from the registers were taken back by their friends, who promised to provide them with the means of subsistence, and gave guarantees for their good conduct. Amongst this number—

133 were reclaimed by the mother only.
72   ,,   ,, the father only.
22   ,,   ,, the mother and father together.
22   ,,   ,, their brothers.
9   ,,   ,, their sisters.
5   ,,   ,, an aunt.
2   ,,   ,, an uncle.

Each of these girls had been inscribed during the following time—

120 from 1 to 6 months
37 more than 6 months
16   ,,   1 year
55   ,,   2 years
9   ,,   3 years
6   ,,   7 years
8   ,,   8 years
3   ,,   9 years

Total—254

The sanitary regulations in Paris are beneficial to the community at large in the highest degree. Physicians are appointed by the prefecture, who make periodical visits, generally twice a month, for the purpose of ascertaining the state of the health of their numerous clients. If they should discover one infected, she is immediately sent to the hospital.

In the foregoing pages we have endeavoured to give a brief exposé of the dark side of the brilliant volatile city of Paris. Such a subject gives ample scope for volumes, but the nature of this work confines us to dry facts and statistics.

PROSTITUTION IN LONDON.*

THE liberty of the subject is very jealously guarded in England, and so tenacious are the people of their rights and privileges that the legislature has not dared to infringe them, even for what by many would be considered a just and meritorious purpose. Neither are the magistracy or the police allowed to enter improper or disorderly houses, unless to suppress disturbances that would require their presence in the most respectable mansion in the land, if the aforesaid disturbances were committed within their precincts. Until very lately the police had not the power of arresting those traders, who earned an infamous livelihood by selling immoral books and obscene prints. It is to the late Lord Chancellor Campbell that we owe this salutary reform, under whose meritorious exertions the disgraceful trade of Holywell Street and kindred districts has received a blow from which it will never again rally.

If the neighbours choose to complain before a magistrate of a disorderly house, and are willing to undertake the labour, annoyance, and expense of a criminal indictment, it is probable that their exertions may in time have the desired effect; but

* We rely for certain facts, statistics, &c., upon Reports of the Society for the Suppression of Vice; information furnished by the Metropolitan Police; Reports of the Society for the Prevention of Juvenile Prostitution; Returns of the Registrar-General; Ryan, Duchatelet, M. les Docteurs G. Richelot, Léon Faucher, Talbot, Acton, &c., &c.; and figures, information, facts, &c., supplied from various quarters: and lastly, on our own researches and investigations.

there is no summary conviction, as in some continental cities whose condition we have studied in another portion of this work.

To show how difficult it is to give from any data at present before the public anything like a correct estimate of the number of prostitutes in London, we may mention (extracting from the work of Dr. Ryan) that while the Bishop of Exeter asserted the number of prostitutes in London to be 80,000, the City Police stated to Dr. Ryan that it did not exceed 7000 to 8000. About the year 1793 Mr. Colquhoun, a police magistrate, concluded, after tedious investigations, that there were 50,000 prostitutes in this metropolis. At that period the population was one million, and as it is now more than double we may form some idea of the extensive ramifications of this insidious vice.

In the year 1802, when immorality had spread more or less all over Europe, owing to the demoralizing effects of the French Revolution, a society was formed, called "The Society for the Suppression of Vice," of which its secretary, Mr. Wilberforce, thus speaks:—

"The particular objects to which the attention of this Society is directed are as follow, viz.—

"1. The prevention of the profanation of the Lord's day.

"2. Blasphemous publications.

"3. Obscene books, prints, etc.

"4. Disorderly houses.

"5. Fortunetellers."

When speaking of the third division a report of the Society says—

"In consequence of the renewed intercourse with the Continent, incidental to the restoration of peace, there has been a great influx into the country of the most obscene articles of every description, as may be inferred from the exhibition of indecent snuff-boxes in the shop windows of tobacconists. These circumstances having tended to a revival of this trade the Society have had occasion within the last twelve months to resort to five prosecutions, which have greatly tended to the removal of that indecent display by which the public eye has of late been too much offended."

Before the dissolution of the Bristol Society for the Suppression of Vice, its secretary, Mr. Birtle, wrote (1808) to London the following letter:—

"Sir,—The Bristol Society for the Suppression of Vice being about to dissolve, and the agents before employed having moved very heavily, I took my horse and rode to Stapleton prison to inquire into the facts contained in your letter. Inclosed are some of the drawings which I purchased in what they call their market, without the least privacy on their part or mine. They wished to intrude on me a variety of devices in bone and wood of the most obscene kind, particularly those representing a crime "*inter Christianos non nominandum,*" which they termed *the new fashion*. I purchased a few, but they are too bulky for a letter. This market is held before the door of the turnkey every day between the hours of ten and twelve."

At the present day the police wage an internecine war with these people, who generally go about from fair to fair to sell indecent images, mostly imported from France; but this traffic is very much on the decline, if it is not altogether extinguished.

The reports of the Society for the Suppression of Vice are highly interesting, and may be obtained gratis on application at the Society's chambers.

Another Society was instituted in May 1835, called "The London Society for the Protection of Young Females, and Prevention of Juvenile Prostitution." We extract a few passages from its opening address.

"The committee cannot avoid referring to the present dreadfully immoral state of the British metropolis. No one can pass through the streets of London without being struck with the awfully depraved condition of a certain class of the youth of both sexes at this period (1835). Nor is it too much to say that in London crime has arrived at a frightful magnitude; nay, it is asserted that nowhere does it exist to such an extent as in this highly-favoured city. Schools for the instruction of youth in every species of theft and immorality are here established * * * * *. It has been proved that 400 individuals procure a livelihood by trepanning females from eleven to fifteen years of age for the purposes of prostitution. Every art is practised, every scheme is devised, to effect this object, and when an innocent child appears in the streets without a protector, she is insidiously watched by one of those merciless wretches and decoyed under some plausible pretext to an abode of infamy and degradation. No sooner is the unsuspecting helpless one within their grasp than, by a preconcerted measure, she becomes a victim to their inhuman designs. She is stripped of the apparel with which parental care or friendly solicitude had clothed her, and then, decked with the gaudy trappings of her shame, she is compelled to walk the streets, and in her turn, while producing to her master or mistress the wages of her prostitution, becomes the ensnarer of the youth of the other sex. After this it is useless to attempt to return to the path of virtue or honour, for she is then watched with the greatest vigilance, and should she attempt to escape from the clutches of her seducer she is threatened with instant punishment, and often barbarously treated. Thus situated she becomes reckless, and careless of her future course. It rarely occurs that one so young escapes contamination; and it is a fact that numbers of these youthful victims imbibe disease within a week or two of their seduction. They are then sent to one of the hospitals under a fictitious name by their keepers, or unfeelingly turned into the streets to perish; and it is not an uncommon circumstance that within the short space of a few weeks the bloom of health, of beauty, and of innocence gives place to the sallow hue of disease, of despair, and of death.

"This fact will be appreciated when it is known that in three of the largest hospitals in London within the last eight years (that is to say, from 1827 to 1835), there have not been less than 2700 cases of disease arising from this cause in children from eleven to sixteen years of age."

Léon Faucher, commenting on this, exclaims with astonishment, mixed with indignation, "Deux mille sept cents enfants visités par cette horrible peste avant l'âge de la puberté! Quel spectacle que celui-là pour un peuple qui a des entrailles! Et comment éprouver assez de pitié pour les victimes, assez d'indignation contre les bourreaux!" A Frenchman, looking at the way in which his own illustrious country is governed, would very naturally exclaim against the authorities for not taking steps to prevent so much crime and misery, but he forgets that although a system may work well in France, it is no criterion of its excellent working among a nation totally dissimilar in their habits and disposition to his own.

All French writers have the profoundest horror of our social economics. MM. Duchatelet, Richelot and Léon Faucher, whom we have just quoted, all unite in condemning our system of blind and wilful toleration. They do not understand the temper of the nation, which would never allow the State to legislate upon this subject. But, nevertheless, we must confess that the profligacy of the metropolis of England, if not so patent and palpable as that of some continental cities we have had occasion to refer to, is perhaps as deeply rooted, and as impossible to eradicate.

The legislature, by refusing to interfere, have tacitly declared the existence of prostitutes to be a necessary evil, the suppression of which would produce alarming and disastrous effects upon the country at large. When any case more than usually flagrant occurs it falls within the jurisdiction of the Society for the Suppression of Vice, and the law is careful to punish anything that can be construed into a misdemeanour or a felony. In cold climates, as in hot climates, we have shown that the passions are the main agents in producing the class of women that we have under consideration, but in temperate zones the animal instinct is less difficult to bridle and seldom leads the female to abandon herself to the other sex. It is a vulgar error, and a popular delusion, that the life of a prostitute is as revolting to herself, as it appears to the moralist sternly lamenting over the condition of the fallen; but, on the contrary, investigation and sedulous scrutiny lead us to a very different conclusion. Authors gifted with vivid imaginations love to pourtray the misery that is brought upon an innocent and confiding girl by the perfidy and desertion of her seducer. The pulpit too frequently echoes to clerical denunciation and evangelical horror, until those unacquainted with the actual facts tremble at the fate of those whose terrible lot they are taught rather to shudder at than commiserate. Women who in youth have lost their virtue, often contrive to retain their reputation; and even when this is not the case, frequently amalgamate imperceptibly with the purer portion of the population and become excellent members of the community. The love of woman is usually pure and elevated. But when she devotes her affections to a man who realizes her ideal, she does not hesitate to sacrifice all she holds dear, for his gratification, ignoring her own interest and her own inclination. Actuated by a noble abnegation of self, she derives a melancholy pleasure from the knowledge that she has utterly given up all she had formerly so zealously guarded, and she feels that her love has reached its grand climacteric, when, without the slightest pruriency of imagination to urge her on to the consummation, without the remotest vestige of libidinous desire to prompt her to self-immolation, without a shadow of meretricious feeling lurking within her, she abandons her person beyond redemption to the idol she has set up in the highest place in her soul. This heroic martyrdom is one of the causes, though perhaps not the primary or most frequently occurring, of the stream

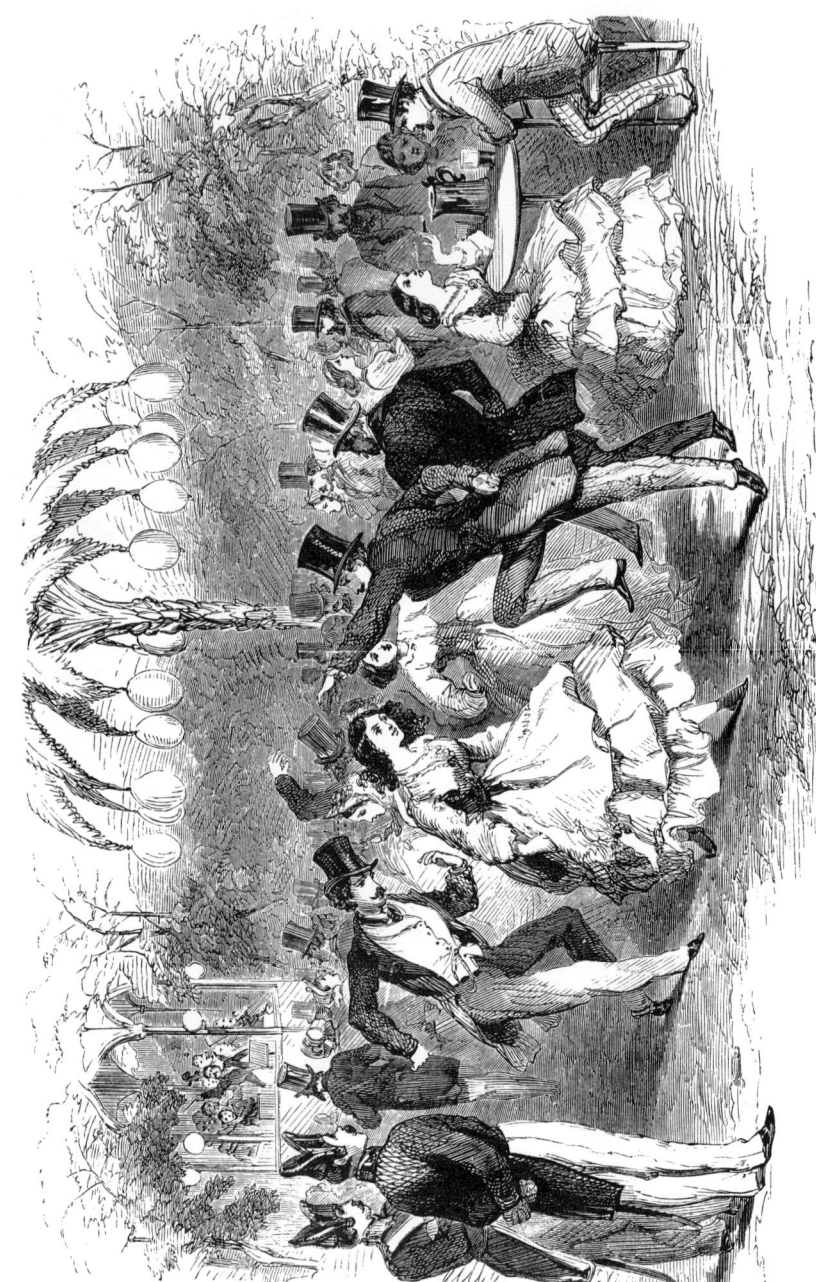

SCENE IN THE GARDENS OF "CLOSERIE DES LILAS." PARIS.

of immorality that insidiously permeates our social system. The greatest, and one equally difficult to combat, is the low rate of wages that the female industrial classes of this great city receive, in return for the most arduous and wearisome labour. Innumerable cases of prostitution through want, solely and absolutely, are constantly occurring, and this will not be wondered at when it is remembered that 105 women in England and Wales are born to every 100 males, which number is further augmented by the dangers to which men are exposed by their avocations, and also in martial service by sea and land. Again, so great are the inducements held out by men of lax morality and loose principles that procuresses find entrapping girls into their abodes a most lucrative and profitable trade. Some are even brought up from their earliest infancy by their pseudo-protectors with the full intention that they shall embark in the infamous traffic as soon as their age will permit them to do so remuneratively. A revolting and horrible case exemplifying the truth of this statement came under our notice some short time back. We were examining a girl, who gave the following replies to the questions put to her.

"My name is Ellen, I have no other. Yes, I sometimes call myself by various names, but rarely keep to one longer than a month or two. I was never baptized that I know of; I don't know much about religion, though I think I know the difference between right and wrong. I certainly think it is wrong to live as I am now doing. I often think of it in secret, and cry over it, but what can I do? I was brought up in the country and allowed to run about with some other children. We were not taught anything, not even to read or write; twice I saw a gentleman who came down to the farm, and he kissed me and told me to be a good girl. Yes, I remember these things very well. I was about eleven the last time he came, and two years after I was sent up to town, carefully dressed and placed in a large drawing-room. After I had been there some time a gentleman came in with the person I had been sent to, and I directly recognized him as the one I had seen in the country. For the first time in my life I glanced at a looking-glass that hung on the wall, they being things we never saw in the country, and I thought the gentleman had changed his place and was standing before me, we were so alike. I then looked at him steadily for a few moments, and at last took his hand. He said something to me which I don't remember, and which I did not reply to. I asked him, when he had finished speaking, if he was my father. I don't know why I asked him. He seemed confused, and the lady of the house poured out some wine and gave me, after that I don't know what happened."

This may be a case of rare occurrence, but it is not so morally impossible as at first it appears.

In 1857, according to the best authorities, there were 8600 prostitutes known to the police, but this is far from being even an approximate return of the number of loose women in the metropolis. It scarcely does more than record the circulating harlotry of the Haymarket and Regent Street. Their actual numerical strength is very difficult to compute, for there is an amount of oscillatory prostitution it is easy to imagine, but impossible to substantiate. One of the peculiarities of this class is their remarkable freedom from disease. They are in the generality of cases notorious for their mental and physical elasticity. Syphilis is rarely fatal. It is an entirely distinct race that suffer from the ravages of the insidious diseases that the licence given to the passions and promiscuous intercourse engender. Young girls, innocent and inexperienced, whose devotion has not yet bereft them of their innate modesty and sense of shame, will allow their systems to be so shocked, and their constitutions so impaired, before the aid of the surgeon is sought for, that when he does arrive his assistance is almost useless.

We have before stated (p. 211) the assumed number of prostitutes in London to be about 80,000, and large as this total may appear, it is not improbable that it is below the reality rather than above it. One thing is certain—if it be an exaggerated statement—that the real number is swollen every succeeding year, for prostitution is an inevitable attendant upon extended civilization and increased population.

We divide prostitutes into three classes. First, those women who are kept by men of independent means; secondly, those women who live in apartments, and maintain themselves by the produce of their vagrant amours; and thirdly, those who dwell in brothels.

The state of the first of these is the nearest approximation to the holy state of marriage, and finds numerous defenders and supporters. These have their suburban villas, their carriages, horses, and sometimes a box at the opera. Their equipages are to be seen in the park, and occasionally through the influence of their aristocratic friends they succeed in obtaining vouchers for the most exclusive patrician balls.

Houses in which prostitutes lodge are those in which one or two prostitutes occupy private apartments; in most cases with the connivance of the proprietor. These generally resort to night-houses, where they have a greater chance of meeting with customers than they would have were they to perambulate the streets.

Brothels are houses where speculators board, dress, and feed women, living upon the farm of their persons. Under this head we must include introducing houses, where the women do not reside, but merely use the house as a place of resort in the daytime. Married women, imitating the custom of Messalina, whom Juvenal so vividly describes in his Satires, not uncommonly make use of these places. A Frenchwoman in the habit of frequenting a notorious house in James Street, Haymarket, said that she came to town four or five times in the week for the purpose of obtaining money by the prostitution of her body. She loved her husband, but he was unable to find any respectable employment, and were she not to supply him with the necessary funds for their household expenditure they would sink into a state of destitution, and anything, she added, with simplicity, was better than that. Of course her husband connived at what she did. He came to fetch her home every evening about ten o'clock. She had no children. She didn't wish to have any.

It must not be supposed that if some, perhaps a majority of them, eventually become comparatively respectable, and merge into the ocean of propriety, there are not a vast number whose lives afford matter for the most touching tragedies,—whose melancholy existence is one continual struggle for the actual necessaries of life, the occasional absence of which entails upon them a condition of intermittent starvation. A woman who has fallen like a star from heaven, may flash like a meteor in a lower sphere, but only with a transitory splendour. In time her orbit contracts, and the improvidence that has been her leading characteristic through life now trebles and quadruples the misery she experiences. To drown reflection she rushes to the gin palace, and there completes the work that she had already commenced so inauspiciously. The passion for dress, that distinguished her in common with her sex in former days, subsides into a craving for meretricious tawdry, and the bloom of health is superseded by ruinous and poisonous French compounds and destructive cosmetics. A hospital surgeon gave us the following description of the death of a French lorette, who at a very juvenile age had been entrapped and imported into this country. She had, according to her own statement, been born in one of the southern departments. When she was fourteen years old, the agent of some English speculator in human beings came into their neighbourhood and proposed that Anille should leave her native country and proceed to England, where he said there was a great demand for female domestic labour, which was much better paid for on the other side of the Channel. The proposition was entertained by the parents, and eagerly embraced by the girl herself, who soon afterwards, in company with several other girls, all deluded in a similar manner, were leaving the shores of their native country for a doubtful future in one with the language of which they were not even remotely acquainted. On their arrival their ruin was soon effected, and for some years they continued to enrich the proprietors of the house in which they resided, all the time remitting small sums to their families abroad, who were unwittingly and involuntarily existing upon the proceeds of their daughters' dishonour, and rejoicing in such unexpected success. After a while Anille was sent adrift to manage for herself. Naturally of a refined and sensitive disposition, she felt her position keenly, which induced a sadness almost amounting to hypochondria to steal over her, and although very pretty, she found this a great obstacle in the way of her success. She knew not how to simulate the hollow laugh or the reckless smile of her more volatile companions, and her mind became more diseased day by day, until she found it impracticable to think of endeavouring to hurl off the morbidity that had taken possession of her very soul. At last she fell a victim to a contagious disorder, the neglect of which ultimately necessitated her removal to the hospital. When there, she was found to be incurable; an operation was performed upon her but without success. She bore her illness with childish impatience, continually wishing for the end, and often imploring me with tearful eyes by the intervention of science to put an end to her misery. One afternoon, as usual, I came to see her. She exclaimed the moment she perceived me, I am cheerful to-day. May I not recover; I suffer no pain. But her looks belied her words; her features were frightfully haggard and worn; her eyes, dry and bloodshot, had almost disappeared in their sockets, and her general appearance denoted the approach of him she had been so constantly invoking. Unwrapping some bandages, I proceeded to examine her, when an extraordinary change came over her, and I knew that her dissolution was not far distant. Her mind wandered, and she spoke wildly and excitedly in her own language. After a while she exclaimed, "J'ignore où je suis. C'en est fait." An expression of intense suffering contracted her emaciated features. "Je n'en puis plus," she cried, and adding, after a slight pause, in a plaintive voice, "Je me meurs," her soul glided impalpably away, and she was a corpse. As a pendant to these remarks, I extract an expressive passage from an old book. "There are also women (like birds of passage) of a migratory nature, who remove after a certain time from St. James's and Marylebone end of the town to Covent Garden, then to the Strand, and from thence to St. Giles and Wapping; from which latter place they frequently migrate much further, even to New South Wales. Some few return in seven years, some in fourteen, and some not at all. During their stay here, like birds they make their nests upon feathers, some higher, some lower than others. At first they generally build them on the first-floor, afterwards on the second, and then up in the cock-loft and garrets, from whence they generally take to the open air, and become ambulatory and noctivagous, and as their price grows less, their wandering increases, when many perish from the inclemency of the weather, and others take their flight abroad."*

Seclusives, or those that live in Private Houses and Apartments.

Two classes of prostitutes come under this denomination—first, kept mistresses, and secondly, prima donnas or those who live in a superior style. The first of these is perhaps the most important division of the entire profession, when considered with regard to its effects upon the higher classes of society. Laïs, when under the protection of a prince of the blood; Aspasia, whose friend is one of the most influential noblemen in the kingdom; Phryne, the chère amie of a well-known officer in the guards, or a man whose wealth is proverbial on the Stock Exchange and the city,—have all great influence upon the tone of morality extant amongst the set in which their distinguished protectors move, and indeed the reflex of their dazzling profligacy falls upon

* Life and Adventures of Col. George Hanger, 1704.

and bewilders those who are in a lower condition of life, acting as an incentive to similar deeds of licentiousness though on a more limited scale. Hardly a parish in London is free from this impurity. Wherever the neighbourhood possesses peculiar charms, wherever the air is purer than ordinary, or the locality fashionably distinguished, these tubercles on the social system penetrate and abound. Again quoting from Dr. Ryan, although we cannot authenticate his statements—"It is computed, that 8,000,000*l*. are expended annually on this vice in London alone. This is easily proved: some girls obtain from twenty to thirty pounds a week, others more, whilst most of those who frequent theatres, casinos, gin palaces, music halls, &c., receive from ten to twelve pounds. Those of a still lower grade obtain about four or five pounds, some less than one pound, and many not ten shillings. If we take the average earnings of each prostitute at 100*l*. per annum, which is under the amount, it gives the yearly income of eight millions.

"Suppose the average expense of 80,000 amounts to 20*l*. each, 1,600,000*l*. is the result. This sum deducted from the earnings leaves 6,400,000*l*. as the income of the keepers of prostitutes, or supposing 5000 to be the number, above 1000*l*. per annum each — an enormous income for men in such a situation to derive when compared with the resources of many respectable and professional men."

Literally every woman who yields to her passions and loses her virtue is a prostitute, but many draw a distinction between those who live by promiscuous intercourse, and those who confine themselves to one man. That this is the case is evident from the returns before us. The metropolitan police do not concern themselves with the higher classes of prostitutes; indeed, it would be impossible, and impertinent as well, were they to make the attempt. Sir Richard Mayne kindly informed us that the latest computation of the number of public prostitutes was made on the 5th of April, 1858, and that the returns then showed a total of 7261.

It is frequently a matter of surprise amongst the friends of a gentleman of position and connection that he exhibits an invincible distaste to marriage. If they were acquainted with his private affairs their astonishment would speedily vanish, for they would find him already to all intents and purposes united to one who possesses charms, talents, and accomplishments, and who will in all probability exercise the same influence over him as long as the former continue to exist. The prevalence of this custom, and the extent of its ramifications is hardly dreamed of, although its effects are felt, and severely. The torch of Hymen burns less brightly than of yore, and even were the blacksmith of Gretna still exercising his vocation, he would find his business diminishing with startling rapidity year by year.

It is a great mistake to suppose that kept mistresses are without friends and without society; on the contrary, their acquaintance, if not select, is numerous, and it is their custom to order their broughams or their pony carriages, and at the fashionable hour pay visits and leave cards on one another.

They possess no great sense of honour, although they are generally more or less religious. If they take a fancy to a man they do not hesitate to admit him to their favour. Most kept women have several lovers who are in the habit of calling upon them at different times, and as they are extremely careful in conducting these amours they perpetrate infidelity with impunity, and in ninety-nine cases out of a hundred escape detection. When they are unmasked, the process, unless the man is very much infatuated, is of course summary in the extreme. They are dismissed probably with a handsome douceur and sent once more adrift. They do not remain long, however, in the majority of cases, without finding another protector.

A woman who called herself Lady —— met her admirer at a house in Bolton Row that she was in the habit of frequenting. At first sight Lord —— became enamoured, and proposed *sur le champ*, after a little preliminary conversation, that she should live with him. The proposal with equal rapidity and eagerness was accepted, and without further deliberation his lordship took a house for her in one of the terraces overlooking the Regent's Park, allowed her four thousand a year, and came as frequently as he could, to pass his time in her society. She immediately set up a carriage and a stud, took a box at the opera on the pit tier, and lived, as she very well could, in excellent style. The munificence of her friend did not decrease by the lapse of time. She frequently received presents of jewelry from him, and his marks of attention were constant as they were various. The continual contemplation of her charms instead of producing satiety added fuel to the fire, and he was never happy when out of her sight. This continued until one day he met a young man in her *loge* at the opera, whom she introduced as her cousin. This incident aroused his suspicions, and he determined to watch her more closely. She was surrounded by spies, and in reality did not possess one confidential attendant, for they were all bribed to betray her. For a time, more by accident than precaution or care on her part, she succeeded in eluding their vigilance, but at last the catastrophe happened; she was surprised with her paramour in a position that placed doubt out of the question, and the next day his lordship, with a few sarcastic remarks, gave her her *congé* and five hundred pounds.

These women are rarely possessed o education, although they undeniably have ability. If they appear accomplished you may rely that it is entirely superficial. Their disposition is volatile and thoughtless, which qualities are of course at variance with the existence of respectability. Their ranks too are recruited from a class where education is not much in vogue. The fallacies about clergymen's daughters and girls from the middle classes forming the majority of such women are long ago exploded; there may be some amongst them, but they are few and far between. They are not, as a rule, disgusted with their way of living; most of them consider it a means to an end, and in no measure degrading or polluting. One and all look forward to marriage and a certain state in society as their ultimate lot. This is their bourne, and they do all in their power to travel towards it.

"I am not tired of what I am doing," a woman once answered me, "I rather like it. I have all I want, and my friend loves me to excess. I am the daughter of a tradesman at Yarmouth. I learned to play the piano a little, and I have naturally a good voice. Yes, I find these accomplishments of great use to me; they are, perhaps, as you say, the only ones that could be of use to a girl like myself. I am three and twenty. I was seduced four years ago. I tell you candidly I was as much to blame as my seducer; I wished to escape from the drudgery of my father's shop. I have told you they partially educated me; I could cypher a little as well, and I knew something about the globes; so I thought I was qualified for something better than minding the shop occasionally, or sewing, or helping my mother in the kitchen and other domestic matters. I was very fond of dress, and I could not at home gratify

A NIGHT HOUSE.—KATE HAMILTON'S.

my love of display. My parents were stupid, easy-going old people, and extremely uninteresting to me. All these causes combined induced me to encourage the addresses of a young gentleman of property in the neighbourhood, and without much demur I yielded to his desires. We then went to London, and I have since that time lived with four different men. We got tired of one another in six months, and I was as eager to leave him as he was to get rid of me, so we mutually accommodated one another by separating. Well, my father and mother don't exactly know where I am or what I am doing, although if they had any penetration they might very well guess. Oh, yes! they know I am alive, for I keep them pleasantly aware of my existence by occasionally sending them money. What do I think will become of me? What an absurd question. I could marry to-morrow if I liked."

This girl was a fair example of her class. They live entirely for the moment, and care little about the morrow until they are actually pressed in any way, and then they are fertile in expedients.

We now come to the second class, or those we have denominated prima donnas. These are not kept like the first that we have just been treating of, although several men who know and admire them are in the habit of visiting them periodically. From these they derive a considerable revenue, but they by no means rely entirely upon it for support. They are continually increasing the number of their friends, which indeed is imperatively necessary, as absence and various causes thin their ranks considerably. They are to be seen in the parks, in boxes at the theatres, at concerts, and in almost every accessible place where fashionable people congregate; in fact in all places where admittance is not secured by vouchers, and in some cases, those apparently insuperable barriers fall before their tact and address. At night their favourite rendezvous is in the neighbourhood of the Haymarket, where the hospitality of Mrs. Kate Hamilton is extended to them after the fatigues of dancing at the Portland Rooms, or the excesses of a private party. Kate's may be visited not only to dissipate ennui, but with a view to replenishing an exhausted exchequer; for as Kate is careful as to who she admits into her rooms— men who are able to spend, and come with the avowed intention of spending, five or six pounds, or perhaps more if necessary— these supper-rooms are frequented by a better set of men and women than perhaps any other in London. Although these are seen at Kate's they would shrink from appearing at any of the cafés in the Haymarket, or at the supper-rooms with which the adjacent streets abound, nor would they go to any other casino than Mott's. They are to be seen between three and five o'clock in the Burlington Arcade, which is a well known resort of cyprians of the better sort. They are well acquainted with its Paphian intricacies, and will, if their signals are responded to, glide into a friendly bonnet shop, the stairs of which leading to the cœnacula or upper chambers are not innocent of their well formed "bien chaussée" feet. The park is also, as we have said, a favourite promenade, where assignations may be made or acquaintances formed. Equestrian exercise is much liked by those who are able to afford it, and is often as successful as pedestrian, frequently more so. It is difficult to say what position in life the parents of these women were in, but generally their standing in society has been inferior. Principles of lax morality were early inculcated, and the seed that has been sown has not been slow to bear its proper fruit.

It is true that a large number of milliners, dress-makers, furriers, hat-binders, silk-binders, tambour-makers, shoe-binders, slop-women, or those who work for cheap tailors, those in pastry-cooks, fancy and cigar shops, bazaars, servants to a great extent, frequenters of fairs, theatres, and dancing-rooms, are more or less prostitutes and patronesses of the numerous brothels London can boast of possessing; but these women do not swell the ranks of the class we have at present under consideration. More probably they are the daughters of tradesmen and of artizans, who gain a superficial refinement from being apprenticed, and sent to shops in fashionable localities, and who becoming tired of the drudgery sigh for the gaiety of the dancing-saloons, freedom from restraint, and amusements that are not in their present capacity within their reach.

Loose women generally throw a veil over their early life, and you seldom, if ever, meet with a woman who is not either a seduced governess or a clergyman's daughter; not that there is a word of truth in such an allegation—but it is their peculiar whim to say so.

To show the extent of education among women who have been arrested by the police during a stated period, we print the annexed table, dividing the virtuous criminals from the prostitutes.

DEGREE OF EDUCATION AMONGST PROSTITUTES.

Degree of Instruction amongst Prostitutes compared with the Degree of Instruction among Women not Prostitutes, arrested for breaking various laws (London). The City not included.

Periods—taking 10,000 in each period. Total of women arrested of both classes 405·362.				Degree of Instruction amongst virtuous women brought up in the Police Courts for various offences during the years elapsing from 1837 to 1854 inclusive.							
					Not able to read or write.		Able to read only, or read and write imperfectly.		Knowing how to read and write well.		Very well instructed.
1st period	6 years	1837–42	10,000		4,813		4,838		327		22
2nd „	6 „	1843–48	10,000		4,167		5,534		279		20
3rd „	6 „	1849–54	10,000		2,802		1,972		209		17
1st period	9 years	1837–45	10,000		4,570		5,098		312		20
2nd „	9 „	1846–54	10,000		3,247		6,504		320		19
Total period	18 „	1837–54	10,000		3,861		5,851		268		20

Periods—taking 10,000 in each period. Total of women arrested of both classes 405·362.				Degree of Instruction among Prostitutes similarly arrested.							
					Not able to read or write.		Able to read only, or read and write imperfectly.		Able to read and write well.		Very well educated.
1st period	6 years	1837–42	10,000		4,524		5,031		432		13
2nd „	6 „	1843–48	10,000		3,672		5,893		425		10
3rd „	6 „	1849–54	10,000		2,305		7,444		212		39
1st period	9 years	1837–45	10,000		4,109		5,424		455		12
2nd „	9 „	1849–54	10,000		2,821		6,910		236		33
Total period	18 „	1837–54	10,000		3,498		6,129		351		22

This table shows us that public women are a little less illiterate than those who together with them form the most infamous part of the population. But we must remember that this is hardly a fair criterion of the education of all the prostitutes, or of prostitutes as a class, because we have only summed up those who were arrested for some crime or offence, so we may justly suppose them to have been the worst of their class in every respect.

We see however that of the total number of women arrested during a period of 18 years, there were in every 10,000—

    3,498 not knowing how to read or write.
    6,129 able to read only, or read and write badly.
    351 able to read and write well.
    22 educated in a superior manner.

10,000

We next come to the consideration of convives, or those who live in the same house with a number of others, and we will commence with those who are independent of the mistress of the house. These women locate themselves in the immediate vicinity of the Haymarket, which at night is their principal scene of action, when the hospitable doors of the theatres and casinos are closed. They are charged enormously for the rooms they occupy, and their landlords defend themselves for their extortionate demands, by alleging that, as honesty is not a leading feature in the characters of their lodgers, they are compelled to protect their own interest by exacting an exorbitant rent. A drawing-room floor in Queen Street, Windmill Street, which is a favourite part on account of its proximity to the Argyll Rooms, is worth three, and sometimes four pounds a-week, and the other *étages* in proportion. They never stay long in one house, although some will remain for ten or twelve months in a particular lodging. It is their principle to get as deeply into debt as they are able, and then to pack up their things, have them conveyed elsewhere by stealth, and defraud the landlord of his money. The houses in some of the small streets in the neighbourhood of Langham Place are let to the people who underlet them for three hundred a-year, and in some cases at a higher rental. This class of prostitutes do not live together on account of a gregarious instinct, but simply from necessity, as their trade would necessarily exclude them from respectable lodging-houses. They soon form an acquaintance with the girls who inhabit the same house, and address one another as "my dear," an unmeaning, but very general epithet, an hour or two after their first meeting. They sometimes prefer the suburbs to reside in, especially while Cremorne is open; but some live at Brompton and Pimlico all the year round. One of their most remarkable characteristics is their generosity, which perhaps is unparalleled by the behaviour of any others, whether high or low in the social scale. They will not hesitate to lend one another money if they have it, whether they can spare it or not, although it is seldom that they can, from their innate recklessness and acquired improvidence. It is very common, too, for them to lend their bonnets and their dresses to their friends. If a woman of this description is voluble and garrulous, she is much sought after by the men who keep the cafés in the Haymarket, to sit decked out in gorgeous attire behind the counters, so that by her interesting appearance and the *esprit* she displays, the *habitués* of those places, but more usually those who pay only a casual visit, may be entrapped into purchasing some of the wares and fancy articles that are retailed at ten times their actual value. In order to effect this they will exert all their talents, and an inexperienced observer would imagine that they indeed entertain some feeling of affection or admiration for their victim, by the cleverness with which they simulate its existence. The man whose vanity leads him to believe that he is selected by the beautiful creature who condescends to address him, on account of his personal appearance, would be rather disgusted if he were to perceive the same blandishments lavished upon the next comer, and would regret the ten shillings he paid with pleasure for a glove-box, the positive market value of which is hardly one-fifth of the money he gave for it.

There is a great abandonment of everything that one may strictly speaking denominate womanly. Modesty is utterly annihilated, and shame ceases to exist in their composition. They all more or less are given to habits of drinking.

"When I am sad I drink," a woman once said to us. "I'm very often sad, although I appear to be what you call reckless. Well! we don't fret that we might have been ladies, because we never had a chance of that, but we have forfeited a position nevertheless, and when we think that we have fallen, never to regain that which we have descended from, and in some cases sacrificed everything for a man who has ceased to love and deserted us, we get mad. The intensity of this feeling does wear off a little after the first; but there's nothing like gin to deaden the feelings. What are my habits? Why, if I have no letters or visits from any of my friends, I get up about four o'clock, dress ("*en dishabille*") and dine; after that I may walk about the streets for an hour or two, and pick up any one I am fortunate enough to meet with, that is if I want money; afterwards I go to the Holborn, dance a little, and if any one likes me I take him home with me, if not I go to the Haymarket, and wander from one café to another, from Sally's to the Carlton, from Barn's to Sam's, and if I find no one there I go, if I feel inclined, to the divans. I like the Grand Turkish best, but you don't as a rule find good men in any of the divans. Strange things happen to us sometimes: we may now and then die of consumption; but the other day a lady friend of mine met a gentleman at Sam's, and yesterday morning they were married at St. George's, Hanover Square. The gentleman has lots of money, I believe, and he started off with her at once for the Continent. It is very true this is an unusual case; but we often do marry, and well too; why shouldn't we, we are pretty, we dress well, we can talk and insinuate ourselves into the hearts of men by appealing to their passions and their senses."

This girl was shrewd and clever, perhaps more so than those of her rank in the profession usually are; but her testimony is sufficient at once to dissipate the foolish idea that ought to have been exploded long ago, but which still lingers in the minds o both men and women, that the harlot's progress is short and rapid, and that there is no possible advance, moral or physical; and that once abandoned she must always be profligate.

Another woman told us, she had been a prostitute for two years; she became so from necessity; she did not on the whole dislike her way of living; she didn't think about the sin of it; a poor girl must live; she wouldn't be a servant for anything; this was much better. She was a lady's maid once, but lost her place for staying out one night with the man who seduced her; he afterwards deserted her, and then she became bad. She was fonder of dress than anything. On an average she had a new bonnet once a week, dresses not so often; she liked the casinos, and was charmed with Cremorne; she hated walking up and down the Haymarket, and seldom did it without she wanted money very much. She liked the Holborn better than the Argyll, and always danced.

Board Lodgers.

Board lodgers are those who give a portion of what they receive to the mistress of the brothel in return for their board and lodging. As we have had occasion to observe before, it is impossible to estimate the number of brothels in London, or even in particular parishes, not only because they are frequently moving from one district to another, but because our system so hates anything approaching to *espionage*, that the authorities do not think it worth their while to enter into any such computation. From this it may readily be understood how difficult the task of the statistician is. Perhaps it will be sufficient to say that these women are much more numerous than may at first be imagined; although those who give the whole of what they get in return for their board, lodging, and clothes are still more so. In Lambeth there are great numbers of the lowest of these houses, and only very recently the proprietors of some eight or ten of the worst were summoned before a police magistrate, and the parish officers who made the complaint bound over to prosecute at the sessions. It is much to be regretted that in dealing with such cases the method of procedure is not more expeditious and less expensive. Let us take for example one of the cases we have been quoting. A man is openly accused of keeping a ruffianly den filled with female wretches, destitute of every particle of modesty and bereft of every atom of shame, whose actual occupation is to rob, maltreat, and plunder the unfortunate individuals who so far stultify themselves as to allow the decoys to entrap them into their snares, let us hope, for the sake of humanity, while in a state of intoxication or a condition of imbecility. Very well; instead of an easy inexpensive process, the patriotic persons who have devoted themselves to the exposure of such infamous rascality, find themselves involved in a tedious criminal prosecution, and in the event of failure lay themselves open to an action. Mysterious disappearances, Waterloo Bridge tragedies, and verdicts of found drowned, are common enough in this great city. Who knows how many of these unfathomable affairs may have been originated, worked out, and consummated in some disgusting rookery in the worst parts of our most demoralized metropolitan parishes; but it is with the better class of these houses we are more particularly engaged at present. During the progress of these researches, we met a girl residing at a house in a street running out of Langham Place. Externally the house looked respectable enough; there was no indication of the profession or mode of life of the inmates, except that, from the fact of some of the blinds being down in the bed rooms, you might have thought the house contained an invalid. The rooms, when you were ushered in, were well, though cheaply furnished; there were coburg chairs and sofas, glass chandeliers, and handsome green curtains. The girl with whom we were brought into conversation was not more than twenty-three; she told us her age was twenty, but statements of a similar nature, when made by this class, are never to be relied on. At first she treated our inquiries with some levity, and jocularly inquired what we were inclined to stand, which we justly interpreted into a desire for something to drink; we accordingly "stood" a bottle of wine, which had the effect of making our informant more communicative. What she told us was briefly this. Her life was a life of perfect slavery, she was seldom if ever allowed to go out, and then not without being watched. Why was this? Because she would "cut it" if she got a chance, they knew that very well, and took very good care she shouldn't have much opportunity. Their house was rather popular, and they had lots of visitors; she had some particular friends who always came to see her. They paid her well, but she hardly ever got any of the money. Where was the odds, she couldn't go out to spend it? What did she want with money, except now and then for a drain of white satin. What was white satin? Where had I been all my life to ask such a question? Was I a dodger? She meant a parson No; she was glad of that, for she hadn't much idea of them, they were a canting lot. Well, white satin, if I must know, was gin, and I couldn't say she never taught me anything. Where was she born?

Somewhere in Stepney. What did it matter where; she could tell me all about it if she liked, but she didn't care. It touched her on the raw—made her feel too much. She was 'ticed when she was young, that is, she was decoyed by the mistress of the house some years ago. She met Mrs. —— in the street, and the woman began talking to her in a friendly way. Asked her who her father was (he was a journeyman carpenter), where he lived, extracted all about her family, and finally asked her to come home to tea with her. The child, delighted at the making the acquaintance of so kind and so well-dressed a lady, willingly acquiesced, without making any demur, as she never dreamt of anything wrong, and had not been cautioned by her father. She had lost her mother some years ago. She was not brought direct to the house where I found her? Oh! no. There was a branch establishment over the water, where they were broken in as it were. How long did she remain there? Oh! perhaps two months, maybe three; she didn't keep much account how time went. When she was conquered and her spirit broken, she was transported from the first house to a more aristocratic neighbourhood. How did they tame her? Oh! they made her drunk and sign some papers, which she knew gave them great power over her, although she didn't exactly know in what the said power consisted, or how it might be exercised. Then they clothed her and fed her well, and gradually inured her to that sort of life. And now, was there anything else I'd like to know particularly, because if there was, I'd better look sharp about asking it, as she was getting tired of talking, she could tell me. Did she expect to lead this life till she died? Well she never did, if I wasn't going to preachify. She couldn't stand that—anything but that.

I really begged to apologize if I had wounded her sensibility; I wasn't inquiring from a religious point of view, or with any particular motive. I merely wished to know, to satisfy my own curiosity.

Well, she thought me a very inquisitive old party, anyhow. At any rate, as I was so polite she did not mind answering my questions. Would she stick to it till she was a stiff un? She supposed she would; what else was there for her? Perhaps something might turn up; how was she to know? She never thought she would go mad; if she did, she lived in the present, and never went blubbering about as some did. She tried to be as jolly as she could; where was the fun of being miserable?

This is the philosophy of most of her sisterhood. This girl possessed a talent for repartee, which accomplishment she endeavoured to exercise at my expense, as will be perceived by the foregoing, though for many reasons I have adhered to her own vernacular. That her answers were true, I have no reason to question, and that this is the fate of very many young girls in London, there is little doubt; indeed, the reports of the Society for the Protection of Young Females sufficiently prove it. Female virtue in great cities has innumerable assailants, and the moralist should pity rather than condemn. We are by no means certain that meretricious women who have been in the habit of working before losing their virtue, at some trade or other, and are able to unite the two together, are conscious of any annoyance or a want of self-respect at being what they are. This class have been called the "amateurs," to contradistinguish them from the professionals, who devote themselves to it entirely as a profession. To be unchaste amongst the lower classes is not always a subject of reproach. The commerce of the sexes is so general that to have been immodest is very seldom a bar to marriage. The depravity of manners amongst boys and girls begins so very early, that they think it rather a distinction than otherwise to be unprincipled. Many a shoeblack, in his uniform and leathern apron, who cleans your boots for a penny at the corners of the streets, has his sweetheart. Their connection begins probably at the low lodging-houses they are in the habit of frequenting, or, if they have a home, at the penny gaffs and low cheap places of amusement, where the seed of so much evil is sown. The precocity of the youth of both sexes in London is perfectly astounding. The drinking, the smoking, the blasphemy, indecency, and immorality that does not even call up a blush is incredible, and charity schools and the spread of education do not seem to have done much to abate this scourge. Another very fruitful source of early demoralization is to be looked for in the quantities of penny and halfpenny romances that are sold in town and country. One of the worst of the most recent ones is denominated, "Charley Wag, or the New Jack Shepherd, a history of the most successful thief in London." To say that these are not incentives to lust, theft, and crime of every description is to cherish a fallacy. Why should not the police, by act of Parliament, be empowered to take cognizance of this shameful misuse of the art of printing? Surely some clauses could be added to Lord Campbell's Act, or a new bill might be introduced that would meet the exigencies of the case, without much difficulty.

Men frequent the houses in which women board and lodge for many reasons, the chief of which is secrecy; they also feel sure that the women are free from disease, if they know the house, and it bears an average reputation for being well conducted. Men in a certain position avoid publicity in their amours beyond all things, and dread being seen in the neighbourhood of the Haymarket or the Burlington Arcade at certain hours, as their professional reputation might be compromised. Many serious, demure people conceal the iniquities of their private lives in this way.

If Asmodeus were loquacious, how interesting and anecdotical a scandal-monger he might become!

Another woman told me a story, varying somewhat from that of the first I examined, which subsequent experience has shown me is slightly stereotyped. She was the victim of deliberate cold-blooded seduction; in course of time a child was born; up to this time her seducer had treated her with affection and kindness, but he now, after presenting her with fifty pounds, deserted her. Thrown on her own resources, as it were, she did not know what to do; she could not return to her friends, so she went into lodgings at a very small rental, and there lived until her money was expended. She then supported herself and her child by doing machine-work for a manufacturer, but at last bad times came, and she was thrown out of work; of course the usual amount of misery consequent on such a catastrophe ensued. She saw her child dying by inches before her face, and this girl, with tears in her eyes, assured me she thanked God for it. "I swear," she added, "I starved myself to nourish it, until I was nothing but skin and bone, and little enough of that; I knew from the first, the child must die, if things didn't improve, and I felt they wouldn't. When I looked at my little darling I knew well enough he was doomed, but he was not destined to drag on a weary existence as I was, and I was glad of it. It may seem strange to you, but while my boy lived, I couldn't go into the streets to save his life or my own—I couldn't do it. If there had been a foundling-hospital, I mean as I hear there is in foreign parts, I would have placed him there, and worked somehow, but there wasn't, and a crying shame it is too. Well, he died at last, and it was all over. I was half mad and three parts drunk after the parish burying, and I went into the streets at last; I rose in the world—(here she smiled sarcastically)—and I've lived in this house for years, but I swear to God I haven't had a moment's happiness since the child died, except when I've been dead drunk or maudlin."

Although this woman did not look upon the death of her child as a crime committed by herself, it was in reality none the less her doing; she shunned the workhouse, which might have done something for her, and saved the life, at all events, of her child; but the repugnance evinced by every woman who has any proper feeling for a life in a workhouse or a hospital, can hardly be imagined by those who think that, because people are poor, they must lose all feeling, all delicacy, all prejudice, and all shame.

Her remarks about a foundling-hospital are sensible; in the opinion of many it *is* a want that ought to be supplied. Infanticide is a crime much on the increase, and what mother would kill her offspring if she could provide for it in any way?

The analysis of the return of the coroners' inquests held in London, for the five years ending in 1860, shows a total of 1130 inquisitions on the bodies of children under two years of age, all of whom had been murdered. The average is 226 yearly.

Here we have 226 children killed yearly by their parents: this either shows that our institutions are defective, or that great depravity is inherent amongst Englishwomen. The former hypothesis is much more likely than the latter, which we are by no means prepared to indorse. This return, let it be understood, does not, indeed cannot, include the immense number of embryo children who are made away with by drugs and other devices, all of whom we have a right to suppose would have seen the light if adequate provision could have been found for them at their birth.

A return has also been presented to Parliament, at the instance of Mr. Kendal, M.P., from which we find that 157,485 summonses in bastardy cases were issued between the years 1845 and 1859 inclusive, but that only 124,218 applications against the putative fathers came on for hearing, while of this number orders for maintenance were only made in 107,776 cases, the remaining summonses, amounting to 15,981, being dismissed. This latter fact gives a yearly average of 1,141 illegitimate children thrown back on their wretched mothers. These statistics are sufficiently appalling, but there is reason to fear that they only give an approximate idea of the illegitimate infantile population, and more especially of the extent to which infanticide prevails.

THE NEW CUT.—EVENING.

Those who live in Low Lodging Houses.

In order to find these houses it is necessary to journey eastwards, and leave the artificial glitter of the West-end, where vice is pampered and caressed. Whitechapel, Wapping, Ratcliff Highway, and analogous districts, are prolific in the production of these infamies. St. George's-in-the-East abounds with them, kept, for the most part, by disreputable Jews, and if a man is unfortunate enough to fall into their clutches he is sure to become the spoil of Israel. We may, however, find many low lodging-houses without penetrating so far into the labyrinth of east London. There are numbers in Lambeth; in the Waterloo Road and contiguous streets; in small streets between Covent Garden and the Strand, some in one or two streets running out of Oxford Street. There is a class of women technically known as "bunters," who take lodgings, and after staying some time run away without paying their rent. These victimise the keepers of low lodging-houses successfully for years. A "bunter," whose favourite promenade, especially on Sundays, was the New Cut, Lambeth, said "she never paid any rent, hadn't done it for years, and never meant to. They was mostly Christ-killers, and chousing a Jew was no sin; leastways, none as she cared about committing. She boasted of it: had been known about town this ever so long as Swindling Sal. And there was another, a great pal of her'n, as went by the name of Chousing Bett. Didn't they know her in time? Lord bless me, she was up to as many dodges as there was men in the moon. She changed places, she never stuck to one long; she never had no things for to be sold up, and, as she was handy with her mauleys, she got on pretty well. It took a considerable big man, she could tell me, to kick her out of a house, and then when he done it she always give him something for himself, by way of remembering her. Oh! they had a sweet recollection of her, some on 'em. She'd crippled lots of the —— crucifiers." "Did she never get into a row?" "Lots on 'em, she believed me. Been quodded no end of times. She knew every beak as sot on the cheer as well as she knew Joe the magsman, who, she *might* say, wor a very perticaler friend of her'n." "Did he pay her well?" This was merely a question to ascertain the amount of remuneration that she, and others like her, were in the habit of receiving; but it had the effect of enraging her to a great extent. My informant was a tall, stout woman, about seven-and-twenty, with a round face, fat cheeks, a rather wheezy voice, and not altogether destitute of good looks. Her arms were thick and muscular, while she stood well on her legs, and altogether appeared as if she would be a formidable opponent in a street-quarrel or an Irish row.

"Did he pay well? Was I a-going to insult her? What was I asking her sich a 'eap of questions for? Why, Joe was good for a —— sight more than she thought I was!—"polite." Then she was sorry for it, never meant to be. Joe worn't a five-bobber, much less a bilker, as she'd take her dying oath I was." "Would she take a drop of summut?" "Well, she didn't mind if she did."

An adjournment to a public-house in the immediate vicinity, where "Swindling Sal" appeared very much at home, mollified and appeased her.

The "drop of summut short, miss," was responded to by the young lady behind the bar by a monosyllabic query, "Neat?" The reply being in the affirmative, a glass of gin was placed upon the marble counter, and rapidly swallowed, while a second, and a third followed in quick succession, much, apparently, to the envy of a woman in the same compartment, who, my informant told me in a whisper, was "Lushing Lucy," and a stunner—whatever the latter appellation might be worth. But the added "Me an' 'er 'ad a rumpus," was sufficient to explain the fact of their not speaking.

"What do you think you make a week?" at last I ventured to ask.

"Well, I'll tell yer," was the response: "one week with another I makes nearer on four pounds nor three—sometimes five. I 'ave done eight and ten. Now Joe, as you 'eered me speak on, he does it 'ansome, he does: I mean, you know, when he's in luck. He give me a fiver once after cracking a crib, and a nice spree me an' Lushing Loo 'ad over it. Sometimes I get three shillings, half-a-crown, five shillings, or ten occasionally, accordin' to the sort of man. What is this Joe as I talks about? Well, I likes your cheek, howsomever, he's a 'ousebreaker. I don't do anything in that way, never did, and shant; it aint safe, it aint. How did I come to take to this sort of life? It's easy to tell. I was a servant gal away down in Birmingham. I got tired of workin' and slavin' to make a livin', and getting a —— bad one at that; what o' five pun' a year and yer grub, I'd sooner starve, I would. After a bit I went to Coventry, cut Brummagem, as we calls it in those parts, and took up with the soldiers as was quartered there. I soon got tired of them. Soldiers is good—soldiers is—to walk with and that, but they don't pay;

cos why, they aint got no money; so I says to myself, I'll go to Lunnon, and I did. I soon found my level there. It is a queer sort of life, the life I'm leading, and now I think I'll be off. Good night to yer. I hope we'll know more of one another when we two meets again."

When she was gone I turned my attention to the woman I have before alluded to. "Lushing Loo" was a name uneuphemistic, and calculated to prejudice the hearer against the possessor. I had only glanced at her before, and a careful scrutiny surprised me, while it impressed me in her favour. She was lady-like in appearance, although haggard. She was not dressed in flaring colours and meretricious tawdry. Her clothes were neat, and evidenced taste in their selection, although they were cheap. I spoke to her; she looked up without giving me an answer, appearing much dejected. Guessing the cause, which was that she had been very drunk the night before, and had come to the public-house to get something more, but had been unable to obtain credit, I offered her half-a-crown, and told her to get what she liked with it. A new light came into her eyes; she thanked me, and, calling the barmaid, gave her orders, with a smile of triumph. Her taste was sufficiently aristocratic to prefer pale brandy to the usual beverage dispensed in gin-palaces. A "drain of pale," as she termed it, invigorated her. Glass after glass was ordered, till she had spent all the money I gave her. By this time she was perfectly drunk, and I had been powerless to stop her. Pressing her hand to her forehead, she exclaimed, "Oh, my poor head!" I asked what was the matter with her, and for the first time she condescended, or felt in the humour to speak to me. "My heart's broken," she said. "It has been broken since the twenty-first of May. I wish I was dead; I wish I was laid in my coffin. It won't be long first. I am doing it. I've just driven another nail in, and 'Lushing Loo,' as they call me, will be no loss to society. Cheer up; let's have a song. Why don't you sing?" she cried, her mood having changed, as is frequently the case with habitual drunkards, and a symptom that often precedes delirium tremens. "Sing, I tell you," and she began,

> The first I met a cornet was
> In a regiment of dragoons,
> I gave him what he didn't like,
> And stole his silver spoons.

When she had finished her song, the first verse of which is all I can remember, she subsided into comparative tranquillity. I asked her to tell me her history.

"Oh, I'm a seduced milliner," she said, rather impatiently; "anything you like."

It required some inducement on my part to make her speak, and overcome the repugnance she seemed to feel at saying any thing about herself.

She was the daughter of respectable parents, and at an early age had imbibed a fondness for a cousin in the army, which in the end caused her ruin. She had gone on from bad to worse after his desertion, and at last found herself among the number of low transpontine women. I asked her why she did not enter a refuge, it might save her life.

"I don't wish to live," she replied. "I shall soon get D. T., and then I'll kill myself in a fit of madness."

Nevertheless I gave her the address of the secretary of the Midnight Meeting Association, Red Lion Square, and was going away when a young Frenchmen entered the bar, shouting a French song, beginning

> Vive l'amour, le vin, et le tabac,

and I left him in conversation with the girl, whose partiality for the brandy bottle had gained her the suggestive name I have mentioned above.

The people who keep the low lodging-houses where these women live, are rapacious, mean, and often dishonest. They charge enormously for their rooms in order to guarantee themselves against loss in the event of their harbouring a "bunter" by mistake, so that the money paid by their honest lodgers covers the default made by those who are fraudulent.

Dr. Ryan, in his book on prostitution, puts the following extraordinary passage, whilst writing about low houses:—

"An *enlightened medical gentleman* assured me that near what is called the Fleet Ditch almost every house is the lowest and most infamous brothel. There is an aqueduct of large dimensions, into which murdered bodies are precipitated by bullies and discharged at a considerable distance into the Thames, without the slightest chance of recovery."

Mr. Richelot quotes this with the greatest gravity, and adduces it as a proof of the immorality and crime that are prevalent to such an awful extent in London. What a pity the enlightened medical gentleman did not affix his name to this statement as a guarantee of its authenticity!

When speaking of low street-walkers, the same author says:—

"These truly unfortunate creatures are closely watched whilst walking the streets, so that it is impossible for them to escape, and if they attempt it, the spy, often a female child, hired for the purpose, or a bully, or procuress, charges the fugitive with felony, as escaping with the clothes of the brothel-keeper, when the police officer on duty immediately arrests the delinquent, and takes her to the station-house of his divison, but more commonly gives her up to the brothel-keeper, who rewards him. This inhuman and infamous practice is of nightly occurrence in this metropolis. When the forlorn, unfortunate wretch returns to her infamous abode, she is maltreated and kept nearly naked during the day, so that she cannot attempt to run away. She is often half starved, and at night sent again into the streets as often as she is disengaged, while all the money she receives goes to her keeper whether male or female. This is not an exaggerated picture, but a fact attested by myself. I have known a girl, aged fifteen years, who in one night knew twelve men, and produced to her keeper as many pounds."

"Paucis horis, hæ puellæ sex vel septem hominibus congruunt, lavant et bibunt post singulum alcoholis paululum (vulgo brandy vel gin) et dein paratæ sunt aliis."

With what a vivid imagination the writer of these striking paragraphs must have been gifted. The Arabian Nights and the Tales of the Genii that are so charmingly improbable, are really matter of fact in comparison. If we multiply 12 by 365, what is the result? We never took such interest in arithmetic before: $12 \times 365 = 4380$. This total of course represents pounds; why, it is nearly equal to the salary of a puisne judge! But perhaps the young lady whose interesting age is fifteen, is not so fortunate every night. Let us reduce it by one half; $4380 \div 2 = 2190$. Two thousand one hundred and ninety pounds per annum is a very handsome income; and after such a calculation, can we wonder that a meretricious career is alluring and attractive to certain members of the fair sex, especially when "hæ puellæ" make it "paucis horis?" So lucrative a speculation cannot be included in the category of those who are "kept nearly naked during the day, and often half starved." We suggest this on our own responsibility, for we have not been an "eye-witness" of such precocious profligacy; but we make the suggestion because it is something like nigger-keeping in the Southern States of America. A full-grown, hearty negro is a flesh and blood equivalent for a thousand or two thousand dollars.

If he were "larruped" and bullied, he would perhaps die, or at any rate not work so well, and a loss to his owner would ensue that Pompey's massa would not be slow to discover. By parity of reasoning the white slave of England must also be treated well, or it naturally follows that she will not be so productive, and the 12*l*. received from as many men in a few hours, may dwindle to as many shillings, gleaned with difficulty in a great number of hours.

Dr. Michael Ryan evidently possesses an extensive acquaintance among remarkable men. Let us examine the statement of "my informant, a truly moral character, a respectable citizen, the father of a family," who gives the following account of bullies:—

"Two acquaintances of his, men of the world" (we submit with all humility that truly moral characters, respectable citizens, and fathers of families ought to be more select in their acquaintance, for birds of a feather, &c.), "were entrapped in one of the Parks by two apparently virtuous females, about twenty years of age, who were driving in a pony phaeton, to accompany them home to a most notoriously infamous square in this metropolis. All was folly and debauchery till the next morning. But when the visitors were about to depart, they were sternly informed they must pay more money. They replied they had no more, but would call again, when their vicious companions yelled vociferously. Two desperate-looking villains, accompanied by a large mastiff, now entered the apartment and threatened to murder the delinquents if they did not immediately pay more money. A frightful fight ensued. The mastiff seized one of the assaulted by the thigh, and tore out a considerable portion of the flesh. The bullies were, however, finally laid prostrate: the assailed forced their way into the street through the drawing-room windows; a crowd speedily assembled, and on learning the nature of the murderous assault, the mob attacked the house and *nearly demolished it before the police arrived*" (where *were* the police?). "The injured parties effected their escape during the commotion."

What a surprising adventure! Haroun Alraschid would have had it written in letters of gold. The man of the world, who had a considerable portion of the flesh torn out of his leg by the terrible mastiff, must have been the model of an athlete to effect his escape and punish his bully after such a catastrophe, more particularly as he jumped out of the drawing-room window.

Then that mob, that ferocious mob that nearly demolished the house before the police arrived! Mob more terrible than any that the faubourgs St. Antoine or St. Jacques could furnish during a bread riot in Paris, to harry the government, and erect barricades. What a horror truly moral characters must entertain of apparently virtuous females driving pony phaetons in the Parks! A little further on the same respectable citizen informs us, in addition, "that in a certain court near another notoriously profligate square, which was pulled down a few years ago, several skeletons were found under the floor, on which inquests were held by the coroner." What ghastly ideas float through the mind and obscure the mental vision of that father of a family!

That rows and disturbances often take place in disorderly houses, is not to be denied. A few isolated instances of men being attacked or robbed when drunk may be met with; but that there are houses whose keepers systematically plunder and murder their frequenters our experience does not prove, nor do we for an instant believe it to be the case. Foreigners who write about England are only too eager to meet with such stories in print, and they transfer them bodily with the greatest glee to their own pages, and parade them as being of frequent occurrence, perhaps nightly, in houses of ill fame.

Prostitutes of a certain class do not hesitate to rob drunken men, if they think they can do so with safety. If they get hold of a gentleman who would not like to give the thief in charge, and bring the matter before the public, they are comparatively safe.

Sailors' Women.

Many extraordinary statements respecting sailors' women have at different times been promulgated by various authors; and from what has gone forth to the world, those who take an interest in such matters have not formed a very high opinion of the class in question.

The progress of modern civilization is so rapid and so wonderful, that the changes which take place in the brief space of a few years are really and truly incredible.

That which ten, fifteen, or twenty years might have been said with perfect truth about a particular district, or an especial denomination, if repeated now would, in point of fact, be nothing but fiction of the grossest and most unsubstantial character. Novelists who have never traversed the localities they are describing so vividly, or witnessed the scenes they depict with such graphic distinctness, do a great deal more to mislead the general public than a casual observer may at first think himself at liberty to believe.

The upper ten thousand and the middle-classes as a rule have to combat innumerable prejudices, and are obliged to reject the traditions of their infancy before they thoroughly comprehend the actual condition of that race of people, which they are taught by immemorial prescription to regard as immensely inferior, if not altogether barbarous.

It is necessary to make these prefatory remarks before declaring that of late years everything connected with the industrious classes has undergone as complete a transformation as any magic can effect upon the stage. Not only is the condition of the people changed, but they themselves are as effectually metamorphosed. I shall describe the wonders that have been accomplished in a score or two of years in and about St. Giles's by a vigilant and energetic police-force, better parochial management, schools, washhouses, mechanics' institutes, and lodging-houses that have caused to disappear those noisome, pestilential sties that pigs would obstinately refuse to wallow in.

The spread of enlightenment and education has also made itself visible in the increased tact and proficiency of the thief himself; and this is one cause of the amelioration of low and formerly vicious neighbourhoods. The thief no longer frequents places where the police know very well how to put their hands upon him. Quitting the haunts where he was formerly so much at home and at his ease, he migrates westwards, north, south, anywhere but the exact vicinity you would expect to meet him in. Nor is the hostility of the police so much directed against expert and notorious thieves. They of course do not neglect an opportunity of making a capture, and plume themselves when that capture is made, but they have a certain sort of respect for a thief who is professionally so; who says, "It is the way by which I choose to obtain my living, and were it otherwise I must still elect to be a thief, for I have been accustomed to it from my childhood. My character is already gone, no one would employ me, and, above all, I take a pride in thieving skilfully, and setting your detective skill at defiance."

It is indeed the low petty thief, the area-sneak, and that *genus* that more especially excites the spleen, and rouses the ire of your modern policeman. The idle, lazy scoundrel who will not work when he can obtain it at the docks and elsewhere, who goes cadging about because his own inherent depravity, and naturally base instincts deprive him of a spark of intelligence, an atom of honest feeling, to point to a better and a different goal. Emigration is as a thing unexisting to them; they live a life of turpitude, preying upon society; they pass half their days in a prison, and they die prematurely unregretted and unmourned.

Whitechapel has always been looked upon as a suspicious, unhealthy locality. To begin, its population is a strange amalgamation of Jews, English, French, Germans, and other antagonistic elements that must clash and jar, but not to such an extent as has been surmised and reported. Whitechapel has its theatres, its music-halls, the cheap rates of admission to which serve to absorb numbers of the inhabitants, and by innocently amusing them soften their manners and keep them out of mischief and harm's way.

The Earl of Effingham, a theatre in Whitechapel Road, has been lately done up and restored, and holds three thousand people. It has no boxes; they would not be patronized if they were in existence. Whitechapel does not go to the play in kid-gloves and white ties. The stage of the Effingham is roomy and excellent, the trap-work very extensive, for Whitechapel rejoices much in pyrotechnic displays, blue demons, red demons, and vanishing Satans that disappear in a cloud of smoke through an invisible hole in the floor. Great is the applause when gauzy nymphs rise like so many Aphrodites from the sea, and sit down on apparent sunbeams midway between the stage and the theatrical heaven.

The Pavilion is another theatre in the Whitechapel Road, and perhaps ranks higher than the Effingham. The Pavilion may stand comparison, with infinite credit to itself and its architect, with more than one West-end theatre. People at the West-end who never in their dreams travel farther east than the dividend and transfer department of the Bank of England in Threadneedle Street, have a vague idea that East-end theatres strongly resemble the dilapidated and decayed Soho in Dean Street, filled with a rough, noisy set of drunken thieves and prostitutes. It is time that these ideas should be exploded. Prostitutes and thieves of course do find their way into theatres and other places of amusement, but perhaps if you were to rake up all the bad characters in the neighbourhood they would not suffice to fill the pit and gallery of the Pavilion.

On approaching the play-house, you observe prostitutes standing outside in little gangs and knots of three or four, and you will also see them inside, but for the most part they are accompanied by their men. Sergeant Prior of the H division, for whose services I am indebted to the courtesy of Superintendent White, assured me that when sailors landed in the docks, and drew their wages, they picked up some women to whom they considered themselves married pro tem., and to whom they gave the money they had made by their last voyage. They live with the women until the money is gone, (and the women generally treat the sailors honourably). They go to sea again, make some more, come home, and repeat the same thing over again. There are perhaps twelve or fifteen public-houses licensed for music in St. George's Street and Ratcliff Highway: most of them a few years ago were thronged, now they can scarcely pay their expenses; and it is anticipated that next year many of them will be obliged to close.

This is easily accounted for. Many sailors go further east to the K division, which includes Wapping, Bluegate, &c.; but the chief cause, the *fons et origo* of the declension is simply the institution of sailors' savings banks. There is no longer the money to be spent that there used to be. When a sailor comes on shore, he will probably go to the nearest sailors' home, and place his money in the bank. Drawing out again a pound or so, with which he may enjoy himself for a day or two, he will then have the rest of his money transmitted to his friends in the country, to whom he will himself go as soon as he has had his fling in town; so that the money that used formerly to be expended in one centre is spread over the entire country, *ergo* and very naturally the public-house keepers feel the change acutely. To show how the neighbourhood has improved of late years, I will mention that six or eight years ago the Eastern Music Hall was frequented by such ruffians that the proprietor told me he was only too glad when twelve o'clock came, that he might shut the place up, and turn out his turbulent customers, whose chief delight was to disfigure and ruin each other's physiognomy.

Mr. Wilton has since then rebuilt his concert-room, and erected a gallery that he sets apart for sailors and their women. The body of the hall is filled usually by tradesmen, keepers of tally-shops, &c., &c.

And before we go further a word

about tally-shops. Take the New Road, Whitechapel, which is full of them. They present a respectable appearance, are little two-storied houses, clean, neat, and the owners are reputed to have the Queen's taxes ready when the collectors call for them. The principle of the tally business is this:—A man wants a coat, or a woman wants a shawl, a dress, or some other article of feminine wearing apparel. Being somewhat known in the neighbourhood, as working at some trade or other, the applicant is able to go to the tally-shop, certain of the success of his or her application.

She obtains the dress she wishes for, and agrees to pay so much a week until the whole debt is cleared off. For instance, the dress costs three pounds, a sum she can never hope to possess in its entirety. Well, five shillings a week for three months will complete the sum charged; and the woman by this system of accommodation is as much benefited as the tallyman.

The British Queen, a concert-room in the Commercial Road, is a respectable, well-conducted house, frequented by low prostitutes, as may be expected, but orderly in the extreme, and what more can be wished for? The sergeant remarked to me, if these places of harmless amusement were not licensed and kept open, much evil would be sown and disseminated throughout the neighbourhood, for it may be depended something worse and ten times lower would be substituted. People of all classes must have recreation. Sailors who come on shore after a long cruise *will* have it; and, added the sergeant, we give it them in a way that does no harm to themselves or anybody else. Rows and disturbances seldom occur, although, of course, they may be expected now and then. The dancing-rooms close at twelve—indeed their frequenters adjourn to other places generally before that hour, and very few publics are open at one. I heard that there had been three fights at the Prussian Eagle, in Ship Alley, Wellclose Square, on the evening I visited the locality; but when I arrived I saw no symptoms of the reported pugnacity of the people assembled, and this was the only rumour of war that reached my ears.

Ship Alley is full of foreign lodging-houses. You see written on a blind an inscription that denotes the nationality of the keeper and the character of the establishment; for instance *Hollandsche lodgement*, is sufficient to show a Dutchman that his own language is spoken, and that he may have a bed if he chooses.

That there are desperate characters in the district was sufficiently evidenced by what I saw when at the station-house. Two women, both well-known prostitutes, were confined in the cells, one of whom had been there before no less than *fourteen times*, and had only a few hours before been brought up charged with nearly murdering a man with a poker. Her face was bad, heavy, and repulsive; her forehead, as well as I could distinguish by the scanty light thrown into the place by the bulls-eye of the policeman, was low; her nose was short and what is called pudgy, having the nostrils dilated; and she abused the police for disturbing her when she wished to go to sleep, a thing, from what I saw, I imagined rather difficult to accomplish, as she had nothing to recline upon but a hard sort of locker attached to the wall, and running all along one side and at the bottom of the cell.

The other woman, whose name was O'Brien, was much better looking than her companion in crime; her hand was bandaged up, and she appeared faint from loss of blood. The policeman lifted her head up, and asked her if she would like anything to eat. She replied she could drink some tea, which was ordered for her. She had met a man in a public-house in the afternoon, who was occupied in eating some bread and cheese. In order to get into conversation with him, she asked him to give her some, and on his refusing she made a snatch at it, and caught hold of the knife he was using with her right hand, inflicting a severe wound: notwithstanding the pain of the wound, which only served to infuriate her, she flew at the man with a stick and beat him severely over the head, endangering his life; for which offence she was taken by the police to the station-house and locked up.

There are very few English girls who can be properly termed sailors' women; most of them are either German or Irish. I saw numbers of German, tall brazen-faced women, dressed in gaudy colours, dancing and pirouetting in a fantastic manner in a dancing-room in Ratcliff Highway.

It may be as well to give a description of one of the dancing-rooms frequented by sailors and their women.

Passing through the bar of the public-house you ascend a flight of stairs and find yourself in a long room well lighted by gas. There are benches placed along the walls for the accommodation of the dancers, and you will not fail to observe the orchestra, which is well worthy of attention. It consists, in the majority of cases, of four musicians, bearded shaggy-looking foreigners, probably Germans, including a fiddle, a cornet, and two fifes or flutes. The orchestra is usually penned up in a corner of the room, and placed upon a dais or raised desk, to get upon which you ascend two steps; the front is boarded up with deal, only leaving a small door at one end to admit the performers, for whose convenience either a bench is erected or chairs supplied. There is a little ledge to place the music on, which is as often as not embellished with pewter pots. The music itself is striking in the extreme, and at all events exhilarating in the highest degree. The shrill notes of the fifes, and the braying of the trumpet in very quick time, rouses the excitement of the dancers, until they whirl round in the waltz with the greatest velocity.

I was much struck by the way in which the various dances were executed. In the first place, the utmost decorum prevailed, nor did I notice the slightest tendency to indecency. Polkas and waltzes seemed to be the favourites, and the steps were marvellously well done, considering the position and education of the company. In many cases there was an exhibition of grace and natural ease that no one would have supposed possible; but this was observable more amongst foreigners than English. The generality of the women had not the slightest idea of dancing. There was very little beauty abroad that night, at least in the neighbourhood of Ratcliff Highway. It might have been hiding under a bushel, but it was not patent to a casual observer. Yet I must acknowledge there was something prepossessing about the countenances of the women, which is more than could be said of the men. It might have been a compound of resignation, indifference, and recklessness, through all of which phases of her career a prostitute must go; nor is she thoroughly inured to her vocation until they have been experienced, and are in a manner mingled together. There was a certain innate delicacy about those women, too, highly commendable to its possessors. It was not the artificial refinement of the West-end, nothing of the sort, but genuine womanly feeling. They did not look as if they had come there for pleasure exactly, they appeared too business-like for that; but they did seem as if they would like, and intended, to unite the two, business and pleasure, and enjoy themselves as much as the circumstances would allow. They do not dress in the dancing-room, they attire themselves at home, and walk through the streets in their ball costume, without their bonnets, but as they do not live far off this is not thought much of. I remarked several women unattached sitting by themselves, in one place as many as half-a-dozen.

The faces of the sailors were vacant, stupid, and beery. I could not help thinking one man I saw at the Prussian Eagle a perfect Caliban in his way. There was an expression of owlish cunning about his heavy-looking features that, uniting with the drunken leer sitting on his huge mouth, made him look but a " very indifferent monster."

I noticed a sprinkling of coloured men and a few thorough negroes scattered about here and there.

The sergeant chanced to be in search of a woman named Harrington, who had committed a felony, and in the execution of his duty he was obliged to search some notorious brothels that he thought might harbour the delinquent.

We entered a house in Frederick Street (which is full of brothels, almost every house being used for an immoral purpose). But the object of our search was not there, and we proceeded to Brunswick Street, more generally known in the neighbourhood and to the police as "Tiger Bay;" the inhabitants and frequenters of which place are very often obliged to enter an involuntary appearance in the Thames police court. Tiger Bay, like Frederick Street, is full of brothels and thieves' lodging houses. We entered No. 6, accompanied by two policemen in uniform, who happened to be on duty at the entrance to the place, as they wished to apprehend a criminal whom they had reason to believe would resort for shelter, after the night's debauch, to one of the dens in the Bay. We failed to find the man the police wanted, but on descending to the kitchen, we discovered a woman sitting on a chair, evidently waiting up for some one.

"That woman," said the sergeant, "is one of the lowest class we have; she is not only a common prostitute herself, and a companion of ruffians and thieves, but the servant of prostitutes and low characters as debased as herself, with the exception of their being waited upon by her."

We afterwards searched two houses on the opposite side of the way. The rooms occupied by the women and their sailors were larger and more roomy than I expected to find them. The beds were what are called "fourposters," and in some instances were surrounded with faded, dirty-looking, chintz curtains. There was the usual amount of cheap crockery on the mantel-pieces, which were surmounted with a small looking-glass in a rosewood or gilt frame. When the magic word "Police" was uttered, the door flew open, as the door of the robbers' cave swung back on its hinges when Ali Baba exclaimed "Sesame." A few seconds were allowed for the person who opened the door to retire to the couch, and then our visual circuit of the chamber took place. The sailors did not evince any signs of hostility at our somewhat unwarrantable intrusion, and we in every case made our exit peacefully, but without finding the felonious woman we were in search of; which might cause sceptical people to regard her as slightly apocryphal, but in reality such was not the case, and in all probability by this time justice has claimed her own.

A glance at the interior of the Horse and Leaping Bar concluded our nocturnal wanderings. This public-house is one of the latest in the district, and holds out accommodation for man and beast till the small hours multiply themselves considerably.

Most of the foreign women talk English pretty well, some excellently, some of course imperfectly; their proficiency depending upon the length of their stay in the country. A German woman told me the following story:—

"I have been in England nearly six years. When I came over I could not speak a word of your language, but I associated with my own countrymen. Now I talk the English well, as well as any, and I go with the British sailor. I am here to-night in this house of dancing with a sailor English, and I have known him two week. His ship is in docks, and will not sail for one month from this time I am now speaking. I knew him before, one years ago and a half. He always lives with me when he come on shore. He is nice man and give me all his money when he land always. I take all his money while he with me, and not spend it quick as some of your English women do. If I not to take care, he would spend all in one week. Sailor boy always spend money like rain water; he throw it into the street and not care to pick it up again, leave it for crossing-sweeper or errand-boy who pass that way. I give him little when he want it; he know me well and have great deal confidence in me. I am honest, and he feel he can trust me. Suppose he have twenty-four pound when he leave his ship, and he stay six week on land, he will spend with me fifteen or twenty, and he will give me what left when he leave me, and we amuse ourself and keep both ourself with the rest. It very bad for sailor to keep his money himself; he will fall into bad hands; he will go to ready-made outfitter or slop-seller, who will sell him clothes dreadful dear and ruin him. I know very many sailors—six, eight, ten, oh! more than that. They are my husbands. I am not married, of course not, but they think me their wife while they are on shore. I do not care much for any of them; I have a lover of my own, he is waiter in a lodging and coffee house; Germans keep it; he is German and he comes from Berlin, which is my town also. I is born there."

Shadwell, Spitalfields, and contiguous districts are infested with nests of brothels as well as Whitechapel. To attract sailors, women and music must be provided for their amusement. In High Street, Shadwell, there are many of these houses, one of the most notorious of which is called The White Swan, or, more commonly, Paddy's Goose; the owner of which is reported to make money in more ways than one. Brothel-keeping is a favourite mode of investing money in this neighbourhood. Some few years ago a man called James was prosecuted for having altogether thirty brothels; and although he was convicted, the nuisance was by no means in the slightest degree abated, as the informer, by name Brooks, has them all himself at the present time.

There are two other well-known houses in High Street, Shadwell—The Three Crowns, and The Grapes, the latter not being licensed for dancing.

Paddy's Goose is perhaps the most popular house in the parish. It is also very well thought of in high quarters. During the Crimean war, the landlord, when the Government wanted sailors to man the fleet, went among the shipping in the river, and enlisted numbers of men. His system of recruiting was very successful. He went about in a small steamer with a band of music and flags, streamers and colours flying. All this rendered him popular with the Admiralty authorities, and made his house extensively known to the sailors, and those connected with them.

Inspector Price, under whose supervision the low lodging-houses in that part of London are placed, most obligingly took me over one of the lowest lodging-houses, and one of the best, forming a strange contrast, and both presenting an admirable example of the capital working of the most excellent Act that regulates them. We went into a large room, with a huge fire blazing cheerily at the furthest extremity, around which were grouped some ten or twelve people, others were scattered over various parts of the room. The attitudes of most were listless; none seemed to be reading; one was cooking his supper; a few amused themselves by criticising us, and canvassing as to the motives of our visit, and our appearance altogether. The inspector was well known to the keeper of the place, who treated him with the utmost civility and respect. The greatest cleanliness prevailed everywhere. Any one was admitted to this house who could command the moderate sum of threepence. I was informed those who frequented it were, for the most part, prostitutes and thieves. That is thieves and their associates. No questions were asked of those who paid their money and claimed a night's lodging in return. The establishment contained forty beds. There were two floors. The first was divided into little boxes by means of deal boards, and set apart for married people, or those who represented themselves to be so. Of course, as the sum paid for the night's lodging was so small, the lodgers could not expect clean sheets, which were only supplied once a week. The sheets were indeed generally black, or very dirty. How could it be otherwise? The men were often in a filthy state, and quite unaccustomed to anything like cleanliness, from which they were as far as from godliness. The floors and the surroundings were clean, and highly creditable to the management upstairs; the beds were not crowded together, but spread over the surface in rows, being a certain distance from one another. Many of them were already occupied, although it was not eleven o'clock, and the house is generally full before morning. The ventilation was very complete, and worthy of attention. There were several ventilators on each side of the room, but not in the roof—all were placed in the side.

The next house we entered was more aristocratic in appearance. You entered through some glass doors, and going along a small passage found yourself in a large apartment, long and narrow, resembling a coffee-room. The price of admission was precisely the same, but the frequenters were chiefly working men, sometimes men from the docks, respectable mechanics, &c. No suspicious characters were admitted by the proprietor on any pretence, and he by this means kept his house select. Several men were seated in the compartments reading newspapers, of which there appeared to be an abundance. The accommodation was very good, and everything reflected great credit upon the police, who seem to have the most unlimited jurisdiction, and complete control over the low people and places in the East-end of London.

Bluegate fields is nothing more or less than a den of thieves, prostitutes, and ruffians of the lowest description. Yet the police penetrate unarmed without the slightest trepidation. There I witnessed sights that the most morbid novelist has described, but which have been too horrible for those who have never been on the spot to believe. We entered a house in Victoria Place, running out of Bluegate, that had no street-door, and penetrating a small passage found ourselves in a kitchen, where the landlady was sitting over a miserable coke fire; near her there was a girl, haggard and woe-begone. We put the usual question, Is there any one upstairs? And on being told that the rooms were occupied, we ascended to the first floor, which was divided into four small rooms. The house was only a two-storied one. The woman of the place informed me, she paid five shillings a-week rent, and charged the prostitutes who lodged with her four shillings a-week for the miserable apartments she had to offer for their accommodation; but as the shipping in the river was very slack just now, times were hard with her.

The house was a wretched tumble-down hovel, and the poor woman complained bitterly that her landlord would make no repairs. The first room we entered contained a Lascar, who had come over in some vessel, and his woman. There was a sickly smell in the chamber, that I discovered proceeded from the opium he had been smoking. There was not a chair to be seen; nothing but a table, upon which were placed a few odds-and-ends. The Lascar was lying on a palliasse placed upon the floor (there was no bedstead), apparently stupefied from the effects of the opium he had been taking. A couple of old tattered blankets sufficed to cover him. By his bedside sat his woman, who was half idiotically endeavouring to derive some stupefaction from the ashes he had left in his pipe. Her face was grimy and unwashed, and her hands so black and filthy that mustard-and-cress might have been sown successfully upon them. As she was huddled up with her back against the wall she appeared an animated bundle of rags. She was apparently a powerfully made woman, and although her face was wrinkled and careworn, she did not look exactly decrepit, but more like one thoroughly broken down in spirit than in body. In all probability she was diseased; and the disease communicated by the Malays, Lascars, and Orientals generally, is said to be the most frightful form of lues to be met with in Europe. It goes by the name of the Dry ——, and is much dreaded by all the women in the neighbourhood of the docks. Leaving this wretched couple, who were too much overcome with the fumes of opium to answer any questions, we went into another room, which should more correctly be called a hole. There was not an atom of furniture in it, nor a bed, and yet it contained a woman. This woman was lying on the floor, with not even a bundle of straw beneath her, rapped up in what appeared to be a shawl, but which might have been taken for the dress of a scarecrow feloniously abstracted from a corn-field, without any very great stretch of the imagination. She started up as we kicked open the door that was loose on its hinges, and did not shut properly, creaking strangely on its rusty hinges as it swung sullenly back. Her face was shrivelled and famine-stricken, her eyes bloodshot and glaring, her features disfigured slightly with disease, and her hair dishevelled, tangled, and matted. More like a beast in his lair than a human being in her home was this woman. We spoke to her, and from her replies concluded she was an Irishwoman. She said she was charged nothing for the place she slept in. She cleaned out the water-closets in the daytime, and for these services she was given a lodging gratis.

The next house we entered was in Bluegate Fields itself. Four women occupied the kitchen on the ground-floor. They were waiting for their men, probably thieves. They had a can of beer, which they passed from one to the other. The woman of the house had gone out to meet her husband, who was to be liberated from prison that night, having been imprisoned for a burglary three years ago, his term of incarceration happening to end that day. His friends were to meet at his house and celebrate his return by an orgie, when all of them, we were told, hoped to be blind drunk; and, added the girl who volunteered the information, "None of 'em didn't care dam for police." She was evidently anticipating the happy state of inebriety she had just been predicting.

One of the houses a few doors off contained a woman well known to the police, and rather notorious on account of her having attempted to drown herself three times. Wishing to see her, the inspector took me to the house she lived in, which was kept by an Irishwoman, the greatest hypocrite I ever met with. She was intensely civil to the inspector, who had once convicted her for allowing three women to sleep in one bed, and she was fined five pounds, all which she told us with the most tedious circumstantiality, vowing, as "shure as the Almighty God was sitting on his throne," she did it out of charity, or she wished she might never speak no more. "These gals," she said, "comes to me in the night and swears (as I knows to be true) they has no place where to put their heads, and foxes they has holes, likewise birds of the air, which it's a mortial shame as they is better provided for and against than them that's flesh and blood Christians. And one night I let one in, when having no bed you see empty I bundled them in together. Police they came and I was fined five pounds, which I borrowed from Mrs. Wilson what lives close to—five golden sovereigns, as I'm alive, and they took them all, which I've paid back two bob a week since, and I don't owe no one soul not a brass farthing, which it's all as thrue as Christ's holiness, let alone his blessed gospel." The woman we came to see was called China Emma, or by her intimate associates Chaney Emm. She was short in stature, rather stout, with a pale face utterly expressionless; her complexion was blonde. There was a look almost of vacuity about her, but her replies to my questions were lucid, and denoted that she was only naturally slow and stupid.

"My father and mother," she said, "kept a grocer's shop in Goswell Street. Mother died when I was twelve years old, and father took to drinking. In three years he lost his shop, and in a while killed himself, what with the drink and one thing and another. I went to live with a sister who was bad, and in about a year she went away with a man and left me. I could not get any work, never having been taught any trade or that. One day I met a sailor, who was very good to me. I lived with him as his wife, and when he went away drew his half-pay. I was with him for six years. Then he died of yellow fever in the West Indies, and I heard no more of him. I know he did not cut me, for one of his mates brought me a silver snuff-box he used to carry his quids in, which he sent me when he was at his last. Then I lived for a bit in Angel Gardens; after that I went to Gravel Lane; and now I'm in Bluegate Fields. When I came here I met with a Chinaman called Appoo. He's abroad now, but he sends me money. I got two pounds from him only the other day. He often sends me the needful. When he was over here last we lived in Gregory's Rents. I've lived in Victoria Place and New Court, all about Bluegate. Appoo only used to treat me badly when I got drunk. I always get drunk when I've a chance to. Appoo used to tie my legs and arms and take me into the street. He'd throw me into the gutter, and then he'd throw buckets of water over me till I was wet through; but that didn't cure; I don't believe anything would; I'd die for the drink; I must have it, and I don't care what I does to get it. I've tried to kill myself more nor once. I have fits at times—melancholy fits—and I don't know what to do with myself. I wish I was dead, and I run to the water and throw myself in; but I've no luck; I never had since I was a child—oh! ever so little. I's always picked out. Once I jumped out of a first-floor window in Jamaica Place into the river, but a boatman coming by hooked me up, and the magistrate give me a month. The missus here (naming the woman who kept the place) wants me to go to a refuge or home, or something of that. P'raps I shall."

The Irishwoman here broke in, exclaiming—

"And so she shall. I've got three or four poor gals into the refuge, and I'll get Chaney Emm, as shure as the Almighty God's sitting on his throne." (This was a favourite exclamation of hers.) "I keeps her very quiet here; she never sees no one, nor tastes a drop of gin, which she shouldn't have to save her blessed life, if it were to be saved by nothink else; leastways, it should be but a taste. It's ruined her has drink. When she got the money Appoo sent her the other day or two back, I took it all, and laid it out for her, but never a drop of the crater passed down Chaney Emm's lips."

This declaration of the avaricious old woman was easily credible, except the laying out the money for her victim's advantage. The gin, in all probability, if any had been bought, had been monopolized in another quarter, where it was equally acceptable. As to the woman's seeing no one, the idea was preposterous. The old woman's charity, as is commonly the case, began at home, and went very little further. If she were excluded from men's society she must have been much diseased.

I find the women who cohabit with sailors are not, as a body, disorderly, although there may be individuals who habitually give themselves up to insubordination. I take them to be the reverse of careful, for they are at times well off, but at others, through their improvidence and the slackness of the shipping, immersed in poverty. The supply of women is fully equal to the demand; but as the demand fluctuates so much I do not think the market can be said to be overstocked. They are unintelligent and below the average of intellectuality among prostitutes, though perhaps on a par with the men with whom they cohabit.

Soldiers' Women.

The evil effects of the want of some system to regulate prostitution in England, is perhaps more shown amongst the army than any other class. Syphilis is very prevalent among soldiers, although the disease is not so virulent as it was formerly. That is, we do not see examples of the loss of the palate or part of the cranium, as specimens extant in our museums show us was formerly the case. The women who are patronized by soldiers are, as a matter of course, very badly paid; for how can a soldier out of his very scanty allowance, generally little exceeding a shilling a day, afford to supply a woman with means adequate for her existence? It follows from this state of things, that a woman may, or more correctly must, be intimate with several men in one evening, and supposing her to be tainted with disease, as many men as she may chance to pick up during the course of her peregrinations, will be incapacitated from serving her Majesty for several weeks.

The following quotation from Mr. Acton's book will suffice to show what I mean. He is speaking of a particular regiment.

"In 1851, Dr. Gordon, surgeon to the 57th, read a paper before the Surgical Society of Ireland, in which he states, (see 'Dublin Medical Press,' February 26th, 1851,) that during the year ending 31st March, 1850, the following number, out of an average strength of 408 men, were treated for venereal diseases in the head-quarters hospital—

"Number admitted . . . 113
Number of days in hospital 2519
Amount of soldiers' pay . £136 10 9

"At the first blush, the economist would be apt to imagine that a very large sum of money is lost to the state annually by the inroads of syphilis. It is but fair to state that this is not the case, as tenpence a day is stopped from each man's pay while he is in hospital, so that about five-sixths of his wages are recovered. The actual loss to the country is his time, which, however during peace, is non-productive.

"From the statistical reports on the sickness, mortality, and invaliding among the troops in the United Kingdom, the Mediterranean, and British America, presented to

Parliament some years ago (1839), it would appear that syphilis is a fatal enemy to the British soldier.

"Total cases during seven and a quarter years 8,072
Total aggregate strength for do. 44,611
Annual mean strength for ditto 6,153
"Thus 181 per 1000, or about one man in five appear to have been attacked.

"Let us compare this with the following statistics extracted from a report on army diseases from 1837 to 1847.

"Aggregate strength :
Cavalry	54,374
Foot-guards	40,120
Infantry	160,103
Total	254,597

"Extent of venereal disease :
Cavalry	11,205
Foot-guards	10,043
Infantry	44,435
Total	65,683
Deaths	17

"Number of men per 1000 of strength admitted during ten years :
"Cavalry	206
Foot-guards	250
Infantry	277

"This report was drawn up by Dr. Balfour and Sir Alexander Tulloch, and the reason that a distinction is made between the line and the foot-guards, is that the line contains a large number of recruits and men returning from foreign service, whereas in the foot-guards, there is usually a much greater proportion of soldiers who have arrived at maturity, on the one hand, and who, on the other, have not served in foreign climates. As these circumstances were likely to have affected the amount of sickness and mortality, the returns of the two classes were kept distinct and separate in preparing the tables.

"Few infected soldiers escape notice, as health inspections are made once a week, which is the general rule in the service. If a soldier is found at inspection to be labouring under disease, he is reported for having concealed it to his superior officer, who orders him punishment drill on his discharge from hospital. In order to induce him to apply early for relief, the soldier is told that if he do so, he may probably be only a few days instead of several weeks under treatment.

"It is contrary to the rules of the service, to treat men out of hospital ; even were it otherwise, the habits of the soldier, and the accommodation in barracks, would not favour celerity of cure."*

In the brigade of Guards, though the average of syphilis primitiva is heavy, as above stated, only 11 per cent. of the cases are followed by secondary symptoms, which, however, follow 33 per cent. of the cases in the line. Dr. Balfour says a mild mercurial system is usually pursued in the army ; and indeed mercury by many surgeons is held absolutely necessary for hard, or Hunterian chancres.

A woman was pointed out to me in a Music Hall in Knightsbridge, who my informant told me he was positively assured had only yesterday had two buboes lanced ; and yet she was present at that scene of apparent festivity, contaminating the very air, like a deadly upas tree, and poisoning the blood of the nation, with the most audacious recklessness. It is useless to say that such things should not be. They exist, and they will exist. The woman was nothing better than a paid murderess, committing crime with impunity. She was so well known that she had obtained the soubriquet of the "hospital" as she was so frequently an inmate of one, and as she so often sent others to a similar involuntary confinement.

Those women who, for the sake of distinguishing them from the professionals, I must call amateurs, are generally spoken of as " Dollymops." Now many servant-maids, nurse-maids who go with children into the Parks, shop girls and milliners who may be met with at the various " dancing academies," so called, are " Dollymops." We must separate these latter again from the "Demoiselle de Comptoir," who is just as much in point of fact a " Dollymop," because she prostitutes herself for her own pleasure, a few trifling presents or a little money now and then, and not altogether to maintain herself. But she will not go to casinos, or any similar places to pick up men ; she makes their acquaintance in a clandestine manner: either she is accosted in the street early in the evening as she is returning from her place of business to her lodgings, or she carries on a flirtation behind the counter, which, as a matter of course, ends in an assignation.

Soldiers are notorious for hunting up these women, especially nurse-maids and those that in the execution of their duty

* Acton.

walk in the Parks, when they may easily be accosted. Nurse-maids feel flattered by the attention that is lavished upon them, and are always ready to succumb to the "scarlet fever." A red coat is all powerful with this class, who prefer a soldier to a servant, or any other description of man they come in contact with.

This also answers the soldier's purpose equally well. He cannot afford to employ professional women to gratify his passions, and if he were to do so, he must make the acquaintance of a very low set of women, who in all probability will communicate some infectious disease to him. He feels he is never safe, and he is only too glad to seize the opportunity of forming an intimacy with a woman who will appreciate him for his own sake, cost him nothing but the trouble of taking her about occasionally, and who, whatever else she may do, will never by any chance infect. I heard that some of the privates in the Blues and the brigade of Guards often formed very reprehensible connections with women of property, tradesmen's wives, and even ladies, who supplied them with money, and behaved with the greatest generosity to them, only stipulating for the preservation of secrecy in their intrigues. Of course numbers of women throng the localities which contain the Knightsbridge, Albany Street, St. George's, Portman, and Wellington Barracks in Birdcage Walk. They may have come up from the provinces; some women have been known to follow a particular regiment from place to place, all over the country, and have only left it when it has been under orders for foreign service.

A woman whom I met with near the Knightsbridge barracks, in one of the beer-houses there, told me she had been a soldiers' woman all her life.

"When I was sixteen," she said, "I went wrong. I'm up'ards of thirty now. I've been fourteen or fifteen years at it. It's one of those things you can't well leave off when you've once took to it. I was born in Chatham. We had a small baker's shop there, and I served the customers and minded the shop. There's lots of soldiers at Chatham, as you know, and they used to look in at the window in passing, and nod and laugh whenever they could catch my eye. I liked to be noticed by the soldiers. At last one young fellow, a recruit, who had not long joined I think, for he told me he hadn't been long at the depot, came in and talked to me. Well, this went on, and things fell out as they always do with girls who go about with men, more especially soldiers, and when the regiment went to Ireland, he gave me a little money that helped me to follow it; and I went about from place to place, time after time, always sticking to the same regiment. My first man got tired of me in a year or two, but that didn't matter. I took up with a sergeant then, which was a cut above a private, and helped me on wonderful. When we were at Dover, there was a militia permanently embodied artillery regiment quartered with us on the western heights, and I got talking to some of the officers, who liked me a bit. I was a—— sight prettier then than I am now, you may take your dying oath, and they noticed me uncommon; and although I didn't altogether cut my old friends, I carried on with these fellows all the time we were there, and made a lot of money, and bought better dresses and some jewellery, that altered me wonderful. One officer offered to keep me if I liked to come and live with him. He said he would take a house for me in the town, and keep a pony carriage if I would consent; but although I saw it would make me rise in the world, I refused. I was fond of my old associates, and did not like the society of gentlemen; so, when the regiment left Dover, I went with them, and I remained with them till I was five-and-twenty. We were then stationed in London, and I one day saw a private in the Blues with one of my friends, and for the first time in my life I fell in love. He spoke to me, and I immediately accepted his proposals, left my old friends, and went to live in a new locality, among strangers; and I've been amongst the Blues ever since, going from one to the other, never keeping to one long, and not particler as long as I get the needful. I don't get much,—very little, hardly enough to live upon. I've done a little needlework in the day-time. I don't now, although I do some washing and mangling now and then to help it out. I don't pay much for my bed-room, only six bob a week, and dear at that. It ain't much of a place. Some of the girls about here live in houses. I don't; I never could abear it. You ain't your own master, and I always liked my freedom. I'm not comfortable exactly; it's a brutal sort of life this. It isn't the sin of it, though, that worries me. I don't dare think of that much, but I do think how happy I might have been if I'd always lived at Chatham, and married as other women do, and had a nice home and children; that's what I want, and when I think of all that, I do cut up. It's enough to drive a woman wild to think that she's given up all chance of it. I feel I'm not respected either. If I have a row with any fellow, he's always the first to taunt me with being what he and his friends have made me. I don't feel it so much now. I used to at first. One dovetails into all that sort of thing in time, and the edge of your feelings, as I may say, wears off by degrees. That's what it is. And then the drink is very pleasant to us, and keeps up our spirits; for what could a woman in my position do without spirits, without being able to talk and blackguard and give every fellow she meets as good as he brings?"

It is easy to understand, the state of mind of this woman, who had a craving after what she knew she never could possess, but which the maternal instinct planted within her forced her to wish for. This is one of the melancholy aspects of prostitution. It leads to nothing—marriage of course excepted; the prostitute has no future. Her life, saving the excitement of the moment, is a blank. Her hopes are all blighted, and if she has a vestige of religion left in her, which is generally the case, she must shudder occasionally at what she has merited by her easy compliance when the voice of the tempter sounded so sweetly.

The happy prostitute, and there is such a thing, is either the thoroughly hardened, clever infidel, who knows how to command men and use them for her own purposes; who is in the best set both of men and women; who frequents the night-houses in London, and who in the end seldom fails to marry well; or the quiet woman who is kept by the man she loves, and who she feels is fond of her; who has had a provision made for her to guard her against want, and the caprice of her paramour.

The sensitive, sentimental, weak-minded, impulsive, affectionate girl, will go from bad to worse, and die on a dunghill or in a workhouse. A woman who was well known to cohabit with soldiers, of a masculine appearance but good features, and having a good-natured expression, was pointed out to me as the most violent woman in the neighbourhood. When she was in a passion she would demolish everything that came in her way, regardless of the mischief she was doing. She was standing in the bar of a public-house close to the barracks talking to some soldiers, when I had an opportunity of speaking to her. I did not allow it to pass without taking advantage of it. I told her I had heard she was very passionate and violent.

"Passionate!" she replied; "I believe yer. I knocked my father down and well-nigh killed him with a flat-iron before I wor twelve year old. I was a beauty then, an I aint improved much since I've been on my own hook. I've had lots of rows with these 'ere sodgers, and they'd have slaughter'd me long afore now if I had not pretty near cooked their goose. It's a good bit of it self-defence with me now-a-days, I can tell yer. Why, look here; look at my arm where I was run through with a bayonet once three or four years ago."

She bared her arm and exhibited the scar of what appeared to have once been a serious wound.

"You wants to know if them rowses is common. Well, they is, and it's no good one saying they aint, and the sodgers is such —— cowards they think nothing of sticking a woman when they'se riled and drunk, or they'll wop us with their belts. I was hurt awful onst by a blow from a belt; it hit me on the back part of the head, and I was laid up weeks in St. George's Hospital with a bad fever. The sodger who done it was quodded, but only for a drag,* and he swore to God as how he'd do for me the next time as he comed across me. We had words sure enough, but I split his skull with a pewter, and that shut him up for a time. You see this public; well, I've smashed up this place before now; I've jumped over the bar, because they wouldn't serve me without paying for it when I was hard up, and I've smashed all the tumblers and glass, and set the cocks agoing, and fought like a brick when they tried to turn me out, and it took two peelers to do it; and then I lamed one of the bobbies for life by hitting him on the shin with a bit of iron—a crow or summet, I forget what it was. How did I come to live this sort of life? Get along with your questions. If you give me any of your cheek, I'll —— soon serve you the same."

It may easily be supposed I was glad to leave this termagant, who was popular with the soldiers, although they were afraid of her when she was in a passion. There is not much to be said about soldiers' women. They are simply low and cheap, often diseased, and as a class do infinite harm to the health of the service.

Thieves' Women.

The metropolis is divided by the police into districts, to which letters are attached to designate and distinguish them. The head-quarters of the F division are at Bow Street, and the jurisdiction of its consta-

* Imprisoned for three months.

bulary extends over Covent Garden, Drury Lane, and St. Giles's, which used formerly to be looked upon as most formidable neighbourhoods, harbouring the worst characters and the most desperate thieves.

Mr. Durkin, the superintendent at Bow Street, obligingly allowed an intelligent and experienced officer (sergeant Bircher) to give me any information I might require.

Fifteen or twenty years ago this locality was the perpetual scene of riot and disorder. The public-houses were notorious for being places of call for thieves, pickpockets, burglars, thieving prostitutes, hangers-on (their associates), and low ruffians, who rather than work for an honest livelihood preferred scraping together a precarious subsistence by any disreputable means, however disgraceful or criminal they might be. But now this is completely changed. Although I patrolled the neighbourhood on Monday night, which is usually accounted one of the noisiest in the week, most of the public houses were empty, the greatest order and decorum reigned in the streets, and not even an Irish row occurred in any of the low alleys and courts to enliven the almost painful silence that everywhere prevailed. I only witnessed one fight in a public-house in St. Martin's Lane. Seven or eight people were standing at the bar, smoking and drinking. A disturbance took place between an elderly man, pugnaciously intoxicated, who was further urged on by a prostitute he had been talking to, and a man who had the appearance of being a tradesman in a small way. How the quarrel originated I don't know, for I did not arrive till it had commenced. The sergeant who accompanied me was much amused to observe among those in the bar three suspicious characters he had for some time "had his eye on." One was a tall, hulking, hang dog-looking fellow; the second a short, bloated, diseased, red-faced man, while the third was a common-looking woman, a prostitute and the associate of the two former. The fight went on until the tradesman in a small way was knocked head over heels into a corner, when the tall, hulking fellow obligingly ran to his rescue, kindly lifted him up, and quietly rifled his pockets. The ecstasy of the sergeant as he detected this little piece of sharp practice was a thing to remember. He instantly called my attention to it, for so cleverly and skilfully had it been done that I had failed to observe it.

When we resumed our tour of inspection, the sergeant, having mentally summed up the three suspicious characters, observed: "I first discovered them in Holborn three nights ago, when I was on duty in plain clothes. I don't exactly yet know rightly what their little game is; but it's either dog-stealing or 'picking up.' This is how they do it. The woman looks out for a 'mug,' that is a drunken fellow, or a stupid, foolish sort of fellow. She then stops him in the street, talks to him, and pays particular attention to his jewellery, watch, and every thing of that sort, of which she attempts to rob him. If he offers any resistance, or makes a noise, one of her bullies comes up, and either knocks him down by a blow under the ear, or exclaims: 'What are you talking to my wife for?' and that's how the thing's done, sir, that's exactly how these chaps do the trick. I found out where they live yesterday. It's somewhere down near Barbican, Golden Lane; the name's a bad, ruffianly, thievish place. They are being watched to-night, although they don't know it. I planted a man on them." Two women were standing just outside the same public. They were dressed in a curious assortment of colours, as the low English invariably are, and their faces had a peculiar unctuous appearance, somewhat Israelitish, as if their diet from day to day consisted of fried fish and dripping. The sergeant knew them well, and they knew him, for they accosted him. "One of these women," he said, "is the cleverest thief out. I've known her twelve years. She was in the first time for robbing a public. I'll tell you how it was. She was a pretty woman—a very pretty woman—then, and had been kept by a man who allowed her 4l. a week for some time. She was very quiet too, never went about anywhere, never knocked about at night publics or any of those places; but she got into bad company, and was in for this robbery. She and her accomplices got up a row in the bar, everything being concerted beforehand; they put out the lights, set all the taps running, and stole a purse, a watch, and some other things; but we nabbed them all, and, strange to say, one of the women thieves died the next day from the effects of drink. All these women are great gluttons, and when they get any money, they go in for a regular drink and debauch. This one drank so much that it positively killed her slick off."

At the corner of Drury Lane I saw three women standing talking together. They were innocent of crinoline, and the antiquity of their bonnets and shawls was really wonderful, while the durability of the fabric of which they were composed was equally remarkable. Their countenances were stolid, and their skin hostile to the application of soap and water. The hair of one was tinged with silver. They were inured to the rattle of their harness; the clank of the chains pleased them. They had *grown grey* as prostitutes.

I learnt from my companion that "that lot was an inexpensive luxury; it showed the sterility of the neighbourhood. They would go home with a man for a shilling, and think themselves well paid, while sixpence was rather an exorbitant amount for the temporary accommodation their vagrant amour would require."

There were a good many of them about. They lived for the most part in small rooms at eighteen pence, two shillings, and half-a-crown a week, in the small streets running out of Drury Lane.

We went down Charles Street, Drury Lane, a small street near the Great Mogul public-house. I was surprised at the number of clean-looking, respectable lodging-houses to be seen in this street, and indeed in almost every street thereabouts. Many of them were well-ventilated, and chiefly resorted to by respectable mechanics. They are under the supervision of the police, and the time of a sergeant is wholly taken up in inspecting them. Visits are made every day, and if the Act of Parliament by the provisions of which they are allowed to exist, and by which they are regulated, is broken, their licences are taken away directly. Some speculators have several of these houses, and keep a shop as well, full of all sorts of things to supply their lodgers.

There is generally a green blind in the parlour window, upon which you sometimes see written, Lodgings for Travellers, 3d. a night; or, Lodgings for Gentlemen; or, Lodgings for Single Men. Sometimes they have Model Lodging-house written in large black letters on a white ground on the wall. There are also several little shops kept by general dealers, in contiguity, for the use of the inmates of the lodging-houses, where they can obtain two pennyworth of meat and "a haporth" of bread, and everything else in proportion.

There are a great number of costermongers about Drury Lane and that district, and my informant assured me that they found the profession very lucrative, for the lower orders, and industrial classes don't care about going into shops to make purchases. They infinitely prefer buying what they want in the open street from the barrow or stall of a costermonger.

What makes Clare Market so attractive, too, but the stalls and barrows that abound there

There are many flower-girls who are sent out by their old gin-drinking mothers to pick up a few pence in the street by the sale of their goods. They begin very young, often as young as five and six, and go on till they are old enough to become prostitutes, when they either leave off costermongering altogether, or else unite the two professions. They are chiefly the offspring of Irish parents, or cockney Irish, as they are called, who are the noisiest, the most pugnacious, unprincipled, and reckless part of the population of London. There is in Exeter Street, Strand, a very old established and notorious house of ill-fame, called the ———, which the police says is always honestly and orderly conducted. Married women go there with their paramours, for they are sure of secrecy, and have confidence in the place. It is a house of accommodation, and much frequented; rich tradesmen are known to frequent it. They charge ten shillings and upwards for a bed. A man might go there with a large sum of money in his pocket, and sleep in perfect security, for no attempt would be made to deprive him of his property.

There is a coffee-house in Wellington Street, on the Covent Garden side of the Lyceum Theatre, in fact adjoining the playhouse, where women may take their men; but the police cannot interfere with it, because it is a coffee-house, and not a house of ill-fame, properly so called. The proprietor is not supposed to know who his customers are. A man comes with a woman and asks for a bed-room; they may be travellers, they may be a thousand things. A subterranean passage, I am told, running under the Lyceum connects this with some supper-rooms on the other side of the theatre, which belongs to the same man who is proprietor of the coffee and chop house.

We have before spoken of "dress-lodgers:" there are several to be seen in the Strand. Any one who does not understand the affair, and had not been previously informed, would fail to observe the badly-dressed old hag who follows at a short distance the fashionably-attired young lady, who walks so gaily along the pavement, and who only allows the elasticity of her step to subside into a quieter measure when stopping to speak to some likely-looking man who may be passing. If her overtures are successful she retires with her prey to some den in the vicinity.

The watcher has a fixed salary of so

much per week, and never loses sight of the dress-lodger, for very plain reasons. The dress-lodger probably lives some distance from the immoral house by whose owner she is employed. She comes there in the afternoon badly dressed, and has good things lent her. Now if she were not watched she might decamp. She might waste her time in public-houses; she might take her dupes to other houses of ill-fame, or she might pawn the clothes she has on, for the keeper could not sue her for a debt contracted for immoral purposes. The dress-lodger gets as much money from her man as she can succeed in abstracting, and is given a small percentage on what she obtains by her employer. The man pays usually five shillings for the room. Many prostitutes bilk their man; they take him into a house, and then after he has paid for the room leave him. The dupe complains to the keeper of the house, but of course fails to obtain any redress.

I happened to see an old woman in the Strand, who is one of the most hardened beggars in London. She has two children with her, but one she generally disposes of by placing her in some doorway. The child falls back on the step, and pretends to be asleep or half-frozen with the cold. Her naturally pale face gives her a half-starved look, which completes her pitiable appearance. Any gentleman passing by being charitably inclined may be imposed upon and induced to touch her on the shoulder. The child will move slowly and rub her eyes, and the man, thoroughly deceived, gives her an alms and passes on, when the little deceiver again composes herself to wait for the next chance. This occurred while I was looking on; but unfortunately for the child's success the policeman on the beat happened to come up, and she made her retreat to a safer and more convenient locality.

Many novelists, philanthropists, and newspaper writers have dwelt much upon the horrible character of a series of subterranean chambers or vaults in the vicinity of the Strand, called the Adelphi Arches. It is by no means even now understood that these arches are the most innocent and harmless places in London, whatever they might once have been. A policeman is on duty there at night, expressly to prevent persons who have no right or business there from descending into their recesses.

They were probably erected in order to form a foundation for the Adelphi Terrace. Let us suppose there were then no wharves, and no embankments, consequently the tide must have ascended and gone inland some distance, rendering the ground marshy, swampy, and next to useless. The main arch is a very fine pile of masonry, something like the Box tunnel on a small scale, while the other, running here and there like the intricacies of catacombs, looks extremely ghostly and suggestive of Jack Sheppards, Blueskins, Jonathan Wilds, and others of the same kind, notwithstanding they are so well lighted with gas. There is a doorway at the end of a vault leading up towards the Strand, that has a peculiar tradition attached to it. Not so very many years ago this door was a back exit from a notorious coffee and gambling house, where parties were decoyed by thieves, blacklegs, or prostitutes, and swindled, then drugged, and subsequently thrown from this door into the darkness of what must have seemed to them another world, and were left, when they came to themselves, to find their way out as best they could.

My attention was attracted, while in these arches, by the cries and exclamations of a woman near the river, and proceeding to the spot I saw a woman sitting on some steps, before what appeared to be a stable, engaged in a violent altercation with a man who was by profession a cab proprietor—several of his vehicles were lying about—and who, she vehemently asserted, was her husband. The man declared she was a common woman when he met her, and had since become the most drunken creature it was possible to meet with. The woman put her hand in her pocket and brandished something in his face, which she triumphantly said was her marriage-certificate. "That," she cried, turning to me, "that's what licks them. It don't matter whether I was one of Lot's daughters afore. I might have been awful, I don't say I wasn't, but I'm his wife, and this 'ere's what licks 'em."

I left them indulging in elegant invectives, and interlarding their conversation with those polite and admirable metaphors that have gained so wide-spread a reputation for the famous women who sell fish in Billingsgate; and I was afterwards informed by a sympathising bystander, in the shape of a stable-boy, that the inevitable result of this conjugal altercation would be the incarceration of the woman, by the husband, in a horse-box, where she might undisturbed sleep off the effects of her potations, and repent the next day at her leisure. "Nec dulces amores sperne puer."

Several showily-dressed, if not actually well-attired women, who are to be found walking about the Haymarket, live in St.

Giles's and about Drury Lane. But the lowest class of women, who prostitute themselves for a shilling or less, are the most curious and remarkable class in this part. We have spoken of them before as growing grey in the exercise of their profession. One of them, a woman over forty, shabbily dressed, and with a disreputable, unprepossessing appearance, volunteered the following statement for a consideration of a spirituous nature.

"Times is altered, sir, since I come on the town. I can remember when all the swells used to come down here-away, instead of going to the Market; but those times is past, they is, worse luck, but, like myself, nothing lasts for ever, although I've stood my share of wear and tear, I have. Years ago Fleet Street and the Strand, and Catherine Street, and all round there was famous for women and houses. Ah! those were the times. Wish they might come again, but wishing's no use, it ain't. It only makes one miserable a thinking of it. I come up from the country when I was quite a gal, not above sixteen I dessay. I come from Dorsetshire, near Lyme Regis, to see a aunt of mine. Father was a farmer in Dorset, but only in a small way—tenant farmer, as you would say. I was mighty pleased, you may swear, with London, and liked being out at night when I could get the chance. One night I went up the area and stood looking through the railing, when a man passed by, but seeing me he returned and spoke to me something about the weather. I, like a child, answered him unsuspectingly enough, and he went on talking about town and country, asking me, among other things, if I had long been in London, or if I was born there. I not thinking told him all about myself; and he went away apparently very much pleased with me, saying before he went that he was very glad to have made such an agreeable acquaintance, and if I would say nothing about it he would call for me about the same time, or a little earlier, if I liked, the next night, and take me out for a walk. I was, as you may well suppose, delighted, and never said a word. The next evening I met him as he appointed, and two or three times subsequently. One night we walked longer than usual, and I pressed him to return, as I feared my aunt would find me out; but he said he was so fatigued with walking so far, he would like to rest a little before he went back again; but if I was very anxious he would put me in a cab. Frightened about him, for I thought he might be ill, I preferred risking being found out; and when he proposed that we should go into some house and sit down I agreed. He said all at once, as if he had just remembered something, that a very old friend of his lived near there, and we couldn't go to a better place, for she would give us everything we could wish. We found the door half open when we arrived. 'How careless,' said my friend, 'to leave the street-door open, any one might get in.' We entered without knocking, and seeing a door in the passage standing ajar we went in. My friend shook hands with an old lady who was talking to several girls dispersed over different parts of the room, who, she said, were her daughters. At this announcement some of them laughed, when she got very angry and ordered them out of the room. Somehow I didn't like the place, and not feeling all right I asked to be put in a cab and sent home. My friend made no objection and a cab was sent for. He, however, pressed me to have something to drink before I started. I refused to touch any wine, so I asked for some coffee, which I drank. It made me feel very sleepy, so sleepy indeed that I begged to be allowed to sit down on the sofa. They accordingly placed me on the sofa, and advised me to rest a little while, promising, in order to allay my anxiety, to send a messenger to my aunt. Of course I was drugged, and so heavily I did not regain my consciousness till the next morning. I was horrified to discover that I had been ruined, and for some days I was inconsolable, and cried like a child to be killed or sent back to my aunt.

"When I became quiet I received a visit from my seducer, in whom I had placed so much silly confidence. He talked very kindly to me, but I would not listen to him for some time. He came several times to see me, and at last said he would take me away if I liked, and give me a house of my own. Finally, finding how hopeless all was I agreed to his proposal, and he allowed me four pounds a week. This went on for some months, till he was tired of me, when he threw me over for some one else. There is always as good fish in the sea as ever came out of it, and this I soon discovered.

"Then for some years—ten years, till I was six-and-twenty,—I went through all the changes of a gay lady's life, and they're not a few, I can tell you. I don't leave off this sort of life because I'm in a manner used to it, and what could I do if I did? I've no character; I've never been used to do anything, and I don't see what employment I stand a chance of getting. Then if I had to sit hours and hours all day long, and part of the night too, sewing or anything like that, I should get tired. It would worrit me so; never having been accustomed, you see, I couldn't stand it. I lodge in Charles Street, Drury Lane, now. I did live in Nottingham Court once, and Earls Street. But, Lord, I've lived in a many places you wouldn't think, and I don't imagine you'd believe one half. I'm always a-chopping and a-changing like the wind as you may say. I pay half-a-crown a week for my bed-room; it's clean and comfortable, good enough for such as me. I don't think much of my way of life. You folks as has honour, and character, and feelings, and such, can't understand how all that 's been beaten out of people like me. I don't feel. *I'm used to it.* I did once, more especial when mother died. I heard on it through a friend of mine, who told me her last words was of me. I did cry and go on then ever so, but Lor', where's the good of fretting? I arn't happy either. It isn't happiness, but I get enough money to keep me in victuals and drink, and it's the drink mostly that keeps me going. You've no idea how I look forward to my drop of gin. It's everything to me. I don't suppose I'll live much longer, and that's another thing that pleases me. I don't want to live, and yet I don't care enough about dying to make away with myself. I arn't got that amount af feeling that some has, and that's where it is I'm kinder 'fraid of it."

This woman's tale is a condensation of the philosophy of sinning. The troubles she had gone through, and her experience of the world, had made her oblivious of the finer attributes of human nature, and she had become brutal.

I spoke to another who had been converted at a Social Evil Meeting, but from a variety of causes driven back to the old way of living.

The first part of her story offered nothing peculiar. She had been on the town for fifteen years, when a year or so ago she heard of the Midnight Meeting and Baptist Noel. She was induced from curiosity to attend; and her feelings being powerfully worked upon by the extraordinary scene, the surroundings, and the earnestness of the preacher, she accepted the offer held out to her, and was placed in a cab with some others, and conveyed to one of the numerous metropolitan homes, where she was taken care of for some weeks, and furnished with a small sum of money to return to her friends. When she arrived at her native village in Essex, she only found her father. Her mother was dead; her sister at service, and her two brothers had enlisted in the army. Her father was an old man, supported by the parish; so it was clear he could not support her. She had a few shillings left, with which she worked her way back to town, returned to her old haunts, renewed her acquaintance with her vicious companions, and resumed her old course of life.

I don't insert this recital as a reflection upon the refuges and homes, or mean to asperse the Midnight Meeting movement, which is worthy of all praise. On the contrary, I have much pleasure in alluding to the subject and acknowledging the success that has attended the efforts of the philanthropic gentlemen associated with the Rev. Mr. Baptist Noel.

I have already described the condition of low and abandoned women in Spitalfields, Whitechapel, Wapping, and Shadwell, although I have not touched very closely upon those who cohabit with thieves and other desperate characters, whose daily means of obtaining a livelihood exposes them to the penalties the law inflicts upon those who infringe its provisions. Their mode of living, the houses they inhabit, and the way in which they pass their time, does not very materially differ from that of other prostitutes, with this exception, they are not obliged to frequent casinos, dancing-rooms, and other places of popular resort, to make acquaintances that may be of service to them in a pecuniary way, although they do make use of such places for the purposes of robbery and fraud. Some women of tolerably good repute—that is, who are regarded as knowing a good set of men, who have admission to the night-houses in Panton Street and the Haymarket —I am informed, are connected with thieves. The night-houses and supper-rooms in the neighbourhood of the Haymarket are for the most part in the hands of a family of Jews. Kate Hamilton's in Princes Street, Leicester Square, belongs to one of this family. She is given a per centage on all the wine that she sells during the course of the evening, and as she charges twelve shillings a bottle for Moselle and sparkling wines, it may readily be supposed that her profits are by no means despicable. Lizzie Davis's, Sams's, Sally's, and, I believe, the Carlton, also belong to this family. One of these Jews, I am told, was some few years back imprisoned for two years on a charge of manslaughter. He was proprietor of a brothel in the vicinity of Drury Lane, and the manslaughter occurred through his instrumentality on the premises. I have been informed by the police that some of the proprietors of these night-houses are well-known receivers of stolen goods, and the assertion is easily credible. To exemplify this I will relate a story told me by a sergeant of the H division. Some two years ago a robbery was committed by a "snoozer," or one of those thieves who take up their quarters at hotels for the purpose of robbery. The robbery was committed at an hotel in Chester. The thief was captured, and the Recorder sentenced him to be imprisoned. This man was a notorious thief, and went under the *soubriquet* of American Jack. He was said to have once been in a very different position. He was polished in his manners, and highly accomplished. He could speak three or four languages with facility, and was a most formidable and dexterous thief, causing much apprehension and trouble to the police. After being incarcerated for a few weeks he contrived in a clever manner to make his escape from one of the London prisons; it was supposed by the connivance of his gaolers, who were alleged to have been bribed by his friends without. Be this as it may, he effected his liberation, and was successfully concealed in London until the hue and cry was over, and then shipped off to Paris. But the night after he escaped he perpetrated the most audacious robbery. He was dressed by his friends, and having changed his prison attire went to B—— Hotel, a well-known place, not far from the Freemasons Tavern, where, singularly enough, the Recorder of Chester, who had sentenced him, chanced to be staying. American Jack had the presumption to enter into conversation with the Recorder, who fancied he had seen his face before, but could not recollect where. The visitors had not long retired to bed before American Jack commenced operations. He was furnished by his accomplice with a highly-finished instrument for housebreaking, which, when inserted in the lock, would pass through and grasp the key on the inside. This done, it was easy to turn the key and open the door. The thief actually broke into sixteen or seventeen rooms that night, and made his exit before daybreak loaded with booty of every description. The proprietors of the hotel would offer no reward, as they feared publicity. The Recorder of Chester, when the robbery was discovered, remembered that the person he had conversed with the night before was the man he had convicted and sentenced at the assizes. He repaired to Bow Street with his information, and the police were put on the scent; but it is well known if no reward is offered for the apprehension of an eminent criminal the police are not so active as they are when they have a monetary inducement to incite them to action. It was imagined that American Jack had taken refuge with his friends near the Haymarket. A waiter who had been discharged from one of the night-houses was known slightly to a sergeant of police, who interrogated him on the subject. This waiter confessed that he could point out the whereabouts of the thief, and would do so for twenty pounds, which reward no one concerned in the matter would offer; and, as I have already stated, the criminal soon after made his escape to Paris, where he continued to carry on his depredations with considerable skill, until one day he mixed himself up in a great jewel robbery, and was apprehended by the *gensdarmes*, and sent to the galleys for some time, where he is now languishing.

This little history is suggestive—why should not Parliament vote every year a small sum of money to form a "Detective and Inquiry Fund," from which the Commissioners of Police at Whitehall and Old Jewry might offer rewards for the capture of offenders? Some spur and inducement surely might be given to our detectives, who take a great deal of trouble, and, if unsuccessful, are almost always out of pocket through their researches.

Cannot Sir Richard Mayne and Mr. Daniel Whittle Harvey improve on this idea?

The police enter the night-houses every evening to see if spirits are sold on the premises; but as there are bullies at all the doors, and a code of signals admirably concerted to convey intelligence of the approach of the officers to those within, everything is carefully concealed, and the police are at fault. They might if they chose detect the practices they very well know are commonly carried on; but they either are not empowered to go to extremities, or else they do not find it their interest so to do. I have heard, I know not with what truth, that large sums of money are paid to the police to insure their silence and compliance; but until this is established it must be received with hesitation, though circumstances do occur that seem strongly to corroborate such suspicions. The women who cohabit with thieves are not necessarily thieves themselves, although such is often the case. Most pickpockets make their women accomplices in their misdeeds, because they find their assistance so valuable to them, and indeed for some species of theft almost indispensable

There are numbers of young thieves on the other side of the water, and almost all of them cohabit with some girl or other. The depravity of our juvenile thieves is a singular feature in their character. It is not exactly a custom that they follow, but rather an inherent depravity on their part. They prefer an idle luxurious life, though one also of ignomy and systematic dishonour, to one of honesty and labour; and this is the cause of their malpractices, perhaps inculcated at first by the force of evil example and bad bringing up, and invigorated every day by independence brought about by the liberty allowed them, the consequence of parental neglect.

It is of course difficult to give the stories of any of these women, as they would only criminate themselves disagreeably by confessing their delinquencies; and it is not easy to pitch upon a thieves' woman without she is pointed out by the police, and even then she would deny the imputation indignantly.

Park Women, or those who frequent the Parks at night and other retired places.

Park women, properly so called, are those degraded creatures, utterly lost to all sense of shame, who wander about the paths most frequented after nightfall in the Parks, and consent to any species of humiliation for the sake of acquiring a few shillings. You may meet them in Hyde Park, between the hours of five and ten (till the gates are closed) in winter. In the Green Park, in what is called the Mall, which is a nocturnal thoroughfare, you may see these low wretches walking about sometimes with men, more generally alone, often early in the morning. They are to be seen reclining on the benches placed under the trees, originally intended, no doubt, for a different purpose, occasionally with the head of a drunken man reposing in their lap. These women are well known to give themselves up to disgusting practices, that are alone gratifying to men of morbid and diseased imaginations. They are old, unsound, and by their appearance utterly incapacitated from practising their profession where the gas-lamps would expose the defects in their personal appearance, and the shabbiness of their ancient and dilapidated attire. I was told that an old woman, whose front teeth were absolutely wanting, was known to obtain a precarious livelihood by haunting the by-walks of Hyde Park, near Park Lane. The unfortunate women that form this despicable class have in some cases been well off, and have been reduced to their present condition by a variety of circumstances, among which are intemperance, and the vicissitudes natural to their vocation. I questioned one who was in the humour to be communicative, and she gave the subjoined replies to my questions:—

"I have not always been what I now am. Twenty years ago I was in a very different position. Then, although it may seem ludicrous to you, who see me as I now am, I was comparatively well off. If I were to tell you my history it would be so romantic you would not believe it. If I employ a little time in telling you, will you reward me for my trouble, as I shall be losing my time in talking to you? I am not actuated by mercenary motives exactly in making this request, but my time is my money, and I cannot afford to lose either one or the other. Well, then, I am the daughter of a curate in Gloucestershire. I was never at school, but my mother educated me at home. I had one brother who entered the Church. When I was old enough I saw that the limited resources of my parents would not allow them to maintain me at home without seriously impairing their resources, and I proposed that I should go out as a governess. At first they would not hear of it; but I persisted in my determination, and eventually obtained a situation in a family in town. Then I was very pretty. I may say so without vanity or ostentation, for I had many admirers, among whom I numbered the only son of the people in whose house I lived. I was engaged to teach his two sisters, and altogether I gave great satisfaction to the family. The girls were amiable and tractable, and I soon acquired an influence over their generous dispositions that afforded great facilities for getting them on in their studies. My life might have been very happy if an unfortunate attachment to me had not sprung up in the young man that I have before mentioned, which attachment I can never sufficiently regret was reciprocated by myself.

"I battled against the impulse that constrained me to love him, but all my efforts were of no avail. He promised to marry me, which in an evil hour I agreed to. He had a mock ceremony performed by his footman, and I went into lodgings that he had taken for me in Gower Street, Tottenham Court Road. He used to visit me very frequently for the ensuing six months, and we lived together as man and wife. At the expiration of that time he took me to the sea-side, and we subsequently travelled on the Continent. We were at Baden when we heard of his father's death. This didn't trouble him much. He did not even go to England to attend the funeral, for he had by his conduct offended his father, and estranged himself from the remainder of his family. Soon letters came from a solicitor informing him that the provisions of the will discontinued the allowance of five hundred a year hitherto made to him, and left him a small sum of money sufficient to buy himself a commission in the army, if he chose to do so. This course he was strongly advised to take, for it was urged that he might support himself on his pay if he volunteered for foreign service. He was transported with rage when this communication reached him, and he immediately wrote for the legacy he was entitled to, which arrived in due course. That evening he went to the gaming table, and lost every farthing he had in the world. The next morning he was a corpse. His remains were found in a secluded part of the town, he having in a fit of desperation blown his brains out with a pistol. He had evidently resolved to take this step before he left me, if he should happen to be unfortunate, for he left a letter in the hands of our landlady to be delivered to me in the event of his not returning in the morning. It was full of protestations of affection for me, and concluded with an avowal of the fraud he had practised towards me when our acquaintance was first formed, which he endeavoured to excuse by stating his objections to be hampered or fettered by legal impediments.

"When I read this, I somewhat doubted the intensity of the affection he paraded in his letter. I had no doubt about the fervour of my own passion, and for some time I was inconsolable. At length, I was roused to a sense of my desolate position, and to the necessity for action, by the solicitations and importunity of my landlady, and I sold the better part of my wardrobe to obtain sufficient money to pay my bills, and return to England. But fate ordered things in a different manner. Several of my husband's friends came to condole with me on his untimely decease; among whom was a young officer of considerable personal attractions, who I had often thought I should have liked to love, if I had not been married to my friend's husband. It was this man who caused me to take the second fatal step I have made in my life. If I had only gone home, my friends might have forgiven everything. I felt they would, and my pride did not stand in my way, for I would gladly have asked and obtained their forgiveness for a fault in reality very venial, when the circumstances under which it was committed are taken into consideration.

"Or I might have represented the facts to the family; and while the mother mourned the death of her son, she must have felt some commiseration for myself.

"The officer asked me to live with him, and made the prospect he held out to me so glittering and fascinating that I yielded. He declared he would marry me with pleasure on the spot, but he would forfeit a large sum of money, that he must inherit in a few years if he remained single, and it would be folly not to wait until then. I have forgotten to mention that I had not any children. My constitution being very delicate, my child was born dead, which was a sad blow to me, although it did not seem to affect the man I regarded as my husband. We soon left Baden and returned to London, where I lived for a month very happily with my paramour, who was not separated from me, as his leave of absence had not expired. When that event occurred he reluctantly left me to go to Limerick, where his regiment was quartered. There in all probability he formed a fresh acquaintance, for he wrote to me in about a fortnight, saying that a separation must take place between us, for reasons that he was not at liberty to apprise me of, and he enclosed a cheque for fifty pounds, which he hoped would pay my expences. It was too late now to go home, and I was driven to a life of prostitution, not because I had a liking for it, but as a means of getting enough money to live upon. For ten years I lived first with one man then with another, until at last I was infected with a disease, of which I did not know the evil effects if neglected. The disastrous consequence of that neglect is only too apparent now. You will be disgusted, when I tell you that it attacked my face, and ruined my features to such an extent that I am hideous to look upon, and should be noticed by no one if I frequented those places where women of my class most congregate; indeed, I should be driven away with curses and execrations."

This recital is melancholy in the extreme. Here was a woman endowed with a very fair amount of education, speaking in a superior manner, making use of words that very few in her position would know how to employ, reduced by a variety of circumstances to the very bottom of a prostitute's career. In reply to my further questioning, she said she lived in a small place in Westminster called Perkins' Rents, where for one room she paid two shillings a week. The Rents were in

Westminster, not far from Palace-yard. She was obliged to have recourse to her present way of living to exist; for she would not go to the workhouse, and she could get no work to do. She could sew, and she could paint in water-colours, but she was afraid to be alone. She could not sit hours and hours by herself, her thoughts distracted her, and drove her mad. She added, she once thought of turning Roman Catholic, and getting admitted into a convent, where she might make atonement for her way of living by devoting the remainder of her life to penitence, but she was afraid she had gone too far to be forgiven. That was some time ago. Now she did not think she would live long, she had injured her constitution so greatly; she had some internal disease, she didn't know what it was, but a hospital surgeon told her it would kill her in time, and she had her moments, generally hours, of oblivion, when she was intoxicated, which she always was when she could get a chance. If she got ten shillings from a drunken man, either by persuasion or threats, and she was not scrupulous in the employment of the latter, she would not come to the Park for days, until all her money was spent; on an average, she came three times a week, or perhaps twice; always on Sunday, which was a good day. She knew all about the Refuges. She had been in one once, but she didn't like the system; there wasn't enough liberty, and too much preaching, and that sort of thing; and then they couldn't keep her there always; so they didn't know what to do with her. No one would take her into their service, because they didn't like to look at her face, which presented so dreadful an appearance that it frightened people. She always wore a long thick veil, that concealed her features, and made her interesting to the unsuspicious and unwise. I gave her the money I promised her, and advised her again to enter a Refuge, which she refused to do, saying she could not live long, and she would rather die as she was. As I had no power to compel her to change her determination, I left her, lamenting her hardihood and obstinacy. I felt that she soon would be—

> "One more unfortunate,
> Weary of breath,
> Rashly importunate,
> Gone to her death."

In the course of my peregrinations I met another woman, commonly dressed in old and worn-out clothes; her face was ugly and mature; she was perhaps on the shady side of forty. She was also perambulating the Mall. I knew she could only be there for one purpose, and I interrogated her, and I believe she answered my queries faithfully. She said:—

"I have a husband, and seven small children, the eldest not yet able to do much more than cadge a penny or so by cater-wheeling and tumbling in the street for the amusement of gents as rides outside 'busses. My husband's bedridden, and can't do nothink but give the babies a dose of 'Mother's Blessing' (that's laudanum, sir, or some sich stuff) to sleep 'em when they's squally. So I goes out begging all day, and I takes in general one of the kids in my arms and one as runs by me, and we sell hartifishal flowers, leastways 'olds 'em in our 'ands, and makes believe cos of the police, as is nasty so be as you 'as nothink soever, and I comes hout in the Parks, sir, at night sometimes when I've 'ad a bad day, and ain't made above a few pence, which ain't enough to keep us as we should be kep. I mean, sir, the children should have a bit of meat, and my ole man and me wants some blue ruin to keep our spirits up; so I'se druv to it, sir, by poverty, and nothink on the face of God's blessed earth, sir, shou'dn't have druv me but that for the poor babes must live, and who 'as they to look to but their 'ard-working but misfortunate mother, which she is now talking to your honour, and won't yer give a poor woman a hap'ny, sir? I've seven small children at home, and my 'usban's laid with the fever. You won't miss it, yer honour, only a 'apny for a poor woman as ain't 'ad a bit of bread between her teeth since yesty morning. I ax yer parding," she exclaimed, interrupting herself—"I forgot I was talking to yourself. I's so used though to this way of speaking when I meant to ax you for summut I broke off into the old slang, but yer honour knows what I mean: ain't yer got even a little sixpence to rejoice the heart of the widow?"

"You call yourself a widow now," I said, "while before you said you were married and had seven children. Which are you?"

"Which am I? The first I toll you's the true. But Lor', I's up to so many dodges I gets what you may call confounded; sometimes I's a widder, and wants me 'art rejoiced with a copper, and then I's a hindustrious needle-woman thrown out of work and going to be druv into the streets if I don't get summut to do. Sometimes I makes a lot of money by being a poor old cripple as broke her arm in a factory, by being blowed hup when a steam-engine blowed herself hup, and I bandage my arm and swell it out hawful big, and when I gets home, we gets in some lush and 'as some frens, and goes in for a reglar blow-hout, and now as I have told yer honour hall about it, won't yer give us an 'apny as I observe before?"

It is very proper that the Parks should be closed at an early hour, when such creatures as I have been describing exist and practise their iniquities so unblushingly. One only gets at the depravity of mankind by searching below the surface of society; and for certain purposes such knowledge and information are useful and beneficial to the community. Therefore the philanthropist must overcome his repugnance to the task, and draw back the veil that is thinly spread over the skeleton.

The Dependants of Prostitutes.

HAVING described the habits, &c., of different classes of prostitutes, I now come to those who are intimately connected with, and dependant upon, them. This is a very numerous class, and includes "Bawds," or those who keep brothels, the followers of dress lodgers, keepers of accommodation houses, procuresses, pimps, and panders, fancy men, and bullies.

Bawds.—The first head in our classification is "Bawds." They may be either men or women. More frequently they are the latter, though any one who keeps an immoral house, or bawdy-house, as it is more commonly called, is liable to that designation. Bawdy-houses are of two kinds. They may be either houses of accommodation, or houses in which women lodge, are boarded, clothed, &c., and the proceeds of whose prostitution goes into the pocket of the bawd herself, who makes a very handsome income generally by their shame.

We cannot have a better example of this sort of thing than the bawdy-houses in King's Place, St. James's, a narrow passage leading from Pall Mall opposite the "Guards Club" into King Street, not far from the St. James's theatre. These are both houses of accommodation and brothels proper. Men may take their women there, and pay so much for a room and temporary accommodation, or they may be supplied with women who live in the house. The unfortunate creatures who live in these houses are completely in the power of the bawds, who grow fat on their prostitution. When they first came to town perhaps they were strangers, and didn't know a soul in the place, and even now they would have nowhere to go to if they were able to make their escape, which is a very difficult thing to accomplish, considering they are vigilantly looked after night and day. They have nothing fit to walk about the streets in. They are often in bed all day, and at night dressed up in tawdry ball costumes. If they ever do go out on business, they are carefully watched by one of the servants: they generally end when their charms are faded by being servants of bawds and prostitutes, or else watchers, or perhaps both.

There are houses in Oxendon Street too, where women are kept in this way.

A victim of this disgraceful practice told me she was entrapped when she was sixteen years old, and prostituted for some time to old men, who paid a high price for the enjoyment of her person.

"I was born at Matlock in Derbyshire," she began; "father was a stonecutter, and I worked in the shop, polishing the blocks and things, and in the spring of '51 we heard of the Great Exhibition. I wished very much to go to London, and see the fine shops and that, and father wrote to an aunt of mine, who lived in London, to know if I might come and stay a week or two with her to see the Exhibition. In a few days a letter came back, saying she would be glad to give me a room for two or three weeks and go about with me. Father couldn't come with me because of his business, and I went alone. When I arrived, aunt had a very bad cold, and couldn't get out of bed. Of course, I wanted to go about and see things, for though I didn't believe the streets were paved with gold, I was very anxious to see the shops and places I'd heard so much about. Aunt said when she was better she'd take me, but I was so restless I would go by myself. I said nothing to aunt about it, and stole out one evening. I wandered about for some time, very much pleased with the novelty. The crowds of people, the flaring gas jets, and everything else, all was so strange and new, I was delighted. At last I lost myself, and got into some streets ever so much darker and quieter. I saw one door in the middle of the street open, that is standing a-jar. Thinking no harm, I knocked, and hearing no sound, and getting no answer, I knocked louder, when some one came and instantly admitted me, without saying a word. I asked her innocently enough where I was, and if she would tell me the way to Bank Place. I didn't know where Bank Place was, whether it was in Lambeth, or Kensington, or Hammersmith, or where; but I have since heard it is in Kensington. The woman who let me in, and to whom I addressed my questions, laughed at this, and said, 'Oh! yes, I wasn't born yesterday.' But I repeated, 'Where am I, and what am I to do?'

"She told me to 'ax,' and said she'd heard that before.

"I suppose I ought to tell you, before I go further," she explained, "that 'ax' meant ask, or find out.

"Just then a door opened, and an old woman came out of a room which seemed to me to be the parlour. 'Come in, my dear,' she exclaimed, 'and sit down.' I followed her into the room, and she pulled out a bottle of gin, asking me if I would have a drop of something short, while she poured out some, which I was too frightened to refuse. She said, 'I likes to be jolly myself and see others so. I'm getting on now. Ain't what I was once. But as I says I likes to be jolly, and I always is. A old fiddle, you know, makes the best music.

"'Market full, my dear,' she added, pushing the wine-glass of gin towards me. 'Ah! I s'pose not yet; too arly, so it is. I's glad you've dropped in to see a body. I've noticed your face lots of times, but I thought you was one of Lotty's girls, and wouldn't condescend to come so far up the street, though, why one part should be better nor another, I'm sure, I can't make out.'

"'Really you must make a mistake,' I interposed. 'I am quite a stranger in London; indeed I have only been three days in town. The fact is, I lost myself this evening, and seeing your door open, I thought I would come in and ask the way.'

"Whilst I was saying this, the old woman listened attentively. She seemed to drink in every word of my explanation, and a great change came over her features.

"'Well, pet,' she replied, 'I'm glad you've come to my house. You must excuse my taking you for some one else; but you are so like a gal I knows, one Polly Gay, I couldn't help mistaking you. Where are you staying?'

"I told her I was staying with my aunt in Bank Place.

"'Oh! really,' she exclaimed; 'well, that is fortunate, 'pon my word, that is lucky. I'm gladder than ever now you came to my shop—I mean my house—cos I knows your aunt very well. Me an' 'er's great frens, leastways was, though I haven't seen her for six months come next Christmas. Is she's took bad, is she? Ah! well, it's the weather, or somethink, that's what it is; we're all ill sometimes; and what is it as is the matter with her? Influenzy, is it? Now, Lor' bless us, the influenzy! Well, you'll stay with me to-night; you's ever so far from your place. Don't say No; you must, my dear, and we'll go down to aunt's to-morrow morning arly; she'll be glad to see me, I know. She always was fond of her old friends.'

"At first I protested and held out, but at last I gave in to her persuasion, fully believing all she told me. She talked about my father, said she hadn't the pleasure of knowing him personally, but she'd often heard of him, and hoped he was quite well, more especially as it left her at that time. Presently she asked if I wasn't tired, and said she'd show me a room up-stairs where I should sleep comfortable no end. When I was undressed and in bed, she brought me a glass of gin and water hot, which she called a night-cap, and said would do me good. I drank this at her solicitation, and soon fell into a sound slumber. The 'night-cap' was evidently drugged, and during my state of insensibility my ruin was accomplished. The next day I was wretchedly ill and weak, but I need not tell you what followed. My prayers and entreaties were of no good, and I in a few days became this woman's slave, and have remained so ever since; though, as she has more than one house, I am occasionally shifted from one to the other. The reason of this is very simple. Suppose the bawd has a house in St. James's and one in Portland Place. When I am known to the habitués of St. James's, I am sent as something new to Portland Place, and so on."

If I were to expatiate for pages on bawds, I don't think I could give a better idea than this affords. Their characteristics are selfishness and avariciousness, combined with want of principle and the most unblushing effrontery.

Followers of Dress-Lodgers.—I have spoken before of dress-lodgers, and I now come to those women who are employed by the keepers of the brothels in which the dress-lodgers live, to follow them when they are sent into the streets to pick up men. They are not numerous. They are only seen in the Strand and about the National Gallery. This species of vice is much magnified by people who have vivid imaginations. It might have assumed larger dimensions, but at the present time it has very much decreased. They follow the dress-lodgers for various reasons, which I have mentioned already. For the sake of perspicuity and putting things in their proper sequence, I may be excused for briefly recapitulating them. If they were not closely watched, they might, imprimis, make their escape with all the finery they have about them, which of course they would speedily dispose of for its market value to the highest-bidding Jew, and then take lodgings and set up on their own account. These unfortunate dress-lodgers are profoundly ignorant of the English law. If they were better acquainted with its provisions, they would know very well that the bawds would have no legal claim against them for money, board, or clothes, for if the bawds could prove any consideration, it would be an immoral one, and consequently bad in law. But the poor creatures think they are completely in the wretch's power, and dare not move hand or foot, or call their *hair* their own. Instances have been known of bawds cutting off the hair of their lodgers when it became long, and selling it if it was fine and beautiful for thirty shillings and two pounds.

There is a dress-lodger who perambulates the Strand every night, from nine, or before that even, till twelve or one, who is followed by the inseparable old hag who keeps guard over her to prevent her going into public-houses and wasting her time and money, which is the second reason for her being watched, and to see that she does not give her custom to some other bawdy-house, which is the third reason.

This follower is a woman of fifty, with grey hair, and all the peculiarities of old women, among which is included a fondness for gin, which weakness was mainly instrumental in enabling me to obtain from her what I know about herself and her class. She wore no crinoline, and a dirty cotton dress. Her bonnet was made of straw, with a bit of faded ribbon over it by way of trimming, fully as shabby and discreditable as the straw itself.

She told me by fits and starts, and by dint of cross questioning, the subjoined particulars.

"They call me 'Old Stock;' why I shan't tell you, though I might easy, and make you laugh too, without telling no lies; but it ain't no matter of your'n, so we'll let it be. They do say I'm a bit cracky, but that's all my eye. I'm a drunken old b—— if you like, but nothing worser than that. I was once the swellest woman about town, but I'm come down awful. And yet it ain't awful. I sometimes tries to think it is, but I can't make it so. If I did think it awful I shouldn't be here now; I couldn't stand it. But the fact is life's sweet, and I don't care how you live. It's as sweet to the w——, as it is to the hempress, and mebbe it's as sweet to me as it is to you. Yes, I was well known about some years ago, and I ain't got bad features now, if it wasn't for the wrinkles and the skin, which is more parchmenty than anything else, but that's all along of the drink. I get nothing in money for following this girl about, barring a shilling or so when I ask for it to get some liquor. They give me my grub and a bed, in return for which in the day-time I looks after the house, when I ain't drunk, and sweeps, and does the place up, and all that. Time was when I had a house of my own, and lots of servants, and heaps of men sighing and dying for me, but now my good looks are gone, and I am what you see me. Many of the finest women, if they have strong constitutions, and can survive the continual racket, and the wear and tear of knocking about town, go on like fools without making any provision for themselves, and without marrying, until they come to the bad. They are either servants, or what I am, or if they get a little money given them by men, they set up as bawdy-house-keepers. I wish to God I had, but I don't feel what I am. I'm past that ever so long, and if you give me half a crown, or five bob, presently, you'll make me jolly for a week. Talking of giving a woman five bob reminds me of having fivers (5*l.* notes) given me. I can remember the time when I would take nothing but paper; always tissue, nothing under a flimsy. Ah! gay women see strange changes; wonderful ups and downs, I can tell you. We, that is me and Lizzie, the girl I'm watching, came out to night at nine. It's twelve now, ain't it? Well; what do ye think we've done? We have taken three men home, and Lizzie, who is a clever little devil, got two pound five out of them for herself, which ain't bad at all. I shall get something when we get back. We ain't always so lucky. Some nights we go about and don't hook a soul. Lizzie paints a bit too much for decent young fellows who've got lots of money. They aren't our little game. We go in more for tradesmen, shopboys, commercial travellers, and that sort, and men who are a little screwy, and although we musn't mention it, we hooks a white choker now and then, coming from Exeter Hall. Medical students are sometimes sweet on Lizzie, but we ain't in much favour with the Bar. Oh! I know what a man is directly he opens his mouth. Dress too has a great deal to do with what a man is—tells you his position in life as it were. 'Meds' ain't good for much; they're larky young blokes, but they've never much money, and they're fond of dollymopping. But talk of dollymopping—lawyers are the fellows for that. Those chambers in the

Inns of Court are the ruin of many a girl. And they are so convenient for bilking, you've no idea. There isn't a good woman in London who'd go with a man to the Temple, not one. You go to Kate's, and take a woman out, put her in a cab, and say you were going to take her to either of the Temples, which are respectable and decent places when compared to the other inns which are not properly Inns of Court, except Gray's Inn and Lincoln's Inn, and she'd cry off directly. I mean Barnard's Inn, and Thavies' Inn, and New Inn, and Clement's Inn, and all those. I've been at this sort of work for six or seven years, and I suppose I'll die at it. I don't care if I do. It suits me. I'm good for nothing else."

I gave her some money in return for her story, and wished her good night. What she says about women who have once been what is called "swell," coming down to the sort of thing I have been describing, is perfectly true. They have most of them been well-known and much admired in their time; but every dog has its day. They have had theirs, and neglected to make hay while the sun was shining. Almost all the servants of bawds and prostitutes have fallen as it were from their high estate into the slough of degradation and comparative despair.

As I have before stated, there are very few dress-lodgers now who solicit in the streets, and naturally few followers of dress-lodgers whose condition does not afford anything very striking or peculiar, except as evidencing the vicissitudes of a prostitute's career, and the end that very many of them arrive at.

Keepers of Accommodation Houses.—Those who gain their living by keeping accommodation houses, or what the French call *maisons de passé*, are of course to be placed in the category of the people who are dependant on prostitutes, without whose patronage they would lose their only means of support.

When you speak of bawds you in a great measure describe this class also, for their avocations are the same, and the system they exist upon very similar. The bawds keep women in their houses, and the others let out their rooms to chance comers, and any one who chooses to take them. The keepers are generally worn-out prostitutes, who have survived their good looks and settled down, as a means of gaining a livelihood; in Oxenden Street and similar places an enormous amount of money is made by these people. The usual charge for rooms of course varies according to the height and the size of the room engaged. A first-floor room is worth seven or ten shillings, then the rooms on the second-floor are five shillings, and three shillings, and so on. The average gains of keepers of accommodation houses in Oxenden Street and James Street, Haymarket, are from two pounds to ten pounds a night; the amount depending a good deal on the popularity of the house, its connection with women, its notoriety amongst men, and its situation. More money is made by bawdy-house keepers, but then the expenses are greater. A story is told of a celebrated woman who kept a house of ill-fame in the neighbourhood of May Fair. The several inmates of her establishment were dilatory on one occasion, and she gave vent to her anger and disapointment by exclaiming, "Twelve o'clock striking. The house full of noblemen, and not a —— girl painted yet." I introduce this anecdote merely to exemplify what I have been advancing, namely, that the best brothels in London, such as Mrs. C—'s in Curzon Street, and others that I could mention, are frequented by men who have plenty of money at their command, and spend it freely.

A Mrs. J—, who kept a house in James Street, Haymarket, where temporary accommodation could be obtained by girls and their paramours, made a very large sum of money by her house, and some time ago bought a house somewhere near Camberwell with her five-shilling pieces which she had the questionable taste to call "Dollar House." A woman who kept a house in one of the small streets near the Marylebone Road told me she could afford to let her rooms to her customers for eighteen pence for a short time, and three and sixpence for all night, and she declared she made money by it, as she had a good many of the low New Road women, and some of those who infest the Edgware Road, as well as several servants and dress-makers, who came with their associates. She added, she was saving up money to buy the house from her landlord, who at present charged her an exorbitant rent, as he well knew she could not now resist his extortionate demands. If he refused to sell it, she should go lower down in the same street, for she was determined before long to be independant.

When we come to touch upon clandestine prostitution we shall have occasion to condemn these houses in no measured terms, for they offer very great facilities for the illicit intercourse of the not yet completely depraved portion of the sexes, such as sempstresses, milliners, servant girls, etc., etc., who only prostitute themselves occasionally to men they are well acquainted with, for whom they may have some sort of a partiality—women who do not lower themselves in the social scale for money, but for their own gratification. They become, however, too frequently insensibly depraved, and go on from bad to worse, till nothing but the *pavé* is before them. The ruin of many girls is commenced by reading the low trashy wishy-washy cheap publications that the news-shops are now gorged with, and by devouring the hastily-written, immoral, stereotyped tales about the sensualities of the upper classes, the lust of the aristocracy, and the affection that men about town—noble lords, illustrious dukes, and even princes of the blood—are in the habit of imbibing for maidens of low degree " whose face is their fortune," shop girls—dressmakers — very often dressmakers and the rest of the tribe who may perhaps feel flattered by reading about absurd impossibilities that their untutored and romantic imaginations suggest may, during the course of a life of adventure, happen to themselves. Well, they wait day after day, and year after year for the duke or the prince of the blood, perfectly ready to surrender their virtue when it is asked for, until they open their eyes, regard the duke and the prince of the blood as apocryphal or engaged to somebody else more fortunate than themselves, and begin to look a little lower, and favourably receive the immodest addresses of a counter-jumper, or a city clerk, or failing those a ruffianly pot-boy may realize their dreams of the ideal; at all events, they are already demoralized by the trash that has corrupted their minds, and perfectly willing at the first solicitation to put money into the pockets of the keepers of accommodation houses.

Procuresses, Pimps, and Panders.—Procuresses are women who in most cases possess houses of their own, where they procure girls for men who employ them. These establishments are called " Introducing Houses," and are extremely lucrative to the proprietors. There are also men who go about for these people, finding out girls, and bringing them to the houses, where they may meet with men. The procuresses who keep introducing houses often take in women to lodge and board. But they are quite independant, and must be well-known about town, and kept by some one, or the procuress, if she is, comparatively speaking, in any position, will not receive them.

To show how the matter is accomplished let us suppose an introducing house of notoriety and good report in its way, somewhere in the nighbourhood of St. George's Road, Pimlico, a district which, I may observe, is prolific in loose women. A well-known professional man, a wealthy merchant, an M.P., or a rich landed proprietor, calls upon the lady of the house, orders some champagne, and enters into conversation about indifferent matters, until he is able delicately to broach the object he has in view. He explains that he wishes to meet with a quiet lady whose secrecy he can rely upon, and whom he can trust in every possible way. He would like her, we will imagine, to be vivacious, witty, and gay.

The lady of the house listens complacently, and replies that she knows some one who exactly answers the description the amorous M.P. has given, and says that she will send a message to her at once if he wishes, but he must take his chance of her being at home; if she is out, an appointment will be made for the next day. In the mean time a messenger is despatched to the lady in question, who in all probability does not reside at any great distance; perhaps in Stanley Street, or Winchester Street, which streets everybody knows are contiguous to St. George's Road, and inhabited by beauty that ridicules decorum and laughs at the virtuous restrictions that are highly conducive to a state of single blessedness and a condition of old-maidism. Some more champagne is ordered and consumed, every bottle of which costs the consumer fifteen shillings, making a profit to the vendor of at least seventy per cent. When the lady arrives, the introduction takes place, and the matter is finally arranged as far as the introducer is concerned. The woman so introduced generally gives half the money she obtains from the man to the keeper of the house for the introduction.

Sometimes these women will write to men who occupy a high position in society, who are well-known at the clubs, and are reputed to be well off, saying that they have a new importation in their houses from the country that may be disposed of for a pecuniary consideration of perhaps fifty or a hundred pounds. This amount of course is readily paid by men who are in search of artificial excitement, and the negotiation is concluded without any difficulty. A woman is usually seduced five or six times. By that I mean she is represented as a maid, and imposed upon men as a virgin, which fabrication, as it is difficult to disprove, is believed, more especially if the girl herself be well instructed, and knows how to carry out the fraud. The Burlington Arcade is a well-known resort of women on the long winter afternoons, when all the men in London walk there before dinner.

It is curious to notice how the places of meeting and appointment have sprung up and increased within the last few years. Not many years ago Kate Hamilton, if I am not misinformed, was knocking about town. Lizzie Davis's has only been open a year or two. Barns's very recently established, and the Oxford and Cambridge last season. The Café Riche three years ago used to be called Bignell's Café. Sams's I believe is the oldest of the night-houses about the Haymarket. The Café Royal, or Kate's, is the largest and the most frequented, but is not now so select as it used formerly to be. Mott's, or the Portland Rooms, used to be the most fashionable dancing place in London, and is now in very good repute. Formerly only men in evening dress were admitted; now this distinction is abolished, and every one indiscriminately admitted. This is beginning to have its effect, and in all likelihood Mott's will in a short time lose its prestige. It is always so with places of this description. Some peculiarity about the house, or some clever and notorious woman, presiding over its destinies, makes it famous; when these vanish or subside, then the place goes down gradually, and some other rival establishment takes its place.

Loose women, as I have before asserted, very often marry, and sometimes, as often as not, marry well. The other day one of the most well-known women about town, Mrs. S—, was married to a German count; a few weeks ago Agnes W—married a member of an old Norfolk family, who settled three thousand a year upon her. This case will most likely come before the public, as the family, questioning his sanity, mean to take out a writ of *de lunatico inquirendo*, when the facts will be elicited by counsel in a court of law. Indeed, so little was the gentleman himself satisfied with the match that a week after marriage he advertised his wife in the newspapers, saying he would not be held responsible for her further debts. These out of many others. A frequenter of the night-houses will notice many changes in the course of the year, although some well-known face will turn up now and then. The habitué may miss the accustomed laugh and unabashed impudence of the "nun," who always appeared so fascinating and piquante in her little "Jane Clarke" bonnet, and demure black silk dress. The "nun" may be far away with her regiment in Ireland, or some remote part of England; for be it known that ladies are attached to the service as well as men, and the cavalry rejoices more than the line in the softening influences of feminine society. Amongst the little scandals of the night, it may be rumoured within the sacred precincts of the Café Royal by "Suppers" of the Admiralty, who has obtained that soubriquet by his known unwillingness to stand these midnight banquets, that the "Baby" was seen at the Holborn with a heightened colour, rather the production of art than nature; *ergo*, the "Baby" is falling off, which remark it is fortunate for "Suppers" the Baby does not overhear. Billy Valentine, of her Majesty's "horse and saddle" department of the Home Office, as is his usual custom, may be seen at Coney's, exchanging a little quiet chaff with "Poodle," whose hair is more crimped than ever, while the "Poodle" is dexterously extracting a bottle of Moselle out of him for the benefit of the establishment. There is a woman of very mature age who goes about from one night-house to another with her betting book in her hand, perhaps "cadging" for men. Then there is Madame S. S.—, who plays the piano in different places, and Dirty Dick, who is always in a state of intoxication; but who, as he spends his money freely, is never objected to.

But the night-houses are carrying me away from my subject.

Pimps are frequently spoken of, and pimping is a word very generally used, but I doubt very much whether many of them exist, at least of the male gender. The women do most of the pimping that is requisite to carry on the amours of London society, and pander is a word that merges into the other, losing any distinctive significancy that it may possess for the eyes of a lexicographer. A woman when she introduces a man to a woman is literally pimping for him, or what I have said about keepers of introducing houses must apply generally to the panders and the pimps. I may add a story I heard of a bully attached to a brothel, who on one occasion acting as a pimp, went into the streets to pick up a woman who was required for the purposes of the establishment. He went some way without success, and at last met a "wandering beauty of the night," whom he solicited; she yielded to his entreaties, and followed him to his brothel. When they reached the light in the passage she raised her veil, when he was as horrified as a man in his position and with his feelings could be to perceive that he had brought his own sister to an immoral house: he had not seen her for some years. His profligacy had killed his father, had brought him to his present degraded position, and in a great measure occasioned his sister's fall and way of living.

Ex uno—the proverb says—a lesson may be taught a great many.

Fancy-men.—Fancy-men are an extremely peculiar class, and are highly interesting to those who take an interest in prostitutes and their associates. They are—that is the best of them—tolerably well-dressed and well-looking, and sufficiently gentlemanly for women to like to be seen about with them. I am now speaking of those who cohabit with the best women about town.

Parent Duchatelet discourses at some length on this subject, and treats it with great perspicuity and succinctness. He asserts that it is a common thing for many law students and medical students to be kept, or semi-supported, by loose women in Paris. This is a state of things that I need hardly say is never observed in England. Yet there is a class who throw all their self-respect into the background, and allow themselves to be partially maintained by loose women who have imbibed a partiality for them. They frequent the night-houses in Panton Street, and often hook gentlemen out of several sovereigns, or by tossing them for champagne make them pay for several bottles in the course of the evening. By this it may be readily understood that they are in league with the proprietor of the establishment; and that this is undeniably the case in one instance I will unhesitatingly declare. It may be so in others, but I am not prepared to say so. I need not mention the name of the house for obvious reasons, but any one who has the slightest knowledge of the subject will be obliged, if he values his veracity, to corroborate my statement. The best, or the aristocracy of fancy-men, are for the most part on the turf. They bet when they have money to bet with, and when they have not they endeavour, without scruple, to procure it from their mistresses, who never hesitate a moment in giving it them if they have it, or procuring it for them by some means, however degrading such means may be. A fancy-man connected with a prostitute who is acquainted with a good set of men will, as the evening advances, be seen in one of the night-houses in Panton Street. His woman will come in perhaps about one o'clock, accompanied by one or two men. Whilst they are talking and drinking he will come up and speak to the woman, as if she was an old flame of his, and she will treat him in the same manner, though more as a casual acquaintance. In the course of time he will get into conversation with her men, and they, taking him for a gentleman, will talk to him in a friendly manner. After a while he will propose to toss them for a bottle of champagne or a Moselle cup. Then the swindling begins. The fancy-man has an infallible recipe for winning. He has in his hand a cover for the half-crown he tosses with, which enables him to win, however the piece falls. It is a sort of "heads I win, tails you lose," a principle with which schoolboys of a speculative disposition bother their friends. Sometimes the proprietor of the house will come up and begin to talk to them, ask them to step upstairs to have supper, and get them into a room where the victim may be legged more quietly, and more at their leisure. The proprietor then says that he must in his turn " stand " a bottle of champagne, but the fancy-man, pretending to be indignant, interposes, and exclaims, " No, let's toss ;" so they toss. The fancy-man loses the toss, pays the proprietor at once with money, with which he has been previously supplied, and the man is more completely gulled than ever. He may be some man in the service up in town on leave for a short while, and determined as long as he stays to go in for some fun, no doubt well supplied with money, and careless how he spends it. He would be very irate if he discovered how he was being robbed, and in all likelihood smash the place up, and the fancy-man into the bargain, for people are not very scrupulous as to what they do in the night-houses. But the affair is managed so skilfully that he loses his four or five pounds at tossing or at some game or other with equanimity, and without a murmur, for he thinks it is his luck which happens to be adverse, and never dreams for one instant that his adversary is not playing on the " square." The rows that take place in the night-houses never find their way into the papers. It isn't the " little game " of the proprietors to allow them, and the police, if they are called in, are too well bribed to take any further notice, without they are particularly requested. I was told of a disturbance that took place in one of the night-houses in Panton Street, not more than a year ago, which for brutality and savage ferocity I should think could not be equalled by a scalping party of North American Red Indians.

Two gentlemen had adjourned there after the theatre, and were quietly drinking some brandy and soda when a woman, with a very large crinoline, came in and went up to one of them, whom we will call A. She asked him for something to drink, and he, perceiving she was very drunk already, chaffed her a little. Angry at his *persiflage*, she leant over and seized his glass, which she threw into a corner of the room, smashing it to atoms, and spilling its contents. While doing so her crinoline flew into the air, and A. put out his hand to keep it down. She immediately began to slang him and abuse him immoderately, declaring that he attempted to take indecent liberties with her, and attempting finally to strike him he good-humouredly held her hands; but she got more furious every moment, and at last he had to push her down rather violently into a chair. A man who was sitting at an opposite table commented upon this in an audible and offensive manner, which excessively annoyed A., who however at first took no notice of his conduct. Presently he handed the woman over to one of the waiters, who with some difficulty turned her out. Then the man who had before spoken said, "D—d plucky thing, by Jove, to strike a woman." A. made some reply to this, and the other man got up, when A. flew at him and knocked him down. Two waiters ran up and seized A. by either arm, when the man got up from his recumbent position and struck A., while he was being retained by the waiters, a tremendous blow in the face, which speedily covered him with blood. A., exerting all his strength, liberated himself, and rushed at the coward, knocking him over a table, jumping over after him, seizing his head and knocking it against the floor in a frightful manner. The door porters were then called in, and A. with great difficulty turned out. A.'s friend had been waiting his opportunity, which had not yet come. When A. was at the door the man he had knocked down raised himself up. A.'s friend seized him by the collar and by one of his legs, and threw him with all his force along the table, which was covered with glass. The velocity with which he was thrown drove everything before him until he fell down on the top of the broken glass in a corner stunned and bleeding. His assailant then put his head down and charged like a battering-ram through the opposing throng, throwing them right and left, till he joined his friend in the street.

Many low betting-men are partially kept by prostitutes—men who frequent Bride Lane and similar places, who, when out of luck, fall back upon their women. Many thieves, too, are fancy-men, and almost all the ruffians who go about "picking up," as the police call it, which I have explained before to be a species of highway robbery. The prostitute goes up to a man, and while she is talking to him the ruffians come up and plunder him. If the victim is drunk so much the better. Most low prostitutes have their fancy-men, such as waiters at taverns, labourers—loose characters, half thieves half loafers. It is strange that such baseness should find a place in a man, but experience proves what I have said to be true; and there are numbers of men in the metropolis who think nothing of being kept by a prostitute on the proceeds of her shame and her disgrace.

Bullies.—Bullies are men attached to brothels and bawdy-houses; but this remark must not be understood to apply to houses of a superior description, for it would not pay them to extort money from their customers, as they have a character and a reputation to support.

The bullies attached to low bawdy-houses are ostensibly kept to perform the functions of door-keepers, but in reality to prevent men from going away without paying enough money; they are in many cases a necessary precaution against "bilking," or going away without paying anything. If a well-dressed man went into an immoral house in Spitalfields, Whitechapel, or Shadwell, he would assuredly be robbed, but not maltreated to any greater extent than was absolutely requisite to obtain his money, and other valuables he might chance to have about him, at the time the depredation was committed.

A man a little tipsy once found himself, he hardly knew how, on the transpontine side of Waterloo Bridge, not far from Stamford Street. It was past twelve, and on being accosted by a woman, he half unconsciously followed her to her rooms in Stamford Street, which were situated about half-way down, near Duke Street, Blackfriars. When upstairs he sent the servant out for some brandy and soda-water, and not having enough silver gave her half-a-sovereign for that purpose, telling her to bring him the change. She soon returned with a bottle of brandy, which she said cost eight shillings, and two bottles of soda-water, and keeping one shilling for herself, told him she had no change to give him: he put up with this extortion, for he was too tipsy to make any resistance. The time passed quickly, and he spent two or three hours in her society, until the soda-water somewhat sobered him, when he put on his hat and declared his intention of going away. The woman sprang up to stop him, and placed her back against the door, meantime calling some one with all her might. Being a strong powerful man, he seized her by the arm and flung her on a sofa. Opening the door, he heard some one rapidly coming up stairs; he rushed back to the room and laid hold of a chair, which he threw at the advancing figure; it missed it, but had the effect of causing it to retreat. Chair after chair followed until the room was nearly denuded of its furniture, the woman being all the time too frightened to take any part in the affray. The man next took the poker in one hand the lamp in the other, and began to descend the stairs, which he did with some difficulty, as the chairs rather impeded his progress. He had no doubt his adversary was waiting for him at the bottom, and it was evident that it was there the real struggle would take place. He descended very cautiously until he was very near the end of the stairs, when he saw a tall strongly-built man awaiting him with a bludgeon in his hand. The gentleman carefully, in the short space he had, reconnoitred the exit to the street by throwing the light of the lamp full into the passage. The bully finding he was discovered began to curse and make demonstrations of hostility, but remained where he was, as he was possessed of the best position. The gentleman when he was within three or four steps of the ground, hurled the lamp with all his force at the bully, striking him on the forehead. The lamp was smashed to atoms, and everything directly plunged in darkness. After this he ran in the direction of the door, but he found the chain up: while he was unfastening this as well as he could in the dark, he heard his antagonist picking himself up and muttering threats of vengeance. In a moment or two he began to grope his way towards the door, but fortunately the gentleman had succeeded in undoing the chain, and flinging the door wide open, he emerged into the street and began to run in the direction of the Waterloo Road as fast as he could. He made his escape; but if he had not had presence of mind, and been strong and powerful enough to fight with the bully, the result might have been very different.

A man who would be a bully at a bawdy-house would stick at nothing. During the daytime they either sleep or lounge about smoking a short pipe, or go to the pawnshops for the women, or else to the public for gin.

The men who used to keep the Cocoa Tree in St. James's Street were two brothers, who, when they were young, held a position of no great importance in their mother's house, which was nothing more than a house of ill fame. They might have degenerated into something of the same sort, but they had a certain amount of talent and opportunities, and once being possessed of this gambling house, which was famous enough in its day, they made money quickly enough.

It is not men though, who have been amongst these scenes when they are young, who take to this sort of life. It is generally returned convicts or gaol birds, who look upon themselves as victims, and get desperate, and do not care very much what they do as long as they can have an easy time of it and enough to eat and drink.

Sometimes, if they watch their opportunity, they may become proprietors of bawdy-houses themselves. Great events spring from little causes; and good management and a good locality will always make a bawdy-house remunerative; but bullies generally have no energy, and are wanting in administrative capability, and more often than not die of disease and excess in the gutter.

The Argyle Rooms were once a small public-house called the "Hall of Rome," where *tableaux vivants* and *poses plastiques* found a home and an audience; but energy and a combination of causes have made it the first casino in London.

A bully in a house in one of the streets near the Haymarket, who was loafing about a public-house, told me in return for some spirits I paid for, that he was a ticket-of-leave man—"he didn't mind saying it, why should he? he'd got his ticket-of-leave, he had, and he'd show it me in two twos.

"When he comed back from Norfolk Island, which he'd been sent to for a term of seven years, he knew no one in town, his pals mostly was lagged by police, and his most hintimit friend was hanged by mistake at the Old Bailey—he knew it was by mistake, as his friend was hincapable of such an act without he was riled extraordinary. Well, he took to the bullying dodge, which paid. He couldn't work, it wornt in his natur, and he took to bullying, kindly —it suited him, it just did, and that was all about it."

The bullies are the lowest ruffians going,

and will not mind doing any act of iniquity, although they stand in great dread of the police, and generally manage matters so as to keep out of their clutches.

Clandestine Prostitutes.

The next division of our subject is clandestine prostitution, whose ramifications are very extensive. In it we must include: 1. Female operatives; 2. Maid-servants, all of whom are amateurs, as opposed to professionals, or as we have had occasion to observe before, more commonly known as "Dollymops"; 3. Ladies of intrigue, who see men to gratify their passions; and 4. Keepers of houses of assignation, where the last-mentioned class may carry on their amours with secresy.

This in reality I regard as the most serious side of prostitution. This more clearly stamps the character of the nation. A thousand and one causes may lead to a woman's becoming a professional prostitute; but if a woman goes wrong without any very cogent reason for so doing, there must be something radically wrong in her composition, and inherently bad in her nature, to lead her to abandon her person to the other sex, who are at all times ready to take advantage of a woman's weakness and a woman's love.

There is a tone of morality throughout the rural districts of England, which is unhappily wanting in the large towns and the centres of particular manufactures. Commerce is incontestably demoralizing. Its effects are to be seen more and more every day. Why it should be so, it is not our province to discuss, but seduction and prostitution, in spite of the precepts of the Church, and the examples of her ministers, have made enormous strides in all our great towns within the last twenty years. Go through the large manufacturing districts, where factory-hands congregate, or more properly herd together, test them, examine them, talk to them, observe for yourself, and you will come away with the impression that there is room for much improvement. Then cast your eye over the statistics of births and the returns of the Registrar-General, and compare the number of legitimate with illegitimate births. Add up the number of infanticides and the number of deaths of infants of tender years—an item more alarming than any. Goldsmith has said that "honour sinks when commerce long prevails," and a truer remark was never made, although the animus of the poet was directed more against men than women.

Female Operatives.—When alluding casually to this subject before, I enumerated some of the trades that supplied women to swell the ranks of prostitution, amongst which are milliners, dress-makers, straw bonnet-makers, furriers, hat-binders, silk-winders, tambour-workers, shoe-binders, slop-women, or those who work for cheap tailors, those in pastry-cook, fancy and cigar-shops, bazaars, and ballet-girls.

I have heard it asserted in more than one quarter, although of course such assertions cannot be authenticated, or made reliable, for want of data, that one out of three of all the female operatives in London are unchaste, and in the habit of prostituting themselves when occasion offers, either for money, or more frequently for their own gratification.

I met a woman in Fleet Street, who told me that she came into the streets now and then to get money not to subsist upon, but to supply her with funds to meet the debts her extravagance caused her to contract. But I will put her narrative into a consecutive form.

"Ever since I was twelve," she said, " I have worked in a printing office where a celebrated London morning journal is put in type and goes to press. I get enough money to live upon comfortably; but then I am extravagant, and spend a great deal of money in eating and drinking, more than you would imagine. My appetite is very delicate, and my constitution not at all strong. I long for certain things like a woman in the family way, and I must have them by hook or by crook. The fact is the close confinement and the night air upset me and disorder my digestion. I have the most expensive things sometimes, and when I can, I live in a sumptuous manner, comparatively speaking. I am attached to a man in our office, to whom I shall be married some day. He does not suspect me, but on the contrary believes me to be true to him, and you do not suppose that I ever take the trouble to undeceive him. I am nineteen now, and have carried on with my 'typo' for nearly three years now. I sometimes go to the Haymarket, either early in the evening, or early in the morning, when I can get away from the printing; and sometimes I do a little in the day-time. This is not a frequent practice of mine; I only do it when I want money to pay anything. I am out now with the avowed intention of picking up a man, or making an appointment with some one for to-morrow or some time during the week. I always dress well, at least you mayn't think so, but I am always neat, and respectable, and clean, if the things I have on ain't worth the sight of money that some women's things cost them. I have good feet too, and as I find they attract attention, I always parade them. And I've hooked many a man by showing my ankle on a wet day. I shan't think anything of all this when I'm married. I believe my young man would marry me just as soon if he found out I went with others as he would now. I carry on with him now, and he likes me very much. I ain't of any particular family; to tell the truth, I was put in the workhouse when I was young, and they apprenticed me. I never knew my father or my mother, although 'my father was, as I've heard say, a well-known swell of capers gay, who cut his last fling with great applause;' or, if you must know, I heard that he was hung for killing a man who opposed him when committing a burglary. In other words, he was 'a macing-cove what robs,' and I'm his daughter, worse luck. I used to think at first, but what was the good of being wretched about it? I couldn't get over for some time, because I was envious, like a little fool, of other people, but I reasoned, and at last I did recover myself, and was rather glad that my position freed me from certain restrictions. I had no mother whose heart I shou'd break by my conduct, or no father who could threaten me with bringing his grey hairs with sorrow to the grave. I had a pretty good example to follow set before me, and I didn't scruple to argue that I was not to be blamed for what I did. Birth is the result of accident. It is the merest chance in the world whether you're born a countess or a washerwoman. I'm neither one nor t'other; I'm only a mot who does a little typographing by way of variety. Those who have had good nursing, and all that, and the advantages of a sound education, who have a position to lose, prospects to blight, and relations to dishonour, may be blamed for going on the loose, but I'll be hanged if I think that priest or moralist is to come down on me with the sledge-hammer of their denunciation. You look rather surprised at my talking so well. I know I talk well, but you must remember what a lot has passed through my hands for the last seven years, and what a lot of copy I've set up. There is very little I don't know, I can tell you. It's what old Robert Owen would call the spread of education."

I had to talk some time to this girl before she was so communicative; but it must be allowed my assiduity was amply repaid. The common sense she displayed was extraordinary for one in her position; but, as she said, she certainly had had superior opportunities, of which she had made the most. And her arguments, though based upon fallacy, were exceedingly clever and well put. So much for the spread of education amongst the masses. Who knows to what it will lead?

The next case that came under my notice was one of a very different description. I met a woman in Leadenhall Street, a little past the India House, going towards Whitechapel. She told me, without much solicitation on my part, that she was driven into the streets by want. Far from such a thing being her inclination, she recoiled from it with horror, and had there been no one else in the case, she would have preferred starvation to such a life. I thought of the motto Vergniaud the Girondist wrote on the wall of his dungeon in his blood, "Potius mori quam fœdari," and I admired the woman whilst I pitied her. It is easy to condemn, but even vice takes the semblance of virtue when it has a certain end in view. Every crime ought to be examined into carefully in order that the motive that urged to the commission may be elicited, and that should be always thrown into the scale in mitigation or augmentation of punishment.

Her father was a dock labourer by trade, and had been ever since he came to London, which he did some years ago, when there was great distress in Rochdale, where he worked in a cotton factory; but being starved out there after working short time for some weeks, he tramped with his daughter, then about fourteen, up to town, and could get nothing to do but work in the docks, which requires no skill, only a good constitution, and the strength and endurance of a horse. This however, as every one knows, is a precarious sort of employment, very much sought after by strong, able-bodied men out of work. The docks are a refuge for all Spitalfields and the adjacent parishes for men out of work, or men whose trade is slack for a time. Some three weeks before I met her, the girl's father had the misfortune to break his arm and to injure his spine by a small keg of spirits slipping from a crane near to which he was standing. They took him to the hospital, where he then was. The girl herself worked as a hat-binder, for which she was very indifferently paid, and even that poor means of support she had lost lately through the failure of the house she worked for. She went to see her father every day, and always contrived to take him something, if it only cost twopence, as a mark of affection on her part, which he was not slow in appreciating, and no doubt found his daughter's kindness a great consolation to him in the midst of his troubles. She said, " I tried everywhere to get employment, and I couldn't. I ain't very good with my needle at fine needlework, and the slopsellers won't have me. I would have slaved for them though, I do assure you, sir; bad as they do pay you, and hard as you must work for them to get enough to live upon, and poor living, God knows, at that. I feel very miserable for what I've done, but I was driven to it; indeed I was, sir. I daren't tell father, for he'd curse me at first, though he might forgive me afterwards: for though he's poor, he's always been honest, and borne a good name; but now—I can't help crying a bit, sir. I ain't thoroughly hardened yet, and it's a hard case as ever was. I do wish I was dead and there was an end of everything, I am so awfully sad and heart-broken. If it don't kill me, I suppose I shall get used to it in time. The low rate of wages I received has often put it into my head to go wrong; but I have always withstood the temptation, and nothing but so many misfortunes and trials coming together could ever have induced me to do it."

This, I have every reason to believe, was a genuine tale of distress told with all simplicity and truth, although everything that a woman of loose morals says must be received with caution, and believed under protest.

Ballet-girls have a bad reputation, which is in most cases well deserved. To begin with their remuneration—it is very poor. They get from nine to eighteen shillings. Columbine in the pantomime gets five pounds a week, but then hers is a prominent position. Out of these nine to eighteen shillings they have to find shoes and petticoats, silk stockings, etc., etc., so that the pay is hardly adequate to their expenditure, and quite insufficient to fit them out and find them in food and lodging. Can it be wondered at, that while this state of things exists, ballet-girls should be compelled to seek a livelihood by resorting to prostitution?

Many causes may be enumerated to account for the lax morality of our female operatives. Among the chief of which we must class—

1. Low wages inadequate to their sustenance.
2. Natural levity and the example around them.
3. Love of dress and display, coupled with the desire for a sweetheart.
4. Sedentary employment, and want of proper exercise.
5. Low and cheap literature of an immoral tendency.
6. Absence of parental care and the inculcation of proper precepts. In short, bad bringing up.

Maid-Servants. — Maid-servants seldom have a chance of marrying, unless placed in a good family, where, after putting by a little money by pinching and careful saving, the housemaid may become an object of interest to the footman, who is looking out for a public-house, or when the housekeeper allies herself to the butler, and together they set up in business. In small families, the servants often give themselves up to the sons, or to the policeman on the beat, or to soldiers in the Parks; or else to shopmen, whom they may meet in the streets. Female servants are far from being a virtuous class. They are badly educated and are not well looked after by their mistresses as a rule, although every dereliction from the paths of propriety by them will be visited with the heaviest displeasure, and most frequently be followed by dismissal of the most summary description, without the usual month's warning, to which so much importance is usually attached by both employer and employed.

Marylebone was lately characterised by one of its vestrymen as being one of the seven black parishes in London. Half the women it is asserted who are sent from the workhouse, and have situations procured for them by the parochial authorities, turn out prostitutes. I have no means of corroborating the truth of this declaration, but it has been made and sent forth to the world through the medium of the public press, though I believe it has been partially contradicted by one of the workhouse authorities; however this may be, there can be no doubt that the tone of morality among servant-maids in the metropolis is low. I will not speak in the superlative—I merely characterise it as low. I had an opportunity of questioning a maid-of-all-work, a simple-minded, ignorant, uneducated, vain little body, as strong physically as a donkey, and thoroughly competent to perform her rather arduous duties, for the satisfactory performance of which she received the munificent remuneration of eight pounds annually, including her board and lodging.

She said: " I came from Berkshire, sir,

near Windsor; father put me to service some years ago, and I've been in London ever since. I'm two and twenty now. I've lived in four or five different situations since then. Are followers allowed? No, sir, missus don't permit no followers. No, I ain't got no perleeceman. Have I got a young man? Well, I have; he's in the harmy, not a hoffisser, but a soldier. I goes out along of him on Sundays, leastways on Sunday afternoons, and missus she lets me go to see a aunt of mine, as I says lives at Camberwell, only between you and me, sir, there ain't no aunt, only a soldier, which he's my sweetheart, as I says to you before, sir."

Maid-servants in good families have an opportunity of copying their mistress's way of dressing, and making themselves attractive to men of a higher class. It is a voluntary species of sacrifice on their part. A sort of suicidal decking with flowers, and making preparations for immolation on the part of the victim herself. Flattered by the attention of the eldest son, or some friend of his staying in the house, the pretty lady's maid will often yield to soft solicitation. Vanity is at the bottom of all this, and is one of the chief characteristics of a class not otherwise naturally vicious. The housemaids flirt with the footmen, the housekeeper with the butler, the cooks with the coachmen, and so on; and a flirtation often begun innocently enough ends in something serious, the result of which may be to blight the prospect of the unfortunate woman who has been led astray.

There are book-hawkers, who go about the country, having first filled their wallets from the filthy cellars of Holywell Street, sowing the seeds of immorality; servants in country houses will pay, without hesitation large prices for improper books. This denomination of evil, I am glad to say, is much on the decrease now, since the Immoral Publications Act has come into operation.

Maid-servants live well, have no care or anxiety, no character worth speaking about to lose, for the origin of most of them is obscure, are fond of dress, and under these circumstances it cannot be wondered that they are as a body immoral and unchaste.

Ladies of Intrigue and Houses of Assignation.—The reader will find more information about "ladies of intrigue" in the annals of the Divorce Court and the pages of the *Causes Célèbres* than it is in my power to furnish him with. By ladies of intrigue we must understand married women who have connection with other men than their husbands, and unmarried women who gratify their passion secretly.

There is a house in Regent Street, I am told, where ladies, both married and unmarried, go in order to meet with and be introduced to gentlemen, there to consummate their libidinous desires. This sort of clandestine prostitution is not nearly so common in England as in France and other parts of the Continent, where chastity and faithfulness among married women are remarkable for their absence rather than their presence. As this vice is by no means common or a national characteristic, but rather the exception than the rule, it can only expect a cursory notice at our hands.

An anecdote was told me illustrative of this sort of thing that may not be out of place here.

A lady of intrigue, belonging to the higher circles of society, married to a man of considerable property, found herself unhappy in his society, and after some time unwillingly came to the conclusion that she had formed an alliance that was destined to make her miserable. Her passions were naturally strong, and she one day resolved to visit a house that one of her female acquaintances had casually spoken about before her some little time before. Ordering a cab, she drove to the house in question, and went in. There was no necessity for her to explain the nature of her business, or the object with which she called. That was understood. She was shown into a handsome drawing-room, beautifully fitted up, for the house was situated in one of the best streets in May Fair, there to await the coming of her unknown paramour. After waiting some little time the door opened, and a gentleman entered. The curtains of the room were partially drawn round the windows, and the blinds were pulled down, which caused a "dim religious light" to pervade the apartment, preventing the lady from seeing distinctly the features of her visitor. He approached her, and in a low tone of voice commenced a conversation with her about some indifferent subject.

She listened to him for a moment, and then with a cry of astonishment recognized her husband's voice. He, equally confused, discovered that he had accidentally met in a house of ill-fame the wife whom he had treated with unkindness and cruelty, and condemned to languish at home while he did as he chose abroad. This strange rencontre had a successful termination, for it ended in the reconciliation of husband

and wife, who discovered that they were mutually to blame.

From the Divorce Court emanate strange revelations, to which the press gives publicity. It reveals a state of immorality amongst the upper and middle classes that is deplorable; but although this unveils the delinquencies of ladies of intrigue, they are not altogether the class we have under discussion. Those who engross our attention are ladies who, merely to satisfy their animal instincts, intrigue with men whom they do not truly love. But though we could multiply anecdotes and stories, it is not necessary to do more than say, they are a class far from numerous, and scarcely deserve to form a distinctive feature in the category of prostitution in London.

Cohabitant Prostitutes.

The last head in our classification is "Cohabitant Prostitutes," which phrase must be understood to include—

1. Those whose paramours cannot afford to pay the marriage fees. This is a very small and almost infinitesimal portion of the community, as banns now cost so very little, that it is next to an absurdity to say "a man and woman" cannot get married because they have not money enough to pay the fees consequent upon publishing the banns, therefore this class is scarcely deserving of mention.

2. Those whose paramours do not believe in the sanctity of the ceremony.

There may be a few who make their religious convictions an objection to marriage, but you may go a very long journey before you will be able to discover a man who will conscientiously refuse to marry a woman on this ground. Consequently we may dismiss these with a very brief allusion.

3. Those who have married a relative forbidden by law. We know that people will occasionally marry a deceased wife's sister, notwithstanding the anathemas of mother church are sure to be hurled at them. Yet ecclesiastical terrors may have weight with a man who has conceived an affection for a sister-in-law, for whom he will have to undergo so many penalties.

Perhaps parliamentary agitation may soon legitimatize these connections, and abolish this heading from our category of Cohabitant Prostitution.

4. Those who would forfeit their income by marrying,—as officers' widows in receipt of pensions, and those who hold property only while unmarried.

This class is more numerous than any of those we have yet mentioned, but it offers nothing sufficiently striking or peculiar to induce us to dwell longer upon it, as it explains itself.

5. Those whose paramours object to marry them for pecuniary or family reasons. This is a subject upon which it has been necessary to dilate; for it includes all the lorettes in London, and the men by whom they are kept. By lorettes, I mean those I have before touched upon as prima donnas, who are a class of women who do not call going to night-houses in Panton Street walking the Haymarket, and feel much insulted if you so characterize their nocturnal wanderings. The best women go to three or four houses in Panton Street, where the visitors are more select than in the other places, where the door porters are less discriminating. Sometimes women who are violent, and make a disturbance, are kept out of particular houses for months.

Of course, the visits of kept women are made by stealth, as the men who keep them would not countenance their going to such places. Perhaps their men are out of town, and they may then go with comparative safety.

Women who are well kept, and have always been accustomed to the society of gentlemen, have an intense horror of the Haymarket women, properly so called, who promenade the pavement in order to pick up men.

And in reality there is a greater distinction between the two classes than would at first appear. Even if a good sort of woman has been thrown over by her man, and is in want of money, she will not pick up any one at a night-house who may solicit her; on the contrary, she will select some fellow she has a liking for: while, on the other hand, the Haymarket women will pick up any low wretch who she thinks will pay her. She will not even object to a foreigner, though all the best women have a great dislike to low foreigners.

Were I to dwell longer upon this subject it is clear I should merely be recapitulating what I have already said in a former portion of this work.

The following narrative was given me by a girl I met in the Haymarket, when in search of information regarding the prostitution of the West-end of London. Her tale is the usual one of unsuspecting innocence and virtue, seduced by fraud and violence. The victim of passion became in time the mistress of lust, and sank from one stage to another, until she found herself compelled to solicit in the streets to obtain a livelihood. She was about twenty-one years of age, beneath the ordinary height, and with a very engaging countenance. She appeared to be a high-spirited intelligent girl, and gave her sad tale with unaffected candour and modesty.

NARRATIVE OF A GAY WOMAN AT THE WEST END OF THE METROPOLIS.

"I was born in the county of ——, in England, where my father was an extensive farmer, and had a great number of servants. I have three brothers and one younger sister. I was sent to a boarding school at B——, where I was receiving a superior education, and was learning drawing, music, and dancing. During the vacations, and once every quarter, I went home and lived with my parents, where one of my chief enjoyments was to ride out on a pony I had, over the fields, and in the neighbourhood, and occasionally to go to M——, a few miles distant. On these occasions we often had parties of ladies and gentlemen; when some of the best people in the district visited us. I had one of the happiest homes a girl could have.

"When I was out riding one day at M——, in passing through the town, my pony took fright, and threatened to throw me off, when a young gentleman who was near rode up to my assistance. He rode by my side till we came to a hotel in town, when we both dismounted. Leaving the horses with the hostlers, we had some refreshment. I took out my purse to pay the expenses, but he would not let me and paid for me. We both mounted and proceeded towards my home. On his coming to the door of the house, I invited him to come in, which he did. I introduced him to my papa and mamma, and mentioned the kind service he had done to me. His horse was put up in our stables, and he remained for some time, and had supper with us, when he returned to M——. He was very wealthy, resided in London, and only visited M—— occasionally with his servants.

"I was then attending a boarding-school at B——, and was about fifteen years of age. A few days after this I left home and returned to B——. We corresponded by letter for nearly twelve months.

"From the moment he rode up to me at M—— I was deeply interested in him, and the attachment increased by the correspondence. He also appeared to be very fond of me. He sometimes came and visited me at home during my school holidays for the next twelve months. One day in the month of May—in summer—he came to our house in his carriage, and we invited him to dinner. He remained with us for the night, and slept with one of my brothers. We were then engaged to each other, and were to be married, so soon as I was eighteen years of age.

"The next day he asked my parents if I might go out with him in his carriage. My mamma consented. She asked if any of our servants would go with us, but he thought there was no occasion for this, as his coachman and footman went along with us. We proceeded to B—— Railway Station. He left his carriage with the coachman and footman, and pressed me to go with him to London. He pretended to my parents he was only going out for a short drive. I was very fond of him, and reluctantly consented to go with him to London.

"He first brought me to Simpson's hotel in the Strand, where we had dinner, then took me to the opera. We went to Scott's supper rooms in the Haymarket. On coming out we walked up and down the Haymarket. He then took me to several of the cafés, where we had wine and refreshments. About four o'clock in the morning he called a Hansom, and drove me to his house; and there seduced me by violence in spite of my resistance. I screamed out, but none of the servants in the house came to assist me. He told his servants I was his young wife he had just brought up from the country.

"I wanted to go home in the morning, and began to cry, but he would not let me go. He said I must remain in London with him. I still insisted on going home, and he promised to marry me. He then bought me a watch and chain, rings and bracelets, and presented me with several dresses. After this I lived with him in his house, as though I had been his wife, and rode out with him in his brougham. I often insisted upon being married. He promised to do so, but delayed from time to time. He generally drove out every day over the finest streets, thoroughfares, and parks of the metropolis; and in the evenings he took me to the Argyle Rooms and to the Casino at Holborn. I generally went there very well dressed, and was much noticed on account of my youthful appearance. We also went to the fashionable theatres in the West-end, and several subscription balls.

"I often rode along Rotten Row with him,

THE HAYMARKET—MIDNIGHT.

and along the drives in Hyde Park. We also went to the seaside, where we lived in the best hotels.

"This lasted for two years, when his conduct changed towards me.

"One evening I went with him to the Assembly Rooms at Holborn to a masked ball. I was dressed in the character of a fairy queen. My hair was in long curls hanging down my back.

"He left me in the supper-room for a short time, when a well-dressed man came up to me. When my paramour came in he saw the young man sitting by my side speaking to me. He told him I was his wife, and inquired what he meant by it, to which he gave no reply. He then asked me if I knew him. I replied no. He asked the gentleman to rise, which he did, apologising for his seating himself beside me, and thereby giving offence. On the latter showing him his card, which I did not see, they sat down and had wine together.

"We came out of the supper-room, and we had a quarrel about the matter. We walked up and down the ball-room for some time, and at last drove home.

"When we got home he quarrelled again with me, struck me, and gave me two black eyes. I was also bruised on other parts of the body, and wanted to leave him that night, but he would not let me.

"In the morning we went out as usual after breakfast for a drive.

"Next evening we went to the Casino at Holborn. Many of the gentlemen were staring at me, and he did not like it. I had on a thick Maltese veil to conceal my blackened eyes.

"The gentleman who had accosted me the previous night came up and spoke to me and my paramour (whom we shall call S.), and had some wine with us. He asked the reason I did not raise my veil. S. said because I did not like to do it in this place. The gentleman caught sight of my eyes, and said they did not look so brilliant as the night before.

"S. was indignant, and told him he took great liberty in speaking of his wife in this manner. The other remarked that no one could help noticing such a girl, adding that I was too young to be his wife, and that he should not take me to such a place if he did not wish me to be looked at. He told him he ought to take better care of me than to bring me there.

"When we got home we had another quarrel, and he struck me severely on the side.

"We did not sleep in the same bed that night. On coming down stairs to breakfast next morning I was taken very ill, and a medical man was sent for. The doctor said I was in a fever, and must have had a severe blow or a heavy fall. I was ill and confined to my bed for three months. He went out every night and left me with a nurse and the servants, and seldom returned till three or four o'clock in the morning. He used to return home drunk; generally came into my bedroom and asked if I was better; kissed me and went downstairs to bed.

"When I got well he was kind to me, and said I looked more charming than ever. For three or four months after he took me out as usual.

"The same gentleman met me again in the Holborn one night while S. had gone out for a short time, leaving me alone. He came up and shook hands with me, said he was happy to see me, and wished me to meet him. I told him I could not. S. was meanwhile watching our movements. The gentleman asked me if I was married, when I said that I was. He admired my rings. Pointing to a diamond ring on his finger, he asked me if I would like it. I said no. He said *your* rings are not so pretty. I still refused it; but he took the ring off his finger and put it on one of mine, and said, 'See how well it looks,' adding, 'Keep it as a memento; it may make you think of me when I am far away.' He told me not to mention it to my husband.

"Meantime S. was watching me, and came up when the man had gone away, and asked what he had been saying to me. I told him the truth, that the same man had spoken to me again. He asked me what had passed between us, and I told him all, with the exception of the ring.

"He noticed the ring on my finger, and asked me where I had got it. I declined at first to answer. He then said I was not true to him, and if I would not tell him who gave me the ring he would leave me. I told him the man had insisted on my having it.

"He thereupon rushed along the room after him, but did not find him. On coming back he insisted on my going home without him.

"He took me outside to his brougham, handed me in it, and then left me. I went home and sat in the drawing-room till he returned, which was about three o'clock in the morning. He quarrelled with me again for not being true to him. I said I was, and had never left his side for a moment from the time I rose in the morning till I lay down at night.

"I then told him I would go home and

tell my friends all about it, and he was afraid.

"Soon after he said to me he was going out of town for a week, and wished me to stop at home. I did not like to remain in the house without a woman, and wished to go with him. He said he could not allow me, as he was to be engaged in family matters.

"He was absent for a week. I remained at home for three nights, and was very dull and wearied, having no one to speak to. I went to my bedroom, washed and dressed, ordered the carriage to be got ready, and went to the Holborn. Who should I see there but this gentleman again. He was astonished to see me there alone; came up and offered me his arm.

"I told him I was wearied at home in the absence of S., and came out for a little relaxation. He then asked to see me home, which I declined. I remained till the dancing was nearly over. He got into the brougham with me and drove to Sally's, where we had supper., after which he saw me home. He bade me 'good-bye,' and said he hoped to see me at the Holborn again some other night.

"Meantime S. had been keeping watch over me, it appears, and heard of this. When he came home he asked me about it. I told him. He swore the gentleman had connexion with me. I said he had not. He then hit me in the face and shook me, and threatened to lock me up. After breakfast he went out to walk, and I refused to go with him.

"When he had gone away I packed up all my things, told the servant to bring a cab, wrote a note and left it on the table. I asked the cabman if he knew any nice apartments a long way off from C——, where I was living. He drove me to Pimlico, and took me to apartments in —— where I have ever since resided.

"When I went there I had my purse full of gold, and my dresses and jewellery, which were worth about 300*l*.

"One evening soon after I went to the Holborn and met my old friend again, and told him what had occurred. He was astonished, and said he would write to my relations, and have S. pulled up for it.

"After this he saw me occasionally at my lodgings, and made me presents.

"He met S. one day in the City, and threatened to write to my friends to let them know how I had been treated.

"I still went to the Holborn occasionally. One evening I met S., who wished me to go home with him again, but I refused, after the ill-usage he had given me.

"I generally spent the day in my apartments, and in the evening went to the Argyle, until my money was gone. I now and then got something from the man who had taken my part; but he did not give me so much as I had been accustomed to, and I used to have strange friends against my own wish.

"Before I received them I had spouted most of my jewellery, and some of my dresses. When I lived with S. he allowed me 10*l*. a week, but when I went on the loose I did not get so much.

"After I had parted with my jewellery and most of my clothes I walked in the Haymarket, and went to the Turkish divans, 'Sally's,' and other cafés and restaurants.

"Soon after I became unfortunate, and had to part with the remainder of my dresses. Since then I have been more shabby in appearance, and not so much noticed."

CRIMINAL RETURNS.

It is very interesting to philanthropists and people who take an interest in seeing human nature improved, and to those who wish to see crime decrease, to notice the fluctuations of crime, its increase, its decrease, or its being stationary, especially among different classes.

Through the kindness of Sir Richard Mayne, and the obliging courtesy of Mr. Yardley, of the Metropolitan Police-Office, Whitehall, I am enabled to show the number of disorderly prostitutes taken into custody during the years 1850 to 1860. Mr. Yardley supplied me with the criminal returns of the Metropolitan Police for the last ten years, from which I have extracted much valuable and interesting information, besides what I have just mentioned.

Number of Disorderly Prostitutes taken into Custody during the years 1850 to 1860, and their Trades.

Year		
1850	- -	2,502
1851	- -	2,573
1852	- -	3,750
1853	- -	3,386
1854	- -	3,764
1855	- -	3,592
1856	- -	4,303
1857	- -	5,178
1858	- -	4,890
1859	- -	4,282
1860	- -	3,734

After some search I have been enabled to give the trades and occupations of those women.

74	were	Hatters and trimmers.
418	,,	Laundresses.
646	,,	Milliners, &c.
400	,,	Servants.
249	,,	Shoemakers.
58	,,	Artificial flower-makers.
215	,,	Tailors.
33	,,	Brushmakers.
42	,,	Bookbinders.
8	,,	Corkcutters.
7	,,	Dyers.
2	,,	Fishmongers.
8	,,	General and marine-store dealers.
24	,,	Glovers.
18	,,	Weavers.

The remainder described themselves as having no trade or occupation.

In ten years then 41,954 disorderly women, who had given themselves up to prostitution, either for their own gratification, because they were seduced, or to gain a livelihood, were arrested by the police. The word disorderly is vague, but I should think it is susceptible of various significations. In one case it may mean drunkenness, in another assaulting the police, in others an offence of a felonious nature may be intended, while in a fourth we may understand a simple misdemeanour, all subjecting the offender, let it be borne in mind, to a fine or incarceration.

Now, 41,954 is an enormous total for ten years. In an unreflective mood I should be inclined to say that prostitutes, taken collectively, were most abandoned, reckless, and wicked; but it is apparent, after a minute's study, that they must not be taken collectively. This forty odd thousand should be understood to represent, for the most part, the very dregs, the lowest, most unthinking, and vilest of the class. We must look for them in the East, in Whitechapel, in Wapping, in transpontine dens and holes, amongst sailors' and soldiers' women. In the Haymarket there is not much drunkenness, and the police are seldom interfered with. If a man, with whom a woman is walking, is drunk, and makes an assault upon the police, the woman will content herself with the innocent, and comparatively harmless amusement of knocking off the policeman's hat, afterwards propelling it gracefully with her foot along the pavement. This pastime is of rather frequent occurrence in nocturnal street rows, and always succeeds in infusing a little comic element into the affray. Amongst the disorderly women of loose habits we see that milliners largely preponderate; 646 in ten years, who have broken the laws in some way, enables us to form, by comparison, a vague idea of the number of milliners, dressmakers, &c., who resort to prostitution; for if so many were disorderly, the number of well-behaved ones must be very large.

Another curious item is laundresses, of whom there were 418 in the hands of the police. Either the influence of their trade is demoralizing in the extreme; or they are underpaid, or else there are large numbers of them; I incline to the latter supposition.

That there should have been only 400 servants is rather a matter of surprise than otherwise, for they are exposed to great temptations, and form a very numerous body.

In our next statistics we are able to be more precise than in the former ones. Peculiar facilities are afforded prostitutes for committing larcenies from the person, and there are annually some hundreds taken into custody, and some few convicted. Only the other day I was passing through Wych Street, on my way from New Inn with a friend, and it so happened that we were instrumental in protecting a gentleman from the rapacity of some men and women of infamous character, by whom he had been entrapped.

In Wych Street there are five or six houses, contiguous to one another, that are nothing more or less than the commonest brothels. The keepers of these places do not in the least endeavour to conceal the fact of their odious occupation; at almost all hours of the day, and till twelve o'clock at night one may perceive the women standing at their doorways in an undress costume, lascivious and meretricious in its nature. Although they do not actually solicit the passer-by with words, they do with looks and gestures.

It might have been a little after twelve o'clock, when, as I was passing one of these houses, a gentleman, with his coat off, and without his hat, rushed out of the doorway and ran up the street. He held a small clasp-knife in his hand, which from his manner I guessed he would not hesitate to use if hard pressed. He was in an instant followed by a pack of men and women, perhaps four or five of each sex, in full cry. They were nearing him, when he turned suddenly round and doubled upon them, which manoeuvre brought him in my direction. I saw, when near enough, that he was intoxicated. Directly he perceived me he implored my protection, saying, "For God's sake keep those fellows off." The noise attracted the attention of a policeman at the end of the street, who came up to see what the origin of the disturbance was, and the crowd fell back at his appearance.

The gentleman said he went into one of the houses to get a cigar, when he was set upon by some women, who attempted to rob him. Although drunk he was able to put his hand in his pocket and take out a small clasp-knife he always carried about with him. He brandished this in their faces, when some bullies descended from the upper regions, and the victim fortunately effected his escape into the street.

This man might have been robbed and subsequently drugged, without much fear of discovery, for the subjoined statistics will prove that such outrages are of frequent occurrence in the metropolis.

LARCENIES from the PERSON by Prostitutes, during the years 1850 to 1860.

	Larcenies.	Convicted.	Total loss.
1850	684	116	£1,814
1851	640	98	1,890
1852	639	97	2,095
1853	605	112	1,578
1854	607	119	2,019
1855	688	96	3,017
1856	780	94	2,668
1857	854	79	2,928
1858	777	39	2,370
1859	681	93	1,743
1860	692	39	1,936

The first thing that strikes us in looking at these figures is the small amount of convictions that followed arrest. For instance in 1850 out of 684 arrested only 116 were convicted. Yet we must not forget the difficulty of proving a charge of this description, and the unwillingness of men to prosecute. It is only natural that a man should have a repugnance to appear in public and mix himself up in a disgraceful affair of this sort. Any one who cared for his character and reputation would at once refuse, and in this repugnance we must look for the cause of the escape of so many offenders.

Whenever an occurrence of this sort takes place in a brothel, one would imagine the police would have some grounds for prosecuting the keeper for harbouring thieves and persons who habitually break the public peace, but the criminal returns of the metropolitan police, from which we have before quoted, do not give one reason to think so.

Let us examine the number of arrests for keeping common brothels, during the last ten years.

NUMBER of PERSONS taken into custody for keeping Common Brothels, during the years 1850 to 1860.

	Females	Males.	Total.
1850	4	4 =	8
1851	12	5	17
1852	4	6	10
1853	9		12
1854	none.		
1855	6	4	10
1856	12	7	19
1857	6	8	14
1858	10	8	18
1859	9	9	18
1860	12	5	17
			143

The largest number (19) was in 1856, while in 1854 there were none at all. But we have already drawn attention to the difficulty the police have in dealing with these cases.

Of those arrested :
1 was a clerk,
1 ,, sailor,
13 were servants,
3 ,, tailors,
1 was a printer,
1 was a sawyer,
1 ,, interpreter,
1 ,, cabinet-maker,
1 ,, brass-founder,
1 ,, green-grocer,
1 ,, butcher,
2 were milliners,
3 ,, laundresses,
9 ,, labourers,
2 ,, smiths,
6 ,, carpenters, [dealers,
3 ,, general and marine store-
1 was a carver and gilder,
4 were shoemakers,
2 ,, watch-makers,
2 ,, painters,
3 ,, bricklayers.

The rest were of no trade or occupation, and depended for a livelihood solely upon this disgraceful means of subsistence.

It is odd to see butchers, printers, tailors, carpenters, brass-founders, interpreters, bricklayers, and cabinet-makers combining this with their own legitimate trades, and if this is a common thing among the trades, how wide-spread the evil must be, for we have only an average of about 12 arrests annually, and this very small amount, with the perhaps light punishment awarded the offender by the sitting magistrate, or if committed by the judge, is evidently purely insufficient and ineffectual to act as a deterrent to others holding the same demoralizing views, and practising the same odious profession.

A few pages back, while commenting upon crime amongst bawds and prostitutes, we took the liberty of criticising some remarks of Dr. Ryan's about the prevalence of murder in immoral houses. The best proof presumptive he could have adduced in support of his theory he utterly neglected to bring forward. I mean the returns of the metropolitan police of the number of persons reported to them annually as missing.

This return, so enormous, so mysterious, so startling, is certainly very alarming before it is analysed. But when with the eye of reflection we calmly and dispassionately look at it, our alarm diminishes as rapidly as it was excited.

NUMBER of PERSONS reported to the Police as lost or missing, and the number found and restored by the Police, during the years 1841 to 1860.

	Reported lost or Missing.	Restored by the Police.
1841	1,000	560
1842	1,179	623
1843	1,218	623
1844	1,111	543
1845	2,201	1,000
1846	2,489	1,082
1847	2,216	1,111
1848	1,866	1,009
1849	1,473	994
1850	2,204	1,137
1851	1,876	928
1852	2,103	1,049
1853	2,034	900
1854	2,286	941
1855	2,178	964
1856	2,371	1,084
1857	2,171	1,198
1858	2,409	1,264
1859	2,374	1,054
1860	2,515	1,164

For twenty years the number of persons reported lost, stolen, strayed, and missing has been steadily increasing.

In 1841 it was 1,000
,, 1851 ,, 1,876
,, 1860 ,, 2,515

Of which

In 1841 560 were restored by the police.
,, 1851 928 ,, ,,
,, 1860 1,164 ,, ,,

Now unscrupulous statisticians and newsmongers would not hesitate to say that the "Fleet Ditch" Dr. Ryan is so fond of might unfold a tale that would elucidate the mystery.

It is surprising that in these enlightened days such monstrosities should be listened to.

How many, I should like to know, disappear from home and enlist in the army? How many run away to sea, and how many commit suicide?

A little reflection shows us that the tales of murder in immoral houses are only bugbears conjured up by moralists to frighten children. Not designedly perhaps, but more through ignorance than anything else.

Perhaps the number of suicides committed annually in London may be of some use in reducing the number of lost and missing.

NUMBER of SUICIDES committed during the years 1841 to 1860.

Year.	Suicides committed.	Year.	Suicides committed.
1841	139	1851	120
1842	134	1852	109
1843	112	1853	131
1844	155	1854	118
1845	144	1855	116
1846	162	1856	127
1847	152	1857	154
1848	100	1858	90
1849	131	1859	180
1850	140	1860	104

I find also that the number of suicides prevented by the police, or otherwise, is on an average nearly equal to the actual number of suicides committed.

Many attempted suicides may not be genuine attempts; for we often hear in the police courts of people endeavouring to make the public believe they wished to destroy themselves, with the sole object of exciting sympathy and drawing attention to their case. However, it is difficult to distinguish, and it is clear there are annually many unhappy wretches who do make away with their lives, and also numbers who are providentially prevented.

Rape is a crime that has not fluctuated to any great extent during the last ten years. I see that in 1850 there were 22 arrests for this offence, and the same number in 1860. Most of the prisoners were in a low station in life; 17 in 1850 only being able to read, or read and write imperfectly, and 15 in 1860 were in the same unintellectual position. In 1855, 21 individuals were given in charge, 16 of whom were imperfectly instructed. It must be remembered that not all those who were charged were convicted, or even committed for trial, because the charge of rape is one easy to trump up, and it requires very sound and unconflicting evidence to bring the charge home.

Concealing the births of infants is a

crime I am glad to perceive of more frequent occurrence, than feloniously attempting to procure abortion; for of two evils it is better the less preponderate.

Year.	Concealing Birth of their Infants.	Feloniously attempting to procure Abortion.
1850	12	1
1855	10	1
1860	17	0

In 1860 there were 2 cases of abduction, and in 1850 none at all; but in the latter year there were 61 cases of indecently exposing the person, which offence had in 1860 attained the dimensions of 103, three only, of which number were females, in the former instance eight.

Of course it is only natural to expect that as the population of the empire increases, crime also will increase; and will more especially show its hideous and unwelcome visage in the metropolis, the centre of a vast and densely-populated kingdom. Where masses of men congregate, there disorder, dissension, and crime will have a place. We have to thank an efficient police force for keeping them within reasonable dimensions.

I have already adverted to the difficulty experienced in even approximating to the actual number of prostitutes existing; but the magisterial authorities are enabled to catalogue and number those who are known to the police and those living in brothels. The subjoined table will be found extremely interesting:

Division and Local Name.	Total.	Well dressed who live in Brothels.	Who walk the Streets. Well dressed.	Who walk the Streets. All others.
A or Whitehall	None.	None.	None.	None.
B or Westminster	469	177	17	275
C or St. James	208	58	150	..
D or St. Mary'bone	428	143	133	152
E or Holborn	511	173	58	280
F or Covent Garden	428	50	204	174
G or Finsbury	225	24	33	168
H or Whitechapel	811	73	82	656
K or Stepney	1015	..	310	705
L or Lambeth	657	147	207	303
M or Southwark	661	53	140	468
N or Islington	441	90	136	215
P or Camberwell	222	44	96	82
R or Greenwich	570	172	124	274
S or Hampstead	331	14	56	261
T or Kensington	97	..	5	92
V or Wandsworth	187	14	40	133
Totals	7,261	1,232	1,791	4,238

This is the latest return that the authorities at Whitehall are in possession of. It will be seen that the largest number of prostitutes are in Stepney; but the prostitution in this district, it would appear, is of a low description, and mostly ambulatory, as no evidence of any women living in brothels is given in the return.

The registered increase since 1857, is in most districts absolutely nothing, whilst the decrease in many localities contrasts very favourably indeed with the increase. For instance:—

	Increase since last return, made in July, 1857.	Decrease since last return, made in July, 1857.
A	None	None
B	..	55
C	..	110
D	..	98
E	..	35
F	..	52
G	..	124
H	..	992
K	..	50
L	..	145
M	..	6
N	..	4
P	..	6
R	169	..
S	100	..
T	..	9
V	..	22
Total	269	1,708

The police have thought it necessary to make special arrangements in special localities, to prevent disorder and enforce the law.

SPECIAL ARRANGEMENTS of POLICE made, and at what places, to prevent disorder and enforce the law.

Division and Local Name.	
A or Whitehall	Cockspur Street—an additional constable occasionally. St. James's, Green, and Hyde Parks—additional constables during summer months.
C—St. James	Regent Street, Waterloo Place, Quadrant, Haymarket, and Coventry Street—four additional constables (and sometimes more) from 3 P M to 5 A.M., daily.

Special Arrangements—continued.	
D—St. Marylebone.	Oxford Street, Edgeware Road. Harrow Road, and Paddington Green—one additional constable from 7 P.M. to 6 A.M., daily. Regent's Park and Bayswater Road—two additional constables from 9 A.M. to 6 A.M., following day. Portland Place — an additional constable from 10 P.M. to 6 A.M.
E—Holborn	Lower Regent Street and Portland Place—one additional constable from 7 P.M. to 10 P.M.; one ditto from 7 P.M. till 2 A.M.; two additional constables from 10 P.M. till 2 A.M., and a sergeant in plain clothes.
F—Covent Garden..	Strand—a sergeant, and occasionally constables. Long Acre—a constable frequently.
H—Whitechapel ..	St. George's Street and High Street, Whitechapel—a constable, and a short beat, each place.
L—Lambeth	Waterloo Road, Herbert's Buildings, and Granby Street—an additional sergeant and two constables patrolling.
S—Hampstead	Regent's Park—an additional constable to patrol. Primrose Hill—two additional constables for eight hours after Park constables go off duty.

COMPARATIVE RETURN of the NUMBER of PROSTITUTES known to the Police, at four different periods, within the last seventeen years.

Division and Local Name.	In 1841	In 1850	In 1857	In 1858
A or Whitehall	...	...	...	...
B „ Westminster ..	...	660	524	469
C „ St. James's ...	...	390	318	208
D „ St. Marylebone	...	429	526	428
E „ Holborn	...	461	546	511
F „ Covent Garden	...	698	480	428
G „ Finsbury	...	320	349	225
H „ Whitechapel ..	...	474	1803	811
K „ Stepney	...	827	965	1015
L „ Lambeth	...	854	802	657
M „ Southwark ...	...	531	667	661
N „ Islington	...	457	445	441
P „ Camberwell ...	...	152	228	222
R „ Greenwich	...	288	401	570
S „ Hampstead	...	216	231	331
T „ Kensington ...	...	92	106	97
V „ Wandsworth ..	...	157	209	187
Totals......	6598	7006	8600	7261

NOTE.—The total number only for 1841 can now be given.

These are the only statistics relative to prostitution that I have been able to procure—indeed I may almost say they are the only ones procurable; and for them I am indebted to the courtesy of the authorities at Whitehall, who, during my researches, have most kindly afforded me every facility that I could wish for.

I dare say that few things contribute so much to the spread of immorality as the sale of indecent and obscene prints and books, which were until lately so widely disseminated over the country by book-hawkers and the filthy traders of Holywell Street. Even now this trade is not entirely suppressed, although the police restrictions are rigorous, and the punishments awarded severe.

Selling obscene prints and exposing for sale:—

In the year	1850	-	1
„	„	1851	-	4
„	„	1852	-	0
„	„	1853	-	0
„	„	1854	-	1
„	„	1855	-	0
„	„	1856	-	5
„	„	1857	-	4
„	„	1858	-	0
„	„	1859	-	3
„	„	1860	-	4
			22

Recently a man called Dugdale, who has grown grey in this disgusting occupation, was brought before a magistrate for selling obscene prints, and also sending some to customers in the country. The magistrate committed him for trial, when he was sent to prison for two years.

It is always more or less interesting to know the extent of instruction among criminals, and with that idea in view I have put together the annexed table, in which I have included all the offences that bear directly and remotely upon the subject I am treating.

As regards the man Dugdale, and the sale of immoral publications, obscene prints, &c., a long account of the prisoner's antecedents was given in the newspaper reports. He had been engaged in this infamous and diabolical traffic nearly forty years, and had spent a great number of them in prison at various times; tons weight of obscene books, pictures, and plates had been seized upon his premises, and he was well known to be the principal instrument for the dissemination of this sort of pollution all over the country. The prosecution was instituted by the meritorious Society for the Suppression of Vice. The judge made a few brief but impressive observations upon the inconceivable enormity of the prisoner's offence, and the whole course of his life, which he said had been one of vice, wickedness, infamy, and villainy, the real extent of which words would fail to describe. From the records of public proceedings for years past the Court had a knowledge of the prisoner's previous history, and it would be a waste of words and the public time to say any thing further to such a person. He was liable to three years' hard-labour, but, considering his age, the Court would refrain from going to extremity, but in the discharge of their duty to society and the rising generation they felt bound to pass upon him a severe sentence, which was that he be kept to hard labour for two years.

TABLE SHOWING THE DEGREE OF INSTRUCTION OF THE PERSONS TAKEN INTO CUSTODY DURING A PERIOD OF TEN YEARS—1850 TO 1860.

OFFENCES.	Years.	Total.	Neither Read nor Write	Read only, or Read and Write imperfectly.	Read and Write well.	Superior Instruction.
Concealing births of their infants	From 1850 to 1860.	167	28	124	15	..
Feloniously attempting to procure abortion		9	..	3	4	2
Rape		324	44	226	97	1
Disorderly Prostitutes		41,914	10,134	30,921	784	75
Indecently exposing the person		1,155	129	785	212	26
Keeping common Brothels		143	22	81	40	..
Selling and exposing obscene prints for sale		22	..	16	6	..

Whilst I am dilating upon statistics it may not be inappropriate to refer to certain figures and facts relating to the Midnight Meeting movement.

By the courtesy of Mr. Theophilus Smith, secretary to the Midnight Meeting movement, I have been furnished with the general statistical results.

20 meetings have been held.
4,000 friendless young women heard the gospel.
23,000 Scripture cards, books, tracts, and Mr. Noel's address at the second meeting circulated.
89 females restored to friends.
75 placed in service.
81 in homes.
1 set up in business.
2 emigrated.
6 married.
1 sent to France.
1 to Holland.
1 to New-York.
30 left homes after a short residence.
———
287

Of this number (287) very many (upwards of thirty) have given evidence of a change of heart.

56 restored at Liverpool.
50 „ Manchester.
130 „ Edinburgh.
30 „ Dundee.
35 „ Dublin.
17 „ Cardiff.
10 „ Ramsgate.
———
358

A total of 645, besides a large number who through the influence of the movement have given up a life of sin, and sought a way of escape for themselves. The committee have heard of many.

I append a list of the metropolitan homes and refuges.

1. British Penitent Female Refuge. Cambridge Heath, Hackney, N E.
2. Female Temporary Home. 218, Marylebone Road, N.W.
3. Guardian Society. 12, North side of Bethnal Green, N.E.
4. Home for Friendless Young Females of Good Character. 17, New Ormond Street, W.C.
5. Home for Penitent Females. White Lion Street, Islington, N.
6. Lock Asylum. Westbourne Green, Paddington.

7. London Diocesan Penitentiary. Park House, Highgate, N.
8. London Female Dormitory. 9, Abbey Road, St. John's Wood.
9. London Female Penitentiary. 166, Pentonville Road, N.
10. London Female Preventive and Reformatory Institution. 200, Euston Road, N.W., and 18, Cornwall Place, Holloway Road, N.
11. London Society for Protection of Young Females. Asylum, Tottenham, N.; Office, 28, New Broad Street, E.C.
12. Magdalen Hospital. 115, Blackfriars Road, S.
13. Refuge for the Destitute. Manor House, Dalston, N.E.
14. Society for the Rescue of Young Women and Children. There are five homes; the office at 11, Poultry, E.C.
15. South London Institution.
16. St. Marylebone Female Protection Society. 157, Marylebone Road, N.W.
17. St. James' Home. Whetstone, Finchley Common, W.
18. Trinity Home. 9, Portland Road, Portland Place, W.
19. Westminster Female Refuge. 44, Vincent Square, S.W.

From February 1860 to February 1861, by contributions and collections the Society, it appears from the balance-sheet, received 2,924*l*. 7*s*. 4*d*.

TRAFFIC IN FOREIGN WOMEN.

ONE of the most disgraceful, horrible and revolting practices (not even eclipsed by the slave-trade), carried on by Europeans is the importation of girls into England from foreign countries to swell the ranks of prostitution. It is only very recently that the attention of Mr. Tyrrwhit, at the Marlborough Police Court, was drawn to the subject by Mr. Dalbert, agent to the "Society for the Protection of Women and Children."

It is asserted that women are imported from Belgium, and placed in houses of ill-fame, where they are compelled to support their keepers in luxury and idleness by the proceeds of their dishonour. One house in particular was mentioned in Marylebone; but the state of the law respecting brothels is so peculiar that great difficulty is experienced in extricating these unfortunate creatures from their dreadful position. If it were proved beyond the suspicion of a doubt, that they were detained against their will, the Habeas Corpus Act might be of service to their friends, but it appears they are so jealously guarded, that all attempts to get at them have hitherto proved futile, although there is every reason to believe that energetic measures will be taken by the above-mentioned Society to mitigate the evil and relieve the victims.

As this traffic is clandestine, and conducted with the greatest caution, it is impossible to form any correct idea of its extent. There are numbers of foreign women about, but it is probable that many of them have come over here of their own free-will, and not upon false pretences or compulsion. One meets with French, Spanish, Italian, Belgian, and other women.

The complaint made before the metropolitan magistrate a short while since was in favour of Belgian women. But the traffic is not confined to them alone. It would appear that the unfortunate creatures are deluded by all sorts of promises and cajolery, and when they arrive in this country are, in point of fact, imprisoned in certain houses of ill-fame, whose keepers derive considerable emolument from their durance. They are made to fetter themselves in some way or other to the trepanner, and they, in their simple-mindedness, consider their deed binding, and look upon themselves, until the delusion is dispelled, as thoroughly in the power of their keepers.

English women are also taken to foreign parts by designing speculators. The English are known to congregate at Boulogne, at Havre, at Dieppe, at Ostend, and other places. It is considered lucrative by the keepers of bawdy-houses at these towns to maintain an efficient supply of English women for their resident countrymen: and though the supply is inadequate to the demand, great numbers of girls are decoyed every year, and placed in the "Maisons de passé," or "Maisons de joie," as they are sometimes called, where they are made to prostitute themselves. And by the farm of their persons enable their procurers to derive considerable profit.

An Englishwoman told me how she was very nearly entrapped by a foreign woman. "I met an emissary of a French bawdy-house," she said, "one night in the Haymarket, and, after conversing with her upon various subjects, she opened the matter she had in hand, and, after a little manœuvring and bush-beating, she asked me if I would not like to go over to France. She specified a town, which was Havre. 'You will get lots of money," she added, and further represented 'that I should have a very jolly time of it.' 'The money you make will be equally divided between yourself and the woman of the house, and when you have made as much as you want, you may come back to England and set up a café or night-house, where your old friends will be only too glad to come and see you. You will of course get lots of custom, and attain a better future than you can now possibly hope for. You ought to look upon me as the greatest friend you have, for I am putting a chance in your way that does not occur every day, I can tell you. If you value your own comfort, and think for a moment about your future, you cannot hesitate. I have an agreement in my pocket, duly drawn up by a solicitor, so you may rely upon its being all on the square, and if you sign this—'

"'To-night?' I asked.

"'Yes, immediately. If you sign this, I will supply you with some money to get what you want, and the day after to-morrow you shall sail for Havre. Madame —— is a very nice sort of person, and will do all in her power to make you happy and comfortable, and indeed she will allow you to do exactly as you please.'"

Fortunately for herself my informant refused to avail herself of the flattering prospect so alluringly held out to her. The bait was tempting enough, but the fish was too wary.

Now let us hear the recital of a girl who, at an early age, had been incarcerated in one of these "Maisons de passé." She is now in England, has been in a refuge, and by the authorities of the charity placed in an occupation which enables her to acquire a livelihood sufficient to allow her to live as she had, up to that time, been accustomed to. Her story I subjoin:—

"When I was sixteen years' old, my father, who kept a public-house in Bloomsbury, got into difficulties and became bankrupt. I had no mother, and my relations, such as they were, insisted upon my keeping myself in some way or other. This determination on their part thoroughly accorded with my own way of thinking, and I did not for an instant refuse to do so. It then became necessary to discover something by which I could support myself. Service suggested itself to me and my friends, and we set about finding out a situation that I could fill. They told me I was pretty, and as I had not been accustomed to do anything laborious, they thought I would make a very good lady's maid. I advertised in a morning paper, and received three answers to my advertisement. The first I went to did not answer my expectations, and the second was moderately good; but I resolved to go to the third, and see the nature of it before I came to any conclusion. Consequently I left the second open, and went to the third. It was addressed from a house in Bulstrode-street, near Welbeck-street. I was ushered into the house, and found a foreign lady waiting to receive me. She said she was going back to France, and wished for an English girl to accompany her, as she infinitely preferred English to French women. She offered me a high salary, and told me my duties would be light; in fact by comparing her statement of what I should have to do with that of the others I had visited, I found that it was more to my advantage to live with her than with them. So after a little consultation with myself, I determined to accept her offer. No sooner had I told her so than she said in a soft tone of voice—

"'Then, my dear, just be good enough to sign this agreement between us. It is merely a matter of form—nothing more, *ma chère*.'

"I asked her what it was about, and why it was necessary for me to sign any paper at all?

"She replied, 'Only for our mutual satisfaction. I wish you to remain with me for one year, as I shall not return to England until then. And if you hadn't some agreement with me, to bind you as it were to stay with me, why, *mon Dieu!* you might leave me directly—oh! *c'est rien.* You may sign without fear or trembling.'

"Hearing this explanation of the transaction, without reading over the paper which was written on half a sheet of foolscap, (for I did not wish to insult or offend her by so doing,) I wrote my name.

"She instantly seized the paper, held it to the fire for a moment or two to dry, and folding it up placed it in her pocket.

"She then requested me to be ready to leave London with her on the following Thursday, which allowed me two days to make my preparations and to take leave of my friends, which I did in very good spirits, as I thought I had a very fair prospect before me. It remained for what ensued to disabuse me of that idea.

"We left the St. Katherine's Docks in the steamer for Boulogne, and instead of going to an hotel, as I expected, we proceeded to a private house in the Rue N— C—, near the Rue de l'Ecu. I have farther to tell you that three other young women accompanied us. One was a housemaid, one was a nursery governess, and the other a cook. I was introduced to them as people that I should have to associate with when we arrived at Madame's house. In fact they were represented to be part of the establishment; and they, poor things, fully believed they were, being as much deluded as myself. The house that Madame brought us to was roomy and commodious, and, as I afterwards discovered, well, if not elegantly, furnished. We were shown into very good bedrooms, much better than I expected would be allotted to servants; and when I mentioned this to Madame, and thanked her for her kindness and consideration, she replied with a smile:—

"'Did I not tell you how well you would be treated? we do these things better in France than they do in England.'

"I thanked her again as she was going away, but she said, '*Tais toi, Tais toi*,' and left me quite enchanted with her goodness."

I need not expatiate on what subsequently ensued. It is easy to imagine the horrors that the poor girl had to undergo. With some difficulty she was conquered and had to submit to her fate. She did not know a word of the language, and was ignorant of the only method she could adopt to insure redress. But this she happily discovered in a somewhat singular manner. When her way of living had become intolerable to her, she determined to throw herself on the generosity of a young Englishman who was in the habit of frequenting the house she lived in, and who seemed to possess some sort of affection for her.

She confessed her miserable position to him, and implored him to protect her or point out a means of safety. He at once replied, "The best thing you can do is to go to the British Consul and lay your case before him. He will in all probability send you back to your own country." It required little persuasion on her part to induce her friend to co-operate with her. The main thing to be managed was to escape from the house. This was next to impossible, as they were so carefully watched. But they were allowed occasionally, if they did not show any signs of discontent to go out for a walk in the town. The ramparts surrounding the "*Haute Ville*" were generally selected by this girl as her promenade, and when this privilege of walking out was allowed her, she was strictly enjoined not to neglect any opportunity that might offer itself. She arranged to meet her young friend there, and gave him notice of the day upon which she would be able to go out. If a girl who was so privileged chanced to meet a man known to the *Bonne* or attendant as a frequenter of the house, she retired to a convenient distance or went back altogether. The plot succeeded, the consul was appealed to and granted the girl a passport to return to England, also offering to supply her with money to pay her passage home. This necessity was obviated by the kindness of her young English friend, who generously gave her several pounds, and advised her to return at once to her friends.

Arrived in England, she found her friends reluctant to believe the tale she told them, and found herself thrown on her own resources. Without a character, and with a mind very much disturbed, she found it difficult to do anything respectable, and at last had recourse to prostitution;—so difficult is it to come back to the right path when we have once strayed from it.

Perhaps it is almost impossible to stop this traffic; but at any rate the infamous wretches who trade in it may be intimidated by publicity being given to their acts, and the indignation of the public being roused in consequence. What can we imagine more dreadful than kidnapping a confiding unsuspecting girl, in some cases we may say child, without exaggeration, for a girl of fifteen is not so very far removed from those who come within the provisions of the Bishop of Oxford's Act? I repeat, what can be more horrible than transporting a girl, as it were, by false representations from her native land to a country of strangers, and condemning her against her will to a life of the most revolting slavery and degradation, without her having been guilty of any offence against an individual or against the laws of the land?

It is difficult to believe that there can be many persons engaged in this white slave-trade, but it is undeniably true.

It is not a question for the legislature; for what could Parliament do? The only way to decrease the iniquity is to widely disseminate the knowledge of the existence of such infamy, that those whom it most nearly concerns, may be put upon their guard, and thus be enabled to avoid falling into the trap so cunningly laid for them.

Much praise is due to those benevolent societies who interest themselves in these matters, and especially to that which we have alluded to more than once—"The Society for the Protection of Women and Children," over which Lord Raynham presides.

Much good may be done by this means, and much misery prevented. The mines of Siberia, with all their terrors, would be preferred—even with the knout in prospective—by these poor girls, were the alternative proffered them, to the wretched life they are decoyed into leading. For all their hopes are blasted, all their feelings crushed, their whole existence blighted, and their life rendered a misery to them instead of a blessing and a means of rational enjoyment.

The idea of slavery of any kind is repulsive to the English mind; but when that slavery includes incarceration, and mental as well as physical subjection to the dominant power by whom that durance is imposed, it becomes doubly and trebly repugnant. If it were simply the deprivation of air and exercise, or even the performance of the most menial offices, it might be borne with some degree of resignation by the sufferer, however unmerited the punishment. But here we have a totally different case: no offence is committed by the victim, but rather by nature, for what is her fault, but being pretty and a woman? For this caprice of the genius of form who presided over her birth she is condemned to a life of misery, degradation, and despair; compelled to receive caresses that are hateful to her, she is at one moment the toy of senile sensuality, and at others of impetuous juvenility, both alike loathsome, both alike detestable. If blandishments disgust her, words of endearment only make her state of desolation more palpable; while profusions of regard serve to aggravate the poignancy of her grief, all around her is hollow, all artificial except her wretchedness. When to this is added ostracism—banishment from one's native country—the condition of the unfortunate woman is indeed pitiable, for there is some slight consolation in hearing one's native language spoken by those around us, and more especially to the class from which these girls are for the most part taken. We must add "*pour comble d' injustice,*" that there is no future for the girl, no reprieve, no hope of mercy, every hope is gone from the moment the prison tawdry is assumed. The condemnation is severe enough, for it is for life. When her beauty and her charms no longer serve to attract the libidinous, she sinks into the condition of a servant to others who have been ensnared to fill her place. Happiness cannot be achieved by her at any period of her servitude; there must always be a restless longing for the end, which though comparatively quick in arriving is always too tardy.

The mind in time in many cases becomes depraved, and the hardness of heart that follows this depravity often prevents the girl from feeling as acutely as she did at first. To these religion is a dead letter, which is a greater and additional calamity. But to be brief, the victim's whole life from first to last is a series of disappointments, combined with a succession of woes that excite a shudder by their contemplation, and which may almost justify the invocation of Death :—

" Death, Death, oh amiable lovely death!
Thou odoriferous stench! sound rottenness!
Arise forth from the couch of lasting night,
Thou hate and terror to prosperity,
And I will kiss thy detestable bones;
And put my eyeballs in thy vaulty brows;
And ring these fingers with thy household worms;
And stop this gap of breath with fulsome dust,
And be a carrion monster like thyself;
Come, grin on me; and I will think thou smil'st,
And kiss thee as thy wife! Misery's love,
O, come to me!
SHAKESPERE, *King John*, Act iii. Scene 4.

THIEVES AND SWINDLERS.

INTRODUCTION.

In tracing the geography of a river it is interesting to go to its source, possibly a tiny spring in the cleft of a rock in some mountain glen. You follow its windings, observing each tributary which flows into its gathering flood until it discharges its waters into the sea. We proceed in a similar manner to treat of the thieves and swindlers of the metropolis.

Thousands of our felons are trained from their infancy in the bosom of crime; a large proportion of them are born in the homes of habitual thieves and other persons of bad character, and are familiarized with vice from their earliest years; frequently the first words they lisp are oaths and curses. Many of them are often carried to the beershop or gin palace on the breast of worthless drunken mothers, while others, clothed in rags, run at their heels or hang by the skirts of their petticoats. In their wretched abodes they soon learn to be deceitful and artful, and are in many cases very precocious. The greater number are never sent to school; some run idle about the streets in low neighbourhoods: others are sent out to beg throughout the city; others go out with their mothers and sit beside their stalls; while others sell a handful of matches or small wares in our public thoroughfares.

One day, in going down a dark alley in the Borough, near Horsemonger Lane Gaol, we saw a little boy—an Irish cockney, who had been tempted to steal by other boys he was in the habit of associating with. He was stripped entirely naked, and was looking over a window on the first floor with a curious grin on his countenance. His mother had kept his clothes from him that day as a punishment for stealing, and to prevent him getting out of the house while she went out to her street-stall.

In our brief sketch of the criminals of the metropolis, we have in the outset directed our attention to the sneaks or common thieves—by far the larger number of our criminal population—from whose ranks the expert pickpockets and the ingenious and daring burglars in most cases emerge. We have treated of the incipient stage of thieving, when the child of five or six years of age steals an apple, or an orange, or a handful of nuts from a stall, or an old pair of boots from a shop door, and then traced the after-stages of more daring crime.

There are thousands of neglected children loitering about the low neighbourhoods of the metropolis, and prowling about the streets, begging and stealing for their daily bread. They are to be found in Westminster, Whitechapel, Shoreditch, St. Giles's, New Cut, Lambeth, the Borough, and other localities. Hundreds of them may be seen leaving their parents' homes and low lodging-houses every morning sallying forth in search of food and plunder. They are fluttering in rags and in the most motley attire. Some are orphans and have no one to care for them; others have left their homes and live in lodging-houses in the most improvident manner, never thinking of to-morrow; others are sent out by their unprincipled parents to beg and steal for a livelihood; others are the children of poor but honest and industrious people, who have been led to steal through the bad companionship of juvenile thieves. Many of them have never been at a day-school nor attended a Sunday or ragged-school, and have had no moral or religious instruction. On the contrary, they have been surrounded by the most baneful and degrading influences, and have been set a bad example by their parents and others with whom they came in contact, and are shunned by the honest and industrious classes of society. The chief agencies which have tended to ameliorate their condition are the ragged-schools, where they receive sound secular and religious instruction; the shoeblacks' brigades, where they are trained in habits of honest industry; and the juvenile reformatories, which have been instituted for their moral and social elevation.

Many of them are hungry, and have no food to eat nor money to purchase it, and readily steal when they find a suitable opportunity. Not having received the benefit of a sound moral training, they have not the conscientious scruples possessed by the children of honest parents; their only care is to avoid being detected in their felonies. When they successfully steal some article from a stall or shop-door, or rifle a till by entering the shop, they are congratulated on their expertness by their companions, and enjoy a larger share of plunder.

The public streets of the metropolis are regarded by these ragged little felons and the children of honest industrious parents in a very different aspect. The latter walk the streets with their eyes sparkling with wonder and delight at the beautiful and grand sights of the metropolis. They are struck with the splendour of the shops and the elegance and stateliness of the public buildings, and with the dense crowds of people of various orders, and trains of vehicles thronging the streets. These little ragged thieves walk along the streets with very different emotions. They, too, in their own way, enjoy the sights and sounds of London. Amid the busy crowds many of them are to be seen sitting in groups on the pavement or loitering about in good-humour and merriment; yet ever and anon their keen roguish eyes sparkle as they look into the windows of the confectioners', bakers', and greengrocers' shops, at the same time keeping a sharp eye on the policeman as he passes on his beat.

These juvenile thieves find an ample field for plunder at the stalls and shop-doors in Whitechapel, Shoreditch, Edgeware Road, and similar localities, where many articles are exposed for sale, which can be easily disposed of to some of the low fences. In this manner thousands of our felons are trained to be expert and daring in crime, and are frequently tried and convicted before the Police Courts.

This is the main source of the habitual felons of the metropolis. As these boys and girls grow up they commence a system of sneaking thefts over the metropolis, some purloining in shops, others gliding into areas and lobbies on various pretences, stealing articles from the kitchen, and when opportunity occurs carrying off the plate.

As these young felons advance in years they branch off into three different classes, determined partly by their natural disposition and personal qualities, and partly by the circumstances in which they are placed. Many of them continue through life to sneak as common thieves, others become expert pickpockets, and some ultimately figure as burglars.

A vast number of juvenile thieves as they grow up continue to carry on a system of petty felonies over the metropolis, and reside in the lowest neighbourhoods. Some pretend to sell laces and small wares to get a pretext to call at the houses of labouring people and tradesmen, and to go down the areas and enter the lobbies in fashionable streets. In addition to the paltry profits arising from these sales they get a livelihood by begging, and as a matter of course do not scruple to steal when they can find an opportunity.

These common thieves are of both sexes, and of various ages, and are often characterized by mental imbecility and low cunning. Many of them are lazy in disposition and lack energy both of body and mind. They go out daily in vast shoals over the metropolis picking up a miserable and precarious livelihood, sometimes committing felonies in the houses they visit of considerable value.

The pickpockets are of various ages and of different degrees of proficiency, from the little ragged urchin in St. Giles's stealing a handkerchief at the tail of a gentleman's coat, to the elegantly dressed and expert pickpocket promenading in the West-end and attending fashionable assemblies. Some are dressed as mechanics, others as clerks, some as smart business men, and others in fashionable attire. They are to be found on all public occasions, some of them clumsy and timid, others daring and most expert. Many of them continue to pursue this class of felonies in preference to any other. They receive a considerable accession to their numbers by young women, frequently servants who have been seduced, and cohabit with burglars, pickpockets, and others, and who are trained to this infamous profession, and in many cases are shoplifters.

Many are trained to commit housebreaking and burglaries from fourteen to fifteen years of age. Boys are occasionally employed to enter through fanlights and windows, and to assist otherwise in plundering dwellings and shops. Some of them commit burglaries of small value in working neighbourhoods, where comparatively little ingenuity and skill are required, others plunder shops and warehouses and fashionable dwellings, which is generally done with greater care and ingenuity, and where the booty is often of higher value.

In addition to the three classes we have named, the common thief, the pickpocket, and the burglar, there is another class of low ruffians who frequently cohabit with low women and prostitutes, and commit highway robberies. They often follow these degraded females on the streets, and attack persons who accost them, believing them to be prostitutes. At other times they garotte men on the street at midnight, or in the by-streets in the evening, and plunder them with violence. This class of persons are generally hardened in crime, and many of them are returned convicts.

The habitual crime of the female portion of the community is in most cases associated with prostitution. We learn from statistics collected by the metropolitan constabulary for 1860, that there are nearly 7000 open prostitutes or street-walkers in London, three fourths of whom we have reason to believe are addicted to stealing. While many of these belong to our native-born felon population, a large proportion have been seduced from the ranks of honest and industrious people in London, or have come up from the provinces, while a few of them are from the Continent.

We believe that the most effective means of checking the crime of the metropolis is to have an efficient machinery of ragged schools in those low neighbourhoods, where neglected children are to be found, similar to the ragged school in George's Yard, and to train them in honest employment, as in the shoeblack brigades or industrial schools.

We learn from the statistics of the constabulary of the metropolis that juvenile crime has been considerably reduced within the past ten years. Several of our police inspectors have laboured with untiring industry to reform the lodging-houses and to introduce cleanliness and decency, where immorality and filth formerly prevailed. And noble exertions have been made by Christian societies to illumine these dark localities with the light of Christian truth.

Yet much still remains to be done. And it is a problem worthy of our highest and wisest statesmen to consider whether adequate means to elevate this abandoned class are to be provided by voluntary effort, or by the paternal care of our Government from the public treasury.

It is far easier to train the young in virtuous and industrious habits, than to reform the grown-up felon who has become callous in crime, and it is besides far more profitable to the State. To neglect them or inadequately to attend to their welfare gives encouragement to the growth of this dangerous class. On the other hand how noble the aim, to adopt wise and vigorous measures to provide for these children of adversity and misfortune, and to transform them into useful members of society!

Our national reformatories are very useful in reclaiming those juveniles who have fallen into crime; but ragged schools efficiently conducted would be of still higher value—as prevention is better than cure. In providing those noble machineries by voluntary effort, or by the State, we would wisely act as the minister of Divine Providence, and would thereby promote the best interests and prosperity of our country.

We have also endeavoured to give a cursory sketch of the swindlers of the metropolis, who are generally of a different class from our felon population. They consist of persons embezzling the property of their employers; of sharpers plundering their dupes by tricks at card-playing, skittles, or otherwise; and of rogues abstracting the property of the public by false pretences. Many of these formerly belonged to the ranks of the honest and industrious working and middle-classes, and not a few of them are well connected, and have lived in fashionable society. By improvidence, extravagance, or dissipation, they have squandered their means, and have now basely adopted a course of systematic dishonesty rather than lead an industrious life. Some of them have led a fast life in the metropolis, and are persons of ruined fortune. Others are indolent in disposition, and carry on a subtle system of public robbery rather than pursue some honest occupation or calling.

It may throw considerable light on the crime of London to look to the criminal statistics of the Metropolitan Police Force. We find a statement of those who were apprehended or proceeded against in the year ending 29th September, 1860.

Under the class of persons proceeded against on indictment there are:—

Known thieves	813
Prostitutes	159
Suspected characters	1,440
	2,412

Under the class of persons proceeded against summarily there are:—

Known thieves	2,850
Prostitutes	7,381
Vagrants, tramps, &c.	2,888
Suspicious characters	7,044
Habitual drunkards	3,661
	23,824

A number of these parties have appeared repeatedly before the Police Courts during the year.

In the return for the month of September, 1860, we find the following statement of depredators, offenders, and suspected persons at large within the districts of the police:—

Known thieves and depredators	2,906
Prostitutes	6,881
Suspicious characters	1,770
Vagrants and tramps	1,461
In all,	13,018

The average number of persons roaming as thieves over the metropolis committing depredations may be safely estimated at from 12,000 to 15,000; a huge army living on the industry of the community.

The amount of property abstracted in the metropolitan districts for the year 1860 - £62,095
Ditto ditto in the City - 9,508
£71,603

This does not give the full amount of the depredations committed by the robbers of the metropolis, as many felonies are not included in the police returns.

In writing this account of the state of crime in London, we have received valuable assistance throughout from the city and metropolitan police force. We have to acknowledge our obligations generally to Sir Richard Mayne and Mr. Yardley at Scotland Yard, and specially to Mr. Jones, of Tower Street Police Station, Lambeth, for information on common thieves; to Mr. Whyte of Marylebone Station on skeleton-key and attic thieves; to Serjeant McVitti of Hoxton; Mr. Ackrill of Fleet Street, and Mr. Jones of Tower Street on pickpockets; to Inspector Foulger of the City police; Mr. Knight, of Fleet Street, and Serjeant Potter of Paddington Station on burglars, forgers, magsmen and skittle-sharps; to Mr. Brennan on coiners; to Inspector Broad of Spitalfields Station on highway robbers; to Inspector Hunt on embezzlers; to Mr. Stubbs on swindlers; and to numerous other officers of the city and metropolitan police for their generous and cordial aid.

THE SNEAKS, OR COMMON THIEVES.

The common thief is not distinguished for manual dexterity and accomplishment, like the pickpocket or mobsman, nor for courage, ingenuity, and skill, like the burglar, but is characterized by low cunning and stealth—hence he is termed the *Sneak*, and is despised by the higher classes of thieves.

There are various orders of Sneaks—from the urchin stealing an apple at a stall, to the man who enters a dwelling by the area or an attic window and carries off the silver plate.

In treating of the various classes of common thieves and their different modes of felony, we shall first treat of the juvenile thieves and their delinquencies, and notice the other classes in their order, according to the progressive nature and aggravation of their crime.

Street-stalls.—In wandering along Whitechapel we see ranges of stalls on both sides of the street, extending from the neighbourhood of the Minories to Whitechapel church. Various kinds of merchandize are exposed to sale. There are stalls for fruit, vegetables, and oysters. There are also stalls where fancy goods are exposed for sale—combs, brushes, chimney-ornaments, children's toys, and common articles of jewellery. We find middle-aged women standing with baskets of firewood, and Cheap Johns selling various kinds of Sheffield cutlery, stationery, and plated goods.

It is an interesting sight to saunter along the New Cut, Lambeth, and to observe the street stalls of that locality. Here you see some old Irish woman, with apples and pears exposed on a small board placed on the top of a barrel, while she is seated on an upturned bushel basket smoking her pipe.

Alongside you notice a deal board on the top of a tressel, and an Irish girl of 18 years of age seated on a small three-legged stool, shouting in shrill tones "Apples, fine apples, ha'penny a lot!"

You find another stall on the top of two tressels, with a larger quantity of apples and pears, kept by a woman who sits by with a child at her breast.

In another place you see a costermonger's barrow, with large green and yellow piles of fruit of better quality than the others, and a group of boys and girls assembled around him as he smartly disposes of pennyworths to the persons passing along the street.

Outside a public-house you see a young man, humpbacked, with a basket of herrings and haddocks standing on the pavement, calling "Yarmouth herrings—three a-penny!" and at the door of a beershop with the sign of the "Pear Tree" we find a miserable looking old woman selling cresses, seated on a stool with her feet in an old basket.

As we wander along the New Cut during the day, we do not see so many young thieves loitering about; but in the evening when the lamps are lit, they steal forth from their haunts, with keen roguish eye, looking out for booty. We then see them loitering about the stalls or mingling among the throng of people in the street, looking wistfully on the tempting fruit displayed on the stalls.

These young Arabs of the city have a very strange and motley appearance. Many of them are only 6 or 7 years of age, others 8 or 10. Some have no jacket, cap, or shoes, and wander about London with their ragged trowsers hung by one brace; some have an old tattered coat, much too large for them, without shoes and stockings, and with one leg of the trowsers rolled up to the knee; others have on an old greasy grey or black cap, with an old jacket rent at the elbows, and strips of the lining hanging down behind; others have on an old dirty pinafore; while some have petticoats. They are generally in a squalid and unwashed condition, with their hair clustered in wild disorder like a mop, or hanging down in dishevelled locks,—in some cases cropped close to the head.

Groups of these ragged urchins may be seen standing at the corners of the streets and in public thoroughfares, with blacking-boxes slung on their back by a leathern belt, or crouching in groups on the pavement; or we may occasionally see them running alongside of omnibuses, cabs, and hansoms, nimbly turning somersaults on the pavement as they scamper along, and occasionally walking on their hands with their feet in the air in our fashionable streets, to the merriment of the passers-by. Most of them are Irish cockneys, which we can observe in their features and accent—to which class most of the London thieves belong. They are generally very acute and ready-witted, and have a knowing twinkle in their eye which exhibits the precocity of their minds.

As we ramble along the New Cut in the dusk, mingled in the throng on the crowded street, chiefly composed of working people, the young ragged thieves may be seen stealing forth: their keen eye readily recognizes the police-officers proceeding in their rounds, as well as the detective officers in their quiet and cautious movements. They seldom steal from costermongers, but frequently from the old women's stalls. One will push an old woman off her seat — perhaps a bushel basket, while the others will steal her fruit or the few coppers lying on her stall. This is done by day as well as by night, but chiefly in the dusk of the evening.

They generally go in a party of three or four, sometimes as many as eight together. Watching their opportunity, they make a sudden snatch at the apples or pears, or oranges or nuts, or walnuts, as the case may be, then run off, with the cry of "stop thief!" ringing in their ears from the passers-by. These petty thefts are often done from a love of mischief rather than from a desire for plunder.

When overtaken by a police-officer, they in general readily go with him to the police-station. Sometimes the urchin will lie down in the street and cry "let me go!" and the bystanders will take his part. This is of frequent occurrence in the neighbourhood of the New-cut and the Waterloo-road—a well-known rookery of young thieves in London.

By the petty thefts at the fruit-stalls they do not gain much money—seldom so much as to get admittance to the gallery of the Victoria Theatre, which they delight to frequent. They are particularly interested in the plays of robberies, burglaries, and murders performed there, which are done in melodramatic style. There are similar fruit-stalls in the other densely populated districts of the metropolis.

In the Mile-end-road, and New Northroad, and occasionally in other streets in different localities of London, common jewellery is exposed for sale, consisting of brooches, rings, bracelets, breast-pins, watch-chains, eye-glasses, ear-rings and studs, &c. There are also stalls for the sale of china, looking-glasses, combs, and chimney-ornaments. The thefts from these are generally managed in this way:—

One goes up and looks at some trifling article in company with his associates. The party in charge of the stall—generally a woman—knowing their thieving propensity, tells them to go away; which they decline to do. When the woman goes to remove him, another boy darts forward at the other end of the stall and steals some article of jewellery, or otherwise, while her attention is thus distracted.

These juvenile thieves are chiefly to be found in Lucretia-street, Lambeth; Union-street, Borough-road; Gunn-street, and Friars-street, Blackfriars-road; also at Whitechapel, St. Giles's, Drury-lane, Somers Town, Anderson Grove, and other localities.

The statistics connected with this class of felonies will be given when we come to treat on "Stealing from the doors and windows of shops."

Stealing from the Tills.—This is done by the same class of boys, generally by two or three, or more, associated together. It is committed at any hour of the day, principally in the evening, and generally in the following way: One of the boys throws his cap into the shop of some greengrocer or other small dealer, in the absence of the person in charge; another boy, often without shoes or stockings, creeps in on his hands and knees as if to fetch it, being possibly covered from without by some of the boys standing beside the shop-door, who is also on the look-out. Any passer-by seeing the cap thrown in would take no particular notice in most cases, as it merely appears to be a thoughtless boyish frolic. Meantime the young rogue within the shop crawls round the counter to the till, and rifles its contents.

If detected, he possibly says, "Let me go; I have done nothing. That boy who is standing outside and has just run away threw in my bonnet, and I came to fetch it." When discovered by the shopkeeper, the boy will occasionally be allowed to get away, as the loss may not be known till afterwards.

Sometimes one of these ragged urchins watches a favourable opportunity and steals from the till while his comrade is observing the movements of the people passing by and the police, without resorting to the ingenious expedient of throwing in the cap.

The shop tills are generally rifled by boys, in most cases by two or more in company; this is only done occasionally. It is confined chiefly to the districts where the working classes reside.

In some cases, though rarely, a lad of 17 or 19 years of age or upwards, will reach his hand over the counter to the till, in the absence of the person in charge of the shop.

These robberies are not very numerous, and are of small collective value.

Stealing from the Doors and Windows of Shops.—In various shopping districts of London we see a great variety of goods displayed for sale at the different shop-doors and windows, and on the pavement in front of the shops of brokers, butchers, grocers, milliners, &c.

Let us take a picture from the New-cut, Lambeth. We observe many brokers' shops along the street, with a heterogenous assortment of household furniture, tables, chairs, looking-glasses, plain and ornamental, cupboards, fire-screens, &c., ranged along the broad pavement; while on tables are stores of carpenters' tools in great variety, copper-kettles, brushes, and bright tin pannikins, and other articles.

We see the dealer standing before his door, with blue apron, hailing the passer-by to make a purchase. Upon stands on the pavement at each side of his shop-door are cheeses of various kinds and of different qualities, cut up into quarters and slices, and rashers of bacon lying in piles in the open windows, or laid out on marble slabs. On deal racks are boxes of eggs, "fresh from the country," and white as snow, and large pieces of bacon, ticketed as of "fine flavour," and "very mild."

Alongside is a milliner's shop with the milliner, a smart young woman, seated knitting beneath an awning in front of her door. On iron and wooden rods, suspended on each side of the door-way, are black and white straw bonnets and crinolines, swinging in the wind; while on the tables in front are exposed boxes of gay feathers, and flowers of every tint, and fronts of shirts of various styles, with stacks of gown-pieces of various patterns.

A green-grocer stands by his shop with a young girl of 17 by his side. On each side of the door are baskets of apples, with large boxes of onions and peas. Cabbages are heaped at the front of the shop, with piles of white turnips and red carrots.

Over the street is a furniture wareroom. Beneath the canvas awning before the shop are chairs of various kinds, straw-bottomed and seated with green or puce-coloured leather, fancy looking-glasses in gilt frames, parrots in cages, a brass-mounted portmanteau, and other miscellaneous articles. An active young shopman is seated by the shop-door, in a light cap and dark apron—with newspaper in hand.

Near the Victoria Theatre we notice a second-hand clothes store. On iron rods suspended over the doorway we find trowsers, vests, and coats of all patterns and sizes, and of every quality dangling in the wind; and on small wooden stands along the pavement are jackets and coats of various descriptious. Here are corduroy jackets, ticketed "15s. and 16s. made to order." Corduroy trowsers warranted "first rate," at 7s. 6d. Fustian trowsers to order for 8s. 6d.; while dummies are ranged on the pavement with coats buttoned upon them, inviting us to enter the shop.

In the vicinity we see stalls of workmen's iron tools of various kinds—some old and rusty, others bright and new.

Thefts are often committed from the doors and windows of these shops during the day, in the temporary absence of the person in charge. They are often seen oy passers-by, who take no notice, not wishing to attend the police court, as they consider they are insufficiently paid for it.

The coat is usually stolen from the dummy in this way: one boy is posted on the opposite side of the street to see if a police-officer is in sight, or a policeman in plain clothes, who might detect the depredation. Another stands two or three yards from the shop. The third comes up to the dummy, and pretends to look at the quality of the coat to throw off the suspicion of any bystander or passer-by. He then unfastens the button, and if the shopkeeper or any of his assistants come out, he walks away. If he finds that he is not seen by the people in the shop, he takes the coat off the dummy and runs away with it.

If seen, he will not return at that time, but watches some other convenient opportunity. When the young thief is chased by the shopkeeper, his two associates run and jostle him, and try to trip him up, so as to give their companion an opportunity of escaping. This is generally done at dusk, in the winter time, when thieving is most prevalent in those localities.

In stealing a piece of bacon from the shop-doors or windows, they wait till the shopman turns his back, when they take a piece of bacon or cheese in the same way as in the case alluded to. This is commonly done by two or more boys in company.

Handkerchiefs at shop-doors are generally stolen by one of the boys and passed to another who runs off with it. When hotly chased, they drop the handkerchief and run away.

These young thieves are the ragged boys formerly noticed, varying from 9 to 14 years of age, without shoes or stockings. Their parents are of the lowest order of Irish cockneys, or they live in low lodging-houses, where they get a bed for 2d. or 3d. a night, with crowds of others as destitute as themselves.

There are numbers of young women of 18 years of age and upwards, Irish cockneys, belonging to the same class, who steal from these shop-doors. They are poorly dressed, and live in some of the lowest streets in Surrey and Middlesex, but chiefly in the Borough and the East end. Some of them are dressed in a clean cotton dress, shabby bonnet and faded shawl, and are accompanied by one or more men, costermongers in appearance. They steal rolls of printed cotton from the outside of linen drapers' shops, rolls of flannel, and of coarse calico, hearthrugs and rolls of oilskin and tablecovers; and from brokers' shops they carry off rolls of carpet, fenders, fire-irons, and other articles, exposed in and around the shop-door. The thefts of these women are of greater value than those committed by the boys. They belong to the felon-class and are generally expert thieves.

The mode in which they commit these thefts is by taking advantage of the absence of the person in charge of the shop, or when his back is turned. It is done very quickly and dexterously, and they are often successful in carrying away articles such as those named without any one observing them.

Another class of Sneaks, who steal from the outsides of shops, are women more advanced in life than those referred to,— some middle-aged and others elderly. Some of them are thieves, or the companions of thieves, and others are the wives of honest, hard-working mechanics and labouring men, who spend their money in gin and beer at various public-houses.

These persons go and look over some pieces of bacon or meat outside of butchers' shops; they ask the price of it, sometimes buy a small piece and steal a large one, but more frequently buy none. They watch the opportunity of taking a large piece which they slip into their basket and carry to some small chandler's shop in a low neigbourhood, where they dispose of it at about a fourth of its value.

We have met some thieves of this order, basket in hand, returning from Drury Lane, who were pointed out to us by a detective officer.

The mechanics' and labourers' wives in many cases leave their homes in the morning for the purpose of purchasing their husband's dinner. They meet with other women fond of drink like themselves. They meet, for example, outside the "Plumb Tree," or such-like public-house, and join their money together to buy beer or gin.

After partaking of it, they leave the house, and remain for some time outside conversing together. They again join their money and return to the public-house, and have some additional liquor: leave the house and separate. Some of them join with other parties fond of liquor as they did with the former. One says to the other: "I have no money, otherwise we would have a drop of gin. I have just met Mrs. So-and-so, and spent nearly all my money." The other may reply: "I have not much to get the old man's dinner, but we can have a quartern of gin." After getting the liquor, they separate. The tradesman's wife, finding that she has spent nearly the whole of her money, goes to a cheesemonger's or butcher's shop, and steals a piece of meat, or bacon, for the purpose of placing it before her husband for dinner, perhaps selling the remainder of the booty at shops in low neighbourhoods, or to lodging-houses.

Such cases frequently occur, and are brought before the police-courts.

These persons sometimes steal flat-irons for ironing clothes at the brokers' shop-doors, which they carry to other pawnbrokers if not detected. At other times they take them to the leaving-shop of an unlicensed pawnbroker. On depositing them, they get a small sum of money. These leaving-shops are in the lowest localities, and take in articles pawnbrokers would refuse. They are open on Sundays, and at other times when no business is done in pawnbrokers' shops.

These shops are well known to the police, and give great assistance to these Sneaks in disposing of their stolen property.

A considerable number of depredations are committed at the doors of shoemakers' shops. They are committed by women of the lower orders, of all ages, some of them very elderly. They come up to the door as tho' they were shopping, attired generally in an old bonnet and faded shawl. The shoes are hanging inside the door, suspended from an iron rod by a piece of string, and are sometimes hanging on a bar outside the shop.

These parties are much of the same order of thieves already described, possibly many of them the mothers and some the grandmothers of the ragged boys referred to. The greater number of them are Irish cockneys. They come up to the shop-door generally in the afternoon, as if to examine the quality of the shoes or boots, but seldom make any purchase. They observe how the articles are suspended and the best mode of abstracting them. They return in the dusk of the evening and steal them.

The shops from which these robberies are committed are to be found in Lambeth-walk, New-cut, Lower Marsh, Lambeth, Tottenham Court-road, Westminster, Drury-lane, the neighbourhood of St. Giles's, Petticoat-lane, Spitalfields, White-cross-street, St. Luke's, and other localities.

Small articles are occasionally taken from shop windows in the winter evenings, by means of breaking a pane of glass in a very ingenious way. These thefts are committed at the shops of confectioners, tobacconists, and watchmakers, &c., in the quiet by-streets.

Sometimes they are done by the younger ragged-boys, but in most cases by lads of 14 and upwards, belonging to the fraternity of London thieves.

In the dark winter evenings we may sometimes see groups of these ragged boys, assembled around the windows of a small grocery-shop, looking greedily at the almond-rock, lollipops, sugar-candy, barley-sugar, brandy-balls, pies, and tarts, displayed in all their tempting sweetness and in all their gaudy tints. They insert the point of a knife or other sharp instrument into the corner or side of the pane, then give it a wrench, when the pane cracks in a semicircular starlike form around the part punctured. Should a piece of glass large enough to admit the hand not be sufficiently loosened, they apply the sharp instrument at another place in the pane, when the new cracks communicate with the rents already made; on applying a sticking-plaster to the pane, the piece readily adheres to it, and is abstracted. The thief inserts his hand through an opening in the window, seizes a handful of sweets or other goods, and runs away, perhaps followed by the shopman in full chase. These thieves are termed star-glazers.

Such petty robberies are often committed by elder lads at the windows of tobacconists, when cigars and pipes are frequently stolen.

They cut the pane in the manner described, and sometimes get a younger boy to commit the theft, while they get the chief share of the plunder, without having exposed themselves to the danger of being arrested stealing the property.

The number of felonies of goods, &c., exposed to sale in the Metropolitan districts for 1860 1671
Ditto   ditto in the City   133
                                              1804

Value of goods thereby stolen in the Metropolitan districts £1487
Ditto   ditto in the City   35
                                                £1522

Stealing from Children.—Children are occasionally sent out by their mothers, with bundles of washing to convey to different persons, or they may be employed to bring clothes from the mangle. They are sometimes met by a man, at other times by a woman, who entices them to go to a shop for a halfpenny or a penny worth of sweets, meanwhile taking care they leave their parcels or bundle, which they promise to keep for them till they return. On their coming out of the shop, they find the party has decamped, and seldom any clue can be got of them, as they may belong to distant localities of the metropolis.

In other cases they go up to the children, when they are proceeding on their way, with a bundle or basket, and say: "You are going to take these things home. Do you know where you are going to take them?" The child being taken off her guard may say. She is carrying them to Mrs. So-and-so, of such a street." They will then say. "You are a good girl, and are quite right. Mrs. So-and-so sent me for them, as she is in a hurry and is going out." The child probably gives her the basket or bundle, when the thief absconds. A case of this kind occurred in the district of Marylebone about six months ago.

A girl was going with two silk-dresses to a lady in Devonshire-street, when she was met by a young woman, who said she was a servant of the lady, and was sent to get the dresses done or undone, and was very glad she had met her. The woman was an entire stranger to the lady. The larceny was detected on the Saturday night, and the lady was put to great inconvenience, as she had not a dress to go out with on the Sunday. Robberies of clothes sent out to be mangled, and of articles of linen are very common. Milliners often send young girls errands who are not old enough to see through the tricks of these parties prowling about the metropolis.

These larcenies are generally committed by vagrants decently dressed, and too lazy to work, who go sneaking about the streets and live in low neighbourhoods, such as St. Giles's, Drury-lane, Short's-gardens, Queen-street, and the Borough. They are in most cases committed in the evening, though sometimes during the day.

Child Stripping.—This is generally done by females, old debauched drunken hags who watch their opportunity to accost children passing in the streets, tidily dressed with good boots and clothes. They entice them away to a low or quiet neighbourhood for the purpose, as they say, of buying them sweets, or with some other pretext. When they get into a convenient place, they give them a halfpenny or some sweets, and take off the articles of dress, and tell them to remain till they return, when they go away with the booty.

This is done most frequently in mews in the West-end, and at Clerkenwell, Westminster, the Borough, and other similar localities. These heartless debased women sometimes commit these felonies in the disreputable neighbourhoods where they live, but more frequently in distant places, where they are not known and cannot be easily traced. This mode of felony is not so prevalent in the metropolis as formerly. In most cases, it is done at dusk in the winter evenings, from 7 to 10 o'clock.

Number of larcenies from children in the Metropolitan districts for 1860 . 87
Ditto   ditto in the City . 10
———
97

Value of property thereby stolen in the Metropolitan districts . . £65 0
Ditto   ditto in the City 5 10
———
£70 10

Stealing from Drunken Persons.—There is a very common low class of male thieves, who go prowling about at all times of the day and night for this purpose.

They loiter about the streets and public-houses to steal from drunken persons, and are called "Bug-hunters" and "mutchers." You see many of them lounging about gin-palaces in the vicinity of the Borough, near St. George's church. We have met them there in the course of our rambles over the metropolis, and at Whitechapel and St. Giles's. They also frequent the Westminster-road, the vicinity of the Victoria Theatre, Shoreditch, and Somers Town. These low wretches are of all ages, and many of them have the appearance of bricklayers', stonemasons', and engineers' labourers. They pretend they are labourers out of work, and are forward in intruding themselves on the notice of persons entering those houses, and expect to be treated to liquor, though entire strangers to them.

They are not unfrequently so rude as to take the pewter-pot of another person from the bar, and pass it round to their comrades, till they have emptied the contents.

If remonstrated with, they return insulting language, and try to involve the person in a broil.

You occasionally find them loafing about the tap-rooms. They watch for drunken people, whom they endeavour to persuade to treat them. They entice him to go down some court or slum, where they strip him of his watch, money, or other valuables he may have on his person. Or they sometimes rob him in the public-house; but this seldom occurs, as they are aware it would lead to detection. They prefer following him out of the public-house. Many of these robberies are committed in the public urinals at a late hour at night.

These men have often abandoned women who cohabit with them, and assist them in these low depredations. They frequently dwell in low courts and alleys in the neighbourhood of gin-palaces, have no settled mode of life, and follow no industrious calling—living as loafers and low ruffians.

Some of them have wives, who go out washing and charing to obtain a livelihood for their children and themselves, as well as to support their brutal husbands, lazzaroni of the metropolis.

This class of persons are in the habit of stealing lead from houses, and copper boilers from kitchens and wash-houses.

There is another class of thieves, who steal from drunken persons, usually in the dusk of the evening, in the following manner: Two women, respectably dressed, meet a drunken man in the street, stop him and ask him to treat them. They adjourn to the bar of a public-house for the purpose of getting some gin or ale. While drinking at the bar, one of the women tries to rob him of his watch or money. A man who is called a "stickman," an accomplice and possibly a paramour of hers, comes to the bar a short time after them. He has a glass of some kind of liquor, and stands beside them. Some motions and signs pass between the two females and this man. If they have by this time secured the booty, it is passed to the latter, who, thereupon slips away, with the stolen articles in his possession.

In some cases, when the property is taken from the drunken man, one of the women on some pretext steps to the door and passes it to the "stickman" standing outside, who then makes off with it. In other cases these robberies are perpetrated in the outside of the house, in some by-street.

Sometimes the man quickly discovers his loss, and makes an outcry against the women; when the "stickman" comes up and asks, "what is the matter?" the man may reply, "these two women have robbed me." The stickman answers "I'll go and fetch a policeman." The property is passed to him by the women, and he decamps. If a criminal information is brought against the females, the stolen goods are not found in their possession, and the case is dropped.

These women seldom or never allow drunken men to have criminal connection with them, but get their living by this base system of plunder. They change their field of operation over the metropolis, followed by the sneaking "stickman."

Some of these females have been known in early life to sell oranges in the street.

The "stickman" during the day lounges about the parlours in quiet public-houses where thieves resort, and the women during the day are sometimes engaged in needlework,—some of the latter have a fair education, which they may have learned in prison, and others are very illiterate.

Though respectable in dress and appearance, they generally belong to the felon class of Irish cockneys, with few exceptions.

They are to be found in Lisson-grove, Leicester-square, Portland-town, and other localities.

Females in respectable positions in society occasionally take too much intoxicating liquor, and are waylaid by old women, gin-drinkers, who frequent publichouses in low neighbourhoods. They introduce themselves to the inebriated woman as a friend, to see her to some place of safety until she has recovered from the effects of her dissipation,—she may have been lying on the pavement, and unable to walk. They lift her up by the hand, and steal the gold ring from her finger.

At other times they take her into some by-court or street in low neighbourhoods, where doors may frequently be seen standing open; they rob her in some of these dark passages of her money, watch, and jewellery, and sometimes carry off her clothes.

If seen by persons in the neighbourhood, it is winked at, and no information given, as they generally belong to the same unprincipled class.

There is another low class of women who prowl about the streets at midnight, watching for any respectable-looking person who may be passing the worse of liquor. If they notice a drunken man, one comes and enters into conversation with him, and while thus engaged, another woman steps up, touches him under the chin, or otherwise distracts his attention. The person who first accosted him, with her companion, then endeavours to pick his pockets and plunder him of his property A case of this kind occurred near the Marble Arch in August 1860.

They have many ingenious ways of distracting the attention of their victim, some of them very obscene and shameless.

They take care to see that no policeman is in sight, and generally endeavour to find out if the person they intend to victimize has something to purloin.

They may ask him for change, or solicit a few coppers to get beer, or inquire what o'clock it is, to see if he is in possession of a watch or money. They abstract the money from the pocket, or snatch the watch from the swivel, which they are adroit in breaking.

Such persons are often seen at midnight in the neighbourhood of Bloomsbury and Oxford-street, the Strand, Lower Thames-street, and other localities.

The most of those engaged in this kind of robbery in Oxford-street come from the neighbourhood of St. Giles's and Lisson-grove.

The number of felonies from drunken persons which occurred in the Metropolitan districts for 1860 were . . . 221
Ditto ditto in the City . 10
———
231

The value of property thereby stolen in the Metropolitan districts . . £867
Ditto ditto in the City . 40
———
£907

Stealing Linen, &c. exposed to dry. This is generally done by vagrants in the suburbs of the metropolis, from 7 to 11 o'clock in the evening; when left out all night, it is often done at midnight.

Linen and other clothes are frequently left hanging on lines or spread out on the grass in yards at the back of the house. Entrance is effected through the street-doors which may have been left open, or by climbing over the wall. In many cases these felonies are committed by middle-aged women. If done by a man, he is generally assisted by a female who carries off the property; were he seen carrying a bundle of clothes, he would be stopped by a vigilant officer, and be called to give an account of it, which would possibly lead to his detection.

These felonies generally consist of sheets, counterpanes, shirts, table-covers, pinafores towels, stockings, and such-like articles.

When any of them are marked, the female makes it her business to pick out the marks, in case it might lead to their detection. Such robberies are often traced by the police through the assistance of the pawnbrokers.

They are very common where there are gardens at the back of the house, such as Kensall Green, Camden Town, Kensington, Battersea, Clapham, Peckham, and Victoria Park.

The clothes are generally disposed of at pawnbrokers or the leaving-shops, commonly called "Dolly Shops." They leave them there for a small sum of money, and get a ticket. If they return for them in the course of a week, they are charged 3d. a shilling interest. If they do not return for them in seven days, they are disposed of to persons of low character. These wretches at the leaving-shops manage to get them into the hands of parties who would not be likely to give information—the articles, from their superior quality, being generally understood to be stolen.

These felonies are also committed by the female Sneaks who call at gentlemen's houses, selling small wares, or on some other similar errand. When they find the door open and a convenient opportunity, they often abstract the linen and other clothes from the lines, and dispose of them in the manner referred to.

They are also stolen by ragged juvenile thieves, who get into the yards by climbing over the wall. This is occasionally done in the Lambeth district, in the dusk of the evening, or early in the morning, and is effected in this way:—Some time previously they commence some boyish game, about half a dozen of them together. They then pretend to quarrel, when one boy will take the others' cap off his head and place it on the garden wall. Another boy lifts him up to fetch it—the object being to reconnoitre the adjacent grounds, and see if there are any clothes laid out to dry, as well as to find out the best mode of stealing them.

When they discover clothes in a yard, they come back at dusk, or at midnight, and carry them off the lines.

They take the stolen property to the receiver's, after having divided the clothes among the party. Some will go off in one direction, and others in another to get them disposed of, which is done to prevent suspicion on the part of the police.

The receiving-houses are opened to them at night, as these low people are very greedy of gain. Sometimes they convey the stolen property to their lodgings, at other times they lodge it in concealment till the next day. These clothes are occasionally of trifling value, at other times worth several pounds, which on being sold bring the thief a very poor return—scarcely the price of his breakfast—the lion's share of the spoil being given to the unprincipled receiver.

They are often encouraged to commit these thefts by wretches in the low lodging-houses, who are aware of their midnight excursions.

Number of felonies of linen, &c., exposed to dry in the Metropolitan districts for 1860 236
Ditto ditto for the City 0
———
236

Value of property thereby abstracted in the Metropolis.. .. .. .. £150

Robberies from Carts and other Vehicles.—There are many depredations committed over the metropolis from carts, carriers' waggons, cabs, railway vans, and other vehicles. Many of those people have the appearance of porters at a warehouse, and are a peculiar order.

At one time they may have been porters at warehouses, or connected with railways, or carmen to large commercial firms. Some have corduroy or moleskin jacket and trowsers, and cloth cap; others have a plain frock-coat and cap.

Many of the robberies from carts are done by the connivance of the carters. They are sent by business establishments to dispose of goods over the metropolis; some of them are connected with the worst class of thieves. They connive with those men in stealing their employers' property, and in rifling other carts, carry the booty away in their own, and always manage to secure a part of the prize.

These carters take thieves occasionally to railway stations to assist them with their work, and when an opportunity occurs, carry off goods from the railway platform, such as bales of bacon, cheese, bags of nails, boxes of tin and copper, and travellers' luggage, which they dispose of to marine-store dealers and at chandlers' shops. The wearing apparel in the trunks they sell at second-hand shops, kept by Jews and others in low neighbourhoods, such as Petticoat-lane, Lambeth, Westminster, and the Borough of Southwark.

Many carts are rifled by persons who represent themselves as hawkers or costermongers—men who have no steady industrious mode of livelihood, and are usually in the company of prostitutes and thieves of the worst description. The carter may have occasion to call at a city house, and to leave his horse and cart in the street, when they steal a whip, coat, or horsecloth, the reins from off the horse, or any portable article they can lay their hands on.

Numbers of hay, straw, and store carmen frequently steal a truss of hay, or clover, or straw, from their employer's cart, and dispose of it to some person who has a horse, or pony, or donkey, for a small sum of money. These dishonest practices are carried on to a far greater extent than the public are aware of, as it is only occasionally they are brought to public notice.

Robberies from cabs and carriages are sometimes effected in the following way: They follow the cab or vehicle with a horse and cart, driving along in its wake—two or three thieves generally in the cart. One of them jumps on the spring of the conveyance while the driver is sitting in front of his vehicle, pulls down the trunk or box, and slips it into the cart, then drives away with the booty.

At other times they run up, and leap on the spring of the conveyance while the driver is proceeding along with his back toward them; lower the trunk or other article from the roof, and walk off with it. These trunks sometimes contain money, silver plate, and other valuable property.

These depredations are always done at night, by experienced thieves, and generally in the winter season. They are common in the fashionable squares of the West-end, at the East-end, toward the Commercial-road and St. George's-in-the-East, at Ratcliffe Highway, the City, the Borough of Southwark, and Lambeth, along the docks, and at the railway stations around the metropolis.

There are a number of laundresses residing at Chelsea, Uxbridge, Hampstead, Holloway, and other districts in the suburbs, who wash large quantities of clothes for the gentry and nobility in the fashionable streets and squares of the metropolis. After washing and dressing the linen, they pack it up in large wicker baskets, and generally convey it in their own carts to the residences of the owners.

A class of people are frequently on the look-out for these carts to plunder them of their linen. The carts are under the management of a man or a woman. The thieves follow the vehicle to a quiet street, one puts his shoulder under a basket while the other cuts the cord which attaches it to the cart, when both make off with the stolen property.

These thieves reside over London in low districts, such as St. Giles's and Shoreditch, and are occasionally brought before the police courts.

There is a class of robberies from gentlemen's carriages about the West-end of the metropolis. In going to the Opera, West-end theatres, or other fashionable places of amusement, the gentleman frequently leaves his valuable overcoat or cloak in the carriage. These thieves follow the conveyance to some quiet street leading to the stables where the vehicle is to remain till the gentleman returns from his evening's amusement. They let down the window of the carriage and carry off any article which is left. The theft is nimbly committed while the vehicle is on its way to the stables, or when it is returning to the Opera, and is done chiefly by young men, experienced thieves. They live in the low neighbourhoods already referred to.

There is a good deal of this mode of thieving carried on in the West-end of London during the winter season.

Number of larcenies from carts and other vehicles in the Metropolitan district for 1860 286
Ditto, ditto, in the City 79
———
365
Value of property thereby stolen in the Metropolis £1075
Ditto, ditto, in the City.. .. 370
———
£1445

Stealing Lead from House-tops, Copper from Kitchens, and Workmen's Tools, &c. in Dwelling-houses.—Of late this mode of thieving has been extensively carried on over the metropolis, chiefly at unoccupied houses. In some cases, a key is obtained by the thief, respectable in appearance, from the gentleman who lets the house, without his accompanying him to the empty dwelling, when he takes the opportunity of stealing the copper boiler from the washing-house, and the lead pipe from the butt or cistern. He passes the stolen property to some of his associates, and returns the key of the dwelling.

This is a peculiar class who make a livelihood by going round empty houses in different districts on similar errands. They do not give their name and address, are strangers in the neighbourhood, and cannot be easily tracked out by the police.

Lead is frequently stolen from the house-tops, by the loafing ruffians, we have before described, who lounge about public-houses, robbing drunken men, and occasionally by boys. Sometimes these robberies are committed by plumbers' workmen and others engaged in repairing the houses.

Lead in most cases is stolen from those dwellings which are under repair, or have been unoccupied for some time. When a house is repaired, it frequently happens the roofs of the adjoining occupied houses are stripped and carried off by unprincipled workmen.

These depredations are often committed by the workmen themselves, or by their connivance. At other times they are done by persons climbing low walls, and clambering up spouts to the roof, and cutting up the sheet lead. This is usually done under night by two or more in company; sometimes, though rarely, by boys. One keeps a look-out to see there is no person near to detect them. This person is termed a "crow." If any one should be near, the "crow" gives a signal, and they decamp. Before commencing their depredations, they generally look out for the means of escape, seldom returning the same way they mounted the roof. They make their way out in another direction. If hard pressed, they sometimes hide themselves on the roof behind chimneys, or lie down in gutters or cisterns or any other likely place of concealment. These felonies are often done by bricklayers' labourers (Irish cockneys) during the winter, and in many cases, as we have said, with the connivance of the workmen engaged in repairing the houses.

There is another class of persons who engage in lead-stealing from the roofs of houses. They were formerly in the service of builders, plumbers, or carpenters, but are out of employment. They go to their late employer's customers, under the pretext that they were sent by him to repair the roof, and meanwhile plunder the sheet lead, which they generally roll up, convey down, and carry off by means of their accomplices, who are hovering in the neighbourhood. They have the appearance and dress of industrious workmen, and may have been lately seen employed in houses in the neighbourhood, so that they are more likely to deceive the unsuspecting people who admit them into their dwellings. This kind of lead-stealing has been lately of very frequent occurrence in the metropolis.

Copper is frequently stolen from the boilers in the kitchens and wash-houses by the same parties. Sometimes they enter by the area door or the window, which is left open. At other times they climb the garden wall at the back of the house, and enter by a window, left unfastened. They take the copper out of the brickwork in the wash-house, or from the kitchen, roll it up and carry it away. This is generally done in unoccupied houses. Sweeps employed cleaning the chimneys sometimes take away copper in like manner in their soot-bags.

In houses under repair, as well as in unfinished houses, they steal carpenters' tools, planes, saws, ploughs, squares, hammers, &c., left by the workmen.

They obtain access to the house by climbing over the wooden enclosure or over garden walls. This is generally done in the evening, between the hours of 9 and 12, and frequently by discharged workmen.

In many cases they are stopped on the way with the tools in their possession. If a proper account is not given, it often leads to the detection of the robbery, which generally puts a stop for the time to such depredations in that neighbourhood.

The stolen tools are taken to pawnbrokers or receiving-shops, and sold at an under price. In some cases the pawnbroker gives notice to the police, but in these other shops, this is seldom or never done.

The thieves generally go to some house where no watchman is employed.

The number of larcenies of tools, lead, glass, &c. from empty or unfinished houes in the Metropolitan districts for 1860, 472
Ditto, ditto, from the City .. 22
———
494

Value of the property thereby abstracted in the Metropolis £462 0
Ditto, ditto, in the City .. 7 10
———
£469 10

Robberies by False Keys.—There are many robberies committed in the metropolis by means of false keys, generally between the hours of seven and nine o'clock in the evening. After nine o'clock they would be considered burglaries. This class of robberies is generally committed by thieves of experience, and frequently, before depredations are committed, persons call at the house in the daytime, who take particular notice of the lock of the street-door, to know the key which opens it, whether a Bramah, Chubb, or other lock. These persons are termed "putters up of robberies," and supply the thieves with the requisite information, when they come in the evening and enter the house. In many cases they get clear off with the booty.

The houses entered are frequently respectable lodging-houses, or houses occupied by one family where there is likely to be no children about the upper rooms. In the case of entering these dwellings they make their way to the bed-rooms above, their chief object being to steal the jewellery and dressing-case left on the dressing-table, often of great value. They also take clothes out of the drawers, and other articles. On coming out they often put on some of the apparel, such as an overcoat, and fill the pockets with stolen property.

In houses in the West-end, single gentlemen, such as government clerks, officers in the army, and others, are often out dining in the evening, or at the clubs; and as the servant is generally engaged downstairs at this time, the thief is frequently not obstructed.

To elude suspicion from the police constables in the street they often have a carpet-bag to carry off the booty. If they meet one of them near the house, they generally ask him some question, such as the way to some street, to take him off his guard.

A case of this kind occurred early this year at the West-end, where four men were engaged in a robbery. On their arriving at the corner of the street where the felony was committed they found two policemen there. They stepped up to them, and conversed for some time, when the constables left, having no suspicion, from their respectable appearance. Two of the thieves crossed the street to a house opposite. Meanwhile their movements were narrowly watched by a keen-eyed detective, who knew the parties, three of the four being returned convicts. Having arrived at the door of the house, they endeavoured to gain an entrance, which, after trying several keys, they effected. The other two confederates had taken up a position opposite the house, being what is termed "lookout," or outside men.

In a short time the two who had entered the house came out and closed the door behind them. They were perceived to have some bulky articles in their possession. The other two men remained for a few minutes in their place on the opposite side of the street, when they followed their companions. When at a short distance from the house, they rejoined them, and the property was divided among them. This was done in the dusk in the quiet street.

The detective officer saw two of the parties with Inverness capes, and carrying umbrellas in their hand they did not have before they entered the house. He went up to them, told them who he was, and arrested one of them; the other was captured a few yards off by another officer when in the act of throwing off the Inverness cape. The other two, meanwhile, escaped. On conducting the two men to the police-station the two capes were taken from them, and in their pockets were found a number of skeleton keys, a waxtaper, and silent lights, along with various small articles, evidently part of the robbery which had just been committed.

Two hours after this a gentleman drove up in a cab to the police-station, and gave information of the robbery, when he identified the articles taken from the prisoners as his property. The two thieves were tried at the sessions, and sentenced to six years' penal servitude. One of the two confederates who escaped was apprehended by the same detective, found guilty, and sentenced to the same punishment, which broke up a gang of thieves who had infested the neighbourhood for several months, and occasioned great alarm.

Robberies from gentlemen's houses by means of false keys are generally put up by some person acquainted with the house, and who may have frequented it under some pretext, such as by courting the servant girl, or by being acquainted with some of the men-servants. They rifle the valuables from wardrobes and drawing-rooms, such as watches, rings, purses, clothes, &c.

Attic thieves chiefly aim at abstracting jewels from ladies' bed-rooms, generally on the second floor; but this class of skeleton-key thieves frequently carry away bundles of stolen goods, and are not so fastidious in their choice.

An instance of a skeleton-key robbery from a gentleman's house occurred lately at the West-end of the metropolis. The two thieves had engaged a cab to carry off the stolen property (the driver of the cab being a confederate), and drove up to the house next door to where the robbery was to be committed. They were seen to leave the cab, to go up to the door of the house, to apply the key to the door, and to walk in. About ten minutes after, they left the house, and walked to the cab with large parcels in their hands, when it drove swiftly away.

On that evening the butler of the house discovered that the whole of his master's clothes had been stolen from his wardrobe, and his dressing-case, with costly articles, his gold watch and chain, and the whole of his linen. Information was given to a detective officer, who in two days after traced the robbery to two well-known thieves, one of them being singularly expert in the use of skeleton keys.

The manner in which it was detected was very ingenious, and reflected high credit on the officer.

On visiting a public-house near Tottenham Court-road, one Saturday night, he saw a middle-aged, intelligent man, like a respectable mechanic, conversing with a person at the bar over a pint of half-and-half. The sharp eye of the detective observed the former with a neckerchief which corresponded with one of the articles of this stolen property. The suspicion of the officer was aroused, and he followed him late at night, and saw where he resided. On the next morning he went with two officers to his house, and found him in bed with his paramour, and arrested him for the robbery. On searching his house a handkerchief was found marked with the crest of the nobleman to whom the property belonged. On a farther search a quantity of other articles were found belonging to this robbery.

On his paramour getting out of bed she was perceived by the detective to conceal something under her petticoats. On being asked to produce it, she denied having anything. On being searched, another handkerchief was found on her person, bearing the nobleman's crest. This man was afterwards identified as one of the two persons who were seen to enter the house where the robbery was committed, and to leave with the cab. He was tried at the Sessions, and sentenced to seven years' penal servitude. This man had for some time been well known to the police, and was suspected of committing a series of large robberies, but he was so dexterous in executing his felonies that his movements had not previously been traced.

Number of felonies in the Metropolitan districts for 1860 by means of false keys 247
Ditto, ditto, in the City .. 17
———
264

Value of property thereby abstracted in Metropolitan districts £1,840
Ditto, diito, in the City .. 160
———
£2,000

Robberies by Lodgers.—Robberies are frequently committed by lodgers in various parts of the metropolis, in low as well as in middle-class localities.

A great many of these are committed in low neighbourhoods, by abandoned women, frequently young. They commit depredations in their own room, or in other rooms in the house in which they lodge, by entering open doors, or by turning the key when the door is locked, while the parties are out. Many of these are done by prostitutes of the lowest order, who sometimes steal the linen, bedding, wearing-apparel, and other property, and pawn or sell it.

Robberies of this kind are sometimes perpetrated by mechanics' wives, addicted to dissipated habits, who steal similar articles from dwelling-houses. Sometimes they are done by servants out of place, driven to steal by poverty and destitution; at other times by sewing girls, often toiling from 4 in the morning to 10 o'clock at night for about 8d. a day—many of whom commit suicide rather than resort to prostitution; and occasionally by clerks and shopmen—fast young men, when in poverty and distress; and by betting-men and skittle-sharps.

In March, 1861, two known prostitutes, lodging together in a house in Charlotte-street, were brought before the Lambeth police court for a felony committed in the room in which they lodged. They abstracted knives and forks, plates and spoons, along with two chairs, rifling the apartment of nearly all it contained. They were convicted and sentenced, the one to three months', and the other to six months', imprisonment—the latter having been previously convicted.

Another felony occurred lately in Isabella-street, Lambeth, where a mechanic's wife stole the bed-clothes and the feathers out of a bed in the house in which she lodged. Her husband was glad to pay the amount to prevent criminal prosecution.

There are many felonies committed by persons lodging in coffee-houses and hotels, some of them of considerable value. The hotel thieves assume the manner and air of gentlemen, dress well, and live in high style. They lodge for an evening or two in some fashionable hotel, frequently near the railway stations. They get up at night, when the house is quiet and business suspended, and commit robberies in the house. They have an ingenious mode of opening the doors, though locked in the inner side, by inserting a peculiar instrument and turning round the key. They go stealthily into the rooms, and abstract silver plate, articles of jewellery, watches, money, and other valuables.

These persons usually leave early in the morning, before the other gentlemen get up. Some of them are young, and others are middle-aged. They have generally some acquaintance with commercial transactions, and conduct themselves like active business men. They are birds of passage, and do not reside long in any one locality, as they would become known to the police.

A very extensive robbery of this kind occurred some time ago at a fashionable hotel in the metropolis, near the Great Northern Railway, to the amount of 700*l*. or 800*l*. The thief was apprehended at York, and committed for trial.

Number of felonies in the Metropolitan districts for 1860, committed by lodgers 1,375
Ditto, ditto, in the City 83
───
1458

Value of property thereby abstracted in the Metropolitan districts .. £3,643
Ditto, ditto, in the City 144
───
£3,787

Robberies by Servants.—There are a great number of felonies committed by servants over the metropolis, many of which might be prevented by prudent precautions on the part of their employers. On this subject we would wish to speak with discrimination. We are aware that many honest and noble-minded servants are treated with injustice by the caprice and bad temper of their employers, and many a poor girl is without cause dismissed from her situation, and refused a proper certificate of character. Being unable to get another place, she is often driven with reluctance from poverty and destitution to open prostitution on the street. On the other hand, many of our employers foolishly and thoughtlessly receive male and female servants into their service without making a proper inquiry into their previous character.

Many felonies are committed by domestic female servants who have been only a month or six weeks in service. Some of them steal tea, sugar, and other provisions, which are frequently given to acquaintances or relatives out of doors. Others occasionally abstract linen and articles of wearing-apparel, or plunder the wardrobe of gold bracelets, rings, pearl necklace, watch, chain, or other jewellery, or of muslin and silk dresses and mantles, which they either keep in their trunk, or otherwise dispose of.

Female domestic servants are often connected with many of the felonies committed in the metropolis. Two of the female servants in a gentleman's family are sometimes courted by two smart dressed young men, bedecked with jewellery, who visit them at the house occasionally. One of them may call by himself on a certain evening, and after sitting with them for some time in the kitchen, may pretend that he is going upstairs to the front door on some errand, such as to bring in some liquor. He goes alone, and opens the door to his companion whom he had arranged to meet him, and who may be hovering in the street. He admits him into the house to rifle the rooms in the floors above. Meantime he comes in with the liquor, and proceeds down stairs, and remains there for some time to occupy the attention of the servants until his companion has plundered the house of money, jewels, or other property.

On other occasions two young men may remain downstairs with the servants, while a third party is committing a robbery in the apartments above.

Some respectable-looking young women, in the service of middle-class and fashionable families, are connected with burglars, and have been recommended to their places through their influence, or that of their acquaintances. Some of these females are usually not a fortnight or a month in service before a heavy burglary is committed in the house, and will remain for two or three months longer to prevent suspicion. They will then take another similar place in a gentleman's family, remain several months there, and by their conduct ingratiate themselves into the good graces of the master and mistress, when another burglary is committed through their connivance. The booty is shared between them and the thieves.

Some continue this system for a considerable time, as their employers have no suspicion of their villainy. They are often Irish cockneys, connected with the thieves, and have been trained with them from their infancy. They generally aim at stealing the silver plate, clothes, and other valuables. In these robberies they are always ready to give the "hue and cry" when a depredation has been committed.

There are often instances of these robberies brought before the police-courts and sessions, where the dishonesty of many servants is brought to light.

There are many felonies committed by the male servants in gentlemen's families; some of them of considerable value. Num bers of these are occasioned by betting on the part of the butlers, who have the charge of the plate. They go and bet on different horses, and pawn a certain quantity of plate which has not the crest of their employer on it, and expect to be able to redeem it as soon as they have got money when the horse has won. He may happen to lose. He bets again on some other horse he thinks will win—perhaps bets to a considerable amount, and thinks he will be able to redeem his loss; he again possibly loses his bet. His master is perhaps out of town, not having occasion to use the plate.

On his coming home there may be a dinner-party, when the plate is called for. The butler absconds, and part of the plate is found to be missing. Information is given to the police; some pawnbroker may be so honourable as to admit the plate is in his possession. The servant is apprehended, convicted, and sentenced possibly to penal servitude. Cases of this kind occasionally occur, and are frequently caused by such betting transactions.

Robberies occasionally are perpetrated by servants in shops and warehouses, clerks, warehousemen, and others, of money and goods of various kinds.

A remarkable case of robbery by a servant occurred lately. A young man, employed by a locksmith, near the West-end of the metropolis, was frequently sent to gentlemen's houses on his master's business to pick locks. In many of the houses where he was employed, money and other property was found missing. He went to pick a lock at a jeweller's shop. After he was gone, the jeweller found a beautiful gold chain missing. As his son was a fast young man, he was afraid to charge the young locksmith with the robbery. Meantime the latter was sent to other houses, and in those places articles were found missing, and servants in the families were discharged on suspicion of committing the robberies.

He went to a solicitor's office to pick the locks of some boxes containing title-deeds and money. From one of the boxes, which he did not require to open, he stole 100l., and locked it up again. The head clerk was then away on business for several days. On his return he found that one of the boxes in the office had been opened and 100l. had been abstracted.

Information was given to Bow-street police office by the solicitor, who offered 5l. as a reward to any one who would give information regarding the robbery. Meantime he stated he would give no one into custody. His clerks had been with him a long time. He had one man employed in the office to pick some locks, but as he belonged to a respectable firm, he did not believe it to be him. Meantime the solicitor discharged his general clerks. His confidential clerk was so indignant at this, that he gave in his resignation.

One of the most accomplished detective officers of the Bow-street police resolved to ferret out the matter. It was arranged the journeyman locksmith was to be sent to a certain house to pick a lock in an apartment where some money was placed which had been marked. The detective watched his movements from the next room. On this occasion also, he not only picked the lock as requested, but picked other locks in the room, and carried off part of the money which was marked.

When he went downstairs, he was detained till it was ascertained if the money had been tampered with. On inspecting it, part was missing. He was taken into custody, and the money got on his person. On searching his house a waggon load of stolen property was found, belonging to a series of robberies he had committed in the houses he visited, amounting in value to 200l. All the charges against him were not investigated. He was tried for nine acts of robbery at Clerkenwell, convicted, and sentenced to six years' penal servitude. He was one of the finest locksmiths in the world, and received from his employer higher wages than the other workmen in the establishment.

Number of cases of felony by servants in the Metropolitan dists. for 1860, 1,790
Ditto, ditto, in the City 199

1,989

Value of property thereby abstracted in the Metropolitan districts .. £13,015
Ditto, ditto, in the City .. 612

£13,627

Area and Lobby Sneaks.—This is a large, and variegated class of thieves, ranging from the little ragged boy of six years of age, to the old woman of threescore and ten. Some are hanging in rags and tatters in pitiable condition; others have a respectable appearance likely to disarm suspicion. Some are ignorant and obtuse; others are intelligent, and have got a tolerable education. Some are skulking and timid; others are so venturesome as to enter dwelling-houses through open windows, and conceal themselves in closets, waiting a favourable opportunity to skulk off, unobserved, with plunder.

Numbers of little ragged boys sneak around the areas of dwellings, where respectable tradesmen reside, as well as in the fashionable streets of the metropolis. We may see them loitering about half-naked, or fluttering in shreds and patches, sometimes alone, at other times in small bands, looking with skulking eye into the areas, as they move along. They are not permitted to beg at the houses, and some of them have no ostensible errand to visit those localities, and are hunted away by the police. During the day they generally sneak in the thoroughfares and quiet by-streets of London.

A few days ago we saw one of them skulking along Blackfriars-road. He was about 13 years of age, and had on an old ragged coat, much too large for him, hanging over his back in tatters, with a string to fasten it round his waist, and a pair of old trowsers and gray cap. He had the air of an old man, as he lazily walked along, and looked a very pitiable object. On seeing us eying him with curiosity, he suddenly laid aside his mendicant air, and with sharp keen eye and startled attitude, appeared to take us for a police officer in undress. We looked over our shoulder, as we moved on, and saw him stand for a time looking after us, when he resumed his former downcast appearance, and sauntered slowly along looking eagerly into the areas as he passed. He appeared to us a very good type of the young area sneak.

These area-divers go down into the areas, and open the safes where provisions are kept, such as roast and boiled beef, butter and bread, and fish, and carry off the spoil. If the door is open, they enter the kitchen, and steal anything they can find, such as clothes, wet and dry linen, and sometimes a copper kettle, and silver spoons; or they will take the blacking-brushes from the boothouse. Nothing comes amiss.

There is another class of area sneaks who make their daily calls at gentlemen's houses, ask the servants when they come in contact with them if they have any kitchen-stuff to sell, or old clothes or glass bottles. Should they not find the servant in the kitchen, they try to make their way to the butler's pantry, which generally adjoins the kitchen, and carry off the basket of plate.

These parties are men from 20 years of age and upwards.

There is a class of women who go down the areas, under pretence of selling combs, stay-laces, boot-laces, and other trifling commodities. When they find a stealthy opportunity, many of them carry off articles from the kitchen, similar to those just described. These people are of all ages, some young, others tottering with old age. They generally belong to London, and go their regular rounds over the streets and squares. Many of them live in Westminster, St. Giles's and Kent-street in the Borough.

There are other sneaks who enter the lobbies of houses, and commit robberies, chiefly in the West-end districts. These persons are of the same class, with the area sneak, but perhaps a step higher in the thievish profession. Their depredations are generally committed in the morning between 7 and 8, when servants are busily engaged dusting furniture and sweeping the hall and rooms. These thieves are then seen loitering about watching a favourable opportunity to steal.

The mode of stealing is the same in the passages of the houses of middle class people, and the entry halls of the elegant mansions of the gentry and aristocracy. Some of these thieves are men respectably dressed while others are in more shabby condition. They are young and middle aged. You may see them in those quiet localities, generally in dark clothing, having the appearance of respectable mechanics, or warehousemen. Others are like men who hang about the streets to run messages and assist men-servants.

They walk into the house, and pilfer any article they can find, such as articles of clothing, umbrellas, and walking-canes. Sometimes they take a coat off the knob and whip it under the breast of their coat, or put it on over their own. They frequently carry off a bundle of clothes, and sell them to some receiver of stolen property.

Such robberies are frequent in the neighbourhood of Brompton, Chelsea, Pimlico, Paddington, Stepney, Hackney, Bayswater, Camberwell, the Kent-road, and other similar districts.

The lobby sneaks are the same class of persons as those who enter the areas, and contrive to get a livelihood in this way. They live in various parts of London, such as the dirty slums, alleys, and by-streets of Covent-garden, Drury-lane, and St. Giles's, Somers Town, Westminster, the Borough, Whitechapel, and Walworth Common, and other similar neighbourhoods.

Sometimes these men are seen in public-houses with large sums of money, no doubt got from the disposal of their plunder; and at other times lounge in low coffee-houses, without even the scanty means of paying for their bed, and are scarcely able to pay a penny for a cup of coffee. They often have to ask assistance from their companions, though a few days previous they may have been seen in possession of handfuls of cash.

They are usually unmarried, and live an uncomfortable, homeless life; often cohabiting with a low class of women, miserably clad, and generally wretched in appearance.

Middle aged and elderly women are occasionally engaged in sneaking depredations from the dwelling-houses of labouring men. An old woman may observe a child standing at her mother's door, and ask if her mother is in. When the child answers, "No," she will say, "I will mind the house, while you go and get a halfpenny worth of sweets," giving the little girl a halfpenny. On the child's return the woman has decamped carrying away with her money, or any other portable article she may have found in the house. This is the class of women we have noticed stealing from the shops of the butchers and cheesemongers.

It is a strange fact, that many of these common thieves, engaged in paltry sneaking thefts, have a more desperate and criminal appearance than most of the daring burglars and highwaymen. Their soft and timid natures feel more poignant misery in their debased and anxious life than the more stern and callous ruffians of a higher class, engaged in more extraordinary adventures.

Another class of larcenies in dwelling-houses are committed *by means of false messages.*

This is a very ingenious mode of thieving, and is done by means of calling at the house, and stating to the servants that they are sent from respectable firms in the neighbourhood for some article of dress to be repaired, or for lamps, fenders, glasses, or decanters to be mended, with other pretences of various descriptions.

Their object is to get the absence of the servant from the hall. While the servant is upstairs, telling a man has called sent by such and such a firm, they walk into the dining-room on the first floor, and abstract any articles of plate that may be exposed, silver-mounted inkstands, books, or other property. If they don't succeed in this, and see no article of value, they will return to the hall, and clear the passages of the coats hanging on the knobs, and the umbrellas and walking-sticks from the stand, while an accomplice is generally outside to receive the property. Should the servant come down too soon, while he has only got a short distance off, no property is found upon his person. They seldom take hats, as these could be easily detected.

They have an endless variety of ingenious expedients to effect this object. A case of this kind occurred in the district of Marylebone a short time ago, where a gentleman was in quest of a lady's maid, and advertised in the 'Times' newspaper, and at the same time answered a number of advertisements by anonymous persons. The next day his house was thronged by a number of people anxious to obtain the situation.

After all had left, a purse containing a large amount of money was missing, consisting partly of bank-notes; when he gave information to the police. Some days after, through the admirable ingenuity and tact of a detective officer at Marylebone, a person was traced out in the locality of Edgware-road, as having been guilty of the felony, and the stolen purse was found on her person. Her apprehension led to the discovery, that she had been pursuing a system of robberies of this description over various parts of the metropolis, for twelve months previously. She was sentenced to three years' penal servitude, and while in Millbank Penitentiary, committed suicide about three months after.

These felonies abound chiefly in the west-end of the metropolis, in the neighbourhood of Belgravia, Russell and Bedford-squares, Oxford-square, Gloucester-square, Seymour-street, Hyde Park-street, Gloucester-terrace, and other fashionable localities. They are often committed by servants of worthless character out of situation, also by lads of respectable appearance, sent out by trainers of thieves, who often begin their despicable life in this manner, and advance to picking of pockets and burglary.

Number of larcenies in the Metropolitan districts for the year 1860, by doors being left open and by false messages .. 2,986
Ditto, ditto, in the City .. 535

3,521

Value of property thereby abstracted in the Metropolitan district .. £9,904
Ditto, ditto, in the City .. 724

£10,628

Stealing by Lifting up Windows or Breaking Glass.—Area-sneaks frequently lift up the kitchen windows to steal. Sometimes they cannot reach the articles through the iron bars, and have recourse to an ingenious expedient to effect their object. They tie two sticks together, and attach a hook to the end, and seize hold of any articles they can find and draw them through the bars; they frequently leave their sticks behind them, which are found by the police.

There is generally an iron fastening in the centre of the window frame. The thief inserts a small thin knife or other sharp instrument in the opening of the frame, and forces back the iron catch. In some instances a fastening or clasp in the inner side of the window is pushed back by means of breaking a pane of glass. These robberies are often committed in dwelling-houses in Queen-street, Mitre-street, and Webber-street, near Blackfriars-road; in Tower-street, Waterloo-road, and similar localities—generally by a man and a young lad. This young lad is employed to enter the window of the house to be robbed, which in these localities is often a front parlour. The window is drawn up softly, not to excite any alarm.

The man generally keeps watch while the lad enters the house, perhaps at the corner of the street, when both decamp with the property.

In some instances they break the glass in the same way that star-glazers do at shop-windows, as already described. This is done either at the front or the back window. They prefer the back window if there is a ready access to it. These robberies are committed in occupied houses as well as in houses while the inmates are absent for a few days. They steal money, trinkets, linen, or anything that is easily carried off.

Similar robberies are perpetrated by two or more persons at the West-end fashionable houses by the area or back windows, when they steal money, jewels, mantel-piece clocks, clothes, linen, and other property.

Sometimes they enter by cutting the window with a diamond. These felonies are often of considerable value.

The parlour windows are sometimes lifted up by young thieves in the morning, when plate is laid on the table for breakfast; the servant frequently leaves the dining-room window open for ventilation, when they effect an entrance in this way:—one throws a cap into the area by way of joke, or through the window into the room; another mounts the railings and enters the window. Should any of the inmates detect him, he will say that "a lad had thrown his cap into the house, and he came in to fetch it." If not disturbed, he carries off the silver plate, and often returns through the window with the plunder without being observed. These thieves take any article easily carried off, such as wearing apparel, work-boxes, or fancy clocks, and are generally Irish cockneys; they are to be found in considerable numbers in the vicinity of King's-cross, Waterloo-road, and other localities. They abstract any valuable property they find lying about, but their chief object is to get the silver plate.

There are few cases of larceny from back bedroom windows, as the servants and inmates are generally hovering about after breakfast. This is sometimes effected, though rarely, by the connivance of the servants.

At other times these robberies from the house are committed by means of breaking a pane of glass, when the thieves undo the fastening of the window and effect an entrance. This is often perpetrated during the temporary absence of the inmates.

The statistics in this class of robberies will be given when we come to treat on "Attic or Garret Thieves."

Attic or Garret Thieves—These are generally the most expert thieves in the metropolis. Their mode of operation is this:—They call at a dwelling-house with a letter, or have communication with some of the servants, for the purpose of discovering the best means of access, and to learn how the people in the house are engaged and the time most suitable for the depredation. They generally come to plunder the house in the evening, when one or two of their accomplices loiter about, watching the movements of the police, the other meanwhile proceeding to the roof of the house.

These attic robberies are generally effected through unoccupied houses—perhaps by the house next door, or some other on the same side of the street. They pass through the attic to the roof, and proceed along the gutters and coping to the attic window of the house to be robbed. They unfasten the attic window by taking the pane of glass out, or pushing the fastening back, and enter the dwelling. This is generally done about 7 or 8 o'clock in the evening, when the family are at dinner—the servants being engaged between the dining-room on the first floor and the kitchen below, serving up the dinner.

The thieves proceed to the bedroom on the second floor, and force open the wardrobe with a short jemmy which they carry, and try to find the jewel-case and any other articles of value. Their object is generally to get valuable jewels.

The dining-room is on the first floor, so that they have often full scope for their operations without being seen or obstructed, while the inmates are engaged below. They return the same way through the attic window on the roof, run along the gutters, and escape by the same house through which they entered.

A very remarkable robbery of this kind occurred in the beginning of 1861 at Loundes-square, where the thieves entered through an attic and obtained jewels to the amount of 3,000*l*.

On their return from the dwelling-house, it being a very windy night, a hat belonging to one of them was blown from the house-top upon one of the slanting roofs he could not reach, which afterwards led to his detection. A short time previously it was in the hands of a hatter for certain repairs, when he inserted a paper marked with his name within it. The thief was arrested, tried, and got ten years' penal servitude.

Some get to the roof by means of a ladder placed outside an unfinished house, or house under repair, and steal in the same manner.

An ingenious attempt at a jewel robbery occurred lately by means of a cab drawing up with a lady before a dwelling-house. The cabman, who was evidently in collusion with the thieves, dismounted, rang the bell, and told the butler who answered the door, that a lady wished to see him. On his coming to the cab, it being about ten or fifteen yards from the street-door, he was kept in conversation by a female. Meantime he observed a respectable-looking man steal into the house from the street, while thus engaged. He left the cab without taking any notice of what he saw, and entered the house, when the cab drove off at a rapid rate, which convinced him that there was something wrong. He made his way up into the bedroom on the second floor, and found a man of respectable appearance concealed in the apartment. An officer was called and the man was searched. There was found on his person a jemmy, a wax taper, and silent lights. He was taken into custody; but no trace of the cabman or woman could be found. He was afterwards committed for the offence.

These attic thieves generally live in Hackney-road and Kingsland-road. On one occasion a gang was discovered in a furnished house in Russell-square. They generally have apartments in respectable neighbourhoods to avoid suspicion, and have servants to attend them, who assist in disposing of the stolen property. The best attic thieves reside in Hackney and Kingsland-roads, and many are to be found in the neighbourhood of Shoreditch church; a few of them are known to be residing in Waterloo-road, but not of so high a class as in the localities referred to.

The women connected with them have an abundance of jewellery; they live in high style, with plenty of cash, but not displayed to any great extent at the time any robbery is committed, as it would excite suspicion.

Many of them have a very gentleman-like appearance, and none but a detective officer would know them. When brought before the police courts for these felonies, it is usual to have constables brought from all the districts to see them and make them known, which very much annoys them.

They generally succeed in making off with their booty, and are seldom caught. Their robberies are skilfully planned, in the same experienced careful manner in which burglaries are effected. They have gone through all grades of thieving from their infancy—through sneaking and picking pockets.

This is a late system of robbery, and has been carried on rather extensively over the west end of the metropolis.

Number of larcenies from dwelling-houses, by lifting up windows, breaking glass, and by attic windows through empty houses, for 1860 515
Ditto, ditto, in the City . . 14
—
529

Value of property thereby abstracted in Metropolitan districts for 1860   £3,962
Ditto, ditto, in the City . .   18
—
£3,980

A Visit to the Rookery of St. Giles and its Neighbourhood.

In company with a police officer we proceeded to the Seven Dials, one of the most remarkable localities in London, inhabited by bird-fanciers, keepers of stores of old clothes and old shoes, costermongers, patterers, and a motley assemblage of others, chiefly of the lower classes. As we stood at one of the angles in the centre of the Dials we saw three young men—burglars—loitering at an opposite corner of an adjoining dial. One of them had a gentlemanly appearance, and was dressed in superfine black cloth and beaver hat. The other two were attired as mechanics or tradesmen. One of them had recently returned from penal servitude, and another had undergone a long imprisonment.

Leaving the Seven Dials and its dingy neighbourhoood, we went to Oxford Street, one of the first commercial streets in London, and one of the finest in the world. It reminded us a good deal of the celebrated Broadway, New York, although the buildings of the latter are in some places more costly and splendid, and some of the shops more magnificent. Oxford Street is one of the main streets of London, and is ever resounding with the din of vehicles, carts, cabs, hansoms, broughams, and omnibuses driving along. Many of the shops are spacious and crowded with costly goods, and the large windows of plate-glass, set in massive brass frames, are gaily furnished with their various articles of merchandise.

On the opposite side of the street we observed a jolly, comfortable-looking, elderly man, like a farmer in appearance, not at all like a London sharper. He was standing looking along the street as though he were waiting for some one. He was a magsman (a skittle-sharp), and no doubt other members of the gang were hovering near. He appeared to be as cunning as an old fox in his movements, admirably fitted to entrap the unwary.

A little farther along the street we saw a fashionably-dressed man coming towards us, arm in arm with his companion, among the throng of people. They were in the prime of life, and had a respectable, and even opulent appearance. One of them was good-humoured and social, as though he were on good terms with himself and society in general; the other was more callous and reserved, and more suspicious in his aspect. Both were bedecked with glittering watch chains and gold rings. They passed by a few paces, when the more social of the two, looking over his shoulder, met our eye directed towards him, turned back and accosted us, and was even so generous as to invite us into a gin-palace near by, which we courteously declined. The two magsmen (card-sharpers) strutted off, like fine gentlemen, along the street on the outlook for their victims.

Here we saw another young man, a burglar, pass by. He had an engaging appearance, and was very tasteful in his dress, very unlike the rough burglars we met at Whitechapel, the Borough, and Lambeth.

Leaving Oxford Street we went along Holborn to Chancery Lane, chiefly frequented by barristers and attorneys, and entered Fleet Street, one of the main arteries of the metropolis, reminding us of London in the olden feudal times, when the streets were crowded together in dense masses, flanked with innumerable dingy alleys, courts, and by-streets, like a great rabbit-warren. Fleet Street, though a narrow, business street, with its traffic often choked with vehicles, is interesting from its antique, historical, and literary associations. Elbowing our way through the throng of people, we pass through one of the gloomy arches of Temple Bar, and issue into the Strand, where we saw two pickpockets, young, tall, gentlemanly men, cross the street from St. Clement's Church and enter a restaurant. They were attired in a suit of superfine black cloth, cut in fashionable style. They entered an elegant dining-room, and probably sat down to costly viands and wines.

Leaving the Strand, we went up St. Martin's Lane, a narrow street leading from the Strand to the Seven Dials. We here saw a young man, an expert burglar, of about twenty-four years of age and dark complexion, standing at the corner of the street. He was well dressed, in a dark cloth suit, with a billicock hat. One of his comrades was taken from his side about three weeks ago on a charge of burglary.

Entering a beershop in the neighbourhood of St. Giles, close by the Seven Dials, we saw a band of coiners and ringers of changes. One of them, a genteel-looking, slim youth is a notorious coiner, and has been convicted. He was sitting quietly by the door over a glass of beer, with his companion by his side. One of them is a moulder; another was sentenced to ten years' penal servitude for coining and selling base coin. A modest-looking young man, one of the gang, was seated by the bar, also respectably dressed. He is generally supposed to be a subordinate connected with this coining band, looking out, while they are coining, that no officers of justice are near, and carrying the bag of base money for them when they go out to sell it to base wretches in small quantities at low prices. Five shillings' worth of base money is generally sold for tenpence. "Ringing the changes" is effected in this way:—A person offers a good sovereign to a shopkeeper to be changed. The gold piece is chinked on the counter, or otherwise tested, and is proved to be good. The man hastily asks back and gets the sovereign, and pretends that he has some silver, so that he does not require to change it. On feeling his pocket he finds he does not have it, and returns a base piece of money resembling it, instead of the genuine gold piece.

We returned to Bow Street, and saw

three young pickpockets proceeding along in company, like three well-dressed costermongers, in dark cloth frock-coats and caps.

Being desirous of having a more thorough knowledge of the people residing in the rookery of St. Giles, we visited it with Mr. Hunt, inspector of police. We first went to a lodging-house in George Street, Oxford Street, called the Hampshire-Hog Yard. Most of the lodgers were then out. On visiting a room in the garret we saw a man, in mature years, making artificial flowers; he appeared to be very ingenious, and made several roses before us with marvellous rapidity. He had suspended along the ceiling bundles of dyed grasses of various hues, crimson, yellow, green, brown, and other colours to furnish cases of stuffed birds. He was a very intelligent man and a natural genius. He told us strong drink had brought him to this humble position in the garret, and that he once had the opportunity of making a fortune in the service of a nobleman. We felt, as we looked on his countenance, and listened to his conversation, he was capable of moving in a higher sphere of life. Yet he was wonderfully contented with his humble lot.

We visited Dyott House, George Street, the ancient manor-house of St. Giles-in-the-Fields, now fitted up as a lodging-house for single men. The kitchen, an apartment about fifteen feet square, is surrounded with massive and tasteful panelling in the olden style. A large fire blazing in the grate—with two boilers on each side—was kept burning night and day to supply the lodgers with hot water for their tea and coffee. Some rashers of bacon were suspended before the fire, with a plate underneath. There was a gas-light in the centre of the apartment, and a dial on the back wall. The kitchen was furnished with two long deal tables and a dresser, with forms to serve as seats. There were about fifteen labouring men present, most of them busy at supper on fish, and bread, and tea. They were a very mixed company, such as we would expect at a London lodging-house, men working in cab-yards assisting cabmen, some distributing bills in the streets, one man carrying advertizing boards, and others jobbing at anything they can find to do in the neighbourhood. This house was clean and comfortable, and had the appearance of being truly a comfortable poor man's home. It was cheerful to look around us and to see the social air of the inmates. One man sat with his coat off, enjoying the warmth of the kitchen; a boy was at his tea, cutting up dried fish and discussing his bread and butter. A young man of about nineteen sat at the back of the apartment, with a very sinister countenance, very unlike the others. There was something about him that indicated a troubled mind. We also observed a number of elderly men among the party, some in jackets, and others in velvet coats, with an honest look about them.

When the house was a brothel, about fifteen years ago, an unfortunate prostitute, named Mary Brothers, was murdered in this kitchen by a man named Connell, who was afterwards executed at Newgate for the deed. He had carnal connexion with this woman some time before, and he suspected that she had communicated to him the venereal disease with which he was afflicted. In revenge he took her life, having purchased a knife at a neighbouring cutler's shop.

We were introduced to the landlady, a very stout woman, who came up to meet us, candle in hand, as we stood on the staircase. Here we saw the profile of the ancient proprietor of the house, carved over the paneling, set, as it were, in an oval frame. In another part of the staircase we saw a similar frame, but the profile had been removed or destroyed. Over the window that overlooks the staircase there are three figures, possibly likenesses of his daughters; such is the tradition. The balustrade along the staircase is very massive and tastefully carved and ornamented. The bed-rooms were also clean and comfortable.

The beds are furnished with a bed-cover and flock bed, with sufficient warm and clean bedding, for the low charge of 2s. a week, or 4d. a night. The first proprietor of the house is said to have been a magistrate of the city, and a knight or baronet.

Leaving George Street we passed on to Church Lane, a by-street in the rear of New Oxford Street, containing twenty-eight houses. It was dark as we passed along. We saw the street lamps lighted in Oxford Street, and the shop-windows brilliantly illumined, while the thunder of vehicles in the street broke on our ear, rolling in perpetual stream. Here a very curious scene presented itself to our view. From the windows of the three-storied houses in Church Lane were suspended wooden rods with clothes to dry across the narrow street, —cotton gowns, sheets, trousers, drawers, and vests, some ragged and patched, and others old and faded, giving a more picturesque aspect to the scene, which was enhanced by the dim lights in the windows, and the groups of the lower orders of al ages assembled below, clustered around the doorways, and in front of the houses, or indulging in merriment in the street. Altogether the appearance of the inhabitants was much more clean and orderly than might be expected in such a low locality. Many women of the lower orders, chiefly of the Irish cockneys, were seated, crouching with their knees almost touching their chin, beside the open windows. Some men were smoking their pipes as they stood leaning against the walls of their houses, whom from their appearance we took to be evidently out-door labourers. Another labouring man was seated on the sill of his window, in corduroy trousers, light-gray coat and cap, with an honest look of good-humour and industry. Numbers of young women, the wives of costermongers, sat in front of their houses in the manner we have described, clad in cotton gowns, with a general aspect of personal cleanliness and contentment. At the corners of the streets, and at many of the doorways, were groups of young costermongers, who had finished their hard day's work, and were contentedly chatting and smoking. They generally stood with their hands in their breeches pockets. Most of these people are Irish, or the children of Irish parents. The darkness of the street was lighted up by the street lamps as well as by the lights in the windows of two chandlers' shops and one public-house. At one of the chandlers' shops the proprietor was standing by his door with folded arms as he looked good-humouredly on his neighbours around his shop-door. We also saw some of the young Arabs bareheaded and barefooted, with their little hands in their pockets, or squatted on the street, having the usual restless, artful look peculiar to their tribe.

Here a house was pointed out to us, No. 21, which was formerly let at a rent of 25*l.* per annum to a publican that resided in the neighbourhood. He let the same in rooms for 90*l.* a year, and these again receive from parties residing in them upwards of 120*l.* The house is still let in rooms, but they are occupied, like all others in the neighbourhood, by one family only.

At one house as we passed along we saw a woman selling potatoes, at the window, to persons in the street. On looking into the interior we saw a cheerful fire burning in the grate and some women sitting around it. We also observed several bushel baskets and sacks placed round the room, filled with potatoes, of which they sell a large quantity.

In Church Lane we found two lodging-houses, the kitchens of which are entered from the street by a descent of a few steps leading underground to the basement. Here we found numbers of people clustered together around several tables, some reading the newspapers, others supping on fish, bread, tea, and potatoes, and some lying half asleep on the tables in all imaginable positions. These, we were told, had just returned from hopping in Kent, had walked long distances, and were fatigued.

On entering some of these kitchens, the ceiling being very low, we found a large fire burning in the grate, and a general air of comfort, cleanliness, and order. Such scenes as these were very homely and picturesque, and reminded us very forcibly of localities of London in the olden time. In some of them the inmates were only half dressed, and yet appeared to be very comfortable from the warmth of the apartment. Here we saw a number of the poorest imbeciles we had noticed in the course of our rambles through the great metropolis. Many of them were middle-aged men, others more elderly, very shabbily dressed, and some half naked. There was little manliness left in the poor wretches as they squatted drearily on the benches. The inspector told us they were chiefly vagrants, and were sunk in profound ignorance and debasement, from which they were utterly unable to rise.

The next kitchen of this description we entered was occupied by females. It was about fifteen feet square, and belongs to a house with ten rooms, part of which is occupied as a low lodging-house. Here we found five women seated around a table, most of them young, but one more advanced in life. Some of them were good-looking, as though they had been respectable servants. They were busy at their tea, bread, and butcher's meat. On the table stood a candle on a small candlestick. They sat in curious positions round the table, some of them with an ample crinoline. One sat by the fire with her gown drawn over her knees, displaying her white petticoat. As we stood beside them they burst out in a titter which they could not suppress. On looking round we observed a plate-rack at the back of the kitchen, and, as usual in these lodging-houses, a glorious fire burning brightly in the grate. An old chest of drawers, surmounted with shelves, stood against the wall. The girls were all prostitutes and thieves, but had no appearance of shame. They were apparently very merry. The old woman sat very thoughtful, looking observant on, and no doubt wondering what errand could have brought us into the house.

We then entered another dwelling-house. On looking down the stairs we saw a company of young women, from seventeen to twenty-five years of age. A rope was hung over the fireplace, with stockings and shirts suspended over it, and clothes were drying on a screen. A young woman, with her hair netted and ornamented, sat beside the fire with a green jacket and striped petticoat with crinoline. Another good-looking young woman sat by the table dressed in a cotton gown and striped apron, with coffee-pot in hand, and tea-cups before her. Some pleasant-looking girls sat by the table with their chins leaning on their hands, smiling cheerfully, looking at us with curiosity. Another coarser featured dame lolled by the end of the table with her gown drawn over her head, smirking in our countenance; and one sat by, her shawl drawn over her head. Another apparently modest girl sat by cutting her nails with a knife. On the walls around the apartment were suspended a goodly assortment of bonnets, cloaks, gowns, and petticoats.

Meantime an elderly little man came in with a cap on his head and a long staff in his hand, and stood looking on with curiosity. On the table lay a pack of cards beside the bowls, cups, and other crockery-ware. Some of the girls appeared as if they had lately been servants in respectable situations, and one was like a quiet genteel shop girl. They were all prostitutes, and most of them prowl about at night to plunder drunken men. As we looked on the more interesting girls, especially two of them, we saw the sad consequences of one wrong step, which may launch the young and thoughtless into a criminal career, and drive them into the dismal companionship of the most lewd and debased.

We then went to Short's Gardens, and entered a house there. On the basement underground we saw a company of men, women, and children of various ages, seated around the tables, and by the fire. The men and women had mostly been engaged in hopping, and appeared to be healthy, industrious, and orderly. Until lately thieves used to lodge in these premises.

As we entered Queen Street we saw three thieves, lads of about fourteen years of age, standing in the middle of the street as if on the outlook for booty. They were dressed in black frock-coats, corduroy, and fustian trousers, and black caps. Passing along Queen Street, which is one of the wings of the Dials, we went up to the central space between the Seven Dials. Here a very lively scene presented itself to our view; clusters of labouring men, and a few men of doubtful character, in dark shabby dress, loitered by the corners of the surrounding streets. We also saw groups of elderly women standing at some of the angles, most of them ragged and drunken, their very countenances the pictures of abject misery. The numerous public-houses in the locality were driving a busy traffic, and were thronged with motley groups of people of various grades, from the respectable merchant and tradesman to the thief and the beggar.

Bands of boys and girls were gamboling in the street in wild frolic, tumbling on their head with their heels in the air, and shouting in merriment, while the policeman was quietly looking on in good humour.

Around the centre of the Dials were bakers' shops with large illuminated fronts, the shelves being covered with loaves, and the baker busy attending to his customers. In the window was a large printed notice advertising the "best wheaten bread at $6d.$" a loaf. A druggist's shop was invitingly adorned with beautiful green and purple jars, but no customers entered during the time of our stay.

At the corner of an opposite dial was an old clothes store, with a large assortment of second-hand garments, chiefly for men, of various kinds, qualities, and styles, suspended around the front of the shop. There were also provision shops, which were well attended with customers. The whole neighbourhood presented an appearance of bustle and animation, and omnibuses and other vehicles were passing along in a perpetual stream.

The most of the low girls in this locality do not go out till late in the evening, and chiefly devote their attention to drunken men. They frequent the principal thoroughfares in the vicinity of Oxford Street, Holborn, Farringdon Street, and other bustling streets. From the nature of their work they are of a migratory character. The most of the men we saw in the houses we visited belong to the labouring class, men employed to assist in cleaning cabs and omnibuses, carriers of advertising boards, distributors of bills, patterers, chickweed sellers, ballad singers, and persons generally of industrious habits, along with a few of doubtful character. They are willing to work, but will steal rather than want.

The lodging-house people here have not been known of late years to receive stolen property, and the inhabitants generally are steadily rising in habits of decency, cleanliness, and morality.

The houses we visited in George Street,

and the streets adjacent, were formerly part of the rookery of St. Giles-in-the-Fields, celebrated as one of the chief haunts of redoutable thieves and suspicious characters in London. Deserted as it comparatively is now, except by the labouring poor vagrants and low prostitutes, it was once the resort of all classes, from the proud noble to the beggar picking up a livelihood from door to door.

We have been indebted to Mr. Hunt, inspector of the lodging-houses of this district, for fuller information regarding the rookery of St. Giles and its inhabitants twenty years ago, before a number of these disreputable streets were removed to make way for New Oxford Street. We quote from a manuscript nearly in his own words:—"The ground covered by the Rookery was enclosed by Great Russell Street, Charlotte Street, Broad Street, and High Street, all within the parish of St. Giles-in-the-Fields. Within this space were George Street (once Dyott Street), Carrier Street, Maynard Street, and Church Street, which ran from north to south, and were intersected by Church Lane, Ivy Lane, Buckeridge Street, Bainbridge Street, and New Street. These, with an almost endless intricacy of courts and yards crossing each other, rendered the place like a rabbit-warren.

"In Buckeridge Street stood the 'Hare and Hounds' public-house, formerly the 'Beggar in the Bush;' at the time of which I speak (1844) kept by the well-known and much-respected Joseph Banks (generally called 'Stunning Joe'), a civil, rough, good-hearted Boniface. His house was the resort of all classes, from the aristocratic marquis to the vagabond whose way of living was a puzzle to himself.

"At the opposite corner of Carrier Street stood Mother Dowling's, a lodging-house and provision shop, which was not closed nor the shutters put on for several years before it was pulled down, to make way for the improvements in New Oxford Street. .... The shop was frequented by vagrants of every class, including foreigners, who, with moustache, well-brushed hat, and seedy clothes—consisting usually of a frock-coat buttoned to the chin, light trousers, and boots gaping at each lofty step—might be seen making their way to Buckeridge Street to regale upon cabbage, which had been boiled with a ferocious pig's head or a fine piece of salt beef. From 12 to 1 o'clock at midnight was chosen by these ragged but proud gentlemen from abroad as the proper time for a visit to Mrs. Dowling's.

"Most of the houses in Buckeridge Street were lodging-houses for thieves, prostitutes, and cadgers. The charge was fourpence a night in the upper rooms, and threepence in the cellars, as the basements were termed. If the beds were occupied six nights by the same parties, and all dues paid, the seventh night (Sunday) was not charged for. The rooms were crowded, and paid well. I remember seeing fourteen women in beds in a cellar, each of whom paid 3*d.* a night, which, Sunday free, amounted to 21*s.* per week. The furniture in this den might have originally cost the proprietor 7*l.* or 8*l.* At the time I last visited it, it was not worth more than 30*s.*

"Both sides of Buckeridge Street abounded in courts, particularly the north side, and these, with the connected back-yards and low walls in the rear of the street, afforded an easy escape to any thief when pursued by officers of justice. I remember on one occasion, in 1844, a notorious thief was wanted by a well-known criminal officer (Restieaux). He was known to associate with some cadgers who used a house in the rear of Paddy Corvan's, near Church Street, and was believed to be in the house when Restieaux and a serjeant entered it. They went into the kitchen where seven male and five female thieves were seated, along with several cadgers of the most cunning class. One of them made a signal, indicating that some one had escaped by the back of the premises, in which direction the officers proceeded. It was evident the thief had gone over a low wall into an adjoining yard. The pursuers climbed over, passed through the yards and back premises of eleven houses, and secured him in Jones Court. There were about twenty persons present at the time of the arrest, but they offered no resistance to the constables. It would have been a different matter had he been apprehended by strangers.

"In Bainbridge Street, one side of which was nearly occupied by the immense brewery of Meux & Co., were found some of the most intricate and dangerous places in this low locality. The most notorious of these was Jones Court, inhabited by coiners, utterers of base coin, and thieves. In former years a bull terrier was kept here, which gave an alarm on the appearance of a stranger, when the coining was suspended till the course was clear. This dog was at last taken away by Duke and Clement, two police officers, and destroyed by an order from a magistrate.

"The houses in Jones Court were connected by roof, yard, and cellar with those in Bainbridge and Buckeridge streets, and with each other in such a manner that the apprehension of an inmate or refugee in one of them was almost a task of impossibility to a stranger, and difficult to those well acquainted with the interior of the dwellings. In one of the cellars was a large cesspool, covered in such a way that a stranger would likely step into it. In the same cellar was a hole about two feet square, leading to the next cellar, and thence by a similar hole into the cellar of a house in Scott's Court, Buckeridge Street. These afforded a ready means of escape to a thief, but effectually stopped the pursuers, who would be put to the risk of creeping on his hands and knees through a hole two feet square in a dark cellar in St. Giles's Rookery, entirely in the power of dangerous characters. Other houses were connected in a similar manner. In some instances there was a communication from one back window to another by means of large spike nails, one row to hold by, and another for the feet to rest on, which were not known to be used at the time we refer to.

"In Church Street were several houses let to men of an honest but poor class, who worked in omnibus and cab-yards, factories, and such other places as did not afford them the means of procuring more expensive lodgings. Their apartments were clean, and their way of living frugal.

"Other houses of a less reputable character were very numerous. One stood at the corner of Church Street and Lawrence Street, occupied by the most infamous characters of the district. On entering the house from Lawrence Lane, and proceeding upstairs, you would find on each floor several rooms connected by a kind of gallery, each room rented by prostitutes. These apartments were open to those girls who had fleeced any poor drunken man who had been induced to accompany them to this den of infamy. When they had plundered the poor dupe, he was ejected without ceremony by the others who resided in the room; often without a coat or hat, sometimes without his trousers, and occasionally left on the staircase naked as he was born. In this house the grossest scenes of profligacy were transacted. In pulling it down a hole was discovered in the wall opening into a timber-yard which fronted High Street—a convenient retreat for any one pursued.

"Opposite to this was the "Rose and Crown" public-house, resorted to by all classes of the light-fingered gentry, from the mobsman and his "Amelia" to the lowest of the street thieves and his "Poll." In the tap-room might be seen Black Charlie the fiddler, with ten or a dozen lads and lasses enjoying the dance, and singing and smoking over potations of gin-and-water, more or less plentiful according to the proceeds of the previous night—all apparently free from care in their wild carousals. The cheek waxed pale when the policeman opened the door and glanced round the room, but when he departed the merriment would be resumed with vigour.

"The kitchens of some houses in Buckeridge Street afforded a specimen of life in London rarely seen elsewhere even in London, though some in Church Lane do so now on a smaller scale. The kitchen, a long apartment usually on the ground-floor, had a large coke fire, along with a sink, water-tap, one or two tables, several forms, a variety of saucepans, and other cooking utensils, and was lighted with a gas jet. There in the evenings suppers were discussed by the cadgers an alderman might almost have envied—rich steaks and onions, mutton and pork chops, fried potatoes, sausages, cheese, celery, and other articles of fare, with abundance of porter, half-and-half, and tobacco.

"In the morning they often sat down to a breakfast of tea, coffee, eggs, rashers of bacon, dried fish, fresh butter, and other good things which would be considered luxuries by working people, when each discussed his plans for the day's rambles, and arranged as to the exchange of garments, bandages, &c., considered necessary to prevent recognition in those neighbourhoods recently worked.

"Their dinners were taken in the course of their rounds, consisting generally of the best of the broken victuals given them by the compassionate, and were eaten on one of the door-steps of some respectable street, after which they would resort to some obscure public-house or beer-shop in a back street or alley to partake of some liquor.

"Heaps of good food were brought home and thrown on a side-table, or into a corner, as unfit to be eaten by those "professional" cadgers,—food which thousands of the working men of London would have been thankful for. It was given to the children who visited these lodging-houses. The finer viands, such as pieces of fancy bread, rolls, kidneys, mutton and lamb, the gentlemen of the establishment reserved for their own more fastidious palates.

"On Sundays many of the cadgers staid at home till night. They spent the day at cards, shove-halfpenny, tossing, and other amusements. Sometimes five or six shillings were staked on the table among a

BOYS EXERCISING AT TOTHILL FIELDS PRISON.

party of about ten of them at cards, although coppers were the usual stakes. . . . The life of a cadger is not in many instances a life of privation. I do not speak (says Mr. Hunt) of the really distressed, to whose wants too little attention is sometimes paid. I allude to beggars by profession, who prefer a life of mendicancy to any other. There are among them sailors, whose largest voyage has been to Tothill Fields prison, or to Gravesend on a pleasure trip. Cripples with their arms in slings, or feet, swathed in blood-stained rags, swollen to double the size, who may be seen dancing when in their lodging at their evening revels. You may see poor Irish with from five to thirty sovereigns in a bag hung round their necks or in the waistband of their trousers; women who carry hired babes, or it may be a bundle of clothing resembling a child, on their back and breast, and other suchlike impostors.

"Between Buckeridge Street and Church Lane stood Ivy Lane, leading from George Street to Carrier Street, communicating with the latter by a small gateway. Clark's Court was on its left, and Rats' Castle on its right. This castle was a large dirty building occupied by thieves and prostitutes, and boys who lived by plunder. On the removal of these buildings, in 1845, the massive foundations of an hospital were found, which had been built in the 12th century by Matilda, Queen of Henry the First, daughter of Malcolm King of Scotland, for persons afflicted with leprosy.

"At this place criminals were allowed a bowl of ale on their way from Newgate to Tyburn.

"Maynard Street and Carrier Street were occupied by costermongers and a few thieves and cadgers. George Street, part of which still stands, consisted of lodging-houses for tramps, thieves, and beggars, together with a few brothels."

From George Street to High Street runs a mews called Hampshire-Hog Yard, where there is an old established lodging-house for single men, poor but honest.

The portion of the rookery now remaining, consisting of Church Lane, with its courts, a small part of Carrier Street, and a smaller portion of one side of Church Street, is now more densely crowded than when Buckeridge Street and its neighbourhood were in existence. The old Crown public-house in Church Lane, formerly the resort of the most notorious cadgers, was in 1851 inhabited by Irish people, where often from twelve to thirty persons lodged in a room. At the back of this public-house is a yard, on the right-hand side of which is an apartment then occupied by thirty-eight men, women, and children, all lying indiscriminately on the floor.

Speaking of other houses in this neighbourhood in 1851, Mr. Hunt states: "I have frequently seen as many as sixteen people in a room about twelve feet by ten, these numbers being exceeded in larger rooms. Many lay on loose straw littered on the floor, their heads to the wall and their feet to the centre, and decency was entirely unknown among them."

Now, however, the district is considerably changed, the inhabitants are rapidly rising in decency, cleanliness, and order, and the Rookery of St. Giles will soon be ranked among the memories of the past.

NARRATIVE OF A LONDON SNEAK, OR COMMON THIEF.

THE following narrative was given us by a convicted thief, who has for years wandered over the streets of London as a ballad singer, and has resided in the low lodging-houses scattered over its lowest districts. He was a poor wretched creature, degraded in condition, of feeble intellect, and worthless character, we picked up in a low lodging house in Drury Lane. He was shabbily dressed in a pair of old corduroy trousers, old brown coat, black shabby vest, faded grey neckerchief, an old dark cap and peak, and unwashed shirt. For a few shillings he was very ready to tell us the sad story of his miserable life.

"I was born at Abingdon, near Oxford, where my father was a bricklayer, and kept the N———n public-house. He died when I was fourteen years of age; I was sent to school and was taught to read, but not to write. At this time I was a steady, well-conducted boy. At fourteen years of age I went to work with my uncle, a basket-maker and rag merchant in Abingdon, and lived with my mother. I wrought there for three years, making baskets and cutting willows for them. I left my uncle then, as he had not got any more work for me to do, and was living idle with my mother. At this time I went with a Cheap John to the fairs, and travelled with him the whole of that season. He was a Lancashire man, between fifty and sixty years of age, and had a woman who travelled the country with him, but I do not think they were married. He was a tall, dark-complexioned man, and was a 'duffer,' very unprincipled in his dealings. He sold cutlery, books, stationery, and hardware.

"When we were going from one fair to another, we would stop on the road and make a fire, and steal fowls and potatoes, or any green-stuff that was in season. We sometimes travelled along with gipsies, occasionally to the number of fifty or sixty in a gang. The gipsies are a curious sort of people, and would not let you connect with any of them unless they saw you were to remain among them.

"I assisted Cheap John in the markets when selling his goods, and handed them to the purchasers.

"The first thing I ever pilfered was a pair of boots and a handkerchief from a drunken man who lay asleep at a fair in Reading, in Berks. He was lying at the back of a booth and no one near him. This was about dusk in September. I pawned the boots at Windsor on the day of a fair for 3s., and sold the handkerchief for 1s.

"I was about seventeen years of age when I went with Cheap John, and remained with him about thirteen weeks, when I left, on account of a row I had with him. I liked this employment very well, got 2s. in the pound for my trouble, and sometimes had from 1l. to 25s. a week. But the fairs were only occasional, and the money I earned was very precarious.

"I left Cheap John at Windsor, and came to Slough with a horse-dealer, where I left him. He gave me 2s. for assisting him. I then came up to London, where I have lived ever since in the lodging-houses in the different localities. I remember on coming to this great city I was much astonished at its wonders, and every street appeared to me like a fair. On coming to London I had no money, and had not any friend to assist me. I went to Kensington workhouse, and got a night's lodging, and lived for about a fortnight at different workhouses in London. They used to give the lodgers a piece of bread at night, and another in the morning, and a night's lodging on straw and boards.

"I then went out singing ballads in the streets of London, and could get at an average from 2s. to 2s. 6d. a night, but when the evenings were wet, I could not get anything. In the winter I sang in the daytime, and in summer I went out in the evening. I have wandered in this way over many of the streets and thoroughfares of London. I sing in Marylebone, Somers Town, Camden Town, Paddington, Whitecross Street, City, Hammersmith, Commercial Road, and Whitechapel, and live at different lodgings, and make them my home as I move along. I sing different kinds of songs, sentimental and comic; my favourites are 'Gentle Annie,' 'She's reckoned a good hand at it,' 'The Dandy Husband,' 'The Week's Matrimony,' 'The Old Woman's Sayings,' and 'John Bull and the Taxes.' I often sing 'The Dark-eyed Sailor,' and 'The Female Cabin Boy.' For many years now I have lived by singing in the public street, sometimes by myself, at other times with a mate. I occasionally beg in Regent Street and Bond Street on the 'fly,' that is, follow people passing along, and sometimes in Oxford Street and Holborn. Sometimes I get a little job to do from people at various kinds of handiwork, such as turning the wheel to polish steel, and irons, &c., and do other kinds of job work. When hard up I pick pockets of handkerchiefs, by myself or with one or two mates. [In the course of our interview we saw he was very clumsy at picking pockets.] I sometimes go out with the young dark-complexioned lad you saw down stairs, who is very clever at pocket picking, and has been often convicted before the criminal courts.

"I have spent many years living in the low lodging-houses of London. The worst I ever saw was in Keat Street, Whitechapel, about nine years ago, before they were reformed and changed. Numbers were then crowded into the different rooms, and the floors were littered with naked people of all ages, and of both sexes, men and women, and boys and girls sleeping alongside indiscriminately. It was very common to see young boys and girls sleeping together. The conversations that passed between them, and the scenes that were transacted, were enough to contaminate the morals of the young.

"In the morning they used to go to their different haunts over the city, some begging, and others thieving.

"On Sunday evenings the only books read were such as 'Jack Sheppard,' 'Dick Turpin,' and the 'Newgate Calendar' they got out of the neighbouring libraries by depositing 1s. These were read with much interest; the lodgers would sooner have these than any other books. I never saw any of them go to church on Sundays. Sometimes one or two would go to the ragged-school, such as the one in Field Lane near Smithfield.

"It often happened a man left his wife, and she came to the lodging-house and got a livelihood by begging. Some days she would glean 2s. or 3s., and at other times would not get a halfpenny.

"The thieves were seldom in the lodging-house, except to meals and at bedtime. They lived on better fare than the beggars. The pickpocket lives better than the sneaking thief, and the pickpocket is thought more of in the lodging-houses and prisons than the beggar.

"The lowest pickpockets often lived in these low lodging-houses, some of them young lads, and others middle-aged men. The young pickpockets, if clever, soon leave the lodging-houses and take a room in some locality, as at Somers Town, Marylebone, the Burgh, Whitechapel, or Westminster. The pickpockets in lodging-houses, for the most part, are stockbuzzers, *i.e.*, stealers of handkerchiefs.

"I have often seen the boys picking each others' pockets for diversion in the lodging-houses, many of them from ten to eleven years of age.

"There are a great number of sneaks in the lodging-houses. Two of them go out together to the streets, one of them keeps a look-out while the other steals some article, shoes, vest, or coat, &c., from the shop or stall. I sometimes go out with a mate and take a pair of boots at a shop-door and sell them to the pawnbroker, or to a labouring man passing in the street.

"Sometimes I have known the lodgers make up a packet of sawdust and put in a little piece of tobacco to cover an opening, leaving only the tobacco to be seen looking through, and sell it to persons passing by in the street as a packet of tobacco.

"When I am hard up I have gone out and stolen a loaf at a baker's shop, or chandler's shop, and taken it to my lodging. I have often stolen handkerchiefs, silk and cambric, from gentlemen's pockets.

"I once stole a silver snuff-box from a man's coat-pocket, and on one occasion took a pocket-book with a lot of papers and postage stamps. I burnt the papers and sold the stamps for about 1s. 6d.

"I never had clothes respectable enough to try purses and watches, and did not have nerve for it. I have seen young thieves encouraged by people who kept the lodging-houses, such as at Keat Street, Whitechapel, and at the Mint. They would ask the boys if they had anything, and wish them to sell it to them, which was generally done at an under-price. In these lodging-houses some lived very well, and others were starving. Some had steaks and pickles, and plenty of drink, porter and ale, eggs and bacon, and cigars to smoke. Some of the poorest go out and get a pennyworth of bread, halfpennyworth of tea, halfpennyworth of butter, and halfpennyworth of sugar, and perhaps not have a halfpenny left to pay for their lodging at night. When they do get money they often go out and spend it in drink, and perhaps the next night are starving again.

"I have been tried for stealing a quart pot and a handkerchief, at Bagnigge Wells police station, and was taken to Vine Street police station for stealing 2s. 6d. from a drunken woman respectably dressed. I took it out of her hand, and was seen by a policeman, who ran after me and overtook me, but the woman refused to prosecute me, and I was discharged. I was also brought before Marylebone police-court for begging.

"In my present lodging I am pretty comfortable. We spend our evenings telling tales and conversing to each other on our wanderings, and playing at games, such as 'hunt the slipper.' I have often been in great want, and have been driven to steal to get a livelihood."

PICKPOCKETS AND SHOPLIFTERS.

IN tracing the pickpocket from the beginning of his career, in most cases we must turn our attention to the little ragged boys living by a felon's hearth, or herding with other young criminals in a low lodging-house, or dwelling in the cold and comfortless home of drunken and improvident parents. The great majority of the pickpockets of the metropolis, with few exceptions, have sprung from the dregs of society—from the hearths and homes of London thieves —so that they have no reason to be proud of their lineage. Fifteen or twenty years ago many of those accomplished pickpockets, dressed in the highest style of fashion, and glittering in gold chains, studs, and rings, who walk around the Bank of England and along Cheapside, and our busy thoroughfares, were poor ragged boys walking barefooted among the dark and dirty slums and alleys of Westminster and the Seven Dials, or loitering among the thieves' dens of the Borough and Whitechapel.

Step by step they have emerged from

their rags and squalor to a higher position of physical comfort, and have risen to higher dexterity and accomplishment in their base and ignoble profession.

We say there are a few exceptions to the general rule, that the most of our habitual thieves have sprung from the loins of felon parents. We blush to say that some have joined the ranks of our London thieves, and are living callous in open crime, who were trained in the homes of honest and industrious parents, and were surrounded in early life with all those influences which are fitted to elevate and improve the mind. But here our space forbids us to enlarge.

The chief sources whence our pickpockets spring are from the low lodging-houses—from those dwellings in low neighbourhoods, where their parents are thieves, and where improvident and drunken people neglect their children, such as Whitechapel, Shoreditch, Spitalfields, New Cut, Lambeth, the Borough, Clerkenwell, Drury Lane, and other localities. Many of them are the children of Irish parents, costermongers, bricklayers' labourers, and others. They often begin to steal at six or seven years of age, sometimes as early as five years, and commit petty sneaking thefts, as well as pick handkerchiefs from gentlemen's pockets. Many of these ragged urchins are taught to steal by their companions, others are taught by trainers of thieves, young men and women, and some middle-aged convicted thieves. They are learned to be expert in this way. A coat is suspended on the wall with a bell attached to it, and the boy attempts to take the handkerchief from the pocket without the bell ringing. Until he is able to do this with proficiency he is not considered well trained. Another way in which they are trained is this: The trainer—if a man—walks up and down the room with a handkerchief in the tail of his coat, and the ragged boys amuse themselves abstracting it until they learn to do it in an adroit manner. We could point our finger to three of these execrable wretches, who are well known to train schools of juvenile thieves—one of them, a young man at Whitechapel; another, a young woman at Clerkenwell; and a third, a middle-aged man residing about Lambeth Walk. These base wretches buy the stolen handkerchiefs from the boys at a paltry sum. We have also heard of some being taught to pick pockets by means of an effigy; but this is not so well authenticated.

Great numbers of these ragged pickpockets may be seen loitering about our principal streets, ready to steal from a stall or shop-door when they find an opportunity. During the day they generally pick pockets two or three in a little band, but at dusk a single one can sometimes do it with success. They not only steal handkerchiefs of various kinds, but also pocketbooks from the tails of gentlemen's coats. We may see them occasionally engaged at this work on Blackfriars Bridge and London Bridge, also along Bishopsgate, Shoreditch, Whitechapel, Drury Lane, and similar localities. They may be seen at any hour of the day, but chiefly from 10 to 2 o'clock. They are generally actively on the look-out on Saturday evening in the shopping streets where the labouring people get their provisions in for the Sunday. At this early stage the boys occasionally pick pockets, and go about cadging and sneaking (begging and committing petty felonies).

The next stage commences—we shall say—about fourteen years of age, when the stripling lays aside his rags, and dresses in a more decent way, though rather shabby. Perhaps in a dark or gray frock-coat, dark or dirty tweed trousers, and a cap with peak, and shoes. At this time many of them go to low neighbourhoods, or to those quieter localities where the labouring people reside, and pick the pockets of the wives and daughters of this class of persons; others steal from gentlemen passing along thoroughfares, while a few adroit lads are employed by men to steal from ladies' pockets in the fashionable streets of the metropolis.

These young thieves seldom commit their depredations in the localities where they are known, but prowl in different parts of the metropolis. They are of a wandering character, changing from one district to another, and living in different lodging-houses—often leaving their parent's houses as early as ten years of age. Sometimes they are driven by drunken loafing parents to steal, though in most cases they leave their comfortless homes and live in lodging-houses.

When they have booty, they generally bring it to some person to dispose of, as suspicion would be aroused if they went to sell or pawn it themselves. In some cases they give it to the trainer of thieves, or they take it to some low receiving house, where wretches encourage them in stealing; sometimes to low coffee-houses, low hairdressers or tailors, who act as middlemen to dispose of the property, generally giving them but a small part of the value.

In the event of their rambling to a distant part of London, they sometimes arrange to get one of their number to convey the stolen goods to these parties. At other times they dispose of them to low wretches connected with the lodging-houses, or other persons in disreputable neighbourhoods.

At this time many of them cohabit with girls in low lodging-houses; many of whom are older than themselves, and generally of the felon class.

These lads frequently steal at the "tail" of gentlemen's coats, and learn the other modes of picking pockets.

Stealing the handkerchief from the "tail" of a gentleman's coat in the street is generally effected in this way. Three or four usually go together. They see an old gentleman passing by. One remains behind, while the other two follow up close beside him, but a little behind. The one walking by himself behind is the looker out to see if there are any police or detectives near, or if any one passing by or hovering around is taking notice of them. One of the two walking close by the gentleman adroitly picks his pocket, and coils the handkerchief up in his hand so as not to be seen, while the other brings his body close to him, so as not to let his arm be seen by any passer by.

If the party feel him taking the handkerchief from his pocket, the thief passes it quickly to his companion, who runs off with it. The looker-out walks quietly on as if nothing had occurred, or sometimes walks up to the gentleman and asks him what is the matter, or pretends to tell him in what direction the thief has run, pointing him to a very different direction from the one he has taken.

They not only abstract handkerchiefs but also pocketbooks from the tail of gentlemen's coats, or any other article they can lay their fingers on.

This is the common way in which the coat-pocket is picked when the person is proceeding along the street. Sometimes it happens that one thief will work by himself, but this is very seldom. In the case of a person standing, the coat-tail pocket is picked much in the same manner.

These boys in most cases confine themselves to stealing from the coat-pocket on the streets, but in the event of a crowd on any occasion, they are so bold as to steal watches from the vest-pocket. This is done in a different style, and generally in the company of two or three in this manner: One of them folds his arms across his breast in such a way that his right hand is covered with his left arm. This enables him to use his hand in an unobserved way, so that he is thereby able to abstract the watch from the vest-pocket of the gentleman standing by his side.

A police-officer informed us, that when at Cremorne about a fortnight ago, a large concourse of people was assembled to see the female acrobat, termed the "Female Blondin," cross the Thames on a rope suspended over the river, he observed two young men of about twenty-four years of age, and about the middle height, respectably dressed, whom he suspected to be pickpockets. They went up to a smart gentlemanly man standing at the riverside looking eagerly at the Female Blondin, then walking the rope over the middle of the river. As his attention was thus absorbed, the detective saw these two men go up to him. One of them placed himself close on the right hand side of him, and putting his right arm under his left, thus covered his right hand, and took the watch gently from the pocket of the gentleman's vest. The thief made two attempts to break the ring attached to the watch, termed the "bowl" or swivel, with his finger and thumb.

After two ineffective endeavours he bent it completely round, and yet it would not break. He then left the watch hanging down in front of the vest, the gentleman meanwhile being unaware of the attempted felony. The detective officer took both the thieves into custody. They were brought before the Westminster police-court and sentenced each to three months' imprisonment for an attempt to steal from the person.

The same officer informed us that about a month or six weeks ago, in the same place, on a similar occasion, he observed three persons, a man, a boy, and a woman, whom he suspected to be picking pockets. The man was about twenty-eight years of age, rather under the middle size. The woman hovered by his side. She was very good-looking, about twenty-four years of age, dressed in a green coloured gown, Paisley shawl, and straw bonnet trimmed with red velvet and red flowers. The man was dressed in a black frock-coat, brown trousers, and black hat. The boy, who happened to be his brother, was about fourteen years old, dressed in a brown shooting-coat, corduroy trousers, and black cap with peak. The boy had an engaging countenance, with sharp features and smart manner. The officer observed the man touch the boy on the shoulder and point him towards an old lady. The boy placed himself on her right side, and the man and woman kept behind. The former put his left hand into the pocket of the lady's gown and drew nothing from it, then left her and went about two yards farther; there he placed himself by other two ladies, tried both their pockets and left them again. He followed another lady and succeeded in picking her pocket of a small sum of money and a handkerchief. The officer took them all to the police station with the assistance of another detective officer, when they were committed for trial at Clerkenwell sessions. The man was sentenced to ten years' penal servitude, the boy to two months' hard labour, and three months in a reformatory, and the woman was sentenced to two years' imprisonment, with hard labour, in the House of Correction at Westminster.

It appeared, in the course of the evidence at the trial, that this man had previously been four years in penal servitude, and since his return had decoyed his little brother from a situation he held, for the purpose of training him to pick pockets, having induced him to rob his employer before leaving service.

The *scarf pin* is generally taken from the breast in this way. The thief generally has a handkerchief in his hand, pretending to wipe his nose, as he walks along the street. He then places his right hand across the breast of the person he intends to rob, bringing his left hand stealthily under his arm. This conceals his movements from the eyes of the person. With the latter hand he snatches out the pin from the scarf. It is sometimes done with the right hand, at other times with the left, according to the position of the person, and is generally done in the company of one or more. The person robbed is rarely aware of the theft. Should he be aware, or should any one passing by have observed the movement, the pin got from the scarf is suddenly passed into the hands of the other parties, when all of them suddenly make off in different directions soon to meet again in some neighbouring locality.

At other times the thief drives the person with a push, in the street, bringing his hands to his breast as if he had stumbled against him, at the same time adroitly laying hold of the pin. This is done in such a way that the person is seldom aware of the robbery until he afterwards finds out the loss of the article.

The *trousers pocket* is seldom picked on the public street, as this is an operation of considerable difficulty and danger. It is not easy to sip the hand into the trousers pocket without being felt by the person attempted to be robbed. This is generally done in crowds where people are squeezed together, when they contrive to do it in this way: They cut up the trousers with a knife or other sharp instrument, lay open the pocket, and adroitly rifle the money from it; or they insert the fingers or hand into it in a push, often without being observed, while the person's attention is distracted, possibly by some of the accomplices or stalls. They often occasion a disturbance in crowds, and create a quarrel with people near them, or have sham fights with each other, or set violently on the person they intend to rob. Many rough expedients are occasionally had recourse to, to effect this object.

Sometimes the pocket is picked in a crowd by means of laying hold of the party by the middle as if they had jostled against him, or by pressing on his back from behind, while the fingers or hand are inserted into the pocket of his trousers to snatch any valuables, money or otherwise, contained therein.

This mode of stealing is sometimes done by one person, at other times by the aid of accomplices. It is most commonly done in the manner now described.

By dint of long experience and natural skill, some attain great perfection in this difficult job, and accomplish their object in the most clever and effective manner. They are so nimble and accomplished that they will accost a gentleman in the street, and while speaking to him, and looking him in the face, will quietly insert their hand into his vest pocket and steal his watch.

In a crowd, the pin is sometimes stolen with dexterity by a person from behind inserting his hand over the shoulder. Sometimes the watch is stolen by a sudden snatch at the guard, when the thief runs off with his booty. This is not so often done in the thoroughfares, as it is attended with great danger of arrest. It is oftener done in quiet by-streets, or by-places, where there are many adjacent courts and alleys intersecting each other, through which the thief has an opportunity of escaping.

These are the various modes by which gentlemen's pockets are generally picked.

A lady's pocket is commonly picked by persons walking by her side, who insert their hand gently into the pocket of her gown. This is often effected by walking alongside of the lady, or by stopping her in the street, asking the way to a particular place, or inquiring if she is acquainted with such and such a person. When the thief is accomplished, he can abstract the purse from her pocket in a very short space of time: but if he is not so adroit, he will detain her some time longer, asking further questions till he has completed his object. This is often done by a man and a woman in company.

A lady generally carries her gold or silver watch in a small pocket in front of her dress, possibly under one of the large flounces. It is often stolen from her by one or two, or even three persons, one of the thieves accosting her in the street in the manner described. They seldom steal the guard, but in most cases contrive to break the ring or swivel by which it is attached. Let us suppose that two pickpockets, a man and a woman, were to see a lady with a watch in the public street; they are possibly walking arm-in-arm; they make up to her, inquire the way to a particular place, and stand in front of her. One of them would ask the way while the other would meantime be busy picking her pocket. If they succeed, they walk off arm-in-arm as they came.

Sometimes two or three men will go up to a lady and deliberately snatch a parcel or reticule-bag from her hand or arm, and run off with it.

At other times a very accomplished pickpocket may pick ladies' pockets without any accomplices, or with none to cover his movements.

Walking along Cheapside one day, toward the afternoon, we observed a well-dressed, good-looking man of about thirty years of age, having the appearance of a smart man of business, standing by the side of an elderly looking, respectably dressed lady at a jeweller's window. The lady appeared to belong to the country, from her dress and manner, and was absorbed looking into the window at the gold watches, gold chains, lockets, pins, and other trinkets glittering within. Meantime the gentleman also appeared to be engrossed looking at these articles beside her, while crowds of people were passing to and fro in the street, and the carts, cabs, omnibuses, and other vehicles were rumbling by, deadening the footsteps of the passers by. Our eye accidentally caught sight of his left hand drooping by his side in the direction of the lady's pocket. We observed it glide softly in the direction of her pocket beneath the edge of her shawl with all the fascination of a serpent's movement. While the hand lay drooping, the fingers sought their way to the pocket. From the movement we observed that the fingers had found the pocket, and were seeking their way farther into the interior. The person was about to plunge his hand to abstract the contents, when we instinctively hooked his wrist with the curve of our walking-stick and prevented the robbery. With great address and tact he withdrew his hand from the lady's pocket, and his wrist from our grasp, and walked quietly away. Meantime a group of people had gathered round about us, and a gentleman asked if we had observed a pocket picked. We said nothing, but whispered to the lady, who stood at the window unaware of the attempted felony, that we had prevented her pocket being picked, and had just scared a thief with his hand in her pocket, then walked over to the other side of the street and passed on.

The more accomplished pickpockets are very adroit in their movements. A young lady may be standing by a window in Cheapside, Fleet Street, Oxford Street, or the Strand, admiring some beautiful engraving. Meantime a handsomely dressed young man, with gold chain and moustache, also takes his station at the window beside her, apparently admiring the same engraving. The young lady stands gazing on the beautiful picture, with her countenance glowing with sentiment, which may be enhanced by the sympathetic presence of the nice looking young man by her side, and while her bosom is thus throbbing with romantic emotion, her purse, meanwhile, is being quietly transferred to the pocket of this elegantly attired young man, whom she might find in the evening dressed as a rough costermonger, mingling among the low ruffians at the Seven Dials or Whitechapel, or possibly lounging in some low beershop in the Borough.

There are various ranks of pickpockets, from the little ragged boy, stealing the handkerchief from a gentleman's coat pocket, to the fashionable thief, promenading around the Bank, or strolling, arm in arm, with his gentlemanly looking companion along Cheapside.

The swell-mob are to be seen all over London, in crowded thoroughfares, at railway stations, in omnibuses and steamboats. You find them pursuing their base traffic in the Strand, Fleet Street, Holborn, Parliament Street, and at Whitehall, over the whole of the metropolis, and they are to be seen on all public occasions looking out for plunder.

Some commence their work at 8 and 9 in the morning, others do not rise till 11 or 12. They are generally seen about 11 or 12 o'clock—sometimes till dusk. Some work in the evening, and not during the day, while others are out during the day, and do nothing in the evening. In times of great public excitement, when crowds are assembled, such as at the late fire at London Bridge, when those great warehouses were burnt down—they are in motion from the lowest to the highest. They are generally as busy in summer time as in the winter. When the gentry and nobility have retired to their country-seats in the provinces, crowds of strangers and tourists are pouring into the metropolis every day.

They often travel into the country to attend races such as Ascot, the Derby at Epsom, and others in the surrounding towns. They go to the Crystal Palace, where the cleverest of them may be frequently seen, also to Cremorne, the Zoological Gardens Regent's Park, the theatres, operas, ball-rooms, casinos, and other fashionable places of amusement—sometimes to the great crowds that usually assemble at Mr. Spurgeon's new Tabernacle.

They also occasionally make tours in different parts of the United Kingdom and to Paris, and along the railways in all directions.

The most accomplished pickpockets reside at Islington, Hoxton, Kingsland Road, St. Luke's, the Borough, Camberwell, and Lambeth, in quiet, respectable streets, and occasionally change their lodging if watched by the police.

They have in most cases been thieves from their cradle; others are tradesmen's sons and young men from the provinces, who have gone into dissipated life and adopted this infamous course. These fast men are sometimes useful as stalls, though they rarely acquire the dexterity of the native-born, trained London pickpocket.

There are a few foreign pickpockets, French and others. Some of them are bullies about the Haymarket. There are also some German pickpockets, but the foreigners are principally French. As a general rule, more of the latter are engaged in swindling, than in picking pockets. Some of the French are considered in adroitness equal to the best of the English. There are also a few Scotch, but the great mass are Irish cockneys, which a penetrating eye could trace by their look and manner. Many of them have a restless look, as if always in dread of being taken, and generally keep a sharp look-out with the side of their eye as they walk along.

They differ a good deal in appearance. The better class dress very fashionably; others in the lower class do not dress so well. The more dexterous they are, they generally dress in higher style, to get among the more respectable and fashionable people. Some of the female pickpockets also dress splendidly, and have been heard to boast of frequently stealing from 20$l.$ to 30$l.$ a-day in working on ladies' pockets. They are sometimes as adroit as the men in stealing ladies' purses, and are less noticed lingering beside them on the streets, by the shop-windows, and in places of public resort.

Yet, though well dressed, there is a peculiarity about the look of most of the male and female pickpockets. The countenance of many of them is suspicious to a penetrating eye. Many of them have considerable mental ability, and appear to be highly intelligent.

The most dexterous pickpockets generally average from twenty to thirty-five years of age, when many of them become depressed in spirit, and "have the steel taken out of them" with the anxiety of the life and the punishments inflicted on them in the course of their criminal career. The restlessness and suspense of their life have the effect of dissipation upon a good many of them, so that, though generally comparatively temperate in the use of intoxicating liquors, they may be said to lead a fast life.

Some of them take a keen bold look, full into your countenance; others have a sneaking, suspicious, downcast appearance, showing that all is not right within.

They dress in various styles; sometimes in the finest of superfine black cloth; at other times in fashionable suits, like the first gentlemen in the land, spangled with jewellery. Some of them would pass for gentlemen—they are so polite in their address. Others appear like a mock-swell, vulgar in their manner—which is transparent through their fine dress, and are debased in their conversation, which is at once observed when they begin to speak.

The female pickpockets dress in fashionable attire; sometimes in black satin dresses and jewellery. Some of them are very lady-like, though they have sprung originally from the lowest class. You may see very beautiful women among them, though vulgar in their conversation. The females are often superior in intellect to the men, and more orderly in their habits. They are seldom married, but cohabit with pickpockets, burglars, resetters, and other infamous characters. Their paramour is frequently taken from them, and they readily go with another man in the same illicit manner.

They are passionately fond of their fancy man in most cases; yet very capricious—so much so that they not unfrequently leave the man they cohabit with for another sweetheart, and afterwards go back to their old lover again, who is so easy in his principles that he often welcomes her, especially if she is a good worker—that is, an expert pickpocket.

The greater part of these women have sprung from the class of Irish cockneys; others have been domestic servants and the daughters of labourers, low tradesmen, and others. This gives us a key to many of these house robberies, done with the collusion of servants—a kind of felony very common over the metropolis. These are not the more respectable genteel class of servants, but the humbler order, such as nursery girls and females in tradesmen's families. Many of them have come from the country, or from labouring people's families over the working neighbourhoods of the metropolis. They are soon taught to steal by the men they cohabit with, but seldom acquire the dexterity of the thief who has been younger trained. They seldom have the acuteness, tact, and dexterity of the latter.

They live very expensively on the best of poultry, butcher-meat, pastry, and wines, and some of them keep their pony and trap; most of them are very improvident, and spend their money foolishly on eating and drinking—though few of them drink to excess,—on dress, amusements, and gambling.

They do not go out every day to steal, but probably remain in the house till their money is nearly spent, when they commence anew their system of robbery to fill their purse.

The female pickpockets often live with the burglars. They have their different professions which they pursue. When the one is not successful in the one mode of plunder, they often get it in the other, or the women will resort to shoplifting. They must have money in either of these ways. The women do not resort to prostitution, though they may be of easy virtue with those they fancy. Some of them live with cracksmen in high style, and have generally an abundance of cash.

Female pickpockets are often the companions of skittlesharps, and pursue their mode of livelihood as in the case of cohabiting with burglars. Their age averages from sixteen to forty-five.

The generality of the pickpockets confine themselves to their own class of robberies. Others betake themselves to card-sharping and skittle-sharping, while a few of the more daring eventually become dexterous burglars.

In their leisure hours they frequently call at certain beershops and public-houses, kept possibly by some old "pals" or connexions of the felon class, at King's Cross, near Shoreditch Church, Whitechapel, the Elephant and Castle, and Westminster, and are to be seen dangling about these localities.

Some of the swell-mobsmen have been well-educated men, and at one time held good situations; some have been clerks; others are connected with respectable families, led away by bad companions, until they have become the dregs of society, and after having been turned out of their own social circle, have become thieves. They are not generally so adroit as the young trained thief, though they may be useful to their gangs in acting as stalls.

Many of them are intelligent men, and have a fund of general information which enables them to act their part tolerably well when in society.

Omnibus Pickpockets.

The most of this class of thieves are well-dressed women, and go out one or two together, sometimes three. They generally manage to get to the farthest seats in the interior of the omnibus, on opposite sides of the vehicle, next to the horses. As the lady passengers come in, they eye them carefully, and one of them seats herself on the right side of the lady they intend to plunder. She generally manages to throw the bottom of her cape or shawl over the lap of the lady, and works with her hand under it, so as to cover her movement.

Her confederate is generally sitting opposite to see that no one is noticing. In abstracting from a lady's pocket, the female thief has often to cut through the dress and pocket, which she does with a pocket-knife, pair of scissors, or other sharp instrument. So soon as she has secured the purse, or other booty, she and her companion leave the omnibus on the earliest opportunity, often in their hurry giving the conductor more than his fare, which creates suspicion, and frequently leads to their detection. Experienced conductors often inquire of the passengers on such occasions if they have lost anything, and if they find they have, they give chase to the parties to apprehend them.

It often happens the thief follows a lady into an omnibus from seeing the lady take out her purse perhaps in some shop. If she could not pick her pocket in the street, she contrives to go into an omnibus, and do it there. These robberies are committed in all parts of London. They generally work at some distance from where they live, so that they are not easily traced if detected at the time.

They invariably give false names and false addresses, when taken into custody. The same women who pick ladies' pockets in the street, perpetrate these felonies in omnibuses, and often travel by railway, pursuing this occupation—sometimes two women together, sometimes one along with a man.

Sometimes gentlemen's pockets are picked in omnibuses by male pickpockets, who also steal from the lady passengers when they find a suitable opportunity, especially at dusk.

RAILWAY PICKPOCKETS.

THIS is the same class of persons who pick pockets on the public street as already described. They often visit the various railway stations, and are generally smartly dressed as they linger there—some of them better than others. Some of the females are dressed like shopkeepers' wives, others like milliners, varying from nineteen to forty years of age, mostly from nineteen to twenty-five; some of them attired in cotton gowns, others in silks and satins.

At the railway stations they are generally seen moving restlessly about from one place to another, as if they did not intend to go by any particular railway train. There is an unrest about the most of them which to a discerning eye would attract attention.

They seldom take the train, but dangle among the throng around the ticket office, or on the platform beside the railway carriages on the eve of the train starting off, as well as when the train arrives. When they see ladies engaged in conversation, they go up to them and plant themselves by their side, while the others cover their movements. There generally are two, sometimes three of them in a party. They place themselves on the right hand side of the ladies, next to their pocket, and work with the left hand. When the ladies move, the thieves walk along with them.

The female pickpockets generally carry a reticule on their right arm so as to take off suspicion, and walk up to the persons at the railway station, and inquire what time the train starts to such a place, to detain them in conversation, and to keep them in their company.

The older female thieves generally look cool and weary, the younger ones are more restless and suspicious in their movements. They sometimes go into first and second class waiting-rooms and sit by the side of any lady they suppose to be possessed of a sum of money, and try to pick her pocket by inserting their hand, or by cutting it with a knife or other sharp instrument. They generally insert the whole hand, as the ladies' pockets are frequently deep in the dress. They often have a large cape to cover their hands, and pick the pocket while speaking to the lady, or sitting by her side. The young pickpockets are generally the most expert.

They seldom take the brooch from the breast, but confine themselves to picking pockets.

After they take the purse, they generally run to some by-place and throw it away, so that it cannot be identified; sometimes they put it into a watercloset, at other times drop it down an area as they pass along.

After taking the purse, the thief hands it to her companion, and they separate and walk away, and meet at some place appointed.

They occasionally travel with the trains to the Crystal Palace and other places in the neighbourhood of London, and endeavour to plunder the passengers on the way. Frequently they take longer excursions—especially during the summer—journeying from town to town, and going to races and markets, agricultural shows, or any places where there is a large concourse of people. Unless they are detected at the time they pick the pocket, they seldom leave any suspicion behind them, as they take care to lodge in respectable places, where no one would suspect them, and have generally plenty of money.

A considerable number of the male thieves also attend the railway stations, and pick pockets in the railway trains. They are generally well dressed, and many of them have an Inverness cape, often of a dark colour, and sometimes they carry a coat on their arm to hide their hand. There are commonly two or more of them together—sometimes women accompanying them. They are the same parties we have already so fully described, who commit such felonies in the streets, thoroughfares, and places of public resort in the metropolis, and their movements are in a great measure the same.

Number of felonies by picking pockets in the Metropolitan dists. for 1860   1,498
Ditto, ditto, in the City 380
                                    1,878

Value of property thereby abstracted in the Metropolitan districts .. £5,819
Ditto, ditto, in the City .. 375
                              £6 194

SHOPLIFTERS.

THERE is a class of women who visit the shops in various parts of the metropolis, sometimes two and at other times three together. They vary their dress according to the locality they visit. Sometimes you find them dressed very respectably, like the wives of people in good circumstances in life; at other times, they appear like servants. They often wear large cloaks, or shawls, and are to be found of different ages, from 14 to 60. They generally call into shops at busy times, when there are many persons standing around the counter, and will stand two or three together. They ask a look of certain articles, and will possibly say, after they have inspected them, that they do not suit them; they will say they are too high in price, or not the article they want, or not the proper colour. They will likely ask to see some other goods, and keep looking at the different articles until they get a quantity on the counter. When the shopman is engaged getting some fresh goods from the window, or from the shelves, one of them generally contrives to slip something under her cloak or shawl, while the other manages to keep his attention abstracted. Sometimes they carry a bag or a basket, and set it down on the counter, and while the shopman is busy, they will get some article and lay it down behind their basket, such as a roll of ribbons, or a half dozen of gloves, or other small portable goods. While the shopman's back is turned, or his attention withdrawn, it is hidden under their shawl or cloak. We frequently find the skirt of their dress lined from the pocket downward, forming a large repository all around the dress, with an opening in front, where they can insert a small article, which is not observed in the ample crinoline. In stealing rolls of silk, or other heavier goods, they conceal them under their arm. Women who engage in shoplifting sometimes pick pockets in the shops. They get by the side of a lady engaged looking over articles, and under pretence of inspecting goods in the one hand, pick their pockets with the other.

We find more of these people living in the east end and on the Surrey side than in the west end of the metropolis. A great many live in the neighbourhood of Kingsland Road and Hackney Road. Some of them cohabit with burglars, others with magsmen (skittle-sharps).

We find ladies in respectable position occasionally charged with shoplifting.

Respectably dressed men frequently go into the shops of drapers and others early in the morning, or at intervals during the day, or evening, to look at the goods, and often manage to abstract one or two articles, and secrete them under their coats. They frequently take a bundle of neckties, a parcel of gloves, or anything that will go in a small compass, and perhaps enter a jeweller's shop, and in this way abstract a quantity of jewellery. On going there, they will ask a sight of some articles; the first will not suit them, and they will ask to look at more. When the shopman is engaged, they will abstract some gold rings or gold pins, or other property, sometimes a watch. Occasionally they will go so far as to leave a deposit on the article, promising to call again. They do this to prevent suspicion. After they are gone, the shopman may find several valuables missing.

Sometimes they will ring the changes. On entering the shop they will bring patterns of rings and other articles in the window, which they have got made as facsimiles from metal of an inferior quality. On looking at the jewellery they will ring the changes on the counter, and keep turning them over, and in so doing abstract the genuine article and leave the counterfeit in its place.

The statistics applicable to this class of felonies are comprised under those given when treating on "stealing from the doors and windows of shops."

A VISIT TO THE DENS OF THIEVES IN SPITALFIELDS AND ITS NEIGHBOURHOOD.

ONE afternoon, in company with a detective officer, we visited Spitalfields, one of the most notorious rookeries for infamous characters in the metropolis. Leaving Whitechapel, we went up a narrow alley called George Yard, where we saw four brothels of a very low description, the inmates being common thieves. On proceeding a little farther along the alley we passed eight or nine lodging-houses. Most of the lodgers were out prowling over the various districts of the metropolis, some picking pockets, others area-sneaking.

On entering into a public-house in another alley near Union Street, we came to one of the most dangerous thieves' dens we have visited in the course of our rambles. As we approached the door of the house, we saw a dissipated looking man stealthily whispering outside the door to the ruffian-looking landlord, who appeared to be a fighting man, from his large coarse head and broken nose. The officer by our side hinted to us that the latter was a fence, or receiver of stolen property, and was probably speaking to his companion on some business of this nature. As we went forward they sneaked away, the one through a neighbouring archway, and the other into his house. We followed the latter into the public house, and found two or three brutal-looking men loafing about the bar. We passed through a small yard behind the house, where we found a number of fighting dogs chained to their kennels. Some were close to our feet as we passed along, and others, kept in an outhouse beside them, could almost snap at our face. We went to another outhouse beyond, where between thirty and forty persons were assembled round a wooden enclosure looking on, while some of their dogs were killing rats. They consisted of burglars, pickpockets, and the associates of thieves, along with one or two receivers of stolen property. Many of them were coarse and brutal in their appearance, and appeared to be in their element, as they urged on their dogs to destroy the rats, which were taken out one after another from a small wooden box. These men apparently ranged from twenty-two to forty years of age. Many of them had the rough stamp of the criminal in their countenances, and when inflamed with strong drink, would possibly be fit for any deed of atrocious villainy. Some of the dogs were strong and vigorous, and soon disposed of the rats as they ran round the wooden enclosure, surrounded by this redoubtable band of ruffians, who made the rafters ring with merriment when the dog caught hold of his prey, or when the rat turned desperate on its adversary. During the brief space of time we were present, a slim little half-starved dog killed several rats. When the rat was first let loose it was very nimble and vigorous in its movements, and the little dog kept for a time at a respectful distance, as the former was ready to snap at it. Sometimes the rat made as though it was to leap over the wooden fence to get away from the dog, but a dozen rough hands were ready to thrust it back. After it had got nearly exhausted with its ineffectual struggles to get away, the little dog seized it by the throat and worried it; when another rat was brought out to take its place, and another dog introduced to this brutal sport.

This is one of the most dangerous thieves' dens we have seen in London. Were any unfortunate man to be inveigled into it in the evening, or at midnight, when the desperadoes who haunt it are inflamed with strong drink, he would be completely in their power, even were he the bravest soldier in the British service, and armed with a revolver. Were he to fight his way desperately through the large ferocious gang in this outhouse, the fighting-dogs in the yard might be let loose on him, and were he to cleave his way through them, he would have to pass through the public-house frequented by similar low characters.

Leaving this alley, we proceeded to Fashion Street, and entered a skittle-ground attached to a low beershop, where we saw another gang of thieves, to the number of about twelve. Some of them, though in rough costermonger's dress, or in the dress of mechanics, are fashionable pickpockets, along with thieves of a coarser and lower description, who push against people in crowds, and snatch away their watches and property. One of them, a tall athletic young man, was pointed out to us as a very expert pickpocket. He was dressed in a dark frock coat, dark trousers and cap, and was busy hurling the skittle-ball with great violence. On our standing by for a little, he slouched his cap sulkily over his eyes and continued at his game. He had an intelligent countenance, but with a callous, bronze-like forbidding expression. Some of his companions were standing at the other end of the skittle-ground engaged in the sport, while the rest of his "pals" sat on a seat alongside and looked on, occasionally eyeing us with considerable curiosity. Some of them were very expert thieves.

In passing through Church Lane we met two young lads dressed like costermongers, and a young woman by their side in a light dirty cotton dress and black bonnet. They were pointed out to us as those base creatures who waylay, decoy, and plunder drunken men at night. We proceeded to Wentworth Street, and entered a large lodging-house of a very motley class of people, consisting of men working at the docks, prostitutes, and area-sneaks. We called at a house in George Street, principally occupied by females from eighteen to thirty years of age, all prostitutes. In Thrall Street we entered a lodging-house where we saw about thirty persons of both sexes, and of different ages, assembled, consisting chiefly of area-sneaks and pickpockets. Here we saw one prostitute, with a remarkably beautiful child on her knee, seated at her afternoon meal. In the tap-room of a public-house in Church Street we found a large party of thieves, consisting of burglars, pickpockets, and area-sneaks, along with several resetters, one or them a Jew. On the walls of the room were pictures of notorious pugilists, Tom

Cribb and others. Several of them had the appearance of pugilists, in their bloated and bruised countenances, and most of them had a rough aspect, which we found to be a general characteristic of the Whitechapel thieves, as well as of most of the thieves we saw in the Borough, and at Lambeth. Two of the resetters, who appeared to be callous, politic men, sneaked off upon our seating ourselves beside them. One of the band, as we found on similar occasions, stood between us and the door flourishing a large clasp knife. We sat for some time over a glass of ale, and he slunk off to a corner and resumed his seat, finding his bullying attitude was of no avail. The Jewish resetter was very social and communicative as he sat on the table. The more daring of the band were also frank and good-humoured.

Being desirous to gain a more intimate acquaintance with the haunts of the London thieves, we were brought into communication with Mr. Price, inspector of the lodging-houses of this district, who accompanied us on several visits over the neighbourhood, one of the chief rookeries of thieves in London.

Before setting out on our inspection he gave us the following information :—

About twenty years ago a number of narrow streets, thickly populated with thieves, prostitutes, and beggars, were removed when New Commercial Street was formed, leading from Shoreditch in the direction of the London Docks, leaving a wide space in the midst of a densely populated neighbourhood, which is favourable to its sanatory condition, and might justly be considered one of the lungs of the metropolis. The rookery in Spitalfields we purposed to visit is comprised within a space of about 400 square yards. It is bounded by Church Street Whitechapel, East Brick Lane, and West Commercial Street, and contains 800 thieves, vagabonds, beggars, and prostitutes, a large proportion of whom may be traced to the old criminal inhabitants of the now extinct Essex Street and old Rose Lane.

For instance, a man and woman lived for many years in George Yard, Whitechapel, a narrow, dirty, and overcrowded street leading from Whitechapel into Wentworth Street. The man was usually seen among crowds of thieves, gambling and associating with them. As his family increased, in the course of time he took a beershop and lodging-house for thieves in Thrall Street. His family consisted of three boys and three girls. His wife usually addressed the young thieves as they left her lodging-house in the morning, in the hearing of her own children, in this manner; "Now, my little dears, do the best you can, and may God bless you!"

The following is a brief account of their children :—

The eldest son married a girl whose father died during his transportation. He and his wife gained their living by thieving, and were frequently in custody. At last he connected himself with burglars, was tried, convicted, and sentenced to six years' penal servitude. He is now at Gibraltar, ten months of his sentence being unexpired. His wife has been left with three young children; since his transportation she has been frequently in custody for robbing drunken men, and has had an illegitimate child since her husband left. Her eldest daughter was taken from her about twelve months ago by Mr. Ashcroft, secretary of the Refuge Aid Society, and placed in a refuge in Albert Street, Mile End New Town, where the Society maintains her. The girl is eleven years of age, and appeared pleased that she was taken away from her filthy abode and bad companions in George Street. The second son has been repeatedly in custody for uttering base coin, and was at last convicted and transported for four years. The eldest daughter married a man, who also was transported, and is now a returned convict. She was apprehended, convicted, and sentenced to four years' penal servitude. While in Newgate jail, she was delivered of twins, and received a reprieve, and has since been in custody for shoplifting.

We went with the inspector to Lower Keat Street, and entered a lodging-house there. Most of the inmates were male thieves, from twelve to nineteen years of age and upwards. The husband of the woman who keeps the house is a returned convict, and has been in custody for receiving stolen property from her lodgers.

We entered another lodging-house in this street, haunted by thieves of a lower class. An old woman was here employed as a deputy or servant, who formerly lived in Kent-street in the Borough, and kept a public-house there, a resort of thieves. She lived with a man there for twenty years and upwards, keeping a brothel, and was then and is now an old fence. We found a number of low thieves in the house at the time of our visit. The landlord has been in custody for having stolen handkerchiefs in his possession, with the marks taken out.

Opposite to this house is a public-house resorted to by thieves.

We then went to Lower George Street, where we entered a registered lodging-house. In three rooms we saw about ninety persons of both sexes and of various ages, many of them thieves and vagrants. This house is not used as a brothel, but some of the lodgers cohabit together as man and wife, which is common in these low neighbourhoods.

We went to a lodging-house in Flower-and-Dean Street, the keeper of which has been recently in prison for receiving from his lodgers. We saw a number of wretched mendicants here. One man had his leg bound up with rags. Many of the inmates gain their livelihood by begging, and others by thieving. Few honest persons reside here.

We next went to a brothel in Wentworth Street, kept by a woman, a notorious character. She has been repeatedly in custody for robbing drunken men, and her husband is now in prison for felony. She is a strong coarse-looking woman, with her countenance bearing marked traces of unbridled passion,—the type of person we would expect as the keeper of a low brothel. She had been stabbed on the cheek a few days previously by another woman, and bore the scar of the fresh wound at the time of our visit. The rooms of her house were wretchedly furnished, suitable to the low orgies transacted in this foul abode. One or two withered prostitutes were lounging about the kitchen.

We passed on to a lodging-house of a very different description, occupied by industrious honest working people, which we shall describe afterwards when we treat of an after-visit.

In this locality we visited the elderly woman living in this neighbourhood whom we have referred to as having blessed the young thieves. She had a very plausible condoling manner, as she sat with her two daughters by her side—one a young auburn-haired girl of about fourteen, with engaging countenance and handsome form, plainly but neatly dressed; the other, an ordinary-looking young woman, with a child in her arms.

We made another visit to this rookery with the inspector of police, and made a more minute survey of this remarkable district.

We went into a lodging-house in George Yard. The kitchen was about 35 feet in length, and had originally consisted of two rooms, the partition between them being removed. There was a fire-place in each; a group of people, men, lads, and boys were ranged along the long tables, many of them labourers at the docks.

The boys were better dressed than the wild young Arabs of the city, some of them in dark and brown coats and tartan and black caps. They sat on the forms along the sides of the tables, or lolled on seats by the fire. The apartments were papered, and ornamented with pictures. A picture of the Great Eastern steamship set in a frame was suspended over the mantelpiece; one boy sat with his head bound up, and another with his jacket off, and his white shirt sleeves exposed. The inmates consisted of beggars and dock-labourers seated around the ample kitchen, some busy at their different meals, and others engaged in conversation, which was suspended on our entrance. At the door we saw the deputy, a young man decently dressed. On our former visit we saw an old man with an ample unshorn beard, who works during the day as a crossing-sweeper. He had when young been engaged in seafaring life, and has now become an admirable picture of Fagin the Jew, as pictured by Charles Dickens. The beds are let here at 3$d.$ a night. The people who usually lodge here are crossing-sweepers, bonepickers, and shoeblacks, &c.

We entered a house in Wentworth Street, and passed through a chandler's shop into the kitchen, which is about 31 feet in length and 15 in breadth. There we found, as is usual in those lodging houses, a large fire blazing in the grate. The room had a wooden floor, and clothes were suspended on lines beneath the rafters. There were two large boilers on each side of the fire to supply the lodgers with hot water for coffee or tea. Tables were ranged around the wall on each side, and a motley company were seated around them. Numbers of them were busy at supper—coffee, bread, fish, and potatoes. An elderly man sat in the corner of the room cobbling a pair of old shoes with a candle nearly burned to the socket placed before him. Groups of elderly women were also clustered around the benches, some plainly but decently dressed, others in dirty tattered skirts and shabby shawls, with careworn, melancholy countenances. Some were middle-aged women, apparently the wives of some of the labourers there. A young man sat by their side, a respectable mechanic out of work.

Two young lads, vagrants, sat squatted by the fire, one of them equipped in dirty tartan trowsers, a shabby black frock-coat sadly torn, and brown bonnet. The other sat in his moleskin trowsers and shirt. At one of the tables several young women were seated at their tea, some good-looking, others very plain, with coarse features.

An elderly woman, the servant of the establishment, stood by the fire with a towel over her bare brown arm.

The tables around were covered with plates, cups, and other crockery; caps, jackets, and other articles of dress.

While in this street the musical band of the ragged school at George Yard passed by, with the teacher at their head, and many of the scholars clustered around them, with other juveniles and people of the district. Knots of people were assembled in the streets as we passed along.

We entered several other lodging-houses in this locality, occupied by beggars, dock-labourers, prostitutes, and thieves, ballad-singers, and patterers of the lowest class.

We went into a house in George Street. The kitchen was also very large, about 36 feet long and 24 feet broad, and had two blazing fires to warm the apartment and cook the food. Tables were ranged round the room as in the other lodging-houses alluded to. There were about twenty-two people here, chiefly young of both sexes. There was one middle-aged bald-headed man among them. Many of them were sad and miserable. A young good-looking girl, not apparently above seventeen years of age, sat by the fire with a child in her arms. Many of the young women had a lowering countenance and dissipated look. Some of the young lads had a more pleasing appearance, dressed as costermongers.

The long tables were strewed with plates and bowls, cups and saucers. Some young men sat by reading the newspapers, others smoking their pipe and whiffing clouds of smoke around them. Some young women were sewing, others knitting; some busy at their supper, others lying asleep, crouching with their arms on the tables.

On going into another lodging-house we saw a number of people of both sexes, and of various ages, similar to those described. There we saw a woman about thirty, also engaged knitting, and another reading Reynolds' Miscellany. A number of young lads of about seventeen years were smoking their pipe; another youth, a pickpocket, was reading a volume he had got from a neighbouring library. Most of the persons here were prostitutes, pickpockets, and sneaks. There were about fifteen present, chiefly young people.

On passing through Flower-and-Dean Street we saw a group of young lads and girls, all of them thieves, standing in the middle of the street.

We passed into another lodging-house, and entered the kitchen, which is about 30 feet long and 18 feet broad. A large fire was burning in the grate. On the one side of the kitchen were tables and forms, and the people seated around them at supper on bread and herring, tea and coffee. There were a number of middle-aged women among them. On the other side of the kitchen were stalls as in a coffee-shop. We saw several rough-looking men here. There was a rack on the wall covered with plates, ranged carefully in order. The tables were littered with heaps of bottles, jugs, books, bonnets, baskets, and shirts, like a broker's shop.

An old gray-headed man sat at one of the tables with his hand on his temples, a picture of extreme misery, his trowsers old, greasy, and ragged, an old shabby ragged coat, and a pair of old torn shoes. His face was furrowed with age, care, and sorrow; his breast was bare, and his head bald in front. He had a long gray beard. His arms were thin and skinny, and the dark blue veins looked through the back of his hands. He was a poor vagrant, and told us he was eighty-eight years of age. There were about forty persons present of both sexes, and of various ages; many of them young, and others very old.

We passed on to Lower Keat Street, and on going into a low lodging-house there we saw a number of young prostitutes, pickpockets, and sneaks.

We visited another lodging-house of the lowest description, belonging to an infamous man whom we have already referred to. We were shown upstairs to a large room filled with beds, by a coarse-featured hideous old hag, with a dark moustache. Her hair was gray, and her face seamed and scarred with dark passions, as she stood before us with her protruding breasts and bloated figure. Her eyes were dark and muddy. She had two gold rings on one of her fingers, and was dressed in a dirty light cotton gown, sadly tattered, a red spotted soiled handkerchief round her neck, and a dirty light apron, almost black. On observing us looking at her, she remarked, "I am an old woman, and am not so young as I have been. Instead of enjoying the fruit of my hard-wrought life, some other person has done it."

On examining one of the beds in the room, we found the bedding to consist of two rugs, two sheets and a flock bed, with a pillow and pillow case, let at 3d. a night. This house is registered for thirty lodgers. Young and middle-aged women, the lowest prostitutes, and thieves frequent this house; some with holes cut with disease into their brow. D--bl--n B--ll is the proprietor of this infamous abode. We saw him as we passed through the house: a sinister-looking, middle-aged man, about 5 feet 7 inches in height. On leaving the house, the old hag stood at the foot of the stair, with a candle in her hand, a picture of horrid misery.

In this locality we went into another infamous lodging-house, a haunt of prostitutes and thieves, mostly young. There was a very interesting boy here, respectably dressed, with a dark eye and well-formed placid countenance, a pickpocket. He told us his parents were dead, and he had no friends and no home. He did not show any desire to leave his disreputable life. Several of them were seated at their supper on herrings, plaice, butter, bread, and coffee.

We visited several of the more respectable lodging-houses in George Yard, to have a more complete view of the dwellings of the poor in this locality. We entered one lodging-house, and passed into the kitchen, 33 feet long by 18 feet broad. There were tables and forms planted round the room, as in the other lodging-houses noticed, and on the walls were shelves for crockery ware. There was a sink in the corner of the kitchen for washing the dishes, and a gasburner in the centre of the apartment. The kitchen was well ventilated at the windows. There was a large fire burning, with a boiler on each side of the fire-place. Over the mantelpiece was a range of bright coffee and tea pots. Coats were hung up on pegs against the wall, and a fender before the fire. Decent-looking men were seated around, some smoking, some writing, others eating a plain, but comfortable supper, others lounging on the seat, exhausted with the labours of the day. In out-houses were ample washing accommodation, and water-closets. Attached to this lodging-house was a reading-room. We went to the bed-rooms, and saw the accommodation and furniture. There were iron bedsteads with flock mattress and bed; on each bed were two sheets, one blanket, and a coverlet, a pillow-case, and a pillow. The bed-rooms were ventilated by a flue.

There is here accommodation for eighty-nine persons at 3d. a night, and there are on an average sixty lodgers each night. The rector of Christ Church visits and supplies the lodgers with tracts and religious services. A register is kept of all the people who lodge here. In this house Karls was apprehended, concerned with another party in the murder of Mrs. Halliday at Kingswood Rectory.

We visited another lodging-house in the same neighbourhood. The kitchen was large, with spacious windows in front. There was a large fireplace, with boiler and oven with a large hot plate. The lodgers had a respectable appearance—some in blue guernseys, and others in respectable dark dresses. There was also a reading-room here, with a dial over the mantelpiece. Some of the men were reading, and others engaged in writing. There was accommodation for washing, water-closets, and excellent beds. This house belongs to the same proprietor as the one already described. It is closed at 12 o'clock, while the others are kept open all night, and is generally frequented by respectable lodgers.

We also inspected another lodging-house in Thrall Street of a superior kind, where beds are to be had at 3½d. a night. There are two superior lodging-houses of the same character, kept by Mr. Wilmot and Mr. Argent, in Thrall Street and Osborne Place, at 3½d. and 4d. a night.

We thus find that alongside those low lodging-houses and brothels, in the very bosom of that low neighbourhood, there are respectable lodging-houses of different gradations in price and position, where working-people and strangers can be accommodated at 3d., 3½d., and 4d. a night, in which decency, cleanliness, and morality prevail.

In the course of our visits to Spitalfields we found two institutions of high value and special interest—a ragged school and a reformatory for young women. The ragged school was instituted by the Rev. Hugh Allen, the incumbent of St. Jude's, in 1853. There are at present 350 ragged children of both sexes attending it, averaging from four to fifteen years of age. They are taught by Mr. Holland, a most intelligent and devoted teacher, who is exercising a powerful influence for good in that dark and criminal locality.

A female reformatory was lately instituted by the Rev. Mr. Thornton, the present incumbent of St. Jude's, who labours with unwearied energy in this district. This asylum is in Wentworth Street, and is fitted to accommodate eighteen persons.

NARRATIVE OF A PICKPOCKET.

THE following recital was given us by a young man who had till lately been an adroit pickpocket in various districts of London, but has now become a patterer for his livelihood. He is about the middle height, of sallow complexion, with a rich dark, penetrating eye, a moustache and beard. He is a man of tolerably good education, and has a most intelligent mind, well furnished with reading and general information. At the time we met him, he was rather melancholy and crushed in spirit, which he stated was the result of repeated imprisonments, and the anxiety and suspense connected with his wild criminal life, and the heavy trials he has undergone. The woman who cohabits with him was then in one of the London prisons, and he was residing in a low lodging-house in the west end of the metropolis. While giving us several exciting passages in his narrative, his countenance lightened up with intense interest and adventurous expression, though his general mien was calm and collected. As we endeavoured to inspire him with hope in an honest career, he mournfully shook his head as he looked forward to the difficulties in his path. He was then shabbily dressed in a dark frock-coat, dark trousers, and cap. We give his narrative almost verbatim:—

"I was born in a little hamlet, five miles from Shrewsbury, in the county of Shropshire, in October 1830, and am now thirty-one years of age. My father was a Wesleyan minister, and died in 1854, after being subject to the yellow jaundice for five or six years, during which time he was not able to officiate. My mother was a Yorkshire woman, and her father kept a shoemaker's shop in the town of Full Sutton. I had two brothers, one of them older and the other younger than I, and a sister two years younger.

"I went to school to learn to write and cipher, and had before this learned to read at home with my father and mother. We had a very happy home, and very strict in the way of religion. I believe that my father would on no account tolerate such a thing as stopping out after nine o'clock at night, and have heard my mother often say that all the time she was wedded to him, she never had known him the worse of liquor. My father had family worship every night between 8 and 9 o'clock, when the curtains were drawn over the windows, the candle was lighted, and each of the children was taught to kneel separately at prayer. After reading the Bible and half an hour's conversation, each one retired to their bed. In the morning my father would get up and attend to a small pony he had, and when I was very young we had a stout girl who milked the cow and did the dairy and household work. The house we lived in was my grandfather's property, but being a man very fond of money, my father paid him the rent as if he had been a stranger.

"There were two acres of land attached to the house, as nearly as I can recollect; about half an acre was kept in cultivation as a garden, and the other was tilled and set apart for the pony and cow.

"Our people were much respected in the neighbourhood. If there were any bickerings among the neighbours, they came to my father to settle them, and anything he said they generally yielded to without a murmur. In the winter time, when work was slack among the poor labouring people, though my father had little himself to give, he got money from others to distribute among those who were the most deserving. I lived very happy and comfortable at home, but always compelled, though against my own inclination, to go twice to service on the Sunday, and twice during the week (Tuesday and Friday). I always seemed to have a rebellious nature against these religious services, and they were a disagreeable task to me, though my father took more pains with me than with my brothers and sister. I always rebelled against this in my heart, though I did not display it openly.

"I was a favourite with my father, perhaps more so than any of the others. For example, if Wombwell's menagerie would come to Shrewsbury for a short time, he would have taken me instead of my brothers to visit it, and would there speak of the wonders of God and of his handiwork in the creation of animals. Everything that he said and did was tinged with religion, and religion of an ascetic argumentative turn. It was a kind of religion that seemed to banish eternally other sects from happiness and from heaven.

"My mind at this time was injured by the narrow religious prejudices I saw around me. We often had ministers to dinner and supper at our house, and always after their meals the conversation would be sure to turn into discussions on the different points of doctrine. I can recollect as well now as though it were yesterday the texts used on the various sides of the question, and the stress laid on different passages to uphold their arguments. At this time I would be sitting there greedily drinking in every word, and as soon as they were gone I would fly to the Bible and examine the different texts of Scripture they had brought forward, and it seemed to produce a feeling in my mind that any religious opinions could be plausibly supported by it. The arguments on these occasions generally hinged on two main points, predestination and election. My father's opinions were those of the Wesleyan creed, the salvation of all through the blood of Christ.

"These continual discussions seemed to steel my heart completely against religion. They caused me to be very disobedient and unruly, and led to my falling out with my grandfather, who had a good deal of property that was expected to come to our family. Though I was young, he bitterly resented this. In 1839 he was accidentally drowned, and it was found when his will was opened that I was not mentioned in it. The whole of his property was left to my father, with the exception of four houses, which he had an interest in till my brothers and sister arrived at the age of twenty-one. Again the property that was left to my father for the whole of his life he had no power to will away at his death, as it went to a distant relative of my grandfather's.

"This was the first cause of my leaving home. It seemed to rankle in my boyish mind that I was a black sheep, something different from my brothers and sister.

"After being several times spoken to by my father about my quarrelsome disposition with my brothers and sister, I threatened, young as I was, to burn the house down the first opportunity I got. This threat, though not uttered in my father's hearing, came to his ear, and he gave me a severe beating for it, the first time he ever corrected me. This was in the summer of 1840, in the end of May. I determined to leave home, and took nothing away but what belonged to me. I had four sovereigns of pocket money, and the suit of clothes I had on and a shirt. I walked to Shrewsbury and took the coach to London. When I got to London I had neither friend nor acquaintance. I first put up in a coffee-shop in the Mile End Road, and lodged there for seven weeks, till my money was nearly all spent.

"During this time my clothes had been getting shabby and dirty, having no one to look after me. After being there for seven weeks I went to a mean lodging-house at Field Lane, Holborn. There I met with characters I had never seen before, and heard language that I had not formerly heard. This was about July, 1840, and I was about ten years of age the ensuing October. I stopped there about three weeks doing nothing. At the end of that time I was completely destitute.

"The landlady took pity on me as a poor country boy who had been well brought up, and kept me for some days longer after my money was done. During these few days I had very little to eat, except what was given me by some of the lodgers when they got their own meals. I often thought at that time of my home in the country, and of what my father and mother might be doing, as I had never written to them since the day I had first left my home.

"I sometimes was almost tempted to write to them and let them know the position I was in, as I knew they would gladly send me up money to return home, but my stubborn spirit was not broke then. After being totally destitute for two or three days, I was turned out of doors, a little boy in the great world of London, with no friend to assist me, and perfectly ignorant of the ways and means of getting a living in London.

"I was taken by several poor ragged boys to sleep in the dark arches of the Adelphi. I often saw the boys follow the male passengers when the halfpenny boats came to the Adelphi stairs, i.e., the part of the river almost opposite to the Adelphi Theatre. I could not at first make out the meaning of this, but I soon found they generally had one or two handkerchiefs when the passengers left. At this time there was a prison-van in the Adelphi arches, without wheels, which was constructed different from the present prison-van, as it had no boxes in the interior. The boys used to take me with them into the prison-van. There we used to meet a man my companions called 'Larry.' I knew him by no other name for the time. He used to give almost what price he liked for the handkerchiefs. If they refused to give them at the price he named, he would threaten them in several ways. He said he would get the other boys to drive them away, and not allow them to get any more handkerchiefs there. If this did not intimidate them, he would threaten to give them in charge, so that at last they were compelled to take whatever price he liked to give them.

"I have seen handkerchiefs, I afterwards found out to be of the value of four or five shillings, sold him lumped together at 9d. each.

"The boys, during this time, had been very kind to me, sharing what they got with me, but always asking why I did not try my hand, till at last I was ashamed to live any longer upon the food they gave me, without doing something for myself. One of the boys attached himself to me more than the others, whom we used to call Joe Muckraw, who was afterwards transported, and is now in a comfortable position in Australia.

"Joe said to me, that when the next boat came in, if any man came out likely to carry a good handkerchief, he would let me have a chance at it. I recollect when the boat came in that evening: I think it was the last one, about nine o'clock. I saw an elderly gentleman step ashore, and a lady with him. They had a little dog, with a string attached to it, that they led along. Before Joe said anything to me, he had 'fanned' the gentleman's pocket, *i.e.*, had felt the pocket and knew there was a handkerchief.

"He whispered to me, 'Now Dick, have a try,' and I went to the old gentleman's side, trembling all the time, and Joe standing close to me in the dark, and went with him up the steep hill of the Adelphi. He had just passed an apple-stall there, Joe still following us, encouraging me all the time, while the old gentleman was engaged with the little dog. I took out a green 'kingsman,' (handkerchief) next in value to a black silk handkerchief. (They are used a good deal as neckerchiefs by costermongers). The gentleman did not perceive his loss. We immediately went to the arches and entered the van where Larry was, and Joe said to him 'There is Dick's first trial, and you must give him a "ray" for it,' *i.e.* 1s. 6d. After a deal of pressing, we got 1s. for it.

"After that I gained confidence, and in the course of a few weeks I was considered the cleverest of the little band, never missing one boat coming in, and getting one or two handkerchiefs on each occasion. During the time we knew there were no boats coming we used to waste our money on sweets, and fruits, and went often in the evenings to the Victoria Theatre, and Bower Saloon, and other places. When we came out at twelve, or half-past twelve at night, we went to the arches again, and slept in the prison-van. This was the life I led till January, 1841.

"During that month several men came to us. I did not know, although I afterwards heard they were brought by 'Larry' to watch me, as he had been speaking of my cleverness at the 'tail,' *i.e.*, stealing from the tails of gentlemen's coats, and they used to make me presents. It seemed they were not satisfied altogether with me, for they did not tell me what they wanted, nor speak their mind to me. About the middle of the month I was seized by a gentleman, who caught me with his handkerchief in my hand. I was taken to Bow Street police-station, and got two months in Westminster Bridewell.

"I came out in March, and when outside the gate of Westminster Bridewell, there was a cab waiting for me, and two of the men standing by who had often made me presents and spoken to me in the arches. They asked me if I would go with them, and took me into the cab. I was willing to go anywhere to better myself, and went with them to Flower-and-Dean Street, Brick Lane, Whitechapel. They took me to their own home. One of them had the first floor of a house there, the other had the second. Both were living with women, and I found out shortly afterwards that these men had lately had a boy, but he was transported about that time, though I did not know this then. They gave me plenty to eat, and one of the women, by name 'Emily,' washed and cleansed me, and I got new clothes to put on. For three days I was not asked to do anything, but in the meantime they had been talking to me of going with them, and having no more to do with the boys at the Adelphi, or with the 'tail,' but to work at picking ladies' pockets.

"I thought it strange at first, but found afterwards that it was more easy to work on a woman's pocket than upon a man's, for this reason:—More persons work together, and the boy is well surrounded by companions older than himself, and is shielded from the eyes of the passers-by; and, besides, it pays better.

It was on a Saturday, in company with three men, I set out on an excursion from Flower-and-Dean Street along Cheapside. They were young men, from nineteen to twenty-five years of age, dressed in fashionable style. I was clothed in the suit given me when I came out of prison, a beaver-hat, a little surtout-coat and trousers, both of black cloth, and a black silk necktie and collar, dressed as a gentleman's son. We went into a pastry-cook's shop in St. Paul's Churchyard about half-past two in the afternoon, and had pastry there, and they were watching the ladies coming into the shop, till at last they followed one out, taking me with them.

"As this was my first essay in having anything to do in stealing from a woman, I believe they were nervous themselves, but they had well tutored me during the two or three days I had been out of prison. They had stood against me in the room while Emily walked to and fro, and I had practised on her pocket by taking out sometimes a lady's clasp purse, termed a 'portemonnaie,' and other articles out of her pocket, and thus I was not quite ignorant of what was expected of me. One walked in front of me, one on my right hand, and the other in the rear, and I had the lady on my left hand. I immediately 'fanned' her (felt her pocket), as she stopped to look in at a hosier's window, when I took her purse and gave it to one of them, and we immediately went to a house in Giltspur Street. We there examined what was in the purse. I think there was a sovereign, and about 17s., I cannot speak positively how much. The purse was thrown away, as is the general rule, and we went down Newgate Street, into Cheapside, and there we soon got four more purses that afternoon, and went home by five o'clock, P.M. I recollect how they praised me afterwards that night at home for my cleverness.

"I think we did not go out again till the Tuesday, and that and the following day we had a good pull. It amounted to about 19l. each. They always take care to allow the boy to see what is in the purse, and to give him his proper share equal with the others, because he is their sole support. If they should lose him, they would be unable to do anything till they got another. Out of my share, which was about 19l., I bought a silver watch and a gold chain, and about this time I also bought an overcoat, and carried it on my left arm to cover my movements.

"A few weeks after this we went to Surrey Gardens, and I got two purses from ladies. In one of them were some French coins and a ring, that was afterwards advertised as either lost or stolen in the garden. We did very well that visit, and were thinking of going again, when I was caught in Fleet Street, and they had no means of getting me away, though they tried all they could to secure my escape. They could not do it without exposing themselves to too much suspicion. I was sentenced to three months' imprisonment in Bridge Street Bridewell, Blackfriars, termed by the thieves the Old Horse.

"This was shortly before Christmas, 1840. During my imprisonment I did not live on the prison diet, but was kept on good rations supplied to me through the kindness of my comrades out of doors bribing the turnkeys. I had tea of a morning, bread and butter, and often cold meat. Meat and all kinds of pastry was sent to me from a cook-shop outside, and I was allowed to sit up later than other prisoners. During the time I was in prison for these three months I learned to smoke, as cigars were introduced to me.

"When I came out we often used to attend the theatres, and I have often had as many as six or seven ladies' purses in the rear of the boxes during the time they were coming out. This was the time when the pantomimes were in their full attraction. It is easier to pick a female's pocket when she has several children with her to attract her attention than if she were there by herself.

"We went out once or twice a week, sometimes stopt in a whole week, and sallied out on Sunday. I often got purses coming down the steps at Spitalfields' Church. I believe I have done so hundreds of times. This church was near to us, and easily got at.

"We went to Madame Tussaud's, Baker Street, and were pretty lucky there. At this time we hired horses and a trap to go down to Epsom races, but did not take any of the women with us.

"I was generally employed working in the streets rather than at places of amusement, &c., and was in dread that my father or some of my friends might come and see me at some of these.

"When at the Epsom races, shortly after the termination of the race for the Derby, I was induced, much against my will, to turn my hand upon two ladies as they were stepping into a carriage, and was detected by the ladies. There was immediately an outcry, but I was got away by two of my comrades. The other threw himself in the way, and kept them back; was taken up on suspicion, committed for trial, and got four months' imprisonment.

"I kept with the other men, and we got another man in his place. When his time was expired they went down to meet him, and he did not go out for some time afterwards—for nearly a fortnight. After that we went out, and had different degrees of luck, and one of the men was seized with a decline, and died at Brompton in the hospital. Like the other stalls, he usually went well-dressed, and had a good appearance. His chief work was to guard me and get me out of difficulty when I was detected, as I was the support of the band.

"About this time, as nearly as I can recollect, when I was two months over thirteen years of age, I first kept a woman. We had apartments, a front and back room of our own. She was a tall, thin, genteel girl, about fifteen years of age, and very good-looking. I often ill-used her and beat her. She bore it patiently till I carried it too far, and at last she left me in the summer of 1844. During the time she was with me—which lasted for nine or ten months—I was very fortunate, and was never without 20l. or 30l. in my pocket, while she had the same in hers. I was dressed in fashionable style, and had a gold watch and gold guard.

"Meantime I had been busy with these

men, as usual going to Cheapside, St. Paul's Churchyard, and Fleet Street. In the end of the year 1844 I was taken up for an attempt on a lady in St. Martin's Lane, near Ben Caunt's. The conviction was brought against me from the City, and I got six months in Tothill-fields Prison.

"This was my first real imprisonment of any length. At first I was a month in Tothill Fields, and afterwards three months in the City Bridewell, Blackfriars, where I had a good deal of indulgence, and did not feel the imprisonment so much. The silent system was strict, and being very wilful, I was often under punishment. It had such an effect on me, that for the last six weeks of my imprisonment I was in the infirmary. The men came down to meet me when my punishment expired, and I again accompanied them to their house.

"During the time I had been in prison they had got another boy, but they said they would willingly turn him away or give him to some other men; but I, being self-willed, said they might keep him. I had another reason for parting with them. When I went to prison I had property worth a good deal of money. On coming out I found they had sold it, and they never gave me value for it. They pretended it was laid out in my defence, which I knew was only a pretext.

"Before I was imprisoned my girl had parted from me, which was the beginning of my misfortunes.

"I would not go to work with them afterwards. I had a little money, and at a public-house I met with two men living down Gravel Lane, Ratcliffe Highway. I went down there, and commenced working with two of them on ladies' pockets, but in a different part of the town. We went to Whitechapel and the Commercial Road; but had not worked six weeks with them before I was taken up again, and was tried at Old Arbour Square, and got three months' imprisonment at Coldbath Fields. If I thought Tothill Fields was bad, I found the other worse.

"When I got out I had no one to meet me, and thought I would work by myself. It was about this time I commenced to steal gentlemen's watches.

"The first I took was from the fob of a countryman in Smithfield on a market day. It was a silver watch, which we called a 'Frying Pan.' It had not a guard, but an old chain and seals. It fetched me about 18s. I took off one of the seals which was gold, which brought me as much as the watch, if not more. I sold it to a man I was acquainted with in Field Lane, where I first lodged, after leaving the coffee-shop when I first came to London, and where the landlady gave me several nights' lodging gratuitously. I repaid her the small sum due her for her former kindness to me.

"I lodged there, and shortly after cohabited with another female. She was a big stout woman, ten years older than I; well-made, but coarse-featured. I did not live with her long—only three or four months. I was then only fifteen years of age. During that time I always worked by myself. Sometimes she would go out with me, but she was no help to me. I looked out for crowds at fairs, at fires, and on any occasion where there was a gathering of people, as at this time I generally confined myself to watches and pins from men.

"I was not so lucky then, and barely kept myself in respectability. My woman was very extravagant, and swallowed up all I could make. I lived with her about four months, when I was taken up in Exmouth Street, Clerkenwell, and got four months' imprisonment in Coldbath Fields Prison.

"When my sentence was expired she came to meet me at the gate of the prison, and we remained together only two days, when I heard reports that she had been unfaithful to me. I never charged her with it, but ran away from her.

"When I left her I went to live in Charles Street, Drury Lane. I stopped there working by myself for five or six months, and got acquainted with a young woman who has ever since been devoted to me. She is now thirty-three years of age, but looks a good deal older than she is, and is about the middle height. We took a room and furnished it. I soon got acquainted with some of the swell-mob at the Seven Dials, and went working along with three of them upon the ladies' purses again. At this time I was a great deal luckier with them than I had been since I had left Tothill-fields Prison. I worked with them till April 1847, visiting the chief places of public resort, such as the Surrey Gardens, Regent's Park, Zoological Gardens, Madame Tussaud's, the Colosseum, and other places. Other two comrades and I were arrested at the Colosseum for picking a lady's pocket. We were taken to Albany Street station-house, and the next day committed for trial at the sessions. I had twelve months' imprisonment for this offence, and the other two got four years' penal servitude, on account of previous convictions. I had only summary convictions, which were not produced at the trial.

"At this time summary convictions were

not brought against a prisoner committed for trial.

"We were frequently watched by the police and detectives, who followed our track, and were often in the same places of amusement with us. We knew them as well as they knew us, and often eluded them. Their following us has often been the means of our doing nothing on many of these occasions, as we knew their eye was upon us.

"I came out of prison three or four days before the gathering of the Chartists on Kennington Common. My female friend met me as I came out.

"I went to this gathering on 10th April, 1848, along with other three men. I took several ladies' purses there, amounting to 3*l*. or 4*l*., when we saw a gentleman place a pocketbook in the tail of his coat. Though I had done nothing at the tail for a long time, it was too great a temptation, and I immediately seized it. There was a bundle of bank-notes in it—7 ten-pound notes, 2 for twenty pounds, and 5 five-pound notes. We got from the fence or receiver 4*l*. 10s. for each of the 5*l*., 8*l*. 10s. for the tens, and 18*l*. for the 20*l*. notes.

"The same afternoon I took a purse in Trafalgar Square with about eighteen sovereigns in it. I kept walking in company with the same men till the commencement of 1849, when I was taken ill and laid up with rheumatism. I lost the use of my legs in a great measure, and could not walk, and paid away my money to physicians. Before I got better, such articles as we had were disposed of, though my girl helped me as well as she could.

"In the early part of 1849, when I was not able to go out and do anything, Sally, who cohabited with me, went out along with another girl and commenced stealing in omnibuses. She was well-dressed, and had a respectable appearance. I did not learn her to pick pockets, and was averse to it at first, as I did not wish to bring her into danger. I think she was trained by my pals. She was very clever, and supported me till I was able to go out again. I had to walk with a crutch for some time, but gradually got better and stronger. Some time after that I got into a row at the Seven Dials, and was sent for a month to Westminster prison for an assault.

"When I came out I was sorry to find that Sally was taken up and committed for trial for an omnibus robbery, and had got six months' imprisonment at Westminster. This was in 1850. I succeeded very well during the time she was in prison in picking ladies' pockets during the time of the Great Exhibition at Hyde Park.

"When she came out, I had nearly 200*l*. by me. I did not go out for some time, and soon made the money fly, for I was then a cribbage player, and would stake as much as 2*l*. or 3*l*. on a game.

"In the end of the year 1851 I was pressed for the first time to have a hand at a crack in the City along with other two men. I was led through their representations to believe they were experienced burglars, but found afterwards, if they *were* experienced they were not very clever. Though they got a plan, they blundered in the execution of it in getting into the place, and went into the wrong room, so that they had to get thro' another wall, which caused us to be so late that it was gray in the morning before we got away; and we did not find so much as we expected.

"At the back of the premises we cut our way into the passage, and, according to the directions given to us in the plan that had been drawn, we had to go up to the second floor, and enter a door there. We found nothing in the room we had entered but neckties and collars, which would not have paid us for bringing them away. We then had to work our way through a back wall, before we got into the apartment where the silks were stored. They cut through the brick wall very cleverly. We had all taken rum to steady our nerve before we went to the work.

"We had gone up the wrong staircase, which was the cause of our having to cut through the wall. There was only one man that slept in the house, and he was in a room on the basement. We at last, after much labour and delay, got into the right room, pressed the bolt back, and found we could get away by the other staircase. We got silks, handkerchiefs, and other drapery goods, and had about 18*l*. each after disposing of them—which was about two-thirds of their value. We had a cab to carry away the things for us to the 'fence' who received them.

"We went to another burglary at Islington, and made an entrance into the house, but were disturbed, and ran away over several walls and gardens.

"We attempted a third burglary in the City. As usual we had a plan of it through a man that had been at work there, who put it up for us. This was a shop in which there were a great many Geneva watches. We got in at this time by the back window, and went upstairs. We were told that the master went away at 11 o'clock. On this occasion he had remained later than usual, looking over his business books. On seeing us, he made an outcry and struggled with us. Assistance came immediately. Two policemen ran up to the house. In the scramble with the man in the house, we tried to make for the door. The police could not get in, as the door was bolted. We were determined to make a rush out. I undid the chain and drew back the bolt. I got away, and had fled along two or three streets, when I was stunned by a man who carried a closed umbrella. Hearing the cry of 'Stop thief!' he drew out the umbrella, and I fell as I was running. I was thereupon taken back by one of the police, and found both of the others in custody. We were committed for trial next day, and sent to Newgate in the meantime for detention.

"My former convictions were not brought against me. My two companions had been previously at Newgate, and were sentenced the one to ten years' and the other to seven years' penal servitude, while I got eighteen months' imprisonment in Holloway prison. I was the younger of the party, and had no convictions. I never engaged in a burglary after this. At this time I was twenty-two or twenty-three years of age.

"I came out of prison in 1853, and was unnerved for some time, though my health was good. This was the effect of the solitary confinement.

"When I came out, I wrote home for the first time since I had been in London, and received a letter back, stating that my father was dead after an illness of several years, and that I was to come home, adding that if I required money, they would send it me. Besides, there were several things they were to give me, according to my father's wishes.

"I went home, and had thoughts of stopping there. My mother was not in such good position as I expected, the property left by my grandfather having gone to a distant relative at my father's death. She was and is still in receipt of a weekly sum from the old Wesleyan fund for the benefit of the widows of ministers.

"I went home in the end of 1853, and had the full intention of stopping there, though I promised to Sally to be back in a few weeks. I soon got tired of country life, though my relations were very kind to me, and after remaining seven weeks at home, came back to London again about the commencement of 1854, and commenced working by myself at stealing watches and breast-pins. I did not work at ladies' pockets, unless I had comrades beside me. I went and mingled in the crowds by myself.

"In the end of 1854 I got another six months' imprisonment at Hicks's Hall police court, and was sent to Coldbath-Fields, and was told that if I ever came again before the criminal authorities, I would be transported.

"I came out in 1855, and have done very little since; acting occasionally as a stall to Sally in omnibuses, and generally carrying a portmanteau or something with me. I would generally sit in the omnibus on the opposite side to her, and endeavour to keep the lady, as well as I could, engaged in conversation, while she sat on her right hand. She got twelve months for this in 1855, and during the time she was in Westminster prison I first commenced pattering in the streets. I did not again engage in thieving till the time of the illumination for the peace in 1856. In Hyde Park on this occasion I took a purse from a lady, containing nine sovereigns and some silver; and was living on this money when Sally was discharged at the expiry of her sentence.

"When she came out, I told her what I had been doing, and found she was much altered, and seemed to have a great disinclination to go out any more. She did not go for some time. I made a sufficient livelihood by pattering in the streets for nearly two years, when I got wet several times, and was laid up with illness again. She then became acquainted with a woman who used to go on a different game, termed shoplifting. While the one kept the shopman engaged, the other would purloin a piece of silk, or other goods. At this time she took to drink. I found out after this she often got things, and sold them, before she came home, on purpose to get drink. News came to me one day that she had been taken up and committed for trial at Marylebone police court. I paid the counsel to plead her case, and she was acquitted.

"I then told her if she was not satisfied with what I was doing as patterer, that I would commence my former employment. So I did for some time during last year, till I had three separate remands at the House of Detention, Clerkenwell. The policeman got the stolen property, but was so much engrossed taking me, he had lost sight of the prosecutor, who was never found, and I got acquitted.

"On this occasion I told Sally I would never engage in stealing again, and I have kept my word. I know if I had been tried at this time, and found guilty, I should have been transported.

"I have since then got my living by pattering in the streets. I earn my 2s., or

2s. 6d. in an hour, or an hour and a half in the evening, and can make a shift.

"For six or seven years, when engaged in picking pockets, I earned a good deal of money. Our house expenses many weeks would average from 4l. to 5l., living on the best fare, and besides, we went to theatres, and places of amusement, occasionally to the Cider Cellars, and the Coal Hole.

"The London pickpockets are acquainted generally with each other, and help their comrades in difficulty. They frequently meet with many of the burglars. A great number of the women of pickpockets and burglars are shoplifters, as they require to support themselves when their men are in prison.

"A woman would be considered useless to a man if she could not get him the use of counsel, and keep him for a few days after he comes out, which she does by shoplifting, and picking pockets in omnibuses, the latter being termed 'Maltooling.'

"I have associated a good deal with the pickpockets over London, in different districts. You cannot easily calculate their weekly income, as it is so precarious, perhaps one day getting 20l., or 30l., and another day being totally unsuccessful. They are in general very superstitious, and if anything cross them, they will do nothing. If they see a person they have formerly robbed, they expect bad luck, and will not attempt anything.

"They are very generous in helping each other when they get into difficulty, or trouble, but have no societies, as they could not be kept up. Many of them may be in prison five or six months of the year; some may get a long penal servitude, or transportation; or they may have the steel taken out of them, and give up this restless, criminal mode of life.

"They do not generally find stealing gentlemen's watches so profitable as picking ladies' pockets, for this reason, that the purse can be thrown away, some of the coins changed, and they may set to work again immediately; whereas, when they take a watch, they must go immediately to the fence with it: it is not safe to keep it on their person. A good silver watch will now bring little more than 25s., or 30s., even if the watch has cost 6l. A good gold watch will not fetch above 4l. I have worked for two or three hours, and have got, perhaps, six different purses during that time, the purses I threw away, so that the robbery may not be traced. Suppose you take a watch, and you place it in your pocket, while you have also your own watch, if you happen to be detected, you are taken and searched, and there being a second watch found on you, the evidence is complete against you.

"The trousers-pockets are seldom picked, except in a crowd. It is almost impossible to do this on any other occasion, such as when walking in the street. A prostitute may occasionally do it, pattering with her fingers about a man's person when he is off his guard.

"I believe a large number of the thieves of London come from the provinces, and from the large towns, such as Leeds, Birmingham, Sheffield, Manchester, and Liverpool; from Birmingham especially, more than any other town in England. There are no foreigners pickpockets in London so far as I know. The cleverest of the native London thieves, in general, are the Irish cockneys.

"I never learned any business or trade, and never did a hard day's work in my life, and have to take to pattering for a livelihood. When men in my position take to an honest employment, they are sometimes pointed out by some of the police as having been formerly convicted thieves, and are often dismissed from service, and driven back into criminal courses.

"I am a sceptic in my religious opinions, which was a stumbling-block in the way of several missionaries, and other philanthropic men assisting me. I have read Paine, and Volney, and Holyoake, those infidel writers, and have also read the works of Bulwer, Dickens, and numbers of others. It gives a zest to us in our criminal life, that we do not know how long we may be at liberty to enjoy ourselves. This strengthens the attachment between pickpockets and their women, who, I believe, have a stronger liking to each other, in many cases, than married people."

HORSE AND DOG STEALERS.

Horse-stealing.—These robberies are not so extensive as they used to be in the metropolitan districts. They are generally confined to the rural districts, where horses are turned out to graze on marshes and in pasture-fields. Horses are stolen by a low unprincipled class of men, who travel the country dealing in them, who are termed " horse coupers," and sometimes by the wandering gipsies and tinkers. They journey from place to place, and observe where there is a good horse or pony, and loiter about the neighbourhood till they get an opportunity to steal it. This is generally done in the night time, and in most cases by one man.

After removing it from the park, they take it away by some by-road, or keep it shut up in a stable or outhouse till the "hue and cry" about the robbery has settled down. They then trim it up, and alter the appearance as much as possible, and take it to some market at a distance, and sell it—sometimes at an under price. This is their general mode of operation. Sometimes they proceed to London, and dispose of it at Smithfield market. The party that steals it does not generally take it to the market, but leaves it in a quiet stable at some house by the way, till he meets with a low horse-dealer. The thief is often connected with horse-dealers, but may not himself be one.

Some Londoners are in the habit of stealing horses. These often frequent the Old Kent-road, and are dressed as grooms or stablemen. They are of various ages, varying from twenty to sixty years. The person who sells the horses gets part of the booty from the horse-stealer.

The mode of stealing by gipsies is somewhat similar. They pitch their tents on some waste ground by the roadside, or on the skirt of a wood, and frequently steal a horse when they get an opportunity. One will take it away who has been keeping unobserved within the tent, and the rest will remain encamped in the locality as if nothing had happened. They may remove it to a considerable distance, and get it into the covert of a wood, such as Epping Forest, or some secluded spot, and take the first opportunity to sell it.

Another class of persons travel about the country, dealing in small wares as Cheap Johns, who occasionally steal horses, or give information to abandoned characters who steal them.

These robberies of horses are generally committed in rural districts, and are seldom done in the metropolis, as horses are in general looked after, or locked up in stables. They are occasionally stolen in the markets in and around the metropolis, such as Smithfield and the new market at Islington.

Sometimes horses in carts, and cabs, and other vehicles are removed by thieves in the streets of the metropolis; but this is only done for a short time until they have rifled the goods. So soon as they have secured them, they leave the horse and vehicle, which come into the hands of the police, and are restored to the owner.

The horses stolen are generally light and nimble, such as those used in phaetons and light conveyances, and not for heavy carts or drays.

These robberies are detected in various ways. For example, sometimes a valuable horse is offered for sale at a reduced price in some market, which excites suspicion. At other times the appearance of the person selling the horse is not consistent with the possession of such an animal. On some occasions these robberies are detected by the police from descriptions forwarded from station to station, and are stopped on the highway.

Horse-stealers generally take the horses through backroads, and never pass through tollbars, if they can avoid it, as they could be traced. The keeper of the toll might give information to the police, and give a clue to the way they had gone.

London thieves have been known to go considerable distances into the country to steal horses—after having learned that horses could easily be taken away. These robberies are generally committed in the spring and summer, when horses are turned out to grass.

Number of cases of horse-stealing in the metropolitan districts for 1860 .. 23
Ditto ditto in the City 0
———
23

Value of property thereby abstracted in the metropolitan districts .. £649

Dog-stealing.—These robberies are generally committed by dog-fanciers and others who confine their attention to this class of felonies. They are persons of a low class.

dressed variously, and are frequently followed by women. They steal fancy dogs ladies are fond of—spaniels, poodles, and terriers, sporting dogs, such as setters and retrievers, and also Newfoundland dogs. These robberies are generally committed by men of various ages, but seldom by boys. Their mode of operation is this:—In prowling over the metropolis, when they see a handsome dog with a lady or gentleman they follow it and see where the person resides. So soon as they have ascertained this they loiter about the house for days with a piece of liver prepared by a certain process, and soaked in some ingredient which dogs are uncommonly fond of. They are so partial to it they will follow the stranger some distance in preference to following their master. The thieves generally carry small pieces of this to entice the dog away with them, when they seize hold of it in a convenient place, and put it into a bag they carry with them.

Another method of decoying dogs is by having a bitch in heat. When any valuable dog follows it is picked up and taken home, when they wait for the reward offered by the owner to return it, generally from 1*l*. to 5*l*. The loss of the dog may be advertized in the Times or other newspapers, or by handbills circulated over the district, when some confederate of the thief will negociate with the owner for the restoration of the dog. Information is sent if he will give a certain sum of money, such as 1*l*., 2*l*., or 5*l*. the dog will be restored, if not it will be killed. This is done to excite sympathy.

Some dogs have been known to be stolen three or four times, and taken back to their owner by rewards. Sometimes when they steal dogs they fancy, they keep them and do not return them to the owner.

There is a class termed dog-receivers, or dog-fanciers, who undertake to return stolen dogs for a consideration. These parties are connected with the thieves, and are what is termed "in the ring," that is, in the ring of thieves. Dogs are frequently restored by agencies of this description. These parties receive dogs and let the owners have them back for a certain sum of money, while they receive part of the price shared with the thief.

Dog-stealing is very prevalent, particularly in the West-end of the metropolis, and is rather a profitable class of felony. These thieves reside at the Seven Dials, in the neighbourhood of Belgravia, Chelsea, Knightsbridge, and low neighbourhoods, some of them men of mature years.

They frequently pick up dogs in the street when their owners are not near. But their general mode is to loiter about the houses and entice them away in the manner described. Sometimes they belong to the felon class, sometimes not. They are often connected with bird-fanciers, keepers of fighting-dogs, and persons who get up rat matches.

Some of those stolen are sent to Germany, where English dogs are sold at a high price.

Number of cases of dog-stealing in the metropolitan districts for 1860 .. 15
Ditto ditto in the City .. 1
—
16

Value of property thereby abstracted in the metropolitan districts .. £134

HIGHWAY ROBBERS.

The highway robbers of the present day are a very different set from the bold reckless brigands who infested the metropolis and the highways in its vicinity in former times. There was a bold dash in the old highwaymen, the Dick Turpins and Claud Du Vals of that day, not to be found in the thieves of our time, whether they lived in the rookeries of St. Giles's, Westminster, and the Borough, nestling securely amid dingy lanes and alleys, densely-clustered together, where it was unsafe for even a constable to enter; or whether they roamed at large on Blackheath and Hounslow Heath, or on Wimbledon Common, and Finchley Common, accosting the passing traveller pistol in hand, with the stern command, ' Stand and deliver.'

The highwaymen of our day are either the sneaking thieves we have described, who adroitly slip their hands into your pockets, or low coarse ruffians who follow in the wake of prostitutes, or garotte drunken men in the midnight street, or strike them down by brutal violence with a life-preserver or bludgeon.

These felonies are generally committed in secluded spots and by-streets, or in the suburbs of the metropolis. Many robberies are committed on the highway by *snatching with violence from the person*. These are generally done in the dusk, and rarely during the day. When committed early in the evening, they are done in secluded places, intersected with lanes and alleys, where the thieves have a good opportunity to escape, such as in the Borough, Spitalfields, Shoreditch, Whitechapel, Drury-lane, West-minster, and similar localities. These are often done by one person, at other times by two or more in company, and generally by young men from nineteen years and upwards. The mode of effecting it is this. They see a person respectably dressed walking along the street, with a silver or gold chain, who appears to be off his guard. One of them as he passes by makes a snatch at it, and runs down one of the alleys or along one of the by-streets.

Sometimes the thief breaks the chain with a violent wrench. At other times the swivel, or ring of the watch may give way; or a piece of the guard breaks off. The thief occasionally fails to get the watch. In these cases he can seldom be identified, because the party may not have had his eye on him, and may lose his presence of mind; and the thief may have vanished swiftly out of his sight.

Should the person to whom the watch belongs run after him, his companions often try to intercept him, and with this view throw themselves in his way. The thief is seldom caught at the time, unless he is pursued by some person passing by, who has seen him commit the robbery, or who may have heard the cry, "Stop thief."

These felonies are committed by men living in low neighbourhoods, who are generally known thieves; and are in most cases done during some disturbance in the street, or in a crowd, or upon a person the worse of liquor.

In September, 1859, Thomas Dalton, alias Thomas Davis, a stout-made man of about thirty years of age, and 5 ft. 6 inches high, in company with another man, went to the regatta at Putney, near London, when Dalton snatched the watch of Mr. Friar, formerly the ballet-master at Vauxhall-gardens. Mr. Friar, being aware of the robbery, suddenly seized hold of both the men, when they wrestled with him. The other man got away, but he retained his hold of Dalton. On a policeman coming up Dalton dropped the watch. He was committed to the Surrey Sessions, tried on 15th September, 1859, and sentenced to ten years' penal servitude.

Dalton was one of five prisoners tried at the Central Criminal Court in December, 1847, for the murder of Mr. Bellchambers, at Westminster, having beaten in his brains with an iron bar in Tothill-street, Westminster during the night. Dalton was then acquitted. Sales, one of the parties charged, was found guilty and hanged at Newgate.

They were seen in the company of the deceased in a public-house in Orchard-street, Westminster on the night of the murder, and had followed him out and robbed him of his money, watch, and seals. Dalton had been several times in custody, for being concerned with other persons in plate robberies; sneaking down into areas and opening the doors by means of skeleton keys, and carrying off the plate. One of the thieves went, dressed as a butcher, with an ox's tail, pretending the lady of the house had ordered it. While the servant went upstairs he put the plate into a basket he carried with him, and carried it away.

On the 23rd of March, 1850, he was in custody with other three notorious house-breakers for attempting to steal plate in Woburn-square by skeleton keys along with other four thieves, when he was found guilty and got three months' imprisonment. One of them opened an area gate about 10 o'clock in the morning, carrying a green-baize cloth containing three French rolls. Finding the servant in the kitchen, cleaning the plate, he told her he had brought the French rolls from the baker. The servant, who was an intelligent shrewd person, refused to go upstairs to her mistress. Meantime two detective officers, who had been on the look-out, arrested the four thieves and prevented the robbery.

On the 6th February, 1854, he was tried at Westminster, for snatching a watch from a gentleman in Parliament-street, while her Majesty was proceeding to open the Houses of Parliament. The gentleman feeling the snatch at his watch laid hold of Dalton, when he threw it down an area in front of the Treasury buildings.

As we have already said, Dalton was afterwards sentenced to transportation.

Another remarkable case of highway robbery took place several years ago by a man of the name of George Morris. He was above five feet nine inches high, stout made, with dark whiskers, and of gentlemanly appearance. He snatched a watch from a man near the Surrey Theatre. Immediately on seizing hold of the watch he ran round St. George's Circus into the Waterloo-road, with the cry of stop thief ringing in his ears. In running down

Waterloo-road he threw himself down intentionally into a heap of dirt in the street, when several people who were chasing him, and also a policeman, stumbled over him. He then got up as they lay on the ground and run down a turning called Webber-row, down Spiller's-court, and got over a closet, then mounted the roof of some low cottages, and jumped off this into the garden at the other side belonging to lofty houses there under repair. Finding a crowd of people and the police close at his heels in the garden below, and being exceedingly nimble, he ran up the ladder like lightning, to the roof of the house. As the policemen were about to follow him he took hold of the ladder and threw it back, preventing all further chase. He disappeared from the top of this house and got to the roof of the Magdalen Institution, and would have made his escape but for the prompt exertions of the police. Some of them ran into a builder's yard and got several ladders and climbed up at different parts of the building and pursued him on the roof of the house—between the chapel and the governor's house. He stood at bay, and threatened to kill the first policeman who approached him, and kept them at defiance for half-an-hour.

Meantime several other policemen had mounted the back part of the chapel by means of a ladder, unperceived by Morris, while the others were keeping him in conversation. On seeing them approach he found all hope of escape was vain, and surrendered himself into the hands of the officers. He was tried at the Central Criminal Court, and sentenced to transportation for ten years.

Not long before he had assaulted a woman in the Westminster-road. There was a cry for the police, and he ran down Duke-street, Westminster-road. On turning the corner of the street he popped into a doorway. This was in the dusk of the evening. His pursuers ran past, thinking he had gone into one of the adjoining streets. As soon as they had passed by he was seen to come out and coolly walk back, as if nothing had occurred. A neighbour who had seen this gave him into the custody of the police about half-an-hour afterwards, and he was fined 40s. for assaulting the woman.

About this time a woman complained to a policeman at the Surrey Theatre that a tall, gentlemanly man had picked her pocket. The constable told her he had seen a well-known thief go into a neighbouring coffee-shop dressed in black. He took the woman over, and she immediately said that was not the man. She was not able to identify him, as he had turned his coat inside out. The coat he had on was black in the inside, and white on the exterior, and could be put on upon either side. He had in the meantime changed the coat, and the woman was thereby unable to recognize him. This enabled him on this occasion to escape the ends of justice.

Highway robberies are also effected by garotting. These are done in similar localities at dusk, frequently in foggy nights at certain seasons of the year, and seldom in the summer time. They are generally done in the by-streets, and in the winter time. A ruffian walks up and throws his arm round the neck of a person who has a watch, or whom he has noticed carrying money on his person. One man holds him tightly by the neck, and generally attacks from behind, or from the side. The garotter tries to get his arm under his chin, and presses it back, while with the other hand he holds his neck firmly behind. He does it so violently the man is almost strangled, and is unable to cry out. He holds him in this position perhaps for a minute or two, while his companions, one or more, rifle his pockets of his watch and money.

Should the person struggle and resist he is pressed so severely by the neck that he may be driven insensible. When the robbery is effected they run off. In general they seize a man when off his guard, and it may be some time before he recovers his presence of mind. These are generally a different class of men from the persons who snatch the watch-chain. They have more of the bull-dog about them, and are generally strong men, and brutal in disposition. Many of them are inveterate thieves, returned convicts, ruffians hardened in crime. Their average age is from twenty-five and upwards, and they reside in low infamous neighbourhoods. Most of these depredations are committed in the East-end of the metropolis, such as Whitechapel and its neighbourhood, or the dark slums in the Borough.

A remarkable case of garotting occurred in the metropolis in July, 1856. Two men went to a jeweller's shop in Mark Lane during the day, when the street was thronged with people. One of them was stout-made, about five feet six inches high, of dark complexion, and about forty-five years of age. The other, named James Hunter, alias Connell, was about five feet ten inches high, of robust frame, with dark whiskers, dressed in the first of fashion

One of the thieves kept watch outside while the other slipped in and laid hold, in the absence of the jeweller, of a lot of valuable jewellery. The shopman, who happened to be in the back parlour, ran into the shop and seized him. On seeing this his companion came in from the street to assist him, knocked the shopman down and gave him a severe wound on the head, when both hastily made their escape. One of them was taken when he had got a small distance off with some of the jewellery on his person, such as watches, rings, brooches, &c., but the other got away. This robbery was daringly done in the very middle of the day, near to the Corn Exchange, while in the heat of business. One of the robbers was taken and tried at the Central Criminal Court in July, 1856, and sentenced to ten years' transportation, having been previously convicted for felony.

From information received by the police, James Hunter alias Clifford alias Connell, the other person concerned in this robbery, was taken afterwards. A good-looking young applewoman swore distinctly he was one of those parties. In running away he had thrown down her stand of apples, and also threw her down when she for a short time had seized hold of him.

He was tried at the Central Criminal Court in August 1856, the following sessions, when the prisoner's counsel proved an alibi by calling his convicted confederate as a witness. His two sisters also swore he was in their house at Lambeth Walk on the day the robbery occurred, and had dinner and tea with his mother, who was an honest and respectable woman.

Other robberies are perpetrated *by brutal violence with a life-preserver or bludgeon*. It is usually done by one or more brutal men following a woman. The men are generally from thirty to forty years of age—some older—carrying a life-preserver or bludgeon. This is termed "swinging the stick," or the "bludgeon business." The woman walks forward, or loiters about, followed by the men, who are hanging in the rear. She walks as if she was a common prostitute, and is often about twenty-six or thirty years of age. She picks up a man in the street, possibly the worse of liquor; she enters into conversation, and decoys him to some quiet, secluded place, and may there allow him to take liberties with her person, but not to have carnal connection. Meantime she robs him of his watch, money, or other property, and at once makes off.

In some instances she is pursued by the person, who may have discovered his loss; when he is met by one of the men, who runs up, stops him, and inquires the direction to some part of London, or to some street, or will ask what he has been doing with his wife, and threaten to punish him for indecent conduct to her. During this delay the woman may get clear away. In somes cases a quarrel arises, and the victim is not only plundered of his money, but severely injured by a life-preserver or bludgeon.

Cases of this kind occasionally occur in the East-end and the suburbs of London. These women and men are generally old thieves, and, when convicted, are often sentenced to transportation, being in most cases well known to the police.

Sometimes these robberies are committed by men without the connivance of women, as in a case which occurred in Drury Lane in August last, when a man was decoyed by several men from sympathy to accompany a drunken man to a public-house, and was violently robbed.

In the month of July 1855 a woman stopt a man in the London-road, Southwark, one evening about twelve o'clock at night, and stole his watch. The party immediately detected the robbery, and laid hold of her. Upon this two men came up to her rescue, struck him in the face, and cut his cheek. They then gave him another severe blow on the head, and knocked him down senseless, while calling out for the police.

A policeman came up at this juncture, and laid hold of Taylor, one of the men, and took him into custody with a life-preserver in his hand. Taylor was tried on 20th August, 1855, at the Central Criminal Court, and was sentenced to fourteen years' penal servitude.

Highway robberies by the pistol are seldom committed, though occasionally such instances do occur. These are seldom committed by professional thieves, as they generally manage to effect their object by picking pockets, and in the modes we have just described.

The old rookeries of thieves are no longer enveloped in mystery as formerly. They are now visited by our police inspectors and constables, and kept under strict surveillance. Our daily press brings the details of our modern highway-men and other thieves clearly to the light of day; and their deeds are no longer exaggerated by fictitious embellishments and exaggerations. Our railways and telegraphs, postal communications and currency arrangements, have put an end to mounted highwaymen.

such as Dick Turpin and Tom King. Were such to appear now, they would furnish a rare piece of sport to our bold and adroit detectives, and would speedily be arrested.

Number of felonies by highway robbery in the metropolitan districts for 1860	21
Ditto ditto in the City	1
	22
Value of property thereby abstracted in the metropolitan districts ..	£98 0
Ditto ditto in the City	2 10
	£100 10

A Ramble among the Thieves' Dens in the Borough.

Leaving the police-office at Stones-end, along with a detective-officer, we went one afternoon to Gunn Street, a narrow by-street off the Borough Road, inhabited by costermongers, burglars, and pickpockets.

Here one of the most daring gangs of burglars and pickpockets in London met our eye, most of them in the dress of costermongers. A professional pickpocket, a well-attired young man, was seated on a costermonger's barrow. He was clothed in a black cloth coat, vest, and trousers, and shining silk hat, and was smoking a pipe, with two or three "pals" by his side. It was then about seven o'clock, P M., and as clear as mid-day. About forty young men, ranging from seventeen to thirty-five years of age, were engaged around a game of "pitch and toss," while others were lounging idle in the street.

We went forward through the crowd, and stood for some time alongside. At first they may have fancied we were come to arrest one or more of them, and were evidently prepared to give us a warm reception. On seeing us standing by smiling, they recovered their good-humour, and most of them continued to cluster together, but numbers sneaked off to their houses out of sight.

Here we saw a tall, robust man, with a dissipated and ruffian look, smoking a long pipe, who had been an accomplice in an atrocious midnight murder.

He had narrowly escaped the gallows by turning Queen's evidence on his companions. He is a determined burglar. We could observe from the brutal, resolute, bull-dog look of the man that he was fit for any deed of heartless villany when inflamed with strong drink.

Three burglars stood in the middle of the crowd, who soon after left it and entered a beershop in the street. One of them was dressed like a respectable mechanic. He was rather beneath the middle height, stout-made, with his nose injured and flattened, possibly done in some broil. Another was more brutal in appearance, and more degraded. The third burglar was not so resolute in character, and appeared to be an associate of the band.

Ten of the persons present had been previously convicted of robberies. The greater part, if not the whole of them, were thieves, or associates of thieves.

We next directed our way to the Mint, a well-known harbour of low characters, passing knots of thieves at the corners of the different streets as we proceeded along. Some were sneaks, and others pickpockets. In the neighbourhood of the Mint we found a number of children gamboling in the streets. One in particular arrested our attention, an interesting little girl of about five years of age, with a sallow complexion, but most engaging countenance, radiant with innocence and hope. Other sweet little girls were playing by her side, possibly the children of some of the abandoned men and women of the locality. How sad to think of these young innocents exposed to the contamination of bad companionships around them, and to the pernicious influence of the bad example of their parents!

We went into Evans's lodging-house, noted as a haunt for thieves. Passing through a group of young women who stood at the doorway, we went downstairs to an apartment below and saw about a dozen of young lads and girls seated around a table at a game of cards. One of these youths was a notorious pickpocket, though young in years, and had twice escaped out of Horsemonger Lane gaol. We were informed there was not a fourth of the persons present who usually frequent the house. After the first panic was over the young people resumed their game, some looking slyly at us, as if not altogether sure of our object. Others were lying extended on the benches along the side of the room. As we were looking on this curious scene the women in the flat above had followed us down and were peering from the staircase into the apartment to try and learn the object of our visit. As we left the house we took a glance over our shoulder and saw them standing at the door, following our movements.

We bent our steps to Kent Street and entered a beershop there. There were a number of thieves and "smashers" (utterers of base coin) hovering round the bar. The "smashers" were ordinary-looking men and women of the lower orders. We saw a party of thieves in the adjoining tap-room, and seated ourselves for a short time among them. One of them was a dexterous swell-mobsman, who has been several times convicted and imprisoned. A dark-complexioned little man, about twenty-one years of age, an utterer of base coin, was lounging in the seat beside us. The swell-mobsman was evidently the leading man among them. He was a good-looking fair-haired youth, about twenty years of age, smart and decided in his movements, and with a good appearance, very unlike a criminal. He occasionally dresses in high style, in a superfine black suit, with white hat and crape, and occasionally drives out in fashionable vehicles.

We also visited Market Street, a narrow by-street off the Borough Road, a well-known rookery of prostitutes. A great number of simple, thoughtless young girls, from various parts of London and the country, leave their homes and settle down here and live on prostitution. Here we saw an organist performing in the street, surrounded by a dense crowd of young prostitutes, middle-aged women, and children of the lower class. Two young women, one with her face painted, and the other a slender girl about seventeen, with an old crownless straw bonnet on her head, and with the crown of it in one hand, and a stick in the other, were dancing in wild frolic to the strains of the organ, amid the merriment of the surrounding crowd, and to the evident amazement of the poor minstrel, while other rough-looking young dames were skipping gaily along the street.

In a brothel in this street an atrocious crime was perpetrated a few days ago by George Philips, a young miscreant, termed the Jew-boy, who resided there. A sailor, recently returned from India, happened to enter this foul den. The inmates consisted of the Jew-boy's sister, a common prostitute, who cohabited with Richard Pitts, a well-known burglar, recently sentenced to transportation for ten years, another prostitute named Irish Julia, and this young villain, the Jew. After remaining for some time the sailor told them he was to leave their company. On hearing this, Philips's sister told her brother to stab him to the heart. He instantly took out a knife from his pocket, opened it, and stabbed the sailor beneath the collar-bone. After committing this atrocious crime he coolly wiped the knife on the cuff of his guernsey, at the same time stating, if the sailor had not got enough he would give him the other end of the knife. The sailor fell, apparently mortally wounded, and was removed to St. Thomas's Hospital.

His sister, on seeing what her brother had done by her order, desperately seized a bottle of laudanum in the room, and drank off part of the contents, and still lies in a precarious state.

In this portion of Market Street we understand every house, from basement to attic, is occupied by prostitutes and thieves.

We entered an adjoining public-house, where three of these young women followed us to the bar, anxious to know the object of our visiting the district. They called for a pint of stout, which they drank off heartily, and stood loitering beside us to hear our conversation, so that they might have something to gossip about to their companions. The girl who frolicked in the street with the old bonnet was one of them, and had now laid this aside. She was fair-haired, and good-looking, but was very foolish and immodest in her movements. One of her companions was taller and more robust, but her conduct showed she was debased in her character, and lost to all sense of propriety. The other girl was tall and dark-eyed, and more quiet and calculating in her manner as she stood, in a light cotton dress, silently leaning against the door-post.

One evening in September, about eight o'clock, we took another ramble over the criminal district of the Borough.

As we went along Kent Street the lamps were lit, and the shops in the adjoining streets were illuminated with their flaring gas lights. On passing St. George's church we saw a crowd collected around a drunken middle-aged Irishwoman. It was one of those motley scenes one often meets in the streets of London. Young people and middle-aged, old women and children were clustered together, some well-dressed, others in mechanics' dress, begrimed with dust and sweat, and others hanging in rags and tatters. They were collected around this woman, who stood on the pavement, while the mass were gathered in the street, many of them looking on anxiously with eyes and mouth open, others grinning with delight, and some with sinister countenance, while she gesticulated wildly, yet in good humour, in a strong Irish accent, amid the applause of the auditory.

We could not hear the subject of her oration. On our coming up to her and remaining for a short time, curious to know the nature of the comedy, the woman went away, followed by part of the crowd, when she appeared to take her station again in the midst of them. We had no time to lose, and passed on.

On our proceeding farther into Kent Street, a good-looking girl, evidently belonging to the lower orders, stood in a doorway, with beaming smile, and beckoned us to enter. She had accosted us in like manner in the light of open day on our previous visit to Kent Street, while another young woman, of her own age and size, apparently her sister, stood by her side. As on the former occasion we did not trust ourselves to these syren sisters, but again passed on, notwithstanding urgent solicitations to enter.

Farther along the street we saw a small group of men and boys—thieves and utterers of base coin. A young woman of about twenty-five years of age stood among them, who was a common prostitute and expert thief, although we could scarcely have known this from her heavy, stupid-looking countenance, which was bloated and dissipated. One of the group was a burglar. He was under the middle size, pockpitted, and had a callous, daring look about him. We had time to study the lines of his face. They soon divined our purpose, and skulked off in different directions, as we found the generality of such persons to do in the course of our visits. The men were of different ages, varying from seventeen to thirty, dressed similar to costermongers.

We bent our way to St. George's New Town, a by-street off Kent Street. On turning the corner from Kent Street, leading into St. George's New Town, we saw a cluster of men and women, varying in age from seventeen to forty, also dressed like those just described. Most of them were convicted thieves.

We then came back to Mint Street, leading out of High Street in the Borough to Southwark Bridge Road, which, as we have said, is very low and disreputable.

Leaving Mint Street and its dark, disreputable neighbourhood, we directed our way to Norfolk Street, a very narrow street, leading into Union Street in the Borough. This locality is much infested with pickpockets and also with "dragsmen," *i. e.* those persons who steal goods or luggage from carts and coaches. At one corner of this street we saw no less than seven or eight persons clustered together, several of them convicted thieves. They were dressed similar to those in the low neighbourhoods already described.

We then went into Little Surrey Street, Borough Road, where we entered a beershop. Here we found four men, from twenty-five to thirty-five years of age—expert burglars. One of them appeared to be a mechanic. He told us he was an engraver. This was the same burglar, with his nose flattened, we had seen on the previous occasion referred to. He was an intelligent, determined man, and acted as the head of the gang. The other two were the companions we had seen with him in Gunn Street. All of them were rather under the middle size. They were now better dressed than formerly, and apparently on the eve of setting out to commit some felony. They appeared trimmed up in working order. A prostitute, connected with them, with her eye blackened, stood by the bar. She was also well-attired, and ready to accompany them. Burglars of this class often have a woman to go before them, to carry their housebreaking tools, to the house they intend to enter, as they might be arrested on the way with the tools in their own possession. The woman was tolerably good-looking, and on setting out, was possibly getting primed with gin. The engraver has been convicted several times for picking pockets as well as for burglary. The other two are convicted burglars. There was a man of about forty years of age seated beside them in the beershop, whom we learned was in a decline. The burglars are often liberal in supporting the invalids connected with them, and the latter lend a subordinate hand occasionally in their nefarious work, such as in assisting to dispose of the stolen property. One of their old "pals" died lately, and the burglars in his neighbourhood raised a subscription between them to defray his funeral expenses.

We proceeded to Market Street, Borough Road, where we had on the former occasion observed the scene of merriment with the organist and the young girls. But the street had now a very different appearance. Instead of the locality ringing with the light-hearted merriment and buffoonery of the young girls and groups of children, the dark pall of night was stretched over it. At every door as we passed we saw a female standing on the outlook for persons to enter their dens of prostitution and crime. They solicited us in whispers to enter, or tapped us gently on the shoulder, or seized us by the skirts of the coat. Some of them were young and good-looking, while others were old and bloated. We looked into several of the houses as we went along, and saw numbers of young prostitutes in their best attire, seated by the tables, or lolling on the seats. This part of Market Street is one of the lowest rookeries of prostitutes and thieves in London. Many a young girl has been ruined by entering these low brothels. She may have been a servant out of place, or she may have left her home in the metropolis, and betaken herself here to a life of infamy.

These prostitutes assist to maintain the burglars, pickpockets, and other thieves, when they are not successful in their lawless calling. Some of them are well-dressed and remarkably good-looking. They occasionally come home with men in cabs from the different theatres, and rob them in their dwellings, and turn them unceremoniously into the street, but do not strip them of their clothing. When their cash is done, they wish their company no longer.

In other low districts in the vicinity of Kent Street, prostitutes have been convicted for stealing the clothes of the unfortunates who have entered their dismal abodes.

Leaving Market Street and the alleys and slums of that locality behind us, we went along Newington Causeway, a far brighter and more salubrious scene. This is a wide business street, and one of the main streets on the Surrey side of the river, where, especially in the evenings, a good deal of shopping is carried on.

The south side of Newington Causeway, from Horsemonger Lane gaol to the Elephant and Castle, is crowded with shops, the street being lit up nearly as clear as day. There are several splendid gin-palaces in this locality, generally crowded with motley groups of people of various ranks and pursuits; and milliners' shops, with their windows gaily furnished with ladies' bonnets of every hue and style, and ribbons of every tint; and drapers' shops with cotton gown pieces, muslins, collars, and gloves of every form and colour. There are many boot- and shoe-shops, with assortments of fancy shoes as well as plain. Upholsterers' shops, with carpets and rugs of every pattern, and chemists, with their gay-coloured jars, flaming like globes of red, blue, green, and yellow fire. The street is filled with incessant tides of mechanics, tradesmen's wives, milliners, dressmakers, and others, going shopping or returning from their daily toil; and many respectable people take their evening's walk along this cheerful and bustling thoroughfare, which is a favourite place for promenading.

In walking along we noticed many young men and women in respectable attire. Here we saw some young, genteel milliners and dressmakers, and girls from other places of business, returning to their homes or lodgings, at the close of the day, and taking an occasional glance at the shop windows, as they passed along. By their side we saw apparently some married women, out shopping with a new bonnet, or other article of dress, carefully wrapt up. In another part of the street we saw a shopman making love to a pretty girl, with clustering ringlets, who looked serenely upon him as he stood bareheaded outside the door of a drapery establishment.

Among the busy throng of people passing to and fro we observed two young women, pickpockets, dressed in brown cloaks, like milliners, and in fancy bonnets, passing quietly along. A person who did not know them personally, could not have detected their criminal character. On following them a short way, they passed over to the other side of the street. From their features and from the similarity of their dress we could have guessed them to be sisters. They were apparently about twenty-five years of age.

As is generally the case with such persons, on being noticed they separated on the other side of the street to prevent our following their movements. One went off in one direction, and the other in another; but meantime they had probably arranged to meet each other when out of the officer's sight.

The Borough is chiefly the locality of labouring people and small shopkeepers— the masses of the people—and has low neighbourhoods in many of the by-streets, infested by the dangerous classes. It contains specimens of almost all kinds of thieves, from the lowest to the most expert, though for the most part few of the swells reside here. Many of them prefer to live about the Kingsland Road.

They occasionally leave their own dwellings in other parts of the city, and come here, and live retired to be away from the surveillance of the police of their own district.

There are some expert "cracksmen" (burglars) here, dressed in fashionable style, who indulge in potations of brandy and champagne, and the best of liquors. In their appearance there is little or no trace of their criminal character. They have the look of sharp business men. They commit burglaries at country mansions, and sometimes at shops and warehouses, often extensive, and generally contrive to get safely away with their booty.

These crack burglars generally live in streets adjoining the New Kent Road and

Newington Causeway, and groups of them are to be seen occasionally at the taverns beside the Elephant and Castle, where they regale themselves luxuriously on the choicest wines, and are lavish of their gold. From their superior manner and dress few could detect their real character. One might pass them daily in the street, and not be able to recognize them.

HOUSEBREAKERS AND BURGLARS.

THE expert burglar is generally very ingenious in his devices, and combines manual dexterity with courage. In his own sphere the burglar in manual adroitness equals the accomplished pickpocket, while in personal daring he rivals our modern ruffians of the highway, who perpetrate garotte robberies, or plunder their victims with open violence.

Many of our London burglars have been trained from their boyhood. Some are the children of convicted thieves; some have for a time lived as sneaks, committing petty felonies when residing in low lodging-houses; others are the children of honest parents, mechanics and tradesmen, led into bad company, and driven into criminal courses.

In treating of sneaks we alluded to the area-sneak, and lobby-sneak, watching a favourable opportunity and darting into the kitchen and pantry, and sometimes entering the apartments on the first floor and stealing the plate. We alluded to the lead-stealer finding his way to the house-top, and to the attic-thief adroitly slipping downstairs to the apartments below, and carrying away valuables, jewellery, plate, and money. Here we see the points of transition, from the petty felon to the daring midnight robber plundering with violence.

We shall in the outset offer a few general remarks on the manner in which housebreaking and burglaries are effected in London, and then proceed to a more detailed account of the various modes pursued in the different districts.

Breaking into houses, shops, and warehouses is accomplished in various ways, such as picking the locks with skeleton keys; inserting a thin instrument between the sashes and undoing the catch of the windows, which enables the thieves to lift up the under sash; getting over the walls at the back, and breaking open a door or window which is out of sight of the street, or other public place; lifting the cellar-flap or area-grating; getting into an empty house next door, or a few doors off, and passing from the roof to that of the house they intend to rob; entering by an attic-window, or trap-door, and if there are neither window nor door on the roof, taking off some of the tiles and entering the house. Sometimes the thieves will make an entry through a brick wall in an adjoining building, or climb the waterspout to get in at the window. These are the general modes of breaking into houses.

Sometimes when doors are fastened with a padlock outside, and no other lock on the door, thieves will get a padlock as near like it as possible. They will then break off the proper lock, one of them will enter the house, and an accomplice will put on a lock as like it as possible to deceive the police, while one or more inside will meantime pack up the goods. Sometimes a well-dressed thief waylays a servant-girl going out on errands in the evening, professes to fall in love with her, and gets into her confidence, till she perhaps admits him into the house when her master and mistress are out. Having confidence in him she shows him over the house, and informs him where the valuables are kept. If the house is well secured, so that there will be difficulty of breaking in by night, he manages to get an accomplice inside to secrete himself till the family has gone to bed, when he admits one or more of his companions into the house. They pack up all they can lay hold of, such as valuables and jewels. On such occasions there is generally one on the outlook outside, who follows the policeman unobserved, and gives the signal to the parties inside when it is safe to come out.

In warehouses one of the thieves frequently slips in at closing-time, when only a few servants are left behind, and are busy shutting up. He secretes himself behind goods in the warehouse, and when all have retired for the night, and the door locked, he opens it and lets in his companions to pack up the booty. Should it consist of heavy goods, they generally have a cart to take it away. They are sometimes afraid to engage a cabman unless they can get him to connive at the theft, and, besides, the number of the cab can be taken. They get the goods away in the following manner. If consisting of bulky articles, such as cloth, silks, &c., they fill large bags, similar to sacks, and get as much as they think the cart can conveniently hold, placed near the door. When the policeman has passed by on his round, the watch stationed outside gives the signal; the door is opened, the cart drives up, and four or five sacks are handed into it by two thieves in about a minute, when the vehicle retires. It is loaded and goes off sooner than a gentleman would take his carpet-bag and portmanteau into a cab when going to a railway-station. The cart proceeds with the driver in one way, while the thieves walk off in a different direction. They close the outer door after them when they enter a shop or warehouse, most of which have spring locks. When the policeman comes round on his beat he finds the door shut, and there is nothing to excite his suspicion. The cart is never seen loitering at the door above a couple of minutes, and does not make its appearance on the spot till the robbery is about to be committed, when the signal is given.

Lighter goods, such as jewellery, or goods of less bulk, are generally taken away in carpet bags in time to catch an early train, often about five or six o'clock, and the robbers being respectably-dressed, and in a neighbourhood where they are not known, pass on in most cases unmolested. Sometimes they pack up the goods in hampers, as if they were going off to some railway-station. When there is no one sleeping on the premises, and when they have come to learn where the party lives who keeps the keys, they watch him home at night after locking up, and set a watch on his house, that their confederates may not be disturbed when rifling the premises. If they are to remove the goods in the morning they do it about an hour before the warehouse is usually opened, so that the neighbours are taken off their guard, supposing the premises are opened a little earlier than usual in consequence of being busy. Sometimes they stand and see the goods taken out, and pay no particular attention to it. In the event of the person who keeps the keys coming up sooner than usual, the man keeping watch hastens forward and gives the signal to his companions, if they have not left the warehouse.

It often happens when they have got an entry into a house, they have to break their way into the apartments in the interior to reach the desired booty, such as wrenching open an inner door with a small crowbar they term a jemmy, cutting a panel out of a door, or a partition, with a cutter similar to a centrebit, which works with two or three knives; this is done very adroitly in a short space of time, and with very little noise. At other times, when on the floor above, they cut through one or more boards in the flooring, and frequently cut panes of glass in the windows with a knife or awl.

They get information as to the property in warehouses from porters and others unwittingly by leading them into conversation regarding the goods on the premises, the silks they have got, &c., and find out the part of the premises where they are to be found. Sometimes they go in to inspect them on the pretence of looking at some articles of merchandise.

It occasionally happens servants are in league with thieves, and give them information as to the hour when to come, and the easiest way to break in. Sometimes servants basely admit the thieves into the premises to steal, and give them impressions of the keys, which enables them to make other keys to enter the house. Thieves sometimes take a blank key without wards, cover it with wax, work it in the keyhole against the wards of the lock, and by that means the impression is left in the wax. They then take it home and make a similar key. When looking into the lock they frequently strike a match on the doorway, and pretend to be lighting a pipe or cigar, which prevents passers by suspecting their object.

These are the general modes of housebreaking and burglary over the metropolis, but in order that we may have a more vivid and thorough conception of the subject, we shall give a more graphic detail of these felonies. We shall first advert to breaking into shops and warehouses, and then proceed to describe burglaries in various parts of the metropolis.

It frequently occurs that a thief enters a warehouse, or large shop, and secretes himself behind some goods, or in the cellar, or up the chimney. This could be done at any hour of the day, but is frequently managed when the servants or shopmen are out dining at mid-day, or towards evening, when the places of business are about to be closed. The thief may be respectably dressed, or not, according to the nature of the place of business. A person may call with some fictitious message, and keep one or more of the servants or shopmen in conversation while a confederate could meantime slip into the shop or warehouse, and if detected would seldom be suspected of being connected with this party. They sometimes hover for days in the neighbourhood of shops and warehouses they intend to plunder, and watch the most favourable opportunity to effect this object.

Towards evening when the servants are all gone, and the place of business closed, the rest of his companions come to the spot, consisting of one or more men, a woman being occasionally employed. While they are aware that one of their gang is secreted on the premises, as a precaution they sometimes knock at the door or ring the bell to ascertain if the servants or shopmen are gone. Should they be lingering in the premises, arranging the goods, engaged with their business-books, accounts, or otherwise, they ask for Mr. So-and-so, or have some other fictitious message.

On the departure of the people belonging to the shop, the thief inside generally opens the door to his companions on the given signal, when they proceed to rifle the premises of Manchester goods, cottons, silks, shawls, satins, or otherwise, and to store them into large bags they bring with them, which they place beside the door, when filled, to be conveniently carried away. They wrench open the desks, money-drawers, and other lockfasts with a jemmy, chisel, or screw-driver, as well as any doors which may be locked, occasionally using the cutter and saw, or other tools, and pierce through brick and other partition walls with an auger or other instrument. In many cases the doors of the apartments in warehouses are left open so that the thief has free access to the property.

Meantime a man or woman is watching outside while the thieves are busy plundering within, keeping a special look-out for the policeman proceeding on his beat. They have many ingenious expedients to decoy him away, by conversation or otherwise. The policeman is generally from fifteen to twenty minutes in going round his beat, so that they have ample time to carry off the booty.

While the thieves are busy collecting their spoil, the door is shut with a spring lock, or fastened with a padlock by means of a key they may have made for the purpose, so that the policeman has no suspicion of what is passing within. The former frequently remain for several hours on the premises, while a person outside is keeping watch, waiting to hear their signal when they have got the booty packed and ready. Should the coast be clear outside, notice is conveyed to the cart or cab, loitering somewhere in the vicinity, or which drives up at a certain hour, when the door opens. The plunder is quickly handed into the vehicle, which drives smartly away. The door is then shut, and the robbers walk off, possibly in a different direction to that in which the conveyance is gone.

Burglaries from *jewellers' shops* are frequently effected by means of skeleton keys, or otherwise, by one or more men. A woman often carries the tools to the shop, and keeps watch. So soon as a favourable opportunity occurs they unlock the door and enter the premises, while a man or woman watches outside, the woman perhaps walking along the street as though she were a common prostitute, or familiarly accosting the policeman or other persons she meets, and decoying them away from the shop. In some cases, when she has not succeeded in getting the policeman away, she pretends to fall down in a fit, when he has possibly to take her to the nearest surgeon. Sometimes the woman feigns to be drunk, and is taken to the police station, which takes him off his beat. In the meanwhile the parties inside, with jemmy, chisel, saw, or other tools, and with silent lights and taper or dark lantern, break open the glass cases and boxes, and steal gold and silver watches, gold chains, brooches, pins, and other jewellery, which they deposit in a small carpet-bag, as well as rifle money from the desk.

Jewellers' shops are sometimes entered by the thief getting into an unoccupied house next door, or two or three houses off, and proceeding along the roofs to the attic or roof of the house to be robbed, and going in by the attic window, or removing a few of the slates. The thieves then go downstairs and cut their way through the door or partition, and effect an entry into the shop.

Most of the robberies in jewellers' shops have of late years been committed by means of false keys, or by cutting out a hole in the door or shutter with a cutter, which is done in a short space of time, and when the instrument is moistened it makes very little noise. This hole is covered with a piece of paper painted of the same colour as the door, and is pasted on, which prevents the police having any suspicion.

Sometimes jewellers' shops are entered by persons lodging in the floor above, or having access to it, and then cutting through the flooring and descending into the jeweller's shop by means of a rope-ladder they attach to the floor. At other times they are entered by cutting through the solid brick wall at the back of the shop.

Several years ago a very remarkable

burglary took place at Mr. Acutt's large linen-drapery establishment in the Westminster Road. About four o'clock in the morning the policeman on duty heard a man give the signal at a shop-door. The constable believing thieves to be on the premises sprung his rattle, roused up the inmates, and got the assistance of several other constables. When they entered the shop they found upwards of 30*l.* worth of silks and satins, and other valuables packed up in bundles ready to be carried off. They found two thieves who had gained an entrance by getting over some closets, scaling a wall by means of the rain-spout, and walking along a high wall about nine inches thick. They then removed the skylight at the back, and let themselves down into the shop by a rope-ladder. By this means they got into the shop of Mr. Acutt.

On being scared by the police they jumped from one house to another, eight feet apart, over a height of about fifty feet, and there concealed themselves behind a stack of chimneys. Several policeman mounted to the roofs, but could not find them; and no one would venture to leap to the adjoining houses, whither the thieves had gone. An inspector of police ordered two men in plain clothes to be on the watch, believing they must be concealed somewhere on the housetops.

About eight o'clock in the morning a man of the name of Fitzgerald was out in a back court of an adjoining house washing himself, when the thieves came down by a spout twenty feet long communicating with the water cistern. On getting down one of them jumped on the back of Fitzgerald. He shouted out "murder and police," when two constables came up and took both of the thieves into custody.

On the trial it was said the prisoners' women had given several pounds to bribe this man, and he pretended he could not identify them, and they were acquitted. They have since been transported for other burglaries.

One of them was a man of thirty years of age, about five feet nine inches high, slim made, with a most daring countenance. The other was of middle stature, about twenty-six years of age, with pleasing appearance.

Another burglary took place in a silk warehouse in Cheapside in 1842. The burglars were admitted into an adjoining carpet warehouse by one of the warehousemen on a Saturday night, and broke through a brick-wall eight or nine inches thick, and made an entry into the silk warehouse. They did not steal any carpets, as they were too bulky. Goods were seen to be taken away by a cab on the Sunday afternoon. The padlock was meantime secure on the outdoor, so that the police had no suspicion.

The robbery was discovered on the Monday morning, when it was found from 1500*l.* to 2000*l.* had been carried off, and that a 100*l.* bank note had also been taken from the desk of the carpet warehouse.

Soon after the foreman of the latter business establishment absconded, and has not since been heard of, and there is strong suspicion he had connived with the burglars.

Number of cases of breaking into shops, &c., in the Metropolitan districts for 1860 104
Ditto ditto in the City .. 20
—
124

Value of property thereby abstracted in the Metropolitan districts .. £1,899 0
Ditto ditto in the City .. 461 10

£2,360 10

We shall now treat of the *burglaries* in the metropolis, commencing with the lower, and proceeding to notice the higher burglars, termed the "cracksmen."

Burglaries in the working districts of the metropolis are effected in various ways—by one man mounting the shoulders of another and getting into a first-floor window, similar to acrobats, by climbing over walls leading to the rear of premises, cutting or breaking a pane of glass, and then unfastening the catch; or by pushing back the catch of the window with a sharp instrument, or by cutting a panel of a door with a sharp tool, such as an American "auger." Frequently they force the lock of the door with a jemmy. The lower class of burglars who have not proper tools sometimes use a screw-driver instead of a jemmy. In the forcing of the locks of drawers or boxes, in search of property, they use a small chisel with a fine edge, and occasionally an old knife.

There are frequently three persons employed in these burglaries—two to enter a house, and one to keep watch outside, to see that there is no person passing likely to detect. This man is generally termed a "crow." Sometimes a woman, called a "canary," carries the tools, and watches outside.

These low burglars carry off a booty of such small value that they are necessitated frequently to commit depredations. They steal male and female wearing apparel, and small articles of plate or jewellery, such as teaspoons or a watch.

They are from seventeen years of age and upwards, and reside in the Borough, Whitechapel, St. Giles, Shoreditch, and other low localities.

There is another kind of burglary committed by persons concealing themselves on the premises, which is often done in public-houses. The parties enter before the house is closed, by concealing themselves in the coal-cellar, skittle-ground, or other place where they are unobserved by those in charge of the house. These burglaries are done by low people, with whose previous mode of living the police are generally not acquainted. Very frequently they steal cigars, money in the till or on the shelves of the bar, left to give change to customers in the morning. There is another mode of entering public-houses, by the cellar flaps from the pavement in front of the house, or by going through the fanlight, and stealing property as before described, and returning the same way, sometimes letting themselves out by the front door, which has often a spring lock.

These burglaries are generally done at midnight, or between 1 and 5 o'clock.

There is a higher class of burglaries committed at fashionable residences over the metropolis, and at the mansions of the gentry and nobility, many of them in the West-end districts.

The houses to be robbed are carefully watched for several weeks, sometimes for months, before the burglary is attempted. The thieves take great precautions in such cases. They glean information secretly as to the inmates of the house; where they sleep, and where valuable property is kept. Sometimes this is done by watching the lights over the house for successive nights. These burglaries are often "put up" by the persons who execute them. They frequently get some of their more engaging companions to court one of the servant girls, give her small presents, and gain her favour, with the ultimate object of gaining access to the house and plundering it. At other times, though more rarely, they endeavour to become acquainted with the male servants of the house—the butler, valet, coachman, or groom. Sometimes they try to learn from the servants through other parties becoming acquainted with them, if they cannot succeed themselves. At other times they gather information from tradesmen who are called to the house on jobbing work, such as painters, plumbers, glaziers, bell-hangers, tinsmiths, and others, some of whom live near the burglars in low neighbourhoods, or are frequently to be seen in the evenings in their company. We can point our finger at three of these base wretches. One of them lives in Whitefriars, Fleet Street, another in Tottenham-court Road, and a third in Newell Street, Wardour Street, Oxford Street. These three persons get up many of the burglaries in the West-end and other parts of the metropolis, where they have work to do, when they find a suitable place. Some of them have put up burglaries for thirteen or fourteen years, and none of them have been detected, though suspected by the police. They never have a hand in the burglaries themselves, but secure a part of the booty. These "putters up" are from thirty to thirty-five years of age, and one of them has been convicted of a felony.

If the burglars cannot enter by the back of the premises, they go to the first-floor window in front, where there are no shutters. It matters not whether it be public or not; they will enter in a couple of minutes the premises by cutting the glass and undoing the catch.

The dwelling-houses in the West-end have often been entered by the first-floor window; and servants have many times been wrongfully charged with these burglaries, and lost their places in consequence.

Burglars generally leave their haunts to plunder about twelve o'clock at midnight, often driving up in a cab to a short distance from the spot where the burglary is to be attempted; but they frequently do not enter the house till one or two in the morning. In general, they take some liquor, such as gin and brandy, to keep up their spirits, as they call it. The one who is to watch outside generally takes up his position first, and the others follow. This is arranged so that the persons who enter —generally two, sometimes three—should not be seen by the policeman or others near the house.

When the latter come up, and find their companion at his post, and see the coast clear, they instantly proceed to enter the house, in front or behind, by the door or windows. Expert burglars go separate, to avoid suspicion.

On entering the house, they go about the work very cautiously and quietly, taking off their shoes, some walking in their stockings, and others with India-rubber overalls. If disturbed they very seldom leave their shoes or boots behind them.

Their chief object is to get plate, jewellery, cash, and other valuables. The drawing-room is usually on the first-floor in front; sometimes the whole of the first-floor is a drawing-room. They often find valuables in the drawing-room. They search parlour, kitchen, and pantry, and even open the servant's workbox for her small savings.

When they cannot get enough jewellery and plate they carry off wearing apparel. They often take money in the drawing-room from writing-desks and ladies workboxes. Experienced burglars do not spare time and trouble to look well for their plunder.

This is the general course adopted on entering a dwelling-house. In entering a shop, if they can find sufficient money to satisfy them, they do not carry off bulky property, but if there is no money in the desk or tills they rifle the goods, if they are of value.

In West-end robberies there are often two good cracksmen, one to keep watch outside, while another is busy at his work of plunder within. The person outside has to be on the alert, as he has generally to keep watch over an experienced officer, and to let his companions know when it is safe for them to work or to come out.

When a catch is in the centre of the window it is opened with a knife. If there should be one on each side they will cut a pane of glass in less than fifteen seconds, and undo them. The burglars seldom think of carrying a diamond with them, but generally cut the glass with a knife, as the starglazers do.

The shutters behind the window frame are often cut with what the burglars term a cutter. It cuts with two knives, with a centrebit stock, and makes a hole sufficiently large to admit the burglar's arm.

When the shutters are opened there are often iron bars to guard the window. The burglars tie a piece of strong cord or rope about two of the bars, and insert a piece of wood about a foot in length between this rope, and twist the wood. The bar is thereby bent sufficient to allow them to enter, or it gives way in the socket. These bars are sometimes forced asunder by a small instrument called a jack, by which a worm worked by a small handle displaces them. The rope and stick are used when they have not a jack. The latter can be conveniently carried in the trousers pocket.

Woodwork, such as shutters, doors, and partitions, is often cut in late years with the cutter, instead of the jemmy, as the former is a more effective tool, and makes an opening more expeditiously. With this instrument a door or shutter can be pierced sufficiently large to admit the arm in a few minutes.

A brick wall requires more time. If there are no persons within hearing, an opening can be made sufficiently large for a man to pass through, in an hour. If there are people near the apartment, it requires to be more softly done, and frequently occupies two or three hours, even when done by an expert burglar. They generally pierce one brick with an auger, and displace it; after the first brick is out, they work with a jemmy, and take the mortar out, then pierce a brick on the other side of the wall.

Burglars cannot pick Chubb's patent locks. The best way to secure premises where no person sleeps is to have a good patent lock on the outer door, with an iron bar outside fastened by a patent Chubb lock. This acts with double safety. If they break it off on the outside, the policeman easily detects it when he comes round on his beat, which he is sure to do before they have got the other lock opened, and this prevents them getting in that way. If they break in from the roof, or from the back, by cutting round the lock of an inside door, they do not get the outside door opened, and cannot get away any bulky goods. By this means the warehouse is more safe than if it were fastened any other way.

Common locks on doors are so easily picked by thieves that no warehouse ought to be left fastened in this way, unless there is a watchman over it.

Some cracksmen have what is called a petter-cutter, that is, a cutter for iron safes; an instrument made similar to a centrebit, in wich drills are fixed. They fasten this into the keyhole by a screw with a strong pressure outside. The turning part is so fixed that the drills cut a piece out over the keyhole sufficiently large to get to the wards of the lock. They then pull the bolt of the lock back and open the door.

Chubb's locks on iron safes are now made drill proof, so that they cannot be pierced.

Any person sleeping in a room, with valuable property in his possession, ought to have a chain on the door, like a street-door chain, as the common locks are so easily picked, and the masked thief, with dark lantern, can creep into the room without being heard. The rattling of the chain is sure to awaken the person sleeping.

Expert burglars are generally equipped with good tools. They have a jemmy, a cutter, a dozen of betties, better known as picklocks, a jack to remove iron bars, a dark lantern or a taper and some silent lights, and a life-preserver, and sometimes have a cord or rope with them, which can be easily converted into a rope ladder. A knife is often used in place of a chisel for opening locks, drawers, or desks. They often carry masks on their face, so that they might not be identified. The dark lantern is very small, with oil and cotton wick, and sometimes only shows a light about the size of a shilling, so that the reflection is not seen on the street without. Burglars often use the jemmy in place of picklocks. When they go out with their tools, they usually carry them wrapped up with list, so that they can throw them away without making a noise, should a policeman stop them, or attempt to arrest them. These are easily carried in the coat pocket, as they are not bulky. There are parties—sometimes old convicts—who lend tools out on hire.

When discovered by the inmates they are generally disposed to make their escape rather than to fight, and try to avoid violence unless hotly pursued. If driven to extremity, they are ready to use the life-preserver, jemmy, or other weapon.

Sometimes they carry a life-preserver of a peculiar style, consisting of a small ball attached to a piece of gut, that fastens round the wrist. With this instrument, easily carried in the palm of the hand, they can strike the persons who oppose them senseless, and severely injure them.

In going up and down stairs, they often creep up not in the centre but the side of the stair, to avoid being heard, as it is apt to creak beneath the footstep, and they generally take off their shoes to move more stealthily along.

They often use the cutter to make an opening in the middle of the panel sufficiently large to admit the arm, to undo locks or bolts they cannot reach outside.

Sometimes when the key is inside, and the door locked, they open it with a small pair of plyers; others use a long piece of wire, with a hoop put through the keyhole to lay hold of the bowl of the key. When the hook is fastened in it, they can as easily undo the lock as if they turned the key from the inside. Some burglars prefer the wire, others use the plyers. They generally prefer the cutter to the centre-bit in removing any woodwork. It resembles the centre-bit, but takes a much larger piece out, and does so more speedily. The cutter costs from 15s. to 1l. In the absence of a cutter, they sometimes work with a couple of gimlets and a knife, but this requires more time and makes more noise, though not sufficient to disturb the inmates of the house, if used expertly.

At the back of the house they enter through the kitchen window on the basement, or by the parlour window above it on the first floor, or by the window of the staircase alongside of the latter.

If experienced burglars, they listen at the doors of the apartments, and know by the breathing in general if the inmates are sound asleep. They sometimes begin their operations by going up to the highest floor, and work their way down, carrying off the plunder. After having finished what they call their work, they await the signal from the "watch" set outside. These signals are sometimes given by one or more coughs; some give a whistle, or sing a certain song, or tap on the door or shutter, or make a particular cry, understood between the parties.

Should the plunder be bulky, they will have a cart or a cab, or a costermonger's barrow, ready on a given signal to carry it away. They in general wait for the time when the police are changed, if the inmates are not getting up, sometimes coming out at the front door, but oftener at the back.

A remarkable case of burglary was committed in a dwelling-house in a fashionable square in the West-end about twelve months ago, and was effected in this manner. One day a well-dressed young man passed by an area and took special notice of the cook, who happened to be looking out of the window. Another day the same young man in passing by accosted this servant, and made an appointment to meet her on a certain occasion to go out to walk. This correspondence lasted for a short time, when the young man was invited to tea at the house, to spend a social evening. He was accompanied by a "pal" of his, a young Frenchman, who courted the housemaid, while the other made love to the cook. During their visit to the house, the family being then absent, one of the young men pretended to be very unwell, and thought a walk in the garden at the back of the house would be beneficial to him, and was accompanied there by one of the servant girls.

Meanwhile the housemaid and her friend had adjourned to one of the upper rooms. It was proposed by the Frenchman that his lady-love should partake of some gin or brandy as refreshment, to which she consented. He went out for the purpose of purchasing it, while she went down stairs to the kitchen. On his going out he left the front-door open, by which one of his confederates, a third party, entered the house, and passed upstairs, broke open several lockfasts, and stole the whole of the plate.

The Frenchman, meanwhile, returned with the liquor, and went downstairs to the kitchen, where he made merry with his fair lady and her companions. When they were seated regaling themselves over this liquor the door-bell rang. One of the girls went to the door and found no person there. This was a signal agreed on between the thieves. One of the young men still pretending to feel unwell proposed to go home with his companion, promising to call on a future occasion, when they would be able to spend a more comfortable evening than they had done on account of his illness.

One of the servants, on going upstairs after their departure, found the plate stolen. Information was given to the police, when these agreeable young men and their unknown friend were found to belong to a gang of most expert thieves. They were tried at Westminster Sessions for this offence, and sentenced to three years' penal servitude.

About eighteen months ago, two desperate burglars attempted to enter a fashionable dwelling-house at Westbourne Park, Paddington, belonging to a merchant in the City. One of them was a tall, raw-boned, muscular man, of about twenty-five years of age, dressed in a blue frock coat, dark cord trousers, black vest and beaver hat. The other was a man of thirty years of age, short and stout, nearly similarly attired. The first had the appearance of a blacksmith, with a determined countenance; the other had a more pleasing aspect, yet resolute. They were armed with a long chisel and heavy crowbar.

They got over several walls, and came up along the back to this dwelling-house in the centre of these villas, situated on the edge of the Great Western Railway. On reaching the garden they went direct to the window of the dining-room on the ground-floor.

As there had been several burglaries committed in the neighbourhood of those villas about this time, an experienced and able detective officer was sent out to watch.

While the detective, a tall, powerful, resolute man, was sitting alone in the dusk under a tree in an adjoining garden, and another criminal officer was stationed a short distance off, at about two o'clock in the morning the former officer heard the shutters crash in the windows of an adjoining house nearly in front of where he stood.

The burglars had approached so softly he did not hear their footsteps, and was not aware of their presence till then. On hearing this noise he drew close to the house, and was seen by one of the thieves—the shortest one called Jack. The detective officer immediately sprung his rattle, rushed on this man and seized him. His companion on this ran from the end of the house and struck the officer across the back with a heavy crowbar. By a sudden movement of his body the latter partially avoided the force of the blow. Had it struck him on the head it would have killed him on the spot; and being a strong muscular man he knocked the shorter man down with a heavy walking-stick he had in his hand, and at the same time rushed on his taller companion, seized him by the throat, and endeavoured to wrench the iron bar from his grasp.

The other burglar had meantime made his escape into an adjoining garden, and was captured, after a desperate struggle, by the other criminal officer, who had come up.

During the scuffle between the officers and burglars the proprietor of the house, in a panic, threw up his bedroom window looking into the garden at the back of the house, and, without giving any call, fired off a pistol. He did this to alarm the neighbourhood, not being aware that the officers were so near him, and supposing that the burglars were in his house.

The other burglar was secured after a determined struggle, and both were with difficulty conveyed to the Marylebone police station by five strong officers. They were next day taken before the magistrates, and charged with attempting to enter this house, and with assaulting the officers in the execution of their duty. They were sentenced to three months each in Clerkenwell prison, with hard labour for the former offence, and with a similar punishment for the latter.

About two years ago a burglary was committed in Charles Street, Gloucester Terrace, Paddington, opposite the Cleveland Arms, by two men and a woman. One of the men was about forty-six years of age, an old desperate burglar, who had been twice transported, and was then on ticket-of-leave. Shortly before, he had been apprehended in St. George's burying-ground, at the rear of some houses in the Bayswater road, with a screw-driver, jemmy, and dark lantern, when he was sentenced to three months' imprisonment as a rogue and vagabond.

He was a stout man, with very bushy whiskers, of a coarse appearance. The other was a young man about nineteen, dressed as a mechanic, of a cheerful countenance, with brown hair and moustache. The woman was about twenty-three years of age, short and stout, with an engaging appearance.

During the night, they had forced open an iron grating in front of a house in Charles Street, Paddington, and had let themselves down into the area. They bored three holes with a centre-bit in the door of the house, then cut the panel, and put their arm through, and undoing the fastening of the door, got into the kitchen. From this they went up to a door leading to the staircase, which was locked. They cut several holes with the centre-bit, and made an opening in this door in like manner. They then went upstairs to the first-floor, and stole a quantity of wearing apparel, and some jewellery, such as rings, studs, &c., and also a watch.

The inmates were sleeping at the top of the house, and had not been disturbed by these operations. The property rifled amounted to about 15*l*.

One of the burglars left his hat behind him and a pair of old boots. The detective officer sent after them knew the hat to belong to this old-returned convict; went to Lisson Grove and arrested both the men, who happened to be together, and found part of the wearing apparel upon them. The remaining part of the property was traced as having been pledged by the woman, who was also apprehended. They were committed for trial for the burglary, and tried at the Old Bailey. The old man being an inveterate offender was sentenced to fifteen years' penal servitude; the others, who had been previously convicted, to four years'; and the girl to twelve months' imprisonment.

In the month of October, 1850, a burglary was committed by three men in the Regent's Park, which attracted considerable attention. One of them, named William Dyson, called the Galloway Doctor, was five feet six inches high, pockpitted, with pale face and red whiskers, and about thirty-two years of age; James Mahon, alias Holmsdale, five feet ten inches high, was robust in form, and aged thirty-four years; John Mitchell was five feet six inches high, stout made, with a pug nose, and aged forty years. They entered the house of Mr. Alford, an American merchant, in Regent's Park, at two o'clock in the morning. They climbed over a back wall into the garden, and got in through a back parlour window by pushing back the catch with a knife. They then forced the shutters open with a jemmy, got into the back-parlour where the butler was lying asleep, and unlocked the door to go through the house, as it was known that Mr. Alford was very wealthy. When they got on the staircase one of their feet slipped, which awoke the butler, who jumped up, and seized Dyson and Mahon, and wrestled with them, at the same time alarming the other inmates of the house. He was knocked down by a blow from a life-preserver, on which the burglars made their escape by jumping out of the back-parlour window again. The butler, on getting up, seized his fowling-piece, which lay loaded beside him, and told them as they were running away to stop, or he would fire upon them. He fired, and shot Mitchell in the back near the shoulder with goose shot, as he was getting over a back wall to make his escape.

The police, on hearing the report of the gun, came up and secured Holmsdale and Dyson in the garden, when they were taken to Marylebone police office.

Soon after an anonymous letter was sent to the police-station of the M division stating there was a man in Surrey Street, Blackfriars Road, lying in bed in a certain house, who had been shot in the back when attempting a burglary in Regent's Park. He had on a woman's nightcap and nightgown, so that if any one went into the room they would fancy him to be a female. Inspector Berry of the M division went to the above house, and found Mitchell in bed in female disguise. He was taken into custody, and made to dress in his own clothes. On examining them there were holes in his fustian frock-coat where the shot had passed through. He was taken to Marylebone police court and put alongside the other two prisoners, and identified as having been seen in the neighbourhood of the Regent's Park on the morning before the burglary was committed. He had been seen by the police to leave a notorious public-house frequented by burglars, at the Old Mint in the Borough. They were committed at the Central Criminal Court, tried on 25th November, 1850, convicted, and sentenced to be transported for life. Holmsdale having been previously transported for ten years, and Mitchell and Dyson also having been formerly convicted.

We took the particulars of the following burglary from the lips of a man who was a few years ago one of the most experienced and expert burglars in the metropolis, and give it as an instance of the ingenuity and daring of this class of London brigands:—

In the year 1850 a burglary was attempted to be committed at a furrier's at the corner of Regent Street near Oxford Street by three cracksmen. One of them, Henry Edgar, was about five feet seven inches high, of fair complexion, with large features, brown hair, and gentlemanly appearance, dressed in elegant style, with jewellery, rings, and chain, and frilled shirt. A second party, Edward Edgar Blackwell, was the son of a respectable cutler in Soho, about five feet two inches high, of fair complexion, teeth out in front, with sullen look, also fashionably dressed, though inferior to the other. The third person was slim made, about five feet six inches high, dark complexion, with dark whiskers and genteel appearance, a gentle, but keen dark eye, and elegantly dressed.

They went to a public-house between ten and eleven o'clock, when the two former went back into a yard with the pretence of going to the water-closet. The publican did not miss them. The house was closed at twelve o'clock, and they were not discovered. The third party went out to give them their signals at the time formerly arranged between them. He did not give them any signal, but they, being impatient and accustomed to the work, thought they would try it themselves. They went up by a fire-escape, and got on to the parapet of the furrier's house, at the corner of Regent Street. Here they cut two panes of glass in a garret window, with a knife, at the same time removing the division between them. The servant going to bed in the dark, discovered the two men. Giving no alarm, she went down stairs to her master. The master came up, with two loaded pistols in his hand, presented them at the garret-window, telling them if they attempted to escape he would shoot them. Edward Edgar Blackwell was so frightened that he lost his presence of mind, and fell from the parapet into the yard, a height of three storeys, and was killed on the spot. Henry Edgar, being more courageous, made a desperate leap to the top of a house in Regent Street, and got through a trap-door, and made his way into a second floor front in Argyle Street, where people were sleeping, and alarmed them. To prevent their taking him, he leaped from a second floor window. Some people, passing-by, saw him jump from the window, and gave information to the police. He was, thereupon, arrested, and conveyed in a cab, with the dead body of his "pal," to Vine Street police station.

It was afterwards ascertained that his ankle was dislocated, and he was removed to Middlesex Hospital, where he was watched eight hours by successive policemen. His friends were allowed to see him, and by ingenious means one of them contrived to effect his escape. They conveyed him from the hospital in a cab to Green Street, Friars Street, Blackfriars Road; then removed him in a cab to the Commercial Road near Whitechapel. Soon after, his companions took a house for him in Corbett's Place, Spitalfields, when he was given into the hands of the police by a brother of one of his "pals," who went to Vine Street station, and lodged information. He was arrested before he could lay his hand on his pistols, committed for trial, and sentenced to penal servitude.

We give the following as an illustration of the ingenuity and perseverance of the cracksmen of the metropolis—

A burglary was committed some years since, at a warehouse in the City, where the premises were securely fastened in front, and the servants were let out by a strong door at the back, secured by three strong locks. There was no one sleeping on the premises. The burglars had first to make keys to get through the outer door into the premises, and had then to get a key to a patent lock for an iron door into a private counting-house. They made another key for a very strong safe which, when opened, had a recess at the bottom enclosed with folding doors also secured by a patent lock. Before they got to the booty they had to make six keys of patent locks.

Not satisfied with this, they made a key for the patent lock of another iron door, leading to another portion of the premises where there was a second iron safe.

They were occupied four months getting the whole of these keys to fit, and had to watch favourable opportunities when the police were absent from that portion of their beat.

The thieves, during the night, carried off two iron boxes containing railway-shares, bills, and similar property to the extent of 13,000*l*., besides other valuable articles.

Through the ingenuity of certain police-officers employed to trace the robbery, the whole of the scrip and documents were recovered while certain unprincipled Jews were negotiating to purchase them.

Some burglars, after they have secured valuable booty, do not attempt another burglary for a time. Others go out the very next night, and commit other depredations, as they are avaricious for money. Some of them lose it by keeping it loosely in the house, or placing it in the bank, when the women they cohabit with reap the benefit. These females often try to induce them to save money and place it in their name in the bank, so that if their paramour gets apprehended, they have the pleasure of spending his ill-gotten wealth.

Some cracksmen succeed occasionally in rifling large quantities of valuable property or money. In such instances they live luxuriously, and spend large sums on pleasure, women, wine, and gambling. Some of them keep their females in splendid style, and live in furnished apartments in quiet respectable streets. Others are afraid to keep women, as the latter are frequently the cause of their being brought to justice.

There are some old burglars at present, keeping cabs, omnibuses, and public houses, whose wealth has been secured chiefly from plunder they have rifled from premises with their own hands, or received from burglars since they have abandoned their midnight work. They had the self-command to abandon their criminal courses after a time, while the most of the others have been more shortsighted. Some of these persons, though abounding in wealth, receive stolen goods, and are ready to open their houses at any hour of the night.

There are great numbers of expert cracksmen known to the police in different parts of the metropolis. Many of these reside on the Surrey side, about Waterloo Road and Kent Road, in the Borough, Hackney and Kingsland Roads, and other localities. Some of them have a fine appearance, and are fashionably dressed, and would not be known, except by persons personally acquainted with them.

A number of most expert cracksmen belonging to the felon class of Irish cockneys, have learned no trade, and have no fixed occupation. Others come to their ranks who have been carpenters and smiths, brass-finishers, shoemakers, mechanics, and even tailors. Sometimes fast young men have taken to this desperate mode of life. Some pickpockets, daring in disposition, or driven to extremity have become burglars. In a short time they learn to use their tools with great expertness; great numbers have been trained by a few leading burglars; some are as young as sixteen or seventeen years; others as old as forty or forty-five—incorrigible old convicts.

Tools are secretly made for them in London, Sheffield, Manchester, Birmingham, and other places. Some burglars keep a set of fine tools of considerable value. Others have indifferent instruments, and are not so expert.

They find very convenient agents in some of the cab-drivers of the metropolis, who for a piece of money are very ready to assist in conveying them at night to the neighbourhood of the houses where they perpetrate their burglaries, and in carrying off the stolen property, and some of the employers of these cab-drivers are as willing to receive it at an underprice.

They have no difficulty in finding unprincipled people to open their houses to receive the stolen property temporarily or otherwise. There are many houses of well-known receivers; then there are hundreds of low public-houses, beer-shops, coffee-shops, brothels, and other places of bad character, where they can leave it for a few hours, or for days, placing one of their gang in the house for a time, until they have arranged with the receivers to purchase it. There are certain well-known beer-shops and public-houses where the burglars meet with the receivers. They meet them in beer-shops in the purlieus of Whitechapel, and in the quieter public-houses and splendid gin-palaces of the West-end.

There are a number of French burglars in London, who are as ingenious, daring, and expert as the English. There are also some Germans and a few Italians, but who are not considered so clever.

Few of the cracksmen in the metropolis are married—though some are. They often live with prostitutes, or with servants, and other females they have seduced. Some have children whom they send to school, but many of them have none. They frequently train up some of their boys to enter the fanlights or windows, and to assist them in their midnight villanies.

While most of the burglars are city-trained, a number come from Liverpool, Manchester, Birmingham, Sheffield, and Bristol. These occasionally work with the London thieves, and the London thieves go occasionally to the provinces to work with them. This is done in the event of their being well known to the police.

For example, a gang of Liverpool thieves might know a house there where valuable property could be conveniently reached. Their being in the neighbourhood might excite suspicion. Under these circumstances they sometimes send to thieves they are acquainted with in London, who proceed thither and plunder the house. Sometimes, in similar circumstances, the London burglars get persons from the provinces to commit robberies in the metropolis—both parties sharing in the booty. In a place where they are not known, they do it themselves.

The burglars in our day are not in general such desperate men as those in former times. They are better known to the

CELL, WITH PRISONER AT "CRANK-LABOUR," IN THE SURREY HOUSE OF CORRECTION.

police than formerly, and are kept under more strict surveillance. Many of the cracksmen have been repeatedly subjected to prison discipline, and have their spirits in a great measure subdued. The crime of our country is not so bold and open as in the days of the redoubtable men whose dark deeds are recorded in the Newgate Calendar. It has assumed more subtle forms, instead of bold swagger and defiance—and has more of the secret, restless, and deceitful character of our great arch-enemy.

Number of burglaries in the Metropolitan districts for 1860 192
Ditto ditto in the City 12
———
204

Value of property abstracted in the Metropolitan districts £2,852
Ditto ditto in the City.. .. 332
———
£3,184

Narrative of a Burglar.

THE following narrative was given us by an expert burglar and returned convict we met one evening in the West-end of the metropolis. For a considerable number of years he had been engaged in a long series of burglareis connected with several gangs of thieves, and had been so singularly cunning and adroit in his movements he had never been caught in the act of plunder; but was at last betrayed into the hands of the police by one of his confederates, who had quarrelled with him while indulging rather freely in liquor. He was often employed as a putter up of burglaries in various parts of the metropolis, and was generally an outsider on the watch while some of his pals were rifling the house. We visited him at his house in one of the gloomiest lanes in a very low neighbourhood, inhabited chiefly by thieves and prostitutes, and took down from his lips the following recital. In the first part of his autobiography he was very frank and candid, but as he proceeded became more slow and calculating in his disclosures. We hinted to him he was "timid." "No," he replied, "I am not timid, but I am cautious, which you need not be surprised at." He was then seated by the fire beside his paramour, a very clever woman, whose history is perhaps as wild and romantic as his own. He is a slim-made man, beneath the middle size, with a keen dark intelligent eye, and about thirty-six years of age. He is good-looking, and very smart in his movements, and was in the attire of a well-dressed mechanic.

"I was born in the city of London in the year 1825. My father was foreman to a coach and harness-maker in Oxford Street. My mother, before her marriage, was a milliner. They had eleven children, and I was the youngest but two. I had six brothers and four sisters. My father had a good salary coming in to support his family, and we lived in comfort and respectability up to his death. He died when I was only about eight years old. My mother was left with eleven children, with very scanty means. Having to support so large a family she soon after became reduced in circumstances. My eldest brother was subject to fits, and died at the age of twenty-four years. He occupied my father's place while he lived. My second brother went to work at the same shop, but got into idle and dissipated habits, and was thrown out of employment. He afterwards got a situation in a lacemaker's shop, and had to leave for misconduct. He then went to a druggist's, and had to leave fo. the same cause. After this he got a situation as potman to a public-house, which completed his ruin. He took every opportunity to lead his younger brothers astray instead of setting us a good example.

"My brother next to him in age did not follow his bad courses, but I was not so fortunate. I went to school at Mr. Low's, Harp Alley, Farringdon Street, but I did not stay there long. At nine years of age I was sent out to work, to help to support myself. I went to work at cotton-winding, and only got 3s. a week. I sometimes worked all night, and had 9d. for it, in addition to my 3s., and often gained 3s. a week besides the six days' wages. I was very happy then to think I could earn so much money, being so young. At this time I was only nine years of age. My brother tried to tempt me to pilfer from my master, but he failed then. I afterwards got a better situation at a trunkmaker's in the City. There my mistress and young master took a liking to me. I was earning 7s. a week, and was only ten years of age. At this time my brother succeeded in tempting me to rob my employers after I had been two months in their service. I carried off wearing apparel and silver plate to the value of several pounds, which my brother disposed of, while he only gave me a few halfpence. I was suspected to be the thief, and was discharged in consequence. I got another situation in a bookbinder's shop, and was not eleven years old then.

My brother did not succeed for two or three months to get me to plunder my master, although he often tried to prevail on me to do so. My master had no plate to lose.

"I used to take out boards of books; one night my brother met me coming from the binder's with a truck loaded with books, stopt me, and pretended to be very kind by giving me money to go and buy a pie at a pie-shop. When I came out I found the books were gone and the truck empty. My brother was standing at the door waiting me, but he had companions who meantime emptied the truck of the whole of the contents. I told him he must know who had taken them, but he told me he did not. He desired me to say to my master that a strange man had sent me to get a pie for him and one for myself, and when I came back the books and the man had both disappeared. He told me if I did not say this I would get myself into trouble and him too. I went and told my master the tale my brother had told me. He sent for a policeman, and tried to frighten me to tell the truth. I would not alter from what I had told him, though he tried very hard to get me to do so. He kept me till Saturday night and discharged me, but endeavoured in the meanwhile to get me to unfold the truth, so I was thrown out of employment again.

"I then went to work at the blacking trade, and had a kinder master than ever. My wages were 7s. a week. I then made up my mind that my brother should not tempt me to steal another time. I was in this situation a year and nine months before my brother succeeded in inducing me to commit another robbery. My master was very kind and generous to me, increased my wages from 7s. to 16s. a week as I was becoming of more service to him.

"We made the blacking with sugar-candy and other ingredients. I was the only lad introduced into the apartment where the blacking was made and the sugar-candy was kept. My brother tempted me to bring him a small quantity of sugar-candy at first. I did so, and he threatened to let my mother know if I did not fetch more. At first I took home 7lbs. of candy, and at last would carry off a larger quantity. I used to get a trifle of money from my brother for this. Being strongly attached to him, up to this time he had great influence over me.

"One day, after bringing him a quantity of sugar-candy, I watched him to see where he sold it. He went into a shop in the City where the person retailed sweets. After he came out of the shop I went in and asked the man in the shop if he would buy some from me, as I was the brother of the young man who had just called in, and had got him the sugar-candy. He told me he would buy as much as I liked to bring.

"I used to bring large quantities to him, generally in the evening, and carried it in a bag. The sugar-candy I should have mixed in the blacking I laid aside till I had an opportunity of carrying it to the receiver. My master continued to be very fond of me, and had strong confidence in me until I got a young lad into the shop beside me, who knew what I had been doing, and informed him of my conduct. He wanted to get me discharged, as he thought he would get my situation, which he did. He told my master I was plundering him; but my master would not believe him until he pointed out a low coffee-house where I used to go, which was frequented by bad characters. My master came into this den of infamy one evening when I was there, and persuaded me to come away with him, which I did. He told me he would forget all I was guilty of, if I would keep better company and behave myself properly in future. I conducted myself better for about a week, but I had got inveigled into bad company through my brother. These lads waited about my employer's premises for me at meal-times and at night. At last they prevailed on me again to go to the same coffee-house. The young lad I had got into the shop beside me soon found means to acquaint my master. He came to see me in the coffee-house again; but I had been prevailed on to drink that evening, and was the worse of intoxicating liquor, although I was not fourteen years of age. My master tried all manner of kind means to persuade me to leave that house, but I would not do so, and insulted him for his kindness.

"On the following morning he paid a visit to my mother's house while I was at breakfast. My mother and he tried to persuade me to go back and finish my week's work, but I was too proud, and would not go back. He then paid my mother my fortnight's wages, and said if I would attend church twice each week he would again take me back into his service. I never attended any church at all, for I had then got into bad habits, and cared no more about work.

"I lived at home with my mother for a short time, and she was very kind to me, and gave me great indulgence. She wished me to remain at home with her to assist in her business as a greengrocer, and used to allow me from 1s. to 1s. 3d. of pocket-money a day. My old companions still followed me about, and prevailed on me to go to the Victoria Theatre. On one of these occasions I was much struck with the play of Oliver Twist. I also saw Jack Sheppard performed there, and was much impressed with it.

"Soon after this I left my mother's house, and took lodgings at the coffee-house, where my master found me, and engaged in an open criminal career. About this time ladies generally carried reticules on their arm. My companions were in the habit of following them and cutting the strings, and carrying them off. They sometimes contained a purse with money and other property. I occasionally engaged in these robberies for about three months. Sometimes I succeeded in getting a considerable sum of money; at other times only a few shillings.

"I was afterwards prevailed on to join another gang of thieves, expert shoplifters. They generally confined themselves to the stationers' shops, and carried off silver pencil-cases, silver and gold mounted scent-bottles, and other articles, and I was engaged for a month at this.

"Being well-dressed, I would go into a shop and price an article of jewellery, or such like valuable, and after getting it in my hand would dart out of the shop with it. I carried on this system occasionally, and was never apprehended, and became very venturesome in robbery.

"I was then about sixteen years of age. A young man came from sea of the name of Philip Scott, who had in former years been a playmate of mine. He requested me to go to one of the theatres with him, when Jack Sheppard was again performed. We were both remarkably pleased with the play, and soon after determined to try our hand at housebreaking.

"He knew of a place in the City where some plate could be got at. We went out one night with a screw-driver and a knife to plunder it. I assisted him in getting over a wall at the back of the house. He entered from a back-window by pushing the catch back with a knife. He had not been in above three quarters of an hour when he handed me a silver pot and cream-jug from the wall. I conveyed these to the coffee-shop in which we lodged, when we afterwards disposed of them. The young man was well acquainted with this house, as his father was often employed jobbing about it.

"After this I cohabited with a female, but my 'pal' did not, although we lived in the same house.

"Soon after we committed another burglary in the south-side of the metropolis, by entering the kitchen window of a private house at the back. I watched while my comrade entered the house. He cut a pane of glass out, and drew the catch back. After gathering what plate he could find lying about, he went up-stairs and got some more plate. We sold this to a receiver in Clerkenwell for about 9l. 18s. From this house we also carried off some wearing apparel. Each of us took three shirts, two coats and an umbrella.

"Some time after this we made up our minds to try another burglary in the city. We secreted ourselves in a brewer's yard beside the house we intended to plunder, about eight o'clock in the evening, before it was shut up. We cut a panel out of a shutter in the dining-room window on the first floor, but were disturbed when attempting this robbery. I ran off and got away. My companion was not so fortunate; he was captured, and got several months' imprisonment.

"A week after I joined two other burglars. We resolved to attempt a burglary in a certain shop in the East-end of the metropolis. There happened to be a dog in the shop. As usual I kept watch outside, while the other two entered from the first-floor window, which had no shutters. So soon as they got in the dog barked. They cut the dog's throat with a knife, and began to plunder the shop of pencil cases, scent-bottles, postage-stamps, &c., and went up-stairs, and carried off pieces of plate. The inmates of the house slept in the upper part of the house. The property when brought to the receiver sold for about 42l.

"Another burglary was committed by us at a haberdasher's shop in the West-end. While I kept watch, the other two climbed to the top of a warehouse at the back of the shop, wrenched open the window on the roof, and having tied a rope to an iron bar, they lowered themselves down, broke open the desks and till, and got a considerable sum of money, nearly all in silver. They then went to the first-floor drawing-room window over the shop, and entered. The door of this room being locked, they cut out a panel, put their arm through and forced back the lock. They found only a small quantity of plate along with a handsome gold watch and chain. The few articles of plate sold for 38s., and the watch and chain for 7l. 15s.

"The thieves entered about one o'clock at midnight, and went out about a quarter past five in the morning.

"These are the only jobs I did with these two men, until my comrade came out of prison, when we commenced again. We committed burglaries in different parts of London, at silk-mercers, stationers' shops, and dwelling-houses—some of considerable value; in others the booty was small.

"In these burglaries numbers of other parties were engaged with us—some of them belonging to the Borough, others to St. Giles's, Golden Lane, St. Luke's, and other localities.

"In 1850 I took a part in a burglary in a shop in the south-side of the metropolis along with two other parties. One went inside, and the others were on the watch without. We got access to the shop by the back-yard of a neighbouring public-house, which is usually effected in this way. One person goes to the bar, and gets into conversation with the barmaid, while one or more of their 'pals' takes a favourable opportunity of slipping back into the yard or court behind the house. This is often done about a quarter of an hour, or half an hour, before the house is shut up. The party who kept the barmaid in conversation, would go to the back of the house, and assist the other burglar who was to enter the house in getting over the wall. So soon as this is effected, his other 'pal' comes out again. If the wall can be easily climbed, the party who enters lurks concealed in the water-closet, or some of the outhouses, till the time of effecting the burglary.

"The house intended to be entered is sometimes five or six houses away from this public-house, and sometimes the next house to it.

"When all is ready, the outside man gives the signal. The signal given from the front, such as a cough or otherwise, can be heard by his confederate behind the house. On hearing it the latter begins his work. In this instance the burglar entered the premises by cutting open the shutters of a window in the first floor to the back. He then cut a pane of glass, and removed the catch, and went down stairs into the shop, and took from a desk about 60*l.* in money, with several valuable snuff-boxes and other articles. He had to wait till the morning before he could get out. The police seemed to have a suspicion that all was not right, but he got out of the shop about the time when the police were changed.

"I was connected with another burglary, committed in the same year in the West-end in a linendraper's shop. It was entered from a public-house in the same manner as in the one described. The same person was engaged inside, while the others were stationed outside. The signal to begin work was given about one o'clock. He had first to remove an iron bar at the first floor landing window to the back, which he did with his jack. (The bars had been seen in the day-time, and we bought this instrument to remove them.) He removed the bar in ten minutes, cut a pane of glass, and removed the two catches. By this means he effected an entry into the house, and to his surprise found the drawing-room was left unlocked. He proceeded there, and got nearly a whole service of plate. After he had gathered the plate up, he made his way toward the shop, cutting through the door which intercepted him. He went to the desk and found 72*l.* in silver money, and 12*l.* in gold. He also packed up half a dozen of new shirts and half a dozen of silk handkerchiefs.

"He was ready to come out of the house, but a coffee-stall being opposite, and the policeman taking his coffee there, the outside man could not give him the signal for some time. To the great surprise of the burglar in the shop, he heard the servant coming down stairs, when he opened the door, and rushed suddenly out, while the policeman was on the kerb near by. He bade the policeman good morning as he passed along with two large bundles in his hands.

"He had not gone fifty yards round the corner of the street, before the servant appeared at the door and asked the policeman as to the person who had just come out. Along with other two constables he gave chase to the burglar, but, being an active, athletic man, he effected his escape.

"I was engaged with two others in another burglary in the West-end soon afterwards. Three persons were engaged in it: one to enter, and other two 'pals' to keep watch. We got access to the house by a mews, and got on the top of a wall, when I gave the end of a rope to my companion to hold by while he slid down on the other side. The house was entered at the kitchen window by removing two narrow bars with the jack, and sliding back the catch. There was no booty to be found in the kitchen. On going up-stairs our 'pal' got several pieces of plate, and other articles. On coming down into the shop, he got a quantity of receipt-stamps with a few postage-stamps.

"The putter up of this robbery was a connection of the people of the house.

"I was connected with another burglary in the south-side of the metropolis. A man who frequented a public-house there put up a burglary in a stationer's shop. Two persons were engaged in it, and got access to the premises to be plundered from the public-house. He then climbed several walls, and got access to the shop by a fanlight from behind. Here we found a large sum of money in gold and silver, which had been deposited in a bureau, some plate, and other articles. His 'pal' went to him at half past three, and gave him the signal. He came out soon after, and had only gone a short distance off when he heard a call for the police, and the rattle of the policeman was sprung.

"After a desperate struggle with two constables, he was arrested and taken to the station, with the stolen property in his possession. He was tried and found guilty of committing the burglary, and for assaulting the constables by cutting and wounding them, and was sentenced to fourteen years' transportation, having been four times previously convicted.

"I have been engaged in many depredations from 1840 to 1851, many of which were 'put up' by myself.

"In the year 1851 I was transported several years for burglary. I returned home on a ticket of leave in 1854, and was sent back in the following year for harbouring an escaped convict. I returned home in 1858, at the expiry of my sentence, and since that time have abandoned my former criminal life."

Narrative of another Burglar.

One evening as we had occasion to be in a narrow dark by-street in St. Giles's, we were accosted by a burglar—a returned convict whom we had met on a former occasion in the course of our rambles. We had repeatedly heard of this person as one of the most daring thieves in the metropolis, and were on the look-out for him at the very time when he fortunately crossed our path. He is a fair-complexioned man, of thirty-two years of age, about 5 feet 2 inches in height, slim made, with a keen grey eye. He was dressed in dark trousers, brown vest, and a grey frock coat buttoned up to the chin, and a cap drawn over his eyes. We hesitated at first as to whether this little man was capable of executing such venturesome feats; when he led us along the dark street to an adjoining back-court, took off his shoes and stockings, and ran up a waterspout to the top of a lofty house, and slid down again with surprising agility. Before we parted that evening, he was recommended to us by another burglar, a returned convict, and by another most intelligent young man, whom we are sorry to say has been a convicted criminal. He afterwards paid us a visit, when we were furnished with the following recital:—

"I was born in the parish of St. Giles's in the Fields, in the year 1828. My father was a soldier in the British service; after his discharge he lived for some time in the neighbourhood of St. Giles's. He was an Irishman from the county of Limerick. My mother belonged to Cork. My eldest sister was married to a plasterer in London; my second sister has been sentenced to four years, and another sister to five years' transportation, both for stealing watches on different occasions. I have another sister, who lately came out of prison after eighteen months' imprisonment, and is now living an honest life.

"I was never sent by my parents to school, but have learned to read a little by my own exertions; I have no knowledge of writing and arithmetic. I was sent out to get my living at ten years of age by selling oranges in the streets in a basket, and was very soon led into bad company. I sometimes played at pitch and toss, which trained me to gamble, and I often lost my money by this means.

"I often remained out all night, and slept in the dark arches of the Adelphi on straw along with some other boys—one of them was a pickpocket who learned me to steal. It was not long before I was apprehended and committed at the Middlesex Assizes, and received six months' imprisonment.

"At this time I learned to swim, and was remarkably expert at it: when the tide was out I often used to swim across the Thames for sport. I continued to pick pockets occasionally for two years, and was at one time remanded for a week on a criminal charge and afterwards discharged. I used to take ladies' purses by myself, and stole handkerchiefs, snuff-boxes, and pocketbooks from the tails of gentlemen's coats.

"I left my home on the expiry of my six months' imprisonment for stealing a pocketbook. My parents would gladly have taken me back, but I would not go. At this time I associated with a number of juvenile thieves. I had a good suit of clothes, which had been purchased before I went to prison, and having a respectable appearance I took to shop-lifting. I worked at this about seven months, when I was arrested for stealing a coat at a shop in the Borough Road, and was sentenced to three months in Brixton Prison.

"When I got out of prison I went to St. Giles's and cohabited with a prostitute. I was then about seventeen years of age. She was a fair girl, about five feet three inches in height, inclined to be stout,—a very handsome girl, about seventeen years of age. Her people lived in Tottenham Court Road, and were very respectable. She had been led astray before I met her, through the bad influence of another girl, and was a common prostitute. She was very kind-hearted. She was not long with me when I engaged with other two persons in a housebreaking in the West-end of the metropolis. On the basement of the house we intended to plunder was a counting-house, while the upper floors were occupied by the family as a dwelling-house. Our chief object was to get to the counting-house, which could be entered from the back. Our mode of entering was this.—At one o'clock in the morning, one of the party was set to watch in the street, to give us the signal when no one was near—a young man was on the watch, while I and another climbed up by a waterspout to the roof of the counting-house. There was no other way of getting in but by cutting the lead off the house and making an opening sufficient for us to pass through.

"The signal was given to enter the house, but at this time the policeman saw our shadow on the roof and sprung his rattle. The party who was keeping watch and my 'pal' on the roof both got away, but I hurt myself in getting down from the house-top to the street. I was apprehended and lodged in prison, and was tried at Middlesex Assizes and sentenced to nine months' imprisonment.

"So soon as the time was expired, I met with another gang of burglars, more expert than the former. At this time I lived at Shoreditch, in the East-end of the metropolis. Four of us were associated together, averaging from twenty-two to twenty-three years of age. We engaged in a burglary in the City. It was hard to do. I was one of those selected to enter the shop; we had to climb over several walls before we reached the premises we intended to plunder. We cut through a panel of the back door. On finding my way into the shop I opened the door to my companions. We packed up some silks and other goods, and remained there very comfortable till the change of the policeman in the morning, when a cart was drawn up to the door, and the outside man gave us the signal. We drew the bolts and brought out the bags containing the booty, put them into the cart, and closed the door after us. We drove off to our lodgings, and sent for a person to purchase the goods. We got a considerable sum by this burglary, which was divided among us. I was then about twenty-two years of age. Our money was soon expended in going to theatres and in gambling, and besides we lived very expensively on the best viands, with wines and other liquors.

"We perpetrated another burglary in the West-end. Three of us were engaged in it; one was stationed to watch, while I and another pal had to go in. We entered an empty house by skeleton-keys, and got into the next house; we lifted the trap off and got under the roof, and found an under-trap was fastened inside. We knew we could do nothing without the assistance of an umbrella. My comrade went down to our pal on the watch, and told him to buy an umbrella from some passer-by, the night being damp and rainy. We purchased one from a man in the vicinity for 2s.; my comrade brought it up to me under the roof. Having cut away several lathes, I made an opening with my knife in the plaster, and inserted the closed umbrella through it, and opened it with a jerk, to contain the falling wood and plaster. I broke some of the lathes off, and tore away some of the mortar, which fell in the umbrella. We effected an entry into the house from the roof. On going over the apartments we did not find what we expected; after all our trouble we only got 35*l.*, some trinkets, and one piece of plate.

"Burglars become more expert at their work by experience. Many of them are connected with some of the first mechanics in the metropolis. Wherever a patent lock can be found they frequently get a key to fit it. In this way even Chubbs and Bramahs can be opened, as burglars endeavour to get keys of this description of locks. They sometimes give 5*l.* for the impression of a single key, and make one of the same description, which serves for the same size of such locks on other occasions. An experienced burglar thereby has more facilities to open locks—even those which are patented.

"I was connected with two pals in another burglary in a dwelling-house at the West-end. It was arranged that I should enter the house. I was lifted to the top of a wall about sixteen feet high, at the back of the premises, and had to come down by the ivy which grew on the garden wall; I had to get across another wall. The ivy was very thick, so that I had to cut part of it away to allow me to get over. I entered the house by the window without difficulty, having removed the catch in the middle with my knife. On a dressing-table in one of the bedrooms I found a gold watch, ring and chain, with 3*l.* 15*s.* in money, and a brace of double-barrelled pistols, which I secured. In the drawing-room I found some desert-spoons, a punch-ladle, and other pieces of silver plate—I looked to them to see they had the proper mark of silver; I found them to be silver, and folded them up carefully and put them into my pocket. On looking into some concealed drawers in a cabinet I found a will and other papers, which I knew were of no use to me; I put them back in their place and did not destroy any of them. I also found several articles of jewellery, and a few Irish one-pound notes. I put them all carefully in my pocket and came to the front-door. The signal was given that the cab was ready; I went out, drew the door close after me, and went away with the booty.

"I entered about half-past eleven o'clock at night, and came out at half-past two o'clock. I saw a servant-girl sleeping in the back-kitchen, and two young ladies in a back-parlour. I did not go up to the top-floors, but heard them snoring. They awoke and spoke two or three times, which made me be careful.

"I went along the passage very softly, in case I should have awakened the two young ladies in the back parlour as well as the servant in the kitchen. All was so quiet that the least sound in the world would have disturbed them.

"I opened the door gently, and came out when the signal was given by my comrades. It was a cold, wet morning, which was favourable to us, as no one was about the street to see us, and the policeman was possibly, as on similar occasions, standing in some corner smoking his pipe. I jumped into the cab along with my two pals, and went to Westminster. The booty amounted to a considerable sum, which was divided among us. We spent the next three or four weeks very merrily along with our girls. On this occasion we gave the cabman two sovereigns for his trouble, whether the burglary came off or not, and plenty of drink.

"A short time after, a person came up to me with whom I had associated, and played cards over some liquor in the West-end. He was a young man out of employment. He thus accosted me, 'Jim, how are you getting on?' I answered, 'Pretty well.' He asked me if I had any job on hand. I said I had not. I inquired if he had anything for me to do. He said he would give me a turn at the house of an old mistress of his. He told me the dressing-case with jewels lay in a back room on a table, but cautioned me to be very careful the butler did not see me, as he was often going up and down stairs. Two of us resolved to plunder the house. My companion was on the outside to watch, while I had to enter the house.

"I got in with a skeleton key while they were at supper, and got up the stairs without any one observing me. On going to the back room I was disturbed by a young lady coming up stairs. I ran up to the second floor above to hide myself, and found a bed in the apartment. I concealed myself underneath the bed, when the lady and her servant came into the room with a light. They closed the door and pulled the curtains down, when the lady began to undress in presence of the servant. The servant began to wash her face and neck. The lady was a beautiful young creature. While lying under the bed I distinctly saw the maid put perfume on the lady's under linen. She then began to dress and decorate herself, and told the servant she was going out to her supper. She said she would not be home till two or three o'clock in the morning, and did not wish the servant to remain up for her, but to leave the lamp burning. As soon as she and the waiting-maid had left the room, I got out of my hiding-place, and on looking around saw but a small booty, consisting of a small locket and gold chain; a gold pencil-case, and silver thimble. As I was returning down stairs with them in my pocket to get to the first floor back, I got possession of a case of jewels, which I thought of great value. I returned to the hall, and came out about twelve o'clock without any signal from my comrade.

"On taking the jewels to a person who received such plunder, he told us they were of small value, and were not brilliants and emeralds as we fancied. They were set in pure gold of the best quality, and only brought us 22*l.*

"To look at them we fancied they would have been worth a much higher sum, and were sadly disappointed.

"Soon after we resolved on another burglary in the West-end. One kept watch without while two of us entered the house by a grating underneath the shop window, and descended into the kitchen by a rope. We got a signal to work. The first thing we did was to lift up the kitchen window. When we got in we pulled the kitchen window down, drew down the blind, and lighted our taper. We looked round and saw nothing worth removing. We went to the staircase to get into the shop. As we were wrenching open a chest of drawers, a big cat which happened to be in the room was afraid of us. We got pieces of meat out of the safe and threw them to the cat. The animal was so excited that it jumped up on the mantelpiece, and broke a number of ornaments. This disturbed an old gentleman in the first-floor front. He called out to his servant, 'John, there is somebody in the house.' We had no means of getting the door open, and had to go out by the window. The old gentleman came down stairs in his nightgown with a brace of pistols, just as we were going out of the window. He fired, but missed us. I jumped so hastily that I hurt my bowels, and was conveyed by my companions in a cab to Westminster, and lay there for six weeks in an enfeebled condition. My money was spent, and as my young woman could not get any, my companions said you had better have a meeting of our "pals." A friendly meeting was held, and they collected about 8*l*. to assist me.

"When I recovered, to my great loss, my companion was taken on account of a job he had been attempting in Regent's Park. He was committed to the Old Bailey, tried, and transported for life. He was a good pal of mine, and for a time I supported his wife and children. On another occasion, I and another comrade met a potman at the West-end. He asked us for something to drink, as he said he was out of work. We did so, and also gave him something to eat. We entered into conversation with him. He told us about a house he lately served in, and said there could be a couple of hundreds got there or more before the brewer's bill was paid. We found out when the brewer's bill was to be paid. We asked the man where this money was kept. He told us that we would find it in the second-floor back.

"We made arrangements as to the night when we would go. Three of us went out as usual. We found the lady of the house and her daughter serving at the bar. We had to pass the bar to go upstairs. There was a row got up in the tap-room with my companions. While the landlady ran in to see what was the matter, and the daughter ran out for the policeman, I slipped upstairs, and got into the room. The policeman knew one of my companions when he came in, and at once suspected there was some design. He asked if there had been any more besides these two. The landlady said there was another. I was coming down stairs with the cash-box when I heard this conversation. The constable asked leave to search the house. I ran with the cash-box up the staircase, and looked in the back room to see if there was any place to get away, but there was none. I took the cash-box up to the front garret, and was trying to break it open, but in the confusion I could not.

"I fled out of the garret window and got on the roof to hide from the policeman. My footsteps were observed on the carpet and on the gutters as I went out and slipped in the mud on the roof. I intended to throw the cash-box to my companions, but they gave me the signal to get away. I had just time to take my boots off, when another constable came out of the garret window of the other house. I had no other alternative but to get along the roof where they could not follow me, and besides I was much nimbler than they. I went to the end of the row of houses, and did not go down the garret window near me. Seeing a waterspout leading to a stable-yard, I slipt down it, and climbed up another spout to the roof of the stable. I lay there for five hours till the police changed.

"I managed to get down and went into the stable-yard, when the stable-man cried out, 'Hollo! here he is.' I saw there was no alternative but to fight for it. I had a jemmy in my pocket. He laid hold of me, when I struck him on the face with it, and he fell to the ground. I fled to the door, and came out into the main street, returned into Piccadilly, and passed through the Park gates. On coming home to Westminster I found one of my comrades had not come home. We sent to the police-station, and learned he was there. We sent him some provisions, and he gave us notice in a piece of paper concealed in some bread that I should keep out of the way as the police were after me, which would aggravate his case.

"I then went to live at Whitechapel. Meantime some clever detectives were on my track, from information they received from the girls we used to cohabit with. We heard of this from a quarter some would not suspect. He told us to keep out of the way, and that he would let us know should he get any further information. At last my companion was committed for trial, tried, and sentenced to seven years' transportation. I did not join in any other burglary for some time after this, as the police were vigilantly looking for me. I kept myself concealed in the house of a cigar-maker in Whitechapel.

"Another pal and I went one evening to a public-house in Whitechapel. My pal was a tall, athletic young fellow, of about nineteen years, handsomely dressed, with gold ring and pin, intelligent and daring. We had gone in to have a glass of rum-and-water, when we saw a sergeant belonging to a regiment of the line sitting in front of the bar. He asked us if we would have anything to drink. We said we would. He called for three glasses of brandy-and-water, and asked my companion if he would take a cigar. He did so. The sergeant said he was a fine young man, and would make an excellent soldier. On this he pulled out a purse of money and looked at the time on his gold watch. My comrade looked to me and gave me a signal, at the same time saying to the soldier, 'Sergeant, I'll 'list.' He took the shilling offered him, and pretended to give him his name and address, giving a false alias, so that he should not be able to trace him.

"He called for half a pint of rum and water, and put down the shilling he received from the sergeant. We took him into the bagatelle-room, and tried to get him to play with us, as we had a number of counterfeit sovereigns and forged cheques about us. He would not play except for a pint of half-and-half. On this he left us, and went in the direction of the barracks in Hyde Park. My comrade said to me, 'We shall not leave him till we have plundered him.' I was then the worse for liquor. We followed him. When he reached the Park gates I whispered to my companion that I would garotte him if he would assist me. He said he would. On this I sprung at his neck. Being a stronger man than I, he struggled violently. I still kept hold of him until he became senseless. My companion took his watch, his pocket-book, papers, and money, consisting of some pieces of gold, and a 5l. note. We sold the gold watch and chain for 8l.

"Along with my pal, I went into a skittle-ground in the City to have a game at skittles by ourselves, when two skittle-sharps who knew us well quarrelled with us about the game. My companion and I made a bet with them, which we lost, chiefly owing to my fault, which irritated him. He said, 'Never mind; there is more money in the world, and we will have it ere long, or they shall have us.' One of the skittle-sharps said to us insultingly, 'Go and thieve for more, and we will play you.' On this we got angry at them. My pal took up his life-preserver, and struck the skittle-sharp on the head.

"A policeman was sent for to apprehend him. I put the life-preserver in the fire as the door was shut on us, and we could not get away. On the policeman coming in my pal was to be given in charge by the landlord and landlady of the house. The skittle-sharp who had been struck rose up bleeding, and said to the landlord and landlady, 'What do you know of the affair? Let us settle the matter between ourselves.' The policeman declined to interfere. We took brandy-and-water with the skittle-sharps, and parted in the most friendly terms.

"One day we happened to see a gentleman draw a pocket-book out of his coat-pocket, and relieve a poor crossing-sweeper with a piece of silver. He returned it into his pocket. I said to my pal, 'Here is a piece of money for us.' I followed after him and came up to him about Regent's Park, put my hand into his coat-pocket, seized the pocket-book, and passed it to my comrade. An old woman who kept an apple-stall had seen me; and when my back was turned went up and told the gentleman. The latter followed us until he saw a policeman, while I was not aware of it; being eager to know the contents of the pocket-book I had handed to my comrade, he being at the time in distress. We went into a public-house to see the contents, and called for a glass of brandy-and-water. We found there were three 10l. notes and a 5l. note, and two sovereigns, with some silver. The policeman meantime came in and seized my hand, and at the same time took the pocket-book from me before I had time to prevent him.

"The gentleman laid hold of my companion, but was struck to the ground by the latter. He then assisted to rescue me from the policeman. By the assistance of the potman and a few men in the taproom, they overpowered me, but my comrade got away. I was taken to the police court and committed for trial, and was afterwards tried and sentenced to seven years transportation.

"On one occasion, after my return from transportation, I and a companion of mine met a young woman we were well acquainted with who belonged to our own class of Irish cockneys. She was then a servant in a family next door to a surgeon. She asked us how we were getting on, and treated us to brandy. We asked her if we could rifle her mistress's house, when she said she was very kind to her, and she would not permit us to hurt a hair of her head or to take away a farthing of her property. She told us there was a surgeon who lived next door—a young man who was out at all hours of the night, and sometimes all night. She informed us there was nobody in the house but an old servant who slept up stairs in a garret.

"The door opened by a latch-key, and when the surgeon was out the gas was generally kept rather low in the hall. We watched him go out one evening at eleven o'clock, applied a key to the door, and entered the house. The young woman promised to give us the signal when the surgeon came in. We had not been long in when we heard the signal given. I got under the sofa in his surgical room; the gas used to burn there all night while he was out. My companion was behind a chest of drawers which stood at a small distance from the wall. As the surgeon came in I saw him take his hat off, when he sat down on the sofa above me.

"As he was taking his boots off, he bent down and saw one of my feet under the sofa. He laid hold of it, and dragged me from under the sofa. He was a strong man, and kneeled on my back with my face turned to the floor. I gave a signal to my companion behind him, who struck him a violent blow on the back, not to hurt him, but to stun him, which felled him to the floor. I jumped up and ran out of the door with my companion. He ran after us and followed us through the street while I ran in my stockings. Our female friend, the servant, had the presence of mind and courage to run into the house and get my boots. She carried them into the house of her employer, and then looked out and gave the alarm of 'Thieves!' We got a booty of 43*l.*

"One night I went to an Irish penny ball in St. Giles's, and had a dance with a young Irish girl of about nineteen years of age. This was the first time she saw me. I was a good dancer, and she was much pleased with me. She was a beautiful and handsome girl—a costermonger, and a good dancer. We went out and had some intoxicating liquor, which she had not been used to. She wished me to make her a present of a white silk handkerchief, with the shamrock, rose, and thistle on it, and a harp in the middle, which I could not refuse her. She gave me in exchange a green handkerchief from her neck. We corresponded after this for some time. She did not know then that I was a burglar and thief. She asked me my occupation, and I told her I was a pianoforte maker. One night I asked her to come out with me to go to a penny Irish ball. I kept her out late, and seduced her. She did not go back to her friends any more, but cohabited with me.

"One night after this we went to a public singing-room, and I got jealous by her taking notice of another young man. I did not speak to her that night about it. Next morning I told her it was better that she should go home to her friends, as I would not live with her any more.

"She cried over it, and afterwards went home. Her friends got her a situation in the West-end as a servant, but she was pregnant at the time with a child to me. She was not long in service before her young master fell in love with her, and kept her in fashionable style, which he has continued to do ever since. She now lives in elegant apartments in the West-end, and her boy, my son, is getting a college education. I do not take any notice of them now.

"One night on my return from transportation I met two old associates. They asked me how I was, and told me they were glad to see me. They inquired how I was getting on. I told them I was not getting along very well. They asked me if I was associated with any one. I told them I was not, and was willing to go out with them to a bit of work. These men were burglars, and wished me to join them in plundering a shop in the metropolis. I told them I did not mind going with them. They arranged I should enter the shop along with another 'pal,' and the other was to keep watch. On the night appointed for the work we met an old watchman, and asked him what o'clock it was. One of our party pretended to be drunk, and said he would treat him to two or three glasses of rum. Meantime I and my companion entered the house by getting over a back wall and entering a window there by starring the glass, and pulling the catch back. When we got in we did not require to break open any lockfast. We packed up apparel of the value of 60*l.* We remained in the shop till six o'clock, when the change of officers took place. The door was then unbolted—a cab was drawn up to the shop. I shut the door and went off in one direction on foot, while one 'pal' went off in a cab, and the other to the receiver at Whitechapel.

"I have been engaged in about eighteen burglaries besides other depredations, some of them in fashionable shops and dwelling-houses in the West-end. Some of them have been effected by skeleton keys, others by climbing waterspouts, at which I am considered to be extraordinary nimble, and others by obtaining an entry through the doors or windows. I have been imprisoned seven times in London and elsewhere, and have been twice transported. Altogether I have been in prison for about fourteen years.

"My first wife died broken-hearted the second time I was transported. Since I came home this last time I have lived an honest, industrious life with my second wife and family."

PROSTITUTE THIEVES.

On taking up this subject, although it is treated comprehensively in another part of this work, we found it impossible to draw an exact distinction between prostitution and the prostitute thieves. Even at the risk of a little repetition we now give a short resumé of the whole subject, dwelling particularly on the part more especially in our province—the Prostitute Thieves of London.

The prostitution of the metropolis, so widely ramified like a deadly upas tree over the length and breadth of its districts, may be divided into four classes, determined generally by the personal qualities, bodily and mental, of the prostitute, by the wealth and position of the person who supports her, and by the localities in which she resides and gains her ignoble livelihood.

The first class consists of those who are supported by gentlemen in high position in society, wealthy merchants and professional men, gentry and nobility, and are kept as *seclusives*.

The second class consists of the better educated and more genteel girls, who live in open prostitution, some of them connected with respectable middle-class families.

The third class is composed of domestic servants and the daughters of labourers, mechanics, and others in the humbler walks in life.

The fourth class comprises old worn-out prostitutes sunk in poverty and debasement.

We may take each class of prostitutes and illustrate it in the order set down, extending our field of observation over the wide districts of the metropolis; or we may select several leading districts as representatives of the whole, and proceed in more minute detail. We adopt the latter plan, as it presents us with a fuller and more graphic view of the subject.

The first class consists of young ladies, in many cases well-educated and well-connected, such as the daughters of professional men, physicians, lawyers, clergymen, and military officers, as well as of respectable farmers, merchants, and other middle-class people, and governesses; also of many persons possessed of high personal attractions —ballet-girls, milliners, dressmakers and shop-girls, chambermaids and table-maids in aristocratic families or at first-class hotels. Many of them are brought from happy homes in the provinces to London by fashionable villains, military or civilian, and basely seduced, and kept to minister to their lust. Others are seduced in the metropolis while residing with their parents, or when pursuing their avocations in shops, dwelling-houses, or hotels.

Many a young lady from the provinces has been entrapped by wealthy young men, frequently young military officers, who have met them at ball-rooms, where they may have shone in all the beauty of health and innocence, the darlings of their home, the pride of their parents' hearts, and the "cynosure of every eye," or these fashionable rakes may have got introduced to their families, and been shown marked kindness. But in return they entice the poor girls from their parents, dishonour them, and destroy the peace of their homes for ever.

Many young ladies possessing fair accomplishments are also entrapped in the metropolis—at the Argyle Rooms, Holborn Assembly-room, and other fashionable resorts. In many cases pretty young girls,—servants in noblemen's families, barmaids, waiting-maids in hotels, and chambermaids, may have attracted the attention of gay gentlemen who had induced them to cohabit with them, or to live in apartments provided for them, where they are kept in grand style. Some are maintained at the rate of 800*l.* a year, keep a set of servants, drive out in their brougham, and occasionally ride in Rotten Row. Others are supported at still greater expense.

As a general rule they do not live in the same house with the gentleman, though sometimes they do. Such women are often kept by wealthy merchants, officers in the army, members of the House of Commons and House of Peers, and others in high life.

As a rule gay ladies keep faithful to the gentlemen who support them. Many of them ride in Rotten Row with a groom behind them, attend the theatres and operas, and go to Brighton, Ramsgate, and Margate, and over to Paris.

When the young women they fancy are not well educated, tutors and governesses are provided to train them in accomplishments, to enable them to move with elegance and grace in the drawing-room, or to travel on the Continent. They are taught French, music, drawing, and the higher accomplishments.

Sometimes these girls belong to the lower orders of society, and may have been selected for their beauty and fascination. The daughter of a labouring man, a beautiful girl, is kept by a gentleman in high position at St. John's Wood at the rate of 800*l.* a year. She has now received a lady's education, rides in Rotten Row, has a set of servants, moves in certain fashionable circles, keeps aloof from the gaiety of the Haymarket, and lives as though she were a married woman.

Let us take another illustration. A young girl was brought up to London several years ago by a military man. He kept her for three weeks, and then left her in a coffee-shop in Panton Street as a dressed lodger. She has since been kept at Chelsea by a gentleman in a Government situation, and occasionally drives out in her chaise with her groom behind. She frequents the Argyle Rooms and the cafés, the Carlton supper-rooms, and Sally's. She was brought away from the provinces when she was seventeen, and is now about twenty-five years of age.

These females are kept from ages varying from sixteen and upwards, and live chiefly in the suburbs of the metropolis—Brompton, Chelsea, St. John's Wood, Haverstock Hill, and on the Hampstead Road.

This class of ladies are often kept by elderly men, military, naval, or otherwise, some of them having wives and families. In such cases the former sometimes have a younger fancy-man. They visit him by private arrangement, and keep it very quiet. Occasionally such things do come to light, and the elderly gentlemen part with them.

They dress very expensively in silks, satins, and muslins, in most fashionable style, glittering with costly jewellery, perhaps of the value of 150*l.*, like the first ladies in the land. Sometimes they become intemperate, and are abandoned by their paramours, and in the course of a short time pawn their jewels and fine dresses, and betake themselves to prostitution in the Waterloo Road, and ultimately go with the most degraded labouring men for a few coppers.

Many of them are very unfortunate, and are discarded by the gentlemen who support them on the slightest caprice, perhaps to give way to some other young woman. To secure his object he occasionally maltreats her, and attempts to create a misunderstanding between them, or he absents himself from her for a time, meantime taking care to introduce some person stealthily into her company to ensnare her, and find some pretext to abandon her, so that her friends may have no ground for an action at law against him.

In some instances these females after having run their fashionable careeer, get married; in others they may have managed to save some money to provide for the future. But in too many cases they are heartlessly abandoned by the men who formerly supported them, and glide down step by step into lower degradation, till many of them come to the workhouse, or the hospital, or to some secluded garret, or it may be rush into a suicide's grave. Volumes might be written on this tragical theme, where fact would far transcend the heart-rending recitals of fiction.

Having briefly adverted to the higher order of prostitutes, kept as seclusives by men of wealth, high station, and title, we shall now turn our attention to the open prostitutes who traverse the streets of the metropolis for their livelihood. With this view, we shall not treat first of the lower order of prostitutes, and proceed to the higher, but keeping in mind the principle with which we started—the progressive downward nature of crime,—we shall commence at the higher order of prostitutes, and afterwards notice the more debased. At the same time we shall select several of the more prominent localities as a sample of the whole districts of this vast metropolis. We shall notice the Haymarket, Bishopgate Street, and Waterloo Road, the Parks, Westminster, and Ratcliff Highway. We shall first advert to

THE PROSTITUTES OF THE HAYMARKET.

A STRANGER on his coming to London, after visiting the Crystal Palace, British

Museum, St. James's Palace, and Buckingham Palace, and other public buildings, seldom leaves the capital before he makes an evening visit to the Haymarket and Regent Street. Struck as he is with the dense throng of people who crowd along London Bridge, Fleet Street, Cheapside, Holborn, Oxford Street, and the Strand, perhaps no sight makes a more striking impression on his mind than the brilliant gaiety of Regent Street and the Haymarket. It is not only the architectural splendour of the aristocratic streets in that neighbourhood, but the brilliant illumination of the shops, cafés, Turkish divans, assembly halls, and concert rooms, and the troops of elegantly dressed courtesans, rustling in silks and satins, and waving in laces, promenading along these superb streets among throngs of fashionable people, and persons apparently of every order and pursuit, from the ragged crossing-sweeper and tattered shoeblack to the high-bred gentleman of fashion and scion of nobility.

Not to speak of the first class of kept women, who are supported by men of opulence and rank in the privacy of their own dwellings, the whole of the other classes are to be found in the Haymarket, from the beautiful girl with fresh blooming cheek, newly arrived from the provinces, and the pale, elegant, young lady from a milliner's shop in the aristocratic Westend, to the old, bloated women who have grown grey in prostitution, or become invalid through venereal disease.

We shall first advert to the highest class who walk the Haymarket, which in our general classification we have termed the second class of prostitutes.

They consist of the better educated and more genteel girls, some of them connected with respectable middle-class families. We do not say that they are well-educated and genteel, but either well-educated or genteel. Some of these girls have a fine appearance, and are dressed in high style, yet are poorly educated, and have sprung from an humble origin. Others, who are more plainly dressed, have had a lady's education, and some are not so brilliant in their style, who have come from a middle-class home. Many of these girls have at one time been milliners or sewing girls in genteel houses in the West-end, and have been seduced by shopmen, or by gentlemen of the town, and after being ruined in character, or having quarrelled with their relatives, may have taken to a life of prostitution; others have been waiting maids in hotels, or in service in good families, and have been seduced by servants in the family, or by gentlemen in the house, and betaken themselves to a wild life of pleasure. A considerable number have come from the provinces to London, with unprincipled young men of their acquaintance, who after a short time have deserted them, and some of them have been enticed by gay gentlemen of the West-end, when on their provincial tours. Others have come to the metropolis in search of work, and been disappointed. After spending the money they had with them, they have resorted to the career of a common prostitute. Others have come from provincial towns, who had not a happy home, with a stepfather or stepmother. Some are young milliners and dressmakers at one time in business in town, but being unfortunate, are now walking the Haymarket. In addition to these, many of them are seclusives turned away or abandoned by the persons who supported them, who have recourse to a gay life in the West-end There are also a considerable number of French girls, and a few Belgian and German prostitutes who promenade this locality. You see many of them walking along in black silk cloaks or light grey mantles—many with silk paletots and wide skirts, extended by an ample crinoline, looking almost like a pyramid, with the apex terminating at the black or white satin bonnet, trimmed with waving ribbons and gay flowers. Some are to be seen with their cheeks ruddy with rouge, and here and there a few rosy with health. Many of them looking cold and heartless; others with an interesting appearance. We observe them walking up and down Regent Street and the Haymarket, often by themselves, one or more in company, sometimes with a gallant they have picked up, calling at the wine-vaults or restaurants to get a glass of wine or gin, or sitting down in the brilliant coffee-rooms, adorned with large mirrors, to a cup of good bohea or coffee. Many of the more faded prostitutes of this class frequent the Pavilion to meet gentlemen and enjoy the vocal and instrumental music over some liquor. Others of higher style proceed to the Alhambra Music Hall, or to the Argyle Rooms, rustling in splendid dresses, to spend the time till midnight, when they accompany the gentlemen they may have met there to the expensive supper-rooms and night-houses which abound in the neighbourhood.

In the course of the evening, we see many of the girls proceeding with young and middle aged, and sometimes silverheaded frail old men, to Oxenden Street, Panton Street, and James Street, near the

Haymarket, where they enter houses of accommodation, which they prefer to going with them to their lodgings. Numbers of French girls may be seen in the Haymarket, and the neighbourhood of Tichbourne Street and Great Windmill Street, many of them in dark silk paletots and white or dark silk bonnets, trimmed with gay ribbons and flowers, or walking up Regent Street in the neighbourhood of All Souls' Church, Langham Place, and Portland Place, or coming down Regent Street to Waterloo Place and Pall Mall, and hovering near the palatial mansions or the Clubs; or they might be seen decoying gents to their apartments in Queen Street, off Regent's Quadrant, from which locality they were lately forcibly ejected by the police. Most of these French girls have bullies, or what they term by a softer term 'fancy men,' who cohabit with them. These base wretches live on the prostitution of these miserable girls,—hang as loafers in their houses or about the streets, and many of them, as we might expect, are gamblers and swindlers. Several of them, we blush to say, are political refugees, exiles for fighting at the barricades of Paris, for the liberty of their country; while they live here with courtesans in the purlieus of Haymarket, in the most infamous and degrading of all bondage.

The generality of the girls of the Haymarket have no bullies, but live in furnished apartments—one or more—in various localities of the metropolis. Many live in Dean Street, Soho, Gerrard Street, Soho, King Street, Soho, and Church Street, Soho, in Tennison Street, Waterloo Road, at Pimlico and Chelsea, several of the streets leading into Fitzroy Square, and other neighbourhoods, and pay a weekly rent varying from seven shillings to a guinea, which has to be regularly paid on the day it is due. In many cases little forbearance is shown by their heartless landladies. Many of these girls have gentlemen who statedly visit them at their lodgings, some of whom are married men. Most of them are very thoughtless and extravagant, with handfuls of money to-day, and in poverty and miserable straits to-morrow, driven to the necessity of pawning their dresses. Hence there are many changes in their life. At one time they are in splendid dress, and at another time in the humblest attire; occasionally they are assisted by men who are interested in them, and restored to their former position, when they get their clothes out of the hands of the pawnbroker. Their living is very precarious, and many of them are occasionally exposed to privation, degradation, and misery, as they are very improvident. They are frequently treated to splendid suppers in the Haymarket and its vicinity, where they sit surrounded with splendour, partaking of costly viands amid lascivious smiles; but the scene is changed when you follow them to their own apartments in Soho or Chelsea, where you find them during the day, lolling drowsily on their beds, in tawdry dress, and in sad dishabille, with dishevelled hair, seedy-looking countenance, and muddy, dreary eyes — their voices frequently hoarse with bad humour and misery.

Large sums of money are spent in luxurious riot in the Haymarket; but it has not been so much frequented by the gentry and nobility for several years past, although considerable numbers are to be seen in the summer and winter seasons.

Strange midnight scenes were wont to be seen occasionally in Queen Street, Regent Street, where the French girls reside. Let us take an illustration. Some fast man—young or middle aged—goes with them to the cafés and music halls, perhaps proceeds to the supper rooms, and after an expensive supper, retires with them to their domicile in Queen Street. Meantime their bully keeps out of sight, or sneaks behind the bed-room door. In many cases, not contented with the half-guinea or guinea given them, their usual hire for prostitution, they demand more money from their victim. On his declining to give it, they refuse to submit to his pleasure, and will not return him his money. The bully is then called up, and the silly dupe is probably unceremoniously turned out of doors.

There are few felonies committed by this class of prostitutes, as such an imputation would be fatal to their mode of livelihood in this district, where they are generally known, and can be easily traced.

The second class of prostitutes, who walk the Haymarket—the third class in our classification—generally come from the lower orders of society. They consist of domestic servants of a plainer order, the daughters of labouring people, and some of a still lower class. Some of these girls are of a very tender age—from thirteen years and upwards. You see them wandering along Leicester Square, and about the Haymarket, Tichbourne Street, and Regent Street. Many of them are dressed in a light cotton or merino gown, and ill-suited crinoline, with light grey, or brown cloak, or mantle. Some with pork-pie hat, and waving feather—white, blue, or red; others with a slouched straw-hat. Some of them walk with a timid look, others with effrontery. Some have a look of artless innocence and ingenuousness, others very pert, callous, and artful. Some have good features and fine figures, others are coarse-looking and dumpy, their features and accent indicating that they are Irish cockneys. They prostitute themselves for a lower price, and haunt those disreputable coffee-shops in the neighbourhood of the Haymarket and Leicester Square, where you may see the blinds drawn down, and the lights burning dimly within, with notices over the door, that "beds are to be had within."

Many of those young girls — some of them good-looking — cohabit with young pickpockets about Drury Lane, St. Giles's, Gray's Inn Lane, Holborn, and other localities—young lads from fourteen to eighteen, groups of whom may be seen loitering about the Haymarket, and often speaking to them. Numbers of these girls are artful and adroit thieves. They follow persons into the dark by-streets of these localities, and are apt to pick his pockets, or they rifle his person when in the bedroom with him in low coffee-houses and brothels. Some of these girls come even from Pimlico, Waterloo Road, and distant parts of the metropolis, to share in the spoils of fast life in the Haymarket. They occasionally take watches, purses, pins, and handkerchiefs from their silly dupes who go with them into those disreputable places, and frequently are not easily traced, as many of them are migratory in their character.

The third and lowest class of prostitutes in the Haymarket — the fourth in our classification—are worn-out prostitutes or other degraded women, some of them married, yet equally degraded in character.

These faded and miserable wretches skulk about the Haymarket, Regent Street, Leicester Square, Coventry Street, Panton Street and Piccadilly, cadging from the fashionable people in the street and from the prostitutes passing along, and sometimes retire for prostitution into dirty low courts near St. James' Street, Coventry Court, Long's Court, Earl's Court, and Cranbourne Passage, with shop boys, errand lads, petty thieves, and labouring men, for a few paltry coppers. Most of them steal when they can get an opportunity. Occasionally a base coloured woman of this class may be seen in the Haymarket and its vicinity, cadging from the gay girls and gentlemen in the streets. Many of the poor girls are glad to pay her a sixpence occasionally to get rid of her company, as gentlemen are often scared away from them by the intrusion of this shameless hag, with her thick lips, sable black skin, leering countenance and obscene disgusting tongue, resembling a lewd spirit of darkness from the nether world.

Numbers of the women kept by the wealthy and the titled may occasionally be seen in the Haymarket, which is the only centre in the metropolis where all the various classes of prostitutes meet. They attend the Argyle Rooms and the Alhambra, and frequently indulge in the gaieties of the supper rooms, where their broughams are often seen drawn up at the doors. In the more respectable circles they may be regarded with aversion, but they here reign as the prima-donnas over the fast life of the West-end.

Occasionally genteel and beautiful girls in shops and workrooms in the West-end, milliners, dressmakers, and shop girls, may be seen flitting along Regent Street and Pall Mall, like bright birds of passage, to meet with some gentleman *on the sly*, and to obtain a few quickly-earned guineas to add to their scanty salaries. Sometimes a fashionable young widow, or beautiful young married woman, will find her way in those dark evenings to meet with some rickety silver-headed old captain loitering about Pall Mall. Such things are not wondered at by those acquainted with high life in London.

We now come to take a survey of the general state of prostitution which prevails over the metropolis, having Bishopgate, Shoreditch, and Waterloo Road more particularly in our eye as a sample of the other districts. These prostitutes in general reside in the dingy lanes and courts off the main streets in these localities, and have small bed-rooms poorly furnished, for which they pay four shillings and upwards a-week. They live in disreputable houses, occupied from the basement to the attics by prostitutes—some young, others more elderly; some living alone, others cohabiting with some low wretch of a man, a "tail" pickpocket, labourer, or low mechanic.

The prostitutes of these localities generally belong to the third and fourth class. The better educated and more genteel girls who live by prostitution in most cases go to the Haymarket. Numbers may occasionally be seen in the neighbourhood of the Bank of England, at Islington, near the Angel tavern, in the City Road, New North Road, Paddington, at the Elephant and Castle, and other localities; though in most cases they only come out occasionally *on the sly*, and are engaged in shops, factories, warerooms, and workrooms, during the day, or secluded in their houses, supported by tradesmen, mechanics, shopmen, clerks, or others, and only live partially by prostitution.

We shall refer to the two classes of open prostitutes generally to be seen over the various districts of the metropolis, such as those residing in the disreputable neighbourhoods we have mentioned. Some of the better class have the appearance of girls who serve in coffee-houses, barmaids, and servants, and others of the lower orders. Numbers of them are good-looking and tolerably well dressed. Some have been ironing girls, and others have sold small wares on the streets, and been engaged in similar employment.

Many of these unfortunate girls have redeeming traits in their character. Some are kind-hearted and honest, and not a few are even generous and self-denying. The great mass, however, are unprincipled and base, ever ready to take an advantage when an opportunity occurs. The vast majority of them are thieves, similar to the third class we have sketched in the Haymarket. They not only steal from the persons they meet on the street under the dark cloud of night in by-streets and courts, but take men to their houses, and plunder them. They rifle the pockets of those who go for a short time with them, and steal their gold pins, watches, and money. This is generally done in low houses of accommodation. They frequently decamp with the clothes of their victim, who has taken a bed with them for the night, and leave him in a strange house in a state of nudity. Married men frequently get into this sad predicament, but the matter is in most cases hushed up. When it does get abroad, the party robbed, to screen his profligacy from his wife and relatives, pretends in many cases that he has been drugged.

These prostitutes, some of them good-looking and handsome, often accost men in the street, retire with them into some by-lane or by-street, and patter about their pockets, while they encourage him to use indecent freedoms with their persons; and while they inflame his passions, rifle his pockets, and decamp with his money. This is frequently done in cases where the man does not have carnal connection with them.

They are generally dressed in a light cotton or merino gown, a light or brown mantle, a straw bonnet trimmed with gaudy ribbons and flowers, and sometimes with a pork-pie hat and white or red feather.

Some of these girls in those lower localities have better traits in their character than many of the more brilliant-dressed girls in the Haymarket, and are sometimes better looking. Not a few of them are very sedate, and will not go with any man whom they do not like. But there are many others more unscrupulous.

When they meet a man the worse of liquor, they decoy him into a brothel and get his money from him, when they try to get up a quarrel with him, and run off crying out they are ill-used by the man. They do this frequently where they do not allow the drunken man to have carnal dealings with them—not from a lustful purpose, but to get his money or other property.

These girls are fifteen years of age and upwards. Some of them, if good-looking, get married, and are rescued from the jaws of prostitution. Others linger on for a time with shattered constitutions, wasted by grief, want, anxiety, and irregular life, and glide into premature graves. Others are sheltered in workhouses, while a considerable number become withered or brutal, and degenerate into the lowest class of abandoned women.

We come now to treat of the lowest class of prostitutes—those old women of the town who prowl about the thorougfares and main streets, chiefly in the evenings and at midnight. They are often dressed in a shabby, dirty cotton skirt, faded dark bonnet, and old shoes; some bloated, dissipated, and brutal in appearance; others pale and wasted by want and suffering Many of them resort to "bilking" for a livelihood, that is, they inveigle persons to low houses of bad fame, but do not allow them to have criminal dealings with them. Possibly the bodies of some may be covered with dreadful disease, which they take care to conceal. While in these houses they often indulge in the grossest indecencies, too abominable to be mentioned, with old grey-headed men on the very edge of the grave. Many of these women are old convicted thieves of sixty years of age and upwards. Strange to say, old men and boys go with these withered crones, and sometimes fashionable gentlemen on a lark are to be seen walking arm in arm with them, and even to enter their houses. Few of these old women are married, though many of them cohabit with low coarse fellows, who wink at their conduct, and live on the proceeds of their obscenities.

For example, in Granby Street, Waterloo Road, there were orgies occasionally indulged in by such women, with persons having the appearance of gentlemen, too abominable to be mentioned.

These belong to the same class of degraded women who walk the Haymarket, and whom we have described as the most abandoned of their sex, who go about cadging and occasionally prostituting themselves to boys and degraded labouring men. They live in the lowest neighbourhoods in the east end of the metropolis, such as Lower Whitecross Street, Wentworth Street, and the low by-streets in Spitalfields, and in the lowest slums and by-streets about the New Cut, Drury Lane, Westminster, and other low localities, with dirty, low fellows, dock-labourers, bricklayers' labourers, and labourers at the workyards and wharfs.

They are in general too ugly to come out during the day with their unwashed slatternly dress, and in the evenings are often seen prowling as cadgers about the streets, and even in the dead of night waylaying and plundering drunken men; sometimes sneaking about alone, at other times two in company, and occasionally with a young simple girl by their side to screen their villainy.

They often resort to prostitution in the dark by-streets and courts with the boys and men who resort to them, which is seldom or never done by the younger girls, except by a few outcast or debased creatures among them, who might justly be comprised in the lowest class.

We now have to notice the "picking-up" women, who generally cohabit with pickpockets, burglars, clerks, shopmen, and others. Their object is to get liquor and money from persons as though they were prostitutes, without resorting to prostitution. For example, we see two well-dressed young women in the attire of milliners or dressmakers proceeding along the City Road in the direction of the Angel tavern, Islington. They see a gentleman pass, and cast a wistful look at him. He returns the glance. They walk on a short distance, and look round. The gentleman in many cases turns round likewise. He will then get a nod or bow from one of them. They will walk slowly, and look round again. On his going up to them, they will enter into conversation. They ask the gentleman to treat them, if he should not first offer to do so. They will then proceed to a gin-palace, where he will give them possibly a glass of wine. He will ask one of them where she lives. She will perhaps reply: "I am afraid to tell you. If you were to come to my house, it might come to the knowledge of my husband, and he would nearly kill me;" adding I don't mind seeing you again, and we will then get better acquainted!" Ultimately it may be arranged to go to some place which she has chanced to know, for the purpose of prostitution, leaving the other young woman to wait for her outside. The gentleman will then possibly give a sum of money. She will either say it is not sufficient, and will not allow him to have connection with her, or she may say she cannot allow him for certain reasons; or she may make an excuse that she requires to go down-stairs on a pressing errand for a moment, or to speak to the landlady, when she decamps. Sometimes robbing him of his watch, or purse, in addition to the sum he gave her.

If he should raise an alarm the occupier of the house will request him to give her a sum of money for the use of the room, and if there is any objection made to pay it, he receives ill-treatment and is turned into the street.

On other occasions a young woman will pretend she is unmarried, and will, in a similar ingenious way, endeavour to get money from parties she meets in the street, and try to escape in a similar way, without allowing him to have connection with her. She frequently manages to steal his watch and to rifle his pockets while he may be off his guard.

The object of these women is to get the wages of prostitution and an opportunity of stealing, without incurring the anger of their paramour by prostituting their bodies to other men. It happens occasionally they are outwitted, as their schemes are beginning to be pretty well known. Their pretexts are sometimes evaded, and cases occur where they yield to prostitution rather than give back the money they have received, which classes them among prostitutes and thieves. Some women resort to this as a shift in case of necessity, while others pursue it as a mode of livelihood in different localities of London.

These persons are to be found over the chief districts of the metropolis; miserable, poorly-dressed females, as well as respectable-looking young women. Some of the poorer sort are to be found about Shoreditch, Whitechapel, Lambeth, and the Borough. Others of the better sort, in appearance, are to be met with in the City Road, New North Road, King's Cross, and Paddington.

Hired Prostitutes.—There are a number of female prostitutes kept by Jewesses and English women of low character. These girls are dressed in good style, in silks and light muslin and cotton dresses, with their hair put up in ringlets or in fancy nets. They are mostly from seventeen to twenty-two years of age, some younger and others older, some with false hair and ringlets. The brothels we refer to are chiefly about the West-end. There is often a cigar-shop attached to them, and the best looking girls are generally found standing by the doors, or ogling through the windows to decoy the passers-by into their infamous dens. Some of these girls have been prostitutes from their girlhood, and belong to the lowest class in society, their mothers having been prostitutes before them. Several have been in these houses for a considerable number of years, who have kept their appearance better than other prostitutes who have had a more changeable and precarious mode of livelihood. Strange to say, some look nearly as young and as fresh as they did ten years ago.

You seldom see the old execrable hags who keep these houses loitering about the doors or standing at the windows. They generally keep out of sight, but are sometimes to be seen peering through the edge of the window-blinds, which are generally drawn down, in the first floor above; or you may occasionally see them in the back parlour, skulking about. They are often very stout, and look like matrons in the maturity of life. They take gentlemen into their houses during the day as well as during the evening, but mostly in the evening.

The girls are then dressed in gaudy finery, with shining head-dresses and jewellery glittering on their breast over their light dresses. Yet there is a low vulgarity in their appearance which repels and disgusts; they look, in many cases, so sensual and debased. They use no art to conceal the life they are leading, as some other prostitutes do, who try so far to screen the baseness of their profligacy.

They generally keep old female servants they call "slaveys" to do the drudgery work of the house. These degraded women live in the house with them, wash their clothes, get their meals ready, clean their boots, brush their clothes, run errands for them out of doors, and show gentlemen into the bed-rooms.

There is often a man in these brothels, a paramour of the old bawd, who is a loafer about the house, and is occasionally employed to act as a bully. These men are in general rough-looking men, dressed in black shabby clothes, and in many cases look more degraded than common thieves. Some are dissipated and pale, others are bloated, their faces covered with pimples and blotches.

As we pass along Wych Street, Strand, in the dark evenings, we see several of the brothels we refer to. There the cigar shops are lit up, and the girls are arrayed in their best attire, and beaming their most inviting smiles to entrap the unwary. We may see brilliant lights in the rooms on the flat above through chinks in the shutters and blinds, where orgies are nightly transacted too gross and disgusting to mention.

Brothels of the same kind are to be found in Exeter Street and Chandos Street, Strand, and other localities of the metropolis.

These girls occasionally walk the Strand and Holborn to decoy gentlemen into their dwellings. They generally belong to the third class of prostitutes and the lowest class of society. Some may have come down through dissipation from the second class, and have formerly been in better positions. They do not steal from persons when sober, as they could be so easily detected, and as this would injure the brothel; but they occasionally pilfer from drunken men, where they are able to do it with impunity. Some of them occasionally get as much money as many of the more genteel girls in the Haymarket.

They never take clothes from the gentlemen who enter their houses, but occasionally give him rough treatment should he enter their house without plenty of money in his purse.

They chiefly confine their pilfering depredations to drunken men. As they walk in the evenings along the crowded thoroughfares lighted up by the street lamps, and the bright illumination of the shop windows, the "slaveys" walk frequently at a short distance behind them, to see that they do not receive gentlemen without the knowledge of the keepers of the brothel, and to watch that they do not run away with the clothes. The slaveys are paid something additional for every gentleman the girls go with, which stimulates them to look better after them, and promotes the selfish ends of the execrable old bawd who hires them.

Park Women.—There are three kinds of women who usually resort to the parks. We find numbers of kept women of the highest class maintained by persons in high life, such as have been governesses, ladies-maids, and the daughters of respectable tradesmen and others, promenading in Hyde Park. They live in fashionable style at Brompton and other localities. In summer they come to the park about half-past five or six in the afternoon. There are not so many in the winter time, when the season is cold, and the landscape faded. While gentlemen and ladies are taking their evening's ride, these ladies often walk along Rotten Row as far as Kensington Gardens, and frequently have a little pet dog, with a ribbon or string attached to it.

These females are dressed in the most fashionable and expensive style, in silk and satin dresses, with expensive shawls, mantles, or paletots, and have light muslin dresses in summer. On such occasions there are great numbers of fashionable gentlemen riding on horseback and walking along the side of the drive.

There are a great many seats placed on the grass at Rotten Row in the summer, where these ladies sit and talk with gentlemen. They are generally from eighteen to twenty-four years of age, in the full bloom of life and beauty. The gentlemen consist of blooming youths and old tottering gallants of sixty, civilians and military, professional men, gentry, and nobility.

These ladies sit chatting together with hundreds of people seated around them in this gay promenade. Many assignations are thus made as to when and where to meet. They are sometimes seated close by the Serpentine under the trees in the dusk of the summer evenings, and middle-aged gentlemen—sometimes elderly—often come and meet them, and sit and converse beside them under the starlit gloom of the park, with few persons near them.

There is another class of females who visit the parks, consisting of servants and the daughters of labouring men and poor mechanics. In general, they are poorly educated, but respectably dressed, and belong, according to our classification, to the third class of prostitutes. They generally come out in the evening for the purpose of prostitution. Many of them are fresh-looking, averaging in age from fifteen to twenty-five, and are to be found all over the park, chiefly from Stanhope Gate to Victoria Gate, where they sit on the seats with men of respectable appearance— tradesmen and others. These females often use indecent liberties with gentlemen without having connexion with them. This is done in the evening from dusk up to the time of shutting the park, and during this sensual excitement robberies are frequently effected by the women of purses, watches, pins, and other property. Information is sometimes given to the police, but these felonies are often concealed by the persons plundered, as they are ashamed to make it known. Many of these dupes are married men, who would be sadly disgraced were the news to come to the ears of their wives and families.

A third class of females who attend the parks are the lowest old prostitutes, dissipated, debased wretches, from twenty-five to fifty years of age. They generally frequent the Lovers' Walk, from Grosvenor Gate to the statue of Achilles, and are to be seen in other parts of the park near the Marble Arch.

They are miserably dressed, many of them having barely rags to cover their wretchedness. They are utterly shameless in their habits. We find them dressed in a dirty cotton gown, nearly black, an old faded ragged shawl and tattered old boots, with scarcely a sole to them. Some are blotched in appearance; others are pale, shrivelled, and haggard, miserable spectacles.

They may sometimes be seen sitting on the settles in the parks from dusk till the time of closing the gates of the park. These women indulge in the same obscene practices as the girls we have already mentioned, with a lower class of people, such as gentlemen's servants, labouring men, and low mechanics, and sometimes have connexion with them in the park. On such occasions, these filthy hags are busy rifling the pockets of their victims.

Soldiers' Women.—There is only one class of prostitutes termed soldiers' women, who live in Westminster. They chiefly reside in the courts leading out of Orchard Street, St. Ann Street, Old Pye Street, New Pye Street, Castle Lane, Gardener's Lane, York Street, and Blue Anchor Yard. They are from sixteen to thirty years of age, and several even older. Some have been in the streets for seventeen years and upwards. They live in the greatest poverty, covered with rags and filth, and many of them covered with horrid sores. and eruptions on their body, arms, and legs, presenting in many cases a revolting appearance. Many of them have not the delicacy of females, and live as pigs in a sty. This is not exaggeration. On the officers of police entering their houses, they often find them in a state of nudity. They have no feeling of shame, and conduct themselves with the greatest indifference. Two of them generally occupy a room. They often take two other lodgers into their room, and lie on the floor. Their furniture consists of an old deal table, one or two old rickety chairs, a few broken cups and saucers, a wooden table, a wash-hand basin and chamber utensil, and an old shattered bedstead with scarcely any bedding. These rooms—generally about ten feet square—

are let under the name of furnished apartments, and there is generally a deputy employed to collect the rents of the house. These girls pay on an average 3s. 6d. or 4s. of weekly rent. Many of them pay 8d. or 10d. for the room per day, as the landladies do not trust them a week's rent. They often come home drunk about twelve or one o'clock at midnight.

They generally get up in the morning about eight or nine o'clock. If they have any coppers they get in something to eat. Food is seldom seen in their cupboards, as they generally have only enough for the occasion. After they have had their breakfast—a cup of tea or coffee and bread—they chat with each other over the past night's adventures, and pass the time till evening.

In the middle of the day they sometimes wash their skirt, the only decent garment many of them have—their under clothing being a tissue of rags—starch and iron it, and get it ready towards the evening, when they wash themselves and sally forth again.

In the evening, most of them go to some low public-house, and sit in company with soldiers, who drink and carouse with them. The soldiers who sit with them generally belong to the Foot Guards, Scots Fusileers, Coldstream, and Grenadier Guards.

The Life Guardsmen do not generally associate with this class. If a stray soldier of the line in other regiments should happen to come on a furlough to this district, some of the prostitutes decoy him to their house, and get money from him professedly for prostitution They slip out of the room while he is asleep in bed, and spend the money they have got with the Foot Guards. Sometimes they bring one of the Foot Guards to bully him out of the room. They treat civilians in a similar manner.

Some of them dress and go out and walk with the soldiers during the day, but this is seldom. In general they do not go out till the evening at dusk.

In some instances the soldiers remain absent in the evening, and manage to avoid the patrols, and stop carousing with these girls till the public-houses close at four o'clock in the morning, when they go with these prostitutes to their dens, and often remain the whole of next day—sometimes remaining for a fortnight with them.

Some of these females are young, strong, healthy girls When they have been for some years in this mode of life, they become dissipated in appearance, and their constitution is often broken up by their irregular wild life. The younger girls keep themselves more reserved for a time, but the bad example of the others very soon induces them to abandon themselves to all kinds of dissipation.

If a young woman is so unfortunate as to come among them and to keep herself reserved, the others bully her out of it, unless she go to the same excess of dissipation as themselves.

Their mode of stealing is to get people to their houses, where they plunder them. A sober man seldom thinks of going to their infamous abodes. In most cases the persons who go are the worse for liquor. On their way home they go into a public-house with the girls, after which they accompany them to their room, where they get some more liquor.

The companions of a girl may see her coming home with a man, and may suppose him, from his appearance, to have money. They come into the house, and get a portion of the drink. In some instances the drunken person gives the woman money to go out for drink, when she decamps, and gets some of the prostitutes in the adjoining room to bully him out of the place. In other instances the girls wait their time till he goes to sleep, when they plunder him.

There are seldom fastenings on their doors, which are never locked. There is an understanding between parties in the same house, and some persons in the adjoining rooms enter while the man is in bed, and carry away his clothes and money. He cannot accuse the girl in the room, as she is lying in bed beside him.

In some cases the girl disappears during the night, and leaves the man naked in the room. She may remove to some other neighbourhood if the booty is of value, and live in some other part of Westminster. The dupe is seldom or never able to identify her, as he may have been much the worse for liquor while in her company.

These prostitutes chiefly look out for drunken men, whom they decoy to their houses, and afterwards plunder. They prowl along Parliament Street and Whitehall Place, and other streets in the vicinity. A great number of them go as far as Knightsbridge, where there are concert rooms. They loiter about these localities till these places close, and are to be seen about the doors of those public-houses where persons resort after leaving the concert rooms. When they pick up a drunken man they bring him home in the manner already described.

Many of these girls come from different parts of the country, and have formerly been servants in town. A good number have been orphans left without friends, and have been basely seduced. The relatives of some have taken them home into the provinces, but they have come back again to London.

The police constables often find as many as four girls in one small room at night—two lying on a miserable bed, and two lying on the hard floor, with scarcely any covering but their petticoat thrown over them. Two soldiers are frequently found lying in the room with them, or one is seen lying between two girls.

It is surprising that any soldiers, however poor, who have an ordinary regard to decency, should lie down among such heaps of filthy rags; far less should we expect such base and unmanly conduct from the Queen's Foot Guards, when we look to the fine appearance and manly bearing of many of them on parade. It kindles our indignation when we learn that not a few of those poor degraded females were formerly in the service of respectable families, and were there seduced and driven to open prostitution by some of these unprincipled soldiers, who still add to their villainy the despicable crime of basely plundering the poor girls they have ruined of the wretched earnings of their dishonour and crime.

To the honour of the regiments of Foot Guards, we are happy to say there are many noble and excellent men in their ranks, who reflect high credit on our army by their exemplary character, and who are as benevolent in heart as they are brave on the battle-field. Some of these go to the other side of the street to avoid meeting with their fellow-soldiers when associated with degraded women. The others we refer to are heartless ruffians in their conduct, and a disgrace to the British service.

Sailors' Women.—There are two classes of prostitutes termed sailors' women to be found in Ratcliff Highway, near the London Docks, at the east end of the metropolis. These belong to the third and fourth classes in our classification of the prostitutes of London.

The better of the two classes are generally composed of younger and more respectable-looking girls, most of them residing in the neighbourhood, others coming from a distance. The generality of them reside in the Highway and in Palmer's Folly, Albert Square, Albert Street, Seven Star Alley, and other adjacent streets and alleys. A few strange girls come occasionally from the Surrey side, such as Kent Street and other localities in the Borough, and remain for a few days only, as they may have committed some depredation in their own district, and wish to be away for a short time from the surveillance of the police. In like manner some of the girls residing in the neighbourhood of Ratcliff Highway, when they have plundered a sailor, leave the locality for a short time, till the ship to which he belonged has set sail, when they return again. There are a number of very good-looking girls of this class, most of them Irish cockneys. There are also a few German and Dutch prostitutes who frequent the Highway who live in Albert Street. These foreign girls do not have bullies or fancy men. Some of them are good looking, and some are not. They generally frequent the German and Dutch music and dancing saloons in Ratcliff Highway. Both of them attend the public-house with the Swedish flag. This class of girls frequents the various saloons in the Highway. They do not generally steal money or watches when they are well paid, and but few steal the sailor's clothes.

They dress tolerably well, in silk and merino gowns with crinolines, and bonnets gaily attired with flowers and ribbons. Many of them have velvet stripes across the breast and back of their gowns, and large brooches with the portrait of a sailor encased in them. They generally lay their hair back in front in the French style.

Some of them have fancy men, and others have not. Their fancy men in many cases are watermen, but being lazy in inclination they hang about as loafers, and live on the prostitution and crime of the girls they cohabit with. These females take their dupes to their own houses or into low coffee-houses and brothels, or other houses of accommodation. Some of them allow the sailors to have connexion with them; others who cohabit with watermen and others, pretend to be prostitutes, and allow men to take indecent liberties with them, but seldom or never allow them to proceed farther.

There is another class of prostitutes to be found in Ratcliff Highway, more dissipated and abandoned than those we have noticed. They reside in or near Bluegate Fields, Angel Gardens, and other streets and lanes in that neighbourhood. Many of them have a robust, coarse, masculine frame, some of them with great protruding breasts. A few of the same class come from a distance, followed by a low, brutal man. The latter are termed "cross-girls." They pick up a sailor, take him into some dark by-street as if for the purpose of prostitution, get all the money they can from him, and seldom allow carnal connexion. If possible, so soon as they have effected their purpose, they run away; this is termed "bilking."

The rough-looking prostitutes of this class seldom attend the music saloons, as they would be far outshone in personal appearance by the younger girls of the other class referred to. We see them late in the evening skulking about the dark lanes, or patrolling the streets, on the watch for drunken sailors, whom they take into low coffee-houses and beer-shops, and sometimes drug by putting snuff, or other ingredients—sometimes laudanum—in his liquor. They look out for north country sea-captains and sailors just come ashore, and sometimes visit their ships lying in the river, at King James's Stair, Wapping, Ratcliff Cross, Horseferry, Regent's Canal Dock, Stone Stairs, or New Crane Stairs, Shadwell.

Some of these brutal women have bullies, convicted thieves, who are sometimes dressed as sailors; some of them are river pirates, and from their childhood have led a criminal life.

The average age of these prostitutes is from twenty to thirty-four. Many are slovenly dressed, and very dissipated and callous in appearance. Some of them are women of colour, whom we have seen brought to the police station at King David's Lane, charged with plundering coloured sailors of their money and clothes.

Number of felonies in the metropolitan districts, by prostitutes, during 1860 692
Ditto, ditto, in the City . . 102
―――
794

Value of property thereby abstracted in the metropolitan districts . £2,651
Ditto, ditto, in the City . . 323
―――
£2,974

FELONIES ON THE RIVER THAMES.

THERE are a great number of robberies of various descriptions committed on the Thames by different parties. These depredations differ in value, from the little ragged mudlark stealing a piece of rope or a few handfuls of coals from a barge, to the lighterman carrying off bales of silk several hundred pounds in value. When we look to the long lines of shipping along each side of the river, and the crowds of barges and steamers that daily ply along its bosom, and the dense shipping in its docks, laden with untold wealth, we are surprised at the comparatively small aggregate amount of these felonies.

THE MUDLARKS.

THEY generally consist of boys and girls, varying in age from eight to fourteen or fifteen; with some persons of more advanced years. For the most part they are ragged, and in a very filthy state, and are a peculiar class, confined to the river. The parents of many of them are coalwhippers—Irish cockneys—employed getting coals out of the ships, and their mothers frequently sell fruit in the street. Their practice is to get between the barges, and one of them lifting the other up will knock lumps of coal into the mud, which they pick up afterwards; or if a barge is ladened with iron, one will get into it and throw iron out to the other, and watch an opportunity to carry away the plunder in bags to the nearest marine-storeshop.

They sell the coals among the lowest class of people for a few halfpence. The police make numerous detections of these offences. Some of the mudlarks receive a short term of imprisonment, from three weeks to a month, and others two months with three years in a reformatory. Some of them are old women of the lowest grade, from fifty to sixty, who occasionally wade in the mud up to the knees. One of them may be seen beside the Thames Police-office, Wapping, picking up coals in the bed of the river, who appears to be about sixty-five years of age. She is a robust woman, dressed in an old cotton gown, with an old straw bonnet tied round with a handkerchief, and wanders about without shoes and stockings. This person has never been in custody. She may often be seen walking through the streets in the neighbourhood with a bag of coals on her head.

In the neighbourhood of Blackfriars Bridge clusters of mudlarks of various ages may be seen from ten to fifty years, young girls and old women, as well as boys.

They are mostly at work along the coal

wharves where the barges are lying a-ground, such as at Shadwell and Wapping, along Bankside, Borough; above Waterloo Bridge, and from the Temple down to St. Paul's Wharf. Some of them pay visits to the City Gasworks, and steal coke and coal from their barges, where the police have made many detections.

As soon as the tide is out they make their appearance, and remain till it comes in. Many of them commence their career with stealing rope or coals from the barges, then proceed to take copper from the vessels, and afterwards go down into the cabins and commit piracy.

These mudlarks are generally strong and healthy, though their clothes are in rags. Their fathers are robust men. By going too often to the public-house they keep their families in destitution, and the mothers of the poor children are glad to get a few pence in whatever way they can.

SWEEPING BOYS.

THIS class of boys sail about the river in very old boats, and go on board empty craft with the pretext of sweeping them. They enter barges of all descriptions, laden with coffee, sugar, rice, and other goods, and steal anything they can lay their hands on, often abstracting headfasts, ropes, chains, &c. In some instances they cut the bags and steal the contents, and dispose of the booty to marine-store-dealers. They are generally very ragged and wretched in appearance, and if pursued take to the water like a rat, splashing through the mud, and may be seen doing so when chased by the police. In general they are expert swimmers. Their ages range from twelve to sixteen. They are dressed similar to the other ragged boys over the metropolis. The fathers of most of them are coalwhippers, but many of them are orphans. They are strong, healthy boys, and some of them sleep in empty barges, others in low lodging-houses at 3d. a night. Some live in empty houses, and many of them have not had a shirt on for six months, and their rags are covered with vermin.

In the summer many sleep in open barges, and often in the winter, when they cover themselves with old mats, sacks, or tarpaulins. Their bodies are inured to this inclement life. They never go to church, and few of them have been to school.

Two little boys of this class, the one nine and the other eleven years of age, lived for six months on board an old useless barge at Bermondsey, and for other five months in an old uninhabited house, and had not a clean shirt on during all that time. At night they covered themselves with old mats and sacks, their clothes being in a wretched state. Seeing them in this neglected condition, an inspector of police took them into custody and brought them before a magistrate, with the view to get them provided for. The magistrate sent them to the workhouse for shelter.

These boys are of the same class with the mudlarks before referred to, but are generally a few years older.

SELLERS OF SMALL WARES.

FELONIES are occasionally committed by boys who go on board vessels with baskets containing combs, knives, laces, &c., giving them in exchange for pieces of rope, sometimes getting fat and bones from the cooks. In many instances the owners are robbed by the crew giving away ropes belonging to the ship for such wares. These parties occasionally pilfer any small article they see lying about the ship, sometimes carrying off watches when they have an opportunity. They generally try to get on board foreign vessels about to sail, so that when robberies are committed the parties do not remain to prosecute them, and the thieves are consequently discharged.

They are generally from fourteen to eighteen years of age, and many of them reside with their parents in Rosemary Lane and other low neighbourhoods about the East-end.

This is a peculiar class of boys who confine their attention to the ships, barges, and coasting vessels, and do not commit felonies in other parts of the metropolis.

LABOURERS ON BOARD SHIP, &c.

THESE men are employed to discharge cargoes on board steam vessels arriving from the coast, and also foreign vessels. They are frequently detected pilfering by the police, and secreting about their clothes small quantities of tallow, coffee, sugar, meat, and other portable goods. These parties abstract articles from the hold, but do not go down into the cabins. They have ample opportunity of breaking open some of the boxes and packages, and of extracting part of the contents. As they have no facility to get large quantities on shore, they confine themselves to petty pilfering. Most of their booty is kept for their own consumption, unless they succeed in carrying off a large quantity, which rarely occurs. In these cases they dispose of it at a chandler's shop.

DREDGEMEN OR FISHERMEN.

THESE are men who are in the habit of coming out early in the morning, as the tide may suit, for the purpose of dredging from the bed of the river coals which are occasionally spilled in weighing when being transferred into the barges. If these parties are not successful in getting coals there, they invariably go alongside of a leaded barge and carry off coals and throw a quantity of mud over them, to make it appear as if they had got them from the bed of the river. The police have made numerous detections. Some have been imprisoned, and others have been transported. The same class of men go alongside of vessels and steal the copper funnels and ropes, and go to the nearest landing place to sell them to marine-store-dealers, who are always in readiness to receive anything brought to them. The doors are readily opened to them, early and late.

To deceive the police these unprincipled dealers have carts calling every morning at their shops to take away the metals and other goods they may have bought during the previous day and night.

SMUGGLING.

NUMEROUS articles of contraband goods are smuggled by seamen on their arrival from foreign ports, such as tobacco, liquors, shawls, handkerchiefs, &c.

Several years ago an officer in the Thames police was on duty at five in the morning. While rowing by the Tower he saw in the dusk two chimney sweeps in a boat leaving a steam vessel, having with them two bags of soot. He boarded the boat along with two officers, and asked them if they had anything in their possession liable to Custom-house duty. They answered they had not. Upon searching the bags of soot he found several packages of foreign manufactured tobacco, weighing 48lbs. The parties were arrested and taken to the police station, and were fined 100*l.* each, or six months' imprisonment. Not being able to pay they, were imprisoned.

These two sweeps had no doubt carried on this illegal traffic for some time, being employed on the arrival of the boats to clean the funnels and the flues of the boilers.

Some time ago a sailor came ashore late at night at the Shadwell Dock, who had just arrived from America. According to the usual custom he was searched, when several pounds of tobacco were found concealed about his person. He was tried at the police court, and sentenced to pay a small fine.

In July, 1858, about midnight, a police constable was passing East Lane, Bermondsey, when he saw a bag at the top of a street, containing something rather bulky, which aroused his suspicions. On proceeding farther he saw a man carrying another bag up the street from a boat in the river. He got the assistance of another constable, and apprehended the man carrying the bag, and also the waterman that conveyed it ashore. The two bags were found to contain 229 lbs. of Cavendish tobacco. Both persons were detained in the Thames police station, and taken before a magistrate at Southwark police court. Prosecution was ordered by the Board of Customs, and both were fined 100*l.* each, and in default sentenced to six months' imprisonment. Being unable to pay the fine, they suffered imprisonment.

In February, 1860, information was given to an inspector of the Thames police of a smuggling traffic which was being carried on in the Shadwell Basin, London Docks, from an American vessel named the Amazon. The steward was in the practice of carrying the tobacco about a certain hour in the morning from the vessel through a private gate at the Shadwell Basin. Vigilant watch was kept over this gate by the inspector, with the assistance of a constable. About eight o'clock in the morning he saw a man coming up who answered the description given him. He followed him into a tobacconist's shop in King David Lane, Shadwell. The officer on going in saw a carpet bag handed over the counter. He seized it, and brought the man with him to the police station. A communication was then made to the Board of Customs, who sent an officer to the Thames police station. On making search on board the ship, they found about two cwt. of tobacco. The man was tried, and sentenced to pay a fine of 100*l.*, or suffer six months' imprisonment.

FELONIES BY LIGHTERMEN.

NUMEROUS depredations are perpetrated by lightermen, employed to navigate barges by the owners of various steam-vessels in the river or in the docks, and are intrusted with valuable cargoes, the value varying from 20*l.* to 20,000*l.* They have been assisted in these robberies by persons little suspected by the public, but well known to the police.

They have got cargoes from vessels in the wharves, or docks, to convey for transshipment and delivery along different parts of the river, and manage on their way to abstract part of the cargo they are in charge of. Sometimes these robberies are effected on the way, sometimes when they are waiting outside the dock for the tide to go in. When they have not such articles on board their own barges, they remove cargoes from other craft while the crew may be on shore at supper, or otherwise. Sometimes they carry away articles about their person, such as tobacco, brandy, wine, opium, tea, &c.

They occasionally steal an empty barge, and go alongside of another barge as if they were legally employed to put the cargo into another craft, and turn the barge into some convenient place, where they may have a cart or van in readiness to remove the property. Sometimes they have a cab for this purpose. Two days often elapse before the police get information of these robberies.

In one instance a barge was taken up Bow Creek, with about twenty bundles of whalebone and twenty bags of saltpetre, which were conveyed away in a van to the city. The police traced the booty to a marine store-dealer. The value of the property was 400*l*. Two well-known thieves were tried for the robbery, but were acquitted.

In April, 1858, Thomas Turnbull and Charles Turnbull, brothers, both lightermen and notorious river thieves, were charged with a robbery from two barges at Wapping. Two lightermen were in charge of two barges laden, the one with lac dye, and the other with cases of wire, near to the entrance of the London Docks. These men having gone on shore for refreshment, the two thieves rowed an empty barge alongside the two barges, and took one chest of lac dye from one of them, and a case of wire card from the other, in value about 25*l*. They took the barge with the stolen property over to Rotherhithe, and landed at the Elephant Stairs, where it was conveyed away in a cart. The property was never recovered, but the police, after making great exertions, got sufficient evidence to convict the parties, who were sentenced to eighteen months each at the Central Criminal Court.

These unprincipled lightermen could get a good livelihood by honest labour, varying from 30*s*. to 2*l*. a week; but they are dissipated and idle in their habits, and resort to thieving. They often spend their time in dancing and concert-rooms, and are to be seen at the Mahagony Bar at Close Square and Paddy's Goose, Ratcliffe Highway. They generally cohabit with prostitutes. They are a different class of men from the tier-rangers, or river pirates, who also live with prostitutes. The lightermen's women are generally smart and well-dressed, and do not belong to the lowest order as those of the tier-rangers do. The ages of this class of thieves generally range from twenty to thirty years.

The River Pirates.

This class of robberies is committed among the shipping on both sides of the river, from London Bridge to Greenhithe, but is most prevalent from London Bridge to the entrance of the West India Dock. The depredations are committed in the docks as well as on the river, but not so much in the former, as they are better protected. Robberies in the docks are generally done in the daytime. In the river, the chief object the thieves have in view is to enter the vessel at midnight, as they know that when vessels arrive the seamen are often fatigued and worn out, and they get a favourable opportunity of getting on board and stealing. They steal from all classes of vessels, but chiefly from brigs and barges. They take any boat from the shore and go on board the vessels, as if they were seamen, being dressed as watermen and seamen. When they get on board they go to the cabin or forecastle. Their chief object is to secure wearing apparel and money. Watches are often to be found hanging up in the cabin, and clothes are also to be found there. In the forecastle the clothes are generally contained in a bag hanging up by the side or bow of the ship. After they have effected their purpose they row ashore and turn the boat adrift.

There is another mode of stealing they adopt. They get on board the ships as if they belonged to some of them, and represent they belong to a certain ship in a line of vessels commonly called a "tier." They proceed to the forecastle, where if they find no one moving about, they go down and plunder. If they are seen by any of the crew they pretend they belong to some other ship, and ask if this ship is named so and so. They then say they cannot get on board their own ship, and wish the crew to allow them to remain for the night.

In many instances the stolen property is found on their person, such as coats, vests, trousers, boots, &c., and their own clothes are left behind. They are generally from eighteen to thirty years of age, and are powerful athletic men.

These robberies are greatly on the decrease, owing to the vigilance of the police.

Several years ago there was a cry of police between twelve and two o'clock midnight on board a vessel lying in Union Tier, Wapping. The crew of a police galley proceeded to the spot, and ascertained that two thieves had been on board a vessel there, and had concealed themselves somewhere in it, or in the barges alongside. After searching some time they discovered a notorious river thief in one of the barges. He was a stout made man, about five feet nine inches in height, and twenty-two years of age. A desperate struggle ensued between him and the police. He struck the inspector with a heavy iron bar on the back a very severe blow, which rendered him henceforth unfit for active duty. The pirate resisted with great desperation, and defied the police for some time.

At last they drew their cutlasses, and succeeded in taking him. He was brought to the police station, convicted, and sentenced to three months' imprisonment. He was afterwards indicted for the assault on the inspector, and sentenced to fifteen months' hard labour. Since that time he has been transported twice for similar offences.

A few years since several river pirates were suspected of being on board a vessel at Bermondsey, where they had stolen a silver watch from the cabin. One of the gang was detected by the crew of the vessel and detained. The crew shouted out for the police, when three of their pals drew up to the side of the vessel in a small boat, representing themselves to be policemen, with numbers chalked on their coats. The captain of the vessel gave the man into their custody, and handed over the watch to one of them. Next morning the captain went to the police-station to see if the party was there. It was then the police heard of the robbery, when it was found the supposed officers and the thief were a party of river pirates who had infested the river for a long time. As the ship was just setting sail the case was dropped.

Some time ago three constables went on duty at midnight in consequence of a number of midnight robberies having been committed all over the river, especially at Deptford, from the ships lying there. They went out in a private boat in plain clothes. On getting to Deptford they proceeded up the creek. After remaining there in the dusk about an hour they heard a loud knocking, and suspected that some one was taking the copper from the bottom of a vessel lying there.

The constables drew up to the vessel with their boat, and found two men with a quantity of copper in a boat, with chisels and a chopper they had been using. They arrested them, and were coming out of the creek with the two boats when they discovered two other notorious river thieves climbing down the chains of a vessel lying alongside the wharf. They had been down in the forecastle, and having disturbed the crew were making their escape when the officers saw them.

The officers thereupon made for the vessel, and succeeded in apprehending them, and took them into their boat after a desperate resistance.

The first two were convicted and sentenced, one to three months, and the other to six months' imprisonment, and the latter were sentenced to three months each in Maidstone gaol.

The Commissioners of Police rewarded the constables with a gratuity for their vigilance and gallant conduct.

Many of these tier-rangers or river pirates have a ruffianly appearance, and generally live with prostitutes, on both sides of the river, at St. George's, Bluegate-fields, the Borough, and Bermondsey.

They confine themselves to robberies on the river, and are frequently transported by the time they are thirty years of age. Occasionally a returned convict comes back for a time, when he generally resumes his former villanies, and is again sent abroad.

These tier-rangers in most cases have sprung from the ranks of the mudlarks, and step by step have advanced further in crime, until they have become callous brutal ruffians, living as brigands on the sides of the river.

Number of felonies, &c., on the river Thames in the metropolitan districts for 1860 - - - - - 203
Value of property abstracted thereby - - - - £712

NARRATIVE OF A MUDLARK.

THE following narrative was given us by a mudlark we found on a float on the river Thames at Millwall, to the eastward of Ratcliffe Highway. He was then engaged, while the tide was in, gathering chips of wood in an old basket. We went to the river side along with his younger brother, a boy of about eleven years of age, we saw loitering in the vicinity. On our calling to him, he got the use of a boat lying near, and came toward us with alacrity. He was an Irish lad of about thirteen years of age, strong and healthy in appearance, with Irish features and accent. He was dressed in a brown fustian coat and vest, dirty greasy canvas trousers roughly-patched, striped shirt with the collar folded down, and a cap with a peak.

"I was born in the county of Kerry in Ireland in the year 1847, and am now about thirteen years of age. My father was a ploughman, and then lived on a farm in the service of a farmer, but now works at loading ships in the London docks. I have three brothers and one sister. Two of my brothers are older than I. One of them is about sixteen, and the other about eighteen years of age. My eldest brother is a seaman on board a screwship, now on a voyage to Hamburg ; and the other is a seaman now on his way to Naples. My youngest brother you saw beside me at the river side. My sister is only five years of age, and was born in London. The rest of the family were all born in Ireland. Our family came to London about seven years ago, since which time my father has worked at the London Docks. He is a strong-bodied man of about thirty-four years of age. I was sent to school along with my elder brothers for about three years, and learned reading, writing, and arithmetic. I was able to read tolerably well, but was not so proficient in writing and arithmetic. One of my brothers has been about three years, and the other about five years at sea.

"About two years ago I left school, and commenced to work as a mudlark on the river, in the neighbourhood of Millwall, picking up pieces of coal and iron, and copper, and bits of canvas on the bed of the river, or of wood floating on the surface. I commenced this work with a little boy of the name of Fitzgerald. When the bargemen heave coals to be carried from their barge to the shore, pieces drop into the water among the mud, which we afterwards pick up. Sometimes we wade in the mud to the ancle, at other times to the knee. Sometimes pieces of coal do not sink, but remain on the surface of the mud ; at other times we seek for them with our hands and feet.

"Sometimes we get as many coals about one barge as sell for 6d. On other occasions we work for days, and only get perhaps as much as sells for 6d. The most I ever gathered in one day, or saw any of my companions gather, was about a shilling's worth. We generally have a bag or a basket to put the articles we gather into. I have sometimes got so much at one time, that it filled my basket twice—before the tide went back. I sell the coals to the poor people in the neighbourhood, such as in Mary Street and Charles Street, and return again and fill my bag or basket and take them home or sell them to the neighbours. I generally manage to get as many a day as sell for 8d.

"In addition to this, I often gather a basket of wood on the banks of the river, consisting of small pieces chipped off planks to build the ships or barges, which are carried down with the current and driven ashore. Sometimes I gather four or five baskets of these in a day. When I get a small quantity they are always taken home to my mother. When successful in finding several basketfuls, I generally sell part of them and take the rest home. These chips or stray pieces of wood are often lying on the shore or among the mud, or about the floating logs ; and at other times I seize pieces of wood floating down the river a small distance off ; I take a boat lying near and row out to the spot and pick them up. In this way I sometimes get pretty large beams of timber. On an average I get 4d. or 6d. a-day by finding and selling pieces of wood ; some days only making 2d., and at other times 3d. We sell the wood to the same persons who buy the coals.

"We often find among the mud, in the bed of the river, pieces of iron ; such as rivets out of ships, and what is termed washers and other articles cast away or dropped in the iron-yards in building ships and barges. We get these in the neighbourhood of Limehouse, where they build boats and vessels. I generally get some pieces of iron every day, which sells at $\frac{1}{4}d$. a pound, and often make 1d. or 2d. a-day, sometimes 3d., at other times only a farthing. We sell these to the different marine store dealers in the locality.

"We occasionally get copper outside Young's dock. Sometimes it is new and at other times it is old. It is cut from the side of the ship when it is being repaired, and falls down into the mud. When the pieces are large they are generally picked up by the workmen ; when small they do not put themselves to the trouble of picking them up. The mudlarks wade into the bed of the river and gather up these and sell them to the marine store dealer. The old copper sells at 1$\frac{1}{2}d$. a pound, the new copper at a higher price. I only get copper occasionally, though I go every day to seek for it.

"Pieces of rope are occasionally dropped or thrown overboard from the ships or barges and are found embedded in the mud

We do not find much of this, but sometimes get small pieces. Rope is sold to the marine store dealers at $\frac{1}{2}d.$ a pound. We also get pieces of canvas, which sells at $\frac{1}{2}d.$ a pound. I have on some occasions got as much as three pounds.

"We also pick up pieces of fat along the river-side. Sometimes we get four or five pounds and sell it at $\frac{3}{4}d.$ a pound at the marine stores; these are thrown overboard by the cooks in the ships, and after floating on the river are driven on shore.

"I generally rise in the morning at six o'clock, and go down to the river-side with my youngest brother you saw beside me at the barges. When the tide is out we pick up pieces of coal, iron, copper, rope and canvas. When the tide is in we pick up chips of wood. We go upon logs, such as those you saw me upon with my basket, and gather them there.

"In the winter time we do not work so many hours as in the summer; yet in winter we generally are more successful than in the long days of summer. A good number of boys wade in summer who do not come in winter on account of the cold. There are generally thirteen or fourteen mudlarks about Limehouse in the summer, and about six boys steadily there in the winter, who are strong and hardy, and well able to endure the cold.

"The old men do not make so much as the boys because they are not so active; they often do not make more than 6d. a day while we make 1s. or 1s. 6d.

"Some of the mudlarks are orphan boys and have no home. In the summer time they often sleep in the barges or in sheds or stables or cow-houses, with their clothes on. Some of them have not a shirt, others have a tattered shirt which is never washed, as they have no father nor mother, nor friend to care for them. Some of these orphan lads have good warm clothing; others are ragged and dirty, and covered with vermin.

"The mudlarks generally have a pound of bread to breakfast, and a pint of beer when they can afford it. They do not go to coffee-shops, not being allowed to go in, as they are apt to steal the men's 'grub.' They often have no dinner, but when they are able they have a pound of bread and 1d. worth of cheese. I never saw any of them take supper.

"The boys who are out all night lie down to sleep when it is dark, and rise as early as daylight. Sometimes they buy an article of dress, a jacket, cap, or pair of trousers from a dolly or rag-shop. They get a pair of trousers for 3d. or 4d., an old jacket for 2d, and an old cap for $\frac{1}{2}d$ or 1d. When they have money they take a bed in a low lodging-house for 2d. or 3d. a night.

"We are often chased by the Thames' police and the watermen, as the mudlarks are generally known to be thieves. I take what I can get as well as the rest when I get an opportunity.

"We often go on board of coal barges and knock or throw pieces of coal over into the mud, and afterwards come and take them away. We also carry off pieces of rope, or iron, or anything we can lay our hands on and easily carry off. We often take a boat and row on board of empty barges and steal small articles, such as pieces of canvas or iron, and go down into the cabins of the barges for this purpose, and are frequently driven off by the police and bargemen. The Thames' police often come upon us and carry off our bags and baskets with the contents.

"The mudlarks are generally good swimmers. When a bargeman gets hold of them in his barge on the river, he often throws them into the river, when they swim ashore and then take off their wet clothes and dry them. They are often seized by the police in boats, in the middle of the river, and thrown overboard, when they swim to the shore. I have been chased twice by a police galley.

"On one occasion I was swimming a considerable way out in the river when I saw two or three barges near me, and no one in them. I leaped on board of one and went down into the cabin, when some of the Thames' police in a galley rowed up to me. I ran down naked beneath the deck of the barge and closed the hatches, and fastened the staple with a piece of iron lying near, so that they could not get in to take me. They tried to open the hatch, but could not do it. After remaining for half-an-hour I heard the boat move off. On leaving the barge they rowed ashore to get my clothes, but a person on the shore took them away, so that they could not find them. After I saw them proceed a considerable distance up the river I swam ashore and got my clothes again.

"One day, about three o'clock in the afternoon, as I was at Young's Dock, I saw a large piece of copper drop down the side of a vessel which was being repaired. On the same evening, as a ship was coming out of the docks, I stripped off my clothes and dived down several feet, seized the sheet of copper and carried it away, swimming by the side of the vessel. As it was dark, I was not observed by the crew nor by any of the men who opened the gates of the dock. I fetched it to the shore, and sold it that night to a marine store dealer.

"I have been in the habit of stealing pieces of rope, lumps of coal, and other articles for the last two years; but my parents do not know of this. I have never been tried before the police court for any felony.

"It is my intention to go to sea, as my brothers have done, so soon as I can find a captain to take me on board his ship. I would like this much better than to be a coal-heaver on the river."

RECEIVERS OF STOLEN PROPERTY.

WHEN we look to the number of common thieves prowling over the metropolis —the thousands living daily on beggary, prostitution, and crime—we naturally expect to find extensive machineries for the receiving of stolen property. These receivers are to be found in different grades of society, from the keeper of the miserable low lodging-houses and dolly shops in Petticoat Lane, Rosemary Lane, and Spitalfields, in the East-end, and Dudley Street and Drury Lane in the West-end of the metropolis, to the pawnbroker in Cheapside, the Strand, and Fleet Street, and the opulent Jews of Houndsditch and its vicinity, whose coffers are said to be overflowing with gold.

Dolly Shops.—As we walk along Dudley Street, near the Seven Dials,—the Petticoat Lane of the West-end,—a curious scene presents itself to our notice. There we do not find a colony of Jews, as in the East-end, but a colony of Irish shopkeepers, with a few cockneys and Jews intermingled among them. Dudley Street is a noted mart for old clothes, consisting principally of male and female apparel, and second-hand boots and shoes.

We pass by several shops without sign boards—which by the way is a characteristic of this strange by-street—where boots and shoes, in general sadly worn, are exposed on shelves under the window, or carefully ranged in rows on the pavement before the shop. We find a middle-aged or elderly Irishman with his leathern apron, or a young Irish girl brushing shoes at the door, in Irish accent inviting customers to enter their shop.

We also observe old clothes stores, where male apparel is suspended on wooden rods before the door, and trousers, vests, and coats of different descriptions, piled on chairs in front of the shop, or exposed in the dirty unwashed windows, while the shopmen loiter before the door, hailing the customers as they pass by.

Alongside of these we see what is more strictly called dolly or leaving shops,—the fertile hot-beds of crime. The dolly shop is often termed an unlicensed pawn-shop. Around the doorway, in some cases of ordinary size, in others more spacious, we see a great assortment of articles, chiefly of female dress, suspended on the wall,—petticoats, skirts, stays, gowns, shawls, and bonnets of all patterns and sizes, the gowns being mostly of dirty cotton, spotted and striped; also children's petticoats of different kinds, shirt-fronts, collars, handkerchiefs, and neckerchiefs exposed in the window. As we look into these suspicious-looking shops we see large piles of female apparel, with articles of men's dress heaped around the walls, or deposited in bundles and paper packages on shelves around the shop, with strings of clothes hung across the apartment to dry, or offered for sale. We find in some of the back-rooms, stores of shabby old clothes, and one or more women of various ages loitering about.

In the evening these dolly shops are dimly lighted, and look still more gloomy and forbidding than during the day.

Many of these people buy other articles besides clothes. They are in the habit of receiving articles left with them, and charge 2d. or 3d. a shilling on the articles, if redeemed in a week. If not redeemed for a week, or other specified time, they sell the articles, and dispose of them, having given the party a miserably small sum, perhaps only a sixth or eighth part of their value. These shops are frequented by common thieves, and by poor dissipated creatures living in the dark slums and alleys in the vicinity, or residing in low lodging-houses. The persons who keep them often conceal the articles deposited with them from the knowledge of the police, and get punished as receivers of stolen property. Numbers of such cases occur over the metropolis in low neighbourhoods. For this reason the keepers of these shops are often compelled to remove to other localities.

The articles they receive, such as old male and female wearing apparel, are also resetted by keepers of low coffee-house and lodging-houses, and are occasionally bought by chandlers, low hairdressers, and others.

They also receive workmen's tools of an inferior quality, and cheap articles of household furniture, books, &c., from poor dissipated people, beggars, and thieves; many of which would be rejected by the licensed pawnbrokers.

They are frequently visited by the wives and daughters of the poorest labouring people, and others, who deposit wearing apparel, or bed-linen, with them for a small piece of money when they are in want of food, or when they wish to get some intoxicating liquor, in which many of them indulge too freely. They are also haunted by the lowest prostitutes on like errands. The keepers of dolly shops give more indulgence to their regular customers than they do to strangers. They charge a less sum from them, and keep their articles longer before disposing of them.

It frequently occurs that these low traders are very unscrupulous, and sell the property deposited with them, when they can make a small piece of money thereby.

There is a pretty extensive traffic carried on in the numerous dolly-shops scattered over the metropolis, as we may find from the extensive stores heaped up in their apartments, in many cases in such dense piles as almost to exclude the light of day, and from the groups of wretched creatures who frequent them — particularly in the evenings.

The principal trade in old clothes is in the East-end of the metropolis—in Rosemary Lane, Petticoat Lane, and the dark by-streets and alleys in the neighbourhood, but chiefly at the Old Clothes Exchange, where huge bales are sold in small quantities to crowds of traders, and sent off to various parts of Scotland, England, and Ireland, and exported abroad. The average weekly trade has been estimated at about 1,500*l*.

Pawnbrokers, &c.—A great amount of valuable stolen property passes into the hands of pawnbrokers and private receivers. The pawnbrokers often give only a third or fourth of the value of the article deposited with them, which lies secure in their hands for twelve months.

A good many of them deal honestly in their way, and are termed respectable dealers; but some of them deal in an illegal manner, and are punished as receivers. Many of those who are reputed as the most respectable pawnbrokers, receive stolen plate, jewellery, watches, &c.

When *plate* is stolen, it is sometimes carried away on the night of the robbery in a cab, or other conveyance, to the house of the burglars. Some thieves take it to a low beershop, where they lodge for the night; others to coffee-shops; others to persons living in private houses, pretending possibly to be bootmakers, watchmakers, copper-plate printers, tailors, marine store-dealers, &c. Such parties are private receivers well-known to the burglars. The doors of their houses are opened at any time of the night.

Burglars frequently let them know previously when they are going to work, and what they expect to get, and the crucible or silver pot is kept ready on a slow fire to receive the silver plate, sometimes marked with the crest of the owner. Within a quarter of an hour a large quantity is melted down. The burglar does not stay to see the plate melted, but makes his bargain, gets his money, and goes away.

These private receivers have generally an ounce and a quarter for their ounce of silver, and the thief is obliged to submit, after he has gone into the house. The former are understood in many cases to keep quantities of silver on hand before they sell it to some of the refiners, or other dealers, who give them a higher price for it, generally 4*s*. 10*d*. per ounce. The burglar himself obtains only from 3*s*. 6*d*. to 4*s*. an ounce.

The receivers we refer to—well-known to the cracksmen of the metropolis—live at White Hart Yard, Catharine Street, Strand; Vinegar Yard, Catharine Street, Strand; Russell Street, Covent Garden; Gravel Lane; Union Street; Friars Street, Blackfriars' Road; Oakley Street, Westminster Road; Eagle Street, Holborn; King Street, Seven Dials; Wardour Street, Oxford Street; Tottenham Place, Tottenham Court Road; Upper Afton Place, Newport Market; George's Street, Hampstead Road; Clarendon Street, Somers Town; Philip's Buildings, Somers Town; New North Place and Judd Street, Gray's Inn Road; Red Lion Street, Clerkenwell; Wilderness Row, Clerkenwell; Golden Lane; Banner Street; Banner Row; Long Alley; Tim Street; Middlesex Street, Whitechapel; Brick Lane, Whitechapel; Halfmoon Passage, Union Street, Spitalfields; Whitechapel Road; Commercial Road; Rosemary Lane, and other localities.

These persons receive plate, silk, satins, and other valuable booty.

There are also several refiners in different parts of the metropolis who generally have silver pots or crucibles on the fire ready to melt whatever plate may be taken in. Some of them are German Jews, others are English people.

These furnaces are generally in a small workshop or parlour at the back of the shop. These receivers profess to sell jewellery, lace, and other articles, which are exposed in the shop windows. They are licensed to buy gold and silver, and offer to give fair value for precious stones.

The *jewellery* stolen is taken to these same fences and sold at less than a third of its value. The names are then erased, and the articles are taken to pieces, and sold to different jewellers over the metropolis. Stolen bank notes and jewellery are often sent abroad by these fences to avoid detection.

The following prices are generally received from the fences for stolen bank-notes:—

For a £5 bank-note, from £4 to £4 10s.
  ,, 10 do. ,, £8 15s. to £9.
  ,, 20 do. about £16 10s.
  ,, 50 do. ,, £35.

As the notes rise in value they give a smaller proportionate sum for them, as they may have more trouble in getting them exchanged.

Silks and satins, and such like goods, are often conveyed to the fence in a cab on the night or morning the robbery is effected; the dealer generally gets previous notice, and expects to receive them.

In addition to the watch set at the house where the robbery is to be committed, there is often a watch stationed near the house of the receiver to look after the movements of the policeman in his locality. One of the burglars goes in the cab direct from the shop or warehouse where the robbery has been committed to the house of the receiver, and possibly at a short distance from the house gets a quiet signal from the watch as to whether it is safe to approach. If not, he can make a detour with the cab, and come back a little afterwards when the coast is clear. The burglar and the cabman remove the bags of goods into the house of the receiver, when the vehicle drives off. The driver of the cab is generally paid according to the value of the booty.

Sometimes these goods are taken to a coffee-house, where the people are acquainted with the burglars, and where one of the burglars remains till the booty is sold and removed, or otherwise disposed of. The fence, who has got notice of the plunder from some of the thieves, often comes and takes it away himself. The keeper of the coffee-house is well paid for his trouble.

Silks and satins are generally sold to the fence at 1s. a yard, whatever the quality of the fabric. Silk handkerchiefs of excellent quality are sold at 1s. each; good broadcloth from 4s. to 5s. a yard, possibly worth from 1l. 1s. to 1l. 5s.; neckties, sold in the shops from 1s. 6d. to 2s. each, are given away for 4d. to 6d. each; kid-gloves, worth from 2s. to 3s. 6d., are sold at 6d. a pair; and women's boots, worth from 6s. 6d. to 10s. 6d., are given for 2s.

Silks and satins of the value of 4,500l. have been sold for 515l., the chief proportion of the spoil thus coming into the hands of the unprincipled receiver.

Numerous cases of receiving stolen property are tried at our police-courts and sessions, as well as at the Old Bailey. We shall only adduce one illustration.

Some time ago a bale of goods was stolen from a passage in a warehouse in the City. The case was put in the hands of the police. They were a peculiar class of goods. Information was given to persons in that line of business. A few weeks after it was ascertained that the stolen property had been offered for sale by a person who produced a sample. They were ultimately traced to a place in the City, not far distant from where they had been stolen. They were seized by two officers of police. The man who was selling them was an agent, and had no hand in the robbery. He would not give up the name of the person who had sent them to him. He was taken into custody, and he and the goods were sent to the police station.

Seeing the dilemma in which he was placed, this man, when in custody, stated that he had received the goods from a well known Jewish dealer, who was thereupon arrested. On searching his premises the officers found a great part of the booty of twelve burglaries, and of three other robberies, one of them being a quantity of jewellery of great value, the whole of the property amounting to from 2000l. to 3000l.

He was tried, convicted, and sentenced to fourteen years' transportation.

From the statistics of the metropolitan police we find the number of houses of bad character, which may be used to receive stolen property, to be as follows:—

163 houses of receivers of stolen goods.
255 public-houses.   ⎫
103 beer-shops.   ⎬ The resort of thieves
154 coffee-shops.   ⎬ and prostitutes.
101 other suspect- ⎭
    ed houses.
1,706 brothels and houses of ill-**fame**.
  361 tramps' lodging-houses.

2 843

NARRATIVE OF A RETURNED CONVICT.

WE give the following brief autobiography of a person who has recently returned from one of our penal settlements, having been transported for life. In character he is very different from the generality of our London thieves, having hot African blood in his veins and being a man of passionate, unbridled character. He was formerly a daring highway robber. He was introduced to us accidentally in Drury-lane, by a Bow-street police officer, who occasionally acts as a detective. On this occasion the latter displayed very little tact and discretion, which made it exceedingly difficult for us to get from him even the following brief tale :—

"I was born in a tent at Southampton, on the skirts of a forest, among the gipsies, my father and mother being of that stock of people. We had generally about seven or eight tents in our encampment, and were frequently in the forest between Surrey and Southampton. The chief of our gang, termed the gipsey king, had great influence among us. He was then a very old, silver-headed man, and had a great number of children. I learned when a boy to play the violin, and was tolerably expert at it. I went to the public-houses and other dwellings in the neighbourhood, with three or four other gipsey boys, who played the triangle and drum, as some of the Italian minstrels do. We went during the day and often in the evening. At other times we had amusement beside the tents, jumping, running, and single-stick, and begged from the people passing by in the vehicles or on foot.

"During the day some of the men of our tribe went about the district, and looked out over the fields for horses which would suit them, and came during the night and stole them away. They never carried away horses from the stables. They generally got their booty along the by-roads, and took them to the fairs in the neighbourhood and sold them, usually for about 10*l*. or 12*l*. The horses they stole were generally light and nimble, such as might be useful to themselves. They disfigured them by putting a false mark on them, and by clipping their mane and tail. When a horse is in good order they keep it for a time till it becomes more thin and lank, to make it look older. They let the horse generally go loose on the side of a road at a distance from their encampment, till they have an opportunity to sell it; and it is generally placed alongside one or two other horses, so that it is not so much observed. The same person who steals it frequently takes it to the fair to be sold.

"The gipsies are not so much addicted to stealing from farms as is generally supposed. They are assisted in gaining a livelihood by their wives and other women going over the district telling fortunes. Some of them take to hawking for a livelihood. This is done by boys and girls, as well as old men and women. They sell baskets, brushes, brooms, and other articles.

"I spent my early years wandering among the gipsies till I was thirteen years of age, and was generally employed going about the country with my violin, along with some of my brothers.

"My father died when I was about six years of age. A lady in Southampton, of the Methodist connexion, took an interest in my brothers and me, and we settled there with our mother, and afterwards learned coach-making. I lived with my mother in Southampton for five or six years. My brothers were well-behaved, industrious boys, but I was wild and disobedient.

"The first depredation I committed was when thirteen years old. I robbed my mother of a box of old-fashioned coins and other articles, and went to Canterbury, where I got into company with prostitutes and thieves. The little money I had was soon spent.

"After this I broke the window of a pawnbroker's shop as a cart was passing by, put my hand through the broken pane of glass, and carried off a bowl of gold and silver coins, and ran off with them and made my way to Chatham.

"Some time after this I was, one day at noon, in the highway between Chatham and Woolwich, when I saw a carriage come up. The postillion was driving the horses smartly along. A gentleman and lady were inside, and the butler and a female servant were on the seat behind. I leaped on the back of the conveyance as it was driving past, and took away the portmanteau with the butler's clothes, and carried it off to the adjoining woods. I sold them to a Jew at Southampton for 3*l*. or 4*l*.

"Shortly after I came up to London, and became acquainted with a gang of young thieves in Ratcliffe Highway. I lived in a coffee-house there for about eighteen months. The boys gained their livelihood picking gentlemen's pockets, at which I soon became expert. After this I joined a gang of men, and picked ladies' pockets, and resided for some time at Whitechapel.

"Several years after I engaged with some

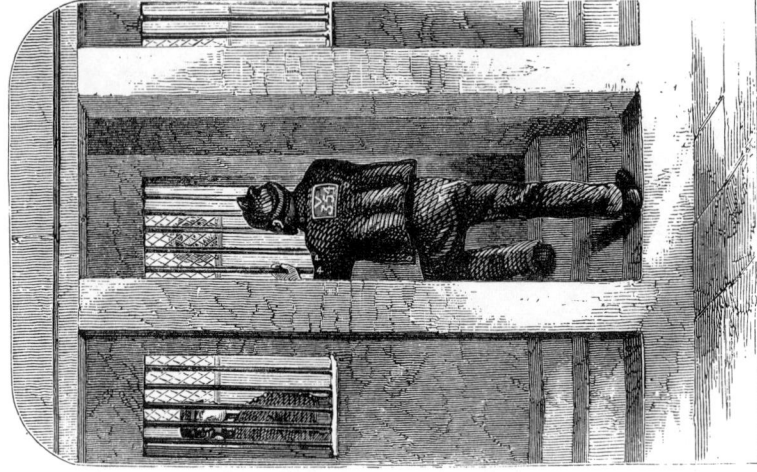
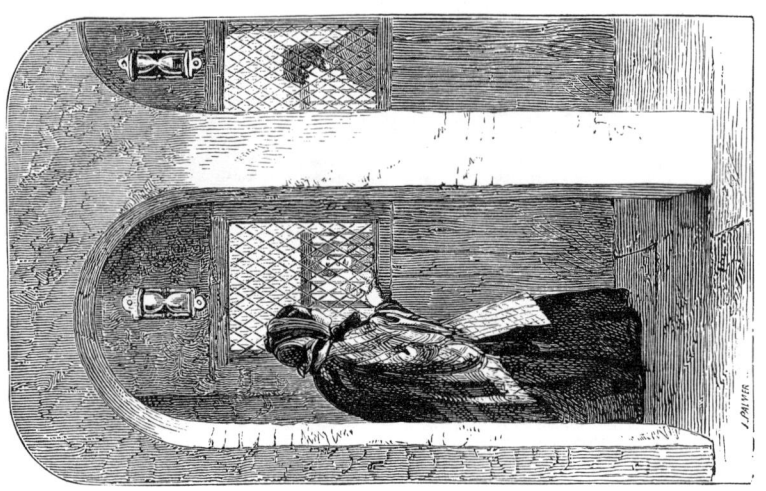

COMPARTMENT ON THE SIDE FOR VISITORS.   COMPARTMENT ON THE SIDE FOR PRISONERS.

FRIENDS VISITING PRISONERS.

other men in highway robbery. I recollect on one occasion we learned that a person was in the habit of going to one of the City banks once a week for a large sum of money—possibly to pay his workmen. He was generally in the habit of calling at other places in town on business, and carried the money with him in a blue serge bag. We followed him from the bank to several places where he made calls, until he came to a quiet by-street, near London bridge. It was a dark wintry night, and very stormy. I rushed upon him and garotted him, while one of my companions plundered him of his bag. He was a stout old man, dressed like a farmer. I was then about twenty-two years of age.

"At this time I went to music and dancing saloons, and played on my violin.

"Soon after I went to a fair at Maidstone with several thieves, all young men like myself. One of us saw a farmer in the market, a robust middle-aged man, take out his purse with a large sum of money. We followed him from the market. I went a little in advance of my companions for a distance of sixteen miles, till we came to a lonely cross turning surrounded with woods. The night happened to be dark. I went up to him and seized him by the leg, and pulled him violently off his horse, and my companions came up to assist me. While he lay on the ground we rifled his pockets of a purse containing about 500*l.* and some silver money. He did not make very much resistance and we did not injure him. We came back to London and shared the booty among us.

"About the time of the great gathering of the Chartists on Kennington Common, in 1848, I broke into a pawnbroker's shop in the metropolis, and stole jewellery to the amount of 2,000*l.*, consisting of watches, rings, &c., and also carried off some money. I sold the jewels to a Jewish receiver for about 500*l.* I was arrested some time after, and tried for this offence, and sentenced to transportation for life.

"I returned from one of the penal settlements about a year ago, and have since led an honest life."

COINING.

THIS class of felonies is as prevalent as ever in the metropolis, and is carried on in many of the low neighbourhoods.

It is generally effected in this way. Take a shilling, or other sterling coin, scour it well with soap and water; dry it, and then grease it with suet or tallow; partly wipe this off, but not wholly. Take some plaster of Paris, and make a collar either of paper or tin. Pour the plaster of Paris on the piece of coin in the collar or band round it. Leave it until it sets or hardens, when the impression will be made. You turn it up and the piece sticks in the mould. Turn the reverse side, and you take a similar impression from it; then you have the mould complete. You put the pieces of the mould together, and then pare it. You make a channel in order to pour the metal into it in a state of fusion, having the neck of the channel as small as possible. The smaller the channel the less the imperfection in the "knerling."

You make claws to the mould, so that it will stick together while you pour the metal into it. But before doing so, you must properly dry it. If you pour the hot metal into it when damp, it will fly in pieces. This is the general process by which counterfeit coin is made. When you have your coin cast, there is a "gat," or piece of refuse metal, sticks to it. You pair this off with a pair of scissors or a knife—generally a pair of scissors—then you file the edges of the coin to perfect the "knerling."

The coin is then considered finished, except the coating. At this time it is of a bluish colour, and not in a state fit for circulation, as the colour would excite suspicion.

You get a galvanic battery with nitric acid and sulphuric acid, a mixture of each diluted in water to a certain strength. You then get some cyanide and attach a copper wire to a screw of the battery. Immerse that in the cyanide of silver when the process of electro-plating commences.

The coin has to pass through another process. Get a little lampblack and oil, and make it into a sort of composition, "slumming" the coin with it. This takes the bright colour away, and makes it fit for circulation. Then wrap the coins up separately in paper so as to prevent them rubbing. When coiners are going to circulate them, they take them up and rub each piece separately. The counterfeit coin will then have the greatest resemblance to genuine coin, if well-manufactured.

While this is the general mode by which it is made, a skilful artificer, or keen-eyed detective can trace the workmanship of different makers.

Counterfeit coin is manufactured by various classes of people—costermongers, mechanics, tailors, and others—and is generally confined to the lower classes of various ages. Girls of thirteen years of age sometimes assist in making it.

It is made in Westminster, Clerkenwell, the Borough, Lambeth, Drury Lane, the Seven Dials, Lisson Grove, and other low neighbourhoods of the metropolis, at all hours of the day and night.

There are generally two persons engaged in making it—sometimes four. In nine cases out of ten, men and women are employed in it together. The man generally holds the mould with an iron clamp, that is an iron hook doubled in the shape of plyers or tongues to prevent the heat from burning their hands. The women generally pour the metal into it. One person could make the coin alone, but this would be too tedious. While engaged in this work, they fasten the doors of their room or dwelling, and have generally a person on the look-out they term a "crow," in case the officers of justice should make their appearance, and detect them in the act.

The officers make a simultaneous rush into the house after having forced open the door with a blow from a sledge-hammer, so as to detect the parties in the very act of coining. On such occasions the men endeavour to destroy the mould, while the women throw the counterfeit coin into the fire, or into the melted metal, which effectually injures it. This is done to prevent the officers getting these articles into their possession, as evidence against them.

The coiners frequently throw the hot metal at the officers, or the acids they use in their coining processes, or they attempt to strike them with a chair or stool, or other weapon that comes in their way. In most cases they resist until they are overpowered and secured.

Counterfeit coin is generally made of Britannia metal spoons and other ingredients, and very seldom of pewter pots, though formerly this was the case.

Sometimes four impressions are cast from each mould at the same instant; in other cases two or three. If too near each other the powerful heat of the metal in casting half-crowns or crowns would make the mould fly. Hence there must be spaces between each impression. Smaller coins, such as sixpences or shillings, can be placed nearer each other in the mould. On each occasion when they cast the coin they blow the dust off the mould to keep it perfectly clear, so as not to injure in the slightest degree the impression. When the latter is imperfect a new mould must be made. The coiner can use the same mould again in less than a minute to make other counterfeit coins.

Sometimes a quart basinful is made on a single occasion; at other times a very small quantity only.

The coiners have agents at different public-houses to dispose of their counterfeit coin, and some of them stand in the street to sell it. Sometimes it is sold to their private agents in their own dwellings, or sent out to parties who purchase it from them. The latter parties generally pay $1d.$ for a shilling's worth, Then these agents sell it to the utterers for $2d.$ a shilling, $3d.$ for two shillings, $3\frac{1}{2}d.$ for a half-crown, and $4d.$ a crown. Some coiners charge $5d.$ for five shillings' worth.

The detection of counterfeit coin in the metropolis is under the able management of Mr. Brennan, a skilful and experienced public officer, who keeps a keen surveillance over this department of crime.

In 1855 Mr. Brennan, along with Inspector Bryant of G division, and other officers, went to the neighbourhood of Kent Street for the purpose of apprehending a person of the name of Green, better known by the cognomen of "Charcoal." The street door was open, and the officers proceeded to the top floor up a winding staircase. The house consisted of three floors. On passing upstairs they were met by three men on the top landing, very robust, their ages averaging from twenty-four to thirty-six. One of them, named Brown, was a noted Devonshire wrestler, and a powerful-bodied man.

These men attempted to force their way down. Mr. Brennan manfully resisted and tried to keep them up, and force them back into the room. Brown leaped over him while struggling with the other two. On Mr. Brennan's son and Inspector Bryant coming up to his assistance, the other two men were arrested and secured in the yard.

A third man came out of the room and was passing by Mr. Brennan, and in doing so hit him on the head with a saucepan, and forced him against the staircase window. His son came up to his assistance, when he struck this new assailant on the arm with a crowbar, and partially disabled him. At this time the frame of the staircase window gave way, and he fell into the court.

One of the men in the house jumped from the window of the staircase on the roof of a shed, and fell right through it, and was followed by Constable Neville of the G division, who jumped after him and secured him. The former was a man of about five feet eight inches high, powerfully built. Other two men were beat back into the room and secured along with two women. Five out of a party of seven men were arrested, and the other two effected their escape. The officers only expected to see one man and a woman coining in this house.

After they succeeded in forcing the two men back into the room, the man named "Charcoal" struggled desperately, and used every effort to smash the mould. They found sufficient fragments of it as evidence against them that they had been making half-crowns, shillings, and sixpences, besides a large quantity of counterfeit coin.

The officers were obliged to remain in the house and yard until they sent to the police station for additional assistance. The prisoners were tried at the Old Bailey and sentenced to various terms of imprisonment, from six months to fourteen years. The Recorder from the bench recommended to Mr. Brennan a compensation of 10*l*. for the manly and efficient part he had acted on this trying occasion.

In 1845 Mr. Brennan received information that a man who resided at Bath Place, Old Street Road, was making counterfeit coin. This house consisted of two rooms, the one above the other. Mr. Brennan went there, accompanied by Sergeant Cole of the G division, leaving a police constable at the end of the court. He broke open the door with a sledge-hammer, and attempted to run upstairs, and was met at the door by the coiner, who tried to rush back into the room, when the former seized him by a leathern apron he had on. In the struggle both he and Mr. Brennan were hurled down to the bottom of the staircase, a distance of eleven steps. The officer was severely injured on the back of the head, and the coiner's knee struck against his belly, yet this brave officer, though severely injured, kept hold of the coiner.

At this time Cole was struggling with the coiner's wife and daughter, while their bull-dog seized him by the leg of his trousers. The dog kept hold of him for about twenty-five minutes. Latterly the three parties were secured.

Meanwhile the constable whom he had left at the end of the court heard the disturbance, and entered and assisted in securing the prisoners.

The woman was tall and masculine in appearance, and the girl was thirteen years of age.

On securing this desperate coiner Mr. Brennan proceeded upstairs, and found four galvanic batteries in full play, and about five hundred pieces of counterfeit coin in various stages of manufacture—crowns, half-crowns, shillings, and sixpences. The prisoner was committed to Newgate for trial. His wife was acquitted, she having acted under his direction. He was sentenced to fifteen years' transportation. The girl was sentenced to two years' imprisonment for the exceedingly active part she had taken in the affair.

Mr. Brennan on this occasion was severely injured in his gallant struggle.

Several years ago Mr. Brennan went to apprehend a man of the name of Morris near Westminster. The street-door of the house, which consisted of three stories, was shut, but was suddenly burst open by the blow of a sledge-hammer. On running up to the top floor he found his hat struck against something, and found there was a flap let down over the "well" of the staircase, which was dreadfully armed with iron spikes of about three or four inches long, and about the same distance apart, and it seemed utterly impossible to force it up.

The man meantime effected his escape through the roof, and ran along the roofs and jumped a depth of twenty-five feet on the roof of a shed, and was much injured. He was carried away by his friends to Birmingham, and kept in an hospital till he recovered. He then left London for two years.

Afterwards he made his appearance in the neighbourhood of Kent Street in the Borough, where Mr. Brennan went to apprehend him, assisted by several other officers. He paid him a visit at seven o'clock on a winter's evening. The coiner was sitting in the middle of the floor making half-crowns. One of the windows of the house was open. On hearing the officers approach he jumped clean out of the window on the back of an officer who was stationed there to watch—the height of one story. Mr. Brennan followed him as he ran off without his coat along some adjoining streets, and caught sight of him passing through a back door that led into some gardens. Here he fled into a house, the floor of which went down a step. There was a bed in the room with three children in it. Mr. Brennan missed his footing, and fell across the bed, and narrowly escaped injuring one of the children by the fall. The father and mother of the children were standing at the fire. The man stepped forward to the officer and was about to use violence, when Mr. Brennan told him who he was and his errand, which quieted him.

Meantime Mr. Brennan tripped up the coiner as he was endeavouring to escape, and threw him on the floor, secured him and put him into a cab, where a low mob, which had meantime gathered in this disreputable neighbourhood, tried to rescue the coiner from the hands of the officers. They threw brickbats, stones, and other missiles to rescue the prisoner.

While the officers were conveying him to the police-station this coiner while handcuffed endeavoured to throw himself in a fit of frantic passion beneath the wheels of a waggon to destroy himself, but was prevented by the officers. When in Horsemonger Gaol he refused for a time to take any food.

He was tried at the Old Bailey, and sentenced to thirty years' transportation for coining and assaulting the officers in the execution of their duty.

Number of cases of coining in the metropolitan districts for 1860 . . . 6
Ditto ditto in the City . 0
—
6
Number of cases of putting or uttering base coin, &c., in the metropolitan districts 616

FORGERS.

FORGERY is the fraudulent making or altering a written instrument, to the detriment of another person. To constitute a forgery it is not necessary that the whole instrument should be fictitious. Making an insertion, alteration, or erasure, on any material part of a genuine document, by which any of the lieges may be defrauded; the insertion of a false signature to a true instrument, or a real signature to a false one, or the altering of the date of a bill after acceptance, are all forgeries. There are different classes of these. For example, there are forgeries of bank notes, of cheques, of acceptances, wills, and other documents.

Bank Notes.—There are many forgeries of Bank of England notes, executed principally at Birmingham. In the engraving and general appearance the counterfeit so closely resembles the genuine note, that an inexperienced eye might be easily deceived. The best way to detect them is carefully to look to the water-mark embossed in the paper, which is not like a genuine note. When the back of the former is carefully inspected, the water-mark will be found to be indented, or pressed into the paper. The paper of a forged note is generally of a darker colour than a good one. To take persons off their guard, forgers frequently make the notes very dirty, so as to give them the appearance of a much-worn good note. They are frequently uttered by pretended horse-dealers, in fairs and markets, and at hotels and public-houses by persons who pretend to be travellers, and who order goods from tradespeople in the provincial towns, and pay them with forged notes. This is often done before banking-hours on the Monday, when they might be detected, but by this time the person who may have offered them has left the town. This is the common way of putting them off in London and the other towns in England. Sometimes they utter them by sending a woman, dressed as a servant, to a public-house or to a tradesman for some article, and in this manner get them exchanged—perhaps giving the address of her master as residing in the vicinity, which is sure to be false. Tradesmen are frequently taken off their guard by this means, and give an article, often of small value, with the change in return for a note. They sometimes do not discover it to be false till several days afterwards, when it is taken to the bank and detected there.

An experienced banking clerk or a keen-eyed detective, accustomed to inspect such notes, know them at once. It sometimes happens they are so well executed that they pass through provincial banks, and are not detected till they come to the Bank of England.

They generally consist of 5*l.* or 10*l.* notes, and are given to agents who sell them to the utterer, and the makers are not known to them. Knowingly to have in our possession a forged bank note, without a lawful excuse, the proof of which lies on the party charged, or to have forging instruments in our possession, is a criminal offence.

There are also forged notes of provincial banks, but these are not so numerous as those of the Bank of England. The provincial banks have generally colours and engine-turned engraving on their notes. Some have a portion of the note pink, green, or other colours, more difficult and expensive to forge than the Bank of England note, which is on plain paper with an elaborate water-mark.

Numerous cases occur before the criminal courts, where utterers of forged notes are convicted and punished.

A case of this kind was tried at Guildhall, in October, 1861. A marine-store dealer in Lower Whitecross-street was charged with feloniously uttering two forged Bank of England notes for 5l. and 10l., with the intent to defraud Mr. Crouch, the proprietor of the "Queen's Head" tavern, in Whitecross Street.

The store-dealer had waited on him to get them exchanged. Mr. Crouch paid them to his distiller, who took them to the Bank of England, when they were sent back, detected as forgeries.

The prisoner was committed to Newgate.

Many forged notes of the Bank of England are now in circulation. They may be detected by wetting them, when the watermark disappears. The vignette is often clumsily engraved. In other respects the forgery is cleverly executed.

Cheques.—A cheque is a draft or order on a banker, by a person who has money in the bank, directing the banker to pay the sum named therein to the bearer or the person named in the cheque, which must be signed by the drawer. Cheques are generally payable to the bearer, but sometimes made payable to the person who is named therein. The place of issue must be named, and the check must bear the date of issue. A *crossed* cheque has the name of a banker written across the face of it, and must be paid through that banker. If presented by any other person it is not paid without rigid inquiry. The word banker includes any person, corporation, or Joint-Stock Company, acting as bankers.

The form of the cheque is seldom forged; it is generally the signature. Sometimes the body of the cheque that contains the genuine signature is forged. For instance, in a cheque for eight pounds the letter " y " may be added to the word " eight," which makes it " eighty ;" and a cypher appended to the figure " 8 " making it " 80," to correspond with the writing. The forms of cheques are frequently obtained by means of a forged order, such as A knowing B to have an account at a bank, A writes a letter to the banker purporting to come from B, asking for a cheque-book, which the banker frequently sends on the faith of the letter being genuine. Sometimes chequebooks are stolen by burglars and other thieves who enter business premises. By some device they get the signature of a person who has money in that bank, and forge it to the stolen cheques. It has been known for forgers who wanted to obtain money from a bank, to go to a solicitor whom they knew kept a bank account. One of them would instruct the solicitor to enter an action against one of his confederates for a pretended debt. After proceedings had been instituted the party would pay the amount claimed to the solicitor; and his companion, who had given instructions in reference to the action, then goes and gets a cheque for the amount, and by that means obtains the genuine signature, and is enabled to insert a facsimile of it in forged cheques. By this means he obtains money from the bank. Cases of this kind very frequently occur.

Sometimes forgeries are done by clerks and others who have an opportunity of getting the signature of their employer. They forge his name, or alter the body of the cheque. In many commercial houses the body of the cheque is filled up by the confidential clerk and taken to the head of the firm, who signs it. These forgeries are sometimes for a small sum, at other times for a large amount.

Several cases of uttering forged cheques were lately tried before the police-courts.

A respectable-looking young woman, who described herself as a domestic servant, was brought before the Lord Mayor, charged with uttering a cheque for 5l. 18s., purporting to be signed by Mr. W. P. Bennett, with intent to defraud a banking firm in London. She had recently been on a visit to London, and had been lent a small sum of money by another servant in town, along with some dresses, amounting to 10s. 6d.

On the 30th October the latter young woman received a letter from the prisoner, enclosing a forged cheque, and at the same time stating that a young man with whom she had been keeping company had died, and had given her this cheque to get cashed. If the servant could not get away to get the cheque cashed, the prisoner wished her to lend her what she was able, to go to the young man's funeral. On presenting the cheque at the banker's the forgery was discovered.

It appeared from the evidence that the prisoner had been lodging in the same house with Mr. Bennett, whose signature she forged.

A young man of respectable appearance residing in the neighbourhood of Fleet Street, was tried at Guildhall lately, charged with uttering a cheque for 6l., well knowing the same to be a forgery. He had gone to the landlord of a public-house in Essex Street, Bouverie Street, and asked him to cash it. It was drawn by Josiah Evans in favour of C. B. Bennett, Esq., and indorsed by the latter. The cheque was on Sir Benjamin Hayward, Bart., & Co., of Manchester. When presented at the bank, it was returned with a note stating that no such person had an account there, and they did not know any of the names. The criminal was then arrested, and committed for trial.

Forged Acceptance.—A bill of exchange is a mercantile contract written on a slip of paper, whereby one person requests another to pay money on his account to a third person at the time therein specified. The person who draws the bill is termed the drawer, the party to whom it is addressed before acceptance is called the drawee—afterwards the acceptor. The party for whom it is drawn is termed the payee, who indorses the bill, and is then styled the indorser, and the party to whom he transfers it is called the indorsee. The person in possession of the bill is termed the holder.

An acceptance is an engagement to pay the bill, the person writing the word accepted across the bill with his name under it. This may be *absolute* or *qualified*. An *absolute* acceptance is an engagement to pay the bill according to its request. A *qualified* acceptance undertakes to do it conditionally.

Bills are either inland or foreign. The inland bill is on one piece of paper; foreign bills generally consist of three parts called a "set;" so that should the bearer lose one, he may receive payment for the other. Each part contains a condition that it shall be paid provided the others are unpaid. These bills require to have a stamp of proper value to make them valid.

Forgeries of bills seldom consist of the whole bill, but either the acceptor's signature, or that of the drawer, or the indorser. Sometimes the contents of the bill is altered to make it payable earlier.

These forgeries are not so numerous, and are frequently done by parties who get the bills in a surreptitious way. It often happens that one party draws the bill in another name, forging the acceptance, and passes it to a third party who is innocent of the forgery. If the person who forged the acceptance, pays the money to the bank where the bill is payable when it is due, the forgery is not detected. When he is not able to pay in the money it is discovered. It happens in this way: A B and C are commercial men, A stands well in the commercial world; B draws a bill in his name, and without his knowledge. The name of A being good, the bill passes to C without any suspicion. If B can meet it at the time it is due, A does not know that his name has been used.

If the bill is not paid at the proper time, C takes it to A, and thus discovers the forgery.

Forged Wills.—A will is a written document in which the testator disposes of his property after his death. It is not necessary that it should be written on stamped paper, as no stamp duty is required till the death of the testator, when the will is proved in court in the district where he resided. The essentials are that it should be legible, and so intelligible, that the testator's intention can be clearly understood.

If the will is not signed by the testator, it must be signed by some other person by his direction, and in his presence; two or more witnesses being present who must attest that the will was signed, and the signature acknowledged by the testator in their presence.

No will is valid unless signed at the foot of the page, or at the end by the testator, or by some other person in his presence, and by his direction. Marriage revokes a will previously made.

A codicil is a supplement, or addition to the will, altering some part, or making an addition. It may be written on the same document, or on another paper, and folded up with the original instrument. There can only be one will, yet there may be a number of codicils attached to it, and the last is equally binding as the first, if they are not contradictory.

Forgeries of wills are generally done by relations, who get a fictitious will prepared in their favour contrary to the genuine will. On the death of the supposed testator, the forged will is put forth as the genuine one, and the other is destroyed.

All parties expecting property on the death of a relative or friend, and finding none, should be careful to have the signatures of the witnesses examined, to test whether they are genuine; and also the signature of the testator.

Every will can be seen at the district court, where they are proved, on the payment of a shilling. Such an examination is the only likely method of detecting the forgery.

There are several other classes of forgery in addition to those already noticed, such as forging certificates of character, and bills of lading.

A case of the latter kind was recently tried at Guildhall. A merchant, near the Haymarket, and an artist also in the West-end, were arraigned with having feloniously forged and altered certain bills of lading;

one of these represented ten casks of alkali amounting to the value of 84*l.*, and another, twenty-six casks of alkali worth 140*l.*, with the intention of defrauding certain merchants in London. All the bills of lading were with one exception to a certain extent genuine, that is, were filled up in the first instance. But after being signed by the wharfinger, they were altered by the introduction of words and figures, to represent a larger quantity of goods than had been shipped. The prisoners were committed for trial.

Number of cases of forgery in the metropolitan districts for the year 1860   27
Ditto ditto in the City   ..   20
—
47

Amount of loss thereby in the metropolitan districts £254
Ditto ditto in the City   ..   736
—
£990

CHEATS.

Embezzlers.

This is the crime of a servant appropriating to his own use the money or goods received by him on account of his master, and is perpetrated in the metropolis by persons both in inferior and superior positions.

Were a party to advance money or goods to an acquaintance or friend, for which the latter did not give a proper return, the case would be different, and require to be sued for in a civil action.

Embezzlement is often committed by journeymen bakers entrusted by their employers with quantities of bread to distribute to customers in different parts of the metropolis, by brewer's draymen delivering malt liquors, by carmen and others engaged in their various errands. A case of this kind occurred recently. A carman in the service of a coal merchant in the West-end was charged with embezzling 6*l.* 1*s.* 6*d.* He had been in the habit of going out with coals to customers, and was empowered to receive the money, but had gone into a public-house on his return, got intoxicated, and lost the whole of his cash. He was tried at Westminster Police Court, and sentenced to pay a fine of 10*l.* with costs. This crime is frequent among this class. The chief inducements which lead to it are the habits of drinking, prevalent among them, gambling in beer-shops, attending music-saloons, such as the Mogul, Drury Lane, and Paddy's Goose, Ratcliffe Highway, and attending running matches. Their pay is not sufficient to enable them to indulge in those habits, and this leads them to commit the crime of embezzlement.

Persons in trade frequently send out their shopmen to receive orders, and obtain payment for goods supplied to families at their residence, and are occasionally entrusted with goods on stalls. In June, 1861, a respectable-looking young man, was placed at the bar of the Southwark Police Court, charged with having embezzled 39*l.*, the property of a bookselling firm in the Strand. He had been entrusted with a stall where he sold books and newspapers, and was called to account for the receipts daily. One day he neglected to send 8*l.*, the receipts of the previous Saturday, and for other seven days he had given no proper count and reckoning. He admitted the neglect, and confessed he had appropriated the money. He was paid at the rate of 1*l.* 10*s.* a month, which with commission amounted to about 6*l.* or 7*l.*

A clerk and salesman in the service of a draper in Camberwell, was charged with embezzling various sums of money belonging to his employer. It was his duty each night to account for the goods he disposed of, and the money he received. One morning he went out with a quantity of goods, and did not return at the proper time, when his employer found him in a beer-shop in the Blackfriars Road. On asking him what had become of the goods, he replied he had left them at a public-house in the Borough, which was untrue. In the account-book found upon him it was ascertained that he had received several sums of money he had not accounted for.

A robbery by a young man of this class was very ingeniously detected a few weeks ago, and brought before the Marlborough Police Court.

A shopman to a cheesemonger in Oxford

Street was charged with stealing money from the till. He had been in his employer's service for ten months, and served at the counter along with three other shopmen. The cheesemonger having found a considerable deficiency in his receipts suspected his honesty, especially as he was in the habit of attending places of amusement, and indulging in other extravagances he knew were beyond his means. He marked three half-crowns, and put them in the till to which the young man had access. Soon after he saw the latter put in his hand, and take out a piece of money. He made an excuse to send the shopman out for a moment, and on examining the till, missed one of the marked pieces of money. He thereupon gave information to the police, and again placed money in the till similarly marked, leaving a police-officer on the watch. The shopman was again detected, he was then arrested, and taken to the police-station.

Many young men of this class are wretchedly paid by their employers, and have barely enough to maintain them and keep them in decent clothing. Many of them spend their money foolishly on extravagant dress, or associating with girls, attending music-saloons, such as Weston's, in Holborn; the Pavilion, near the Haymarket; Canterbury Hall; the Philharmonic, Islington; and others. Some frequent the Grecian Theatre, City Road, and other gay resorts, and are led into crime. In one season eighteen girls were known to have been seduced by fast young men, and to become prostitutes through attending music-saloons in the neighbourhood of Tottenham Court Road.

Embezzlements are occasionally committed by females of various classes. Some of them, by fraudulent representations, obtain goods from various tradesmen, consisting of candles, soap, sugar, as on account of their customers. Some women of a higher class, such as dressmakers, and others, are entrusted with merinos, silks, satins, and other drapery goods which they embezzle.

A young married woman was lately tried at Guildhall, on a charge of disposing of a quantity of silk entrusted to her. It appeared from the evidence of the salesman of the silk manufacturer, that this female applied to him for work, at same time producing a written recommendation, purporting to come from a person known by the firm. Materials to the value of 5l. 15s. were given her to be wrought up into an article of dress. On applying for it at the proper time, he found she had sold the materials, and had left her lodging. While the work was supposed to be in progress, the firm had also given her 2l. 13s., on partial payment. She pleaded poverty as the cause of her embezzling the goods.

Parties connected with public societies occasionally embezzle the money committed to their charge. The secretary of a friendly society in the east-end, was brought before the Thames Police Court, charged with embezzling various sums of money he had received on account of the society. The secretary of another friendly society on the Surrey side, was lately charged at Southwark Police Court with embezzling upwards of 100l. This society has branches in all parts of the kingdom, but the central office is in the metropolis. The secretary had been in their service for upwards of two years, at a fixed salary. It was his duty to receive contributions from the country, and town members; and to account for the same to the treasurer. He recently absconded, when large defalcations were discovered amounting to upwards of 100l.

A considerable number of embezzlements are committed by commercial travellers, and by clerks in lawyers' offices, banks, commercial firms, and government offices. Some of them of great and serious amounts.

Tradesmen and others in the middle class, and some respectable labouring men, and mechanics, place their sons in counting-houses, or other establishments superior to their own position; these foolishly try to maintain the appearance of their fellow-clerks who have ampler pecuniary means. This often leads to embezzling the property of the employer or firm.

Crimes of this class are occasionally committed by lawyers' clerks, who are in many cases wretchedly paid, as well as by some who have handsome salaries. Numerous embezzlements are also perpetrated in commercial firms, by their servants; some of them to the value of many thousand pounds.

A commercial traveller was lately brought up at the Mansion House, charged with embezzlement. It appears he travelled for a firm in the City, and had been above ten years in their service at a salary of 1l. 1s. per day. It was his duty to take orders and collect accounts as they became due. Some days he received from the customers certain sums and afterwards paid a less amount to the firm, keeping the rest of the money in his hands, which he appropriated. Another day he received a sum of money he never accounted for. He was committed for trial.

An embezzlement was committed by a cashier to a commercial firm in the City.

It appeared from the evidence, he had been in the service of his employers for ten years, and kept the petty cash-book; with an account of all sums paid. He had to account for the amounts given him as petty cash, and for disbursements whenever he should be called.

From the extravagant style in which he was living, which reached the ear of the firm, their suspicions were aroused, and one of them asked him to bring his books into the counting-house, and render the customary account of the petty cash. His employer discovered the balance of some of the pages did not correspond with the balance brought forward, and asked the cashier to account for it; when he acknowledged that he had appropriated the difference to his own use.

Several items were then pointed out, ranging over a number of months, in which he had plundered his employers of several hundred pounds. This was effected in a very simple way; by carrying the balance of the cash in hand to the top of next page 100*l*. less than it was on the preceding page, and by calling the disbursements when his employers checked the accounts, 100*l*. more than they really were.

The books of commercial firms are frequently falsified in other modes, to effect embezzlements.

These defalcations often arise from fast life, extravagant habits, and gambling. Many fashionable clerks in lawyers' offices, banks, and Government offices, frequent the Oxford and Alhambra music halls, the West-end theatres, concerts, and operas. They attend the Holborn Assembly-room and the Argyle Rooms, and are frequently to be seen at masked balls, and at Cremorne Gardens during the season. They occasionally indulge in midnight carousals in the Turkish divans and supper-rooms. Some Government clerks have high salaries, and keep a mistress in fashionable style, with brougham and coachman, and footman; others maintain their family in a style their salary is unable to support, all of which lead them step by step to embezzlement and ruin.

Number of cases of embezzlement in the
Metropolitan districts for 1860 .. 223
Ditto ditto in the City .. 70
———
293

Value of money and property abstracted thereby in the Metropolitan districts—
£5,271
Ditto ditto in the City .. 2,660
———
£7,931

MAGSMEN, OR SHARPERS.

THIS is a peculiar class of unprincipled men, who play tricks with cards, skittles, &c. &c., and lay wagers with the view of cheating those strangers who may have the misfortune to be in their company.

Their mode of operation is this: There are generally three of them in a gang—seldom or never less. They go out together, but do not walk beside each other when they are at work. One may be on the one side of the street, and the other two arm-in-arm on the other. They generally dress well, and in various styles, some are attired as gentlemen, others as country farmers. In one gang, a sharper is dressed as a coachman in livery, and in another they have a confederate attired as a parson, and wearing green spectacles.

Many of them start early in the morning from the bottom of Holborn Hill, and branch off in different directions in search of dupes. They frequent Fleet Street, Oxford Street, Strand, Regent Street, Shoreditch, Whitechapel, Commercial Road, the vicinity of the railway stations, and the docks. They are generally to be seen wandering about the streets till four o'clock in the afternoon, unless they have succeeded in picking up a stranger likely to be a victim. They visit the British Museum, St. Paul's, Westminster Abbey, and the Crystal Palace, &c., and on market days attend the fairs.

The person who walks the street in front of the gang, is generally the most engaging and social; the other two keep in sight, and watch his movements. As the former proceeds along he keenly observes the persons passing. If he sees a countryman or a foreigner pass who appears to have money, or a person loitering by a shop-window, he steps up to him and probably enters into conversation regarding some object in sight.

For instance, in passing Somerset House in the Strand, he will go up to him and ask what noble building that is, hinting at the same time that he is a stranger in London. It frequently occurs that the individual he addresses is also a stranger in London. Having entered into conversation, the first object he has in view is to learn from the person the locality to which he belongs. The sharp informs him he has some relation there, or knows some person in the town or district. (Many of the magsmen have travelled a good deal, and are acquainted with many localities, some of them speak several foreign languages.) He may then represent that he has a good deal of property, and is going back to this village to give so much money to the poor. It sometimes occurs in the course of conversation he proposes to give the stranger a sum of money to distribute among the poor of his district, as he is specially interested in them, and may at the same time produce his pocket-book, with a bundle of flash notes. This may occur in walking along the street. He will then propose to enter a beer-shop, or gin-palace to have a glass of ale or wine. They go in accordingly. When standing at the bar, or seated in the parlour, one of his confederates, enters, and calls for a glass of liquor.

This party appears to be a total stranger to his companion. He soon enters as it were casually into conversation, and they possibly speak of their bodily strength. A bet is made that one of them cannot throw a weight as many yards as the other. They make a wager, and the stranger is asked to go with them as a referee, to decide the bet. They may call a cab, and adjourn to some well-known skittle-alley. On going there they find another confederate, who also pretends to be unacquainted with the others. One of the two who made the wager as to throwing the weight may pace the skittle-ground to find its dimensions, and pretend it is not long enough.

They will then possibly propose to have a game at skittles, and will bet with each other that they will throw down the pins in so many throws.

The sharp who introduced the stranger, and assumes to be his friend, always is allowed to win, perhaps from 5s. to 10s., or more, as the case may be. He plays well, and the other is not so good. Up to this time the intended victim has no hand in the game. Another bet is made, and the stranger is possibly induced to join in it with his agreeable companion, and it is generally arranged that he wins the first time.

He is persuaded to bet for a higher amount by himself, and not in partnership, which he loses, and continues to do so every time till he has lost all he possessed.

He is invariably called out to the bar by the man who introduced him to the house, when they have a glass together, and in the meantime the others escape.

The sharp will say to the victim after staying there a short time, " I believe these men not to be honest; I'll go and see where they have gone, and try and get your money back." He goes out with the pretence of looking after them, and walks off. The victim proceeds in search of them, and finds they have decamped leaving him penniless.

They have a very ingenious mode of finding out if the person they accost has money in his pocket. This is done after he is introduced into the public-house when getting a glass of ale. The second confederate comes in invariably. The two magsmen begin to converse as to the money they have with them. One pretends he has so much money, which the other will dispute. They possibly appear to get very angry, and one of them makes a bet that he can produce more money than any in the company. They then take out their cash, and induce the stranger to do so, to find which of them has got the highest amount. They thus learn how much money he has in his possession.

When they find he has a sufficient sum, they adjourn to a house they are accustomed to use for the purpose of paying the sum lost by the wager. It generally happens the stranger has most, and wins the bet.

On arriving at this house they wish a stamped receipt for the cash. Being a stranger he is asked as a security to leave something as a deposit till he returns. At the same time this sharp takes out a bag of money containing medals instead of sovereigns, or a pocket-book with flash notes.

He soon comes back with a receipt stamp, but a dispute invariably arises whether it will do. He suggests that some one else should go and get one. The stranger is urged to go for one. In the same manner he leaves money on the table as a security that he will return.

He may not know where to get the receipt stamp, and one of them proposes to accompany him. They walk along some distance together, when this man will say, "I don't much like these two men you have left your money with; do you know them?" He will then advise him to go back, and see if his cash is all right. On his return he finds them both gone, and his money has also disappeared.

We shall now notice several of the tricks they practise to delude their victims.

The Card tricks.—These are not often practised in London but generally at racecourses and country fairs, or where any pastime is going on. Only three cards are used. There is one picture card along with two others. They play with them generally on the ground or on their knee. There are always several persons in a gang at this game. One works the cards, shuffling them together, and then deals them on the ground. They bet two to one no one will find the picture card (the Knave, King, or Queen). One of the confederates makes a bet that he can find it, and throws down

LIBERATION OF PRISONERS FROM COLDBATH FIELDS HOUSE OF CORRECTION.

a sovereign or half-sovereign, as the case may be.

He picks up one of the cards, which will be the picture card, or the one they propose to find. The sharp dealing the cards bets that no one will find the same card again. Some simpleton in the crowd will possibly bet from 1*l.* to 10*l.* that he can find it. He picks up a card, which is not the picture card and cannot be, as it has been secretly removed from the pack, and another card has been substituted in its place.

Skittles.—They generally depend on the ability of one of their gang when engaged in this game, so that he shall be able to take the advantage when wanted. When they bet and find their opponent is expert, he is expected to be able to beat him. In every gang there is generally one superior player. He may pretend to play indifferently for a time, but has generally superior skill, and wins the bet.

Thimble and Pea.—It is done in this way. There are three thimbles and a pea. These are generally worked by a man dressed as a countryman, with a smock-frock, at country fairs, race-courses, and other places without the metropolitan police district. They commence by working the pea from one thimble to another, similar to the card trick, and bet in the same way until some person in the company—not a confederate—will bet that he can find the pea. He lifts up one of the thimbles and ascertains that it is not there. Meantime the pea has been removed. It is secreted under the thumb nail of the sharp, and is not under either of the thimbles.

The Lock.—While the sharps are seated in a convenient house with their dupe, a man, a confederate of theirs, may come in, dressed as a hawker, offering various articles for sale. He will produce a lock which can be easily opened by a key in their presence. He throws the lock down on the table and bets any one in the room they cannot open it. One of his companions will make a bet that he can open it. He takes it up, opens it easily, and wins the wager.

He will show the stranger how it is opened; after which, by a swift movement of his hand, he substitutes another similar lock in its place which cannot be opened. The former is induced possibly to bet that he is able to open it.

The lock is handed to him; he thinks it is the same and tries to open it, but does not succeed, and loses his wager.

There are various other tricks somewhat of a similar character, on which they lay wagers and plunder their dupes. They have a considerable number of moves with cards, and are ever inventing new dodges or "pulls" as they term them.

They chiefly confine themselves on most occasions to the tricks we have noticed. Sometimes, however, they play at whist, cribbage, roulette, loo, and other card games, and manage to get the advantage in many ways. One of them will look at the cards of his opponent when playing, and will telegraph to some of the others by various signs and motions, understood among themselves, but unintelligible to a stranger.

The same sharpers who walk the streets of London attend country fairs and race-courses, in different dress and appearance, as if they had no connexion with each other.

It often happens one of them is arrested for these offences and is remanded. Before the expiry of the time his confederates generally manage to see the dupe, and restore his property on the condition he shall keep out of the way and allow the case to drop. The female who cohabits with him, or possibly his wife, may call on him for this purpose, and give him part or the whole of his money.

Their ages average from twenty to sixty years. Many of them are married and have families; others cohabit with well-dressed women—pickpockets and shoplifters.

Some are in better condition than others. They are occasionally shabbily dressed and in needy condition; at other times in most respectable attire—some appear as men of fashion.

They are generally very heartless in plundering their dupes. Not content with stripping him of the money he may have on his person—sometimes a large sum—they try to get the cash he has deposited in the bank, and strip him of his watch and chain, leaving him without a shilling in his pocket.

There is no formal association between the several gangs, yet from their movements there appears to be an understanding between them. For example, if a certain gang has plundered a victim in Oxford Street, it will likely remove to another district for a time, and another party of magsmen will take their place.

Magsmen are of various grades. Some are broken-down tradesmen, others have been brokers and publicans and french-polishers, while part of their number are convicted felons. Numbers of them are betting-men and attend races; indeed most of them are connected with this disreputable class. Many of them reside in the neighbourhood of Waterloo Road and King's

Cross, and in quiet streets over the metropolis.

They are frequently brought before the police-courts, charged with conspiracy with intent to defraud; but the matter is in general secretly arranged with the prosecutor, and the case is allowed to drop.

Sometimes when the sharps cannot manage to defraud the strangers they meet with, they snatch their money from them with violence.

In the beginning of November, 1861, two sharps were brought before the Croydon police-court, charged with being concerned, with others not in custody, in stealing 116*l*., the property of a baker, residing in the country.

As the prosecutor, a young man, was going along a country road he met one of the sharps and a man not in custody. At this time there were four men on the road playing cards. He remained for a few minutes looking at them. The man who was the companion of the sharp asked him to accompany him to a railway hotel, and ordered a glass of ale for himself.

A man not in custody then asked a sharp to lend him some money, saying he would get him good security; upon which the latter offered to lend him the sum of 50*l*. at five per cent. interest. On the stranger being represented to this person as a friend, he offered to lend him as large a sum of money as he could produce himself, to show that he was a respectable and substantial person. The sharp then told the baker to go home and get 100*l*. and he would lend him that sum. He did so, one of the sharps accompanying him nearly all the way to his house. The dupe returned with a 10*l*. note. They told him it was not enough, and wished him to leave it in their hands and to bring 100*l*. He went out leaving the 10*l*. on the table as security for his coming back with more money.

He returned with 100*l*. in bank notes and gold and counted it out on the table. The sharp pretended then to be willing to lend 100*l*. at five per cent., but added that he must have a stamped receipt. The dupe left his money on the table covered with his handkerchief, and went out to get a stamp, and on his return found the sharps and his money had disappeared.

A few days after, the victim happening to be in London, saw one of them in the street, and gave him into custody.

A few weeks ago three skittle-sharps, well-dressed men, were brought before the Southwark police court, charged with robbing a country waiter of 40*l*. in Bank of England notes. It appeared from the evidence, that the prosecutor met a man in High Street, Southwark, on an afternoon, who offered to show him the way to the Borough Road. They entered a public-house on the way, when the other prisoners came in. One of them pulled out a number of notes, and said he had just come into possession of a fortune. It was suggested, in the course of conversation, they should go to another house to throw a weight, and the prosecutor was to go and see they had fair play.

They accordingly went to another house, but instead of throwing the weight, skittles were introduced, and they played several games. The prosecutor lost a sovereign, which was all the money he had with him. One of the sharps bet 20*l*. that the waiter could not produce 60*l*. within three hours. He accepted the bet and went with two of them to Blackheath, and returned to the public house with the money, amounting to 40*l*. in bank notes and 20*l*. in gold. They went to the skittle-ground, when one of them snatched the notes out of his hand, and they all decamped.

They were apprehended that night by Mr. Jones, detective at Tower Street station.

The statistics of this class of crime will be given when we come to treat of swindlers.

SWINDLERS.

SWINDLING is carried on very extensively in the metropolis in different classes of society, from the young man who strolls into a coffeehouse in Shoreditch or Bishopsgate, and decamps without paying his night's lodging, to the fashionable rogue who attends the brilliant assemblies in the West-end. It occurs in private life and in the commercial world in different departments of business. Large quantities of goods are sent from the provinces to parties in London, who give orders and are entirely unknown to those who send them, and fictitious references are given, or references to confederates in town connected with them.

We select a few illustrations of various modes of swindling which prevail over the metropolis.

A young man calls at a coffeehouse, or hotel, or a private lodging, and represents that he is the son of a gentleman in good position, or that he is in possession of certain property, left him by his friends, or that he has a situation in the neighbourhood, and after a few days or weeks decamps without paying his bill, perhaps leaving behind him an empty carpet bag, or a trunk, containing a few articles of no value.

An ingenious case of swindling occurred in the City some time since. A fashionably attired young man occupied a small office in White Lion Court, Cornhill, London. It contained no furniture, except two chairs and a desk. He obtained a number of bracelets from different jewellers, and quantities of goods from different tradesmen to a considerable amount, under false pretences. He was apprehended and tried before the police court, and sentenced to twelve months' imprisonment with hard labour.

At the time of his arrest he had obtained possession of a handsome residence at Abbey Wood, Kent, which was evidently intended as a place of reference, where no doubt he purposed to carry on a profitable system of swindling.

Swindlers have many ingenious modes of obtaining goods, sometimes to a very considerable amount, from credulous tradesmen, who are too often ready to be duped by their unprincipled devices. For example, some of them of respectable or fashionable appearance may pretend they are about to be married, and wish to have their house furnished. They give their name and address, and to avoid suspicion may even arrange particulars as to the manner in which the money is to be paid. A case of this kind occurred in Grove Terrace, where a furniture-dealer was requested to call on a swindler by a person who pretended to be his servant, and received directions to send him various articles of furniture. The goods were accordingly sent to the house. On a subsequent day the servant called on him at his premises, with a well-dressed young lady, whom she introduced as the intended wife of her employer, and said they had called to select some more goods. They selected a variety of articles, and desired they should be added to the account. One day the tradesman called for payment, and was told the gentleman was then out of town, but would call on him as soon as he returned. Soon after he made another call at the house, which he found closed up, and that he had been heartlessly duped. The value of the goods amounted to 58*l*. 18*s*. 4*d*.

Swindling is occasionally carried on in the West-end in a bold and brilliant style by persons of fashionable appearance and elegant address. A lady-like person who assumed the name of Mrs. Gordon, and sometimes Mrs. Major Gordon, and who represented her husband to be in India, succeeded in obtaining goods from different tradesmen and mercantile establishments at the West-end to a great amount, and gave references to a respectable firm as her agents. Possessing a lady-like appearance and address, she easily succeeded in obtaining a furnished residence at St. John's Wood, and applied to a livery stable-keeper for the loan of a brougham, hired a coachman, and got a suit of livery for him, and appeared in West-end assemblies as a lady of fashion. After staying about a fortnight at St. John's Wood she left suddenly, without settling with any of her creditors. She addressed a letter to each of them, requesting that their account should be sent to her agents, and payment would be made as soon as Captain Gordon's affairs were settled. She expressed regret that she had been called away so abruptly on urgent business.

She was usually accompanied by a little girl, about eleven years of age, her daughter, and by an elderly woman, who attended to domestic duties.

She was afterwards convicted at Marylebone police court, under the name of Mrs. Helen Murray, charged with obtaining large quantities of goods from West-end tradesmen by fraudulent means.

A considerable traffic in commercial swindling in various forms is carried on in London. Sometimes fraudulently under the name of another well-known firm; at other times under the name of a fictitious firm.

A case of this kind was tried at the Liverpool assizes, which illustrates the fraudulent system we refer to. Charles Howard and John Owen were indicted for obtaining goods on false pretences. In other counts of their indictment they were charged with having conspired with another man named Bonar Russell—not in custody—with obtaining goods under false pretences. The prosecutor Thomas Parkenson Luthwaite, a currier at Barton in Westmoreland, received an order by letter from John Howard and Co. of Droylesden, near Manchester, desiring him to send them a certain quantity of leather, and reference was given as to their respectability. The prosecutor sent the leather and a letter by post containing the invoice. The leather duly arrived at Droylesden; but the police having received information gave notice to the railway officials to detain it, until they got further knowledge concerning them. Howard and Russell went to the station, but were told they could not get the leather, as there was no such firm as

Howard and Co. at Droylesden. Howard replied that there was—that he lived there. It was subsequently arranged that the goods should be delivered, on the party producing a formal order. On the next day, Owen came with a horse and cart to Droylesden station, and asked for the goods, at the same time producing his order.

They were delivered to him, when he put them in his cart and drove off. Two officers of police in plain clothes accosted him, and asked for a ride in his cart which he refused. The officers followed him, and found he did not go to Droylesden, but to a house at Hulme near Manchester, as he had been directed. This house was searched, and Howard and Russell were arrested. Howard having been admitted to bail, did not appear at the trial.

On farther inquiries it was found there was no such firm as John Howard and Co. at Droylesden, but that Howard and Russell had taken a house there which was not furnished, and where they went occasionally to receive letters addressed to Howard and Co., Droylesden. Owen was acquitted; Howard was found guilty of conspiracy with intent to defraud.

A number of cases occur where swindlers attempt to cheat different societies in various ways. Two men were tried at the police court a few days ago for unlawfully attempting to cheat and defraud a loan society to obtain 5l. The prisoners formed part of a gang of swindlers, who operated in this way:—Some of them took a house for the purpose of giving references to others, who applied to loan societies for an advance of money, and produced false receipts for rent and taxes. They had carried on this system for years, and many of them had been convicted. Some of the gang formerly had an office in Holborn, where they defrauded young men in search of situations by getting them to leave a sum of money as security. They were tried and convicted on this charge.

There is another heartless system of base swindling perpetrated by a class of cheats, who pretend to assist parties in getting situations, and hold out flaming inducements through advertisements in the newspapers to working men, servants, clerks, teachers, clergymen, and others; and contrive to get a large income by duping the public.

A swindler contrived to obtain sums of 5s. each in postage stamps, or post-office orders, from a large number of people, under pretence of obtaining situations for them as farm bailiffs. An advertisement was inserted in the newspaper, and in reply to the several applicants, a letter was returned, stating that although the applicant was among the leading competitors another party had secured the place. At the same time another attempt was made to inveigle the dupe, under the pretence of paying another fee of 5s., with the hope of obtaining a similar situation in prospect. The swindler intimated that the only interest he had in the matter was the agent's fee, charged alike to the employer and the employed, and generally paid in advance. He desired that letters addressed to him should be directed to 42, Sydney Street, Chorlton-upon-Medlock. He had an empty house there, taken for the purpose, with the convenience of a letter-box in the door into which the postman dropped letters twice a day. A woman came immediately after each post and took them away.

On arresting the woman, the officers found in her basket 87 letters, 44 of them containing 5s. in postage stamps, or a post-office order payable to the swindler himself. Nearly all the others were letters from persons at a distance from a post office, who were unable to remit the 5s., but promised to send the money when they got an opportunity.

On a subsequent day, 120 letters were taken out of the letter-box, most of them containing a remittance, This system had been in operation for a month. One day 190 letters were delivered by one post. It was estimated that no fewer than 3000 letters had come in during the month, most of them enclosing 5s.; and it is supposed the swindler had received about 700l., a handsome return for the price of a few advertisements in newspapers, a few lithographed circulars, a few postage-stamps, and a quarter of a year's rent of an empty house.

Another case of a similar kind, occurred at the Maidstone assizes. Henry Moreton, aged 43, a tall gentlemanly man, and a young woman aged 19 years, were indicted for conspiring to obtain goods and money by false pretences. The name given by the male prisoner was known to be an assumed one. It was stated that he was well connected and formerly in a good position in society,

At the trial, a witness deposed that an advertisement had appeared in a Cornish newspaper, addressed to Cornish miners, stating they could be sent out to Australia by an English gold-mining company, and would be paid 20l. of wages per month, to commence on their arrival at the mines. The advertisement also stated that if 1s. or twelve postage stamps were sent to Mr. Henry Moreton, Chatham, a copy of the stamped agreement and full particulars as to the company, would be given.

The prisoner was arrested, and 41 letters found in his possession, addressed to "Mr. H. Moreton, Chatham:" 25 of the letters contained twelve postage stamps each and some of them had 1s. inside. It was ascertained the female cohabited with him. It appeared that he had pawned 482 stamps on the 14th February, for 1l. 15s., 289 on the 21st, for 1l., and 744 on another day.

Eighty-two letters came in one day chiefly from Ireland and Cornwall.

On searching a box in his room they found a large quantity of Irish and Cornish newspapers, many of them containing the advertisement referred to.

He was found guilty, and was sentenced to hard labour for fifteen months. The young woman was acquitted.

The judge, in passing sentence, observed that the prisoner had been convicted of swindling poor people, and his being respectably connected aggravated the case.

We give the following illustration of an English swindler's adventures on the Continent.

A married couple were tried at Pau, on a charge of swindling. The husband represented himself to be the son of a colonel in the English army and of a Neapolitan princess. His wife pretended to be the daughter of an English general. They said they were allied to the families of the Dukes of Norfolk, Leinster, and Devonshire. They came in a post-chaise to the Hotel de France, accompanied by several servants, lived in the style of persons of the highest rank, and run up a bill of 6000 francs. As the landlord declined to give credit for more, they took a château, which they got fitted up in a costly way. They paid 2500 francs for rent, and were largely in debt to the butcher, tailor, grocer, and others. The lady affected to be very pious, and gave 895 francs to the abbé for masses.

An English lady who came from Brussels to give evidence, stated that her husband had paid 50,000 francs to release them from a debtors' prison at Cologne, as he believed them to be what they represented. It was shown at the trial that they had received letters from Lord Grey, the King of Holland, and other distinguished personages. They were convicted of swindling, and condemned to one year's imprisonment, or to pay a fine of 200 francs.

On hearing the sentence the woman uttered a piercing cry and fainted in her husband's arms, but soon recovered. They were then removed to prison.

The assumption of a variety of names, some of them of a high-sounding and pretentious character, is resorted to by swindlers giving orders for goods by letter from a distance—an address is also assumed of a nature well calculated to deceive: as an instance, we may mention that an individual has for a long period of time fared sumptuously upon the plunder obtained by his fraudulent transactions, of whose aliases and pseudo residences the following are but a few:—

Creighton Beauchamp Harper; the Russets, near Edenbridge.

Beauchamp Harper; Albion House, Rye.

Charles Creighton Beauchamp Harper; ditto.

Neanberrie Harper, M. N. I.; The Broadlands, Winchelsea.

Beauchamp Harper; Halden House, Lewes.

R. E. Beresford; The Oaklands, Chelmsford.

The majority of these residences existed only in the imagination of this indefatigable cosmopolite. In some cases he had christened a paltry tenement let at the rent of a few shillings per week "House;" a small cottage in Albion Place, Rye, being magnified into "Albion House." When an address is assumed having no existence, his plan is to request the postmaster of the district to send the letters, &c., to his real address—generally some little distance off—a similar notice also being given at the nearest railway station. The goods ordered are generally of such a nature as to lull suspicion, viz., a gun, as "I am going to a friend's grounds to shoot and I want one immediately;" "a silver cornet;" "two umbrellas, one for me and one for Mrs. Harper;" "a fashionable bonnet with extra strings, young looking, for Mrs. Harper;" "white lace frock for Miss Harper, immediately;" "a violet-coloured velvet bonnet for my sister," &c., &c., &c., ad infinitum.

A person, pretending to be a German baron, some time ago ordered and received goods to a large amount from merchants in Glasgow. It was ascertained he was a swindler. He was a man of about forty years of age, 5 feet 8 inches high, and was accompanied by a lady about twenty-five years of age. They were both well-educated people, and could speak the English language fluently.

A fellow, assuming the name of the Rev. Mr. Williams, pursued a romantic and adventurous career of swindling in different positions in society, and was an adept in deception. On one occasion, by means of forged credentials, he obtained an appointment as curate in Northamptonshire, where he conducted himself for some time with a most sanctimonious air. Several marriages were celebrated by him, which were apparently satisfactorily performed. He obtained many articles of jewellery from firms in London, who were deceived by his appearance and position. He wrote several modes of handwriting, and had a plausible manner of insinuating himself into the good graces of his victims.

He died a very tragical death. Having been arrested for swindling he was taken to Northampton. On his arrival at the railway station there, he threw himself across the rails and was crushed to death by the train.

There is a mode of extracting money from the unwary, practised by a gang of swindlers by means of *mock auctions*. They dispose of watches, never intended to keep time, and other spurious articles, and have confederates, or decoys, who pretend to bid for the goods at the auctions, and sometimes buy them at an under price; but they are by arrangement returned soon after, and again offered for sale.

We have been favoured with some of the foregoing particulars by the officials of Stubbs' Mercantile Offices; the courtesy of the secretary having also placed the register of that extensive establishment at our service.

Number of cases of fraud and conspiracy with intent to defraud in the Metropolitan districts for 1860 325
Ditto ditto in the City .. 51
———
376
Value of property thereby abstracted in the Metropolitan district .. £3,443
Ditto ditto in the City .. 2,429
———
£5,872

BEGGARS AND CHEATS.

In primitive times beggars were recognised as a legitimate component part in the fabric of society. Socially, and apart from state government, there were, during the patriarchal period, three states of the community, and these were the landowners, their servants. and the dependants of both —beggars. There was no disgrace attached to the name of beggar at this time, for those who lived by charity were persons who were either too old to work or were incapacitated from work by bodily affliction. This being the condition of the beggars of the early ages, it was considered no less a sacred than a social duty to protect them and relieve their wants. Many illustrious names, both in sacred and profane history, are associated with systematic mendicancy, and the very name of "beggar" has derived a sort of classic dignity from this circumstance. Beggars are frequently mentioned with honour in the Old Testament; and in the New, one of the most touching incidents in our Lord's history has reference to "a certain beggar named Lazarus, which was laid at the rich man's gate." Nor must it be forgotten that the father of poetry, the immortal Homer, was a beggar and blind, and went about singing his own verses to excite charity. The name of Belisarius is more closely associated with the begging exploits ascribed to him than with his great historical conquests. "Give a halfpenny to a poor man" was as familiar a phrase in Latin in the old world as it is to-day in the streets of London. It would be tedious to enumerate all the instances of honourable beggary which are celebrated in history, or even to glance at the most notable of them; it will be enough for the purpose we have in view if I direct attention to the aspects of beggary at a few marked periods of history.

It will be found that imposture in beggary has invariably been the offspring of a high state of civilization, and has generally had its origin in large towns. When mendicancy assumes this form it becomes a public nuisance, and imperatively calls for prohibitive laws. The beggar whose poverty is not real, but assumed, is no longer a beggar in the true sense of the word, but a cheat and an impostor, and as such he is naturally regarded, not as an object for compassion, but as an enemy to the state. In all times, however, the real beggar—the poor wretch who has no means of gaining a livelihood by his labour, the afflicted outcast, the aged, the forsaken, and the weak—has invariably commanded the respect and excited the compassion of his more fortunate fellow-men. The traces of this consideration for beggars which we find in history are not a little remarkable. In the early Saxon times the relief of beggars was one of the most honourable duties of the mistress of the house. Our beautiful English word "lady" derives its origin from this practice. The mistress of a Saxon household gave away bread with her own hand to the poor, and thence she was called "*lef day*," or bread giver, which at a later period was rendered into *lady*. A well-known incident in the life of Alfred the Great shows how sacred a duty the giving of alms was regarded at that period. In early times beggary had even a romantic aspect. Poets celebrated the wanderings of beggars in so attractive a manner that great personages would sometimes envy the condition of the ragged mendicant and imitate his mode of life. James V. of Scotland was so enamoured of the life of the gaberlunzie man that he assumed his wallet and tattered garments, and wandered about among his subjects begging from door to door, and singing ballads for a supper and a night's lodging. The beggar's profession was held in respect at that time, for it had not yet become associated with imposture; and as the country beggars were also ballad-singers and story-tellers, their visits were rather welcome than otherwise. It must also be taken into account that beggars were not numerous at this period.

It would appear that beggars first began to swarm and become troublesome and importunate shortly after the Reformation. The immediate cause of this was the abolition and spoliation of the monasteries and religious houses by Henry VIII. Whatever amount of evil they may have done, the monasteries did one good thing—they assisted the poor and provided for many persons who were unable to provide for themselves. When the monasteries were demolished and their revenues confiscated, these dependent persons were cast upon the world to seek bread where they could find it. As many of them were totally unaccustomed to labour, they had no resource but to beg. The result was that the country was soon overrun with beggars, many of whom exacted alms by violence and by threats. In the course of the next reign we hear of legislative enactments for the suppression of beggary. The first efforts in this direction wholly failed to abate the nuisance, and more stringent acts were passed. In the reign of Charles II. begging had become so profitable that a great many Irish came over to this country to pursue it as a trade.

The evil then became so intolerable that a royal proclamation was issued, specially directed to check the importation of beggars from Ireland. It is intituled "A Proclamation for the speedy rendering away of the Irishe Beggars out of this Kingdome into their owne Countrie and for the Suppressing and Ordering of Rogues and Vagabonds according to the Laws," which recites that: "Whereas this realme hath of late been pestered with great numbers of Irishe beggars who live here idly and dangerously, and are of ill example to the natives of this kingdome; and, whereas the multitude of English rogues and vagabonds doe much more abound than in former tymes—some wandering and begging under the colour of soldiers and mariners, others under the pretext of impotent persons, whereby they become a burthen to the good people of the land, all which happeneth by the neglect of the due execution of the lawes, formerly with great providence made, for relief of the true poore and indigent, and for the punishment of sturdy rogues and vagabonds; for the reforming therefore of soe great a mischiefe, and to prevent the many dangers which will ensue by the neglect thereof, the king, by the advice of his privy council and of his judges, commands that all the laws and statutes now in force for the punishment of rogues and vagabonds be duly putt in execution; and more particularly that all Irishe beggars, which now are in any part of this kingdome, wandering or begging, under what pretence soever, shall forthwith depart this realme and return to their owne countries, and there abide." And it is further directed that all such beggars "shall be conveyed from constable to constable to Bristoll, Mynhead, Barstable, Chester, Lyrepool, Milford-haven, and Workington, or such of them as shall be most convenient."

We see by this that the state of mendicancy in 1629, was very much what it is now, and that the artifices and dodges resorted to at that period were very similar to, and in many cases, exactly the same, as the more modern impostures which I shall have to expose in the succeeding pages.

THE ORIGIN AND HISTORY OF THE POOR LAWS.

An Act passed in 1536 (27 Henry VIII. c. 25) is the first by which voluntary charity was converted into compulsory payment. It enacts that the head officers of every parish to which the impotent or able-bodied poor may resort under the provisions of the Act of 1531, shall receive and keep them, so that none shall be compelled to beg openly. The able-bodied were to be kept to constant labour, and every parish making default, was to forfeit 20s. a month. The money required for the support of the poor, was to be collected partly by the head officers of corporate towns and the churchwardens of parishes, and partly was to be derived from collections in the churches, and on various occasions where the clergy had opportunities for exhorting the people to charity. Almsgiving beyond the town or parish was prohibited on forfeiture of ten times the amount given. A "sturdy beggar" was to be whipped the first time he was detected in begging; to have his right ear cropped for the second offence; and if again guilty of begging was to be indicted for "wandering, loitering, and idleness," and if convicted was "to suffer execution of death as a felon and an enemy of the Commonwealth." The severity of this act prevented its execution, and it was repealed by 1 Edward VI. c. 3 (1547). Under this statute, every able-bodied person who should not apply himself to some honest labour, or offer to serve for even meat and drink, was to be taken for a vagabond, branded on the shoulder and adjudged a slave for two years to any one who should demand him, to be fed on bread and water and refuse meat and made to work by being beaten, chained, or otherwise treated. If he ran away during the two years, he was to be branded on the cheek and adjudged a slave for life, and if he ran away again he was to suffer death as a felon. If not demanded as a slave he was to be kept to hard labour on the highway in chains. The impotent poor were to be passed to their place of birth or settlement from the hands of one parish constable to those of another.

The statute was repealed three years afterwards and that of 1531 was revived. In 1551 an Act was passed which directed that a book should be kept in every parish containing the names of the householders and of the impotent poor; that collectors of alms should be appointed who should "gently ask every man and woman what they of their charity will give weekly to the relief of the poor." If any one able to give should refuse, or discourage others from giving, the ministers and churchwardens were to exhort him, and failing of success, the bishop was to admonish him on the subject. This Act, and another made to enforce it, which was passed in 1555, were wholly ineffectual, and in 1563 it was re-enacted (5 Elizabeth c. 3), with the addition that any person able to contribute and refusing should be cited by the bishop to appear at the next sessions before the justices, where if he would not be persuaded to give, the justices were to tax him according to their discretion, and on his refusal he was to be committed to gaol until the sum taxed should be paid, with all arrears.

The next statute on the subject, which was passed in 1572 (14 Eliz. c. 5), shows how ineffectual the previous statutes had been. It enacted that all rogues, vagabonds and sturdy beggars, including in this description "all persons whole and mighty in body, able to labour, not having land or master, nor using any lawful merchandise, craft or mystery, and all common labourers, able in body, loitering and refusing to work for such reasonable wage as is commonly given," should "for the first offence be grievously whipped and burned through the gristle of the right ear with a hot iron of the compass of an inch about;" for the second should be deemed felons; and for the third should suffer death as felons without benefit of clergy.

For the relief and sustentation of the aged and impotent poor, the justices of the peace within their several districts were "by their good discretion" to tax and assess all the inhabitants dwelling therein. Any one refusing to contribute was to be imprisoned until he should comply with the assessment. By the statutes 39 of Elizabeth, c. 3 and 4 (1598,) every able-bodied person refusing to work for the ordinary wages was to be "openly whipped until his body should be bloody, and forthwith sent from parish to parish, the most strait way to the parish where he was born, there to put himself to labour as a true subject ought to do."

The next Act, the 43 Elizabeth, c. 2, has been in operation from the time of its enactment in 1601 to the present day. A change in the mode of administration was, however, effected by the Poor Law Amendment Act (4 and 5 Wm. IV. c. 76) which was passed in 1834. During that long period many abuses crept into the administration of the laws relating to the poor, so that in practice their operation impaired the character of the most numerous class, and was injurious to the whole country. In its original provisions the Act of Elizabeth directed the overseers of the poor in every parish to "take order for setting to work the children of all such parents as shall not be thought able to maintain their children," as well as all such persons as, having no means to maintain them, use no ordinary trade to get their living by. For this purpose they were empowered to raise weekly, or otherwise, by "taxation of every inhabitant, parson, vicar, and other; and of every occupier of lands, houses, tithes, mines, &c., such sums of money as they shall require for providing a sufficient stock of flax, hemp, wool and other ware, or stuff to set the poor on work; and also competent sums for relief of lame, blind, old and impotent persons, and for putting out children as apprentices." Power was given to the justices to send to the house of correction or common gaol all persons who would not work. The churchwardens and overseers were further empowered to build poor houses at the charge of the parish for the reception of the impotent poor only. The justices were further empowered to assess all persons of sufficient ability for the relief and maintenance of their children, grandchildren, and parents. The parish officers were also empowered to bind as apprentices any children who should be chargeable to the parish.

These simple provisions were in course of time greatly perverted, and many abuses were introduced into the administration of the poor law. One of the most mischievous practices was that which was established by the justices for the county of Berks in 1795, when, in order to meet the wants of the labouring population, caused by the high price of provisions, an allowance in proportion to the number of his family was made out of the parish fund to every labourer who applied for relief. This allowance fluctuated with the price of the gallon loaf of second flour, and the scale was so adjusted as to return to each family the sum which in given number of loaves would cost beyond the price in years of ordinary abundance. This plan was conceived in a spirit of benevolence; but the readiness with which it was adopted in all parts of England clearly shows the want of sound views on the subject. Under the allowance system the labourer received a part of his means of subsistence in the form of a parish gift, and as the fund out of which it was provided was raised from the contributions of those who did not employ labourers, as well as of those who did, their employers being able in part to burthen others with the payment for their labour had a direct interest in perpetuating the system. Those who employed labourers looked upon the parish contribution as part of the fund out of which they were to be paid, and accordingly lowered their rate of wages. The labourers also looked on the fund as a source of wage. The consequence was, that the labourer looked to the parish, and as a matter of right, without any regard to his real wants, and he received the wages of his labour as only one and a secondary source of the means of subsistence. His character as a labourer became of less value, his value as a labourer being thus diminished, under the combined operation of these two causes.

In 1832 a commission was appointed by the Crown, under whose direction inquiries were made through England and Wales, and the actual condition of the labouring classes in every parish was ascertained, with the view of showing the evils of the existing practice and of suggesting some remedy.

The labour of this inquiry was great; but in a short time a report was presented by the commissioners, which explained the operation of the law as administered, with its effects upon different classes, and suggested remedial measures. This report was presented in 1834, and was followed by the passing of the Poor Law Amendment Act (4 and 5 Wm. IV. c. 76) in August of the same year. This Act was again amended by the 7 and 8 Victoria, c. 101 (9th August 1844).

The chief provisions of this law are the appointment of a central board of three commissioners in London for the general superintendence and control of all bodies charged with the management of funds for the relief of the poor. There are nine assistant commissioners; each of whom has a district; the assistant commissioners are appointed by and removable by the commissioners; and the whole is under the direction of the President of the Poor Law Board. The administration of relief to the poor is under the control of the commissioners, who make rules and regulations for the purpose. They are empowered to order workhouses to be built, hired, altered, or enlarged, with the consent of a majority of a board of guardians. They have the power of uniting several parishes for the purposes of a more effective and economical administration of poor relief, but so that the actual charge in respect to its own poor is defrayed by each parish. These united parishes or unions are managed by Boards of Guardians, annually elected by the rate-payers of the various parishes; but the masters of the workhouses and other paid officers are under the orders of the commissioners, and removable by them. The system of paying wages partly out of poor-rates is discontinued, and, except in ordinary cases, of which the commissioners are the judges, the relief is only to be given to able-bodied persons, or to their families, within the walls of the workhouse.

A glance at some of the clauses of the Act 7 and 8 Victoria will show the present condition of the machinery of the Poor Law, as regards the latest reforms.

Chapter 101, sect. 12, empowers the Poor Law Commissioners to prescribe the duties of the masters to whom poor children may be apprenticed, and the terms and conditions of the indentures of apprenticeship: and no poor children are in future to be apprenticed by the overseers of any parish included in any union, or subject to a Board of Guardians under the provisions of the 4 and 5 Wm. IV. c. 76; but it is declared to be lawful for the guardians of such union or parish to bind poor children apprentices. The 13th section abolishes so much of the 43 Eliz., c. 2, and of the 8 and 9 William III. c. 3, and of all other Acts, as compels any person to receive any poor child as an apprentice.

The 14th and following sections make some new regulations as to the number of votes of owners of property and rate-payers in the election of guardians and in other cases where the consent of the owners and rate-payers is required for any of the purposes of the 4 and 5 Wm. IV. c. 76.

The 18th section empowers the commissioners, having due regard to the relative population or circumstances of any parish, included in a union, to alter the number of guardians to be elected for such parish without such consent as is required by the Act of William.

This section also empowers the commissioners to divide parishes which have more than 20,000 inhabitants, according to the census then last published, into wards for the purpose of electing guardians, and to determine the number of guardians to be elected for each ward.

The 25th section provides that so long as any woman's husband is beyond the seas, or in custody of the law, or in confinement in a licensed house or asylum as a lunatic or idiot, all relief given to such a woman, or to her child or children, shall be given in the same manner, and subject to the same conditions as if she was a widow; but the obligation or liability of the husband in respect of such relief continues as before.

The 26th section empowers the guardians of a parish or union to give relief to widows under certain conditions, who at the time of their husband's death were resident with them in some place other than the parish of their legal settlement, and not situated in any union in which such parish is comprised.

The 32nd section provides that the commissioners may combine parishes and unions in England for the audit of accounts. By the 40th section the commissioners may, subject to certain restrictions there mentioned, combine unions or parishes not in union, or such parishes and unions, into school districts for the management of any class or classes of infant poor not above the age of 16 years, being chargeable to any such parish or union, or who are deserted by their parents, or whose parent, or surviving parent, or guardians are consenting to the placing of such children in the school of such district.

By the 41st section the commissioners are empowered to declare parishes, or unions, or parishes and unions within the district of the metropolitan police, or the city of London, &c., to be combined into districts for the purpose of founding and managing asylums for the temporary relief and setting to work therein of destitute homeless poor who are not charged with any offence, and who may apply for relief, or become chargeable to the poors' rates within any such parish or union.

STATISTICS OF THE POOR LAWS.

The salaries and expenses of the commissioners for carrying into execution the Poor Law Acts in England and Ireland amount to about 56,000*l.*

The following statements will show the number of paupers, and the amounts expended in relieving their wants at various periods since the year 1783.

The average sum expended for the years 1783, 1784, and 1785, was £1,912,241

Year	£
1801	4,017,871
1811	6,656,105
1821	6,959,249
1831	6,798,888
1832	7,036,969
1833	6,790,799
1834	6,317,254
1835	5,526,418
1836	4,717,630
1837	4,044,741
1838	4,123,604
1839	4,421,714
1840	4,576,965
1841	4,760,929
1842	4,911,498
1843	5,208,027
1844	4,976,093
1860	5,454,964

Number of indoor and outdoor paupers relieved during the following years:

Year	Paupers	Proportion per cent. to Population
1803	1,040,716	12
1815	1,319,851	13
1832	1,429,356	9
1844	1,477,561	9·3
1860	844,633	4·3

In the last report of the Poor Law Board (that for 1860) it is stated that for twenty-two years preceding the Poor Law Amendment Act in 1834 the average annual disbursement for the relief of the poor was 6,505,037*l.*, while for the subsequent 25 years it has only been 5,169,073*l.*, the supposed annual saving by the new law being 1,335,964*l.* The average annual cost of the new union-workhouses has been about 200,000*l.*, and the salaries of the paid Union-officers about 600,000*l.*

The strikes of 1860 told severely upon the returns. On July 1st, 1860, there were 1,751 able-bodied men receiving relief more than on the same day of the previous year. On new year's day of 1860 there were 40,972 more persons of all classes in receipt of relief than on the first day of the preceding year. There were 6,720 more able-bodied men in receipt of relief, and 7,026 more able-bodied women.

REPORT OF THE POOR LAW BOARD (1860).

The usual statistics of this report show that in the year 1860 the sum of 5,454,964*l.* was expended for the relief of the poor in England and Wales, being at the rate per head of the estimated population, of 5s. 6d. The net annual value of the rateable property at the present time (1860) is 71 millions.

The inefficiency of the Poor Law to meet the wants of the destitute in times of great and prevailing distress has been demonstrated over and over again, and at no period more pointedly and decisively than during the year 1860. On this subject we subjoin the remarks of a writer in the *Times* (Feb. 11, 1861). "It is an admitted and notorious fact, that after a fortnight's frost the police courts were besieged by thousands who professed to be starving; the magistrates and officers of the court undertook the office of almoners in addition to their other laborious duties; the public poured in their contributions as they would for the victims of a terrible disaster; for a time we had in a dozen places a scene that rather took one back to the indiscriminate dole before the convent door, or the largess flung by the hand among the crowd at a royal progress than to an institution or custom of this sensible age. To some it naturally occurred that the Poor Law ought to have dispensed with this extraordinary exhibition; to others that no law could meet the emergency. . . . . It was the saturnalia if not of mendicancy, at least of destitution. The police stood aside while beggars possessed the thoroughfares on the sole plea of an extraordinary visitation. There was a fortnight's frost, so it was allowable to one class to hold a midnight fair on the Serpentine, and to another to insist on being maintained at the expense of the public. Was all this right and proper? We had thought that the race of sturdy vagrants and valiant beggars was extinct, or at least that they dared no longer show themselves. But here they were in open day like the wretches which are said to emerge out of darkness on the day of a revolution. . . . . When such is the fact, and when it is now admitted by all to have been not only exceptional, but highly exceptionable, we may leave others to find out the right shoulders on which the blame should be laid. For our part we hold that a Poor Law ought to be as proof against a long frost, or any other general visitation—and there are many more serious—as a ship ought to be against a storm, or an embankment against an inundation."

On the occasion here referred to the Poor Law gave relief to 23,000; but sent away 17,000 empty-handed, who would have starved but for the open-handed charity of the public, dispensed in the most liberal spirit by the metropolitan magistrates.

Mendicancy has always increased to an alarming extent after a war, and during the time of war, if it has been protracted. There is no doubt that the calamities of war reduce many respectable persons to want; but at the same time the circumstances which attend a period of commotion and trouble always afford opportunities to impostors. Mendicancy had reached a fearful pitch during the last great war with France; and in 1816, the year after the battle of Waterloo, the large towns were so infested by beggars of every description that it was deemed necessary to appoint a select committee of the House of Commons to consider what could be done to abate the nuisance. The report of this committee furnishes some interesting particulars of the begging impostures of the time and of the gains of beggars.

STREET BEGGARS IN 1816.

It was clearly proved that a man with a dog got 30s. in one day.

Two houses in St. Giles's frequented by from 200 to 300 beggars. It was proved that each beggar made on an average from 3s. to 5s. a day. They had grand suppers at midnight, and drank and sang songs until day-break.

A negro beggar retired to the West Indies, with a fortune of 1,500l.

The value of 15s. 20s. and 30s. found upon ordinary street beggars. They get more by begging than they can by work; they get so much by begging that they never apply for parochial relief.

A manufacturer in Spitalfields stated that there were instances of his own people leaving profitable work for the purpose of begging.

It was proved that many beggars paid 50s. a week for their board.

Beggars stated that they go through 40 streets in a day, and that it is a poor street that does not yield 2d.

Beggars are furnished with children at houses in Whitechapel and Shoreditch; some who look like twins.

A woman with twins who never grew older sat for ten years at the corner of a street.

Children let out by the day, who carried to their parents 2s. 6d. a day as the price paid by the persons who hired them.

A little boy and a little girl earned 8s. a day. An instance is stated of an old woman who kept a night school for instructing children in the street language, and how to beg.

The number of beggars infesting London at this time (1816) was computed to be 16,000, of which 6,300 were Irish. We glean further from the report respecting them.

It appears by the evidence of the person who contracts for carrying vagrants in and through the county of Middlesex, that he has passed as many as 12,000 or 13,000 in a year; but no estimate can be formed from that, as many of them are passed several times in the course of the year. And it is proved that these people are in the course of eight or ten days in the same situation;

as they find no difficulty in escaping as soon as they are out of the hands of the Middlesex contractor.

A magistrate in the office at Whitechapel, thinks there is not one who is not worthless.

The rector of Saint Clement Danes describes them as living very well, especially if they are pretty well maimed, blind, or if they have children.

Beggars scarify their feet to make the blood come; share considerable sums of money, and get scandalously drunk, quarrel, and fight, and one teaches the other the mode of extorting money; they are the worst of characters, blasphemous and abusive; when they are detected as impostors in one parish they go into another.

They eat no broken victuals; but have ham, beef, &c.

Forty or fifty sleep in a house, and are locked in lest they should carry anything away, and are let out in the morning all at once.

Tear their clothes for an appearance of distress.

Beggars assemble in a morning, and agree what route each shall take. At some of the houses, the knives and forks chained to the tables, and other articles chained to the walls.

Mendicant Pensioners.

Some who have pensions as soldiers or sailors were among those who apply by letters for charity; one sailor who had lost a leg is one of the most violent and desperate characters in the metropolis.

Among beggars of the very worst class there are about 30 Greenwich pensioners, who have instruments of music, and go about in parties.

A marine who complained that he had but 7*l.* a year pension, said he could make a day's work in an hour in any square in London.

A pensioner who had 18*l.* a year from Chelsea, when taken up for begging had bank-notes concealed in his waistcoat, and on many of that description frequently 8*s.* 10*s.* or 12*s.* are found, that they have got in a day.

Chelsea pensioners beg in all directions at periods between the receipts of their pensions.

A Chelsea pensioner who receives 1*s.* 6*d.* a day is one of the most notorious beggars who infest the town.

A Greenwich pensioner of 7*l.* a year, gets from 5*s.* to 10*s.* for writing begging letters.

Begging Letter Writers in 1816.

Some thousand applications by letters are made for charity to ladies, noblemen, and gentlemen in the metropolis; two thousand on an average were within the knowledge of one individual who was employed to make inquiries. Several persons subsist by writing letters; one woman profits by the practice, who receives a guinea a week as a legacy from a relation, and has laid out 200*l.* in the funds. Letters have been written by the same person in five or six different hands.

Persons who write begging letters are called twopenny-post beggars.

A man who keeps a school writes begging letters for 2*d.* each.

These extracts, culled here and there from a voluminous report, will suffice to give an idea of the state of mendicancy in the metropolis at the beginning of the century. The public were so shocked and startled by the systematic impostures that were brought to light that an effort was made to protect the charitable by means of an organized system of inquiry into the character, and condition of all persons who were found begging. The result of this effort was the establishment in 1818 of the now well-known

Mendicity Society.

The object of this Society was to protect noblemen, gentlemen, and other persons accustomed to dispense large sums in charity from being imposed upon by cheats and pretenders, and at the same time to provide, on behalf of the public, a police system, whose sole and special function should be the suppression of mendicancy.

The plan of the Society is as follows:— The subscribers receive printed tickets from the Society, and these they give to beggars instead of money. The ticket refers the beggar to the Society's office, and there his case is enquired into. If he be a deserving person relief is afforded him from funds placed at the disposal of the Society by its subscribers. If he is found to be an impostor he is arrested and prosecuted at the instance of the Society. Governors of this Society may obtain tickets for distribution at any time. The annual payment of one guinea constitutes the donor a governor, and the payment of ten guineas at one time, or within one year, a governor for life. A system of inquiry into the merits of persons who are in the habit of BEGGING BY LETTER has been incorporated with the Society's proceedings, and the following persons are entitled to refer such letters to the office for investigation, it being understood that the eventual grant of relief rests with the subscriber sending the case:—

I. All contributors to the general funds of the Society to the amount of twenty guineas.
II. All contributors to the general funds of the Society to the amount of ten guineas, and who also subscribe ONE GUINEA annually.
III. All subscribers of two guineas and upwards per annum.

So successful have been the efforts of this Society in protecting the charitable from the depredations of begging-letter writers and other mendicants, that now almost every public man whose prominent position marks him out for their appeals, contributes to the Society, either by subscriptions or donation. The Queen herself is the Patron; the President is the Marquis of Westminster, and among the Vice-Presidents may be counted three dukes, three marquises, eight earls, one viscount, a bishop, and a long list of lords and members of parliament. Altogether the Society has about 2,400 subscribers, whose donations and subscriptions range from 100*l.* and 50*l.* to 2*l.* and 1*l.* The total amount of the Society's income for 1860 was 3,913*l.* 14*s.* 2*d.*, of which 3,010*l* 13*s.* 9*d.* was derived from subscriptions and donations, the remainder being derived from legacies, interest on stock and the profits of the Society's works. The expenditure for the same year was 3,169*l.* 16*s.* 10*d.*, and the amount expended in the relief of mendicants, 906*l.* 9*s.*

The meals given in 1860 to persons who were found to be deserving were 42,192.

The unregistered cases (that is, those not thought to require a special investigation) were 4,224, and the registered cases 430.

The vagrants apprehended were 739; of whom 350 were convicted,

The following Table sets forth the whole of the cases that came under the notice of the Society in 1860.

Number of registered cases in 1860 . . 430
Of which there appeared to belong—
To parishes in London . . . 151
Country 142
Ireland 82
Scotland 0
Wales 8
France 2
East Indies 7
West Indies 2
America 1
Italy 5
Africa 1
China 1
Switzerland 2
Germany 2
Poland 1
Unknown 7
—— 430

Alleged causes of distress.
Want of employment . . . 395
Age and infirmity 1
Failure in business 1
Foreigners and others desirous of returning home . . . 22
Sickness and accidents . . . 2
Want of clothing 3
Loss of stock, tools, &c. . . . 1
Loss of character 1
Loss of relations and friends by death, desertion, imprisonment, &c. . . 4
—— 430

The various cases were disposed of as follows :—

Referred to London parishes; most of whom were admitted into workhouses, or obtained relief through the interference of the Society, some being previously relieved with money, food, and clothing 15
Relieved with clothing and sent to their respective parishes 9
Provided with situations, clothing, tools, goods, or other means of effectually supporting themselves 8
New apprehended cases by the Society's constables during 1860: a large number of whom were committed by the magistrates as vagrants; others were referred to the Society, and sent to work, the men at the mill, and stone-breaking, and the women at oakum-picking; and several were assisted with the means of returning home . . . 376
Proved on investigation to be undeserving . 4
Employed at the mill and oakum picking (not apprehended cases) 1
Placed in hospitals and assisted with clothing 4
Relieved weekly, where distress appeared temporary, and clothes, blankets, shoes, &c. given 13

Total . . . 430

The following Table exhibits a statement of the Society's proceedings from the first year of its formation to the year 1860:—

Years.	Cases registered.	Vagrants committed.	Meals given.
1818	3,284	385	16,827
1819	4,682	580	33,013
1820	4,546	359	46,407
1821	2,339	324	28,542

Years.	Cases registered.	Vagrants committed.	Meals given.
Brought ford.			
1822	2,235	287	22,232
1823	1,493	193	20,152
1824	1,441	195	25,396
1825	1,096	381	19,600
1826	833	300	22,972
1827	806	403	35,892
1828	1,284	786	21,066
1829	671	602	26,286
1830	848	—	105,488
1831	1,285	—	79,156
1832	1,040	—	73,315
1833	624	—	37,074
1834	1,226	652	30,513
1835	1,408	1,510	84,717
1836	946	1,004	68,134
1837	1,087	1,090	87,454
1838	1,041	873	155,348
1839	1,055	962	110,943
1840	706	752	113,502
1841	997	1,119	195,625
1842	1,233	1,306	128,914
1843	1,148	1,018	167,126
1844	1,184	937	174,229
1845	1,001	868	165,139
1846	980	778	148,569
1847	910	625	239,171
1848	1,161	979	148,661
1849	1,043	905	64,251
1850	787	570	94,106
1851	1,150	900	102,140
1852	658	607	67,985
1853	419	354	62,788
1854	332	326	52,212
1855	235	239	52,731
1856	325	293	49,806
1857	354	358	54,074
1858	329	298	43,836
1859	364	305	40,256
1860	430	350	42,192
	51,016	24,773	3,357,834

Total number of apprehended cases in 1860:—
Committed 350
Discharged 389
——— 739
Non-registered cases during the year 4,224
Registered cases 430
——— 4,654

I will now give a few examples of the cases which ordinarily come under the notice of the Society.

A Deserving Case.

A. L. and her sister, the one a widow, 70, the other a single woman, 55, applied for relief under the following circumstances. They had for many years been supporting themselves by making children's leather-covered toy balls, at one time earning a comfortable living; but their means were reduced from time to time by the introduction of India-rubber and gutta-percha, until at last five pence per dozen was all they could obtain for their labour; and it required both to apply themselves for many hours to earn that small amount; still, to avoid the workhouse, they toiled on, until the destruction of Messrs. Payne's toy warehouse in Holborn, which threw them entirely out of work, and reduced them to absolute want. It was thus they were found in the winter having been frequently without food, fire, or candle, nearly perishing with cold, and in fear of being turned into the streets for arrears of rent. Inquiry having been instituted as to their character, which was found to be exceedingly good, they were relieved for three months with money and food weekly, besides bedding and clothing being given to them from the Society's stores.

Another.

E. W., the applicant, a widow of a journeyman carpenter, who, in consequence of his protracted illness and want of employment, was at the time of his death destitute, and in her confinement at the time she was visited by the Society. She had three young children incapable of contributing to their own support, and the parish officers in consequence were relieving her with a trifle weekly; but she was in a very low state for want of nourishment. The referee expressed it as his opinion that she was a very deserving woman, and that on two or three occasions he had afforded her assistance, and had much pleasure in recommending her case. Assistance was in consequence given her for several weeks, for which she appeared very grateful.

An Impostor.

J. C. This man, who has been seventeen times apprehended by the Society's constables, and as many more by the police, was taken into custody for begging. He is an old man, and his age usually excites the sympathy of the public; but he is a gross impostor, and for the last fifteen years has been about the streets, imposing upon the benevolent. He has been convicted of stealing books, newspapers, and on one occasion an inkstand from a coffee house. His appeals to the benevolent in the streets are very pertinacious, and persons frequently give him money for the purpose of getting rid of him. He had, when last taken into custody, 2l. 9s. 4d. secreted about his person, part in his stockings, which he stated had been given to him to enable him to leave the country, and a variety of what he represented to be original verses was found in his possession and produced before the magistrate, to whom he appealed to sympathise with a poor author. "Pray, sir," said he, "look at my verses: you will find that they are such as would be written by a man of scholastic attainments; they breathe a sentiment of love and charity, and of generosity to the poor; they are of scientific interest, and fit for the perusal of royalty." His sentence to a month's imprisonment only evidently surprised him, for which he thanked the magistrate; but he continued in a suppressed tone of voice: "But, sir, what about my money?" On being informed that, on account of his age, it should be returned to him when his time of imprisonment expired, he indulged in a rhapsody of delight, but begged that his emotion might not be misconstrued. "It is not the love of money, sir," addressing the magistrate, "that moves me thus; it is a far higher feeling; I have an affectionate heart, sir,—it is gratitude."

Another Impostor.

E. M. C. This man applied for relief during the severity of the winter of 1860-1, representing himself as in much distress for want of employment; that he had a wife ill at home, confined to her bed, and having been for a long time out of work, his three children were wanting food. Work was accordingly given to him at the Society's mill, and he was supplied with food for the immediate wants of his family, pending inquiry into the truthfulness of his story. It was found that he was a single man, who, for deceptive purposes, had adopted the name of a woman with whom he was living, and who had separated from her husband but a short time previously, and was tutoring her children in all imaginable kinds of vice. It was also ascertained that the police had strict orders to watch the man's movements, for he was known as an associate of characters of the worst description. He was consequently discharged from the Society's works, with a caution against applying to the benevolent for their sympathy in the future.

The following is the case of a person who applied for charity by letter, whose case was found to be a deserving one:—

J. W. A middle-aged man of creditable appearance, who had for many years obtained a livelihood for himself and family (consisting of his wife and six children) as a clerk and salesman to a respectable firm, being thrown out of his situation through his employer's embarrassed circumstances, became gradually reduced to destitution, and therefore made application for assistance to a subscriber to the Society. It appeared upon investigation that he had been most regular in his attention to his duties, strictly honest, industrious, and sober, and just at the time of the inquiry it fortunately happened that he procured another situation, but was hampered with trifling debts which he incurred while out of employment, which it was necessary to discharge, as well as procure suitable clothing. His character having proved satisfactory, the subscriber applied to directed a handsome donation to be appropriated to his assistance, whereby he was enabled to overcome his difficulties. He showed himself most grateful for the assistance.

I shall now, by way of contrast, give the case of two beggars by letter, who were found to be rank impostors:—

H. G. This man and his wife have been known to the Society for many years as two of the most persevering and impudent impostors that ever came under its cognizance. The man, although possessing considerable ability, and having a respectable situation as a clerk in a public institution, had become such an habitual drunkard as to be quite reckless as to what false representations he put forth to obtain charitable assistance; and finding himself detected in his various fabricated tales of distress, had the impudence to apply to a subscriber by letter, wherein he represented that his wife had died after several months' severe affliction, which upon inquiry turned out untrue, his wife being alive and well, and they were living together at the very time the letter was written. Notwithstanding he was thus foiled in his endeavours to impose, a few weeks afterwards the wife had the assurance to send a letter to another subscriber, craving assistance on account of the death of her husband, and in order to carry out the deception she dressed herself in widow's weeds. The gentleman applied to, however, having some misgivings as to her representations, fortunately forwarded her appeal to the Society, where it was ascertained that her husband was also alive and well.

A Well-Educated Beggar.

J. R. P. F. A man about 45 years of age, the son of a much respected clergyman in Lancashire, who had received a good classical education, and was capable of gaining an excellent livelihood, applied to various persons for aid, in consequence, as he said, of being in great distress through want of a situation. He carefully selected those gentlemen who were well acquainted with, and respected, his father, some of whom, mistrusting his representations, forwarded the letters to the Mendicity Society for inquiry, which proved the applicant to be a most depraved character, who had been a source of great trouble to his parents for many years, they having provided him with situations (as teacher in various respectable establishments) from time to time, and also furnished him with means of clothing himself respectably; but on every occasion he remained in his employment but a very short time, before he gave way to his propensity to drink, and so disgraced himself that his employers were glad to get rid of him; whereupon he made away with his clothing to indulge his vicious propensity.

I will now proceed to give an account of the beggars of London, as they have come under my notice in the course of the present inquiry.

BEGGING-LETTER WRITERS.

Foremost among beggars, by right of pretension to blighted prospects and correct penmanship, stands the Begging-Letter Writer. He is the connecting link between mendicity and the observance of external respectability. He affects white cravats, soft hands, and filbert nails. He oils his hair, cleans his boots, and wears a portentous stick-up collar. The light of other days of gentility and comfort casts a halo of "deportment" over his well-brushed, white-seamed coat, his carefully darned black-cloth gloves, and pudgy gaiters. He invariably carries an umbrella, and wears a hat with an enormous brim. His once raven hair is turning grey, and his well-shaved whiskerless cheeks are blue as with gunpowder tattoo. He uses the plainest and most respectable of cotton pocket-handkerchiefs, and keeps his references as to character in the most irreproachable of shabby leather pocket-books. His mouth is heavy, his under-lip thick, sensual, and lowering, and his general expression of pious resignation contradicted by restless, bloodshot eyes, that flash from side to side, quick to perceive the approach of a compassionate-looking clergyman, a female devotee, or a keen-scented member of the Society for the Suppression of Mendicity.

Among the many varieties of mendacious beggars, there is none so detestable as this hypocritical scoundrel, who, with an ostentatiously-submissive air, and false pretence of faded fortunes, tells his plausible tale of undeserved suffering, and extracts from the hearts and pockets of the superficially good-hearted their sympathy and coin. His calling is a special one, and requires study, perseverance, and some personal advantages. The begging-letter writer must write a good hand, speak grammatically, and have that shrewd perception of character peculiar to fortune-tellers, horoscopists, cheap-jacks, and pedlars. He "must read and write, and cast accounts;" have an intuitive knowledge of the "nobility and landed gentry;" be a keen physiognomist, and an adept at imitation of handwritings, old documents, quaint ancient orthography, and the like. He must possess an artistic eye for costume, an unfaltering courage, and have tears and hysterics at immediate command.

His great stock-in-trade is his register. There he carefully notes down the names, addresses, and mental peculiarities of his victims, and the character and pretence under which he robbed them of their bounty. It would not do to tell the same person the same story *twice*, as once happened to an unusually audacious member of the fraternity, who had obtained money from an old lady for the purpose of burying his wife, for whose loss he, of course, expressed the deepest grief. Confident in the old lady's kindness of heart and weakness of memory, three months after his bereavement he again posted himself before the lady's door, and gave vent to violent emotion.

"Dear me!" thought the old lady, "there's that poor man who lost his wife some time ago." She opened the window, and, bidding the vagabond draw nearer, asked him what trouble he was in at present.

After repeated questioning the fellow gurgled out, "That the wife of his bosom, the mother of his children, had left him for that bourne from which no traveller returns, and that owing to a series of unprecedented and unexpected misfortunes he had not sufficient money to defray the funeral expenses, and—'

"Oh, nonsense!" interrupted the old lady. "You lost your wife a quarter of a year ago. You couldn't lose her twice; and as to marrying again, and losing again in that short time, it is quite impossible!"

I subjoin some extracts from a Register kept by a begging-letter writer, and who was detected and punished:—

Cheltenham.   *May* 14, 1842.
Rev. John Furby.—Springwood Villa.—Low Church.—Fond of architecture—Dugdale's Monastica—Son of architect—Lost his life in the "Charon," U.S. packet—£2, and suit of clothes —Got reference.

Mrs. Branxholme.—Clematis Cottage—Widow —Through Rev. Furby, £3 and prayer-book.

Gloucester.   *May* 30
Mrs. Captain Daniels.—— —— Street.—Widow —Son drowned off Cape, as purser of same ship, "The Thetis"—£5 and old sea-chest. N.B.: Vamosed next day—Captain returned from London—Gaff blown in county paper. Mem.: Not to visit neighbourhood for four years.

Lincoln.   *June* 19.
Andrew Taggart.—— street.— Gentleman— Great abolitionist of slave trade—As tradesman from U.S., who had lost his custom by aiding slope of fugitive female slave—By name Naomi Brown—£5. N.B.: To work him again, for he is good.

Grantham.   *July* 1.
Charles James Campion.—Westby House.— Gentleman—Literary—Writes plays and novels— As distant relative of George Frederick Cooke, and burnt-out bookseller—£2 2s. N.B.: Gave me some of his own books to read—Such trash— Cadger in one—No more like cadger than I'm like Bobby Peel—Went to him again on 5th— Told him thought it wonderful, and the best thing out since Vicar of Wakefield—Gave me £1 more—Very good man—To be seen to for the future.

Huntingdon.   *July* 15.
Mrs. Siddick.— —— Street.—Widow—Cranky —Baptist—As member of persuasion from persecution of worldly-minded relatives—£10—Gave her address in London—Good for a £5 every year—Recognized inspector—Leave to-night.

There are, of course, many varieties of the begging-letter writer; but although each and all of them have the same pretensions to former respectability, their mode of levying contributions is entirely different. There are but few who possess the versatility of their great master— Bampfylde Moore Carew; and it is usual for every member of the fraternity to chalk out for himself a particular "line" of imposition—a course of conduct that renders him perfect in the part he plays, makes his references and certificates continually available, and prevents him from "jostling" or coming into collision with others of his calling who might be "on the same lay as himself, and spoil his game!" Among the many specimens, one of the most prominent is the

Decayed Gentleman.

The conversation of this class of mendicant is of former greatness, of acquaintance among the nobility and gentry of a particular county—always a distant one from the scene of operations—of hunting, races, balls, meets, appointments to the magistracy, lord-lieutenants, contested elections, and marriages in high life. The knowledge of the things of which he talks so fluently is gleaned from files of old county newspapers. When at fault, or to use his own phrase, "pounded," a ready wit, a deprecating shrug, and a few words, such as, "Perhaps I'm mistaken—I used to visit a good deal there, and was introduced to so many who have forgotten me now —my memory is failing, like everything else" — extricate him from his difficulty, and increase his capital of past prosperity and present poverty. The decayed gentleman is also a great authority on wines—by right of a famous sample—his father "laid down" in eighteen eleven, "the comet year you know," and is not a little severe upon his past extravagance. He relishes the retrospection of the heavy losses he endured at Newmarket, Doncaster, and Epsom in "forty-two and three," and is pathetic on the subject of the death of William Scott. The cause of his ruin he attributes usually to a suit in the Court of Chancery, or the "fatal and calamitous Encumbered Irish Estates Bill." He is a florid impostor, and has a jaunty sonorous way of using his clean, threadbare, silk pocket-handkerchief, that carries conviction even to the most sceptical.

It is not uncommon to find among these degraded mendicants one who has really been a gentleman, as far as birth and education go, but whose excesses and extravagances have reduced him to mendicity. Such cases are the most hopeless. Unmindful of decent pride, and that true gentility that rises superior to circumstance, and finds no soil upon the money earned by labour, the lying, drunken, sodden wretch considers work " beneath him;" upon the shifting quicksands of his own vices rears an edifice of vagabond vanity, and persuades himself that, by forfeiting his manhood, he vindicates his right to the character of gentleman.

The letters written by this class of beggar generally run as follows. My readers will, of course, understand that the names and places mentioned are the only portions of the epistles that are fictitious.

"*Three Mermaids Inn, Pond Lane.*
           April —, 18

"Sir, or Madam,
"Although I have not the honour to

be personally acquainted with you, I have had the advantage of an introduction to a member of your family, Major Sherbrook, when with his regiment at Malta; and my present disadvantageous circumstances emboldens me to write to you, for the claims of affliction upon the heart of the compassionate are among the holiest of those kindred ties that bind man to his fellow-being.

"My father was a large landed proprietor at Peddlethorpe, ——shire. I, his only son, had every advantage that birth and fortune could give me claim to. From an informality in the wording of my father's will, the dishonesty of an attorney, and the rapacity of some of my poor late father's distant relatives, the property was, at his death, thrown into Chancery, and for the last four years I have been reduced to—comparatively speaking—starvation.

"With the few relics of my former prosperity I have long since parted. My valued books, and, I am ashamed to own, my clothes, are gone. I am now in the last stage of destitution, and, I regret to say, in debt to the worthy landlord of the tavern from which I write this, to the amount of eight and sixpence. My object in coming to this part of the country was to see an old friend, whom I had hoped would have assisted me. We were on the same form together at Rugby—Mr. Joseph Thurwood of Copesthorpe. Alas! I find that he died three months ago.

"I most respectfully beg of you to grant me some trifling assistance. As in my days of prosperity I trust my heart was never deaf to the voice of entreaty, nor my purse closed to the wants of the necessitous; so dear sir, or madam, I hope that my request will not be considered by you as impertinent or intrusive.

"I have the honour to enclose you some testimonials as to my character and former station in society; and trusting that the Almighty Being may never visit you with that affliction which it has been His all-wise purpose to heap on me, I am
 "Your most humble and
  "Obliged servant,
 "FREDERICK MAURICE STANHOPE,
"Formerly of Stanhope House, ——shire."

THE BROKEN-DOWN TRADESMAN

is a sort of retail dealer in the same description of article as the decayed gentleman. The unexpected breaking of fourteen of the most respectable banking-houses in New York, or the loss of the cargoes of two vessels in the late autumnal gales, or the suspension of payment of Haul, Strong, and Chates, "joined and combined together with the present commercial crisis, has been the means of bringing him down to his present deplorable situation," as his letter runs. His references are mostly from churchwardens, bankers, and dissenting clergymen, and he carries about a fictitious set of books—day-book, ledger, and petty-cash-book, containing entries of debts of large amounts, and a dazzling display of the neatest and most immaculate of commercial cyphering. His conversation, like his correspondence, is a queer jumble of arithmetic and scripture. He has a wife whose appearance is in itself a small income. She folds the hardest-working-looking of hands across the cleanest of white aprons, and curtseys with the humility of a pew-opener. The clothes of the worthy couple are shabby, but their persons and linen are rigorously clean. Their cheeks shine with yellow soap, as if they were rasped and bee's-waxed every morning. The male impostor, when fleecing a victim, has a habit of washing his hands "with invisible soap and imperceptible water," as though he were waiting on a customer. The wedded pair—and, generally, they are really married—are of congenial dispositions and domestic turn of mind, and get drunk, and fight each other, or go half-price to the play according to their humour. It is usually jealousy that betrays them. The husband is unfaithful, and the wife "peaches;" through her agency the police are put upon the track, and the broken-down tradesman is committed. In prison he professes extreme penitence, and has a turn for scriptural quotation, that stands him in good stead.

On his release he takes to itinerant preaching, or political lecturing. What becomes of him after those last resources it is difficult to determine. The chances are that he again writes begging letters, but "on a different lay."

THE DISTRESSED SCHOLAR

is another variety of the same species, a connecting link between the self-glorification of the decayed gentleman and the humility of the broken-down tradesman. He is generally in want of money to pay his railway-fare, or coach-hire to the north of England, where he has a situation as usher to an academy—or he cannot seek for a situation for want of "those clothes which sad necessity has compelled him to part with for temporary convenience." His letters, written in the best small hand, with the finest of upstrokes and fattest of downstrokes, are after this fashion:

"*Star Temperance Coffee House,*
"*Gravel Walk.*

"Sir, or Madam,
"I have the honour to lay my case before you, humbly entreating your kind consideration.

"I am a tutor, and was educated at St. ——'s College, Cambridge. My last situation was with the Rev. Mr. Cross, Laburnum House, near Dorking. I profess English, Latin, Greek, mathematics, and the higher branches of arithmetic, and am well read in general literature, ancient and modern. 'Rudem esse omnino in nostris poetis est inertissimæ signitiæ signum.'

"I am at present under engagement to superintend the scholastic establishment of Mr. Tighthand of the classical and commercial academy ——, Cumberland, but have not the means of defraying the expenses of my journey, nor of appearing with becoming decency before my new employer and my pupils.

"My wardrobe is all pledged for an amount incommensurate with its value, and I humbly and respectfully lay my case before you, and implore you for assistance, or even a temporary accommodation.

"I am aware that impostors, armed with specious stories, often impose on the kindhearted and the credulous. 'Nervi atque artus est sapientiæ—non temere credere.' I have therefore the honour to forward you the enclosed testimonials from my former employers and others as to my character and capacity.

"That you may never be placed in such circumstances as to compel you to indite such an epistle as the one I am at present penning is my most fervent wish. Rely upon it, generous sir—or madam—that, should you afford me the means of gaining an honourable competence, you shall never have to repent your timely benevolence. If, however, I should be unsuccessful in my present application, I must endeavour to console myself with the words of the great poet. 'Ætas ipsa solatium omnibus affert,' or with the diviner precept: 'And this too shall pass away.'

"I have, sir—or madam—the honour to be
"Your humble and obedient servant,
"Horace Humm."

A gracefully flourished swan, with the date in German text on his left wing, terminates the letter.

The Kaggs Family.

This case of cleverly organized swindling fell beneath the writer's personal observation.

In a paved court, dignified with the name of a market, leading into one of the principal thoroughfares of London, dwelt a family whom, from fear of an action for libel which, should they ever read these lines, they would assuredly bring, I will call Kaggs. Mr. Kaggs, the head of the family, had commenced life in the service of a nobleman. He was a tall, portly man, with a short nose, broad truculent mouth, and a light, moist eye. His personal advantages and general conduct obtained him promotion, and raised him from the servants' hall to the pantry. When he was thirty years of age, he was butler in the family of a country gentleman, whose youngest daughter fell in love, ran away with, and—married him. The angry father closed his doors against them, and steeled his heart to the pathetic appeals addressed to him by every post. Mr. Kaggs, unable to obtain a character from his last place, found himself shut out from his former occupation. His wife gave promise of making an increase to the numbers of the family, and to use Mr. Kaggs's own pantry vernacular, "he was flyblown and frostbitten every joint of him."

It was then that he first conceived the idea of making his wife's birth and parentage a source of present income and provision for old age. She was an excellent penwoman, and for some months had had great practice in the composition of begging letters to her father. Mr. Kaggs's appearance being martial and imposing, he collected what information he could find upon the subject, and passed himself off for a young Englishman of good family, who had been an officer in the Spanish army, and served "under Evans!" Mrs. Kaggs's knowledge of the county families stood them in good stead, and they begged themselves through England, Scotland, and Wales, and lived in a sort of vulgar luxury, at no cost but invention, falsehood, and a ream or so of paper.

It was some few years ago that I first made their acquaintance. Mrs. Kaggs had bloomed into a fine elderly woman, and Mr. Kaggs's nose and stomach had widened to that appearance of fatherly responsibility and parochial importance that was most to be desired. The wife had sunk to the husband's level, and had brought up her children to tread in the same path. Their family, though not numerous, was a blessing to them, for each child, some way or other, contrived to bring in money. It was their parents' pride that they had given their offspring a liberal education. As soon as they were of an age capable of receiving instruction, they were placed at a respectable boarding-school, and, although they only stayed in it one half-year, they went to another establishment for the next half-year, and so managed to pick up a good miscellaneous education, and at the same time save their parents the cost of board and lodging.

James Julian Kaggs, the eldest and only son, was in Australia, "doing well," as his mamma would often say—though in what particular business or profession was a subject on which she preserved a discreet silence. As I never saw the young man in question, I am unable to furnish any information respecting him.

Catherine Kaggs, the eldest daughter, was an ugly and vulgar girl, on whom a genteel education and her mother's example of elegance and refinement had been thrown away. Kitty was a sort of Cinderella in the family, and being possessed of neither tact nor manner to levy contributions on the charitable, was sentenced to an out-door employment, for which she was well fitted. She sold flowers in the thoroughfare, near the market.

The second daughter, Betsey, was the pride of her father and mother, and the mainstay of the family. Tall, thin, and elegant, interesting rather than pretty, her pale face and subdued manners, her long eyelashes, soft voice, and fine hands, were the very requisites for the personation of beggared gentility and dilapidated aristocracy. Mrs. Kaggs often said, "That poor Kitty was her father's girl, a Kaggs all over—but that Bessie was a Thorncliffe (her own maiden name) and a lady every inch!"

The other children were a boy and girl of five and three years old, who called Mrs. Kaggs "Mamma," but who appeared much too young to belong to that lady in any relation but that of grand-children. Kitty, the flower girl, was passionately fond of them, and "Bessie" patronized them in her meek, maidenly way, and called them her dear brother and sister.

In the height of the season Miss Bessie Kaggs, attired in shabby black silk, dark shawl, and plain bonnet, would sally forth to the most aristocratic and fashionable squares, attended by her father in a white neck-cloth, carrying in one hand a small and fragile basket, and in the other a heavy and respectable umbrella. Arrived at the mansion of the intended victim, Miss Bessie would give a pretentious knock, and relieve her father of the burthen of the fragile basket. As the door opened, she would desire her parent, who was supposed to be a faithful retainer, to wait, and Mr. Kaggs would touch his hat respectfully and retire meekly to the corner of the square, and watch the placards in the public-house in the next street.

"Is Lady —— within?" Miss Betsey would inquire of the servant.

If the porter replied that his lady was out, or that she could not receive visitors, except by appointment, Miss Betsey would boldly demand pen, ink, and paper, and sit down and write, in a delicate, lady's hand, to the following effect:—

"Miss Thirlbrook presents her compliments to the Countess of ——, and most respectfully requests the honour of enrolling the Countess's name among the list of ladies who are kindly aiding her in disposing of a few necessaries for the toilette.

"Miss Thirlbrook is reduced to this extreme measure from the sad requirements of her infirm father, formerly an officer in his Majesty's ——d Regiment, who, from a position of comfort and affluence, is now compelled to seek aid from the charitable, and to rely on the feeble exertions of his daughter: a confirmed cripple and valetudinarian, he has no other resource.

"The well-known charity of the Countess of —— has induced Miss Thirlbrook to make this intrusion on her time. Miss T. will do herself the honour of waiting upon her ladyship on Thursday, when she *earnestly entreats* the favour of an interview, or an inspection of the few articles she has to dispose of."

Monday.

This carefully concocted letter—so different from the usual appeals—containing no references to other persons as to character or antecedents, generally had its effect, and in a few days Miss Betsey would find herself tête-à-tête with the Countess ——.

On entering the room she would make a profound curtsey, and, after thanking her ladyship for the honour, would open the fragile basket, which contained a few bottles of scent, some fancy soaps, ornamental envelopes, and perforated notepapers.

"Sit down, Miss Thirlbrook," the Countess would open the conversation. "I see the articles. Your note, I think, mentioned something of your being in less fortunate——"

Miss Betsey would lower her eyelashes and bend her head—not *too* deferentially, but as if bowing to circumstances for her father—her dear father's sake—for this was implied by her admirably concealed histrionic capability.

The lady would then suggest that she had a great many claims upon her consideration, and would delicately inquire into the pedigree and circumstances of Lieutenant Thirlbrook, formerly of his Majesty's —d Regiment.

Miss Betsey's replies were neither too ready nor too glib. She suffered herself to be drawn out, but did not advance a statement, and so established in her patroness's mind the idea that she had to deal with a very superior person. The sum of the story of this interesting scion of a fallen house was, that her father was an old Peninsular officer—as would be seen by a reference to the Army List (Miss Betsey had found the name in an old list); that he had left the service during the peace in 1814; that a ruinous lawsuit, arising from railway speculations, and an absconding agent, had reduced them to—to—to their present position—and that six years ago, an old wound—received at Barossa—had broken out, and laid her father helpless on a sick bed. "I know that these articles," Betsey would conclude, pointing to the fancy soaps and stationery, "are not such perhaps as your ladyship is accustomed to; but if you would kindly aid me by purchasing some of them—if ever so few—you would materially assist us; and I hope that—that we should not prove—either undeserving or ungrateful."

When, as sometimes happened, ladies paid a visit to Lieut. Thirlbrook, everything was prepared for their reception with a dramatic regard for propriety. The garret was made as clean and as uncomfortable as possible. Mr. Kaggs was put to bed, and the purpled pinkness of his complexion toned down with violet powder and cosmetics. A white handkerchief, with the Thirlbrook crest in a corner, was carelessly dropped upon the coverlid. A few physic bottles, an old United Service paper, and a ponderous Bible lay upon a ricketty round table beside him. Mrs. Kaggs was propped up with pillows in an arm-chair near the fireplace, and desired to look rheumatic and resigned. Kitty was sent out of the way; and the two children were dressed up in shabby black, and promised plums if they would keep quiet. Miss Betsey herself, in grey stuff and an apron, meek, mild, and matronly beyond her years, glided about softly, like a Sister of Mercy connected with the family.

My readers must understand that Mr. Kaggs was the sole tenant of the house he lived in, though he pretended that he only occupied the garrets as a lodger.

During the stay of the fashionable Samaritans Lieut. Thirlbrook—who had received a wound in his leg at Barossa, under the Duke—would say but little, but now and then his mouth would twitch as with suppressed pain. The visitors were generally much moved at the distressing scene. The gallant veteran—the helpless old lady—the sad and silent children—and the ministering angel of a daughter, were an impressive spectacle. The ladies would promise to exert themselves among their friends, and do all in their power to relieve them.

"Miss Thirlbrook," they would ask, as Miss Betsey attended them to the street-door, "those dear children are not your brother and sister, are they?"

Betsey would suppress a sigh, and say, "They are the son and daughter of my poor brother, who was a surgeon in the Navy—they are orphans. My brother died on the Gold Coast, and his poor wife soon followed him. She was delicate, and could not bear up against the shock. The poor things have only us to look to, and we do for them what little lies in our power."

This last stroke was a climax. "She never mentioned them before!" thought the ladies. "What delicacy! What high feeling! These are not common beggars, who make an exaggerated statement of their griefs."

"Miss Thirlbrook, I am sure you will pardon me for making the offer; but those dear children upstairs do not look strong. I hope you will not be offended by my offering to send them a luncheon now and then—a few delicacies—nourishing things—to do them good."

Miss Betsey would curtsey, lower her eyelids, and say, softly, "They are not strong."

"I'll send my servant as soon as I get home. Pray use this trifle for the present," (the lady would take out her purse,) "and good morning, Miss Thirlbrook. I must shake hands with you. I consider myself fortunate in having made your acquaintance."

Betsey's eyes would fill with tears, and as she held the door open, the expression of her face would plainly say: "Not only for myself, oh dear and charitable ladies, but for my father—my poor father—who was wounded, at Barossa, in the leg—do I thank you from the depths of a profoundly grateful heart."

When the basket arrived, Miss Betsey would sit down with her worthy parents and enjoy whatever poultry or meat had not been touched; but anything that had been cut, anything "second-hand," that dainty and haughty young lady would instruct her sister Kitty to give to the poor beggars.

This system of swindling could not, of course, last many years, and when the west end of London became too hot to hold them, the indefatigable Kaggses put an advertisement into the *Times* and *Morning Post*, addressed to the charitable and humane, saying that "a poor, but respectable family, required a small sum to enable them to make up the amount of their passage to Australia, and that they could give the highest references as to character.

The old certificates were hawked about, and for more than two years they drove a roaring trade in money, outfits, and necessaries for a voyage. Mr. Kaggs, too, made a fortunate hit. He purchased an old piano, and raffled it at five shillings a head. Each of his own family took a chance. At the first raffle Miss Betsey won it, at the second, Miss Kitty, on the third, Mr. Kaggs, on the fourth, his faithful partner, and on the fifth and last time, a particular friend of Miss Kitty's, a young lady in the greengrocery line. This invaluable piece of furniture was eventually disposed of by private contract to a dealer in Barret's Court, Oxford Street, and, a few days after, the Kaggs family really sailed for Melbourne, and I have never since heard of them.

Among the begging-letter fraternity there are not a few persons who affect to be literary men. They have at one time or another been able to publish a pamphlet, a poem, or a song—generally a patriotic one, and copies of these works—they always call them "works"—they constantly carry about with them to be ready for any customer who may turn up. I have known a notable member of this class of beggars for some years. He was introduced to me as a literary man by an innocent friend who really believed in his talent. He greeted me as a brother craftsman, and immediately took from the breast-pocket of his threadbare surtout a copy of one of his works. "Allow me," he said, "to present you with my latest work; it is dedicated, you will perceive, to the Right Honourable the Earl of Derby—here is a letter from his lordship complimenting me in the most handsome terms;" and before I could look into the book, the author produced from a well-worn black pocket-book a dirty letter distinguished by a large red seal. Sure enough it was a genuine letter beginning "The Earl of Derby presents his compliments," and going on to acknowledge the receipt of a copy of Mr. Driver's work.

Mr. Driver—I will call my author by that name—produced a great many other letters, all from persons of distinction, and the polite terms in which they were expressed astonished me not a little. I soon, however, discovered the key to all this condescension. The work was a political one, glorifying the Conservative party, and abounding with all sorts of old-fashioned Tory sentiments. The letters Mr. Driver showed me were of course all from tories. The "work" was quite a curiosity. It was called a political novel. It had for its motto, "Pro Rege, Lege, Aris et Focis," and the dedication to the Right Honourable the Earl of Derby was displayed over a whole page in epitaph fashion. At the close of our interview Mr. Driver pointed out to me that the price of the work was two shillings. Understanding the hint, I gave him that amount, when he called for pen and ink, and wrote on the fly leaf of the work, "To ——, Esq., with the sincere regards of the author.—J. Fitzharding Driver." On looking over the book—it was a mere paper-covered pamphlet of some hundred pages—I found that the story was not completed. I mentioned this to Mr. Driver the next time I met him, and he explained that he meant to go to press—that was a favourite expression of his—to go to press with the second volume shortly. Ten years, however, have elapsed since then, and Mr. Driver has not yet gone to press with his second volume. The last time I met him he offered me the original volume as his "last new work," which he presumed I had never seen. He also informed me that he was about to publish a patriotic song in honour of the Queen. Would I subscribe for a copy—only three-and-sixpence—and he would leave it for me? Mr. Driver had forgotten that I had subscribed for this very song eight years previously. He showed me the selfsame MS. of the new national anthem, which I had perused so long ago. The paper had become as soft and limp and dingy as a Scotch one-pound note, but it had been worth a good many one-pound notes to Mr. Fitzharding Driver. Mr. Driver has lived upon this as yet unpublished song, and that unfinished political novel, for ten years and more. I have seen him often enough to know exactly his *modus operandi*. Though practically a beggar Mr. Driver is no great rogue. Were you to dress him well, he might pass for a nobleman. As it is, in his shabby genteel clothes he looks a broken-down swell. And so in fact he is. In his young days he had plenty of money, and went the pace among the young bloods of Bond Street. Mr. Driver's young days were the days of the Regent. He drove a dashing phaeton-and-four then, and lounged and gambled, and lived the life of a man about town He tells you all that with great pride, and also how he came to grief, though this part of the story is not so clear. There is no doubt that he had considerable acquaintance among great people in his prosperous days. He lives now upon his works, and the public-house parlours of the purlieus of the west-end serve him as publishing houses. He is a great political disputant, and his company is not unwelcome in those quarters. He enters, takes his seat, drinks his glass, joins in the conversation, and, as he says himself, shows that he is a man of parts. In this way he makes friends among the tradesmen who visit these resorts. They soon find out that he is poor, and an author, and moved both to pity and admiration, each member of the company purchases a copy of that unfinished political novel, or subscribes for that new patriotic song, which I expect will yet be in the womb of the press when the crack of doom comes. I think Mr. Driver has pretty well used up all the quiet parlours of W. district by this time. Not long ago I had a letter from him enclosing a prospectus of a new work to be entitled "Whiggery, or the Decline of England," and soliciting a subscription to enable him to go to press with the first edition. I have no doubt that every conservative member of both houses of Parliament has had a copy of that prospectus. Mr. Fitzharding Driver will call at their houses for an answer, and some entirely out of easy charity, and others from a party feeling of delight at the prospect of the Whigs being abused in a book even by this poor beggar, will send him down half-crowns, and enable the poor wretch to eat and drink for a few months longer. On more than one occasion while I have known him, Mr. Driver has been on the point of " being well off again," to use his own expression. His behaviour under the prospect was characteristic of the man, his antecedents, and his mode of life. He touched up his seedy clothes, had some cotton-velvet facings put to his threadbare surtout, revived his hat, mounted a pair of shabby patent-leather boots, provided himself with a penny cane, adorned with an old silk tassel, and appeared each day with a flower in his button-hole. In addition to these he had sewn into the breast of his surtout a bit of parti-coloured ribbon to look like a decoration. In this guise he came up to me at the Crystal Palace one day, and appeared to be in great glee. His ogling and mysterious manner puzzled me. Judge of my astonishment when this hoary, old, tottering, toothless beggar informed me, with many self-satisfied chuckles, that a rich widow, " a fine dashing woman, sir," had fallen in love with him, and was going to marry him. The marriage did not come off, the pile is worn away from the velvet facings, the patent-leather boots have become mere shapeless flaps of leather, the old broad-brimmed hat is past the power of reviver, and the Bond Street buck of the days of the Regent now wanders from public-house to public-house selling lucifer-matches. He still however carries with him a copy of his "work," the limp and worn MS. of his anthem, and the prospectus of " Whiggery, or the Decline of England." These and the letters from distinguished personages stand him in better stead than the lucifer-matches, when he lights upon persons of congenial sympathies.

ADVERTISING BEGGING-LETTER WRITERS.

Among many begging-letter writers who appealed to sentiment, the most notorious and successful was a man of the name of Thomas Stone, alias Stanley, alias Newton. He had been in early life transported for forgery, and afterwards was tried for perjury; and when his ordinary methods of raising money had been detected and exposed, he resorted to the ingenious expedient of sending an advertisement to the *Times*, of which the following is a copy:—

"To the Charitable and Affluent.

" At the eleventh hour a young and most unfortunate lady is driven by great distress to solicit from those charitable and humane persons who ever derive pleasure from benevolent acts, some little *pecuniary assistance*. The advertiser's condition is almost hopeless, being, alas! friendless, and reduced to the last extremity. The smallest aid would be most thankfully acknowledged, and the fullest explanation given. Direct Miss T. C. M., Post-office, Great Randolph St., Camden New Town."

This touching appeal was read by a philanthropic gentleman, who sent the advertiser 5*l*., and afterwards 1*l*. more, to which he received a reply in the following words:—

"SIR,—I again offer my gratitude for your charitable kindness. I am quite unable to speak the promptings of my heart for your great goodness to me, an entire stranger, but you may believe me, sir, I am very sincerely thankful. You will, I am sure, be happy to hear I have paid the few trifling demands upon me, and also obtained sufficient of my wearing apparel to make a decent appearance; but it has swallowed up the whole of your generous bounty, or I should this day have moved to the Hampstead Road, where a far more comfortable lodging has been offered me, and where, sir, if you would condescend to call I would cheerfully and with pleasure relate my circumstances in connexion with my past history, and I do hope you might consider me worthy of your further notice. But it is my earnest desire to support myself and my dearest child by my own industry. As I mentioned before, I have youth and health, and have received a good education, but alas! I fear I shall have a great difficulty in obtaining employment such as I desire, for I have fallen! I am a mother, and my dear poor boy is the child of sin. But I was deceived—cruelly deceived by a base and heartless villain. A licence was purchased for our marriage; I believed all; my heart knew no guile; the deceptions of the world I had scarcely ever heard of; but too soon I found myself destroyed and lost, the best affections of my heart trampled upon, and myself infamous and disgraced. But I did not continue to live in sin. Oh no! I despised and loathed the villain who so deceived me. Neither have I received, nor would I, one shilling from him. I think I stated in my first letter I am the daughter of a deceased merchant; such is the case; and had I some friends to interest themselves for me, I do think it would be found I am entitled to some property; however, it would be first necessary to explain personally every circumstance, and to you, sir, I would unreservedly explain all. And oh! I do earnestly hope you would, after hearing my sad tale, think there was some little palliation of my guilt.

"In answer to the advertisement I had inserted, I received many offers of assistance, but they contained overtures of such a nature that I could not allow myself to reply to any of them. You, sir, have been my best friend, and may God bless you for your sympathy and kindness. I am very desirous to remove, but cannot do so without a little money in my pocket. Your charity has enabled me to provide all I required, and paid that which I owed, which has been a great relief to my mind. I hope and trust that you will not think me covetous or encroaching upon your goodness, in asking you to assist me with a small sum further, for the purpose named. Should you, however, decline to do so, believe me, I should be equally grateful; and it is most painful and repugnant to my feelings to ask, but I know not to whom else to apply. Entreating your early reply, however it may result, and with every good wish, and the sincerest and warmest acknowledgments of my heart, believe, sir, always your most thankful and humble servant,
"FRANCES THORPE.

"Please direct T. C. M., Post-office, Crown Street, Gray's Inn Road."

With the same sort of tale, varying the signature to Fanny Lyons, Mary Whitmore, and Fanny Hamilton, &c., Mr. Stone continued to victimize the public, until the Society for the Suppression of Mendicity laid him by the heels. He was committed for trial at Clerkenwell Sessions, and sentenced to transportation for seven years.

I must content myself with these few specimens of the begging-letter impostors; it would be impossible to describe every variety. Sometimes they are printers, whose premises have been destroyed by fire; at others, young women who have been ruined by noblemen and are anxious to retrieve themselves; or widows of naval officers who have perished in action or by sickness. There was a long run upon "aged clergymen, whose sands of life were fast running out," but the fraud became so common that it was soon "blown."

The greatest blow that was ever struck at this species of imposition was the establishment of the Begging-Letter Department by the Society for the Suppression of Mendicity. In the very first case they investigated they found the writer—who had penned a most touching letter to a well-known nobleman—crouching in a fireless garret in one of the worst and lowest neighbourhoods of London. This man was discovered to be the owner and occupier of a handsomely-furnished house in another part of the town, where his wife and family lived in luxury. The following is a specimen of a most artful begging letter from America.

Ellicot's Mills, Howard Co., Maryland, United States,
June 6, 1859.

"MY DEAREST FRIEND,

"Why—why have you not written, and sent me the usual remittances? Your silence has caused me the greatest uneasiness. Poor dear Frederick is dying and we are in the extremest want. The period to hear from you has past some time, and no letter. It is very strange! What can it mean?

"In a short time your poor suffering son will be at rest. I shall then trouble you no more; but—oh! I beseech you, do not permit your poor son to die in want. I have expended my last shilling to procure him those little necessaries he must and shall have. Little did I think when, long, long years ago, I deserted all, that you might be free and happy, that you would fail me in this terrible hour of affliction—but you have not—I know you have not. You must have sent, and the letter miscarried. Your poor dying son sends his fondest love. Poor dear fellow!—he has never known a father's care; still, from a child, he has prayed for, revered, and loved you —he is now going to his Father in heaven, and, when he is gone my widowed heart will break. When I look back upon the long past, although broken-hearted and crushed to the earth, yet I cannot tutor my heart to regret it, for I dearly loved you. Yes, and proved it, dearest friend, by forsaking and fleeing with my poor fatherless boy to this strange and distant land, that you might be free and happy with those so worthy of you; and, believe me when I say, that your happiness has been my constant prayer. In consequence of poor dear Frederick's sickness we are in the greatest distress and want. I have been compelled to forego all exertion, and attend solely upon him; therefore, do, I pray you, send me, without an instant's delay, a 10*l*. note. I must have it, or I shall go mad. Your poor suffering boy must not die in misery and want. Send the money by return mail, and send a Bank of England note, for I am now miles away from where I could get a draught cashed. I came here for the benefit of poor dear Frederick, but I fear it has done him no good. We are now among strangers, and in the most abject distress, and unless you send soon, your afflicted unoffending boy will starve to death. I can no longer bear up against poverty, sickness, and your unkindness; but you must have sent; your good, kind heart would not permit you to let us die in want. God bless you, and keep you and yours. May you be supremely happy! Bless you! In mercy send soon, for we are in extremest want.

"Remaining faithfully,
"Your dearest friend,
"Kate Stanley.

"Pay the postage of your letter to me, or I shall not be able to obtain it, for I am selling everything to live."

The above affecting letter was received by the widow of a London merchant six months after his death. The affair was investigated and proved to be an imposture. The moral character of Mr. —— had been irreproachable. American begging-letter writers read the obituaries in English newspapers and ply their trade, while the loss of the bereaved relatives of the man whose memory they malign is recent.

Ashamed Beggars.

By the above title I mean those tall, lanthorn-jawed men, in seedy well-brushed clothes, who, with a ticket on their breasts, on which a short but piteous tale is written in the most respectable of large-hand, and with a few boxes of lucifer-matches in their hands, make no appeal by word of mouth, but invoke the charity of passers-by by meek glances and imploring looks—fellows who, having no talent for "patter," are gifted with great powers of facial pathos, and make expression of feature stand in lieu of vocal supplication. For some years I have watched a specimen of this class, who has a regular "beat" at the west end of London. He is a tall man, with thin legs and arms, and a slightly-protuberant stomach. His "costume" (I use the word advisedly, for he is really a great actor of pantomime,) consists of an old black dress-coat, carefully buttoned, but left sufficiently open at the top to show a spotlessly white shirt, and at the bottom, to exhibit an old grey waistcoat; and a snowy apron, which he wears after the fashion of a Freemason, forgetting that real tradesmen are never seen in their aprons except behind the counter. A pair of tight, dark, shabby trousers, black gaiters without an absent button, and heavy shoes of the severest thickness, cover his nether man. Round his neck is a red worsted comforter, which neatly tied at the throat, descends straight and formally beneath his coat, and exhibits two fringed ends, which fall, in agreeable contrast of colour, over the before-mentioned apron. I never remember seeing a beggar of this class without an apron and a worsted comforter—they would appear to be his stock-in-trade, a necessary portion of his outfit; the white apron to relieve the sombre hue of his habiliments, and show up their well-brushed shabbiness; the scarlet comforter to contrast with the cadaverous complexion which he owes to art or nature. In winter the comforter also serves as an advertisement that his great-coat is gone.

The man I am describing wears a "pad" round his neck, on which is written—

> Kind Friends and Christian Brethren!
> I was once a
> Respectable Tradesman,
> doing a Good Business;
> till Misfortune reduced me to
> this Pass!
> Be kind enough to Buy
> some of the Articles I offer,
> and you will confer a
> Real Charity!

In his hands, on which he wears scrupulously-darned mittens, he carries a box or two of matches, or a few quires of note-paper or envelopes, and half-a-dozen small sticks of sealing-wax. He is also furnished with a shabby-genteel looking boy of about nine years old, who wears a Shakesperian collar, and the regulation worsted comforter, the ends of which nearly trail upon the ground. The poor child, whose features do not in the least resemble the man's, and who, too young to be his son, is too old to be his grandson, keeps his little hands in his large pockets, and tries to look as unhappy and half-starved as he can.

But the face of the beggar is a marvellous exhibition! His acting is admirable! Christian resignation and its consequent fortitude are written on his brow. His eyes roll imploringly, but no sound escapes him. The expression of his features almost pronounces, "Christian friend, purchase my humble wares, for *I scorn to beg*. I am starving, but tortures shall not wring the humiliating secret from my lips." He exercises a singular fascination over old ladies, who slide coppers into his hand quickly, as if afraid that they shall hurt his feelings. He pockets the money, heaves a sigh, and darts an abashed and grateful look at them that makes them feel how keenly he appreciates their delicacy. When the snow is on the ground he now and then introduces a little shiver, and with a well-worn pocket-handkerchief stifles a cough that he intimates by, a despairing dropping of his eyelids, is slowly killing him.

THE SWELL BEGGAR.

A singular variety of this sort of mendicant used to be seen some years ago in the streets of Cambridge. He had been a gentleman of property, and had studied at one of the colleges. Race-courses, billiard-tables, and general gambling had reduced him to beggary; but he was too proud to ask alms. As the "Ashamed Beggar" fortifies himself with a "pad," this swell-beggar armed himself with a broom. He swept a crossing. His clothes—he always wore evening-dress—were miserably ragged and shabby; his hat was a broken Gibus, but he managed to have good and fashionable boots; and his shirt collar, and wristbands were changed every day. A white cambric handkerchief peeped from his coat-tail pocket, and a gold eye-glass dangled from his neck. His hands were lady-like; his nails well-kept; and it was impossible to look at him without a mingled feeling of pity and amusement.

His plan of operations was to station himself at his crossing at the time the ladies of Cambridge were out shopping. His antics were curiously funny. Dangling his broom between his fore-finger and thumb, as if it were a light umbrella or riding-whip, he would arrive at his stand, and look up at the sky to see what sort of weather might be expected. Then tucking the broom beneath his arm he would take off his gloves, fold them together and put them into his coat-pockets, sweep his crossing carefully, and when he had finished, look at it with admiration. When ladies crossed, he would remove his broken hat, and smile with great benignity, displaying at the same time a fine set of teeth. On wet days his attentions to the fair sex knew no bounds. He would run before them and wipe away every little puddle in their path. On receiving a gratuity, which was generally in silver, he would remove his hat and bow gracefully and gratefully. When gentlemen walked over his crossing he would stop them, and, holding his hat in the true mendicant fashion, request the loan of a shilling. With many he was a regular pensioner. When a mechanic or poor-looking person offered him a copper, he would take it, and smile his thanks with a patronising air, but he never took off his hat to less than sixpence. He was a jovial and boastful beggar, and had a habit of jerking at his stand-up collar, and pulling at his imperial coxcombically. When he considered his day's work over, he would put on his gloves, and, dangling his broom in his careless elegant way, trip home to his lodging. He never used a broom but one day, and gave the old ones to his landlady. The undergraduates were kind to him, and encouraged his follies; but the college dons looked coldly on him, and when they passed him he would assume an expression of impertinent indifference *as if he cut them*. I never heard what became of him. When I last saw him he looked between forty and fifty years of age.

CLEAN FAMILY BEGGARS.

Clean Family Beggars are those who beg or sing in the streets, in numbers varying from four to seven. I need only particularize one "gang" or "party," as their appearance and method of begging will do as a sample of all others.

Beggars of this class group themselves artistically. A broken-down looking man, in the last stage of seediness, walks hand-in-hand with a pale-faced, interesting little girl. His wife trudges on his other side, a baby in one arm; a child just able to walk steadies itself by the hand that is disengaged; two or three other children cling about the skirts of her gown, one occasionally detaching himself or herself—as a kind of rear or advanced guard from the main body—to cut off stragglers and pounce upon falling halfpence, or look piteously into the face of a passer-by. The clothes of the whole troop are in that state when seediness is dropping into rags; but their hands and faces are perfectly clean—their skins literally shine—perhaps from the effect of a plentiful use of soap, *which they do not wash off before drying themselves with a towel*. The complexions of the smaller children, in particular, glitter like sand-paper, and their eyes are half-closed, and their noses corrugated, as with constant and compulsory ablution. The baby is a wonderful specimen of washing and getting-up of ornamental linen. Altogether, the Clean Family Beggars form a most attractive picture for quiet and respectable streets, and "pose" themselves for the admiration of the thrifty matrons, who are their best supporters.

Sometimes the children of the Clean Family Beggars sing—sometimes the father "patters." This morning a group passed my window, who both sang and "pattered." The mother was absent, and the two eldest girls knitted and crochetted as they walked along. The burthen of the song which the children shrieked out in thin treble, was,

" And the wild flowers are springing on the plain."

The rest of the words were undistinguishable. When the little ones had finished, the man, who evidently prided himself upon his powers of eloquence, began, in a loud, authoritative, oratorical tone :—

"My dear friends,—It is with great pain, and affliction, and trouble, that I present myself and my poo—oor family before you, in this wretched situation, at the present moment; but what can I do? Work I cannot obtain, and my little family ask me for bread! Yes, my dear friends—my little family ask me for bread! Oh, my dear friends, conceive what your feelin's would be, if, like me, at the present moment your poo—oor dear children asked for bread, and you had it not to give them! **What** then could you do? God send, my dear friends, that no individual, no father of a family, nor mother, nor other individual, *with* children, will ever, or ever may be drove to do what—or, I should say, that which I am now a-doing of, at the present moment. If any one in this street, or in the next, or in any of the streets in this affluent neighbourhood, had found theirselves in the situation, in which I was placed this morning, it would be hard to say what they could, or would have done; and I assure you, my dear friends,—yes, I assure you, from my heart, that it is very possible that many might have been drove to have done, or do worse, than what I am a doing of, for the sake of my poo—oor family, at the present moment, if they had been drove, by suffering, as I and my poo—oor wife have been the morning of this very day. My wife, my kind friends, is now unfortunately ill through unmerited starvation, and is ill a-bed, from which, at the present moment, she cannot rise. Want we have known together, my dear friends, and so has our poo—oor family, and baby, only eight months old. God send, my dear friends, that none of you, and none of your dear babes, and families, that no individual, which now is listening to my deep distress, at the present moment, may ever know the sufferin's to which we have been reduced, is my fervent prayer! All I want to obtain is a meal's victuals for my poo—oor family!"

(Here the man caught my eye, and immediately shifted his ground.)

"You will ask me, my dear friends," he continued, in an argumentative manner, "you will ask me how and why it is, and what is the reason, which I cannot obtain work? Alas! my dear friends, it is unfortunately so at the present moment. I am a silk-weaver in Bethnal Green, by trade, and the noo International Treaty with France, which Mr. Cobden—" (here he kept his eye on me, as if the political reason were intended for my especial behoof)—"which *Mr. Cobden*, my dear friends, was depooted to go to the French emperor, Louis Napoleon, to agree upon, betwixt this country and France, which the French manufacturers sends goods into this country, without paying no dooty, and undersells the native manufacturers, though, my dear friends, our workmanship is as good, and English silk as genuine as French, I do assure you. Leastways, there is no difference, except in pattern, and, through the neglect of them as ought to look after it better, that is, to see we had the best designs; for design is the only thing—I mean design and pattern—in which they can outdo us; and also, my dear friends, ladies as go to shops will ask for foreign goods—it is more to their taste than English, at the present moment; and so it is, that many poo—oor families at Bethnal Green and Spitalfields—and Coventry likewise, is redooced to the situation which I myself—that is, to ask your charity—am a doing of—at the present moment."

I gave a little girl a penny, and the man, still fixing me with his eye, continued—

"You will ask me, my dear friends, praps, how it is that I do not apply to the parish? why not to get relief for myself, my de—ar wife, and little family? My kind friends, you do not know the state in which things is with the poor weavers of Bethnal Green, and, at the present moment, Spitalfields likewise. It comes of the want of knowledge of the real state of this rich and 'appy country, its material prosperity and resources, which you, at this end of the town, can form no idea of. There is now sixteen or seventeen thousand people out of work. Yes, my dear friends, in about two parishes, there is sixteen or seventeen thousand individuals—I mean, of course, counting their poo—oor families and all, which at the present moment, cannot obtain bread. Oh, my dear friends, how grateful ought you be to God that you and your dear families, are not out of work, and can obtain a meal's victuals, and are not like the sufferin' weavers of Bethnal Green—and Spitalfields, and Coventry likewise, through the loss of trade; for, my dear friends, if you were like me, forced to what I am doing now at the present moment, &c., &c., &c."

NAVAL AND MILITARY BEGGARS

are most frequently met with in towns situated at some distance from a seaport or a garrison. As they are distinct specimens of the same tribe, they must be separately classified. The more familiar nuisance is the

Turnpike Sailor.

This sort of vagabond has two lays, the "merchant" lay, and the "R'yal Navy" lay. He adopts either one or the other according to the exigencies of his wardrobe, his locality, or the person he is addressing. He is generally the offspring of some inhabitant of the most notorious haunts of a seaport town, and has seldom been at sea, or when he has, has run away after the first voyage. His slang of seamanship has been picked up at the lowest public-houses in the filthiest slums that offer diversion to the genuine sailor.

When on the "merchant lay" his attire consists of a pair of tattered trousers, an old guernsey-shirt, and a torn straw-hat. One of his principal points of "costume" is his bare feet. His black silk handkerchief is knotted jauntily round his throat after the most approved models at the heads of penny ballads, and the outsides of songs. He wears small gold earrings, and has short curly hair in the highest and most offensive state of glossy greasiness. His hands and arms are carefully tattooed—a foul anchor, or a long-haired mermaid sitting on her tail and making her toilette, being the favourite cartoons. In his gait he endeavours to counterfeit the roll of a true seaman, but his hard feet, knock-knees, and imperceptibly acquired turnpike-trot betray him. His face bears the stamp of diabolically low cunning, and it is impossible to look at him without an association with a police-court. His complexion is coarse and tallowy, and has none of the manly bronze that exposure to the weather, and watching the horizon give to the real tar.

I was once walking with a gentleman who had spent the earlier portion of his life at sea, when a turnpike sailor shuffled on before us. We had just been conversing on nautical affairs, and I said to him—

"Now, there is a brother sailor in distress; of course you will give him something?"

"*He* a sailor!" said my friend, with great disgust. "Did you see him spit?"

The fellow had that moment expectorated.

I answered that I had.

"He spit to wind'ard!" said my friend.

"What of that?" said I.

"A regular landsman's trick," observed my friend. "A real sailor never spits to wind'ard. *Why, he could'nt.*"

We soon passed the fellow, who pulled at a curl upon his forehead, and began in a gruff voice, intended to convey the idea of hardships, storms, shipwrecks, battles, and privations. "God—bless—your—'onors—give—a—copper—to — a — poor—sailor—as—hasn't—spliced—the — main—jaw—since—the—day—'fore—yesterday—at—eight—bells—God—love—yer—'onors—do! — I—avent—tasted—sin'—the—day—'fore — yesterday—so—drop—a — cop—poor—seaman—do."

My friend turned round and looked the beggar full in the face.

"What ship?" he asked, quickly.

The fellow answered glibly.

"What captain?" pursued my friend.

The fellow again replied boldly, though his eyes wandered uneasily.

"What cargo?" asked my inexorable companion.

The beggar was not at fault, but answered correctly.

The name of the port, the reason of his discharge, and other questions were asked and answered; but the man was evidently beginning to be embarrassed. My friend pulled out his purse as if to give him something.

"What are you doing here?" continued the indefatigable inquirer. "Did you leave the coast for the purpose of trying to find a ship *here*?" (We were in Leicester.)

The man stammered and pulled at his useful forelock to get time to collect his thoughts and invent a good lie.

"He had a friend in them parts as he thought could help him."

"How long since you were up the Baltic?"

"Year—and—a—arf,—yer—'onor."

"Do you know Kiel?"

"Yes,—yer—'onor."

"D'ye know the 'British Flag' on the quay there?"

"Yes,—yer—'onor."

"Been there often?"

"Yes,—yer—'onor."

"Does Nick Johnson still keep it?"

"Yes,—yer—'onor."

"Then," said my friend, after giving vent to a strong opinion as to the beggar's veracity, "I'd advise you to be off quickly, for there's a policeman, and if I get within hail of him I shall tell him you're an impostor. There's no such house on the quay. Get out, you scoundrel!"

The fellow shuffled off, looking curses, but not daring to express them.

On the "R'yal Navy" lay, the turnpike sailor assumes different habiliments, and altogether a smarter trim. He wears coarse blue trousers symmetrically cut about the hips, and baggy over the foot. A "jumper," or loose shirt of the same material, a tarpaulin hat, with the name of a vessel in letters of faded gold, is struck on the back of his neck, and he has a piece of whipcord, or "lanyard" round his waist, to which is suspended a jack-knife, which if of but little service in fighting the battles of his country has stood him in good stead in silencing the cackling of any stray poultry that crossed his road, or in frightening into liberality the female tenant of a solitary cottage. This "patter," or "blob," is of Plymouth, Portsmouth, Cawsen' Bay, Hamoaze—ships paid off, prize-money, the bo'sen and the first le'tenant. He is always an able-bodied, never an ordinary seaman, and cannot get a ship "becos" orders is at the Hadmiralty as no more isn't to be put into commission. Like the fictitious merchant-sailor he calls every landsman "your honour," in accordance with the conventional rule observed by the jack tars in nautical dramas. He exhibits a stale plug of tobacco, and replaces it in his jaw with ostentatious gusto. His chief victims are imaginative boys fresh from "Robinson Crusoe," and "Tales of the Ocean," and old ladies who have relatives at sea. For many months after a naval battle he is in full force, and in inland towns tells highly-spiced narratives of the adventures of his own ship and its gallant crew in action. He is profuse in references to "the cap'en," and interlards his account with, "and the cap'en turns round, and he says to me, he says—" He feels the pulse of his listener's credulity through their eyes, and throws the hatchet with the enthusiasm of an artist. "When we boarded 'em," I heard one of these vagabonds say—"oh, when we boarded 'em!" but it is beyond the power of my feeble pen to relate the deeds of the turnpike true blue, and his ship and its gallant, gallant crew, when they boarded 'em, I let him run out his yarn, and then said, "I saw the account of the action in the papers, but they said nothing of boarding. As I read it, the enemy were in too shallow water to render that manœuvre possible; but that till they struck their flag, and the boats went out to take possession, the vessels were more than half a mile apart."

This would have posed an ordinary humbug, but the able-bodied liar immediately, and with great apparent disgust, said, "The papers! the noo—o—o—s-papers! d——n the noo—o—o—s—papers. You don't believe what they says, sure*ly*. Look how they sarved out old Charley Napier. Why, sir, *I was there, and I ought to know*."

At times the turnpike sailor roars out a song in praise of British valour by sea; but of late this "lay" has been unfrequent. At others he borrows an interesting-looking little girl, and tying his arm up in a sling, adds his wounds and a motherless infant to his other claims upon the public sympathy. After a heavy gale and the loss of several vessels, he appears with a fresh tale and a new suit of carefully chosen rags. When all these resources fail him he is compelled to turn merchant, or "duffer," and invests a small capital in a few hundred of the worst, and a dozen or two of the very best, cigars. If he be possessed of no capital he steals them. He allows his whiskers to grow round his face, and lubricates them in the same liberal manner as his shining hair. He buys a pea-coat, smart waistcoat, and voluminous trousers, discards his black neckerchief for a scarlet one, the ends of which run through a massive ring. He wears a large pair of braces over his waistcoat, and assumes a half-foreign air, as of a mariner just returned from distant climes. He accosts you in the streets mysteriously, and asks you if you want "a few good cigars?" He tells you they are smuggled, that he "run" them himself, and that the "Custom-'us horficers" are after him. I need hardly inform my reader that the cigar he offers as a sample is excellent, and that, should he be weak enough to purchase a few boxes he will not find them "according to sample." Not unfrequently, the cigar-"duffer" lures his victim to some low tavern to receive his goods, where in lieu of tobacco, shawls, and laces, he finds a number of cut-throat-looking confederates, who plunder and illtreat him.

It must not be forgotten that at times a begging sailor may be met, who has really been a seaman, and who is a proper object of benevolence. When it is so, he is invariably a man past middle age, and offers for sale or exhibition a model of a man-of-war or a few toy yachts. He has but little to say for himself, and is too glad for the gift of a pair of landsmen's trousers to trouble himself about their anti-nautical cut. In fact, the real seaman does not care for costume, and is as frequently seen in an old shooting-coat as a torn jacket; but despite his habiliments, the true salt oozes out in the broad hands that dangle heavily from the wrists, as if wanting to grip a rope or a handspike; in the tender feet accustomed to the smooth planks of the deck, and in the settled, far-off look of the weather-beaten head, with its fixed expression of the aristocracy of subordination.

In conclusion, a real sailor is seldom or never seen inland, where he can have no chance of employment, and is removed from the sight of the sea, docks, shipmates, and all things dear and familiar to him. He carries his papers about him in a small tin box, addresses those who speak to him as "sir" and "marm," and never as "your honour" or "my lady;" is rather taciturn than talkative, and rarely brags of what he has seen, or done, or seen done. In these and all other respects he is the exact opposite of the turnpike sailor.

STREET CAMPAIGNERS.

Soldier beggars may be divided into three classes: those who really have been soldiers and are reduced to mendicancy, those who have been ejected from the army for misconduct, and those with whom the military dress and bearing are pure assumptions.

The difference between these varieties is so distinct as to be easily detected. The first, or soldier proper, has all the evidence of drill and barrack life about him; the eye that always "fronts" the person he addresses; the spare habit, high cheekbones, regulation whisker, stiff chin, and deeply-marked line beneath from ear to ear. He carries his papers about him, and when he has been wounded or seen service, is modest and retiring as to his share of glory. He can give little information as to the incidents of an engagement, except as regards the deeds of his own company, and in conversation speaks more of the personal qualities of his officers and comrades than of their feats of valour. Try him which way you will he never will confess that he has killed a man. He compensates himself for his silence on the subject of fighting by excessive grumbling as to the provisions, quarters, &c., to which he has been forced to submit in the course of his career. He generally has a wife marching by his side—a tall strapping woman, who looks as if a long course of washing at the barracks had made her half a soldier. Ragged though he be, there is a certain smartness about the soldier proper, observable in the polish of his boots, the cock of his cap, and the disposition of the leather strap under his lower lip. He invariably carries a stick, and when a soldier passes him, casts on him an odd sort of look, half envying, half pitying, as if he said, "Though you are better fed than I, you are not so free!"

The soldier proper has various occupations. He does not pass all his time in begging: he will hold a horse, clean knives and boots, sit as a model to an artist, and occasionally take a turn at the wash-tub. Begging he abhors, and is only driven to it as a last resource.

If my readers would inquire why a man so ready to work should not be able to obtain employment, he will receive the answer that universally applies to all questions of hardship among the humbler classes—the vice of the discharged soldier is intemperance.

The second sort of soldier-beggar is one of the most dangerous and violent of mendicants. Untamable even by regimental discipline, insubordinate by nature, he has been thrust out from the army to prey upon society. He begs but seldom, and is dangerous to meet with after dark upon a lonely road, or in a sequestered lane. Indeed, though he has every right to be classed among those who will not work, he is not thoroughly a beggar, but will be met with again, and receive fuller justice at our hands, in the, to him, more congenial catalogue of thieves.

The third sort of street campaigner is a perfect impostor, who being endowed, either by accident or art, with a broken limb or damaged feature, puts on an old military coat, as he would assume the dress of a frozen-out gardener, distressed dock-yard labourer, burnt-out tradesman, or scalded mechanic. He is imitative, and in his time plays many parts. He "gets up" his costume with the same attention to detail as the turnpike sailor. In crowded busy streets he "stands pad," that is, with a written statement of his hard case slung round his neck, like a label round a decanter. His bearing is most military; he keeps his neck straight, his chin in, and his thumbs to the outside seams of his trousers; he is stiff as an embalmed preparation, for which, but for the motion of his eyes, you might mistake him. In quiet streets and in the country he discards his "pad" and begs "on the blob," that is, he "patters" to the passers-by, and invites their sympathy by word of mouth. He is an ingenious and fertile liar, and seizes occasions such as the late war in the Crimea and the mutiny in India as good distant grounds on which to build his fictions.

I was walking in a high-road, when I was accosted by a fellow dressed in an old military tunic, a forage-cap like a charity boy's, and tattered trousers, who limped along barefoot by the aid of a stick. His right sleeve was empty, and tied up to a button-hole at his breast, à la Nelson.

"Please your honour," he began, in a doleful exhausted voice, "bestow your charity on a poor soldier which lost his right arm at the glorious battle of Inkermann."

I looked at him, and having considerable experience in this kind of imposition, could at once detect that he was "acting."

"To what regiment did you belong?" I asked.

"The Thirty —, sir."

I looked at his button and read Thirty —

"I haven't tasted bit o' food, sir, since yesterday at half-past four, and then a lady give me a cruster bread," he continued.

"The Thirty —!" I repeated "I knew the Thirty —. Let me see—who was the colonel?"

The man gave me a name, with which I suppose he was provided.

"How long were you in the Thirty — ?" I inquired.

"Five year, sir."

"I had a schoolfellow in that regiment, Captain Thorpe, a tall man with red whiskers—did you know him?"

"There was a captain, sir, with large red whiskers, and I think his name was Thorpe; but he warn't captain of my company, so I didn't know for certain," replied the man, after an affected hesitation.

"The Thirty — was one of the first of our regiments that landed, I think?" I remarked.

"Yes, your honour, it were."

"You impudent impostor!" I said; "the Thirty — did not go out till the spring of '55. How dare you tell me you belonged to it?"

The fellow blenched for a moment, but rallied and said, "I didn't like to contradict your honour for fear you should be angry and wouldn't give me nothing."

"That's very polite of you," I said, "but still I have a great mind to give you into custody. Stay; tell me who and what you are, and I will give you a shilling and let you go."

He looked up and down the road, measured me with his eye, abandoned the idea of resistance, and replied:

"Well, your honour, if you won't be too hard on a poor man which finds it hard to get a crust anyhow or way, I don't mind telling you I never was a soldier."

I give his narrative as he related it to me.

"I don't know who my parents ever was. The fust thing as I remember was the river side (the Thames), and running in low tide to find things. I used to beg, hold hosses, and sleep under dry arches. I don't remember how I got any clothes. I never had a pair of shoes or stockings till I was almost a man. I fancy I am now nearly forty years of age.

"An old woman as kep a rag and iron shop by the water-side give me a lodging once for two years. We used to call her 'Nanny;' but she turned me out when she caught me taking some old nails and a brass cock out of her shop; I was hungry when I done it, for the old gal gi' me no grub, nothing but the bare floor for a bed.

"I have been a beggar all my life, and begged in all sorts o' ways and all sorts o' lays. I don't mean to say that if I see anything laying about handy that I don't mouch it (i. e. steal it). Once a gentleman took me into his house as his servant. He was a very kind man; I had a good place, swell clothes, and beef and beer as much as I liked; but I couldn't stand the life, and I run away.

"The loss o' my arm, sir, was the best thing as ever happen'd to me: it's been a living to me; I turn out with it on all sorts o' lays, and it's as good as a pension. I lost it poaching; my mate's gun went off by accident, and the shot went into my arm, I neglected it, and at last was obliged to go to a orspital and have it off. The surgeon as ampitated it said that a little longer and it would ha' mortified.

"The Crimea's been a good dodge to a many, but it's getting stale; all dodges are getting stale; square coves (*i. e.*, honest folks) are so wide awake."

"Don't you think you would have found it more profitable, had you taken to labour or some honester calling than your present one?" I asked.

"Well, sir, p'raps I might," he replied; "but going on the square is so dreadfully confining."

FOREIGN BEGGARS.

These beggars appeal to the sympathies as "strangers"—in a foreign land, away from friends and kindred, unable to make their wants known, or to seek work, from ignorance of the language.

In exposing the shams and swindles that are set to catch the unwary, I have no wish to check the current of real benevolence. Cases of distress exist, which it is a pleasure and a duty to relieve. I only expose the "dodges" of the beggar by profession—the beggar by trade—the beggar who lives by begging, and nothing else, except, as in most cases, where he makes the two ends of idleness and self-indulgence meet,—by thieving.

Foreign beggars are generally so mixed up with political events, that in treating of them, it is more than usually difficult to detect imposition from misfortune. Many high-hearted patriots have been driven to this country by tyrants and their tools, but it will not do to mistake every vagabond refugee for a noble exile, or to accept as a fact that a man who cannot live in his own country, is necessarily persecuted and unfortunate, and has a claim to be helped to live in this.

The neighbourhood of Leicester Square is, to the foreign political exile, the foreign political spy, the foreign fraudulent tradesman, the foreign escaped thief, and the foreign convict who has served his time, what, in the middle-ages, sanctuary was to the murderer. In this modern Alsatia—happily for us, guarded by native policemen and detectives of every nation in the world—plots are hatched, fulminating powder prepared, detonating-balls manufactured, and infernal machines invented, which, wielded by the hands of men whose opinions are so far beyond the age in which they live, that their native land has cast them out for ever; are destined to overthrow despotic governments, restore the liberty of the subject, and, in a wholesale sort of way, regenerate the rights of man.

Political spies are the monied class among these philanthropic desperadoes. The political regenerators, unless furnished with means from some special fund, are the most miserable and abject. Mr. Thackeray has observed that whenever an Irishman is in difficulties he always finds another Irishman worse off than himself, who talks over creditors, borrows money, runs errands, and makes himself generally useful to his incarcerated fellow-countryman. This observation will apply equally to foreigners.

There is a timid sort of refugee, who lacking the courage to arrive at political eminence or cash, by means of steel, or poison, is a hanger-on of his bolder and less scrupulous compatriot. This man, when deserted by his patron, is forced to beg. The statement that he makes as to his reasons for leaving the dear native land that the majority of foreigners are so ready to sing songs in praise of, and to quit, must be, of course, received with caution.

The French Beggar.

My reader has most likely, in a quiet street, met a shabby little man, who stares about him in a confused manner, as if he had lost his way. As soon as he sees a decently-dressed person he shuffles up to him, and taking off a "casquette" with considerably more brim than body, makes a slight bow, and says in a plaintive voice, "Parlez Français, m'sieu?"

If you stop and, in an unguarded moment, answer "Oui," the beggar takes from his breast-pocket a greasy leather book, from which he extracts a piece of carefully folded paper, which he hands you with a pathetic shrug.

The paper, when opened, contains a small slip, on which is written in a light, foreign hand—

"You are requested to direct the bearer to the place to which he desires to go, as he cannot speak English!"

The beggar then, with a profusion of bows, points to the larger paper.

"Mais, m'sieu, ayez la bonté de lire. C'est Anglais."

The larger paper contains a statement in French and English, that the bearer Jean Baptiste Dupont is a native of Troyes, Champagne, and a fan-maker by trade; that paralysis in the hand has deprived him of the power of working; that he came to England to find a daughter, who had married an Englishman and was dwelling in Westminster, but that when he arrived he found they had parted for Australia; that he is fifty-two years of age, and is a deserving object of compassion, having no means of returning to Troyes, being an entire stranger to England, and having no acquaintances or friends to assist him.

This statement is without any signature, but no sooner have you read it than the beggar, who would seem to have a blind credence in the efficacy of documents, draws from his pocket-book a certificate of birth, a register of marriage, a passport, and a permission to embark, which, being all in a state of crumpled greasiness, and printed and written in French, so startles and confounds the reader, that he drops something into the man's hand and passes on.

I have been often stopped by this sort of beggar. In the last case I met with I held a long talk with the man—of course, in his own language, for he will seldom or never be betrayed into admitting that he has any knowledge of English.

"Parlez Français, m'sieu?"

"Yes, I do," I answered. "What do you want?"

"Deign, monsieur, to have the bounty to read this paper which I have the honour to present to monsieur."

"Oh, never mind the papers!" I said, shortly. "Can't you speak English?"

"Alas, monsieur, no!"

"Speak French, then!"

My quick speaking rather confused the fellow, who said that he was without bread, and without asylum; that he was a tourneur and ebeniste (turner, worker in ebony and ivory, and cabinet-maker in general) by trade, that he was a stranger, and wished to raise sufficient money to enable him to return to France.

"Why did you come over to England?" I asked.

"I came to work in London," he said, after pretending not to understand my question the first time.

"Where?" I inquired.

At first I understood him to answer Sheffield, but I at last made out that he meant Smithfield.

"What was your master's name?"

"I do not comprehend, monsieur—if monsieur will deign to read—"

"You comprehend me perfectly well; don't pretend that you don't—that is only shuffling (tracasserie).

"The name of my master was Johnson."

"Why did you leave him?" I inquired.

"He is dead, monsieur."

"Why did you not return to France at his death?" was my next question.

"Monsieur, I tried to obtain work in England," said the beggar.

"How long did you work for Mr. Johnson?"

"There was a long time, monsieur, that—"

"How long?" I repeated. "How many years?"

"Since two years."

"And did you live in London two years, and all that time learn to speak no English?"

"Ah, monsieur, you embarrass me. If monsieur will not deign to aid me, it must be that I seek elsewhere—"

"But tell me how it was you learnt no English," I persisted.

"Ah, monsieur, my comrades in the shop were all French."

"And you want to get back to France?"

"Ah, monsieur, it is the hope of my life."

"Come to me to-morrow morning at eleven o'clock—there is my address." I gave him the envelope of a letter. "I am well acquainted with the French Consul at London Bridge, and at my intercession I am sure that he will get you a free passage to Calais; if not, and I find he considers your story true, I will send you at my own expense. Good night!"

Of course the man did not call in the morning, and I saw no more of him.

Destitute Poles.

It is now many years since the people of this country evinced a strong sympathy for Polish refugees. Their gallant struggle, compulsory exile, and utter national and domestic ruin raised them warm friends in England; and committees for the relief of destitute Poles, balls for the benefit of destitute Poles, and subscriptions for the relief of the destitute Poles were got up in every market-town. Shelter and sustenance were afforded to many gentlemen of undoubted integrity, who found themselves penniless in a strange land, and the aristocracy fêted and caressed the best-born and most gallant. To be a Pole, and in distress, was almost a sufficient introduction, and there were few English families who did not entertain as friend or visitor one of these unfortunate and suffering patriots.

So excellent an opportunity for that class of foreign swindlers which haunt roulette-tables, and are the pest of second-rate hotels abroad, was of course made use of. Crowds of adventurers, "got up" in furs, and cloaks, and playhouse dresses, with padded breasts and long moustachios, flocked to England, and assuming the title of count, and giving out that their patrimony had been sequestered by the Emperor of Russia, easily obtained a hearing and a footing in many English families, whose heads would not have received one of their own countrymen except with the usual credentials.

John Bull's partiality for foreigners is one of his well-known weaknesses; and valets, cooks, and couriers in their masters clothes, and sometimes with the titles of that master whom they had seen shot down in battle, found themselves objects of national sympathy and attention. Their success among the fair sex was extraordinary; and many penniless adventurers, with no accomplishments beyond card-sharping, and a foreign hotel waiter's smattering of continental languages, allied themselves to families of wealth and respectability. All, of course, were not so fortunate; and after some persons had been victimized, a few inquiries made, and the real refugee gentlemen and soldiers had indignantly repudiated any knowledge of the swindlers or their pretensions, the pseudo-Polish exiles were compelled to return to their former occupations. The least able and least fortunate were forced to beg, and adopted exactly the same tactics as the French beggar, except that instead of certificates of birth, and passports, he exhibited false military documents, and told lying tales of regimental services, Russian prisons, and miraculous escapes.

The "destitute Pole" is seldom met with now, and would hardly have demanded a notice if I had not thought it right to show how soon the unsuccessful cheat or swindler drops down into the beggar, and to what a height the "Polish fever" raged some thirty years ago. It would be injustice to a noble nation if I did not inform my reader that but few of the false claimants to British sympathy were Poles at all. They were Russians, Frenchmen, Hungarians, Austrians, Prussians, and Germans of all sorts.

The career of one fellow will serve to show with what little ingenuity the credulous can be imposed on. His real name is lost among his numerous aliases, neither do I know whether he commenced life as a soldier, or as a valet; but I think it probable that he had combined those occupations and been regimental servant to an officer. He came to London in the year 1833 under the name of Count Stanislas Soltiewski, of Ostralenka; possessed of a handsome person and invulnerable audacity, he was soon received into decent society, and in 1837 married a lady of some fortune, squandered her money, and deserted her. He then changed his name to Levieczin, and travelled from town to town, giving political lectures at town-halls, assembly-rooms, and theatres. In 1842 he called himself Doctor Telecki, said he was a native of Smolensk, and set up a practice in Manchester, where he contracted a large amount of debts. From Manchester he eloped with one of his patients, a young lady to whom he was married in 1845, in Dublin, in which place he again endeavoured to practise as a physician. He soon involved himself in difficulties, and quitted Dublin, taking with him funds which had been entrusted to him as treasurer of a charitable institution. He left his second wife, and formed a connexion with another woman, travelled about, giving scientific lectures, and sometimes doing feats of legerdemain. He again married a widow lady who had some four or five hundred pounds, which he spent, after which he deserted her. He then became the scourge and terror of hotel-keepers, and went from tavern to tavern living on every luxury, and, when asked for money, decamping, and leaving behind him nothing but portmanteaus filled with straw and bricks. He returned to England and obtained a situation in a respectable academy as a teacher of French and the guitar. Here he called himself Count Hohenbreitenstein-Boitzenburg.

Under this name he seduced a young lady, whom he persuaded he could not marry on account of her being a Protestant, and of his being a Count of the Holy Roman Empire in the pontifical degree. By threatening exposure he extracted a large sum of money from her friends, with which he returned to London, where he lived for some time by begging letters, and obtaining money on various false pretences. His first wife discovered him, and he was charged with bigamy, but owing to some technical informality was not convicted. He then enlisted in the 87th regiment, from which he shortly after deserted. He became the associate of thieves and the prostitutes who live in the neighbourhood of Waterloo Road. After being several times imprisoned for petty thefts he at length earned a miserable living by conjuring in low public-houses, where he announced himself as the celebrated Polish professor of legerdemain, Count Makvicz.

He died in August, 1852, and, oddly enough, in a garret in Poland Street, Oxford Street.

Of modern Polish swindlers and beggars, the most renowned is Adolphus Czapolinski. This "shabby genteel man of military appearance"—I quote the daily papers,—" has been several times incarcerated, has again offended, and been again imprisoned. His fraudulent practices were first discovered in 1860." The following is from the *Times*, of June the 5th of that year :—

"Bow Street.—A military-looking man, who said his name was Lorenzo Noodt, and that he had served as captain in one of our foreign legions during the Crimean war, was brought before Mr. Henry on a charge of attempting to obtain money by false and fraudulent pretences from the Countess of Waldegrave."

Mr. George Granville Harcourt (the husband of Lady Waldegrave, deposed :

"I saw the prisoner to-day at my house in Carlton Gardens, where he called by my request in reference to a letter which Lady Waldegrave had received from him. It was a letter soliciting charitable contributions, and enclosing three papers. The first purported to be a note from Lady Stafford, enclosing a post-office order for 3*l*. I know her ladyship's handwriting, and this is like it, but I cannot say whether it is genuine. The second is apparently a note from Colonel Macdonald, sending him a post-office order for 4*l*. on the part of the Duke of Cambridge. The third is a note purporting to be written by the secretary of the Duke d'Aumale. This note states that the duke approves this person's departure for Italy, and desires his secretary to send him 5*l*. We were persuaded that it could not be genuine, in the first place, as we have the honour of being intimate with the Duke d'Aumale. We perfectly well knew that he would not say to this individual, or to any one else, that he approved his departure for Italy ; in the second place, there are mistakes in the French which render it impossible that the duke's secretary should have written it ; in the third place, the name is not that of the secretary, though resembling it. Under all the circumstances, I took an opportunity of asking both the secretary and the Duke d'Aumale whether they had any knowledge of this communication, and they stated that they knew nothing of it. The duke said that it was very disagreeable to him that he should be supposed to be interfering to forward the departure of persons to Italy, which would produce an impression that he was meddling in the affairs of that country. I wrote to the prisoner to call on me, in order to receive back his papers. At first another man called, but on his addressing me in French I said, 'You are an Italian, not a German. I want to see the captain himself.' To-day the prisoner called. I showed the papers, and asked him if they were the letters he had received, and if he had received the money referred to in those letters. To both questions he replied in the affirmative. The officer Horsford, with whom I had communicated in the meanwhile, was in the next room. I called him in, and he went up to Captain Noodt, telling him he was his prisoner. He asked why ? Horsford replied, for attempting to obtain money by means of a forged letter. He then begged me not to ruin him, and said that the letter was not written by him."

The prisoner's letter to Lady Waldegrave was then read as follows :—

"Milady Countess,

"I am foreigner, but have the rank of captain by my service under English colours in the Crimean war, being appointed by her Majesty's brevet. I have struggled very hard, after having been discharged from the service, but, happily, I have been temporarily assisted by some persons of distinction, and the Duke of Cambridge. To-day, milady Countess, I have in object to ameliorate or better my condition, going to accept service in Italian lawful army, where by the danger I may obtain advancement. Being poor, I am obliged to solicit of my noble patrons towards my journey. The Duc d'Aumale, the Marchioness of Stafford, &c., kindly granted me their contributions. Knowing your ladyship's connexion with those noble persons, I take the liberty of soliciting your ladyship's kind contribution to raise any funds for my outfit and journey. In 'appui' of my statements I enclose my captain's commission and letters, and, in recommending myself to your ladyship's consideration, I present my homage, and remain,

"Your humble servant,
"Captain L. B. Noodt."

The letter of the pretended secretary was as follows :—

"Monsieur le Capitaine,

"Son altesse Monseigneur le Duc d'Aumale approuve votre départ pour l'Italie, et pour vous aider dans la dépense de votre voyage m'a chargé de vous transmettre 5*l.*, ci inclus, que vous m'obligerez de m'en accuser la reception.

"Agréez, monsieur le capitaine, l'assurance de ma consideration distinguée.

"Votre humble serviteur,
"Chs. Couleuvrier, Sec."

The prisoner, *who appeared much agitated*, acknowledged the dishonesty of his conduct, but appealed to the pity of Mr. Harcourt, saying that he had suffered great hardships, and had been driven to this act by want. *It was sad that an officer bearing the Queen's commission should be so humiliated.* The letter was not written by himself, but by a Frenchman who led him into it.

Mr. Henry said he had brought the humiliation on himself. He must be well aware that the crime of forgery was punished as severely in his own country as here. The prisoner should have the opportunity of producing the writer of the letter, or of designating him to the police. On the recommendation to mercy of Mr. Harcourt, he was only sentenced to one month's imprisonment.

On July the 9th he was brought up to Marlborough Street by Horsford, the officer of the Mendicity Society, charged with obtaining by false and fraudulent pretences the sum of 3*l.* from Lady Stafford. Since his imprisonment it had been discovered that his real name was Adolphus Czapolinski, and that he was a Pole. The real Captain Noodt was in a distant part of the kingdom, and Czapolinski had obtained surreptitious possession of his commission, and assumed his name. The indefatigable Mr. Horsford had placed himself in communication with the secretary of the Polish Association, who had known the prisoner (Czapolinski) for twenty-five years. It would seem that in early life he had been engaged under various foreign powers, and in 1835 he came to this country and earned a scanty maintenance as a teacher of languages; that he was addicted to drinking, begging, and thieving, and upon one occasion, when usher in a school, he robbed the pupils of their clothes, and even fleeced them of their trifling pocket-money. While in the House of Detention he had written to Captain Wood, the secretary of the Mendicity Society, offering to turn approver. The letter in question ran thus:—

"Sir,—Permit me to make you a request, which is, not to press your prosecution against me, and I most solemnly promise you that for this favour all my endeavours will be to render you every assistance for all the information you should require. I was very wrong to not speak to you when I was at your office, but really I was not guilty of this charge, because the letter containing the post-office order was delivered to Captain Noodt. I was only the messenger from Lady Stafford.

"Look, Captain Wood, I know much, and no one can be so able to render you the assistance and information of all the foreigners than me. Neither any of your officers could find the way; but if you charge me to undertake to find I will, on only one condition—that you will stop the prosecution. The six weeks of detention were quite sufficient punishment to me for the first time; and let it be understood that for your condescension to stop the prosecution all my services shall be at your orders, whenever you shall require, without any remuneration. My offers will be very advantageous to you under every respect. Send any of your clerks to speak with me to make my covenant with you, and you will be better convinced of my good intentions to be serviceable to you.

"I am, &c.,
"A. Czapolinski."

He was sentenced to three months' imprisonment and hard labour.

Czapolinski is one of the most extraordinary of the beggars of the present day. He raises money both by personal application and by letter. He has been known to make from 20*l.* to 60*l.* per day. He is a great gambler, and has been seen to lose —and to pay—upwards of 100*l.* at a gambling house in the neighbourhood of Leicester Square in the course of a single night and morning.

Hindoo Beggars

Are those spare, snake-eyed Asiatics who walk the streets, coolly dressed in Manchester cottons, or chintz of a pattern commonly used for bed-furniture, to which the resemblance is carried out by the dark, polished colour of the thin limbs which it envelopes. They very often affect to be converts to the Christian religion, and give away tracts; with the intention of entrapping the sympathy of elderly ladies. They assert that they have been high-caste Brahmins, but as untruth, even when not acting professionally, is habitual to them, there is not the slightest dependence to be placed on what they say. Sometimes, in the winter, they "do shallow," that is, stand on the kerb-stone of the pavement, in their thin, ragged clothes, and shiver as with cold and hunger, or crouch against a wall and whine like a whipped animal; at others they turn out with a small, barrel-shaped drum, on which they make a monotonous noise with their fingers, to which music they sing and dance. Or they will "stand pad with a fakement," *i. e.* wear a placard upon their breasts, that describes them as natives of Madagascar, in distress, converts to Christianity, anxious to get to a seaport where they can work their passage back. This is a favourite artifice with Lascars—or they will sell lucifers, or sweep a crossing, or do anything where their picturesque appearance, of which they are proud and conscious, can be effectively displayed. They are as cunning as they look, and can detect a sympathetic face among a crowd. They never beg of soldiers, or sailors, to whom they always give a wide berth as they pass them in the streets.

From the extraordinary mendacity of this race of beggars—a mendacity that never falters, hesitates, or stumbles, but flows on in an unbroken stream of falsehood,—it is difficult to obtain any reliable information respecting them. I have, however, many reasons for believing that the following statement, which was made to me by a very dirty and distressed Indian, is moderately true. The man spoke English like a cockney of the lowest order. I shall not attempt to describe the peculiar accent or construction which he occasionally gave to it.

"My name is Joaleeka. I do not know where I was born. I never knew my father. I remember my mother very well. From the first of my remembrance I was at Dumdum, where I was servant to a European officer—a great man—a prince—who had more than a hundred servants beside me. When he went away to fight, I followed among others—I was with the baggage. I never fought myself, but I have heard the men (Sepoys) say that the prince, or general, or colonel, liked nothing so well as fighting, except tiger-hunting. He was a wonderful man, and his soldiers liked him very much. I travelled over a great part of India with Europeans. I went up country as far as Secunderabad, and learned to speak English very well—so well that, when I was quite a young man, I was often employed as interpreter, for I caught up different Indian languages quickly. At last I got to interpret so well that I was recommended to ——, a great native prince who was coming over to England. I was not his interpreter, but interpreter to his servants. We came to London. We stopped in an hotel in Vere-street, Oxford-street. We stayed here some time. Then my chief went over to Paris, but he did not take all his servants with him. I stopped at the hotel to interpret for those who remained. It was during this time that I formed a connexion with a white woman. She was a servant in the hotel. I broke my caste, and from that moment I knew that it would not do for me to go back to India. The girl fell in the family-way, and was sent out of the house. My fellow-servants knew of it, and as many of them hated me, I knew that they would tell my master on his return. I also knew that by the English laws in England I was a free man, and that my master could not take me back against my will. If I had gone back, I should have been put to death for breaking my caste. When my master returned from France, he sent for me. He told me that he had heard of my breaking my caste, and of the girl, but that he should take no notice of it; that I was to return to Calcutta with him, where he would get me employment with some European officer; that I need not fear, as he would order his servants to keep silent on the subject. I salaamed and thanked him, and said I was his slave for ever; but at the same time I knew that he would break his word, and that when he had me in his power, he would put me to death. He was a very severe man about caste. I attended to all my duties as before, and all believed that I was going back to India—but the very morning that my master started for the coast, I ran away. I changed my clothes at the house of a girl I knew—not the same one as I had known at the hotel, but another. This one lived at Seven Dials. I stopped in-doors for many days, till this girl, who could read newspapers, told me that my master had sailed away. I felt very glad, for though I knew my master could not force me to go back with him, yet I was afraid for all that, for he knew the King and the Queen, and had been invited by the Lord Mayor to the City. I liked England better than India, and English women have been very kind to me. I think English women are the handsomest in the world. The girl in whose house I hid, showed me how to beg. She persuaded me to turn Christian, because she thought that it would do me good—so I turned Christian. I do not know what it means, but I am a Christian, and have been for many years. I married that girl for some time. I have been married several times. I do not mean to say that I have ever been to church as rich folks do; but I have been married without that. Sometimes I do well, and sometimes badly. I often get a pound or two by interpreting. I am not at all afraid of meeting any Indian who knew me, for if they said anything I did not like, I should call out "Police!" I know the law better than I did. Every thing is free in England. You can do what you like, if you can pay, or are not found out. I do not like policemen. After the mutiny in 1857 I did very badly. No one would look at a poor Indian then—much less give to him. I knew that the English would put it down soon, because I know what those rascals over there are like. I am living now in Charles Street, Drury Lane. I have been married to my present wife six years. We have three children and one dead. My eldest is now in the hospital with a bad arm. I swept a crossing for two years; that was just before the mutiny. All that knew me used to chaff me about it, and call me Johnny Sepoy. My present wife is Irish, and fought two women about it. They were taken to Bow-street by a policeman, but the judge would not hear them. My wife is a very good wife to me, but she gets drunk too often. If it were not for that, I should like her better. I ran away from her once, but she came after me with all the children. Sometimes I make twelve shillings a week. I could make much more by interpreting, but I do not like to go among the nasty natives of my country. I believe I am more than fifty years of age."

NEGRO BEGGARS.

The negro beggar so nearly resembles the Hindoo that what I have said of one, I could almost say of the other. There are, however, these points of difference. The negro mendicant, who is usually an American negro, never studies the picturesque in his attire. He relies on the abject misery and down-trodden despair of his appearance, and generally represents himself as a fugitive slave—with this exception, his methods of levying contributions are precisely the same as his lighter-skinned brother's.

Some years ago it was a common thing to see a negro with tracts in his hand, and a placard upon his breast, upon which was a wood-cut of a black man, kneeling, his wrists heavily chained, his arms held high in supplication, and round the picture, forming a sort of proscenium or frame, the words: "Am I not a man and a brother?" At the time that the suppression of the slave trade created so much excitement, this was so excellent a "dodge" that many white beggars, fortunate enough to possess a flattish or turned-up nose, *dyed themselves black* and "stood pad" as real Africans. The imposture, however, was soon detected and punished.

There are but few negro beggars to be seen now. It is only common fairness to say that negroes seldom, if ever, shirk work. Their only trouble is to obtain it. Those who have seen the many negroes employed in Liverpool, will know that they are hard-working, patient, and, too often, underpaid. A negro will sweep a crossing, run errands, black boots, clean knives and forks, or dig, for a crust and a few pence. The few impostors among them are to be found among those who go about giving lectures on the horrors of slavery, and singing variations on the "escapes" in that famous book 'Uncle Tom's Cabin.' Negro servants are seldom read of in police reports, and are generally found to give satisfaction to their employers. In the east end of London negro beggars are to be met with, but they are seldom beggars by profession. Whenever they are out of work they have no scruples, but go into the streets, take off their hats, and beg directly.

I was accosted by one in Whitechapel, from whom I obtained the following statement:—

"My father was a slave, so was my mother. I have heard my father say so. I have heard them tell how they got away, but I forget all about it. It was before I was born. I am the eldest son. I had only one brother. Three years after his birth my mother died. My father was a shoe-black in New York. He very often had not enough to eat. My brother got a place as a servant, but I went out in the streets to do what I could. About the same time that my father, who was an old man, died, my brother lost his place. We agreed to come to England together. My brother had been living with some Britishers, and he had heard them say that over here niggers were as good as whites; and that the whites did not look down on them and illtreat them, as they do in New York. We went about and got odd jobs on the quay, and at last we hid ourselves in the hold of a vessel, bound for Liverpool. I do not know how long we were hid, but I remember we were terribly frightened lest we should be found out before the ship got under weigh. At last hunger forced us out, and we rapped at the hatches; at first we were not heard, but when we shouted out, they opened the hatches, and took us on deck. They flogged us very severely, and treated us shamefully all the voyage. When we got to Liverpool, we begged and got odd jobs.

At last we got engaged in a travelling circus, where we were servants, and used to ride about with the band in beautiful dresses, but the grooms treated us so cruelly that we were forced to run away from that. I forget the name of the place that we were performing at, but it was not a day's walk from London. We begged about for some time. At last, my brother—his name is Aaron—got to clean the knives and forks at a slap-bang (an eating-house) in the city. He was very fortunate, and used to save some bits for me. He never takes any notice of me now. He is doing very well. He lives with a great gentleman in Harewood-square, and has a coat with silver buttons, and a gold-laced hat. He is very proud, and I do not think would speak to me if he saw me. I don't know how I live, or how much I get a week. I do porter's work mostly, but I do anything I can get. I beg more than half the year. I have no regular lodging. I sleep where I can. When I am in luck, I have a bed. It costs me threepence. At some places they don't care to take a man of colour in. I sometimes get work in Newgate-market, carrying meat, but not often. Ladies give me halfpence oftener than men. The butchers call me 'Othello,' and ask me why I killed my wife. I have tried to get aboard a ship, but they won't have me. I don't know how old I am, but I know that when we got to London, it was the time the Great Exhibition was about. I can lift almost any weight when I have had a bit of something to eat. I don't care for beer. I like rum best. I have often got drunk, but never when I paid for it myself."

The following cases of genuine distress fell under my notice. My readers will observe the difference of tone, the absence of clap-trap, and desire to enlarge upon a harrowing fact of those unfortunates who have been reduced to beggary, compared with the practised shuffle and conventional whine of the mendicant by profession.

I was standing with a friend at the counter of a tavern in Oxford Street, when a man came in and asked me to help him with a penny.

I saw at a glance that he was a workman at some hard-working trade. His face was bronzed, and his large, hard hands were unmistakably the hands of a labourer. He kept his eyes fixed on me as he spoke, and begged with a short pipe in his mouth.

I asked him if he would have some beer?

"Thank ye, sir, I don't want beer so much as I want a penny loaf. I haven't tasted since morn, and I'm not the man I was fifteen year ago, and I feel it."

"Will you have some bread-and-cheese and beer?" I asked.

"Thank ye, sir; bread-and-cheese and beer, and thank ye, sir; for I'm beginning to feel I want something."

I asked the man several questions, and he made the following statement:—

"I'm a miner, sir, and I've been working lately five mile from Castleton in Darbyshire. Why did I leave it? Do you want me to tell the truth, now—the real truth? Well then I'll tell you the real truth. I got drunk—you asked me for the real truth, and now you've got it. I've been a miner all my life, and been engaged in all the great public works. I call a miner a man as can sink a shaft in anything, barring he's not stopped by water. I've got a wife and two children. I left them at Castleton. They're all right. I left them some money. I've worked in eighteen inches o' coal. I mean in a chamber only eighteen inches wide. You lay on your side and pick like this. (Here he threw himself on the floor, and imitated the action of a coal-miner with his pick.) I've worked under young Mr. Brunel very often. He were not at all a gentleman unlike you, sir, only he were darker. My last wages was six shilling a-day. I expect soon to be in work again, for I know lots o' miners in London, and I know where they want hands. I could get a bed and a shilling this minute if I knew where my mates lived; but to-day, when I got to the place where they work, they'd gone home, and I couldn't find out in what part of London they lived. We miners always assist each other, when we're on the road. I've worked in lead and copper, sir, as well as coal, and have been a very good man in my time. I am just forty year old, and I think I've used myself too much when I were young. I knows the Cornish mines well. I'm sure to get work in the course of the week, for I'm well known to many on 'em up at Notting Hill. I once worked in a mine where there were a pressure of fifty pound to the square foot of air. You have to take your time about everything you do there—you can't work hard in a place like that. Thank you, sir, much obliged to you."

One evening in the parish of Marylebone an old man who was selling lucifer-matches put his finger to his forehead, and offered me a box. "Ha'penny a box, sir," he said.

I told him to follow me; an old woman also accompanied us. He made the following statement:—

"My name is John Wood—that's my wife. I am sixty-five years of age; she's seventy-five—ten years older than I am. I kept a shop round this street, sir, four-and-twenty years. I've got a settlement in this parish, but we neither of us like to go into the union—they'd separate us, and we like to be together for the little time we shall be here. The reason we went to the bad was, I took a shop at Woolwich, and the very week I opened it, I don't know how many hundred men were not discharged from the Arsenal and Dockyard. I lost £350 there; after that we tried many things; but everything failed. This is not a living. I stood four hours last night, and took twopence-ha'penny. We lodge in Warde's Buildings. We pay one and ninepence a-week. We've got sticks of our own,—that is a bed, and a table. We are both of us half-starved. It is hard—very hard. I'm as weak as a rat, and so is my wife. We've tried to do something better, but we can't. If I could get some of the folks that once knew me to assist me, I might buy a few things, and make a living out of them. We've been round to 'em to ask 'em, but they don't seem inclined to help us. People don't, sir, when you're poor. I used to feel that myself one time, but I know better now. Good night, sir, and thank you."

In the same neighbourhood I saw an elderly man who looked as if he would beg of me if he dared. I turned round to look at him, and saw that his eyes were red as if with crying, and that he carried a rag in his hand with which he kept dabbing them. I gave him a few pence.

"Thank you, sir," he said; "God bless you. Excuse me, sir, but my eyes is bad—I suffer from the erysipelas—that is what brought me to this. Kindness rather overcomes me—I've not been much used to it of late."

He made the following statement:

"I have been a gentleman's servant, sir, but I lost my place through the erysipelas. I was mad with it, and confined in Bedlam for four years. The last place I was in service at was Sir H—— H——'s (he mentioned the name of an eminent banker). Sir H—— was very kind to me. I clean his door-plate now, for which I get a shilling a-week—that's all the dependence I have now. The servants behave bad to me. Sir H—— said that I was to go into the kitchen now and then; but they never give me anything. I don't get half enough to eat, and it makes me very weak. I'm weak enough naturally, and going without makes me worse. I lodge over in Westminster. I pay threepence a-night, or eighteenpence a-week. There are three others in the same room as me. I hold horses sometimes, and clean knives and forks when I can get it to do; but people like younger men than me to do odd jobs. I can't do things quick enough, and I'm so nervous that I ain't handy. I can go into the workhouse, and I think I shall in the winter; but the confinement of it is terrible to me. I'd like to keep out of it if I can. My shilling a-week don't pay my rent, and I find it very hard to get on at all. Nobody can tell what I go through. I suppose I must go into the workhouse at last. They're not over kind to you when you're in. Every day the first thing I try to get is the threepence for my lodging. I pay nightly, then I don't have anything to pay on Sundays. I don't know any trade; gentlemen's servants never do. I used to have the best of everything when I was in service. God bless you, sir, and thank you. I'm very much obliged to you.

DISASTER BEGGARS.

This class of street beggars includes shipwrecked mariners, blown-up miners, burnt-out tradesmen, and lucifer droppers. The majority of them are impostors, as is the case with all beggars who pursue begging pertinaciously and systematically. There are no doubt genuine cases to be met with, but they are very few, and they rarely obtrude themselves. Of the shipwrecked mariners I have already given examples under the head of Naval and Military Beggars. Another class of them, to which I have not referred, is familiar to the London public in connection with rudely executed paintings representing either a shipwreck, or more commonly the destruction of a boat by a whale in the North Seas. This painting they spread upon the pavement, fixing it at the corners, if the day be windy, with stones. There are generally two men in attendance, and in most cases one of the two has lost an arm or a leg. Occasionally both of them have the advantage of being deprived of either one or two limbs. Their misfortune so far is not to be questioned. A man who has lost both arms, or even one, is scarcely in a position to earn his living by labour, and is therefore a fit object for charity. It is found, however, that in most instances the stories of their misfortunes printed underneath their pictures are simply inventions, and very often the pretended sailor has never been to sea at all. In one case which I specially investigated, the man had been a bricklayer, and had broken both his arms by falling from a scaffold. He received some little compensation at the time, but when that was spent he went into the streets to beg, carrying a paper on his breast describing the cause of his misfortune. His first efforts were not successful. His appearance (dressed as he was in workman's clothes) was not sufficiently picturesque to attract attention, and his story was of too ordinary a kind to excite much interest. He had a very hard life of it for some length of time; for, in addition to the drawback arising from the uninteresting nature of his case, he had had no experience in the art of begging, and his takings were barely sufficient to procure bread. From this point I will let him tell his own story:—

A Shipwrecked Mariner.

"I had only taken a penny all day, and I had had no breakfast, and I spent the penny in a loaf. I was three nights behind for my lodging, and I knew the door would be shut in my face if I did not take home sixpence. I thought I would go to the workhouse, and perhaps I might get a supper and a lodging for that night. I was in Tottenham Court-road by the chapel, and it was past ten o'clock. The people were thinning away, and there seemed no chance of anything. So says I to myself I'll start down the New Road to the work'ouse. I knew there was a work'ouse down that way, for I worked at a 'ouse next it once, and I used to think the old paupers looked comfortable like. It came across me all at once, that I one time said to one of my mates, as we was sitting on the scaffold, smoking our pipes, and looking over the work'ouse wall, 'Jem, them old chaps there seems to do it pretty tidy; they have their soup and bread, and a bed to lie on, and their bit o' baccy, and they comes out o' a arternoon and baskes in the sun, and has their chat, and don't seem to do no work to hurt 'em.' And Jem he says, 'it's a great hinstitooshin, Enery,' says he, for you see Jem was a bit of a scollard, and could talk just like a book. 'I don't know about a hinstitooshin, Jem,' says I, 'but what I does know is that a man might do wuss nor goe in there and have his grub and his baccy regular, without nought to stress him, like them old chaps.' Somehow or other that 'ere conversation came across me, and off I started to the work'ouse. When I came to the gate I saw a lot of poor women and children sitting on the pavement round it. They couldn't have been hungrier than me, but they were awful ragged, and their case looked wuss. I didn't like to go in among them, and I watched a while a little way off. One woman kep on ringing the bell for a long time, and nobody came, and then she got desperate, and kep a-pulling and ringing like she was mad, and at last a fat man came out and swore at her and drove them all away. I didn't think there was much chance for me if they druv away women and kids, and such as them, but I thought I would try as I was a cripple, and had lost both my arms. So I stepped across the road, and was just agoing to try and pull the bell with my two poor stumps when some one tapped me on the shoulder. I turned round and saw it was a sailor-like man, without ne'er an arm like myself, only his were cut off short at the shoulder. 'What are you agoing to do?' says he. 'I was agoing to try and ring the work'ouse bell,' says I. 'What for?' says he. 'To ask to be took in,' says I. And then the sailor man looks at me in a steady kind of way, and says, 'Want to get into the work-'ouse, and you got ne'er an arm? Your'e a infant,' says he. 'If you had only lost one on 'em now, I could forgive you, but—' 'But surely,' says I, 'it's a greater misfortune to lose two nor one; half a loaf's better nor no bread, they say.' 'You're a infant,' says he again. 'One off aint no good; both on 'em's the thing. Have you a mind to earn a honest living,' says he, quite sharp. 'I have,' says I; 'anything for a honest crust.' 'Then,' says he, 'come along o' me.' So I went with the sailor man to his lodging in Whitechapel, and a very tidy place it was, and we had beefsteaks and half a gallon o' beer, and a pipe, and then he told me what he wanted me to do. I was to dress like him in a sailor's jacket and trousers and a straw 'at, and stand o' one side of a picture of a shipwreck, vile he stood on the 'tother. And I consented, and he learned me some sailors' patter, and at the end of the week he got me the togs, and then I went out with him. We did only middlin the first day, but after a bit the coppers tumbled in like winkin'. It was so affectin' to see two mariners without ne'er an arm between them, and we had crowds round us. At the end of the week we shared two pound and seven shillings, which was more nor a pound than my mate ever did by his self. He always said it was pilin' the hagony to have two without ne'er an arm. My mate used to say to me, 'Enery, if your stumps had only been a trifle shorter, we might ha' made a fortun by this time; but you waggle them, you see, and that frightens the old ladies.' I did well when Trafalgar

Jack was alive. That was my mate, sir; but he died of the cholera, and I joined another pal who had a wooden leg; but he was rough to the kids, and got us both into trouble. How do I mean rough to the kids? Why, you see, the kids used to swarm round us to look at the pictur just like flies round a sugar-cask, and that crabbed the business. My mate got savage with them sometimes, and clouted their heads, and one day the mother o' one o' the brats came up a-screaming awful and give Timber Bill, as we called him, into custody, and he was committed for a rogue and vagabond. Timber Bill went into the nigger line arterwards and did well. You may have seen him, sir. He plays the tambourine, and dances, and the folks laugh at his wooden leg, and the coppers come in in style. Yes, I'm still in the old line, but it's a bad business now."

BLOWN-UP MINERS.

These are simply a variety of the large class of beggars who get their living in the streets, chiefly by frequenting public-houses and whining a tale of distress. The impostors among them—and they are by far the greater number—do not keep up the character of blown-up miners all the year round, but time the assumption to suit some disaster which may give colour to their tale. After a serious coal-mine accident "blown-up miners" swarm in such numbers all over the town that one might suppose the whole of the coal-hands of the north had been blown south by one explosion. The blown-up miner has the general appearance of a navvy; he wears moleskin trousers turned up nearly to the knees, a pair of heavy-laced boots, a sleeved waistcoat, and commonly a shapeless felt hat of the wide-awake fashion. He wears his striped shirt open at the neck, showing a weather-browned and brawny chest. The state of his hands and the colour of his skin show that he has been accustomed to hard work, but his healthy look and fresh colour give the lie direct to his statement that he has spent nearly the whole of his life in working in the dark many hundred feet beneath the surface of the earth. Many of them do not pretend that they have been injured by the explosion of the mine, but only that they have been thrown out of work. These are mostly excavators and bricklayers' labourers, who are out of employ in consequence of a stoppage of the works on which they have been engaged, or more often, as I have proved by inquiry, in consequence of their own misconduct in getting drunk and absenting themselves from their labour. These impostors are easily detected. If you cross-question them as to the truth of their stories, and refer to names and places which they ought to be acquainted with if their representations were genuine, they become insolent and move away from you. There are others, however, who are more artful, and whose tales are borne out by every external appearance, and also by a complete knowledge of the places whence they pretend to have come. These men, though sturdy and horny-fisted, have a haggard, pallid look, which seems to accord well with the occupation of the miner. They can converse about mining operations, they describe minutely the incidents of the accident by which they suffered, and they have the names of coal-owners and gangsmen ever ready on their tongues. In addition to this they bare some part of their bodies—the leg or the arm—and show you what looks like a huge scald or burn. These are rank impostors, denizens of Wentworth-street and Brick-lane, and who were never nearer to Yorkshire than Mile-end gate in their lives. Having met with one or two specimens of "real" distressed miners, I can speak with great certainty of the characteristics which mark out the impostor. For many years past there has always been an abundance of work for miners and navigators; indeed the labour of the latter has often been at a premium; cases of distress arise among them only from two causes—ill-health and bodily disaster. If they are in health and found begging it is invariably during a long journey from one part of the country to another. The look and manner of these miners forbids the idea of their being systematic mendicants or impostors. They want something to help them on the road, and they will be as grateful for a hunck of bread and cheese as for money. If you cross-question these men they never show an uncomfortable sense of being under examination, but answer you frankly as if you were merely holding a friendly conversation with them. Miners are very charitable to each other, and they think it no shame to seek aid of their betters when they really need it. Of the device called the "scaldrum dodge," by which beggars of this class produce artificial sores, I shall have to treat by-and-bye.

BURNT-OUT TRADESMEN.

With many begging impostors the assumption of the "burnt-out tradesman" is simply a change of character to suit circumstances; with others it is a fixed and settled rôle. The burnt-out tradesman does not beg in the streets by day; he comes out at night, and his favourite haunts are the private bars of public-houses frequented by good company. In the day-time he begs by a petition, which he leaves at the houses of charitable persons with an intimation that he will call again in an hour. In the evening he is made up for his part. He lurks about a public-house until he sees a goodly company assembled in the private bar, and then, when the "gents," as he calls them, appear to be getting happy and comfortable, he suddenly appears among them, and moves them by the striking contrast which his personal appearance and condition offers to theirs. Like many others of his class he has studied human nature to some purpose, and he knows at a glance the natures with which he has to deal. Noisy and thoughtless young men, like clerks and shopmen, he avoids. They are generally too much occupied with themselves to think of him or his misfortunes; and having had no experience of a responsible position, the case of a reduced tradesman does not come home to them. A quiet and sedate company of middle-aged tradesmen best suits his purpose. They know the difficulties and dangers of trade, and maybe there are some of them who are conscious that ruin is impending over themselves. To feeling men of this class it is a terrible shock to see a man, who has once been well-to-do like themselves, reduced to get a living by begging. The burnt-out tradesman's appearance gives peculiar force to his appeal. He is dressed in a suit of black, greasy and threadbare, which looks like the last shreds of the dress suit which he wore on high days and holidays, when he was thriving and prosperous. His black satin stock, too, is evidently a relict of better days. His hat is almost napless; but it is well brushed—indicating care and neatness on the part of its owner. His shoes are mere shapeless envelopes of leather, but the uppers are carefully polished, and the strings neatly tied. When the burnt-out tradesman enters a bar he allows his appearance to have its due effect before he opens his mouth, or makes any other demonstration whatever. In this he seems to imitate the practice of the favourite comedian, who calculates upon being able to bespeak the favour of his audience by merely showing his face. The beggar, after remaining motionless for a moment, to allow the company fully to contemplate his miserable appearance, suddenly and unexpectedly advances one of his hands, which until now has been concealed behind his coat, and exposes to view a box of matches. Nothing can surpass the artistic skill of this mute appeal. The respectable look, and the poor, worn clohes, first of all—the patient, broken-hearted glance accompanied by a gentle sigh—and then the box of matches! What need of a word spoken. Can you not read the whole history? Once a prosperous tradesman, the head of a family, surrounded by many friends. Now, through misfortune, cast out of house and home, deserted by his friends, and reduced to wander the streets and sell matches to get his children bread. Reduced to sell paltry matches! he who was in a large way once, and kept clerks to register his wholesale transactions! It is seldom that this artist requires to speak. No words will move men who can resist so powerful an appeal. When he does speak he does not require to say more than—" I am an unfortunate tradesman, who lost everything I possessed in the world by a disastrous fire—" Here the halfpence interrupt his story, and he has no need to utter another word, except to mutter his humble thanks.

There are a great many beggars of this class, and they nearly all pursue the same method. They are most successful among tradesmen of the middle class, and among the poor working people. One of them told me that the wives of working men were, according to his experience, the most tender-hearted in London. "The upper classes, the swells, aint no good," he said; " they subscribe to the Mendicity Society, and they thinks every beggar an imposture. The half-and-half swells, shopmen and the likes, aint got no hearts, and they aint got no money, and what's the good. Tradesmen that aint over well off have a fellow feeling; but the workmen's wives out a-marketing of a Saturday night are no trouble. They always carries coppers—change out of sixpence or a something—in their hands, and when I goes in where they are a havin' their daffies—that's drops o' gin, sir—they looks at me, and says, ' Poor man !' and drops the coppers, whatever it is, into my hand, and p'raps asks me to have a half-pint o' beer besides. They're good souls, the workmen's wives."

There is a well-known beggar of this class who dresses in a most unexceptionable manner. His black clothes are new and glossy, his hat and boots are good, and to heighten the effect he wears a spotless white choker. He is known at the west end by the name of the "Bishop of

London." His aspect is decidedly clerical. He has a fat face, a double chin, his hat turns up extensively at the brim, and, as I have said, he wears a white neck-cloth. When he enters a bar the company imagine that he is about to order a bottle of champagne at least; but when he looks round and produces the inevitable box of matches, the first impression gives way either to compassion or extreme wonder. So far as my experience serves me, this dodge is not so successful as the one I have just described. A person with the most ordinary reasoning powers must know that a man who possesses clothes like those need not be in want of bread; but if the power of reasoning were universally allotted to mankind, there would be a poor chance for the professional beggar. There never was a time or place in which there were not to be found men anxious to avoid labour, and yet to live in ease and enjoyment, and there never was a time in which other men were not, from their sympathy, their fears, or their superstition, ready to assist the necessitous, or those who appeared to be so, and liable to be imposed upon or intimidated, according as the beggar is crafty or bold.

As a rule the burnt-out tradesmen whom I have described are impostors, who make more by begging than many of those who relieve them earn by hard and honest labour. The petitions which they leave at houses are very cleverly drawn out. They are generally the composition of the professional screevers, whose practices I shall have to describe by-and-by. They have a circumstantial account of the fire by which the applicant "lost his all," and sometimes furnish an inventory of the goods that were destroyed. They are attested by the names of clergymen, churchwardens, and other responsible persons, whose signatures are imitated with consummate art in every variety of ink. Some specimens of these petitions and begging letters will be found under the head of "Dependants of Beggars."

LUCIFER DROPPERS.

The lucifer droppers are impostors to a man—to a boy—to a girl. Men seldom, if ever, practise this "dodge." It is children's work; and the artful way in which boys and girls of tender years pursue it, shows how systematically the seeds of mendicancy and crime are implanted in the hearts of the young Arab tribes of London. The artfulness of this device is of the most diabolical kind; for it trades not alone upon deception, but upon exciting sympathy with the guilty at the expense of the innocent. A boy or a girl takes up a position on the pavement of a busy street, such as Cheapside or the Strand. He, or she—it is generally a girl—carries a box or two of lucifer matches, which she offers for sale. In passing to and fro she artfully contrives to get in the way of some gentleman who is hurrying along. He knocks against her and upsets the matches which fall in the mud. The girl immediately begins to cry and howl. The bystanders, who are ignorant of the trick, exclaim in indignation against the gentleman who has caused a poor girl such serious loss, and the result is that either the gentleman, to escape being hooted, or the ignorant passers-by, in false compassion, give the girl money. White peppermint lozenges are more often used than lucifers. It looks a hopeless case, indeed, when a trayful of white lozenges fall in the mud.

BODILY AFFLICTED BEGGARS.

Beggars who excite charity by exhibiting sores and bodily deformities are not so commonly to be met with in London as they were some years ago. The officers of the Mendicity Society have cleared the streets of nearly all the impostors, and the few who remain are blind men and cripples. Many of the blind men are under the protection of a Society, which furnishes them with books printed in raised type which they decipher by the touch. Others provide their own books, and are allowed to sit on door steps or in the recesses of the bridges without molestation from the police. It has been found on inquiry that these afflicted persons are really what they appear to be—poor, helpless, blind creatures, who are totally incapacitated from earning a living, and whom it would be heartless cruelty to drive into the workhouse, where no provision is made for their peculiar wants.

The bodily afflicted beggars of London exhibit seven varieties. 1. Those having real or pretended sores, vulgarly known as the "Scaldrum Dodge." 2. Having swollen legs. 3. Being crippled, deformed, maimed, or paralyzed. 4. Being blind. 5. Being subject to fits. 6. Being in a decline. 7. "Shallow Coves," or those who exhibit themselves in the streets, half-clad, especially in cold weather.

First, then, as to those having real or pretended sores. As I have said, there are few beggars of this class left. When the officers of the Mendicity Society first directed their attention to the suppression of this form of mendicancy, it was found that the great majority of those who exhibit sores were unmitigated impostors. In nearly all the cases investigated the sores did not proceed from natural causes, but were either wilfully produced or simulated. A few had lacerated their flesh in reality; but the majority had resorted to the less painful operation known as the "Scaldrum Dodge." This consists in covering a portion of the leg or arm with soap to the thickness of a plaister, and then saturating the whole with vinegar. The vinegar causes the soap to blister and assume a festering appearance, and thus the passer-by is led to believe that the beggar is suffering from a real sore. So well does this simple device simulate a sore that the deception is not to be detected even by close inspection. The "Scaldrum Dodge" is a trick of very recent introduction among the London beggars. It is a concomitant of the advance of science and the progress of the art of adulteration. It came in with penny postage, daguerreotypes, and other modern innovations of a like description. In less scientific periods within the present century it was wholly unknown; and sores were produced by burns and lacerations which the mendicants inflicted upon themselves with a ruthless hand. An old man who has been a beggar all his life, informed me that he had known a man prick the flesh of his leg all over, in order to produce blood and give the appearance of an ulcerous desease. This man is a cripple and walks about upon crutches, selling stay laces. He is now upwards of seventy years of age. At my solicitation he made the following statement without any apparent reserve.

Seventy Years a Beggar.

"I have been a beggar ever since I was that high—ever since I could walk. No, I was not born a cripple. I was thirty years of age before I broke my leg. That was an accident. A horse and cart drove over me in Westminster. Well; yes I was drunk. I was able-bodied enough before that. I was turned out to beg by my mother. My father, I've heard, was a soldier; he went to Egypt, or some foreign part, and never came back. I never was learnt any trade but begging, and I couldn't turn my hand to nothing else. I might have been learnt the shoemaking; but what was the use? Begging was a better trade then; it isn't now though. There was fine times when the French war was on. I lived in Westminster then. A man as they called Copenhagen Jack, took a fancy to me, and made me his valet. I waited upon, fetched his drink, and so forth. Copenhagen Jack was a captain; no not in the army, nor in the navy neither. He was the captain of the Pye-Street beggars. There was nigh two hundred of them lived in two large houses, and Jack directed them. Jack's word was law, I assure you. The boys—Jack called them his boys, but there was old men among them, and old women too—used to come up before the captain every morning before starting out for the day, to get their orders. The captain divided out the districts for them, and each man took his beat according to his directions. It was share and share alike, with an extra for the captain. There was all manner of "lays;" yes, cripples and darkies. We called them as did the blind dodge, darkies,—and "shakers" them as had fits,—and shipwrecked mariners, and — the scaldrum dodge, no; that's new; but I know what you mean. They did the real thing then—scrape the skin off their feet with a bit of glass until the blood came. Those were fine times for beggars. I've known many of 'em bring in as much as thirty shillings a day, some twenty, some fifteen. If a man brought home no more than five or six shillings, the captain would enter him, make a note of him, and change his beat. Yes, we lived well. I've known fifty sit down to a splendid supper, geese and turkeys, and all that, and keep it up until daylight, with songs and toasts. No; I didn't beg then; but I did before, and I did after. I begged after, when the captain came to misfortune. He went a walking one day in his best clothes, and got pressed, and never came back, and there was a mutiny among them in Pye-Street, and I nearly got murdered. You see, they were jealous of me, because the captain petted me. I used to dress in top-boots and a red coat when I waited on the captain. It was his fancy. Romancing? I don't know what you mean. Telling lies, oh! It's true by ——. There's nothing like it nowadays. The new police and this b—— Mendicity Society has spoilt it all. Well, they skinned me; took off my fine coat and boots, and sent me out on the orphan lay in tatters. I sat and cried all day on the door steps, for I was really miserable now my friend was gone, and I got lots of halfpence, and silver too, and when I took home the swag, they danced round me and swore that they would elect me captain if I went on like that; but there was a new captain made, and when they had their fun out, he came and took the money away, and kicked me under the table. I ran away the next day, and went to a house in St. Giles's, where I was better treated. There was no captain there; the landlord managed the house, and nobody was master but him. There was nigh a hundred beggars in that house, and some two or three hundred more in the houses next it. The houses are not standing now. They were taken down when New Oxford-street was built; they stood on the north side. Yes; we lived well in St. Giles's—as well as we did in Westminster. I have earned 8, 10, 15, ay, 30 shillings a day, and more nor that sometimes. I can't earn one shilling now. The folks don't give as they did. They think everybody an imposture now. And then the police won't let you alone. No; I told you before, I never was anything else but a beggar. How could I? It was the trade I was brought up to. A man must follow his trade. No doubt I shall die a beggar, and the parish will bury me."

Having Swollen Legs.

Beggars who lie on the pavement and expose swollen legs, are very rarely to be met with now. The imposture has been entirely suppressed by the police and the officers of the Mendicity Society. This is one of the shallowest of all the many "dodges" of the London beggars. On reflection any one, however slightly acquainted with the various forms of disease, must know that a mere swelling cannot be a normal or chronic condition of the human body. A swelling might last a few days, or a week; but a swelling of several years' standing is only to be referred to the continued application of a poisonous ointment, or to the binding of the limb with ligatures, so as to confine the blood and puff the skin.

Cripples.

Various kinds of cripples are still to be found, begging in the streets of London. As a rule the police do not interfere with them, unless they know them to be impostors. A certain number of well-known cripples have acquired a sort of prescriptive right to beg where they please. The public will be familiar with the personal appearance of many of them. There is the tall man on crutches, with his foot in a sling, who sells stay laces; the poor wretch without hands, who crouches on the pavement and writes with the stumps of his arms; the crab-like man without legs, who sits strapped to a board, and walks upon his hands; the legless man who propels himself in a little carriage, constructed on the velocipede principle; the idiotic-looking youth, who "stands pad with a fakement," shaking in every limb as if he were under the influence of galvanism. These mendicants are not considered to be impostors, and are allowed to pursue begging as a regular calling. I cannot think, however, that the police exercise a wise discretion in permitting some of the more hideous of these beggars to infest the streets. Instances are on record of nervous females having been seriously frightened, and even injured, by seeing men without legs or arms crawling at their feet. A case is within my own knowledge, where the sight of a man without legs or arms had such an effect upon a lady in the family way that her child was born in all respects the very counterpart of the object that alarmed her. It had neither legs nor arms. This occurrence took place at Brighton about eleven years ago. I have frequently seen ladies start and shudder when the crab-like man I have referred to has suddenly appeared, hopping along at their feet. I am surprised that there is no home or institution for cripples of this class. They are certainly deserving of sympathy and aid; for they are utterly incapacitated from any kind of labour. Impostors are constantly starting up among this class of beggars; but they do not remain long undetected. A man was lately found begging, who pretended that he had lost his right arm. The deception at the first glance was perfect. His right sleeve hung loose at his side, and there appeared to be nothing left of his arm but a short stump. On being examined at the police office, his arm was found strapped to his side, and the stump turned out to be a stuffing of bran. Another man simulated a broken leg by doubling up that limb and strapping his foot and ankle to his thigh. Paralysis is frequently simulated with success until the actor is brought before the police surgeon, when the cheat is immediately detected.

A Blind Beggar.

A blind beggar, led by a dog, whom I accosted in the street, made the following voluntary statement. I should mention that he seemed very willing to answer my questions, and while he was talking kept continually feeling my clothes with his finger and thumb. The object of this, I fancy, must have been to discover whether I was what persons of his class call a "gentleman" or a poor man. Whether he had any thoughts of my being an officer I cannot say.

"I am sixty years of age: you wouldn't think it, perhaps, but I am. No, I was not born blind; I lost my sight in the small-pox, five and twenty years ago. I have been begging on the streets eighteen years. Yes, my dog knows the way home. How did I teach him that? why, when I had him first, the cabmen and busmen took him out to Camden Town, and Westminster, and other places, and then let him go. He soon learnt to find his way home. No, he is not the dog I had originally; that one died; he was five and twenty years old when he died. Yes, that was a very old age for a dog. I had this one about five years ago. Don't get as much as I used to do? No, no, my friend. I make about a shilling a-day, never—scarcely never—more, sometimes less—a good deal less; but some folks are very kind to me. I live at Poole's-place, Mount Pleasant. There are a good many engineers about there, and their wives are very kind to me; they have always a halfpenny for me when I go that way. I have my beats. I don't often come down this way (Gower-street), only once a month. I always keep on this side of Tottenham Court-road; I never go over the road; my dog knows that. I am going down there," (pointing); "that's Chenies-street. Oh, I know where I am: next turning to the right is Alfred-street, the next to the left is Francis-street, and when I get to the end of that the dog will stop; but I know as well as him. Yes, he's a good dog, but never the dog I used to have; he used always to stop when there was anybody near, and pull when there was nobody. He was what I call a steady dog, this one is young and foolish like; he stops sometimes dead, and I goes on talking, thinking there is a lady or gentleman near; but it's only other dogs that he's stopping to have a word with. No, no, no, sir." This he said when I dropped some more coppers into his hat, having previously given him a penny. "I don't want that. I think I know your voice, sir; I'm sure I've heard it before. No! ah, then I'm mistaken." Here again he felt my coat and waistcoat with an inquiring touch: apparently satisfied, he continued, "I'll tell you, sir, what I wouldn't tell to every one; I've as nice a little place at Mount Pleasant as you would desire to see. You wouldn't think I was obliged to beg if you saw it. Why, sir, I beg many times when I've as much as sixteen shillings in my pocket; leastwise not in my pocket, but at home. Why you see, sir, there's the winter months coming on, and I lays by what I can against the wet days, when I can't go out. There's no harm in that, sir. Well, now, sir, I'll tell you: there's a man up there in Sussex-street that I know, and he said to me just now, as I was passing the public house, 'Come in, John, and have a drop of something.' 'No, thank ye,' says I, 'I don't want drink; if you want to give me anything give me the money.' 'No,' says he, 'I won't do that, but if you come in and have something to drink I'll give you sixpence.' Well, sir, I wouldn't go. It wouldn't do, you know, for the likes of me, a blind man getting his living by begging, to be seen in a public-house; the people wouldn't know, sir, whether it was my money that was paying for it or not. I never go into a public-house; I has my drop at home. Oh, yes, I am tired—tired of it; but I'll tell you, sir, I think I'll get out of it soon. Do you know how that is, sir? Well, I think I shall get on to Day and Martin's Charity in October; I'm promised votes, and I'm in hopes this time. God bless you, sir."

There was for many years in the city a blind man with a dog, who was discovered to be a rank impostor. The boys found it out long before the police did. They used to try and take the money out of the little basket that the dog carried in his mouth, but they never succeeded. The moment a boy approached the basket the blind man ran at him with his stick, which proved, of course, that the fellow could see. Some of my readers may recollect seeing in the papers an account of a respectable young girl who ran away from her home and took up with this blind man. She cohabited with him, in fact, and it was found that they lived in extravagance and luxury on the blind beggar's daily takings.

Beggars subject to Fits

are impostors, I may say, wholly without exception. Some of them are the associates and agents of thieves, and fall down in the street in assumed fits in order to collect a crowd and afford a favourable opportunity to the pickpockets, with whom they are in league. The simulation of fits is no mean branch of the beggar's art of deception. The various symptoms—the agitation of the muscles, the turning up of the whites of the eyes, the pallor of the face and the rigidity of the mouth and jaw—are imitated to a nicety; and these symptoms are sometimes accompanied by copious frothing at the mouth. I asked Mr. Horsford, of the Mendicity Society, how this was done, and received the laconic answer—"Soap." And this brought to my memory that I had once seen an actor charge his mouth with a small piece of soup to give due *vraissemblance* to the last scene of *Sir Giles Overreach*. I was shown an old woman who was in the habit of falling down in assumed fits simply to get brandy. She looked very aged and poor, and I was told she generally had her fits when some well-dressed gentleman was passing with a lady on his arm. She generally chose the scene of her performance close to the door of a public-house, into which some compassionate person might conveniently carry her. She was never heard to speak in her fits except to groan and mutter " brandy," when that remedy did not appear to suggest itself to those who came to her aid. An officer said to me, " I have known that old woman have so many fits in the course of the day that she has been found lying in the gutter dead drunk from the effect of repeated restoratives. She has been apprehended and punished over and over again, but she returns to the old dodge the minute she gets out. She is on the parish; but she gets money as well as brandy by her shamming."

I have heard that there are persons who purposely fall into the Serpentine in order to be taken to the receiving-house of the Humane Society, and recovered with brandy. One man repeated the trick so often that at last the Society's men refused to go to his aid. It is needless to say that he soon found his way out of the water unaided, when he saw that his dodge was detected.

Being in a Decline.

No form of poverty and misfortune is better calculated to move the hearts of the compassionate than this. You see crouching in a corner, a pale-faced, wan young man, apparently in the very last stage of consumption. His eyes are sunk in his head, his jaw drops, and you can almost see his bones through his pallid skin. He appears too exhausted to speak; he coughs at intervals, and places his hand on his chest as if in extreme pain. After a fit of coughing he pants pitifully, and bows his head feebly as if he were about to die on the spot. It will be noticed, however, as a peculiarity distinguishing nearly all these beggars, that the sufferers wear a white cloth bound round their heads overtopped by a black cap. It is this white cloth, coupled with a few slight artistic touches of colour to the face, that produces the interesting look of decline. Any person who is thin and of sallow complexion may produce the same effect by putting on a white night-cap, and applying a little pink colour round the eyes. It is the simple rule observed by comedians, when they make up for a sick man or a ghost. These beggars are all impostors; and they are now so well known to the police that they never venture to take up a fixed position during the day, but pursue their nefarious calling at night at public-houses and other resorts where they can readily make themselves scarce should an officer happen to spy them out.

"Shallow Coves."

This is the slang name given to beggars who exhibit themselves in the streets half clad, especially in cold weather. There are a great many of these beggars in London, and they are enabled to ply their trade upon the sympathies of the public with very little check, owing to the fact that they mostly frequent quiet streets, and make a point of moving on whenever they see a policeman approaching. A notorious "shallow cove," who frequents the neighbourhood of the Strand and St. Martin's Lane, must be well known to many of my readers. His practice is to stand at the windows of bakers and confectioners, and gaze with an eager famished look at the bread and other eatables. His almost naked state, his hollow, glaring eye, like that of a famished dog, his long thin cheek, his matted hair, his repeated shrugs of uneasiness as if he were suffering from cold or vermin, present such a spectacle of wretchedness as the imagination could never conceive. He has no shirt, as you can see by his open breast; his coat is a thing of mere shreds; his trousers, torn away in picturesque jags at the knees, are his only other covering, except a dirty sodden-looking round-crowned brown felt hat, which he slouches over his forehead in a manner which greatly heightens his aspect of misery. I was completely taken in when I first saw this man greedily glaring in at a baker's window in St. Martin's Lane. I gave him twopence to procure a loaf, and waited to see him buy it, anxious to have the satisfaction of seeing him appease such extreme hunger as I had never—I thought—witnessed before. He did not enter the shop with the alacrity I expected. He seemed to hesitate, and presently I could see that he was casting stealthy glances at me. I remained where I was, watching him; and at last when he saw I was determined to wait, he entered the shop. I saw him speak to the woman at the counter and point at something; but he made no purchase, and came out without the bread, which I thought he would have devoured like a wolf, when he obtained the money to procure it. Seeing me still watching him, he moved away rapidly. I entered the shop, and asked if he had bought anything. "Not he, he don't want any bread," said the mistress of the shop, "I wish the police would lock him up, or drive him away from here, for he's a regular nuisance. He pretends to be hungry, and then when people give him anything, he comes in here and asks if I can sell him any bits. He knows I won't, and he don't want 'em. He is a regular old soldier, he is, sir."

I received confirmation of this account from Mr. Horsford, who said that the fellow had been sent to prison at least thirty times. The moment he gets out he resorts to his old practices. On one occasion, when he was taken, he had thirteen shillings in his pocket,—in coppers, sixpences and threepenny and fourpenny bits. Softhearted old ladies who frequent the pastrycooks are his chief victims.

"Shallow coves" have recently taken to Sunday begging. They go round the quiet streets in pairs, and sing psalm tunes during church hours. They walk barefooted, without hats, and expose their breasts to show that they have no under clothing.

The "shallow cove" is a very pitiable sight in winter, standing half naked, with his bare feet on the cold stones. But give him a suit of clothes and shoes and stockings, and the next day he will be as naked and as wretched-looking as he is to-day. Nakedness and shivers are his stock in trade.

Famished Beggars.

The famished beggars, that is, those who "make up" to look as if they were starving, pursue an infinite variety of dodges. The most common of all is to stand in some prominent place with a placard on the breast, bearing an inscription to the effect that the beggar is "starving," or that he has "a large family entirely dependent upon him." The appeal is sometimes made more forcible by its brevity, and the card bears the single word, "Destitute." In every case where the beggar endeavours to convey starvation by his looks and dress it may be relied upon that he is an impostor, a lazy fellow, who prefers begging to work, because it requires less exertion and brings him more money. There are some, however,—blind men and old persons—who "stand pad," that is to say, beg by the exhibition of a written or printed paper, who are not impostors; they are really poor persons who are incapacitated from work, and who beg from day to day to earn a living. But these beggars do not get up an appearance of being starved, and indeed some of them look very fat and comfortable.

The beggars who chalk on the pavement "I am starving," in a round scholastic hand, are not of this class. It does not require much reflection to discern the true character of such mendicants. As I have frequently had occasion to observe, the man who begs day after day, and counts his gains at the rate of from twelve to twenty shillings a week, cannot be starving. You pass one of these beggars in the morning, and you hear the coppers chinking on the pavement as they are thrown to him by the thoughtless or the credulous; you pass him again in the evening, and there is still the inscription "I am starving." This beggar adds hypocrisy to his other vices. By his writing on the pavement he would give you to understand that he is too much ashamed to beg by word of mouth. As he crouches beside his inscription he hides his head. The writing, too, is a false pretence. "I am starving" is written in so good a hand that you are led to believe that the wretch before you has had a good education, that he has seen better days, and is now the victim of misfortune, perhaps wholly undeserved. It should be known, however, that many of these beggars cannot write at all; they could not write another sentence except "I am starving" if it were to save their lives. There are persons who teach the art of writing certain sentences to beggars, but their pupils learn to trace the letters mechanically. This is the case with the persons who draw in coloured chalk on the pavement. They can draw a mackerel, a broken plate, a head of Christ, and a certain stereotyped sea-view with a setting sun, but they cannot draw anything else, and these they trace upon a principle utterly unknown to art. There is one beggar of this class who frequents the King's-Cross end of the New Road, who writes his specimens backwards, and who cannot do it any other way. He covers a large flag-stone with "copies" in various hands, and they are all executed in the true "copperplate" style. They are all, however, written backwards.

The distinction made by the magistrates and the police between those who draw coloured views and those who merely write "I am starving" in white chalk, exhibits a nicety of discrimination which is not a little amusing. When the officers of the Mendicity Society first began to enforce their powers with rigour (in consequence of the alarming increase of mendicancy) they arrested these flag-stone artists with others. The magistrates, however, showed an unwillingness to commit them, and at length it was laid down as a rule that these men should not be molested unless they obstructed a thoroughfare or created a disturbance. This decision was grounded upon the consideration that these street artists did some actual work for the money they received from the public; they drew a picture and exhibited it, and might therefore be fairly regarded as pursuing an art. So the chalkers of mackerel were placed in the category of privileged street exhibitors. The "I am starving" dodge, however, has been almost entirely suppressed by the persevering activity of Mr. Horsford and his brother officers of the Mendicity Society.

One of the latest devices of famished beggars which has come under my notice I shall denominate

The Choking Dodge.

A wretched-looking man, in a state of semi-nudity, having the appearance of being half starved and exhausted, either from want of food or from having walked a long way, sat down one day on the doorstep of the house opposite mine. I was struck by his wretched and forlorn appearance, and particularly by his downcast looks. It seemed as if misery had not only worn him to the bone, but had crushed all his humanity out of him. He was more like a feeble beast, dying of exhaustion and grovelling in the dust, than a man. Presently he took out a crust of dry bread and attempted to eat it. It was easy to see that it was a hard crust, as hard as stone, and dirty, as if it had lain for some days in the street. The wretch gnawed at it as a starved dog gnaws at a bone. The crust was not only hard, but the beggar's jaws seemed to want the power of mastication. It seemed as if he had hungered so long that food was now too late. At length he managed to bite off a piece; but now another phase of his feebleness was manifested—he could not swallow it. He tried to get it down, and it stuck in his throat. You have seen a dog with a bone in his throat, jerking his head up and down in his effort to swallow: that was the action of this poor wretch on the door-step. I could not but be moved by this spectacle, and I opened the window and called to the man. He took no heed of me. I called again. Still no heed; misery had blunted all his faculties. He seemed to desire nothing but to sit there and choke. I went over to him, and, tapping him on the shoulder, gave him twopence, and told him to go to the public house and get some beer to wash down his hard meal. He rose slowly, gave me a look of thanks, and went away in the direction of the tavern. He walked more briskly than I could have conceived possible in his case, and something prompted me to watch him. I stood at my door looking after him, and when he got near the public-house he turned round. I knew at once that he was looking to see if I were watching him. The next minute he turned aside as if to enter the public-house. The entrance stood back from the frontage of the street, and I could not tell, from where I stood, whether he had gone into the house or not. I crossed to the other side, where I could see him without being noticed. He had not entered the house, but was standing by the door. When he had stood there for a few minutes he peeped out cautiously, and looked down the street towards the place where he had left me. Being apparently satisfied that all was right, he emerged from the recess and walked on. I was now determined to watch him further. I had not long to wait for conclusive evidence of the imposture which I now more than suspected. The man walked slowly along until he saw some persons at a first-floor window, when he immediately sat down on a door-step opposite and repeated the elaborate performance with the hard crust which I have already described. This I saw him do four times before he left the street, in each case getting money. It is needless to say that this fellow was a rank impostor. One of his class was apprehended some time ago—it might have been this very man—and no less than seven shillings were found upon him. These men frequent quiet bye-streets, and never, or rarely, beg in the busy thoroughfares. I will give another case, which I shall call

The Offal-Eater.

The most notable instance of this variety of the famished beggars which has come under my notice is that of a little old man who frequents the neighbourhood of Russell-square. I have known him now for two years, and I have seen him repeat his performance at least a score of times. The man has the appearance of a cutler. He wears a very old and worn, but not ragged, velveteen coat with large side pockets, a pair of sailor's blue trousers a good deal patched, a very, very bad pair of shoes, and a chimney-pot hat, which seems to have braved the wind and rain for many years, been consigned to a dust-bin, and then recovered for wear. He is below the average height, and appears to be about seventy years of age. This little old man makes his appearance in my street about eleven o'clock in the forenoon. He walks down the pavement listlessly, rubbing his hands and looking about him on every side in a vacant bewildered manner, as if all the world were strange to him, and he had no home, no friend, and no purpose on the face of the earth. Every now and then he stops and turns his face towards the street, moving himself uneasily in his clothes, as as if he were troubled with vermin. All this time he is munching and mumbling some food in a manner suggestive of a total want of teeth. As he pauses he looks about as if in search of something. Presently you see him pick up a small piece of bread which has been thrown out to the sparrows. He wipes it upon his velveteen coat and begins to eat it. It is a long process. He will stand opposite your window for full ten minutes mumbling that small piece of bread, but he never looks up to inspire compassion or charity; he trusts to his pitiful mumblings to produce the desired effect, and he is not disappointed. Coppers are flung to him from every window, and he picks them up slowly and listlessly, as if he did not expect such aid, and scarcely knew how to apply it. I have given him money several times, but that does not prevent him from returning again and again to stand opposite my windows and mumble crusts picked out of the mud in the streets. One day I gave him a lump of good bread, but in an hour after I found him in an adjacent street exciting charity in the usual way. This convinced me that he was an artful systematic beggar, and this impression was fully confirmed on my following him into a low beer-shop in St. Giles's and finding him comfortably seated with his feet up in a chair, smoking a long pipe, and discussing a pot of ale. He knew me in a moment, dropped his feet from the chair, and tried to hide his pipe. Since that occasion he has never come my way.

PETTY TRADING BEGGARS.

This is perhaps the most numerous class of beggars in London. Their trading in such articles as lucifers, boot-laces, cabbage-nets, tapes, cottons, shirt-buttons, and the like, is in most cases a mere "blind" to evade the law applying to mendicants and vagrants. There are very few of the street vendors of such petty articles as lucifers and shirt-buttons who can make a living from the profits of their trade. Indeed they do not calculate upon doing so. The box of matches, or the little deal box of cottons, is used simply as a passport to the resorts of the charitable. The police are obliged to respect the trader, though they know very well that under the disguise of the itinerant merchant there lurks a beggar.

Beggars of this class use their trade to excite compassion and obtain a gift rather than to effect a sale. A poor half-clad wretch stands by the kerb exposing for sale a single box of matches, the price being "only a halfpenny." A charitable person passes by and drops a halfpenny or a penny into the poor man's hand, and disdains to take the matches. In this way a single box will be sufficient for a whole evening's trading, unless some person should insist upon an actual "transaction," when the beggar is obliged to procure another box at the nearest oilman's. There are very few articles upon which an actual profit is made by legitimate sale. Porcelain shirt-buttons, a favourite commodity of the petty trading beggars, would not yield the price of a single meal unless the seller could dispose of at least twenty dozen in a day. Cottons, stay-laces, and the like, can now be obtained so cheaply at the shops, that no one thinks of buying these articles in the streets unless it be in a charitable mood. Almost the only commodities in which a legitimate trade is carried on by the petty traders of the streets are flowers, songs, knives, combs, braces, purses, portmonnaies. The sellers of knives, combs, &c., are to a certain extent legitimate traders, and do not calculate upon charity. They are cheats, perhaps, but not beggars. The vendors of flowers and songs, though they really make an effort to sell their goods, and often realize a tolerable profit, are nevertheless beggars, and trust to increase their earnings by obtaining money without giving an equivalent. A great many children are sent out by their parents to sell flowers during the summer and autumn. They find their best market in the bars of public-houses, and especially those frequented by prostitutes. If none else give prostitutes a good character, the very poor do. "I don't know what we should do but for them," said an old beggar-woman to me one day. "They are good-hearted souls—always kind to the poor. I hope God will forgive them." I have had many examples of this sympathy for misfortune and poverty on the part of the fallen women of the streets. A fellow feeling no doubt makes them wondrous kind. They know what it is to be cast off, and spurned, and despised; they know, too, what it is to starve, and, like the beggars, they are subject to the stern "move on" of the policeman.

The relations which subsist between the prostitutes and the beggars reveal some curious traits. Beggars will enter a public-house because they see some women at the bar who will assist their suit. They offer their little wares to some gentlemen at the bar, and the women will say, "Give the poor devil something," or "buy bouquets for us," or if the commodity should be laces or buttons, they say, "Don't take the poor old woman's things; give her the money." And the gentlemen, just to show off, and appear liberal, do as they are told. Possibly, but for the pleading of their gay companions, they would have answered the appeal with a curse and gruff command to begone. I once saw an old woman kiss a bedizened prostitute's hand, in real gratitude for a service of this kind. I don't know that I ever witnessed anything more touching in my life. The woman, who a few minutes before had been flaunting about the bar in the reckless manner peculiar to her class, was quite moved by the old beggar's act, and I saw a tear mount in her eye and slowly trickle down her painted cheek, making a white channel through the rouge as it fell. But in a moment she dashed it away, and the next was flaunting and singing as before. Prostitutes are afraid to remain long under the influence of good thoughts. They recal their days of innocence, and overpower them with an intolerable sadness—a sadness which springs of remorse. The gay women assume airs of patronage towards the beggars, and as such are looked up to; but a beggar-woman, however poor, and however miserable, if she is conscious of being virtuous, is always sensible of her superiority in that respect. She is thankful for the kindness of the "gay lady," and extols her goodness of heart; but she pities while she admires, and mutters as a last word, "May God forgive her." Thus does one touch of nature make all the world akin, and thus does virtue survive all the buffets of evil fortune to raise even a beggar to the level of the most worthy, and be a treasure dearer and brighter than all the pleasures of the world.

The sellers of flowers and songs are chiefly boys and young girls. They buy their flowers in Covent Garden, when the refuse of the market is cleared out, and make them up into small bouquets, which they sell for a penny. When the flower season is over they sell songs—those familiar productions of Ryle, Catnach and company, which, it is said, the great Lord Macaulay was wont to collect and treasure up as collateral evidences of history. Some of the boys who pursue this traffic are masters of all the trades that appertain to begging. I have traced one boy, by the identifying mark of a most villanous squint, through a career of ten years. When I first saw him he was a mere child of about four years of age. His mother sent him with a ragged little girl (his sister) into public-house bars to beg. Their diminutive size attracted attention and excited charity. By-and-by, possibly in consequence of the interference of the police, they carried pennyworths of flowers with them, at other times matches, and at others halfpenny sheets of songs. After this the boy and the girl appeared dressed in sailor's costume, (both as boys,) and sung duets. I remember that one of the duets, which had a spoken part, was not very decent; the poor children evidently did not understand what they said; but the thoughtless people at the bar laughed and gave them money. By-and-by the boy became too big for this kind of work, and I next met him selling fuzees. After the lapse of about a year he started in the shoe-black line. His station was at the end of Endell Street, near the baths; but as he did not belong to one of the regularly organized brigades, he was hunted about by the police, and could not make a living. On the death of the crossing-sweeper at the corner he succeeded to that functionary's broom, and in his new capacity was regarded by the police as a useful member of society. The last time I saw him he was in possession of a costermonger's barrow selling mackerel. He had grown a big strong fellow, but I had no difficulty in identifying the little squinting child, who begged, and sold flowers and songs in public-house bars, with the strong loud-lunged vendor of mackerel. I suppose this young beggar may be said to have pursued an honourable career, and raised himself in the world. Many who have such an introduction to life finish their course in a penal settlement.

There are not a few who assume the appearance of petty traders for the purpose of committing thefts, such as picking a gentleman's pocket when he is intoxicated, and slinking into parlours to steal bagatelle balls. Police spies occasionally disguise themselves as petty traders. There is a well-known man who goes about with a bag of nuts, betting that he will tell within two how many you take up in your hand. This man is said to be a police spy. I have not been able to ascertain whether this is true or not; but I am satisfied that the man does not get his living by his nut trick. In the day-time he appears without his nuts, dressed in a suit of black, and looking certainly not unlike a policeman in mufti.

Among the petty trading beggars there are a good many idiots and half-witted creatures, who obtain a living—and a very good one too—by dancing in a grotesque and idiotic manner on the pavement to amuse children. Some of them are not such idiots as they appear, but assume a half-witted appearance to give oddness to their performance, and excite compassion for their misfortune. The street boys are the avengers of this imposition upon society.

The idiot performer has a sad life of it when the boys gather about him. They pull his clothes, knock off his hat, and pelt him with lime and mud. But this persecution sometimes redounds to his advantage; for when the grown-up folks see him treated thus, they pity him the more. These beggars always take care to carry something to offer for sale. Halfpenny songs are most commonly the merchandise.

The little half-witted Italian man who used to go about grinding an organ that "had no inside to it," as the boys said, was a beggar of this class, and I really think he traded on his constant persecution by the *gamins*. Music, of course, he made none, for there was only one string left in his battered organ; but he always acted so as to convey the idea that the boys had destroyed his instrument. He would turn away at the handle in a desperate way, as if he were determined to spare no effort to please his patrons; but nothing ever came of it but a feeble tink-a-tink at long intervals. If his organ could at any time have been spoiled, certainly the boys might have done it; for their great delight was to put stones in it, and batter in its deal back with sticks. I am informed that this man had a good deal more of the rogue than of the fool in his composition. A gentleman offered to have his organ repaired for him; but he declined; and at length when the one remaining string gave way he would only have that one mended. It was his "dodge" to grind the air, and appear to be unconscious that he was not discoursing most eloquent music.

Tract-selling in the streets is a line peculiar to the Hindoos. I find that the tracts are given to them by religious people, and that they are bought by religious people, who are not unfrequently the very same persons who provided the tracts.

Very few petty trading beggars take to tract-selling from their own inspiration; for in good sooth it does not pay, except when conducted on the principle I have just indicated. Some find it convenient to exhibit tracts simply to evade the law applying to beggars and vagrants; but they do not use them if they can procure a more popular article. In these remarks it is very far from my intention to speak of "religious people" with any disrespect. I merely use the expression "religious people" to denote those who employ themselves actively and constantly in disseminating religious publications among the people. Their motives and their efforts are most praiseworthy, and my only regret is that their labours are not rewarded by a larger measure of success.

AN AUTHOR'S WIFE.

In the course of my inquiry into the habits, condition, and mode of life of the petty trading beggars of London, I met with a young woman who alleged that the publications she sold were the production of her husband. I encountered her at the bar of a tavern, where I was occupied in looking out for "specimens" of the class of beggars, which I am now describing. She entered the bar modestly and with seeming diffidence. She had some printed sheets in her hand. I asked her what they were. She handed me a sheet. It was entitled the *Pretty Girls of London*. It was only a portion of the work, and on the last page was printed "to be continued." "Do you bring this out in numbers?" I asked. "Yes, sir," she replied, "it is written by my husband, and he is continuing it from time to time." "Are you then his publisher?" I inquired. "Yes, sir, my husband is ill a-bed, and I am obliged to go out and sell his work for him?" I looked through the sheet, and I saw that it was not a very decent work. "Have you ever read this?" I enquired. "Oh yes, sir, and I think it's very clever; don't you think so, sir?" It certainly was written with some little ability, and I said so; but I objected to its morality. Upon which she replied, "But it's what takes, sir." She sold several copies while I was present, at twopence each; but one or two gave her fourpence and sixpence. As she was leaving I made further inquiries about her husband. She said he was an author by profession, and had seen better days. He was very ill, and unable to work. I asked her, to give me his address as I might be of some assistance to him. This request seemed to perplex her; and at length she said, she was afraid her husband would not like to see me; he was very proud. I have since ascertained that this author's pretty little wife is a dangerous impostor. She lives, or did live at the time I met her, at the back of Clare Market, with a man (not her husband) who was well known to the police as a notorious begging-letter writer. He was not the author of anything but those artful appeals, with forged signatures, of which I have given specimens under the heading of "Screevers." I was also assured by an officer that the pretended author's wife had on one occasion been concerned in decoying a young man to a low lodging near Lincoln's Inn Fields, where the unsuspecting youth was robbed and maltreated.

DEPENDANTS OF BEGGARS.

The dependants of beggars may be divided into screevers proper; i. e., writers of "slums and fakements" for those who live by "screeving," and referees, or those who give characters to professional beggars when references are required. Beggars are generally born and bred to the business. Their fathers and mothers were beggars before them, and they have an hereditary right to the calling. The exceptions to this rule are those who have fallen into mendicancy, and follow it from necessity, and those who have flown to it in a moment of distress, and finding it more lucrative than they supposed, adopted it from choice. Hence it follows that the majority are entirely destitute of education; and by education I mean the primary arts of reading and writing. Where there is demand there is supply, and the wants of mendicants who found their account in "pads," and "slums," and "fakements," created "screevers."

The antecedents of the screever are always more or less—and generally more —disreputable. He has been a fraudulent clerk imprisoned for embezzlement; or a highly-respected treasurer to a philanthropic society, who has made off with the funds entrusted to him; or a petty forger, whose family have purchased silence, and "hushed up" a scandal; or, more frequently, that most dangerous of convicts, the half-educated convict—who has served his time or escaped his bonds.

Too proud to beg himself, or, more probably, too well known to the police to dare face daylight; ignorant of any honest calling, or too idle to practise it; without courage to turn thief or informer; lazy, dissolute, and self-indulgent, the screever turns his little education to the worst of purposes, and prepares the forgery he leaves the more fearless cadger to utter.

The following are specimens of the screever's work, copied from the original documents in the possession of Mr. Horsford, of the Mendicity Society :—

"Parish of Battersea;
County of Surrey.

"This memorial sheweth that Mr. Alexander Fyfe, a native of Port Glasgow N.B. and for several years carrying on the business of a NURSERY and SEEDSMAN in this parish, became security for his son in law Andrew Talfour of Bay st. Port Glasgow who in October last privately disposed of his effects and absconded to the colonies, leaving his wife and six children totally unprovided for and the said Mr. Alexander Fyfe responsible for the sum of £1350. the sudden reverse of fortune together with other domestic afflictions so preyed on the mind of Mr. Fyfe that he is now an inmate of a LUNATIC ASYLUM.

"The said Mr. Fyfe together with his family have hitherto maintained the character of HONESTY and INDUSTRY in consideration of which I have been earnestly solicited by a few Benevolent persons to draw up this statement on behalf of the bereaved family. I have therefore taken on myself the responsibillity of so doing trusting those whom Providence has given the means will lend their timely aid in rescuing a respectable family from the ruin that inevitably awaits them.

"GIVEN under my Hand at the VESTRY in the aforesaid parish of Battersea and County of Surrey this Twenty-Fourth day of February in the year of Our Lord 1851."

John Thomas Freeman, Vestry Clerk.	£3
J. S. Jenkinson Vicar of Battersea.	£5 0 0
Watson and Co.	£5
John Forster & Co.	5
Revd. J. Twining	2 2
Alderman J. Humphery	5
Sir George Pollock Southlands.	5
	£.
Henry Mitton	2
Wm. Downs Oak wharf.	2
Mrs. Broadley Wilson	1
Sir Henry B. Houghton	£5
Mrs. Adml Colin Campbell	1..1
Col. J. Mc Donall	£5 paid.
Anonymous	2

Mrs. Col. Forbes	£3
Col. W. Mace paid	5
P. H. Gillespie	5
Minister of the Scotch Church Battersea Rise 3d March /51	
Messrs. Moffat, Gillespie & Co. 5 pd.	

My readers will perceive that the above document is written in a semi-legal style, with a profuse amount of large capitals, and minute particularity in describing localities, though here and there an almost ostentatious indifference exists upon the same points. Thus we are told that the parish of Battersea is in the county of Surrey, and that Port Glasgow is in North Britain, while on the other hand we are only informed that the absconding Andrew Talfour, of Bay Street, Port Glasgow, N.B., made off to the *colonies*, which, considering the vast extent of our colonial possessions, is vague, to say the least of it. It must also be allowed that, the beginning the word "benevolent" in the second paragraph with a capital B is equally to the credit of the writer's head and heart. It is odd that after having spelt "responsible" so correctly, the writer should have indulged a playful fancy with "responsibi*ll*ity;" but perhaps trifling orthographical lapses may be in keeping with the assumed character of vestry-clerk. Critically speaking, the weak point of this composition is its punctuation; its strong point the concluding paragraph, "the GIVEN under my hand at the VESTRY," which carries with it the double weight of a royal proclamation, and the business-like formality of an Admiralty contract; but the composition and caligraphy are trifles—the real genius lies in the signatures.

I wish my readers could see the names attached to this "Memorial" as they lay before me. The first, "J. S. Jenkinson," is written in the most clerical of hands; "Watson and Co." is round and commercial; "John Forster & Co." the same; the "Revd J. Twining" scholarly and easy; "Alderman J. Humphery" stiff and upright. These names are evidently copied from the Red Book and Directory; some are purely fictitious; many are cleverly executed forgeries.

The ingenuity of the concocter and compiler—of the sympathiser with the woes of Mr. Alexander Fyfe of Port Glasgow, N.B.—was exercised in vain. The imposture was detected; he was taken to a police-court, condemned, and sentenced.

Here is the case of another unfortunate Scotchman from the pen of the same gifted author. The handwriting, the wording, the capitals, and the N.B.'s, are identical with those of the warm-hearted vestry-clerk of Battersea.

"These are to certify that Mr. Alexr. Malcolm Ship-Owner and General Merchant, was on his passage from FRASERBURGH. ABERDEENSHIRE. N.B. on the night of the 3d. inst when his vessel the Susan and Mary of Fraserburgh laden with Corn was run down by a "steamer name unknown" the Crew consisting of Six persons narrowly escaping with their lives.

"Mr. Malcolm sustained a loss of property by the appalling event to the amount of £370. and being a person of exemplary character with a numerous family entirely depending upon him for support his case has excited the greatest sympathy, it has therefore been proposed by a few of his friends to enter into a subscription on his behalf with a view of raising by voluntary contributions a sufficient sum to release him from his present embarrassed situation.

"I have known him for several years a constant trader to this wharf, and consider him worthy of every sympathy."

Leith and Glasgow Wharf London May 6th. 1847	Joseph Adams	£5 0 0
	Geo. Carroll	5
A. Nichol & Sons pd.		5
P. Laurie		5
Vivian & Sons		3
J. H. Petty		2 pd
Messrs. Drummond		£5 pd.
Cranford Colvin & Co.		£3
Baring Brothers		5
Curries & Co.		3
Jono. Price		5 5
Reid, Irving & Co.		£5

The signatures attached to this are imitations of the handwriting of various firms, each distinct, individual, and apparently genuine.

The next "screeve" takes the form of a resolution at a public meeting:—

"Notting-Hill, District
Parish of Kensington
August 6th, 1857

"The Gentry and Clergy of this neighbourhood will no doubt remember that the late Mr. Edward Wyatt, (for many years a respectable tradesman in this parish) died in embarrassed circumstances in 1855, leaving a Widow and Seven Children totally unprovided for, the eldest of whom a fine Girl 19 years of age having been a Cripple from her Birth has received a liberal education and is considered a competent person to superintend a SEMINARY for the tuition of young females which would materially assist her Mother in supporting a numerous family.

"A meeting was convened on Monday evening the 3rd inst (the Revd J. P. Gall, Incumbent of St. Johns, in the Chair) when it was unanimously proposed to enter into a subscription with a view of raising by voluntary contributions the sum of £40 in order to establish the afflicted girl in this praiseworthy undertaking, I have been instructed by the Parochial Authorities to draw up this statement and therefore take upon myself the responsibility of so doing knowing the case to be one meriting sympathy.

"Signed
By order of the Chairman
Reüben Green
Vestry Clerk"

Subscriptions received at the Meeting, £11 13 6

Revd J. P. Gill	...	£1 0 0
Mrs. W. Money	...	10 0 pd
Chushington	...	£1
Mrs Coventry paid	...	10/
J. & W. S. Huntley Addison Terrace Notting Hill	pd	1 1
Mrs. Cribb pd	...	5 0
The Misses Shorland	...	7 6
Mrs Harris	...	5 0
Miss Hall Lansdowne Crescent	...	10/
W. Atkinson pd	...	5 0
Thos Jacomb	...	5 0
Miss J. Robertson paid	...	5 0
The Misses Howard	...	5 0

The above letter is written in a better style than those preceding it. Great talent is exhibited in the imitations of "lady's-hand." The signatures "Mrs. Coventry," "Mrs. Cribb," "The Misses Howard," and "Mrs. Harris" (surely this screever must have been familiar with the works of Dickens), are excellently done, but are surpassed by the clever execution of the letters forming the names, "The Misses Shorland" and "Miss Hall Lansdowne Crescent," which are masterpieces of feminine caligraphy.

The following note was sent to its address, accompanied by a memorial in one of the House of Commons envelopes, but the faulty grammar, so unlike the style in which a member of Parliament ought to write, betrayed it.

"Committee Room No. 3
House of Commons

"Mr. J. Whatman presents his respectful compliments to the Revd. W. Smith Marriott at the earnest request of the poor families (whose case will be fully explained on perusal of the accompanying document in the bearer's possession), begs to submit it for that gentlemen's charitable consideration.

"The persons whom this concerns are natives of Cranbrook Gondhurst, Brenchley &c and bears unexceptionable characters, they have the honor of knowing Mr. Marriott at Worsmorden and trust he will add his signature to the list of subscribers, for which favour they will feel grateful.

"J. Whatman takes more than ordinary interest in this case having a knowledge of its authenticity, he therefore trusts that the motives which actuates him in complying with the request will be deemed a sufficient apology.

Friday Evening
May 28, 1858"

"This Memorial sheweth that Mr. Henry Shepherd a General Carrier from EWELL, CHEAM, SUTTON &c. to LONDON VIA Mitcham, Morden, Tooting and Clapham, was returning home on the Evening of Thursday the 26th inst when near the Elephant and Castle, his Horse took fright at a Band of street Musicians and ran off at a furious pace, the Van coming in contact with a Timber carriage was dashed to pieces, the Animal received such injuries as caused its death, and Mr. SHEPHERD endeavouring to save the property entrusted to his care for delivery had his Right Leg fractured and is now an inmate of GUYS HOSPITAL.

"On further investigation We find his loss exceeds £70. and knowing him to be an Industrious, Honest man, with a large family depending upon his exertions for support We earnestly beg leave to recommend his case to the notice of the Gentry and Clergy of his neighbourhood, trusting their united Donations in conjunction with our mutual assistance will release a deserving family from their present unfortunate position in life.

"GIVEN under Our Hands this 30th day of August in the Year of Our Lord 1858" } William Harmer £2

Geo. Stone Ewell	...	£2
Sir Geo. L. Glyn	...	2 2
F. Gosling	...	2 2
Revd W. H. Vernon	...	£1
Morton Stubbs Sutton	...	1 1
Edmund Antrobus pd to Bearer 2d/9th/58	...	£2 2
W. R. G. Farmer	...	£2 2 pd.
Revd. R. Bouchier	...	£2 pd.

My readers must admire the ingenuity of this letter. The VIA Mitchem looks so formal and convincing. The grouping of the circumstances—the "local colouring," as the critics would call it, which contributed to the ruin of the ill-fated general carrier Henry Shepherd—is excellent.—"Near the Elephant and Castle his horse took fright at a band of street musicians." What more natural? "Ran off at a furious pace. The van, coming in contact with a timber carriage, was *dashed to pieces*. The Animal," not the horse—that would have been tautological, and Animal with a capital A. "The Animal received such injuries as *caused its death*, and Mr. Shepherd, endeavouring to save the property entrusted to his care—." Admirable man! Devoted carrier!—leaving his van to smash—his horse to perish as they might, that the goods confided to him might receive no hurt. ". . . . endeavouring to save the property entrusted to his care for delivery, had his *right leg fractured*, and is now an inmate of Guy's Hospital."

This is as well conceived and carried out as Sheridan's pistol-bullet that misses its mark, "strikes a bronze Hercules in the mantel-piece, glances off through the window, and wounds the postman who was coming to the door with a double letter from Northamptonshire!"

The word "Paid" and its abbreviation pd. is scattered here and there artistically among the subscriptions. A small note in a different hand, in a corner of the last page shows the fate of industry and talent misapplied. It runs:—

"Taken from Thos. Shepherd, Sept. 13. Mansion House. Lord Mayor Sir A. Carden. Committed for 3 months.
"J. W. HORSFORD."

The last instance I shall cite is peculiar, from the elaborate nature of the deception, and from containing a forgery of the signature of Lord Brougham. The screever, in this case, has taken a regularly printed Warrant, Execution, or Distress for Rent, filled it up with the name of Mrs. Julia Thompson, &c., and placed an imaginary inventory to a fictitious seizure. The word "Patent" is spelt "Pattent," which might be allowable in a broker's man, but when "Ewer" is written "Ure," I think he is too hard upon the orthography peculiar to the officers of the Sheriff of Middlesex, particularly as it is evident from the rest of the filling-in of the form that the error is intentional. Not only law but science is invoked in aid of this capital case of sham real distress. "Pleuro-Pneumonia" looks veterinary and veracious enough to carry conviction to the hearts of the most sceptical.

"TAKE NOTICE, That by the authority and on the behalf of your Landlord, Thos. Young, I have this Sixteenth day of April in the year of Our Lord One thousand eight hundred and fifty-six distrained the several goods and chattels specified in the Schedule or Inventory hereunder written in

19 Praed Street
in the Parish of Paddington in the County of Middlesex, for Twenty-nine pounds, being Twelve Months and arrears Rent due to the said Mr. Thos. Young
at Ninth Febry last
and if you shall not pay the said Twelve Months and Arrears Rent so due and in arrear as aforesaid together with the costs and charges of this distress or replevy the said goods and chattels within five days from the date hereof I shall cause the said goods and chattels to be appraised and sold, pursuant to the statute in that case made and provided.

"Given under my hand the day and year above written.
"J. W. RUSSELL.
"Sworn Broker, &c.
"To Mrs. Julia Thompson."

Removing any goods off the premises to avoid a distress or any person aiding, assisting, or concealing the same, will subject themselves to double the value of such effects so removed or concealed, or suffer imprisonment in the House of Correction, there to be kept to hard labour without Bail or Mainprize for Six Months, pursuant to the Act 11th George 2nd.

Sold by G. H. Beckford, Law Stationer, 122, Chancery Lane.

The Schedule or Inventory above referred to:—
Mahogany Drawers
Mahogany Dining Tables
Six Mahogany Seated Chairs
Two Arm Do. Do.
One Eight-Day clock
Six Oil Paintings Gilt Frames
One Large Pier Glass
Carpet and Hearthrug
Fender and Fire-irons
Quantity of Chimney Ornaments
Six Kitchen Chairs
One Long Table Deal
One Large Copper Boiler
Two Copper Kettles
Pattent Mangle
One Large Water Butt
Two Washing Tubs
1½ Doz. of Knifes and Forkes
Quantity of Earthenware &c. &c.
Two Feather Beds & Bedding
One Flock Do. Do.
Two Mahogany Bedsteads
One French Do

Washhand stand Ure &c.
Two Hair Mattresses
Three Bedroom Chairs
One set of Bedroom Carpeting
Staircase Carpeting, Brass Rods &c
One Milch Cow
One Cart Mare
One Dung Cart
One Wheelbarrow
Three Cwt. of Hay
Quantity of Manure
And Sundry Dairy Utensils
&c. &c. &c.

On the back of this legal document is written:

"This memorial sheweth that Mrs. Julia Thompson, widow, Cowkeeper and Dairywoman has since the demise of her husband which took place in 1849 supported a family consisting of six children by the assistance of a small Dairy the Pleuro-Pneumonia a disease Among Cattle has prevailed in the neighbourhood for several weeks during which time she has lost five Milch Cows estimated at £75. ,, ,, which will end in her entire ruin unless aided by the Hands of the Benevolent whose Donations in conjunction with Our mutual assistance will We trust enable Mrs. Thompson to realize some part of her lost property to follow her Business As before.

		H. Peters	£3	3	0
April 17th, 1856					
Chaplin & Horne	..	..	£2		
Mrs. Gore	..	..	1		
Revd J. W. Buckley	..	..	2		
Revd John Miles	..	..	1		
Mrs. J. Shaw	..	..	2		paid
C. Lushington	..	..	3	3	
W. H. Ormsby	..	..	2		
C. Molyneux	..	..	1		
Miss Ferrers	..	..	2		paid
W. Emmitt	..	..	2	2	
Anonymous	..	..	2	0	
Misses Gregg	..	..	2	2	
Miss Browne	..	..	1		
J. B. White & Bros	..	..	3		pd
Thos Slater	..	..	2		
W. T. Bird	..	..	2		pd.
Miss Hamilton	..	..	3		paid
Revd. J. A. Toole	..	..	2		paid
Mr. Hopgood	..	..	2		Paid
A Friend to the Widow		..	3	3	
Paid to Mr. Pegg					
Richd Green	..	..	£2		pd
Revd A. M. Campbell		..	3		
W. P. France	..	..	1		
W. M. N. Reilly	..	..	2	2	
Mrs. Forbes	..	..	2		pd
R. Gurney	..	..	1		
J. Spurling	..	..	2		pd
Geo. R. Ward	..	..	1		
Miss Brown	..	..	2		
Mrs Needham	..	..	2		Paid
Mr Davidson	..	..	£2		
Mrs. H. Scott Waring		..	3	3	
Mrs Hall	..	..	1	1	
Saml. Venables	..	..	2		
Revd. A. Taylor	..	..	1		
Revd. H. V. Le Bas	..	..	1		
Thomas Bunting	..	..	2		pd
Mrs & Miss Vullamy		..	3		
Revd. C. Smalley	..	..	5		
Miss Smalley	..	..	3		
Lord Brougham	..	..	2		

The two most notorious "screevers" of the present day are Mr. Sullivan and Mr. Johnson of Westminster, or as he is proud of being called, "Johnson the Schemer."

REFEREES

are generally keepers of low lodging-houses, brothels, &c., or small tradesmen who supply thieves and beggars with chandlery, &c. When applied to for the character of any of their friends and confederates, they give them an excellent recommendation—but are careful not to *overdo* it. With that highest sort of artfulness that conceals artfulness, they know when to stop, and seldom or never betray themselves by saying too much.

"Mrs. Simmons!" said one of them in answer to an application for character—"ah, yes, sir, I knowed her a good many years, and a very honest, hard-working, industrious, sober sort of a person I always knowed her to be, at least as far as *I* see—I never see nothing wrong in the woman for *my* part. The earliest-uppest, and downest-latest woman I ever see, and well she need be, with that family of hers—nine on 'em, and the eldest girl a idiot. When first I knew her, sir, her husband was alive, and then Susan—that's the idiot, sir, were a babe in arms—her husband was a bad man to her, sir—the way that man drunk and spent his money among all the lowest girls and corner-coves was awful to see,—I mean by corner-coves them sort of men who is always a standing at the corners of the streets and chaffing respectable folks a passing by—we call them corner-coves about here; but as to poor Mrs. Simmons, sir, that husband of hers *tret* her awful—though he's dead and gone now, poor man, and perhaps I have no right to speak ill on the dead. He had some money with her too—two hundred pound I heard—her father was a builder in a small way—and lived out towards Fulham—a very deserving woman I always found her, sir, and I have helped her a little bit myself, not much of course, for my circumstances would not allow of it; I've a wife and family myself—and I have often been wishful I could help her more, but what can a man do as has to pay his rent and taxes, and bring up his family respectable? When her last baby but two had the ring-worm we helped her now and then with a loaf of bread—poor thing—it ran right through the family, that ring-worm did—six on 'em had it at the same time, she told us—and then they took the measles—the most unluckiest family in catching things as goes about I never saw—but as to Mrs. Simmons herself, sir, poor thing—a more hard-workinger and honester woman I never, &c., &c., &c."

DISTRESSED OPERATIVE BEGGARS.

All beggars are ingenious enough to make capital of public events. They read the newspapers, judge the bent of popular sympathy, and decide on the "lay" to be adopted. The "Times" informs its readers that two or three hundred English navigators have been suddenly turned adrift in France. The native labourers object to the employment of aliens, and our stalwart countrymen have been subjected to insult as well as privation. The beggar's course is taken; he goes to Petticoat Lane, purchases a white smock frock, a purple or red plush waistcoat profusely ornamented with wooden buttons, a coloured cotton neckerchief, and a red nightcap. If procurable "in the Lane," he also buys a pair of coarse-ribbed grey worsted-stockings, and boots whose enormous weight is increased by several pounds of iron nails in their thick soles; even then he is not perfect, he seeks a rag and bottle and old iron shop—your genuine artist-beggar never asks for what is new, he prefers the worn, the used, the ragged and the rusty—and bargains for a spade. The proprietor of the shop knows perfectly well that his customer requires an article for show, not service, and they part with a mutual grin, and the next day every street swarms with groups of distressed navigators. Popular feeling is on their side, and halfpence shower round them. Meanwhile the poor fellows for whom all this generous indignation is evoked are waiting in crowds at a French port till the British Consul passed them over to their native soil as paupers.

The same tactics are pursued with manufactures. Beggars read the list of patents, and watch the effect of every fresh discovery in mechanics on the operatives of Lancashire and Yorkshire. A new machine is patented. So many hands are thrown out of work. So many beggars, who have never seen Lancashire, except when on the tramp, are heard in London. A strike takes place at several mills, pretended "hands" next day parade the streets. Even the variability of our climate is pressed into the "cadging" service; a frost locks up the rivers, and hardens the earth, rusty spades and gardening tools are in demand, and the indefatigable beggar takes the pavement in another "fancy dress." Every social shipwreck is watched and turned to account by these systematic land-wreckers, who have reduced false signals to a regular code, and beg by rule and line and chart and compass.

STARVED-OUT MANUFACTURERS

parade in gangs of four and five, or with squalid wives and a few children. They wear paper-caps and white aprons with "bibs" to them, or a sort of cross-barred pinafore, called in the manufacturing districts a "chequer-brat." Sometimes they make a "pitch," that is, stand face to face, turning their backs upon a heartless world, and sing. The well-known ditty of

"We are all the way from Manches-ter
And we've got no work to do!"

set to the tune of, "Oh let us be joyful," was first introduced by this class of beggars. Or they will carry tapes, stay-laces, and papers of buttons, and throw imploring looks from side to side, and beg by implication. Or they will cock their chins up in the air, so as to display the unpleasantly prominent apples in their bony throats, and drone a psalm. When they go out "on the blob," they make a long oration, not in the Lancashire or Yorkshire dialects, but in a cockney voice, of a strong Whitechapel flavour. The substance of the speech varies but slightly from the "patter" of the hand-loom weaver; indeed, the Nottingham "driz" or lace-man, the hand on strike, the distressed weaver, and the "operative" beggar, generally bear so strong a resemblance to each other, that they not only look like but sometimes positively *are* one and the same person.

UNEMPLOYED AGRICULTURISTS and FROZEN-OUT GARDENERS

are seen during a frost in gangs of from six to twenty. Two gangs generally "work" together, that is, while one gang begs at one end of a street, a second gang begs at the other. Their mode of procedure their "programme," is very simple. Upon the spades which they carry is chalked " frozen-out!" or " starving!" and they enhance the effect of this "slum or fakement," by shouting out sturdily "frozen out," "We're all frozen-out!" The gardeners differ from the agriculturists or "navvies" in their costume. They affect aprons and old straw hats, their manner is less demonstrative, and their tones less rusty and unmelodious. The "navvies" roar; the gardeners squeak. The navvies' petition is made loud and lustily, as by men used to work in clay and rock; the gardeners' voice is meek and mild, as of a gentle nature trained to tend on fruits and flowers. The young bulky, sinewy beggar plays navvy; the shrivelled, gravelly, pottering, elderly cadger performs gardener.

There can be no doubt that in times of hardship many honest labourers are forced into the streets to beg. A poor hard-working man, whose children cry to him for food, can feel no scruple in soliciting charity,—against such the writer of these pages would urge nothing; all credit to the motive that compels them unwillingly to ask alms; all honour to the feeling that prompts the listener to give. It is not the purpose of the author of this work to write down every mendicant an impostor, or every almsgiver a fool; on the contrary, he knows how much real distress, and how much real benevolence exist, and he would but step between the open hand of true charity, and the itching palm of the professional beggar, who stands between the misery that asks and the philanthropy that would relieve.

The winter of 1860-61 was a fine harvest for the "frozen out" impostors, some few of whom, happily, reaped the reward of their deserts in the police-courts. Three strong hearty men were brought up at one office; they said that they were starving, and they came from Horselydown; when searched six shillings and elevenpence were found upon them; they reiterated that they were starving and were out of work, on which the sitting magistrate kindly provided them with both food and employment, by sentencing them to seven days' hard labour.

The "profits" of the frozen-out gardener and agriculturist are very large, and generally quadruples the sum earned by honest labour. In the February of 1861, four of these "distressed navvies" went into a public-house to divide the "swag" they had procured by one day's shouting. Each had a handkerchief filled with bread and meat and cheese. They called for pots of porter and drank heartily, and when the reckoning was paid and the spoils equally divided, the share of each man was seven shillings.

The credulity of the public upon one point has often surprised me. A man comes out into the streets to say that he is starving, a few halfpence are thrown to him. If really hungry he would make for the nearest baker's shop; but no, he picks up the coppers, pockets them, and proclaims again that he is starving, though he has the means of obtaining food in his fingers. Not that this obvious anachronism stops the current of benevolence or the chink of coin upon the stones—the fainting, famished fellow walks leisurely up the street, and still bellows out in notes of thunder, "I am starving!" If one of my readers will try when faint and exhausted to produce the same tone in the open air, he will realize the impossibility of shouting and starving simultaneously.

HAND-LOOM WEAVERS AND OTHERS DEPRIVED OF THEIR LIVING BY MACHINERY.

As has been before stated, the regular beggar seizes on the latest pretext for a plausible tale of woe. Improvements in mechanics, and consequent cheapness to the many, are usually the causes of loss to the few. The sufferings of this minority is immediately turned to account by veteran cadgers, who rush to their wardrobes of well-chosen rags, attire themselves in appropriate costume, and ply their calling with the last grievance out. When unprovided with "patter," they seek the literati of their class, and buy a speech; this they partly commit to memory, and trust to their own ingenuity to improvise any little touches that may prove effective. Many "screevers, slum-scribblers, and fakement-dodgers" eke out a living by this sort of authorship. Real operatives seldom stir from their own locality. The sympathy of their fellows, their natural habits, and the occasional relief afforded by the parish bind them to their homes, and the "distressed weaver" is generally a spurious metropolitan production. The following is a copy of one of their prepared orations:

"My kind Christian Friends,

"We are poor working-men from —— which cannot obtain bread by our labour, owing to the new alterations and inventions which the master-manufacturers have introduced, which spares them the cost of employing hands, and does the work by machinery instead. Yes, kind friends, machinery and steam-engines now does the work, which formerly was done by our hands and work and labour. Our masters have turned us off, and we are without bread and knowing no other trade but that which we was born and bred to, we are compelled to ask your kind assistance, for which, be sure of it, we shall be ever grateful. As we have said, masters now employs machinery and steam-engines instead of men, forgetting that steam-engines have no families of wives or children, and consequently are not called on to provide for them. We are without bread to put into our mouths, also our wives and children are the same. Foreign competition has drove our masters to this step, and we working-men are the sufferers thereby. Kind friends, drop your compassion on us: the smallest trifle will be thankfully received, and God will bless you for the relief you give to us. May you never know what it is to be as we are now, drove from our work, and forced to come out into the streets to beg your charity from door to door. Have pity on us, for our situation is most wretched. Our wives and families are starving, our children cry to us for bread, and we have none to give them. Oh, my friends, look down on us with compassion. We are poor working-men, weavers from —— which cannot obtain bread by our labour owing to the new inventions in machinery, which, &c. &c. &c.

In concluding this section of our work, I would commend to the notice of my readers the following observations on almsgiving:—

The poor will never cease from the land. There always will be exceptional excesses and outbreaks of distress that no plan could have provided against, and there always will be those who stand with open palm to receive, in the face of heaven, our tribute of gratitude for our own happier lot. Yet there is a duty of the head as well as of the heart, and we are bound as much to use our reason as to minister of our abundance. The same heaven that has rewarded our labours, and filled our garners or our coffers, or at least, given us favour in the sight of merchants and bankers, has given us also brains, and consequently a charge to employ them. So we are bound to sift appeals, and consider how best to direct our benevolence. Whoever thinks that charity consists in mere giving, and that he has only to put his hand in his pocket, or draw a check in favour of somebody who is very much in want of money, and looks very grateful for favours to be received, will find himself taught better, if not in the school of adversity, at least by many a hard lesson of kindness thrown away, or perhaps very brutishly repaid. As animals have their habits, so there is a large class of mankind whose single cleverness is that of representing themselves as justly and naturally dependent on the assistance of others, who look paupers from their birth, who seek givers and forsake those who have given as naturally as a tree sends its roots into new soil and deserts the exhausted. It is the office of reason—reason improved by experience—to teach us not to waste our own interest and our resources on beings that will be content to live on our bounty, and will never return a moral profit to our charitable industry. The great opportunities or the mighty powers that heaven may have given us, it never meant to be lavished on mere human animals who eat, drink and sleep, and whose only instinct is to find out a new caterer when the old one is exhausted.

APPENDIX.

MAPS AND TABLES

ILLUSTRATING THE CRIMINAL STATISTICS OF EACH OF THE COUNTIES OF ENGLAND AND WALES IN 1851.

	PAGE
MAP SHOWING THE DENSITY OF THE POPULATION	451
Table of ditto	452
MAP SHOWING THE INTENSITY OF CRIMINALITY	455
Table of ditto	456
MAP SHOWING THE INTENSITY OF IGNORANCE	459
Table of ditto	460
Table of Ignorance among Criminals	462
Table of Relative Degrees of Criminality	464
Comparative Educational Tables	465
MAP SHOWING THE NUMBER OF ILLEGITIMATE CHILDREN	467
Table of ditto	468
MAP SHOWING THE NUMBER OF EARLY MARRIAGES	471
Table of ditto	472
MAP SHOWING THE NUMBER OF FEMALES	475
Table of ditto	476
MAP SHOWING COMMITTALS FOR RAPE	477
Table of ditto	479
MAP SHOWING COMMITTALS FOR CARNALLY ABUSING GIRLS	481
Table of ditto	482
MAP SHOWING COMMITTALS FOR DISORDERLY HOUSES	485
Table of ditto	486
MAP SHOWING CONCEALMENT OF BIRTHS	489
Table of ditto	490
MAP SHOWING ATTEMPTS AT MISCARRIAGE	493
Table of ditto	494
MAP SHOWING ASSAULTS WITH INTENT	497
Table of ditto	498
MAP SHOWING COMMITTALS FOR BIGAMY	499
Table of ditto	500
MAP SHOWING COMMITTALS FOR ABDUCTION	501
Table of ditto	502
MAP SHOWING THE CRIMINALITY OF FEMALES	503
Table of ditto	504

APPENDIX

MAPS AND TABLES

ILLUSTRATING THE VITAL STATISTICS OF EACH OF THE COUNTIES
OF ENGLAND AND WALES IN 1841.

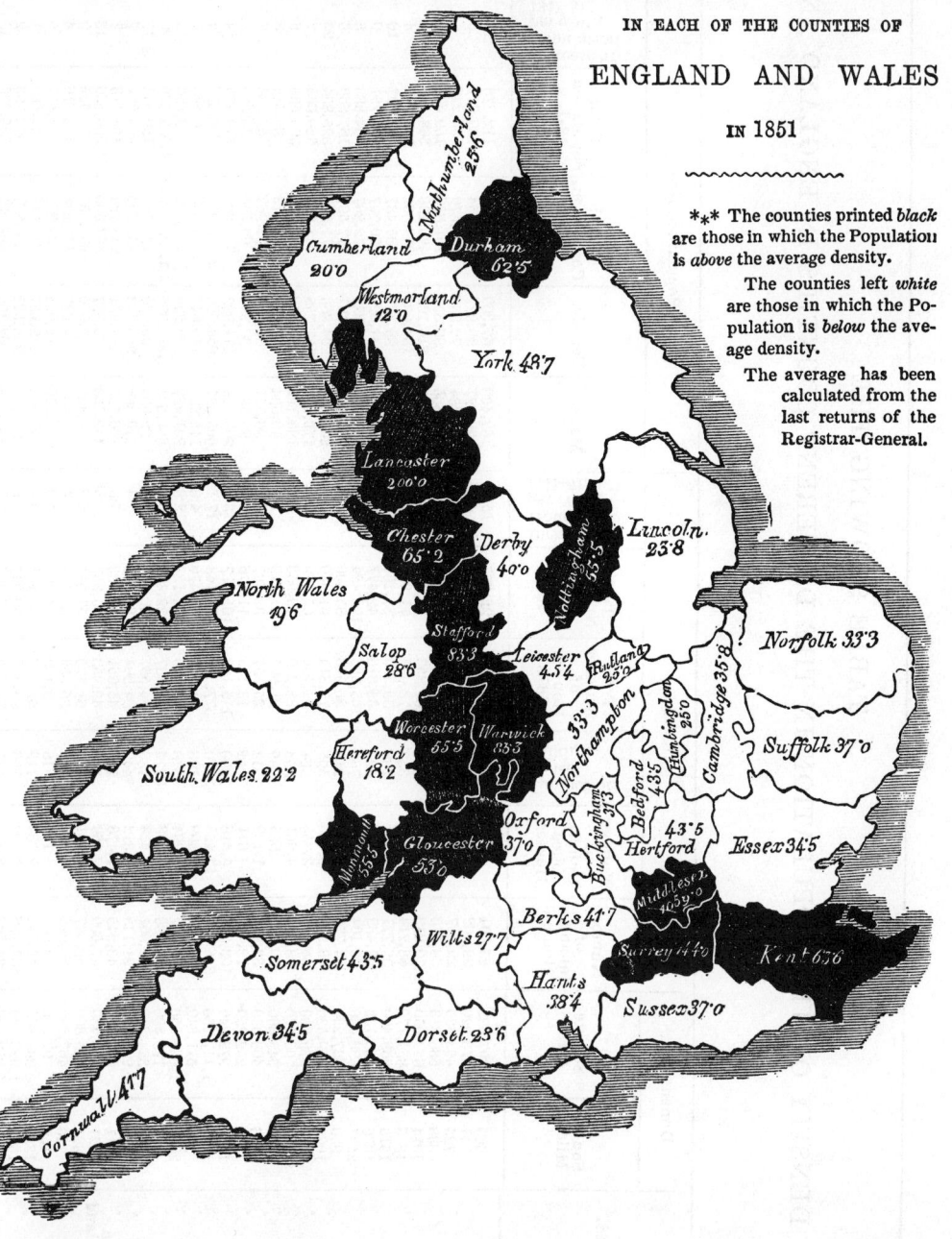

TABLE SHOWING THE DENSITY OF THE POPULATION IN THE DIFFERENT COUNTIES IN ENGLAND AND WALES IN 1851.

COUNTIES.	Dimensions.		Houses.						Population, 1851.					Density.			
	Square Miles.	Statute Acres.	Number of Inhabited Houses.	Number of Uninhabited Houses.	Number of Houses Building.	Total Number of Houses, 1851.	Total Number of Houses, 1841.	Increase of Houses per cent., 1841–51.	Males.	Females.	Total Population, 1851.	Total Population, 1841.	Increase of Population per cent., 1841–51.	No. of Persons to each 100 acres.	No. of acres to each Person.	No. of acres to each House.	No. of Persons to each Inhabited House.
Bedford	465	297,632	25,694	676	126	26,496	22,877	15·8	62,420	67,369	129,789	112,378	16	43·5	2·3	11·2	5·1
Berks	741	473,920	39,462	1,563	211	41,236	39,660	4·0	99,227	99,927	199,154	189,927	5	41·7	2·4	11·5	5·0
Bucks	725	463,880	29,217	1,103	89	30,409	28,860	5·4	70,784	72,886	143,670	138,248	4	31·3	3·2	15·2	4·9
Cambridge	838	536,313	38,773	1,777	204	40,754	35,799	13·8	96,351	96,351	191,856	169,638	13	35·8	3·1	13·1	4·9
Chester	1014	649,050	79,850	4,248	756	84,853	75,103	13·0	206,715	216,723	423,438	368,115	15	65·2	1·5	7·6	5·3
Cornwall	1336	854,770	68,214	4,528	353	73,095	71,913	1·6	171,979	184,683	356,662	343,265	4	41·7	2·4	11·6	5·2
Cumberland	1515	969,490	36,771	1,531	238	38,540	37,160	3·7	96,106	99,381	195,487	177,807	10	20·0	5·0	25·1	5·3
Derby	1036	663,180	52,482	2,411	423	55,316	49,477	1·2	129,379	131,328	260,707	239,791	9	40·0	2·5	12·6	5·0
Devon	2557	1,636,450	99,104	6,016	765	105,885	102,424	3·4	271,579	300,628	572,207	534,883	8	34·5	2·9	16·5	5·7
Dorset	980	627,220	34,771	1,554	218	36,543	35,400	3·2	85,816	91,781	177,597	167,689	6	28·6	3·5	17·1	5·1
Durham	1062	679,530	68,989	3,030	595	72,614	61,940	17·2	206,666	204,866	411,532	325,334	26	62·5	1·6	9·3	5·9
Essex	1530	979,000	68,383	3,353	364	72,100	65,570	10·0	172,161	171,755	343,916	320,605	7	34·5	2·9	13·5	5·0
Gloucester	1235	790,470	78,385	4,961	393	83,739	79,953	4·7	198,122	221,353	419,475	395,533	6	53·0	1·9	9·4	5·3
Hereford	850	543,800	20,453	983	69	21,505	21,119	1·8	49,694	49,418	99,112	96,515	3	18·2	5·5	25·3	4·8
Hertford	626	400,350	33,954	1,189	214	35,357	32,687	8·2	86,331	87,632	173,963	162,394	7	43·5	2·3	11·3	5·1
Hunts	379	242,250	12,472	641	62	13,175	11,676	12·8	29,984	30,336	60,320	55,565	9	25·0	4·0	18·3	4·8
Kent	1519	972,240	108,386	5,516	1290	115,192	101,717	13·3	308,115	311,092	619,207	540,275	14	63·6	1·6	8·4	5·7
Lancaster	1746	1,117,260	356,436	17,453	3470	377,359	322,148	17·1	1,005,627	1,058,286	2,063,913	1,696,377	22	200·0	·5	2·9	5·8
Leicester	799	511,340	49,968	1,599	198	51,765	49,470	4·6	115,295	119,643	234,938	220,263	7	45·4	2·2	9·9	4·7
Lincoln	2600	1,663,850	79,667	3,394	579	83,640	74,138	12·8	201,027	199,239	400,266	356,226	12	23·8	4·2	19·9	5·0
Middlesex	280	179,590	242,798	12,213	3276	258,287	222,443	16·1	885,614	1,010,096	1,895,710	1,582,538	20	1059·0	·09	·7	7·9
Monmouth	507	324,310	32,901	1,473	183	34,557	30,099	4·8	92,095	85,070	177,165	150,544	17	55·5	1·8	9·3	5·4
Norfolk	2019	1,292,300	91,143	3,312	449	94,904	88,378	7·4	210,360	223,443	433,803	404,971	7	33·3	3·0	13·6	4·8
Northampton	1011	646,810	43,945	1,478	238	45,661	42,358	7·8	106,533	107,251	213,784	198,518	7	33·3	3·0	14·1	4·9
Northumberland	1821	1,165,430	47,509	2,060	384	49,953	55,337	10·8*	149,158	154,377	303,535	265,636	13	25·6	3·9	23·3	6·3
Nottingham	822	525,800	59,427	1,481	267	61,175	57,611	6·2	144,428	150,010	294,438	270,535	9	55·5	2·7	8·6	5·0
Oxford	730	467,230	34,922	1,323	105	36,350	34,151	6·4	85,449	84,837	170,286	163,216	4	37·0	2·7	12·8	4·9
Rutland	152	97,500	4,961	153	18	5,132	4,899	4·8	12,270	12,002	24,272	23,151	5	25·0	4·0	19·0	4·9
Salop	1351	864,360	48,842	2,184	112	51,138	50,131	2·0	122,022	122,997	245,019	241,685	1	28·6	3·5	16·9	5·0
Somerset	1606	1,028,090	87,776	5,090	396	93,252	90,947	2·6	216,716	239,521	456,237	443,793	2	43·5	2·3	11·0	5·2
Southampton	1591	1,018,550	74,588	3,471	617	78,676	69,807	12·7	199,834	202,199	402,033	348,298	13	38·4	2·6	12·9	5·3
Stafford	1150	736,290	120,501	4,526	962	125,989	107,941	16·7	320,394	310,112	630,506	528,867	20	83·3	1·2	5·8	4·8
Suffolk	1436	918,760	69,479	3,098	424	73,001	67,050	8·9	165,267	170,724	335,991	314,467	7	37·0	2·7	12·5	4·8
Surrey	741	474,480	109,453	5,717	1663	116,838	101,121	15·6	325,155	359,650	684,805	586,816	17	144·0	·7	4·0	6·3

Warwick	887	567,930	4,609	977	103,909	90,868		14·6	5·7
Westmorland	759	485,990	530	94	11,871	11,783		·54	4·9
Wilts	1356	8,060	2,923	171	51,455	49,918		40·9	5·2
Worcester	718	9,710	2,753	362	55,170	49,371		16·8	4·9
York	5733	3,669,510	16,469	3244	378,417	341,147		8·5	5·0
Travelling						5,016		9·7	4·9
North Wales	3194	2,044,160	3,720	522	87,333	85,847		23·2	4·9
South Wales	4231	2,707,840	5,269	844	125,620	115,822		21·5	5·1
TOTAL FOR ENGLAND AND WALES	57,067	36,522,615	152,898	26,534	3,460,393	3,144,626		10·5	5·5

* In 1841 *Flats* were returned in Northumberland as separate Houses; this accounts for the decrease in 1851.

LIST OF COUNTIES IN THE ORDER OF THE DENSITY OF THEIR POPULATION, AS SHOWN BY THE NUMBER OF PERSONS TO EVERY 100 ACRES.

Counties above the Average.
Middlesex .... 1059·0
Lancaster .... 200·0
Surrey .... 144·0
Stafford .... 83·3
York, West Riding .... 83·3
Berks .... 65·2
Chester .... 63·6
Kent .... 62·5
Durham .... 55·5
Worcester .... 55·5
Warwick .... 83·3
Nottingham .... 55·5
Monmouth .... 55·5
Gloucester .... 53·0
Average for England and Wales .... 49·7

Counties below the Average.
Leicester .... 45·4
Bedford .... 43·5
Hertford .... 43·5
Somerset .... 43·5
Derby .... 41·7
Cornwall .... 40·0
Southampton .... 38·4
Oxford .... 37·0
Suffolk .... 37·0
Sussex .... 37·0
Cambridge .... 35·8
Devon .... 34·5
Essex .... 34·5
Norfolk .... 33·3
York, East Riding .... 33·3
Bucks .... 31·3
Dorset .... 28·6
Shropshire .... 28·6
Wilts .... 27·7
Northumberland .... 25·6
Huntingdon .... 25·0
Rutland .... 23·8
Lincoln .... 22·2
South Wales .... 20·0
Cumberland .... 20·0
North Wales .... 19·6
Hereford .... 18·2
York, North Riding .... 15·2
Westmorland .... 12·0

COMPARISON OF THE DENSITY OF THE POPULATION IN 1841 AND 1851.

	1841.	1851.
Agricultural Counties.		
Lincoln	21·7	23·8
Rutland	22·7	25·0
Huntingdon	25·0	25·0
Cambridge	30·3	35·8
Essex	35·7	34·5
Sussex	32·2	37·0
Hereford	20·8	18·2
Agricultural and Sub-Manufacturing Counties.		
Westmorland	11·6	12·0
Norfolk	32·2	33·3
Suffolk	33·3	37·0
Hertford	40·0	43·5
Bedford	37·0	43·5
Buckingham	33·3	31·3
Northampton	31·2	33·3
Oxford	34·4	37·0
Berks	34·4	41·7
Hants	47·6	38·4
Wilts	30·3	27·7
Dorset	27·7	28·6
Somerset	41·6	43·5
Devon	32·2	34·5
Sub-Agricultural and Sub-Manufacturing County.		
Gloucester	55·5	26·1
Manufacturing Counties.		
Lancaster	166·6	200·0
Yorkshire	42·6	48·7
Chester	58·8	65·2
Nottingham	47·6	55·5
Leicester	43·0	45·4
Warwick	71·4	83·3
Worcester	52·6	55·5
Mining Counties.		
Durham	47·6	62·5
Cornwall	41·6	41·7
Manufacturing and Sub-Mining Counties.		
Derby	41·6	40·0
Stafford	71·4	83·3
Agricultural and Sub-Mining Counties.		
Shropshire	28·5	28·6
North Wales	19·3	19·6
South Wales	19·0	22·2
Sub-Agricultural and Sub-Mining Counties.		
Northumberland	21·2	25·6
Cumberland	18·5	20·0
Monmouth	43·0	55·5
Metropolitan County.		
Middlesex	1000·0	1059·0
Sub-Metropolitan Counties.		
Surrey	125·0	141·0
Kent	55·5	63·6

NOTE.—An *Agricultural* county has *more than* 10 per cent., and a *Sub-Agricultural* county *less than* 10 per cent. of its population employed in agriculture. A *Manufacturing* county has *more than* 15 per cent., and a *Sub-Manufacturing* county *less than* 15 per cent. of its population employed in manufacture. A *Mining* county has *more than* 5 per cent., and a *Sub-Mining* county *less than* 5 per cent. of its population employed in mining.

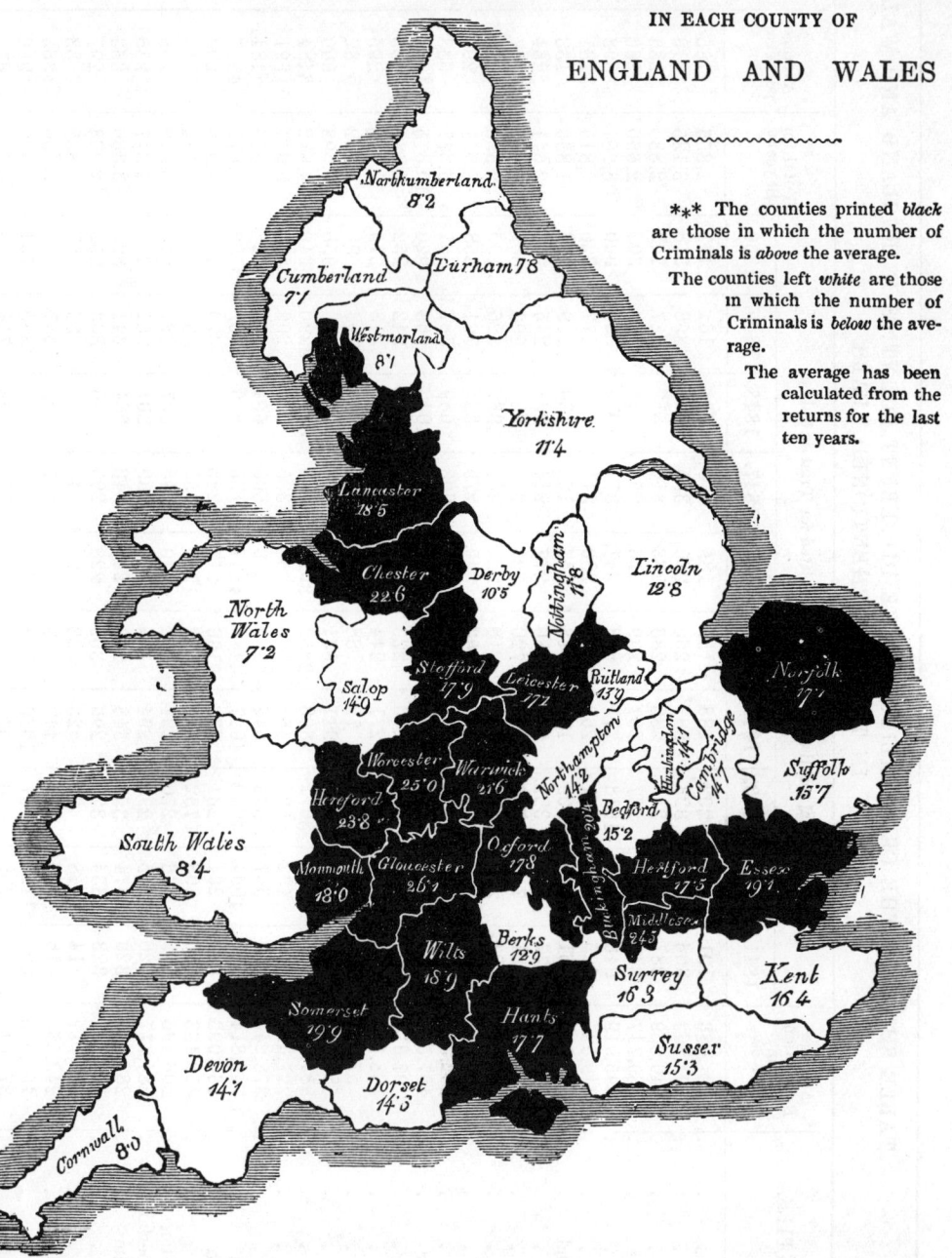

TABLE SHOWING THE CRIMINALITY OF THE DIFFERENT COUNTIES IN ENGLAND AND WALES IN THE UNDERMENTIONED YEARS.

COUNTIES.	Average Population from 1841-50.	Total number of Persons committed for Trial or Bailed.										Total for 10 years.	Average per Year	Proportion to the Population	Number of Criminals to every 10,000 of Population.
		1841.	1842.	1843.	1844.	1845.	1846.	1847.	1848.	1849.	1850.				
Bedford	121,083	191	229	202	188	155	185	178	204	162	161	1,855	185	1 in 654	15·2
Berks	194,763	306	333	328	287	260	250	335	360	358	318	3,135	313	,, 622	16·0
Bucks	140,959	287	277	313	280	286	283	315	310	287	242	2,880	288	,, 489	20·4
Cambridge	180,747	240	241	257	297	239	276	255	244	309	302	2,660	266	,, 679	14·7
Chester	395,919	943	1086	1018	777	688	767	871	1070	861	900	8,981	898	,, 440	22·6
Cornwall	349,991	295	282	301	269	272	280	341	272	277	226	2,815	281	,, 1245	8·0
Cumberland	186,762	151	115	109	138	118	147	210	130	159	146	1,333	133	,, 1404	7·1
Derby	250,249	277	322	322	279	186	277	214	264	245	255	2,641	264	,, 947	10·5
Devon	554,738	687	716	740	715	720	721	949	924	893	807	7,872	787	,, 704	14·1
Dorset	172,736	284	241	252	203	218	225	307	287	326	190	2,533	253	,, 682	14·6
Durham	368,787	215	266	300	376	203	249	279	334	321	358	2,901	290	,, 1271	7·8
Essex	332,363	647	758	710	596	554	602	603	689	587	631	6,377	638	,, 520	19·1
Gloucester	407,504	1236	1252	1186	1071	929	884	1092	1042	1063	920	10,675	1067	,, 381	26·1
Hereford	97,813	245	259	238	230	226	158	212	270	242	252	2,332	233	,, 419	23·8
Hertford	168,178	319	338	265	271	244	243	291	348	318	315	2,952	295	,, 570	17·5
Hunts	57,942	62	68	68	79	88	81	89	104	93	90	822	82	,, 706	14·1
Kent	585,249	962	1155	977	911	831	815	889	1020	980	958	9,598	960	,, 609	16·4
Lancaster	1,881,261	3987	4497	3677	2893	2852	3072	3456	3778	3290	3340	34,842	3484	,, 539	18·5
Leicester	227,621	466	492	509	481	328	358	335	346	299	300	3,914	391	,, 582	17·1
Lincoln	378,246	349	507	563	542	389	419	506	504	529	528	4,836	484	,, 781	12·8
Middlesex	1,740,814	3586	4094	4260	4027	4440	4641	5175	4856	3861	3732	42,672	4267	,, 407	24·5
Monmouth	164,093	364	264	261	278	196	217	282	298	370	433	2,963	296	,, 554	18·0
Norfolk	419,463	666	808	782	788	642	720	751	689	633	705	7,184	718	,, 584	17·1
Northampton	206,496	342	346	270	294	302	270	243	307	327	248	2,949	295	,, 699	14·2
Northumberland	284,777	226	245	290	294	189	169	189	201	261	283	2,347	235	,, 1211	8·2
Nottingham	282,584	329	374	353	348	267	286	343	364	341	325	3,330	333	,, 848	11·8
Oxford	166,751	323	334	328	296	309	228	299	296	303	252	2,968	297	,, 591	17·8
Rutland	23,711	14	48	39	23	28	26	41	52	35	27	333	33	,, 718	13·9
Salop	243,352	416	470	534	449	308	227	267	305	347	307	3,630	363	,, 670	14·9
Somerset	452,515	991	1148	967	1039	873	701	774	888	885	754	9,020	902	,, 501	19·9
Southampton	377,040	677	702	676	517	619	608	737	728	751	686	6,701	670	,, 562	17·7
Stafford	579,686	1059	1485	1175	885	717	851	1028	1120	1009	1053	10,382	1038	,, 558	17·9
Suffolk	325,336	482	527	585	630	407	471	505	495	537	472	5,111	511	,, 636	15·7
Surrey	635,917	923	1017	867	941	942	958	1315	1296	1109	1030	10,398	1040	,, 611	16·3

Sussex														
Warwick	320,944		559	550	493	409	409	468	522	546	502	480	4918	492 ,, 652	15·3
	444,558		1046	1003	1045	894	769	799	998	1257	910	880	9601	960 ,, 463	21·6
Westmoreland	57,494		33	39	44	24	46	74	33	47	57	70	467	47 ,, 1223	8·1
Wilts	241,887		506	548	464	432	379	436	502	465	452	386	4570	457 ,, 529	18·9
Worcester	244,574		566	609	679	603	563	535	620	681	653	607	6116	612 ,, 399	25·0
York	1,686,461		1895	2598	2304	1691	1417	1560	1794	2036	2022	1915	19,232	1923 ,, 876	11·4
North Wales	396,161		251	279	294	283	269	220	307	332	338	316	2889	289 ,, 1370	7·2
South Wales	568,430		377	387	546	514	426	350	471	590	514	613	4788	479 ,, 1186	8·4
TOTAL FOR ENGLAND AND WALES	16,918,458		27,760	31,309	29,591	26,542	24,303	25,107	28,833	30,349	27,816	26,813	278,423	27,842 ,, 607	16·4

THE YEARS OF CRIME.

Years.	Number of Criminal Offenders.	Population.	Number of Criminals to every 10,000 people.	Years.	Number of Criminal Offenders.	Population.	Number of Criminals to every 10,000 people.
1811	5,337	10,150,615	5·2	1831	19,647	13,897,187	14·1
1812	6,576	10,332,441	6·3	1832	20,829	14,088,142	14·7
1813	7,164	10,515,267	6·8	1833	20,072	14,299,097	14·0
1814	6,390	10,689,093	5·9	1834	22,451	14,500,052	15·4
1815	7,818	10,881,919	7·3	1835	20,731	14,701,007	14·1
1816	9,091	11,064,745	8·2	1836	20,984	14,901,962	14·1
1817	13,932	11,247,571	11·5	1837	23,612	15,102,917	15·6
1818	13,567	11,430,397	11·8	1838	23,094	15,303,872	15·1
1819	14,254	11,613,223	12·2	1839	24,443	15,504,827	15·7
1820	13,710	11,796,049	11·6	1840	27,187	15,705,782	17·3
Total for 10 years	97,839	109,630,320		Total in 10 years	223,050	148,114,825	
Average ditto.	9,783	10,963,032	8·9	Average ditto	22,305	14,811,482	15·0
1821	13,115	11,978,875	10·9	1841	27,750	15,914,148	17·4
1822	12,241	12,170,706	10·0	1842	31,309	16,115,010	19·4
1823	12,263	12,362,537	9·9	1843	29,591	16,315,872	18·1
1824	13,698	12,554,368	10·9	1844	26,542	16,516,734	16·0
1825	14,437	12,746,199	11·3	1845	24,303	16,717,596	14·5
1826	16,164	12,938,030	12·5	1846	25,107	16,918,458	14·9
1827	17,924	13,129,861	13·6	1847	28,833	17,119,320	16·8
1828	16,564	13,321,692	12·4	1848	30,349	17,320,182	17·5
1829	18,675	13,531,523	13·8	1849	27,816	17,521,044	15·9
1830	18,107	13,705,354	13·2	1850	26,813	17,721,906	15·1
Total for 10 years	153,188	128,421,145		Total for 10 years	278,413	168,180,270	
Average ditto	15,318	12,842,114	11·9	Average ditto	27,841	16,818,027	**16·5**

LIST OF COUNTIES IN THE ORDER OF THEIR CRIMINALITY, AS SHOWN BY THE NUMBER OF CRIMINALS TO EVERY 10,000 OF THE POPULATION.

Counties above the Average in Crime.		Counties below the Average in Crime.	
Gloucester	26·1	Kent	16·4
Worcester	25·0	Surrey	16·3
Middlesex	24·5	Berks	16·0
Hereford	23·8	Suffolk	15·7
Chester	22·6	Sussex	15·3
Warwick	21·6	Bedford	15·2
Bucks	20·4	Salop	14·9
Somerset	19·9	Cambridge	14·7
Dorset	19·1	Northampton	14·6
Essex	18·9	Devon	14·2
Wilts	18·9	Rutland	14·1
Lancaster	18·5	Lincoln	13·9
Monmouth	18·0	Nottingham	12·8
Stafford	17·9	York	11·8
Oxford	17·8	Derby	11·4
Southampton	17·7	Leicester	10·5
Hertford	17·5	Northumberland	8·4
Leicester	17·1	Westmorland	8·2
Norfolk	17·1	Cornwall	8·1
Average for all England and Wales	16·4	Durham	8·0
		North Wales	7·8
		Cumberland	7·2
			7·1

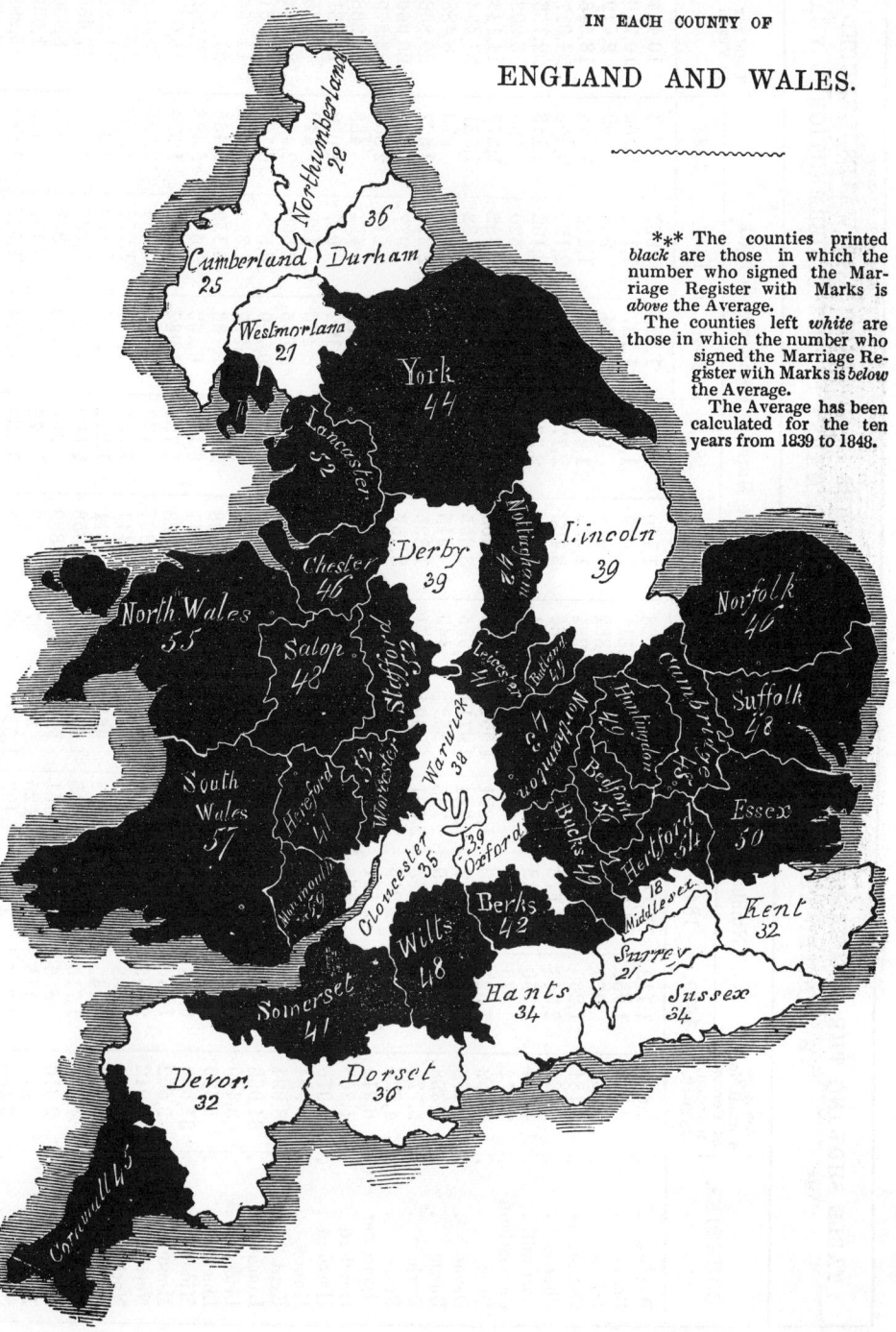

TABLE SHOWING THE IGNORANCE OF THE DIFFERENT COUNTIES IN ENGLAND AND WALES, DEDUCED FROM THE NUMBER WHO SIGNED THE MARRIAGE REGISTER WITH MARKS IN THE UNDERMENTIONED YEARS.

COUNTIES.	Average Annual No. of Persons married, 1839-48.	Number of Males and Females who signed the Marriage Register with Marks.										Total for 10 Years.	Annual Average.	No. of Persons who signed with Marks in every 100 married.	Per Cent. above and below the Average.
		1839.	1840.	1841.	1842.	1843.	1844.	1845.	1846.	1847.	1848.				
Bedford	1,850	1,112	1,148	956	921	1,028	1,110	1,095	1,124	957	1,003	10,454	1,045	56	+40·0
Berks	2,588	1,036	1,131	1,061	1,063	1,111	1,079	1,070	1,137	1,118	1,164	10,970	1,097	42	+ 5·0
Bucks	1,920	979	1,008	820	918	882	918	975	1,074	906	999	9,479	948	49	+22·5
Cambridge	2,784	1,269	1,372	1,495	1,389	1,281	1,330	1,471	1,398	1,213	1,328	13,546	1,355	45	+12·5
Chester	5,160	2,343	2,510	2,350	2,096	2,366	2,403	2,777	2,608	2,121	2,503	24,017	2,408	46	+15·0
Cornwall	4,894	2,150	2,148	2,128	2,312	2,284	2,141	2,338	2,407	2,102	2,146	22,156	2,216	45	+12·5
Cumberland	2,072	470	563	527	539	506	500	581	647	520	350	5,203	520	25	*37·5
Derby	3,652	1,521	1,490	1,321	1,061	1,351	1,455	1,642	1,544	1,382	1,377	14,144	1,414	39	* 2·5
Devon	8,678	2,603	1,817	2,744	2,971	2,995	3,055	3,312	3,224	2,782	1,981	27,484	2,748	32	*20·0
Dorset	2,358	725	930	785	852	449	945	1,033	905	941	923	8,488	849	36	*10·0
Durham	5,770	1,900	2,083	2,001	1,830	1,771	1,825	2,375	2,378	2,376	2,327	20,866	2,087	36	*10·0
Essex	4,228	1,964	2,215	2,103	2,062	2,110	2,157	2,246	2,163	1,977	1,963	20,960	2,096	50	+25·0
Gloucester	6,918	2,329	2,541	2,347	2,197	2,393	2,277	2,578	2,698	2,215	2,304	23,879	2,388	35	*12·5
Hereford	1,268	462	463	522	548	609	516	598	576	424	488	5,206	521	41	+ 2·5
Hertford	1,976	1,189	1,045	1,057	954	1,083	1,038	1,153	1,102	947	1,013	10,581	1,058	54	+35·0
Hunts	904	391	465	453	446	439	413	434	466	438	440	4,385	439	49	+22·5
Kent	8,094	2,431	2,382	2,476	2,488	2,556	2,502	2,944	2,855	2,569	2,481	25,684	2,568	32	*20·0
Lancaster	34,068	16,411	15,793	16,096	14,626	17,820	19,850	22,177	20,709	16,588	18,161	178,231	17,823	52	+30·0
Leicester	3,460	1,494	1,504	1,281	1,189	1,416	1,505	1,518	1,579	1,329	1,441	14,256	1,426	41	+ 2·5
Lincoln	5,530	1,944	2,209	2,174	2,082	1,959	1,998	2,232	2,166	2,159	2,436	21,359	2,136	39	* 2·5
Middlesex	31,590	5,134	5,569	5,242	5,045	5,416	6,141	6,456	6,163	5,666	5,433	56,265	5,627	18	*55·0
Monmouth	2,562	1,646	1,697	1,283	1,091	1,110	1,228	1,722	1,982	1,720	1,574	15,053	1,505	59	+47·5
Norfolk	6,042	2,485	2,772	2,514	2,832	2,816	2,901	3,120	2,964	2,783	2,855	28,042	2,804	46	+15·0
Northampton	3,194	1,338	1,489	1,377	1,220	1,404	1,441	1,504	1,467	1,253	1,332	13,825	1,383	43	+ 7·5
Northumberland	4,094	1,149	1,264	1,108	965	1,013	811	1,214	1,244	1,190	1,328	11,286	1,129	28	*30·0
Nottingham	4,168	1,715	1,724	1,645	1,642	1,742	1,953	2,000	1,834	1,635	1,760	17,650	1,765	42	+ 5·0
Oxford	2,316	826	961	951	957	929	889	831	880	869	843	8,936	894	39	* 2·5
Rutland	216	115	92	125	99	97	69	73	99	152	118	1,039	104	49	+22·5
Salop	3,180	1,647	1,568	1,497	1,533	1,392	1,496	1,428	1,544	1,532	1,661	15,298	1,530	48	+20·0
Somerset	6,226	2,300	2,608	2,705	2,643	2,654	2,643	2,598	2,632	2,183	2,360	25,326	2,533	41	+ 2·5
Southampton	5,768	1,614	1,801	2,049	1,959	1,910	1,977	2,181	2,185	2,019	1,875	19,570	1,957	34	*15·0
Stafford	8,292	3,886	4,045	3,552	3,065	3,335	3,937	5,091	4,920	6,423	5,263	43,517	4,352	52	+30·0
Suffolk	4,728	2,172	2,253	2,349	2,057	2,124	2,304	2,436	2,389	2,325	2,354	22,857	2,286	48	+20·0

Sussex	4,268	1,452	1,480	1,400	1,364	1,443	1,427	1,534	1,594	1,512	2,218	21	*47·5
Warwick	6,494	1,512	2,470	2,294	2,052	2,415	2,516	2,958	2,670	2,870	1,458	34	*15·0
Westmorland	780	195	191	177	185	193	225	321	237	220	2,461	38	+ ·5·0
Wilts	3,236	1,495	1,603	1,550	1,487	1,522	1,527	1,642	1,685	1,481	208	27	*32·5
Worcester	5,536	3,201	3,098	2,934	2,588	2,528	2,974	4,192	3,744	1,871	1,552	48	†20·0
York	26,664	11,439	11,899	10,726	10,503	11,099	12,970	12,688	13,395	11,797	2,877	52	†30·0
North Wales	5,164	3,028	3,022	2,999	2,925	2,694	2,737	3,219	2,916	2,904	11,845	44	†10·0
South Wales	8,152	4,382	4,532	4,378	4,093	4,190	4,617	5,565	4,978	4,703	2,840	55	†37·5
											4,625	57	†42·5
Total for England and Wales	261,340	100,616	104,335	99,684	94,996	101,235	107,985	117,633	118,894	104,306	105,937	1,050,907	105,091	40

LIST OF COUNTIES IN THE ORDER OF THEIR IGNORANCE, AS SHOWN BY THE NUMBER WHO SIGNED THE MARRIAGE REGISTER WITH MARKS IN EVERY 100 PERSONS MARRIED.

Counties above the Average, or most Ignorant.		Counties below the Average, or least Ignorant.	
Monmouth	59	Derby	39
South Wales	57	Lincoln	39
Bedford	56	Oxford	39
North Wales	55	Warwick	38
Hertford	54	Dorset	36
Lancaster	52	Durham	36
Stafford	52	Gloucester	35
Worcester	52	Southampton	34
Essex	50	Sussex	34
Bucks	49	Devon	32
Hunts	49	Kent	32
Rutland	49	Northumberland	28
Salop	48	Westmorland	27
Suffolk	48	Cumberland	25
Wilts	48	Surrey	21
Chester	46	Middlesex	18
Norfolk	46		
Cambridge	45		
Cornwall	45		
York	44		
Northampton	43		
Berks	42	Average for England and Wales	40
Nottingham	42		
Hereford	41		
Leicester	41		
Somerset	41		

THE CRIME AND IGNORANCE OF THE SEVERAL COUNTIES COMPARED.

	Percentage above and below the Average.				Percentage above and below the average.		
	In No. of Criminals.	In No. signing Register with Marks.	In No. of Criminals unable to read and write.		In No. of Criminals.	In No. signing Register with Marks.	In No. of Criminals unable to read and write.
Counties having great Crime and great Ignorance.				*Counties having great Crime and little Ignorance.*			
Worcester	†52·4	†36·0	† 8·5	Gloucester	†59·1	*12·5	*11·9
Hereford	†45·1	† 2·5	†41·5	Middlesex	†49·4	*55·0	*21·7
Chester	†37·8	†15·0	† 9·4	Oxford	† 8·5	* 2·5	* ·9
Bucks	†24·4	†22·5	† 6·9	Southampton	† 7·9	*15·0	*13·5
Somerset	†21·3	† 2·5	† 7·2				
Essex	†16·4	†25·0	†24·2				
Lancaster	†12·8	†30·0	†22·0				
Stafford	† 6·7	†35·0	†29·8				
Hertford	† 4·2	†15·0	†19·1				
Norfolk							
Counties having little Crime and little Ignorance.				*Counties having little Crime and great Ignorance.*			
Cumberland	*56·7	*37·5	*15·4	North Wales	†20·4	†37·5	†20·4
Westmorland	*50·6	*32·5	*38·6	South Wales	*48·7	†42·5	†14·7
Northumberland	*50·0	*30·0	*19·1	Hants	*14·0	†22·5	† 1·9
Derby	*36·0	* 2·5	*93·5	Northampton	*13·4	† 7·5	† 1·5
Lincoln	*22·0	* 2·5	*14·8	Salop	* 9·1	†20·0	†25·8
Devon	*14·0	*20·0	*12·9	Bedford	* 7·3	†40·0	†28·3
Sussex	* 6·7	*15·0	* 4·0	Suffolk	* 4·2	†20·0	† 8·1
Surrey	* ·6	*47·5	*13·8				
Counties having great Crime, and in which the Ignorance Tests are contradictory.				*Counties having little Crime, and in which the Ignorance Tests are contradictory.*			
Warwick	†31·7	* 5·0	† 9·7	Durham	*51·8	*10·0	† 1·5
Wilts	†15·2	†20·0	*20·4	Cornwall	*51·2	*12·5	* 6·9
Monmouth	† 9·7	†47·0	*12·2	York	*30·5	*10·0	* 8·5
Stafford	† 9·1	†30·0	* 3·4	Nottingham	*28·0	* 5·0	* 5·6
Leicester	† 4·2	† 2·5	*11·6	Berks	*21·4	*22·5	* 4·7
				Rutland	*15·2	*12·5	* 2·5
				Cambridge	*10·3	*10·0	* 4·7
				Dorset	*10·0	*20·0	† 6·3
				Kent			

N.B. The † prefixed to a number denotes that it is *above*, the * that it is *below* the average by the percentage which it expresses.

TABLE SHOWING THE AMOUNT OF IGNORANCE AMONGST THE CRIMINALS IN THE DIFFERENT COUNTIES OF ENGLAND AND WALES IN THE UNDERMENTIONED YEARS.

COUNTIES.	Average Annual Number of Criminals from 1839-48.	Number of Criminals who could neither read nor write.										Total for 10 years.	Average Number per Year.	No. of Criminals who can neither read nor write in every 100.	Per Cent. above and below the Average. † denotes above. * denotes below.
		1839.	1840.	1841.	1842.	1843.	1844.	1845.	1846.	1847.	1848.				
Bedford	181	39	72	90	110	80	81	64	66	64	79	745	74	40·8	†28·3
Berks	313	103	121	97	113	48	75	79	88	100	127	951	95	30·3	* 4·7
Bucks	285	89	107	87	112	113	91	95	89	105	82	970	97	34·0	† 6·9
Cambridge	249	79	65	90	78	80	77	69	78	75	81	772	77	30·9	* 2·5
Chester	904	285	370	334	333	336	259	230	296	336	371	3,150	315	34·8	† 9·4
Cornwall	294	81	95	82	80	82	65	90	89	125	86	875	87	29·6	† 6·9
Cumberland	130	39	30	26	45	37	41	21	46	32	37	354	35	26·9	*15·4
Derby	263	74	48	66	92	77	61	53	63	41	64	642	64	24·3	*23·5
Devon	755	143	154	146	144	204	235	211	248	307	295	2,087	209	27·7	*12·9
Dorset	258	84	107	96	75	95	73	83	64	93	84	864	86	33·3	† 4·7
Durham	260	70	33	56	88	96	138	66	78	97	120	842	84	32·3	† 1·5
Essex	638	213	297	302	295	290	219	188	242	254	224	2,524	252	39·5	†24·2
Gloucester	1067	326	322	370	414	330	211	210	235	293	276	2,987	299	28·0	*11·9
Hereford	229	102	120	121	107	107	83	96	64	112	115	1,027	103	45·0	†41·5
Hertford	288	147	133	146	119	98	111	90	82	121	148	1,195	119	41·3	†29·8
Hunts	77	20	33	21	22	26	27	32	14	21	36	252	25	32·4	† 1·9
Kent	942	348	251	353	371	330	301	301	267	305	368	3,195	319	33·8	† 6·3
Lancaster	3462	1143	1391	1556	1947	1423	992	1023	1097	1283	1389	13,444	1344	38·8	†22·0
Leicester	419	141	159	135	141	137	135	87	96	66	82	1,179	118	28·1	*11·6
Lincoln	458	117	119	99	133	131	134	112	125	136	137	1,243	124	27·1	*14·8
Middlesex	4230	927	882	980	800	1033	933	1230	1177	1280	1322	10,564	1056	24·9	*21·7
Monmouth	272	83	94	112	73	79	67	34	45	81	95	763	76	27·9	*12·2
Norfolk	727	285	266	258	308	284	290	254	271	293	247	2,756	276	37·9	†19·1
Northampton	291	96	92	118	111	92	90	107	86	56	93	941	94	32·3	† 1·5
Northumberland	214	24	57	45	58	75	96	44	45	49	57	550	55	25·7	*19·1
Nottingham	333	104	108	91	102	112	115	79	88	95	106	1,000	100	30·0	* 5·6
Oxford	308	113	134	106	99	117	84	93	64	90	73	973	97	31·5	† ·9
Rutland	29	4	—	1	11	13	8	12	8	15	17	89	9	31·0	* 2·5
Salop	367	136	176	182	173	215	164	104	89	112	119	1,470	147	40·0	†25·8
Somerset	935	281	410	352	363	333	360	298	224	266	313	3,200	320	34·1	† 7·2
Southampton	664	215	207	188	186	159	126	153	193	213	194	1,834	183	27·5	†13·5
Stafford	1017	233	271	324	465	313	304	212	263	354	387	3,126	313	30·7	† 3·4
Suffolk	511	187	201	184	188	195	198	113	159	159	179	1,763	176	34·4	† 8·1

Sussex . . .	498	173	173	176	191	143	111	97	151	136	168	1,519	152	30·5	* 4·0
Warwick . . .	959	293	396	403	363	392	267	237	234	324	440	3,349	335	34·9	+ 9·7
Westmorland . .	41	8	6	5	5	6	3	11	20	5	9	78	8	19·5	*38·6
Wilts . . .	462	132	145	146	127	116	100	85	101	118	104	1,174	117	25·3	*20·4
Worcester . . .	594	169	275	244	250	242	204	210	195	229	232	2,250	225	34·5	+ 8·5
York . . .	1878	553	572	531	776	621	444	378	453	528	619	5,475	547	29·1	* 8·5
North Wales . .	274	84	110	92	122	116	107	81	79	126	136	1,053	105	38·3	+20·4
South Wales . .	435	108	136	135	138	174	188	183	108	187	240	1,593	159	36·5	+14·7
TOTAL FOR ENGLAND AND WALES .	27,542	8196	9058	9220	10,128	9173	7901	7438	7698	9050	9691	87,553	8755	31·8	

LIST OF COUNTIES IN THE ORDER OF THE IGNORANCE AMONGST THEIR CRIMINALS, AS SHOWN BY THE NUMBER OF PERSONS WHO COULD NEITHER READ NOR WRITE IN EVERY 100 CRIMINALS.

Counties above the Average.		*Counties below the Average.*	
Hereford	45·0	Oxford	31·5
Hertford	41·3	Rutland	31·0
Bedford	40·8	Cambridge	30·9
Salop	40·0	Stafford	30·7
Essex	39·5	Sussex	30·5
Lancaster	38·8	Berks	30·3
North Wales	38·3	Nottingham	30·0
Norfolk	37·9	Cornwall	29·6
South Wales	36·5	York	29·1
Warwick	34·9	Leicester	28·1
Chester	34·8	Gloucester	28·0
Worcester	34·5	Monmouth	27·9
Suffolk	34·4	Devon	27·7
Somerset	34·1	Southampton	27·5
Bucks	34·0	Surrey	27·4
Kent	33·8	Lincoln	27·1
Dorset	33·3	Cumberland	26·9
Hunts	32·4	Northumberland	25·7
Durham	32·3	Wilts	25·3
Northampton	32·3	Middlesex	24·9
		Derby	24·3
Average for England and Wales	31·8	Westmorland	19·5

THE COUNTIES ARRANGED CRIMINALLY AND TOPOGRAPHICALLY (*to show the local association of crime*).

DIVISION I.—*Northern, Welsh, and Cornish Counties.*

	No. of Criminals in 10,000.
Cumberland	7·1
Durham	7·8
Westmorland	8·1
Northumberland	8·2
North Wales	7·2
South Wales	8·4
Cornwall	8·0

DIVISION II.—*York and N. Midland Counties.*

York	11·4
Derby	10·5
Nottingham	11·8
Lincoln	12·8
Rutland	13·9

DIVISION III.—*S. Midland & Eastern Counties.*

Hunts	14·1
Northampton	14·2
Cambridge	14·7
Bedford	15·2
Suffolk	15·7
Norfolk	17·1
Essex	19·1
Oxford	17·8
Herts	17·5
Bucks	20·4

DIVISION IV. — *South Eastern and South Western.*

	No. of Criminals in 10,000.
Berks	12·9
Devon	14·1
Dorset	14·8
Sussex	15·3
Surrey	16·3
Kent	16·4
Hants	17·7
Wilts	18·9
Somerset	19·9
Monmouth	18·0

DIVISION V. — *Western and North Western.*

Shropshire	14·9
Leicestershire	17·1
Stafford	17·9
Lancaster	18·5
Chester	22·6
Warwick	21·6
Hereford	23·8
Worcester	25·0
Gloucester	26·1

DIVISION VI. — *Metropolitan.*

Middlesex	24·5

The Northern, Welsh, and Cornish Counties range in criminality from 7·1 to 8·4 in 10,000.
York and the N. Midland Counties, from 11·4 to 13·9.
The S. Midland and Eastern Counties, from 14·1 to 20·4.
The S. Eastern and S. Western, from 12·9 to 19·9.
The Western and N. Western, from 14·9 to 26·1.
The Metropolitan, 24·5.

TABLE SHOWING THE RELATIVE CRIMINALITY AND IGNORANCE OF THE SEVERAL COUNTIES, ARRANGED ACCORDING TO THE OCCUPATION OF THEIR INHABITANTS.

	No. of Criminals in every 10,000 of Pop.	No. of Persons who signed with Marks in every 100 married.		No. of Criminals in every 10,000 of Pop.	No. of Persons who signed with Marks in every 100 married.
Agricultural Counties.					
Lincoln	12	39	Chester	22	46
Rutland	13	49	Nottingham	11	42
Huntingdon	14	49	Leicester	17	41
Cambridge	14	45	Warwick	21	38
Essex	19	50	Worcester	25	52
Sussex	15	34	*Mining Counties.*		
Hereford	23	41	Durham	7	36
Agricultural and Sub-Manufacturing Counties.			Cornwall	8	45
			Manufacturing and Sub-Mining Counties.		
Westmorland	8	27			
Norfolk	17	46	Derby	10	39
Suffolk	15	48	Stafford	17	52
Hertford	17	54	*Agricultural and Sub-Mining Counties.*		
Bedford	15	56			
Buckingham	20	49	Salop	14	48
Northampton	14	43	North Wales	7	55
Oxford	17	39	South Wales	8	57
Berks	12	42	*Sub-Agricultural and Sub-Mining Counties.*		
Hants	17	34			
Wilts	18	48	Northumberland	8	28
Dorset	14	36	Cumberland	7	25
Somerset	19	41	Monmouth	18	59
Sub-Agricul. and Sub-Manufact. County.			*Metropolitan County.*		
			Middlesex	24	18
Gloucester	26	35	*Sub-Metropolitan Counties.*		
Manufacturing Counties.					
Lancaster	18	52	Surrey	16	21
Yorkshire	11	44	Kent	16	32

For definition of Agricultural, Manufacturing, and Mining Counties, see Table of Density of Population, No. 37.

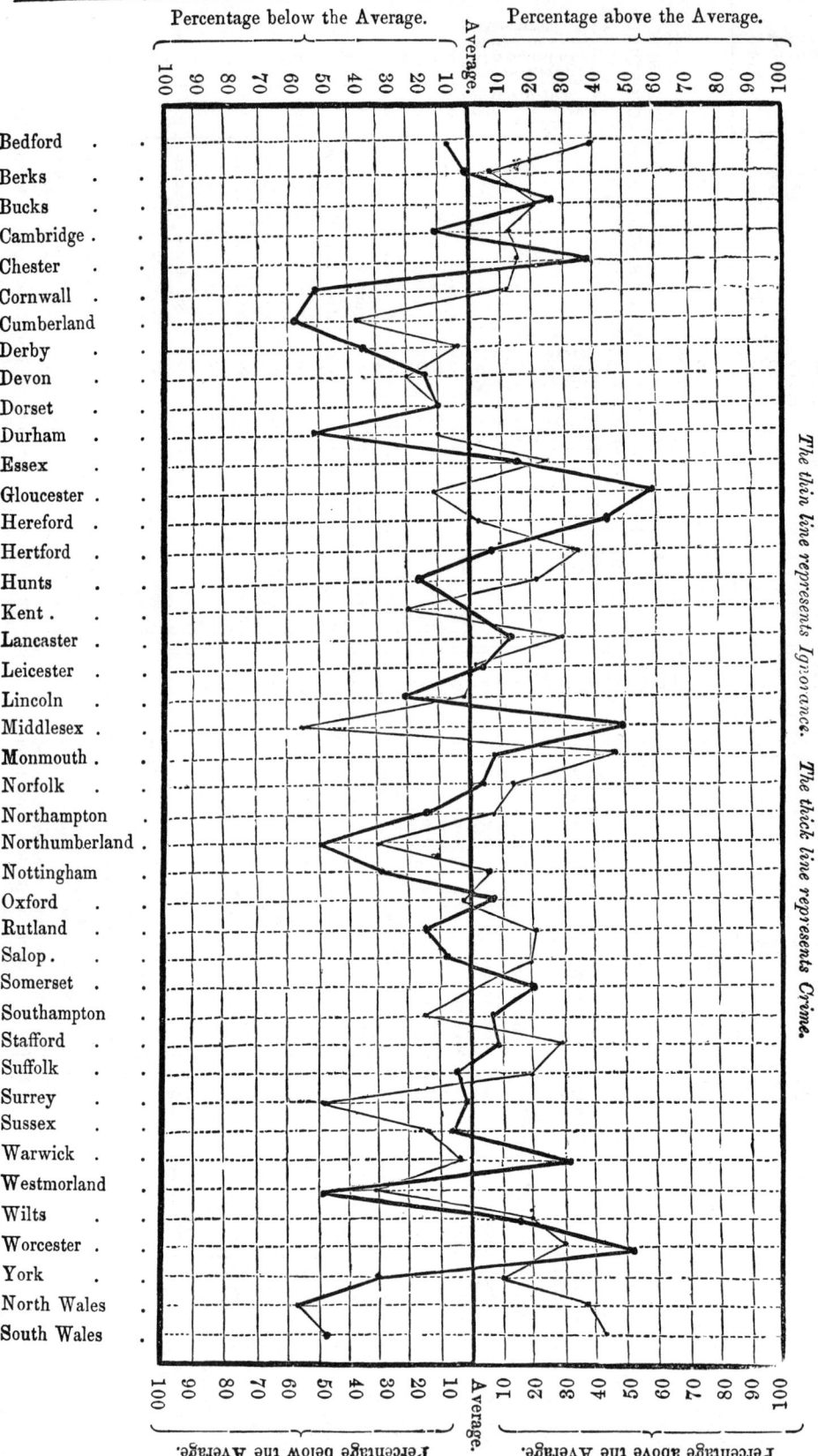

EDUCATION OF CRIMINALS (ENGLAND AND WALES).

TABLE SHOWING THE DEGREES OF INSTRUCTION OF PERSONS OF ALL AGES COMMITTED TO PRISON FROM 1839 TO 1848.

Years.	Unable to read or write.	Able to read and write imperfectly.	Able to read and write well.	Superior Instruction.	Instruction could not be ascertained.	Total.
1839	8,196	13,071	2462	78	636	24,443
1840	9,058	15,109	2253	101	666	27,187
1841	9,220	15,732	2053	26	629	27,760
1842	10,128	18,260	2121	69	731	31,309
1843	9,173	17,045	2371	140	862	29,591
1844	7,901	15,735	2165	111	639	26,542
1845	7,438	14,179	2037	89	560	24,303
1846	7,698	14,942	1936	85	446	25,107
1847	9,050	16,980	2245	82	476	28,833
1848	9,691	17,111	2984	81	482	30,349

TABLE SHOWING THE CENTESIMAL DEGREES OF INSTRUCTION OF PERSONS OF ALL AGES COMMITTED TO PRISON FROM 1839 TO 1848.

Years	Unable to read or write.	Able to read and write imperfectly.	Able to read and write well.	Superior Instruction.	Instruction could not be ascertained.
1839	33·53	53·48	10·07	0·32	2·60
1840	33·32	55·57	8·29	0·37	2·45
1841	33·21	56·67	7·40	0·45	2·27
1842	32·35	58·32	6·77	0·22	2·34
1843	31·00	57·60	8·02	0·47	2·91
1844	29·77	59·28	8·42	0·42	2·41
1845	30·61	58·34	8·38	0·37	2·30
1846	30·66	59·51	7·71	0·34	1·78
1847	31·39	58·89	7·79	0·28	1·65
1848	31·93	56·38	9·83	0·27	1·59

*** "The instruction of the offenders," say the Criminal Returns of 1848, "has been without much variation, exhibiting, on a comparison of the last ten years, a *decreased* proportion of those entirely uninstructed;" and it may be added a corresponding *increase* of those who are able to read and write imperfectly.

THE STATE OF EDUCATION AND DENSITY OF THE POPULATION IN THE SEVERAL COUNTIES COMPARED.

Counties having great Ignorance and great density of Population.	Percentage above and below the Average.		Counties having little Ignorance and great density of Population.	Percentage above and below the Average.	
	In No. signing register with Marks.	In No. of Persons to 100 Acres.		In No. signing register with Marks.	In No. of Persons to 100 Acres.
Monmouth	†47	9	Middlesex	*55	†2030
Lancaster	†30	†270	Surrey	*47	†189
Stafford	†30	†72	Kent	*20	†28
Worcester	†30	†13	Gloucester	*12	†6
Chester	†15	†31	Durham	*10	†21
Nottingham	†5	†12	Warwick	*5	†70

Counties having little Ignorance and little density of Population.			Counties having great Ignorance and little density of Population.		
Cumberland	*37	*59	South Wales	†42	*55
Westmorland	*32	*75	Bedford	†40	*12
Northumb.	*30	*48	North Wales	†37	*60
Devon	*20	*30	Hertford	†35	*12
Sussex	*15	*25	Essex	†25	*29
Southampton	*15	*20	Bucks	†22	*37
Dorset	*10	*43	Hunts	†22	*49
Oxford	*2	*26	Rutland	†22	*49
Lincoln	*2	*51	Salop	†20	*42
Derby	*2	*20	Wilts	†20	*44
			Norfolk	†15	*32
			Cambridge	†12	*28
			Cornwall	†12	*16
			York	†10	*2
			Northampton	†7	*33
			Berks	†5	*15
			Hereford	†2	*63
			Leicester	†2	*7
			Somerset	†2	*10

*** The rule appears to be, that those counties are the *most* ignorant in which the population is the *least* dense.

THE CRIME AND DENSITY OF THE POPULATION OF THE SEVERAL COUNTIES COMPARED.

Counties having great Crime and great density of Population.	Percentage above and below the Average.		Counties having great Crime and little density of Population.	Percentage above and below the Average.	
	In Number of Criminals.	In No. of Persons to 100 Acres.		In Number of Criminals.	In No. of Persons to 100 Acres.
Gloucester	†59·1	64	Hereford	†45·1	*63·4
Worcester	†52·4	13·3	Bucks	†24·4	*37·0
Middlesex	†49·4	†2030·8	Somerset	†21·3	*10·9
Chester	†37·8	†31·2	Essex	†16·4	*29·6
Warwick	†31·7	†70·0	Wilts	†15·2	*44·1
Lancaster	†12·8	†270·6	Oxford	†8·5	*26·8
Monmouth	†9·7	†9·9	Southampton	†7·9	*20·7
Stafford	†9·1	†72·2	Hertford	†6·7	*12·5
			Leicester	†4·2	*7·4
			Norfolk	†4·2	*32·6

Counties having little Crime and little density of Population.			Counties having little Crime and great density of Population.		
Cumberland	*56·7	*59·6	Durham	*51·8	†21·9
North Wales	*56·1	*60·4	Nottingham	*28·0	†12·7
Cornwall	*51·2	*16·3	Surrey	*6	†189·7
Westmorland	*50·6	*75·9	Kent		†28·0
Northumb.	*50·0	*48·1			
South Wales	*48·7	*55·1			
Derby	*36·0	*20·9			
York	*30·5	*2·0			
Lincoln	*22·0	*51·7			
Berks	*21·4	*15·5			
Hunts	*14·0	*49·9			
Devon	*14·0	*30·0			
Rutland	*15·2	*49·9			
Northampton	*13·4	*33·4			
Cambridge	*10·3	*28·2			
Dorset	*10·0	*43·1			
Salop	*9·1	*42·9			
Bedford	*7·3	*12·3			
Sussex	*6·7	*25·0			
Suffolk	*4·2	*26·6			

*** The rule appears to be, that those counties are the least criminal in which the population is the least dense.

N.B. The † prefixed to a number denotes that it is *above*, the * that it is *below* the average by the percentage which it expresses.

MAP

SHOWING

THE NUMBER OF ILLEGITIMATE CHILDREN

IN EVERY 1000 BIRTHS,

IN EACH COUNTY OF

ENGLAND AND WALES.

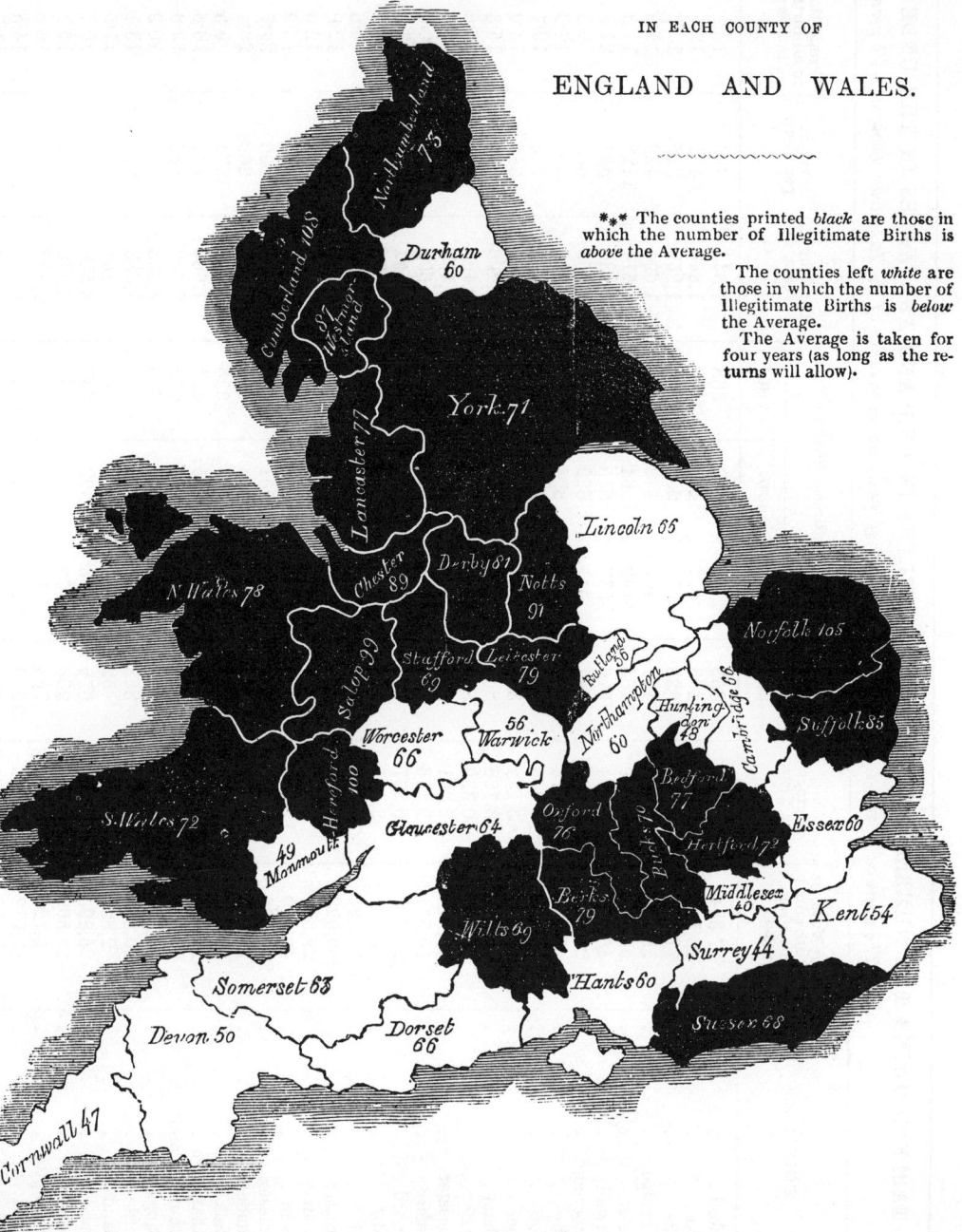

⁎ The counties printed *black* are those in which the number of Illegitimate Births is *above* the Average.

The counties left *white* are those in which the number of Illegitimate Births is *below* the Average.

The Average is taken for four years (as long as the returns will allow).

The Average for all England and Wales is 67 in every 1000.

A TABLE SHOWING THE NUMBER OF ILLEGITIMATE BIRTHS IN ENGLAND AND WALES IN THE UNDERMENTIONED YEARS.

* *The average is calculated for as long a series of years as the returns of the Registrar General will permit.*

COUNTIES.	Total Number of Births for 4 Years, from 1845-48.	Average per Year.	Number of Illegitimate Births.					Total for 4 Years.	Average per Year.	Proportion to all Births, 1 in every	Number of illegitimate in every 1000 Births.	Per Cent. above and below the Average. †denotes above " below
			1845.	1846.	1847.	1848.					
Bedford	17,384	4,346	355	349	302	338	1,344	336	12·9	77	†14·9
Berks	23,195	5,799	463	472	438	470	1,843	461	12·5	79	†17·9
Bucks	17,984	4,496	328	329	296	306	1,259	315	14·2	70	†4·4
Cambridge	25,546	6,386	441	407	442	404	1,694	423	15·0	66	*1·5
Chester	51,396	12,599	1188	1190	1064	1072	4,514	1128	11·3	89	†32·8
Cornwall	45,017	11,254	576	537	515	508	2,136	534	21·0	47	*29·8
Cumberland	23,541	5,885	647	641	629	638	2,555	639	9·2	108	†61·2
Derby	32,295	8,074	672	670	674	610	2,626	656	12·2	81	†20·9
Devon	64,802	16,200	789	889	758	837	3,273	818	19·7	50	*25·3
Dorset	20,529	5,132	364	331	309	366	1,370	342	14·9	66	*1·5
Durham	54,916	13,729	804	821	812	859	3,296	824	16·3	60	*10·4
Essex	41,356	10,339	588	673	590	634	2,485	621	16·6	60	*10·4
Gloucester	49,444	12,361	811	855	720	767	3,153	788	15·6	64	*4·5
Hereford	10,984	2,746	273	305	254	263	1,095	274	10·0	100	†49·2
Hertford	21,590	5,397	402	414	368	367	1,551	388	13·9	72	†7·4
Hunts	8,179	2,045	116	100	80	98	394	98	20·7	48	*28·3
Kent	73,836	18,459	1015	1008	976	995	3,994	998	14·8	54	*19·4
Lancaster	293,023	73,256	5929	5897	5477	5384	22,687	5672	12·9	77	†14·9
Leicester	29,512	7,378	640	624	531	536	2,331	583	12·6	79	†17·9
Lincoln	49,546	12,386	843	845	773	821	3,282	820	15·0	66	*1·5
Middlesex	217,523	54,381	2048	2254	2201	2298	8,801	2200	24·7	40	*40·3
Monmouth	21,995	5,499	247	266	253	309	1,075	269	20·4	49	*26·8
Norfolk	52,387	13,097	1424	1440	1295	1336	5,495	1374	9·5	105	†56·7
Northampton	27,674	6,918	440	420	395	411	1,666	416	16·6	60	*10·4
Northumberland	37,523	9,381	668	678	715	679	2,740	685	13·6	73	†8·9
Nottingham	35,244	8,811	895	827	775	736	3,233	808	10·9	91	†35·8
Oxford	20,886	5,221	368	468	386	361	1,583	396	13·1	76	†13·4
Rutland	2,825	706	52	34	30	45	161	40	17·5	56	*16·4
Salop	25,899	6,475	676	658	593	632	2,559	640	10·1	99	†47·7
Somerset	53,509	13,377	903	860	796	830	3,389	847	15·7	63	*6·0
Southampton	46,726	11,681	704	711	688	709	2,812	703	16·6	60	*10·4
Stafford	77,972	19,493	1240	1283	1409	1433	5,365	1341	14·5	69	†8·0
Suffolk	42,055	10,514	937	950	849	846	3,582	895	11·7	85	†26·8
Surrey	81,068	20,402	855	911	930	915	3,611	903	22·6	44	*34·3

Sussex	...	557	695	626	2,647	14·5	68	†1·5
Warwick	...	779	830	879	3,323	17·7	56	*16·4
Westmorland	...	179	149	149	624	11·3	87	†29·8
Wilts	...	521	485	469	2,024	14·3	69	†3·0
Worcester	...	768	549	553	2,718	14·9	66	*1·5
York	...	4266	4030	4106	16,619	13·9	71	†6·0
North Wales	...	872	830	832	3,388	12·7	78	†16·4
South Wales	...	1407	1271	1300	5,234	13·7	72	†7·4
Total for England and Wales	...	38,241	36,125	36,747	149,642	14·8	67	

LIST OF COUNTIES IN THE ORDER OF THEIR ILLEGITIMATE BIRTHS, AS SHOWN BY THE NUMBER OF ILLEGITIMATES IN EVERY 1000 CHILDREN BORN.

Counties above the Average.		Counties below the Average.	
Cumberland	108	Cambridge	66
Norfolk	105	Dorset	66
Hereford	100	Lincoln	66
Salop	99	Worcester	66
Nottingham	99	Gloucester	64
Chester	89	Somerset	63
Westmorland	87	Southampton	60
Suffolk	85	Northampton	60
Derby	81	Essex	60
Berks	79	Durham	58
Leicester	79	Warwick	56
North Wales	79	Rutland	56
Lancaster	78	Kent	54
Bedford	77	Devon	50
Oxford	77	Monmouth	49
Northumberland	76	Hunts	48
Hertford	73	Cornwall	47
South Wales	72	Surrey	44
York	72	Middlesex	40
Bucks	71		
Wilts	70	Average for England and Wales	67
Stafford	69		
Sussex	68		

THE EARLY MARRIAGES AND THE INCREASE OF THE POPULATION IN EACH COUNTY COMPARED.

Counties in which the Increase of the Population and the number of Early Marriages are both above the Average.	Rate of Increase of the Population from 1841 to 1851 per cent.	Annual No. of Early Marriages in every 1000 Marriages, from 1844-48.	
		Among Males.	Among Females.
Lancaster	22	50	139
Stafford	20	62	176
Bedford	16	109	235
Chester	15	64	151

Counties in which the Increase of the Population and the number of Early Marriages are both below the Average.			
Northumberland	13	39	124
Southampton	13	25	118
Cumberland	10	33	105
Gloucester	6	42	104
Devon	6	22	82
Rutland	5	36	128
Cornwall	4	32	131
North Wales	4	27	77
Hereford	3	17	79
Westmorland	3	32	128
Salop	1	29	95

Counties in which the Increase of the Population and the Early Marriages among Females are above the Average and those among Males below it.			
Durham	26	35	142
Kent	14	46	140

County in which the Increase of the Population and Early Marriages among Females are below the Average, and those among Males above.			
Warwick	18	46	131

Counties in which the Increase of the Population is below the Average, and the number of Early Marriages are above it.			
Cambridge	13	73	227
Worcester	13	56	151
York	13	57	187
Hunts	9	99	336
Nottingham	9	60	153
Derby	9	46	138
Essex	7	57	204
Hertford	7	75	210
Norfolk	7	50	148
Suffolk	7	52	162
Northampton	7	71	190
Leicester	7	79	179
Berks	5	148	143
Bucks	4	94	74
Oxford	4	46	151
Wilts	0·7	68	164

Counties in which the Increase of Population is above the Average, and the number of Early Marriages is below it.			
Middlesex	20	18	85
Surrey	17	16	91
Monmouth	17	28	105
South Wales	14	30	82

Counties in which the Increase of the Population and the Early Marriages among Males are below the Average and those among Females above it.			
Lincoln	12	39	153
Sussex	12	38	160

Counties in which the Increase of the Population and Early Marriages among Females is below the Average and those among Males above it.			
Somerset	2	47	112
Dorset	6	47	125

TABLE SHOWING THE NUMBER OF EARLY MARRIAGES OF MALES AND FEMALES IN THE SEVERAL COUNTIES FOR THE UNDERMENTIONED YEARS.

** The returns of the Registrar do not admit of the average being calculated from a longer series of years.

COUNTIES.	Annual Average Number of Marriages from 1844–48.	Number of Early Marriages.										Total for 5 years.		Average per year.		Proportion to all Marriages, 1 in every		Number of early Marriages to every 1000.		℗ Cent. above and below the Average. † denotes above ,, ,, below	
		1844.		1845.		1846.		1847.		1848.											
		Males	Females	Males	Females	Males	Females	Males	Females	Males	Females	Males	Females	Males	Females	Males	Females	Males	Females	Males	Females
Bedford	960	102	237	103	216	108	238	115	221	96	218	524	1,130	105	226	9·1	4·2	109	235	†153	†74
Berks	1,322	52	186	61	182	62	201	74	204	70	171	319	944	64	189	20·6	6·9	48	143	†12	†6
Bucks	974	66	181	66	175	87	196	76	179	67	213	362	944	72	189	13·5	5·1	74	194	†72	†44
Cambridge	1,428	115	324	89	308	112	349	96	311	115	328	527	1,620	105	324	13·6	4·4	73	227	†70	†68
Chester	2,764	153	393	175	427	154	455	132	372	136	446	750	2,093	150	419	18·4	6·5	54	151	†25	†12
Cornwall	2,510	86	312	84	348	80	334	86	313	68	341	404	1,648	81	330	30·9	7·6	32	131	*25	*3
Cumberland	1,060	31	88	54	145	28	133	23	94	38	97	174	557	35	111	30·2	9·5	33	105	*23	*22
Derby	1,954	86	276	76	243	104	289	82	270	109	275	457	1,353	91	271	21·4	7·2	46	138	†7	†2
Devon	4,574	84	324	95	352	104	367	97	401	124	430	504	1,874	101	375	45·2	12·1	22	82	*49	*39
Dorset	1,209	62	155	64	161	46	130	57	166	57	147	286	759	57	152	21·2	7·9	47	125	†9	*7
Durham	3,137	82	353	110	468	118	463	124	462	115	489	549	2,235	110	447	28·5	7·0	35	142	*19	†5
Essex	2,154	125	454	133	436	116	415	123	411	121	462	618	2,178	124	436	17·3	4·9	57	202	†33	†50
Gloucester	3,568	133	350	162	378	180	414	114	340	163	372	752	1,854	150	371	23·7	9·6	42	104	*32	*23
Hereford	648	15	47	10	61	11	60	14	47	7	42	57	257	11	51	58·9	12·7	17	79	*60	†41
Hertford	1,009	86	218	77	229	83	227	68	193	68	192	382	1,059	76	212	13·2	4·7	75	210	†74	†56
Hunts	455	77	370	41	91	29	110	42	94	37	102	226	767	45	153	10·1	2·9	99	336	†130	†149
Kent	4,339	98	584	112	614	128	659	108	567	128	625	574	3,049	115	610	37·7	7·1	26	140	*40	†4
Lancaster	18,785	831	2310	1040	2729	1005	2784	773	2330	1100	2864	4749	13,017	950	2603	19·7	7·2	50	139	†16	†3
Leicester	1,827	160	330	168	359	150	321	125	277	124	347	727	1,634	145	327	12·6	5·5	79	179	†84	†33
Lincoln	2,862	112	393	115	430	82	453	110	417	138	509	557	2,202	111	440	25·7	6·5	39	153	*9	†13
Middlesex	16,859	249	1262	360	1477	329	1606	322	1428	286	1437	1546	7,210	309	1442	54·5	11·6	18	85	*58	*37
Monmouth	1,395	28	119	38	149	43	147	44	157	44	165	197	737	39	147	35·7	9·4	28	105	*35	†22
Norfolk	3,189	164	467	173	448	158	472	144	444	164	504	803	2,335	161	467	19·8	6·8	50	146	†16	†81
Northampton	1,648	109	317	136	354	112	326	110	287	119	281	586	1,565	117	313	14·0	5·2	71	190	†65	†41
Northumberland	2,161	68	219	79	283	98	310	97	255	77	278	419	1,345	84	269	24·5	8·0	39	124	*9	*81
Nottingham	2,204	148	369	133	365	139	365	113	302	130	341	663	1,742	133	348	16·5	6·3	60	158	†40	†17
Oxford	1,154	53	172	52	190	56	156	51	163	57	196	269	877	54	175	21·3	6·5	46	151	†7	†12
Rutland	164	2	10	5	16	4	14	11	34	6	33	28	107	6	21	27·3	7·8	36	128	*16	*5
Salop	1,596	36	144	32	118	62	165	52	151	55	177	237	755	47	151	33·9	10·5	29	95	*33	*30
Somerset	3,159	144	375	159	328	166	385	116	319	159	371	744	1,778	149	356	21·2	8·8	47	112	†9	*17
Southampton	3,085	77	370	81	414	100	370	67	304	70	367	395	1,825	79	365	39·0	8·4	25	118	*42	*13

LIST OF COUNTIES IN THE ORDER OF THEIR EARLY MARRIAGES, AS SHOWN BY THE NUMBER OF MARRIAGES, UNDER TWENTY-ONE YEARS OF AGE, IN EVERY 1000 MARRIAGES.

AMONGST MALES.		AMONGST FEMALES.	
Counties above the Average.	Counties below the Average.	Counties above the Average.	Counties below the Average.
Bedford 109	Gloucester ... 42	Huntingdon 336	Warwick .. 131
Hunts 99	Lincoln 39	Bedford 235	Cornwall .. 131
Leicester 79	Northumb. ... 39	Cambridge .. 227	Westmor. .. 128
Hertford 75	Sussex 38	Hertford 210	Rutland ... 128
Bucks 74	Rutland 36	Essex 204	Dorset 125
Cambridge 73	Durham 35	Bucks. 194	Northumb.. 124
Northamp. 71	Cumberland .. 33	Northamp. .. 190	Southamp. . 118
Wilts 68	Cornwall 32	York 187	Somerset ... 112
Stafford 62	Westmor. 32	Leicester ... 179	Monmouth . 105
Nottingham ... 60	S. Wales 30	Stafford 176	Cumberland 105
Essex 57	Salop. 29	Wilts 164	Gloucester . 104
York 57	Monmouth ... 28	Suffolk 162	Shropshire . 95
Worcester 56	N. Wales 27	Sussex 160	Surrey 91
Chester 54	Kent 26	Nottingham . 158	Middlesex .. 85
Suffolk 52	Southamp. 25	Lincoln 153	Devon 82
Lancaster 50	Devon 22	Oxford 151	S. Wales ... 82
Norfolk 50	Middlesex 18	Chester 151	Hereford ... 79
Berks 48	Hereford 17	Worcester ... 151	N. Wales .. 77
Dorset 47	Surrey 16	Norfolk 148	
Somerset 47		Berks. 143	Average for
Derby 46	Average for	Durham 142	England
Oxford 46	England	Kent 140	and Wales 135
Warwick 46	and Wales 43	Lancaster ... 139	
		Derby. 138	

*** The rule is, that where the greatest number of males marry at an early age, the greatest number of females do so likewise—the exceptions being Dorset, Somerset, and Warwick, among the males, and Sussex, Lincoln, Durham, and Kent among the females.

††† There are, on an average, rather more than 3 females married at an early age to every male.

THE ILLEGITIMATE BIRTHS AND EARLY MARRIAGES IN THE SEVERAL COUNTIES COMPARED.

(† denotes plus.)   (* denotes minus.)

Counties in which the Illegitimate Births and the Early Marriages are both above the Average.	Percent. above & below the Aver.			Counties in which the Illegitimate Births are above the Average and the Early Marriages below it.	Percent. above & below the Aver.		
	In No. of Illegitimate Births.	In No. of Early Marriages.			In No. of Illegitimate Births.	In No. of Early Marriages.	
		Among Males.	Among Females.			Among Males.	Among Females.
Norfolk........	†56	† 16	†81	Cumberland ...	†61	*23	*22
Nottingham ..	†35	† 40	†17	Hereford	†49	*60	*41
Suffolk........	†26	† 21	†21	Salop..........	†47	*33	*30
Derby	†20	† 7	† 2	Westmorland ..	†29	*25	*5
Chester	†32	† 25	†12	North Wales ..	†18	*37	*43
Leicester	†17	† 84	†33	Northumberland	† 8	* 9	*81
Berks	†17	† 12	† 6	South Wales ..	† 7	*30	*39
Lancaster	†14	† 16	† 3				
Bedford	†14	†153	†74	*** In the majority of these counties some peculiar form of courtship (as "night courtship" and "bundling") prevails.			
Oxford	†13	† 7	†12				
Hertford	† 7	† 74	†56				
York	† 6	† 33	†39				
Bucks	† 4	† 72	†44				
Stafford	† 3	† 44	†30				
Wilts..........	† 3	† 58	†21				

Counties in which the Illegitimate Children and Early Marriages are both below the Average.				Counties in which the Illegitimate Children are below the Average, and the Early Marriages above it.			
Middlesex......	*40	† 58	*37	Hunts	*28	†130	†149
Surrey........	*34	† 63	*25	Northampton ..	*10	† 65	† 41
Cornwall......	*29	† 25	* 3	Essex	*10	† 33	† 50
Monmouth	*26	† 35	*22	Worcester	* 1	† 30	† 12
Devon	*25	† 49	*39	Cambridge	* 1	† 70	† 68
Rutland	*16	† 16	* 5				
Southampton ..	*10	† 42	*13				
Gloucester	* 4	† 2	*23				

Counties in which the Illegitimate Children and Early Marriages among Males are both below the Average, and those among Females above it.				Counties in which there are the greatest number of Early Marriages, and those among Females are both below the Average, and those among Males above it.			
Kent...........	*19	† 40	† 4	Warwick	*16	† 7	* 3
Durham	*10	† 19	† 5	Somerset	* 6	† 9	*17
Lincoln........	* 1	† 9	†13	Dorset	* 1	† 9	* 7

Exceptional County.			
Sussex	† 1	* 12	†19

*** The rule appears to be, that in those counties in which there are the greatest number of Illegitimate Children, there are (generally) the greatest number of Early Marriages, and vice versâ.

TABLE No. VIII. — LONDON LABOUR AND THE LONDON POOR.

THE EXCESS OF FEMALES AND ILLEGITIMATE BIRTHS COMPARED.

Counties in which the Number of Females and Illegitimate Births are both above the Average.	Percentage above and below the Average. † denotes above and * below.		Counties in which the Number of Females is above and of the Illegitimate Births below the Average.	Percentage above and below the Average. † denotes above and * below.	
	In No. of Females to Males.	In No. of Illegitimate Births.		In No. of Females to Males.	In No. of Illegitimate Births.
Bedford	†3	†14	Middlesex	†8	*3
Norfolk	†1	†56	Gloucester	†6	*4
			Devon	†5	*25
			Surrey	†5	*34
			Somerset	†5	*6
			Cornwall	†2	*29
			Dorset	†1	*1

Counties in which the Number of Females and Illegitimate Births are both below the Average.			Counties in which the Number of Females is below in proportion to the males, and the Illegitimate Births above it.		
Monmouth	*12	*26	Stafford	*7	†3
Rutland	*6	*16	Oxford	*5	†13
Lincoln	*5	*1	Hereford	*5	†49
Durham	*5	*10	Westmorland	*3	†29
Essex	*4	*10	Salop	*3	†47
Hunts	*3	*28	Derby	*3	†20
Northampton	*3	*10	Berks	*3	†17
Kent	*3	*19	York	*2	†6
Cambridge	*3	*1	Hertford	*2	†7
Southampton	*3	*10	South Wales	*2	†6
Warwick	*1	*16	North Wales	*2	†8
Worcester	*1	*1	Northumb.	*1	†61
			Cumberland	*1	†3
			Wilts	*1	†26
			Suffolk	*1	†4
			Bucks	*1	†35
			Nottingham	*1	†17
			Leicester	*1	†6
			Sussex	*1	†14
			Lancaster	..	†32
			Chester	..	†32

*** The rule appears to be, that in those counties in which the number of females, in proportion to the males, is the *smallest*, the number of illegitimate births is the *greatest*, and where it is the *greatest*, the illegitimate births are the *smallest*.

LIST OF COUNTIES IN THE ORDER OF THEIR PROPORTION OF FEMALE TO MALE POPULATION, AS SHOWN BY THE NUMBER OF FEMALES TO EVERY 100 MALES.

COUNTIES ABOVE THE AVERAGE.		COUNTIES BELOW THE AVERAGE.	
Middlesex	114	Chester	105
Gloucester	112	Lancaster	105
Devon	111	Leicester	104
Somerset	111	Nottingham	104
Surrey	111	Warwick	104
Bedford	108	Worcester	104
Cornwall	107	Bucks	103
Dorset	107	Cumberland	103
Norfolk	106	Northumb.	103
		Suffolk	103
		Sussex	103
		Wilts	102
		Hertford	102
		York	102
		North Wales	102
		South Wales	102
		Berks	101
		Cambridge	101
		Derby	101
		Hunts	101
		Kent	101
		Northampton	101
		Salop	101
		Southampton	101
		Westmorland	101
		Essex	100
		Durham	99
		Hereford	99
		Lincoln	99
		Oxford	99
		Rutland	98
		Stafford	97
		Monmouth	92

Average for England & Wales 105

TABLE SHOWING THE PROPORTION OF FEMALES TO MALES IN THE DIFFERENT COUNTIES OF ENGLAND AND WALES.

COUNTIES.	1851.		Number of Females to every 100 Males.	Proportion per Cent. above and below the Average. † denotes above. * denotes below.
	Male Population.	Female Population.		
Bedford	62,420	67,369	108	†2·9
Berks	99,227	99,927	101	*3·8
Bucks	70,784	72,886	103	*1·9
Cambridge	95,505	96,351	101	*3·8
Chester	206,715	216,723	105	
Cornwall	171,979	184,683	107	†1·9
Cumberland	96,106	99,381	103	*1·9
Derby	129,379	131,328	101	*3·8
Devon	271,579	300,628	111	†5·7
Dorset	85,816	91,781	107	†1·9
Durham	206,666	204,866	99	*5·7
Essex	172,161	171,755	100	*4·8
Gloucester	198,192	221,353	112	†6·7
Hereford	49,694	49,418	99	*5·7
Hertford	86,331	87,632	102	*2·9
Hunts	29,984	30,336	101	*3·8
Kent	308,115	311,092	101	
Lancaster	1,005,627	1,058,286	105	*1·0
Leicester	115,295	119,643	104	*5·7
Lincoln	201,027	199,239	99	*8·6
Middlesex	885,614	1,010,096	114	†12·4
Monmouth	92,095	85,070	92	*1·0
Norfolk	210,360	223,443	106	*3·8
Northampton	106,533	107,251	101	*1·9
Northumberland	144,428	150,010	104	*1·0
Nottingham	149,158	154,377	103	*5·7
Oxford	85,449	84,837	99	*6·7
Rutland	12,270	12,002	98	*3·8
Salop	122,022	122,997	101	*5·7
Somerset	216,716	239,521	111	*3·8
Southampton	199,834	202,199	101	*7·6
Stafford	320,394	310,112	97	*1·9
Suffolk	165,267	170,724	103	†5·7
Surrey	325,155	359,650	111	*1·0
Sussex	166,828	172,600	103	*1·9
Warwick	235,263	244,716	104	*3·8
Westmorland	29,064	29,316	101	*1·9
Wilts	113,839	122,164	103	*1·0
Worcester	126,739	132,023	104	*2·9
York	886,845	901,922	102	*2·9
North Wales	200,538	203,622	102	*2·9
South Wales	300,645	306,851	102	
TOTAL FOR ENGLAND AND WALES	**8,762,588**	**9,160,180**	**105**	

MAP No. VII.

MAP

SHOWING

THE NUMBER OF PERSONS COMMITTED FOR RAPE

IN EVERY 10,000,000 OF THE POPULATION,

IN THE SEVERAL COUNTIES OF

ENGLAND AND WALES.

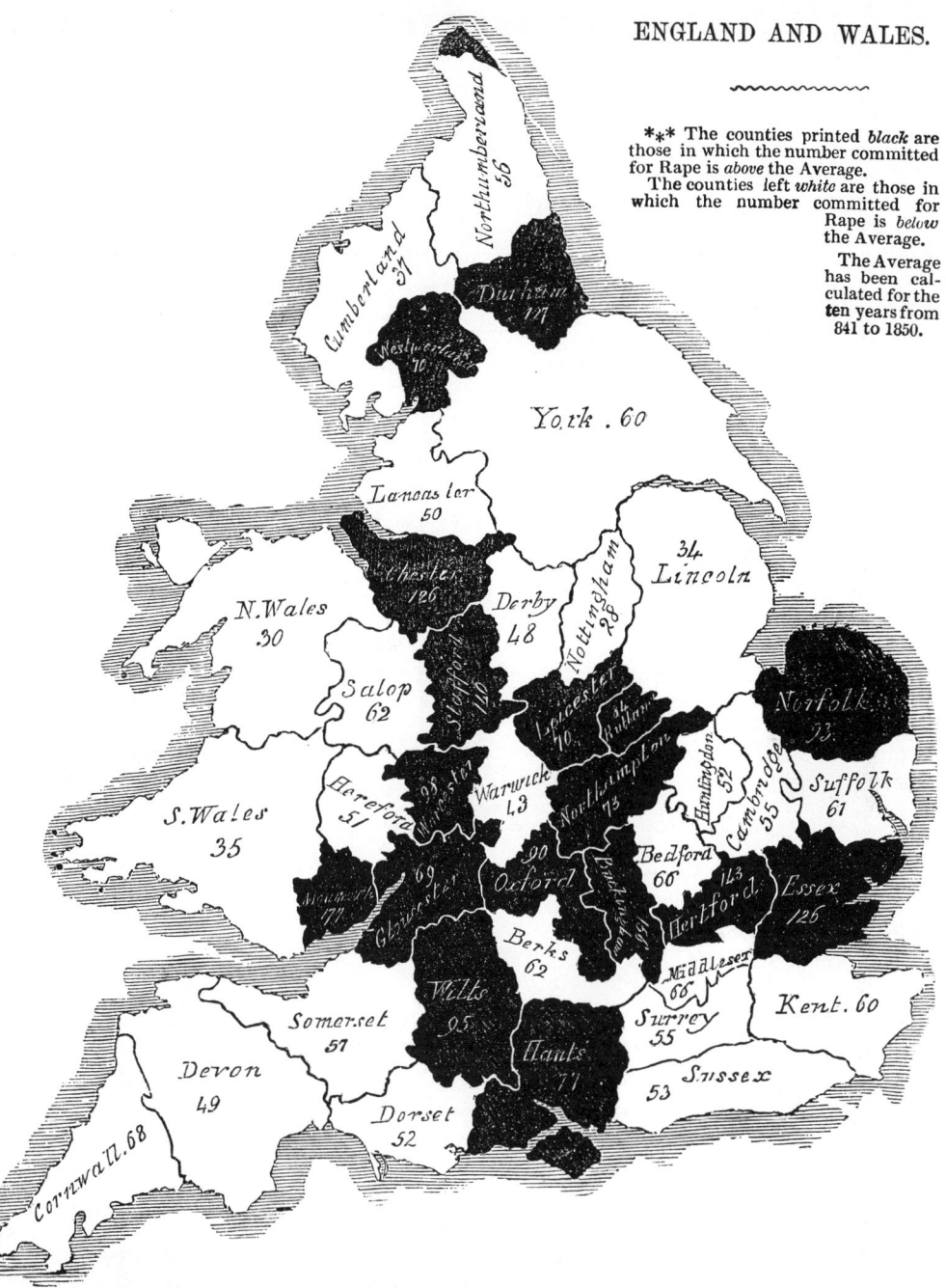

*** The counties printed *black* are those in which the number committed for Rape is *above* the Average.
The counties left *white* are those in which the number committed for Rape is *below* the Average.
The Average has been calculated for the **ten** years from 841 to 1850.

The Average for all England and Wales is 68 in every 10,000,000 People.
Monmouth (the highest)   171   ,,   ,,
Nottingham (the lowest)   28   ,,   ,,

TABLE IX.   LONDON LABOUR AND THE LONDON POOR.

TABLE SHOWING THE CRIMINALITY OF THE DIFFERENT COUNTIES OF ENGLAND AND WALES WITH REGARD TO RAPE.

COUNTIES.	Average Population from 1841–50.	Total Number Committed for Rape.										Total for 10 Years.	Annual Average.	No. committed annually for Rape in every 10,000,000 Persons.	Proportion per Cent above and below the Aver. † denotes above. * ,, below.
		1841.	1842.	1843.	1844.	1845.	1846.	1847.	1848.	1849.	1850.				
Bedford	121,083	2	2	…	…	1	…	…	1	1	1	8	·8	66	*2·9
Berks	194,763	1	1	1	3	…	…	…	3	1	2	12	1·2	62	*8·8
Bucks	140,959	1	1	2	7	2	…	2	…	5	2	22	2·2	156	†129·4
Cambridge	180,747	1	…	…	…	1	2	2	1	1	2	10	1·0	55	*19·1
Chester	395,919	1	9	7	6	…	7	2	11	2	6	50	5·0	126	†85·3
Cornwall	349,991	7	1	1	2	1	3	1	5	2	2	24	2·4	68	…
Cumberland	186,762	…	…	…	3	…	2	…	…	1	…	7	·7	37	*45·6
Derby	250,249	1	1	5	2	1	2	1	…	…	5	12	1·2	48	*29·4
Devon	554,738	…	1	5	3	…	2	4	4	5	1	27	2·7	49	*27·9
Dorset	172,736	…	1	3	2	2	5	1	1	2	4	9	·9	52	*23·5
Durham	368,787	2	2	8	5	1	…	7	4	4	2	47	4·7	127	†86·8
Essex	332,363	2	10	2	12	1	9	2	4	2	7	42	4·2	126	†85·3
Gloucester	407,504	…	1	2	7	2	4	2	1	4	…	28	2·8	69	†1·5
Hereford	97,813	…	…	…	…	1	2	1	…	1	…	5	·5	51	*25·0
Hertford	168,178	…	6	…	5	2	3	…	4	2	1	24	2·4	143	†110·3
Hunts	57,942	1	…	…	…	…	…	…	1	…	1	3	·3	52	*23·5
Kent	585,249	1	10	7	8	1	1	1	1	2	3	35	3·5	60	*11·8
Lancaster	1,881,261	8	8	11	12	10	8	12	12	4	9	94	9·4	50	*26·5
Leicester	227,621	1	3	2	2	…	2	1	…	4	1	16	1·6	70	†2·9
Lincoln	378,246	…	1	2	1	2	…	3	4	…	2	13	1·3	34	*50·0
Middlesex	1,740,814	9	13	11	8	12	12	15	15	11	9	115	11·5	66	*2·9
Monmouth	164,093	3	2	2	5	4	…	1	…	5	5	29	2·9	177	†145·6
Norfolk	419,463	2	1	4	3	2	6	…	4	2	9	39	3·9	93	†36·8
Northampton	206,496	3	…	1	2	3	7	2	1	3	4	15	1·5	73	†7·4
Northumberland	284,777	1	…	6	3	…	1	…	4	1	…	16	1·6	56	*17·6
Nottingham	282,584	…	1	2	1	2	1	1	1	1	…	8	·8	28	*58·8
Oxford	166,751	1	…	2	1	…	…	…	3	3	1	15	1·5	90	†32·4
Rutland	23,711	…	…	1	…	…	…	…	1	1	…	2	·2	84	†23·5
Salop	243,352	2	2	3	2	1	1	2	…	2	5	15	1·5	62	*8·8
Somerset	452,515	4	1	3	6	…	4	3	3	5	3	26	2·6	57	*16·2
Southampton	377,040	6	1	4	4	2	1	3	4	1	1	29	2·9	77	†13·2
Stafford	579,686	1	4	8	…	5	10	8	6	17	13	81	8·1	140	†105·9
Suffolk	325,336	…	3	2	…	2	3	2	2	3	2	20	2·0	61	*10·3
Surrey	635,917	5	1	6	…	7	3	4	5	4	4	35	3·5	55	*19·1

Westmorland	57,494	...	...	...	...	...	...	4	†2·9
Wilts	241,887	3	2	2	1	1	2	23	+39·7
Worcester	244,574	1	2	4	1	3	2	24	+44·1
York	1,686,461	5	3	3	3	15	...	102	*11·8
Hertford	396,161	3	2	15	15	2	14	12	*55·9
North Wales	568,430	...	2	...	2	2	2	20	*48·5
South Wales									
Total for England and Wales	16,918,458	78	118	127	127	86	139	97	124	121	137	1154	1154	68

*** The proportionate number of persons perpetrating this crime has been calculated with reference to the *entire* population, instead of the *male part of it only*, as at the first glance might seen necessary, males only being capable of committing the above offence. But it was found, on examination, that the intensity of the criminality in the several counties in this respect was influenced by the relative number of females. Monmouth contains the greatest number of males in proportion to females; so that, were the male population alone considered, the criminality of that county in the above respect would be considerably decreased. But the fact of there being more rapes in Monmouth than elsewhere would appear to be owing to the very excess of males over females in that county; the average, therefore, has been calculated from the entire population.

LIST OF COUNTIES IN THE ORDER OF THEIR CRIMINALITY WITH REGARD TO RAPE, AS SHOWN BY THE NUMBER COMMITTED FOR THIS OFFENCE IN EVERY 10,000,000 OF THE POPULATION.

Counties above the Average.		Counties below the Average.	
Monmouth	177	Cornwall	68
Bucks	156	Bedford	66
Hertford	143	Middlesex	66
Stafford	140	Berks	62
Durham	127	Salop	62
Chester	127	Suffolk	61
Essex	126	Kent	60
Worcester	98	York	60
Wilts	95	Somerset	57
Norfolk	93	Northumb.	56
Oxford	90	Cambridge	55
Rutland	84	Surrey	55
Southamp.	77	Sussex	53
Northamp.	73	Dorset	52
Leicester	70	Hunts.	52
Westmor.	70	Hereford	51
Gloucester	69	Lancaster	50
		Devon	49
		Derby	48
		Warwick	43
		Cumberland	37
		S. Wales	35
		Lincoln	34
		N. Wales	30
Average for England and Wales	68	Nottingham	28

THE CRIME OF RAPE COMPARED WITH THE NUMBER OF ILLEGITIMATE CHILDREN IN EACH COUNTY.

Counties in which the Number of Rapes and the Number of Illegitimate Births are both above the Average.	Percentage above and below the Average. * denotes above, † below.		Counties in which the Number of Rapes is above and the Number of Illegitimate Births below the Average.	Percentage above and below the Average. * denotes above, † below.	
	In Number of Rapes.	In No. of Illegitimate Births.		In Number of Rapes.	In No. of Illegitimate Births.
Bucks	†129·4	† 4·4	Monmouth	†145·6	*26·8
Hertford	†110·3	† 7·4	Durham	86·8	*10·4
Stafford	†105·9	† 3·0	Essex	85·3	*10·4
Chester	85·3	*32·8	Worcester	44·1	* 1·5
Wilts	39·7	† 3·0	Rutland	23·5	*16·4
Norfolk	36·8	*56·7	Southampton	13·2	*10·4
Oxford	32·4	*13·4	Northampton	7·4	*10·4
Rutland	2·9	*17·9	Gloucester	1·5	* 4·5
Leicester	2·9	*29·8			
Westmorland					
Counties in which the Number of Rapes and the Number of Illegitimate Births are both below the Average.			Counties in which the Number of Rapes is below and the Number of Illegitimate Births above the Average.		
Lincoln	*50·0	* 1·5	Nottingham	*58·8	*35·8
Warwick	*36·8	*16·4	North Wales	*55·9	*16·4
Devon	*27·9	*25·3	South Wales	*48·5	* 7·4
Hunts	*23·5	*28·3	Cumberland	*45·6	*61·2
Dorset	*23·5	* 1·5	Derby	*29·4	*20·9
Surrey	*19·1	*34·3	Lancaster	*26·5	*14·9
Cambridge	*19·1	* 1·5	Hereford	*25·0	*49·2
Somerset	*16·2	* 6·0	Sussex	*22·1	* 1·5
Kent	*11·8	*19·4	Northumb.	*17·6	* 8·9
Middlesex	* 2·9	*40·3	York	*11·8	* 1·60
Cornwall	*	*29·8	Suffolk	*10·3	*26·8
			Salop	* 8·8	*47·7
			Berks	* 8·8	*17·9
			Bedford	* 2·9	*14·9

*** The rule appears to be, that the crime of Rape is (in the majority of cases) the *least* where the number of Illegitimate Children is the *greatest*.

THE CRIME OF RAPE COMPARED WITH THE RELATIVE NUMBER OF FEMALES TO MALES IN EACH COUNTY.

Counties in which the Number of Rapes and the Number of Females are both above the Average.	Percentage above and below the Average. * denotes above, † below.		Counties in which the Number of Rapes is above and the Number of Females below the Average.	Percentage above and below the Average. * denotes above, † below.	
	In Number of Rapes.	In No. of Females to Males.		In Number of Rapes.	In No. of Females to Males.
Norfolk	†36·8	†1·0	Monmouth	†145·6	*12·4
Gloucester	† 1·5	†6·7	Bucks	†129·4	* 1·9
Counties in which the Number of Rapes and the Number of Females are both below the Average.			Hertford	†110·3	* 2·9
			Stafford	†105·9	* 7·6
			Durham	† 86·8	* 5·7
Nottingham	*58·8	*1·0	Chester	† 85·3	*
North Wales	*55·9	*2·9	Essex	85·3	* 4·8
Lincoln	*50·0	*5·7	Worcester	44·1	*1·0
South Wales	*48·5	*2·9	Wilts	39·7	*1·9
Cumberland	*45·6	*1·9	Oxford	32·4	*5·7
Warwick	*36·8	*1·0	Rutland	23·5	*6·7
Derby	*29·4	*3·3	Southampton	13·2	*3·8
Lancaster	*26·5		Northampton	7·4	*3·8
Hereford	*25·0	*5·7	Leicester	2·9	*1·0
Sussex	*23·5	*1·9	Westmorland	2·9	*3·8
Cambridge	*22·1	*3·8	Counties in which the Number of Rapes is below and the Number of Females above the Average.		
Northumb.	*19·1	*1·9	Devon	*27·9	* 5·7
York	*17·6	*2·9	Dorset	†23·5	* 1·9
Kent	*11·8	*3·8	Surrey	*19·1	* 5·7
Suffolk	*10·3	*1·9	Somerset	*16·2	* 5·7
Salop	* 8·8	*3·8	Middlesex	* 2·9	* 8·6
Berks	* 8·8	*3·8	Bedford	* 2·9	* 2·9
			Cornwall	*	† 1·9

*** The rule appears to be, that the number of Rapes is the *greatest* in those counties where the number of Females is the *least*.

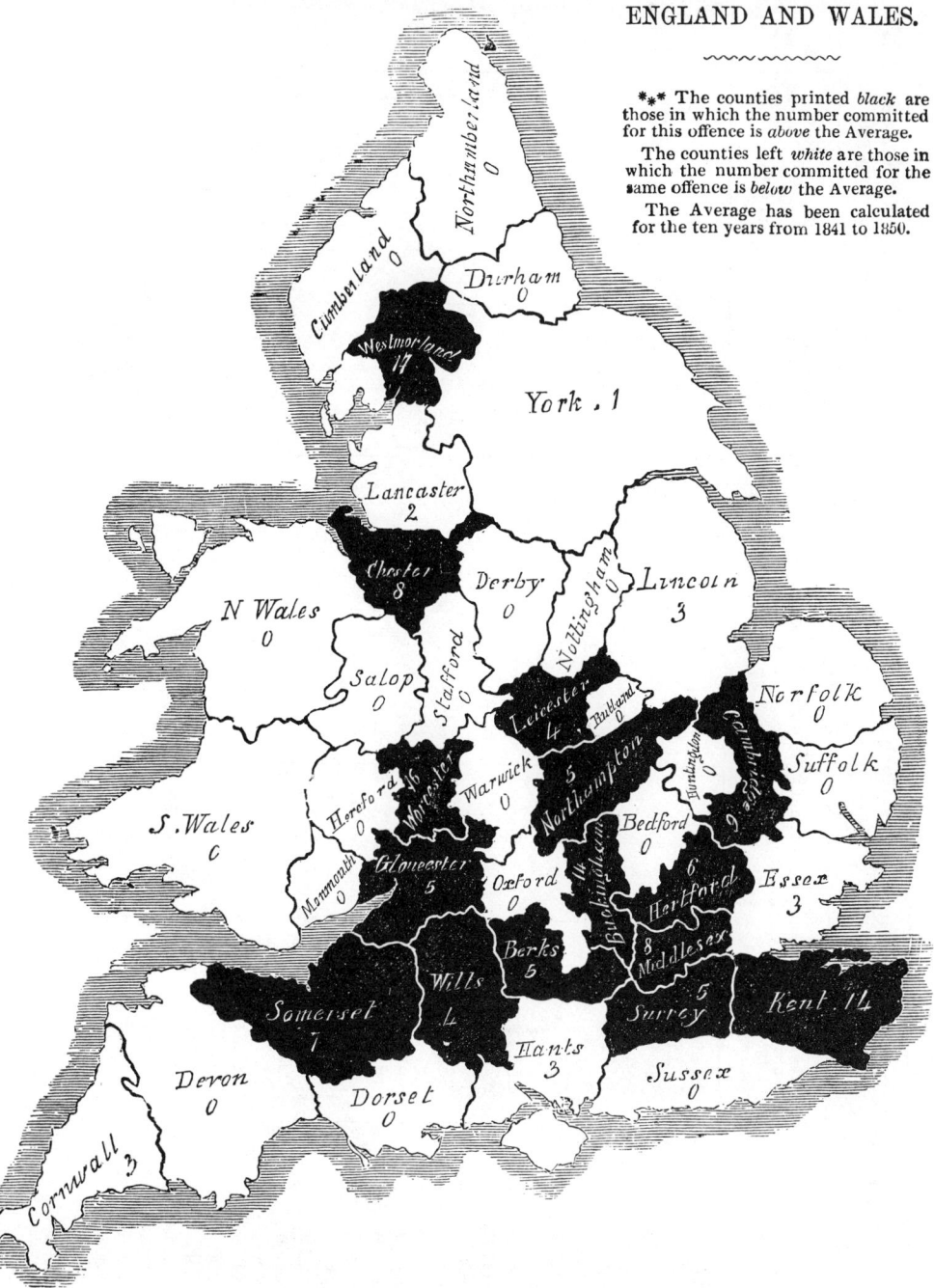

482　TABLE X.　　LONDON LABOUR AND THE LONDON POOR.

TABLE SHOWING THE CRIMINALITY OF THE DIFFERENT COUNTIES OF ENGLAND AND WALES WITH REGARD TO CARNALLY ABUSING GIRLS BETWEEN THE AGE OF 10 AND 12 YEARS.

COUNTIES.	Average Population from 1841-50.	Total number committed for carnally abusing girls between the age of 10 and 12 years.										Total for 10 Years.	Annual Average.	No. committed annually in every 10,000,000 Persons.	Proportion per Cent. above and below the Aver. † denotes above. * „ below.
		1841.	1842.	1843.	1844.	1845.	1846.	1847.	1848.	1849.	1850.				
Bedford . .	121,083	...	...	...	...	...	...	...	...	...	...	...	...	...	†100·0
Berks . .	194,763	...	...	1	...	...	...	...	...	...	...	1	·1	5	†66·7
Bucks . .	140,959	...	...	1	...	...	...	2	...	...	...	2	·2	14	†366·7
Cambridge .	180,747	...	...	...	...	...	...	...	...	...	...	1	·1	6	†100·0
Chester . .	395,919	...	...	...	2	...	1	...	...	...	...	3	·3	8	†100·0
Cornwall .	349,991	...	...	...	...	1	...	...	...	...	...	1	·1	3	†166·7
Cumberland .	186,762	...	...	...	...	...	...	...	...	...	...	...	...	...	†100·0
Derby . .	250,249	...	...	...	...	...	...	...	...	...	...	...	...	...	†100·0
Devon . .	554,738	...	...	...	...	...	...	...	...	...	...	...	...	...	*100·0
Dorset . .	172,736	...	...	...	...	...	...	...	...	...	...	...	...	...	*100·0
Durham . .	368,787	...	...	...	...	...	...	...	...	...	...	...	...	...	*100·0
Essex . .	332,363	1	...	...	...	...	1	...	...	...	1	1	·1	3	†66·7
Gloucester .	407,504	...	...	...	...	...	...	...	...	...	...	2	·2	5	*100·0
Hereford .	97,813	...	...	...	...	...	...	...	...	...	...	...	...	...	*100·0
Hertford .	168,178	...	...	...	...	...	1	...	...	...	...	1	·1	6	†100·0
Hunts . .	57,942	...	...	...	...	...	...	...	...	...	...	...	...	...	*100·0
Kent . .	585,249	...	...	2	...	1	1	1	3	...	...	8	·8	14	†366·7
Lancaster .	1,881,261	...	...	...	...	...	...	...	1	2	1	4	·4	2	*33·3
Leicester .	227,621	...	...	...	...	...	...	...	...	1	...	1	·1	4	†33·3
Lincoln .	378,246	...	...	2	1	...	1	...	1	2	...	1	1	3	†166·7
Middlesex .	1,740,814	...	1	...	1	4	...	2	1	...	...	14	1·4	8	†166·7
Monmouth .	164,093	...	...	...	...	...	...	...	...	...	...	...	...	...	*100·0
Norfolk .	419,463	...	...	...	...	...	...	...	1	...	...	1	·1	5	†66·7
Northampton .	206,496	...	...	...	...	...	...	...	...	...	...	...	...	...	*100·0
Northumberland	284,777	...	...	...	...	...	...	...	...	...	...	...	...	...	*100·0
Nottingham .	282,584	...	...	...	...	...	...	...	...	...	...	...	...	...	*100·0
Oxford . .	166,751	...	...	...	...	...	...	...	...	...	...	...	...	...	*100·0
Rutland .	23,711	...	...	...	...	...	...	...	...	...	...	...	...	...	*100·0
Salop . .	243,352	...	...	...	1	...	...	...	1	1	...	3	·3	7	†133·3
Somerset .	452,515	1	...	...	...	...	...	...	...	...	...	1	·1	3	...
Southampton .	377,040	...	...	...	...	...	...	...	...	...	...	...	...	...	*100·0
Stafford .	579,686	...	...	...	...	...	...	...	...	...	...	...	...	...	*100·0
Suffolk . .	325,336	...	...	...	...	...	...	...	1	...	...	3	·3	5	†66·7
Surrey . .	635,917	...	1	...	...	...	...	...	1	1	...	...	...	...	*100·0

Warwick	444,558	...	...	...	...	...	...	...	...	*100·0
Westmorland	57,494	1	...	...	1	...	...	...	17	†466·7
Wilts	241,887	...	...	1	1	...	...	·1	4	†83·3
Worcester	244,574	4	...	...	4	...	2	·1	16	†433·3
York	1,686,461	1	1	...	2	...	...	·4	1	*66·7
North Wales	396,161	...	...	...	...	2	...	·2	...	*100·0
South Wales	568,430	...	...	...	...	...	...	...	...	*100·0
Total for England and Wales	16,918,458	4	2	8	6	5	9	8	2	56	56·6	3

** The proportionate number of persons perpetrating the above crime has been calculated with reference to the *entire* population, instead of the *male part of it only*, as at the first glance might seem necessary, males only being capable of committing the above offence. But it was found, on examination, that the intensity of the criminality in the several counties in this respect was influenced by the relative number of females (see comparative table below); the average, therefore, has been calculated from the entire population.

LIST OF COUNTIES IN THE ORDER OF THEIR CRIMINALITY WITH REGARD TO CARNALLY ABUSING GIRLS BETWEEN THE AGE OF 10 AND 12 YEARS, AS SHOWN BY THE NUMBER COMMITTED FOR THIS OFFENCE IN EVERY 10,000,000 OF THE POPULATION.

Counties above the Average.
Westmor. 17
Worcester 16
Kent 14
Bucks 14
Middlesex 8
Chester 8
Somerset 7
Cambridge 6
Hertford 6
Surrey 5
Gloucester 5
Dorset 5
Berks 5
Durham 5
Northamp. 5
Hereford 4
Leicester 4
Hunts 4
Wilts 4
 —
Monmouth
Norfolk
Northumb.
Nottingham
Oxford
Rutland
Salop
Stafford
Suffolk
Sussex
Warwick
N. Wales
S. Wales 3

Counties below the Average.
Cornwall. 3
Essex 3
Lincoln 3
Southamp. 3
Lancaster. 2
York 1
Bedford
Cumberland
Derby
Devon

Average for England and Wales 3

THE CRIME OF RAPE COMPARED WITH THAT OF CARNALLY ABUSING CHILDREN IN EACH COUNTY.

Counties in which the Number of Rapes is above the Number of Cases of Carnal Abuse are both above the Average.	Percentage above and below the Average. * denotes above. † denotes below.	
	In Number of Rapes.	In No. of Cases of Carnal Abuse.
Bucks	*129·4	†366·7
Hertford	†110·3	*100·0
Chester	† 85·3	†166·7
Worcester	† 44·1	†433·3
Wilts	† 39·7	† 33·3
Northampton	† 7·4	† 66·7
Leicester	† 2·9	† 33·3
Westmorland	† 2·9	†466·6
Gloucester	† 1·5	† 66·7

Counties in which the No. of Rapes and the No. of Cases of Carnal Abuse are both below the Average.

Nottingham	*58·8	*100·0
North Wales	*55·9	*100·0
Lincoln	*50·0	*
South Wales	*48·5	*100·0
Cumberland	*45·6	*100·0
Warwick	*36·8	*100·0
Derby	*29·4	*100·0
Devon	*27·9	*100·0
Lancaster	*26·5	* 33·3
Hereford	*25·0	*100·0
Hunts	*23·5	*100·0
Dorset	*23·5	*100·0
Sussex	*22·1	*100·0
Northumb.	*17·6	* 66·7
York	*11·8	*100·0
Suffolk	*10·3	*100·0
Salop	* 8·8	*100·0
Bedford	* 2·9	*100·0
Cornwall	*	*

Counties in which the Number of Rapes is below the Number of Cases of Carnal Abuse is below the Average.

Monmouth	†145·6	*100·0
Stafford	†105·9	*100·0
Durham	† 86·8	*100·0
Essex	† 85·3	*
Norfolk	† 32·4	*100·0
Oxford	† 7·4	*100·0
Rutland	† 23·5	*100·0
Southampton	† 13·2	*

Counties in which the No. of Rapes is below and the No. of Cases of Carnal Abuses above the Average.

Surrey	*19·1	† 66·7
Cambridge	*19·1	*100·0
Somerset	*16·2	†133·3
Kent	*11·8	†366·7
Berks	* 8·8	† 66·7
Middlesex	* 2·9	†166·7

** The rule appears to be, that where the Number of Rapes is the *greatest*, the Number of Cases of Carnally Abusing Children is (generally speaking) the greatest also; and *vice versâ*, where the Rapes are the *least*, the carnal abuse of Children is the *least* likewise.

THE CRIME OF CARNALLY ABUSING CHILDREN COMPARED WITH THE NUMBER OF FEMALES TO MALES IN EACH COUNTY.

Counties in which the Carnal Abuse of Children and the Number of Females to Males are both above the Average.	Percentage above and below the Average. * denotes above. † denotes below.	
	In No. of Cases of Carnal Abuse.	In No. of Females to Males.
Middlesex	†166·7	*8·6
Somerset	†133·3	†5·7
Worcester	† 66·7	*6·7
Gloucester	† 66·7	*5·7
Surrey	† 66·7	*5·7

Counties in which the Carnal Abuse of Children and the No. of Females to Males are both below the Average.

South Wales	*100·0	*2·9
North Wales	*100·0	*2·9
Warwick	*100·0	*1·0
Sussex	*100·0	*1·9
Suffolk	*100·0	*1·9
Stafford	*100·0	*7·6
Salop	*100·0	*3·8
Rutland	*100·0	*6·7
Oxford	*100·0	*5·7
Nottingham	*100·0	*1·0
Northumb.	*100·0	*12·4
Monmouth	*100·0	*
Hunts	*100·0	*3·8
Hereford	*100·0	*5·7
Durham	*100·0	*3·8
Derby	*100·0	*1·9
Cumberland	*100·0	*2·9
York	* 66·7	*3·8
Lancaster	* 33·3	*4·8
Southampton	*	*
Lincoln	*	*
Essex	*	*

Counties in which the Carnal Abuse of Children is below and the No. of Females to Males above the Average.

Norfolk	*100·0	†1·0
Dorset	*100·0	†1·9
Devon	*100·0	†5·7
Bedford	*100·0	†2·9
Cornwall	*	†1·9

Counties in which the Carnal Abuse of Children is above, and the Number of Females to Males below the Average.

Westmorland	†466·6	*3·8
Worcester	†433·3	*1·0
Bucks	†366·7	*1·9
Kent	†366·7	*3·8
Chester	†166·7	*
Cambridge	*100·0	*3·8
Hertford	*100·0	*2·9
Berks	† 66·7	*3·8
Northampton	† 66·7	*1·0
Leicester	† 33·3	*
Wilts	† 33·3	*1·9

** The rule appears to be, that the crime of Carnally Abusing is (generally speaking) the *greatest* in those Counties where the number of Females is the *least*.

MAP No. IX.

MAP

SHOWING THE NUMBER OF

PERSONS COMMITTED FOR KEEPING DISORDERLY HOUSES IN EVERY 10,000,000 OF THE POPULATION,

IN THE SEVERAL COUNTIES OF

ENGLAND AND WALES.

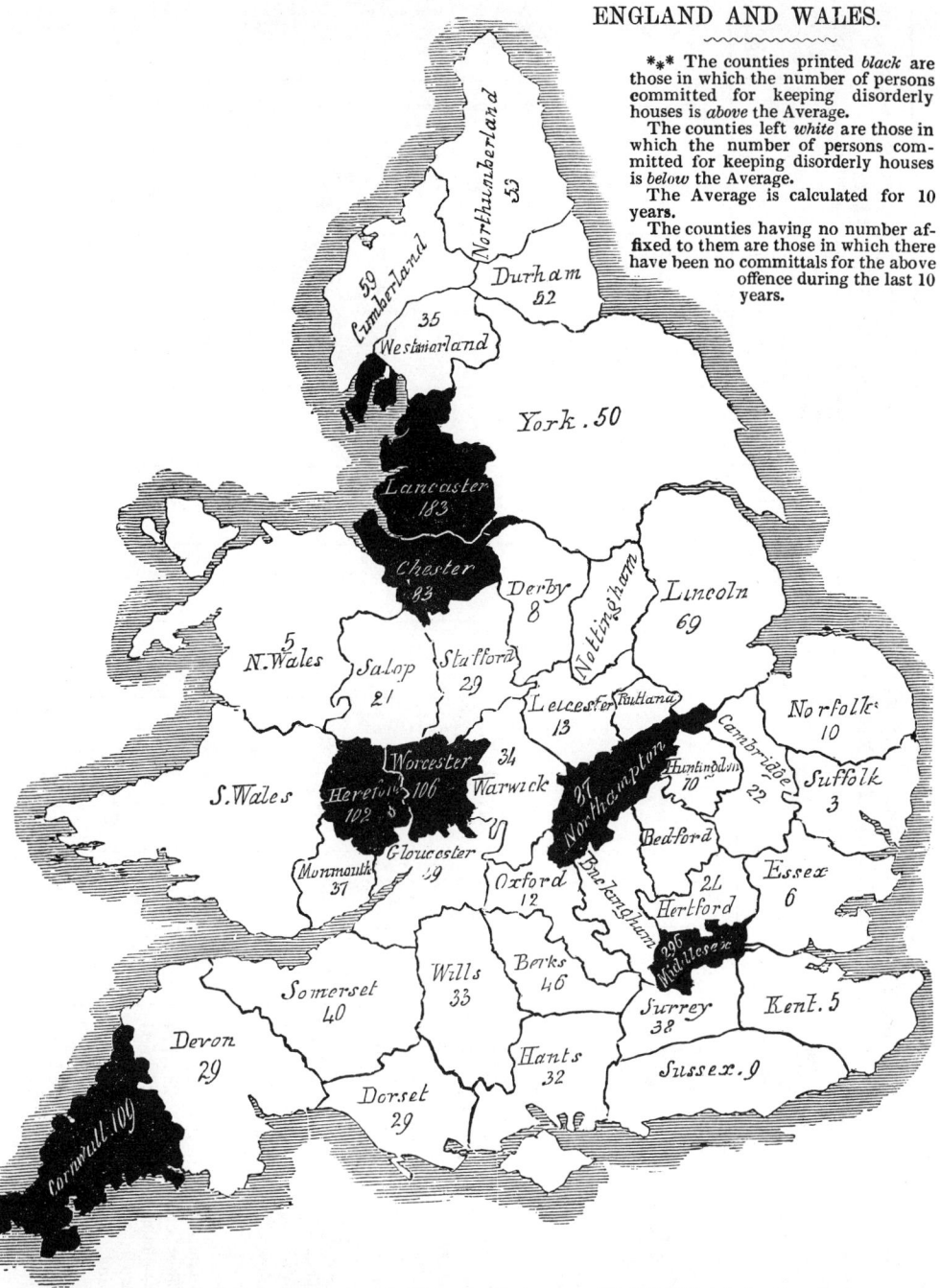

** The counties printed *black* are those in which the number of persons committed for keeping disorderly houses is *above* the Average.

The counties left *white* are those in which the number of persons committed for keeping disorderly houses is *below* the Average.

The Average is calculated for 10 years.

The counties having no number affixed to them are those in which there have been no committals for the above offence during the last 10 years.

The Average for England and Wales is 79 in every 10,000,000 of the Population.
" Middlesex (the highest) is 296   "   "

TABLE XI.

TABLE SHOWING THE NUMBER OF PERSONS COMMITTED FOR KEEPING DISORDERLY HOUSES IN THE DIFFERENT COUNTIES OF ENGLAND AND WALES FOR THE UNDERMENTIONED YEARS.

COUNTIES.	Average Population from 1841-50.	Number Committed for keeping Disorderly Houses.										Total for 10 Years.	Annual Average.	No. committed annually in every 10,000,000 of the Population.	Proportion per Cent above and below the Aver. * denotes above. † denotes below.
		1841.	1842.	1843.	1844.	1845.	1846.	1847.	1848.	1849.	1850.				
Bedford	121,083	...	...	...	...	...	...	...	...	...	...	...	...	...	*100·0
Berks	194,763	...	4	...	1	...	...	...	...	...	...	9	·9	46	*41·8
Bucks	140,959	...	...	...	...	...	...	...	...	...	...	...	...	...	*100·0
Cambridge	180,747	...	...	...	...	...	4	...	1	...	...	4	·4	22	*72·2
Chester	395,919	4	12	3	4	2	1	1	1	2	3	33	3·3	83	†5·1
Cornwall	349,991	4	3	7	1	2	6	5	4	4	2	38	3·8	109	†38·0
Cumberland	186,762	7	1	1	...	...	...	2	...	...	...	11	1·1	59	*25·3
Derby	250,249	...	...	1	...	...	...	...	...	1	...	2	·2	8	*89·9
Devon	554,738	2	3	...	2	...	...	4	4	1	1	16	1·6	29	*63·3
Dorset	172,736	3	...	...	...	...	...	...	1	...	1	5	·5	29	*63·3
Durham	368,787	...	3	...	5	...	...	...	...	...	14	19	1·9	52	*34·2
Essex	332,363	...	2	2	2	2	...	2	2	...	...	2	·2	6	*92·4
Gloucester	407,504	5	9	1	...	...	2	...	...	...	...	24	2·4	59	*25·3
Hereford	97,813	3	...	2	5	2	16	1	...	1	...	10	1·0	102	†29·1
Hertford	168,178	...	...	...	...	...	...	1	...	...	...	4	·4	24	*69·6
Hunts	57,942	...	...	...	2	4	...	...	2	...	...	4	·4	70	*11·4
Kent	585,249	...	1	...	...	...	2	...	...	...	...	3	·3	5	*93·7
Lancaster	1,881,261	85	55	45	27	24	16	14	32	42	4	344	34·4	183	†131·6
Leicester	227,621	...	...	...	...	...	2	...	...	1	...	3	·3	13	*83·5
Lincoln	378,246	1	3	2	2	...	7	1	7	3	...	26	2·6	69	*12·7
Middlesex	1,740,814	36	67	31	114	37	31	51	42	79	27	515	51·5	296	†274·7
Monmouth	164,093	...	...	...	2	1	1	2	...	...	...	6	·6	37	*53·2
Norfolk	419,463	...	...	...	2	...	...	...	...	...	...	4	·4	10	*87·3
Northampton	206,496	8	5	...	...	...	...	...	1	1	1	18	1·8	87	†10·1
Northumberland	284,777	...	...	2	3	...	1	...	...	1	13	15	1·5	53	*32·9
Nottingham	282,584	...	...	...	...	...	...	...	...	...	...	...	...	...	*100·0
Oxford	166,751	...	1	...	...	...	1	...	...	...	...	2	·2	12	*84·8
Rutland	23,711	...	...	...	...	...	...	...	...	...	...	...	...	...	*100·0
Salop	243,352	2	1	1	1	...	...	...	...	...	...	5	·5	21	*72·4
Somerset	452,515	7	...	1	5	2	...	1	...	1	1	18	1·8	40	*49·4
Southampton	377,040	...	3	...	1	2	...	...	...	...	8	12	1·2	32	*59·5
Stafford	579,686	1	2	...	...	2	...	1	4	5	2	17	1·7	29	*63·3
Suffolk	325,336	...	...	...	...	...	...	...	...	...	1	1	·1	3	*96·2
Surrey	635,917	...	1	15	3	2	3	...	...	...	...	24	2·4	38	*51·9
Sussex	320,944	2	...	1	...	...	...	...	...	...	...	3	·3	9	*88·6

Warwick .	444,558		2	6	...	1	...	2	...	15	1.5	34	*57.0
Westmorland .	57,494	...	...	...	...	...	1	...	2	.2	35	*55.7
Wilts .	241,887	...	1	1	...	...	2	1	8	.8	33	*58.2
Worcester .	244,574	11	3	5	11	...	3	2	26	2.6	106	†34.2
York .	1,686,461	21	21	1	1	5	...	4	85	8.5	50	*36.7
Northampton .	396,161	...	...	...	...	1	7	...	2	.2	5	*93.7
North Wales .												
South Wales .	568,430	...	...	...	...	...	...	...	...	...	...	*100.0
Total for England and Wales	16,918,458	198	186	145	187	86	84	99	190	148	1335	133.5	79

THE NUMBER OF DISORDERLY HOUSES COMPARED WITH THE NUMBER OF ILLEGITIMATE BIRTHS IN EACH COUNTY.

	Percentage above and below the Average. † denotes above. * „ below.	
	In No. of Disorderly Houses.	In No. of Illegitimate Children.
Counties in which the Number of Disorderly Houses and the Number of Illegitimate Children are both above the Average.		
Lancaster	†131·	†14
Hereford	†29·	†49
Chester	† 5·	†32
Counties in which the Number of Disorderly Houses and the Number of Illegitimate Children are both below the Average.		
Rutland	*100·	*16
Kent	* 93·	*19
Essex	* 92·	*10
Cambridge	* 72·	* 1
Dorset	* 63·	*25
Devon	* 63·	*10
Southampton	* 59·	*16
Warwick	* 57·	*26
Monmouth	* 53·	*34
Surrey	* 51·	* 6
Somerset	* 49·	*10
Durham	* 34·	* 4
Gloucester	* 25·	* 1
Lincoln	* 12·	*28
Hunts	* 11·	

** The rule appears to be, that the number of Disorderly Houses is the *least* in those Counties where the number of Illegitimate Births is the *greatest*, and, *vice versâ*, the *greatest* where the Illegitimates are the *least*.

	Percentage above and below the Average. † denotes above. * „ below.	
	In No. of Disorderly Houses.	In No. of Illegitimate Children.
Counties in which the Number of Disorderly Houses is above and the Number of Illegitimate Children below the Average.		
Middlesex	†274·	*40
Cornwall	† 38·	*29
Worcester	† 34·	* 1
Northampton	† 10·	*10
Counties in which the Number of Disorderly Houses is below and the Number of Illegitimate Children above the Average.		
South Wales	*100·	† 7
Nottingham	*100·	†35
Bucks	*100·	† 4
Bedford	*100·	†14
Suffolk	* 96·	†26
North Wales	* 93·	† 6
Derby	* 89·	†20
Sussex	* 88·	† 1
Norfolk	* 87·	†56
Oxford	* 84·	†13
Leicester	* 83·	†17
Salop	* 73·	†47
Hertford	* 69·	† 7
Stafford	* 63·	† 3
Wilts	* 58·	† 3
Westmorland	* 55·	†29
Berks	* 41·	†17
York	* 36·	† 6
Northumberland	* 32·	† 8
Cumberland	* 25·	†61

LIST OF COUNTIES IN THE ORDER OF THEIR BROTHELS, AS SHOWN BY THE NUMBER OF PERSONS COMMITTED FOR KEEPING DISORDERLY HOUSES IN EVERY 10,000,000 OF THE POPULATION.

Counties above the Average.		Counties below the Average.	
Middlesex	296	Hunts	70
Lancaster	183	Lincoln	69
Cornwall	109	Gloucester	59
Worcester	106	Cumberland	59
Hereford	102	Northumberland	53
Northampton	87	Durham	52
Chester	83	York	50
		Berks	46
		Somerset	40
		Surrey	38
		Monmouth	37
		Westmorland	35
		Warwick	34
		Wilts	33
		Southampton	32
		Devon	29
		Dorset	29
		Stafford	29
		Hertford	24
		Cambridge	22
		Salop	21
		Leicester	13
		Oxford	12
		Norfolk	10
		Sussex	9
		Derby	8
		Essex	6
		Kent	5
		North Wales	5
		Suffolk	3
		Bedford	0
		Bucks	0
		Nottingham	0
		Rutland	0
		South Wales	0
Average for England and Wales	79		

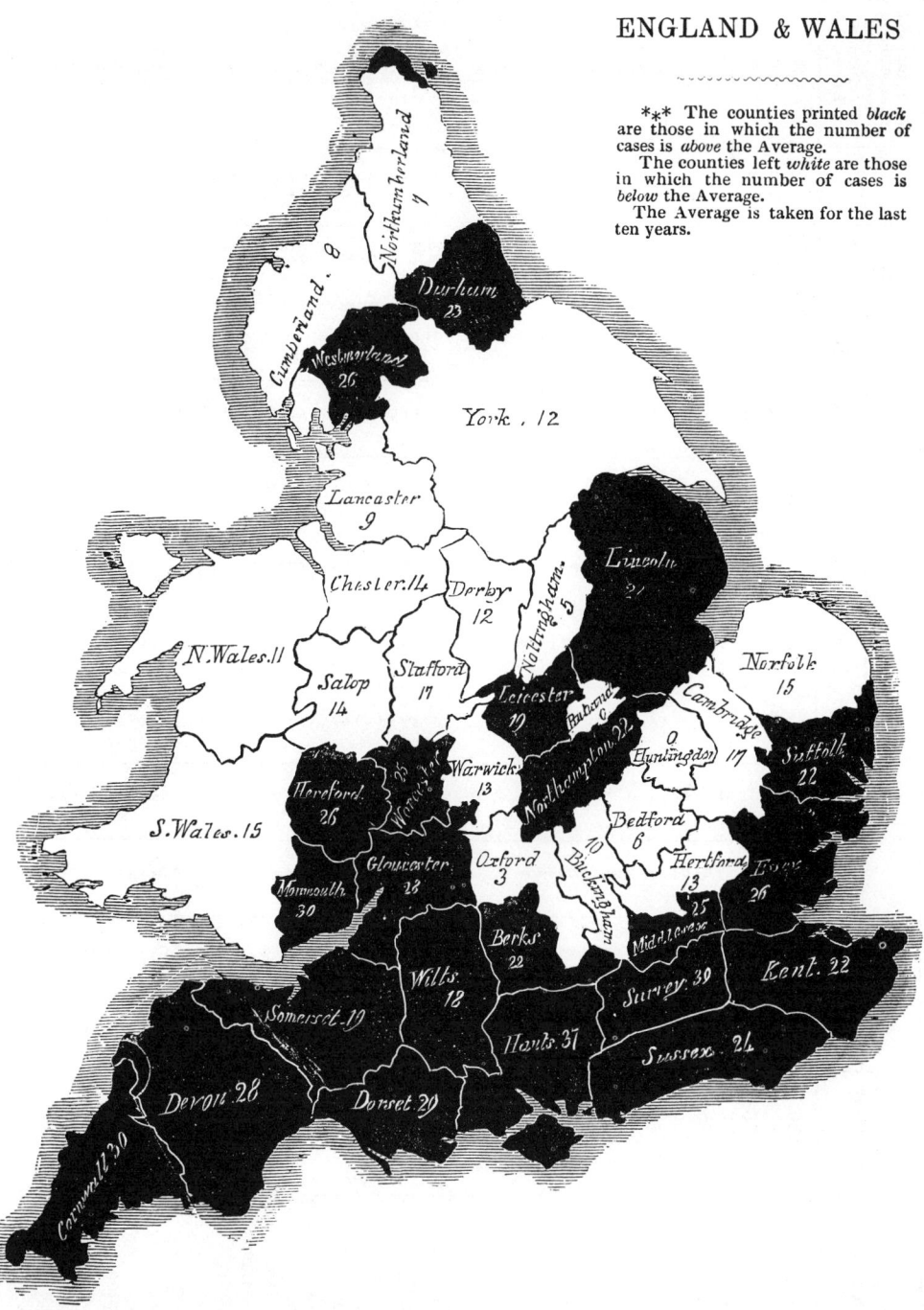

TABLE XII.

TABLE SHOWING THE CRIMINALITY OF THE DIFFERENT COUNTIES OF ENGLAND AND WALES WITH REGARD TO THE CONCEALMENT OF THE BIRTHS OF INFANTS.

COUNTIES.	Average Yearly No. of Illegitimate Births.	1841.	1842.	1843.	1844.	1845.	1846.	1847.	1848.	1849.	1850.	Total for 10 Years.	Annual Average.	No. committed for concealments in every 10,000 Illegitimate Births.	Proportion per Cent. above and below the Aver. † denotes above. * ,, below.
Bedford	836	...	...	...	1	...	...	...	...	1	...	2	.2	6	*64·7
Berks	461	...	...	...	2	2	...	...	1	3	2	10	1·0	22	†29·5
Bucks	315	...	...	...	...	...	...	1	...	...	1	3	·3	10	*41·2
Cambridge	423	...	...	1	2	1	1	...	3	3	...	7	·7	17	......
Chester	1128	3	2	2	2	1	1	...	...	...	5	16	1·6	54	*17·6
Cornwall	534	2	3	2	1	1	1	1	3	4	1	16	1·6	30	†76·9
Cumberland	639	...	...	...	...	...	...	...	1	1	1	5	·5	8	*52·9
Derby	656	...	...	...	...	...	3	2	1	...	4	8	·8	12	*29·4
Devon	818	2	2	8	7	2	2	2	1	...	3	23	2·3	28	†64·8
Dorset	342	1	1	...	5	1	4	1	1	5	1	10	1·0	29	†70·6
Durham	824	...	1	2	4	2	1	...	1	2	...	19	1·9	23	†35·3
Essex	621	1	1	1	...	2	1	...	1	1	...	16	1·6	26	†53·0
Gloucester	788	1	1	...	...	...	1	5	...	4	...	22	2·2	28	†64·8
Hereford	274	1	...	...	...	...	...	2	2	3	...	7	·7	26	†53·0
Hertford	388	2	2	...	...	...	...	1	...	1	...	5	·5	13	*23·5
Hunts	98	...	...	...	...	...	...	...	...	...	...	...	...	...	*100·0
Kent	998	...	...	...	...	3	...	5	5	3	2	22	2·2	22	†29·5
Lancaster	5672	2	4	2	4	7	7	6	5	5	3	50	5·0	9	*47·1
Leicester	583	4	4	4	5	1	1	...	2	2	1	11	1·1	19	†11·8
Lincoln	820	2	...	2	1	2	1	...	2	1	4	23	2·3	28	†64·8
Middlesex	2200	1	4	1	7	5	8	7	5	6	4	54	5·4	25	†47·1
Monmouth	269	2	...	6	7	2	...	...	...	3	4	8	·8	30	†76·9
Norfolk	1374	2	4	2	3	1	6	3	2	3	2	21	2·1	15	†11·8
Northampton	416	1	...	1	2	2	3	1	...	3	...	9	·9	22	†29·5
Northumberland	685	...	...	1	2	1	...	...	1	1	...	5	·5	7	*58·8
Nottingham	808	1	...	1	...	...	...	...	1	1	...	4	·4	5	†70·6
Oxford	896	...	1	...	...	...	1	...	...	...	...	1	·1	3	*82·4
Rutland	40	...	...	...	...	...	...	...	...	...	...	...	...	...	*100·0
Salop	640	3	2	2	2	1	2	1	4	1	2	19	1·9	14	*17·6
Somerset	847	3	1	1	1	3	2	4	3	3	2	16	1·6	19	†11·8
Southampton	703	1	2	5	...	1	5	2	2	1	2	26	2·6	37	†117·7
Stafford	1341	2	...	2	6	1	2	3	1	3	2	23	2·3	17	......
Suffolk	895	3	...	2	5	1	4	2	4	1	2	20	2·0	22	†29·5
Surrey	903	4	6	3	5	1	5	3	1	3	3	35	3·5	39	†129·5
Sussex	662	2	2	1	2	1	...	1	4	1	...	16	1·6	24	†41·2
Warwick	831	1	...	1	1	1	...	1	...	...	2	11	1·1	13	*23·5
Westmorland	156	...	...	1	...	...	...	...	...	2	1	4	·4	26	†53·0
Wilts	506	...	1	1	1	2	1	1	1	2	...	9	·9	18	†4·1
Worcester	679	1	...	3	1	...	3	1	2	2	3	17	1·7	25	†47·1

York	4155	3	3	5	3	5	7	49	49	12	*29.4
North Wales	847	...	...	2	2	1	2	9	.9	11	*35.3
South Wales	1308	2	1	2	1	4	3	19	1.9	15	*11.8
Total for England and Wales	37,410	51	49	66	87	60	75	650	65.0	17	

LIST OF COUNTIES, IN THE ORDER OF THEIR CRIMINALITY WITH REGARD TO THE CONCEALMENT OF THE BIRTHS OF INFANTS, AS SHOWN BY THE NUMBER COMMITTED FOR THIS OFFENCE IN EVERY 10,000 ILLEGITIMATE BIRTHS.

Counties above the Average.

Surrey	39
Southampton	37
Cornwall	30
Monmouth	30
Dorset	29
Devon	28
Gloucester	28
Lincoln	28
Essex	26
Hereford	26
Westmorland	26
Middlesex	25
Bucks	25
Worcester	25
Sussex	24
Durham	23
Berks	22
Kent	22
Northampton	22
Suffolk	22
Leicester	19
Somerset	19
Wilts	18

Counties below the Average.

Cambridge	17
Stafford	17
Norfolk	15
South Wales	15
Chester	14
Salop	14
Hertford	13
Warwick	13
Derby	12
York	12
North Wales	11
Lancaster	10
Cumberland	9
Northumberland	8
Bedford	7
Nottingham	5
Oxford	3
Hunts	0
Rutland	0

Average for England and Wales 17

THE ATTEMPTS AT CONCEALING THE BIRTHS OF INFANTS AND ILLEGITIMATE BIRTHS COMPARED.

Counties in which the Number of cases of Concealing Births and Number of Illegitimate Births are both above the Average.

County	Percentage above and below the Average. † denotes above. * " below.	
	In No. of Cases of Concealing Births.	In No. of Illegitimate Births.
Hereford	†53.0	†49.2
Westmorland	†53.0	†29.8
Sussex	†41.2	† 1.5
Berks	†29.5	†17.9
Suffolk	†29.5	†26.8
Leicester	†11.8	†17.9
Wilts	† 4.1	† 3.0

The Average for the whole of the above Counties is †29.4 †31.4
(The Number of cases of Concealing Births is 22 in every 10,000 Illegitimate Births, and the Number of Illegitimate Births 88 in every 1000 Births.)

Counties in which the No. of cases of Concealing Births and No. of Illegitimate Births are both below the Average.

County	In No. of Cases of Concealing Births.	In No. of Illegitimate Births.
Rutland	*	* 1.5
Hunts	* 23.5	*16.4
Warwick	*100.0	*28.3
Cambridge	*100.0	*16.4

The Average for the whole of the above Counties is *23.5 *13.4
(The Number of cases of Concealing Births is 13 in every 10,000 Illegitimate Births, and the Number of Illegitimate Births 58 in every 1000 Births.)

Counties in which the Number of Concealing Births is above the Average and the Number of Illegitimate Births below it.

County	In No. of Cases of Concealing Births.	In No. of Illegitimate Births.
Surrey	†129.5	*34.3
Southampton	†117.7	*10.4
Cornwall	† 76.9	*29.8
Monmouth	† 76.9	*26.8
Dorset	† 70.6	* 1.5
Devon	† 64.8	*25.3
Gloucester	† 64.8	* 4.5
Lincoln	† 64.8	* 1.5
Essex	† 53.0	*10.4
Middlesex	† 47.1	*40.3
Worcester	† 47.1	* 1.5
Durham	† 35.3	*10.4
Kent	† 29.5	*19.4
Northampton	† 29.5	*10.4
Somerset	† 11.8	* 6.0

The Average for the above Counties is †58.9 *20.9
(The Number of cases of Concealing Births is 27 in every 10,000 Illegitimate Births, and the Number of Illegitimate Births 53 in every 1000 Births.)

Counties in which the No. of cases of Concealing Births is below the Average and the No. of Illegitimate Births above it.

County	In No. of Cases of Concealing Births.	In No. of Illegitimate Births.
Oxford	*82.4	†13.4
Nottingham	*70.6	†35.8
Bedford	*64.7	†14.9
Northumberland	*58.8	† 8.9
Cumberland	*52.9	†61.2
Lancaster	*47.1	†14.9
Bucks	*35.3	†16.4
North Wales	*29.4	† 6.0
York	*29.4	†20.9
Derby	*23.5	† 7.4
Hertford	*17.6	†47.7
Salop	*17.6	†32.8
Chester	*11.8	† 7.4
South Wales	*11.8	†56.7
Norfolk	—	† 3.0
Stafford	*	†17.9

The Average for the whole of the above Counties is *29.4 †17.9
(The Number of cases of Concealing Births is 12 in every 10,000 Illegitimate Births, and the Number of Illegitimate Births 79 in every 1000 Births.)

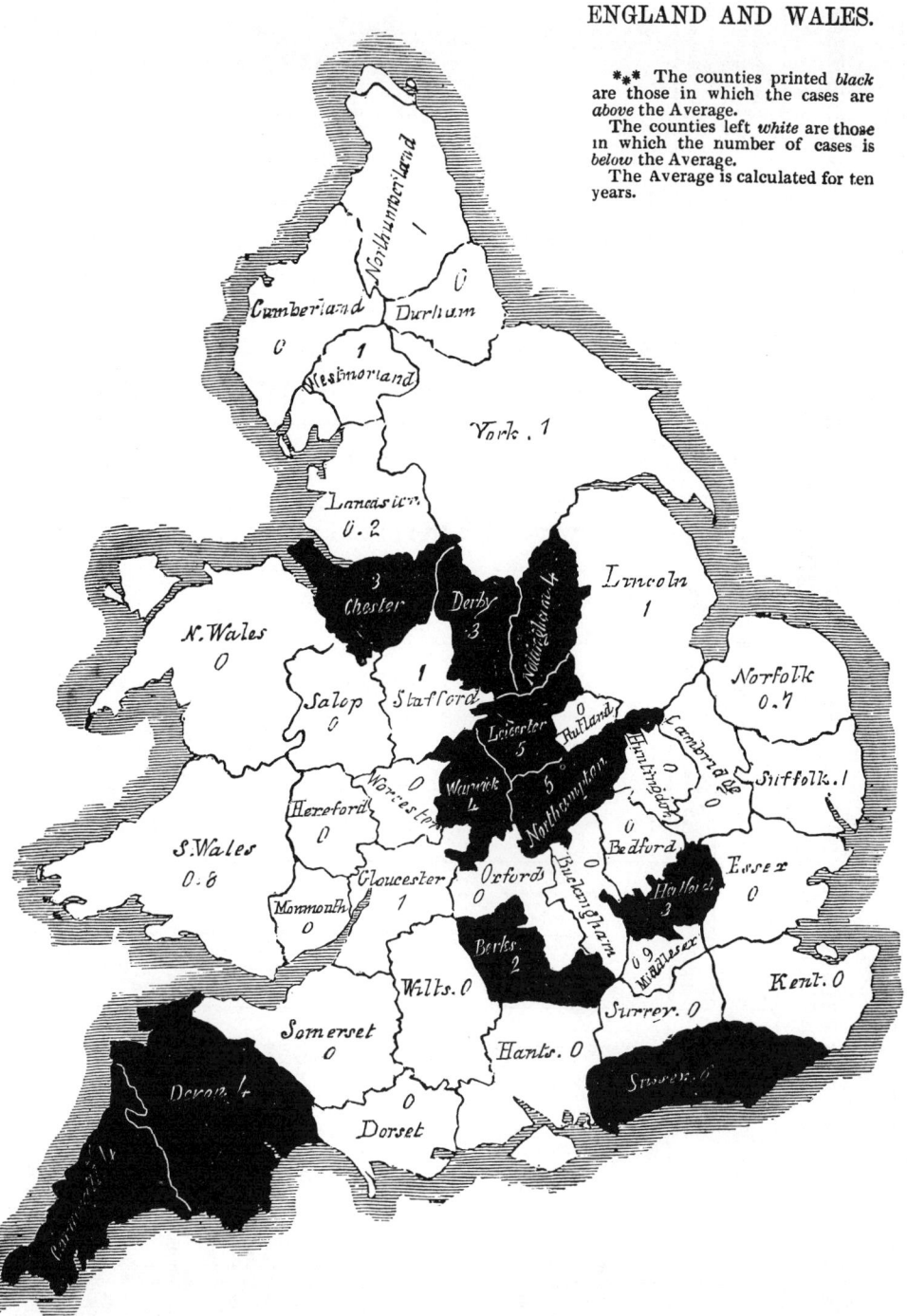

TABLE XIII.

TABLE SHOWING THE CRIMINALITY OF THE DIFFERENT COUNTIES OF ENGLAND AND WALES, WITH REGARD TO THE ATTEMPTS TO PROCURE THE MISCARRIAGE OF WOMEN.

COUNTIES.	Average Yearly No. of Illegitimate Births.	Total number committed for attempting to procure the miscarriage of women.										Total for 10 Years.	Annual Average.	No. committed annually in every 10,000 Illegitimate Births.	Proportion per Cent. above and below the Aver. * denotes above. † denotes below.
		1841.	1842.	1843.	1844.	1845.	1846.	1847.	1848.	1849.	1850.				
Bedford	336	...	...	...	...	...	...	...	...	...	...	...	...	...	*100·0
Berks	461	...	...	...	...	...	1	...	...	...	...	1	·1	2	†100·0
Bucks	315	...	...	...	...	...	...	...	...	...	...	...	...	...	*100·0
Cambridge	423	...	2	1	...	...	...	...	...	...	...	3	·3	3	†200·0
Chester	1128	...	2	...	1	...	...	...	...	...	...	3	·3	4	†300·0
Cornwall	534	...	...	...	...	...	...	...	...	...	...	...	...	...	*100·0
Cumberland	639	...	...	2	...	...	...	...	...	...	...	2	·2	3	†200·0
Derby	656	...	...	...	3	...	...	...	...	...	...	3	·3	4	†300·0
Devon	818	...	...	...	...	...	...	...	...	...	...	...	...	...	*100·0
Dorset	342	...	...	...	...	...	...	...	...	...	...	...	...	...	*100·0
Durham	824	...	...	...	...	...	...	...	...	...	...	...	...	...	*100·0
Essex	621	...	1	...	...	...	...	...	...	...	...	1	·1	1	......
Gloucester	788	...	...	...	...	...	...	...	...	...	...	...	...	...	*100·0
Hereford	274	1	...	1	...	...	1	...	...	...	...	3	·3	3	†200·0
Hertford	388	...	...	...	...	...	...	...	...	...	...	...	...	...	*100·0
Hunts	98	...	...	...	...	...	...	...	...	...	...	...	...	...	*100·0
Kent	998	...	...	...	...	...	...	...	...	...	...	1	·1	0·2	†80·0
Lancaster	5672	...	...	1	1	...	1	...	...	...	...	3	·3	5	*400·0
Leicester	583	...	...	1	...	...	...	...	...	...	...	1	·1	1	...
Lincoln	820	...	...	...	1	...	1	...	...	...	...	2	·2	0·9	†10·0
Middlesex	2200	...	...	...	...	...	...	...	...	...	...	...	...	...	*100·0
Monmouth	269	...	...	...	...	...	...	...	...	...	...	1	·1	0·7	*30·0
Norfolk	1374	...	...	...	...	...	1	1	...	...	...	2	·2	5	†400·0
Northampton	416	...	...	1	...	...	...	...	...	...	...	1	·1	1	...
Northumberland	685	...	...	...	...	...	1	1	1	...	1	3	·3	4	†300·0
Nottingham	808	...	...	...	...	...	...	...	...	...	...	...	...	...	*100·0
Oxford	396	...	...	...	...	...	...	...	...	...	...	...	...	...	*100·0
Rutland	40	...	...	...	...	...	...	...	...	...	...	...	...	...	*100·0
Salop	640	...	...	...	...	...	...	...	...	...	...	...	...	...	*100·0
Somerset	847	...	...	...	1	...	...	...	1	...	...	2	·2	1	......
Southampton	703	1	...	...	...	...	...	...	...	...	...	1	·1	1	*100·0
Stafford	1341	...	...	...	...	...	...	...	...	...	...	...	...	...	*100·0
Suffolk	895	...	...	4	...	...	...	...	...	...	...	4	·4	6	*500·0
Surrey	903	...	1	1	1	...	...	1	...	...	...	3	·3	4	†300·0
Sussex	662	...	...	...	...	...	...	...	...	...	...	...	...	...	*100·0
Warwick	831	...	...	...	...	...	...	...	...	...	...	...	...	...	*100·0
Westmorland	156	...	...	...	...	...	...	...	...	...	...	...	...	...	*100·0
Wilts	506	...	...	...	...	...	...	...	...	...	...	...	...	...	*100·0
Worcester	679	...	...	2	...	1	1	1	...	1	...	6	·6	6	*100·0
York	4155	2	...	...	...	...	...	...	...	...	...	1	·1	1	...
North Wales	847	...	...	...	...	...	...	...	...	...	...	...	...	...	*100·0
South Wales	1308	...	...	...	...	...	...	...	...	...	...	...	...	0·8	*20·0
Total for England and Wales	37,410	3	5	13	6	1	4	3	3	3	3	44	4·4	1	

LIST OF COUNTIES, IN THE ORDER OF THEIR CRIMINALITY WITH REGARD TO ATTEMPTING TO PROCURE THE MISCARRIAGE OF WOMEN, AS SHOWN BY THE NUMBER COMMITTED FOR THIS OFFENCE IN EVERY 10,000 ILLEGITIMATE BIRTHS.

Counties above the Average.

County	
Sussex	6
Leicester	5
Northampton	5
Devon	4
Nottingham	4
Warwick	4
Cornwall	3
Chester	3
Derby	3
Hertford	3
Berks	2

Counties below the Average.

County	
York	1
Stafford	1
Gloucester	1
Lincoln	1
Northumb.	1
Suffolk	0.9
Middlesex	0.9
S. Wales	0.3
Norfolk	0.7
Lancaster	0.2
Bedford	0
Bucks	0
Cambridge	0
Cumberland	0
Dorset	0
Durham	0
Essex	0
Hereford	0
Hunts	0
Kent	0
Monmouth	0
Oxford	0
Rutland	0
Salop	0
Somerset	0
Southamp.	0
Surrey	0
Westmor.	0
Wilts	0
Worcester	0
N. Wales	0

Average for England and Wales 1

THE CONCEALMENT OF THE BIRTHS OF INFANTS AND THE ATTEMPTS TO PROCURE THE MISCARRIAGE OF WOMEN COMPARED.

Counties in which the Concealment of Births and attempts to procure Miscarriage are both above the Average.

County	Percentage above and below the Average. * denotes above. † below.	
	In No. of Concealment of Births.	In No. of Attempts at Miscarriage
Cornwall	†76·9	†300·0
Devon	†64·8	†300·0
Sussex	†41·2	†500·0
Northampton	†29·5	†400·0
Leicester	†11·8	†400·0

The Average for the whole of the above Counties is .. †41·1 †300·0
(The Number of cases of Concealing Births is 24, and of Attempts at Miscarriage 4 in every 10,000 Illegitimate Births.)

Counties in which the Concealment of Births and Attempts to procure Miscarriage are both below the Average.

County	In No. of Conceal.	In No. of Attempts
Rutland	*100·0	*100·0
Hunts	*100·0	*100·0
Oxford	*82·4	*100·0
Bedford	*64·7	*100·0
Northumb.	*58·8	*
Cumberland	*52·9	*100·0
Lancaster	*47·1	*80·0
Bucks	*41·2	*100·0
N. Wales	*35·3	*100·0
York	*29·4	*
Salop	*17·6	*100·0
Derby	*11·8	*20·0
Warwick	*11·8	*30·0
Stafford	*	*100·0
Cambridge	—	

The Average for the whole of the above Counties is .. *29·4 *30·0
(The Number of cases of Concealing Births is 14, and Attempts at Miscarriage 0·7, in every 10,000 Illegitimate Births.)

Counties in which the Concealment of Births is above the Average, and the attempts to procure Miscarriage below.

County	In No. of Concealment of Births.	In No. of Attempts at Miscarriage
Surrey	†129·5	*100·0
Southampton	†117·7	*100·0
Monmouth	†76·9	*100·0
Dorset	†70·6	*100·0
Gloucester	†64·8	*
Lincoln	†64·8	*100·0
Essex	†53·0	*100·0
Hereford	†53·0	*100·0
Westmorland	†47·1	* 100·0
Middlesex	†47·1	*100·0
Worcester	†35·3	*100·0
Durham	†29·5	*100·0
Kent	†29·5	*100·0
Suffolk	†11·8	*100·0
Somerset	†4·1	*100·0

The Average for the whole of the above Counties is .. †53·0 * 60·0
(The Number of Concealing Births is 26, and Attempts at Miscarriage 0·4 in every 10,000 Illegitimate Births.)

Counties in which the Concealment of Births is below the Average, and the Attempts to procure Miscarriage above it.

County	In No. of Conceal.	In No. of Attempts
Nottingham	*70·6	†300·0
Derby	*29·4	†200·0
Warwick	*23·5	†300·0
Hertford	*23·5	†200·0
Chester	*17·6	†100·0

The Average for the whole of the above Counties is .. * 29·4 †200·0
(The Number of cases of Concealing Births is 12, and Attempts at Miscarriage 3 in every 10,000 Illegitimate Births.)

THE ATTEMPTS TO PROCURE THE MISCARRIAGE OF WOMEN AND ILLEGITIMATE BIRTHS COMPARED.

Counties in which the Number of cases of Attempts at Miscarriage and Number of Illegitimate Births are both above the Average.

County	In No. of Attempts at Miscarriage	In No. of Illegitimate Births
Sussex	†500·0	† 1·5
Leicester	†400·0	†17·9
Nottingham	†300·0	†35·8
Chester	†200·0	†32·8
Derby	†200·0	†20·9
Hertford	†200·0	† 7·4
Berks	†100·0	†17·9

The Average for the whole of the above Counties is .. †300·0 †20·9
(The number of cases of Attempts at Miscarriage is 4 in every 10,000 Illegitimate Births, and Number of Illegitimate Births 81 in every 1000 Births.)

Counties in which the cases of Attempts at Miscarriage and Number of Illegitimate Births are both below the Average.

County	In No. of Attempts	In No. of Illegit. Births
Cambridge	*100·0	* 1·5
Dorset	*100·0	*10·4
Durham	*100·0	*10·4
Essex	*100·0	*28·3
Hunts	*100·0	*19·4
Kent	*100·0	*26·8
Monmouth	*100·0	*16·4
Rutland	*100·0	* 6·0
Somerset	*100·0	*10·4
Southampton	*100·0	*34·3
Surrey	*100·0	*40·3
Worcester	*100·0	*
Middlesex	*100·0	* 4·5
Lincoln	*	
Gloucester	—	

The Average for the whole of the above Counties is .. * 60·0 *19·4
(The Number of cases of Attempts at Miscarriage is ·4 in every 10,000 Illegitimate Births, and Number of Illegitimate Births 54 in every 1000 Births.)

Counties in which the cases of Attempts at Miscarriage are above the Average and the Number of Illegitimate Births below it.

County	In No. of Attempts	In No. of Illegit. Births
Northampton	†400·0	*10·4
Devon	†300·0	*25·3
Warwick	†300·0	*16·4
Cornwall	†300·0	*29·8

The Average for the whole of the above Counties is .. †300·0 *20·9
(The Number of cases of Attempts at Miscarriage is 4 in every 10,000 Illegitimate Births, and Number of Illegitimate Births 53 in every 1000 Births.)

Counties in which the cases of Attempts at Miscarriage are below the Average and the Number of Illegitimate Births above it.

County	In No. of Attempts	In No. of Illegit. Births
Bedford	*100·0	†14·9
Bucks	*100·0	† 4·4
Cumberland	*100·0	†61·2
Hereford	*100·0	†49·2
Oxford	*100·0	†13·4
Salop	*100·0	†47·7
Westmorland	*100·0	†29·8
Wilts	*100·0	†16·4
North Wales	*80·0	† 6·0
Lancaster	* 60·0	†14·9
Norfolk	* 30·0	†56·7
South Wales	* 20·0	† 7·4
Suffolk	*	†26·8
Northumb.	*	† 8·9
Stafford	*	† 3·0
York	*	† 6·0

The Average for the whole of the above Counties is .. † 40·0 †16·4
(The Number of cases of Attempts at Miscarriage is ·6 in every 10,000 Illegitimate Births, and Number of Illegitimate Births 78 in every 1000 Births.)

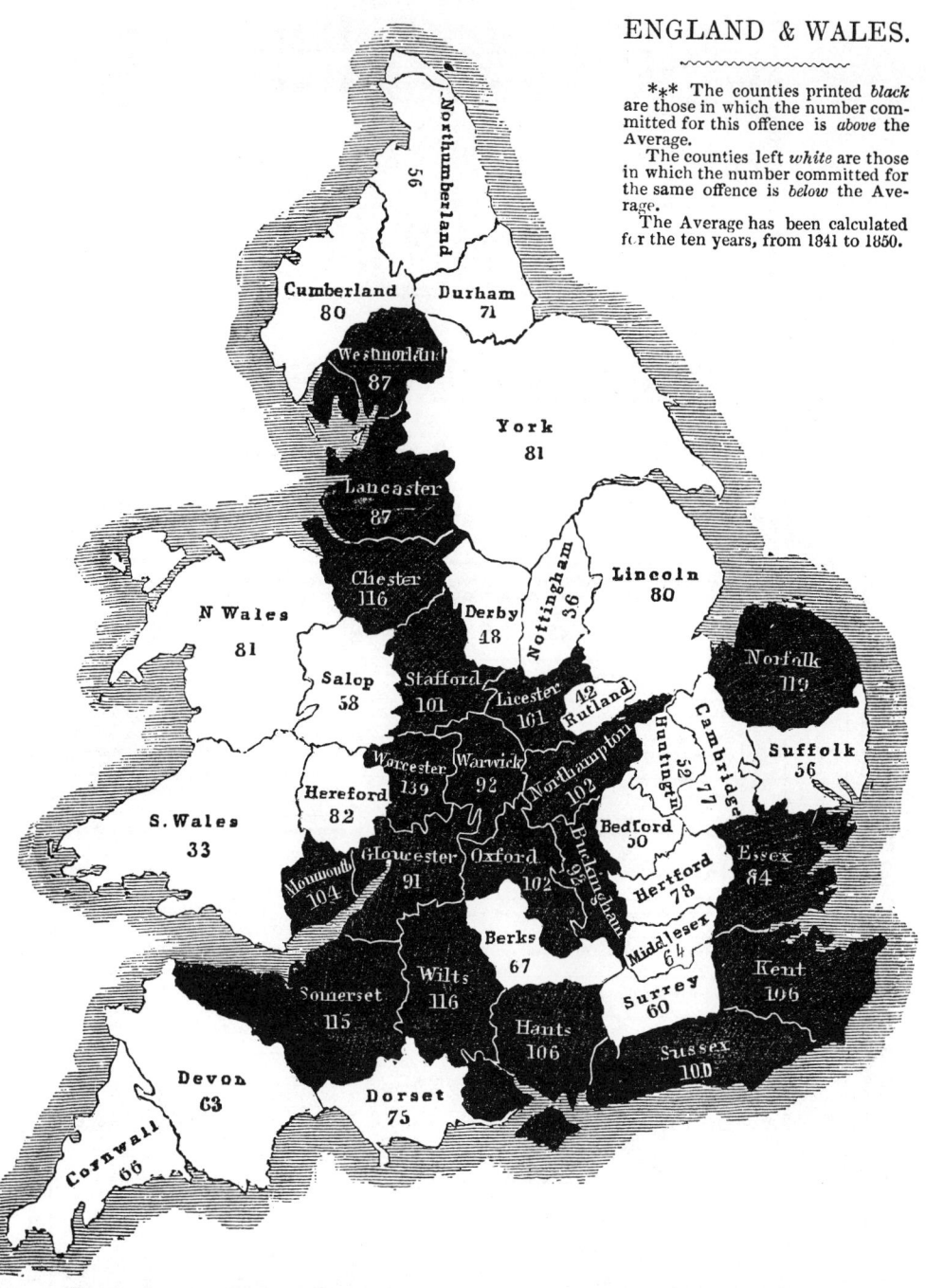

MAP No. XII.

MAP
SHOWING THE NUMBER OF PERSONS COMMITTED FOR
ASSAULTS, WITH INTENT TO RAVISH AND CARNALLY ABUSE,
IN EVERY 1,000,000 OF THE POPULATION,
IN THE SEVERAL COUNTIES OF
ENGLAND & WALES.

⁎ The counties printed *black* are those in which the number committed for this offence is *above* the Average.

The counties left *white* are those in which the number committed for the same offence is *below* the Average.

The Average has been calculated for the ten years, from 1841 to 1850.

The Average for all England and Wales is .... 83 in every 1,000,000 *people*.
 ,,   ,,   Worcester (*the highest*)   139   ,,   ,,
 ,,   ,,   South Wales (*the lowest*)   33   ,,   ,,

TABLE XIV.

TABLE SHOWING THE CRIMINALITY OF THE DIFFERENT COUNTIES OF ENGLAND AND WALES, WITH REGARD TO ASSAULTS WITH INTENT TO RAVISH AND CARNALLY ABUSE.

COUNTIES.	Average Population 1841-50.	Total Number Committed for Assaults, with intent to Ravish and Carnally Abuse.										Annual Average.	No. Committed Annually in every 1,000,000.	Percentage above and below the Average. † denotes above. * denotes below.
		1841	1842	1843	1844	1845	1846	1847	1848	1849	1850	Total for 10 Years.			
Bedford	121,083	. .	. .	1	. .	. .	2	1	1	1	1	6	0·6	50	*39·3
Berks	194,763	1	. .	1	4	2	1	1	1	1	1	13	1·3	67	*19·2
Bucks	140,959	1	1	4	3	1	. .	1	2	1	. .	13	1·3	92	†10·8
Cambridge	180,747	3	1	1	2	2	. .	. .	3	. .	3	14	1·4	77	*7·2
Chester	395,919	7	5	2	5	7	5	4	3	5	3	46	4·6	116	†39·8
Cornwall	349,991	2	6	1	4	. .	2	2	3	4	2	23	2·3	66	*20·5
Cumberland	185,762	1	3	2	2	1	3	1	1	2	. .	15	1·5	80	*3·6
Derby	250,249	2	. .	1	3	1	1	. .	1	2	1	12	1·2	48	*42·2
Devon	554,738	3	2	3	3	3	5	3	3	7	3	35	3·5	63	*24·7
Dorset	172,736	. .	. .	2	. .	1	4	. .	1	2	3	13	1·3	75	*9·6
Durham	368,787	1	3	7	. .	3	3	3	. .	4	. .	26	2·6	71	*14·5
Essex	332,363	2	6	1	. .	1	2	5	4	6	1	28	2·8	84	†1·2
Gloucester	407,504	6	2	4	4	3	3	3	3	. .	5	37	3·7	91	†9·6
Hereford	97,813	1	. .	. .	. .	1	2	. .	. .	. .	5	8	0·8	82	*1·2
Hertford	163,178	. .	. .	. .	. .	. .	2	2	4	. .	1	13	1·3	78	*6·0
Hunts	57,942	. .	. .	3	1	. .	1	1	. .	. .	. .	3	0·3	52	*37·4
Kent	585,249	3	8	8	9	7	5	5	5	5	. .	62	6·2	106	†27·7
Lancaster	1,881,261	13	19	21	21	26	15	15	15	11	6	162	16·2	87	†4·8
Leicester	227,621	2	5	4	. .	4	3	. .	. .	1	4	23	2·3	102	†21·7
Lincoln	378,246	2	6	2	6	2	4	1	. .	3	2	29	2·9	101	†3·6
Middlesex	1,740,814	14	10	10	11	9	12	6	20	8	11	111	11·1	64	*22·9
Monmouth	164,093	. .	1	2	4	1	2	1	4	. .	2	17	1·7	104	†25·3
Norfolk	419,463	3	3	7	3	9	7	6	1	3	5	50	5·0	119	†43·4
Northampton	206,496	. .	1	1	. .	. .	2	7	5	1	1	21	2·1	102	†22·9
Northumberland	284,777	1	3	3	4	7	7	7	. .	1	1	16	1·6	56	*32·5
Nottingham	282,584	. .	1	4	3	3	3	3	5	. .	. .	36	3·6	36	*56·6
Oxford	166,751	1	1	. .	2	1	2	3	. .	2	. .	10	1·0	87	†22·9
Rutland	23,711	. .	4	. .	1	. .	1	. .	. .	. .	. .	17	1·7	102	†49·4
Salop	243,352	. .	. .	. .	. .	. .	. .	. .	. .	. .	. .	14	1·4	58	*30·1
Somerset	452,515	5	3	5	6	6	6	2	3	4	2	51	5·1	115	†38·6
Southampton	377,040	2	7	7	7	7	7	5	4	3	2	40	4·0	106	†27·7
Stafford	579,686	4	3	11	4	2	5	1	7	1	11	58	5·8	101	†21·7
Suffolk	325,336	1	7	1	3	2	4	7	2	4	3	18	1·8	56	†32·5
Surrey	635,917	2	1	1	10	. .	4	2	5	5	4	38	3·8	60	†27·7
Sussex	320,944	. .	5	5	. .	2	5	4	4	6	. .	32	3·2	100	†20·5
Warwick	444,558	. .	7	. .	4	3	4	3	5	7	4	41	4·1	92	†10·8
Westmorland	57,494	. .	3	. .	. .	. .	. .	1	2	1	. .	5	0·5	87	†4·8
Wilts	241,887	3	3	3	3	3	. .	1	3	. .	3	28	2·8	116	†39·8
Worcester	244,574	3	3	5	4	1	5	1	6	5	. .	34	3·4	139	†67·5
York	1,686,461	16	14	15	16	12	19	16	6	8	14	136	13·6	81	*2·4
North Wales	396,161	5	2	2	2	1	6	7	4	1	4	32	3·2	81	*2·4
South Wales	568,430	1	1	. .	3	3	3	2	1	2	2	18	1·8	33	*60·2
Total for England and Wales	16,918,458	118	141	158	167	123	164	131	133	112	122	1369	137·0	83	

LIST OF COUNTIES, IN THE ORDER OF THEIR CRIMINALITY WITH REGARD TO ASSAULTS WITH INTENT TO RAVISH AND CARNALLY ABUSE, AS SHOWN BY THE NUMBER COMMITTED FOR THIS OFFENCE IN EVERY 1,000,000 OF THE POPULATION.

Counties above the Average.

Worcester	139
Norfolk	119
Chester	116
Wilts	116
Somerset	115
Kent	106
Southampton	106
Monmouth	104
Northampton	102
Oxford	102
Stafford	101
Leicester	101
Sussex	100
Warwick	92
Bucks	92
Gloucester	91
Lancaster	87
Westmorland	87
Essex	84

Counties below the Average.

Hereford	82
York	81
North Wales	81
Lincoln	80
Cumberland	80
Hertford	78
Cambridge	77
Dorset	75
Durham	71
Berks	67
Cornwall	66
Middlesex	64
Devon	63
Surrey	60
Salop	58
Suffolk	56
Northumberland	56
Hunts	52
Bedford	50
Derby	48
Rutland	42
Nottingham	36
South Wales	33

Average for England and Wales 83

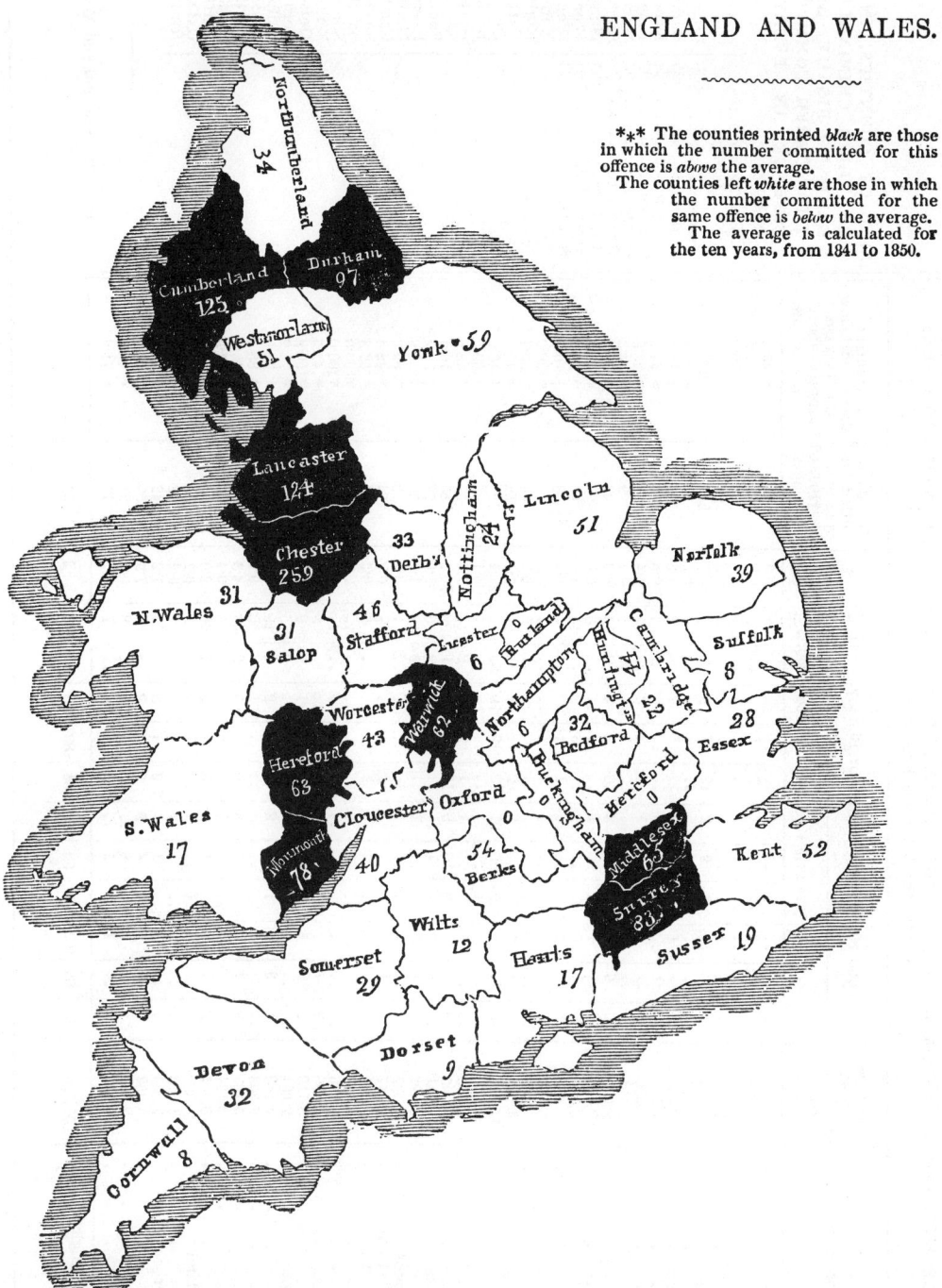

MAP No. XIII.

MAP
SHOWING THE NUMBER OF PERSONS COMMITTED FOR
BIGAMY
IN EVERY 100,000 MARRIAGES,
IN THE SEVERAL COUNTIES OF
ENGLAND AND WALES.

*** The counties printed *black* are those in which the number committed for this offence is *above* the average.
The counties left *white* are those in which the number committed for the same offence is *below* the average.
The average is calculated for the ten years, from 1841 to 1850.

The average for all England and Wales is 59 in every 100,000 Marriages.
  "   "   Chester (the highest)   259   "   "

TABLE XV. LONDON LABOUR AND THE LONDON POOR.

LIST OF COUNTIES, IN THE ORDER OF THEIR CRIMINALITY WITH REGARD TO BIGAMY, AS SHOWN BY THE NUMBER COMMITTED FOR THIS OFFENCE IN EVERY 100,000 MARRIAGES.

Counties above the Average.		Counties below the Average.	
Chester	259	York	59
Cumberland	125	Berks	54
Lancaster	124	Kent	52
Durham	97	Lincoln	51
Surrey	83	Westmorland	51
Monmouth	78	Stafford	46
Middlesex	65	Hunts	44
Hereford	63	Worcester	43
Warwick	62	Gloucester	40
		Norfolk	39
		Northumberland	34
		Derby	33
		Devon	32
		Bedford	32
		North Wales	31
		Salop	31
		Somerset	29
		Essex	28
		Nottingham	24
		Cambridge	22
		Sussex	19
		South Wales	17
		Southampton	17
		Wilts	12
		Dorset	9
		Cornwall	8
		Suffolk	8
		Leicester	8
		Northampton	6
		Bucks	6
		Hertford	0
		Oxford	0
		Rutland	0

Average for England and Wales 59

TABLE SHOWING THE CRIMINALITY OF THE DIFFERENT COUNTIES OF ENGLAND AND WALES WITH REGARD TO BIGAMY.

COUNTIES.	Average Marriages for 10 years, from 1839-48.	1841	1842	1843	1844	1845	1846	1847	1848	1849	1850	Total for 10 Years.	Annual Average.	No. committed Annually in every 100,000 Marriages.	Percentage above and below the Average. † denotes above, * below.
Bedford	925	1	.	.	1	.	.	.	.	1	.	3	0·3	32	* 45·8
Berks	1,294	1	1	2	.	2	2	2	1	1	.	7	0·7	54	* 8·5
Bucks	960	.	.	.	.	.	.	.	.	.	.	.	.	.	.
Cambridge	1,392	.	1	1	.	.	.	.	.	.	.	3	0·3	22	*100·0
Chester	2,580	.	7	11	6	2	2	12	6	9	8	67	6·7	259	†338·9
Cornwall	2,447	4	.	.	1	2	.	.	1	.	.	13	1·3	8	* 86·4
Cumberland	1,036	.	1	1	3	2	2	.	1	.	2	.	0·2	125	† 11·2
Derby	1,826	2	.	.	.	.	3	1	1	3	.	6	0·6	33	* 44·1
Devon	4,339	.	1	2	2	1	1	3	3	3	2	14	1·4	32	* 45·8
Dorset	1,174	1	.	.	.	.	.	.	.	.	.	.	0·1	9	* 4·8
Durham	2,885	.	6	3	1	2	3	3	3	4	2	28	2·8	97	† 64·4
Essex	2,114	2	.	1	2	.	1	1	.	.	.	6	0·6	28	* 52·5
Gloucester	3,459	2	1	5	1	2	.	.	3	.	.	14	1·4	40	* 32·2
Hereford	634	1	.	1	.	1	1	.	1	.	.	4	0·4	63	† 6·8
Hertford	988	.	.	.	.	.	.	.	.	.	.	.	.	.	*100·0
Hunts	452	.	.	2	.	.	2	.	.	.	.	2	0·2	44	* 25·4
Kent	4,047	2	5	3	2	2	3	2	.	1	1	21	2·1	52	* 11·9
Lancaster	17,034	13	11	35	19	20	27	29	19	19	20	212	21·2	124	†110·2
Leicester	1,730	.	.	.	1	.	.	.	.	.	.	.	0·1	6	* 89·8
Lincoln	2,765	.	.	.	4	2	3	2	1	1	1	14	1·4	51	† 13·6
Middlesex	15,795	8	8	10	9	16	9	12	10	9	11	102	10·2	65	† 10·2
Monmouth	1,981	.	.	2	1	1	.	1	2	2	2	10	1·0	78	† 32·2
Norfolk	3,021	.	2	3	2	.	.	2	2	.	1	12	1·2	39	† 33·9
Northampton	1,597	.	1	1	.	1	3	.	2	.	.	1	0·1	6	* 89·8
Northumberland	2,047	.	.	.	1	.	3	.	3	4	.	7	0·7	34	* 42·4
Nottingham	2,084	.	1	.	1	.	1	1	1	.	.	5	0·5	24	* 59·3
Oxford	1,158	.	.	.	.	.	.	.	.	.	.	.	.	.	*100·0
Rutland	158	.	.	.	.	.	.	.	.	.	.	.	.	.	*100·0
Salop	1,590	2	1	.	.	.	.	1	.	1	.	5	0·5	31	* 47·5
Somerset	2,884	1	.	2	1	1	1	1	2	.	.	9	0·9	29	* 50·9
Southampton	3,113	.	3	1	.	.	2	.	3	1	.	5	0·5	17	* 71·2
Stafford	4,146	1	.	.	4	4	2	1	.	2	2	19	1·9	46	* 22·0
Suffolk	2,369	.	.	.	.	.	.	.	3	.	4	.	0·2	8	* 86·4
Surrey	5,187	2	7	5	9	3	3	4	4	5	.	43	4·3	83	† 40·7
Sussex	2,134	.	1	.	1	1	1	.	2	.	8	4	0·4	19	† 67·8
Warwick	3,247	3	.	2	2	.	3	3	4	2	1	20	2·0	62	* 5·1
Westmorland	390	.	.	.	.	.	.	.	.	.	.	2	0·2	51	† 13·6
Wilts	1,618	.	.	.	.	1	1	.	1	.	.	2	0·2	12	* 79·7
Worcester	2,769	.	.	3	.	4	2	2	3	3	1	12	1·2	43	* 27·1
York	13,332	3	6	6	8	9	14	7	14	9	13	79	7·9	59	* 5·1
North Wales	2,582	.	1	1	.	2	.	.	2	1	.	8	0·8	31	* 47·5
South Wales	4,076	1	.	.	.	.	.	1	1	2	1	7	0·7	17	* 71·2
Total for England and Wales	130,670	50	65	107	69	62	82	84	88	83	82	772	·2	59	

TABLE XVI.   LONDON LABOUR AND THE LONDON POOR.

LIST OF COUNTIES, IN THE ORDER OF THEIR CRIMINALITY WITH REGARD TO ABDUCTION, AS SHOWN BY THE NUMBER COMMITTED FOR THIS OFFENCE IN EVERY 10,000,000 OF THE MALE POPULATION.

Counties above the Average.		Counties below the Average.	
Nottingham	14	Kent	3
Bucks	14	Middlesex	2
Cambridge	11	Bedford	0
Stafford	10	Chester	0
Berks	10	Cornwall	0
Warwick	9	Cumberland	0
Lancaster	8	Derby	0
Northumberland	7	Devon	0
Surrey	7	Dorset	0
		Durham	0
		Essex	0
		Gloucester	0
		Hereford	0
		Hertford	0
		Hunts	0
		Leicester	0
		Lincoln	0
		Monmouth	0
		Norfolk	0
		Northampton	0
		Oxford	0
		Rutland	0
		Salop	0
		Somerset	0
		Southampton	0
		Suffolk	0
		Sussex	0
		Westmorland	0
		Wilts	0
		Worcester	0
		York	0
		North Wales	0
		South Wales	0

Average for England and Wales 3

TABLE SHOWING THE CRIMINALITY OF THE DIFFERENT COUNTIES OF ENGLAND AND WALES WITH REGARD TO ABDUCTION.

Counties.	Average Male Population 1841-50.	Total Number committed for Abduction.										Total for 10 Years.	Annual Average.	No. committed Annually in every 10,000,000 Males.	Percentage above and below the Average. * denotes above. † " below.
		1841	1842	1843	1844	1845	1846	1847	1848	1849	1850				
Bedford	58,372	..	..	..	..	..	..	..	..	..	..	..	..	..	*100·0
Berks	97,055	..	..	..	1	..	..	..	..	..	..	1	·1	10	†233·3
Bucks	69,226	..	..	..	..	..	..	1	..	..	..	1	·1	14	†366·7
Cambridge	89,762	..	..	..	..	..	..	..	1	..	..	1	·1	11	†266·7
Chester	193,728	..	..	..	..	..	..	..	..	..	..	..	..	..	*100·0
Cornwall	168,854	..	..	..	..	..	..	..	..	..	..	..	..	..	*100·0
Cumberland	91,199	..	..	..	..	..	..	..	..	..	..	..	..	..	*100·0
Derby	124,224	..	..	..	..	..	..	..	..	..	..	..	..	..	*100·0
Devon	263,055	..	..	..	..	..	..	..	..	..	..	..	..	..	*100·0
Dorset	82,998	..	..	..	..	..	..	..	..	..	..	..	..	..	*100·0
Durham	183,956	..	..	..	..	..	..	..	..	..	..	..	..	..	*100·0
Essex	166,255	..	..	..	..	..	..	..	..	..	..	..	..	..	*100·0
Gloucester	192,960	..	..	..	..	..	..	..	..	..	..	..	..	..	*100·0
Hereford	48,985	..	..	..	..	..	..	..	..	..	..	..	..	..	*100·0
Hertford	83,264	..	..	..	..	..	..	..	..	..	..	..	..	..	*100·0
Hunts	28,761	..	..	..	..	..	..	..	..	..	..	..	..	..	*....·.
Kent	294,219	..	..	..	..	..	1	..	..	..	..	1	·1	3	†166·7
Lancaster	917,922	1	6	..	..	..	..	..	..	..	..	7	·7	8	*100·0
Leicester	111,629	..	..	..	..	..	..	..	..	..	..	..	..	..	*100·0
Lincoln	189,768	..	..	..	1	..	..	..	1	..	..	2	·2	2	*33·3
Middlesex	815,107	..	..	..	..	..	..	..	..	..	..	..	..	..	*100·0
Monmouth	85,564	..	..	..	..	..	..	..	..	..	..	..	..	..	*100·0
Norfolk	202,811	..	..	..	..	..	..	..	..	..	..	..	..	..	*100·0
Northampton	102,853	..	..	..	..	..	..	..	..	..	..	..	..	..	*100·0
Northumberland	139,028	..	..	..	..	..	..	1	..	..	..	1	·1	7	*100·0
Nottingham	138,413	2	..	..	..	..	..	..	..	..	..	2	·2	14	†366·7
Oxford	83,290	..	..	..	..	..	..	..	..	..	..	..	..	..	*100·0
Rutland	11,937	..	..	..	..	..	..	..	..	..	..	..	..	..	*100·0
Salop	121,316	..	..	..	..	..	..	..	..	..	..	..	..	..	*100·0
Somerset	216,177	..	..	..	..	..	..	..	..	..	..	..	..	..	*100·0
Southampton	186,661	..	..	..	..	..	..	..	..	..	..	..	..	..	*100·0
Stafford	294,120	..	..	..	..	..	1	1	..	..	1	3	·3	10	†233·3
Suffolk	159,561	..	..	..	..	..	..	..	..	..	..	..	..	..	*100·0
Surrey	303,083	..	1	..	..	..	..	1	..	..	..	2	·2	7	†133·3
Sussex	157,915	..	..	..	..	..	..	..	..	..	..	..	..	..	*100·0
Warwick	217,569	..	..	..	1	..	..	..	1	..	..	2	·2	9	†200·0
Westmorland	28,680	..	..	..	..	..	..	..	..	..	..	..	..	..	*100·0
Wilts	119,598	..	..	..	..	..	..	..	..	..	..	..	..	..	*100·0
Worcester	119,808	..	..	..	..	..	..	..	..	..	..	..	..	..	*100·0
York	835,816	..	..	..	..	..	..	..	..	..	..	..	..	..	*100·0
North Wales	196,064	..	..	..	..	..	..	..	..	..	..	..	..	..	*100·0
South Wales	279,818	..	..	..	..	..	..	..	..	..	..	..	..	..	*100·0
Total for England and Wales	8,270,087	3	7	..	4	..	1	2	2	..	4	23	2·3	3	

MAP No. XV.   503

MAP

SHOWING

THE CRIMINALITY OF FEMALES

IN EVERY 100,000 OF THE FEMALE POPULATION,

IN EACH COUNTY OF

ENGLAND AND WALES.

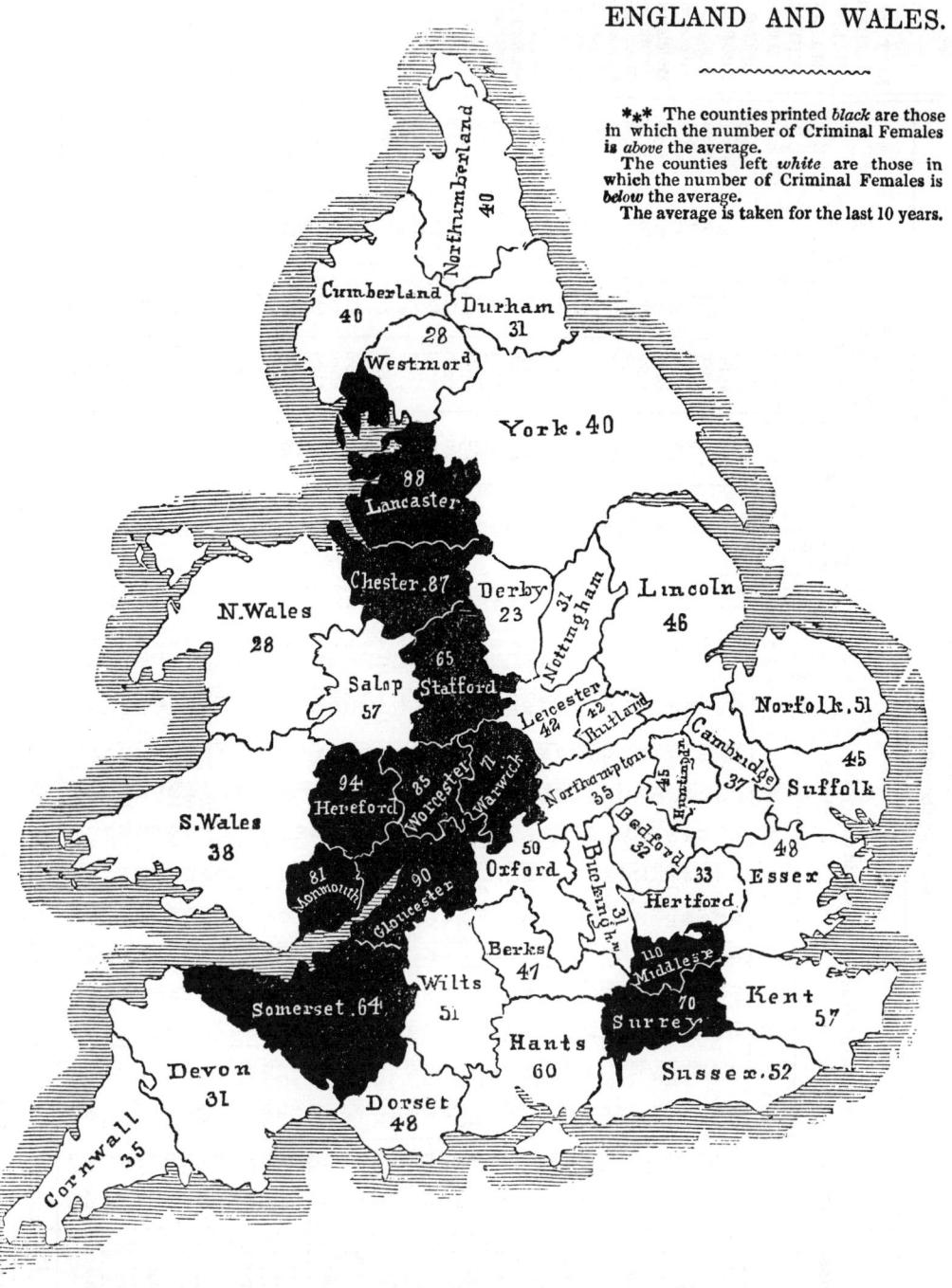

*** The counties printed *black* are those in which the number of Criminal Females is *above* the average.
The counties left *white* are those in which the number of Criminal Females is *below* the average.
The average is taken for the last 10 years.

The Average for all England and Wales is 62 in every 100,000 of the Female Population.
     ,,   ,, *Middlesex (the highest)*   110   ,,   ,,
     ,,   ,, *Derby (the lowest)*   23   ,,   ,,

TABLE XVII. — TABLE SHOWING THE RELATIVE AMOUNT OF FEMALE AND MALE CRIMINALITY IN THE SEVERAL COUNTIES OF ENGLAND AND WALES.

† denotes above the average, * below it.

Counties	Average Female Population, 1841–50.	Number of Female Criminals in each year.										Total Female Criminals in Ten Years.	Average No. of Female Criminals per year, 1841–50.	Average No. of Male Criminals per year, 1841–50.	No. of Female Criminals in every 100,000 of Female Population.	No. of Male Criminals in every 100,000 of Male Population.	Percentage above and below the Average of Female Criminals.	Percentage above and below the Average of Male Criminals.	No. of Female Criminals to every 100 Male Criminals.	Average of Female to Male Criminals.
		1841	1842	1843	1844	1845	1846	1847	1848	1849	1850								
Bedford	62,711	11	36	22	20	15	20	21	22	17	19	203	20·3	166	32	284	*48·4	†4·4	11	*52·2
Berks	97,708	45	55	43	44	42	43	55	43	47	39	455	45·5	268	47	276	*24·2	†1·5	17	*26·1
Bucks	71,732	20	23	31	17	25	21	22	21	27	16	223	22·3	266	31	384	*50·0	†41·2	8	*65·2
Cambridge	90,945	29	28	33	23	34	34	44	32	34	44	340	34·0	232	37	258	*40·3	*5·2	14	*39·1
Chester	202,190	195	181	170	147	139	183	197	209	169	184	1764	176·4	722	87	373	†40·3	†37·1	23	*—
Cornwall	181,137	61	67	75	56	62	67	78	64	64	46	649	64·9	217	35	128	†43·6	*52·9	27	†17·4
Cumberland	95,563	39	38	38	40	37	36	37	34	39	41	379	37·9	95	40	104	†35·5	*61·8	38	†65·2
Derby	126,025	21	26	34	33	28	47	24	25	27	25	290	29·0	235	23	189	*20·0	*30·5	12	†47·8
Devon	291,683	171	194	177	151	184	183	206	226	224	193	1910	191·0	596	31	227	*20·0	*16·5	14	†39·1
Dorset	89,738	46	34	42	41	33	35	37	38	61	38	434	43·4	210	48	253	†22·6	†7·0	19	†17·4
Durham	184,931	46	57	53	65	40	55	51	72	45	97	581	58·1	787	31	436	†50·0	†53·7	25	†8·7
Essex	166,108	82	85	99	89	75	69	61	82	64	82	787	78·7	559	48	336	†22·6	†23·5	14	†39·1
Gloucester	214,544	193	221	224	198	178	190	204	188	188	148	1932	193·2	875	90	453	†45·2	†66·6	20	†8·7
Hereford	48,828	64	49	45	38	39	34	52	52	44	45	462	46·2	187	94	382	†51·6	†40·4	24	†13·0
Hertford	84,914	35	34	24	27	30	27	28	30	29	23	281	28·1	267	33	321	†46·8	†18·0	10	†4·4
Hunts	29,181	7	8	10	15	19	14	12	15	15	13	128	12·8	69	45	240	*8·1	†11·8	19	†56·5
Kent	294,029	161	156	147	156	151	161	171	182	200	167	1679	167·9	792	57	272	*8·1	*—	21	†17·4
Lancaster	963,338	927	947	847	689	698	826	882	902	819	950	8487	848·7	2635	88	287	†41·9	†5·5	31	*8·7
Leicester	115,991	56	69	55	56	30	61	49	37	38	41	492	49·2	342	42	306	*32·3	†12·5	14	†34·8
Lincoln	188,477	74	100	86	92	71	78	106	87	91	72	857	85·7	398	46	210	*25·8	†22·8	22	†39·1
Middlesex	926,007	869	989	980	948	1102	1118	1176	1223	945	882	10232	1023·2	3244	110	398	†77·4	†46·3	28	†21·7
Monmouth	78,528	63	51	53	77	41	64	67	64	78	79	637	63·7	232	81	271	†30·4	†0·4	30	†4·4
Norfolk	216,652	112	127	117	77	101	120	143	78	100	97	1114	111·4	607	51	299	*17·7	†9·9	17	†30·4
Northampton	103,642	45	38	25	34	47	41	32	38	24	38	362	36·2	259	35	252	†43·6	†7·4	14	†26·1
Northumb.	145,749	54	52	77	52	46	43	50	44	61	37	579	57·9	177	40	127	†35·5	*53·3	31	†39·1
Nottingham	144,171	38	49	43	51	42	45	64	33	37	34	436	43·6	289	31	209	*50·0	*23·2	15	†34·8
Oxford	82,461	46	48	52	37	44	43	41	37	34	34	411	41·1	256	50	307	†19·4	†12·9	16	†30·4
Rutland	11,774	6	4	7	3	3	4	7	10	4	2	50	5·0	28	42	235	*—	†13·6	18	†21·7
Salop	122,035	80	75	89	84	73	48	62	65	61	59	696	69·6	293	57	242	†8·1	†11·0	24	†4·4
Somerset	236,337	172	166	136	160	143	150	145	145	159	134	1506	150·6	751	64	347	†3·2	†27·6	20	*21·7
Southampton	190,379	102	127	124	93	115	94	137	115	120	120	1147	114·7	555	60	297	*3·2	*9·2	20	†13·0
Stafford	285,566	179	190	197	175	161	188	221	176	189	193	1869	186·9	851	65	289	*4·8	†6·2	22	*4·4
Suffolk	165,775	77	80	68	77	66	77	82	78	76	68	749	74·9	436	45	273	†27·4	†0·4	16	†30·4
Surrey	332,838	212	236	177	194	215	200	316	278	275	237	2340	234·0	806	70	266	†12·9	*2·2	26	†13·0
Sussex	163,028	61	81	83	81	86	83	83	83	101	83	832	83·2	409	52	259	*16·1	*4·8	20	†17·4
Warwick	226,969	168	157	177	119	144	163	179	199	142	162	1610	161·0	799	71	367	†14·5	†34·9	19	†8·7
Westmorland	23,814	9	8	7	6	7	6	8	4	9	7	76	7·6	39	28	136	†54·9	†50·0	21	†34·8
Wilts	122,359	65	57	65	57	52	60	86	59	78	47	626	62·6	394	51	330	†17·7	†21·3	15	†13·0
Worcester	124,766	75	102	104	87	75	105	141	116	112	109	1059	105·9	506	85	422	†37·1	†55·1	20	*4·4
York	850,625	331	375	375	323	290	294	351	344	347	321	3356	335·6	1587	40	190	†35·5	†30·7	21	†43·5
North Wales	200,096	60	56	43	45	49	47	68	65	63	62	563	56·3	233	28	119	†54·9	*56·3	21	†43·5
South Wales	288,612	93	79	84	117	84	91	127	145	134	151	1105	110·5	368	38	132	*38·7	†51·5	29	†26·1
Total for England & Wales	8,648,371	5200	5569	5340	4993	4962	5257	5930	5763	5401	5265	53680	5368·0	22474	62	272			23	

[a] The average number of Male Criminals has been arrived at in the same manner as that for Female Criminals, but the table itself is reserved for another place.

LIST OF COUNTIES, IN THE ORDER OF THEIR CRIMINALITY AMONGST FEMALES, AS SHOWN BY THE NUMBER OF FEMALE CRIMINALS IN EVERY 100,000 OF THE FEMALE POPULATION.

Counties above the Average.

Middlesex	110
Hereford	94
Gloucester	90
Lancaster	88
Chester	87
Worcester	85
Monmouth	81
Warwick	71
Surrey	70
Stafford	65
Somerset	64

Counties below the Average.

Southamp.	60
Kent	57
Salop	57
Sussex	52
Norfolk	51
Wilts	51
Oxford	50
Essex	48
Dorset	48
Berks	47
Lincoln	46
Suffolk	45
Hunts	45
Leicester	42
Rutland	42
York	40
Northumb.	40
Cumberland	40
S. Wales	38
Cambridge	37
Cornwall	35
Northampton	35
Hertford	33
Bedford	32
Devon	31
Durham	31
Nottingham	31
Bucks	31
N. Wales	28
Westmor.	28
Derby	23

Average for England and Wales 62